Hippocrene Standard Dictionary

Tagalog-English
English-Tagalog

Revised and Expanded Edition

Tagalog-English
English-Tagalog

DICTIONARY

* * *

TALÁHULUGANANG

Pilipino-Ingglés
Ingglés-Pilipino

Revised and Expanded Edition

compiled by

Carl R. Galvez Rubino, Ph.D.

with the assistance of

Maria Gracia Tan Llenado, Chief Consultant

HIPPOCRENE BOOKS
New York

This book was compiled with the assistance of Maria Gracia Tan Llenado, Chief Consultant, and Kenneth Chang, Computer Consultant.

Front cover: "Come to paradise." Photograph by Karie Garnier from his award-winning website http://www.sfu.ca/fuga

Revised and Expanded Edition, 2002.
Ninth printing, 2010.

For information, address:
HIPPOCRENE BOOKS, INC.
171 Madison Avenue
New York, NY 10016

Library of Congress Cataloging-in-Publication Data

Rubino, Carl R. Galvez
Tagalog-English, English-Tagalog dictionary = Pilipino-Inggĺés, Inggĺés-Pilipino Taláhuluganang / compiled by Carl R. Galvez Rubino with the assistance of Maria Gracia Tan Llenado.
p. cm.
ISBN-10: 0-7818-0961-4 (hb)
ISBN-10: 0-7818-0960-6 (pb)
ISBN-13: 978-0-7818-0960-3 (pb)
1. Tagalog language--Dictionaries--English. 2. English language--Dictionaries--Tagalog. I. Title: Pilipino-Inggĺés, Inggĺés-Pilipino Taláhuluganang. II. Llenado, Maria Gracia Tan. III. Title.

PL6056 .R83 2002
499'.211321--dc21 2002068848

Printed in the United States of America.

CONTENTS

PREFACE

This Tagalog-English dictionary was written to serve two audiences, speakers of Tagalog who need access to a bilingual dictionary and students of Tagalog (Pilipino), the national language of the Philippines.

To be as comprehensive as possible for its size, the dictionary is root based, as are most dictionaries of languages with a complex morphological typology. It is assumed that the majority of Tagalog speakers will be able to use this format, as they are usually easily able to parse complex words into roots and affixes and have been taught in school to do so. For non-native speakers and beginning learners, a chart of Tagalog affixes (prefixes, suffixes, infixes, and reduplication) is provided to help them identify the proper way to look up the more complex (polymorphemic) entries. The relatively simple nature of Tagalog affixation (with minimal morphophonemics) should not make this a difficult task.

The grammar outline included herein also serves as a concise introduction to acquaint the users to the fundamentals of Tagalog morphology and syntax to further aid them in using this dictionary as well as entertain the curious philologist. More comprehensive treatments are available for linguists and listed in the Reference section.

I would like to thank a few people who have been most instrumental in my work on Tagalog and on this dictionary. First, I thank Maria Gracia Tan Llenado who patiently served as my chief consultant and helped translate the many words and idioms I have collected for this dictionary. I would like to thank my parents, Ralph and Erlinda Rubino, and friends Melissa Deleissegues, Robert Newman, Marianne Mithun, Laurie Reid, Nikolaus Himmelmann, David Zorc, Jean Paul Potet, Agnes Kang, Alex Gonzales, Paul Barthmaier, and Alec Coupe for all their support over the years, as well as my family in America and the Philippines: the Rubinos (Paul, Alan, and Earl), Galvezes, Villanuevas, Carbonells, and Konvalinkas. I greatly appreciate all the help of Jose Sabado, Jr., Alexis Racelis, and Carol Genetti for initiating and supporting the campaign to start a Tagalog program at the University of California, Santa Barbara. Many thanks to Kenneth Chang for helping me with the dictionary program used for the layout of this book and to Kenneth Ilio for his untiring work for the Philippine community outside their homeland. I would also like to thank the members of the Department of Linguistics at UCSB, and the Monterey Institute of International Studies, and the Australian National University RSPAS. *Maraming salamat* to the following who have helped me in my research: Dexina Llenado, Avelino Llenado, Cesar J. Gonzales Jr., Antonio Llenado, Chris Sundita, Larry Candido, and Emmanuel Esguerra.

In closing, I would like to acknowledge all those who dedicate their lives to helping endangered species, native cultures, and virgin rainforests. They are the true children of the earth.

I lovingly dedicate this work to
my two grandmothers:

Florence Tomisek Konvalinka and Josefa Mallare Galvez
they have supported me in all my dreams and aspirations

Maraming salamat sa inyóng lahát, Carl

http://tagalog.org
http://iloko.tripod.com

NOTE ON TAGALOG ORTHOGRAPHY

Prior to the arrival of the Spanish, Tagalogs used an Indic syllabary consisting of three vowels and fifteen consonants. Final consonants (syllable codas) were not represented in the system, e.g. ᜄᜎᜓᜄᜓ 'galunggóng,' ᜐᜎᜋ 'salamat,' ᜑᜓᜋᜑᜈ 'humahanap.' True to the phonological nature of the pre-Hispanic Tagalog language, the consonants /d/ and /r/ were represented by the same symbol (ᜇ), as were the vowels /e/, /i/ (ᜁ); and /o/, /u/ (ᜂ). Diacritics were used to distinguish vowels 6 ᜄ ga, ᜄᜒ ge/gi, ᜄᜓ go/gu. The Ilocano innovation to the syllabary which reflects coda consonants by placing a 'stop' diacritic under the consonant is often used in modern renditions of the ancient script, e.g. ᜄᜎᜓᜅ᜔ᜄᜓᜅ᜔ 'galunggóng,' ᜐᜎᜋᜆ᜔ 'salamat,' ᜑᜓᜋᜑᜈᜉ᜔ 'humahanap.' The ancient syllabary was quickly replaced with the Latin script based on Spanish orthography.

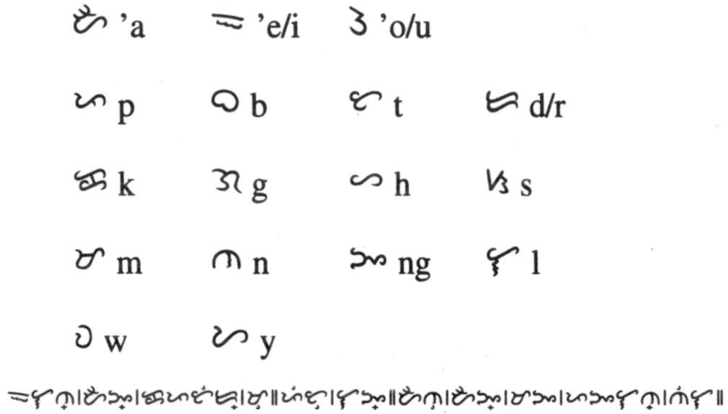

ᜀ 'a   ᜁ 'e/i   ᜂ 'o/u

ᜉ p   ᜊ b   ᜆ t   ᜇ d/r

ᜃ k   ᜄ g   ᜑ h   ᜐ s

ᜋ m   ᜈ n   ᜅ ng   ᜎ l

ᜏ w   ᜌ y

ᜁᜎᜈ᜔᜵ᜀᜅ᜔᜵ᜃᜉᜆᜒᜇ᜔᜵ᜋᜓ᜶ᜉᜒᜆᜓ᜵ᜎᜅ᜔᜶ᜀᜈᜓ᜵ᜀᜅ᜔᜵ᜋᜅ᜵ᜉᜅᜎᜈ᜔᜵ᜈᜒᜎ᜶
Ilán ang kapatid mo? Pito lang. Ano ang mga pangalan nila?

Figure 1. The ancient Tagalog script and sample sentences

Modern Tagalog now employs a Tagalicized spelling system which has replaced the previous Spanish one, as an attempt to avoid certain ambiguities of consonant representation, notably the confusing use of the consonant symbols /c/, /f/, /j/, /q/, /v/, /x/, and /z/.

The Tagalog alphabet used today is as follows. Note that the letter [k] is third in the alphabet, and the velar nasal segment /ng/ is treated as a separate letter. The Tagalog-English section of this dictionary is alphabetized following standard Tagalog practice.

The modern Tagalog alphabet (*abakada*):

A B K D E G H I L M N NG O P R S T U W Y

The old symbols /x/ and /ch/ have been replaced by /ks/ and /ts/, respectively, and the voiced alveo-palatal affricate sound of the letter 'j' as in 'judge' is now represented by /dy/.

AFFIX CROSS-REFERENCE LIST FOR WORD SEARCHES

Successful searching in a root-based dictionary of a morphologically complex language such as Tagalog requires the ability to separate, where applicable, the root morpheme from the affixes. Native speakers of Tagalog and trained linguists are usually able to do this quite easily in most cases, but for students of the language, this cross-reference list may prove most helpful. The affixes alphabetized below are separated by category: prefixes, infixes, and suffixes. Users of this dictionary must also keep in mind that many of these affixes may be used with root reduplication. The reduplicated form of the root must also be simplified to its original form before word searching. Remember also that the phoneme /u/ is usually written [o] in word-final syllables, and [d] and [r] are variants of the same underlying sound. An intervocalic [r] may actually be a [d]. It may also help to keep in mind that roots that can take derivation in Tagalog are minimally two syllables.

i.e.	For the word	Meaning	Search for the root
	darating	'will arrive'	*dating* (CV-dating)
	dumiskarte	'pave the way; make a move'	*diskarte* (diskarte + -um-)
	kalayuan	'distance'	*layô* (ka- layô + -(h)an)
	marumí	'dirty'	*dumi* (ma- + dumí)
	habulin	'chase, pursue'	*habol* (habol- + (h)in)

The following is a list of the common affixes used in the Tagalog:

Infixes (placed before first vowel of root)

-in-	b*in*asa, h*in*intáy, s*in*ilág
-um-	s*um*ará, p*um*arito, l*um*abás

Suffixes

-(h)an	tingnán, sarhán, sulatan, tawagan
-(h)in	linisin, tugtugin, hiramín
-ero, -era (Spanish)	basurero, alahero
-ado (Spanish)	muskulado, kontrolado, iletrado

Prefixes (N = homorganic nasal: m, n, ng)

di- (with hyphen)	di-matabâ, di-maaarì, di-malayò
ka-	katuwaan, káloobán, kapangalan
kasiN-	kasimpobre, kasinggandá
i-	ihadláng, igalang, idamít, ikulay
ika-	ikaduda, ikáhintô, ikagutom, ikagalit
ikapag-	ikapag-antók, ikapag-away
ikapagpa-	ikapagpapayaman, ikapagpapalakí
ikapaN-	ikapanglimá, ikapampitó
ikina-	ikinabúbuhay, ikinahíhiyâ, ikinagulat
ipa-	ipamana, ipakasál, ipakilala, ipaalaala
ipaki-	ipakiabót, ipakisama, ipakiusap
ipag-	ipagtagumpáy, ipagtawá, ipagbuwís
ipagka-	ipagkabuhay, ipagkaloób, ipagkámalî

ipagpa-	ipagpagawâ, ipagpaaral, ipagpáhulí
ipaN-	ipanggapas, ipanganib, ipangaral, ipamilí, ipamangkâ
ipapaN-	ipapangpunas, ipapamingwít
isa-	isa-Tagalog, isaulì, isaayos
ma-	malagkít, malayò, mahinà, malakás
maka-	makadatíng, mákalarô, makasigáw
makapag-	makapágpayo, makapágsugál, makapág-ingat
makapaN-	makapandayà, makapanlamíg, makapangyari
maki-	makitulad, makilinyá, makihamok
makipag-	makipág-away, makipágbálitaán, makipágkamáy
mag-	magsipà, magpalít, magtubò, mag-aral
magka-	magkasalapî, magkasarili, magkásubuán
magkanda-	magkandarapà, magkandahulog
magkaN-	magkanghuhulog, magkáng-aantók
magkasing-	magkasínggandá, magkasíngpangit
magiN- (from *maging* 'become')	magimbatà, magimpalikero, magingkarpintero
magpa-	magpalambót, magpalinaw, magpalayà
magpaka-	magpakatao, magpakatiwalà, magpakasuyà
magsa-	magsápanahón, magsapanganib
magsi-	magsitulong, magsisama, magsimulâ
magsipag-	magsipaglarô, magsipag-away
mai-	maipiraso, máiyák, maitupî
maipa-	maipahusto, maipakatawán, máipakain
maipag-	maipagbawal, maipagbayad, maipaglutò
maipagpa-	maipagpasalamat, maipagpaliban
maipaN-	maipamatò, maipanlapì, maipangakò
maipapang-	maipapangkublí
mala-	malahiningá, malasakit, malasarili
maN-	manudyó, manursí, mamarîl, mamayong, mangitlóg
manga-	mangawalâ, mangalarô
mangaka-	mangakaríníg, magakagawâ
mangag-	mangagtawá, mangagbasa, mangaglulutò
mapa-	mapasali, mapatakas, mapaupô
mapag-	mapágnais, mapágkalingà, mápagkilala
mapagpa-	mapagpabayâ, mapagpakunwarî
mapaN-	mapanirà, mápamaskó, mapanágutan
mapapag-	mapapág-ayos, mapapág-usapan, mapapág-araro
may-	maylupà, maybahay, may-mana, may-nais
na-	nasawî, násuso, naibá, náhamon
naka-	nakábuwaya, nakábalità, nakatayâ
nakaka-	nakakabingí, nakakabisita, nakaka
nakapag-	nakapag-áalaalá, nakapagtagò
nakapagpa(pa)-	nakapagpápainit, nakapagpápatulog
nakapaN-	nakapang-aral, nakapangúngusap
naki-	nakitulad, nakilinyá, nakihamok
nakipag-	nakipág-away, nakipágbálitaán, nakipágkamáy
nakipagsa-	nakipagsápalarán
nag-	nagmulto, nagkantá, naglarô, nagsimbá
nagiN- (from *maging* 'become')	nagimbatà, nagimpalikero, nagingkarpintero
nagpa-	nagpaalís, nagpaani, nagpaahit

nagpaka-	nagpakasirà, nagpakasipag, nagpakapagod
nagsa-	nagsaparì, nagsapagóng
nai-	natítindíg, naisabáy, naiwasan
naipa-	náipakain, naipabutas, naipabukas
naipag-	naipagbigáy-alám, naipaglihim, naipagdalá
naipaN-	naipanulat, naipangakò
nang-	nangahoy, nanggaling, nangaral
napa-	napakita, napabuti, napaabót
napaka-	nápakamura, napakaitím, napakalapit
ni- (infix -in- before [l])	nilutò, nilagà, nilinaw, nilikhâ
pa-	pagawaín, pabalát, paayos, pababâ, patulong
paka-	pakabiglâ, pakababaan, pakabusugín
paki-	pakiabót, pakialám, pakibasa, pakikuha
pakiki-	pakikidamay, pakikibasa, pakikikain
pakikipag-	pakikipagbalak, pakikipagbabuyan
pag-	pag-andár, pagmana, paglalampín,
pagka-	pagkabilád, pagkaburá, pagkalayô
pagkaka-	pagkakasirâ, pagkakásamâ, pagkakápatáy
pagpa-	pagpasubalian, pagparito, pagpasiyahán
pagpapa-	pagpapalayag, pagpapalapit, pagpapasuót
pagpapaka-	pagpapakadami, [illegible]
pala-	palasumpaan, palásuwáy, palátulóng
paN-	pambansâ, pandarayà, pandagat, pang-alís
papag-	papágbuhatin, papág-isipin, papáglalaín
papagka-	papagkagalitín, papagkagastusín
papaN-	papangusinaan, papanganakín
pina-	pinalipat, pinalambót, pinahintô
puma-	pumarito, pumagitnâ, pumalagì
saN-	sandaígdigan, sambúwanan, sangkabán
siN-	simpobre, sintaás, singgandá
tag-	tag-ulán, taggutom, tag-ampalayá
taga-	tagabanyagà, tagabayad, taga-Manila
tagapag-	tagapággatas, tagapágkulay, tagapágsará
tala-	taláarawan, talátinigan
tig-	tig-apat, tig-isa, tiglimá

Reduplication (Reduplicated segment is italicized)

CV	*ta*takbó, *sa*sayáw, *i*iwan, nag-*a*aral, mag*sa*saká
CVCV (non-full)	*hiwa*-hiwalay, pa*singa*-Singapore, *bali*-baliktád
Full	ma*lakí*-lakí, *bahay*-bahayan, *oras*-oras, mag*sama*-sama

The enclitic *-ng*

The linker (ligature) *na* has an enclitic variant *-ng* after vowels (including glottal vowels) and the consonant [*n*]. Students of Tagalog will have to know when a word ends in a velar nasal if the *-ng* is part of the root or not.

i.e.	*murang bahay = bahay na murà*	'cheap house'
	masayáng batà = batang masayá	'happy child'
	pandák na pinsán = pinsáng pandák	'short cousin'

ABBREVIATIONS

adj.	adjective
adv.	adverb
alt.	alternate form
AmSp.	American Spanish
art.	grammatical article
Aus.	Australian English
aux.	auxiliary
C	consonant
Ch.	Chinese
coll.	colloquial
conj.	conjunction
dem.	demonstrative
Eng.	English
expr.	expression
f.	from
fig.	figurative
gram.	grammatical/linguistic term
id.	idiom
interrog.	interrogative
Ilk.	Ilocano
Jap.	Japanese
lig.	ligature/grammatical linker
lit.	literary; literally
n.	noun
N	nasal
obs.	obsolete
Pam.	Kapampangan
part.	particle
Pil.	Pilipino (widely shared)
pl.	plural
pref.	prefix
prep.	preposition
pron.	pronoun
PSp.	Philippine Spanish
refl.	reflexive
reg.	regional
rt.	root
sp.	species
Sp.	Spanish (Spanish spellings are given for words only if they differ from the Tagalog)
v.	verb
V	vowel
var.	variant
Vis.	Visayan
vulg.	vulgar

INTRODUCTION TO TAGALOG GRAMMAR

Tagalog, the basis of the national language of the Philippines since 1939, is an Austronesian language of the Philippine type spoken natively by about fifteen million speakers. It is also used and understood by about 70 percent of the Philippine population as the official language of the country, propagated considerably by its use in the media and increased function in education.

The original homeland of the Tagalog people encompasses the mid southern regions of the island of Luzon, around the capital city of Manila, but Tagalog people have migrated also to the islands of Mindoro, Mindanao, and Palawan and have sizable communities in most urban centers of the developed world.

This grammar outline is meant to serve as an introductory reference to facilitate the use of this dictionary. For more extensive coverage of the topics discussed herein, or for more information on topics excluded from this outline, please refer to the Tagalog grammars listed in the Reference section.

1. Phonology and Pronunciation

1.1 The Consonants

Tagalog has the following contrastive consonant sounds (shown in the table by their orthographic symbols). Stops in Tagalog are unaspirated, and unreleased in final position. The voiceless velar stop (k) often slightly fricates before vowels. The alveolar trill (r) has various pronunciations from a simple flap to a trill, closely resembling its Spanish counterpart. The orthographic sequences /ts/ and /dy/ represent the English sounds [ch] and [j], respectively. In the table below, Alibata (native syllabary) equivalents are given after each phoneme.

	Voicing	Bilabial	Dental/ Alveolar	Alveo-palatal	Velar	Glottal
Stops	- +	p b	t d	(ts, t(i)y) [tʃ] (dy) [dʒ]	k g	,' (-) [ʔ]
Fricatives	-		s			h
Nasals	+	m	n	(ny)	ng [ŋ]	
Laterals	+		l			
Trill/Flap	+		(r)			
Glides	+	w	y			

1.1.1 Consonant Morphophonemics

Glottal stop. The glottal stop [ʔ] is not represented in modern orthography, other than word-medially following a consonant with a hyphen (-) → *pag-asa* 'hope' [*pag.'á:.sa*], *mag-amóy* 'to smell' [*mag.'a.móy*]. Vowel-initial words are pronounced with an initial glottal stop → *aso* 'dog' [*'á:.so*]. Glottal stops may also occur word finally (in conversation, phrase-finally). This dictionary follows the orthography of the *balarilà* (Tagalog official grammar) in which a final glottal stop is represented two ways: 1. with words with final stress, with a circumflex accent (^) → *mukhâ* 'face' [*muk.há'*], *sirâ* 'broken; bad' [*si.rá'*], and 2. with words with penultimate stress, with a grave accent → *silò* 'noose' [*sí:.lo'*], *bahalà* 'responsibility' [*ba.há:.la'*].

Word final h. Tagalog words are not written with the glottal fricative [*h*] word finally. An *h* does appear, however, when the suffixes *-in* or *-an* are attached to a root ending in a vowel (non-glottal stop). Notice the *h* insertion with the following suffixed roots:

Root	Root with suffix *-in* or *-an*
linis 'clean'	*linisin* 'to clean'
sama 'accompany'	*samahan* 'to accompany'
guló 'confusion'	*guluhín* 'to confuse'
tagò 'hide' [*tá:.go'*]	*taguán* 'hide and seek'
mukhâ 'face' [*muk.há'*]	*mukhaán* 'recognize by the face'

D and R. The consonants [d] and [r] often appear in native words as variants of the same underlying consonant. The consonant [d] may become [r] in vowel medial environments → *daratíng* 'will come' comes from *da-dating*, *makiramay* 'to sympathize' comes from *maki-damay*, *karapatán* 'right' comes from *ka-dapat-an*, *hubarán* 'to undress someone' comes from *hubád-an*.

Palatalization. The dental obstruents [t], [d], and [s] palatalize to [ch], [j], and [sh], respectively, before a palatal glide [y] or its orthographic equivalent [the unstressed vowel *i* followed by the glide y] → *tiyán* 'stomach' [*chan*], *siyá* 's/he' [*sha*], *dyús* 'juice' [*jus*], *diyós* 'god' [*jos*], *diyeta* 'diet' [*jé:.ta*], *diyán* 'there' [*jan*]. They do not palatalize before a stressed vowel [*i*] → *tíya* 'aunt' [*tí:.ya*].

Nasal assimilation. The velar nasal [ng or (N)] in the prefixes *kasing-* (*kasiN-*), *mang-* (*maN-*), *nang-* (*naN-*) and *pang-* (*paN-*) assimilates to the place of articulation of the first consonant of the root to which they attach. Before the labial consonants *m*, *p*, and *b*, the nasal is labial [m] and before the dental consonants *t*, *d*, *l*, and *s*, the nasal is dental [n], with the velar consonants, before vowels (underlying glottal stop), and in all other environments, i.e. before velar or glottal stops, and glides, the nasal is velar [ng].

pang- + *sindí*	*panindí*	lighter
mang- + *buhay*	*mamuhay*	to live; manage
mang- + *pilì*	*mamilì*	to choose
mang- + *palò*	*mamalò*	to beat; spank
pang- + *talì*	*panalì*	string
pang- + *kontra*	*pangontra*	proof; preventative
mang- + *'aso*	*mangaso*	to hunt with dogs

Metathesis. The infix *-in-* metathesizes to *ni-* before the lateral [l] → *niluto* = */l{in}uto/*, *nilabaán* = */l{in}aba-an/*. Metathesis also occurs with certain roots, e.g. in the root *taním* 'plant,' the [n] and [m] metathesize before the suffix *-(h)an* → *tamnán* 'to plant.'

N insertion. In a few lexicalized cases, the nasal [n] may appear at the end of a few vowel-final roots before the suffixes *-(h)in* or *-(h)an*, sometimes accompanied by vowel loss → *kasarinlán* 'independence, individuality' = *ka-sarili-(h)an*, *sarilinin* 'to monopolize, appropriate' = *sarili* + *-(h)in*, *kunin* 'to get' = *kuha* + *-(h)in*, *halinhán* 'to replace; relieve' = *halili* + *-(h)an*, and *pagtawanin* 'to amuse' = *pag-tawa* + *-(h)in*.

1.2 Vowels and Stress

Tagalog has five vowels in the native orthography. They are often compared phonetically to the vowels of Spanish or Italian, /a/ a low, central vowel, /e/ a front mid vowel, /i/ a high front vowel, /o/ a mid back vowel, and /u/ a high back vowel. Before the arrival of the Spanish and Spanish loanwords, Tagalog was essentially a three-vowel language, [i] and [e], as [o] and [u] were alternative pronunciations of the same phoneme (contrastive vowel). The high variants /i/ and /u/ occurred in all places except word finally, where they dropped considerably to /e or lax i/ and /o/ respectively. As a language with a borrowed orthographic system, this phenomenon is represented in the orthography. This can be seen with the following derivations of the root *guló* 'confusion; commotion; trouble' → *gumuló* 'to trouble, molest' /*g{um}uló*/, *guluhín* 'to trouble, molest something' /*gulo-(h)ín*/.

Two adjacent vowels will each comprise their own syllable. A glottal stop is usually inserted in careful speech between the vowels to separate the syllables, careful speech will reveal that there are no vowel-initial syllables in the language → *saán* 'where' [*sa.'án*], *buô* 'whole' [*bu.'ó'*], *maamò* 'tame' [*ma.'á:.mo'*].

Stress. Stress (syllable prominence) is contrastive in Tagalog → *bagà* 'lung' [*bá:.ga'*] ≠ *bagâ* [*ba.gá'*] 'tumor,' *gábi* 'taro' [*gá:.bi*] ≠ *gabí* 'night' [*ga.bí*]. Words in this dictionary will bear an accent mark on the final vowel for words with final stress. Words without an accent mark bear stress on the penultimate syllable. Words ending in a glottal stop show stress by the circumflex accent (â) for final stress and grave accent (*à*) for penultimate stress. When stress falls on an open syllable (syllable not closed with a consonant), the stressed vowel is lengthened (v:) → *kalakal* 'merchandise' [*ka.lá:.kal*], *halaman* 'plant' [*ha.lá:.man*].

In addition to final and penultimate stress, Tagalog has what is called antepenultimate accompanying stress. Words with this stress type bear stress on the final or penultimate syllable, but also have an additional prominent syllable (marked by pitch prominence or vowel length). Note that in this dictionary, words with penultimate stress are not marked → *íisá* 'only one,' *áanim* 'only six,' *úpuan* 'seat,' *táhanan* 'home,' *kútuhin* 'one affected with lice,' *máunawaan* 'to understand,' *mápaluhód* 'fall on one's knees.' The following minimal pairs will acquaint the reader with the various stress patterns in Tagalog:

kaibigan [*ka.'i.bí:.gan*]	'friend' (penultimate)
kaibigán [*ka.'i.bi.gán*]	'desire; preference' (final)
kaibigán [*ká:.'i.bi.gán*]	'mutual consent' (final + antepenultimate)
kaíbigan [*ka.'í:.bí:.gan*]	'sweetheart' (penultimate + antepenultimate)
baga [*bá:.ga*]	'glowing ember' (penultimate)
bagá [*ba.gá*]	'interrogative particle' (final)
bagà [*bá:.ga'*]	'lung' (penultimate glottal)
bagâ [*ba.gá'*]	'breast tumor' (final glottal)

Stress shift. Stress may shift due to grammatical factors or with the addition of a suffix *-(h)an*, or *-(h)in* → *súkat* 'measure, root' [*sú:.kat*] vs. *sukát* 'measured, adjective' [*su.kát*]; *tagpî* 'patch, noun' [*tag.pí'*] vs. *tagpián* 'to patch, verb' [*tag.pi.'án*], *kuyóm* 'clenched, adjective' [*ku.yóm*] vs. *kuyumín* 'to clench, verb' [*ku.yu.mín*].

Vowel loss. With the addition of the suffixes *-(h)in* and *-(h)an*, final root vowels are lost in a few common cases, i.e. *dalá* + *-(h)an* = *dalhán* 'to carry,' *sakáy* + *-(h)an* = *sakyán* 'to ride,' *tirá* + *-(h)an* = *tirhán* 'to spare,' *tingín* + *-(h)an* = *tingnán* 'to look at, examine,' *bigáy* + *-(h)an* = *bigyán* 'to give,' *gawâ* + *-(h)in* = *gawín* 'to do,' *bilí* + *-(h)in* = *bilhín* 'to buy,' *kain* + *-(h)in* = *kanin* 'to eat,' *tikím* + *-(h)an* = *tikmán* 'to taste,' *bukás* + *-(h)an* = *buksán* 'to open.'

Syllabification. Syllabification in Tagalog is relatively simple. For native words, the basic syllable shape is CV(C). Syllables consist minimally of a vowel and consonantal onset (consonant before the vowel), two vowels cannot share a syllable. In orthographic vowel-initial syllables, a glottal stop (') is pronounced to provide the syllable with an onset. Consonant clusters are broken between syllables, but remember that the velar nasal [ng] is one consonantal segment that cannot be broken. → *aandáp-andáp* 'flickering' [*'a.'an.dáp.'an.dáp*], *dagildilín* 'shove with the elbow' [*da.gil.di.lín*], *maglambingan* 'to caress each other' [*mag.lam.bí:.ngan*], *naráraanan* 'passable' [*ná.rá:.ra.'á:.nan*], *makapág-aral* 'be able to study' [*ma.ka.pág.'á:.ral*].

Reduplication. Reduplication (repetition of a word or word segment) is a common morphological device in Tagalog. Tagalog has both full reduplication (reduplication of the entire root word) and partial reduplication. Words with full reduplication include *mahiyá-hiyâ* 'to be a little ashamed' from *hiyâ* 'shame,' *bahíd-bahíd* 'full of stains' from *bahid* 'stain, smear,' *baháy-baháy* 'from house to house' from *bahay* 'house,' *bahay-bahayan* 'toy house,' from *bahay* 'house,' *hati-hatì* 'divided into equal parts,' from *hatì* 'divide,' and *araw-araw* 'every day' from *araw* 'day.'

Words with partial reduplication only reduplicate the first segment of the stem. There are no reduplicative suffixes in the language. Initial CV (consonant vowel) reduplication is the most common, but there is also disyllabic reduplication (CVCV). Examples of CV reduplication include → *iitlóg* 'will lay an egg' [*'i.'it.lóg*] from *itlóg* 'egg,' *kakantá* 'will sing' from *kantá* 'sing,' *nagbibigáy* 'is giving' from *bigáy* 'give,' and *pagbabago* 'change' from *bago* 'new.' Examples of disyllabic partial reduplication (CVCV) include → *pa-Singa-Singapore* 'keep going to Singapore,' *magkahiwa-hiwaláy* 'to get thoroughly separated,' and *magpakatahi-tahimik* 'try to be very quiet.'

2. Overview of Tagalog Grammar

2.1 Syntactic Overview

The predicate. Tagalog, like all its sister Philippine languages, is a predicate-initial language. The initial position is reserved for the predicate → *Kumakain silá*. They are eating; *Malungkót silá*. They are sad.

Predicates may consist of a verb phrase, noun phrase, prepositional phrase, or adjective phrase. Tagalog does not have a copula verb ("to be") → *Nasa bahay si Beng*. Beng is at home; *Siruhano ang kapatíd ko*. My brother is a surgeon; *Dalawa ang kamáy ko*. I have two hands (my hands are two); *Mayaman akó*. I am rich.

Predicate inversion. In certain cases, the topic noun (subject of the predicate) may precede the predicate in which the inverse particle *ay* ('y after vowels) identifies the non-initial predicate. *Si Beng* ***ay*** *nasa bahay; Ang kapatíd ko***'y** *siruhano; Ang kamáy ko***'y** *dalawá; Akó***'y** *mayaman.*

Identificational predicates. When noun phrases are used as predicates, they are identificational (serve to identify or contrast referents). Note the differences between the following sentences (predicates are underlined).

Magandá siyá.
'She is beautiful.' Simple declarative sentence; Predicate is *magandá* 'beautiful.'

Siyá ang magandá.
'She is the one who is beautiful, The one who is beautiful is she (as opposed to them).' Identificational or contrastive sentence where *siyá* 'she' is the predicate.

The linker *na/-ng*. Tagalog, like all Philippine languages has a linker which serves various purposes in the syntax of the language. The linker has two phonologically conditioned variants, *na* after consonants and *-ng* after vowels, *n*, or a final glottal stop [ʔ]. The linker is used to connect adjectives and nouns → *murang bahay (bahay na murà)* 'cheap house,' *masayáng buhay (buhay na masayá)* 'happy life.' It is also used in relative clauses and to introduce some subordinate clauses, i.e. complement clauses → *Mayaman ang lalaking nakita niyá.* 'The man *that* she saw is rich'; *Gusto kong sumayáw.* 'I want to dance.' *Alam ni Bong na malayò.* 'Bong knows that it is far.'

Negation. Tagalog sentences are negated simply by placing the negative adverb *hindî* 'no' before the negated predicate → *Mayabang ang gurò natin.* 'Our teacher is boastful,' *Hindî mayabang ang gurò natin.* 'Our teacher is not boastful,' *Kumakain ang mga batà.* 'The children are eating,' *Hindî kumakain ang mga batà.* 'The children are not eating.' Commands are negated with *huwág* (see COMMANDS below). The verb *gustó* 'like' is negated with *ayaw* 'like.' *Alám* 'know' may be negated with *hindí alám* 'not know' or *aywán* 'not know.' *Hindí ko alám* 'I don't know.' *Aywan ko.* 'I don't know.'

With second position enclitic pronouns, the pronouns immediately follow *hindî* (in second position) → *Hayop ka.* 'You are an animal,' *Hindî ka hayop.* 'You are not an animal,' *Matalino silá.* 'They are intelligent' *Hindî silá matalino.* 'They are not intelligent.'

Questions. There are two types of questions in Tagalog, information questions and polar (yes/no) questions. Yes/no questions are formed either simply by imposing question intonation on a simple declarative phrase, or with the insertion of the second position interrogative enclitic *ba* → *Pilipino ang sundalo.* 'The soldier is Filipino.' *Pilipino ba ang sundalo?* Is the soldier Filipino?

Information questions consist of an interrogative adverb in predicate (initial) position. The common interrogative words in Tagalog are *anó* 'what,' *sino* 'who,' *paano* 'how,' *bakit* 'why,' *kailan* 'when,' *ilán* 'how many,' *magkano* 'how much does it cost,' *saán* 'where (action),' *nasaán* 'where (located),' *alín* 'which,' *taga-saán* 'where from,' *gaanó* 'how much, what quantity or amount,' *pang ilán* 'in which order (first, second, etc.).' *Sino, anó,* and *alín* have reduplicated plural forms, *sinu-sino, anú-anó,* and *alín-alín*, respectively.

Ano ang pangalan niyá?	What is her name?
Sino ang kasama mo?	Who is your companion?
Ilán ang kapatíd mo?	How many brothers do you have?
Saán ka pupuntá?	Where are you going?
Bakit umiiyák si Elena?	Why is Elena crying?
Taga-saán ang nanay mo?	Where is your mother from?
Kailán ang kasál?	When is the wedding?
Magkano ang niyóg?	How much are the coconuts?
Pang-ilán ka?	In which order are you?
Nasaán ang pera ko?	Where is my money?
Gaanó ka kataás?	How tall are you?

Commands. Positive imperatives (commands) are formed with the infinitive form of the verb, or bare root → *Tulog na* '(Go to) sleep', *Tumayô ka!* 'Stand up!' *Kunin mo ang pagkain.* 'Get the food.' *Kumain kayó*! 'Eat (you plural)!'

Negative commands are formed with *huwág* and the linker *na/-ng*, not *hindî* → *Huwág kang tumayô*. 'Don't stand up!,' *Huwág mong kunin ang pagkain.* 'Don't get the food,' *Huwág kayóng kumain.* 'Don't eat.'

Polite requests are formed with the prefix *paki-* and adverb *ngâ* 'please' → *Pakikuha mo ngâ ang pagkain.* 'Please get the food,' *Pakiabót mo ngâ ang asín.* 'Please pass the salt.'

Exclamatory Sentences. Adjectival predicates may be turned into exclamatory utterances in two ways, 1) with the article *ang*, and 2) with the oblique noun marker *kay*. These exclamatory sentences take arguments in the genitive case: *Magandá ang buhay ko.* 'My life is beautiful.' *Ang gandá ng buhay ko*! *Kay gandá ng buhay ko*! 'How beautiful my life is!' *Ang gutóm ko*! 'How hungry I am!'

2.2 Lexical Classes

2.2.1 Nouns

Nouns in Tagalog may be simple roots or morphologically complex (derived) lexemes (root with one or more affixes). Simple nouns include *buhay* 'life,' *araw* 'sun,' *aklát* 'book,' and *isip* 'mind,' while complex nouns are morphologically derived with affixes → *kabuhayan* 'livelihood' */ka-buhay-an/*, *talaarawán* 'diary' */tala-araw-án/*, *aklatan* 'library' */aklat-an/*, and *kaisipán* 'intellect; opinion' */ka-isip-an/*.

Derivational affixes for nouns. There are a number of affixes used to derive nouns. The suffix *-(h)an* may be used to express source or location → *aklatan* 'library, place of books,' *láruan* 'playground, where one plays,' *húkuman* 'courtroom, place of judgment,' *tindahan* 'store,' *gúpitan* 'barbershop.'

The prefixes *mag-* and *mang-* (*maN-*) with CV reduplication indicate occupation or the person responsible for performing the action expressed by the root → *mag-aalahás* 'jeweler, dealer in jewels,' *maglalabá* 'clothes washer,' *magsasaká* 'farmer,' *magbibibingká* 'rice cake vendor, rice cake maker,' *magbibigas* 'rice dealer,' *manghahabi* 'weaver,' *manggagawà* 'laborer,' *manggagaod* 'oarsman, rower,' *manggagaway* 'witch, one who practices witchcraft,' *manggagamot* 'doctor, one who practices medicine.' *Mag-* without CV reduplication is also used to express a reciprocal relationship → *mag-asawa* 'husband and wife,' *mag-iná* 'mother and child,' *magpanginoón* 'master and servant,' *magtiyá* 'aunt and niece/nephew.'

The affix combination *ka- -an* is used to derive abstract nouns or locative nouns → *kasamaán* 'evilness,' *kabáitan* 'virtue,' *karapatán* 'right, privilege,' *kapootán* 'hatred,' *katámaran* 'laziness,' *kagubatan* 'forest region,' *kabundukan* 'mountain region,' *katagalugan* 'region where Tagalogs predominate,' *kabahayan* 'residential area, place with many houses.'

The prefix *tag-* is used to indicate a season or period of time → *taglamíg, taggináw* 'cold season, winter,' *taggutom* 'famine, period of starvation,' *tag-ulán* 'rainy season,' *taghálalan* 'election time,' *taglagás* 'autumn, fall,' *tagkamatis* 'period in which tomatoes are in season,' *tagkampanya* 'campaigning time,' *tag-unós* 'typhoon season.'

The prefix *pa-* is used to form causative nouns or nouns of utility → *patabâ* 'fertilizer,' *pahatíd* 'message, something delivered,' *palipas-uhaw* 'thirst quencher,' *pahila* 'load to be pulled,' *pabalato* 'money given to gambling losers by winner.'

The infix *-in-* (past form of *-(h)in*) forms nouns made by the process expressed by the root → *tinapá* 'smoked fish or meat,' *sinigáng* 'stew,' *sinaing* 'boiled rice,' *linagà* 'boiled dish,' *inihaw* 'something barbecued,' *inuyat* 'taffy made by boiling molasses,' *ginataán* 'cooked in coconut milk.'

The prefix *sang-* (*saN-*), from the cardinal number *isá* 'one' and the linker *-ng* form nouns that express oneness, wholeness, or completeness → *sangyutà* 'one hundred thousand,' *sampû* 'ten, one group of ten,' *sanlinggó* 'one week,' *sanlibután, sandaigdíg, santinakpán* 'the whole universe,' *sandiwà* 'one soul,' *sanduguán* 'alliance (one blood).' *Sangka- -an* indicates the whole expanse → *sangkatauhan* 'all humanity,' *sangkalangitán* 'all of heaven,' *sangkalupaán* 'the whole Earth,' *sangkapuluan* 'the whole archipelago,' *sangkakristiyanuhan* 'the entire Christendom.'

Pala- -(h)an is used to indicate the method, art, rules or basis of what is denoted by the root → *palábantasan* 'punctuation rules,' *palátandaan* 'indication, sign,' *palátauhan* 'anthropogenesis,' *paláisipan* 'riddle,' *palápantigan* 'rules of syllabification,' *palátinigan, palátunugan* 'phonetics,' *palátuldikan* 'accent rules,' *palátumbasan* 'rate of exchange.'

The affix combination *tala- -(h)an* comes from *talâ* 'note, record, list' and is used to indicate lists → *taláaklatan* 'book list,' *taláarawan* 'diary, journal; calendar (list of days),' *taláhuluganan, talatinigan* 'dictionary, vocabulary,' *taláawitan* 'songbook.'

Finally, a few nouns have been recently converted into prefixes to coin new terms. From the noun *aghám* 'science,' originate the prefixes *ag-* and *aghám-*: *agbuhay, aghámbuhay* 'biology,' *aglipunan, aghám-lipunan* 'social science,' *agtao, aghámtao* 'anthropology.' The prefix *dalub-* from *dalubhasà* 'expert' is used for professions: *dalubwikà* 'linguist,' *dalub-aghamtao* 'anthropologist.'

For more nominal derivation patterns and the prefix *pag-*, see **Nominalization**.

Gender. Native nouns do not express gender. However, there are a few words borrowed from Spanish or recently coined in which masculine forms end a consonant, *-o* (Spanish) or *-oy* (Tagalog), and feminine forms end in *-a* (Spanish) *-ay* (Tagalog). Nouns with no gender include *asawa* 'husband, wife,' *kapatíd* 'brother, sister,' *kambíng* 'goat.' Some animate nouns have inherent gender → *kuya* 'older brother' vs. *ate* 'older sister,' *nanay* 'mother' vs. *tatay* 'father.' Nouns that express gender morphologically include *Doktór / doktora* 'doctor / female doctor,' *Pilipino / Pilipina* 'Filipino man / woman,' *alahero / alahera* 'male jeweler / female jeweler,' *bungagero / bungangera* 'male / female braggart,' and *Pinóy / Pináy* 'Filipino man / woman.'

Pluralization. Nouns may be pluralized with the particle *mga* (pronounced *mangá*) placed immediately before the noun → *pusò* 'heart,' *mga pusò* 'hearts,' *Silá ang mga kapatíd ko*. 'They are my brothers.' The particle *mga* is normally not used with numbers; plural reference is understood by the number → *tatlong araw* 'three days,' *apat na babae* 'four girls.'

Nominalization. In all Philippine languages, verbs may be used as nouns simply by putting them in a nominal position (in topic position or after a noun marker) → *sumayáw* 'danced, verb,' *ang sumayáw* 'the one who danced,' *Si Milette ang sumayáw*. 'Milette is the one who danced.'

There are also certain affixes responsible for nominalizing actor focus verbs (see Sec. 2.2.7), as shown in the following table.

Verb affix	Nominalization Affix	Example
mag-	pagCV-	pag-sa-salitâ
-um-	pag-	pag-ibig
ma-	pagka(CV)-	pagka-(tu)-tulog
maN-	paNCV-	pang-ku-kulam
maki-	pakiki-	pakiki-sama
magpa-	pagpapa-	pagpapa-sulát
magsi-	pagsisi-	pagsisi-tulong

i.e. *pag-asa* 'hope,' *paglipat* 'act of transferring,' *pagliwanang* 'act of explaining,' *pagkauháw* 'state of being thirsty,' *pagkagamót* 'manner of treatment,' *pagkaulól* 'insanity,' *panganganib* 'exposure to danger,' *pangangakò* 'act of promising,' *pangguguIay* 'act of gathering vegetables,' *pakikidalamhatì* 'condolence, sharing of sympathy,' *pakikikamáy* 'act of shaking hands,' *pakikiaway* 'act of quarreling,' *pagpapahatíd* 'act of sending to someone,' *pagpapahayag* 'proclamation, act of expressing one's views,' *pagpapahingá* 'act of resting,' *pagsisiwalat* 'act of revealing a secret,' *pagsisitulong* 'mutual help, cooperation.'

2.2.3 Noun markers

Tagalog has a class of non-deriving words that mark nouns. These may be called articles, determiners, or simply, noun markers. Noun markers come immediately before the nouns they qualify. Like pronouns, they inflect for case, but the cases are somewhat different in the noun markers and pronouns. Noun markers come in three cases: topic, non-topic, and oblique. The topic category is the same in noun markers and pronouns. The non-topic markers precede possessors, objects of actor focus verbs, and actors of goal focus verbs (see verbs), and the oblique markers mark everything else, functioning similarly to prepositions in English.

Noun markers may be common or personal. Common noun markers precede inanimate nouns or generic animate nouns. Personal articles precede names, terms of address, and animate nouns which the speaker and addressee can readily identify with (known kinterms). The noun marker *ng* is pronounced [*nang*].

	Topic	Non-topic	Oblique
Common (sg) (pl)	 ang ang mga	 ng [nang] ng mga	 sa sa mga
Personal (sg) (pl)	 si siná	 ni niná	 kay kiná

Magandá ang nanay ko.	My mother is beautiful.
Mayaman si Tatay.	Father is rich.
Ito ang palda ni Maria.	This is Maria's skirt.
Sumasayáw ang mga batà.	The children are dancing.
Kinain ko ang saging.	I ate the banana.
Kumain ako ng saging.	I ate bananas.
Matalino sina Kiki at Lulu.	Kiki and Lulu are intelligent.
Nasaan ang bahay nina Jun?	Where is Jun & company's house?

Locative markers. Location may be expressed in Tagalog with the marker *nasa*, for common nouns, and *na kay, na kiná* for personal nouns → *nasa bahay* 'at home,' *nasa Amerika* 'in America,' *nasa inyó* 'with you, in your possession,' *na kay Gracia* 'with Grace, in Grace's possession.'

2.2.4 Pronouns

Tagalog pronouns do not encode the same personal concepts as English ones. Gender, for instance, is not encoded in the pronouns, and there are two ways to encode the first person plural (we).

Politeness is shown in the second person with three degrees of respect.

The Tagalog topic pronouns are: *akó* 'I,' *ikáw* (*independent*) or *=ka* (*suffixal*) 'you, familiar,' *siyá* 's/he,' *kamí* 'we, not including you (*exclusive*),' *tayo* 'we, including you (*inclusive*),' *kayó* 'you (plural or polite),' and *silá* 'they; you (very polite).' The topic pronouns are enclitics, usually occurring in the second position of their clause.

Ikáw ang Amerikano.	'You are the one who is American'
Bahalà ka.	'It's up to you.'
Amerikano akó.	'I am American'
Hindî akó Amerikano.	'I am not American'

Like the noun markers, Tagalog pronouns inflect for case. Topic pronouns correspond to the topic (basic complement) of the predicate, genitive pronouns correspond to possessors or actors of goal focus verbs, and oblique pronouns correspond to nouns that are not verbal arguments, often translated in English by prepositional phrases.

Pronoun	Topic	Genitive	Oblique
I	akó	=ko	sa akin
you (fam.)	ikáw, =ka	=mo	sa iyo
s/he	siyá	niyá	sa kaniyá
we (excl.)	kamí	namin	sa amin
we (incl.)	tayo	natin	sa atin
you (pl, pol.)	kayó	ninyó	sa inyó
they	silá	nilá	sa kanilá

Gusto ko silá.	I like them.
Ipakita mo ang ibon sa akin.	Show the bird to me.
Mahal ka namin.	We love you.
Ninakaw ng batà ang kendi.	The child stole the candy.
Nagnakaw ang batà ng kendi.	The child stole some candy.
Nasaán ang bahay ninyó?	Where is your house?
Magandá ang kapatíd nilá.	Their sibling is beautiful.

The monosyllabic pronouns *ko, mo,* and *ka* behave like suffixes. They must always follow a constituent and cannot stand alone like the independent pronouns. The independent second person pronoun is *ikáw*. The suffixal behavior of these three pronouns is shown below as they interact with the adverbial clitic *na* 'already.' *Na* cannot separate a monosyllabic pronoun from its host.

Kumain na akó.	I already ate.
Kumain =ka na.	You already ate.
Kinain na natin.	We already ate it.
Kinain =mo na.	You already ate it.
Nakita =ko na.	I already saw it.
Nakita na nilá.	They already saw it.

The portmanteau pronoun *kitá* replaces *ko + ka*, which is ungrammatical. *Mahal kita.* 'I love you (you are my love),' *Gurò kita.* 'You are my teacher,' *Hindí kitá nakíta.* 'I didn't see you.'

Deictic pronouns. Tagalog separates space into three domains, the proximate (close to the speaker), the medial (close to the addressee, or not too far from either), and the distal (far from the speech event). To express location, Tagalog has *dito* 'here,' *diyán* 'there (medial),' and *doón* 'there (distal).'

The deictic pronouns inflect for four cases, simple locative (here, there), *nasa* locative (is here, is there), topic (this, that), and genitive (of this, of that) as shown in the following table.

	Locative here, there	*nasa* Locative is here, is there	Topic this, that	Genitive of this, of that
Proximate	dito	nandito, ná(ri)ritó	itó	nitó
Medial	diyán	nandiyán, nari(ri)yán	iyán	niyán
Distal	doón	nandoón, ná(ro)roón	iyón	noón

Nandito ang opisina ko.	My office is here.
Sino ang nanay nitó?	Who is the mother of this (child)?
Gusto ko itó.	I like this.
Mayaman ang mga tao dito.	The people are rich here.
Diyán ka lang.	Goodbye (stay there).

2.2.5 Adjectives

Tagalog adjectives may be simple or complex. Simple (monomorphemic) adjectives include *murà* 'cheap,' *ulól* 'crazy,' *pangit* 'ugly,' *kalbó* 'bald,' *bago* 'new,' *payát* 'slender,' and *lasíng* 'drunk.'

Derived adjectives. Derived adjectives are those that consist of a root with affixation. They may have a number of forms. Many adjectives are formed by shifting the root stress to the final syllable → *gútom* 'hunger' vs. *gutóm* 'hungry,' *habà* 'length' vs. *habâ* 'long,' and *sirà* 'break' vs. *sirâ* 'broken.'

A large number of adjectives are formed with the prefix *ma-* → *malakás* 'strong,' *matalino* 'intelligent,' *mahinà* 'weak,' *mataás* 'high,' *mabuti* 'good,' *masamâ* 'bad,' *mabahò* 'foul smelling,' *mabangó* 'fragrant,' *masayá* 'happy,' *malungkót* 'sad,' *maluwáng* 'wide,' *matigás* 'hard,' *malutóng* 'brittle,' and *magandá* 'beautiful.'

The prefix *maka-* may be used to indicate support for the referent expressed by the root, or non-active causation → *maka-Hapón* 'pro-Japan,' *makatao* 'humanitarian,' *makahapis* 'causing grief,' *maka-mantsa* 'staining, able to cause a stain,' *makainggít* 'causing envy,' *makatakot* 'frightful, causing fear.'

The prefixes *mapag-* and *pala-* form adjectives of a habitual (frequent) nature → *mapágsalitâ* 'talkative, always talking,' *mapágsuhól* 'inclined to giving bribes,' *mapágpagód* 'always tired,' *mapáglasíng* 'habitually drunk,' *mapágmatigás* 'stubborn,' *mapágkunwarî* 'always pretending,' *paláutang* 'frequently borrowing money,' *paláutós* 'always commanding,' *palátutól* 'in the habit of objecting or opposing,' *palátulóg* 'always sleeping.'

The prefix *pang-* (*paN-*) forms adjectives (and nouns) denoting instrument, use, or intention → *panggabí* 'for nighttime use,' *pansulat* 'for writing,' *panlahát* 'universal; for everyone,' *pang-adorno* 'for decorative use,' *pang-aghám* 'scientific, having to do with science.'

The prefix *tagá-* indicates origin → *tagá-Amerika* 'from America,' *tagá-Hapón* 'from Japan,' *tagabundók* 'from the mountains,' *tagailog* 'from the river.'

Some adjectives end in the borrowed Spanish suffix *-ado* → *nibelado* 'leveled,' *aminado* 'admitted,' *kalmado* 'calmed,' *deklarado* 'declared,' *pirmado* 'signed,' *parado* 'stopped,' *sarado* 'closed,' and *muskulado* 'muscular.'

Comparatives and Superlatives. Comparative adjectives are formed with the borrowed Spanish adverb *mas* placed immediately before the adjective. Superlative adjectives are formed with the prefix *pinaka-* → *mabuti* 'good,' *mas mabuti* 'better,' *pinakamabuti* 'best;' *matandá* 'old,' *mas matandá* 'older,' *pinakamatandá* 'oldest.'

Mas matalino siyá kay Jhun.	'She is smarter than Jhun.'
Si Juana ang pinakamagandáng katulong.	'Juana is the most beautiful maid.'

Intensification. Adjectives may be intensified with the prefix *napaka-* → *masayá* 'happy,' *napakasayá* 'very happy, quite happy,' *magandá* 'beautiful,' *napakagandá* 'very beautiful.' They may also be intensified by full reduplication after the article *ang* → *ang sayá-sayá* 'very happy, how happy!' In both cases if there is a subject noun, it occurs in the genitive case.

Napakapangit ng kapatíd mo.	'Your sibling is very ugly.'
Ang saya-saya namin.	'How happy we are!'

Adjective repetition (separated by the linker *na/-ng*) also indicates an intense degree → *pagód na pagód* 'very tired,' *murang-murà* 'very cheap,' *tamád na tamád* 'very lazy,' as does reduplication of the first two syllables → *butas-butas* 'full of holes,' *bali-baliktád* 'topsy turvy,' *basag-basag* 'broken to pieces,' *hiwa-hiwaláy* 'scattered everywhere.'

Equalitives. The prefix *kasing-* is used to express equality. *Kasingtamád ni Jorge si Diana.* 'Diana is as lazy as Jorge,' *Kasinggandá akó ng mga putî.* 'I am as beautiful as the fair complexioned ones.' The prefix *magkasing-* is used to express the same concept in verbs → *Magkasingtalino silá.* 'They are equally smart.'

Similarity. The word *gaya* 'like, as' is used to express phrases of similarity. *Gaya* (or *kagaya*) is used with *ng* phrases or genitive pronouns → *Gaya ng damít ko ang damít mo*. 'My clothes are like your clothes,' *Kagaya ko silá*. 'I am like them.'

Gaya contracts with the deictic pronouns *itó, iyán,* and *iyón* to form *ganitó* 'like this,' *ganyán* 'like that (medial),' *ganoón* 'like that (distal).'

Ganyán ang mga Pinóy.	'Filipinos are like that.'
Ah, ganoón ba?	'Oh, is that the way it goes?'

Like *gaya*, *parang* and *(ka)tulad* may also express phrases of similarity.

Walá kang katulad.	'No one is like you.'
Parang ako silá.	'They are like me.'
Katulad ka ng ate ko.	'My older sister is like you.'

2.2.6 Numbers

Speakers of Tagalog use two number systems: a native one for simple counting, and a borrowed Spanish system used for telling time, dates, calculations, monetary transactions, and advanced counting:

	Tagalog	Spanish		Tagalog	Spanish
1	isá	uno	20	dalawampû	beinte
2	dalawá	dos	21	dalawampú't isá	beintiuno
3	tatló	tres	30	tatlumpû	treinta
4	apat	kuwatro	40	ápatnapû	kuwarenta
5	limá	singko	50	limampû	singkuwenta
6	anim	seis, sais	60	animnapû	sesenta
7	pitó	siyete	70	pitúmpû	setenta
8	waló	otso	80	walúmpû	otsenta
9	siyám	nuwebe	90	siyámnapû	nobenta
10	sampû	diyes	100	sandaán	siyento
11	labíng-isá	onse	101	sandaá't isá	siyentouno
12	labíndalawá	dose	110	sandaá't sampû	siyento diyes
13	labíntatló	trese	200	dalawandaán	dosiyentos
14	labíng-apat	katorse	300	tatlón daán	tresiyentos
15	labínlimá	kinse	1,000	sanlibo	mil
16	labíng-anim	diesisais	10,000	sanlaksá	diyes mil
17	labímpitó	diesisiyete	100,000	sangyutà, sandaáng libo	siyento mil
18	labíngwaló	diesiotso	1,000,000	sang-angaw	milyón
19	labíngsiyám	diesinuwebe	1,000,000,000	sanlibong angaw	bilyón

Ordinal numbers over one are formed with the prefix *ika-* or *pang-* → *una* 'first,' *ikalawá (ika-2), pangalawá* 'second,' *ikatló (ika-3), pangatló* 'third,' *ikapat (ika-4), pang-apat* 'fourth,' *ikalimá (ika-5), panlimá* 'fifth,' *ika-anim (ika-6), pang-anim* 'sixth.' The prefix *tig-* is used to form distributive numbers → *tig-isá* 'one each,' *tigalawá* 'two each,' *tigatló* 'three each,' *tig-apat* 'four each,' *tiglimá* 'five each,' *tig-isáng daán* 'one hundred each.'

The numbers may be restricted with initial CV reduplication → *iisá* 'only one,' *dadalawá* 'only two,' *tatatló* 'only three,' *aapat* 'only four,' *lilimá* 'only five.'

2.2.7 Verbs

One notable thing about Tagalog is that all nouns may be verbalized with affixes. An interesting feature about Tagalog verbs is that they derive for 'focus,' in which the semantic relationship between the topic (*ang* phrase or *topic* pronoun) is specified by the morphology of the verb.

Actor focus verbs (formed with the affixes *mag-, -um-, mang-, ma-*, past forms *nag- -um-, nang-, na-*, respectively) indicate that the topic is an actor (instigator or experiencer of the action). (*-Um-* is a verbalizing infix which goes before the first vowel of the root.) *Matulog ka na!* 'Sleep!' *Pumuntá akó ng*

Manila. 'I went to Manila,' *Kumain ka pa*. 'Eat (you) more,' *Nagsinungaling silá sa kaniyá*. 'They lied to her,' *Dumatíng si Carmen*. 'Carmen arrived,' *Umuwî siyá*. 'She went home.'

Object focus verbs (formed with the suffix *-(h)in*, past form *-in-*) indicate that the topic is a patientive argument, directly affected by the action expressed by the verb → *Hinubad niyá ang suot na damít*. 'She took off the clothes she had on,' *Ginawâ niyá ang lahát*. 'She did everything,' *Dadalhín ka namin sa ospitál*. 'We will take you to the hospital.'

Directional focus verbs (formed with the suffix *-(h)an*, past form *-in- -an*) indicate that the topic is the direction of the action or a partially affected patient → *Tinikmán niyá ang niluto ko*, 'She tried what I cooked,' *Nilagyán niyá ng kanin ang plato ko*. 'She put the rice on my plate,' *Bigyán mo akó ng sapatos*,' 'Give the shoes to me.'

Instrumental focus verbs (formed with the prefix *ipaN-*, past form *ipinaN-*) indicate that the topic is the instrument used to perform the action → *Ipinampunas ko ang panyo*. 'I wiped with the handkerchief,' *Ipinampalò niyá sa kanilá ang batutà*. 'He hit them with the club.' *Ipinambilí niyá ang kaniyáng káluluwá*. 'He bought (paid for) it with his soul.'

Benefactive focus verbs (formed with the prefix *i-/ipag-*, past form *i- -in-, ipinag-*) indicate that the topic of the verb is the beneficiary of its action → *Ibinilí niyá akó ng aklát*. 'She bought a book for me.' The prefix *i-* is also widely used to indicate the moving or transference → *iuwî* 'to bring home,' *itaás* 'to raise, put up,' *itagò* 'to hide,' *ilabás* 'to put outside,' *isará* 'to close,' *ilagáy* 'to put,' *isama* 'to bring along with,' and *isakáy* 'to take along in a vehicle.'

The major focuses can be summarized by the following sentences (in focus topics are underlined, and the verbal morphology is in bold):

__Bum__ilí ka ng manggá sa palengke para sa akin.
You bought mangos at the market for me. (actor)
Bil__hín__ mo ang manggá sa palengke para sa akin.
Buy the mangos at the market for me. (object)
Bil__hán__ mo akó ng manggá sa palengke.
Buy mangos from me at the market. (direction)
__I__bilí mo akó ng manggá sa palengke.
Buy mangos for me at the market. (beneficiary)
__Ipam__bilí mo ng manggá ang pera ko.
Buy mangos with my money. (instrument)

Potentive mode. Tagalog has the potentive affixes *maka-* (actor focus) and *ma-* (goal focus) which specify abilitative, accidental, or coincidental actions → *makainúm* 'to be able to drink,' *makatulong* 'to be able to help,' *makatakbó* 'to be able to run,' *makapulot* 'to find (accidentally),' *makabunggô* 'to bump accidentally,' *makasagasa* 'to run over accidentally,' *mahanap* 'to find,' *maringíg* 'to hear.' We can contrast the notion of control or volition by the following sentences → *Hinahanap ko ang relos ko*. 'I am looking for my watch (+ control).' vs. *Nahanap mo ba ang sapatos mo*? 'Did you find your shoes (- control),' *Binanggâ ko ang trak nilá* 'I crashed into their truck (on purpose).' vs. *Nabanggâ ko ang trak*. 'I accidentally crashed into the truck.'

Ma- verbs may also specify actions without an actor, similar to the English passive voice → *Mabubulgár ang lahát*. 'Everything will be revealed.'

Causation and Direction. The derivational prefix *pa-* is used with verbs to indicate both direction and indirect action (causation). The prefix *pa-* is used with a variety of other verbal affixes to indicate indirect action, depending on the relationship between the topic (noun in focus) and the causative verb:

Topic noun	Causative affix	Example	Gloss
Causer	mag-pa-	mag-pa-lutò	to have someone cook
Actor	pa- -in	pa-tulug-in	to put someone to sleep
Object	i-pa-, pa- -an	i-pa-kita	to show, cause to see something
Location	pa-pag- -an	pa-pag-sayaw-án	to have people dance at a place
Benefactor	ipag-pa-	ipag-pa-linis	to cause to clean for

Examples of *pa-* indirect action verbs with their corresponding direct action verbs include the following:

Direct Action Verbs		Indirect Action Verbs	
mag-labá	wash clothes	*mag-pa-labá*	have someone wash clothes, have the clothes washed
t{um}abâ	get fat	*mag-pa-tabâ*	to fatten up
maligò	take a bath	*paliguan*	bathe someone else
mag-buhát	lift, carry	*ipabuhat*	get someone to carry
s{um}ulat	write	*pa-sulat-an*	have someone write to someone else
p{um}asok	enter	*pa-pasuk-an*	allow to enter, let in
ma-tulog	sleep	*pa-tulug-in*	put to sleep

i.e. *Nagpapalutò akó ng manók kay Cesar.* 'I had Cesar cook chicken,' *Ipinadalá ko ang pera sa kaniyá.* 'I sent the money to him,' *Papasukin mo siyá.* 'Let her come in.'

Pa- is also used to indicate direction → *dito* 'here,' *parito* 'come here,' *doón* 'there,' *paroón* 'go there,' *pa-Manila* 'go to Manila,' *pa-singa-Singapore* 'keep going back and forth to Singapore.'

Social verbs. The prefix *maki-* is used to form 'social verbs,' verbs that indicate that an action is performed in the company of another person or other people, or that an action is requested to be done → *kumain* 'to eat' vs. *makikain* 'to eat with someone, share food' *dumaán* 'to pass' vs. *makiraán* 'to request to be allowed to pass,' *matulog* 'sleep' vs. *makitulog* 'to sleep with someone, share a bed,' *magsindí* 'to light, set fire to' vs. *makisindí* 'to borrow fire, ask for a light.' The prefixes *makipag-* and *makipang-* may be used instead of *maki-* for *mag-* and *mang-* (*maN-*) verbs respectively → *mamilí* 'to buy, go shopping,' vs. *makipamilí* 'to go shopping with,' *maglutò* 'to cook' vs. *maki(pag)lutò* 'to cook with.'

Nakikain siyá sa amin. 'She ate with us,' *Nakikidalamhatì akó sa iyó* 'I sympathize, share in your grief, grieve with you (expression of bereavement),' *Makipagkumpetensiya pa silá sa kaniyá.* 'They are still competing with each other for her.'

Aspect. Tagalog verbs inflect for four aspects 1.) infinitive aspect, which includes commands (i.e. *maglarô*: play); 2.) perfective aspect (past) for completed actions (i.e. *naglarô*: played); 3.) imperfective aspect for actions that are initiated but not yet complete (*naglalarô*: is playing), and 4.) contemplative aspect for future actions (*maglalarô*: will play). The infinitive forms are the least morphologically marked. Perfective and imperfective verbs in Tagalog take a form of the realis (+initiated) infix *–in-* (prefix *n-* for *mag-*, *ma-*, *maka-*, and *mang-* (*maN-*) verbs; this infix is lost with *–um-* verbs). Contemplated (future) actions are indicated by CV reduplication.

Aspects of major actor focus verbs

Aspect	Verb class **mag-**	**-um-**	**maN-**	**maka-**	**ma-**
Infinitive	mag-	-um-	maN-	maka-	ma-
Perfective	nag-	-um-	naN-	naka-	na-
Imperfective	nagCV-	-CumV-	naNCV-	nakaka-	naCV
Contemplated	magCV-	CV-	maNCV-	makaka-	maCV-

i.e. **mag- verbs**: magpunas, nagpunas, nagpupunas, magpupunas
um verbs: bumasa, bumasa, bumabasa, babasa
maN- verbs: mamilì, namilì, namimilì, mamimilì
maka- verbs: makagising, nakagising, nakakagising/ nakagigising, makakagising/ makagigising
ma- verbs: matulog, natulog, natutulog, matutulog

Aspects of major goal focus verbs

Aspect	Verb class **-in**	**-an**	**i-**	**ika-**	**ipag-**
Infinitive	-in	an	i	ika	ipag
Perfective	-in-	-in- -an	i- -in-	ikina-	ipang-
Imperfective	CinV-	CinV- -an	i- -CinV-	ikinaka , ikinaCV	ipinapag
Contemplated	CV- -in	CV- -an	iCV-	ikaka-, ikaCV-	ipagCV-

i.e. **-in verbs**: gulatin, ginulat, ginugulat, gugulatin
-an verbs: tawagan, tinawagan, tinatawagan, tatawagan
I- verbs: ibigáy, ibinigáy, ibinibigáy, ibibigáy
ika- verbs: ikagulό, ikinagulό, ikinakagulό/ikinagugulό, ikakagulό/ikagugulό
ipa- verbs: ipatulόy, ipinatulόy, ipinapatulόy, ipapatulόy
ipag- verbs: ipagdalá, ipinagdalá, ipinagdadalá, ipagdadalá
ipang- verbs: ipambilí, ipinambilí, ipinapambilí, ipapambilí

Recent past. Tagalog verbs also inflect for a recent past form, as shown in the following table:

Basic form Affix	Recent Past Affix	Example
-um-, ma-, maka-	kaCV-	kaaakyát, kagugupít
mag-	kaCV-, kapagCV-	katatapos, kapagbabasa
mang- (maN-)	kapaNCV-, kapapaN-	kapapanguha, kapangunguha

The actor of the recent past verb is encoded with a genitive noun phrase → *Kaiihì ko lang*. 'I just urinated,' *Kakakain ko ng tinapay*. 'I just ate some bread,' *Kapapalò lang kamí ni lolo*. 'Grandpa just spanked us.'

2.2.8 Adverbs

Tagalog has three kinds of adverbs, simple monomorphemic adverbs, derived adverbs (often used also as adjectives), and enclitic non-deriving particles.

Simple monomorphemic adverbs include *halos* 'almost,' *agád* 'immediately,' *ganáp* 'completely,' *bakâ, siguro* 'maybe, perhaps,' *talagá* 'really,' *bahagyâ* 'slightly,' *kusà* 'willingly, voluntarily,' *unti-untî* 'gradually, little by little,' *lalò* 'especially,' and *biglâ* 'suddenly.' Simple adverbs may or may not be linked to their verbs with the linker *na*: *Unti-untî nag-alisan na ang mga usyosero*. 'The curious bystanders left gradually,' *Halos hindî kitá napansín*. 'I almost didn't notice you.' *Bigláng binawì ang kamáy sa matandâ*. 'He took back his hand suddenly from the old man.' *Ayaw mo talagáng ngumitî, ha*? 'You really don't want to smile, do you?'

Adjectives do not change their form when they modify a verb → *Siyá'y magandáng sumayáw*. 'She dances beautifully,' *Lumakad silá nang marahan*. 'They walk softly.'

Adverbs of time include (simple and derived): *ngayón* 'now, today,' *bukas* 'tomorrow,' *kahapon* 'yesterday,' *tuwina, lagì* 'always,' *birihà, madalang* 'seldom,' *noón* 'then (in the past),' *(m)ulî, ulít* 'again,' *malimit, madalás* 'often.' Many temporal nouns may be reduplicated to indicate 'every + N' → *araw-araw* 'every day,' *gabí-gabí* 'every night,' *oras-oras* 'every hour,' *taún-taón* 'every year.'

Adverbial particles. Adverbial particles are non-inflecting words that occur in a fixed position. Initial adverbs are those that precede the rest of the sentence. Some of them require the linker *na/-ng* before the rest of the sentence like *bakâ sakali* 'maybe,' *pambihirà* 'seldom,' and *totoó* 'it's true that,' while others do not, i.e. *bakâ* 'maybe,' *di* 'then,' *tila* 'it seems.' *Tila uulán*. 'It seems it's going to rain,' *Totoóng Amerikano siyá*. 'It's true that he is American.'

Enclitic adverbs also occur in a fixed position, but cannot be the first constituent of a phrase. They function grammatically between the levels of a full word and a suffix. These adverbs include (with inexact translations) → *na* 'already, now,' *pa* 'still, yet,' *ngâ* 'please, indeed,' *din* 'also, too,' *daw* 'it is said,' *pô* 'polite particle,' *ba* 'question particle,' *lang* 'only, just,' *namán* 'too,' *palá* 'so,' *yatà* 'maybe.'

Monosyllabic (one-syllable) adverbs precede disyllabic ones when both types occur in the same sentence. The fixed order for the mono-syllabic adverbial particles is:

<table>
<tr><td>na</td><td rowspan="2">ngâ</td><td rowspan="2">din</td><td rowspan="2">daw</td><td rowspan="2">pô, hô</td><td rowspan="2">ba</td></tr>
<tr><td>pa</td></tr>
</table>

i.e. *Sandalî, magbibihis lang akó*. 'Just a second, I'll just get dressed,' *Bagay ngâ kayó*! 'You go well together indeed!' *Pinapapasok lang sa isáng tenga't pinalalabás din sa kabilá*. 'It just went in one ear and out the other.' *Sino pô ba silá*? 'Who are they, sir?' *Kayó hô palá*. 'So it's you, sir (I didn't realize it before).' *Papasok ka na ba?* 'Are you going to school / work (going to enter)?'

2.2.9 Existentials

Tagalog has two existential particles that are used to indicate both possession and existence: *may, mayroón* 'have; there is' and *walâ* 'don't have; there isn't.' *Marami* 'many' also has similar syntactic behavior.

Mayroón, marami, and *walâ* are used with the linker *na/-ng*, while *may* is not. They may indicate existence (i.e. 'there is, there are').

May batà sa kusinà.	'There is a child in the kitchen.'
Waláng batà sa kusinà.	'There isn't a child in the kitchen.'
Mayroon ding pansít.	'There are noodles also.'
Maraming serbesa.	'There is a lot of beer.'
Waláng pagbabago sa mukhâ niyá.	'Nothing changed in her face (there is no change..).'
Marami akóng kaibigan.	'I have many friends.'

May, mayroón and *walâ* are also used to indicate possession. *May pera akó.* 'I have money,' *Walâ akóng pera.* 'I don't have money.' *Mayroón ka bang bahay?* 'Do you have a house?' *May eroplano si Jessica.* 'Jessica has an airplane.' *Waláng aklát si Angela.* 'Angela doesn't have a book.'

In indefinite phrases with inflected verbs, existentials may appear in predicate position, in which they act as indefinite pronouns corresponding to what would be the topic nominal (in focus) → *May ginawâ siyá.* 'She did something,' *May sumisigáw.* 'Someone is screaming,' *May sinulat akó.* 'I wrote something,' *May sinulatan akó.* 'I wrote someone,' *Walá akóng sinulat.* 'I didn't write anything.'

2.2.10 Prepositions

Aside from the articles, Tagalog has a class of words responsible for relating the function of a noun to the rest of sentence. As these words precede the nouns they modify, they are called 'prepositions.' The most common prepositions are → *sa* 'in, at, to,' *para* 'for,' *ukol* 'about,' *tungkól* 'about,' *laban* 'against,' *alinsunod* 'according to.'

Prepositions take nouns in the oblique case → *ukol sa iyo* 'it is about you,' *sumama ka sa akin* 'come with me,' *itó ang para sa kanilá* 'this is for them.'

Prepositions which express location in English are expressed in Tagalog with locator (relational) nouns, not prepositions. The most common relational nouns include *dulo* 'end,' *gitnâ* 'middle,' *haráp* 'front,' *ibabâ* 'lower part, below,' *ibabaw* 'place above,' *ilalim* 'place beneath,' *itaás* 'upper part,' *labás* 'exterior, outside,' *likód, likuran* 'back,' *loób* 'interior,' and *tabí* 'side.'

Sino ang nasa gitnâ ng mga babae?	'Who is between (in the center of) the girls?'
Naglalarô silá sa tabí ng daán.	'They are playing beside (at the side of) the road.'
Nasa ilalim ng lamesa ang manók.	'The chicken is (in the space) under the table.'

2.2.11 Conjunctions and Subordinators

Tagalog has a wealth of conjunctions and subordinators. Coordinating conjunctions such as *at* 'and,' *o* 'or,' go between two coordinated constituents, and subordinators immediately precede subordinate phrases. Some common Tagalog subordinators are *pero* 'but,' *nguni't* 'but,' *subali't* 'but,' *datapuwá't* 'but,' *kung* 'if,' *habang* 'while,' *samantalang* 'while,' *bago* 'before,' *kundî* 'but; except,' *maliban* 'except,' *pag* 'if, when,' *kapág* 'when, whenever,' *nang* 'when,' *ni.. ni..* 'neither... nor...,' *o... o...* 'either... or...'

May sasabihin akó sa iyó, pero kundî ka ngingitî, hindî ko sasabihin. 'I have something to tell you, but if you don't smile I won't say it,' *Nagyakapan silá habang nakamasíd lang si Terence.* 'They embraced each other while Terence just stared,' *Anó ang ginagawâ mo kapág may pasok?* 'What do you do when you have class?'

Kung introduces conditional clauses → *Kung umuwî na silá, bakit ba nandito pa ang aso nilá*? 'If they already went home, why is their dog still here?' *Kung* also introduces subordinate phrases headed by indefinite (interrogative) pronouns → *Hindî ko alám kung sino ang nanay niyá* 'I don't know who her mother is,' *Alam mo ba kung bakit akó nagbago*? 'Do you know why I changed?' To express hypothetical (or counterfactual) conditionals, *sana* is used with *kung* → *Kung mayaman ka, mas masayá sana tayo*. 'If you were rich, we would be happier.'

Pag 'if, when' may introduce both temporal clauses and conditional ones → *Pag magandá ang panahón, aalís akó*. 'If/when the weather is good, I'll leave,' *Pag datíng niyá, aalís akó*. 'When he arrives, I'll leave.'

TAGALOG – ENGLISH

TAGALOG – INGGLÉS

A

a: *excl.* ah! oh!

aâ: (Ch. *child talk*) dirt, filth.

aák: *n.* ripping; slashing. **aakán.** *v.* to rip; slash.

aám: (Ch.) rice broth; **aamín** *v.* to scoop out rice broth.

aáp: *n.* wholesale purchase of harvest; **aapín** *v.* to purchase the entire harvest.

abá: *interj.* well!; hey!

abâ: *adj.* wretched, poor; **abaín** *v.* to mistreat, treat miserably; despise.

abaká: *n.* Manila abaca hemp.

abakada: *n.* alphabet (*coined from first four letters of the Tagalog alphabet*). **abakadahin.** *v.* to alphabetize.

ábakó: (Sp. *ábaco*) *n.* abacus.

abád₁: (Sp.) *n.* abbot.

abád₂: *adj.* foiled; thwarted.

abadesa: (Sp.) *n.* mother superior; abbess.

abadyá: (Sp. *abadía*) *n.* abbey; abbacy.

abala: *n.* delay; trouble, bother; inconvenience; **umabala** *v.* to delay, hinder; **maabala** *v* to be inconvenienced.

abal-abal: *n.* fuss; knickknacks.

abalá: *adj.* busy, occupied.

abaloryo: (Sp.) *n.* glass bead.

abandono: (Sp.) *n.* abandonment; neglect.

abaniko: (Sp. *abaniko*) fan; black berry lily.

abano: (Sp. *havano*) *n.* cigar

abanse: (Sp. *avance*) *coll. n.* something stolen; act of taking surreptitiously.

abante: (Sp. *avante*) *interj.* forward; proceed; *n.* moving forward, proceeding.

abáng: *n.* watcher; act of waiting and watching.

abangabang: *n.* prickly heat rash. (*bungang-araw*)

abang-abang: *n.* *Leea manillensis* shrub.

abaserya: (Sp. *abacería*) *n.* grocery.

abasero: (Sp. *abacero*) *n.* grocer.

abasto: (Sp.) *n.* baggage.

abát: *n.* ambush; person lying in wait; keeping watch. **abatan** *v.* to ambush; intercept; keep watch over.

abay: *n.* escort; best man; maid of honor; **abayan** *v.* act as an escort; **pang-abay** adverb. **abay sa kasál** *n.* groomsman; bridesmaid.

abáy: *adj.* close to each other. **abay-abay** *adj.* side by side.

abe: (Kpm.) *n.* friend; pal. (*kaibigan, katoto*)

abéha: (Sp. *abeja*) *n.* bee (*pukyutan, laywán*). **abeha maestra, abeha reyna** *n.* queen bee.

abehera: (Sp. *avejera*) *n.* beehive (*pugad-pukyutan*); apiary.

abehero: *n.* beekeeper.

abelyana: (Sp. *avellana*) *n.* tan colored, brown.

abenida: (Sp. *avenida*) *n.* avenue.

abér: (Sp. *a ver*) *interj.* okay; let's see.

aberasyón: (Sp. *aberración*) *n.* mental disorder; mechanical trouble; aberration.

aberiya: (Sp. *avería*) *n.* mechanical trouble; mental disorder.

abese: (*obs.*) *n.* alphabet (*abakada*); rudiments.

abesedaryo: *n.* alphabet (*abakada*).

abilidád: (Eng.) *n.* ability; cunningness. **abilidarín** *v.* to do by cunningness.

abiso: (Sp. *aviso*) *n.* notice, information.

ábitó: (Sp. *hábito*) *n.* cassock of a priest; **abituhan** *v.* to ordain as a priest.

abitsuwelas: (Sp. *habichuela*) *n.* kidney bean.

ablá: (Sp. *habla*) *n.* idle talk, babble.

ablada: (Sp. *hablada*) *n.* chatter.

ablatibo: (Sp.) *n.* ablative case.

abo: *n.* croaker fish; porgy fish.

abó: *n.* ash, ashes; **abuhan** ashtray; **abó ang lamán ng ulo** *id.* stupid (ash headed).

abók: *n.* dust. (*alikabók*)

abóg: *n.* hollow noise; **waláng-abóg** without notice or warning.

abogado: (Sp.) *n.* lawyer.

abogago: (*slang, abogado + gago*) *n.* stupid lawyer.

abogasyá: *n.* study of law; law profession.

abonado: (Sp.) *adj.* fertilized; reimbursed; having incurred a loss in business.

abono: (Sp.) *n.* fertilizer; reimbursing; amount of money paid as a reimbursement.

abong: *n.* dense blown smoke or dust.

abot: **abutan, abutin** *v.* to overtake, catch up with.

abót: *n.* reach; power, range; capacity; *adj.*

within reach; **iabot, abután** to hand something over; **umabót, abutín** *v.* to reach for; **mag-abót** *v.* to hand over; **abot-dilì** *id.* could hardly reach (in a critical or serious condition); **abót-agaw** *id.* hovering between life and death; exhausted; **abot-kisáp, abot-kuráp** *n.* continuous winking; **abot-siko** *adj.* with the elbows held tightly at the back; **pag-aabót ng kamáy** *id.* offering help (reaching of hands); **di maabot-tanáw, di maabot ng tingín** *id.* can't be seen; vast; **inabot ng kaliwá't kanan** *id.* beat up (reached by left and right).

abót-agawin: *n.* region of the back that cannot be reached by one's hands.

abot-kisáp, abot-kuráp: *n.* continuous winking.

abot-dilì: *adj.* hovering between life and death; exhausted; barely enough to reach or touch.

abot-hiyáw: *adj.* within reach of one's shout; *n.* continuous shouting.

abot-siko: *adj.* with the elbows held tightly together at one's back.

abot-sigáw: *adj.* within reach of one's shout; *n.* continuous shouting.

abot-tanáw: *n.* casting one's eyes off in the distance; *adj.* within a visible distance.

abot-tingín: *adj.* within a visible distance.

abóy: *n.* driving away.

abra: (Sp.) *n.* ravine.

abrasadór: (Sp.) *n.* leg pillow. (*dantayanan*)

abrasete: (Sp. *de bracete*) *adj.* walking arm-in-arm.

abré: (Sp. *abrir*) *adj.* open; not locked; *n.* act of opening. (*bukás*) **abrihán** *v.* to open; provide with a hole for opening.

abrelata: (Sp.) *n.* can opener.

abrigo: (Sp.) *n.* overcoat.

Abríl: (Sp.) *n.* April.

abrilata: (Sp. *abrelatas*) *n.* can opener.

absíng: *n.* species of flea.

absoluto: (Sp.) *adj.* complete; full; without limit; absolute; pure.

absuweltado: (Eng). *adj.* absolved, acquitted.

absuwelto: (Sp. *absuelto*) *adj.* acquitted, absolved; *n.* acquittal.

abu-abo: mist, haze; drizzle. (*abong*)

abubot: *n.* knickknacks, trinkets.

abuhín: (rt. *abó*) *a.* ashen, ashy.

abukanin: *n.* homeless person.

abukay: *n.* white parrot.

abuloy: *n.* subsidy, contribution; aid; help; alms. **ábuluyán** *n.* fund raising.

aburido: (Sp. *aburrido*) *adj.* worried, disturbed; depressed; obsessed.

abusero: (Sp.) *adj.* abusive; *n.* abusive man.

abusiyón: *n.* superstition. (*pamahiin*)

abuso: (Sp.) *n.* abuse, maltreatment. **abusuhin** *v.* to abuse; mistreat; rape.

abuwáb: *n.* arrow poison.

abyád: *n.* duty, obligation that must be attended to. **abyarín** *v.* to attend to one's duty.

abyérta: (Sp. *abierta*: open) *n.* man's open coat; *adj.* open (*bukás*).

abyóg: *n.* swinging, dangling; bending due to a heavy load.

abyón: *n.* swaying to and fro.

akab: **akáb** *adj.* tight fitting, tightly set.

akademya: (Sp. *academia*) *n.* academy; academic institution; association.

akag: *n.* act of inviting a person for a certain purpose. **akagán** *n.* cooperative work; invitational labor.

akalà: *n.* idea, belief; *v.* to think; **akalain** *v.* to think, assume; suppose, presume; **mag-akalà** *v.* to think, consider; **pag-aakalà** *n.* way of thinking; belief; **pag-akalaan** *v.* to plan to do something about.

akap: *n.* tight embrace. **akapan** *v.* attach; fasten; **akapán** *n.* mutual embracing. **akapin** *v.* to embrace; hold tightly in one's arms.

akapará: (Sp. *acaparar*) *n.* acquisition; exclusive control. **akaparahín** *v.* to hoard; monopolize.

akaparadór: (Sp. *acaparador*) *n.* monopolizer.

akapulko: (Sp.) *n.* ringworm bush.

akat: *n.* transplanting seedlings. **akát** *adj.* transplanted. **akatán** *n.* seedbed; transplanting time.

akay: *adj.* led by the hand; *n.* leading, conducting, guiding. **akayán** *n.* hatch; brood.

akbá: *adj.* peeled too thick. **akbahín** *v.* to peel too thick.

akbáy: *adj.* with the arm over another's shoulder.

akdâ: *n.* literary work, play. **akdaín** *v.* to compose. **akdáng-buhay** *n.* novel. **akdáng-gurò** *n.* masterpiece. **akdáng-sining** *n.* literary work of art.

akibat: *n.* carrying over the shoulder and across the body.

akin: *pron.* my, mine; belonging to me.

akiná: (*akin* + *na*) give it to me.

akinse-katapusan: (*slang, a* + *kinse* + *katapus-an*: on fifteenth and end) *n.* payday.

akip: *n.* enclosing.

akit: **akitin** *v.* to attract, charm; tempt, persuade; **kaakit-akit** *adj.* attractive, charming, fascinating; interesting.

aklahà: *n.* cry of monkeys.

Aklanon: *n.* language and ethnic group of Aklan province, Panay.

aklás: *n.* strike (*of workers*). (*welga*)

aklát: *n.* book; **aklatan** *n.* bookstore, library. **aklatín** *v.* to bind into a book; publish a manuscript. **aklát-pampáaralán** *n.* textbook. **aklát-sulatán** *n.* notebook. **aklát-taláarawán** *n.* diary. **aklát-tuusán** *n.* journal, record book.

aklé: *n.* species of tree (*Ablzzlu acle*).

akmâ₁: *adj.* proper, suited, fitting; **iakmâ** to fit, adjust; adapt; to be on the point of doing something; to threaten to do something. **akmaán** *v.* to fit, adjust; threaten with a blow; **magkáakmá-akmâ** *v.* to fit exactly; **pagkaakmâ** *n.* agreement, accordance.

akmâ₂: *adj.* on the verge of doing; *n.* threatening gesture; **umakmâ** *v.* to threaten to do; be on the verge of doing.

akó: *pron.* I; me; **makaakó** *adj.* selfish; **akó na rin** I myself.

akò: **pangakò** *n.* promise; **ipangakò** *v.* to promise, engage.

akompanya(miyento): (Sp. *acompaña(miento)*) *n.* accompaniment.

akompanyante, akompanyadór: (Sp. *acompañante, acompañador*) *n.* accompanist.

aksayá: *n.* waste, extravagance; **mag-aksayá** *v.* to waste, throw away; lose; **aksayado** *adj.* wasteful. **aksayahín** *v.* to waste, squander.

aksesorya: (Sp. *accesoria*) *n.* apartment house, tenement.

aksesoryo: (Sp. *accesorio*) *n.* spare parts; accessory; accomplice.

aksibál: *n.* aloe tree.

aksíp: *n* species of rice worm.

aksiw: *n.* carrying on the shoulder. **áksiwan** *n.* pole used for carrying over the shoulder.

aksiyón: (Sp. *acción*) *n.* movement; motion; share of stock; attitude; decision on a case; effect; reaction.

aksiyonista: (Sp. *accionista*) *n.* stock holder.

akta: (Sp. *acta*) *n.* minutes of a meeting (*katitikan*); proceedings of a conference.

aktitúd: (Sp. *actitud*) *n.* manner of thinking or dealing with others, attitude.

akto: (Sp. *acto*) *n.* act; law, decree.

akurdiyón: (Sp. *acordeón*) *n.* accordion.

akusado: (Sp. *acusado*) *adj.* accused.

akusatíbo: (Sp. *acusativo*) *n.* accusative case; direct object.

akwáryo: (Sp. *acuario*) *n.* aquarium; Aquarius.

akyát: *n.* rise, climb; **umakyát** *v.* to ascend, climb; **akyát-bahay** (*slang*) *n.* burglar.

ada: (Sp. *hada*) *n.* fairy. (*diwatà*)

ad-ád: act of scraping or rubbing.

Adán: (Sp.) *n.* Adam.

adarga: (Sp.) *n.* leather shield. (*kalasag*)

Adasen: *n.* ethnic group and language from Abra, NE Luzon.

adegón: (brand name; *slang*) *n.* old radio.

adelantado: (Sp.) *adj.* in advance, ahead of time; progressive.

adelantera: (Sp.)

adelanto: (Sp.) *n.* down payment; progress; progressiveness; brazenness.

adelpa: *n.* oleander shrub.

adhikâ: (Sp.) *n.* aim, intention, objective, goal; desire; ambition; wish. **adhikaín** *v.* to strive to attain or accomplish.

adidas: (brand name; *slang*) *n.* barbecued chicken feet.

adobe: (Sp.) *n.* sundried brick; adobe stone.

adobo: (Sp.) *n.* pork or chicken pickled with vinegar, garlic, pepper and bay leaf.

adorno: (Sp.) *n.* adornment; ornament.

adsi: (*slang, adobo* + *sinangág*) *n.* fried rice with *adobo*.

aduladór: (Sp.) *n.* flatterer.

adultero: (Sp.) *adj.* adulterous (*mápangalunyà*); *n.* adulterer.
adulto: (Sp.) *n.* adult. (*nasa-gulang*)
aduwana: (Sp. *aduana*) *n.* customs. **aduwanero** *n.* customs officer.
adwâ: *n.* nausea. (*duwál*)
adyá: *n.* protection, defense; salvation.
adyó: *n.* climbing, ascending; mounting.
adyós: (Sp. *adiós*) good bye; **mag-adyusan** *v.* to say goodbye to one another.
aga: *n.* earliness; **maaga** *adj.* early; **káumagahan** *n.* early morning; **kinámagahan** *n.* the next morning; **maagahan** *v.* to feel that it is too early (for an event); **magpaaga** *v.* to advance in time, make earlier; **mápaagá** *v.* to occur too early, be premature; **umaga** *n.* morning; **umagang-umaga** *adv.* very early in the morning; **umagahin** *v.* to be overtaken by the morning; **agahan** *n.* breakfast; *v.* to make something early; **mag-agahan** *v.* to take breakfast; **maaga pa sa lamók** *id.* too early.
agaak: *n.* four-barred grunt fish.
agaas: *n.* rustling sound; soft breeze.
agák: *n.* quack of ducks; sound of hitting a stomach.
agád: *adv.* immediately, at once; quickly.
ag-ag, agág: *n.* sifting. **ágagan** *n.* sifter.
agahan: (rt. *aga*) *n.* breakfast; *v.* to start early.
agahás: *n.* wheeze.
agal-agal: *n.* hard core of root stocks.
agalya: (Sp. *agalla*) *n.* gill; tonsils.
agam: **agam-agam**. *n.* doubt; suspicion.
agang: *n.* buzzing sound of a swarm of bees.
agap: *n.* quickness, alertness; anticipation; **maagap** *adj.* quick, prompt.
agapay: *adv.* side by side; *n.* escort; bodyguard; support or reinforcement. **agapáy** *adj.* parallel; side by side.
agar-agar: *n.* agar-agar, seaweed jello.
agas: *n.* miscarriage. (*hulog*)
agasás, agas-ás: *n.* rustling sound.
agatát, agat-át: *n.* grating sound.
agaw: **agawan** to snatch, grab; rob; **~-tulog** half-asleep; **umagaw** *v.* to deprive; **nag-aagaw-buhay** *id.* in a serious condition (snatching life); **inagaw ang buhay** *id.* saved from death; **nag-aagaw-dilím** *id.* twilight (snatching darkness). **agaw-liwanag** *n.* daybreak, dawn.
agay-áy: *n.* breeze.
agbilang: (coined from *aghám* + *bilang*) *n.* mathematics.
agbuhay: (coined from *aghám* + *buhay*) *n.* biology, life science.
agdinigan: (coined from *aghám* + *diníg*) *n.* acoustics; speech recognition.
aghám: *n.* science. **aghámbilang** *n.* mathematics; **aghámbuhay** *n.* biology; **aghámlipunán** *n.* sociology, social science; **aghámtao** *n.* anthropology; **aghámwikà** *n.* linguistics.
agik-ik: *n.* giggle.
agihap: *n.* sore at the corner of the mouth.
ágila: (Sp. *águila*) *n.* eagle.
agimat: *n.* amulet; economy.
aginaldo: (Sp.) *n.* Christmas present.
agipó: short firewood brand.
agit-it: *n.* squeaking sound.
agiw: *n.* soot; cobwebs.
aglahì: *n.* joke, jest; insult; mockery.
aglipunan: (*aghám* + 'science' *lipunan* 'society') *n.* sociology; social science.
agnás: *n.* erosion; **umagnás** *v.* to erode.
agnós: (Sp.) *n.* locket; small religious medallion.
agong: *n.* Chinese bell.
agos: *n.* current of water, flow; **agusan** *v.* to flow.
Agosto: (Sp.) *n.* August.
agoy: *n.* poorly constructed building; difficult movements of a weak or sick person.
agpáng: *adj.* exact, fitted; adequate.
agrabyado: (Sp. *agraviado*) *adj.* injured, offended.
agridulse: (Sp. *agridulce*) *adj.* sweet and sour.
agrimensór: (Sp.) *n.* land surveyor.
Agta: *n.* language and ethnic group of the Negritos of Luzon.
aguha: (Sp. *aguja*) *n.* needle; hand of watch or clock. **aguhón** *n.* large needle; compass needle.
aguhò: *n.* pine tree.
agulo: *n.* concubinage (*pakikiapíd*).
agunyás: (Sp. *agonías*) *n.* tolling bells for the

dead.

aguot: *n.* spotted silver grunt fish.

agusíl: (Sp. *alguacil*: constable) *n.* constable, peace officer.

Agutaynen: *n.* ethnic group and language of Palawan.

agwa: (Sp. *agua*) *n.* water; ~ **bendita** *n.* holy water; ~ **plorida** scented water; **agwadór** water carrier; **agwa puwerte** nitric acid; **agwa dulse** fresh water.

agwádo: (Sp. *aguado*) *adj.* watery; liquefied.

agwadór: (Sp. *aguador*) *n.* water carrier.

agwahe: (Sp. *aguaje*) *n.* wake of a ship; tidal wave.

agwanta: (Sp. *aguanta*) *n.* endurance; patience; fortitude.

agwarás: (Sp. *aguarras*) *n.* turpentine.

agwardiyente: (Sp. *aguardiente*) *n.* hard liquor; alcohol.

agwás: *n.* mullet fish.

agwasa: (Sp. *aguaza*) *n.* pus secretion; decay of a corpse.

agwát: *n.* gap, distance; space; **umagwát** *v.* become separated, leave a gap. **agwat-agwát**. *adj.* with gaps in between.

ahang: *n.* vainglory.

ahà: (*coll.*) *n.* idea; supposition.

ahan: (*dial.*) *var.* of *nahan*: where (to be located).

ahang: *n.* boastfulness; vainglory.

ahas: *n.* snake; **ahas-bahay** *id.* house snake (person who is always at home; **ahas na tulóg** *id.* sleepy snake (lazybum, slowfoot); **ahas sa damó** *id.* snake in the grass (treacherous person); **ahas na sawá** *n.* python; *id.* traitor; **ahas na ulupóng** *n.* cobra; *id.* dangerous (cobra).

ahat: (OTag.) *adj.* forbidden; prohibited.

ahedrés: (Sp. *ajedrez*) *n.* chess.

ahente: (Sp. *agente*) *n.* agent, salesperson; middleman.

ahit: *n.* act of shaving; **mag-ahit** *v.* to shave oneself; **umahit** *v.* to shave (someone else).

ahon: *n.* going up; trip for the village to down; disembarking form a boat; removal of food from the stove; **ahunin** *v.* to remove cooked food from the stove; **umahon** to go up.

aíng: *n.* moan.

ala: (Sp.) *n.* wing.

alaala: *n.* memory; keepsake; souvenir; **maalaala** *v.* to remember; **magpaalaala** *v.* to remind.

alaalá: *adj.* worried; anxious.

alab: *n.* blaze; **mag-alab** *v.* to flare up.

alabastro: (Sp.) *n.* alabaster.

alabát: *n.* doorway railing used to obstruct the passage of babies.

alabók: *n.* dust (*abó*, *alikabók*).

alak: *n.* wine, alcohol; **alakán** *n.* distillery, wine factory; wine store; **alák-alakan** *n.* cheap wine; ~**-bigás** *n.* rice wine.

alakaak: *n.* plain croaker fish.

alak-alakán: *n.* calf of the leg; hock.

alakbát: *n.* shoulder strap; *adj.* slung from the shoulder.

alakbáy: *var.* of *akbáy*.

alakdán: (Sp. *alacrán*) *n.* scorpion. (*atang-atang*, *pitong-bukó*)

alakom: *n.* handful, amount or quantity that a hand can hold (*dakót*).

alagà: *n.* ward; **alagâ** *adj.* careful; well-taken care of; **alagaan** *v.* to attend to, care for; nurse; take care of; protect; **pangangalagà** *n.* conservation; **alagang kulasisi** *n.* concubine.

alagád: *n.* follower; disciple; minister; **alagád ng batás** *n.* law enforcement worker (disciple of the law).

alagatâ: *n.* constant caution; constant desire; concern; **alagataín** *v.* to mind; be concerned about; think about.

alagáw: *n.* kind of shrub used in medicine.

alahas: (Sp. *alajas*) *n.* jewels; **álahasán** *n.* jewelry store.

alahero: (Sp. *alajero*) *n.* jeweler.

alál, al-ál *n.* widening of a hole by dibbling.

alalá: *adj.* worried, anxious; **mag-alalá** *v.* to worry; **alalahanin** *v.* to recall; remember; think about, take into consideration; **álalahanín** *n.* cause of worry; worry; responsibility.

alalad: *n.* echo, resonance.

álalaón: **álalaón ko** what I mean; **álalaóng bagá** therefore; that is; **álalaón sana** should have; might have.

alalay: *n.* support, prop; holding something with care; (*slang*) right-hand man; yes-man.

alam: *n.* knowledge; *v.* to know; **alám** *adj.* known; understood; **alamín** *v.* to investigate; find out; **kaalamán** *n.* information; view; understanding; **kinálàman** *n.* knowledge of an event or deed. **ipaalám** *v.* to inform, enlighten. **makaalám** *v.* to know; **makialám** *v.* to meddle, interfere. **makipag-alám** *v.* to contact, deal with. **máláman** *v.* to know, be aware of; learn; keep in touch; **pakialám, pakialamero** *n.* meddler, busybody; **pakialamán** *v.* to meddle with; take charge of something undesirable. **pakikipag-alám** *n.* contact (with people). **pagkáalám** *n.* knowledge; consciousness; **may kinálàman** concern, relate to, have to do with.

alama: *n.* siganid, *Teuthis sp.*

alamaam: *adj.* cloudy.

alamáng: *n.* species of small shrimp; (*fig.*) unimportant person.

alamát: *n.* tradition, legend, folklore; myth.

alambre: (Sp.) *n.* wire.

alambrera: (Sp.) *n.* wire screen, wire netting.

alamíd: *n.* raccoon.

alamó: (*coll.*, *alám mo*) *expr.* you know.

alampáy: *n.* shoulder kerchief.

alang: **alang-alang** regard, esteem, consideration; respect; **mag-alang-alang** to consult; consider, regard. **isaalang-alang** *v.* to care for, regard; consider.

alangaang: *n.* space; atmosphere; ebb of a normal tide.

Alangan: *n.* ethnic group and language of Northern Mindoro.

alangán: *adj.* irregular, abnormal; improper; **mag-alangán** *v.* to hesitate; **alanganin** *adj.* doubtful; insufficient; (*slang*) homosexual; **naaalangán ho akó** I feel uncomfortable (not at ease); I'm not sure about it.

alangás: *adj.* conceited; daring.

alap: *n.* turn, shift (of workers); cut tips of grass. **umalap** *v.* to take one's turn.

alapaap: *n.* cirrus cloud; (*fig.*) doubt.

alap-ap, alapáp: *n.* doubt; uncertainty.

alapaw: *n.* climbing clumsily on top; spreading over (vines); animal coitus.

alapot: *n.* saddlebag, knapsack; *adj.* untidily dressed.

alas: *n.* aligning, leveling.

alás: (Sp.) *n.* ace; o'clock; **alas singko** *id.* five o'clock (drunk).

alasás: *n.* screw pine.

alaskadór: (*slang*) *n.* tease.

alat: *n.* saltiness; (*fig.*) bad luck; (*slang*) police. **maalat** *adj.* salty; **alatan** *n.* honey-combed grouper.

alatiit: *n.* squeaking sound.

alatwát, alatuwát: *n.* dull echo.

alawák: *n.* bubbling gush, sudden gush.

alawáb: *n.* slime.

alawas: *n.* long-handed fishing net.

alawás: *adj.* derailed; out of alignment; awkward; wayward.

alay: *n.* offering; victim; **ialay** *v.* to offer.

alay-ay: *n.* scarecrow; row, file.

albakora: *n.* yellowfin tuna, albacore.

albanaka: *n.* species of aromatic shrub.

albay: *n.* support at the side of a house.

alboroto: (Sp.) *n.* outcry, tumult (*guló*).

alkabala: *var.* of *arkabala*: market fee.

alkalde: (Sp. *alcalde*) *n.* mayor.

alka(g)wete: (Sp. *alcahuete*) *n.* pimp.

alkampór: (Sp. *alcanfor*) *n.* camphor, mothball. **alkamporado** *adj.* camphorated.

alkansiyá: (Sp. *alcancia*) *n.* piggy bank.

alkantarilya: (Sp. *alcanarilla*) *n.* culvert, sewer. **alkantarilyado** *n.* sewer system.

alkayde: (Sp. *alcaide*) *n.* warden.

alkilá: (Sp. *alquilar*) *n.* hire, rent; **alkilahín** *v.* to rent; **ipaalkilá** *v.* to hire, rent out to.

alkitrán: (Sp. *alquitrán*) *n.* tar; asphalt.

aldaba: (Sp.) *n.* latch.

aldabís: (Sp. *al revés*: back handed slap) *n.* slap with the back of the hand.

ale: *var.* of *ali*: aunt; stepmother; term of respect for a woman one generation older than the speaker.

alegato: (Sp.) *n.* brief (*law*); plea. (*ulat*)

Alemán: (Sp.) *n.*, *adj.* German.

alembong: (*slang*) *n.* flirtatious woman.

alero: (Sp.) *n.* eaves.

algodón: (Sp. *algodón*: cotton) *n.* lactarid fish;

milkfish.

ali: *n.* stepmother; aunt; mistress, miss.

alí: *n.* evil influence.

alibadbád: *n.* nausea.

alibangbáng: *n.* kind of tree with long pods and pink to purple flowers; (*coll.*) flirt; small yellow winged butterfly.

alibangon: *n.* species of creeping plant.

alibughâ: *n.* wasteful; irresponsible.

alikabók: *n.* dust.

alikbangon: *n.* kind of weed with oval leaves that secrete a sticky, slimy fluid.

alik-ík: *n.* giggle, chuckle.

alikmatà: *n.* confused state; loss of one's sense of direction.

alikmatá: *n.* pupil of the eye (*balintatáw*).

alikót: *n.* laziness; fooling around idly.

aliktiyâ: *n.* offensive words; insult.

aligasín: *n.* mullet fish, *Mugil ceramensis*.

aligatâ: *n.* concern; considerateness; forethought; ambition.

aligbangon: *var.* of *alikbangon*.

aligí: *n.* ovary of crustaceans.

aligíd: *adj.* circling around, hovering. **aligiran** *v.* to surround, encircle

aligutgót: *adj.* entangled; *n.* trouble; mischief.

alilà: *n.* servant; **mang-alilà** *v.* treat like a servant. **alilang-kanin** *id.* servant who works without pay.

alilis: *n.* milling sugar cane. **álilisán** *n.* sugar cane mill.

alim: *n.* species of tree, *Adella monoica Blanco*.

alimango: *n.* species of crab; (*zodiac*) Cancer.

alimasag: *n.* species of crab smaller than the *alimango*.

alimbukáy: *n.* nausea; swell of water.

alimbuyugin: *n.* red-colored rooster with black spots on the wings.

alimís: *adj.* secret, furtive.

alimpapayaw: *n.* gliding flight.

alimpungát: *adj.* half-awake.

alimpusò: *n.* knot of wood.

alimpuyó: *n.* whirl, eddy.

alimpuyók: *n.* strong emission of steam or smoke.

alimulón: *adj.* cone shaped.

alimuóm: *n.* vapor rising from the ground; *id.* gossip.

alimurà: *n.* insult, criticism; scornful remarks; **alimurahin** *v.* to criticize; vilify.

alimuranin: *n.* species of large snake.

alimusod: *n.* cone; funnel shaped object.

alimusom: *n.* fragrance.

alimuwáng: *n.* occultism.

alín: *pron* which.

alinagnág: *adj.* seen through haze; *n.* hazy visibility.

alindayag: *adj.* floating in the air.

alindóg: *n.* charm, great beauty; **maalindóg** *adj.* charming.

alinmán: *pron.* whichever.

alinlangan: *n.* doubt.

alinsabay: **alinsabay** *adj.* contemporary, of the same era.

alinsangan: *n.* sultry weather.

alinsunod: *prep.* according to; following; **álinsunuran** *n.* precedent; model; statute; basis.

alintana: *n.* care; attention; concern; **alintanahin** *v.* to notice or consider in passing; be aware of.

alinugnóg: *n.* spinning.

alíng: *var.* of *saling*: light touch.

alingahit: (Ch.) *n.* hot weather; **alingahít** *adj.* hot (weather).

alingaling: *adj.* fickle, changeable.

alingaro: *n.* species of climbing shrub with sweet fruit, *Eleaeagnus philippinsis*.

alingasaw: *n.* reeking, giving off an odor; odor.

alingasngás: *n.* scandal, rumor; tumult.

alingawngáw: *n.* echo; reverberation; (*fig.*) rumor; noise, clamor.

alingayngáy: *n.* echo, reverberation.

alipalà: *adv.* suddenly, instantly; at the present moment.

alipangyán: *n.* species of snake. (*bibitunan*)

alipapâ: *n.* flat roof.

aliparó: *n.* species of small butterfly with bright multi-colored wings.

alipato: *n.* flying ember.

alipin: *n.* slave; **alipinin** *v.* to enslave.

alip-ip: *adj.* anxious, in suspense.

alipunyâ: *n.* indentured servant.

alipungá: *n.* Athlete's foot.

alipuris: *n*. blind follower.
alipustâ: *n*. insult; **alipustaín** *v*. to insult.
alipuyó: *n*. whirlpool.
alipuypóy: *n*. act of sneaking around for attention or to get one's way.
alirang: *adj*. dehydrated.
alís: *n*. departure; **umalís** *v*. to leave, depart; **alisán** *v*. to uncover, take away, pick out; drop; dismantle; **makaalís** *v*. to be able to depart; **mag-alís** *v*. to remove, take away; take off (clothes); dismiss; (coll.) fire; **magpaalís** *v*. to evict, send someone away; **paalís** *adj*. outgoing, outward bound; about to leave; **pag-aalís** *n*. removal; taking away; **pagpapaalís** *n*. dismissal; **alisín sa isip** *id*. to forget.
alisagâ: *adj*. lazy; fickle, inconsistent.
alisagság: *adj*. lazy; neglectful.
alisangsáng: *n*. strong, offensive odor.
alis-is: *n*. intense heat.
aliso: *n*. gray snapper fish.
alisto: (Sp. *listo*) *adj*. alert; ready; sharp (*mentally*).
alisuwág: *n*. humidity.
alit: **alitan** *n*. quarrel; clash, conflict; friction; faction.
alitaptáp: *n*. firefly.
alitbangon: *n*. species of succulent herb, *Cyanetis axillaris*.
alituntunin: *n*. regulation, law.
aliw: *n*. comfort, consolation; **álíwan** *n*. entertainment, amusement, relaxation; **aliwín** *v*. to console; **mag-alíw** *v*. to relax; entertain oneself; **pag-aalíw** *n*. recreation. **tagaalíw** *n*. comforter; **umaliw** *v*. to comfort, cheer up..
aliwalas: *n*. clearness; brightness; fineness; serenity. **maaliwalas** *adj*. bright; pleasant (weather); serene; **umaliwalas** *v*. to become bright.
aliwaswás: *n*. scandal; dishonor; malicious gossip; (*coll*.) capricious person.
aliw-iw: *n*. sound of flowing water.
almá: (Sp. *armar*) *n*. rising on the hind legs; bucking (*horses*); tantrum, fit of temper (*alboroto*, *sumpóng*, *ligalig*).
almagre: (Sp.) *n*. red ochre.
almasén: (Sp. *almacén*) *n*. department store.
almasiga: (Sp. *almáciga*) *n*. mastic tree; resin from the mastic tree.
almasón: (Sp. *armazón*) *n*. framework, frame.
almendras: (Sp.) *n*. almond.
almendrilya: (Sp. *almendrilla*) *n*. almond shaped file.
almete: *n*. helmet.
almirante: (Sp.) *n*. admiral.
almirés: (Sp.) *n*. stone mortar. (*lusúnglusungan*)
almiról: (Sp. *almidón*) *n*. laundry starch. (*panggás*)
almo: (*slang*, f. *almoranas*) *n*. hemorrhoids.
almohadón: (Sp.) *n*. cushion.
almoneda: (Sp.) *n*. bargain sale; public auction.
almuhasa: (Sp.) *n*. horse comb, currycomb.
almúndigás: (Sp. *albóndigas*) *n*. meatball.
almuranas: (Sp. *almorranas*) *n*. hemorrhoids.
almusál: (Sp. *almorzar*) *n*. breakfast.
almuseda: (Sp.) *n*. tax on water for land irrigation.
alò: *n*. lullaby, something that consoles or cheers up.
alob: *n*. sharpening tools (*hasà*, *tagís*, *lagís*); purification.
alod: *n*. small creek.
alók: *n*. offer, bid; **alukín** *v*. to offer.
alóg: *n*. shake, jerk; **umalóg** *v*. to shake; **alóg na ang babà** *id*. already old (chin is shaking already); **ináalóg sa bumbóng** *id*. fooling.
alogbati: *n*. kind of vine with reddish stems and edible leaves.
alon: *n*. wave; **ináalon ang dibdíb** *id*. nervous (wavy chest).
alongbani: *n*. whirlpool in water.
aloy: *n*. lullaby (*uyayi*).
alpá: (Sp. *arpa*) *n*. harp.
alpabeto: (Sp. *alfabeto*) *n*. alphabet.
alpahól: *n*. sweet potatoes cooked in syrup.
alpalpa: (Sp. *alfalfa*) *n*. alfalfa.
alpargatas: (Sp. *alpargata*) *n*. fiber sandal.
alpás: *adj*. loose (*animal*). **alpasán** *v*. set free, release from captivity.
alpilér: (Sp. *alfiler*) *n*. pin, brooch.
alpombra: (Sp. *alfombra*) *n*. rug, carpet.
alponsino: (Sp. *alfonsino*) *n*. style of haircut with close shaved sides.

alporhas: (Sp. *alforjas*) *n.* saddlebag.

alsá: (Sp. *alzar*) *n.* rousing, rebellion; **alsahan** *n.* strike, walkout; rebellion, revolt. **ialsá** *v.* to lift, raise; **alsá-balutan** *id.* changing residences (lift package). **alsahín** *v.* to cut cards; lift up slightly.

alsamiyento: (Sp. *alzamiento*) *n.* rebellion.

alsis: *n.* snapper fish.

alsó: *n.* silver-spotted gray snapper.

alta: (*slang, almusal* + *tanghalian*) *n.* brunch.

Alta: *n.* ethnic group and language of South and Eastern Luzon.

áltanghap: (*slang, almusál, tangalian, hapunan*) *n.* three meal restaurant; single meal of the day.

altapresiyón: (Sp. *alta presión*) *n.* high blood pressure.

altár: (Sp.) *n.* altar. (*dambanà*)

altura: (Sp.) *n.* altitude; summit; height of a mountain.

alubo: (OTag) *n.* foster child. (*anák-anakan*)

alugbati: *n.* Malabar night shade herb with red stems and edible spinach like leaves.

álulusán: *n.* gutter; canal (*páagusán*).

alulód: *n.* rain gutter.

alulóng: *n.* distant howling.

alulós: *n.* current of a river; **álulusán** *n.* waterway, riverbed.

alumahan: *n.* mackerel.

alumana: *adj.* noticed, attended to; *n.* care; attention.

alumbiberas: *n.* silvery pomfret fish.

alumihit: *n.* restlessness.

aluminyo: (Sp. *aluminio*) *n.* aluminum.

alumpihit: *n.* restlessness; **alumpihít** *adj.* restless; twisting.

alunigníg: *n.* faint echo or idea.

aluningníng: *n.* brilliance, resplendence.

alupág: *n.* species of tree, *Nephelium glabrum*.

alupihan: *n.* centipede (*ulupihan*).

alusiksík: *n.* resourcefulness; intensive search.

alusiman: *n.* purslane.

alusithâ: *n.* affidavit; certificate; proof.

alwán: *n.* ease (*gaán*); comfort (*ginhawà*).

alwás: *n.* unloading; unharnessing; emptying a container (*halwát*). **alwasán** *v.* to unload; empty the contents of.

alyabó: *n.* embers; gust of smoke or dust.

alyado: (Sp. *aliado*) *n.* ally.

alyamás: (obs.) *n.* paint; varnish.

alyansa: (Sp. *alianza*) *n.* alliance.

alyás: (Sp. *alias*) *n.* alias.

am: (Ch.) *var. of aám*: rice broth.

ama: (Sp.) *n.* mistress, housewife; caretaker of children.

ama: (Ch.) *adv.* seldom, rarely.

amá: *n.* father; founder; **amaín** *n.* uncle; **amáng kahoy** *id.* negligent father (wood father). **amá-amahan** *n.* foster father. **amáng-bayan** *n.* town official. **amáng-binyág** *n.* baptismal godfather. **amáng-kumpíl** *n.* male sponsor at confirmation. **amáng-lalawigan** *n.* provincial official. **amáng-lungsod** *n.* city official; mayor. **amáng-pangumán** *n.* stepfather.

amak: *n.* domestication; taming of an animal; small hut in the woods. **amák** *adj.* tame, domesticated. **amakin** *v.* to tame; befriend.

amák: *n.* hut in the forest.

amakan: *n.* species of snail.

amag: *n.* mildew, mold. **amagin** *v.* to be covered with mildew, become moldy. **amagín** *adj.* prone to become moldy.

amagong: *n.* species of shrub whose bark is used to make rope and whose fruits are used to treat gonorrhea and syphilis.

amahong: *n.* species of salt water mussel.

amaín: (rt. *ama*) *n.*uncle.

amánamin: (*ama namin*) *n.* Our Father prayer.

amanos: *adj.* on even terms.

amang: *n.* boy; daddy.

amapola: (Sp.) *n.* poppy.

amargóso: (Sp.) *n.* bittermelon. (*ampalayá*)

amarilis: *n.* goatfish.

amarilyo: (Sp.) *n.* yellow.

amasona: (Sp. *amazona*) *n.* Amazon.

amatista: (Sp.) *n.* amethyst.

amatóng: *n.* type of granary.

ambâ: *n.* uncle; threatening gesture.

ambág: *n.* contribution; **ambagán** *v.* to contribute.

ambíl: *n.* pet name; different interpretation.

Ambo: (*slang*) *n.* American male.

ambón: *n.* shower, drizzle; species of banana;

(*coll.*) giving winnings in gambling; **pa-ambón** *v.* to give out (usually gambling winnings).
ambós: (Sp.) *n.* consolation prize; both, together.
ambulog: *n.* soaring flight.
ambuwáng: *n.* large beetle.
amerikana: (Sp. *americana*) *n.* American female; coat.
amerikano: (Sp. *americano*) *n.*, *adj.* American.
ametralyadora: (Sp. *ametralladora*) *n.* machine gun.
amihan: *n.* cool northeast wind; **umamihan** to blow from the northeast.
amíl: *n.* mumble, murmur.
amilyaramyento: (Sp.) *n.* land tax.
amin: *pron.* our, ours (*exclusive*).
amin: **aminin** *v.* to confess; admit, acknowledge; **aminado** *adj.* admitted; confessed.
amiról: (Sp.) *n.* starch.
amís: *adj.* offended; oppressed.
amistád: (Sp.) *n.* friendship.
amo: (Sp.) *n.* master, employer; *id.* appellation to anyone who always gives support.
amò: **maamò** *adj.* tame, domestic; docile; meek, gentle; **amuin** *v.* to tame, coax; **ma-among kalapati** *id.* well behaved (tame dove).
amók: (Eng.) *n.* amuck, murderous frenzy; **mag-amók** *v.* to run amuck.
amol: *n.* dirt on the face.
among: (Sp. *amo*) *n.* master, boss.
amór: (Sp.) *n.* love, affection.
amorseko: (Sp. *amor seco*) *n.* burry lovegrass, *Chrysopogon aciculatus*.
amortisasyón: (Sp.) *n.* mortgage.
amot: **umamot**, **amutin** *v.* to buy at cost; **mag-amot** *v.* to sell at cost.
amóy: *n.* smell, odor; **amuyan** *v.* to smell; **pangamóy** *n.* sense of smell; scent; **amóy-kambíng** *id.* armpit odor (smell of a goat); **amóy-tsiko** *id.* drunk (smell of *chico* fruit); **naamuyán** *v.* was smelled; *id.* heard from someone.
ampalayá: *n.* bitter melon.
ampáng: *n.* toddle.
ampát: *adj.* stopped (bleeding); dammed up.
ampáw: *n.* puffed rice or corn; (*coll.*) weak.
ampáy: *n.* umpire. (*tagahatol*)
ampibyán: (Eng.) *n.*, *adj.* amphibian.
ampiyas: *n.* rain entering through cracked walls; **umampias** *v.* to leak (roof).
ampolyas: (Sp. *ampolla*) *n.* ampoule, glass vial.
ampón: *n.* adopted child; **mag-ampón** *v.* protect; **ampunan**: *n.* orphanage; asylum; **ampunín** *v.* to adopt; **tagaampón** *n.* adoptive father, benefactor.
amukì: *n.* persuasion, urging.
almusál: (Sp. *almorzar*) *n.* breakfast.
-an: *suffix.* Transitive verb suffix; nominalizing suffix, whose variant is *-han* after words ending in vowels (non-glottal stop).
anak: **kamag-anak** *n.* family, relative; **mag-kamag-anak** *adj.* related.
anák: *n.* child; offspring; **anakán** *adj.* with many children; **anák-anakan** *n.* foster child; **anakín** *v.* to adopt; **ipanganák** *v.* to be born; **kaanak** *n.* relative; **kaánákan** *n.* expected month of delivery (ninth month); **kapangá-nakan** *n.* birthday; birth; **mag-anák** *v.* to breed; **magkaanák** *v.* to breed; **magpaanák** *v.* to propagate; deliver (a child); **manganák** *v.* to give birth; deliver; **palaanák** *adj.* prolific; **panganganák** *n.* giving birth; **anák sa labás** *n.* illegitimate child; **anák-araw** (*slang*) mestizo, Eurasian; **anák-pawis** *n.* child born to the lower (laboring) class.
anakì: *adv.* apparently; seemingly.
anakláng: (Sp. *alacran*) *n.* scorpion.
anag-ag: *n.* glimmer.
anahaw: *n.* kind of palm, *Livistona rotundifolia*.
anán, an-an: *n.* patches of discolored (light) skin.
anáng: *part.* it is said; according to.
anás: *n.* whisper, low tone of speech; **ianas** *v.* to whisper.
anay: *n.* termite, white ant; (*fig.*) traitor; smallpox.
anayad: *adj.* serene, suave.
anayò, anayo: *n.* urticaria; allergy.
andadór: (Sp.) *n.* stroller; rolling walker.
andám: *n.* intuition, premonition.

andamyo: (Sp. *andamio*) *n.* gangplank.
andana: *n.* tier.
andáp: *n.* glimmer, shimmer; flicker.
andár: (Sp.) *n.* working, operation; function; development, progress. **magpaandár** *v.* to cause to run, set in action or motion; **umandar** *v.* to work, function.
andás: (Sp.) *n.* pedestal, bier with shafts.
andén: (Sp.) *n.* platform at a railway station.
ander: (Eng. under) *n.* henpecked husband.
anduk(h)â: *n.* care; protection. (*arugâ*)
anémiko: (Sp. *anémico*) *adj.* anemic.
angkohan: *n.* Palawan cherry tree.
anhín: (rt. *ano*) *v.* to do something to someone.
ani: *n.* crop, harvest; **anihin** *v.* to harvest, reap; **umani ng papuri** reaped praises
aní$_1$: (*wikà ni*) said by: **anikó** I said; **anilá** they said; **aniyá** s/he said.
aní$_2$: *n.* disgust; **maaní** to feel disgusted.
anib: **aniban** *v.* to be joined, affiliated with; **kaanib** *n.* adherent, ally, person of the same party; **umanib** *v.* to join.
anikó: [*aní* + =*ko*] I said.
anilá: [*aní* + =*nila*] they said.
aniyá: [*aní* + =*niyá*] he said, she said.
anluwagi: *n.* carpenter.
anilyo: (Sp. *anillo*) *n.* ring.
anim: *num.* six.
animado: (Sp.) *adj.* lively; encouraged.
animál: (Sp.) *n.* animal (*hayop*); (*fig.*) brute.
ánimas: (Sp. *ánimas*) *n.* ringing of church bells for the dead.
animo: *prep.* it seems.
ánimó: (Sp.) *n.* spirit, soul; courage.
aninag: *adj.* transparent; **aninagin** *v.* to look closely as, to squint; **maaninag** *v.* to be able to perceive.
aninaw: *n.* examining, inspecting; clarifying.
anináw: *adj.* shortsighted.
anino: *n.* shadow; image, reflection.
anís: (Sp.) *n.* anise.
anisado: (Sp.) *n.* anise liqueur.
anit: *n.* scalp; **umanit** *v.* to shave the head.
anito: *n.* idol, idolatry.
anlalawà, alalawà: *n.* spider.
anláw: *n.* last rinsing of clothes.
anluwagi: *n.* carpenter.

anó: *pron.* what; any; **anuhin** to do something; **dî umanó** it is said; **kaanu-ano** *interrog.* what relationship; **kahit anó** any; **ikaano** *pron.* in what order; **pang-anó** *interrog.* for what use; **magíng anumán** no matter; regardless; **magkaánúhan** *v.* to have a misunderstanding; **umanó** *v.* to do; **waláng-anumán** you're welcome; **waláng-anú-anó** all of a sudden; **maanó(ng)** please; may it be; **maanó kung** so what if; **sa anumáng paraán** in any way; at all; **Maanó ka na?** How are you? [Reduplicated form *anó-anó* used for plural/distributive subjects].
anod: *n.* flotsam; **anurin** *v.* to be carried away by the current; **maanod** *v.* to drift.
anomalya: (Sp. *anomalia*) *n.* anomaly.
anopá't: (*ano* + *pa*) in short.
anós: *adj.* overcooked, burnt.
anót: *adj.* close-cut.
ansikót: *n.* loitering; **~ero** slacker.
antá: **maantá** *adj.* rancid; **umantá** *v.* to become rancid.
antabay: *n.* slowing down in order for someone to catch up.
anták: *n.* stinging pain.
antala: *n.* delay; **maantala** *v.* to be delayed.
antandâ: *n.* sign of the cross.
antás: *n.* step; degree; grade; circumference; rim of a wheel. **antasín** *v.* to classify, grade.
antáy: *n.* brief wait; **antayín** *v.* to wait for.
antemano: (Sp.) *adv.* beforehand.
antíg: *n.* friendly reminder; **antigín** *v.* to affect; arouse.
antigo: (Sp.) *adj.* antique, ancient.
antíng-antíng: *n.* amulet, talisman.
antipátiko: (Sp. *antipático*) *adj.* displeasing, unfriendly; (*coll.*) wise guy, smart aleck.
antipolo: *n.* species of tree, *Artocarpus incisa*.
antisipo: (Sp. *anticipo*) *n.* advance payment.
antók: *n.* sleepiness; **antúkin** *adj.* always sleepy; **mag-antók** *v.* to feel drowsy; **pampaantók** *adj.* lethargic, causing drowsiness..
antót: *n.* odor of stagnant water.
antropólogo: (Sp.) *n.* anthropologist.
anubíng: *n.* species of tree, *Artocarpus cumingiana*.
anunas: *n.* pineapple.

anúnsiyo: (Sp. *anuncio*) *n.* announcement, ad.
anuwáng: *n.* water buffalo. (*kalabáw*)
anyaya: *n.* invitation; **anyayahan** *v.* to invite.
anyayà: *n.* accident; disgrace; misfortune; neglect. **manganyayà** *v.* to sabotage.
anyeho: (Sp. *añejo*) *adj.* stale, musty.
anyo: (Sp. *año*) *n.* year; **anyo-bisyesto** leap year.
anyô: *n.* form, appearance, likeness; figure; **magpaanyô** *v.* to prepare.
ang: *art.* topic marking article for general (non-personal) nouns.
angá: *adj.* agape.
angal: *n.* prolonged crying; **umangal** *v.* to cry, bawl.
ang-ang: *n.* stutter, stammer.
angás: *adj.* arrogant; proud.
angát: *adj.* somewhat higher, slightly raised; **iangát** *v.* to raise slightly.
ang-ang: *n.* stuttering.
angaw: (Ch.) *n.* million; **sanlibong-angaw** *n.* one billion.
angkák: (Ch.) *n.* kind of leaven, reddish leaves for fermentation purposes; flatulence.
angkán: *n.* clan, group; tribe; parentage; **ka-angkán** *adj.* of the same clan or group; **tala-angkanan** *n.* family tree, list of descendants.
angkás: **angkasán** *v.* to ride with someone; **iangkás** *v.* to give someone a ride.
angkát: *n.* import; **angkatín** *v.* to import.
angkín: *n.* claim; **angkinín, umangkín** *v.* to claim; demand.
angkla: (Sp. *ancla*) *n.* anchor.
angkladero: (Sp. *ancladero*) *n.* anchorage.
angklahe: (Sp. *anclaje*) *n.* anchoring; anchoring place; anchoring fee.
angkóp: *adj.* suitable, fitting, apt; appropriate; **iangkóp** *v.* to adapt to, make suitable for; **kaangkupán** *n.* suitability; pertinence; **pang-angkóp** *n.* (*gram.*) ligature.
angkora: (Sp.) *n.* anchor.
anggarilyas: (Sp. *angarillas*) *n.* handbarrow. (*arag-arag*)
anggí: *n.* spatter of rain indoors.
anggó: *n.* smell of fermenting milk.
ánggulo: (Sp. *ángulo*) *n.* angle.
angháng: *n.* pungency; **maangháng** *adj.* pungent, peppery; (*coll.*) sensual.
anghél: (Sp. *ángel*) *n.* angel; (*fig.*) patron, financier; **anghél ng tahanan** *id.* small children (angel of the home).
anghina: (Sp. *angina*) *n.* angina.
anghít: *n.* smell of underarms.
angí: *n.* smell of burnt rice.
angil: *n.* growl of a dog; **umangil** *v.* to growl.
angís: *n.* smell of excreta or putrefied food.
angít: **inangít** *n.* sticky rice cooked with salt and coconut milk.
angláw: *n.* rinsing of clothes.
anglít: (Ch.) *n.* small clay cooking pot.
anglô: (Ch.) *n.* rattan holder for jars.
angó: *n.* odor of fresh meat or fish.
angót: *n.* stench, odor.
apa: (Jap.) *n.* rice starch wafer; *id.* fragile.
apâ: *n.* groping; stolen; **apaín** *v.* to grope; steal.
apak: *n.* tread, step; **apák** *adj.* barefooted.
apad: *n.* flank; ribs; pain in the side.
apahap: *n.* silver sea bass.
apalit: *n.* sandalwood.
apalyá: *var.* of *ampalayá*: bitter melon.
apanas: *n.* kind of small red ant.
aparadór: (Sp.) *n.* dresser.
aparatista: (Sp.) *n.* machine operator.
aparato: (Sp.) *n.* apparatus, equipment.
apartado: *adj.* distant, secluded; separated.
apat: *n.* four; **apatin** *v.* divide into four parts; **labing-apat** *n.* fourteen; **ikaapat, pang-apat** *adj.* fourth; **makaapat** *adj.* four times; **mag-apat** *v.* to divide into four; **apatán** *n.* one-fourth a *gatang*; **apatin** *v.* to quarter, divide into four parts; **sangkapat** *n.* one fourth, quarter; **tig-apat** *adj.* four each.
apatiya: (Sp. *apatía*) *n.* apathy; indifference.
apaw: *n.* overflow, flood; **umapaw** *v.* to overflow.
apdó: *n.* bile; gall bladder.
apelá: (Sp. *apelar*) **iapela** *v.* to appeal.
apelyido: (Sp. *apellido*) *n.* surname. (*pamanság*)
apí: *n.* oppression; **apihín** *v.* to oppress, offend; injure.
apì: **apiapì** *n.* type of shrub that grows near the seashore with small yellow flowers and bark used for dyeing, *Avicinnia officinalis*.

apian: (Sp. *anfion*) *n.* opium.
apíd: **pakikiapíd** *n.* fornication.
apitong: *n.* species of tree, *Dipterocarpus grandiflorus*.
apiyà: (*coll.*) *n.* flatterer.
aplâ: *n.* whitish flesh under the thorax of cat-fish.
aplaya: (Sp. playa) *n.* beach.
apò: *n.* patriarch; term used to express respect. **apuin** *v.* to regard with respect.
apó: *n.* grandchild; ~ **sa talampakan** *n.* great-great grandchild; ~ **sa tuhod** *n.* great grand-child; **inapó** *n.* descendent, offspring.
apog: *n.* lime.
aporo: (Sp. *aforro*) *n.* lining (*of clothes*). (*tutóp*)
apostola: *n.* Palawan cherry tree.
apóy: *n.* fire; *id.* angry; **apuyan** *n.* fireplace; **mag-apóy** *v.* burst into flames; **magpaapóy** *v.* to ignite; **pag-apuyín** *v.* to set on fire; **pamatáy-apóy** *n.* fire extinguisher; **ináapóy ng lagnát** *id.* hot with fever.
apritada: (Sp. *fritada*) *n.* meat stew.
apulà: *n.* checking, controlling; **apulain** *v.* to check, control; **pang-apulà** *adj.* preven tative.
apulid: *n.* member of the serge family, *Eleocharis dulcis*.
apura: (Sp.) **apurahín** *v.* to hurry; **mag-apurá** *v.* to be in a hurry.
apurado: (Sp.) *adj.* in a hurry.
apyák: *n.* yolk.
apyan: (Sp. *anfion*) *n.* opium.
apyo: (Sp.) *n.* celery.
arabál: (Sp. *arrabal*) *n.* suburb.
arag-arag: *n.* handbarrow.
arahan: *n.* sea catfish, *Arius manillensis*.
aral: *n.* lesson, learning; **áralan** *n.* place for studying, school; *v.* to teach; **aralán** *n.* apprentice; **aralin** *v.* to study; **mag-aral** *v.* to study; **mag-aarál** *n.* student; **páaralán** *n.* school; **pang-aral** *n.* sermon; **kaaral** *n.* study mate; **kamag-aarál** *n.* schoolmate; **ipangaral** *v.* to preach; give advice; **mángangaral** *n.* preacher; **mangaral** *v.* to preach; give advice to; **nápag-aralan** *n.* training; education; **páaralán** *n.* school; **pag-aaral** *n.* study; observation; **pag-aralan** *v.* to study a specific subject; **pinag-aralan** *n.* education, training (in a specific field); **pampáaralán** *adj.* for use in school; **pangaral** *n.* sermon; **palaarál** *adj.* studious; **papag-aralin** *v.* to have someone study; educate; **aralíng-pambahay** *n.* homework; **bayad sa pag-aaral** *n.* tuition; **silíd-aralán** *n.* study room.
aransél: (Sp. *arancel*) *n.* tariff; custom's duty.
aranyá: (Sp. *araña*) *n.* chandelier.
arangká(da): (Sp. *arranca(da)*) *n.* spurt, bust of speed; sudden start.
arap: **mangarap** *v.* to dream; **mángangaráp** *n.* dreamer; **mapangarapín** *adj.* dreamy; **pangarap** *n.* dream, ambition; vision; **pangarapin** *v.* to dream of; **mangarap nang gising** *v.* to daydream.
araro: (Sp. *arado*) *n.* plow; **mag-araro** *v.* to plow, cultivate the soil; **mag-aararó** *n.* plowman.
aras: (Sp. *arras*) *n.* coins used in the wedding ceremony.
arastre: (Sp. *arrastrar*: drag) *n.* haulage; crawling.
araw: *n.* day; sun; **aráw, arawán** *adj.* daily; **anak-araw** *n.* albino; **kaarawán** *n.* birthday; **maaraw** *adj.* sunny; **madalíng-araw** *n.* dawn, daybreak; **magpaaraw** *v.* to put under the sun; **naáarawan** *adj.* sunny **tag-aráw** *n.* summer; **taláarawán** *n.* diary; **pang-araw-araw** *adj.* daily, every day; **umaraw** *v.* to be sunny; **bungang-araw** *n.* prickly heat; **araw na kasunód** the next day; **araw na dáratíng** future; **pagsikat ng araw** *n.* sunrise; **paglubóg ng araw** *n.* sunset; **sunog ng araw** *n.* sunburn.
aráy: *interj.* ouch.
arbularyo: (Sp. *erbulario*) *n.* quack doctor, herbalist.
arka: (Sp. *arca*) *n.* ark.
arkilá: (Sp. *alquilar*) *n.* rent.
ardilya: (Sp. *ardilla*) *n.* squirrel.
areglado: (Sp. *arreglado*) *adj.* arranged; orderly.
areglo: (Sp. *arreglo*) *n.* arrangement, agreement.
argamasa: (Sp.) *n.* mortar.

argolya: (Sp.) *n.* hoop.
aroma: *n.* kind of small spiny tree.
arì$_1$: *n.* property; **arí-arian** *n.* possessions, property; goods; **ariin** *v.* to consider; acknowledge; **may-arì** *n.* owner; **paarî** *adj.* possessive; **pag-aarì** *n.* property; **pagka-may-arì** *n.* ownership; possession.
arì$_2$: **maáarì** *adj.* possible; likely; liable; might; **di-maáarì** *adj.* impossible.
arí: *pron.* this one.
ariba: (Sp. *arriba*) *interj.* Long live!
aribaybaho: (Sp. *arriba y abajo*) *n.* sickness involving vomiting and diarrhea.
árimuhunán: *adj.* worth taking although not needed; **mag-árimuhunán** *v.* to be thrifty.
arina: (Sp. *harina*) *n.* flour.
arindá: *n.* renting, leasing.
aringkín: *n.* sudden trip, somersault.
arirà: **pangangarirà** *n.* taunting; cunning extraction of information; **arirain** *v.* to cunningly extract information; taunt; **maarirà** *adj.* cunningly inquisitive.
arisgá: (Sp.) *n.* risk; **iarisga** *v.* to risk.
arisgado: (Sp. *arriesgado*) *adj.* risky.
armás: (Sp.) *n.* weapons, arms.
arnibal: (Sp.) *n.* syrup.
arnís: (Sp. *arnés*) *n.* fencing; swordplay.
aró: (*coll.*) *interj.* is that so?
arô: *n.* my dear.
aroba: (Sp. *arroba*) *n.* measure equivalent to 25 pounds.
arók: *n.* measure for water depth; **maarok** *v.* to be able to measure the depth of.
aroskaldo: (Sp. *arroz caldo*) *n.* chicken broth with rice.
arpa: (Sp.) *n.* harp.
arpón: (Sp.) *n.* harpoon.
arsobispo: *n.* archbishop.
arte: (Sp.) *n.* art; **maarte** *adj.* artistic; insincere, artificial; **umarte** *v.* to act artificially.
artikulante: (Sp. *articulante*) *adj.* loquacious.
artista: (Sp.) *n.* actor, actress; artist.
arugâ: *n.* nurture, tender care.
arupél: *n.* tinsel, tinfoil.
aruró: *n.* arrowroot.
arúy: *interj.* ouch!
arya: (Sp. *arriar*) **aryahán** *v.* to let hang, let hang loose; strike; continue to go ahead.
asa: **pag-asa** *n.* hope; chance; **asahan** *v.* to hope for; expect; bargain for; **maáasahan** *adj.* dependable; **maasahín** *adj.* hopeful; **mapag-asa** *adj.* hopeful; **paasahin** *v.* to give someone hope; **umasa** *v.* to hope; expect; count on, depend on; trust.
asák: *adj.* in vogue.
asad: *n.* small bamboo strips woven together.
asada: (Sp. *azada*) *n.* hoe.
asado: (Sp.) *adj.* roasted.
asahár: (Sp.) *n.* orange blossoms.
asal: *n.* behavior, conduct; **asalin** *v.* to act; behave; **mag-asal, umasal** *v.* to behave; **kaasalán** *n.* behavior; conduct; **magmasamáng-asál** *v.* to misbehave; **asal-hudas** *id.* treacherous behavior (Judas' character).
asalto: (Sp.) *n.* assault.
asám: **pag-asám** *n.* longing for something; prospect; **asamín** *v.* to long for.
asanâ: *n.* species of *narra* tree.
asanorya: (Sp. *zanahoria*) *n.* carrot.
asáp: *n.* irritation of the eyes caused by smoke.
asár: (Sp. *asar*: roast) *adj.* offensive, infuriating.
asaról: (Sp. *azadón*) *n.* large hoe.
asawa: *n.* spouse; **mag-asawa** *n.* married couple; *v.* to marry; **may-asawa** *adj.* married; **magkápangasawahán** *v.* to intermarry; **mangasawa** *v.* to court someone for marriage; **pag-aasawa** *n.* getting married; **pangangasawa** *n.* courting; **papag-asawahin** *v.* to marry off; **mag-asawang kalapati** *id.* always together (dove couple); **buhay may-asawa** *n.* married life.
asbar: **asbarán** *v.* to whip, spank.
asbesto: (Sp.) *n.* asbestos.
asbók: *n.* sudden gust of smoke.
askád: **maaskád** *adj.* bitter, acrid; (*slang*) ugly; shameless, rude.
asegurá: (Sp. *asegurar*) **asegurahín** *v.* to insure.
aseleradór: (Sp. *acelerador*) *n.* accelerator.
asendero: (Sp. *hacendero*) *n.* plantation owner.
asenso: (Sp. *ascenso*) *n.* promotion, increase in salary.
asensór: (Sp. *ascensor*) *n.* elevator.

asero: (Sp. *acero*) *n.* steel.
aseyte: (Sp. *aceite*) *n.* cooking oil.
asikaso: (Sp. *hacer caso*) *n.* attention, act of paying attention; **asikasuhin** *v.* to pay attention; **maasikaso** *adj.* attentive; **mag-asikaso** *v.* to attend to; take care of.
asikót: *n.* loitering.
asignatura: (Sp.) *n.* subject in school.
asilo: (Sp.) *n.* asylum.
asim: *n.* sourness; **maasim** *adj.* sour; **umasim** *v.* to become sour.
asín: *n.* salt; **ásínan** *n.* salt bed, salty land; **as(i)nán** *v.* to pour salt on, salt; **maasín** *adj.* salty; **mag-asín** *v.* to use salt; make salt.
asintá: (Sp. *asentar*) **asintahín** *v.* to adjust; **asintado** *adj.* adjusted.
asisti: (Sp. *asistir*) **asistihán** *v.* to attend; go with; assist.
asiwà: see *ngasiwà*: administer.
asiwâ: *n.* clumsy, awkward; uneasy.
asnán: (rt. *asín*) *v.* to salt, pour salt on.
asno: (Sp.) *n.* donkey.
asngál: *n.* palate, roof of the mouth.
asngáw: *n.* smell of liquor.
aso: *n.* dog, canine; **mag-aso** *v.* to care for dogs; **mang-aso** *v.* to hunt with dogs; **asong ulól** *n.* mad dog; **parang aso't pusà** *id.* always quarreling.
asó: *n.* smoke; **umáasó ang ulo** *id.* brag.
asód: *n.* successive blows; **asuran** *n.* anvil; **asurín** *v.* to deliver successive blows to; **pang-asód** *n.* hammer.
asog: *adj.* sterile, asexual.
asoge: (Sp. *azogue*) *n.* mercury.
asotea: (Sp.) *n.* second floor veranda, roofless balcony.
aspalto: (Sp.) *n.* asphalt; **aspaltado** *adj.* paved; asphalted.
aspáragus: (Eng.) *n.* asparagus.
aspekto: (Sp. *aspecto*) *n.* aspect; (*gram.*) tense.
aspilí: (Sp. *alfiler*) *n.* pin.
aspirante: (Sp.) *n.* aspirant; candidate.
asta₁: (*slang*) *n.* brat.
asta₂: (Sp. *hasta*) **asta sa** even in; **asta sa pagsasalitâ** even in speaking.
astâ: *n.* posture, pose; bearing; action; **umastâ** *v.* to pose.
astakà: *n.* mold for making lead fishing weights.
astakâ: *adj.* eroded by water.
astíg: (*slang*, f. *tigás*) *n.* show-off, braggart; *adj.* shameless; macho; proud; successful; *interj.* fantastic.
astinggál: *n.* harquebus.
astrólogo: (Sp.) *n.* astrologer.
asuáng: see *aswang*.
asubi: *n.* mullet fish.
asugon: *n.* barracuda fish.
asukal: (Sp. *azúcar*) *n.* sugar; **asukalan** *v.* to put sugar on.
asuhos: *n.* whiting fish, sillago fish; **~-bulik** banded sillago.
asúl: (Sp. *azul*) *n.* blue; **asúl-marino** *n.* navy blue; **asulán** *v.* to add blue to; **asulín** *v.* to color blue.
asuleho: (Sp. *azulejo*) *n.* blue glazed tile.
asunto: (Sp.) *n.* lawsuit, affair; **ásuntuhan** *n.* lawsuit; litigation; **asuntuhín** *v.* to file a case against someone in court.
asungot: (*slang*) *n.* irritating person.
asuos: *n.* sillago fish, sand borer.
asupre: (Sp.) *n.* sulfur.
asusena: (Sp. *azucena*) *n.* white lily; (*coll., from aso 'dog' + cena, Spanish for dinner*) *n.* dog meat for eating.
as(u)wáng: *n.* kind of mythological creature; (*slang*) mother-in-law.
asyenda: (Sp. *hacienda*) *n.* estate, plantation, hacienda.
at: *conj.* and; **at iba pa** et cetera.
ata: *pron.* our, ours.
Ata: *n.* ethnic group and language of Negros Oriental.
atà: *var.* of *yatà*: perhaps.
atab: (*slang*, f. *batà*) *n.* sweetheart; child.
atabâ: *n.* archer fish, blowgun fish.
atake: (Sp. *ataque*) *n.* attack; seizure; breakdown; **~ serebrál** *n.* stroke.
atado: (Sp.) *n.* bundle, things tied together.
atag: *adv.* repeatedly, always; *n.* community work on making roads.
atang: (Ch.) **iatang** *v.* to help someone else put a load on their shoulders or head; **iniatang sa balikat** *id.* gave the responsibility to (placed on shoulder).

atang-atang: *n.* scorpion. (*alakdán*)
atangyá: (Ch.) *n.* smelly rice insect.
ataraya: (Sp., Vis.) *n.* cast net.
atas: *n.* command, order; mandate; **mag-atas** *v.* to command, order; impose; bid; bind, oblige by law.
atát: *n.* stutterer; stuttering. **atát na atát** (*slang*) *adj.* eager; excited; lustful, horny; impatient.
ataúl: (Sp. *ataúd*) *n.* coffin, casket.
atáy: *n.* liver; arch of the sole of the foot.
atay-atay: *adv.* little by little, slowly; *n.* cooking over a slow fire.
ate: *n.* elder sister (term used towards elder females of the speaker's generation).
ateismo: (Sp.) *n.* atheism.
ateista: (Eng.) *n.* atheist.
atento: (Sp.) *adj.* attentive.
ateo: (Sp.) *n.* atheist.
Ati: *n.* ethnic group and language of the Negritos of Panay Island; **ati-atihan** *n.* festival of the *Ati* people.
atibán: (*slang*) *n.* thief, bag snatcher.
atík: (*slang*) *n.* money.
atikabó: *n.* sudden surge; **umatikabó** *v.* to surge; burst (applause, smoke).
atikhâ: *n.* gradual accumulation of money by saving, thrift; **atihaín** *v.* to save for the future; endeavor to attain one's desire.
atíg: *n.* gentle persuasion.
atím: *n.* tolerance; **atamín** *v.* to allow; tolerate.
atin: *pron.* our, ours (*inclusive of addressee*); **atin-atin** *pron.* between us only; **ating-atin** *pron.* definitely ours; **sa atin** to us; for us; at our place; **sumaatin** *v.* to be in us; to be with us.
atindí: (Sp.) *n.* attention; **atindihín** *v.* to attend to.
atíp: *n.* thatch roof; **at(i)pán** *v.* to thatch.
atis: *n.* custard apple, sweetsop; (*slang*) hand grenade; tiled roof.
atleta: (Sp.) *n.* athlete. (*manlalarò*)
ato: **pag-ato** *n.* attempt; **umato** *v.* to attempt.
atô: *n.* familiar way of addressing someone.
atole: (Sp.) *n.* flour paste; glue.
atrakadero: (Sp. *atracadero*) *n.* dock.
atrás: (Sp.) *n.* backward movement; **atrasán** *v.* to move backward, withdraw support.
atrasado: (Sp.) *adj.* late, delinquent; behind; backward.
atraso: (Sp.) *n.* arrears, lateness; (*slang*) inconvenience; gang war; **atrasuhin** *v.* to delay.
atrebido: (Sp. *atrevido*) *adj.* daring, bold. (*marahás*)
atríl: (Sp.) *n.* easel, music stand.
atrilyadora: (Sp. *trilladora*) *n.* threshing machine.
atrosidád: (Sp. *atrocidad*) *n.* atrocity.
atsara: (Sp. *achara*) *n.* pickles. (*buro*)
atsáy: (*slang*) *n.* maid.
atsè: (*baby talk*) *n.* dirt.
atse: (Sp. *hache*) *n.* the letter *h* in the Spanish alphabet.
atséng: (*slang*) *n.* homosexual male.
atsóy: *n.* jeer; (*slang*) houseboy; **umatsóy** *v.* to jeer at.
atsuete: (Sp. *achiote*) *n.* annatto, plant whose red seeds are used in coloring food.
Atta: *n.* ethnic group and language of Cagayan Province, Luzon.
atubilí, atubilì: *n.* hesitation, reluctance; *adj.* doubtful; **mag-atubilí** *v.* to hesitate, waver; be reluctant.
atulay: *n.* hardtail fish.
atungal: *n.* cry of cattle.
atupag: *n.* regular chore; **umatupag** *v.* to do a regular chore.
auditibo: (Sp.) *n.* telephone receiver.
aumento: (Sp.) *n.* addition, increase; **aumentuhán** *v.* to increase.
autór: (Sp.) *n.* author. (*may-akdâ*)
autoridád: (Sp.) *n.* authority. (*kapangyarihan*)
awà: *n.* mercy, compassion, pity; **maawà** *v.* to have mercy on; *adj.* compassionate; **maawaín** *adj.* merciful; **kaawaan** *v.* to pity, have mercy on; **kaawa-awà, káwawà** *adj.* pitiful; wretched; **káwanggawâ** *n.* charity; **ipagmakaawà** *v.* to beg for mercy on behalf of someone; **magmakaawà** *v.* to beg for; ask earnestly; **mapagkáwanggawâ** *adj.* charitable; **nakaáawà** *adj.* arousing pity; **pagkakáwanggawâ** *n.* benevolence, charity; **pagkamaawaín** *n.* mercifulness; **pagmamakaawà** *n.* begging for mercy; **waláng-**

awà *adj.* ruthless, cruel.
awak: *n.* large body of water.
awák: *n.* overflow of water.
awáng: *n.* gap, crack, space between; *adj.* slightly open, ajar; **iawang** *v.* to leave slightly open; **nakaawáng** *adj.* ajar.
awas: *n.* overflow; **umawas** *v.* to overflow.
awás: *adj.* deducted, subtracted; dismissed; **awasan** *n.* dismissal time; **awasán** *v.* to deduct, subtract; **awasín** *v.* to unload an animal.
awat: *n.* weaning of a baby; pacification of people; **umawat, awatin** *v.* to pacify; break up a fight; **awatin sa iná** *v.* to wean; **awatan** *v.* to reduce a fire.
aw-aw: *n.* barking of dogs; (*coll.*) *n.* dog meat; **umaw-aw** *v.* to bark.
away: *n.* fight, quarrel, dispute; **mag-away** *v.* to fight, quarrel; **kaaway** *n.* enemy; **pala-awáy** *adj.* inclined to fighting; **kaaway ng liwanag** *id.* thief (enemy of light).
awditibo: (Sp. *auditivo*) *n.* earpiece; telephone receiver.
awi: **awiawi** *n.* petty merchandise.
awíng: *n.* swaying, dangling.
awit: *n.* song; anthem; **umawit** *v.* to sing; (*slang*) confess, squeal; **awitán** *n.* singing contest; **awitin** *v.* to sing; **awitín** *n.* common songs, hits; **awiting-bayan** *n.* folksong.
ay: *inversion marker used to signal non-initial predicate, contracts to 'y after vowels.* **Maganda sila = Sila'y maganda** They are beautiful.
ayà: *n.* delight; charm, beauty. **kaaya-aya** *n.* pleasant, delightful.
aya: *var. of yaya*: nursemaid.
ayaas: *n.* soft rustling sound.
ayán: *interj.* There!
ayap: **paayap** *n.* string beans. (*sitaw*)
ayát: **ayát ang bulsá** (*coll.*) *adj.* penniless.
ayaw: *n.* dislike; *v.* to not like, loathe; **umayáw** *v.* to dislike; **pag-ayaw** *n.* aversion.
ayáw-ayáw: *adj.* proportionately distributed; **ayáw-ayawang takaw** *id.* hypocrisy.
ayò: *n.* favor, partiality; bias.
ayô: *n.* tendril-bearing wooden vine, *Vitis capriolata.*
ayoko: (*ayaw + ko*) *v.* I don't want/like.
ayon: *adj.* in agreement; **ayunan** *v.* to agree with; approve; **ayon sa** according to; **kaayon ng** in agreement with; **kasang-ayon** *adj.* in agreement with; sympathetic; approving; **iayon** *v.* to correlate with; **makaayon** *v.* to be able to agree; **magkaayon** *adj.* agreeing; concurrent; **paayón** *adj.* affirmative; parallel; **sang-ayon** *adj.* disposed, willing; **pasang-ayon** *n.* act of agreeing, approval; **mapasang-ayon** *v.* to be convinced, persuaded; **umayon** *v.* to agree with; sympathize; conform; **sumang-ayon** *v.* to agree with; side with.
ayóp: **ayupín**. *v.* to humiliate; offend.
ayos: *n.* order, arrangement; ok; tidiness; condition; **ayusin** *v.* to settle; arrange, put in order; **kaayusan** *n.* order, neatness; **iayos** *v.* to fix, put in order; **isaayos** *v.* to arrange; **maayos** *adj.* orderly; **nasa ayos** *adj.* neat, in order, well-formed.
Ayta: *n.* Negrito, Aeta (language and ethnic group).
ayudante: (Sp.) *n.* assistant.
ayuno: (Sp.) *n.* fast; **mag-ayuno** *v.* to fast.
ayungin: *n.* silver perch fish.
aywán: *n.* ignorance; denial of knowledge; *v.* I don't know. (*ewan*)

B

ba: *interrogative particle.*
bâ: *n.* term of address for an elderly man.
baák: *adj.* divided into two; **kabaák** *n.* the other half.
baang: *n.* beard. (*bungót, balbás*)
baát: *n.* rattan reinforcement band.
babà$_1$: *n.* chin.
babà$_2$: *n.* lowness; descent; landing place; **bumabà** *v.* to descend, go down; **ibabà** *v.* to lower; let down; demote; degrade; put down; deposit; **pababâ** *adv.* down, downward; downstairs; **pababaín** *v.* to make lower; drop; **mababà** *adj.* low; **bábaan** *n.* place of alighting (airfield, bus station,

loading dock); harvest season of fruits; **magbabâ** *v.* to bring down; lower; harvest fruits; **magpakumbabâ** *adj.* humble; *v.* to humiliate oneself; **pagbabâ** *n.* descent; landing; **ang ibabâ** *n.* lower part; downstairs; downtown; distance of a drop; **sa ibabâ** below, beneath; underneath; downstairs; **kababaang-loób** *n.* humbleness; **mababà ang luhà** *id.* crybaby (tear is low); **pagbabâ-pagtaás** *n.* fluctuation.

babá: *n.* coitus of animals; piggy back.

babâ: *n.* descent; fruit picking season; **bumabâ** *v.* to descend; drop; **ibabâ** *v.* to take down; **tagababâ** *n.* fruit picker.

babad: *n.* soaking; (*fig.*) overstaying, staying a long time; **ibabad** *v.* to soak; **mamád** *adj.* softened and swollen from being immersed in liquid.

babadlóng: *n.* cavalla fish, *Caranx* sp.

babae: *n.* girl, female; (*fig.*) concubine; **babaero** *n.* ladies' man; **babaihin** *v.* to take a mistress; **binabae** *n.* effeminate man; **kababaihan** *n.* womanhood; **kilos-babae** *adj.* effeminate; **magpakababae** *v.* to be womanly; **mambabae** *v.* to have elicit affairs with women; **mambababae** *n.* womanizer; **pagkababae** *n.* woman-ness; **pambabae** *adj.* feminine; **babaeng ermita** (*coll.*) entertainment girl; **sakít sa babae** *n.* venereal disease.

babag: *n.* bump, impact; **ibabag ang katawán** *id.* to try hard to do (hit the body on).

babág: *n.* quarrel, fight.

babalâ: *n.* caution, warning, notice; **ibabalâ** *v.* to warn, advise, inform.

babansî: *n.* grunt fish.

babaw: *n.* shoal, shallowness; **mababaw** *adj.* shallow.

babayáw: *n.* spotted goatfish.

babayo: *n.* barracuda.

babero: (Sp.) *n.* bib.

baboy: *n.* pig, hog; **babuyan** *n.* piggery; **kababuyan** *n.* dirtiness, moral filth; **magbababoy** *n.* swine dealer.

baboy-ramó: *n.* wild hog.

badlaan: *n.* yellowfin tuna.

baka: (Sp. *vaca*) *n.* cow; **baka-baka** *n.* cowfish; **baka-bakahan** *n.* trunkfish; **bakang gatasán** *id.* backer (milk cow).

baka: **pagbabaka** *n.* battle, conflict.

bakâ: *adv.* perhaps, maybe, might.

bakal: *n.* iron; (*slang*) firearm; **magbabakal** *n.* blacksmith; **mambabakal** *n.* dishonest person; chiseler; **bakal na kalooban** *id.* brave (iron will).

bakál: *n.* pointed stick used in planting seeds; **bakalan** (*coll.*) *v.* to ask for money.

bakaláw: (Sp. *bacalao*) *n.* cod.

bakám: *n.* join, mortise, notch; cupping glass used to extract pus from boils.

bakante: (Sp. *vacante*) *adj.* vacant.

bakas: *n.* partnership; pool of money; **kabakas** *n.* shareholder; business partner; **magbakas** *v.* to pool (put money together).

bakás: *n.* print, mark; track, imprint; trace; **bakasán** *v.* to mark; **bakás-dalirì** fingerprint; **bumakas, bakasín** *v.* to trace; follow tracks; **kabakasán** *v.* to give a trace of; color; **may bakás** to have a trace of.

bakásakalì: [*baká* + *sakalì*] *adv.* by chance; possibly; **magbakásakalì** *v.* to take a chance; **pabakásakalì** *adj.* random, haphazard; **pagbabakásakalì** *n.* taking a chance.

bakasyón: (Sp. *vacación*) *n.* vacation.

bakat: *n.* impress, mark.

bakaw: (*slang*) stealing, pilfering. **bákawan** *n.* mangrove.

bakáw: *n.* heron, crane.

bakay: *n.* ambusher; **bumakay** *v.* to ambush.

bakbák: *adj.* detached; **bakbakan** *n.* fight, serious quarrel; **bakbakán** *v.* to remove the skin or bark from; flay, chastise.

baketa: (Sp. *baqueta*) *n.* drumstick; ramrod.

bakikong: *n.* catfish trap.

bakid: *n.* large basket used for carrying produce.

bakin: (*obs.*) *adv.* why.

bakit: *adv.* why.

baklá: *n.* perplexity.

baklâ: *n.* homosexual male; **pagkabaklâ** *n.* homosexuality. [Slang variants: *baklê*, *baklita*, *balalaika*]

baklád: *n.* fish corral.

baklás: *adj.* uprooted; forcibly opened.

baklî: **bakliin**: *v.* to break off snapping.
baklís: *adj.* stripped off, scratched off.
bakô: *n.* unevenness of roads.
bakod: *n.* fence; **bakuran** *n.* yard; *v.* to enclose with a fence; **magbakod ang may masisira** *id.* referring to parents with grown up daughters (one who has something that may be destroyed must fence).
bakoko: *n.* porgy fish.
bakol: *n.* fish basket; **isáng bakol ang mukhâ** *id.* with a pouting face (basket face).
bakong: *n.* species of lily-like plant, *Crinum asiaticum.*
bakood: *n.* highland, plateau.
baksâ: *n.* shoulder kerchief.
baksyô: (*slang*) *v.* to try; share.
baktáw: *n.* carpenter's line drawing instrument.
baktót: *n.* bulge.
bakulaw: *n.* ape; (*fig.*) oaf; *adj.* long-haired.
bakuli: *n.* goby; murrel fingerling; **bakulihan** *n.* sleeper fish.
bakuna: *n.* vaccine; **bakunahan** *v.* to vaccinate.
bakunót: *adj.* bent from a heavy load.
bakutot: *n.* four banded cardinal fish, mackerel scad.
bakwít: *n.* evacuation; defective pronunciation.
bakyâ: *n.* clog, wooden shoe; (*slang*) old fashioned, out of date thing; **mamamakyâ** *n.* wearers of clogs; people of a lower social level.
badáng: (*slang*) *n.* breast; wealthy girl.
badáp: (*slang*) *n.* homosexual male [Variants include: *badapdidáp, badapsíng, badapski*].
badíng: (*slang*) *n.* homosexual male.
badinga: (*slang*) *n.* hog.
badinggáy: (*slang*) *adj.* out of fashion.
badóng: (*slang*) *n.* high society male.
badúy: (*coll.*) *adj.* unkempt; not in style.
badyá: *n.* assertion, expression; mimicry; **bumadyá, badyahín** *v.* to mimic.
baga: *n.* ember, live coal; *bisugo* fish.
bagà: *n.* lung.
bagâ: *n.* abscess; tumor.
bagá: *part.* interrogative particle.
bagabag: *n.* trouble, restlessness; anxiety; **bagabagin** *v.* to distress.
bagabaga: *n.* soldierfish.
bagabundo: (Sp. *vagabundo*) *n.* vagabond.
bagakbák: *n.* pouring or flowing out.
bagahe: (Sp. *bagaje*) *n.* baggage.
bagal: *n.* sloth, tardiness; delay; **bagalan** *v.* to make slower, slacken; **mabagal** *adj.* slow.
bagamán: *conj.* although, in spite of; while.
bagamundo: *var. of bagabundo*: vagabond, tramp.
bagansyá: (Sp. *vagancia*) *n.* vagrancy; (*slang*) police.
bagáng: *n.* molar tooth; **magkabagáng** *adj.* compatible.
bagangán: *n.* mojarras fish.
bagaong: *n.* convex-lined grunt fish.
bagasbás: *n.* deep-bodied sardine fry.
bagaso: (Sp. *bagazo*) *n.* bagasse of sugar cane.
bagay: *n.* thing, object; matter; item, article; *adj.* suiting, appropriate; fitting, apropos; **bumagay** *v.* to suit, conform to, agree; **maibagay** *v.* to adapt, adjust; **pakikibagay** *n.* conformity. **bagay-bagay** various things.
bagbág: *adj.* broken up; shipwrecked; **bagbagín** *v.* to undermine; **mabagbág** *v.* to be worn away by water.
bagkát: *n.* molasses candy.
bagkô: *n.* impediment.
bagkós: *adv.* even more; on the contrary.
bagets: (*slang*) *n.* teenager.
baghán: *n.* bewilderment, stupor; **mabaghán** *adj.* stunned.
baging: *n.* vine; **magbaging** *v.* to grow vines.
bagisbís: *n.* flowing of tears; **bumagisbís** *v.* to trickle.
bagitò: *n.* inexperienced person, novice; push-over.
bagnâ: *adj.* piled in a disorderly fashion; **ibagnâ** *v.* to pile in a disorderly fashion.
bago: *adj.* new; fresh; modern, recent; *adv.* before, earlier; recently; **bagong-tao** *n.* bachelor; amateur; newcomer; **baguhin** *v.* to change, alter; renovate; **bumago** *v.* to change, alter; **magbago** *v.* to reform, get better; change; change one's attitude; **pagbabago** *n.* change; **bagong-ahon** *n.* newcomer; **bagong-bakal** *id.* new pair of

shoes (new iron); **nababago sa matá** *id.* new thing just seen (new to the eye); **pagbabagong-loób** *n.* change of opinion or attitude (changing inside); **bagong saltá** (*slang*) *n.* newcomer; **bagong tasa** (*slang*) sporting a new haircut.

bagók: *n.* thump.

bagól: *adj.* uncouth, awkward; *n.* five centavo coin.

bagón: (Sp. *vagón*) *n.* wagon.

bagoneta: (Sp.) *n.* pushcart.

bagoóng: *n.* salted fish in brine, salted shrimps in brine; **nabagoóng** *id.* has remained in the same place long (was made into *bagoóng*).

bagót: *adj.* impatient, fed up; tired out; **kabagután** *n.* exasperation.

bagsák: *n.* sudden fall or crash; kind of shark; *adj.* failed; defeated; (*slang*) very drunk; bribe; **ibagsák** *v.* to upset, defeat; put down; overthrow; flunk; **pabagsák** *id.* bribe money (in a falling manner); **ibagsák ang sisi** *id.* to blame; **bagsák-pako** (*slang*) turned down.

bagsík: **mabagsík** *adj.* brutal, ferocious.

bagtás: *n.* trail through rough country; **bagtasín** *v.* to cut through (*in passing*).

bagtíng: *n.* chord; obstacle; *adj.* taut; **bagtingín** *v.* to tighten.

baguhan: (rt. *bago*) *n.* novice.

bagumbahay: [*bago-ng bahay*] *n.* new life.

bagumbóng: *n.* shuttle; species of mite.

baguntao: [*bago-ng + tao*] *n.* bachelor.

Baguntaón: [*bago-ng taón*] *n.* New Year.

bagwís: *n.* soft feathers; **magbagwís** *v.* to grow wings; become independent; **murà pa ang bagwís** *id.* can't live independently.

bagyó: *n.* storm, typhoon; (*slang*) boasting; sexually attractive; talented, successful.

bahâ: *n.* flood; (*slang*) short pants; **bumahâ** *v.* to flood; **babahâ ang dugô** *id.* blood will flow (there will be bloodshed).

bahada: (Sp. *bajada*; *slang*) *adj.* never giving up, refusing to surrender.

bahág: *n.* G-string, loin cloth; **bahág ang buntót** *id.* coward.

bahágharì *n.* rainbow.

bahagi: *n.* part; fraction; section; element; segment; **ipamahagi** *v.* to share; distribute; **bumahagi**: *v.* to participate, share in something.

bahagyâ: *adv.* slightly; a little, somewhat; scarcely; *adj.* scant.

bahalà: *n.* responsibility; care; **kabahalà** *n.* fellow trustee; **ikabahalà** *v.* to cause concern; **ipabahalà** *v.* to leave the responsibility for something to someone else; **mabahalà** *v.* to be concerned, worried; **mamahalà** *v.* to be in charge of, manage; control, supervise; **pabahalà** *n.* trust; **pábahalaán** *n.* board of trustees; **pamahaláan** *v.* to govern; direct, manage, control; regulate; **pámahalaán** *n.* government; management; **pamamahalà** *n.* rule; supervision; direction; **pagkabahalà** *n.* worry, anxiety; trusteeship; **tagapamahalà** *n.* manager; **magwaláng-bahalà** *v.* to disregard; **bahalà na** come what may.

bahaw: *n.* left-over rice; healing; **baháw** *adj.* healed; **mamahaw** *v.* to eat leftovers.

baháw₁: *n.* mountain owl.

baháw₂: *adj.* low pitched (voice).

bahay: *n.* house, residence; **baháy-baháy** *adj.* house to house; **bahayán** *n.* community of homes; **kabahay, kasambaháy** *n.* housemate; **kabahayan** *n.* village; **kapitbahay** *n.* neighbor; **mabahay** *adj.* having many homes (in one place); **makibahay** *v.* to lodge with others; **makipamahay** *v.* to live with others (in one house); **magbahay** *v.* to build a house; **magkakapitbahay** *n.* neighborhood; **mamahay** *v.* to set up a residence; reside in a certain place; **maybahay** *n.* wife; **pabahay** *n.* house expenses; **pagpapabahay** *n.* housing; **pambahay** *adj.* household; **pamahayan** *v.* to reside in a certain place; **pámahayán** *adj.* residential; **bahay na pulá** *id.* red lighthouse, whorehouse; **bahay-bahayan** *n.* doll house; **bahay at paligid** *n.* premises; **taong-bahay** *n.* housekeeper.

bahay-aklatan: *n.* library.

bahay-áliwan: *n.* amusement house.

bahay-ampunan: *n.* asylum, orphanage.

bahay-anilan: *n.* beehive.

bahay-baboy: *n.* pig pen.

bahay-bákasyunan: *n.* vacation home.

bahay-batà: *n.* uterus, womb.

bahay-kalakal: *n.* business firm.
bahay-katayán: *n.* slaughterhouse.
bahay-kubo: *n.* nipa hut.
bahay-gagambá: *n.* spider web.
bahay-harì: *n.* royal palace.
bahay-langgám: *n.* ant nest.
bahay-manók: *n.* chicken coop; **bahay-manukan** *n.* poultry house.
bahay-páaralán: *n.* school.
bahay-págamutan: *n.* hospital.
bahay-pámahalaán: *n.* town building, municipal hall.
bahay-pánuluyan: *n.* boarding house.
bahay-parì: *n.* monastery.
bahay-pukyutan: *n.* beehive.
bahay-putaktí: *n.* wasp hive.
bahay-sanglaan: *n.* pawnshop.
bahay-sáyawan: *n.* dance hall; cabaret.
bahay-súgalan: *n.* casino, gambling house.
bahay-tubig: *n.* urinary bladder; small body of stagnant water; sinkhole.
bahid: *n.* blot, stain, spot; **bahid-dungis** *n.* dirt stain; stain on one's name; **waláng bahid** *id.* with reputable character (no stains). **bahid-pulitika** *n.* dirty politics.
bahilya: (Sp. *vajilla*) *n.* dinner set.
bahín: *n.* sneeze; **bumahín** *v.* to sneeze.
bahiti: (Sp. *bajete*) *adj.* financially broke; short.
baho: (Sp. *bajo*) *n.* bass.
bahò: *n.* bad odor; **mabahò** *adj.* foul, smelly; fetid; **mamahò** *v.* to smell, emit a foul odor; **mabahuan** *v.* to be affected by a bad odor.
bahóg: *n.* pig feed, slops; broth with rice.
bahón: (Sp. *bajón*) *n.* bassoon.
baikì: *n.* mumps.
baile, bayle: (Sp. *baile*) *n.* dance.
baimbî: (Ch.) *n.* jingle bell.
bainát: *n.* relapse.
bainó: *n.* lotus plant.
baisán: *n.* relationship between the parents of a married couple; **baisanan** *n.* wedding reception.
baít: *n.* kindness; **mabaít** *adj.* kind, good natured, virtuous; mild, amiable; *n.* euphemism for rats; **bumaít** *v.* to become good.
baitang: *n.* step; stair; grade, degree.
bala: (Sp.) *n.* bullet (*punglô*); slug; (*slang*) answer sheet; money; **bala-balahan** *n.* blank cartridge; **pambala sa kanyón** *id.* useless person (bullet for the canon).
balà: *n.* thread; warning; caution; **balaan** *v.* to warn, caution.
balaat: *n.* metal reinforcement for tool handles; inside headband of a helmet.
balabà: *n.* whole leaf or joint of bananas or palms.
balaát: *n.* metal ring around a barrel.
balabág: *n.* cast, throw; **balabagín** *v.* to throw, cast.
balabal: *n.* shawl; cloak.
balabala: *n.* decussated snapper fish.
balábalâ: *n.* pretense, make-believe.
balabalakì: *n.* potpourri.
balak: *n.* plan, idea; purpose, aim; **bumalak** *v.* to study, calculate; verify.
balakáng: *n.* hip; loin, pelvis.
balakás: *n.* strips of rattan wound around something to fortify it.
balakbák: *n.* dried bark.
balakì: *n.* variety; *adj.* mixed.
balakíd: *n.* obstacle; **balakirán** *v.* to stumble.
balakilan: *n.* rafter, crossbeam.
balaklaót: *n.* northwest wind.
balaksilà: *n.* obstacle.
balakubak: *n.* dandruff.
balakwít: *n.* species of heart-shaped mollusk, *Strombus canarium*.
balakyót: *adj.* wicked, deceitful.
baladre: *n.* oleander type shrub.
balae: *n.* parent-in-law.
balag: *n.* trellis.
balagat: *n.* collarbone, shoulder blade.
balagbág: *n.* crossbeam; **bumalagbág** *v.* to lie across, intersect.
balaghán: *n.* wonder, amazement; **kababalaghán** *n.* mystery; miracle; marvel; phenomenon; **mabalaghán** *v.* to be astonished.
balagtás$_1$: **bálagtasan** *n.* poetical joust (coined after Tagalog literary figure).
balagtás$_2$: *n.* direct path, short cut; crossing the street; **balagtasín** *v.* to take a short cut; utter directly.
balagwít: *adj.* carried on two ends of a bamboo

pole.
balahibo: *n.* fine body hair; feather; plumage; fur; **walâ sa balahibo** *id.* cannot compare to.
balahò: *n.* swamp, bog.
balahurà: (*slang*) *adj.* dirty; **balahurain** *v.* to slander, disparage.
balaíd: *n.* hemorrhoids.
balaís: *adj.* restless; worried.
balam: *n.* delay; **balám** *adj.* delayed.
balambán: *n.* membrane.
bálaná: *pron.* anyone, anybody.
balanan: *n.* small fish basket.
balandra: *n.* bouncing; (*fig.*) defeat.
balanì: *n.* magnetism; charm; **batubalanì** *n.* magnet; **mabalanì** *v.* to be attracted to; **kabalanian** *n.* magnetism; **mabalanian** *v.* to be magnetized; **may-balanì** *adj.* magnetic.
balanoy: *n.* sweet basil.
balansa: (Sp.) *n.* weighing scale; balance.
balansáng: *n.* confusion; overthrow; disorder; **balabalansangín** *v.* to upset, overthrow something.
balanse: (Sp. *balance*) *n.* balance.
balantáy: **kabalantáy** *adj.* adjacent, close.
balantók: *n.* span; bamboo arch; **balantukan** *n.* partially healed wound.
balanyâ: *n.* theft.
balang[1]: *pron.* each; each one; any.
balang[2]: *n.* locust; flying fish.
balangâ: *n.* wide-mouthed earthen jar.
balangáw: *n.* rainbow. (*bahaghari*)
Balangáo: *n.* ethnic group and language from Eastern Bontoc Province, Luzon.
balangay: *n.* community of people; sailboat.
balangáy: *n.* backstroke; swoon, fainting spell.
balangkás: *n.* framework; frame; structure, outline; profile; **magbalangkás** *v.* to plan, plot; frame.
balangkát: *n.* ring; rim, edge, border to reinforce torn objects.
balangkawitan: *n.* species of brown migratory pond bird with long legs and a long bill, *Numenius madagascariensis*.
balangkinitan: *adj.* slender.
balanggót: *n.* species of aquatic reed.
balangwán: *n.* mackerel scad fish.
balaong: *n.* kind of large bamboo basket.
balaráw: *n.* dagger.
balariid: **mabalariid** *v.* to choke.
balarilà: *n.* grammar; **pambalarilà** *adj.* grammatical.
balás: *n.* north wind; coarse grains of starch.
balasa: (Sp.) *n.* shuffling; (*slang*) street fight; **bumalasa** *v.* to misdeal; **magbalasa** *v.* to shuffle.
balasaw: *n.* riot, tumult.
balasik: *n.* **mabalasik** *adj.* fierce, stern; brave.
balasubas: *n.* swindler; tightwad; (*slang*) *adj.* rude; antisocial; bad credit risk.
bálat: *n.* birthmark, blotch on the skin. [Denotes unluckiness, e.g. **may balat sa puwít** He is unlucky].
balát: *n.* skin, hide, pelt; peel, rind; wrapper (*for lumpiya*); cover of a book; **balatan** *v.* to skin, bark, peel; bind a book; **magbalát** *v.* to take the skin off; bind (a book); **pabalát ng aklát** *n.* jacket of a book; **balát-kalabáw** *id.* thick skinned (water buffalo hide); **balát-sibuyas** *id.* thin and smooth skin (onion skin); (*fig.*) *adj.* oversensitive; **pabalát-bunga** *id.* not sincere as in inviting (skin-fruit); **pabalát-bunga** *id.* only for the sake of courtesy.
balatay: *n.* stripe; *adj.* lying stretched out flat; **balatayan** (*coll.*) *v.* to court, woo.
balatbát: *n.* careless binding; binding materials; **balatbatán** *v.* to tie, bind (carelessly).
balat-kayô: *n.* disguise, camouflage; mask; transformation.
balato: (Sp. *barato*) *n.* share of money given by a gambling winner to the losers; **balatuhan** *v.* to give a share of one's winnings.
balatok: *n.* gold ore.
balatók: *n.* hitting with a short stick.
balatong: *n.* mungo bean, *Phaseolus mungo*.
balatóng: *n.* obstacle; guess work.
balaw-baláw: *n.* boiled rice and anchovies.
balawbáw: *adj.* full, overflowing.
balawís: *n.* rebel, scoundrel; *adj.* fierce.
baláy: *n.* small flag; pole with a trap to catch birds.
balayág: **balayagán** *v.* to investigate someone, interrogate; **mambabalayág** *n.* inquisitor.
balaybáy: *n.* cluster; fallen palm leaves; bed-

time stories.
balayong: *n.* species of tree, *Pahudia rhomboidea* (*tindalo*)
balayubay: *n.* dark dandruff.
balbál: *adj.* vulgar word; slang expression; broken pieces of pottery or glass.
balbás: (Sp. *barba*) *n.* beard; **balbás-pusà** *id.* thin moustache.
balbino: (*slang*) *n.* idiot.
balbón: (Sp. *barbón*) *adj.* with a heavy heard, hairy.
bálbula: (Sp. *válvula*) *n.* valve.
balkón: (Sp. *balcón*) *n.* balcony.
balkonahe: (Sp. *balconaje*) *n.* small porch.
baldá: (Sp. *falta*) *n.* failure, lack; omission.
baldakín: (Sp. *baldaquín*) *n.* canopy.
baldado: (Sp.) *adj.* defective; crippled, disabled.
baldé: (Sp.) *n.* bucket, pail. (*taóng*)
baldóg: (*slang*) *n.* valium (*bulyúm*); stealing.
baldosa: (Sp.) *n.* tile.
baldukín: (Sp. *baldaquín*) *n.* canopy, dais.
bale: (Sp. *vale*) *n.* promissory note; **bale-bale** *adj.* valuable; **di bale** it doesn't matter. **balihin** *v.* to buy on credit. **balihan** *v.* to buy on credit from.
balewalâ: *var.* of *baliwalâ*: of no value.
baléy: (Eng.) *n.* ballet.
bali: *n.* bamboo granary for unhusked rice.
balì: *n.* fracture; **balî** *adj.* fractured, broken; (*slang*) crazy; **baliin** *v.* to break. **balî ang kamáy** *id.* doesn't know how to write.
baliad-ád: *adj.* bent backwards.
balián: *n.* scarecrow made of hay.
balibág: **ibalibág** *v.* to cast, hurl.
balibang: **ibalibang** *v.* to throw upward.
balibát: *adj.* contradictory.
balibid: *n.* wound reinforcement.
balibol: *n.* auger, drill; volleyball.
balík: *n.* return; **bumalik** *v.* to return; **balikán** *v.* to go back for; **balikín** *v.* to turn over (to the reverse side); **ibalik** *v.* to return; replace; extradite; **pabalik** *adv.* on the way back, backward; **pabalikín** *v.* to recall, call someone back; **kabalikán** *n.* usual return time; opposite, reverse; **ipabalík** *v.* to have something sent back; **magbalík** *v.* to return; give back; **magpabalík** *v.* to throw back; reflect (light); **magpapanumbalik** *v.* to restore; **nagbalík ang hangin** *id.* the happenings were reversed (wind returned); **papanumbalikin** *v.* to renew; restore.
balík-aral: *n.* review of previous lesson(s).
balikaró: *n.* swelling of lips; thickening of the edges (wounds).
balikaskás: *adj.* flayed, peeled off; **balikbayan** *n.* person who returns to the Philippines after a long absence.
balikat: *n.* shoulder; **bálikatán** *adj.* with all one's efforts. **balikatin** *v.* to shoulder; carry on one's shoulder. **bálikatín** *n.* shouldered work (performed single-handedly). **pinakibít ang balikat** *id.* didn't care (shrugged the shoulders).
balikawkáw: *adj.* twisted out of shape.
balikbayan: [*balik* + *bayan*] *n.* Philippine returnee; (*slang*) multiple offender.
baliktád: *var.* of *baligtád.*
balikukô: *adj.* twisted; **balikukuín** *v.* to twist, bend.
balikungkóng: *n.* curving upward.
balikuskós: *n.* scales, scurf.
balikutsá: (Sp. *mecocha*) *n.* taffy; state of being completely dry.
balikwás: *n.* sudden jumping; **bumalikwás** *v.* to spring up.
balidasyón: (Sp. *validación*) *n.* validation (*pagbibigáy-bisà*); confirmation.
bálido: (Sp. *válido*) *adj.* valid. (*may-bisà*)
baliga: *n.* eel goby.
balighô: *adj.* absurd; impossible.
baligtád, baliktád: *adj.* inside-out; upside-down; **baligtarín** *v.* to reverse, turn inside-out, upside-down; **báligtaran** *n.* paying back of a loan by contract; *adj.* reversible (jacket); **bumaligtád** *v.* to turn upside down; reverse oneself; change to an opposite side; **kabaligtarán** *n.* opposite, contrary; **ibaligtád** *v.* to reverse; turn over; turn inside out or upside down; **pabaligtád** *adv.* in reverse; upside down; **pagbaligtád** *n.* reversal; **pambabaligtád** *n.* irony; **baligtád ang bulsá** *id.* penniless.
baligyâ: *n.* peddler; hawker.

balihandâ: *n.* loiterer; lascivious woman.
balila: *n.* cutlass fish, hairtail fish; (*slang*) punishment paddle.
baliling: *n.* twisted neck.
balimbíng: *n.* star fruit; (*fig.*) turncoat, traitor.
balindáng: *n.* water hose; coarse cloth; **balindangan** (*coll.*) *n.* gossip.
balino: *n.* restlessness, anxiety.
balinô: *n.* act of misleading; **magbalinô** *v.* to mislead, deceive.
balinsasayaw: *n.* kind of small bird.
balinsusô: *n.* ringlet, curl of hair.
balintatáw: *n.* pupil of the eye.
balintawák: *n.* butterfly sleeve dress.
balintiyák: *adj.* passive (verbs); doubtful.
balintóng: *n.* somersault.
balintunà: *adj.* unnatural; contradictory; ironic.
balintunay: *n.* paradox, irony.
balintuwád: *adj.* upside-down.
balintuwáng: *n.* falling head first.
baling: *n.* turn; **balingan** *v.* to turn.
balingadngád: *adj.* twisted backward. **balingadngarín** *v.* to twist backward.
balingangà: *adj.* with a twisted neck. **balingangain** *v.* to twist someone's neck.
balingkinitan: *adj.* slender.
balinghád: *adj.* partially rolled upward (edge of a leaf, pages of a book).
balinghát: *adj.* blown inside-out (umbrella).
balinghóy: *n.* species of cassava.
balingót: *adj.* half-deaf.
balingus: **balingusan** *n.* bridge of the nose.
balingusngós: *n.* bad mood.
balingót: *adj.* partially deaf.
balíng-uwáy: *var.* of *balingwáy*: species of rattan.
balinguyngóy: *n.* nose bleed; uneasiness, anxiety.
balingwáy: *n.* species of rattan; tendril climbing reed-like plant.
balisa: *n.* anxiety, uneasiness; concern; **balisá** *adj.* worried, anxious.
balisakáng: *n.* hips; pain in the hips.
balisaksák: *adj.* robust, vigorous.
balisasa: (Pam.) *n.* large cone-shaped fish net.
balisawsáw: *n.* painful discharge of urine; (*fig.*) caprice, whim; **bálisawsawin** *adj.* Capricious; prone to painful urination.
balisbís: **bálisbisan** *n.* eaves of a roof.
baliskád: *adj.* bristling, standing on end (hair).
balisóng: *n.* butterfly knife; **bumalisóng** *v.* to strike with a butterfly knife.
balisungsóng: *n.* funnel.
balisusô: *adj.* curled (like a shell).
balità: *n.* news, information; item; advice, notice; *adj.* renowned, famous; known; **balitaan** *v.* to inform someone of the news; **kabálitaan** *n.* newspaper correspondent; **ipabalità** *v.* to get the news from someone; **ipamalità** *v.* to spread the news around; **mabalità** *adj.* newsworthy; **mábalità** *v.* to be passed around (news); be rumored; **magbalità** *v.* to relay news; **mamalità** *v.* to proclaim; **pabalità** *n.* news sent to someone; **pagbalità** *n.* relaying the news; **tagapagbalità** *n.* reporter, announcer; **walâ kang balità** *id.* you don't know; **balitang-kutsero, balitang-barbero** *n.* hearsay, false report; **balitang-balità** *adj.* widely known.
balitakták: *n.* heated debate.
balitang: *n.* land measure of one thousand square fathoms.
balitaw: (Bis.) *n.* love song; fandango.
balitì: *n.* manacle; species of tree; **balitiin** *v.* to hold someone behind his back.
balitók: *n.* gold ore.
balíw: *adj.* lunatic, crazy, insane.
baliwag: *adj.* profound.
baliwalâ: *adj.* of no value. **baliwalaín** *v.* to disregard.
baliwasnán: *n.* fishing rod.
baliwis: *n.* siganid fish.
balo: *n.* garfish, billfish.
balok: *n.* thin membrane inside the shell of an egg; membrane.
balón: *n.* water well; **balon-balón** *adj.* uneven.
balong: *n.* spring of water, small stream; **bumalong** *v.* to ooze out, flow.
balór: (Sp. *valor*) *n.* value; importance; power; courage.
balot: *n.* wrapper, wrapping; **balutan** *n.* bundle, pack; *v.* to wrap; **balót sa putî** *id.* heavily in debt (wrapped in white).
balót: *n.* duck egg with a developed embryo;

(*slang*) zero score (*itlóg*).
balota: (Sp.) *n.* ballot.
balsá: (Sp.) *n.* ferry, raft.
balse: (Sp. *valse*) *n.* waltz.
balták: *n.* hitch, yank, strong pull.
baltík: *n.* stubbornness; (*slang*) craziness.
baluán: *n.* wavy-lined grouper.
balubad: *n.* cashew.
balubalô: *n.* pretense; fiction.
balubatà: *adj.* middle-aged.
balukag: **bumalukag** *v.* to stand on end, bristle.
balukanád: *n.* species of tree whose seeds are used for oil, *Aleurites moluccana.*
balukas: *n.* escape; fugitive.
balukaskás: *n.* roughness of a surface.
balukaykáy: *n.* imperfect or unequal circle, spiral.
balukì: **balukî** *adj.* crooked; twisted.
balukiskís: *adj.* peeled off.
balukol: *n.* act of twisting the neck to kill (fish).
baluktót: *adj.* crooked, bent; wicket; *n.* kink, curl; distortion; **bumaluktót** *v.* to bend, bow; submit; **mamaluktót** *v.* to huddle up; curl up; **mabaluktót** *v.* to curl up; buckle; *adj.* pliable, flexible, bendable.
baludbód: *n.* scattering things sparingly.
balugà: *n.* half-breed Aeta; (*slang*) ugly, dark person.
balugbóg: *n.* nape of the neck of fowls; spine.
balugo: *n.* St. Thomas bean.
balulang: *n.* rooster not trained for cock-fighting; chicken coop.
balumbalunan: *n.* gizzard of fowls.
balumbón: *n.* roll; wad; thick crowd.
balumbóng: *n.* holder for the wick in a gas lamp.
balungain: *n.* mullet.
balunglugód: *n.* pride.
balungos: *n.* snout of fish; **kuskus** ~ empty talk; ado.
balusbós: **mamalusbós** *v.* to be spilled (grains).
balustrada: (Sp.) *n.* balustrade, banner.
balutan: (rt. *balot*) *n.* package.
balutbót: **balutbutín** *v.* to pry into, examine.
balutì: *n.* armor, breast plate.
balwarte: (Sp. *baluarte*) *n.* bulwark, defense.
balwég: [*slang*, f. *Father Balweg*] *n.* priest
balyena: (Sp. *ballena*) *n.* whale.
balyós: *n.* barracuda.
bambakì: *n.* interior pellicle of bamboo.
bambán: *n.* inner membrane of fruits; *adj.* hollow.
bambáng: *n.* canal, ditch.
bambangin: *n.* flame-colored snapper.
bambangon: *n.* red snapper.
bambú: *n.* club, cudgel.
bamì: (Ch.) *n.* flour noodles cooked with meat or shrimp.
banâ: *n.* marsh, swamp; pool.
banaag: *n.* glimmer, ray.
banabá: *n.* tree with purple flowers, *Lagerstroemia speciosa.*
banakal: *n.* rind of fruit.
banahan: *n.* yellow-margined grouper fish.
banak: *n.* mullet.
banakal: *n.* rind of trees.
banál: *adj.* holy; virtuous; blessed; **banalín** *v.* to sanctify, make holy; **kabánálan** *n.* virtue, sanctity, piety; **magpabanál** *v.* to bless; sanctify; **magbanál-banalan** *v.* to pretend to be holy; **banál banayod sa ilalim ang kayod** *id.* sinner who pretends to be just.
banalo: *n.* kind of shrub with large flowers, *Cordia subcordata.*
banás: *n.* sultry weather; **kabanasán** *n.* sultry weather; **mabanás** *adj.* sultry; **makabanás** *v.* to be affected by sultry weather.
banat: *n.* act of stretching by pulling, act of hitting; (*slang*) sexual experience of women (stretched vagina); *v.* shoot, hit; copulate; **banát** *adj.* tense, stretched; **banatin** *v.* to stretch by pulling; **mabanatan** *v.* to be mauled, beat up; **magbanat ng ugát** *v.* to do physical exercise; **magbanat ng butó** *id.* work hard for a living (stretch the bone).
banay-banay: *n.* acting in moderation.
banayad: *adj.* soft, gentle; **kabanayaran** *n.* modesty, dignity; **magbanayad** *v.* to behave with dignity; **banayaran** *v.* to do slowly.
banban: *n.* kind of shrub with large leaves, *Dona cannaeformis.*
bankutà: *n.* large squid.
banda: (Sp.) *n.* band.

bandá: *n.* place, part; **banda sa** towards; **sa may bandá** towards; **banda alas siyete** around seven o'clock..

bandahalì: *n.* majordomo; manager.

bandáy: *adj.* stupid; depraved.

bandeha: (Sp. *bandeja*) *n.* tray; **pabandeha** *n.* passing of a (church) collection tray; (*fig.*) customary offering of food by the family of a prospective groom to the family of the bride.

bandehado: (Sp. *bandejado*) *n.* platter.

bandera: (Sp.) *n.* flag (*watawat*); **bumandera** *v.* to win (in horseracing); to show oneself openly.

bandereta: (Sp.) *n.* pennant; streamer; army camp colors.

banderín: (Sp.) *n.* camp colors; railway flag.

bandido: (Sp.) *n.* bandit; **kabandiduhan** *n.* banditry.

bandilà: (Sp. *bandera*) *n.* flag.

bandó: (Sp.) *n.* proclamation; **ipagbandó** *v.* to proclaim.

bandolero: (Sp.) *n.* bandit.

bandurya: (Sp. *bandurria*) *n.* small guitar, mandolin.

banháy: *var.* of *bangháy*: rough draft, outline.

banidád: (Sp. *vanidad*) *n.* vanity.

banidoso: (Sp.) *adj.* vain.

baníg: *n.* sleeping mat; (*slang*) drug addict with ample supplies; **baníg-usá** *n.* kind of hairy grass.

banil: *n.* welt; dirt on the neck; swollen veins.

banilya: (Sp. *vainilla*) *n.* vanilla.

banlág: *adj.* squint-eyed.

banlát: *n.* pigpen; fish corral.

banláw: *n.* first rinsing; **banlawan** *v.* to rinse.

banlî: *n.* scalding; **banlian** *v.* to scald.

banlík: *n.* slime; silt.

banlók: *n.* hole in the ground.

bangág: (*slang*) *adj.* high on drugs.

banglóg: *n.* spotted cavalla fish.

banluág: *adj.* adulterated; *n.* cocktail.

banô: (*slang*) *adj.* stupid.

banoglawin: *n.* weathercock.

banos: *n.* long piece of farmland.

banoy: *n.* eagle.

bansâ: *n.* nation; state; **isabansâ** *v.* to nationalize; **makabansâ** *adj.* nationalistic; **pambansâ** *adj.* national; **pagkabansâ** *n.* nationality; **pagkakásabansâ** *n.* nationalization; **kapit-bansâ** *n.* neighboring country.

banság: *n.* motto, slogan; surname; *adj.* famous; **bansagán** *v.* to give a name to; be boastful to; **magbanság** *v.* to divulge, make known; **magpabanság** *v.* to censure, ridicule; **ipabanság** *v.* to make known; **pamamanság** *n.* public declaration.

bansî: *n.* drinking straw; native flute.

bansíw: *n.* taste or stench of fermented broth.

bansót: *adj.* stunted in growth.

bantâ: *n.* threat; suspicion; **magbantâ** *v.* to threaten; **pagbantaán** *v.* to threaten someone.

bantád: *adj.* familiar, accustomed; bored, tired of; weary.

bantás: *n.* punctuation; **bantasan** *v.* to punctuate.

bantáy: *n.* guard, sentry; **bantayán** *v.* to guard, watch over; **bantayan** *n.* watchtower, sentry box; arms of a balance; **magbantáy** *v.* to keep watch; guard; **bantáy-salakay** *n.* dishonest guard (attacking guard).

bantayog: *n.* monument, memorial.

bantíl: *n.* light slap with the open hand.

bantilan: *n.* wharf, pier; dock.

bantiláw: *adj.* half-cooked; uncertain.

bantíng: *n.* rope, cable.

bantitì: (Ch. *bân* t^h*î* t^h*î*: very slow) *n.* delay; hesitation, doubt.

bantô: *n.* dilution; immigrant; **bantuán** *v.* to dilute, adulterate.

Bantoanon: *n.* ethnic group and language from Romblon Province.

bantód: *n.* diameter.

bantóg: *adj.* famous; distinguished; shining; **kabantugán** *n.* fame.

bantót: *n.* stench.

bantulót: *adj.* hesitant; **bumantu-bantulot** *v.* to sneak around.

banuyo: *n.* species of tree, *Wallaceodrendron celebicum.*

banyadero: (Sp. *bañadero*) *n.* bathing resort.

banyagà: *n.* foreigner, alien.

banyás: *n.* boa.

banyera: (Sp. *bañera*) *n.* bathtub, washtub.
banyo: (Sp. *baño*) *n.* bathroom.
banyós: (Sp. *baños*) *n.* sponge bath.
banyuháy: (*coined: bago + anyo + buhay*: new + form + life) **magbanyuháy** *v.* to metamorphose.
bangà: *n.* fan palm.
bangâ: *n.* earthen jar.
bangág: (*slang*) *adj.* high on drugs.
bangál: *adj.* torn off, lopped off; *n.* mouthful.
bangán: *n.* granary, barn.
bangas: *n.* bruise on the face. **bangás** *adj.* wounded on the face; harelipped.
bangaw: *n.* blowfly; (*slang*) eating; wearing thick sunglasses; pest; **binangaw** *adj.* infested with flies; **binangaw sa takilya** (*slang*) *n.* flop movie.
bang-aw: *adj.* crazy, demented, insane.
bangay: *n.* noisy quarrel; **magbangay** *v.* to squabble, quarrel; **magbangayán** *v.* to squabble with others.
bangayngáy: *n.* ornate sleeper fish.
bangbáng: *n.* drain.
bangbangin: *n.* red snapper, *Lutianus sp.*
bangkâ: *n.* native canoe; **magbangkâ** *v.* to ride in a *bangkâ*; **mámamangkâ** *n.* boatman, ferryman; **mamangkâ** *v.* to go by boat; go boating; **pamamangkâ** *n.* riding by boat.
bangkál: (Sp. *bancal*) *n.* terrace.
bangkaláng: *n.* salamander.
bangkarota: (Sp. *bancarrota*) *adj.* bankrupt.
bangkás: *n.* multicolored fighting cock.
bangkaso: *n.* semi-spherical hamper.
bangkát: *n.* rope reinforcement, plaited rope; **bangkatín** *v.* to reinforce (by tying).
bangkáy: *n.* corpse.
bangkero: (Sp. *banquero*) *n.* banker; boatman; dealer in cards; (*slang*) life of the party.
bangketa: (Sp. *banqueta*) *n.* sidewalk; footpath.
bangkete: (Sp.) *n.* banquet; **magpabangkete** *v.* to give a banquet.
bangkîl: *n.* large round basket.
bangkilas: *n.* raft; fluvial parade float; glimmer of sun rays.
bangkilíng: *adj.* slightly twisted, turned.
bangkitò: (Sp. *banquito*) *n.* small bench, stool.
bangkiyáw: *n.* torn mat used as a flag to scare birds away from grains.
bangko: (Sp. *banco*) *n.* bank; **papel-de-bangko** *n.* banknote.
bangkô: (Sp. *banco*) *n.* bench.
bangkóng: *n.* concavity.
bangkoro: *n.* Indian mulberry, *Morinda citrifolia.*
bangkukang: *n.* ulcerous wound.
bangkúlit: *n.* superficially healed wound.
bangkulóng: *n.* trap; **bangkulungín** *v.* to trap, blockade.
bangkutà: *n.* kind of large squid; coral reef.
bangkuwáng: *n.* kind of coarse mat.
bangê: *adj.* high on drugs.
banggâ: *n.* automobile accident, collision; impact; **banggaín** *v.* to collide; **bumanggâ** *v.* to crash into; **kabanggaín** *v.* to oppose (in a competition); **bumanggâ sa padér** *id.* fought against a powerful opponent (bumped the wall).
banggera: *n.* extension of a kitchen where china is kept.
banggít: *n.* mention; **banggitín** *v.* to cite; mention; **bumanggít** *v.* to mention; **pamanggít** (*gram.*) *adj.* relative.
bangháy: *n.* draft, outline; plot, project; plan; conjugation; framework; **bangháy-aralín** *n.* lesson plan.
bangí: *adj.* broiled; **ibangí** *v.* to broil.
bangibang: *n.* head plumage.
bangibáng: *adj.* overloaded.
bangín: *n.* abyss, gorge; ravine, precipice.
bangís: **mabangís** *adj.* savage, fierce, ferocious; **bumangís** *v.* to become fierce.
banglát: *n.* hog sty; small fish corral in a river.
bangó: *n.* aroma, fragrance; **mabangó** *adj.* fragrant; **pabangó** *n.* perfume; **bangong-puri** *n.* redemption from dishonor.
bangokngók: *n.* small pomadasid fish.
bangon: **bumangon** *v.* to rise, get up; **pagbabangon** *n.* uprising; **ibangon ang puri** *id.* to regain lost honor.
bangós: *n.* milkfish.
bangrís: (*reg.*) var. of *bangós*: milkfish.
bangungon: *n.* cone-shaped snail, *Potamides telescopium.*

bangungot: *n.* nightmare; **bángungutín** *adj.* prone to having nightmares.
banguyngóy: *n.* continuous sobbing.
bangyáw: *n.* species of blowfly.
bao: *n.* coconut shell; cranium; *adj.* widowed.
baóg: *adj.* sterile; unproductive; **pamaog** *n.* sterilizer.
báol: *n.* trunk of a tree.
baúl: (Sp. *baúl*) *n.* chest, trunk.
baon: *n.* provisions; **magbaon** *v.* to carry provisions, bring food.
baón: *adj.* buried; embedded; **baón sa utang** *id.* buried in debt; **ibaón sa limot** *v.* to forget.
bapór: (Sp. *vapor*) *n.* steamship; vapor; (*slang*) large person; **magbapór** *v.* to ride a ship, go by ship; **bapór-de-gera** warship.
bará: *n.* stoppage, block; **barahán** *v.* to block; **ipagbará ng ilóng** *id.* cause for losing one's temper; **madalíng-magbará** *id.* easily irritated (blocked); **nagbará ang ilóng** *id.* irritated.
barabás: (Sp. *barrabás*) *n.* fiend.
barák: *adj.* pale, pallid; faded.
baraka: (Sp. *barraca*) *n.* market.
barakilan: *n.* beam of a house.
barako: (Sp. *barraco*) *n.* breeding boar, bully; species of native coffee; philanderer.
baradero: (Sp. *varadero*) *n.* shipyard.
barado: *adj.* clogged, blocked.
baraha: (Sp. *baraja*) *n.* deck of cards.
barál: (Sp.) *n.* peg, pin; latch.
barandál: (Sp.) *n.* banister; railing.
barandilya: (Sp. *barandilla*) *n.* railing; balustrade.
barang: *n.* small biting insect.
barangan: *n.* siganid fish.
barangka: (Sp. *barranca*) *n.* ravine, gorge; climbing a cliff.
barangko: (Sp. *barranco*) *n.* cliff.
baranggáy: *n.* community of people, neighborhood; (*slang*) *v.* solicit money.
baraungan: *n.* gruntfish, *Therapon sp.*
baras: (Sp. *barra*) *n.* bar, rod.
barasan: *n.* sawfish, *Pritis microdon.*
baraso: (Sp. *brazo*) *n.* arm.
barasot: *n.* halfbeak fish.
barát: (Sp. *baratar*) *n.* haggler; (*slang*) *adj.* irritating; stingy; **baratín** *v.* to haggle.
baratilyo: (Sp. *baratillo*) *n.* bargain sale.
barbaridád: (Sp.) *n.* brutality, barbarity.
bárbaró: (Sp.) *adj.* barbarous, savage.
barbero: (Sp.) *n.* barber. (*manggugupit*)
bárbikyó: (Eng.) *n.* barbecue.
barbón: (Sp.) *adj.* hairy; thick-bearded.
barkada: *n.* clique, group of friends.
barkero: (Sp. *barquero*) *n.* ferryman.
barkílyos: (Sp. *barquillo*) *n.* rolled wafer.
barkó: (Sp. *barco*) *n.* ship.
bardagól: (*slang*) *adj.* fat and awkward.
barena: (Sp. *barrena*) *n.* auger, drill.
barera: (Sp.) *n.* tollgate.
bareta: (Sp. *barreta*) *n.* crowbar.
bargás: (Sp. *parga*) *adj.* coarse in speech and manner.
barik: *n.* alcoholic beverage; **baríк** *adj.* drunk; **barikán** *n.* bar. **bumarik** *v.* to drink wine.
bariga: (Sp. *barriga*) *n.* bigger end of an egg shell; (*coll.*) throwing down in wrestling.
baríl: (Sp. *barril*) *n.* gun; **bumaril** *v.* to shoot; **mamamaril** *n.* hunter; **mamaríl** *v.* to hunt; **nábaríl ng asín** *id.* bribed.
bariles: (Sp. *barril*) *n.* barrel.
barimbaw: (Sp. *birimbao*) *n.* Jew's harp.
barit: *n.* kind of grass used as fodder.
barnís: (Sp. *barniz*) *n.* varnish.
barò: *n.* dress, apparel; **magbarò** *v.* to wear a dress; **babaruin** *n.* dress materials; **barong-pamparti** *n.* party dress; **isáng baro't isáng saya ang dalá** *id.* very poor woman (one dress and a skirt); **isáng baro't isáng salawál** *id.* very poor man.
baro-baro: *var. of paruparo*: butterfly fish.
barok: *n.* small pillow.
barók: (*slang*) *n.* drug addict; someone with a speech defect.
baróg: (*slang*) *n.* wrestling to the ground; ganging up on.
barón: (Sp.) *n.* baron.
baronesa: (Sp.) *n.* baroness.
barong-barong: *n.* makeshift shack.
barong-Tagalog: *n.* kind of native shirt made of pineapple cloth.
bartolina: (Sp.) *n.* dungeon; (*slang*) bad

situation; *adj.* grounded.

barumbado: *adj.* coarse, uncouth.

barungbarung: *n.* hut.

barurot: (*slang*) *adj.* fast; *v.* to copulate.

baruso: (Sp.) *adj.* reddish (pimpled face).

barutbót: *n.* sound of continuous farting.

baryá: (Sp. *varia*) *n.* loose change, coins; small denomination bills; **baryahín** *v.* to change money into smaller denominations.

baryo: (Sp. *barrio*) *n.* outlying district of a town.

basa: *n.* reading; **bumasa, magbasá** *v.* to read.

basâ: *adj.* wet; **basaín** *v.* to wet; **basâ ang papél** *id.* with a bad record (paper is wet); **basáng-sisiw** *id.* pitiful (wet chick).

basabasa: *n.* re cooked wet rice.

basakay: *n.* species of iguana.

basag: *n.* crack; **baság** *adj.* cracked, broken; (*fig.*) de-virginized; (*slang*) high on drugs; **bumasag** *v.* to break, smash; **mabasag** *adj.* broken; **basag-ulo** *id.* quarrel (broken head), **basag-uluero** *n.* trouble maker; **maka-basag-kampanà** *n.* grand affair (can break the bell); **baság ang pulá** *adj.* crazy.

basahan: *n.* rag.

basal: *adj.* youthful; virgin.

basalyo: (Sp. *vasallo*) *n.* vassal; subordinate.

basanlót: *n.* rag.

basangál: *n.* heated dispute.

basbás: *n.* blessing; **basbasán** *v.* to bless.

baskág: *n.* frame, framework.

basketbol: (Eng.) *n.* basketball.

báskula: (Sp. *báscula*) *n.* weighing scale.

basí: (*slang*, *BBQ* + *sinangág*) *n.* meal of barbecued meat and fried rice.

basì: *n.* sugarcane wine.

basig: *adj.* castrated.

basio: (Sp. *vacío*) *adj.* empty.

baso: (Sp. *vaso*) *n.* drinking glass; **sambaso** *n.* one glassful.

baso: (Sp. *bazo*) *n.* spleen.

basò: *n.* test; assay.

basó: *n.* target practice.

basta: (Sp.) *interj.* enough! stop! **basta-basta** *adj.* lightly, poor.

bastâ: *n.* bundle; packaging; **magbastâ** *v.* to pack.

bastág: *n.* frame. **bastagan** *n.* frame.

bastéd: (*coll.*) *adj.* rejected, turned down; broken hearted; flat broke.

bastidór: (Sp.) *n.* embroidery hoop.

bastipór: *n.* helmet.

bastón: (Sp.) *n.* walking cane.

bastonera: (Sp.) *n.* majorette.

bastonero: (Sp.) *n.* bandmaster, leader of an orchestra; prison warden.

bastós: *adj.* rude; crude; unrefined.

basura: (Sp.) *n.* trash.

basurero: (Sp.) *n.* garbage collector.

baswás: *adj.* disobedient.

basyada: (Sp. *vaciada*) *n.* sharpening blades by machine.

basyo: (Sp. *vacío*) *n.* empty bottle; (*slang*) broke, empty-handed; caught in the act.

bata: (Sp.) *n.* gown; **~-de-banyo** *n.* bathrobe.

batà: *n.* child, infant; youngster; sweetheart; employee; *adj.* young; **bumatà** *v.* to rejuvenate; **kabataan** *n.* childhood; *adj.* youthful; **magbatá-bataan**, **magpakabatà** *v.* to act childishly; **nakákabatà** *adj.* rejuvenating; younger (sibling); **pabatain** *v.* to make young again, **pagkabatà** *n.* childhood; **pag papabatà** *n.* rejuvenation; **pambatà** *adj.* infantile, juvenile; **pilyong batà** *n.* brat; **batang lansangan** *n.* homeless child.

batá: **bathín** *v.* to endure; tolerate; **magbatá** *v.* to bear, endure; **ipabatá** *v.* to inflict hardship on; **mapagbatá** *adj.* enduring.

bataan: (rt. *bata*) *n.* servant; **magbataan** *v.* to employ a servant; **mambataan** *v.* to treat as a servant.

batak: *n.* pull; *adj.* well-exercised; **batakin** *v.* to pull, tug; (*fig.*) cheat on an exam; **baták ang katawan** *id.* accustomed to working; healthy (stretched body); **kabatakán** *id.* friend (one with whom one pulls); **mag-batak ng butó** *id.* work (pull the bones).

Batak: *n.* ethnic group and language from North Central Palawan.

batád: *n.* coarse variety of sorghum.

batalán: *n.* bamboo back porch.

batalay: *n.* garfish, *Tylosurus strongylurus*.

batangán: *n.* outrigger.

batas: *n.* shortcut.

batás: *n.* law, decree; command; **bátásan** *n.* legislature; congress; **dalub-batás** *n.* law expert; **ibatás** *v.* to decree a law; **isabatás** *v.* to put into a law; **mambabatás** *n.* lawmaker; **pagbabatás** *n.* legislation; **pambatás** *adj.* legal; **pambátásan** *adj.* legislative; **alagád ng batás** *n.* police, agent of the law; **batás militár** *n.* martial law; **labág sa batás** *adj.* illegal; **lumabág sa batás** *v.* to break the law; **panukalang-batás** *n.* bill, proposed law; **takdâ ng batás** *adj.* statutory.

bataw: *n.* species of bean; swarm of bees; buoy.

batay: *adj.* based on, by; with; **bátáyan** *n.* ground, basis; cause; **batayán** *adj.* fundamental; primary, original; *n.* ground, basis; foundation; **ibatay** *v.* to base on; **mábátay** *v.* to base; depend on; **pagkábátay** *n.* rest, support; **pinagbatayan** *n.* basis; foundation.

batbát: *adj.* covered with.

baté: (*slang*) **magbaté** *v.* masturbate.

batél: *n.* small sailing boat.

Bathalà: *n.* God.

bathín: (rt. *batá*) *v.* to endure; tolerate.

batì: *n.* greeting, greetings; **bumatì, batiin** *v.* to greet, salute; address; **kabátían** *n.* casual acquaintance; **magbatì** *v.* to greet each other; **magbatián** *v.* to greet one another; **pagbatì** *n.* greeting.

batí: (Sp. *batir*) *adj.* churned, beaten; **batihín** *v.* to beat (eggs); churn; **pambatí** *n.* beater.

batibot: *adj.* strong, robust.

batik: *n.* spot, stain; blemish. **batikán** *adj.* spotted; tried, tested; expert.

Batikano: (Sp. *vaticano*) *n.* Vatican.

batikola: (Sp. *baticola*) *n.* crupper.

batikos: *n.* criticism; hit with a cudgel; **batikusin** *v.* to hit with a cudgel; (*fig.*) criticize severely; **pambatikos** *n.* cudgel.

batikulíng: *n.* kind of tree, *Litsea glutinosa.*

batíd: *adj.* known, aware of; **kabátíran** *n.* information; **ipabatíd** *v.* to inform; **mabatíd** *v.* to be informed, acquainted; **pabatíd** *n.* information; **pagkabatíd** *n.* awareness.

batidór: (Sp.) *n.* mixing bowl.

batino: *n.* kind of tree with small yellowish-white flowers.

batíng: *n.* trap for animals.

batingáw: *n.* large bell.

batingtíng: *n.* musical triangle bar.

batis: *n.* spring of water; **magbatis** *v.* to form a spring (gushing water).

bató$_1$: *n.* stone; knot in wood; kidney; **bátúhan** *n.* stone fight; **batuhán** *n.* stony place; reef; **batuhín** *v.* to stone; hurl; **bumató** *v.* to stone; **ibató** *v.* to throw; **mabató** *v.* to be hit accidentally by something thrown; **magbató** *v.* to turn to stone; harden; **magbabató** *n.* stonecutter; **bató sa lansangan** *id.* useless person (stone in the street); **nagíng bató** *id.* turned into stone; became valueless; lost; froze; **batóng-tampók** *n.* stone set in a ring.

bató$_2$: (*slang*) *n.* dope; *adj.* stoned; boring; stingy; **bató-bató** *adj.* muscular.

batò: *n.* chief piece in the game of *tangga*; **pambatò** *n.* most valuable player.

batok: *n.* nape; **pamatok** *n.* yoke.

batóg: **binatóg** *n.* boiled corn with salt and coconut.

batón: (Eng.) *n.* conductor's rod.

batotoy: *n.* species of clam, *Arca antiquata.*

batsóy: (Ch. *bàq cuì*) *n.* copped and sautéed entrails of pig with soup; (*slang*) fat.

batubalanì: *n.* magnet.

batúbató: *n.* wild pigeon.

batugan: *adj.* lazy.

batuláng: *n.* chicken coop; bell-shaped basket.

batutà: (Sp.) *n.* policeman's club, cudgel; conductor's wand; (*slang*) penis; **batutain** *v.* to hit with a club.

batutay: *n.* pork sausage.

batyâ: (Sp. *batea*) *n.* tub; **batyaan** *n.* wash tub.

batyág: *see matyág*: observe.

batyáw: *n.* spy, informer; **batyawán** *v.* to spy on; **pagbatyáw** *n.* espionage.

baúl: (Sp. *baúl*) *n.* chest, trunk.

bautismo: (Sp.) *n.* baptism. (*binyág*)

bawa: *n.* relaxation; **magbawa** *v.* to lessen, decrease; become less intense; **magpabawa** *v.* to relieve, alleviate.

bawà, bawa't *pron.* each; all, every.

bawal: *adj.* prohibited, forbidden; **kabawalan** *n.* restriction; **magbawal** *v.* to forbid; condemn, outlaw; ban.

bawang: *n.* garlic; (*slang*) fat person; **parang bawang** *id.* go getter.

bawas: *n.* discount, reduction; **bawasan** *v.* to reduce, decrease, deduct; cut.

bawa't: *pron.* each; all.

baway: *n.* fishing rod.

bawì: *n.* recovery; retraction; **bumawì, bawiin** *v.* to recover, regain; take back; reclaim; **makabawì** *adj.* to recover; **palabawî** *n.* Indian giver; **pagkabawì** *n.* recovery; **mambabawî, pamamawì** *n.* taking back (what was given); recovery; **binawian ng buhay** *id.* died (life was retracted).

bayà: **bayaan** *v.* to allow, let; **magpabayà** *v.* to fail to do, neglect; **magpabayà** *v.* to neglect; fail to do; **napabayaan** *adj* neglected; **pabayaan** *v.* to abandon, neglect; disregard; **pagkapabayà, kapabayaán** *n.* negligence; carelessness.

bayâ: (Marinduque) *adv.* particle expressing sureness of speaker.

bayabag: *n.* support, reinforcement.

bayabas: *n.* guava; **namayabas** *id.* frustrated.

bayakan: *n.* species of large bat.

bayakid: *n.* stumbling block; act of stumbling; **bayakirín** *v.* to trip.

bayakís: *n.* act of gathering together the ends of a skirt.

bayad: *n.* payment; admission; rate; **bayád** *adj.* paid; **magbayad** *v.* to pay; settle; **bayaran** *v.* to pay; repay; recompense; reimburse; **bayarán** *n.* payment due date; **kabayaran** *n.* payment, settlement; price; **ibayad** *v.* to pay with; **ipagbayad** *v.* to pay for something for someone; **makabayad** *v.* to be able to pay; **pagbayaran** *v.* to pay for; atone; **páunáng-bayad** *n.* advance payment; **pambayad-utang** *id.* refers to a daughter whose father used to be a playboy; **waláng-ibábáyad** *adj.* unable to pay one's debts.

bayág: *n.* testicle; **waláng bayág** *id.* referring to a coward; **batág-kambíng** kind of prickly shrub.

bayambáng: *n.* thorny amaranth weed.

bayan: *n.* town; country; **kababayan** *n.* townmate; **makabayan** *adj.* nationalistic; patriotic; **makipamayan** *v.* to settle a town; **magbayan** *v.* to establish a town; **mamayan** *v.* to live in a town; **mámamayán** *n.* resident; **pambayan** *adj.* civic; **pagkamakabayan** *n.* patriotism, nationalism; **pagkamámamayán** *n.* citizenship; **pamamayan** *n.* residence in a town; **pámayanán** *n.* community; **pangmámamayán** *adj.* civil; **sambayanán** *n.* townspeople; **kurong-bayan** *n.* public opinion.

bayani: *n.* hero; **bayanihan** *n.* mutual aid; cooperation.

bayang: *n.* leaf-fish, *Platax orbicularis*.

bayáw: *n.* brother-in-law.

bayawak: *n.* iguana; (*slang*) brother-in-law.

bayawáng: *n.* waist.

baybáy: *n.* edge, border; coast; **mamaybáy** *v.* to coast, go along the edge of; **baybayín** *v.* to enumerate; **palabaybayan** *n.* spelling.

bayì: *n.* princess; royal lady of the court.

bayle: (Sp. *baile*) *n.* dance. (*sayáw*)

bayná: (Sp. *vaina*) *n.* scabbard. (*kaluban*)

baynika: (Sp. *vainica*) *n.* hemstitch.

baynilya: (Sp. *vainilla*) *n.* vanilla.

bayo: (Sp.) *n.* bay color (horses).

bayó: *n.* act of pounding; **báyúhan** *n.* mortar; **pambayó** *n.* pestle.

bayók: *n.* act of shaking, vibration; **pambayók** *n.* vibrator.

bayoneta: (Sp.) *n.* bayonet.

bayóng: *n.* bag made from palm leaves.

bayot: (*slang*) *n.* homosexual male.

baysá: *n.* granary, barn.

baysán: *n.* in-law.

bayubay: *adj.* dangling, hanging.

bayubò: *n.* screen.

bayugo: *n.* kneecap; fruit of the *gugò* tree; St. Thomas bean.

bayumbóng: *n.* cylindrical bamboo container.

bayuot: **bayuót** *adj.* crumpled and rolled. **bayuutin** *v.* to crumple; wrinkle.

baywáng: *n.* waist; **nakapamaywáng** *adj.* akimbo.

Bb. *abbr.* for *binibini*: Miss.

beateryo: (Sp. *beaterio*) *n.* institution for religious women.

bebot: (*slang*) *n.* girl, woman.

beha: *n.* old Chinese woman; cigarette stub.

behíkulo: (Sp. *vehículo*) *n.* vehicle.
beho: *n.* old Chinese man.
beinte: (Sp. *veinte*) *n.* twenty; **beinte nuebe** (*slang*) nine inch switchblade.
belada: (Sp.) *n.* entertainment; concert.
belat: (*coll.*) *n.* contemptuous term for female genitalia; *interj.* expresses disdain.
Belén: (Sp.) *n.* Bethlehem; nativity scene.
belo: (Sp. *velo*) *n.* veil. (*talukbóng*)
belosidád: (Sp. *velocidad*) *n.* velocity; speed. (*kabilisán, katulinan*)
belosimetro: (Sp. *velocímetro*) *n.* speedometer.
belyako: (Sp. *vellaco*) *adj.* sly, cunning.
belyas: (*slang*) *n.* bar hostess; prostitute.
belyas artes: (Sp. *bellas artes*) *n.* fine arts.
bembè: *n.* cascabel, jingle bell.
bena: (Sp. *vena*) *n.* vein. (*ugát*)
benda: (Sp. *venda*) *n.* bandage, dressing.
bendahe: (Sp. *vendaje*) *n.* bandage; dressing for a wound.
bende Kristo (Sp. *vende Cristo*: sell Christ) *n.* one who sells inherited properties to the dismay of his family.
bendisiyón: (Sp. *bendición*) *n.* blessing. (*basbás*)
bendita: (Sp.) **agua bendita** *n.* holy water; **benditahán** *n.* font, basin.
beneno: (Sp. *veneno*) *n.* venom (*kamandág*); poison (*lason*)
benepisyo: (Sp. *beneficio*) *n.* benefit. (*pakinabang*)
bensido: (Sp. *vencido*) *adj.* due; subdued.
benta: (Sp. *venta*) *n.* sales; ready made clothes.
bentaha: (Sp. *ventaja*) *n.* advantage.
bentiladór: (Sp. *ventilador*) *n.* electric fan.
bentosa: (Sp. *ventosa*) *n.* suction glass used to improve circulation of the blood.
bengga: (*slang*) *adj.* fired from office.
benggadór: (Sp. *vengador*) *n.* avenger.
benggala: *n.* pheasant.
benggansa: (Sp. *venganza*) *n.* revenge. (*higantí*)
benggatibo: (Sp. *vengativo*) *adj.* vindictive.
beranda: (Eng.) *n.* veranda.
berbal: (Sp. *verbal*) *adj.* verbal; frank. **berbalín** *v.* to speak frankly.
berbena: (Sp.) *n.* verbena.
berbo: (Sp. *verbo*) *n.* verb. (*pandiwà*)
berde: (Sp. *verde*) *n.* green (*luntî*); **berdeng lumot** *n.* moss green.
berdugo: (Sp. *verdugo*) *n.* hangman, executioner. (*tagabitay*)
berhas: (Sp. *verja*) *n.* grating.
beripikado: (Sp. *verificado*) *adj.* verified; without doubt. (*napatunayan*)
berlina: (Sp.) *n.* closed carriage.
bersíkuló: (Sp. *versículo*) *n.* line of verse. (*taludtód*)
bértebrá: (Sp. *vertebra*) *n.* vertebra. (*butó sa gulugód*)
besbol: (Eng.) *n.* baseball.
beses: (Sp. *veces*) *n.* times, instances.
betamax: (Eng. *betamax*) *n.* chicken intestines.
betchot: (*slang*) *n.* sexual intercourse.
betka: (*slang*) *n.* common-law wife, lover.
beterano: (Sp. *veterano*) *n.* veteran.
beto: (Eng.) *n.* veto; game of dice.
betlóg: (*slang*) *n.* male genitals.
betún: (Sp. *bitón*) *n.* shoe polish.
biâ: *var. of biyâ*: goby.
biâ: *n.* goby fish.
biák: *adj.* divided into halves, split; (*slang*) *v.* make love.
biás: internode of bamboo or cane.
biáy: *n.* keeping live fishes in a temporary vessel before selling or cooking.
Biba!: (Sp. *viva*) Long Live!
bibero: (Sp.) *n.* bib.
biberón: (Sp) *n.* nursing bottle.
bibi: *n.* duckling.
bibíg: *n.* mouth; **mabigbig** *adj.* talkative; **magbibíg-anghél** *v.* to have what was said come true (be the mouth of an angel); **waláng-bibíg** *id.* timid; with no right to interfere (no mouth); **waláng bukáng bibíg** *id.* favorite expression (no open mouth).
bibinga: *n.* shard.
bibingka: *n.* rice cake; **bibingkang-galapóng** *n.* rice cake cooked with *malagkít*.
bibít: *n.* phantom.
Bibliyá: *n.* Bible.
bibo: (Sp. *vivo*) *adj.* alert, active.
bikâ: *adj.* not sharp, obtuse.
bikakâ: *adj.* wide apart; forked.

bikangkáng: *adj.* forced open at one end.

bikas: *n.* posture; bearing; **kabikasan** *n.* elegance; **mabikas** *adj.* with an attractive figure; well-dressed.

bikat: *n.* scar on the face.

bikaw: *n.* four-fingered threadfin fish.

bikì: *n.* mumps.

bikíg: *n.*. something stuck in the throat (fish-bone).

bikil: *n.* bulge; **nakabikil** *adj.* bulging.

bikláng: *adj.* bowlegged; astride.

biklát: *n.* spread open, unfolded; disjointed.

biklíng: *n.* small hoop, curtain ring.

biko: (Ch. *bì ko*: rice cake) *n.* rice cake sweetened with brown sugar.

Bikol: *n.* language and ethnic group of Southeastern Luzon. The people are also called **Bikolano**.

bíktima: (Sp. *víctma*) *n.* victim.

bikuda: *n.* barracuda.

bida: (Sp. *vida*) *n.* story; main character in a story, protagonist.

bidbíd: *n.* convulsion; spool; ten-pounder fish; **bidbiran** *n.* spool; *v.* to wind yarn.

bidlawan: *n.* kind of fish, *Caesio sp.*

bidyá: *n.* fret of a stringed instrument.

bienes: (Sp.) *n.* real estate.

bigà: **malabigà** *adj.* glib; fault-finding.

bigan: (*slang*, f. *kaibigan*) *n.* friend, mate.

bigás: *n.* husked rice; **magbigás** *v.* to mill unhusked rice. **bígasan** *n.* rice mill.

bigát: *n.* heaviness; seriousness; **mabigát** *adj.* heavy; **bumigát** *v.* to become heavy; to become serious (sickness); **bigatin** *adj.* heavy; (*fig.*) intelligent; influential; well-to-do; **mabigát ang bibíg** *id.* proud (heavy mouth); **mabigát ang kamáy** *id.* lazy (hand is heavy); **mabigát ang katawán** *id.* sick, indisposed (body is heavy); **mabigát ang dibdíb** *adj.* with ill feeling (chest is heavy); **mabigát ang dugô** *id.* with dislike (blood is heavy); **mabigát ang loób** *id.* in dis-agreement (inside is heavy); **mabigát ang paá** *id.* always at home (foot is heavy); **mabigát ang salapî** *id.* hard to earn money (money is heavy); **mabigát ang timbáng** *id.* powerful, influential (weight is heavy); **mabigát ang ulo** *id.* with headache (head is heavy); **mabigát panimbangán** *id.* hard to get along with (heavy to weigh with).

bigáw: *adj.* stunned; thunderstruck; **bigawín** *v.* to deafen.

bigáy: *n.* giving; gift; **ibigáy, bigyán** *v.* to give, offer; **bumigáy** *v.* to give in (under pressure); give up; **bigayan** *n.* act of giving, attitude of reciprocity; **kabígáyan** *n.* person with whom one exchanges gifts; **ipamigáy** *v.* to give out, distribute; **magbigáy** *v.* to give; emit, give off; **magbígáyan** *v.* to compromise, meet half way; **magbigáy-daán** *v.* to give way to, give a chance to; **mamigáy** *v.* to give out; distribute; **mapagbigáy** *adj.* generous; **mapagbigyán** *v.* to give, accommodate; **bigáy-alám** *n.* notice, notification. **pagbigyán** *n.* to grant, gratify; indulge; **pagkamapagbigáy** *n.* generosity; **pamimigáy** *n.* disposal, giving away; **tagapamigáy** *n.* distributor; **bigáy-bahalà** *n.* assigned responsibility; delegation. **bigáy-dapat** *n.* recognition of someone's right. **bigay-kaya** *n.* dowry; exertion of all one's efforts; **bigáy hilig** *n.* indulgence; **bigáy-loób** *id.* something given to please (give inside); **bigáy-lugód** *n.* something that satisfies; **bigáy-palà** *n.* reward; gratuity; **bigáy-sala** *n.* accusation; **bigay-sisi** *n.* blaming. **bigáy-todo** *n.* giving one's all, exertion of all one's efforts and knowledge; **bigáy-tulot** *n.* permission.

bigkás: *n.* pronunciation; recitation **bumigkás** *v.* to pronounce; recite.

bigkís: *n.* girdle; bond; bundle; **bigkisín** *v.* to bind.

bighanì: *n.* charm; **pambighanì** *n.* fascination. **bighaniin** *v.* to charm, seduce.

bigì: *n.* grain, kernel. (*butil*)

biglâ: *adv.* sudden, quick; unexpected, impromptu; **biglaín** *v.* to startle, surprise; **pagbibiglâ** *n.* speed, haste. **biglaan** *adj.* sudden, unexpected; abrupt; *adv.* suddenly. **bigláng-yaman** *n.* someone who has suddenly become rich, usually with negative connotations; **bigláng-likô** (*slang*) *n.* hourly motel for sexual encounters.

bigláw: *adj.* immature; unsuccessful.

bignáy: *n.* kind of tree.

bigô: *adj.* disappointed, frustrated; useless; **biguín** *v.* to disappoint, frustrate; fail; **kabiguán** *n.* disappointment; failure; **mabigô** *v.* to be disappointed; fail; **pagkabigô** *n.* disappointment.

bigonya: (Eng.) *n.* begonia.

bigote: (Sp.) *n.* mustache. (*misáy*, *bungot*)

bigotilyo: (Sp. *bigotillo*) *n.* thin mustache.

bigtál: *adj.* unstitched, detached; **bigtalín** *v.* to unstitch, detach.

bigtás: *n.* rip; unseaming, unstitching.

bigtí: *adj.* strangled; **bigtihan** *n.* gallows; **bumigtí** *v.* to strangle; **magbigtí** *v.* to hang oneself.

bigtíng: *n.* forceps, tongs.

bigwás: *n.* blow with the fist; jerk on a fishing line; **pamigwás** *n.* fishing rod and line.

bigwela: (Sp. *vihuela*) *n.* old fashioned guitar.

bigyán: (*rt. bigáy*) *v.* to give.

biha: *n.* cigarette butt.

bihag: *n.* captive, prisoner; **bihagin** *v.* to capture, allure; charm.

bihasa: *adj.* used to, accustomed to; accomplished; skilled; **bihasahin** *v.* to acquaint; **kabihasnán** *n.* civilization; **mamihasa** *v.* to get used to; **pamihasnín** *v.* to accustom, habituate; **pinagkábihasnán** *n.* tradition.

bíhay: *n.* strip of cloth; **biháy** *adj.* rumpled; destroyed.

bihilya: (Sp. *vigilia*) *n.* vigil; abstinence.

bihirà: *adv.* rarely, seldom; scarcely; **bihíbihirà** *adv.* very seldom; **bihirain** *v.* to take as an exception; **nápakapambihirà** *adj.* very unusual; **pambihirà** *adj.* rare; abnormal; unique; extraordinary.

bihis: *n.* clothing; **magbihis** *v.* to dress. **bihís** *adj.* dressed up. **bihisan** *n.* reserved clothes for traveling; **bihís na bihís** *adj.* dressed to kill.

bihon: (Ch. *bî hùn*: rice flour) *n.* rice noodles.

biík: *n.* young suckling pig. (*kulíg*, *buwík*)

bila: *n.* reinforcing bamboo splits fastened horizontally along a fence.

bilád: *adj.* exposed to the sun (to dry); **ibilád** *v.* to put out in the sun to dry; **magbilád ng asín** *id.* to brag.

bilada: (Sp. *velada*) *n.* entertainment program.

bilang₁: *n.* number; count; **bilangin** *v.* to count; **kabilang** *adj* among; including; **ibilang** *v.* to count, consider; **pagbilang** *n.* count; **pamilang** *n.* counter; figure representing a number; **tambilang** *n.* digit; **nagbibiláng ng bitwín** *id.* dreaming, hopeless; counting gain in advance (counting stars); **nagbibiláng ng poste** *id.* jobless (counting posts); **ibilang sa walâ** *id.* to forget; **dî mabilang ng ulól** *id.* innumerable.

bilang₂: *prep.* as, in the capacity as.

bilanggô: *n.* prisoner; **bílangguan** *n.* prison, jail. **ibilanggô** *v.* to jail; **mábilanggô** *v.* to be imprisoned; **pagbibilanggô** *n.* imprisonment; **pagpapabilanggóng mulî** *n.* remand; sending back to prison; **ibilanggô sa mga bisig** *id.* embrace.

bilao: *n.* winnowing basket.

bilaok: **mabilaokan** *v.* to get stuck in one's throat.

bilás: *n.* the husband of one's sister-in-law; the wife of one's brother-in-law.

bilasà: **bilasâ** *adj.* spoiled, putrid; (*slang*) sexually promiscuous; **bilasà na** *id.* sleepy.

bilasyón: (Sp. *velaciones*) *n.* nuptial Mass.

bilát: (*slang*) *n.* vagina.

bilbíl: *n.* dropsy.

bilhán: (rt. *bilí*) *v.* to buy (something) from.

bilhín: (rt. *bilí*) *v.* to buy something.

bilí: *n.* purchase price; buying; **bumilí, bilhín** *v.* to buy; **magbilí** *v.* to sell; (*coll.*) handle; **bílíhan** *n.* market; selling price; **ipagbilí** *v.* to sell; put for sale; part with; **maipagbíbilí** *adj.* marketable; **magbibíli** *n.* seller; **mámimili** *n.* shopper; **nápagbilhán** *n.* amount sold, total sales; **pagbilí** *n.* buying; **pagbilhán** *v.* to sell to someone; **pagkakápagbilí** *n.* sale; **pámilihan** *n.* exchange, place of trade; **pinamilí** *n.* purchases; **tagapagbilí** *n.* seller; **ipagbilí nang buô** *id.* fool, cheat (sell whole); **binilí ang tindá** *id.* believed everything (bought the store).

bilíb: (Eng. *believe*) *v.* to be impressed, admire.

bilibid₁: *n.* prison; **ibilibid** *v.* to send to prison.

bilibid₂: *n.* twine, cord; **bílibirán** *n.* spool;

bilibirin *v.* to wind around; **mábilibid** *adj.* wound; twisted.
bilík: *n.* temporary shelter; annex; small room.
bilíg₁: *n.* embryo.
bilíg₂: *n.* cataract of the eye.
bilin: *n.* request; directions, instructions; order; advice; **ipagbilin** *v.* to give instructions; **magbilin** *v.* to order; request; **tagubilin** *n.* instructions, orders; recommendation. **bilinan** *v.* to leave instructions.
biling: *n.* rotation, turn; restlessness; **biling-bilingan** *n.* windlass.
bilíg: *adj.* lost, strayed.
bilís: *n.* speed, pace; herring; **bumilís** *v.* to speed; **kabilisán** *n.* speed, rapidity; **mabilís** *adj.* fast; **pagkamabilís** *n.* quickness; promptness; **magpabilís** *v.* to speed up; **pabilisín** *v.* to speed up something; **mabilís ang kamáy** *id.* quick in stealing (hand is fast).
biló: *n.* roll; pill; **biluhín** *v.* to roll; **biniló** *n.* pellets; pills; **pambiló** *n.* rolling pin; **biló-biló** *n.* kneaded rice flour balls used in *ginataán*.
bilog: *n.* circle; **bilóg** *adj.* round; (*slang*) *n.* liquor; **bilugan** *n.* mullet fish; **bilugán** *adj.* rounded; **kabilugan** *n.* roundness; **pabilóg** *adv.* in a circle; **bilugin ang ulo** *id.* to make fun of (make the head round).
bilot: *n.* small package; **magbilot** *v.* to roll cigars; **bilutin** *v.* to roll up.
bilót: *n.* puppy. (*tutà*, *kuwâ*)
biloy: *n.* dimple. (*turupyâ*)
bilukaw: *n.* species of tree, *Garcinia cambogia*.
bilyano: (Sp. *villano*) *n.* villain.
bilyár: (Sp. *billar*) *n.* billiards.
bilyete: (Sp. *billete*) *n.* ticket.
bilyón:(Eng.) *n.* billion. (*sanlibong angaw*)
bimáy: (*slang*) *n.* female house help.
bimbáng: *n.* blow with the fist.
bimbín: *adj.* delayed.
bimól: (Sp.) *adj.* flat (in music).
bimóy: (*slang*) *n.* male house help.
bimpo: (Ch.) *n.* face towel.
binabae: *n.* sissy, homosexual male.
binagre: (Sp. *vinagre*) *n.* vinegar. (*sukà*)
binalaki: *n.* tomboy, mannish woman; lesbian.
binanalak: (*rt. balalak*) *n.* hammer.
binalangkát: *n.* gold bracelet.
binalatán: *n.* false gold; *adj.* bound (books).
binat: *n.* relapse; (*slang*) grudge.
binatà: (*rt. batà*) *n.* bachelor.
binatilyo: *n.* male adolescent, teenager.
bintaok: *n.* gold bracelet or ring.
binay: *n.* goodness, kindness.
binayuyò: *n.* species of rice plant.
binbín: *n.* delay.
binhî: *n.* seed; **bibinhiin** *n.* seeds for planting; **binhiín** *v.* to select seeds suitable for planting. **binhian** *n.* nursery, seed plot.
binì: *n.* modesty; **mabinì** *adj.* modest.
binibini: *n.* young lady.
bíniboy: (*slang*) *n.* male homosexual.
binigsá: *n.* collar.
binit: *n.* tension; **binít** *adj.* tense, stretched, taut.
binlaók: *n.* lump in the throat.
binlíd: *n.* small broken particles of milled rice.
bino: (Sp. *vino*) *n.* wine.
binsâ: *adj.* stupid.
binta: (Sp. *vinta*) *n.* small sailboat.
bintád: *adj.* stretched out; **bintarín** *v.* to stretch out.
bintanà: (Sp. *ventana*) *n.* window; **bintanilya** *n.* small window, ticket window.
bintáng: *n.* accusation; rash judgement; **magbintáng** *v.* to detract, accuse of; **mapagbintangán** *v.* to be accused of; **pagbintangán** *v.* to accuse (falsely).
bintáy₁: *n.* relapse; **mabintáy** *v.* to suffer a relapse.
bintáy₂: *n.* estimation of the weight of something; **bintayín** *v.* to guess the weight of something.
bintî: *n.* calf of the leg.
bintóg: *n.* inflation, swelling; **bumintóg** *v.* to swell; **pabintugín** *v.* to inflate.
bintól: *n.* crabnet.
Binukid: *n.* language of the *Bukidnon* people of Mindanao.
binusá: *n.* toasted grains.
binya: (Sp. *viña*) *n.* vineyard.
binyág: *n.* baptism; **magbinyág** *v.* to baptize.

binyeta: (Sp. *viñeta*) *n.* vignette.
bingá: *n.* mother-of-pearl shell.
bingal: *n.* broken off portion; **bingál** *adj.* broken at the tip.
bingas: *n.* chip; **bingás** *adj.* chipped.
bingaw: *n.* notch; **bingáw** *adj.* notched.
bingká(n)g: *adj.* forced open; bowlegged.
bingkás: *adj.* unraveled.
bingkóng: *adj.* warped.
bingkungan: *n.* hammerhead shark.
bingí: *adj.* deaf; *n.* deaf person; (*fig.*) married woman who does not give birth; **bingihín** *v.* to deafen; **makabingí** *v.* to cause deafness, deafen; **magbingí-bingihan** *v.* to pretend to be deaf; **bingí't pipi** *adj.* deaf-mute.
bingit: *n.* edge, rim; brink; verge; **bumingit** *v.* to border on, to be on the verge of.
bingot: *n.* harelip; notch in chinaware.
bingwít: *n.* fishing tackle; **mamingwít** *v.* to fish with tackle; **mámimingwít** *n.* angler, fisherman.
biólogo: (Sp.) *n.* biologist.
bir: (Eng.) *n.* beer. (*serbesa*)
birá: (Sp. *virar*) *n.* strike with the fist; turning a crank; **birahán** *v.* to strike with the fist; **halá birá** *interj.* inciting exclamation.
biradór: (Sp.) *n.* wrench; screwdriver.
birago: (Sp. *virago*) *n.* virago; amazon.
birám: (*slang*) *v.* to say, tell.
birang: *n.* kerchief for the head.
biráy: *n.* kind of flat-bottomed rowing boat.
birete: (Sp. *birrete*) *n.* small cap.
birgo: (Sp. *virgo*) *adj.* virgin; chaste; Virgo.
birhen: (Sp. *virgen*) *n.* virgin.
birì: *n.* parrot seed, wild saffron.
birimbáw: (Sp. *birimbao*) *n.* Jew's harp.
birina: (Sp. *virina*) *n.* glass shade for candles.
biringki: (*slang*) *adj.* upside-down.
birò: *n.* joke; jest; **biruán** *n.* joking with one another; **bumirò, biruin** *v.* to joke, poke fun at; tease, fool; **kabiruán** *n.* person with whom one exchanges jokes; **magbiruán** *v.* to joke with one another; **pabirô** *adj.* joking, facetious; **birò ng tadhanà** *id.* mishap, misfortune (joke of nature).
birtúd: (Sp. *virtud*) *n.* virtue; strength (of liquor or medicine); efficacy; **mabirtud** *adj.* strong, effective, powerful (medicine); virtuous.
birus: (Eng.) *n.* virus.
bisa: (Sp. *visa*) *n.* visa.
bisà: *n.* power; force; effect; strength; **bigyáng-bisà** *v.* to validate; **kabisaan** *n.* effectiveness; **mabisà** *adj.* effective, potent; influential, valid; **magkabisà** *v.* to take effect; influence, have an effect on; **kawaláng-bisà** *n.* ineffectiveness; inefficiency; **magpawaláng-bisà** *v.* to annul, repeal; **magbigáy-bisà** *v.* to validate; **may-bisà** *adj.* in force, binding; **pagkamabisà** *n.* effectiveness; power to convince; **waláng-bisà** *adj.* useless; void; valueless; without effect.
bisaklát: *adj.* astride.
bisagra: (Sp.) *n.* hinge.
bisalà: *n.* fault, defect; error.
Bisayà: *n.*, *adj.* Visayan; **bisayain** *v.* to say in Visayan; translate in Visayan.
biskonde: (Sp. *vizconde*) *n.* viscount.
biskondesa: (Sp. *vizcondesa*) *n.* viscountess.
biskotso: (Sp. *bizcocho*) *n.* toasted bread.
bise- (Sp. *vice-*) *pref.* vice; (*coll.*) *n.* assistant deputy.
bisebersa: (Eng.) *adj.* vice-versa.
bisì: *n.* drought.
bisikleta: (Sp. *bicicleta*) *n.* bicycle.
bisig: *n.* forearm, arm; manpower; laborer; **bisig ng batás** *id.* authorities (arm of the law); **orasan pambisig** *n.* wristwatch.
bisiro: (Sp. *becerro*) *n.* calf, young of cattle.
bisita: (Sp. *visita*) *n.* guest, visitor; visit; **magbisita** *v.* to visit; **magbisitahán** *v.* to visit each other; **ang maybisita** *n.* host, hostess; **bisitahin** *v.* to visit.
bisláд: *n.* dried fish.
bisnis: (*slang*, Eng. *business*) *n.* prostitute.
bisô: *n.* error, mistake; **magkabisô** *v.* to err.
bísperas: (Sp. *víspera*) *n.* eve.
bista: (Sp. *vista*) *n.* court hearing; view; landscape; eyesight; **bistahín** *v.* to try a case in court.
bistado: (Sp.) *adj.* obvious; exposed.
bistáy: (Ch.) *n.* sieve; careful examination; **bistayín** *v.* to sift.
bistí: (Sp. *vestir*) *n.* dressy apparel; **bisting-**

bistí *adj.* well-dressed.
bisto: (Sp. *visto*) *adj.* obvious; discovered.
bisugo: *n.* red gilthead fish.
bisyo: (Sp. *vicio*) *n.* vice.
bisyoso: *adj.* wicked; vicious.
biták: *n.* crack; chink; crevice; **bumiták** *v.* to split, crack; **mamiták** *v.* to dawn; **pamimiták** *n.* dawning.
bitád: *n.* jerked meat; **bitarín** *v.* to jerk meat or fish.
bitadtád: *adj.* spread out.
bitag: *n.* snare; **bitagan** *v.* to snare.
bitamina: (Sp. *vitamina*) *n.* vitamin.
bitáw: **bitawan, ibitaw** *v.* to release, let go; let two roosters fight each other.
bitay: *n.* execution; **bibitayán** *n.* scaffold; **bitayin** *v.* to execute, hang; (*fig.*) cheat; **mambibitay** *n.* executioner; **pagbitay** *n.* executing, putting to death.
bitbít: *adj.* hand carried; **bitbitin** *adj.* portable; *v.* to hand carry.
bitháy: (Ch.) *n.* bamboo sieve, screen; type of fishing gear.
bitík: *n.* garter; anklet.
bitig: *n.* muscular tension, cramp; **mamitig** *v.* to tense up (*muscles*); **pamitigan** *v.* to experience cramps.
bitíg: *n.* fishbone in the throat.
bitilya: *n.* porgy fish; pampano.
bitin: *n.* hanging; **nakabitin** *adj.* hanging; **magbitin, ibitin** *v.* to hang; **bitín** *adj.* hanging; left hanging (in suspense).
bitíw₁: **bitiwan, ibitíw** *v.* to let go of; disengage; **makabitíw** *v.* to fumble, accidentally let go; **magbitiw** *v.* to resign from office; **nakabitíw sa tulos** *id.* let slip out of the tongue (secret).
bitíw₂: *n.* resignation; **magbitíw** *v.* to resign.
bitlág: *n.* bamboo seats in boats.
bitlíg: *n.* painful spasm.
bitlíng: *n.* metal or rattan ring around the handle of knives.
bitô: *n.* dot; point.
bitones: *var.* of *botones*: button.
bitoó: *n.* kind of edible freshwater snail.
bitsín: (Ch.) *n.* monosodium glutamate.
bitso: (Ch. *bí cò*: rice balls) *n.* fried cake made of rice flour.
bituka: *n.* intestine, entrails; **bitukang-manók** *n.* chicken entrails; *id.* crooked; windy (roads).
bitungol: *n.* species of tree with toothed leaves.
bituín: *n.* star; **kabituinán** *n.* stardom; **mabituín** *adj.* starry; **Pulóng-Bituín** *n.* Milky Way.
biwás: **biwasín** *v.* to jerk on a fishing line.
biyâ: *n.* goby fish.
biya: (Sp. *vía*) *n.* way, route; **Biya Krusis** *n.* way of the Cross.
biyák: *n.* split, crack; division; (*slang*) sexual intercourse; **biyakín** *v.* to divide, split; **kabiyák** *n.* mate, one of a pair; **kabiyák ng dibdíb** *id.* wife (half of the breast); **kákabiyák** *adj.* odd, with pair missing; **biniyák na bunga** *id.* similar, alike (split fruit); **magkabiyák na bao** *id.* two friends with the same interests (divided coconut shell); **pabiyák** (*slang*) sex crazy; nymphomaniac.
biyakís: *adj.* rolled up (trousers).
biyada: (Sp. *viada*) *n.* wiggling of wheels.
biyahe: (Sp. *viaje*) *n.* trip; **magbiyahe** *v.* to travel; **ibiyahe** *v.* to take on a trip.
biyahero: (Sp. *viajero*) *n.* traveler; traveling merchant.
biyanán: *n.* parent-in-law.
biyás: *n.* internode; joint of arms or legs.
biyáy: *n.* shallow tray filled with water surrounding a bowl of food which prevents ants from reaching the food; act of keeping shellfish in a container with water before cooking.
biyayà: *n.* blessing, grace; favor; **magbiyayà** *v.* to give lavishly as a favor; **mapagbiyayà** *adj.* generous.
biyenán: *var.* of *biyanán*: parent-in-law.
biyenes: (Sp. *bienes*) *n.* real estate, property.
Biyernes: (Sp. *viernes*) *n.* Friday; **Biyernes Santo** Good Friday; **mukháng Biyernes Santo** *adj.* with a gloomy face.
biyola: (Sp. *viola*) *n.* viola.
biyoleta: (Sp. *violeta*) *n.*, *adj.* violet.
biyolín: (Sp. *violín*) *n.* violin.
biyukos: *n.* crushing, crumpling.
biyuda: (Sp. *viuda*) *n.* widow. (*balong babae*)

biyudo: (Sp. *viudo*) *n.* widower. (*balong lalake*)
biyumbo: (Sp. *biombo*) *n.* folding screen.
Blaan: *n.* ethnic group and language from South Cotabato Province, Mindanao.
blaha: (*slang*, f. *bahalà na*) come what may.
blangka: (Sp. *blanca*) *n.* blank; zero score.
bloke: (Sp. *bloque*) *n.* block.
blokeo: (Sp. *bloqueo*) *n.* blockade.
blusa: (Sp. *blusa*) *n.* blouse.
blusil: (*slang*, Eng. *blue seal*) *n.* smuggled goods; imported cigarettes; pretty woman; fair-skinned woman.
bobo: (Sp.) *adj.* stupid, idiotic.
bóbida: (Sp. *boveda*) *n.* cupola.
bobina: (Sp.) *n.* spool, reel.
bokado: (Sp. *bocado*) *n.* bit, bridle of a horse.
bokadura: (Sp. *bocadura*) *n.* bridle of a horse; ability to speak well.
boka-inséndiyo: (Sp. *boca incendio*) *n.* fire hydrant.
bokál: (Sp. *vocal*) *n.* vowel; third-ranking member of a provincial board.
bokilya: (Sp. *boquilla*) *n.* mouthpiece.
boksing: (Eng.) *n.* boxing.
bokyâ: (*slang*) *adj.* out of fashion; zero, nothing.
boda: (Sp.) *n.* wedding.
bódabíl: (Sp. *vodevil*) *n.* vaudeville.
bodega: (Sp.) *n.* warehouse.
bog: (*slang*, f. *talbog*) *n.* loser; *v.* lose.
bogá: (*slang*) *n.* shotgun.
bogák: (*slang*) *n.* gun.
bogaris: (*slang*) *n.* cigarette.
bogli: (*slang*, *baliktád* of *libóg*) *adj.* horny.
bogok: (*slang*) *adj.* foolish; stupid.
bohemyo: (*slang*) *n.* playboy.
bohól: *n.* species of thorny shrub.
bola: (Sp.) *n.* ball; joke; (*fig*,) chubby; **bolada** *n.* bluff; short flight.
boladór: (Sp. *volador*) *n.* kite; flying fish.
bolante: (Sp. *volante*) *n.* fly-wheel; circular.
bolero: *n.* habitual joker, flatterer; bluffer.
bóliból: (Eng.) *n.* volleyball.
Bolinao: *n.* ethnic group and language from Western Pangasinan.
bolitas: (Sp.) *n.* pellets, ballbearings.
bolsa: (Sp.) *n.* stock exchange.
boltahe: (Sp. *voltage*) *n.* voltage.
bomba: (Sp.) *n.* pump; Artesian well; bomb; (*fig*.) big, important secret; (*slang*) X-rated movie.
bombero: (Sp.) *n.* fireman.
bombilya: (Sp. *bombilla*) *n.* light bulb.
bombo: (Sp.) *n.* a big drum; (*slang*) a pregnant mother.
bonito: *n.* bonito fish.
Bontok: *n.* ethnic group and language from the Mountain Province, Luzon.
bono: (Sp.) *n.* bond, certificate.
bonggá: (*slang*) *adj.* good looking; stylish; **bónggahan** *n.* shindig.
bonggalís: (*slang*) *adj.* pock-marked.
bopol: (slang, *bobo* + *pulpól*) *adj*. stupid.
boradór: (Sp. *borrador*) *n.* rough draft, outline.
boratso: (Sp. *borracho*) *adj.* drunk.
borlas: (Sp.) *n.* tassel, tuft; ruffle.
boro: *n.* kind of fish, *Pisodonophis boro*.
bos: (*slang*) *vocative* sir.
bosero: (*slang*) *n.* diver; peeping Tom, voyeur.
boses: (Sp. *voz*) *n.* voice; **boses-ipis** *id.* soft voice (voice of a cockroach).
boso: (*slang*) *n.* peeping Tom.
bosyò: (Sp.) *n.* goiter.
botas: (Sp.) *n.* boot.
botante: (Sp. *votante*) *n.* voter.
bote: (Sp.) *n.* bottle; lifeboat; **ibote** *v.* to bottle.
botelya: (Sp. *botella*) *n.* bottle.
botete: *var. of butete*: puffer fish.
boto: (Sp. *voto*) *n.* vote.
botón: (Sp. *botón*) *n.* button.
botonsilyo: *n.* kind of plant with a flower head resembling a button.
boya: (Sp.) *n.* buoy.
braso: (Sp. *brazo*) *n.* arm.
bragada: (Sp.) *n.* brigade.
brilyante: (Sp. *brillante*) *n.* diamond; *adj.* brilliant.
brilyo: (Sp. *brillo*) *n.* luster, brilliance.
brio: (Sp.) *n.* enterprise; life, animation.
brotsa: (Sp. *brocha*) *n.* large paint brush; (*slang*) cunnilingus, oral sex.
bruas: (Sp. *broa*) *n.* ladyfinger cookie.
bruha: (Sp. *bruja*) *n.* witch.

bruho: (Sp. *brujo*) *n.* warlock, sorcerer.
brúhula: (Sp. *brújula*) *n.* compass.
buáng: (*slang, Visayan*) *adj.* crazy.
buay: **mabuay** *adj.* unstable, unsteady; weak, prone to collapse.
buaya: *n.* alligator, crocodile.
bubas: (Sp.) *n.* pustule.
bubelya: (*slang*) *n.* breast.
bubo: *n.* fishtrap; clown.
bubò: **bubuan** *n.* cast; mold.
bubô: *adj.* overflowing; **magbubô** *v.* to spill deliberately.
bubó: **bumubó** *v.* to drive away (animals).
bubog: *n.* crystal; broken glass.
bubón: *n.* shallow well, cistern.
bubóng: *n.* roof.
bubot: (*slang*) *n.* girl, female.
bubót: *adj.* small unripe fruit.
buboy: *n.* cotton tree, kapok.
bubule: *n.* lizard fish, *Lygosona smaragdinum.*
bubulusan: *n.* bellows.
bubuntís: *n.* molly fish.
bubungán: *n.* roofing.
bubuwít: *n.* newly born mouse.
bubuyog: *n.* bumblebee; (*fig.*) young bachelor.
bubwít: (*slang*, f. *bubuwít*) *n.* short person.
buká: *adj.* open; **bukhín** *v.* to open; **bukáng-liwaywáy** *n.* daybreak; **bukáng-bibíg** *id.* common expression (open mouth).
bukakâ: *adj.* with the legs astraddle.
bukád: *adj.* open (flowers).
bukadkád: *adj.* fully opened (flowers).
bukahag: *n.* whale.
bukál: (Sp.) *n.* spring, fountain; source; **bumukal** *v.* to spring; **bukál sa isip** *id.* inborn, by nature (spring in the mind).
bukalkál: *n.* act of overturning, digging up.
bukambibíg: *n.* common saying.
bukana: *n.* front, threshold.
bukáng-bibíg: *n.* favorite word or expression.
bukáng-isip: *adj.* broad minded.
bukáng-liwaywáy: *n.* daybreak, dawn.
bukas: *adv.* tomorrow; **kinabukasan** *n.* the day after; **pagpapabukas-bukas** *n.* procrastination. **bukas-makalawá** some day, some time in the future.
bukás: *adj.* open; **buksán** *v.* to open; **magbukás ng dibdíb** *id.* reveal one's feelings (open the breast); **bukás-palad** *id.* generous (open palm); **bukás na aklát** *id.* known to all (open book); **bukás na dibdíb** *id.* accommodating (open breast); **nabuksán ang langit** *id.* became happy, mind became clear (sky opened); **bukás-bukasin** *v.* to put off until tomorrow; **bukás-loób** *adj.* wholehearted, sincere; **bukás-kotse** (*slang*) *n.* car thief.
bukaskás: *adj.* open; uncovered.
bukawal: *n.* porgy fish.
bukawi: *n.* species of bamboo.
bukayò: *n.* coconut caramel.
bukaypato: (Sp. *boca y pato*) *n.* pliers.
bukbók: *n.* weevil; decay (*of teeth*); (*slang*) *adj.* pimpled; pock-marked.
buke: (Sp. *buque*) *n.* ship; steamship.
bukhín: (rt. *buká*) *v.* to open.
bukid: **kabukiran** *n.* farm, country; **tagabukid** *n.* country fellow; **magbukid** *v.* to farm; **magbubukíd** *n.* farmer.
bukitkít: *n.* turning over carefully during a search.
bukíng (*coll.*) **mabukíng** *adj.* caught red handed.
buklát: *adj.* open.
bukláw: *n.* goiter; mumps.
buklíg: *n.* cyst; small pimple.
buklód: *n.* hoop around a barrel.
buko: *n.* young coconut; **mamuko** *v.* to bud.
bukò: *n.* intent, purpose.
bukó: *n.* node; knot in wood; knuckle; **bukuhín** *v.* to oppose; criticize; **nabukó** *adj.* disappointed; **ibukó** *v.* to tell, squeal; embarrass.
bukód: *adj.* separate; apart; in addition to; **bukod-tangì** *adj.* unique; **ibukod** *v.* to set apart, segregate; **bukúd-bukurin** *v.* to classify; separate.
bukol: *n.* lump, swelling, tumor.
bukóng: *n.* bone joint.
bukongbukong: *n.* internal and external malleolus.
bukót: *n.* hunchback.
buksán: (rt. *bukás*) *v.* to open, open up.
buktót: *adj.* wicked, corrupt; infamous.

bukung-bukong: *n.* ankle.
budbód: *n.* sprinkle; distribution of small quantities to many; **ibudbód** *v.* to sprinkle.
budhî: *n.* conscience; intuition.
budlóng: *n.* shove.
bugà, búgaan: *n.* pumice.
bugá: *n.* belch; spout; puff; **ibugá** *v.* to expel, drive out with force; **mamugá** *v.* to snort.
bugál: *n.* hard lump of earth.
bugalwák: **bumugalwák** *v.* to gush forth.
bugambílya: (Sp.) *n.* bougainvillea.
bugang: *n.* bragging; bickering.
búgaret: (*slang*) *n.* cigarette.
bugasok: *n.* large bamboo basket used for storing grain.
bugasók: *adj.* abrupt.
bugaw: *n.* go-between; pimp; **bumugaw** *v.* to shoo away.
bugáw: (*derogatory*) *n.* term for a small girl.
bugbóg: *n.* wallop; clubbing; *adj.* swollen from beating.
bugháw: *n.* blue.
bughô: **panibughô** *n.* jealousy.
bugíng: *n.* half-beak fish.
bugnít: *n.* hip.
bugnós: *adj.* disentangled, untied; **ibugnós** *v.* to untie.
bugnót: *n.* exasperation; *adj.* exasperation.
bugnóy: *n.* fallen coconut fruit.
bugók: *adj.* rotten (eggs); (*fig.*) weak headed.
bugóy: (*slang*) *adj.* deceptive; incompetent.
bugsô: *n.* crowd of people; flush; blast.
bugsók: *n.* kind of bamboo basket.
bugtóng: *adj.* sole, lone; *n.* riddle.
bugwák: **bumugwák** *v.* to gush, spurt out.
buhag: *n.* swarm of bees.
buhaghág: *adj.* spongy, porous.
buhalhál: *adj.* disorderly.
buhangin: *n.* sand; **kastilyong-buhangin** *n.* sand castle.
buhat[1]: *prep.* from; **pámuhatan** *n.* source, origin; **pinagbuhatan** *n.* descent.
buhat[2]: **bumuhat, magbuhát, buhatin** *v.* to lift, raise; **búhátin** *adj.* moveable; **pambuhat** *n.* crane, tool used for lifting; **nagbubuhát ng sariling bangkô** *id.* egoistic (carrying one's own bench); **pagbuhatan ng kamáy** *v.* to lift the hand against someone, hurt, injure.
buhawì: *n.* waterspout; whirlwind; cyclone.
buhay: *n.* life; **buhay-buhay** *n.* one's daily life; **buháy** *adj.* alive; **mabuhay** *excl.* Long live!; *v.* remain alive; live; **bumuhay, buhayin** *v.* to reanimate; bring back to life; support one's dependents, nourish; **buhayín** *n.* dependent; **bumuhay** *v.* to vitalize, give life to; **ikabuhay** *n.* means of livelihood; reason for living; **kabuhayan** *n.* livelihood; belongings; **bigyán-buhay** *v.* to animate, give life to; **magbuhay** *v.* to take care of something to keep it alive; **magbagong-buhay** *v.* to regenerate, rehabilitate; **mamuhay** *v.* to live (a certain way); manage, get along; **nakabúbuhay** *adj.* giving life, sustaining life; **pagbabaong-buhay** *n.* revival; rehabilitation; **buháy ang loób** *id.* brave (inside is alive); **habang-buhay** *adj.* lifelong; perpetual; **nabuhayan siyá ng loób** He was given hope; **buhay alamáng pagluksó'y patáy** *id.* one who lives an uncertain life. **buhay-alamáng** *n.* short life; **hanap-buhay** *n.* profession, trade; **maghanap-buhay** *v.* to earn a living; **talambuhay** *n.* biography; **urì ng pamumuhay** *n.* way of life.
buhaya: (*slang*, f. *buwaya*) *adj.* selfish; greedy.
Buhid: *n.* ethnic group and language from Southern Mindoro.
buhíya: (Sp. *bujía*) *n.* spark plug.
buho: (Sp.) *n.* owl.
buhò: *n.* species of bamboo.
buhók: *n.* hair; **buhukán** *v.* to pull someone by the hair; **mabuhók** *adj.* hairy. **buhúk-buhukan** *n.* wig, artificial hair; **gabuhók lamang** close shave, narrow escape; **gagabuhók** *n.* hairbreadth.
buhól: *n.* knot; union; **talimbuhól** *n.* betrothal; **nagkabuhúl-buhól ang hiningá** *id.* gasping for breath; exerting oneself (knotted breath).
buhóng: *n.* rascal; *adj.* deceitful; cunning, sly.
buhos: *n.* pouring; baptism; flow; **buhós na buhós** *adj.* intent; **ibuhos** *v.* to pour; **ibuhos ang kalooban** *id.* to trust completely.
bulà: *n.* fib; **bulaan** *n.* liar; **bulaanin** *v.* to

contradict.

bulâ: *n.* foam, bubbles; (*slang*) beer; **bumulâ** *v.* to bubble, foam. **buláng-gugò** (*fig.*) generous.

bulabod: *n.* sprinkling; sowing.

bulabog: *n.* disturbance, tumult; **bulabugin** *v.* to rout, drive away; annoy.

buladas: (*slang*) *v.* cheat, deceive.

buladór: *var. of boladór*: flying fish.

buladas: (*slang*) *n.* cheating; deceiving.

bulak: *n.* cotton.

bulák: **bumulák** *v.* to bubble when boiling.

bulakán: *n.* kind of vine whose leaves are used as a shampoo.

bulakból: *adj.* vagabond, truant.

bulaklák: *n.* flower; blossom; **mamulaklák** *v.* to blossom; **bulaklák ng dilà** *id.* flattering words (flower of the tongue); **bulaklák-bulaklakan** *n.* artificial flower; **mabulaklák ang landás** *id.* happy life (flowery path); **namúmulaklák ang tanrangkahan** *id.* will soon marry (gate is blooming); **tsitsarón-bulaklák** crunchy fried intestines.

buladór: (Sp. *volador*) *n.* flying fish; skyrocket; kite.

bulag: *n.* blindness; **bulág** *adj.* blind; **magbulág-bulagan** *v.* to pretend not to see; **nabulag sa salapî** *id.* influenced by money.

bulagâ: *interj.* Used with children, Boo!

bulagáw: *adj.* with gray eyes.

bulagsák: *adj.* careless; wasteful.

bulagtâ: *adj.* fallen flat.

bulahaw: *n.* tumult.

bulaid: *n.* hemorrhoids.

bulalakaw: *n.* shooting star.

bulalás: *n.* ejaculation; outburst; storm; **ibulalás** *v.* to exclaim.

bulalay: *n.* elephant's trunk.

bulalô: *n.* kneecap.

bulandál: *n.* old bachelor, old spinster.

buláng-gugò: *n.* generous person; *adj.* generous with others.

bulangláng: *n.* vegetable stew.

bulaos: *n.* path, trail.

bularit: *n.* kind of card game.

bulas: *n.* robustness; severe scolding.

bulastóg: *adj.* boastful; lying, bluffing; rash.

bulati: *n.* earthworm; ~ **sa bituka** *n.* hookworm; **parang bulati** *id.* seldom away from home.

bulatlát: *n.* careful search for something by removing the contents of a container.

buláw: *n.* suckling pig; *adj.* reddish colored.

bulay₁: *n.* strip of palm leaf.

bulay₂: **bulayin** *v.* to contemplate; **bulay-bulay** *n.* contemplation; reflection, meditation.

bulbók: *n.* bubbling of liquids.

bulbóg: *adj.* bruised.

bulból: *n.* pubic hair; armpit hair.

bulkán: (Sp. *volcán*) *n.* volcano.

buldét: (*slang, Pampango buldít*) *n.* anus.

buli: *n.* act of polishing, polish; **pambuli** *n.* polisher; **bulihin** *v.* to polish.

bulik: *adj.* speckled; *n.* black and white chicken.

bulikil: (*slang*) *n.* male.

bulíd: **ibulid** *v.* to hurl down from a height.

bulíg: *n.* mudfish not yet fully grown.

buligà: *n.* eyeball; mound of earth.

buligáw: *adj.* with no sense of direction; shortsighted.

buliglíg: *n.* swelling of the eyes (of fowls).

bulihalà: *n.* a fowl with ashy feathers and black legs; (*slang*) management; care; responsibility.

bulilít: *adj.* tiny, dwarfish; *n.* pygmy.

bulilyaso: (*slang*) *adj.* failed, thwarted.

bulilyo: (Sp. *bolillo*) *n.* bowling pin; lace bobbin.

bulinaw: *n.* anchovy; transparent sardine; (Vis.) species of bamboo.

buling: *n.* smear, smudge.

bulingbuling: *n.* Ash Wednesday; carnival.

bulingbuling: *n.* custom of throwing water at people on the feast of St. John the Baptist.

bulisik: **mabulisik** *adj.* mean, vile.

bulislís: *adj.* with the sleeves rolled up, with the skirt tucked up.

bulo: *n.* hairy covering of some fruits; **kabuluhán** *n.* value, worth.

bulô: *n.* calf; young water buffalo.

bulók: *adj.* rotten, putrid; (*slang*) not reliable; **mabulók** *v.* to decompose.

bulog: *n.* virility; **bulugan** *n.* breeding boar.

bulón: *n.* act of choking; **mabulunán** *v.* to be choked (by food).
bulóng: *n.* whisper, murmur; **bulungán** *v.* to whisper; **ibulóng nang malakás** *id.* expose a secret (whisper loudly).
bulos₁: *n.* harpoon.
bulos₂: *n.* second helping of food; gut of air; **bulusan** *n.* bellows.
bulos₃: **kabulusan** *n.* open space; public place; **pamulos** *n.* harpoon.
bulos₄: **panibulos** *n.* complete trust or confidence.
bulós: *adj.* complete, perfect; consumed, used up; fallen out; *n.* bold of cloth; contents of a container that have fallen out.
bulsá: (Sp. *bolsa*) *n.* pocket; **mamulsá** *v.* to put one's hands in one's pockets.
bulsilyo: (Sp. *bolsillo*) *n.* small pocket, side pocket.
bulto: (Sp.) *n.* bundle; religious image.
bulubok: **bumulubok** *v.* to bubble; gurgle.
bulubuktó: *n.* cavalla fish, *Caranx sp.*
bulubod: **buluburan** *n.* nursery garden, seed plot; **ibulubod** *v.* to scatter seeds.
bulubundukin: *n.* mountainous landscape.
bulukabok: *n.* gurgling sound.
bulugan: *n.* breeding male.
bululós: *n.* diarrhea.
bulung-ita: *n.* kind of shrub with edible fruits, *Diospyros philosanthera.*
bulusan: *n.* bellows.
bulusok: **ibulusok** *v.* to sink the feet into soft mud.
bulusok: **pagbulusok** *n.* nose dive; swishing sound of a bullet.
bulutong: *n.* pockmarks; smallpox; **bulutung-tubig, bulutong-manók** *n.* chicken pox.
bulutunggó: *adj.* pockmarked.
bulwák: *n.* gush of water.
bulwág: *adj.* wide open.
bulwagan: *n.* porch, entrance of a building.
bulwáng: *adj.* forced open, burst open.
bulyáw: *n.* loud rebuke; **bulyawán** *v.* to shout at.
bumbero: (Sp. *bombero*) *n.* fireman; (*slang*) cigarette lighter.
bumbón: *n.* twig dam; pond.
bumbóng: *n.* cylindrical container.
bumbunan: *n.* crown of the head.
bundaki: *n.* murrel fish.
bundalag: *n.* murrel fish.
bundát: *adj.* full from eating; (*slang*) *n.* beer belly; *adj.* pregnant.
bundók: *n.* mountain; **mamundók** *v.* to travel in the mountains, mountain-climb; **bundók na buhangin** *id.* success of short duration (mountain of sand).
bundól: **bundulín** *v.* to ram.
buni: *n.* herpes, shingles.
bunlag: *n.* ruins.
bunlót: **bumunlót** *v.* to uproot.
bunô: *n.* wrestling; **bunuín** *v.* to wrestle with; **kabunô** *n.* wrestling opponent. **búnuan** *n.* wresting match.
bunot: **bumunot** *v.* to pull up, uproot.
bunót: *n.* coconut husk.
bunsô: *adj.* youngest (child).
bunsód: *n.* boom; launching; **ibunsód** *v.* to launch.
bunsól: *n.* swoon, fainting fit; **mabunsól** *v.* to be bewitched.
buntál: *n.* buri fiber; blow with the fist; **buntalan** *n.* fist fight.
buntalà: *n.* comet.
buntís: *adj.* pregnant; **buntisín** *v.* to impregnate.
buntó: *n.* pressure; **ibuntó** *v.* to focus one's emotion on; disclose one's troubles.
buntón: *n.* heap; pile; (*coll.*) undetermined amount; **ibunton** *v.* to pile up; **buntunan** *n.* dump site. **buntunán** *v.* to dump; pile things up. **buntóng-hiningá** *id.* strong sigh (piled breath). **buntóng-galit** *n.* inner feeling of anger.
buntót: *n.* tail; rear end; trail; train of a dress; (*fig.*) tagalong; result; overcome. **bumuntót** *v.* to trail behind; **buntót-pusà** *n.* cat's tail. **buntót-pagi** *n.* tail of a ray used as a whip. **buntót-baláy** *n.* species of long-necked clam.
bunutan: *n.* big-eyed scad; **nagbuntót ng masamâ** *id.* caused something bad (tailed something bad).
bunyág: *n.* disclosure, revelation; *adj.* disclo-

sed, revealed. **ibunyág** *v.* to reveal, expose; divulge, disclose.

bunyagáw: (*slang*) *n.* initiation into a fraternity.

bunyî: *n.* fame, renown; exaltation. **mabunyî** *adj.* famous, illustrious; distinguished. **bunyiín** *v.* to exalt, honor.

bunga: *n.* fruit; produce; (*fig.*) child; **magbunga** *v.* to bear fruit; **bungang-araw** *n.* prickly heat rash (fruit of the sun); **bungang-isip** *n.* creative works (fruit of the mind); **bungang-tulog** *n.* dream (fruit of sleep); **bunga't ngangà** *id.* merely words. **bungahan** *n.* betel palm plantation; *v.* to chew betel nut. **búngahin** *adj.* prolific (plant or tree).

bungad: *n.* front; threshold; **ibungad** *v.* to put in the front.

bungal: *n.* extraction of the front teeth; **bungál** *adj.* toothless in front.

bungalngál: *n.* crybaby; complainer. **mabungalngál** *adj.* vociferous.

bungantulog: *n.* daydream; ambition, dream.

bungang-araw: *n.* prickly heat, a kind of tropical itchy rash.

bungangà: *n.* gullet; mouth; **magbungangâ** *v.* to shout; brag; **mabungangà** *adj.* loquacious; **waláng bungangà** *id.* timid. **bungangero** *n.* talkative man.

bungat: *n.* wrasse fish.

bungáw: *adj.* toothless; blunt; Jarbua gruntfish.

bunghá: *n.* cardinal fish.

bungkál: *n.* makeshift roof; tilling the soil; **dinabubungkál** *adj.* uncultivated.

bungkós: *n.* bundle; batch; bunch.

bunggalán: *adj.* having many nodes.

bunggô: *n.* collision; bump; **bumunggô nang maraham** *v.* to nudge; **magkabunggô** *v.* to collide, bump into; **kabungguang-balikat** *id.* constant companion (one with whom another rubs shoulders).

bunghalit: **bumunghalit** *v.* to burst (into laughter).

bungì: *n.* notch in the teeth; **bungî** *adj.* with a missing tooth; **mabungian** *v.* to lose a tooth.

bungisngís: *n.* giggle; **bumungisngís** *v.* to giggle.

bungô: *n.* skull.

bungót: *n.* beard; **bungot-bungot** *n.* ocellated plesiops fish.

bungsód: *n.* fish corral.

bunguán: *n.* smooth-headed sea catfish, *Arius leiotetocephalus*.

bungulan: *n.* species of banana.

buô: *adj.* complete; entire; whole; perfect; all; **bumuô** *v.* to form; constitute; **buuín** *v.* to consist of; develop; complete; **buóng-buô** *adj.* completely intact; **kabuuán** *n.* composition; entirety; **mabuô** *v.* to shape, develop; **magbuô** *v.* to assemble, put together; integrate; **mamuô** *v.* to solidify; congeal; coagulate. **nakabúbuô** *adj.* constructive (helpful); **pag(bu)buô** *n.* organization; development; **pagkabuô** *n.* integrity, wholeness; **sa kabuuan** for the most part; on the whole; **buóng-galang** *adv.* very respectfully; **buóng-giting** *adv.* bravely; **buóng-loób** *adj.* courageous; *adv.* courageously; **buóng-pusò** *adj.* sincere; earnest; **buóng-tiwalà** *n.* complete trust or confidence; *adv.* with complete trust.

buô and loób *id.* brave (inside is complete)

buód: **kabuuran** *n.* abstract; résumé, summary, synopsis; **buurín** *v.* to summarize; **binuô sa isip** *id.* made a personal decision (put in the mind).

buóg: *adj.* often sleepy.

buól: *n.* ankle.

buóng *pref.* [*buô* + *ng*] whole, full; **buóng buhay** whole life; **buóng-araw** whole day. **buóng-giting** *adv.* bravely. **buóng-loób** *adj.* brave, courageous. **buóng-pusò** *adv.* wholeheartedly, sincerely. **buóng-tiwalà** *n.* complete trust or confidence.

bupanda: (Sp. *bufanda*) *n.* muffler.

bupete: (Sp. *bufete*) *n.* lawyer's office.

bopis: (Sp. *bofes*) *n.* dish of lungs and intestines.

burá: (Sp. *borrar*) **burahín** *v.* to erase; **pamburá** *n.* eraser. **burado** *adj.* erased.

burak: *n.* muddy place.

buradól: *n.* kite.

buradór: (Sp. *borrador*) *n.* draft; rough copy.

burál: *n.* embossing; **maburál** *v.* to be em-

bossed.
burang: *n.* outburst of anger.
burarâ: *adj.* sloppy, untidy.
burát: *n.* act of rolling up the foreskin; (*slang*) testicle.
buratso: (Sp. *borracho*) *adj.* drunk. **buratsero** *n.* drunkard.
burdá: (Sp. *borda*) *n.* embroidery; **burdado** *adj.* embroidered; **magburdá** *v.* to embroider.
burikák: *n.* prostitute, whore.
burikì: *n.* probe used to sample rice in sacks.
buriko: (Sp. *borrico*) *n.* donkey.
buririì: *n.* excessive care. **buririin** *v.* to do with excessive care or attention.
burisingkáw: (*coll.*) *adj.* ungrateful.
burlés: (Eng.) *adj.* burlesque; (*slang*) naked.
burloloy: (*slang*) *n.* accessories, decoration; *adj.* wearing a lot of jewelry.
burník: (*slang*) *n.* booger. (*kulangot*)
buro$_1$: *n.* pickled meat; buro snake eel; **buruhin** *v.* to salt meat, pickle; **maburo** (*slang*) to be an old maid.
buro$_2$: (Sp. *burro*) *n.* donkey.
buro$_3$: (Eng.) *n.* bureau.
burok: **maburok** *adj.* chubby.
burol: **pagkaburol** *n.* lying in state; **pamburol** *adj.* suitable for burial; *id.* most elegant clothing; **kinabuburulan** *n.* tomb.
buról: *n.* hill; **maburól** *adj.* hilly.
burot: *adj.* pompous.
buruba: *n.* kind of fish, *Scolopsis sp*.
bursigí: (Sp. *borcegui*) *n.* shoe with laces, half-boot.
burubót: *n.* watery stool; **magburubót** *v.* to have loose bowel movements.
buryóng: (*slang*) *adj.* desperate, hopeless; insane.
busà: *n.* angry quarrel.
busá: *n.* popped corn or rice; **magbusá** *v.* to toast corn or rice; **mamusá** *v.* to sputter.
busabos: *n.* slave; **busabusin** *v.* to enslave.
busaksák: *adj.* very full.
busagság: *adj.* split open (bamboo).
busal: *n.* corncob.
busál: (Sp. *bozal*) *n.* muzzle; gag.
busalsál: *adj.* slovenly, slipshod.
busan: (rt. *buhos*) *v.* to pour on.
busangsáng: *adj.* fully opened (flowers).
busarga: *adj.* swollen (lips).
busbós: *n.* cutting open; surgical operation.
buskád: *adj.* open; unrolled.
busiksík: *adj.* full to bursting; stocky.
busil: *n.* corncob; core of wood.
busilak: *adj.* immaculate.
busilig: *n.* white of the eye; eyeball.
busilsíl: *adj.* blunted.
busina: (Sp. *bocina*) *n.* car horn; **bumusina** *v.* to blow the horn.
busisì: *adj.* fastidious; *n.* foreskin; **pagbubusisì** *n.* masturbation; **busisiin** *v.* to roll up the foreskin.
busiyô: *n.* goiter.
buslô: *n.* small woven basket; **buslóng butás** *id.* with a poor memory.
buslóg: *adj.* cocked (trigger).
buslót: *n.* small hole in the floor.
buso: (Sp. *buzo*) *n.* sea diver.
busog: *n.* bow (for shooting an arrow).
busóg: *adj.* full, satiated, satisfied; **pambusóg** *n.* something that satisfies the hunger.
busól: *n.* doorknob; **busulán** *n.* latch.
busón: (Sp. *buzón*) *n.* mailbox.
busong: *adj.* ungrateful; **kabusungan** *n.* ingratitude.
busto: (Sp.) *n.* bust.
buswáng: *n.* wound on the sole of the foot.
busyò: *n.* goiter.
butâ: (*slang*) *n.* zero.
butabutà: *n.* tree with lives in brackish water, *Excoecari agallocha*.
butaka: (Sp. *butaca*) *n.* orchestra seat.
butál: *adj.* odd, extra, left-over.
butangál: *n.* gray snapper fish.
butangero: *n.* goon, hoodlum, gangster.
butas: *n.* hole; opening; aperture; **butás** *adj.* perforated; (*fig.*) no longer a virgin; **bumutas** *v.* to pierce; **butasan** *v.* to bore a hole in; **butás ang bulsá** *id.* penniless; spendthrift (pocket has a hole); **nagbubutás ang silya** *id.* wallflower, person who doesn't dance at a party (making holes in the chair); **waláng butas** *id.* can't see a reason (no hole); **butas-ahas** *n.* snake pit. **butas-**

karayom *n.* eye of the needle; **butas-ilóng** *n.* nostril; **may butas sa tuktók** *id.* idiotic.
butatâ: (*slang*) *n.* cutting someone off; stopping the ball (in sports).
butaw: *n.* membership fee.
butáw: *n.* pitting roosters against each other in cockfighting; (*slang*) *adj.* useless.
butbót: *n.* thorough search; cry of the owl.
butete: *n.* puffer fish; (*fig.*) large-bellied person; **buteteng-laut** *n.* porcupine fish; *id.* person with a large belly.
buti: **mabuti** *adj.* good; **pinakamabuti** *adj.* best, finest; **bumuti** *v.* to get better, improve; get well; **butihin** *adj.* gentle, charming (women); **kabutihan** *n.* goodness; benefit; **buti ngâ** that's what you get, you asked for it; **makabuti** *v.* to benefit; **mabutihin** *v.* to favor; think well of; approve of; **mapabuti** *v.* to improve; **mabutí-butí** *adj.* a little better; **pagbuti** *n.* improvement; **pagbutihin** *v.* to perfect; strive to do something well; **magpakabuti** *v.* to strive to improve oneself; **pabutihin** *v.* to improve, make better; **ikabuti** *v.* to be advantageous; **mabuting-kamáy** *id.* good caretaker (good hands).
butikaryo: (Sp. *boticario*) *n.* chemist, druggist.
butikî: *n.* house lizard, gecko; **parang butikî** *id.* doing something outside of ones range of capabilities.
butiktík: *adj.* teeming with; **mamutiktík** *v.* to teem with, abound.
butíg: *n.* wart.
butihin: (rt. *buti*) *n.* modest, gentle lady.
butil: *n.* grain, kernel, seed; bead; pill;
butingtíng: *n.* fastidiousness; **mabutingtíng** *adj.* detailed, fastidious.
butiti: *see butete.*
butitos: (Sp.) *n.* high-heeled shoes.
butlíg: *n.* small cyst.
butó: *n.* bone; hard seed (as in the mango); **mabutó** *adj.* bony; seedy; **butó't balát** *adj.* skin and bones; **waláng butó** *id.* weak.
(butod, ibutod): **káibuturan** *n.* innermost part, very center; utmost depth.
butón: (Sp. *botón*) *n.* press button; stud, knob.
butones: (Sp. *botón*) *n.* button (for clothes).
butsé: (Sp. *buche*) *n.* crop or first stomach of a bird; (*slang*) anger.
butsí: (Ch.) *n.* sesame rice cake filled with bean paste.
butuan: *n.* species of banana with seeds, *Musa sapientum.*
Butuanon: *n.* ethnic group and language of Butuan City, Mindanao.
butukán: *n.* store.
butyóg: (Ilk. *buttióg*) *adj.* having a big belly.
buwà: *n.* prolapsed uterus.
buwág: *adj.* dissolved; demolished; **bumuwág, buwagín** *v.* to topple; demolish, disband; **pagbuwág** *n.* dissolution, breaking up.
buwál: *adj.* fallen flat; **mabuwál** *v.* to fall down, tumble; **ibuwál** *v.* to pull down.
buwán: *n.* moon; month; (*slang*) bald head; **kabilugan ng buwán** *n.* full moon; **bubuwanin** *adj.* crazy; **buwán-buwán** tarpon fish, ox-eyed herring, *Megalops cyprinoides*; *adv.* monthly. **buwanin** *id.* moody (going with the moon); **kabuwanán** *n.* maturity (of pregnancy, loans, harvest, etc.).
buwang: (*slang*) *adj.* crazy.
buwáy: *n.* unsteadiness; instability; **mabuwáy** *adj.* unbalanced, unsteady; **kabuwayán** *n* instability.
buwaya: *n.* crocodile, alligator; (*fig.*) *adj.* tricky; greedy; **buwayang-lubóg** *id.* traitor pretending to be good; usurer (crocodile staying underwater); **nabuwaya** *adj.* cheated.
buwelo: (Sp. *vuelo*) *n.* swaying; flare; spurt.
buwelta: (Sp. *vuelta*) *n.* return; turn over; **bumuwelta** *v.* to return; **ibuwelta** *v.* to cause to turn back.
buwenas: (Sp. *buenas*) *n.* good luck; **buwenasin** *v.* to enjoy good luck.
buweno: (Sp. *bueno*) *interj.* Good!
buwéy: (Sp. *buey*) *n.* ox.
buwík: *n.* young pig, piglet.
buwíg: *n.* bunch of fruits.
buwís: *n.* tax, tariff; cropshare; **magpabuwís** *v.* to tax; **bumuwís** *v.* to pay taxes; **mámumuwisan** *n.* taxpayer.
buwisit: (Ch. *bo uî sít*: no clothes food) *n.* bad luck; nuisance; **mambuwisit** *v.* to annoy.
buwisita: (*slang, buwisit + bisita*) *n.* unwanted visitor.

buwitre: (Sp. *buitre*) *n.* vulture.
buyà₁: **pabuyà** *n.* tip (given to a waiter); **magpabuyà** *v.* to give a tip to. [Root not used alone]
buyà₂: *n.* satiation, glut; **buyaan** *v.* to satiate.
buyág: *adj.* loose (soil); **buyagín** *v.* to loosen the soil.
buyangyáng: *adj.* loose; unprotected.
buyayà: *n.* spendthrift, wasteful person. **buyayâ** *adj.* wasteful, extravagant with money.
buyo: *n.* betel leaf; yellow-fin tuna; **buyo-anís** betel leaf pepper.
buyó: **nabuyó** *adj.* seduced, induced; **magbuyó** *v.* to incite, urge on; motivate. **buyúng-buyó** *adj.* deeply engrossed in.
buyón: *n.* paunch, belly; (*slang*) toilet; *adj.* big bellied.
buyóy: (*slang*) *adj.* tongue twisted.
buyuyoy: *n.* appellation given to a small boy.
bweno: (Sp. *bueno*) *interj.* all right.

C

The letter *c* is no longer used in modern (phonetic) Tagalog alphabet. To avoid ambiguity, the letters ***k*** and ***s*** have taken its place. There are a few languages and ethnic groups in the Philippine archipelago, however, that continue to use the letter *c*. The following languages from the Philippines start with the letter *c*. For words originally starting with *ch*, search under **ts**.

Caluyanun: *n.* language and ethnic group from Caluya Islands, Antique.
Capiznon: *n.* language and ethnic group from Northeast Panay Island.
Cebuano: *n.* language and ethnic group from Cebu Island and Northern Mindanao.
Chavacano: *n.* pidgin Spanish (language of Zamboanga city, Mindanao).
Cuyonon: *n.* language and ethnic group of the Cuyo Islands between Panay and Palawan.

K

ka: *enclitic.* you (familiar). Independent form is *ikáw*. [See also *kitá*]
ka₁-: *prefix.* forms abstract nouns of size, distance or time: **kalayò** *n.* distance; **kalakí** *n.* largeness, bigness; **katagál** *n.* duration. See also *ka- -an*:
ka₂-: *prefix.* forms comitative nouns: **kabario** *n.* person from the same neighborhood; **kababayan** *n.* townmate; **kaklase** *n.* classmate; **kakampón** *n.* fellow gang member. **kalakbáy** *n.* traveling companion; **kaliga** *n.* person from the same league; **kamay-akdâ** *n.* co-author.
ka- -an₁: *affix.* 1. Forms abstract nouns: **kalambután** *n.* softness; weakness; **kalahian** *n.* ancestry, lineage; nationality; **kalasingán** *n.* drunkenness, intoxication; **kalungkutan** *n.* sadness; **kabubú't-hubarán** *n.* nudity; 2. Forms locative nouns, where the entity denoted by the stem exists: **kakahuyan** *n.* forest, woods; **kalangitan** *n.* the entire sky; heavens.
ká- -an₂-: 1. forms nouns that represent reciprocal or simultaneous acts: **kátuwaan** *n.* joyful merrymaking. 2. Forms superlatives, used with certain roots: **kálaliman** *adj.* deepest; *n.* deepest part; **káduluhan** *n.* farthest point; **kálakihán** *adj.* largest, biggest; 3. with temporal roots, denotes relative time: **kágabihán** *adv.* the next night; **káhapunan** *adv.* the very afternoon; the next afternoon.
kaCV-: *prefix.* forms verbs in the recent past: **kabibilí** *v.* just bought. This form takes actors in the genitive case: **Kabibilí ko lang.** I just bought it.
káCV-: *prefix.* denotes continuous acts: **kásisigáw** *n.* continuous shouting.
kaagád: (*rt. agád*) *adv.* immediately.

kaáng: *n.* large earthen jar with a wide mouth; *adj.* with the legs spread wide apart.
kabá: *n.* palpitation; premonition; **kabahán** *n.* palpitation.
kababayan: (*rt. bayan*) *n.* townmate, countryman.
kabado: *adj.* in doubt; nervous.
kabag: *n.* gas pain.
kabág: *n.* fruit bat.
kabál: *n.* potion; talisman; **kabál sa sakít** *n.* immunity; **may-kabál** *adj.* immune.
kabalyas: (Sp. *caballa*) *n.* saddlebag; short-bodied mackerel.
kabalyerisa: (Sp. *caballeriza*) *n.* cavalry.
kabalyero: (Sp. *caballero*) *n.* gentleman; knight.
kabalyete: (Sp. *caballete*) *n.* sawhorse.
kabán: *n.* chest for clothes; dry measure of 25 gantas.
kabanatà: *n.* chapter.
kabanya: (Sp. *cabaña*) *n.* cabin, hut.
kabáng: *adj.* multi-colored; *n.* whiskered-croaker fish.
kabaong: *n.* coffin.
kabasi: *n.* short-finned gizzard shad.
kabatsóy: *n.* kind of frog.
kabayo₁: (Sp. *caballo*) *n.* horse; **kabayo-kabayuhan** *n.* sea horse.
kabayo₂. (*slang*) *n.* big woman; police car.
kabkáb: *n.* big bite; peeling off (with the teeth); species of frog; **kabkabín** *v.* to take a big bite.
kabesera: (Sp. *cabecera*) *n.* capital; head of the table.
kabibi: *n.* species of clam; valve.
kabikî: *n.* species of tree.
kabig: *n.* winnings in gambling; vassal, follower; act of pulling towards oneself; **kabigin** *v.* to draw towards oneself.
kabil: *n.* double chin.
kabilâ: *n.* the other side; **sa kabilâ ng** instead of, in spite of; in the face of; **magkabilâ** either; **kabilaan** *adj.* reversible.
kabilya: (Sp. *cabilla*) *n.* dowel, rod.
kabisa: (Sp. *cabeza*) *n.* head, chief.
kabisada: (Sp. *cabezada*) *n.* bridle.
kabisado: (*f. kabisa*) *adj.* memorized.
kabisera: (Sp. *cabecera*) *n.* capital city.
kabisî: *n.* Chinese store owner.
kabisilya: (Sp. *cabecilla*) *n.* banker in gambling; chief investor.
kabisote: (Sp. *cabezote*) *adj.* mentally retarded; obstinate.
kabít: *adj.* attached, connected; (*fig.*) common-law wife; concubine; **ikabít** *v.* to fix, fasten; **magkabít** *v.* to connect, install; **pinakabít** *n.* money given by winners in gambling to losers so they can continue betting.
kabiyâ: *n.* species of clam.
kable: (Sp. *cable*) *n.* cable.
kabo: (Sp. *cabo*) *n.* corporal; (*slang*) zero.
kabód: *adv.* abruptly.
kabóg: *n.* loud thump.
kabonegro: (Sp. *cabo negro*) *n.* sago palm.
kabrá: (Sp. *cabra*) *n.* female goat.
kabrón: (Sp. *cabrón*) *n.* male goat.
kabutí: *n.* mushroom.
kabutíng-ahas: *n.* toadstool.
kabuwal: **mangabuwál** *v.* to fall; **nangabuwál sa dilím** *id.* died a hero (fell in the dark).
kabuyaw: *n.* species of citrus tree.
kabyás: **kabyawan** *n.* sugarcane mill.
káka-: [*kaCV*] *prefix.* forms limitatives of time or quantity: **kákauntî** very little bit; **kákahapon** just yesterday.
kaka: *n.* name for eldest uncle or aunt.
kakâ: *n.* name of eldest sibling.
kakáb: *adj.* hollow; empty; *n.* notch.
kakabit. *n.* big spine flathead fish.
kakak: *n.* cackling; (*slang*) *adj.* scared to death; **kumakak** *v.* to cackle.
kakaníng itík: (*slang*) *n.* coward; controlled person.
kakanggatâ: [*kaka* + *gatâ*] *n.* first undiluted coconut milk; gist, substance, essence.
kakap-bató: *n.* triple tail fish.
kakapsóy: *n.* species of frog.
kakas: *n.* abrasion.
kakáw: *n.* cacao.
kakawag: *n.* milkfish fry.
kakawate: *n.* species of tree used for lumber (*madrekakaw*)
kaki: *n.* khaki cloth or color.
kakí: **pagkakí** *n.* keeping time with the feet

(while listening to music).
kako: [*wikà ko*] I said, as I say.
kakusa: (*slang*) *n*. companion.
kada: (Sp. *cada*) *adv*. each (used with time expressions); every. (*bawa't*)
kadáng-kadáng: *n*. disease of coconut trees.
kadkád: *adj*. unfurled; spread out.
kadena: (Sp. *cadena*) *n*. chain.
kadilakad: (*slang*) *n*. going on foot.
kadíri: (*slang*) *n*. loathing.
kadlít: *n*. vaccination; incision.
kadlô: **kadluín** *v*. to scoop out.
kadyós: *n*. pigeon pea, *Cajanus cajan*.
kadyót: *n*. upward thrust or stab, jerk; (*slang*) have sex.
kaembang: (*slang*) *n*. wide pants.
kagalkál: *n*. whirring sound.
kagáng: *n*. hard soil; *adj*. hard (soil); overdried.
kagaskás: *n*. rattling sound.
kagát: *n*. bite; exact fit (clothes); **kumagát** *v*. to bite; (*fig*.) to be in conformity with; **kumagát sa halagá (pakò)** *id*. paid the high price (bit the cost (nail)); **kumagát sa pain** *id*. was fooled (bit the bait); **kumagát sa patalím** *id*. to try everything when in a desperate situation (bit the sharp weapon); **kumagát sa pain** *id*. trapped; **pagkagát ng dilím** *id*. at nightfall (when darkness bites); **dî makagát** *id*. sold at cost; **pakagát** *n*. bait.
kagaw: *n*. mite.
kagawad: (*rt. gawad*) *n*. member of a committee. **kagawarán** *n*. governmental department.
Kagayanen: *n*. ethnic group and language from Cagayan Island, between Negros and Palawan.
kagkág: *n*. scratching to relieve the itch; *adj*. spread out (wings).
kagingkíng: *n*. tinkling sound.
kagitnâ: (*rt. gitnâ*) *n*. half a pint.
kagód: *n*. grating sound.
kagugkóg: *n*. sound of thunder; explosion.
kagungkóng: *n*. clamor.
kagyát: *adv*. instantly; immediate.
kagyós: *n*. pigeon pea.
kaha: (Sp. *caja*) *n*. box; packet.
kahang: *n*. species of small mollusk.
kahapon: (*rt. hapon*) *adv*. yesterday.
kahat: **makakahat** *adj*. acrid.
kahatì: (*rt. hatì*) *n*. one-half; **kahati't-waló** thirty centavos.
kahél: *n*. species of orange tree.
kahero: (Sp. *cajero*) *n*. cashier.
kahì, kahi't: *conj*. even if, although.
kahig: **kahigan** *v*. to scrape off something; scratch off; **kahig nang kahig** *id*. continuously looking for means of livelihood (always scratching); **kumakahig** *id*. conversing with (scratching); **parang kinahig ng manók** *id*. chicken scratches (bad writing); **isáng kahig isáng tukâ** *id*. income just is enough for food (one scratch, one peck); **panáy na pakahíg** *id*. always scratching, refers to someone who always wants to receive but doesn't give.
kahig: *n*. inciting two roosters to fight.
kahiman: *conj*. although.
kahimanawarì: *interj*. may it come true.
káhinatnán: *v*. to end up with, result in.
kahista: (Sp. *cajista*) *n*. typesetter.
kahit na: *conj*. although.
kahita: (Sp. *cajita*) *n*. small box.
kahók: *n*. act of dipping fingers in liquid (holy water).
kahog: *n*. haste.
kahól: **kumahól** *v*. to bark (dogs).
kahón: (Sp. *cajón*) *n*. box, chest; (*slang*) *adj*. persistent.
kahoy: *n*. wood; lumber; **mangahoy** *v*. to gather firewood; **magkahoy** *v*. to deal in lumber; **kahuyan** *n*. woods, woodlands; **bungang-kahoy** *n*. fruit.
kaibigan: (*rt. ibig*) *n*. friend; **pakikipagkaibigan** *n*. friendship; **kaibigang putik** *id*. insincere friend.
káibuturan: *n*. very center, innermost part; utmost depth.
kailâ: *adj*. unknown, hidden, secret. **ikailâ** *v*. to keep secret; hide; **pagkailaán** *v*. to hide from someone.
kailán: *adv*. when; **kahit kailan** any time; **kailanmán** *adv*. whenever.
kailangan: *v*. to need; *adj*. be necessary; *n*. need; **pangangailangan** *n*. necessity.

kaimito: *n.* star apple.
kain: *n.* eating; **kainán** *n.* dining room; restaurant; **káinan** *n.* banquet, dinner party; **kanin** *v.* to eat; *n.* rice; food; **kakanín** *n.* edible tidbits; **kumain** *v.* to eat; **magkaín** *v.* to devour, eat voraciously; **manginain** *v.* to graze; **makikain** *v.* to join others in eating; **pakain** *n.* ration of food; **pagkain** *n.* food; **pakainin** *v.* to feed; **kinakain ang salitâ** *id.* not speaking clearly (eating the words); **kumakain ng pangaral** *id.* attentive to other's advice (eating the advice); **pakakanin ng bala** *id.* shoot (feed bullets); **pakanin sa palad** *id.* treat nicely (feed on the palm); **hindî makain** *id.* can't believe it (can't eat); **kinain ang lahò** *id.* disappeared; **magkaín ang barò (basahan)** *id.* to become poor; **nápakain ng laway** *id.* persuaded.
kaíng: *n.* woven bamboo basket.
kaingin: *n.* opening in the forest for cultivation; **kaingero** *n.* slash and burn farmer.
kaít: **ikaít** *v.* to withhold, deny, refuse.
kala: *n.* tortoise.
kalâ: **kumalâ** *v.* to gargle.
kalaanan: *n.* abandoned land.
kalabà: *n.* white spots on the eyeball, cataract.
kalabasa: (Sp. *calabaza*) *n.* squash, pumpkin; (*slang*) failure in school; idiot; **kalabasang pulá** *id.* fire; **nangálabasa** *id.* failed in an exam.
kalabáw: *n.* water buffalo; **magkalabáw** *v.* to ride a water buffalo.
kalabít: *var. of kalbít*: touch with the tip of the finger.
kalabóg: *n.* thump, thud.
kalaboso: (Sp.) *n.* prison.
kalabukab: *n.* species of water snake.
kalakukab: *reg. var.* of *kalabukab*.
kalabyáng: *n.* kind of large bat.
kalakal: *n.* merchandise; commodity; business; **kalakalan** *n.* trade, commerce; **kalakalin** *v.* to commercialize; **kalakal-saria** *id.* losing in business.
kalakatak: **parang kalakatak ang bibíg** *id.* talking loudly.
kalakatì: *n.* tool used for cutting betel nuts.
kalakhán: (rt. *lakí*) *n.* bigness, largeness; greatness; magnitude.
kalakuwerda: **parang kalakuwerda** *id.* talking loudly.
kalakyán: *n.* adult male water buffalo.
kaladkád: *n.* dredge net; act of dragging; **kaladkarín** *v.* to drag.
kalado: (Sp. *calado*) *n.* open work.
kalág: *adj.* loose; free; untied; **kalagín** *v.* to untie, undo.
Kalagan: *n.* ethnic group and language from Mindanao.
kalagkág: *n.* gargle; hard scratching.
kalaghalâ: *n.* phlegm.
kalaguman: (*rt. lagom*) *n.* confederation.
kalaguyò: *n.* intimate friend.
kalahatì: *n.* one half.
kalaháy: *n.* fervent desire; loud shriek.
kalám: *n.* remorse; feeling of hunger.
kalamák: *n.* resin, gum; pitch, tar.
kalamansî: *n.* kind of tree which bears small sour fruits.
kalamay: *n.* confection made with flour, coconut milk and sugar; **kalamayin ang loób** *id.* to calm one's self (make the inside into *kalamay*).
kalamayo: *n.* dropsy.
kalambâ: (Sp. *caramba*) *n.* kind of large jar.
kalambigas: *n.* gold bracelet with three strands.
kalambigì: *n.* bracelet.
kalambóg: *n.* heavy thumping.
kalambre: (Sp. *calambre*) *n.* cramp; **kinakalambre ang tiyán** *id.* very hungry (cramp in stomach).
kalamkám: *n.* tingling sensation.
kalamidád: (Sp. *calamidad*) *n.* calamity.
kalamita: (Sp. *calamita*) *n.* loadstone.
kalampág: *n.* clanking noise; (*fig.*) speaking in a loud voice.
kalamundíng: *n.* species of citrus fruit.
kalamyás: *n.* kind of sour fruit.
kalán: *n.* stove.
kalandák: *n.* act of boasting; spreading rumors.
kalandóng: *n.* awning; arbor.
kalandra: *n.* bier; hearse.
kalansáy: *n.* skeleton.
kalansíng: *n.* jingling sound.

kalantarì: *n.* idle gossip.
kalantás: *n.* species of tree with red aromatic wood.
kalantís: *n.* swishing sound.
kalantóg: *n.* rattling sound.
kalang: (Sp. *calar*) *n.* wedge; **kalangan** *v.* to wedge.
kalangay: *n.* cockatoo.
kalangkáng: *n.* disorderly pile.
kalangkáw: *n.* Indian turbot fish.
kalap: *n.* log, lumber; **pagkalap** *n.* campaigning, recruitment; **kalapin** *v.* to recruit.
kalapâ: *n.* careful consideration.
kalapati: *n.* dove, pigeon; **kalapating mababà ang lipád** *n.* loose woman, prostitute (low flying dove).
kalapato: *n.* cavalla fish, *Caranx sp.*
kalapáy: *n.* tassel; fin.
kalapit-: *pref.* neighboring; near.
kalapnít: *n.* species of small bat.
kalás: *adj.* detached, disconnected; (*slang*) brave; *v.* resign.
kalasag: *n.* coat of arms; shield.
kalasáw: *n.* wriggling movement.
kalasíng: *n.* clinking sound.
kalasò: *n.* lizard fish.
kalatsutsi: *n.* frangipani tree.
kalat: *n.* litter; disorder; spread out; **kalát** *adj.* stray; sporadic; scattered; (*slang*) flirtatious; careless; **kumalat** *v.* to circulate, scatter, spread; sprawl; **nagkalát ng bahò** *id.* exposed one's own defects (spread foul odor).
kalatas: *n.* written message, letter.
kalatkát: *n.* act of spreading out.
kalatís: *n.* sound, noise.
kalatóg: *n.* knocking sound; **kalatóg-pinggán** *n.* uninvited party crasher (noise of the plate).
kalatóng: *n.* small drum; clash.
kalatsutsî: *n.* temple flower tree.
kalatuwát: *n.* echo.
kalaw: *n.* hornbill.
kalawà: *n.* taro.
kalawang: *n.* rust; **kinakalawang na** already rusty.
kalawat: **ikalawat** *v.* to tie to a stake.
kalawkáw: **kumalawkáw** *v.* to stir with a stick (liquids).
kalawili: *n.* accord, harmony.
kalawit: *n.* hook; gaff.
kaláy: *adj.* with weak knees.
kalaykáy: *n.* rake.
kalbáng: *n.* species of bamboo.
kalbaryo: (Sp. *calvario*) *n.* (Bible) Cavalry; (*fig.*) extreme sacrifice.
kalbít: *n.* light touch; **kalbitín** *v.* to touch; pluck; tap.
kalbó: (Sp. *calvo*) *adj.* bald.
kalburo: (Sp. *carburo*) *n.* carbide.
kalkál: **kumalkál** *v.* to scratch.
kaldera: (Sp. *caldera*) *n.* caldron; steam boiler.
kaldereta: (Sp. *caldereta*) *n.* kettle; meat stew (usually goat meat).
kaldero: (Sp. *caldero*) *n.* cauldron, kettle.
kalderón: (Sp. *calderón*) *n.* cauldron.
kaldo: (Sp. *caldo*) *n.* broth; rice soup.
kalembang: (*slang*) *n.* wide pants.
kalendaryo: (Sp. *calendario*) *n.* calendar.
kalengkláng: (*slang*) *n.* sloppy walking.
kalesa: (Sp. *calesa*) *n.* horse carriage; **magkalesa** *v.* to ride a carriage; **kalesero** *n.* carriage driver; carriage maker.
kalesín: (Sp. *calesín*) *n.* two-wheeled chaise.
kalí: *n.* peace, quiet.
kalibkíb: *n.* copra.
kalibo: *n.* kind of cloth made in Kalibo, Aklan.
kalibre: (Sp. *calibre*) *n.* caliber; capacity.
kalibungbóng: *n.* group of people, crowd. **magkalibungbóng** *v.* to crowd around.
kalikaw: **kalikawin** *v.* to poke and stir liquid.
kalikol: **pangkalikol** *n.* probe.
kalikot: *n.* act of poking in a hole.
kalidád: (Sp. *calidad*) *n.* quality.
kaligay: *n.* species of snail, cowry.
kaligkíg: *n.* shiver.
kalilya: (Sp. *candelilla*) *n.* catheter.
kaling: *n.* steering handle, rudder; tiller.
Kalinga: *n.* ethnic group and language from Kalinga-Apayao Province, North Central Luzon.
kalingà: *n.* support, patronage; refuge; solicitude.
kalingkingan: *n.* little finger; **walâ sa kalingkingan** *id.* not of the same ability (not in the little finger); **ganggákalingkingan** *id.* very

small when compared to another (as big as the small finger).
kalipkíp: *n.* kind of creeping vine.
kalipunan: *n.* federation.
kalís: *adj.* scraped clean; **kalisán** *v.* scrape off.
kalisag: *n.* spine; bristles; **mangalisag** *v.* to bristle.
kaliskís: *n.* scales of fish.
kalít: *n.* creaking sound.
kaliwâ: *n.* left side; **kaliwain** *v.* to use the left hand; to double cross; **mangaliwâ** *v.* to double cross; **magpakaliwâ** *v.* to go left; **pumakaliwâ** *v.* to turn left.
kaliwete: *adj.* left-handed; (*slang*) unfaithful partner.
Kallahan: *n.* language and ethnic group from Western Nueva Viscaya and north-eastern Pangasinan.
kalma: (Sp. *calm*) *adj.* calm.
kalmante: (Sp. *calmante*) *n.* sedative.
kalmen: (Sp. *carmen*) *n.* scapular; scapulary.
kalmín-kalmín: *n.* drepane fish.
kalmós: *n.* scratch.
kalmót: *n.* harrow; **kalmutín** *v.* to scratch; paw.
kalò: *n.* bowl.
kalô: *n.* pulley.
kalóg₁: **kumalóg** *v.* to shake; **kalóg** *adj.* wobbly, shaky; mentally unbalanced, *n.* **kakalúg-kalóg** *id.* too few for a big house (shaking); **kalóg ang utak** *id.* foolish, idiot.
kalóg₂: (*slang*) extortion; joker; good sport; *adj.* crazy; hyperactive; happy go lucky.
kalong: *adj.* held in one's lap; **kalungan** *n.* lap; **kumalong** *v.* to hold in the lap.
kaloób: *n.* gift, offering; **loobín** *v.* to grant, bestow.
kalop: *n.* thin metal lining or embossing.
kalos: *n.* strickle, instrument used to level grains.
kalós: *adj.* shaky; unstable; **mangalós** *v.* to shake; be unsteady..
kalot: *n.* residue after extraction of coconut oil.
kalót: *adj.* nude; **kakalót** *n.* nudist.
kalsá: (Sp. *calza*) *n.* wedge.
kalsada: (Sp. *calzada*) *n.* street.
kalsado: (Sp. *calzado*) *n.* footwear.
kalsadór: (Sp. *calzador*) *n.* shoehorn.
kalsó: (Sp. *calzo*) *n.* wedge; chock; shoes.
kalsón: (Sp. *calzón*) *n.* breeches, trousers.
kalták: *n.* snapping of the fingers.
kaltáng: *n.* grouper fish.
kaltás: *adj.* removed; detached; canceled; **kumaltás** *v.* to remove, delete; **kaltasín** *v.* to deduct, subtract; lay off. **kaltasán** *v.* to cut on; subtract from; reduce; lay off.
kaltís: *n.* clicking sound.
kaluban: *n.* scabbard, sheath. (*baina*)
kalubkób: *n.* coating on vegetables (onions).
kalùkadídang: (slang) *n.* mistress.
kalugay: *n.* ravine, gorge.
kalugkóg: *n.* muffled sound; distant roll of thunder.
kalugdán: (rt. *lugód*) *v.* to be delighted with.
kalugó: *n.* large wart.
kaluluwá: *n.* soul, spirit; **nangáluluwá** *v.* serenading house to house at night during All Saint's Day.
kalumatá: *n.* dark rings around the eyes from lack of sleep.
kalumbibít: *n.* kind of prickly vine.
kalumismís: *n.* species of sand clam.
kalumpáng: *n.* wild almond tree.
kalumpít: *n.* kind of tree.
kalunuran: (*rt. lunod*) *n.* west.
kalunyâ: (*rt. alunyâ*) *n.* concubine.
kalupkóp: *n.* metal hoop; inlay, overlay; **kalupkupán** *v.* to overlay.
kalupi: *n.* wallet; portfolio.
kaluskós: *n.* rustling sound.
kalutkót: *n.* act of searching through contents.
kalyâ: (Ch. *kâ liaq*) *n.* kind of fruit basket.
kalye: (Sp. *calle*) *n.* street.
kalyehero: (Sp. *callejero*) *n.* loiterer.
kalyehón: (Sp. *callejón*) *n.* lane, alley.
kalyo: (Sp. *callo*) *n.* callus.
kalyos: (Sp. *callo*) *n.* tripe dish.
kama: (Sp. *cama*) *n.* bed.
kamá: *adj.* well adjusted.
kamâ: *n.* touching something dirty.
kamakalawá: (*rt. dalawá*) *n.* the day before yesterday.
kamakatló: (*rt. tatló*) *n.* three days ago.
kamada: (Sp. *camada*) *n.* litter, brood; band

of robbers; flock, herd; well arranged pile.
kamado: *adj.* well-adjusted.
kamag-anak: *n.* family, relatives.
kamagsá: *n.* species of vine with pink flowers.
kamál$_1$: *n.* large handful; **magkamál** *v.* to hold a handful of something; (fig.) acquire many possessions; **mapagkamál** *adj.* fortunate to have plenty of something.
kamál$_2$: *n.* kneading of dough; **kamalín** *v.* to knead.
kamalán: *see under malî.*
kamaleón: (Sp. *camaleón*) *n.* chameleon.
kamalig: *n.* warehouse.
kamamalò: *n.* species of poisonous snake.
kamámbabatas: (rt. *batás*) *n.* fellow lawmaker.
kamáNCV: *pref.* denotes a mutual relationship: **kamámbabatas** *n.* fellow lawmaker; **kamánananggól** *n.* fellow lawyer; **kamándaragát** *n.* fellow fisherman; **kamánunulát** *n.* co-author, fellow writer; **kamáng-aagham** *n.* fellow scientist; **kamángangalakál** *n.* fellow businessman.
kamandág: *n.* venom.
kamantigì: *n.* species of herb, balsam.
kamangâ: *n.* whetstone.
kamaó: *n.* back of the hand, fist.
kamápaniwalaín: (rt. *paniwalà*) *n.* credulity, tendency to believe too readily.
kámara: *n.* legislative chamber; camera.
kamarero: (Sp. *camarero*) *n.* waiter.
kamarín: (Sp. *camarín*) *n.* small storehouse.
kamariya: *n.* maidenwort herb, mugwort.
kamarote: (Sp.) *n.* stateroom.
kamás: *adj.* mashed with the hands.
kamatis: *n.* tomato; (*slang*) abscess.
kamatsilé: (Sp.) *n.* guamachil tree.
kámay: *adj.* accustomed to handling.
kamáy: *n.* hand; **kamayán** *v.* to shake someone's hand; **kamáyan** *n.* using hands in eating; **kamayín** *v.* to do with the hands; **kumamáy** *v.* to shake hands; **pang-kamáy** *adj.* manual; **magkamáy** *v.* to shake hands; eat with the hands; use the hands; **magkakamáy** *adj.* holding hands; **nápasakamáy** *adj.* put in the hands of; fell in the hands of; **nasa kamáy** on hand; **pagkamáy** *n.* handshake; **pagkakamáy** *n.* shaking hands; **pangkamáy** *adj.* manual, done with the hands; **maglipat-kamáy** *v.* to change hands; **kamáy na bakal** *id.* strict in punishing (iron hand); **nasa kanyáng kamáy** *id.* at his mercy (in his hands); **nasa mabuting kamáy** *id.* in good hands; **waláng kamáy** *id.* not knowing how to do any type of work (no hand); **sa kamáy lamang** freehand.
Kamayo: *n.* ethnic group and language from Surigao del Sur, Mindanao.
kambabalò: *n.* species of garfish.
kambál: *n.* twins; **kakambal** *n.* fellow twin; **kambál-kambál.** *adj.* joined, attached (fruits); **kambál-patinig** *n.* diphthong; **magkakambál** *n.* twins; being alike.
kambáng: *n.* opening of the petals of flowers; bulge.
kambás: (Eng.) *n.* canvas; campaign; investigation.
kambíl: *n.* spool.
kambíng: *n.* goat; (*slang*) pimp.
kambyo: (Sp. *cambio*) *n.* gear shift; **magkambyo** *v.* to change gears.
kambóg: *n.* splashing sound.
kambray: *n.* cambric.
kamkám: **kumamkám** *v.* to claim without rights; **kamkamín** *v.* to seize without rights; usurp; **mangangamkám** *n.* usurper; **makamkám** *adj.* greedy.
kamelyo: (Sp. *camello*) *n.* camel.
kamí: *pron.* we (*exclusive*): we excluding you. [Genitive forms: *namin*, *amin*; Oblique: *sa amin*]
kamigíng: *n.* species of yam.
kaminero: (Sp. *caminero*) *n.* street sweeper.
kamisa: (Sp. *camisa*) *n.* shirt.
kamiseta: (Sp. *camiseta*) *n.* undershirt.
kamisón: (Sp. *camisón*) *n.* chemise, slip; petticoat.
kamít: **kamtán** *v.* to get; **makamít** *v.* to obtain.
kamo: [*wikà mo*] you said, as you said.
kamot: *n.* scratch; **magkamót** *v.* to scratch; **magkamót ng tiyán** *id.* to be lazy (scratch the belly); **magkamót-pusà** *id.* to work alone.
kamote: (Sp. *camote*) *n.* sweet potato; (*fig.*)

flunking, doing poorly; **kamutihan** *n.* lizard fish; **nangamote** *id.* frustrated.
kamoteng-kahoy: *n.* cassava.
kampág: *adj.* slow, sluggish.
kampamento: (Sp. *campamento*) *n.* military camp.
kampanà: (Sp. *campana*) *n.* bell; **parang kampanà ang bibíg** *id.* talking noisily.
kampanaryo: (Sp. *campanario*) *n.* bell tower.
kampanera: (*slang*) *n.* hunchback.
kampante: (Sp. *campante*) *adj.* unconcerned.
kampanula: (Eng.) *n.* campanula, bellflower.
kampanya: (Sp. *campaña*) *n.* campaign.
kampáng: *n.* swaying motion in walking.
kampapalis: *n.* swallow-like bird.
kampáy: *n.* swing of the arms; flapping of the wings.
kampeón: (Sp. *campeón*) *n.* champion.
kampeonato: (Sp. *campeonato*) *n.* championship.
kampí: **kakampí** *n.* ally; **kampihán** *v.* to take someone's side.
kampilan: *n.* saber.
kampíng: *n.* languor, weariness.
kampít: *n.* small kitchen knife.
kampo: (Sp. *campo*) *n.* camp, field.
kampón: *n.* disciple; vassal.
kamposanto: (Sp. *campo santo*) *n.* cemetery.
kampupot: *n.* double-petalled *sampaguita*; Arabian jasmine.
kamtán: [*kamit* + *-an*] *v.* to get, obtain.
kamumo: *n.* species of small bee.
kamunukalà: *n.* co-author; co-sponsor.
kamyás: *n.* kind of sour fruit.
kanâ: *adj.* fixed, in place; *n.* exertion, effort; (*coll.*) assault, attack; sexual assault; (*slang, amerikana*) *n.* American female; coat, suit, jacket. **ikanâ** *v.* to set a trap; **kanaán** *v.* to fix in place, adjust; set a trap; **kánaan** *n.* fistfight; quarrel; (*fig.*) coitus.
kanaghalâ: *n.* phlegm.
kanál: *n.* canal, gutter; drain; groove.
kanalado: *adj.* grooved; *n.* groove; furrow.
kanan₁: *adj.* right, right-handed; *n.* right side; right hand; turn to the right; blow with the right hand; **kumanan, pumakanan** *v.* to make a right turn; **kananin** *v.* to keep on the right side; **pakanán** *adv.* right, going right; **paikót sa kanan** *adv.* clockwise.
kanan₂: (rt. *kain*) *v.* to eat from; **pákakanán** *n.* feeding trough.
kanapé: (Sp. *canapé*) *n.* sofa.
kanasta: (Sp. *canasta*) *n.* canasta; hamper.
kanáw: *adj.* diluted, dissolved.
kanawa-nawà: *adj.* easily done, easily obtained; *adv.* naturally; instantly.
Kankanaey: *n.* ethnic group and language from Northern Benguet Province and SE Mountain Province.
Kankanáy: *n.* ethnic group and language from Western Mountain Province.
kandabulól: **magkandabulól** *v.* to be tongue tied, be at a loss for words.
kandado: (Sp. *candado*) *n.* lock.
kandahulog: see *hulog*.
kandalapák: *n.* prostitute.
kandáng: *n.* wingspread of birds.
kandanggaok: *n.* heron.
kandarapà: *n.* eared nightjar bird.
kandelabro: (Sp. *candelabro*) *n.* candelabrum.
kandelero: (Sp. *candelero*) *n.* candlestick.
kandidato: (Sp. *candidato*) *n.* candidate.
kandi: *n.* estrus.
kandilà: (Sp. *candela*) *n.* candle.
kandili: *n.* caring for the poor; protection.
kandirít: *n.* hop, jump.
kandóng: *adj.* held in the lap.
kandós: *n.* species of squash.
kandulì: *n.* species of sea catfish.
kandurô: *n.* woodcock bird.
kanela: (Sp. *canela*) *n.* cinnamon.
kanilá: *pron.* their, theirs.
kanin: (*rt. kain*) *n.* rice; food; *v.* to eat; **kakaníng-itik** *id.* one who is often belittled or victimized (food for the duck); **hindî kaning isusubò** *id.* not easily done (not rice put in the mouth).
kanina: *adv.* a while ago.
kanino: *pron.* whose; whom.
kanipay: *n.* poison ivy.
kanitá: *pron.* our (dual).
kaniyá: *pron.* his, her, its; hers; **kaniyá-kaniyá** to each his own; **sumakaniyá** *v.* to be in him/her.

kanlíng: *n.* pantry.
kanlóng: *adj.* sheltered; **kanlungán** *v.* to shelter someone.
kanluran: (*rt. lunod*) *n.* west.
Kanô: (*coll.*) *n.* American.
kanós: *n.* odor of burnt food.
kansáw: **makansáw** *v.* to be moved (said of water with jumping fish).
kanselado: (Sp. *cancelado*) *n.* cancelled.
kansíng: *n.* gold brooch.
kansóg: *n.* gurgling sound.
kansora: *n.* species of banana.
kansót: *n.* jerk, jerking.
kansusuwit: *n.* halfbeak fish.
kantá: (Sp. *canta*) *n.* song, chant; **kumanta** *v.* to sing; **magkantá** *id.* sing; (*fig.*) confess.
kantero: (Sp. *cantero*) *n.* mason.
kantî: *n.* light tap.
kantidád: (Sp. *cantidad*) *n.* quantity.
kantín: (*slang*, Eng.) *n.* cafeteria; snack bar.
katingan, katingán: *n.* large, earthen cooking pot.
kantíw: *n.* light touch.
kantiyáw: *n.* banter, joking; **kantiyawán** *v.* to joke, tease.
kanto: (Sp. *canto*) *n.* corner, chant.
kantoboy: (*kanto* + *boy*: corner boy) *n.* idle, jobless person.
kantód: *n.* limping; **kumantod** *v.* to limp.
kantóg: *n.* tottering.
kantonero: (Sp. *cantonero*) *n.* loafer.
kantór: (Sp. *cantor*) *n.* singer.
kantót: (*vulg.*) **magkantót** *v.* to copulate.
kanturî: *n.* species of sand clam.
kanugnóg: *n.* suburb.
kanugtóg: *n.* chicken-like bird whose cries foretell rain.
kanuló: *n.* betrayal; **magkanuló** *v.* to betray.
kanuping: *n.* porgy fish.
kanyá: *var.* of *kaniyá*.
kanyamaso: (Sp. *cañamazo*) *n.* canvas.
kanyáng: *n.* strut.
kanyód: *n.* movement of the male body in coitus.
kanyóg: *n.* jerky movement (rickety cart).
kanyón: (Sp. *cañón*) *n.* cannon.
kang: (Ch.) *n.* uniform design in mahjong.
kangay: (Ch.) *n.* wedding party.
kangkáng: *n.* yelping sound of dogs.
kangkóng: *n.* river spinach.
kanggâ: *n.* sled like cart.
kanggreho: (Sp. *cangrejo*) *n.* crab.
kanggrena: (Sp. *cangrena*) *n.* gangrene.
kaoba: (Sp. *caoba*) *n.* mahogany.
kaón$_1$: **kumaón** *v.* to fetch someone.
kaón$_2$: (*slang*) *adj.* abundant.
kaong: *n.* palm fruit.
kapa: (Sp. *capa*) *n.* cape; layer of dirt or fat on the top of liquids.
kapâ: *adj.* grouping; touching a sexual organ; **kumapâ, kapaín** *v.* search for, grope; **mangapâ** *v.* to grope; fish with bare hands.
kapak: *n.* mullet fish; **parang kapak** *id.* nice in appearance.
kapakanán: *n.* welfare, health; interest.
kapág: *conj.* if; when; whenever.
kapagdaka: *adv.* at once, immediately.
kapál$_1$: *n.* thickness; wealth; **makapál** *adj.* thick; dense; **kapalin** *id.* rich, wealthy (may thicken); **kumapál** *v.* to thicken; **pakapál** *n.* padding; **makapál ang mukhâ** *id.* shameless (face is thick); overconfident; **makapál ang palad** *id.* hard-working (palm is thick).
kapál$_2$: *n.* creature; *adj.* created; **kumapál, kapalín** *v.* to create; **sangkinapál** *n.* creation.
kapalang: *adj.* inexact.
kapalaran: (*rt. palad*) *n.* fortune, luck.
Kapampangan: *n.* native of Pampanga province; the Pampango language.
kapansanan: *n.* impediment; inconvenience.
kapangyarihan: (rt. *yari*) *n.* power; authority.
kapara: (rt. *para*) *adj.* similar, like.
kapararakan: *n.* value; use, utility.
kapás: (Sp. *capaz*) *adj.* capable; enough.
kapasidád: (Sp. *capacidad*) *n.* capacity.
kapatás: (Sp. *capataz*) *n.* overseer, foreman.
kapatíd: (*rt. patíd*) *n.* sibling; **kapatiran** *n.* fraternity; brotherhood; **kinákapatíd** *n.* stepsibling; **magkapatíd** *n.* siblings; **kapatíd sa hupaw** *id.* illegitimate sibling.
kapatin: (rt. *apat*) *v.* to divide into four.
kapaw: *n.* removal of scum off the surface of a liquid.

kapáy: *n.* flapping of wings; swinging of arms.

kapkáp: *n.* frisking; **kapkapín** *v.* to feel for, grope for; **kapkapán** *v.* to frisk someone.

kapé: (Sp. *café*) *n.* coffee; **kápíhan** *n.* coffee pot; **magkakapé** *n.* coffee addict; coffee dealer; coffee planter.

kapelyán: (Sp.) *n.* chaplain.

kapetera: (Sp. *cafetera*) *n.* coffee pot.

kapilya: (Sp. *capilla*) *n.* chapel.

kapís: *n.* scallop.

kapit: *n.* hold; grasp; *adj.* suited; **kapitán** *n.* holder; handle bar; **kumapit** *v.* to hold on; cling to; **kapít** *adj.* stuck, sticking; **kapit-bayawak, kapit-tukô** *id.* firm hold (grasp of lizard); **pampakapit** *n.* binder; **hindî kakapitan ng alikabók** *id.* well dressed (the dust will not cling); **kumapit sa patalím** *id.* forced by necessity; **waláng mákapitan** *id.* without a protector (nothing to cling to).

kapitál: *n.* capital.

kapitbahay: *n.* neighbor; **mangapitbahay** *v.* to visit a neighbor; **kapitbahayan** *n.* neighborhood.

kapitbansâ: *n.* neighboring country.

kapítulo: (Sp. *capítulo*) *n.* chapter.

kaple: *n.* sleeper fish, *Butis amboinensis*.

kaplog: (*slang*) *v.* have an affair; **kaplugin** *adj.* sexually loose (woman)

kapol: *n.* smear, smudge.

kapón: (Sp. *capón*) *n.* castrated animal; goatfish.

kaporál: (Sp. *caporal*) *n.* ringleader; mastermind.

kapós: *adj.* insufficient, inadequate; **kapóspalad** *id.* unfortunate (palm is lacking).

kapote: (Sp. *capote*) *n.* raincoat.

kapré: (Sp. *cafre*) *n.* folklore giant.

kapritso: (Sp. *capricho*) *n.* caprice, whim.

kapsâ: *n.* earthen jar.

kápsula: (Sp. *cápsula*) *n.* capsule; cartridge.

kaputsa: (Sp. *capucha*) *n.* hood.

kapuwâ: *var. of kapwà.*

kapwà: *n.* fellow human; neighbor; *adj.* both, the two; *pron.* others; **kapwa-tao** *n.* one's relations with others; **makipagkapwà** *v.* to get along with others, be sociable; **pakikipagkapwà** *n.* sociability; **sírkulo ng pakikipagkapwà** *n.* social circle.

kara: (Sp. *cara*) *n.* head side of a coin; (*slang*) manners, behavior; character; **karakrus** *n.* coin toss.

kará: *n.* repeated stamping of feet.

karaka: *adv.* at once.

karakás: (*slang*) *n.* face.

karakót: *n.* small handful.

karakrús: (Sp. *caracruz*) *n.* heads or tails; coin toss.

karág: *n.* sound of heavy footsteps, restlessness.

karagatan: (rt. *dagat*) *n.* ocean, high seas.

karagdagan: (f. *dagdág*) *adj.* additional; extra; *n.* addition; enlargement.

karahasán: (f. *dahás*) *n.* violence; force; cruelty.

karaháy: *n.* large frying pan.

karaingan: (rt. *daíng*) *n.* complaint.

karambola: (Sp.) *n.* carom (in billiards).

karamelo: (Sp. *caramelo*) *n.* caramel.

karaniwan: (rt. *daniw*) *adj.* common, ordinary, normal; customary; simple; prevailing.

karang: *n.* awning; nipa roofing; float.

karáng: *n.* coral reef, atoll.

karangalan: (rt. *dangál*) *n.* honor; dignity.

karangkál: *n.* distance between thumb and middle finger when stretched apart.

karangkáng: *n.* loud boasting; kind of vine, *Shefflera odorata*.

karangyaán: (rt. *dangyâ*) *n.* lavishness; pompositv.

Karao: *n.* ethnic group and language from Eastern Benguet Province.

karapatán: (*rt. dapat*) *n.* right, privilege.

karapdáp: *n.* kind of tree with red flowers.

karate: (Jap.) *n.* karate; **karatista** *n.* karate artist.

karátula: (Sp. *carátula*: mask) *n.* sign board.

karawit: (*rt. dawit*) *adj.* implicated; involved.

karay: (Sp. *carey*) *n.* tortoise shell.

karáy: *n.* leather bag for blacksmith's tools.

karayama: *n.* intermingling; constant companion.

karaykrús: (Sp. *cara y cruz*) *n.* coin toss.

karayom: *n.* needle; **di-mahulugang karayom** *id.* crowded (could not drop a needle).

karburo: (Sp. *carburo*) *n.* carbide.

kardelina: (Sp. *cardelina*) *n.* goldfinch.
kareo: (Sp. *careo*) *n.* testing cocks to see if they can fight.
karera: (Sp. *carrera*) *n.* race; career; profession.
kareta: (Sp. *carreta*) *n.* small cart.
karete: (Sp. *carrete*) *n.* spool; bobbin.
karetilya: (Sp. *carretilla*) *n.* pushcart.
karga: (Sp. *carga*) *n.* load, cargo; tax; **kargahan** *v.* to load; **kargado** *adj.* loaded; *n.* caretaker; **kargada** *adj.* (*slang*) loaded, with a weapon.
kargadór: (Sp. *cargador*) *n.* baggage carrier, porter.
kargamento: (Sp. *cargamento*) *n.* cargo.
karí-karí: *n.* dish of oxtail, vegetables, peanuts and annatto seeds.
karikitán: (rt. *dikit*) *n.* beauty.
karíg: *n.* gallop.
karíl: (Sp. *carril*) *n.* rail, track.
karilyo: (Sp.) *n.* shadow play.
karilyón: *n.* carillon.
karimlán: (rt. *dilím*) *n.* darkness.
karinderia: *n.* cafeteria, pick and choose restaurant.
karinyo: (Sp. *cariño*) *n.* affection.
karis-karis: *n.* sardine; young cavalla fish.
karit: *n.* sickle; gash; **kumarit** *v.* to gash; cut with a sickle.
kariwasaan: *n.* riches, wealth.
karnabál: (Sp. *carnaval*) *n.* carnival.
karné: (Sp. *carne*) *n.* meat; **karne norte** *n.* corned beef.
karnero: (Sp. *carnero*) *n.* sheep.
karnerong-dagat: *n.* seal.
karnisero: (Sp. *carnicero*) *n.* butcher.
karo: (Sp. *carro*) *n.* hearse.
Karolanos: *n.* ethnic group and language from mid-central Negros.
karomata: (Sp.) *n.* horse-drawn two-wheeled vehicle.
karós: *n.* recklessness.
karosa: (Sp. *carroza*) *n.* float in a parade.
karpentado: (*slang*) *adj.* marked by a tattoo.
karpeta: (Sp. *carpeta*) *n.* letter file; portfolio; small carpet.
karpintero: (Sp. *carpintero*) *n.* carpenter.
kárpiyó: (Eng.) *n.* curfew.
karsél: (Sp. *cárcel*) *n.* jail.
karsonsilyo: (Sp. *calzoncillos*) *n.* underpants.
karta: (Sp. *carta*) *n.* map, playing cards; letter; (*slang*) personality.
kartada: (*slang*) *n.* figure.
karte: (*slang*, f. *deskarte*) *n.* strategy.
kartelón: (Sp. *cartelón*) *n.* poster, placard.
kartera: (Sp. *cartera*) *n.* portfolio, wallet.
kartero: (Sp. *cartero*) *n.* mailman.
kartilya: (Sp. *cartilla*) *n.* primer book.
kartón: (Sp. *cartón*) *n.* carton; cardboard.
kartulina: (Sp. *cartulina*) *n.* thin cardboard.
kartutso: (Sp. *cartucho*) *n.* cartridge.
karugô: (*rt.* *dugô*) *n.* blood relative.
karwahe: (Sp. *carruaje*) *n.* carriage.
kasa: (Sp. *casa*) *n.* house; firm; suit of playing cards; *adj.* cocked and ready to fire; **pangasá** *n.* cock of a gun.
kasá: *n.* acceptance of a challenge or bet; cocking a gun; *adj.* cocked (firearm).
kasâ: (*slang*) *n.* gang fight.
kasáb: *n.* movement of the jaw in eating.
kasabá: (Eng.) *n.* cassava, tapioca.
kasablangka: (*slang*, Sp. *casa blanca*) *n.* pub, beer house.
kasado: (Sp. *casado*, *cazado*) *adj.* married; set, cocked (firearm).
kasadór: (Sp. *cazador*) *n.* man in charge of placing bets in cockfighting.
kasadores: (Sp. *cazadores*: hunters) *n.* light infantry men who fought the revolutionary guerillas during the Spanish regime.
kaság: *n.* sound of heavy footsteps.
kasál: (Sp. *casar*) *n.* wedding; **magkasál** *v.* to marry; **kasál-parè** *n.* marriage solemnized by a priest.
kasalanan: (rt. *sala*) *n.* guilt, fault; blame; sin; offense, crime; **makasalanan** *adj.* wrong; guilty; corrupt; wicked; *n.* sinner; **waláng-kasalanan** *adj.* innocent; sinless.
kasama: (*rt sama*) *n.* companion.
kasambaháy: [*kasama ng bahay*] *n.* housemate.
kasangkapan: *n.* instrument, utensil.
kasarinlán: *n.* liberty; individuality.
kasaykasay: *n.* jinx; white-collared kingfisher

bird.

kaskabél: (Sp. *cascabel*) *n.* jingle bell.

kaskaho: (Sp. *cascajo*) *n.* gravel.

kaskás: *n.* spurt; rush; *adj.* scraped off; **pakaskás** *n.* molasses candy; **pangaskás** *n.* scraper.

kaskasero: *n.* speed maniac.

kasko: (Sp. *casco*) *n.* river boat.

kasera: (Sp. *casera*) *n.* landlady; **mangasera** *v.* to board; **bahay-pangaserahán** *n.* boarding house.

kasero: (Sp. *casero*) *n.* landlord.

kaserola: (Sp. *cacerola*) *n.* stew pan, sauce pan; casserole.

kasi. *n.* dear, loved one.

kasí: *conj.* because.

Kasiguranin: *n.* ethnic group and language from Quezon Province, Luzon.

kasim: (Ch.) *n.* back portion of a pig.

kasin: (*slang*) *n.* girlfriend; boyfriend.

kasindáp: *n.* kind of tree with red flowers.

kasíng- *prefix.* makes comparative adjectives: **kasing-gandâ** as beautiful as.

kasirola: *var.* of *kaserola*: stew pan.

kasisung: *n.* leather jacket fish.

kaslág: *n.* canopy, awning.

kaslóg: *n.* rumbling of the bowels.

kasmód: *n.* puckering of the nose.

kasmurà: (*coll.*) var. of *sikmurà*.

kaso: (Sp. *caso*) *n.* court case; case; value; **makasuhan** *v.* to be charged (in court); **kasuhan** *v.* to charge someone.

kastá: (Sp. *casta*) *n.* breed, caste.

kastanyas: (Sp. *castaña*) *n.* chestnut.

kastanyetas: (Sp. *castañedas*) *n.* castanets.

kastanyo: (Sp. *castaño*) *n.* hazel; chestnut.

kastigado: (Sp. *castigado*) *adj.* punished.

kastigo: (Sp. *castigo*) *n.* punishment.

Kastilà: (Sp. *castellana*) *n.* Spanish.

Kastilalóy: *n.* derogatory term for Spanish mestizo.

kastilyo: (Sp. *castillo*) *n.* castle.

kasubhâ: *n.* kind of herb used for coloring food.

kasúy: *n.* cashew.

katâ: *n.* fiction, make-believe; start of bubbling of boiled rice.

katá: *pron.* we (dual).

katabâ: *n.* archer fish.

katabay: *adj.* slow; slowly; carefully.

katad: *n.* tanned hide, leather.

katagâ: *n.* grammatical particle; word.

katál: **magkatál** *v.* to tremble.

katalà: *n.* white parrot.

katali: *n.* species of cooking banana.

kataló: *n.* loser in gambling.

katám: *n.* carpenter's plane; (*slang*) laziness; **pinagkatamán** *n.* wood shaving.

katang: (Ch. *kâq tang*: carry heavy) *n.* support, stand; **katangan** *v.* to put a support under.

katáng: *n.* kind of small fresh-water crab.

katarata: (Sp. *catarata*) *n.* cataract.

katarungan: (*rt. taróng*) *n.* justice; equity.

katás: *n.* sap, juice; (*slang*) fruit of one's labors (from working overseas.

katastro: (Sp. *catastro*) *n.* list of real properties in a town.

katawán: *n.* body; figure; shaft; **kinatawán** *n.* representative, delegate; **katawanín** *v.* to represent; **kumatawán** *v.* to represent; **pagkatawán** *n.* proxy; **pangkatawán** *adj.* physical; **pangangatawán** *n.* physique, build; exertion of efforts; **pangatawanán** *v.* to stand by; **ipakatawán** *v.* to delegate.

katay: (Ch.) *n.* slice of meet; butchering; **magkakatay** *n.* butcher.

katkát: *adj.* blotted out, erased.

katedrál: (Sp. *catedral*) *n.* cathedral.

kathâ: *n.* literary composition; **mangangathâ** *n.* novel.

kati: *n.* low tide.

katí: *n.* itch; **kumatí** *v.* to itch. **makatí** *adj.* itchy; **makatí ang kamáy** *id.* thief (hand is itchy); **makatí ang dilà** *id.* gossiper (tongue is itchy); **makatí ang paá** *id.* always going somewhere (feet are itchy); **makatí sa gabí** *id.* lascivious.

katî: *n.* clicking sound; **pangatî** *n.* decoy.

katig: *n.* outrigger; support; **kumatig** *v.* to favor, back.

katigbí: *n.* Job's tears.

katipáw: *n.* kind of small quail.

katipunan: *n.* society, association.

katitíng: *adj.* tiny, minute; particle.

katiwalà: *n.* manager.
kátiyáw: *var.* of *katyáw*: young rooster.
katlabì: *n.* biting the lips.
katlô: (rt. *tatlô*) *adj.* triple; *n.* triplicity; **katluín** *v.* to divide into three parts.
katmón: *n.* species of tree that bears a sour fruit.
katníg: *adj.* joined; siding with; **katnigán** *v.* to attach, join to; favor, side with.
katô: *n.* mite; (*fig.*) spurt of mischief; **may katô sa katawán** *id.* astute.
katók: *n.* knock; (*fig.*) crazy; naughty; **kumatók** *v.* to knock; **may katók sa ulo** *id.* crazy (had a knock in the head).
katóg: *n.* trembling, shaking.
katóliko: (Sp. *católico*) *n.* Catholic.
katón: (Sp. *catón*) *n.* primer spelling book.
katorse: (Sp. *catorce*) *n.* fourteen.
katoto: *n.* chum, pal.
katre: (Sp. *catre*) *n.* bed.
katsá: *n.* muslin cloth.
katsáng: *n.* empty boasting.
katsarita: *n.* Oceanic bonito fish. (*katsót*)
katsaro: (Sp. *cacharro*) *n.* worthless thing; broken piece of earthenware.
katsót: *n.* bonito fish.
katuga: (*slang*, *kain*, *tulog*, *galâ*) *n.* eating, sleeping and wandering (without working); lazybones.
katulad: (*rt. tulad*) *adj.* like, similar.
katuyot: *n.* sea bass, *Lates calcarifer*.
katyáw: *n.* young rooster; (*fig.*) neophyte, novice, beginner.
kauntî: (rt. *untî*) *adj.* small, little; some; *n.* bit, small amount; **kákauntî** *adj.* small; few, very little; scant; **kakauntián** *n.* scarcity; fewness; smallness; **kákauntî kaysa** less than; **pinakakauntî** *adj.* minimum; least possible in quantity.
kawa: *n.* large cauldron.
kawad: *n.* wire.
kawág: *n.* helpless flapping; **kawag-kawág** *n.* milkfish fry; **kumawág** *v.* to flap the arms and legs (as in swimming); **magkakawág** *v.* to thrash about; **kakawág-kawág na magisá** *id.* working alone.
kawal: *n.* soldier.
kawaláng-: *pref.* prefix forming abstract nouns that denote lack **kawaláng-baít** *n.* senselessness; **kawaláng-katapusan** *n.* endlessness.
kawalì: *n.* frying pan.
kawan: *n.* herd, flock.
kawang: *adj.* detached, apart; *n.* crack.
káwanggawâ: *n.* charity; act of service. **káwanggawaán** *v.* to give a contribution to.
kawas: *n.* forgiveness, emancipation; **kawás** *adj.* freed.
kawasà: **di-kawasà** *adj.* intolerable; right away, immediately.
kawat: (*Vis.*) *n.* stealing. theft. **kawatin** *v.* to steal. **kawatan** *v.* to rob. **kawatán** *n.* thief.
kawawà: (*rt. awà*) *adj.* poor, pitiful.
kawáy: *n.* waving of the hand; **kumawáy** *v.* to wave.
kawayan: *n.* bamboo.
kawboy: (Eng. *cowboy*) *n.* good sport; person who is at ease in any situation.
kawkáw: *n.* dipping of the hand in liquid; barking of a dog; **magkawkáw** *v.* to play with water with the hands.
kawíl: *n.* fish hook.
kawíng: *n.* link of a chain.
kawit: *n.* hook; fastener; **kawit-kawit** *adj.* hinge.
kawot: *n.* ladle. (*kaot*)
kay: *prep.* for, to, towards (precedes proper names); precedes adjectives to express admiration *kay gandá* how beautiful!
kaya: *n.* ability, power; aptitude; **may-kaya** *adj.* capable; **walang-kaya** *adj.* helpless, incompetent; **hindî kaya ng bulsá** *id.* can't afford it (wallet is not capable).
kayâ: *conj.* that's why; therefore, hence, so; particle expressing reason.
kayakas: *n.* fallen dried leaves; kind of fishing net.
kayag: *n.* invitation, inducing.
kayas: **kayasan** *v.* to scrape off nodes.
kayat: *n.* trickling.
kayá't: [*kayâ* + *at*] *conj.* that's why; therefore.
kayawà: *n.* disease of the spleen. (*kiyawà*)
kaykáy: **kumaykáy** *v.* to scratch the soil (chickens).
kayo: *n.* cloth, fabric.

kayó: *pron.* you (plural or polite). **kayú-kayó lang** only you.
kayod: *n.* grating, scraping; (*fig.*) hard work; **kayurán** *n.* grater, scraper; **kayurin** *v.* to scrape; grate; **kayuran** *v.* to scrape off from; **panay ang ~** *id.* always working; **kumakayod** *v.* to work hard; **magkumayod** *v.* to flounder; keep working.
kayóg: *adj.* lopsided.
kaypalà: *adv.* perhaps.
kayrél: (Sp. *kairel*) *n.* watch chain.
kaysá: *conj.* than; rather than.
kayugkóg: *n.* sound of thunder.
kayumád: *n.* young of head louse.
kayumanggí: *adj.* brown (said of skin).
kayumkóm: *n.* clenched fist.
kayungkóng: *adj.* carried close to the chest.
kayuyò: *n.* belly, abdomen.
ke: (Sp. *que*) *conj.* whether, even if.
kekok: (babytalk) *n.* chicken.
keha: (Sp. *queja*) *n.* complaint; grumble.
kelot: (*slang*) *n.* guy, single man.
kembóng: (*slang*) *n.* bad girl; flirt.
kembot: (*coll.*) *n.* shaking of the hips.
keme: (*slang*) *n.* for example; *var.* of *arte*.
kendéng: *n.* exaggerated wiggling of the hips; **magkendéng-kendéng** *v.* to wiggle the hips (while walking, etc.).
kendi: (Eng.) *n.* candy.
kengkóy: (*slang*) *n.* joker; comedian; stupid person; cartoons.
kepay: (*slang*) *n.* vagina.
kepo: (*slang*) *n.* busybody.
kepweng: (*slang*) *n.* faith healer.
kerelya: (Sp. *querella*) *n.* complaint in court. (*sakdál*)
kerida: (Sp. *querida*, *coll.*) *n.* mistress.
kerido: (Sp. *querido*) *n.* lover; darling.
kerubín: (Sp. *querubín*) *n.* cherub.
keso: (Sp. *queso*) *n.* cheese.
kesyo: (*coll.*) *conj.* that, for that reason.
ketong: *n.* leprosy.
ketsap: (Eng.) *n.* catsup.
kiáy: *n.* swaggering movement.
kibal: *n.* string bean; warping.
kibkíb: **kibkibín** *v.* to gnaw.
kibít: *n.* jerk, twitch; shrug of the shoulders.
kibô: *n.* motion, movement; breaking of silence; **maikibô** *v.* to move.
kibót: *n.* twitch, jerk; **muntíng kibót** *id.* at every moment, always (small jerk).
kikay: (*slang*) *adj.* flirtatious.
kikì: *n.* vulva.
kikig: **kumikig** *v.* to clean the ears.
kikil: *n.* carpenter's file; (*slang*) extortion; **kikilan** *v.* to file down; **mangikil** *v.* to chisel; (*coll*) ask for money..
kikinsót: *n.* mosquito larva (*kitikití*); **parang kikínsot** *id.* restless.
kikiro: *n.* spadefish, *Scatophagus argus.*
kikiyo: *n.* mosquito larva; species of restless bird.
kikyám: (Ch.) *n.* fried meat loaf sandwich; (*slang*) vagina.
kidkíd: *n.* spool; **ikidkid** *v.* to wind.
kidlát: *n.* lightning; **kumidlát** *v.* to flash (lightning).
kigtíng: *n.* grouper fish.
kiím: *n.* iron tongs.
kilá: (*coll.*) third person plural oblique personal noun marker. [*Kiná*]
kilabot: *n.* goose bumps; terror, fear; (*coll.*) loafer; **kakilá-kilabot** *adj.* terrifying; unnatural.
kilala: **kilalá** *adj.* familiar, known; *v.* to know a person; **kakilala** *n.* acquaintance; **ipakilala** *v.* to introduce; **kilalanin** *v.* to acknowledge; consider; **kumilala** *v.* to respond, react; **makilala** *v.* to know, recognize; **magkilala** *v.* to become acquainted; **magpakilala** *v.* to reveal, indicate; denote; **pagkakilalá** *n.* prestige, reputation; **pagkikilala** *n.* meeting; mutual knowledge of each other; **kiníkilala** *adj.* titular; **pagkilala** *n.* acknowledgement; identification; **mapagkíkilanlán** *v.* to be identified; **pagkakákilala** *n.* knowledge; recognition; **pagkakákilanlán** *n.* identity; individuality; *adj.* characteristic, distinguishing; **pagpapakilala** *n.* making known; introduction; **tagapagpakilala** *n.* toastmaster; **hindî nakakakilala ng hiyâ** *id.* shameless (doesn't recognize shame).
kilatis: (Sp. *quilate*) *n.* carat; **kilatisin** *v.* to appraise.

kiláw: *adj.* juvenile, youthful; *n.* raw meat; colic pain; **kilawín** *v.* to prepare raw meat for eating.

kilay: *n.* eyebrow.

kilik: *n.* carrying under the armpit or astride the hip. **kilik-kilik** *adj.* carried along under the armpit or astride the hip wherever one goes.

kilikid: *n.* thread.

kilikili: *n.* armpit.

kilíg: *n.* tremble, shudder. **kiligín** *v.* to shake.

kililíng: *n.* small bell.

kiling: *n.* bias, partiality; inclination; **kumiling** *v.* to tilt, incline. **kilíng** *adj.* partial, biased; *n.* twisted neck.

kilíng: *n.* mane of a horse.

kilís: *n.* shrinking (wood).

kilít: *n.* hunching of the shoulders.

kilitî: *n.* ticklish feeling; **makilitî** *v.* to have a ticklish feeling.

kilo: *n.* kilogram; rafter of a roof.

kilô: *adj.* bent, crooked.

kilos: *n.* movement, motion; behavior, conduct; attitude; manner; way; **kumilos** *v.* to act, behave, be active; **di-pagkilos** *n.* inertia, state of being inactive; **pagkilos** *n.* action.

kiluwâ: (Ch. *kaî luáq*) *n.* powdered mustard.

kilwà: *var. of kiluwâ*: powdered mustard.

kilya: (Sp. *quilla*) *n.* keel.

kilyóng: *n.* drepane fish, *Drepane punctata*.

kimáw: *adj.* with a defective arm or hand; clumsy.

kimbót: *n.* throb; slight muscular spasm, twitch.

kimkím: *adj.* held in the fist; **kimkimín** *v.* to clench; **pakimkím sa kamáy** *id.* money given by a godparent to godchild (put on the hand).

kimî: *adj.* shy; bashful; **kakimián** *n* shyness; embarrassment; **mangimî** *v.* to be hesitant; be timid.

kímika: (Sp. *química*) *n.* chemistry.

kimís: *adj.* squeezed in the fist; *n.* subordinate person.

kimót: *n.* handicraft; unconscious movement of the hand or feet by a seated person.

kimpál: *n.* lump; clod.

kimpáy: *adj.* crippled in the hands or feet.

kimpót: *n.* shrimp trap; *adj.* narrower than usual.

kiná: *prep.* oblique preposition for plural personal nouns. [Colloquial variant *kilá*]

kinábukasan: (rt. *bukas*) *n.* the next day; future; (*fig.*) hope.

kinákapatíd: (rt. *patíd*) *n.* godsibling; stepsibling.

kinákaribdíb: (rt. *dibdíb*) *adj.* nervous.

kinágabihán: (rt. *gabí*) *n.* the next night.

kinágawián: : (rt. *gawî*) *adj.* usual; habitual; referring to one's habit or way.

kinágis(g)nán: (rt. *gising*) *adj.* already present at birth; existing when one is born.

kinához apunan: (rt. *hapon*) *n.* the following afternoon.

kináhinatnán: (rt. *dating*) *n.* outcome, result; consequence.

kináhiratihan: (rt. *dati*) *adj.* referring to the habit or way acquired through experience.

kinálabasán: (rt. *labás*) *n.* outcome; result.

kináláman: (rt. *alám*) *n.* knowledge of an event or deed; **may kináláman** to concern, have a connection with; relate to.

kinamatayán: (rt. *patáy*) *n.* place of death.

kinámihasnán: (rt. *bihasa*) *n.* practice to which one is accustomed.

kinandá: *n.* variety of highland rice.

kináng: *n.* shine; **kumináng** *v.* to shine; **makináng** *adj.* shiny, brilliant.

Kinaray-á: *n.* ethnic group and language from Western Panay.

kinatawán: (rt. *katawán*) *n.* representative; agent; Congressman.

kindát: *n.* wink; **magkindatan** *v.* to wink at each other; **kumindát sa dilím** *id.* hopeless (wink in the darkness).

kindáy: *n.* strut.

kindíng: *see kendéng*.

kini: *n.* remora fish.

kiníg$_1$: *n.* **manginíg** *v.* to tremble, shiver.

kiníg$_2$: *n.* something heard; **makiníg** *v.* to hear; **dinggín, pakinggán** *v.* to listen to; **pandiníg** *n.* sense of hearing.

kinina: (Sp. *quinina*) *n.* quinine.

kinis: *n.* polish; smoothness; **makinis** *adj.* smooth, soft.

kinse$_1$: (Sp. *quince*) *n.* fifteen.

kinse$_2$: (Ch. *kièn cì*) *n.* foreshank of cow (for soup).

kinsena: (Sp. *quincena*) *n.* fortnight.

kinseñera: (Sp. *quinceñera*) *n.* debutante ball (traditionally held for girls at fifteen years of age).

kinsíkinsí: *n.* balustrade; spokes.

kintáb: *n.* gloss; glaze; polish; **makintáb** *adj.* glossy, shiny; sleek.

kintál: (Sp. *quintal*) *n.* 100 kilograms; seal, mark; impression; **ikintál** *v.* to seal.

kintáy: *adj.* coagulated.

kintsáy: (Ch.) *n.* Chinese celery.

kinyentos: (Sp. *quinientos*) *n.* five hundred.

kingké: (Sp. *quinque*) *n.* wick lamp.

kiolay: (*slang*) *n.* eyebrows.

kiosko: (Sp. *quiosco*) *n.* kiosk.

kipkíp: **kumipkíp** *v.* to carry under the armpit.

kipit: *n.* money stolen in small amounts; **kipit-kipit** *adj.* carried under the arm.

kipot: *n.* strait; narrowness; **pakiputin** *v.* to make narrow; pretend to be uninterested.

kirapo: *n.* giant grouper fish.

kirát: *adj.* with a squint in one eye; scar on eyelid.

kirí: *n.* flirt; *adj.* flirtatious.

kiriray: (*slang*) *adj.* flirtatious.

kirót: *n.* sharp pain; **makirót** *adj.* aching, painful.

kiruhe: *n.* species of bird, *Cacomantis merulinus*.

kisà: *n.* corn or other grains mixed with rice.

kísame: *n.* ceiling.

kisáp: *n.* wink, blink; **kisáp-matá** *n.* wink of an eye, moment.

kisaw: *n.* ruffling of water.

kisáy: *n.* convulsions; death throes.

kiskís: *n.* milling of rice; friction; **kiskisan** *n.* rice mill; striking surface of a matchbox; **ikiskís** *v.* to strike, set on fire by rubbing; **pakiskís** *n.* bribe, tip.

kisig: *n.* elegance.

kisíg: *n.* convulsive spasm; cramp.

kisíw: *n.* bird trap that snaps when stepped on.

kisláp: *n.* sparkle, glitter; twinkle.

kislíg: *n.* stiffening of the body.

kislót$_1$: **kumislót** *v.* to wriggle.

kislót$_2$: *n.* muscular quivering in the flesh of newly slaughtered animals.

kita$_1$: *adj.* seen; obvious; **mákíta** *v.* to see; **makákíta** *v.* to see; happen to see; **kitang-kita** *adj.* prominent; obvious; **ipakita** *v.* to show, indicate; **magkita** *v.* to meet each other; **magpakita** *v.* to show; display; reveal; **magpangita** *v.* to happen to meet; **mákiní-kinitá** *v.* to foresee; **pakita** *n.* demonstration; sample; **pagkákíta** *n.* observation; **pagpapakita** *n.* show, showing; demonstration; **makipagkita** *v.* to meet someone; receive (a visitor); **pakitang-tao** *id.* pretense, for show; **pángitáin** *n.* omen; apparition; **hanggáng sa mulíng pagkikita** until we meet again.

kita$_2$: *n.* wages, income; **kumita** *v.* to earn.

kitá: *pron.* we (dual); portmanteau of enclitic pronouns *ko* with *ka*: I to you (transitive verbs); You are my. **Mahal kita** I love you (You are my love). **Gurò kitá**. You are my teacher.

kitang: *n.* fishing line with many hooks; spadefish.

kitî$_1$: *n.* ticklish feeling.

kitî$_2$: (Ch.) *n.* young chick.

kitikití: *n.* mosquito larva.

kitid: *n.* narrowness; **makitid ang kumot** *id.* destitute (blanket is narrow); **makitid ang noó** *id.* not intelligent (forehead is narrow).

kitíg: *n.* throb, pulsation.

kitil: *n.* barracuda; **kitlín, kumitil** *v.* to nip off; kill; **kitlán** *v.* to take away from; kill; nip.

kiwâ: *adj.* embarrassed; twisted, crooked.

kiwal: *n.* warp; wobbly condition.

kiwít: *adj.* bend, crooked; twisted.

kiyà: (Ch. *kiá*: walk) *n.* manner of walking, characteristic gesture.

kiyakis, kiyakos: *n.* friction.

kiyakoy: *n.* dangling the feet.

kiyamlo: (Ch. *kiâm lò*) *n.* noodle dish with eggs.

kiyáng: (Ch.) *n.* walking with the legs apart.

kiyapò: *n.* duckweed.

kiyás: *n.* physical posture; attitude.

kiyáw: (Ch. *kiaù kiaù* + k^h*au*: incessant cry) *n.*

swarming; wriggling movements; **kiyáw-kiyáw** *n.* useless fretting.
kiyáy: (Ch.) *adj.* with dislocated hips; lame.
kiyeme: (*coll.*) **kiyeme-kiyeme** *n.* pretending to be disinterested (when truly interested); **magpakiyeme** *v.* to play hard to get; pretend to dislike.
klabe: (Sp. *clave*) *n.* clue.
klabete: (Sp. *clavete*) *n.* tack, small nail.
klabiha: (Sp. *clavija*) *n.* peg.
klarín: (Sp. *clarín*) *n.* bugle.
klarinete: (Sp. *clarinete*) *n.* clarinet.
klaro: (Sp. *claro*) *n.* white of an egg.
klase: (Sp. *clase*) *n.* class; kind; sort; rate; grade.
klero: (Sp. *clero*) *n.* clergy.
kliyente: (Sp. *cliente*) *n.* client.
ko: my; I (agent of transitive). [First person singular genitive enclitic pronoun. See also *kitá*]
koboy: (Eng.) *n.* cowboy.
kobradór: (Sp. *cobrador*) *n.* collector.
kobransa: (Sp. *cobranza*) *n.* money collected.
kokak: *n.* croaking; (*slang*) prostitute.
koko: *n.* kind of muslin.
kokomo: *n.* kind of crawfish.
kodak: *n.* camera.
kódigo: (Sp. *código*) *n.* code; cheat sheet.
kola: (Sp. *cola*) *n.* trail of a dress; glue, paste.
kolado: *n.* uninvited guest, gate crasher.
kolekta: (Sp. *colecta*) *n.* collection in church.
kolehiyala: *n.* female collegian.
kólera: (Sp. *cólera*) *n.* cholera.
koliplór: (Sp. *coliflor*) *n.* cauliflower.
kolitis: *n.* spinach weed; colitis.
kolonyado (ng asawa): *id.* hen pecked.
kolorete: (Sp. *colorete*) *n.* rouge.
kolorum: (*slang*) *adj.* without license.
kolyár: (Sp. *collar*) *n.* collar for animals, neck chain.
komadre: (Sp. *comadre*) *n.* female sponsor.
komadrona: (Sp. *comadrona*) *n.* midwife.
kombento: (Sp. *convento*) *n.* convent.
komedór: (Sp. *comedor*) *n.* dining room.
komersyo: (Sp. *comercio*) *n.* business, trade.
kómiko: (Sp. *cómico*) *n.* clown, comedian.
komida: (Sp. *comida*) *n.* meal.
komilyas: (Sp. *comillas*) *n.* quotation marks.
kómoda: (Sp. *cómoda*) *n.* chest of drawers.
kómodo: (Sp. *cómodo*) *adj.* comfortable.
kompadre: (Sp. *compadre*) *n.* male sponsor at a baptism, godfather.
kompanya: (Sp. *compañía*) *n.* company.
kompanyero: (Sp. *compañero*) *n.* colleague; companion.
komparsa: (Sp. *comparsa*) *n.* string band.
kompermiso: (Sp. *con permiso*) Excuse me.
kompeténsiya: (Sp. *competencia*) *n.* competition.
kompiyansa: (Sp. *confianza*) *n.* confidence, trust; courage.
komplót: (Eng.) *n.* plot, scheme; conspiracy.
komporme: (Sp. *conforme*) *adj.* agreeable.
komprobante: (Sp. *comprobante*) *n.* voucher.
komprometido: (Sp. *comprometido*) *adj.* engaged, pledged.
kompromiso: (Sp. *compromiso*) *n.* pledge, engagement; commitment.
komunidád: (Sp. *comunidad*) *n.* community; society.
konde: (Sp. *conde*) *n.* count.
kondenado: (Sp. *condenado*) *adj.* condemned.
kondisyón: (Sp. *condición*) *n.* condition.
kondól: *n.* white gourd melon.
koneho: (Sp. *conejo*) *n.* rabbit.
konsehál: (Sp. *consejal*) *n.* councilor.
konseho: (Sp. *consejo*) *n.* counsel; *n.* council.
konsilyo: (Sp. *concillo*) *n.* high council.
konsiyénsiya: (Sp. *conciencia*) *n.* conscience.
konsiyerto: (Sp. *concierto*) *n.* concert; agreement.
konsorte: (Sp. *consorte*) *n.* escort, consort.
konsulado: (Sp. *consulado*) *n.* consulate.
konsulta: (Sp. *consulta*) *n.* consultation.
konsumido: (Sp. *consumido*) *adj.* exhausted, exasperated.
konsumisyón: (Sp. *consumisión*) *n.* exasperation.
konsuwelo: (Sp. *consuelo*) *n.* comfort; **konsuwelo de bobo** *n.* fool's consolation.
kontodo: (Sp. *con todo*: with everything) complete with; laden with; **kontodo-pabangó** doused in perfume.
kontra: (Sp. *contra*) *n.* vote against; negative;

opponent; **kontrahín** *v.* to oppose; **pangkontra** *n.* proof against something.
kontrabando: (Sp. *contrabando*) *n.* smuggled goods.
kontrabida: (Sp. *contra vida*) *n.* villain, antagonist.
kontrapeso: (Sp. *contrapeso*) *n.* counterweight.
kontrasenyas: (Sp. *contraseñas*) *n.* countersign; password.
kontratista: (Sp. *contratista*) *n.* contractor.
kontsa: (Sp. *concha*) *n.* conch.
konya: (Sp. *coño*: vagina) *n.* (*slang*) rich, spoiled social lady (demeaning term).
konyo: *n.* classy person; socialite.
kongkreto: (Sp. *concreto*) *n.* concrete.
kongreso: (Sp. *congreso*) *n.* congress.
kopa: (Sp. *copa*) *n.* cup, glass.
kopita: (Sp. *copita*) *n.* small wine glass.
kopla: (Sp. *copla*) *n.* couplet.
koplang: (*slang*) *n.* oral sex; breast.
kopo: *n.* sweep, winning all games.
kopon: *n.* group of friends; **koponán** *n.* team.
kopón: (Eng.) *n.* coupon.
kopong: (*slang*) *n.* member of the group.
kopra: (Sp. *copra*) *n.* dried coconut meat, copra.
kopya: (Sp. *copia*) *n.* copy.
koral: (Sp. *coral*) *n.* coral.
korál: (Sp. *corral*) *n.* pen, corral.
korkobado: (Sp. *corcovado*) *n.* humpbacked. (*kubà*)
kordero: (Sp. *cordero*) *n.* lamb.
kordón: (Sp. *cordón*) *n.* cord; shoelace.
korea: (Sp. *correa*) *n.* machine belt; leash.
koredór: (Sp. *corredor*) *n.* broker.
koreo: (Sp. *correo*) *n.* post, mail.
korida: (Sp. *corrida*) *n.* bullfight; routine.
korneta: (Sp. *corneta*) *n.* bugle.
koro: (Sp. *coro*) *n.* choir.
korona: (Sp. *corona*) *n.* crown; wreath. (*putong*)
korta-bista: (Sp. *corta vista*) *adj.* near sighted.
kortadura: (Sp. *cortadura*) *n.* cuttings.
kortapluma: (Sp. *cortapluma*) *n.* pocketknife.
korte: (Sp. *corte*) *n.* shape; court.
kortesa: (Sp. *corteza*) *n.* bark of a tree. (*balakbák*)
kortsetes: (Sp. *corchetes*) *n.* hook and eye.
koryente: (Sp. *corriente*) *n.* current, electricity; **makoryente** *v.* to be electrocuted.
kosa: (Sp. *cosa*) *n.* companion; friend; gang mate; gang.
kosido: (Sp. *cocido*) *n.* Spanish stew.
kosinero: (Sp. *cocinero*) *n.* cook.
kosinilya: (Sp. *cocinilla*) *n.* small cooking stove.
kosíng: (*slang*) *n.* five centavos.
kostál: (Sp. *costal*) *n.* jute sack.
kostas: (Sp. *costas*) *n.* expenses.
kostilyas: (Sp. *costillas*) *n.* ribs.
kostumbre: (Sp. *costumbre*) *n.* custom.
kostura: (Sp. *costura*) *n.* needlework, stitching; suture.
koteho: (Sp. *cotejo*) *n.* comparison; canvassing; list of winning numbers in the lottery.
koto: (Sp. *coto*) *n.* bet limit in cards.
kotong: (*slang*) *n.* bribe; **pulis-kotong** *n.* corrupt police officer.
kotse: (Sp. *coche*) *n.* automobile; coach.
koyáng: (*slang*) *n.* respect.
koyat: (*slang*) *n.* sexual intercourse.
koyò: (*slang*) *n.* ex-convict.
krayola: *n.* crayon.
krema: (Sp. *crema*) *n.* cream.
krimen: (Sp. *crimen*) *n.* crime.
kristiyano: (Sp. *cristiano*) *n.* Christian.
kritikón: (Sp. *criticón*) *n.* one who excessively criticizes.
krokis: (Sp. *croquis*) *n.* sketch, rough draft; plan.
krosing: (Eng.) *n.* crossroads; crossing.
krudo: (Sp. *crudo*) *adj.* crude; coarse.
krus: (Sp. *cruz*) *n.* cross; **Krus Roha, Krus na Pulá** Red Cross.
krusada: (Sp. *cruzada*) *n.* crusade.
krusan: *n.* hammerhead shark.
krusipiho: (Sp. *crucifijo*) *n.* crucifix.
kubà: *adj.* hunchbacked; **kubâ** (*slang*) *n.* Volkswagen bug; **magkangkukubà sa paggawâ** *id.* working alone.
kubabang: *adj.* lying face down.
kubabaw: *adj.* lying face down while astride; *n.* position of male animal while copulating.

kubakob: *n.* hut without posts; **kubakób** *adj.* surrounded; blocked.
kubáw: *n.* species of banana; species of water buffalo with horns curved in front of the face.
kubkób: *adj.* enclosed; surrounded; besieged; *n.* kind of fishing gear.
kubeta: (Sp. *cubeta*) *n.* water closet, latrine.
kublí: *adj.* hidden; secret; **kumublí** *v.* to conceal.
kubo: (Sp. *cubo*) *n.* cube, hut.
kuból: *n.* temporary shelter; (*slang*) prison showers.
kubón: (*slang*) *n.* bed covered with clothing for privacy.
kubóng: *n.* shawl.
kúbong-kúbong: *n.* mosquito net.
kubót: *n.* wrinkle, rumple.
kubyerta: (Sp. *cubierta*) *n.* deck of a ship.
kubyertos: (Sp. *cubiertos*) *n.* silverware.
kukaok: *n.* crow of a rooster.
kukó: *n.* fingernail, claw; **walâ sa kukó** *id.* very different from (not in the fingernail).
kukób: *adj.* curved out, convex.
kukok: *n.* cackling of fowls.
kukót: *n.* nibble.
kukote: (Sp. *cocote*) *n.* back part of the head; (*fig.*) brain, mind.
kudkód: *adj.* grated; **kudkuran** *n.* grater.
kudeta: (Eng.) *n.* coup d'état.
kudlís: *n.* line, fine mark.
kudlít: *n.* small mark; apostrophe; small incision.
kudlóng: *n.* bamboo guitar.
kudra: (*slang*) *n.* father.
kudyapî: *n.* lyre.
kugkóg: *n.* hollow sound produced by bamboo instruments.
kugità: *n.* octopus.
kugon: *n.* species of tall grass, cogon grass.
kugtóng: *n.* giant grouper fish.
kuha: *n.* act of getting; **kukunán** *n.* source of supply; **kunin, kumuha** *v.* to get, take; **kunan** *v.* to get from; **nakuha sa bibíg** *id.* able to convince verbally (taken by the mouth).
kuhilâ: *n.* scoundrel, traitor.
kuhit: *n.* extraction (of a sticky substance).
kuhól: *n.* species of edible snail.
kulá: (Sp. *colar*) **kulahín** *v.* to bleach.
kulabà: *n.* white film over the eyes, film over liquids.
kulabat: *n.* walking with the help of the arms and furniture (babies).
kulabô: *adj.* faded; hazy.
kulaklíng: *n.* dapple gray color.
kulado: (Sp. *colado*) *adj.* refined; bleached; uninvited.
kulag: *n.* goose flesh.
kulagó: *n.* monkey eagle.
kulagyâ: *n.* species of small shrimp.
kulam: *n.* witchcraft; **mangkukulam** *n.* witch.
kulambô: *n.* mosquito net.
kulamós: *n.* scratch on the face.
kulanì: *n.* swelling of a lymph gland; (*slang*) unwanted pregnancy.
kulandóng: *n.* canopy; head covering.
kulang: *adj.* deficient, short in supply; inadequate; incomplete; lacking; lacking in intelligence; *n.* deficit; **kulangin** *v.* to lack; **kulang sa pansín** *adj.* lacking attention; **waláng-kulang** *adj.* complete.
kulangot: *n.* dried snot.
kulap: *n.* mist, fog.
kulapó: *n.* sea perch; kind of mildew.
kulapol: *n.* smear.
kulas: *n.* banker's share in bets.
kulasa: (*slang*) *n.* maid.
kulasím: *adj.* acrid, sour.
kulasiman: *n.* species of purslane.
kulasisì: *n.* parrot; mistress.
kulasyón: (Sp. *colación*) *n.* partial fasting.
kulat: *n.* kind of fungus. (*taingang-dagâ*)
kulata: (Sp. *culata*) *n.* butt of a rifle.
kulatad: *n.* the bottom.
kulatay: *n.* Bermuda grass.
kulatkulat: *n.* species of fungus.
kuláw: *adj.* pilfered; *n.* species of small monkey.
kulawít: *n.* act of tripping over something.
kulay: *n.* color; **makulay** *adj.* colorful; **kulay-abó** gray, ashen; **kulay-gatas** milk colored.
kulbít: *var.* of *kalbit*: touch.
kulbót: *var.* of *kulubót*: wrinkled.

kulkól: *n.* shallow digging.
kuleta: (Sp. *coleta*) *n.* small tail; postscript.
kulì: *n.* retraction.
kulíg: *n.* suckling pig.
kuliglíg: *n.* cricket; **kinúkuliglíg ang tainga** *id.* see *kinukulilì ang tainga*.
kulilì: *n.* burnt food stuck to the bottom of the pot; **kinukulilì ang tainga** *id.* tired of hearing the same thing over and over (ear filled with burned substance).
kulilíng: *n.* small bell; **kulilíng sa ulo** *adj.* crazy.
kulimbáng: *n.* act of ringing a big bell.
kulimbát: *n.* act of stealing; *adj.* stolen.
kulimlím: *adj.* dark, overcast; **kumulimlím** *v.* to be cloudy.
kulindáng: *n.* machine belting used in the foot treader of a sewing machine.
kulintáng: *n.* musical instrument composed of eight gongs.
kuliró: *adj.* false, counterfeit.
kulis: *n.* kind of shrub whose roots are used for certain irregularities in menstruation.
kulisap: *n.* insect; young louse.
kulisaw: *n.* school of fish.
kulit: *adj.* stubborn.
kulít: **makulít** *adj.* repetitive.
kulitì: *n.* sty in the eye.
kulitis: *n.* nettle; kind of weed.
kulitiw: *var.* of *kulìti*: sty.
kulmá: (Sp. *corma*) *n.* stocks, pillory.
kulo: *n.* pointed end of an egg.
kuló: *n.* coconut shell plate.
kulô: *n.* boiling, simmering; **kumukulô ang dugô** *id.* angry (boiling blood); **nasa loób ang kulô** *id.* unpredictable; outwardly good but inwardly naughty (boiling inside); **kukulú-kulô ang tiyán** *id.* incapable.
kulób-: *pref.* used to form the following indefinite pronouns and conjunction: **kulób-alín** whichever; **kulób-anó** whatever; **kulób-man** although, even though; **kulób-sino** whoever, anyone.
kulob: **kuluban** *n.* pressure cooker; **magkulob** *v.* to cook meat long and slowly in a covered pan; **pagkukulob** *n.* act of having a person perspire by wrapping him in blankets.
kulób: *var. of maski.*
kulubót: *adj.* wrinkled (old skin).
kulóg: *n.* thunder; **kumulóg** *v.* to thunder.
kulogó: (*slang*) *n.* crazy person.
kulóng: *adj.* surrounded; jailed; caged; *n.* prison, cage; **ikulóng** *v.* to cage, shut in.
kulop: *n.* thin metal protective lining.
kulós: *n.* rustling sound.
kulót: *n.* curl; (*slang*) passing fancy; *adj.* curly; **kúlutan** beauty shop; **kulután** to curl someone's hair; **kulutan** Chinese burr shrub.
kultá: (Sp. *cortar*) *adj.* curdled.
kultí: (Sp. *curtir*) *adj.* tanned.
kulto: (Sp. *culto*) *n.* cult; religious meeting.
kultura: (Sp. *cultura*) *n.* culture. (*kalinangán*)
kulumbóng: *n.* head wrap.
kulubót: *n.* wrinkle.
kulukay: (*coll.*) *n.* derogatory term for a female.
kulukoy: (*coll.*) *n.* derogatory term for a male.
kulukutô: *n.* whim.
kulughóy: *n.* numb state caused by the cold.
kulumós: *adj.* crumpled.
kulumot: *n.* crowd; congestion.
kulumpól: *n.* shoal.
kulunóy: *n.* quagmire, swamp.
kuluntóy: *adj.* faded and withered; **nangunguluntóy** feeling weak.
kulungkót: (*rt. lungkot*) *n.* low spirits.
kuluóm: *adj.* stagnant (water); not ventilated.
kulupón: *n.* crowd, swarm (of children).
kulutan: *n.* Chinese burr shrub.
kulutkutan: *n.* kind of shrub with reddish branches.
kulutrang: (*slang*) *n.* curly hair.
kulya: *n.* shove with the elbow.
kulyát: *n.* black hardwood.
kulyawan: *n.* golden oriole.
kumag: *n.* small insect; fine powder on grains of rice.
kumág: (*slang*) *adj.* innocent; unworldly; lazy person; money changer.
kumantà: (*slang*, f. *kanta*) *n.* stool pigeon.
kumbabâ: **mapagpakumbabâ** *adj.* humble.
kumbagá: (*kung bagá*) *adv.* like, as.
kumbád: *n.* kindling.

kumbidá: (Sp. *convidar*) *n.* invitation.
kumbinsí: (Sp. *convencer*) **kumbinsihín** *v.* to convince.
kumbite: (Sp. *convite*) *n.* invitation only event.
kumkóm: *adj.* held against the chest.
kuminóy: *n.* quicksand.
Kumintáng: *n.* Tagalog epic.
kumón: (Sp. *común*) *n.* water closet.
kumós: *adj.* crumpled.
kumot: *n.* blanket; bed sheet.
kumpare: (Sp. *compadre*) *n.* godfather.
kumpás: (Sp. *compas*) *n.* rhythm, beat; gesture; whip.
kumpáy: *n.* fodder.
Kumpíl: (Sp. *confirmar*) *n.* sacrament of Confirmation.
kumpís: *adj.* deflated.
Kumpisál: (Sp. *confesar*) *n.* Confession; **kumpisalan** *n.* confessional.
kumpít: *n.* sailboat used by Philippine Muslims.
kumpites: (Sp. *confite*) *n.* bonbons.
kumpitis: (Sp. *confites*) *n.* confetti.
kumpiyansa: (Sp. *confianza*) *n.* confidence.
kumpleanyo: (Sp. *cumpleaño*) *n.* birthday.
kumpól: *n.* bunch, cluster.
kumpuní: (Sp. *componer*) **kumpunihín** *v.* to repair, renovate.
kumustá: (Sp. *cómo está*) how are you; *n.* regards; **pakumusta** *n.* good wishes.
kuna: (Sp. *cuna*) *n.* cradle, crib.
kunan: (*rt. kuha*) *v.* to get from.
kunat: **makunat** *adj.* flexible; hard to chew; leathery; **makunat sa pera** *id.* stingy; mean.
kundangan: *n.* respect; regard; *conj.* because of.
kundáy: *n.* dance movements made by the wrist; **kumundáy** *v.* to move the hands and wrists in dancing.
kundî: [*kung* + *dî*] *prep.* except.
kundilát: *n.* big eyed herring.
kundiman: *n.* lovesong; red muslin.
kundít: **pakundít-kundít** *n.* talking with many hedges.
kundól: *n.* white gourd melon.
kuneho: (Sp. *conejo*) *n.* rabbit.
kunin: (*rt. kuha*) *v.* to get; take something.
kunó: (*slang*) *adj.* pretense; false; artificial.
kunót: *n.* wrinkle, crease; **magkunót** *v.* to pucker.
kunsî: *n.* bolt, latch.
kunsintidór: (Sp. *consentidor*) *n.* one who consents to bad things.
kunsintimiyento: (Sp. *consentimiento*) *n.* consent.
kunsumisyón: (Sp. *consumición*) *n.* exasperation; angered state.
kuntíl: *n.* uvula; protruding wart; **kuntíl-butil** with too many unnecessary details.
kunwâ, kunwarì: *adj.* pretended, fake; **magkun-warî** *v.* to pretend; fake; impersonate; **pakunwarî** *adj.* pretended; artificial; **pagkukunwarî** *n.* pretense.
kunyapit: *n.* climbing of trees.
kung: *prep.* if, in the case that; also precedes interrogative indefinite pronouns; **kung sa bagay** as a matter of fact; **Alam mo ba kung anóng pangalan niyá?** Do you know what his name is?
kungkáy: *n.* female genital organ.
kungkóng: *n.* chimes.
kupad: **makupad** *adj.* sluggish, slow.
kupal: *n.* dried semen under the foreskin.
kupang: *n.* counterweight; species of tree.
kupás: *adj.* faded; (*slang*) out of date; **kumupas** *v.* to fade, lose color; **mangupas** *v.* to fade, discolor.
kupkóp: *adj.* held against one's chest; **kupkupín** *v.* to take care of; protect; harbor.
kupete: (Sp. *copete*) *n.* feeling of inferiority or timidity.
kupí: *n.* nit.
kupì: *n.* dent; **kupî** *adj.* dented.
kupíng: *adj.* irregularly shaped (ears); dented; (*slang*) oral sex.
kupís: *adj.* deflated; thin.
kupit: *n.* pilfering.
kupón: (Eng.) *n.* coupon.
kupyâ: *n.* hat; helmet; circumflex accent (^).
kura: (Sp. *cura*) *n.* priest.
kurà: *n.* outdoor picnic.
kurá: (Jap.) *interj.* Attention! Stand Straight!
kurakot: (*slang*) *n.* stealing.
kurakoy: (*slang*) *n.* corrupter.

kuráp: *n.* wink, blink; **kumuráp** *v.* to wink; blink.
kurba: (Sp. *curva*) *n.* curve, bend; (*slang*) common, ordinary.
kurbata: (Sp. *corbata*) *n.* necktie.
kurkubado: (Sp. *corcovado*) *adj.* humpbacked.
kuringdíng: *n.* two-finned bonito fish.
kuripot: *adj.* stingy; *n.* miser.
kurirì: *n.* fuss.
kurit: *n.* small pinch.
kurò: **kumurò** *v.* to think; **magkurô** *v.* to reflect, ponder; **pagkukurò** *n.* opinion, point of view; belief.
kurók: *n.* clucking sound.
kurós: (Sp. *cruz*) *n.* cross; **ikurós sa noó** *id.* to remember (make the sign of the cross on one's forehead).
kurót: *n.* pinch.
kursilyo: (Sp. *cursillo*) *n.* short course of study.
kurso: (Sp. *curso*) *n.* course of study.
kursó: *n.* diarrhea.
kursonada: (Sp. *corazonada*) *n.* feeling of interest towards someone; impulse.
kurtina: (Sp. *cortina*) *n.* curtain.
kurukutók: *n.* cooing of doves.
kuryénte: *var.* of *koryente*: electricity; (*slang*) venereal disease; electric shock torture.
kusà: *adj.* deliberately, on purpose, voluntarily; **kusang-palò** *id.* doing voluntarily (deliberate whip); **waláng kusang-palò** *adj.* having no initiative; **kusang-loób** *n.* free will.
kuskós: *n.* scrubbing, rubbing, **kuskús-balungos** *n.* unnecessary details; fuss, ado.
kusilba: *n.* sweet fruit preserves.
kusinà: (Sp. *cocina*) *n.* kitchen.
kusinero: (Sp. *cocinero*) *n.* cook.
kusinilya: (Sp. *cocinilla*) *n.* gas stove.
kusíng: *n.* one half a centavo.
kusot: (Ch. *kù sùt*) *n.* sawdust.
kusót: *adj.* crumpled.
kutà: *n.* fort, bulwark; **magkutà** *v.* to entrench; **kutaan** *v.* to fortify a place.
kutab: *n.* notch, groove; barren land.
kutamaya: (Sp. *cota de malla*) *n.* coat of arms; armor. (*balutì*)
kutiltíl: **magkutí-kutiltíl** *v.* to tinker with.
kutím: (*slang*) *n.* dark person.
kutíng: *n.* kitten.
kutipáw: *n.* young quail.
kuktipyó: *adj.* bald.
kutis: *n.* complexion.
kutitap: *n.* flickering, blinking.
kuto: *n.* louse; **kutong-lupà** *id.* short person (ground louse).
kutô: *n.* swarm, crowd.
kutób: *n.* hunch, feeling; foreboding; premonition.
kutód: *n.* short pants.
kutóg: *n.* pulsation, throb.
kutón: *n.* gold; pleat, fold; **kutong-lupà** *n.* bug; (*id.*) small, unimportant person.
kutong: (*slang*) *adj.* short of money, *n.* inexact change.
kutós: **kutusán** *v.* to hit with the knuckles.
kutsaba: (*coll.*) *n.* accomplice; conniver; **maki-pagkutsaba** *v.* conspire, plot; **pakikipag-kutsabahan** *n.* conspiring, conspiracy, plot.
kutsara: (Sp. *cuchara*) *n.* spoon; trowel; **may kutsarang gintô sa bibíg nang isilang** *id.* born rich (had a golden spoon in mouth when born).
kutsarita: (Sp. *cucharita*) *n.* teaspoon; bonito fish.
kutsaról, kutsarón: (Sp. *cucharón*) *n.* ladle, large spoon.
kutsáy: (Ch. k^h*û* c^h*ai*) *n.* green leek.
kutsero: (Sp. *cochero*) *n.* driver, coachman.
kutsilyo: (Sp. *cuchillo*) *n.* knife.
kutsino: (Sp. *cochino*) *adj.* shameless.
kutsinta: *n.* sticky rice flour cake.
kutso: *n.* thick-soled lady's slippers.
kutso-kutso: (*coll.*) *n.* idle talk.
kutsón: (Sp. *colchón*) *n.* mattress.
kutukuto: *n.* mullet fry.
kutúkutô: *n.* water spider.
kutyâ: *n.* scorn, ridicule.
kutyám: (Ch. *kù tiam*: sawing board) *n.* anvil-like block of iron with graduated grooves used to shape or round rings.
kutyog: *n.* shaved haircut.
kuwâ: *n.* puppy.
kuwako: (Ch.) *n.* tobacco pipe; (*slang*) revolver.

kuwa-kuwa: *n.* threadfin fish.
kuwaderno: (Sp. *cuaderno*) *n.* notebook.
kuwadra: (Sp. *cuadra*) *n.* stable.
kuwadrado: (Sp. *cuadrado*) *adj.* square.
kuwadrante: (Sp. *cuadrante*) *n.* sundial; quadrant.
kuwadrilya: (Sp. *cuadrilla*) *n.* squad, patrol.
kuwadro: (Sp. *cuadro*) *n.* frame; canvas for painting.
kuwago: *n.* owl; (*slang*) fool, crazy person.
kuwaho: (Ch.) *n.* gambling card game.
kuwalta, kuwarta: (Sp. *cuarta*) *n.* money (*pera*); **manguwalta** *v.* to deprive of money fraudulently; **kuwalta na'y nagíng bató pa** *id.* disillusionment, frustration (money already but turned to stone); **kuwarta na** *id.* okay.
kuwán: (Sp. *cuál*?) hedge (uh, um..), expression of indefiniteness; **kakuwanán** *n.* peculiar behavior, antics; **kapagkuwán** *adv.* then; later; afterwards.
kuwarenta: (Sp. *cuarenta*) *n.* forty.
kuwarentenas: (Sp. *cuarentena*) *n.* quarantine.
kuwaresma: *n.* lent.
kuwarta: *var. of kuwalta*: money.
kuwartél: (Sp. *cuartel*) *n.* barracks.
kuwarto: (Sp. *cuarto*) *n.* room; one fourth.
kuwatro: (Sp. *cuatro*) *n.* four; **kuwatro kantos** (*slang*) *n.* gin, liquor.
kuwatsóy: (Ch. *k^{h}uâq c^{h}ui*: broad mouth) *n.* broad-bladed pick used in quarrying.
kuweba: (Sp. *cueva*) *n.* cave.
kuwekong: (Ch.) *n.* pimp.
kuwela: (*slang*) *n.* funny remark.
kuwelyo: (Sp. *cuello*) *n.* collar.
kuwenta: (Sp. *cuenta*) *n.* account, bill; value; **waláng kuwenta** *adj.* no value; not nice.
kuwento: (Sp. *cuento*) *n.* story, tale.
kuwengka: (Sp. *cuenca*) *n.* basin of a river, deep valley.
kuwerdas: (Sp. *cuerda*) *n.* string, chord.
kuwerna: (*slang*) *n.* new prisoner.
kuwero: (Sp. *cuero*) *n.* leather.
kuwidáw: (Sp. *cuidado*) *interj.* be careful!
kuwintás: *n.* necklace.
kuwít: *n.* comma.
kuwitib: *n.* small red ant.
kuwitis: (Sp. *cohetes*) *n.* rocket.
kuya: (Ch.) *n.* older brother.
kuyakos: *n.* rubbing the body against something.
kuyakoy: *n.* swinging the legs when sitting.
kuyad: *n.* slowness of action.
kuyagot: *n.* rubbish; useless stuff.
kuyapí: (*slang*) *adj.* on the verge of insanity.
kuyapit: *n.* clinging on tightly.
kuyapós: *adj.* overwhelmed.
kuyaw: *n.* swarm; throng.
kuykóy: **kuykuyín** *v.* to dig out.
kuyò: (Ch. *ko ióq*: ointment medicine) *n.* kind of Chinese plaster applied to boils.
kuyob: *n.* act of attacking or surrounding an enemy.
kuyog: *n.* siganid fry; swarm; **kuyóg** (*slang*) *adj.* having many enemies.
kuyóm: *adj.* closed (fist), clenched.
kuyop: *n.* taking care of a parentless child.
kuyukót: *n.* coccyx.
kuyumád: *n.* young louse.
kuyumós: *adj.* clenched.
kuyumpís: *adj.* deflated; thin.
kuyumpít: *adj.* dented; crumpled.
kuyupì: **kuyupî** *adj.* smashed; dented.
kwekong: (*slang*, Ch.) *n.* pimp.
kwidáw: (*slang*, Sp. *cuidado*) *interj.* be careful, look out.
kyawkyáw: (*slang*) *n.* incessant nagging.
kyondî: (*slang*) *n.* flirt.

D

dâ: (*f. indâ*) *n.* appellation for an elderly woman.
da: (Eastern Marinduque) *art.* plural of the personal topic marker *si*. [*siná*]
daán$_1$: *n.* hundred; **dantaón** *n.* century; **sandaán** *n.* one hundred; **dáan-dáan** *adj.* hundreds; **dadaanin** *n.* hundred peso bill.
daán$_2$: *n.* road, street; way; **daanán** *n.* path; access; *v.* to pass; fetch someone; **daáng tuwiran** *n.* shortcut; **dumaán** *v.* go through, pass by; drop by, visit; **magparaán** *v.* to let

pass; **maraanan, madaanan** *v.* to be able to pass; **nakaraán** *adj.* past, former; recent; **nakaráraán** *adj.* past; ago; **nagdaán** *adj.* passed, past. **karapatáng-dumaán.** *n.* right of way. **magbigáy-daán** *v.* to yield, give way. **paraán** *n.* way, course of action; mode, process; **nasa paraán** methodical; **pagdaán** *n.* passing; **pagdaanan** *v.* to pass over, pass through; experience; **paraanán** *v.* to pass over. **pamamaraán, kaparaanán.** *n.* method; specific way of doing something. **pinagdaanán, pinagdáraanán** *n.* path of movement; **daang-bakal** *n.* railroad tracks; **daanín sa tigás ng butó** *id.* to take through force (pass by the hardness of the bone); **dinaán sa bibíg** *id.* quarreling with words (passed with mouth); **magdáraán sa ibabaw ng bangkáy** *id.* would rather die than have a particular thing done (will pass over the corpse); **nagdaán sa bitháy** *id.* studied carefully (passed through the sieve); **Pakiraán pô (Makikiraán ngâ pô)** Excuse me (may I pass).

dabaw: *n.* ford.

dabdáb: *n.* glow, glitter.

dabog: *n.* stamping of the feet.

dabyana: (*slang*) *n.* fat girl.

daka: **pagdaka, pagkaraka** *adv.* instantly, immediately; **kará-karaka, kapagdaka** *adv.* immediately; **kapagkaraka** *adv.* suddenly; immediately; already.

dakdák: (*slang*) *n.* speaking out of turn; nonstop talk about irrelevant matters.

dakikong: *n.* baited pot for catching catfish.

dakilà: *adj.* great; distinguished; extreme; notable; illustrious.

dakíp: *n.* catch; **dumakíp, dakpín** *v.* to catch, arrest.

daklót: *n.* snatching; grabbing.

dakmâ: *n.* sudden seizure; arrest.

dako: *n.* direction, way; region; spot, place; **idako** *v.* to turn, direct.

dakô: (*slang*) *n.* large penis. [Alt: *dakota*]

dakól: *n.* large handful.

dakót: *n.* handful.

dakpín: (rt. *dakíp*) *v.* to catch; arrest.

dakumô: *n.* species of crab.

dakunót: *adj.* stooped, bent (body).

dado: (Sp.) *n.* dice.

daga: (Sp.) *n.* dagger.

dagâ: *n.* rat, mouse; **dagáng-putî** guinea pig; **dagáng-dindíng** *id.* nocturnal petty thief.

dagabdáb: *n.* blaze, conflagration.

dagadagaan: *n.* biceps.

dagaldál: *n.* rumbling noise of dragging.

dagán: *n.* paperweight; **idagan** *v.* to press down with a weight; **dagán-dagán** *adj.* placed one over another. **máraganán** *v.* to be pressed by a weight.

dagandáng: *n.* heat; heating.

dagás: *n.* emergency call.

dagasâ: *adj.* sudden; impetuous, rash.

dagasdás: *n.* sudden action.

dagat₁: *n.* sea, ocean; **tabing-dagat** *n.* beach. **karagatan** *n.* ocean, high seas; **pagdaragat** *n.* flooding; fishing in the ocean sea; **pandaragat** *n.* sea voyage; sea fishing.

dagat₂: **karagatan** *n.* ancient poetic drama.

dagdág: *n.* extension, increase; addition; **idagdág** *v.* to add to, append. **karagdagan** *n.* increase; addition; enlargement; *adj.* extra, additional. **maragdagán** *v.* to be able to increase.

dagil: *n.* sideswipe; light touch in passing.

dagím: *n.* rain cloud; **pagdaragím** *n.* formation of rain clouds.

dagindíng: *n.* droning sound.

dagisdís: *n.* continuous blowing of a strong wind.

dagison: **idagison** *v.* to move things closer together.

dagit: *n.* swooping, sudden snatching; **pandaragit** *n.* swooping prey.

dagitab: *n.* spark.

daglát: *n.* abbreviation.

daglî: *adv.* immediately.

dagok: *n.* blow with the fist on the nape; **dagok ng kapalaran** *id.* misfortune (slap of fate).

dagól: (*slang*) *n.* tough man.

dagos: *n.* sudden departure.

dagsâ: *n.* violent forward rush; glut; influx; **pagdagsaán** *v.* to be crowded with, to be beset; to be flooded. **karagsaán** *n.* condition of being glottal. **maragsâ** *adj.* glottal

(ending in a glottal stop). **maragsaán** *v.* to be flooded with goods.
dagtâ: *n.* resin, sap.
dagubáng: *n.* thumping sound.
dagubdób: *n.* noisy blaze.
daguldól: *n.* grinding sound.
dagundóng: *n.* peal, rumble.
dagunót: *n.* sound of traffic.
dagusdós: *n.* downward slip, glide.
dahak: **dumahak** *v.* to clear the throat of phlegm.
dahan: **marahan** *adj.* gently, softly; **dahanan** *v.* to soften, lower (the voice); **nádahan-dahan** *id.* asked; taken surreptitiously; **kadahanan** *n.* slowness.
dahás: *n.* force; ferocity; **mandahás** *v.* to use force against, violate; **marahás** *adj.* drastic, severe, violent; ruthless. **karahasán** *n.* violence, force; audacity; cruelty; **pandarahás** *n.* use of force or violence; rape.
dahik: **dahikan** *n.* shipyard.
dahil: *prep.* because of; **dahilan** *n.* reason, means; origin; alibi, excuse; **idahilán** *v.* to attribute, blame, be the cause of; adduce. **marahil** *adv.* perhaps, possibly.
dahilig: *n.* slope; inclination.
dahol: *n.* water snake.
dahon: *n.* leaf; **magdahon** *v.* to grow leaves; **dahong-gabi** *n.* leaf-fish; **may dahong kawayang tuyô sa ulo** *id.* husband with an unfaithful wife; **dahon ng ala-ala** *id.* memories.
dahong-: *pref.* leaf of; **dahong-gabi** *n.* taro leaf; leaf fish, *Platax orbicularis.*
dahóp: *adj.* needy; insufficient; destitute; **magdahóp** *v.* to be in want; **kadahupán** *n.* lack, shortage.
dáhumpaláy: *n.* species of green, poisonous snake.
dahunán: *n.* blue spotted sting ray.
daig: *n.* live embers; starting a fire; **magdaig** *v.* to kindle.
daíg: *adj.* defeated, surpassed; better; **daigín** *v.* to outdo; **madaíg** *v.* to excel, overcome; **makadaíg** *v.* to be able to surpass; **manaíg** *v.* to prevail; override; **mapanaigán** *v.* to overcome; surmount; **pananaíg** *n.* preponderance; supremacy; **pandaraíg** *n.* domineering; surpassing; taking advantage of someone's weakness.
daigdíg: *n.* world, earth; **sandaigdigan** *n.* the whole world; universe; **háting-daigdíg** *n.* hemisphere; **pandaigdíg** *adj.* universal; mundane.
dáing: *n.* dried fish; **daing-gusong** *n.* big-scaled sillago fish.
daíng: *n.* moan, complaint; lament; **dumaíng** *v.* to complain; **idaíng** *v.* to complain; plead for; **maraingán** *v.* to be able to beg for. **karáíngan** *n.* request; complaint; **madáíngin, paladaíng** *adj.* prone to complaining.
daís: **daís-daís** *adj.* close together; **idaís** *v.* to move close together; **dumaís** *v.* to get close to; **magdaís** *v.* to move close to someone.
daít: **idaít** *v.* to place something so it touches something else; **magdaít** *v.* to be very close to another or others.
daiti: *var. of daít.*
dala: *n.* dragnet, cast net.
dalá: *adj.* carried; brought; **dalhán** *v.* to bring; **dalhín** *v.* to carry, bring, deliver; **ipadalá** *v.* to send, deliver; **ipagdalá** *v.* to carry on behalf of someone else; **magdalá** *v.* to carry, bring; **padalá** *n.* thing sent; consignment; *adj.* sent; **padalhán** *v.* to send to someone; **pagdadalá** *n.* delivery; **pagdádalhán** *n.* destination of a thing being sent; **taga-pagdalá** *n.* carrier; **nagdadaláng-tao** *adj.* pregnant; **magdadalá ng bigát** *id.* will shoulder the responsibility (will carry the weight); **magdaláng-habág** *id.* to take pity, sympathize (bring pity); **napadádalá sa mga balí-balità** *id.* believing in gossip (carried by news); **napadádalá sa agos** *id.* Docile; **huwág padalá sa nadaramá** don't be swept away by emotions; **waláng kadalá-dalá** *id.* doesn't learn.
dalâ: *adj.* wary; **dalâ na** *id.* no longer a virgin; widow.
dalág: *n.* mudfish; **dalagan** *n.* sleeper fish; **dalág-dagat** *n.* sergeant fish.
dalaga: *n.* maiden, unmarried woman; **dumalaga** *n.* young fowl; young female animal that has not borne any young; **kadalagahan**

n. maidenhood; virginity; group of maidens; **dálagahín** *adj.* beginning puberty (girls); **magdalagá** *v.* to grow into a teenage girl; **pagkadalaga** *n.* maidenhood; **matandáng dalaga** *n.* old maid; **pagdadalagá** *n.* female adolescence; **dalagang bukid** *n.* Caesio fish; maiden from the village; **dalagang-iná** *n.* unwed mother.

dalagdág: (*reg.*) *n.* species of vine also called *kulambibíg*.

dalagindáy: (*coll.*) *n.* teenage girl.

dalagindíng: (*coll.*) *n.* teenage girl.

dalagita: *n.* young maid.

dalahik: *n.* point reached on the seashore by the waves; intense coughing attack; **dalahikan** *n.* isthmus; small dock for boats.

dalahirà: *adj.* gossipy; provocative.

dalahit: *n.* intense coughing attack.

dalamhatì: *n.* grief, sorrow; **ipagdalamhatì** *v.* to mourn; **makidalamhatì** *v.* to condole, sympathize; **pakikidalamhatì** *n.* condolence; **papagdalamhatiin** *v.* to cause extreme sorrow.

dalampasigan: *n.* seashore; bank of a river.

dalandán: (Sp. *naranja*) *n.* orange; **kulay-dalandán** *adj.* orange colored.

dalang: **madalang** *adv.* rarely; **dumalang** *v.* to become fewer; to become sparse; **pandaralang** *n.* become sparse; **kadalangan** *n.* infrequency; sparseness.

dalangát: *n.* black-finned slipmouth fish.

dalanghita: (Sp. *naranjita*) *n.* tangerine, mandarin orange.

dalangin: **panalangin** *n.* prayer; **manalangin** *v.* to pray.

dalapdáp: *n.* pruning of trees.

dalás: *n.* frequency; rapidity; **madalás** *adj.* frequently, rapidly; **dumalás** *v.* to occur frequently; **kadalásan** *n.* frequency; *adv.* often; usually; **kadalasán** *n.* frequency, frequent occurrence.

dalasà: *n.* attack, assault; piece, bit.

dalatan: *n.* cultivated highland.

dalaw: *n.* visitor, guest; **dalawin** *v.* to visit someone; drop by.

dalawá: *n.* two; couple; double; **dalawampû** *n.* twenty; **magdalawá** *v.* to be two; **makalawá** *adv.* twice, two times; **ikalawá** *adj.* second; **nagdadalawáng-isip** *id.* in a state of indecision (having two minds).

dalawit: *n.* lever; **dalawitin** *v.* to pry up, raise; **madalawit** *v.* to become involved in a questionable affair.

dalaydáy: *n.* fluid motion of liquids.

dalaydayan: *n.* framework used for drying fish nets.

daldál: *n.* gossip; *adj.* talkative; **daldalero** *n.* gossiper, newsmonger.

daldalkina: (*slang*) *adj.* talkative.

dale: (Sp.) Go ahead!

dali: *n.* attack; **dalihin** *v.* to hit, attack.

dalhán, dalhín: *see dalâ.*

dalì: *n.* inch; measure equal to the breadth of a finger.

dalî: *n.* quickness, rapidity; ease; *interj.* quick, hurry; **daliín** *v.* to hurry; **madalî** *adj.* easy; quickly; rush; **madalíng-araw** *n.* dawn; **padaliín** *v.* to make easy, facilitate; **sandalî** *n.* moment; **madalíng-magbará** *adj.* easily irritated.

dalimanok: *n.* eagle ray.

daling: *n.* fastening.

dalin(g)síl: *adj.* lost, astray; wrong, incorrect.

dalirì: *n.* digit: (finger or toe); (*coll.*) pointing things out in detail. **daliriin** *v.* to point things out. **dálirián** *n.* poking fingers at each other; (*fig.*) exchange of reminders about each other's debts of gratitude; **taták ng dalirì** *n.* fingerprint. [Fingers in Tagalog are: *hinlalakí* (thumb); *hintuturò* (index finger); *datò, hinlalatò* (middle finger); and *kálingkingan* (little finger)]

dalirot: *n.* poking; **dalirutin** *v.* to poke.

dalisay: *adj.* pure, unadulterated; immaculate.

dalisdís: *n.* slope.

dalit: *n.* slice.

dalít: *n.* psalm.

dalitâ: *n.* extreme poverty; **máralitâ** *adj.* indigent; **karálitaán** *n.* misery; poverty.

daló: *n.* presence; **daluhán** *v.* to attend; **dumaló** *v.* to attend.

daló: *n.* help; **magpadaló** *v.* to ask for help.

dalók: *n.* pickled fruits.

dalos: **magpadalus-dalos** *v.* to do rashly.

daloy: *n.* flow; oozing; **daluyan** *v.* to flow or ooze from; *n.* tube for liquids, conductor of electricity; **daluyang-uhog** *n.* mucus gland; **dumaloy** *v.* to ooze, flow, trickle.

dalub- *prefix.* denoting expertise: **dalubaghám** *n.* scientist; **dalubhasà** *n.* expert; **dalubwikà** *n.* language expert; **dalúbgurò** *n.* professor emeritus.

dalubhasà: *n.* expert; connoisseur.

dalugdóg: *n.* beating of drums.

daluhong: *n.* assault, onslaught.

dalulong: *n.* safe-conduct.

dalumat: *n.* deep thought.

dalumog: *n.* sudden attack. **dalumugin** *v.* to attack.

dalumos: *n.* sudden lurching of a crowd.

dalumóy: *n.* low, dark clouds.

dalungdóng: *n.* grass hut in the forest.

dalupanì: *n.* wily slipmouth fish.

dalupang: *n.* kind of shrub with reddish branches.

dalurò: *n.* cork tree.

dalusapì: *n.* rooster with blackish-yellow feathers.

dalusdós: *n.* slope; slipping downward.

dalusong: *n.* attack from a high place.

dalutdót: *n.* poking with the finger. **dalutdutín** *v.* to poke with the finger.

daluyong: *n.* surge of the sea, large wave.

dama: (Sp.) *n.* checkers; maid of honor; **damahán** *n.* checkerboard.

damá: *adj.* perceived, felt; perceptible; **damahín, damhín.** *v.* to perceive; understand; touch, feel. **máramá** *v.* to feel, experience.

damák: *n.* palm; *adj.* open-handed.

damág: **magdamág** *adv.* all night; overnight.

damagan: *n.* mountain bass.

damay₁: **pagdamay** *n.* sympathetic aid; **karamay** *n.* sympathizer; **kadamay-damay** *adj.* constantly helping; **dumamay** *v.* to sympathize with, aid a bereaved person; **makiramay** *v.* to sympathize. **maramayan** *v.* to be able to give help.

damay₂: **karamay** *n.* accomplice; **idamay** *v.* to involve someone in a crime. **máramay** *v.* to be implicated.

dambá: *n.* rising on the hind legs; movement of rowers.

dambanà: *n.* altar, shrine.

dambáng: *n.* trough.

dambo: (*slang*) *adj.* large.

dambóng: *n.* loot, plunder; **dumambóng** *v.* to loot; **pandarambóng** *n.* pillage, plundering.

dambuhalà: *n.* whale.

damdám: *n.* feeling; **damdamin** *n.* feelings; sympathy; (*coll.*) resentment; **damdamín** *v.* to feel sorry, hurt; resent, take offense; **iparamdám** *v.* to hint; **makáramdám** *v.* to feel; be aware of; **makipagdamdám** *v.* to identify with; feel one with; **madamdamin** *adj.* emotional; **magdamdám** *v.* to feel (pain); **máramdamán** *v.* to be felt; **pakiramdám** *n.* feeling, emotion; **paramdám** *n.* hint. **karamdaman** *n.* sickness, illness; confinement; **káramdamán** *v.* to sense something from; **kadamdamin** *adj.* congenial; with similar interests or beliefs; **máramdamán** *v.* to feel, experience; be aware of; **pagkamapagdamdám** *n.* sensitiveness; **pandamdám** *n.* sense of touch; **di-maramdamin** *adj.* insensitive.

damhín: *see damá.*

dami: *n.* amount; quantity; **karamihan** *n.* majority; crowd; bulk; **dumami** *v.* to increase in number; **marami** *adj.* many, much, plenty. **maramihan** *v.* to consider more than what is needed. **máramihán** *adj.* in large numbers.

damirâ: *adj.* thick and sticky.

damis: *n.* jackfish; **damis-lawin** *n.* threadfish.

damít: *n.* clothes, garment; costume; **karamtám** *n.* garment; **damtín** *v.* to wear, use as clothing; **damtán** *v.* to put clothes on; **madamít** *adj.* having many clothes. **maram(i)tán** *v.*to be able to clothe; **damít-pambahay** *n.* house clothes; **damít-pantrabaho** *n.* work clothes. **damít-pangkasál** *n.* wedding gown; **damít-panggabí** *n.* evening dress.

damó: *n.* grass; garbage in the form of peelings; (*slang*) marijuana; **damóng-makahiyâ** *n.* sensitive plant, *Mimosa asperata*; (*slang*) timid; **damó-ligáw** *n.* lost soul; **damóng-Maryá** *n.* maidenwort, worm wood.

damot: **karamutan** *n.* stinginess, selfishness.

dampâ: *n.* hut, cabin. (*kubo*)
dampalít: *n.* samphire shrub with purple flowers.
dampî: *n.* light touch; applying powder on; **dampián** *v.* to apply on gently; touch lightly.
dampól: *n.* tan dye.
dampót: **dumampót** *v.* to pick up something (from the ground); **karampót** *n.* small quantity; pinch (of salt); **patáy-dampót** *id.* unconscious (dead lifted).
damsák: *n.* wet soil.
damtán: (rt. *damít*) *v.* to put clothes on.
damtín: (rt. *damít*) *v.* to wear, use as clothing.
damukô: *n.* species of crab. (*dakumô*)
damuhò: *adj.* rough, brutal; rustic; savage; stupid.
damulag: *n.* beast; water buffalo.
danak: *n.* spilling (of blood); (*slang*) gang war; **dumanak** *v.* to flow; pour out; **padanakin** *v.* to spill.
danas: **karanasán** *n.* experience; **káranasan** *v.* to experience from, learn from. **dumanas** *v.* to undergo, experience; **maranasan** *v.* to feel, experience.
danaw: *n.* pond, lake.
dandáng: *n.* act of warming by the fire.
Danés: *n.* Danish.
danî: *adj.* lying side by side.
daniw: *adj.* common, ordinary; *n.* customary usage. **daníw** *adj.* accustomed to. **karaniwan** *adj.* common, ordinary; customary; *n.* custom, practice; mode, vogue.
dantáy: **dumantáy** *v.* to rest one's leg over something; **danyayan** *n.* leg pillow.
danyos: (Sp. *daños*) *n.* damage, injury.
dangál: *n.* honor, integrity; **marangál** *adj.* honorable; honest; polite; reputable; **karángálan** *n.* honor, dignity; **magparangál** *v.* to honor; **pagkamarangál** *n.* honesty; righteousness; **pagpaparangál** *n.* testimonial; **pandangál** *adj.* honorary; **parangál** *n.* celebration in the honor of; testimonial; **parangalán** *v.* to honor.
dangan: **dangan at** *conj.* if it were not for.
dangat: *n.* act of piercing, stabbing.
dangát: *n.* cardinal fish.
dangkál: *n.* span, area between the extended thumb and index finger.
dangláy: *n.* fine strips of bamboo.
dangyâ: see *rangyâ*: pomp.
daó: *n.* species of hardwood tree.
daóng: *n.* ship; **daungán** *v.* to dock.
daóp: *adj.* joined closely together.
daos: **pagdaraos** *n.* celebration; **idaraos** *v.* to celebrate; hold a meeting; take the time and energy to do. **máraos** *v.* to be celebrated, finished; **karáráos** *adj.* just held; just celebrated; **pinagdárausan** *n.* place of assembly.
daot: (*slang*, Ceb.) *adj.* unfortunate.
dapâ₁: *adj.* lying on one's stomach; **maparapâ** *v.* to fall prostrate; **padapâ** *adj.* lying prostrate; **ikatlóng pagkárapâ** *id.* third misfortune, third strike without success. **márapâ** *v.* to stumble.
dapâ₂: *n.* flounder; **dapang-bilóg** *n.* brill fish.
dapâ₃: (*slang*) *n.* pair of shoes.
dapak: *n.* red snapper.
dapal: *n.* white goby, *Glossogobius giurus*.
dapat: *v.* should, ought to, must; **karapat-dapat** *adj.* worthy, deserving; **karapatán** *n.* right; authority; **marapat** *adj.* proper, right, appropriate; necessary, essential. **marapatin** *v.* to consider something proper; **karapat-dapat** *adj.* deserving; worthy; **karampatan** *adj.* proper; worthy; **magindapat** *v.* to become worthy; **pagindapatin** *v.* to deign; consider as worthy; **pagkamarapat** *n.* qualification; **papagindapatin** *v.* to try to make someone worthy.
dapdáp: *n.* Indian coral tree.
dapil, dapilpil: *adj.* flat (nose).
dapilos: *n.* act of skidding.
dapit: *n.* act of carrying a dead body to church; *prep.* towards; near; **dapit-hapon** *n.* dusk; **dapit-umaga** *n.* daybreak.
daplás: *n.* climbing.
daplís: *adj.* grazing, just hitting; **dumaplís** *v.* to just miss the target, to graze, glance off.
dapò: *n.* air plant; orchid; parasite; act of alighting; **dapuán** *n.* roost, bar on which birds perch; **dinapuan ng karamdaman** *id.* fell in (perched by sickness); **dî padapuan sa langaw** *id.* priceless.

dapóg: *n.* open fire.
dapulak: *n.* aphid, plant louse.
dapwâ: *conj.* but.
dapyó: *n.* light touch of air; (*fig.*) attack of an illness.
darák: *n.* bran.
darág: *n.* stamping of the feet in anger.
daragís: *n.* dysentery. [Coll. var: *darag-ís*]
darandáng: *n.* kamala tree.
daráng: **darangán** *n.* live coals; **idaráng** *v.* to roast over live coals.
darapâ: (*rt. dapâ*) *n.* flat fish; **darapáng-habâ** *n.* tongue fish; **darapáng-talangkáw** *n.* Indian turbot fish.
darapugan: *n.* leaf fish, *Platax orbicularis*.
darás: *n.* carpenter's adz.
daratíng: (*rt. datíng*) *adj.* coming; *n.* future; *v.* will arrive.
dasa: (Sp. *raza*) *n.* race, breed.
dasál: (Sp. *rezar*) *n.* prayer; **dásálan** *n.* prayer book; place of prayer; rosary beads; **magdasál** *v.* to pray; **madásálin** *adj.* habitually praying; **ipagdasál** *v.* to pray for something; **ipagdasál mo na** pray for it; (*fig.*) give it up.
daskól: **padaskól** *n.* something done in a careless manner; **dumaskól** *v.* to do in a careless manner.
dasdás: *n.* act of sanding the surface of wood.
dasig: **dumasig** *v.* to move nearer.
dastô: *n.* trace, vestige.
datà: *n.* body dirt.
datál: **dumatál** *v.* to arrive; **idatál** *v.* to bring.
datapwâ: *conj.* but, however.
datay: **nararatay, máratay** *adj.* bedridden. **máratay sa baníg** *adj.* confined to the bed.
dati: *adj.* former, previous; old; ex-; **datihan** *adj.* used to, accustomed; **dati-rati** *adv.* formerly, previously; **parati** *adv.* always. [See also *hirati*: accustomed]
datig: *n.* cloth lining; **karatig** *adj.* adjoining, neighboring, adjacent.
dátiles: (Sp. *dátil*) *n.* date (fruit).
datíng: *n.* arrival; **dumatíng** *v.* to arrive, come; **datnán** *v.* to visit; find on arrival; **datnín** *v.* to reach; **magparatíng** *v.* to send; give a bribe to; **paratíng** *n.* message sent. **karáratíng** *v.* just arrived. **kararatnán** *n.* time of menstruation; **kárаratnán** *n.* result, expected consequence. **maratíng** *v.* to be able to reach (a destination); **makaratíng** *v.* to be able to attain; to be able to reach.
dating-: [*dati* + *=ng*] *pref.* ex-, former.
datò: *n.* middle finger; Moro chief.
datóng: (*slang*) *adj.* rich; *n.* money.
daungan: *n.* pier.
dausdós: **idausdós** *v.* to slide something down.
Davawenyo: *n.* ethnic group and language from Davao Oriental and Davao del Sur, Mindanao.
daw: (*raw after vowels*) *part.* it is said, he said, she said, they said.
dawa: *n.* common millet; cross strips in latticework; **dawa-dawa** *n.* latticework.
dawak: **marawak** *adj.* immense, vast.
dawag: *n.* spine of rattan.
dawal: **marawal** *adj.* low, unworthy; degraded, despicable. **karawalan** *n.* indignity.
dawdáw: **idawdáw** *v.* to dip into a liquid.
dawi: **dumawi** *v.* to bite the bait.
dawil: *n.* act of forcing blood out of a wound.
dawis: *n.* anguish, dismay.
dawit: *n.* entanglement; Indian arm wrestling; **madawit** *adj.* entangled. **karawit** *adj.* implicated (in a crime).
dayà: *n.* deceit, fraud; *adj.* fake, cheating; **magdayà** *v.* to cheat, beguile, delude, trick; **parayâ** *n.* advantage allowed to others. **karayaan** *n.* deceit, dishonesty; **pandarayà** *n.* cheating, swindling.
dayag: *n.* front, façade. **karayagán** *n.* right side (of a cloth).
dayami: *n.* rice straw, hay.
dayán: *n.* festive decor.
dayandáng: *n.* faint echoes; exposure to heat.
dayangdayang: *n.* noble lady; brown-striped snapper fish, *Lutianus vitta*.
dayap: *n.* lime tree.
dayaw: *n.* bird song.
dayikdík: *n.* skin eruption.
dayo: *n.* visitor; stranger; foreigner, alien; **dayuhan** *adj.* foreign, alien; **dumayo** *v.* to go to a faraway place; migrate.
dayukdók: *adj.* extremely hungry; (*slang*) rape; abuse.

dayupay: *n.* emaciated locust; *adj.* financially broke.
de- (Sp. *de* "of") *pref.* having, wearing; concerning; **de-koryente** *adj.* electric; **de-abaniko** *adj.* using a fan; **de-mesa** *adj.* having a table; using a table.
debér: (Sp.) *n.* right, obligation.
deboto: (Sp. *devoto*) *n.* devotee.
debuwenas: (*de-* + *buwenas*) *adj.* lucky.
dekahón: (Sp. *cajón*) *adj.* bookish.
dekalibre: (Sp. *de calibre*) *n.* gentleman; *adj.* having ethics.
dekampanilya: (Sp. *de campanilla*) *n.* trustworthy lawyer.
deklibe: (Sp. *declive*) *n.* slope.
dekoro: (Sp.) *n.* decorum, propriety.
dekwat: (*slang*) *n.* pilfering. [Alt: *dengwat*]
dedmá: (*slang*, Eng. *dead* + *malisya* < *patáy malisya*) **magdedmá, dumedmá, dedmahín** *v.* to ignore completely; snub.
dedo: (*slang*, Eng.) *adj.* dead; caught (in trouble).
dehado: (Sp. *dejado*) *n.* underdog (in gambling); being at a disadvantage.
delantál: (Sp.) *n.* apron.
delantera: (Sp.) *n.* façade.
delagado: (Sp.) *n.* delegate.
delikadesa: (Sp. *delicadeza*) *n.* refinement; prudishness; fastidiousness; **kadelikadesahan** *n.* fastidiousness.
delikado: (Sp. *delicado*) *adj.* delicate; serious, crucial; important; fussy; sensitive; fragile.
delikadesa: (Sp. *delicadeza*) *n.* refinement.
deliryo: (Sp. *delirio*) *n.* delirium.
delito: (Sp.) *n.* evidence; proof. (*katibayan*)
delpín: (Sp. *delfín*) *n.* dolphin.
demanda: (Sp.) *n.* demand; legal accusation.
demandadór: (Sp.) *n.* accuser (in court).
demandante: (Sp.) *n.* accuser, complainant.
deménsiya: (Sp. *demencia*) *n.* dementia, insanity.
de-mesa: (Sp.) *adj.* having a table, using a table; *n.* flat top haircut.
demonyo: (Sp. *demonio*) *n.* devil, demon.
dentadura: (Sp.) *n.* dentures.
denggóy: (*slang*) *n.* fooling.
depende: (Sp.) *v.* it depends.
depensór: (Sp. *defensor*) *n.* defender.
depinido: (Sp. *definido*) *adj.* definite, certain.
depósito: (Sp.) *n.* deposit; pocket; reservoir.
deretsa: (Sp. *derecha*) *n.* right side.
deretso: (Sp. *derecho*) *adj.* straight, direct.
deretsos: (Sp. *derechos*) *n.* fees, dues.
desapiyo: (Sp. *desafío*) *n.* challenge, duel.
desaprobado: (Sp.) *adj.* disapproved.
desbentaha: (Sp.) *n.* disadvantage.
deskarga: (Sp. *descarga*) *n.* unloading.
deskargo: (Sp. *descargo*) *n.* excuse, apology; **magdiskargo** *v.* to apologize.
deskaríl: (Sp. *descarril*) *n.* derailment.
deskarte: *var. of diskarte.*
deskompasado: (Sp. *descompasado*) *adj.* out of rhythm.
deskuwento: (Sp. *descuento*) *n.* discount.
desenso: (Sp. *descenso*) *n.* demotion.
desetso: (Sp. *desecho*) *n.* rejected product.
desgaste: (Sp.) *n.* wear and tear.
desgrasya: (Sp. *desgracia*) *n.* misfortune, mishap, automobile accident; disgrace; **madesgrasya** *v.* to be disgraced.
despalko: (Sp. *desfalco*) *n.* embezzlement.
despatsado: (Sp. *despachado*) *adj.* dispatched.
despatso: (Sp. *despacho*) *n.* dispatch; office.
despedida: (Sp.) *n.* farewell party.
despertadór: (Sp.) *n.* alarm clock.
destino: (Sp.) *n.* destiny, fate.
destornilyadór: (Sp. *destornillador*) *n.* screwdriver.
detalye: (Sp. *detalle*) *n.* detail.
dî: *adv.* not, no.
di- negative prefix, short for *hindî*: no.
dialekto: (Sp. *dialecto*) *n.* dialect.
diantre: (Sp.) *n.* devil.
dibdíb: *n.* chest, bosom; (*fig.*) heart; **dibdibín** *v.* to brood, think seriously about.
dibinidád: (Sp. *divinidad*) *n.* divinity.
dibuhante: (Sp. *dibujante*) *n.* draftsman.
dibuho: (Sp. *dibujo*) *n.* drawing; design, pattern.
dikay: *n.* species of sour rattan.
dikdík: *n.* pulverization.
dikín: *n.* circular rattan hat.
dikít₁: **dumikít** *v.* to stick to, adhere; **pandikít** *n.* paste, glue; **dikitán** *v.* to attach to, stick

on; **nakadikít sa balintatáw** *id.* always present in the imagination (pasted in the pupil).

dikít$_2$: *n.* loveliness; magnificence; **marikít** *adj.* beautiful, lovely.

dikít$_3$: **marikít** *adj.* flammable. **pagdidikít** *n.* act of kindling; **pamparikít** *n.* kindling.

dikláp: *n.* spark.

diko: (Ch. *di kô*) *n.* second eldest brother.

diktá: (Sp. *dicta*) *n.* dictation.

diktadór: (Sp. *dictador*) *n.* dictator.

dikyâ: *n.* jellyfish.

dikyám: (Ch.) *n.* salted, preserved plums.

didál: (Sp.) *n.* thimble.

diés: (Sp. *diez*) *n.* ten.

dieta: (Sp. *dieta*) *n.* diet.

diga: *n.* idle talk; **dumidiga** (*coll.*) courting.

digkál: *n.* crowbar.

dighál: *n.* belch.

digló: (*slang*) *n.* fart.

digmâ: *n.* war, warfare, battle; **digmaín** *v.* to wage war on.

dignidád: (Sp. *dignidad*) *n.* dignity.

diín: *n.* pressure; emphasis; stress; **bigyáng-diín** *v.* to emphasize, stress; accentuation; **idiín** *v.* to press, accent, stress. **mariín** *adj.* emphatic; stressed on the last syllable.

diít: *n.* slight pressure; thumb mark. **máriít** *v.* to happen to touch lightly.

dilà: *n.* tongue; **dilaan** *v.* to lick; stick out the tongue at; **dilang gintô** *id.* eloquent speaker (golden tongue); **nasa dulo ng dilà** *id.* at the tip of one's tongue; **dilá-dilà** *n.* tongue shaped rice cake; **waláng dilà** *id.* shy.

dilang-baka: *n.* species of cactus-like plant.

diläg: **mariläg** *adj.* splendid, exquisite.

dilán: *adj.* any, all; whatever.

dilat: **dilát** *adj.* aware; trained; open-eyed; big-eyed herring fish; **dumilat** *v.* to open the eyes; **dilatan** *v.* to stare, glare; **mádílat** *adj.* aware; **mandilat** *v.* to stare at with wide-opened eyes; **pandidilat** *n.* glare; **magdilát ng matá** *id.* to think carefully (open eyes); **dilát ang matá, panís ang laway** *id.* insensitive to what is happening around.

diláw: *n.* yellow; turmeric; **mariláw** *adj.* yellow; **dumiláw** *v.* to turn yellow; **mag-diláw** *v.* to wear yellow.

dildíl: **idildíl** *v.* to insist; press; **magdildíl ng asín** *id.* to live a wretched life (press salt).

dilì: *adv.* seldom, rarely; **paroón-dilì** *adj.* undecided, hesitant; **abot-dilì** *id.* in a serious condition (could hardly reach).

dilíg: *n.* watering of plants; **pandilíg** *n.* sprinkler.

dilihénsiya$_1$: (Sp.) *n.* diligence; **dilihensiyáng patáy** *id.* last resort; **waláng dilihénsiya** *id.* doesn't know how to look for subsistence.

dilihénsiya$_2$: (slang) *n.* extortion; collecting money.

dilím: *n.* darkness; **madilím** *adj.* dark, dim; obscure; **dilimán** *v.* to darken; **dumilím** *v.* to become dark; **nagdilím ang paningín** *id.* became angry (sight became dark). **karimlán** *n.* darkness; (*fig.*) obscurity. **marimlán** *v.* to darken; become confused.

dilis: *n.* long-jawed anchovy.

dilís: *n.* chord or string for the guitar.

dimapigil: (*slang, hindî mapigil*) *n.* flirt.

dimaporo: (*slang*) *n., adj.* Muslim.

dimig: **dimíg** *adj.* humid, damp.

dimití: **magdimití** *v.* to resign.

dimol: **dumimol** *v.* to lick.

dimón: *n.* period of convalescence of a mother after delivery; delivery bed of sows.

din: (*rin after vowels*) *adv.* also, too.

dindíng: *var.* of *dingdíng*: wall, partition.

dini, dine: *adv.* here; **dumine** *v.* to be here; **pumarine** *v.* to come here.

diníg: *adj.* audible; **dinggín** *v.* to listen to; **paringgán** *v.* to allude, refer to, mention; **pariníg** *n.* hint; **pandiníg** *n.* sense of hearing. **máriníg** *v.* to hear.

dingal: **maringal** *adj.* magnificent, grand; proud. **karingalan** *n.* splendor; pomp.

dingas: *n.* flame, blaze; **maningas** *v.* to set on fire.

dingat: **karingat-dingat** *adv.* unexpectedly; without notice.

dingdíng: *n.* wall.

dinggá: (*slang*) *n.* homosexual.

dinggín: (*rt. diníg*) *v.* to listen to.

dingíg: *adj.* audible.

Diós: (Sp.) *n.* god.

dipá: *n.* fathom, length of extended arms; **dumipá** *v.* to extend the arms.
diperensyá: (Sp. *diferencia*) *n.* difference; aberration; accident; defect, disability.
diputado: (Sp.) *n.* deputy.
dirà: *n.* watery discharge of the eye.
direksyón: (Sp. *dirección*) *n.* direction; address; order, command; instruction.
direktiba: (Sp. *directiva*) *n.* management, board of directors.
diri: *n.* loathing; **mandiri** *v.* to loathe.
dirihí: (Sp. *dirigir*) **magdirihí** *v.* to direct.
diskanso: (Sp. *descanso*) *n.* rest; relief.
diskarga: (Sp. *descarga*) *n.* unloading; **diskargahín** *v.* to unload.
diskargado: (Sp. *descargado*) *adj.* unloaded.
diskargo: (Sp. *descargo*) *n.* apology; excuse; **diskarguhán** *v.* to ask for an apology from.
diskarte: (Sp. *descarte*: discarding) *n.* appeal; way one can attract a member of the opposite sex; **dumiskarte** *v.* to charm; make a move on; woo; pave the way.
disko: (Sp. *disco*) *n.* disk.
diskurso: (Sp. *discurso*) *n.* speech.
disenyo: (Sp. *diseño*) *n.* design, sketch.
disgusto: *n.* disgust.
disimulado: (Sp.) *adj.* pretended.
disín: *part.* used to express hypothetical conditions.
disiotso: (Sp. *dieciocho*) *n.* eighteen.
disiplina: (Sp.) *n.* discipline.
dismenorea: (Sp. *dismenorrea*) *n.* painful menstruation.
disparate: (Sp.) *n.* blunder, mistake.
dispatsadór: (Sp. *despachador*) *n.* counter salesman.
dispensa: (Sp.) *n.* pantry, dispensation.
disprás: (Sp. *disfraz*) *n.* mask, disguise.
dispuwesto: (Sp. *dispuesto*) *adj.* disposed, ready.
distrito: (Sp.) *n.* district.
distrungká: (Sp. *destroncar*) **distrungkahín** *v.* to break a lock.
distrungkado: (Sp. *destroncado*) *n.* broken (locks).
Disyembre: (Sp. *diciembre*) *n.* December.
dità: *n.* poison.
ditdít: *adj.* torn into strips.
dito: *adv.* here; **dumito** *v.* to be here; stay here; **pumarito** *v.* to come here; **pagparito** *n.* coming here; **náritó** *adj.* here, present.
ditóy: (*slang*) *n.* child.
ditsé: (Ch.) *n.* second eldest sister.
ditso: (Sp. *dicho*) *n.* lines of an actor.
ditsóy: (Ch. *díq* c^{h}*ui*: slit mouth) *n.* shoemaker's welting awl.
diwà: *n.* essence, meaning; spirit; sense; central point, meaning; **pandiwà** *adj.* mental; *v.* verb; **waláng-diwà** *adj.* senseless.
diwang: **pandiriwang** *n.* celebration, ceremony, event, occasion.
diwarà: *n.* setback, misfortune; **mádiwarà** *adj.* attentive to details; meet a misfortune; **mápariwarà** *v.* to meet a misfortune, suffer a setback; **kariwaraan** *n.* misfortune; calamity, adversity; **mápariwarà ang puri** to be disgraced (woman's honor).
diwasâ: *n.* opulence; **mariwasâ** *adj.* well-off, opulent. **kariwasaán** *n.* wealth, opulence.
diwatà: *n.* muse, nymph, fairy.
diway: (*slang*) *adj.* beautiful.
diyablo: (Sp. *diablo*) *n.* devil.
diyán: *adv.* there (near person addressed); **dumiyán** *v.* to be there, stay there (near addressee); **náriyán** *adj.* is/are there (near addressee); **pumariyán** *v.* to go there (near addressee); **Diyan ka na** See you later.
diyana: (Sp. *diana*) *n.* reveille.
diyaryo: (Sp. *diario*) *n.* daily paper; *adj.* daily.
diyatà: *adv.* really.
diyeta: (Sp. *dieta*) *n.* diet.
diyós: (Sp. *dios*) *n.* God; **diyosa** *n.* goddess.
doblado: (Sp.) *adj.* doubled; folded.
doble: (Sp.) *adj.* double; **doblihín** *v.* to double; **doble-karera** *adj.* double-breasted; **doble kara** *adj.* two-faced; *n.* traitor.
dokléng: (*slang*) *adj.* cross-eyed. [Var: *dok*]
doktór: (Sp. *doctor*) *n.* doctor; **doktór-laway** *n.* quack doctor.
doktrina: (Sp. *doctrina*) *n.* doctrine.
dokumento: (Sp. *documento*) *n.* document.
dodô: (*slang*) *adj.* stupid.
dodoy: (*slang*) *n.* mistress.
doloroso: (Sp.) *adj.* sorrowful.

dolyár: (Sp. *dollar*) *n.* dollar.
domadór: (Sp.) *n.* animal trainer.
dominante: (Sp.) *adj.* domineering, dominant.
dominyo: (Sp. *dominio*) *n.* dominion.
donadór: (Sp.) *n.* donor.
donselya: (Sp. *doncella*) *n.* maiden, virgin.
donya: (Sp. *doña*) *n.* madam; rich woman; **donya klara** (*slang*) *n.* budding homosexual.
doón: *adv.* there (distal form); **dumoón** *v.* to be there; stay there; **magkaroón** *v.* to have; be affected; **pagkakaroón** *n.* existence; having; **nároón, nároroón** *v.* is there (far from speaker); **paroonán** *v.* to go to a certain place; **pumaroón** *v.* to go there; **kinároroonán** *n.* whereabouts; **bukod sa roón** in addition; **para doón** therefore; **paroó't-parito** *adv.* to and fro, here and there; **sa malapit doón** thereabout.
dorado: (Sp.) *adj.* golden.
dormitoryo: (Sp. *dormitorio*) *n.* dormitory.
dorobo: (*slang*, Jap.) *n.* bum; pickpocket.
dos: (Sp.) *n.* two; **dos-por-dos** *n.* two by two piece of lumber.
dosena: (Sp. *docena*) *n.* dozen.
dosis: (Sp.) *n.* dose.
dosyentos: (Sp. *doscientos*) *n.* two hundred.
dote: (Sp.) *n.* dowry; **dotehan** *v.* to give a dowry to. (*bigáy-kaya*)
draga: (Sp.) *n.* dredge.
dragón: (Sp.) *n.* dragon. (*dambuhalà*)
drama: (Sp.) *n.* drama, play.
dramaturgo: (Sp.) *n.* playwright.
drástikó: (Sp. *drástico*) *adj.* drastic.
drenahe: (Sp. *drenaje*) *n.* drainage.
drowing: (Eng.) *n.* drawing; **drowingin** *v.* to draw; **drowingan** *v.* to draw on.
duakang: (*slang*) *n.* coward.
dubdób: **karubdubán** *n.* intensity of a fire; **marubdób** *adj.* blazing; ardent; enthusiastic.
dublí: (Sp. *doble*) *adj.* double; **dublihín** *v.* to fold.
dukál: *n.* shallow digging; **dukalín** *v.* to excavate.
dukdók: *adj.* crushed flat.
dukesa: (Sp. *duquesa*) *n.* duchess.
dukhâ: *adj.* poor, needy; **karukhaán** *n.* poverty; lack, deficiency.
dukit: *n.* carving.
dukláy: *adj.* hanging, drooping (branches); extending the arms to reach for something.
dukmô: *adj.* resting the head on both arms.
dukot: *n.* pull; kidnapping; **dukutin** *v.* to draw, pull out; kidnap; **dukutan** *v.* to pickpocket; **nagdukót sa palayók** *id.* became hungry.
dukrót: (*slang*) *n.* fresh cadet.
dukuson: *n.* grunt fish.
dukwáng: **dumukwáng** *v.* to stretch the arm in order to reach.
duda: (Sp.) *n.* doubt; **dudoso** *adj.* doubtful.
dugô: *n.* blood; **kadugô** *n.* blood relative; **marugô** *adj.* bloody; **magdugô** *v.* to bleed; **magkadugô** *adj.* of the same blood; **mandurugô** *n.* blood sucker, vampire; **dinuguán** *n.* dish made from blood; **kulang sa dugô** *adj.* anemic; **duguín** *v.* to have a hemorrhage; **pagdurugô** *n.* hemorrhage; **sanduguan** *n.* blood pact; **dugô sa kanyáng dugô** *id.* child (blood of his blood); **kumúkulô ang dugô** *id.* very angry (blood is boiling); **dugóng-mahál** *id.* royal blood (costly blood); **nagdurugô ang pusò** *id.* with an ill-feeling (heart is bleeding); **dugóng aso** *id.* traitor (dog blood). **karuguán** *n.* bloodiness; **uhaw sa dugô** *adj.* bloodthirsty.
dugsô: *n.* swordfish.
dugsóng: *n.* addition.
dugtóng: *n.* annex; **karugtóng** *n.* continuation, sequel; **dugtungán** *v.* to lengthen; add to; **idugtóng** *v.* to attach, annex, add; **magdugtóng** *v.* to join together; splice; **karugtóng ng buhay** *id.* spouse (extension of life). **karugtóng-bituka** *n.* sibling of the same parents; **pagkakádugtóng** *n.* joint; **pinagdugtungán** *v.* to join.
duhagi: *n.* oppression, maltreatment.
duhapang: **dumuhapang** *v.* to lurch forward in order to grab.
duhat: *n.* Java plum, *Syzygium cumini.*
duhay: *n.* black pomfret; butter fish.
duhól: *n.* species of river snake.
duít: *n.* act of pilfering.
dulà, dulâ: *n.* drama, play; **dulaan** *n.* play-

house; **pandulà** *adj.* dramatic.

dulámbuhay: (*coined: dulà + buhay*: poem + life) *n.* biography.

dulang: *n.* low dining table.

dularo: *n.* leather jacket fish.

dulás: *n.* slipperiness; **dumulás** *v.* to slide, slip; **madulás, marulás** *adj.* slippery; **madulás ang dilà** *id.* talkative; **dulasan** *n.* cavalla fish; **padulás** *n.* bribe; tip.

dulay: *n.* climbing from branch to branch; beating around the bush.

duldól: *n.* act of shoving; **iduldól** *v.* to shove.

dulíng: *adj.* cross-eyed; (*slang*) *n.* counterfeit money; **nagkákandududuling sa salapî** *id.* in great need of money.

dulingás: *adj.* perplexed.

dulis: *n.* anchovy; **dulisan** *n.* decussated snapper.

dulit: *n.* fright.

dulo: *n.* end, result; tip; point; **magdulo** *v.* to result in, end up; **pandulo** *adj.* terminal.

dulók: *n.* act of digging and burning small sticks left after a slash and burn fire is out.

dulóg: *n.* attendance; recourse, resort; kind of fish; **dulungán** *v.* to resort to; have recourse to; appear before; **dumulóg** *v.* to turn to for help, resort to.

dulong: *n.* lake goby, *Mirogobius lacustris*.

dulós: *n.* trowel.

dulot: *n.* offer, offering; **dulutan** *v.* to offer.

dulse: (Sp. *dulce*) *n.* dessert.

dulsera: (Sp. *dulcera*) *n.* dessert dish.

duluhan: *n.* backyard.

Dumagat: *n.* tribe living along the Pacific Ocean in Quezon province.

dumal: **karumal-dumal** *adj.* dirty; **marumal** *adj.* shameful.

dumarás: *n.* mallard.

dumat: *n.* taking a long time to do something; **marumat** *adj.* sluggish; **magparumat-dumat** *v.* to take a long time in doing.

dumbusan: *n.* barracuda.

dumí: *n.* feces, excreta; dirt; **dumumí** *v.* to move the bowels; **dum(i)hán** *v.* to dirty; **magdumí** *v.* to soil; **magparumí** *v.* to contaminate; stain; **marumí** *adj.* dirty; nasty; indecent; **márumihán** *v.* to become dirty or polluted; to be affected (disgusted) by dirt; **marumíng-basahan** *id.* worthless (dirty rag); **márumihán** *v.* to become dirty; **pag-dumí** *n.* bowel movement; **pampadumí** *n.* laxative.

dumóg: *adj.* addicted, given to; **dumumog** *v.* to crowd, mob; **magpakadumog** *v.* to become absorbed in (work).

dumpilás: *n.* herring.

dunong: *n.* knowledge; **marunong** *adj.* learned, intelligent; *v.* to know. **karunungan** *n.* wisdom, knowledge; talent; ability.

dungaw: **dumungaw** *v.* to look out a window. **márungawan** *v.* to happen to see out the window.

dungkál: *n.* digging.

dunggíl: *n.* hitting with the tip of the finger.

dunggít: *n.* point, extremity; insinuation, allusion; innuendo; **magparunggít** *v.* to insinuate; make an indirect reference to.

dunggól: *n.* jab, light bump.

dunggót: *n.* point, tip.

dunghál: **dumunghál** *v.* to stretch the neck in order to see.

dungis: *n.* dirt, stain; **marungis** *adj.* dirty, stained. **karungisan** *n.* dirtiness.

dungô: *adj.* timid; stupid.

dungon: *n.* species of tree.

duól: *n.* misfortune, failure.

duóng: *n.* prow of a boat.

duóp: *adj.* joined closely together.

dupang: (*slang*) *adj.* greedy; selfish.

dupikál: *var. of repikál*: ringing of church bells.

dupil: *n.* amulet.

dupilas: *n.* skidding; stumbling; tripping.

dupók: **karupukán** *n.* instability; **marupók** *adj.* flimsy, fragile, frail, weak.

dupong: *n.* firebrand; cinder; (*fig.*) person with a dark complexion.

durâ: spit, saliva; **dumurâ** *v.* to spit; **dur(a)án** *v.* to spit on.

durado: *n.* leather jacket fish; *adj.* golden.

durián: *n.* durian fruit.

durò: *n.* prick; **duruán** *n.* skewer, spit.

durok: **karurukan** *n.* climax (of a story); summit, highest point. **karurukán** *n.* being very high. **marurok** *adj*. lofty, high.

durog: **dumurog** *v*. to crush; grind; pound; **madurog** *adj*. to be split; to be broken, crushed; **durugin ang pusò** *id*. inflict mental pain (pound the heart); **makadurog-pusò** *adj*. heartbreaking.

duróg: (*slang*) *n*. drug addict; **durugan** *n*. drug session; **durugista** *n*. drug addict.

dusa: *n*. suffering, grief; **magdusa** *v*. to suffer; grieve; **maparúrusahan** *adj*. penal; **pagdusahan** *v*. to suffer for; **parusa** *n*. punishment; **parusahan** *v*. to punish; **párusahán** *n*. place for punishment; **magsadusa** *v*. to put into a dramatic form.

dusdós: *n*. mange; scab.

dusing: *n*. dirt on the face; **karusingan** *n*. dirtiness.

dustâ: *adj*. insulted; oppressed, debased; **kadustá-dustâ** *adj*. disgraceful; **dustaín** *v*. to oppress, treat badly; **mapangdustâ** *adj*. insulting; **pandurustâ, pagdustâ** *n*. insulting; disgraceful action; condemnation; censure.

dutdót: **idutdót** *v*. to poke.

dutsa: (Sp. *ducha*) *n*. shower.

duwák: *n*. retching.

duwág: *n*. coward; *adj*. cowardly; **karuwagan** *n*. cowardice. **maruwagán** *v*. to fear.

duwál: *n*. retching; garfish; **dumuwál** *v*. to retch. **máruwál** *v*. to retch, vomit.

duwelo: (Sp. *duelo*) *n*. duel.

duwende: (Sp. *duende*) *n*. mythological dwarf, elf; hobgoblin.

duwít: *n*. pilfering; **duwitín** *v*. to pilfer.

duyan: *n*. cradle; hammock; **iduyan** *v*. to rock, swing.

duyo: *n*. dead end; principal part of a church.

duyong: *n*. manatee.

dyakol: (*slang*) *n*. masturbation.

dyagan: (*slang*) *adj*. beautiful.

dyahe: (*slang*) *adj*. shameful; embarrassing; shy.

dyani: (*slang*) *n*. janitor.

dyeproks: (*slang*) *n*. spoiled brat.

dyinggel: (*slang*, Eng. *jingle*) *n*. urinating.

dyip: (Eng.) *n*. jeep.

dyipni: (Eng. *jeepney*) *n*. passenger vehicle jeep used for public transportation.

dyokan: (*slang*) *n*. sex.

dyoker: (Eng.) *n*. joker.

dyoklâ: (*slang*) *n*. homosexual male.

dyoga: (*slang*) *n*. breast.

dyorangka: (*slang*) *adj*. frank, open.

dyukaka: (*slang*) *n*. face.

dyugdyóg: (*slang*) **pakikipagdyugdyugan** *n*. sexual intercourse.

dyús: (Eng.) *n*. juice.

dyutay: (*slang*, Vis.) *adj*. small.

E

ebak: (*slang*) *n*. excrement. (*tae*)

ebaporada: (Sp. *leche evaporada*) *n*. evaporated milk.

ebobot: (*slang*) *n*. girl, woman. [Alt: *ebong, ebot*]

ek-ék: (*slang*) *n*. et cetera; vagina.

ekipáhe: (Sp. *equipaje*) *n*. baggage.

ekipo: (Sp. *equipo*) *n*. equipment.

ekis: (Sp. *equis*) *n*. letter x; **rayo-ekis** *n*. x-ray.

eklat: (*slang*) *n*. pretending; acting coy.

eksamen: (Sp. *examen*) *n*. test, exam.

ekskomulgado: (Sp. *excomulgado*) *n*. excommunicated.

ektarya: (Sp. *hectaria*) *n*. hectare.

ekups: (*slang*) *n*. vagina.

ekwadór: (Sp. *ecuador*) *n*. equator.

edád: (Sp.) *n*. age; **mayor-de-~** *n*. of legal age; **may edád** *adj*. middle aged.

egat, egay: (*slang*) *n*. dark female, black female.

egot, egoy: (*slang*) *n*. dark male, black male.

ehang: (*slang*) *n*. wife with unfaithful husband.

ehe: (Sp. *eje*) *n*. axle.

ehemplár: (Sp. *ejemplar*) *n*. model, example.

ehemplo: (Sp. *ejemplo*) *n*. example.

ehersisyo: (Sp. *ejercicio*) *n*. exercise.

ehong: (*slang*) *n*. husband with unfaithful wife.

elado: (Sp. *helado*) *adj*. frozen.

élise: (Sp. *hélice*) *n*. propeller; screw.

embahada: (Sp. *embajada*) *n*. embassy.

embahadór: (Sp. *embajador*) *n*. ambassador.

embalsamado: (Sp.) *adj.* embalmed.
embargo: (Sp.) *n.* seizure of goods.
embés: (Sp. *en vez (de)*) *prep.* instead of.
embestidura: (Sp. *envestidura*) *n.* investiture.
embudo: (Sp.) *n.* funnel; (*slang*) *adj.* irritated.
embutido: (Sp.) *n.* sausage.
empanada: (Sp.) *n.* meat pie.
empatso: (Sp. *empacho*) *n.* indigestion.
empenyo: (Sp. *empeño*) *n.* request, favor asked.
emperadór: (Sp.) *n.* emperor.
emperdible: (Sp. *enferdible*) *n.* safety pin.
emplasto: (Sp.) *n.* plaster.
empleado: (Sp.) *n.* employee.
empleyo: (Sp. *empleo*) *n.* employment.
emporyo: (Sp. *emporio*) *n.* emporium.
enano: (Sp.) *n.* dwarf.
enkahe: (Sp. *encaje*) *n.* lace.
Enero: (Sp.) *n.* January.
ensalada: (Sp.) *n.* salad; **ensaladera** salad bowl.
ensayado: (Sp.) *adj.* rehearsed.
ensaymada: (Sp.) *n.* puff cake.
ensayo: (Sp.) n rehearsal.
entablado: (Sp.) *n.* stage.
entendido: (Sp.) *adj.* learned.
entero: (Sp.) *adj.* entire, whole.
entrada: (Sp.) *n.* entry; entrance.
entreakto: (Sp.) *n.* intermission.
entrega: (Sp.) *n.* delivery; surrender.
entremés: (Sp.) *n.* appetizer, canapé.
entrepanyo: (Sp. *entrepaño*) *n.* panel.
entresuwelo: (Sp. *entresuelo*) *n.* mezzanine.
entsupe: (Sp. *enchufe*) *n.* electric socket.
engkahe: (Sp. *encaje*) *n.* lace.
engkanto: (Sp. *encanto*) *n.* charm, spell.
eng-éng: (*slang*) *adj.* stupid.
engganyo: (Sp. *engaño*) *n.* deceit, fraud.
enggot: (*slang*) *adj.* drunk.
engganahe: (Sp. *engranaje*) *n.* gear.
enggrande: (Sp. *en grande*) *adj.* grand.
engot: (*slang*) *adj.* stupid.
epda: (*slang*) *n.* shoplifting.
epekto: (Sp. *efecto*) *n.* effect.
epektos: (*slang*) *n.* smuggled goods.
eprot: (*slang*) *adj.* timid with women.
erkon: (Eng.) *n.* air conditioning.
erbularyo: (Sp. *herbolario*) *n.* quack doctor, herb doctor, herbalist.
ere: (*slang*) **maere** *adj.* proud, boastful.
eredero: (Sp. *heredero*) *n.* heir.
erehe: (Sp. *hereje*) *n.* heretic.
erlat: (*slang*) *n.* sister.
erlot: (*slang*) *n.* brother.
ermat: (*slang*) *n.* mother.
ermita: (Sp.) *n.* hermitage.
ermitanyo: (Sp. *ermitaño*) *n.* hermit.
eroplano: (Eng.) *n.* airplane.
erpat: (*slang*) *n.* father.
eskabetse: (Sp. *escabeche*) *n.* pickled fish; (*slang*) mistress.
eskala: (Sp. *escala*) *n.* scale (music).
eskaparate: (Sp. *escaparate*) *n.* showcase.
eskarlata: (Sp. *escarlata*) *n.* scarlet.
eskayola: (Sp. *escayola*) *n.* plaster of Paris.
eskina: (Sp. *esquina*) *n.* street corner.
eskinita: (Sp. *esquinita*) *n.* street corner turning into an alley; alley.
eskiról: (Sp. *esquirol*) *n.* scab, strike breaker.
eskoba: (Sp. *escoba*) *n.* brush.
eskola: (*slang*) *n.* social climber.
eskolta: (Sp. *escolta*) *n.* convoy, military escort.
eskombro: (Sp. *escombro*) *n.* crushed stones for pavement.
eskopeta: (Sp. *escopeta*) *n.* rifle.
eskorbuto: (Sp. *escorbuto*) *n.* scurvy.
Eskosés: (Sp. *eskosés*) *n.* Scotch.
eskribano: (Sp.) *n.* clerk.
eskribyente: (Sp. *escribiente*) *n.* clerk.
eskrima: (Sp. *esgrima*) *n.* fencing (fight).
eskudero: (Sp. *escudero*) *n.* squire.
eskudo: (Sp. *escudo*) *n.* shield; coat of arms.
eskultór: (Sp. *escultor*) *n.* sculptor.
eskultura: (Sp. *escultura*) *n.* sculpture.
eskupidór: (Sp. *escupidor*) *n.* spittoon.
eskuwadra: (Sp. *escuadra*) *n.* squad.
eskuwala: (Sp. *escuala*) *n.* carpenter's square.
eskuwater: (Eng.) *n.* squatter, makeshift house on someone else's property. [Slang Alt: *eskwakwa*]
eseng: (*slang*) *n.* marijuana.
esmalte: (Sp.) *n.* enamel.
esmeralda: (Sp.) *n.* emerald.

esópago: (Sp. *esófago*) *n.* esophagus.
espada: (Sp.) *n.* sword; hairtail fish; (*slang*) heavy kissing; **espadahán** *n.* swordplay.
Espanya: (Sp. *España*) *n.* Spain.
Espanyol: (Sp. *español*) *n.*, *adj.* Spanish.
espanyola: (Sp. *española*) *n.*, *adj.* Spanish female; species of banana with many seeds.
espáragó: (Sp. *espárrago*) *n.* asparagus.
espeho: (Sp. *espejo*) *n.* mirror. (*salamín*)
esperansa: (Sp. *esperanza*) *n.* hope. (*pag-asa*)
esperma: (Sp.) *n.* sperm, sperm whale; candle made from the sperm of a whale.
espesyalidád: (Sp. *especialidad*) *n.* specialty.
espiga: (Sp.) *n.* spike of grain.
espina: (Sp.) *n.* thorn, spine.
espináka: (Sp. *espinaca*) *n.* spinach.
espinghe: (Sp. *esfinge*) *n.* sphinx.
espioháhe: (Sp. *espionaje*) *n.* espionage.
espiritísmo: (Sp. *espiritismo*) *n.* spiritualism, the belief that the dead can communicate with the living.
espiritísta: (Sp. *espiritista*) *n.* spiritualist, one who believes that the dead can communicate with the living.
espíritu: (Sp. *espíritu*) *n.* spirit; soul; **espíritu sánto** *n.* holy spirit.
esplika: (Sp. *explica*) **iesplika** *v.* to explain.
esponsáles: (Sp. *esponsales*) *n.* espousal or betrothal ceremonies.
espóngha: (Sp. *esponja*) *n.* sponge; powder puff.
esporádiko: (Sp. *esporádico*) *adj.* sporadic.
espósa: (Sp. *esposa*) *n.* wife. (*asáwa*)
esposas: (Sp.) *n.* handcuffs; manacles.
espóso: (Sp. *esposo*) *n.* husband.
espuélas: (Sp. *espuelas*) *n.* spur.
espúma: (Sp. *espuma*) *n.* foam; lather; spume.
espóngha: (Sp. *esponja*) *n.* sponge.
estabilidád: (Sp. *estabilidad*) *n.* stability.
establesimiénto: (Sp. *establecimiento*) *n.* establishment.
establo: (Sp.) *n.* stable.
estaka: (Sp. *estaca*) *n.* stake; pale.
estakada: (Sp. *estacada*) *n.* stockade.
estádiyo: (Sp. *estadio*) *n.* stadium.
estadísta: (Sp. *estadista*) *n.* statesman.
estadístika: (Sp. *estadística*) *n.* statistics.
estádo: (Sp. *estado*) *n.* state; situation; estate; **Estados Unídos** The United States.
estámbre: (Sp. *estambre*) *n.* yarn, spun thread; stamen (botany).
estámpa: (Sp. *estampa*) *n.* image, dry seal; picture of a saint.
estampíta: (Sp. *estampita*) *n.* holy picture, small religious picture or holy card. (*búlto*)
estandárte: (Sp. *estandarte*) *n.* banner.
estaniadór: (Sp. *estañador*) *n.* welder, solderer; tinsmith.
estánio: (Sp. *estaño*) *n.* tin (used in soldering).
estánte: (Sp. *estante*) *n.* bookshelf, showcase.
estangkádo: (Sp. *estancado*) *adj.* stagnant; checked.
estápa: (Sp. *estafa*) *n.* swindle.
estapadór. *n.* swindler.
estasión: (Sp. *estación*) *n.* station.
estátua: (Sp. *estatua*) *n.* statue. (*búlto*)
éste$_1$: (Sp. *éste*) *n.* east.
éste$_2$: (Sp. *este*: this (used as a hedge)) hedge used in speaking: um.
estebedór: (Sp. *estibador*) *n.* stevedore; longshoreman.
estéla: (Sp. *estela*) *n.* wake of a ship.
esteremenggoles: (*slang*) *n.* woman who continually changes lovers.
esterlína: (Sp. *esterlina*) *adj.* sterling; **libra esterlina** *n.* pound sterling.
estero: (Sp.) *n.* foul ditch; slum.
estéropon: (f. English) *n.* Styrofoam.
estetoskópio: (Sp. *estetoscopio*) *n.* stethoscope.
estibadór: (Sp. *estibador*) *n.* longshoreman, cargo man, stevedore, man who loads and unloads ships.
estílo: (Sp. *estilo*) *n.* style.
estimá(r): (Sp. *estimar*: estimate) *n.* esteem; entertaining visitors; **magestimar** *v.* to take care of; **estimado** *adj.* esteemed, respected; entertained.
estimulánte: (Sp. *estimulante*) *adj.* stimulating, exciting; *n.* stimulant.
estímulo: (Sp. *estímulo*) *n.* stimulus; prompt; encouragement.
estudiyánte: (Sp. *estudiante*) *n.* student.
estúdio: (f. English) *n.* studio.
estoisísmo: (Sp. *estoicismo*) *n.* stoicism.

estokáda: (Sp. *estocada*) *n.* parry and thrust, lunge in fencing.
estóla: (Sp.) *n.* stole (worn by clergy).
estopa: *n.* burlap; stuffing material.
estopádo: (Sp. *estofado*) *n.* stew.
estúpido: (Sp. *estúpido*) *adj.* stupid.
estórbo: var. of *istorbo*: bother, nuisance; hindrance.
estória: (Sp. *historia*) *n.* story.
estoriyadór: (Sp. *historiador*) *n.* historian; story teller.
estútse: (Sp. *estuche*) *n.* case or bag for instruments, usually surgical instruments.
estráda: (Sp. *estrada*) *n.* paved road.
estranghéro: (Sp. *estrangero*) *n.* stranger; foreigner. (*gannaet*)
estratéhia: (Sp. *estrategia*) *n.* strategy. (*síkap*)
estrélya: (Sp. *estrella*) *n.* star; **estrelyado** *n.* fried egg whose yoke is intact.
estrelyádo: (Sp. *estrellado*) *n.* fried egg.
estríbo: (Sp. *estribo*) *n.* spur; stirrup.
estribór: (Sp. *estribor*) *n.* starboard, right side of a ship.
estríkto: (Sp. *estricto*) *adj.* strict.
estrópa: (Sp. *estrofa*) *n.* stanza; verse of a poem.
etat: (*slang*) *n.* feces, stool.
eternidád: (Sp. *eternity*) *n.* eternity.
étika: (Sp. *ética*) *n.* ethics, the principles or science of proper conduct.
etikéta: (Sp. *etiqueta*) *n.* label; ticket indicating price; etiquette.
étikó: (Sp. *ético*) *adj.* ethical, moral.
etimolohía: (Sp. *etimología*) *n.* etymology, an account of the origin and history of a word.
etnak: (*slang*) *n.* sex.
étnikó: (Sp. *étnico*) *adj.* ethnic.
etnólogó: (Sp.) *n.* ethnologist.
etnolohiya: (Sp. *etnología*) *n.* ethnology, science dealing with the origin, customs, beliefs, etc. of different ethnic groups.
eto: *var.* of *heto*: here it is; here.
etsas: (*slang*) *n.* excrement.
etseng: (*slang*) *n.* homosexual male.
etséterá: (Eng.) *n.* et cetera. (*at ibá pa*)
etsos: (*slang*, Sp. *hecho*) *n.* homosexual male.
etsosero: (*slang*) *n.* joker; liar.
eukalipto: (Sp. *eucalipto*) *n.* eucalyptus.
ewan: *v.* I don't know. (*ewan ko*) [see *aywán*]
ewang: *var.* of *iwang*: wiping the anus.

G

ga: *part.* contraction of *bagá*, interrogative particle.
ga: (*reg.*) *pref.* prefix used to express equality in size or shape: **gasantól** as big as a *santól.*
gaán: *n.* lightness in weight; **magaán** *adj.* light (in weight); **gaanán** *v.* to lighten; simplify; **pagaanín** *v.* to lighten the weight of; **magaanán** *v.* to find something light or easy; **magpagaán** *v.* to make easier, facilitate; **kagaanán ng loób** *n.* willingness; readiness; **magaán ang bibíg** *id.* friendly (mouth is light); **magaán ang dugô** *id.* sympathetic (blood is light); **magaán ang kamáy** *id.* green thumb; tender touch; quickness in punishing.
gaanó: *pron.* how much (what quantity); **gaano man** however; **tiggagaanó** how many for each one; **waláng-gaanó** *adj.* rare; thin, not dense.
gabán: (Sp.) *n.* overcoat.
gabarero: (Sp. *gabarrero*) *n.* barge man.
gabáy: *n.* handrail, banisters; **gabáy ng magulang** *id.* main support of parents in their old age (rail of parents).
gabi: *n.* taro.
gabí: *n.* night; evening; **kagabí** *adv.* last night; **kinágabihán** *adv.* on that night; **gabí-gabí** *adv.* nightly, every night; **hatinggabí** *n.* midnight; **gumabí** *v.* to fall (said of the night); **magabihán** *v.* to be overtaken by the night; **magpakagabí** *v.* to wait until late at night; **magpagabí** *v.* to wait until evening; **panggabi** *adj.* for the evening.
gabinete: (Sp.) *n.* cabinet.
gabo: (*slang*) *n.* gun; police; *v.* shoot.
gabók: *n.* settled dust.
gabos: (*slang*) *adj.* high on drugs.
gabot: **gabutin** *v.* to pull, uproot.

gabya: (Sp. *gavia*) *n.* main topsail.
gakgák: *n.* babbling.
Gaddang: *n.* ethnic group and language from North Central Luzon.
gadgád: *adj.* shelled, threshed; **gadgaran** *n.* grater.
gadyá: (*obs.*) *n.* elephant.
gaga- *pref.* as little as, as small as.
gaga: (*fem.*) *adj.* stupid. [See *gago*]
gagá: **gaghán** *v.* to rape; **gagahín** *v.* to usurp.
gagad: *n.* imitation, mimic.
gagambá: *n.* spider.
gagaong: *n.* convex-lined theraponid fish.
gagapang: *n.* mullet fish.
gago: *adj.* stammering; stupid.
gahak: *n.* long rip, forceful rip.
gahamán: *adj.* threatening.
gahang: *n.* long crack, rip.
gahasà: *adj.* impetuous, rash; **gumahasà, gahasain** *v.* to assault; **kagahasaan** *n.* violence; **paggahasà** *n.* assault (crime).
gahî: *adj.* slightly withered.
gahís: *adj.* subdued, overpowered; **gahisín** *v.* to overpower, overcome; rape; **panggagahís** *n.* violation; use of force; rape.
gahò: (Sp. *gajo*) *n.* division of an orange.
gahól: *adj.* pressed for time.
gala: *adj.* gala.
galà: **paggagalâ** *n.* travelling, roving; *adj.* migrant; **gumalà** *v.* to rove, wander; stray; roam; **pagalà** *n.* wanderer; circular (letter); *adj.* stray; **palagalâ** *adj.* fond of wandering or traveling.
galabók: *n.* dust, fine powder.
galák: *n.* joy; **galakín** *v.* to cheer up someone; **magalák** *v.* to rejoice; **kagalakán** *n.* joy.
galakgák: *n.* loud laughter.
galagalá: *n.* caulker, tar plaster.
galatán: *n.* bamboo basket.
galamáy: *n.* tentacle; extensions; hands and feet; **magalamáy** *adj.* with many appendages.
galamgám: *n.* ticklish feeling.
galán: (Sp.) *n.* ladies' man; leading man in a performance.
galante: (Sp.) *adj.* gallant.
galantirya: (Sp. *galantería*) *n.* gallantry.
galang: *n.* reverence; respect, honor; homage; **kagalangan** *n.* courtesy; **kagalang-galang** *adj.* honorable, respectable; **gumalang** *v.* to respect; **igalang** *v.* to honor, respect; **magalang** *adj.* respectful; **magalang** *adj.* respectful, well-mannered; **paggalang** *n.* esteem, honor; **pagkakágálang-galang** *n.* respectability; **pagkawaláng-galang** *n.* lack of respect; profanity.
galáng: *n.* bracelet; **nakagaláng** *adj.* wearing a bracelet.
galanggalangán: *n.* wrist.
galapóng: *n.* rice flour.
galas: *n.* roughness, harshness.
galasgás: **magalasgás** *adj.* rough.
galauran: *n.* rowboat.
galáw: *n.* movement; **igaláw** *v.* to move; **magaláw** *adj.* constantly moving; **mágaláw** *v.* to be moved; **gumaláw**, **galawín** *v.* to move; disturb; displace; **pagalawín** *v.* to move, put into motion; **di-magágaláw** *adj.* immovable.
galawád: *n.* armful; stretching or swinging of the arms.
galawgáw: *n.* ticklish feeling; restlessness; **galawgawín** *v.* to tickle; go over a place extensively.
galaygáy: *n.* going from one to another (houses).
galbanisado: (Sp. *galvanizado*) *adj.* galvanized.
galbót: *n.* uprooting, pulling.
galema: (*slang*) *n.* traitor.
galera: (Sp.) *n.* galley.
galgál: *adj.* foolish, silly.
galing: *v.* to come from; derive; result; **galing sa ibá** *adj.* second hand; **pinanggalingan** *n.* cause, source; root; **saán galing** from where.
galíng1: *n.* merit, perfection; utility; benefit; **kágalingan** *n.* welfare; **kagalingán** *n.* excellence, goodness; **kágalíng-galingan** *adj.* the very best; **galingán** *v.* to do with great skill; **galingín** *v.* to be lucky; **magalíng** *adj.* good, expert; **magalingín** *v.* to approve; **gumalíng** *v.* to improve; heal; get better; **ipagmagalíng** *v.* to boast about; **makagalíng** *v.* to cure; **magmagalíng** *v.* to boast,

brag; **magpakagalíng** *v.* to try to improve; **mapagmagalíng** *adj.* proud; conceited; **nápakagalíng** *adj.* fine, excellent, very good; first class; **pagmamagalíng** *n.* pride; **pagpapagalíng** *n.* making something better, curing; convalescence; **magalíng ang kamáy** *adj.* skilled.

galíng₂: *n.* amulet.

galís: *n.* sarna infection.

galit: *n.* anger; **galitin** *v.* to provoke, enrage, make angry; **galít** *adj.* angry, mad; **makagalit** *v.* to irritate; **kagalitan** *v.* to scold; rebuke; be angry with; **kagalit-galit, nakagágálit** *adj.* causing anger; **magagalitín** *adj.* hot headed; **magkánggagalit** *v.* to become furious; **maggalít-galitan** *v.* to pretend to be angry; **pagalít** *adj.* angrily, **pagkamagagalitín** *n.* irritability; **pagpapagalit** *n.* provocation; **pampagalit** *n.* provocation.

galmós: *n.* scratch, wound on skin.

galón: (Sp.) *n.* gallon; chevron.

galong: *n.* earthen jar.

galope: (Sp.) *n.* gallop.

galos: *n.* slight scratch.

galót: *adj.* tattered; crumpled.

galpóng: *n.* rice flour.

galukgók: *n.* trembling; rumbling noise of a hungry stomach.

galugad: *n.* exploration; **galugarin** *v.* to explore.

galunggóng: *n.* big-bodied round scad fish.

galyetas: (Sp. *galleta*) *n.* cookie.

gamas: *n.* weeding of plants; **gamasán** *v.* to weed.

gamay: *adj.* accustomed to, used to.

gambúgambá: *n.* spider. (*gagambá*)

gambalà: **gambalain** *v.* to disturb; delay; interrupt now and then.

gamból: *adj.* badly bruised; **gambulín** *v.* to beat up, maul; shake up.

gamít: *n.* use; utilization; *adj.* used; **gamitin** *v.* to use, apply; **pagkakagamit** *n.* usage.

gamlay: *n.* power of movement; **makagamláy** *v.* to be able to move.

gamót: *n.* cure; medicine; drug; **magpagamót** *v.* to consult a doctor; **gumamót, gamutín** *v.* to cure, treat. **maggamót** *v.* to treat oneself; **manggagamót** *n.* doctor; **manggamót** *v.* to practice medicine; **igamót** *v.* to administer a drug to; **ipaggamót** *v.* to have a sickness cured; **kagamután** *n.* cure, remedy; **panggamót** *adj.* medicinal; *n.* medicine. **panggágamót** *n.* practice of medicine; **págamutan** *n.* clinic; infirmary; **gamót na pampasiglá** *n.* dope; **gamót na pampadumí** *n.* laxative; **gamót na pampaantók** *n.* narcotic; sleeping pill.

gampán: (rt. *ganáp*) *n.* fulfilling of one's duty; assuming one's role. **gámpanan** *n.* mutual fulfillment of duties (in a contract). **gampanán** *v.* to fulfill; play the role of; perform the duty of; keep a promise.

gamugamó: *n.* small moth.

gamusa: (Sp. *gamuza*) *n.* chamois; suede.

gana: (Sp.) *n.* appetite; enthusiasm, interest; earnings, pay, wages; functioning of a machine; profit; gain; **pampagana** *n.* appetizer; **waláng-kagana-gana** *adj.* not interested at all.

ganado: (Sp.) *n.* livestock, cattle; *adj.* interested; enthusiastic; with a good appetite; **ganadero** *n.* rancher.

ganadór: (Sp.) *n.* breeding bull.

ganán: *n.* share, portion, party.

ganansiya: (Sp. *ganancia*) *n.* profit, gain

ganáp: *adj.* complete; perfect; total; thorough; *adv.* fully, completely, entirely; **kaganapan** *n.* fulfillment; **ganapín** *v.* to fulfill; perform; carry out, accomplish; **tagapagpaganáp** *adj.* executive. [See also *gampán*]

gandá: *n.* beauty; loveliness; **kagandahan** *n.* beauty; **magandá** *adj.* beautiful; **gandahán** *v.* to beautify; **gumandá** *v.* to become beautiful; **magandahán** *v.* to be attracted (by beauty); **magandahín** *v.* to consider beautiful; **pagandá** *n.* something used to beautify; **pagandahín** *v.* to beautify; **págandahan** *n.* beauty contest.

ganháw: *adj.* watery.

ganid: *n.* brute, beast; stingy person.

ganirí: *adj.* like this.

ganít: **maganít** *adj.* tough, hard; stiff.

ganitó: *adj., adv.* like this; in this manner; **sa ganitó** thus, to this degree.

ganoón: *adv.* in that way, like that; such.
ganot: **ganutin** *v.* to pull out, uproot; cut off (hair).
gansâ: (Sp.) *n.* goose.
gansál: *adj.* uneven, odd.
gansilyo: (Sp. *ganchillo*) *n.* crochet.
ganso: (Sp. *gancho*) *n.* hook.
gansua: (Sp. *ganzua*) *n.* skeleton key.
ganta: *n.* unit of dry measure equivalent to 3 liters.
gantáy: (*slang*) *n.* flirt.
gantí: *n.* return, requital; reward; retribution; **gantihan** *n.* reciprocity; **gantihán** *v.* to reward; make amends; **gantihín** *v.* to render; repay; pay back; return; **gantimpagál** *n.* repayment, recompense; **gumantí** *v.* to get even with; **gantim-parusa** *n.* reprisal.
gantimpalà: *n.* reward; compensation; premium.
gantsilyo: *var. of gansilyo*: crochet.
gantso: *var. of ganso*: hook.
ganyák: **ganyakín** *v.* to induce to do; **maganyák** *adj.* to be induced.
ganyán: *adv.* like that, such, in that case.
gangkuling: *n.* dusky chromis fish.
gangga-: (*pl. of ga*) as big as; **ganggákalingkingan** *adj.* as big as the small finger; **gangganitó** as big as these.
gangga: (Sp. *ganga*) *n.* bargain.
ganggrena: (Sp. *gangrena*) *n.* gangrene.
gaod: *n.* oar; **gauran** *v.* to row.
gapak: *n.* part of a tree where a branch was broken off; **gapák** *adj.* broken off.
gapang: *n.* act of crawling; (*slang*) rape; **gumapang** *v.* to crawl, creep; **gágapang na parang ahas** *id.* will lead a miserable life (will crawl like a snake); **igagapang** *id.* to assiduously support (crawl for someone).
gapas₁: (Sp. *gafas*) *n.* goggles.
gapas₂: *n.* cutting of grass or rice stalks; **gapasin** *v.* to mow; reap; **panggapas** *n.* mower.
gapì: *n.* act of overwhelming; **gapiin** *v.* to overwhelm; overpower.
gapô: *adj.* decayed, rotten.
gapók: *adj.* rotten inside; fragile.
gapóng: *adj.* amputated.
gapos: *n.* manacle; **igapos** *v.* to bind, tie up.
garà: **magarà** *adj.* dashing, sharp, elegant; **garaan** *v.* to make elegant.
garahe: (Sp. *garaje*) *n.* garage.
garagál: *n.* gargling sound.
garantíya: (Sp. *garantía*) *n.* guarantee; collateral; warrant.
garantisado: (Sp. *garantizado*) *adj.* guaranteed.
garapa: (Sp. *garrafa*) *n.* decanter, jar.
garapál: (Sp. *garrafal*) *adj.* openly shameless.
garapata: (Sp.) *n.* tick.
garapetse: (Sp. *garrapeche*) *n.* golden jack fish.
garapinyera: (Sp. *garapiñera*) *n.* ice-cream freezer.
garapita: (Sp.) *n.* small bottle.
garapito: (Sp. *garafito*) *n.* tick, dog lice.
garapón: (Sp. *garrafón*) *n.* large jar.
garáy: *n.* kind of ancient sailboat.
garbansos: (Sp. *garbanzo*) *n.* chickpea, garbanzo bean.
garbo: (Sp.) **magarbo** *adj.* graceful, elegant.
gargantilya: (Sp. *gargantilla*) *n.* choker.
garil: *n.* speech defect. **garíl** *adj.* defective in pronunciation.
garing: *n.* ivory. **garingan** *n.* variety of rice of poor quality.
gárisón: (Eng.) *n.* garrison.
garol: *n.* sexual erection; catch in a padlock.
garote: (Sp. *garrote*) *n.* club, cudgel.
garsa: (Sp. *garza*) *n.* heron.
garungin: *n.* milkfish fingerling.
garupa: *n.* marbled grouper fish; grand slam.
gasa: (Sp.) *n.* gauze; arm band; mantle.
gasà: *n.* reprimand, scolding.
gasák: *adj.* pruned; ripped, torn.
gasang: *n.* small chip, small pieces of stone; undertow; surf.
gasera: *n.* gas lamp; **gáserahán** *n.* gas lamp.
gaseta: (Sp. *gazeta*) *n.* gazette.
gasgás: *n.* abrasion; **gasgasín** *v.* to scratch; **magasgás** *adj.* chafed, sore by rubbing; worn out through friction; **gasgás ang bulsá** *id.* spent heavily (pocket is scratched).
gasino: *adj.* not much; *pron.* somebody.
gasláw: *n.* vulgarity; (*slang*) flirt; **magasláw**

adj. rough, harsh, rude.

gasmaytu: (*slang*, cf. *tumigás*) *n.* erect penis.

gasó: *n.* restlessness; wildness; **magasó** *adj.* restless.

gasolina: (Sp.) *n.* gasoline.

gaspáng: *n.* coarseness; **gumaspáng** *v.* to become rough, coarse; **magaspáng** *adj.* rough, coarse; vulgar.

gastado: (Sp.) *adj.* worn out.

gastadór: (Sp.) *n.* spendthrift.

gastá: (Sp.) **gastahán** *v.* to spend on; **gumastá** *v.* to spend money.

gastos: (Sp.) *n.* expenses; cost.

gatâ: *n.* coconut milk; **ginataan** *n.* dish made from coconut milk; **gataán** *v.* to extract coconut milk.

gatang: *n.* chupa (.37 liter).

gatas: *n.* milk; **gatasan** *v.* to milk; **may gatas pa sa labì** *id.* still young (still has milk on the lips).

gatas-gatas: *n.* Australian asthma weed.

gatgát: *n.* groove; indentation; **gatgatán** *v.* to indent, make notches in.

gatlâ: *n.* mark, notch.

gatláng: *n.* mark, notch.

gato: (Sp.) *n.* vise, lifting jack.

gatô: *adj.* rotten; weakened structurally.

gatod: **magatod** *adj.* lascivious; luxury-loving; overdressed.

gatól: *n.* sudden stop; **pagatúl-gatól** *adv.* in a stammering way.

gatong: *n.* fuel.

gatós: *n.* one billion.

gaud-gaod: *n.* porgy fish.

gawâ: *n.* act, action; work; turn, deed; product; play; task, duty; *adj.* made, manufactured; due to; **kagagawán** *n.* act, deed; responsibility for an undesirable act; **gáwáin** *n.* assignment, work assigned, employment; activity; enterprise; undertaking; **gawín** *v.* to do, perform; adapt; make; **gáwáan** *n.* workshop; simultaneous working; **gaw(a)án** *v.* to do for; perform an act for; make in; **gumawâ** *v.* to make, do; produce; form; **igawâ** *v.* to make something for someone; **ipagawâ** *v.* to have done; assign; **isagawâ** *v.* to push, urge; effect; put into effect; **makagawâ** *v.* to be able to do; **magágawâ** *adj.* able to be done; available; accessible; **magawâ** *v.* to be able to do; *adj.* doable; **maggawâ** *v.* to make, manufacture; **magsagawâ** *v.* to carry out; perpetrate; prosecute; **maisagawâ** *v.* to be able to carry out, implement; **manggagawà** *n.* worker, laborer; **maygawâ** *n.* owner; actor, doer; author; **págawaan** *n.* factory; **pagkakágawâ** *n.* workmanship; **pagsasagawâ** *n.* implementation; **panggawâ** *n.* tool, apparatus; **tagagawâ** *n.* doer; workman; **waláng-gawâ** *adj.* unemployed, idle; leisure; **gawáng-kamáy** *adj.* handmade; **gawáng-aso** *n.* shameful act; **di-magágawâ** *adj.* impossible; **di-maisásagawâ** *adj.* impractical; **gawá-gawâ lamang** not real, made up, fictitious; **may-kagagawán** *adj.* responsible.

gawak: *n.* ripping, tearing; wasting of funds.

gawad: *n.* award; gift; prize; **kagawad** *n.* fellow, member; **gawaran** *v.* to award, bestow; declare; **igawad** *v.* to give, grant, bestow.

gaway: *n.* witchcraft; **gawayin** *v.* to bewitch; **manggagaway** *n.* witch.

gawgáw: (Ch.) *n.* starch.

gawì, gawî[1]: custom, habit; tendency; **gawî** *adj.* accustomed to; **kagawian** *n.* mannerism.

gawì[2]: *n.* direction. **igawì** *v.* to move something in a certain direction.

gawín: (*rt.* *gawâ*) *v.* to do; make.

gaya: *n.* imitation; *adj.* like, similar; **kagaya** *adj.* similar; **gayahan** *v.* to copy; **paggaya** *n.* imitation; **gaya-gaya puto maya** *exp.* saying which ridicules copycats.

gayák: *n.* decoration; trimmings; intention; **gayák** *adj.* prepared; dressed up; ornate.

gayad: *n.* dragging a dress on the floor.

gayán: *adv.* like that, in that way.

gayáng: *n.* spear.

gayarí: *adv.* in this way, like this.

gayas: *n.* lace.

gayás: *n.* sandy soil.

gaygáy: *n.* travelling around.

gayón: *pron.* such, like that; **kung gayón** then, therefore, in that case; **gayón din namán**

vice-versa; **gayón man** however, nevertheless; **sa gayón** thereby; **gayón palá** so that's it; **gayundín** *adv.* likewise, in the same way; **pagkakágayón** *n.* manner of becoming that way; **pagkagayón** *n.* being that way.

gayót: **magayót** *adj.* tough to the bite.

gayuma: *n.* love charm, love potion; allurement; **magayuma** *v.* to be charmed; **gayumaan** *v.* to attract someone; use a love potion on.

gera: (Sp. *guerra*) *n.* war.

gerero: (Sp. *guerrero*) *n.* warrior.

gerilya: (Sp. *guerilla*) *n.* guerilla fighter.

Giangan: *n.* ethnic group and language from Davao del Sur, Mindanao.

gibâ: *adj.* demolished.

gibalang: (*slang*) *adj.* beaten up.

gibang: *n.* swaying sideways.

gibay: *n.* balancing.

gibík: *n.* aid; **gibikán** *v.* to come to the aid of.

gikgík: *n.* giggle; grunting of young pigs.

giggî: (Pil.) *n.* Philippine squirrel.

gigì: *n.* moving slow; **magigì** *adj.* slow-acting.

gigí: *adj.* prone to giggle.

gigil: *n.* trembling; gritting of the teeth.

gigintô: *n.* gold bug; iron pyrite.

gihà: *n.* division in fruits (oranges).

gihò: *n.* kind of tree.

giík: *n.* threshing of grain; **panggiík** *n.* thresher.

giít: *n.* assertion, insistence; **igiít** *v.* to insist, assert; **gumiít** *v.* to insist; persist; force one's way through a ground.

gilà: *n.* motion of boats riding waves.

gilagid: *n.* gum of the teeth.

gilagiran: *n.* support for flooring.

gilalas: *n.* amazement, astonishment.

gilas: *n.* elegance, gallantry; angry stare.

gilê: *n.* sergeant fish.

gilgíl: *n.* cutting while applying pressure.

gilí: *n.* rolling with the hand.

gilid: *n.* edge, border; margin; **kagiliran** *n.* surroundings, environment; horizon; **giliran** *n.* edge, border; **gumilid** *v.* to approach the edge; take a boat to shore; **tagilid** *n.* tilt, slant; **tagilíd** *adj.* tilted, slanted, crooked; **tagiliran** *n.* side; **tumagilid** *v.* to lean to one side; slant; tilt; **pagilid** *n.* border, edge; **patagilíd** *adv.* sideways; **nakatagilid** *adj.* askew; tilted; **buóng gilid** *n.* perimeter; **mangilid ang luhà** *v.* to be about to tear up (cry).

giling: *n.* grinding, milling; **gilingán** *n.* grinding machine; mill; **giniling** *n.* ground meat; ground substances.

gilit: *n.* seaweed, algae; moss.

gilít: *n.* cut, incision; **gilitan** *v.* to cut, slice, incise; **panggilít** *n.* cutting tool.

giliw: *n.* darling; affection; **kagiliwan** *n.* fondness, affection; **giníglíliw** *adj.* beloved; **giliwin** *v.* to act affectionately towards; be fond of; **gumiliw** *v.* to love; **magkágiliwán** *v.* to be fond of each other; **magiliw** *adj.* affectionate, loving; friendly; **pagkamagiliw** *n.* friendliness, cordiality.

gimbál: *n.* clatter.

gimbuló: *n.* secret envy.

Ginang: *n.* Mrs., appellation for a married woman; matron. [Abbreviated as *Gng.*]

gináw: *n.* cold, chill; **maginaw** *adj.* cold, chilly; **ginawín** *v.* to chill.

gindá: *n.* act of going to a certain place; change of course.

gindáy: *n.* swaying, wobbling.

ginhawa: *n.* comfort, ease; wealth; convenience; **maginhawa** *adj.* comfortable; convenient; **makaginhawa** *v.* to comfort, relieve; ease; **nakagíginhawa** *adj.* relieving.

gining: *n.* young woman.

ginip: *see panaginip.*

Ginoó: *n.* Mister; sir; **kaginoohan** *n.* men (collectively); gentlemanliness; **máginoó** *n.* gentleman; **máginoohín** *adj.* gentlemanly; **pagkamáginoó** *n.* manliness; gentlemanliness; sportsmanship; dignity.

ginsá: **kaginsá-ginsá** *adj.* all at once; **di-kaginsá-ginsá** *adv.* all of a sudden, unexpectedly.

gintíng: *adj.* unlike, unequal (threads).

gintô: *n.* gold, wealth; **pandáy-gintô** *n.* goldsmith; **ginintuáng pusò** *id.* sympathetic, kind-hearted (golden heart). **gintuín** *v.* to gild, make with gold; *adj.* prosperous, abundant.

gintsám: (Ch. *gín câm*: silver cut) *n.* goldsmith's chisel.

gingging: (Ch.) *n.* shrub with sweet fleshy fruit.

gipalpál: *n.* thick, slimy dirt.

gipít: *adj.* hard, severe; pressed for time; in difficult circumstances; **gipitín, gumipít** *v.* to put someone in a difficult situation, cause a crisis; **ikagipít** *v.* to be the reason for a difficulty; **kagípitán** *n.* crisis; emergency. **kagipitán** *n.* lack of room; lack of time; **magipít** *v.* to be in difficulty; suffer a crisis; **panahón ng kagípitan** *n.* crisis.

gipô: *adj.* decayed; broken off (from decay).

gipós: *adj.* reduced to a stub (cigars).

gipuspós: *adj.* low-spirited.

giray: *n.* staggering, tottering.

girì: *n.* strutting around; **gumirì** *v.* to strut.

girimpulá: *n.* weathercock, weathervane.

gisá: (Sp. *guisar*) **igisa** *v.* to sauté, stir fry; **igisá sa sariling mantikà** *id.* to invite someone and make them pay their own way (to fry in one's own lard).

gisado: (Sp. *guisado*) *adj.* sautéed, stir fried.

gisantes: (Sp. *guisante*) *n.* pea.

gisap: *n.* bristling.

gisaw: *n.* abatement of fever; sore in the mouth caused by fever.

gisì: *n.* tear in cloth; **gisiin** *v.* to tear.

gising: *n.* waking up from sleep; **gisíng** *adj.* awake; **gumising** *v.* to wake up.

gisok: *n.* grain; vein.

gitáng: *n.* crack in metal.

gitara: (Sp. *guitarra*) *n.* guitar.

gitatà: *n.* wet, sticky mud.

gitaw: *n.* appearance; coming into view.

gitgít₁: *n.* welt; notch; gnashing of teeth; **gitgitán** *v.* to make a welt or notch on.

gitgít₂: *n.* hustling, jostling; **gumitgít** *v.* to hustle, elbow one's way through a crowd.

gitî: *n.* breaking out of sweat; **gumitî** *v.* to break out in a sweat; exude.

gitil: *n.* gritting of the teeth.

giting: *n.* heroism; **magiting** *adj.* heroic, brave.

gitlá: *n.* scare, fright.

gitlapì: *n.* infix.

gitlíng: *n.* hyphen.

gitnâ: *n.* center, middle; **panggitnâ** *adj.* middle; **sa gitnâ ng** among, amid; **gitnaín** *v.* to surround.

giwà: *n.* red owl.

giwang: *n.* wobbling.

giya: (Sp. *guía*) *n.* guide.

giyagis: *adj.* afflicted by; restless.

giyán: (Ch.) *n.* developed fondness or propensity for an activity.

giyera: (Sp. *guerra*) *n.* war; **giyera patanì** *n.* free for all fight.

giyón: (Sp. *guión*) *n.* hyphen; dash; (*mil.*) flag bearer; pennant.

glab: (Eng.) *n.* glove.

gladyola: (Sp. *gladiola*) *n.* gladiolus.

glándula: (Sp.) *n.* gland.

glasé: (Sp.) *n.* glacé silk.

glilserina: (Sp. *glicerina*) *n.* glycerin.

globo: (Sp.) *n.* globe, sphere.

gloripiká: (Sp. *glorificar*) **gloripikahín** *v.* to glorify. **gloripikasyón** *n.* glorification.

glorya: (Sp. *gloria*) *n.* glory; fame, honor; (*fig.*) paradise, heaven.

gloryeta: (Sp. *glorieta*) *n.* arbor; bandstand.

gloryoso: (Sp. *glorioso*) *adj.* glorious.

glosaryo: (Sp. *glosario*) *n.* glossary.

glukosa: (Sp. *glucosa*) *n.* glucose.

Gng.: abbreviation of *Ginang*: Mrs.

gob.: abbreviation of *Gobernador*: Governor.

gobyerno: (Sp. *gobierno*) *n.* government.

gol: (Eng.) *n.* goal (in games).

golgoreta: *n.* narrow-necked earthen pitcher.

golondrina: (Sp.) *n.* swallow; swallow-shaped kite.

golp: (Eng.) golf.

golpe: (Sp.) *n.* hit, stroke; **golpe-de-estado** *n.* coup-d'état; **golpe-de-gulat** *n.* impressive show of force or ability from the start. **gulpihín** *v.* to hit, whip.

golpo: (Sp. *golfo*) *n.* gulf.

goma: (Sp. *goma*) *n.* rubber; eraser; condom; **gomang pandilíg** *n.* rubber hose. **gomahan** *n.* rubber plantation; *v.* to provide with rubber.

gonorea: (Sp.) *n.* gonorrhea.

gonggóng: *n.* grunt fish (*Theraponidae*).

gora: (Sp. *gorra*) *n.* cap.

gorilya: (Sp. *gorila*) *n.* gorilla.
goryon: (Sp. *gorrión*) *n.* sparrow; kind of small kite.
gota: (Sp.) *n.* drop (of medicine); gout.
gotera: (Sp.) *n.* dropper, pipette.
gótikó: (Sp. *gótico*) *adj.* Gothic.
goto: (Ch. *gu tô* ox stomach) *n.* ox tripe, rice mixed with tripe.
goyò: (*slang*) *n.* cheating; swindling. ~ **lang** just a joke.
graba: (Sp. *grava*) *n.* gravel.
grabado: (Sp.) *n.* engraving, cut.
grabadór: (Sp.) *n.* engraver.
grabadora: (Sp.) *n.* tape recorder.
grabadura: (Sp.) *n.* engraving.
grabe: (Sp. *grave*) *adj.* serious; extreme; exceptional.
grabedád: (Sp. *gravedad*) *n.* seriousness, gravity.
grado: (Sp.) *n.* grade, degree, scale.
gradwado: (Sp. *graduado*) *adj.* graduated.
granada: (Sp.) *n.* pomegranate; hand grenade.
granadero: (Sp.) *n.* grenadier.
granadilya: (Sp. *granadilla*) *n.* passion flower.
granate: (Sp.) *n.* garnet.
granitó: (Sp.) *n.* small pimple.
grano: (Sp.) *n.* grain, cereal.
grasa: (Sp.) *n.* grease; soft animal fat.
grasya: (Sp. *gracia*) *n.* grace.
gratis: (Sp.) *adj.* free, gratis.
greta: (*slang*) *n.* marijuana.
Griyego: (Sp. *griego*) *n.* Greek.
gripe: (Sp.) *n.* influenza, grippe.
gripo: (Sp. *grifo*) *n.* faucet; (*coll.*) artesian well; **gripuhan** *v.* (*coll.*) to stab.
gris: (Sp.) *n.* gray.
grua: (Sp.) *n.* crane (machine for lifting).
grupo: (Sp.) *n.* group.
gruta: (Sp.) *n.* grotto.
guantes: (Sp.) *n.* gloves.
guáng: *adj.* hollow.
guapo: (Sp.) *adj.* good looking, handsome. [Variants: *guaping, guapito*]
guayabano: (Sp. *guanabano*) *n.* soursop.
gubat: *n.* forest; jungle; (*slang*) pubic hair; **tanod-gubat** *n.* forest ranger; **saanmáng gubat ay may ahas** *id.* there is always a bad one in the group.
gukgók: *n.* grunt.
gugò: *n.* large tree whose bark is made into shampoo; **guguan** *v.* to shampoo the hair.
gugol: *n.* expense; **gugulan** *v.* to spend.
guhám: *n.* skin eruption, rash.
guhit: *n.* line; stripe, mark; **guhitan** *v.* to draw lines on; **salangguhit** *n.* underline; **guhit ng palad** *n.* fate, destiny; **iguhit sa noó** *id.* to remember (draw a line on the forehead); **i-guhit sa tubig** *id.* to not consider, not count (draw a line on the water).
guhít: (*slang*) *n.* 100 grams of marijuana.
guhò: *n.* collapse; ruins; landslide; **gumuhò** *v.* to cave in, crumble.
gulaman: *n.* seaweed gelatin.
gulanít: *adj.* in rags, threadbare.
gulantáng: *n.* startled state; **gulantangín** *v.* to startle.
gulang: *n.* age; **magulang** *n.* parent; *adj.* mature; (*fig.*) cunning, tricky; **gulangan** *v.* to take advantage of an inexperienced person; **may-gulang** *adj.* adult.
gulapay: *n.* labored movement, weakness; **di-makagulapay** *adj.* hardly able to move.
gulat: *n.* shock, surprise; **kagulat-gulat** *adj.* startling, amazing; **gulát** *adj.* scared, frightened, shocked; **gulatin** *v.* to scare, frighten; **parang nágulat sa kulóg** *id.* absent-minded.
guláw: **maguláw** *adj.* rough, turbulent.
gulay: *n.* vegetable; (*fig.*) weak person; **gulayan** *n.* vegetable garden; **parang gulay ang katawán** *id.* feeble.
gulayláy: *n.* rest, relaxation.
gulgól: *n.* by-products.
gulilat: *n.* state of fright.
gulis: *n.* claw mark.
gulitî: *n.* sty on the eyelid.
gulό: *n.* tumult, commotion; panic; riot; **maguló** *adj.* confused, muddled; disorderly; complex; involved; **manggugúlo** *n.* trouble maker; **pangguló** *n.* molestation.
gulô: *n.* amulet.
gulok: *n.* bolo.
gulód: *n.* hilltop.
gulong: *n.* roll, rolling; **igulong** *v.* to cause something to roll.

gulóng: *n.* wheel.
gulonggulungan: *n.* windpipe.
gulót: *adj.* ripped, ragged.
gulpi: *var. of golpe*: hit, strike.
gulugód: *n.* spine, spinal column. **waláng-gulugód** *id.* spineless, weak character.
gulumihan: **kagulumihan** *n.* baffled state of mind.
gulunggulungan: *n.* Adam's apple; larynx.
gulyabaw: *n.* thick-lipped grunt fish.
gulyasan: *n.* striped tuna fish.
gumaka: *n.* species of small palm.
gumamela: (Sp.) *n.* hibiscus.
gumì: *n.* beard; kind of weed.
gumok: *n.* turning around; moving to and fro.
gumon: *n.* wallowing; **gumúng-gumón** *adj.* addicted; **gumumon** *v.* to wallow.
gunaguná: *n.* enjoyment.
gunamgunam: *n.* reflection, meditation.
gunaw: *n.* deluge.
guníguní: *n.* feeling, presentiment; illusion.
gunitâ: *n.* memory, recollection; **magunitâ** *v.* to remember; **ipagunitâ** *v.* to remind. **taga-pagpagunitâ** *n.* souvenir.
gunó: *n.* silversides fish.
gunók: *var. of gunó*: silversides fish.
guntíng: *n.* scissors.
gunggóng: (Ch.) *adj.* stupid; gruntfish.
gupiling: (*lit.*) *n.* light but restful sleep.
gupilpil: *n.* pressing down something to make it thinner.
gupít: *n.* haircut; **gupitan** *n.* barbershop.
gupò: *n.* ruin, ruins; **gupô** *adj.* shattered, ruined; **iginupò ng sariling bigát** *id.* lost one's pride (subdued by one's own weight).
gura: (Sp. *gorra*) *n.* crested wild pigeon.
gurami: *n.* species of fresh-water fish.
guráng: (*slang*) *adj.* old, elder; forgetful.
gurdoy: (*slang*) *adj.* out of fashion.
gurlís: *n.* light scratch.
gurò: *n.* teacher, instructor.
guryón: (Sp. *gorrión*) *n.* small kite.
gusád: *n.* clearing ground by cutting weeds.
gusalì: *n.* building; structure.
gusanilyo: (Sp. *gusanillo*) *n.* small worm; twist-stitch; auger bit; spring of a watch.
gusano: (Sp.) *n.* worm; small winding spring in clocks.
gusgós: *adj.* in rags.
gusì: (Ch.) *n.* large vase.
gusilaw: *n.* eye shade, visor.
gusót: *n.* tangle; difficulty; *adj.* wrinkled, crumpled; confused; unkempt; **gusutín** *v.* to rumple; make uneven.
gusto: (Sp.) *n.* likes, preference; *v.* to like; want. **gustuhín** *v.* to will; **magustuhán** *v.* to care for, like.
gutáy: *adj.* torn to pieces; shredded.
gutgót: *adj.* torn to pieces.
gutingtíng: *adj.* fastidious.
gutláy: *n.* strip of paper.
gutlî: *n.* indentation, nick.
gutól: *n.* cutting off with the fingernails.
gutom: *n.* hunger; **gutom** *adj.* hungry; **gutumin** *v.* to starve; **paggutom** *n.* starvation.
guwano: (Sp. *guano*) *n.* guano.
guwantes: (Sp. *guante*) *n.* glove.
guwáng: *n.* hollow; crevice.
guwapo: (Sp. *guapo*) *adj.* handsome.
guwaratsa: (Sp. *guaracha*) *n.* Spanish clog dance.
guwardakosta: (Sp. *guardacosta*) *n.* coast-guard.
guwardado: (Sp. *guardado*) *adj.* guarded.
guwardiya: (Sp. *guardia*) *n.* guard, watchman.
guwarnisiyón: (Sp. *guarnición*) *n.* harness.
guyà: (Ch. *gú à*: cow son) *n.* young water buffalo.
guyam: (*Bat.*) *n.* species of small ant.
guyod: *n.* bundle of rattan sticks; herd; throng; thick rope; **taguyod** *n.* united support for a cause.
guyón: *n.* cord, rope; rein.

H

ha?: Interrogative particle.
habà: *n.* length; garfish; **habâ** *adj.* long, elongated; **habaan** *v.* to elongate, prolong; **humabà** *v.* to become long; stretch; **mahabà** *adj.* long; **pahabâ** *adj.* lengthwise, longitudinal; **parihabâ** *adj.* rectangular;

mahabà ang buntót *id.* spoiled child (tail is long); **mahabà ang dilà** *id.* gossiper (tongue is long); **mahabà ang kamáy** *id.* thief (hand is long); **sa hinabá-habà** *adv.* ultimately, in the long run.
habâ: *n.* garfish.
habád: (*slang*) *n.* leaving hastily.
habág: *n.* pity, sorrow; compassion; **kahabagán** *v.* to have pity on; **mahabág** *v.* to feel pity, sorrow for.
habagat: *n.* west or Southwest wind; **habagatán** *n.* west; **hinahabagat** *id.* with a slight ailment (with west wind).
habambuhay: *var.* of *habang-buhay*: lifelong.
habampanahón: *var.* of *habang-panahón*: always, eternally, forever.
habán: *adj.* purple.
Habanés: (Sp. *javanés*) *n.* Javanese.
habang: *conj.* while, during; as long as; **habang daán** along the way; **habang-buhay** *adj.* lifelong; **habang-buháy** *adj.* while alive.
habáng: *adj.* unsymmetrical.
habas: *n.* prudence; discretion; **waláng-habas** *adj.* reckless, careless.
habháb: *n.* dog or pig attack; biting with the lips; unpolished rice; noisy eating.
habi: *n.* weaving pattern; texture of a fabric; **habingan** *n.* loom; **humabi** *v.* to weave; **habi ng dilà** *id.* result of indiscriminate speech (weaving of the tongue).
habì: *interj.* get out of the way; **humabì** *v.* to step aside.
habíd: *n.* entangling obstacle.
habilin: *n.* last will and testament of a dying person; something given for safekeeping; **ihabilin** *v.* to commend, entrust, commit to the care of.
habilóg: *adj.* oval.
habín: *n.* yarn; braid, thread used in nets.
habíng: *adj.* twisted, twined.
habitswelas: (Sp. *habicheulas*) *n.* kidney bean.
hablá: (Sp. *habla*) *n.* accusation, charge; **máhablá** *adj.* accused; **ihablá** *v.* to accuse.
habol: *n.* object of pursuit; postscript; demand; appeal; hurrying; **habulin** *v.* to chase, pursue; **maghabol** *v.* to protest, appeal; **tighaból** *adj.* belated; **paghahabol** *n.* demand, claim; **hináhabol na ng sabón** *id.* dirty (is being chased by soap).
habonera: (Sp. *jabonera*) *n.* soap dish.
habonero: (Sp. *jabonero*) *n.* soap maker.
habonete: (Sp. *jabonete*) *n.* toilet soap.
habong: *n.* annex; temporary shelter.
habsô: *adj.* easily untied.
habubos: *adj.* big and strong.
habyóg: *n.* bending of a branch.
hakà: *n.* idea, supposition; suspicion; **hakain** *v.* to suspect something; suppose.
hakab: (Ch.) *adj.* tight fitting; held on by suction; clinging closely to.
hakbáng: *n.* step, footstep; stride; course; **hakbangán** *v.* to step over; **hakbáng-hakbáng** step by step; **humakbáng** *v.* to step.
hakbót: *n.* sudden pulling or grabbing.
hakdáw: *n.* step, pace.
hakhák: *n.* gobbling.
hakhakan: *n.* species of sugarcane.
haklít: *n.* sudden pull with the mouth.
hakot: *n.* load, quantity; **humakot** *v.* to transport, carry; **tagahakot** *n.* carrier, transporter.
hadhád: *n.* rubbing; **hadhád** *adj.* scraped off, rubbed off.
hadláng: *n.* obstacle, hindrance; **humadláng** *v.* to obstruct, block; prevent, hinder; **paghadláng** *n.* obstruction.
hadlikâ: *n.* nobility; **mahadlikâ, maharlika** *adj.* noble.
hadyi: *n.* royalty; Muslim that has made a pilgrimage to Mecca.
haén: (Sp. *jaen*) *n.* large white grape.
hagabháb: *n.* sound of sharp inhalation.
hagak: *n.* gasp, pant.
hagák: *n.* cackling.
hagakhák: *adj.* coarse (said of the voice).
hagad: *n.* pursuer, traffic policeman; **manghagad, hagarin** *v.* to run after, chase; **paghagad** *n.* pursuit.
hagahál: *adj.* insulting, disrespectful; *n.* outburst of laughter.
hagahás: *n.* raspy breathing.
hagallhál: *n.* loud laughter; sound of waterfall.
hagap: *n.* idea; vague opinion.
hagayháy: *n.* gentle breeze; spreading of grains

under the sun to dry.

hagkán: *n.* kiss; **mahagkán** *v.* to be kissed.

hagkís: *n.* emphasis, stress; hint; stroke of a whip.

hagdán: *n.* ladder, stairs; **hagdanan** *n.* staircase.

hagibis: *n.* rapidity; whizzing sound of fast cars; **humagibís** *v.* to flash by; move fast.

hagikgík: *n.* snicker, suppressed laughter.

hagilap: *n.* groping; **hagilapin** *v.* to grope for; **hagilapin sa alaala** *id.* to exert the effort to try to remember (grope in the memory).

haginít: *n.* cracking sound; swishing sound; **humaginít** *v.* to whine, swish by; whistle; **pahaginitín** *v.* to crack, cause to make a sharp noise.

haging: *n.* buzz, whiz, something heard indistinctly; **mahagingan** *v.* to be heard indistinctly.

hagingchíng: *n.* whizzing sound; howl of the wind.

hagíp: *adj.* within reach; hit by something moving; **mahagíp** *v.* to be hit by something moving; **hagipín** *v.* to seize while passing.

hagis: *n.* throw; cast; **ihagis** *v.* to throw, fling; **paghahagis** *n.* pitching, throwing; **hagisan ng tuwalya** *id.* making the opponent surrender (throw the towel).

hagok: *n.* snore. (*harok, hilik*)

hagod: *n.* rubbing; stroke of a pen; **hagurin** *v.* to massage; **hagód** *adj.* tired in appearance; polished; massaged.

hagot: *adj.* tired in appearance; stripping of abaca palm fibers.

hagpís: *n.* grief, affliction.

hagpós: *n.* gentle rubbing; *adj.* free, loose, slack.

hagudhód: *adj.* finished, exhausted.

haguhap: *n.* groping in the dark.

hagulhól: *n.* loud weeping.

hagunhón: *n.* pushing to the side (to make space); *adj.* pushed to one side.

hagunót: *n.* loud whining, roaring.

hagunoy: *n.* kind of climbing vine.

hagunghóng: *n.* reverberating sound.

hagupít: *n.* lash, whip; **hagupitín** *v.* to whip, flog.

haguták: *n.* sound of feet walking through mud.

haguthót: *n.* swift speed.

hagwáy: **mahagwáy** *adj.* tall and well-proportioned.

hahà: *n.* big rip or tear.

hain: **magpahain** *v.* to set the table.

Hal.: *abbrev.* of *halimbawà*: example.

halà: (*slang*) *n.* dating other men.

halá: *interj.* go ahead; **halá birá** *interj.* inciting exclamation.

halaan: *n.* species of mussel.

halabas: *n.* long, thin bolo.

halabíd: *n.* entangling.

halabók: *adj.* pulverized.

halabós: *n.* slightly cooking shrimps in salty water.

halabót: *var.* of *halbót*: taking out contents of a drawer; drawing a revolver.

halák: *n.* raspy voice.

halakhák: *n.* loud laughter; **maghalakhák** *v.* to laugh loudly.

halagá: *n.* price, cost; charge; value; sum; **mahalagá** *adj.* costly, valuable; important; serious, grave; outstanding; substantial; **halagahán** *v.* to give the price of; assess; **maghalagá** *v.* to appraise, estimate the value of; **bigyáng-halagá** *v.* to attach importance to; **mahalagahín** *v.* to value, treasure, appreciate; **halagáng-gintô** *id.* very costly (gold's cost).

halagap: *n.* matter that forms on the surface of something; **halagapan** *v.* to remove matter from the surface of.

halaghág: *adj.* careless, negligent.

halaháb: *adj.* singed, scorched.

halál: *n.* vote; *adj.* elective; **mahalál** *adj.* to be elected.

halaman: *n.* plant, bush; **maghahalamán** *n.* gardener; **halamanin** *v.* to cultivate plants; **halamanan** *n.* garden.

halambát: *n.* provisional fence.

halang: *n.* barrier, barricade; crossbeam; substitute, alternate; **haláng** *adj.* placed crosswise, transverse; (*slang*) *n.* sinner; **halangan** *v.* to block; substitute for someone; **haláng ang bituka** *id.* cruel, not afraid to die or kill (intestine is inverted).

haláp: *n.* hope.

halapáw: *n.* removing the top layer.

halapót: *n.* money purse.

halas: *n.* scratch on skin from grass.

halatâ: *adj.* obviously; noticeable; apparent, visible; **humalatâ** *v.* to notice, detect; **hálatain** *adj.* noticeable; **halataín** *v.* to take notice of; **ipahalatâ** *v.* to manifest; show; **makáhalatâ** *v.* to be able to notice, perceive; **magpahalatâ** *v.* to attract notice; **máhalatâ** *v.* to notice, detect; **mahalatâ** *v.* to be able to notice, detect; **mapanghalatâ** *adj.* with sharp perception; **nakáhalatâ** *adj.* noticeable, perceptible; **madalíng káhalataán** *adj.* sensitive; easily influenced.

haláw: *n.* digest, excerpt, condensed book; *adj.* condensed, abridged; superficial; **halawín** *v.* to condense; excerpt.

halawán: *adj.* half-gray (hair).

halawháw: *adj.* disorderly.

halay: **humalay** *v.* to insult; **kahalayan** *n.* obscenity, lewdness; **kahalay-halay** *adj.* indecent, obscene; **mahalay** *adj.* immoral, indecent; vile; improper.

halayá: (Sp. *jalea*) *n.* jelly; dessert made from mashed yam.

halayháy: *n.* row, line.

halbós: *adj.* half boiled (usually referring to shrimps).

halbót: *n.* sudden pulling.

halea: (Sp. *jalea*) *n.* jelly.

halgá: (*slang*, f. *halagá*) *adj.* expensive.

hali: *interj.* go ahead; **halika** come here.

halhál: *n.* person who talks too much; person prone to laughing.

halibas: *n.* hurl; **halibasin** *v.* to hurl.

halibhíb: *n.* decorticating.

halibukáy: *n.* nausea; surge of waves.

halibuyak: *n.* diffusion of fragrance.

halík: *n.* kiss; **halikán** *v.* to kiss; **humahalík sa yapak** *id.* worshipping (kissing the footsteps).

halika: [*hali* + =*ka*] Come here.

halíkayó: [*hali* + =*kayo*] Come here (plural).

halikhík: *n.* subdued laughter.

halikwát: *n.* lifting with a lever; turning things over in a pile.

haligayót: *adj.* flexible, pliant.

haligi: *n.* post, column, pole; **haligi ng tahanan** *id.* father (post of the house).

haligutgót: *adj.* naughty, mischievous.

halihaw: *n.* ransacking; repeated stabbing.

halili: *n.* replacement, substitute; successor; **hali-halili** *adj.* alternating; **halinhán** *v.* to replace someone; **humalili** *v.* to substitute, succeed; supplant; **maghalilí** *v.* to alternate; **ang hinalinhán** *n.* predecessor.

halimaw: *n.* wild beast.

halimbawà *n.* example, model; pattern; **kahalimbawà** *adj.* similar; **halimbawaan** *v.* to give an example to; **halimbawain** *v.* to use as an example.

halimbukáy: *n.* nausea; surge of sea waves.

halimhím: *n.* brooding of eggs; **halimhimán** *v.* to sit on eggs to brood.

halimunmón: *n.* fragrance, sent, aroma.

halimuyák: *n.* fragrance; whiff; **humalimuyak** *v.* to give off a scent; **mahalimuyak** *adj.* fragrant.

halina: *v.* Come on, Let's go.

halina: *n.* glamour; attraction; *adj.* attractive, charming; alluring; **mahalina** *v.* to be charmed, fascinated; **halinahin** *v.* to charm, fascinate.

halinhán: (rt. *halili*) *v.* to replace; substitute.

halintulad: **ihalintulad** *v.* to compare.

halíng: *adj.* extremely fond of, doting; crazy about; **kahalingán** *n.* mania, craze, passion; **nakaháhalíng** *adj.* infatuated; **pagkahalíng** *n.* infatuation.

halinghíng: *n.* neigh, whinny; moan, groan.

halíp: *n.* stead; alternate, substitute; *prep.* in place of, instead of; **ihalíp** *v.* to replace; **halipán** *v.* to replace. **panghalíp** *n.* pronoun.

haliparót: *adj.* flirtatious.

halipáw: *n.* surface matter (on liquids).

haliryóng: *n.* transporting little by little.

halít: *adj.* torn, detached.

halo: *n.* pestle.

halò: *n.* mixture; **haluan** *v.* to temper, add something to a mixture; **haluán** *adj.* mixed; **halo-halò** *n.* mixture of different ingredients (usually shaved ice, ice cream and sweets);

makihalò *v.* to mingle; **halu-halong kalamay** *id.* mixed up without order (mixed jam); **naghalò ang balát sa tinalupan** *id.* serious fight (the skin was mixed with the thing skinned); **parang hinalong kalamay** *id.* disarranged.

halubaybáy: *n.* deep-bodied sardine.

halos: *adj.* nearly, almost; approximately; about; **halos sumalo sa pusà** *id.* indigent.

halpók: *adj.* putrid.

halták: *n.* jerk, sudden pull.

halubíd: *n.* spanking, flogging; tripping the feet.

halubidbíd: *n.* winding around, coiling around.

halubilo: *n.* mingling with the crowd; **humalubilo** *v.* to mingle, intermingle.

halukay: *n.* digging; **halukayin** *v.* to turn upside down, upset.

halukipkíp: *adj.* with folded arms.

haludhód: *n.* scratching, rubbing.

halughóg: *n.* close examination, search; ransacking search.

halumigmíg: *adj.* humid, damp.

halungkál: *n.* turning over contents while searching for something.

halungkát: *n.* meticulous search; rummaging.

halusán: *n.* drinking straw.

halutakták: *n.* arrowhead, point of a spear.

haluyhóy: *n.* moan, groan.

halwát. *n.* searching by emptying the contents.

halyás: *n.* inner part of the banana plant used to feed hogs.

hamak: *adj.* lowly, humble; mean; petty; shabby; **kapahamakán** *n.* catastrophe, injury; damnation; **hamakin** *v.* to degrade, despise, look down on; belittle; scorn; **humamak** *v.* to treat with contempt; **manghamak** *v.* to insult, disparage; **paghamak** *n.* insult; contempt; belittling.

hamaka: (Sp. *hamaca*) *n.* hammock.

hamalit: *n.* light-colored garfish.

hambá: (Sp. *jamba*) *n* door jamb.

hambál: *n.* doleful feeling; melancholy; **hambalín** *v.* to despise, look down upon.

hambalang: *adj.* fallen across a path (tree).

hambalos: *n.* flogging, beating, caning.

hambáw: *adj.* superficial.

hambíng: *adj.* similar; **hambingan** *n.* comparison; **ihambíng** *v.* to contrast, compare.

hambó: *n.* bath.

hambóg: *adj.* boastful; proud; **maghambóg** *v.* to brag, boast.

hambulà: *n.* mixing with bad people.

hamig: *n.* collecting of the winnings.

hamít: *n.* unsatisfactory reward for a well-intentioned act.

Hamo: [*Hayaan mo*] Don't worry about it.

hamok: *n.* fight, brawl (hand to hand).

hamóg: *n.* dew; **hamóg sa tag-araw** *id.* relief for the poor (dew in the summer).

hamon: *n.* dare; **hamunin** *v.* to dare, challenge.

hamón: (Sp. *jamón*) *n.* ham; challenge.

hampás: *n.* blow, strike; lash, flogging; **hampasán** *v.* to flog, beat, scourge, whip; hit, swat; **hampas-lupà** *n.* vagabond, tramp; **hampás-bató, hampás-palò** *id.* jobless; **humampás-hampás sa kalye** *id.* loafing around without work; **hampasang-alon** *n.* seashore; breakwater; **hampás-kalabáw** *n.* beating without mercy; **hampás-tikín** *n.* afternoon sun inclined towards the west; **hampás-tigbalang** *n.* species of woody vine.

hampíl: *n.* sudden stop when crashing against something.

hampilà: *n.* piling up soil at the base of a plant; **hampás ng langit** *id.* God's punishment (strike of heaven).

hampól: *n.* highest point of a wave.

Han: *interj.* used to stop cattle.

-han: *suff.* variant of the suffix *-an* after vowels.

hanâ: **pagkahanâ** *n.* weakness due to hunger.

haná: *interj.* Let's go, go ahead.

hanap: *n.* search, quest; **hanapan** *v.* to look for; **mahanap** *v.* to find; **hanapbuhay** *n.* means of livelihood, occupation; **maghanáp** *v.* to search, pursue; **mapaghanáp** *adj.* making hard demands, hard to please; **hanáp-hanapin** *v.* to miss (the absence of a person); **humahanap ng katí ng katawán** *id.* looking for trouble (looking for the itch in the body); **humanap ng batóng ipinukók sa ulo** *id.* did something self-destructive (looked for a stone to strike the head); **hanap-patáy** *id.* begging.

hanay: *n.* row, line; rank; **humanay** *v.* to line up; **ihanay** *v.* to put in a row, arrange; **pagkakahanay** *n.* alignment; series.

handâ: *adj.* ready, prepared; handy; alert; *n.* prepared food; **handaan** *n.* party with food; **handaán** *v.* to prepare for; reserve something for; **humandâ** *v.* to prepare; **paghahandâ** *n.* preparation, provision.

handák: *adj.* greedy; lustful, lewd.

handalapák: *adj.* gossipy; disrespectful.

handóg: *n.* gift, present; treat; **ihandóg** *v.* to offer, dedicate; **maghandóg** *v.* to hand over, offer, present.

handulan: *n.* rustic coffin.

handulong: *n.* sudden attack, aggressiveness.

handusáy: *adj.* lying prostrate and sprawling.

hanép: (*slang*) *adj.* awesome, amazing; wow.

hánimún. (Eng.) *n.* honeymoon. (*pulutgatâ*)

hanip: *n.* chicken flea.

hanís: (*slang*) **hanís-hanís** *adj.* affectionate.

hantád: *adj.* exposed; **hantaran** *adj.* in full view.

hantík: *n.* large, red poisonous ant.

hantóng: *n.* destination; **hantungan** *n.* terminal, stopping place; **hantungán** *v.* to stop, end; result in; arrive, land.

Hánunuo: *n.* highland ethnic group and language of Mindoro.

hangà: *n.* admiration; amazement; **hangaan** *v.* to admire, marvel at; **pahangain** *v.* to impress; **tagahangà** *adj.* admirer.

hangád: *n.* desire, ambition; intention; **hangarín** *v.* to desire, seek; woo; **mapaghangád ng masamâ sa kapwà** *adj.* spiteful, showing ill will.

hangál: *adj.* stupid, idiotic.

hanggá: *n.* result, outcome; **kahanggá** *adj.* adjacent; **hanggahan** *n.* boundary, end; destination; **humanggá** *v.* to end; culminate.

hanggán: *n.* end, boundary, limit; side line; **kahanggán** *n.* neighbor; **waláng-hanggán** *adj.* infinite, boundless.

hanggáng: *prep.* until, till, up to; **hanggáng bibíg** *id.* referring to things said but not done (until the mouth); **hanggáng-piyér** *id.* referring to Philippine ladies that are left behind by their American boyfriends (until the pier); **hanggáng sa labì ng hukay** *id.* till death (until the lips of the ditch).

hanggód: *n.* spiky herb.

hangháng: *n.* pungency; **mahangháng** *adj.* pungent.

hangin: *n.* wind, air; **hanginán** *n.* draft of air; **hanging-amihan** *n.* breeze; **humangin** *v.* to blow (wind); **mahangin** *adj.* windy; **mahangin ang tiyán** *fig.* person who laughs or talks excessively; **mahangin ang ulo** *fig.* conceited; **pananggáng-hangin** *n.* windshield.

hangláy: *n.* sour taste of uncooked vegetables.

hangò: *n.* removal of something from the fire; extract, literary adaptation; *adj.* derived, adapted, extracted; **humangò** *v.* to extricate, reclaim, redeem.

hangos: *n.* gasp, pant; *adj.* out of breath.

hangyód: *n.* offensive odor.

haot: *n.* dried sardine.

hapák: *adj.* chopped.

hapád: *var.* of *sapád*: lopsidedly flat.

hapág: *n.* table; **hapág-kainán** *n.* dining table; **hapág-pulungán** *n.* conference table; **hapág-sulatán** *n.* writing table, desk.

hapaw: *n.* excess liquid in boiling rice that is removed, dirt-like formation on the surface of broth; **hapawin** *v.* to skim, remove from the top; report something in an superficial manner; **pahapáw** *adj.* done in a superficial manner.

hapay: *adj.* tilted, leaning; bankrupt; **humapay** *v.* to lean, bend; become bankrupt; **humapay-hapay** *v.* to wobble.

hapdî: *n.* stinging pain; **humapdî** *v.* to sting (pain); **mahapdî** *adj.* very painful; prickly; **mahapdî ang bituka** *id.* hungry (gut is painful).

hapilà: *n.* breakwater; small dike in rice fields; **hapilâ** *n.* something used to prevent piled grains from scattering.

hapín: *n.* string, twine; **hapín ng buhay** *id.* help to one's livelihood (twine of life); **may hapín** *id.* reversible.

hapis: *n.* anguish, distress; grief; **hapís** *adj.*

sorrowful, gloomy; **nakahahapis** *adj.* distressful.

hapit: **mahapit** *v.* to be able to contract; **humapit** *v.* to tighten; **hapít** *adj.* tight fitting, tense, taut.

haplás: **panghaplás** *n.* liniment, balm; **haplasán** *n.* to apply ointment to.

haplít$_1$: *n.* stroke of a whip; reprimand; **haplitín** *v.* to whip; direct a sarcastic remark to.

haplít$_2$: *n.* final burst of energy when trying to win a race.

haplós: **humaplós** *v.* to massage tenderly, pet.

haplót: *n.* washing of the face with hands.

hapò$_1$: *n.* asthma. (*hikà*)

hapò$_2$: *n.* panting; **hapô** *adj.* tired out, fatigued; **matagál sa hapò** *adj.* long-winded, enduring.

hapon$_1$: *n.* afternoon; **hapunin** *v.* to be late in the afternoon; **hapunan** *n.* dinner; **hapunanin** *v.* to eat dinner; **kahapon** *n.* yesterday; **maghapon** *adv.* the whole day; **maghapunan** *v.* to eat dinner.

hapon$_2$: *n.* perching of birds; **hapunan** *v.* to perch on; **humapon** *v.* to roost.

Hapón: (Sp. *japón*) *n.* Japan; Japanese.

Haponesa: (Sp. *japonesa*) *adj.* Japanese (fem.); *n.* female Japanese.

hapuhap: *var.* of *apuhap*: grope.

harà: **humara-harà** *v.* to block others; meddle, hinder.

harabe: (Sp. *jarabe*) *n.* syrup; (*coll.*) striking violently.

haragán: (Sp.) *n.* idler; *adj.* disrespectful.

harana: (Sp. *jarana*) *n.* serenade; **haranahin** *v.* to serenade someone.

harang: *n.* bar, obstacle; (*slang*) *adj.* overpriced; **harangan** *v.* to block; waylay, intercept; **humarang** *v.* to block the way; **panghaharang** *n.* hold up.

haráp: *n.* front, façade; presence; sex organ; **kaharáp** *adj.* facing, opposite; **haharapín** *n.* future; outlook; **harapán** *v.* to face, be present at; **humaráp** *v.* to show oneself, confront, deal with; **harapín** *v.* to face, confront; attend to; **iharáp** *v.* to present; hand over; confront; submit; **magharáp** *v.* to introduce; present; **paharapín** *v.* to summon; **haráp-haráp** *adj.* facing each other; with everyone concerned present; **sa hinaharap** in the future; **panghinaharáp** *n.* future tense; **haharáp sa dambanà** *id.* will get married (face the altar); **harapín ang sinaing** *id.* to watch closely what is cooking (face the rice).

harayà: (Vis.) *n.* imagination.

hardín: (Sp. *jardín*) *n.* garden; **hardinero** *n.* gardener.

hardol: (Eng.) *n.* hurdle.

harì: *n.* king, ruler; **kaharián** *n.* kingdom; **magharì** *v.* to reign, rule; control; **pangharì** *adj.* regal; **harí-harian** *n.* false king; puppet king; bully, domineering person; **harì ng maibigan** *id.* doing whatever is desired (king of whatever is liked); **haring-bastos** *n.* king of clubs; **haring-kopas** *n.* king of goblets; **haring-ispada** *n.* king of spades; **haring-oros** *n.* king of diamonds.

Harimanawarì: *interj.* May God make it so!

harina: (Sp. *harina*) *n.* flour.

harinangâ: *interj.* May it be so!

harinawâ: *interj.* May it be so!

haringgá: (Sp. *jeringa*) *n.* syringe.

haro: (Sp. *jarro*) *n.* jug, pitcher.

harok: *n.* snoring; **humarok** *v.* to snore.

harós: *n.* frolic; mischief.

harót: *adj.* very fast, quick to make decisions; (*slang*) *n.* kiss; *adj.* flirtatious.

harurot: **paharurutin** *v.* to rev up an engine.

hasà: *n.* whetting; practice; **hasâ** *adj.* sharp, well-trained; **hasahasà** *n.* species of mackerel; **hasáng-hasâ** *id.* well accustomed (well-sharpened).

hasang: *n.* gill. **hasangan.** *v.* to take out the gills (of fish).

hasap: **hasapin** *v.* to suffocate.

hasi: *n.* collecting winnings after each game (cards); acceptance of banker of all the bets.

hasík: *adj.* sown. **hasikán** *v.* to sow a place with seeds.

hasô: *adj.* loosely tied.

hasinto: (Sp. *jacinto*) *n.* hyacinth.

hasmín: (Sp. *jasmín*) *n.* jasmine.

hasô: *var.* of *habsô*: easily untied.

haspé: (Sp.) *n.* grain in wood; jasper.

hatak: *n.* pulling; **haták** *adj.* tight, taut; well-trained; well-experienced; **humatak** *v.* to pull; haul; train.

hataw: *n.* thrashing, beating; (*slang*) eat with gusto; go faster; food; **hatawin** *v.* to thrash; **hataw na** *id.* give it all you got.

hatdán: (rt. *hatíd*) *v.* to deliver to.

hatì: *n.* dividing line, part; division; **kahatì** *n.* 25 centavos; **kalahatì** *n.* one half; **kalahatián** *n.* center; **hatî** *adj.* divided in two equal parts; **tigkalahatì** *adv.* half and half, with equal shares; **hating-demonyo** *n.* unequal sharing; **háting-daigdíg** *n.* hemisphere.

hatíd: *n.* escorting; **hatíd-dumapit** *n.* gossip; **hatirang-karera** *n.* relay race; **ihatíd** *v.* to escort; bring; **hat(i)dán** *v.* to deliver to; **maghatíd** *v.* to conduct; escort; survey; **pahatíd** *n.* message, dispatch; **páhatiran** *n.* communication; **pahatirán, pahatdán** *v.* to send someone something. **tagahatíd** *n.* messenger, usher; **ihatíd sa dambanà** *id.* to marry (take to church); **hatíd-dumapit** *adj.* gossipy.

hatinggabí: *n.* midnight.

hatirin: *n.* milkfish fingerling.

hatol: *n.* decision, sentence, judgment; medical prescription; **hatulan** *v.* to judge, pass sentence; condemn; **paghatol** *n.* conviction; condemnation; judgment; **tagahatol** *n.* referee, umpire, judge.

hatsa: (*slang*) *n.* flirtatious woman.

hatsét: (*slang*) *n.* food, meal; eating.

hatsíng: *n.* sound of a sneeze.

hawa: *n.* infection, contagion; (*slang*) *adj.* lousy; nasty; **hawa-hawa** *adj.* infected; **mahawa** *v.* to become infected; **nakakahawa** *adj.* infectious, contagious.

hawak: *n.* hold, grasp; *adj.* held in the hand; **hawakan** *v.* to take hold of; **humawak** *v.* to hold, grasp; manipulate; **may-hawak** *v.* to have control of, have possession of; **hawak sa tainga** *id.* obeying everything (held by the ears).

hawan: *n.* clearing made in the forest.

hawás: *adj.* with fine posture; slender build; oval.

haway: *n.* searching under water with a drag hook.

hawáy: **hakahawáy** *adj.* floating in the air; hanging from above.

hawháw: *n.* third rinsing of clothes; (*slang*) fooling, joking.

hawì: *n.* making a clearing in the forest to pass through; parting of the hair.

hawig: **hawíg** *adj.* similar, like; **hawigan** *v.* to copy, imitate.

hawil: *n.* small part that holds an almost severed part of an object; being almost cut off.

hawili: *n.* small tree with shiny leaves.

hawla: (Sp. *jaula*) *n.* birdcage.

hawóng: (Ch.) *n.* wooden soup bowl.

hawot: *n.* dried *tinsoy* fish.

hayà: *n.* threatening gesture; tolerance of an act; **hayaan** *v.* to leave alone, let be.

hayag: **hayág** *adj.* easily seen; public, exposed to view; **maghayág** *v.* to reveal; **pahayag** *n.* proclamation, public announcement, declaration; **ihayág** *v.* to disclose, reveal, divulge; **ipahayag** *v.* to announce, proclaim, express; **malabong pahayag** *n.* generality; **mamamahayág** *n.* newspaper reporter; **pamahayag** *n.* proclamation.

hayán: *interj.* There!

hayáng: *adj.* spread out (grains).

hayap: *n.* sharpness, keenness; **mahayap** *adj.* sharp, keen.

hayku: (Jap.) *n.* haiku.

hayháy: *n.* breeze, fresh air; row, file; **ihayháy** *v.* to hang under the sun to dry or to air out.

hayin: *n.* tribute, offering; **ihayin** *v.* to offer in sacrifice.

hayo: *interj.* Go ahead!

hayok: *adj.* extremely hungry; greedy.

hayón: *interj.* There it is!

hayón: *n.* farthest distance that can be reached, capacity for travel.

hayop: *n.* animal, beast; **hayupan** *n.* zoo; domestic animals; animal farm; **hayupán** (*coll.*) *n.* exchanging jokes; **maghayop** *v.* to take care of animals; **malahayop** *adj.* like an animal; **pagkakahayop** *n.* bestiality; **hayóp** (*slang*) *adj.* fantastic.

hayuhay: *n.* drooping and swaying.
hayuma: *n.* mending of fishing nets.
hebilya: (Sp. *hebilla*) *n.* buckle, clasp.
heko: (Ch.) *n.* dark sauce made from salted shrimps.
helat: *var.* of *belat.*
helatina: (Sp. *gelatina*) *n.* gelatin.
hele: *n.* lullaby; **helehele** *n.* pretending not to like something; **helehele bago kiyere** *id.* saying the opposite of what one means.
hemelo: (Sp. *gemelo*) *n.* cuff links.
henerál: (Sp. *general*) *n.* general.
hénero: (Sp. *género*) *n.* textile, woven fabric.
henyo: (Sp. *genio*) *n.* genius.
Hep: *interj.* Present! Here!; Stop!
hepà: (*coll.*) *n.* hepatitis.
hepe: (Sp. *jefe*) *n.* chief, boss.
heranyo: (Sp. *geranio*) *n.* geranium.
herarkiya: (Sp. *jerarquía*) *n.* hierarchy.
heringga: (Sp. *jeringa*) *n.* syringe.
heringgilya: (Sp. *jeringuilla*) *n.* hypodermic syringe.
hero: (Sp. *hierro*) *n.* brand on cattle; **maghero** *v.* to brand; **panghero** *n.* branding iron.
heto: *intrj.* Here it is.
hibáng: **nahihibáng** *adj.* delirious, crazy, mad; **máhibáng** *adj.* delirious, crazy; **pagkahibáng** *n.* delirium.
hibás: *adj.* reduced in intensity; *n.* low tide.
hibasbás: *n.* regaining consciousness.
hibát: *n.* proverb, enigma.
hibay: **humihay** *v.* to sway due to weakness.
hibaybáy: *n.* region bordering a body of water; border, boundary; surrounding region.
hibi: (Ch.) *n.* small dried shrimps.
hibî: *n.* pouting of the lips.
hibík: *n.* pleading, supplication; sob.
hibilya: (Sp. *hebilla*) *n.* buckle.
hiblá: (Sp. *hebra*) *n.* strand.
hibò: *n.* flattery; temptation; **hibuin** *v.* to flatter.
hibok: *n.* persuasion by flattery.
hikà: *n.* asthma.
hikáb: *n.* yawn; **humikáb** *v.* to yawn.
hikahós: *adj.* needy, destitute; broke.
hikap: *n.* travelling from place to place.
hikaw: (Ch.) *n.* earring.
hikayat: *n.* persuasion; **humikayat** *v.* to persuade.
hikbî: *n.* sob.
hikit: *n.* making of nets.
hiklás: *adj.* torn apart. **hiklasín** *v.* to rip apart.
hiklát: **hiklatín** *v.* to open forcibly.
hikog: *n.* type of snare used to catch prawns.
hikwát: *adj.* raised by levers.
hidhíd: *adj.* frugal, stingy.
hidwâ: *adj.* contrary, irregular; **hidwaan** *n.* discord, disagreement, rift.
higâ: *adj.* horizontal, lying down; **higaan, higán** *v.* to lie on, repose; **nahihigâ sa salapî** *id.* wealthy (lying on money).
higáb: *n.* gaping the mouth; kind of black caterpillar; tusk, fang.
higad: *n.* kind of small worm with long, sharp hair; (*fig.*) tightwad, selfish person; (*slang*) moustache; **higád-higaran** *n.* Indian turnsole (hairy plant).
higante: (Sp. *gigante*) *n.* giant.
higantí: *n.* revenge; **ipaghigantí** *v.* to avenge, take revenge; **mapaghigantí** *adj.* revengeful, vindictive.
Higaonon: *n.* ethnic group and language from North Central Mindanao.
higkót: *n.* tightening of a knot.
higik: *n.* snore.
higing: *n.* humming sound, drone, buzz.
higing: *n.* cue to start singing, tune, tone; something vaguely heard.
higít: **mahigít sa** *adv.* more, more than, over, plus; **kahigtán** *n.* excess; **higít pa** *adv.* rather; **higitín** *v.* to surpass, excel; **hig(i)tán** *v.* to exceed; **humigít** *v.* to outnumber, exceed, outweigh.
higláw: *var.* of *hugláw*: cessation of intensity.
hignáw: **mahignáw** *adj.* calm, serene.
higop: *n.* sip; (*slang*) sycophant; **higupan** *v.* to sip.
higpít₁: *n.* closeness in a contest; tightness; **mahigpít** *adj.* firm; close (in competition; tight; **humigpít** *v.* to tighten; **mahigpít ang hawak sa bulsá** *id.* stingy (holds the pocket tightly); **nahihigpít ng sinturón** *id.* economizing.
higpít₂: *n.* strictness, severity; **mahigpít** *adj.*

strict, severe, drastic, rigorous.
higtán: (rt. *higít*) *v.* to exceed.
hihip: *n.* blowing; blowpipe; **hihipán** *n.* mouth-piece; **hipán** *v.* to blow into.
hila: (Sp. *girar*) *n.* pulling, dragging, hauling; **hilahin** *v.* to drag, pull; trail; **hiníhila ang dilà** *id.* fatigued (dragging the tongue).
hilab: *n.* swell, bulge; spasm.
hilabó: *adj.* free for all.
hilakbót: *n.* terror, fright.
hilakô: *adj.* poorly made.
hilagà: *n.* north; **pahilagâ** *adj.* northward.
hilagpós: *n.* getting loose; **makahilagpós** *v.* to be able to break loose (from a bind).
hilagyô: *n.* spirit, affinity; namesake; essence.
hilahid: *n.* smear.
hilahil: *n.* hardship; grief.
hilahod: *n.* shuffling of the feet; limping.
hilam: *n.* skin blemish on the face; pain in the eyes; turbidity.
hilamos: **maghilamos** *v.* to wash one's face; **hilamos-pusà** *id.* slightly washing the face.
hilantád: *adj.* lying on one's back without any clothes.
hilat: *n.* stretching of an opening.
Hilat! *interj.* That's what you get!
hilatà: *adj.* sprawled; **humilatà** *v.* to sprawl, lie in a wanton manner.
hilatlát: *n.* making a hole wider.
hilatsá: (Sp. *hilacha*) *n.* unraveled thread from cloth.
hiláw: *adj.* raw, uncooked; unripe; immature.
hilbana: (Sp. *hilvana*) *n.* basting, temporary stitching; **hilbanahan** *v.* to baste, stitch.
hilera: (Sp.) *n.* row, file; **hilé-hilera** *adj.* arranged in rows.
hilhíl: *n.* loud laughter.
hilí: *n.* lullaby.
hilì: **mahilì** *adj.* envious; **pananaghilì** *n.* envy.
hilík: *n.* snore; **humilík** *v.* to snore.
hilig: *n.* liking, appetite; desire; slant, inclination; **mahilig** *adj.* liking, prone; fond of; **humilig** *v.* to recline, slant, slope; **hiligan** *v.* to lean on; **pahilíg** *adj.* slantwise.
Hiligaynon: *n.* ethnic group and language from Panay Island and Negros Occidental.
hilihid: *n.* panorama.
hilihíd: *adj.* awry, twisted to one side.
hilíng: *n.* request; claim; application; **hilingín** *v.* to petition, ask earnestly.
hilis: **hilisin** *v.* to cut slantingly; to press and squeeze (pimple).
hiliwíd: *adj.* slanting, inclined.
hilo: (Sp. *giro*) **hiló** *adj.* dizzy, confused; **hiluhin** *v.* to make someone dizzy; **hilóng-talilong** *id.* confused (dizzy mullet).
hilod: **hiluran** *v.* to scrub the skin of someone to remove the dirt; **panghilod** *n.* sponge used to scrub off dirt.
hilom: **maghilom** *v.* to heal (wound); close up (opening).
hilot: *n.* midwife; **hilutin** *v.* to massage.
hilukâ: *adj.* languished, pale.
himà: *n.* whitish vaginal secretion.
himakás: *n.* last farewell; *adj.* farewell.
himagal: *n.* payment for services rendered; *adj.* slightly tired.
himagas: *n.* dessert.
himagáw: *adj.* hoarse.
himago: *n.* being unfamiliar with a new place.
himagod: *n.* slight fatigue.
himagsík: *n.* revolt, rebellion; **naghihimagsík** *adj.* rebel.
himalâ: *n.* miracle; **mapaghimalâ** *adj.* miraculous.
himalay: *n.* second threshing of rice; **himalayin** *v.* to glean.
himaling: *n.* obsession.
himamat: *n.* weeding; **himamatan** *v.* to remove small weeds around a plant.
himan: **mahiman** *adj.* slow and gentle.
himantíng: *n.* scraping off small branches or thorns.
himangláw: *n.* feeling of loneliness.
himas: *n.* caressing, gentle massage.
himasmás: **mahimasmasán** *adj.* to regain consciousness.
himasok: *n.* interference; **mapanghimasok** *adj.* meddlesome, intrusive.
himat: *n.* excessive carefulness.
himatáy: *n.* fainting.
himatlóg: *n.* languor.
himaton: *n.* information, verbal help; showing the directions to a place; denunciation.

himatong: *var.* of *himaton*: information given.
himay: *n.* shelling grains; **maghimay** *v.* to shell; string (remove strings from beans).
himay: *n.* rest after work.
himaymay: *n.* fiber; tranquility.
himaynát: *n.* slight sign of relapse.
himbabaó: *n.* species of tree used in making clogs.
himbák: *n.* jump over an obstacle.
himbalangáy: *n.* backstroke.
himbíng: *n.* deep sleep. **mahimbíng** *adj.* deep (sleep). **náhihimbíng** *adj.* fast asleep.
himbubulí: *n.* species of lizard.
himbubuyog: *n.* bumblebee.
himelo: (Sp. *gemelo*) *n.* cufflink.
himig$_1$: *n.* tune, melody; note; **ihimig** *v.* to hum; sing.
himig$_2$: *n.* humidity.
himláy: **himlayan** *n.* place of rest; cemetery; *v.* to rest on something.
himnasyo: (Sp. *gimnasio*) *n.* gymnasium.
himno: (Sp.) *n.* hymn.
himo: **maghimo** *v.* to anoint with oil.
himok: *n.* persuasion; **humimok** *v.* to persuade.
himod: **himuran** *v.* to lap up with the tongue, lick; **humihimod sa pundiryá** *id.* flattering.
himpak: *adj.* deflated; emaciated; emptied.
himpapalis: *n.* species of swallow.
himpapawíd: *n.* space overhead, sky; **hukbong-panghimpapawíd** *n.* air force; **isahimpapawíd** *v.* to air; broadcast; **sa himpapawíd** in the air.
himpíl: *n.* stop; parking; **humimpil** *v.* to stop, park.
himukas: **paghihimukas** *n.* removal of small fish adhering to a net.
himukó: *n.* pruning.
himuktô: *n.* swelling around the eyes due to crying.
himugtô: *n.* sigh.
himulá: *n.* blushing.
himulmól: *n.* plucking of feathers; raveled thread.
himutà: *n.* removing gum from the eyes.
himuti: *n.* final picking of fruits.
himutî: *n.* slight fading of colors.
himutlâ: *adj.* pallid (from fear, etc.).
himutmót: *n.* raveled thread.
himutók: *n.* outcry.
-hin: *var.* of the suffix *-in* after vowels.
hinà: **mahinà** *adj.* weak; soft (bones); frail; **huminà** *v.* to weaken; **hinaan** *v.* to soften; decrease (volume); **panghihinà** *n.* fatigue; languor; deterioration; **panghinain** *v.* to weaken; waste; **panghinaan** *v.* to feel weakness in; **mahinà ang kapit** *id.* with little influence (grasp is weak); **mahinà ang loób** *id.* coward (inside is weak); **mahinà ang tuhod** *id.* weakness of the body (knee is weak); **mahinà ang ulo** *id.* feeble-minded (head is weak).
hinabáng: *n.* loss of interest; indifference.
hinakdál: *n.* complaint, resentment.
hinakot: *n.* misgiving.
hinagap: *n.* idea, notion; **hinagapin** *v.* to imagine.
hinagpís: *n.* sorrow, displeasure.
hináharáp: (*rt. haráp*) *n.* future.
hinahon: **kahinahunan** *n.* self-control, composure; restraint, prudence; **huminahon** *v.* to compose oneself; **mahinahon** *adj.* calm, prudent; mild, gentle; moderate.
hinaíng: (*rt. daíng*) **kahinaingán** *n.* supplication.
hinalà: (*rt. sala*) **paghihinalà** *n.* suspicion; **hinalain** *v.* to suspect.
hinalig: *n.* belief; trust; reliance.
hinamád: (*rt. tamád*) **paghinamád** *n.* stretching of one's arms.
hinampó: (*rt. tampó*) **paghihinampó** *n.* hurt feeling toward a loved one.
hinanakít: (*rt. sakít*) *n.* resentment; **hínanakitan** *n.* mutual resentment; **paghihinanakít** *n.* complaint; gripe; ill will.
hinang: *n.* weld, solder; **hinangin** *v.* to weld, solder together. **hinangán** *n.* welding shop.
hinas: *n.* ointment.
hináw: *n.* washing of the hands of feet; **hínawan** *n.* washbowl. **hinawán** *v.* to wash (hands or feet).
hinawà: (*rt. sawà*) **paghihinawà** *n.* loss of interest, surfeit; boredom.
hinay: *n.* slowness; **huminay** *v.* to slow down.
hinayang: (*rt. sayang*) **panghihinayang** *n.*

regret; **manghinayang, panghinayangan** *v.* to regret.

hindarà: **hindarâ** *adj.* seated flat on the floor with legs stretched wide apart.

hindî: *adv.* no; not [negator of statements]; **hindián** *v.* to answer negatively; **hindî na** no more, not any more; **magpahindî** *v.* to refuse; **kung hindî** if not; otherwise. [See also *huwág*]

hindík: *n.* breathing of a person in agony; gasping from sudden fear.

hindót: *n.* copulation, casual sex.

hindulós: *adj.* lying flat with the arms stretched horizontally with the body.

hindusáy: *var.* of *handusáy*: prostrate and sprawling.

hinebra: (Sp. *ginebra*) *n.* gin.

hinete: (Sp. *ginete*) *n.* jockey.

hinhín: **kahinhinán** *n.* modesty, refinement; **mahinhíng-talipandás** *id.* modest at first sight but actually flirtatious (modest, imprudent).

hiniksík: **paghihiniksík** *n.* picking of nits from the hair.

hininga: (*rt.* *hingá*) *n.* breath; (*fig.*) life; **malahiningá** *adj.* of body temperature.

hinlalakí: (*rt.* *lakí*) *n.* thumb, big toe.

hinlalatò: *n.* middle finger.

hinlaláy: **pahinlaláy** *n.* hopping on one foot.

hinlóg: *n.* kin, relative.

hinóg: *adj.* ripe; mature; **mahinóg** *v.* to ripen; **hinóg sa pilit** *id.* forced to agree (ripened by force); **magpahinóg ka na** *id.* face the consequences (become ripe already); **nagpapahinóg** *id.* waiting for the hour of death, be in agony (waiting to be ripe).

hintakot: *n.* slight fear; **hintakót** *adj.* slightly afraid.

hintáy: **maghintáy** *v.* to wait; **maghintayan** *v.* to wait for each other; **paghihintáy** *n.* waiting; **hintayan** *n.* waiting place; **hintayán** *v.* to expect something from; **hintayín** *v.* to wait for; anticipate; **paghihintáy** *n.* waiting; **hinihintáy na ng mga bulati** *id.* dying (earthworms already awaiting).

hintô: *n.* halt, stop; intermission; **hintuan** *n.* stopping place; **hintuán** *v.* to stop at a place; **humintô** *v.* to cease, stop; **ihintô** *v.* to cause to stop; **pagkáhintô** *n.* standstill, halt; **pahintú-hintô** *adv.* intermittent; **pahintuín at tanungín** to stop and question; challenge.

hintutubí: *n.* large dragonfly.

hintutulí: *n.* earwax.

hintuturò: *n.* index finger.

hinukó: **paghihinukó** *n.* cutting of fingernails or toenails; **maghinukó** *v.* to cut the nails.

hinukod: (*rt.* *tukod*) *n.* posture, stature; appearance; being submissive.

hinuhà: *n.* deduction, inference; **hinuhain** *v.* to deduce.

hinuhod: **paghinuhod** *n.* assent.

hinulí: (*rt.* *tutulí*) *n.* removal of earwax; **hinulihán** *v.* to remove earwax.

hinyangò: *n.* chameleon.

hinyayangò: *n.* species of poisonous snake.

hingá: **paghingá** *n.* respiration; wind; **hiningá** *n.* breath; **humingá** *v.* to breathe; **maghingá** *v.* to unburden, let out suppressed feelings; **waláng-pahingá** *adj.* without resting; **pahingahan** *n.* rest house; **pahingá** *n.* resting; **magpahingá** *v.* to rest; **nakahingá ng maluwag** *id.* surmounted difficulties.

hingál: **humingál** *v.* to gasp, pant; **híngalin** *adj.* easily fatigued.

hingalay: *n.* nap, short rest.

hingalô: (*rt.* *ngalô*) *n.* agony, death pangs; **maghingalô** *v.* to be on the verge of death.

hingán: *var.* of *hingián*: request.

hingasing: *n.* growl; hard breathing.

hingkód: *adj.* lame, crippled.

hinggíl: *prep.* regarding, concerning; *n.* purpose.

hinggíw: *n.* woody vine, *Streptocaulon baumii.*

hingî: *n.* request; requesting; requirement; thing requested or required; *adj.* given for free. **humingî** *v.* to ask for, request; **hing(i)án** *v.* to request from; **híngian** *n.* person from whom one usually requests something; **hing(i)ín** *v.* to request, ask for; require. **paghingî** *n.* act of requesting; **paghingî ng kamáy** *id.* asking for one's hand (in marriage). **híngiang-tawad** *n.* mutual asking of forgiveness.

hingukó: (*rt.* *kukó*) *n.* cutting of the finger or

toe nails.

hinguto: (*rt. kuto*) *n.* picking of lice from the hair.

hingutóng: *n.* playing with the nipples of their mothers (babies).

hipâ: *n.* decrease (in intensity).

hipák: *adj.* hollow, caved-in; shrunken.

hipag: (Ch.) *n.* sister-in-law. [Masc: *bayáw*]

hipan: (rt. *hihip*) *n.* blowing (a fire, musical instrument); **hipán** *v.* to blow into.

hiphíp: *n.* drinking by means of a straw; forced, deep breathing.

hipík: *n.* the movements of the abdomen when breathing.

hipíg: *n.* nap.

hipnó: *n.* copy; translation.

hipnotisadór: (Sp. *hipnotizador*) *n.* hypnotist.

hipò: *n.* touch; **hipuan** *v.* to touch a person (indecently); **hipuin** *v.* to touch, feel; **mahipuan** *v.* to be touched indecently.

hipon: *n.* shrimp; **palahipunan** *n.* shrimp pond; **hipong tulóg** *id.* slowfoot (sleeping shrimp).

hipopotamo: (Eng.) *n.* hippopotamus.

hirá(do): (Sp. *gira(do)*) *n.* confusion; *adj.* confused.

hirám: *adj.* borrowed; not inborn (talent); *n.* borrowing. **hiramán** *v.* to borrow from a person; **hir(a)mín** *v.* to borrow; adopt. **ipahirám** *v.* to lend, **hirám-kantores** *id.* no returning (choir's loan).

hirang: *n.* choice; appointee; **hirangin** *v.* to appoint, choose; delegate; **mahirang** *v.* to be able to choose.

hirap: *n.* difficulty; trail, trouble; **mahirap** *adj.* difficult, arduous; poor; awkward; **hiráp** *adj.* tired, poor, suffering; **pahirap** *n.* burden, strain; **magpahirap** *v.* to make matters difficult; **mahirap pa sa dagâ** *id.* indigent.

hirasól: (Sp. *girasol*) *n.* sunflower.

Hirat! *interj.* That's what you get!

hirati: (*rt. dati*) **hiratí** *adj.* accustomed; acquainted. **mahirati** *v.* to become accustomed to, get used to.

hiraw: *n.* rooster with white feathers and green spots.

hirayà: *n.* imagination; vision.

hirin: *n.* lump in the throat; choking; **mahirinan** *v.* to be choked.

hiringgilya: (Sp. *jeringuilla*) *n.* syringe.

hirís: *adj.* slanting; out of alignment.

hirit: *n.* full force (strike of blow); (*slang*) *n.* talking out of turn; asking for something.

hiro postal: (Sp. *giro postal*) *n.* money order.

hirol: *n.* squirming in pain.

hisò: *n.* brushing of the teeth. **hisuin** *v.* to brush the teeth.

hitâ: *n.* benefit, gain; advantage; unworthy reward. **mahitâ** *v.* to benefit.

hità: *n.* thigh. **hitaán** *adj.* having large thighs.

hitád: *n.* flirt. *adj.* flirtatious; (*slang*) selfish, greedy.

hitano: (Sp. *gitano*) *n.* gypsy.

hithít: *n.* absorption of liquid; inhalation; (*slang*) smoking of illegal drugs; **humithít** *v.* to inhale smoke; smoke.

hitík: **mahitík** *adj.* laden with fruit; filled; loaded; pregnant.

hitò: *n.* catfish.

hitsó: (Ch.) *n.* betel nut wrapped in betel leaf.

hitsura: (Sp. *hechura*) *n.* form, figure, look; appearance.

hiwà: *n.* cut; wound; slice; **hiwaan** *v.* to cut a mark; **hiwain** *v.* to slice, cut.

hiwagà: *n.* mystery. (*himalâ, kababalaghán*)

hiwalay: (*rt. walay*) *n.* separating; separation. **hiwaláy** *adj.* separated; apart. **ihiwalay** *v.* to separate; **maghiwaláy** *v.* to diverge, separate from each other. **hiwalayan** *v.* to separate from; divorce. **hiwá-hiwaláy** *adj.* far from each other.

hiwás: *n.* moonfish; slipmouth fish; *adj.* tilted, slanting; biased.

hiwatig: **pahiwatig** *n.* hint, suggestion; insinuation; **ipahiwatig** *v.* to hint, imply; indicate; show, reveal; **pahiwatíg** *adj.* implicit, implied; figuratively.

hiwî: *n.* pursing the lips; *adj.* wry.

hiwíd: *adj.* twisted; slanting.

hiwís: *adj.* slanting.

hiyâ: *n.* shame; disgrace; humiliation; **kahiyá-hiyâ** *adj.* shameful, disgraceful; **káhiyaan** *n.* something done to save face; **hiyaín** *v.* to shame, disgrace; dishonor; embarrass; **híyaan** *n.* embarrassing each other; **ipagmakahiyâ** *v.* to avoid doing something to avoid embarrassment; **mahiyâ** *v.* to feel ashamed; be shy; be embarrassed; **makahiyâ** *v.* to be ashamed of; *n.* the *mimosa* plant that curls up upon touch; **mahiyain** *adj.* shy, bashful, timid; **mápahiyâ** *v.* to be put to shame, embarrassed, humiliated; **nakákahiyâ** *adj.* shameful; disgraceful; **pagkahiyâ** *n.* shame; disgrace; humiliation; embarrassment; **pagkamahíyáin** *n.* bashfulness, timidity; modesty; **paghiyâ** *n.* humiliation; **daláng-hiyâ** *n.* embarrassment; **waláng-hiyâ** *adj.* shameless; **waláng kahiyá-hiyâ** *adj.* completely shameless; **huwág kang mahihiyâ** don't be bashful (said when offering food); **magbigáy-hiyâ** *v.* to show respect for.

hiyá: *interj.* used to speed up horses.

hiyád: **nakahiyád** *adj.* with protruding stomach.

hiyáng: **kahiyáng** *adj.* suited, agreeable.

hiyás: (Sp. *joyas*) *n.* gem, jewel; (*slang*) virginity; **hiyás ng pagkababae** *id.* honor (jewel of womanhood); **hiyás ng tahanan** *id.* maiden (jewel of the home); **mumurahing hiyás** *n.* trinket.

hiyáw: *n.* scream, yell; **humiyáw** *v.* to yell; **maghumiyáw** *v.* to shout at the top of one's voice.

hô: *part.* polite particle, less honorific than *pô*.

holen: (Eng. hole in) *n.* marble.

hopyà: (Ch. *hò pià*: good cake) *n.* cake stuffed with sweetened mashed beans.

hormonada: (*slang*) *n.* homosexual male who wants to have big breasts.

hornál: (Sp. *jornal*) *n.* daily wage; day work; installment; paying by installment.

hota: (Sp. *jota*) *n.* the letter *j*.

hothot: *n.* honking sound.

hototay: (Ch.) *n.* chicken soup with eggs and vegetables.

hoya: (Sp. *jolla*) *n.* jewel, gem; **hoyero** *n.* jeweler; **hoyeriya** *n.* jewelers.

hoyo: (Sp.) *n.* golf hole.

hu: *interj.* exclamation used to scare animals.

hubád: *adj.* naked from the waist up; **hubarín, hubdín** *v.* to disrobe; **hubarán, hubdán** *v.* to strip (of clothes); **hubú't-hubád** *adj.* completely naked; **hubád sa katotohanan** *id.* far from the truth (nude in truth); **habádbaro** *adj.* naked.

hubero: *adj.* piebald.

hubélyo: (Sp. *jubileo*) *n.* jubilee.

hublî: **paghublî** *n.* cash payment with discount for a crop share.

hubô: *adj.* naked, nude (from the waist down); **maghubò** *v.* to undress.

hubog: *n.* shape of an arch; **hubóg** *adj.* slightly bent, curved; **hubugin** *v.* to curve; bend; form, shape; train someone.

hubyâ: (*slang*, Waray) *adj.* lazy.

Huk: *n.* member of guerilla organization, *Hukbalahap*.

hukab: *var.* of *hukag*: big hole.

hukag: *n.* big hole, hollow.

hukáy: *n.* hole, pit; excavation; **humukay, maghukáy** *v.* to dig; **humuhukay ng sariling libingan** *id.* doing something self-destructive (digging one's own grave).

Hukbalahap: *n.* guerilla organization.

hukbó: *n.* army; **panghukbó** *adj.* military; **hukbóng-katihan** *n.* army, land troops; **hukbóng-karagatan** *n.* navy; **hukbóng-himpapawíd** *n.* air force. **hukbóng-lakad** *n.* infantry, foot soldiers. **hukbóng-sandatahán** armed forces.

hukbót: *n.* ducking the head (to avoid a blow).

hukhók: *adj.* sunken; caved in.

hukláy: *adj.* drooping; insipid.

huklô: *n.* ducking of the head.

huklób: *adj.* senile; decrepit.

huklót: *var.* of *huklô*: ducking the head (to avoid a blow, etc.).

hukóm: *n.* judge; **húkúman** *n.* law court; courthouse; **hukumán** *v.* to pass sentence; **paghuhukóm** *n.* trial; passing of judgment; **Hukóm-Tagapamayapà** Justice of the Peace; **Húkuman sa Paghahabol** *n.* Court of Appeals; **Húkumang Unang Dulugan** *n.* Court of First Instance; **Kátaás-taasang Húkúman** *n.* Supreme Court.

hukóng: *adj.* hunchbacked.

hukót: *adj.* round-shouldered, stooped.

Hudas: *n.* Judas; (*fig.*) traitor, one who betrays; **yakap-Hudas** *id.* pretension (embrace of Judas); **mag-Hudas** *v.* to double cross.

hudhód: **paghuhudhód** *n.* scrubbing off dirt from the skin.

hudikatura: (Sp. *judicatura*) *n.* magistracy.

hudyát: *n.* alert, signal; password; **hudyatán** *v.* to signal someone; **maghudyát** *n.* to signal; alert beforehand.

Hudyó: (Sp. *judío*) *n.* Jew; Jewish.

hugák: *n.* hollow sound.

hugadór: (Sp. *jugador*) *n.* gambler.

hugas: **maghugas** *v.* to wash (body, dishes); **hugasan** *v.* to wash; bathe; **hugasán** *n.* washtub; **hugas-bigás** *n.* water used to wash rice; **tagahugas ng pinggán** *n.* dishwasher; **naghuhugas ng kamáy** *id.* denying doing bad things (washing the hands).

hughóg: **hughugán** *v.* to rinse; **paghughóg** *n.* ransacking a placc; **pagkahughóg** *n.* falling off (loose clothes).

hugis-: *pref.* from *hugis*: shaped like: **hugis-kandilà** shaped like a candle; **hugis-tao** shaped like a man.

hugis: *n.* shape, form; figure; mold; model; **humugis** *v.* to form, shape.

hugláw: *var.* of *hugnáw*.

hugnáw: *var.* of *hignáw*: serene; abating.

hugnáy: *n.* combined clause.

hugók: *var.* of *ugók*.

hugnós: *var.* of *bugnós*: untangling a knot

hugong: *n.* buzzing sound, murmur.

hugos: **ihugos** *v.* to let down a rope.

hugot: **hugutin** *v.* to pull out, unsheathe.

hugpóng: *n.* juncture; **ihugpóng** *v.* to join.

huhô: **huhuán** *v.* to pour; **pagkahuhô** *n.* leakage; landslide; overflow.

hulà: *n.* forecast; guess; **mahulaan** *v.* to anticipate; foretell; **hulaan** *v.* to guess; **manghuhulà** *n.* fortune teller; **magpahulà** *v.* to have one's fortune told.

hulab: *var.* of *hilab*: swell, bulge.

hulagpós: *adj.* untied.

hulapì: *n.* suffix.

hulás: *adj.* liquefied, melted; lowered (fever).

hulaw: *n.* abating.

huli: *n.* catch (in fishing); **humuli** *v.* to catch; **hulihin** *v.* to catch, capture; **hulihán** *n.* game of catching each other; **magpahuli** *v.* to allow oneself to get caught; **máhúli** *v.* to be caught, seized, arrested; **mahuli** *v.* to be able to catch; **manghuli** *v.* to catch many (fish, etc.); **mapanghuli** *adj.* sly; **pagkakáhúli** *n.* arrest, seizing; **panghuli** *n.* means of catching; trap; **nahuli sa bibíg** *id.* unintentionally revealed a secret (caught in the mouth); **nahuli sa kamáy** *id.* thing lost found in the hands of the thief (caught in the hand).

hulì: **mahulì, hulî** *adj.* senile; **kahulian** *n.* senility.

hulí: *n.* tail, tail end; rear; *adj.* late, final, last; behind; **kahulihán** *n.* lateness; **káhulí-hulihan** *adj.* latest; farthest behind; *adv.* last; **hulihan** *n.* balance left to pay on a loan; **hulihán** *n.* tail end; back; rear; **ipahulí, ipagpáhulí** *v.* to put at the end; **máhulí** *adj.* late; **pagkáhulí** *n.* lateness; falling behind; **pamáhulihán** *n.* hind, rear; **hulíng hantungan** *id.* grave (last goal); **hulíng-habilin** *n.* last will and testament; **hulíng-paalam** *n.* last farewell; **sa hulí** in back, behind.

hulilip: **waláng-kahulilip** *adj.* incomparable.

hulímbuhay: (*huling-buhay*) *n.* end of one's life.

hulímpatì: (*huling-pati*) *n.* last turn in a debate.

hulíng-: *pref.* last: **hulíng-kabít** *n.* last common law spouse, **hulíng-katagâ** *n.* last words, closing remarks; **hulíng-habilin** *n.* last will and testament.

hulip: *n.* substitution of a worn-out object or dying plant.

hulmá: (Sp. *horma*) *n.* molded shape; **hulmado** *adj.* molded; **hulmahan** *n.* mold; **hulmahín** *v.* to mold.

hulò: **kahuluan** *n.* source of river; uppermost end of town.

hulò: *n.* rationalization; **mahulò** *v.* to deduce.

hulog$_1$: *n.* fall; deposit (in a bank); **mahulog** *v.* to fall, drop; flunk; **magpakahulog, magpatihulog** *v.* to fall down intentionally; **hulugan** *v.* to let fall, throw down; **hulog ng langit** *n.* gift from heaven; **nahuhulog ang**

katawán *id.* becoming weak (body is falling); **parang nahulog sa balóng katawán** *id.* unfortunate; **maghulog sa koreo** *v.* to mail.
hulog₂: **kahulugan** *n.* meaning, significance; intent, purpose; sense; **mangahulugán** *v.* to mean; suppose, imply; **kasingkahulugán** *adj.* synonymous; **ipakahulugán** *v.* to give as an interpretation; **makahulugán** *adj.* meaningful; **magpakahulugán** *v.* to interpret; **pakahulugán** *n.* interpretation; **singkahulugán** *n.* synonym; **tálahuluganán** *n.* glossary.
hulog₃: *n.* translation; **ihulog** *v.* to translate.
hulog₄: **paghuhulog** *n.* installment payment; **hulog-sapì** *n.* fee in a membership organization.
hulog₅: **panghulog** *n.* plumb line (used to test the depth of water).
hulog₆: (*slang*) *n.* game fixing (in gambling).
Hulyo: (Sp. *julio*) *n.* July.
huma: **paghuma** *n.* talk, speech.
humál: *adj.* with a nasal twang (voice).
humaymáy: **pagkahumaymáy** *n.* peacefulness, tranquility.
humbá: (Ch. *hông bàq*: saucy meat) *n.* highly spiced dish of pork or chicken.
humbák: *n.* trough between waves.
humigít-kumulang: *adv.* more or less.
humpák: *adj.* hollow, concave.
humpáy: *n.* pause, stop; **maghumpáy** *v.* to pause.
hunâ: **humunâ** *v.* to become frail; **mahunâ** *adj.* frail.
hunab: *n.* scum, fatty substance on the surface of a liquid; **hunaban** *v.* to remove the fatty substance off the surface of a liquid.
hunáb: *n.* vapor rising from the ground; drops of moisture on the surface of glass.
hunhón: *n.* pushing to the side.
huni: *n.* hoot, chirping sound.
hunos: *n.* skin peeling; **maghunos** *v.* to molt, shed one's skin; **hunos-dilì** *n.* self-control; **maghunos-dilì** *v.* to control one's self.
hunós: *n.* share of the crop being harvested.
hunta: (Sp. *junta*) *n.* board, council; **paghuhuntahan** *n.* conversation; **huntahín** *v.* to converse with.
hunusdilì: *n.* prudence, careful consideration; **maghunusdilì** *v.* to reflect, meditate; reconsider.
hunyangò: *n.* chameleon; (*slang*) fool.
Hunyo: (Sp. *junio*) *n.* June.
hungkág: *adj.* hollow, empty; concave.
hungkóy: (Ch.) **hungkuyan** *n.* winnowing mill.
hungháng: *adj.* foolish, senseless.
hungot: *n.* coconut shell used as a dipper.
hupâ: **pahupaín** *v.* to make less intense, diminish; **humupâ** *v.* to decrease; subside.
hupák: *var.* of *himpák*: deflated.
hupaw: *n.* lessening of the intensity of.
hupyák: *adj.* hollow; sunken.
hura: (Sp. *jura*) **humura** *v.* to take an oath; **paghura** *n.* oath.
hurado: (Sp. *jurado*) *n.* jury; board of judges; *adj.* sworn in.
huramentado: (Sp. *juramentado*) *adj.* amuck.
huramento: (Sp. *juramento*) *n.* oath.
hurisprudensiyá: (Sp. *jurisprudencia*) *n.* jurisprudence; legal profession, law.
hurista: (Sp. *jurista*) *n.* jurist.
hurnál: (Sp. *jornal*) *n.* installment; daily wage; journal.
hurnó: (Sp. *horno*) *n.* oven; **maghurnó** *v.* to bake.
huróg: (*slang*) *adj.* high on drugs.
hurung-huróng: *n.* crowd; throng.
husay: **mahusay** *adj.* skillful, capable; methodical; **kahusayan** *n.* skill, efficiency; orderliness; **husayin** *v.* to put in order.
husgá: (Sp. *juzgar*) **humusgá** *v.* to pass judgement.
husgado: (Sp. *juzgado*) *n.* court of justice; tribunal.
husi: *n.* pineapple fabric.
husô: *adj.* disentangled.
hustisya: (Sp. *justicia*) *n.* justice.
hustó: (Sp. *justo*) *adj.* enough, sufficient; adequate; up-to-date; correct; complete; **di-hustó** *adj.* inadequate, not enough, inexact; **hustuhín** *v.* to complete; **maghustó** *v.* to fit, be exact; suffice.
huták: *n.* sound of walking in the mud.

hután: *n.* handle.

huthót: **huthután** *v.* to profiteer; extort; **humuthót** *v.* to suck; **paghuthót** *n.* sucking, suction.

hutok: **humutok** *v.* to weigh down; to train.

huwád: *adj.* counterfeit, dummy; fake; false; **huwarín** *v.* to copy, imitate, counterfeit.

huwág: *aux.* do not, don't. Verb used in negative commands. **Huwag kayong kumain!** Don't eat.

huwaling: *n.* banded slipmouth fish.

huwana: (Ch. *huân à*: foreign son) *n.* derogatory term for Filipinos (used by Chinese).

huwasò: *adj.* lacking refinement.

Huwebes: (Sp. *jueves*) *n.* Thursday.

huwego: (Sp. *juego*) *n.* gambling game; set; **maghuwego** *v.* to gamble; **huwego de toro** *n.* bullfight; **huwego-de-anilyo** *n.* ring game played on horses; **huwego-de-prenda** *n.* game of forfeits.

huwepe: (Ch.) *n.* resin torch wrapped in palm leaves.

huwés: (Sp. *juez*) *n.* judge (*hukóm*); **Huwés-de-Pas** *n.* Justice of the Peace.

huweteng: (Ch. *huê tng*: flower space) *n.* form of lottery gambling.

huwipe: (Ch. *huè pe*: fire bundle) *n.* torch.

huwisyo: (Sp. *juicio*) *n.* court trial; judgement; common sense.

huyad: **paghuyad** *n.* walking with difficulty (obese person).

huyok: **huyók** *adj.* bent down.

huyong: (*obs.*) *n.* hunger; **huyóng** *adj.* hungry.

I

i-: *pref.* prefix used to form theme focus verbs.

ibà: *n.* species of tree with acidic fruits.

ibá: *pron.* other, another; different; else; **ibahín** *v.* to make different, alter, revise; **ibá't-ibá** *adj.* different, various; **ikaibá** *v.* to differentiate; **mag-ibá-ibá** *v.* to keep changing; **maibá** *v.* to feel out of place; **pagkakaibá** *n.* difference; diversity.

ibabâ: *n.* lower part, underpart; **ibabâ** *v.* to put lower, take downstairs; **sa ibabâ** *adj.* below, underneath.

ibabaw: *n.* top, surface; **sa ibabaw** *prep.* on top, over, on the surface of; **magpaibabaw** *v.* to surface; **mamaibabaw, pumaibabaw** *v.* to rise above; **mangibabaw** *v.* to rise to the top; surmount; dominate; predominate; **nakapangíngibabaw** *adj.* dominant, prevailing; **paibabawan** *v.* to put over, put on top of; **pang-ibabaw** *n.* veneer; **pang-ibabawan** *v.* to wear something with an outer garment; cover the surface with; **pangibabawan** *v.* to dominate; overwhelm; **pangingibabaw** *n.* predominance; excellence.

ibag: **pag-ibag** *n.* dodging, evading, eluding; **umibag** *v.* to dodge, jump to avoid; elude.

ibalay: *n.* spotted pomadasid fish.

Ibalóy: *n.* ethnic group and language from Benguet Province and western Nueva Vizcaya Province.

Ibanág: *n.* ethnic group and language from Isabela and Cagayan Provinces.

Ibatán: *n.* ethnic group and language from Batanes Islands.

ibay: *n.* dizziness caused by chewing betel nut.

ibayo$_1$: *adj.* double, as large as; *adv.* doubly; **mag-ibayo** *v.* to double, increase greatly.

ibayo$_2$: *n.* opposite side; *adv.* across; **ibayong dagat** *n.* foreign land.

ibig: **pag-ibig** *n.* love, fondness; whim, caprice; **kaibigan** *n.* friend; **pagkakaibigan** *n.* friendship; **umibig** *v.* to fall in love, love; **palaibig** *adj.* amorous; **pangingibig** *n.* wooing, suit; **ibigin** *v.* to love; **ibig na ayaw** *id.* undecided; **ibig sabihin** *v.* to mean.

ibís$_1$: **ibisán** *v.* to unload; get down to (when getting off a vehicle); **umibís** *v.* to get off a vehicle.

ibís$_2$: **pagkaibís** *n.* relief from pain; **maibsán** *v.* to be relieved from.

ibô: *n.* action, movement.

ibok: (*slang*) *n.* helplessness.

ibon: *n.* bird; (*slang*) rank in the military; **ibunan** *n.* aviary; **palaibunan** *n.* ornithology; **ibong mababà ang lipád** *id.* prostitute (bird

with low flight); **ibong malayà** *id.* bachelor (free bird).
ibos: *n.* buri palm.
ibot: *n.* croaker fish, dusummier's drumfish.
ibsán: (rt. *ibís*) *v.* to unload; get down to (when getting off a vehicle).
ibutud: **ibuturan, káibuturan** *n.* innermost center; utmost depth.
ikà: *contr.* of *wikà*: said (by): *wikà ko* > *ikà ko.* said by me, as I said.
ikâ: **umikâ** *v.* to walk with a limp.
ika- *pref.* 1. forms ordinal numbers; 2. forms nominals out of stative roots that indicate non-volitional cause or reason: **ikabagal** *v.* to cause or be the cause of delay; **ikabulag** *v.* to be the cause of one's blindness.
ikáw: *pron.* you (singular, familiar).
ikay: **ikáy** *adj.* done thoroughly.
ikì: *n.* mythological nocturnal creature with a long tongue that sucks blood and fetuses from pregnant woman.
ikid: *n.* roll, coil; **ikirin** *v.* to spin, wind.
ikit: *n.* turn, gyration, rotation; **umikit** *v.* to whirl, twirl, spin.
iklî: **maiklî** *adj.* brief, short; **mangiklî** *v.* to shrink, become short; **umiklî** *v.* to contract, shrink; **maiklî ang pisì** *id.* with little money (thread is short).
ikmó: *n.* betel pepper.
ikód: *n.* limping.
ikóm: **nakaikóm** *adj.* closed (hand, flowers).
ikot: **umikot** *v.* to revolve, turn around, rotate; **paikutin** *v.* to spin something around.
iksamen: (Sp. *examen*) *n.* test, exam.
iksî: **maiksî** *adj.* short.
ikuran: *n.* silver gruntfish.
ikwál: **pag-ikwál** *n.* wriggling.
idlíp: *n.* nap, snooze; **umidlíp** *v.* to doze, take a nap.
ídolo: (Sp.) *n.* idol; pimp.
Ifugáo: *n.* ethnic group and language from Ifugao Province.
igá: **naigá** *adj.* dried up, evaporated.
igan: (*slang*, *kaibigan*) *n.* friend.
igat: *n.* black eel, freshwater eel; (*slang*) black complexioned.
igaya: **kaigayahan** *n.* delight; charm; **maigaya** *v.* to be attracted, induced.
igkás: **umigkás** *v.* to recoil, spring back.
igera: (Sp. *higuera*) *n.* fig tree.
igi: **maigi** *adj.* good, fine; **kaigihan** *n.* goodness, excellence.
igíb: **umigíb** *v.* to get water from a well.
igík: *n.* grunt.
igíg: **igigín** *v.* to shake something.
igláp: *n.* instant, brief moment.
iglesya: (Sp. *iglesia*) *n.* church.
igos: (Sp. *higo*) *n.* fig.
igpáw: *n.* leap over an obstacle.
igsî: **maigsî** *adj.* short; **umigsî** *v.* to become shorter.
igtád: **umigtád** *v.* to dodge, move to the side quickly; (*slang*) escape.
igting: **maigting** *adj.* tight, taut; **igtingán** *v.* to tighten.
iha: (Sp. *hija*) *n.* daughter.
ihaw: **ihawán** *n.* roaster; **pag-ihaw** *n.* roasting; **inihaw** *adj.* roasted; **parang iníihaw** *id.* restless.
ihì: *n.* urine; **kaiihì** *n.* frequent urination; **ihian** *v.* to urinate on; **maihî** *v.* to urinate involuntarily; **ihî** *adj.* incontinent.
ihip: *n.* blow, gust, breeze.
ihít: **pag-iihít** *n.* fit, convulsion (of laughter, anger or sadness).
iho: (Sp. *hijo*) *n.* son.
iim: *n.* common spotted slipmouth fish.
iít: *n.* humorous nickname; signal given during hide and seek game to start looking for the hiding players.
iito: *n.* plotosid catfish.
iлák: *n.* striped rudder fish.
ilak: **mangilak** *v.* to raise funds.
ilado: (Sp. *helado*) *adj.* frozen.
ilag: **ilagan** *v.* to avoid, dodge; **umilag** *v.* to shun, dodge; avoid.
ilalim: *n.* bottom; **pailalim** *v.* to go under; **pailalím** *adv.* towards the bottom; secretly; slyly; **pang-ilalim** *adj.* under, below; **sa ilalim** *prep.* at the bottom; **sa ilalim ng** *prep.* under, beneath; **ipailalim** *v.* to put under; subordinate; **isailalim** *v.* to put under; **mangilalim** *v.* to be underneath; be underlying; **sumailalim, pumailalim** *v.* to

submit, go under; **káilaliman** *n.* the very bottom.

ilán: *pron.* few, some; how many?; **kailanán** *n.* grammatical number; **kailan** when? **íilán** *adv.* few (*ilán lamang*; *kákauntî*); **Ílánan**? How many in each group?

ilandáng: *n.* shooting up of water from a fountain.

iláng: *n.* desert, wasteland.

ilang-ilang: *n.* kind of fragrant flower.

ilangláng: *n.* soaring. **pumailangláng** *v.* to soar, ascend.

iláp: *n.* wild state; **mailáp** *adj.* wild, unbroken, not tame. **kailapán** *n.* wildness; elusiveness.

ilat: *n.* dry bed of a rivulet.

ilaw: *n.* light; **ilawán** *n.* lamp; **iláwan** *v.* to illuminate, give light; **umilaw** *v.* to light up; **waláng ilaw ang mga matá** *id.* blind (eyes have no light).

ilay: **pagkailay** *n.* motion sickness.

ilaya: *n.* interior part of country, upper part of town.

iletrado: (Sp.) *adj.* illiterate.

ilíg: **umilíg** *v.* to shake.

ilihán: *n.* shelter against wind or rain; mountain retreat.

ilíng: *n.* shaking of the head; **umilíng** *v.* to shake the head.

ilit: **pag-ilit** *n.* confiscation; **umilit, ilitin** *v.* to confiscate.

iliw: *n.* flying fish, Family *Exocoetidae*.

ilo: (Sp. *hilo*) *n.* thread; yarn; fiber.

iló: **pag-iló** *n.* crushing of sugar cane; **iluhan** *n.* machine used to crush sugarcane.

Ilokano: *n.* ethnic group from Northern Luzon (Ilocos region); language of Ilocano people.

Iloko: *n.* language of the Ilocano people.

ilog: *n.* river; **ilug-ilugan** *n.* rivulet; **mag-ilog** *v.* to turn into a river.

ilóng: *n.* nose; **butas ng ilóng** *n.* nostril; **sarát na ilóng** *n.* pug nose, flat nosed; **malambót ang ilóng** *id.* easily fooled; not witty (nose is soft); **nagsisikíp ang ilóng** *id.* filled with hatred (nose is choked).

Ilongot: *n.* ethnic group and language from Eastern Nueva Vizcaya and Western Quirino Provinces, Luzon.

ilustrado: (Sp.) *adj.* illustrated; learnèd, educated; accomplished.

imahen: (Sp. *imagen*) *n.* image. (*larawan*)

imahinasyon: (Sp. *imaginación*) *n.* imagination.

imán: (Sp.) *n.* magnet. (*batubalanì*)

imbabáw: **kaimbabawan** *n.* exterior; **mapagpa-imbabáw** *adj.* superficial; hypocritical.

imbák: **imbakan** *n.* storage place; **mag-imbák** *v.* to store, conserve.

imbálido: (Sp. *inválido*) *adj.* invalid.

imbáw: *n.* leap; lump. **umimbáw** *v.* to leap.

imbáy: *n.* trot of a horse; swinging movement of the arms.

imabayog: *n.* swaying, swinging; **umimbayog** *v.* to swing, sway.

imbentaryo: (Sp. *inventario*) *n.* inventory.

imbento: (Sp. *invento*) *n.* invention; **umimbento** *v.* to invent, fabricate.

imberna: var. of *imbierna*: irritated, disturbed.

imbestidura: (Sp. *investidura*) *n.* investiture.

imbestigá: (Sp. *investigar*) **mag-imbestigá** *v.* to investigate.

imbí: *adj.* mean, low; ignoble.

imbierna: (Sp. *envenenar*) **maimbierna** (*slang*) *v.* to be irritated.

imbót: **maimbót** *adj.* covetous, greedy, selfish; **mag-imbót** *v.* to covet.

imbubuyog: *n.* wasp, hornet.

imbudo: (Sp. *embudo*) *n.* funnel; (*slang*) annoyance.

imbulóg: **pag-imbulóg** *n.* soaring.

imbulsá: (Sp. *embolso*) **pag-iimbulsá** *n.* reimbursement; **imbulsahán** *v.* to reimburse.

imburnál: (Sp. *embornal*) *n.* culvert, sewer.

imbutido: (Sp. *embutido*) *n.* stuffed sausage; inlaid work, mosaic.

imî: *n.* cry of goats.

imík: **umimík** *v.* to speak, talk, utter; **pag-imík** *n.* talk; replay.

imíd: **umimíd, imirán** *v.* to look askance.

imis: **imisin** *v.* to put things in order; **maimis** *adj.* neat and orderly.

imno: (Sp. *himno*) *n.* hymn.

imot: **maimot** *adj.* mean, stingy.

impake: (Sp. *empaque*) *n.* packing.

impakto: *n.* evil spirit, spook.

impatso: (Sp. *empacho*) *n.* indigestion; **impatsado** *adj.* with indigestion.
imperdible: (Sp.) *n.* safety pin.
imperyo: (Sp. *imperio*) *n.* empire.
impís: *adj.* flat; deflated; **umimpís** *v.* to become deflated.
impít: *adj.* compressed, pressed; **paimpít** *adj.* glottal, guttural.
impiyerno: (Sp. *infierno*) *n.* hell.
impluensya: (Sp. *influencia*) *n.* influence; **maimpluwensiya** *adj.* influential.
impo: (*slang*, Eng.) *n.* police informer
impó: (Ch.) *n.* grandmother.
impók: **mag-impók** *v.* to save, store up.
importante: (Sp.) *adj.* important.
impotente: (Sp.) *adj.* impotent.
imprenta: (Sp.) *n.* printing shop; printing press.
imus: *n.* cape (land).
-in-: *infix.* forms perfective forms of patient focus verbs: **ginawâ** did, make; **sinampál** slapped.
-in: *suffix.* forms patient focus verbs, variant *-hin* after vowels: **bagtíng** *adj.* tight, **bagtingín** *v.* to tighten something.
iná: *n.* mother; **mag-iná** *n.* mother and child; **inahán** *n.* safety point of the game of hide and seek; **inahín** *n.* mother hen; **makainá** *adj.* very fond of one's mother.
inaamá: (*rt. amá*) *n.* godfather.
inaanák: (*rt. anák*) *n.* godchild.
inakáy: *n.* young bird, birdling.
inam: **mainam** *adj.* nice, neat; good; respectable; temperate; modest; **kainaman** *n.* sufficient quantity; mildness; **pinakamainam** *adj.* prime, first-rate.
inambayan: [*iná=ng bayan*] *n.* mother country.
inampalán: *n.* jury.
inanák: (*rt. anák*) *n.* descendant.
ináng: *n.* appellation for one's mother; **inánghagdán** *n.* two parallel boards of a stepcase to which the stairs are joined.
inat: **mag-inát** *v.* to stretch (oneself).
ináy, inang: *n.* appellation for one's mother.
inkilino: (Sp. *inquilino*) *n.* tenant.
indá: **di-indá** *adj.* not noticing, not feeling.
indâ: *n.* term of respect for an old woman.
indák: **umindák** *v.* to tap dance.
indangan: *n.* surgeon fish.
indáy: (*Vis.*) *n.* young woman; sweetheart.
indayog: *n.* rhythm.
índise: (Sp. *índice*) *n.* index.
indiyán: (*slang*, Eng. *indian*) **iyindiyán** *v.* to fail to show up, stand up a person.
indóy: (*slang*) *adj.* ugly.
indulto: (Sp.) *n.* amnesty, pardon.
indungan: *n.* siganid fish.
indyán: (Eng. *indian*) *n.* trickster; failing to meet an appointment.
Inglés: (Sp.) *n.* English.
inhenyero: (Sp. *ingeniero*) *n.* engineer.
inhenyoso: (Sp. *ingenioso*) *adj.* ingenious.
inhusto: (Sp. *injusto*) *adj.* unjust.
iniksiyón: (Eng.) *n.* injection.
in-in: *adj.* fully cooked; **in-inín** *v.* to keep something cooking.
iníng: *n.* term of address for young girls.
iníp: **mainíp** *adj.* bored; **kainipán** *n.* boredom.
inís$_1$: **pagkainís** *n.* disgust; **nakakainís** *adj.* disgusting; **mainís** *v.* to be disgusted.
inís$_2$: **mainís** *adj.* to be suffocated; **pag-inís** *n.* suffocation.
init: *n.* heat; **mainit** *adj.* hot; **magpainit** *v.* to warm oneself; **mainit ang ulo** *id.* easily angered (head is hot); **mainit sa kamáy** *id.* easily spent (hot in the hand); **mainit ang dugô** *id.* antipathetic; **mainit ang matá** *id.* angry; desirous.
inlá: *n.* pupil of the eye.
inlís: *n.* inermid fish.
inó: **inuhin** *v.* to take notice of.
inodoro: (Sp.) *n.* toilet.
inog: **uminog** *v.* to whirl, spin, rotate.
inóm: *n.* drinking; **uminom** *v.* to drink; **maginuman** *v.* to drink together; **inumin** *n.* drink, beverage.
Inonhan: *n.* ethnic group and language from Southern Tablas Island, Romblon Province and Mindoro.
inót: **inút-inután** *v.* to do little by little.
insán: (*coll.*) *n.* cousin.
insayo: (Sp. *ensayo*) *n.* rehearsal.
insensaryo: (Sp. *incensario*) *n.* incense con-

tainer.

Insík: *n.*, *adj.* Chinese.

insó: (Ch.) *n.* appellation for the wife of an elder brother or cousin.

instinto: (Sp.) *n.* instinct.

instituto: (Sp.) *n.* institute.

instrumento: (Sp.) *n.* instrument.

insulá: **insulahín** *v.* to insulate.

insulares: (Sp., *obs.*) *n.* Spanish people born in the Philippines. [Contrast *peninsulares*]

insulto: (Sp.) *n.* insult.

integridád: (Sp.) *n.* integrity.

interés: (Sp.) *n.* interest; concern.

intindí: (Sp. *entiende*) **intindihín** *v.* to pay attention to; **maintindihán** *v.* to understand.

intriga: (Sp.) *n.* intrigue; (*slang*) daily rent money paid by a jeepney driver to the vehicle owner.

intrimitido: (Sp. *entremetido*) *n.* busybody, meddler.

Intsik: *var. of Insik*: Chinese.

inupas: *n.* dry leaves of sugarcane.

inutil: (Sp.) *adj.* useless; helpless.

inyó: *adj.* your (plural or polite).

ingat: *n.* care, carefulness; **ingatan, mag-ingat** *v.* to beware, be careful about; watch out; guard; take care of; **maingat** *adj.* careful; prudent; vigilant; **tagapag-ingat** *n.* caretaker; **ingat-yaman** *n.* treasurer.

ingáw: *n.* meow of cats.

ingay: **kaingayan** *n.* noise, fuss, ado; **mag-ingáy** *v.* to make a noise; blare; **maingay** *adj.* noisy.

ingkáng: **paingkáng-ingkáng** *adj.* unbalanced when walking (with the feet apart).

Inkóng: (Ch.) *n.* term of address for an elderly man.

inggít: *n.* envy; grudge; **mainggít** *v.* to envy, be jealous of; **naiinggít** *adj.* envious.

inggreso: (Sp. *intreso*) *n.* ledger entry, receipts, income.

ingil: *n.* snarl, growl.

ing-ing: *n.* sound of the violin.

ingít: *n.* sob, whimper; creaky sound.

Inglatera: (Sp. *Inglaterra*) *n.* England.

ipá: *n.* chaff of rice grains.

ipa- *pref.* forms causative transitive verbs (indicating indirect action): **ipalinis** *v.* to cause/permit to clean; **ipakita** *v.* to show, cause to see; **ipabigáy** *v.* to have someone give something.

ipaki: *pref.* forms polite *i-* verbs: **ipakibigáy** *v.* to please give.

ipag-: *pref.* forms transitive benefactive verbs: **ipaglabá** *v.* to do the laundry for; **ipag-ihaw** *v.* to broil for someone; **ipagbuwís** *v.* to pay the taxes for.

ipang-: *pref.* forms transitive benefactive or instrumental verbs from *mang-* verbs: **ipanguha** *v.* to gather for; **ipanahi** *v.* to sew for; **ipanggapos** *v.* to use to tie up.

ipil: *n.* large tree.

ipis: cockroach; **parang ipis** *id.* speaking softly; always getting food in the cupboard (like a cockroach).

ipit: *n.* hairclip; tweezers; **ipitin** *v.* to squeeze; **maipit** *v.* to be crushed, squeezed, pinned down.

ipo: *n.* kind of evergreen tree.

ipókrita: (Sp. *hipócrita*) *n.* hypocrite.

ipod: **pag-ipod** *n.* moving a little, budging.

ipon: **ipunin** *v.* to gather, collect; **kaipunan** *n.* collection, gathering.

ipot: *n.* fowl droppings.

ipuipo: *n.* whirlwind.

iral: **umiral** *v.* to exist, prevail; operate, be effective; **pag-iral** *n.* existence; prevalence; **magpairal**, **pairalin** *v.* to put into effect; **mapaiíral** *adj.* enforceable, applicable, **pagpapairal** *n.* application, putting into effect; maintenance.

irap: **irapan** *v.* to give a nasty look to, sneer at; **mag-írápan** *v.* to sneer at each other; **pairáp** *adj.* sullen; **umirap** *v.* to sneer.

Iraya: *n.* ethnic group and language from Northern Mindoro.

irí: *pron.* this; **ganirí** *adv.* like this.

irí: **umirí** *v.* to expel from the body, grunt when giving birth or defecating.

iríng: *n.* disdain; **iringín** *v.* to treat with disdain; **mapang-iríng** *adj.* prone to be disdainful.

irit: **umirit** *v.* to shriek, scream; give a signal.

Irlanda: (Sp.) *n.* Ireland; **Irlandés** *n.* Irish.

irog: *n.* darling, beloved; **kairug-irog** *adj.* likeable; beloved; **mairog** *adj.* fond, loving; **mairugín** *adj.* gracious, affectionate; **magpairog** *v.* to be gracious to grant a favor; **pag-irog** *n.* affection; **pairog** *n.* giving in, indulgence.

isa-: *pref.* forms transitive verbs rendering transference, or translation of the stem: **isaisip** *v.* to put in one's mind; **isa-Tagalog** *v.* to translate into Tagalog; **isaaklát** *v.* to make into a book.

isá: *n.* one; **bawa't isá** each; **kaisá-isá** *adj.* only one; **kaisá** *adj.* united with; **kaisahán** *n.* unity, solidarity; oneness; **íisáhan** *adv.* one by one; **isahín** *v.* to unite, make one; **isá't-isá** everyone; **mákaisá** *v.* to agree; **makapag-íisá** *adj.* self-sufficient; **makipagkáisá** *v.* to enter an agreement; **magkaisá** *adj.* united, joined; **mag-isá** *v.* to be alone, do alone; **maisahán** *v.* to do something that is better than someone else; **mangisá-ngisá** *adv.* rarely; **nag-íisá** *adj.* alone; **mápagkáisahán** *v.* to be judged; **nagkakáisá** *adj.* firmly united; **pakikipag-isá** *n.* being one with; communion; **pagkakáisá** *n.* solidarity; union; **pagkaíisá** *n.* oneness; **pagkáisahán** *v.* to agree on one thing; **pag-iisá** *n.* solitude; **pang-isá** *adj.* single; **pag-isahín** *v.* to combine, unite; unify; **pang-isá** *adj.* single; singular; **sang-ísáhan** *n.* unity; union; **tig-(i)isá** *adj.* one each; **iisá ang tugtugin** *id.* two persons with the same character (only one music); **magkaisáng-pusò** *id.* to marry (able to unite heart); **nakaisáng-palad** *id.* married (had palms united).

isaw: *n.* small intestine.

iskala: (Sp. *escala*) *n.* scale; stop during travelling, stop over.

iskaparate: (Sp. *escaparate*) *n.* showcase.

iskape: (Sp. *escape*) *n.* gallop.

iskarlata: (Sp. *escarlata*) *n.* scarlet.

iskerda: *var.* of *iskiyerda*: leave.

iskiyerda: (Sp. *izquierda*: left, as opposed to right) *v.* go home; leave.

iskombro: (Sp. *escombro*) *n.* rubble.

iskurukutóy: (*slang*) *n.* fool; dunce.

isdâ: *n.* fish; **mangisdâ** *v.* to fish; **mag-isdâ** *v.* to deal in fish; **mangingisdâ** *n.* fisherman; **tiník ng isdâ** *n.* fishbone; **isdáng-ilóng** *n.* nosefish; **isdáng-buaya** *n.* flathead fish; **isdáng-laring-laring** *n.* shrimp fish; **isdáng-lawin** *n.* flying fish; **isdáng-sikwán** *n.* shrimp fish.

isdantukô: *n.* white shark.

isil: *n.* nudge, light touch.

Isináy: *n.* ethnic group and language from Nueva Vizcaya.

isip: *n.* mind, intellect; thought, judgement; **kaisipán** *n.* the mind, intellect; attitude; opinion; **makaisip** *v.* to be able to think; **isaisip** *v.* to bear in mind; think of; **isipan** *n.* mind; **isipin** *v.* to think about; consider; **mag-isíp** *v.* to think; plan; contemplate on; **nasa isip** *adj.* in one's head; imaginary, not real; **palaisipán** *n.* mind puzzle; enigma; **umisip** *v.* to think of; **abót ng isip** *n.* extent of view, scope of one's intelligence; **bukás ang isip** *adj.* open-minded; **isip-ipis, isip-lamók** *n.* ignorant person.

is-is: *n.* species of shrub whose rough leaves are used for scrubbing; **is-isín** *v.* to scour, scrub.

isla: (Sp.) *n.* island.

ismíd: **ismirán** *v.* to sneer at, sniff at; scoff.

ismól: (*slang*, Eng. *small*) **ismolin** *v.* to belittle.

isnabero: (*slang*) *n.* snob.

Isnág: *n.* ethnic group and language from Northern Apayao, Luzon.

iso: *n.* silver spotted gray snapper fish.

isod: **umisod** *v.* to move on one's buttocks.

isoy: (*slang*) *n.* cigarette.

ispada: (Sp. *espada*) *n.* sword; spade; swordfish; hairtail fish.

ispirikitik: (*slang*) *n.* surprise action.

ispiya: (Sp. *espía*) *n.* spy.

isputing: (*slang*, Eng. *sporting*) **nakaisputing** *adj.* dressed up.

istakada: (Sp. *estacada*) *n.* stockade.

istambay: (Eng. stand by) *n.* idle person; **istambayan** *n.* hang out.

istampa: (Sp. *estampa*) *n.* holy picture.

istariray: (*slang*) *n.* attracting attention.

istante: (Sp. *estante*) *n.* bookcase, shelf.

istanyo: (Sp. *estaño*) *n.* solder.

istorya: (Sp. *historia*) *n.* history; story.
iswád: *adj.* with prominent buttocks.
isyu: (Eng.) *n.* issue.
Ita: (*also Aeta*) *n.* Negrito.
itaás: (*rt.* *taás*) **sa itaás** *adv.* up, upstairs, above.
iták: *n.* machete.
Italyano: (Sp. *italiano*) *n.* Italian.
Itawit: *n.* ethnic group and language from Southern Cagayan, Luzon.
Itáy: *n.* Father. (*tatay*)
iti: **pag-iiti** *n.* dysentery.
itib: **pagitib** *n.* sipping liquids through a straw.
itik: *n.* species of duck; **itik-itik** *n.* native folkdance which imitates the movements of a duck.
itím: *n.* black; *adj.* black; dark skinned; **umitím** *v.* to become black; to get a sun tan; **mag-itím** *v.* to wear black; **maitím ang budhî** *id.* traitor (conscience is black); **maitím ang butó** *id.* bad person (bone is black); **maitím na binabalak** *id.* deadly plan (black plan).
iting: *adj.* pressed tight (set teeth).
itnéb: (*slang*) *n.* twenty pesos.
itlóg: *n.* egg; (*slang*) zero score; **paitlugan** *n.* nest (for eggs); **maitlóg** *adj.* with many eggs; **mag-iitlóg** *n.* egg dealer; *v.* to lay eggs; **umitlóg** *v.* to lay an egg.
Itnég: *n.* ethnic group and language from Northern Luzon.
Itóy: *n.* term of address for a young boy.
itsá: (Sp. *echar*) *n.* hurling, throwing; **mag-itsá** *v.* to throw, hurl, toss.
itsura: (Sp. *hechura*) *n.* shape, form; the way someone looks.
Ivatán: *n.* ethnic group and language from the Batanes Islands.
iwà: *n.* stab; **iwaan** *v.* to stab someone.
I-wak: *n.* ethnic group and language from Benguet Province.
iwan: *v.* to leave; abandon; omit; **maiwan** *v.* to be left, abandoned; **magpaiwan** *v.* to stay, remain; **mang-iwan** *v.* to leave behind; **mapag-iwanan** *v.* to be left behind; **waláng-iniwan** *id.* like, similar (left nothing).
iwang: *n.* wiping the anus after defecation; **iwangan** *v.* to wipe the anus.
iwas: **umiwas, iwasan** *v.* to avoid; flee; escape; evade; **maiiwasan** *adj.* avoidable.
iwi: **mag-iwi** *v.* to take care of an animal for someone else; **ipaiwi** *v.* to give an animal to someone else to take care of.
iyák: *n.* cry; **umiyák** *v.* to cry; **mag-umiyák** *v.* to cry at the top of one's voice; **paiyakan** (*coll.*) *n.* buying something in installments.
iyág: **maiyág** *adj.* lustful, sexy.
iyán: *pron.* that (medial); **ganyan** like that; **niyán** of that; **iyáng-iyán** exactly that.
iyó: *pron.* your (plural or polite).
iyók: *n.* cry of poultry.
iyón: *pron.* that (distal); it; **iyón din** same, very (identical); **niyón** of that.
iyot: (*slang*) *n.* sexual intercourse.

L

l: **ma-l** (*pron.* *maél*) abbreviation of *malibóg*: lustful, sexually excited.
laab, laáb: *n.* flame, blaze; **magláab** *v.* to burst into flames.
laán: **paglalaán** *n.* dedication; reserve, setting aside; devotion; **nakalaán** *adj.* reserved for; destined for, intended for; meant for; **ilaán** *v.* to provide; reserve; devote; **laáng-gugulín** *n.* something set aside for a purpose.
laang: *var.* or *lang*: only.
laás. *adj.* cracked (wood).
laaw: *n.* shrill from a distance.
labá: (Sp. *lavar*) *n.* laundry; **maglabá** *v.* to wash clothes.
labâ: *n.* increase, growth; usurious interest.
lababo: (Sp. *lavabo*) *n.* sink; washbasin.
labák: *n.* hole in ground; low region; (*slang*) homosexual; **labák-labák** *adj.* full of holes.
labakara: (Sp. *lava cara*: wash face) *n.* face towel.
labada: (Sp. *lavada*) *n.* laundry.
labág: *adj.* against; contrary to; **labagín** *v.* to go against; transgress; invade.
labaha: (Sp. *navaja*) *n.* razor.
labahita: *n.* blue-line surgeon fish.

laban: *n.* fight; duel; race, contest; **kalaban** *n.* opponent; enemy; *adj.* rival, hostile; **labanán** *v.* to oppose; fight against; **maglaban** *v.* to fight, compete; **palaban** *n.* competition; **waláng-laban** *adj.* defenseless; **labanán ng mga pusò** *id.* avoiding conversation between two lovers (conflict of the hearts).

labadera: (Sp. *lavadera*) *n.* laundry woman.

labanderiya: (Sp. *lavandería*) *n.* place where clothes are washed.

labanós: (Sp. *rábanos*) *n.* radish.

labáng: *n.* groove in wood; hole in the ground.

labangán: *n.* trough.

labangko: (Sp. *lavanco*) *n.* wild duck.

lábas: *n.* species of water lily.

labás: *adj.* outside; *n.* installment; issue; edition; **ilabás** *v.* to take out; **lumabás** *v.* to go out; come out; prove; appear in a show; **maglabás** *v.*to take out; draw out; **makalabás** *v.* to get out (without control); leak out; **palabás** *n.* show; **paglabás** *n.* exit; appearance; **panlabás** *adj.* external; **tagalabás** *n.* outsider; **k(in)álabasán, kálalabasán** *n.* development; effect, result; **kálabás-labás** *n.* unexpected outcome; **labasán** *v.* to bring out; discharge; **lábásan, pálabasan** *n.* exit; outlet; vent; **labasín** *v.* to go out to get something; **manlalabás** *n.* actor, actress; **pagkakápagpalabás** *n.* representation; **paglalábásan** *n.* exodus; **pagpapalabás** *n.* expulsion; representation; **palabasín** *v.* to let out; send out; screen (a movie); **tagalabás** *n.* outsider; **labás-masok** *id.* more or less (going in and out); **labás sa bakuran** *id.* out of one's jurisdiction (out of the yard); **lálabasán** *id.* has ability or intelligence (something will come out); **anák sa labás** *n.* illegitimate child; **labás sa panganib** out of danger.

labasa: *var. of labaha*: razor; **labasang-pulpól** *id.* arrogant.

labatiba: (Sp. *lavatiba*) *n.* enema.

labay₁: *n.* skein, hank; leafiness; **malabay** *adj.* leafy.

labay₂: **maglabay** *v.* to eat rice with broth; eat viands with rice.

labayan: *n.* slippery duck fish.

labaylabay: *n.* horse trot; breast stroke.

labì: (Sp. *labio*) *n.* lip; brim; **labián** *adj.* thick lipped; *n.* thick-lipped grunt fish; **lumabi** *v.* to pout; **labì ng hukay** *id.* grave (lip of dug soil).

labí: *n.* remains; excess; survival; wreck; relic; **nalalabí** *adj.* remaining, residual; **labí ng aso** *id.* lady who eloped with a man and then returned to her parents (left-over of the dog).

labintadór: (Sp. *reventador*) *n.* firecracker.

labíng: *n.* ravine.

labíng- *prefix-* over ten; **labing-isá** eleven.

labis: *n.* surplus, extra, excess; *adj.* excessive; too much; leftover; *adv.* greatly, deeply, intensely; **kalabisan** *n.* surplus; redundancy; **lumabis** *v.* to exceed, overdo; overflow; **magpalabis, palabisin** *v.* to exaggerate; **magmalabís, magpakalabis** *v.* to overdo, exaggerate; overindulge; **palabis** *n.* extra amount; margin; **palabisan** *v.* to add to; **pagmalabisán** *v.* to abuse; take advantage of; **pagmamalabís** *n.* excessive use; abuse; **kulang sa pitó, labis sa waló** *exp.* crazy; **waláng-labis, waláng-kulang** *exp.* exact.

labíw: *n.* kind of weed.

labláb: *n.* mud; marshy land; swamp.

labnát: (*slang*) *n.* love, need for loving.

labnáw: **malabnáw** *adj.* watery, diluted; **malabnáw ang utak** *id.* simpleton (watery brain).

labnít: *n.* species of rattan; **malabnit** *v.* to peel off (skin).

labnóg: **malabnóg** *adj.* turbid, muddy (water).

labnós: **pagkalabnós** *n.* peeling off of the skin.

labnót: *adj.* plucked out; uprooted; **labnután** *v.* to pull out from, pluck out; **labnutín** *v.* to tweak, twist and pull.

labò: **malabò** *adj.* unclear, hazy; obscure; blurred; cloudy; turbid; foggy; (*slang*) impossible; **lumabò** *v.* to fade; become dim.

labog: **labóg** *adj.* over boiled to the point of being to soft, mushy; turbid.

labon: *n.* boiling tubers. **maglabon** *v.* to boil tubers.

labón: *n.* silt.

labóng: *n.* bamboo shoot.

labór: (Sp.) *n.* decorative design.

labos: *n.* skinning of animals.
labot: **paglalabot** *n.* weaning young animals; pulling out plants.
labót: *n.* tripe; stomach of ruminant animals.
laboy₁: **lumaboy** *v.* to bum; loaf, wander; **palaboy** *n.* vagrant person, bum; **palabuyin** *v.* to let animals graze anywhere.
laboy₂: *n.* flabby flesh; **malaboy** *adj.* flabby.
labrá: (Sp. *labra*) *n.* carving of wood.
labradór: (Sp. *labrador*) *n.* wood carver.
labsák: **malabsák** *adj.* soft and mushy from overcooking.
labsáw: **nalabsáw** *adj.* melted.
labsô: *adj.* slippery and difficult to hold; easily untied.
labtík: *n.* crack of the whip.
labulabò: *n.* brawl; free-for-all fight.
labusák: *n.* spendthrift; *adj.* prodigal.
labusáw: *n.* turbidity due to sediment stirring.
labuyaw: **nalabuyaw** *adj.* gone wild (animal that was once tame).
labuyò: *n.* wild chicken; act of growing wild (plants).
labyú: *n.* kind of weed.
lakad: *n.* walking; march; start, beginning to go; trend; mission; **may lakad akó** I have an appointment, somewhere to go; **lakád** *adj.* barefooted; on foot, walking; **lumakad** *v.* to walk; begin to move; **maglakad** *v.* to engage in business; hand carry (documents); **maglakád** *v.* to go on foot; **maglakád-lakád** *v.* to promenade; **magpalakad** *v.* to run (a business); **makalakad** *v.* to be able to walk; **ilakad** *v.* to use for walking; negotiate; carry a proposal; **lakarin** *v.* to walk (a distance); **lakarín** *n.* walk (distance); errands; **kalakad** *n.* walking companion; **kalakarán** *n.* current practice or custom; rule of the day; **lakaran** *v.* to tread, walk on; **lakarán** *n.* walking in groups; walkway; using influence to get something approved; **nilálákad** *n.* mission; errand; **palakad, pamamalakad** *n.* policy; errand; regulation; **paglalakád** *n.* walk; **lakad-susò, lakad-pagóng** *id.* slowfoot; **naglálakád sa liwanag ng buwán** *id.* walking slowly (under the light of the moon); **lakad-kalabáw** *id.* slow movement; **karaniwan palakad** *n.* routine; **pamamalakad na pangkabuhayan** *n.* economy; **taong naglálakád** *n.* pedestrian.
lakambini: *n.* muse.
lakán: *n.* title of nobility.
lakandiwà: *n.* poetical joust.
lakás: *n.* strength, vigor; **malakás** *adj.* strong, powerful, potent; sturdy; *adv.* loudly; aloud; **malakás ang kapit** *adj.* influential; **lakás-loób** *n.* courage; **lumakás** *v.* to become stronger; recuperate; boom; **lak(a)sán** *v.* to make something stronger or louder; **kalakasán** *n.* strength; **ilakás** *v.* to make louder; **maglakás-lakasan** *v.* to pretend to be strong; **makapagpalakás** *v.* to invigorate; **magpalakás, palakasín** *v.* to strengthen, aggrandize; reinforce; **pagkamalakás** *n.* being strong; being influential; **pálakasan** *n.* athletics; contest in strength; **pampalakás** *adj.* strengthening; **may lakás ng bibíg** *id.* justified (has strength in the mouth); **nagpapalakás** *v.* (*slang*) trying to please; **daanin sa lakás** *v.* to get by force.
lakatán: *n.* species of banana.
lakayo: (Sp. *lacayo*) *n.* clown.
lakbáy: *n.* travel, voyage, journey; **maglakbáy** *v.* to tour; travel; **manlalakbáy** *n.* traveler.
lakdáng: *n.* stride.
lakdáw: *n.* step, omission; **lakdawán** *v.* to step over, omit; override.
lakí: *n.* size; bulk; amount; extent; **lumakí** *v.* to grow big; grow up; develop; **malakí** *adj.* large, big; great; **manlakí** *v.* to enlarge (eyes); **nápakalakí** *adj.* huge, giant, enormous; **lakihán, lakhán** *v.* to enlarge; **ilakí** *v.* to cause to grow; **kalak(i)hán** *n.* largeness, bigness; magnitude; greatness. **ipagmalakí** *v.* to brag, boast; pride oneself in; **magkasinlakí** *adj.* equal in size; **magmalakí** *v.* to be proud; **malakihán** *v.* to outgrow (faster than expected); **malakhín** *v.* to value, appreciate; **mapagkalakhán** *v.* to outgrow; **mapagmalakí** *adj.* proud; smug; **pagmamalakí** *n.* pride; **paglakí** *n.* growth; swelling; **palakí** *n.* animal or child that is reared by someone; **pagkalakhán** *v.* to grow up (with a certain situation); **pagmalakhán** *v.* to act with con-

tempt, treat coldly; **pagpapalakí** *n.* enlargement; expansion; upbringing; **lakí sa lansangan** *id.* bad mannered (grew up in the street); **lakí sa nunò** *id.* pampered (grew up with grandparents); **lumálakí ang ulo** *id.* arrogant (growing head); **lakí sa layaw** *id.* brought up spoilt; **may-kalakihán** *adj.* sizeable, large; **sinlakí ng tao** *adj.* life-size.

lakiérda: (*slang*) *v.* to leave. [see *iskiyerda*]

lakíp: *n.* enclosure; **kalakíp** *adj.* enclosed; included; **lakipan** *v.* to enclose in, include.

lakít: *adj.* widespread.

laklák: *n.* voracious eating; (*slang*) high on drugs; drinking session; **lumaklák** *v.* to lick; guzzle; gulp.

lakmáy: **nilakmáy** *n.* small bundle of rice stalks.

lakmít: *n.* species of vine.

lakò: *n.* peddled goods; **ilakò** *v.* to peddle; **manlalakò** *n.* peddler; **maglakò** *v.* to offer for sale; **palakò** *n.* goods consigned to a peddler.

lakó: *n.* part of arm opposite the elbow.

lakom: *n.* gathering with one sweep of the arm.

lakorya: (*slang*) *n.* play time.

lakre: (Sp. *lacre*) *n.* sealing wax.

laksâ: *n.* ten thousand.

laksán: (rt. *lakás*) *v.* to strengthen; make louder.

laksante: (Sp. *laxante*) *n.* laxative.

laktá: *n.* clearing of land for cultivation.

laktâ: *n.* omission, skipping; carry over in addition.

laktáw: *n.* species of lobster; **lumaktáw** *v.* to skip, omit.

lakukuwít: (*slang*) *n.* coward.

lakwatsa: (Sp. *lacuacha*) *n.* truancy, being absent from school; **lakwatsero** *n.* frequently truant person, wandering person.

ladlád: *adj.* unfolded; unfurled; **magladlád ng kapa** *id.* show one's true colors.

ladrilyo: (Sp. *ladrillo*) *n.* brick.

lagà: **ilagà, maglagâ** *v.* to boil; **nilagà** *adj.* boiled; **lagaán** *n.* boiler.

lagabláb: *n.* blaze, burst of flames.

lagak: *n.* money deposit; bail, bond; mortgage; **maglagak** *v.* to deposit; put up the bail; **magpalumagak** *v.* to stay indefinitely.

lagaklák: *n.* gushing sound of water.

lagadlád: *n.* flotsam; bobbing up and down; *adj.* spread out; unfurled, unrolled.

lagalág: *adj.* well-traveled; nomadic; *n.* rover, wanderer.

laganap: *adj.* widespread; general; common; **lumaganap** *v.* to spread around; pervade; **malaganap** *adj.* current.

lagáp: *adj.* common, readily available.

lagapák: **lumagapák** *v.* to crash, clatter; fail an exam.

lagarì: *n.* carpenter's saw; (*slang*) excessive work; **lumagarì** *v.* to saw; **lagaring-patíng** *n.* sawfish; **parang lagarì** *id.* going back and forth.

lagas: **malagas** *v.* to fall off, fall out; **taglagás** *n.* autumn, fall.

lagasáw: *n.* sound of flowing water.

lagaslás: *n.* babble, sound of rippling or running water.

lagaták: *n.* leaking through a roof.

lagáy$_1$: *n.* condition, status; way; situation; (*coll.*) bribe; tip; bet in gambling; **ilagáy** *v.* to put, place; set; **lagyán** *v.* to put, place; add to, put with. **maglagáy** *v.* to put; (*coll.*) give a bribe; **paglalagáy** *n.* putting; application; **palagáy** *n.* opinion; outlook; attitude; belief; **magpalagáy** *v.* to suppose; form an opinion of; **málagáy** *v.* to be placed, put in a certain position. **ipalagáy** *v.* to consider, regard as; suppose; **ipinalálagáy** *adj.* supposed; presumable; **ipagpalagáy** *v.* to take for example, suppose; take for grated; **magpálagayan** *v.* to treat (in a certain capacity); consider as; **kalágayan** *n.* condition, rank; position; status; situation; **lalagyán** *n.* container; **kinálalagyán** *n.* presence; location; position; **lumagáy sa estado/ tahimik/ panatag** *v.* to get married; **pagpapalagáy** *n.* opinion, presupposition; **lagáy ng loób** *n.* attitude; mood; **lagáy na loób** *n.* tranquility; confidence. **dî pagkápalagáy** *n.* unrest, restlessness; **gipít na kalágayan** *n.* tight situation. **mahirap na kalágayan** *n.* dilemma. **matigás sa kanyáng palagáy** obstinate; opinionated.

lagáy$_2$: *n*. unit of size or number.
lagayláy: *adj*. hanging, drooping (palm leaves).
lagkít: **malagkít** *adj*. sticky, adhesive.
lagdâ: *n*. signature; rule; decision of a court; **ilagdâ** *v*. to sign, endorse; **waláng-lagdâ** *adj*. anonymous.
lagete: *n*. species of vine.
lagì: **palagì** *adv*. always, forever; constantly; **lumagì** *v*. to remain, abide; **pamalagiin** *v*. to stabilize; **palagian** *adj*. regular, steady; stable; **magpamalagì** *v*. to establish.
lagibás: *adj*. stale.
lagidlíd: *n*. mackerel or cavalla young.
lagím: **malagím** *adj*. gloomy.
laginít: *n*. crack of a whip; noise of splitting wood.
laginlíng: *adj*. tight in the middle; with a narrow waist.
lagís: *n*. honing, whetting.
lagislís: *n*. noise of falling branches.
lagitik: *n*. click; creak.
lagitlít: *n*. creak.
lagläg: (Ch.) *adj*. fallen, fallen off; (*slang*) captured; bribe; **malagläg** *v*. to fall off, drop off; **pagkalaglág** *n*. miscarriage; **pagpapalaglág** *n*. abortion (deliberate); **lagláglukså** *n*. last day of mourning period; death anniversary; **makalaglág-matsing** *id*. beautiful eyes (can make the monkey fall).
lagmák: *adj*. prostrate.
lagnát: *n*. fever.
lago: *n*. whole length; lake.
lagô: *n*. luxuriant growth; **lumagô** *v*. to develop; flourish; **malagô** *adj*. lush.
lagók: *n*. gulp, swallow.
lagom: **lumagom** *v*. to assimilate; absorb; summarize; **paglagom** *n*. merger; monopoly.
lagunlóng: *n*. anchovy.
lagong: *n*. low voice.
lagós: *adj*. pierced through; **lumagós** *v*. to penetrate, pierce through.
lagót$_1$: *adj*. cut off, broken; **lagutín** *v*. to snap, break; **malagután ng hiningá** (*fig*.) *v*. to die, be finished; **lagót ang pisì** *id*. penniless (thread is cut).
lagót$_2$: *adj*. obsessed.
lagpák: *n*. thud, crash, fall; failure; **lumagpák** *v*. to thud; fail an exam; **lagpakán** *v*. to fall on.
lagpás: *adj*. surpassed; gone beyond the limit; survived a critical situation; (*fig*.) successful in an exam; *n*. going beyond; passing unnoticed; surpassing; **lagpasán** *v*. to go beyond, surpass; be successful in; survive through; penetrate through.
lagpáw: *n*. surpassing; overcoming a hurdle or obstacle; **lagpawán** *v*. to surpass; overcome.
lagpî: **nalagpî** *adj*. torn off; disrupted; **lagpiín** *v*. to tear off; disrupt work.
lagpós: *adj*. loose, free; **lagpusán** *v*. to penetrate.
lagsáng: *adj*. just delivered (babies).
lagtás: **lagtasín** *v*. to detach, cut off.
lagublób: *n*. sudden crowding around something; sound of a bonfire.
laguklók: **lumaguklók** *v*. to gurgle; to make a noise (as water out of a bottle).
laguma: **paglaguma** *n*. act of joining others in a party although uninvited.
lagumbá: *n*. draw-well.
lagundî: *n*. kind of shrub with blue flowers.
lagunlón: *adj*. drawn together; drawn aside (curtains); crowded; *n*. sound of falling water.
lagunós: *n*. sudden rushing (flowing water).
lagunót: *n*. sound of a whip.
laguplóp: *n*. monopoly; everything within reach; *adj*. including all within one's reach.
lagusan: (rt. *lagós*) *n*. underpass, tunnel; passageway.
lagusáw: *n*. sound of splashing water.
lagutók: *n*. click, snap; **lumagutók** *v*. to crack, snap.
laguyò: *n*. paramour; intimate friendship.
lagwát: *n*. basting stitch.
lagwerta: (Sp. *la huerta*) *n*. orchard.
lagyán: (rt. *lagáy*) *v*. to put/place in/on.
lagyô: *n*. essence; spirit; name; **kalagyô** *n*. namesake; **palagyô** *adj*. nominative.
laha: (Sp. *laja*) *n*. slab; flagstone.
lahab: *n*. mark caused by a punch or blow.
lahad: *n*. opening of the hand (palm up); **ilahad** *v*. to offer, expose; **paglalahad** *n*. exposition.

lahang: *n.* crack.

lahát: *pron., adj.* all; everyone, everybody; everything; **kalahatán** *n.* generality; the whole; **láhátan** *adv.* entirely, as a whole; *adj.* all inclusive; **lahatín** *v.* to include everything; **panlahát** *adj.* universal; general; public; collective; **pangkalahatán** *adj.* broad; general; **sa kalahatán** in general; at large; **halos lahát** mostly, mainly; **sumalahát** *v.* to be received by all.

lahaw: **palahaw** *n.* loud shout in the wilderness.

lahì: *n.* race, people, breed; lineage; **kalahì** *n.* someone of the same race; **pagkalahì** *n.* strain; **panlahì** *adj.* racial.

lahid: *n.* smear, strain.

lahò: **maglahò** *v.* to dissolve, vanish; fade away; **paglalahò** *n.* disappearance; eclipse.

lahók: *n.* mixture; entry in a contest; **paglahók** *n.* entry; **lahukán** *adj.* mixed; **ihalók** *v.* to add, to mix.

lahoy: **paglahoy** *n.* drip, flow (blood).

laib: **paglalaib** *n.* softening of leaves by exposure to the sun.

laing: (*Bicol*) *n.* dish made with taro leaves and coconut milk.

laíng: *adj.* dried and withered.

lait: **lumait** *v.* to vilify, revile, blaspheme; **kalait-lait** *adj.* mean; **paglait** *n.* insult; blasphemy.

lala: *n.* weave; **maglala** *v.* to weave; interlace.

lalâ: **malalâ** *adj.* serious, acute (illness); **lumalâ** *v.* to get worse; **pampalalâ** *n.* aggravation.

lalab: *n.* shroud.

lalake: *n.* male, man; **manlalaki** *v.* to take a husband; **maglalaki** *v.* to act like a man, take the role of a man; **panlalaki** *adj.* masculine.

lalakwè: (*slang*) *n.* homosexual.

lalád: *adj.* carried away by the wind or current.

lalág: **lalagín** *v.* to dismantle; tear off; undo.

lalagukán: (*rt. lagók*) *n.* trachea; Adam's apple.

lalagyán: (*rt. lagáy*) *n.* container.

lalamunan: (*rt. lamon*) *n.* throat.

lalamyâ-lamyâ: *n.* person who acts like a baby.

laláng$_1$: *n.* creation, creature; **lalangín** *v.* to create; **nilaláng** *adj.* created.

laláng$_2$: *n.* hoax, trick; trap, stratagem; **mapaglalangán** *v.* to play a trick on.

lalanghutan: *n.* kitchen utensils.

lalás: **nilalás** *adj.* blown off (roofs); stripped off (palm leaves).

lalawà: *n.* species of spider.

lalawigan: *n.* province; **lalawiganín** *adj.* provincial; *n.* provincialism; **panlalawigan** *adj.* provincial.

laláy: *adj.* gradually sloping; unstressed (pronunciation).

lalik: *n.* lathe work.

lalim: *n.* depth; distance down; **lumalim** *v.* to get deep; **malalim** *adj.* deep; profound; **malalim na ang gabí** *id.* late midnight (deep night).

lalin: *n.* contagion; spot caused by staining; **maglalin** *v.* to pour in, infuse; **nakakalalin** *adj.* contagious.

lalò: *adv.* more, increasingly; **lalo't lalò** more and more; **lalò na** especially; **lumalò nang higít** *v.* to overshadow.

lalós: *adv.* all together.

lamad: *n.* membrane.

lamán: *n.* meat, flesh; body, substance; contents; worldliness; **kalamnán** *n.* substance; **lam(a)nán** *v.* to fill; stuff; **maglamán** *v.* to accommodate; develop flesh; **malamán** *adj.* fleshy; venereal, pertaining to sexual acts; **makapaglamán** *v.* to be able to contain, hold; **nilálamán** *n.* contents; **lamáng-lupà** *n.* tuber; **palamán** *n.* stuffing; **lamáng-loób** *n.* guts, intestines, innards; **lamáng-tiyán** *n.* edible things; **ubusin ang lamán** *v.* to empty out; **lamáng-kati** *id.* meat of butchered animals (contents of low tide); **lamán ng lamán** *id.* son, daughter; **lamán ng kapitbahay** *id.* always at the neighbor's house.

lamang: *adv.* only; alone; merely; mere.

lamáng: **kalamangán** *n.* advantage; lead; majority; **malamáng** *adj.* probably; likely; **ipalamáng** *v.* to give up something in favor of something else; **palamáng** *n.* handicap (advantage); *v.* yield, give an advantage to; **palamangín** *v.* to give someone a handicap;

mapagpalamáng *adj*. self-sacrificing; self-accommodating; **malamáng na hindî** *adv*. most unlikely. **nápakalakíng kalamangán** *n*. landslide, huge advantage.

lamas$_1$: *n*. mashing; **lamasin** *v*. to mash.

lamas$_2$: *n*. hand to hand combat; mojarra fish.

lamat: *n*. crack.

lamay: *n*. night vigil for the dead, wake; overtime work; **lamayán** *n*. wake to honor the dead; **maglamay** *v*. to go to a wake; stay up all night; **luksáng-lamayán** *n*. prearranged night work.

lamayan: *n*. mountain bass fish.

lambâ: **malambâ** *adj*. overgrown (weeds).

lambák: *n*. valley, plain.

lambál: *adj*. doubled (thread); *n*. wick; **lambalín** *v*. to fold; double.

lambanóg: *n*. coconut whisky; long sling shot; (*coll.*) whipping.

lambáng$_1$: *n*. guess; **lámbangan** *n*. guesswork; guessing contest; **lambangín** *v*. to guess.

lambáng$_2$: **kalambangán** *n*. rudeness, impoliteness.

lambát: *n*. fishing net; **lambát-lambát** *adj*. netted; made like a net; checkered; **lambatín** *v*. to snare, catch with a net.

lambayog: *n*. hanging fruit cluster; swaying.

lambî: *n*. excess appendage (second chin; dewlap of cattle; flesh that hangs from the throat of chickens; feelers on the lips of certain fish.)

lambíng: **malambíng** *adj*. affectionate; melodious (music); **lumambíng** *v*. to act in a loving way, caress.

lambís: *n*. extension of the lower lip to show disapproval; **malambís** *adj*. meticulous.

lambitin: **maglambitin** *v*. to hang from tree branches.

lambó: *n*. tassel; fringe.

lambô: *n*. leafiness.

lambód: *n*. fresh growth of grasses, shoots, weeds, etc.

lambóg: *n*. act of whipping.

lambóng: *n*. black covering, veil; spreading out; **lumambóng** *v*. to spread out; **lambungán** *v*. to cover something with a mantle.

lambót$_1$: **malambót** *adj*. soft, tender; flabby; **lumambót** *v*. to become soft; **malambót ang pusò** *adj*. considerate, kind-hearted; **malambót ang ulo** *adj*. obedient, easily persuaded.

lambót$_2$: *n*. weakness of the body; **malambót** *adj*. limp; soft, languid.

lamesa: (Sp. *la mesa*) *n*. table.

lamî: *n*. species of plant with edible roots.

lamikmík: *n*. tranquility; repose.

lamíg: *n*. coldness; **malamíg** *adj*. cold, cool; **manlamíg** *v*. to be cold to someone; **palamigan** *n*. cooler; **palamigín** *v*. to chill, refrigerate; **pantaglamíg** *n*. winter; **taglamíg** *n*. winter.

lamirâ: *adj*. filthy and sticky; viscous.

lamiran: *n*. wild cat.

lamirát: *adj*. mashed to a soft pulp, overhandled.

lamlám: *n*. dimness; languidness; lifelessness; **malamlám** *adj*. lifeless; languid; **lumamlám** *v*. to become glaring; soften up.

lamnán: (rt. *lamán*) *v*. to fill; stuff.

lamò: *n*. raft.

lamók: *n*. mosquito; **isip-lamók** *adj*. weak-minded; **nilálamók** *id*. poor sale.

lamod: *n*. soft, mucus-like substance found around the seeds of fruits.

lamóg: *adj*. softened by too much handling; squashed; beat to a pulp; **lamugín** *v*. to press until soft.

lamon: *n*. gorging, voracious eating; eel grass; **lamunin** *v*. to devour, gobble up; **palamunin** *v*. to give too much to eat; engulf.

lampá: *adj*. weak and feeble; awkward and unsteady.

lámpará: (Sp.) *n*. lamp.

lamparilya: (Sp. *lamparilla*) *n*. small night lamp.

lampás-: *prep*. over, exceeding → **lampás-baywáng** *adj*. higher than the waist; **lampás-tao** *adj*. taller than a person.

lampás: *adj*. overdone, excessive; beyond; **i-lampás** *v*. to do over or beyond; **lampasán** *v*. to pass over; **lampás-tao** *adj*. exceeding the normal height of an average person; **palampasín** *v*. to overdo.

lampaso: (Sp.) *n*. mop; **maglampaso** *v*. to

mop; scour.
lampík: *n.* dewlap of cattle, wattle. (*lambî*)
lampín: *n.* diaper.
lampóng: *n.* whining of cats.
lampós: *adj.* passed (in time).
lampót: *adj.* weak; flabby.
lamukós: *adj.* crushed; **lamukusin** *v.* to crush, crumple.
lamukot: *n.* fleshy part of fruits around the seeds.
lamugà: *n.* display of fondness.
lamuráy: *adj.* mangled to pieces; **malamuray** *adj.* mangled.
lamurít: *adj.* broken from over-handling.
lamusak: *adj.* mashed, crushed; dirty.
lamuymóy: *n.* tassel; fringe; filament; hanging threads.
lamuyot: *n.* seduction, persuasion; **lamuyutin** *v.* to seduce, persuade, entice; squeeze or crush.
lamyerda: (*slang*, Sp. *la mierda*: shit) *n.* strolling; having a good time.
lamyós: *n.* caressing.
lana: (Sp.) *n.* wool; sesame oil.
lanap: *adj.* inundated.
lanaw: *n.* pool, lake, pond.
lanáy: *adj.* spread out.
landás₁: *n.* path; pass; trail; orbit; **landás na matiník** *id.* difficulties (thorny path).
landás₂: **malandás** *adj.* slippery.
landáy: **malandáy** *adj.* shallow (pots).
landî: *adj.* flirtatious, sensuous (women); **maglandî** *v.* to act sensuously; flirt; **paglalandî** *n.* playing with things.
landít: *adj.* lustful. (*landî*)
landók: *n.* crowbar.
lanilya: (Sp. *lanilla*) *n.* crowbar.
lanitì: *n.* kind of tall tree.
lanolina: (Sp.) *n.* lanolin.
lanót: *adj.* raveled.
lansá₁: *n.* smell of fish; (*fig.*) obscenity; **malansá** *adj.* fishy, with a fishy odor or taste.
lansá₂: (Sp. *lanza*) *n.* lance.
lansák: *adj.* open, frank; **lansakín** *v.* to treat with frankly; **palansák** *adj.* collective (grammatical term).
lanság: *adj.* disorganized, dissolved; dismantled; **lansagín** *v.* to dismantle, put an end to; dissolve.
lansáng: *adj.* forward in manner.
lansangan: *n.* street, road. **lansangan-bayan** *n.* highway; **taong-lansangan** *n.* street person.
lanseros: (Sp. *lanceros*) *n.* square dance.
lansí: (Sp. *lance*) *n.* trick, cunning; **lumansí** *v.* to deceive; feign; trick.
lansinà: *n.* castor oil plant; **lansi-lansinaan** *n.* kind of shrub with purple flowers.
lansita: (Sp. *lanceta*) *n.* pocketknife.
lansones: *n.* kind of native fruit tree with sweet, grape-like fruit.
lantá: *adj.* withered, wilted; **lumantá** *v.* to wither; shrivel up; **malantá** *v.* to wither; wilt; languish; dry up; **lantáng bulaklák** *id.* disgraced woman (withered flower); **lantáng kulangót** *id.* exhausted.
lanták: *n.* violent attack.
lantakà: *n.* small brass cannon.
lantád: **nakalantád** *adj.* in full view; exposed; prominent; **kalantarán** *n.* prominence; publicity; **paglantád** *n.* exposure; (*slang*) showing off one's body; **malantád** *v.* to be exposed.
lantanà: *n.* kind of ornamental shrub.
lantáy: *n.* pure, unalloyed; positive (grammatical term).
lantík: *n.* graceful curve (hips, eyelashes, etc.).
lantíng: *n.* part of a plow that is attached to the harness.
lantód: *adj.* indecently dressed (women); flirtatious.
lantóng: *n.* stench of rotten fish.
lantót: *n.* stench of stagnant water.
lantsa: (Sp. *lancha*) *n.* launch; motorboat.
lantutay: *n.* idler; *adj.* lazy.
lanubò: *n.* young tree branch.
lanyâ: *n.* lustfulness; indecency.
lanyán: *n.* species of snake.
lang: *adv.* only. (*lamang*)
langaray: *n.* glassfish; **langaray-pakò** silversides fish.
langasngás: *n.* gnashing of the teeth.
langatngát: *n.* creaking sound.
langaw: *n.* housefly; **langaw at gatas** *id.* applies to a couple where the man is ugly and

the woman is beautiful (fly and milk); **langawin** *adj.* infested with flies; (*slang*) *v.* to avoid people.

langaylangayan: *n.* species of swallow; **nilá-langaw** *id.* poor sale.

langkâ: *n.* jackfruit.

lankág: *n.* empty; hollow; bulky but light in weight.

langkáp: *adj.* joined with; incorporated.

lankayan: *n.* stretcher, bier; stand for images.

langgám: *n.* ant.

langgás: **langgasán** *v.* to wash a wound; **pan-langgás** *n.* antiseptic for wounds.

langgotse: (Ch.) *n.* jute fiber; jute sack.

langguwáy: *n.* box for chewing tobacco, betel nuts, etc.; betel leaves.

langháp: *n.* inhaling; **lumangháp** *v.* to inhale.

langíb: *n.* scab of wounds; **maglanbíb** *v.* to scab.

langís: *n.* oil; unction; (*slang*) money; sycophants; **langís at tubig** *id.* rivals; people that don't match (oil and water); **langís-langisán** *id.* to win the favor (oil up); **parang langís** *id.* always on top, superior.

langit: *n.* sky; heaven; (*slang*) ecstasy; **maka-langit** *adj.* celestial; **langit-langit** *n.* canopy, pallium; **langitin** *v.* to idolize; **sumalangit** *v.* to be in heaven; **langit at lupà** *id.* opposites (heaven and earth); **langit ng buhay** *id.* complete happiness (heaven of life); **hulog sa langit** *id.* gift from heaven, heaven sent (fell from heaven).

langitngít: *n.* creak; squeak.

langláng: *n.* spice; Chinese cooking.

langó: *adj.* tipsy, drunk; **maglangó** *v.* to get drunk.

langóy: *n.* swimming; **maglangóy, lumangóy** *v.* to swim; **lánguyan** *n.* swimming pool; swimming contest; **languyín** *v.* to get by swimming, swim (a distance).

langutngót: *n.* crunching of the teeth; gritting.

laóg: *adj.* wild (cats); vagrant.

laon: *n.* long time; **malaon** *adj.* long (time); **malaunan** *v.* to take a long time; last a long time.

laón: (Ch.) *adj.* vintage; of a previous harvest.

laot: *n.* middle; ocean; (*fig.*) eternity; **pumalaot** *v.* to steer into the open sea.

lapà: **lapain** *v.* to butcher; (*slang*) rape; **lapaan** *n.* slaughterhouse.

lapák: *adj.* torn off, disjointed.

lapad: *n.* width, breadth; spread; deep-bodied sardine; **lapád** *adj.* broad and flat; **laparan** *v.* to spread, widen; **malapad ang papél** *id.* influential (role is wide); **nagpapalapad** *id.* trying to please.

lapád: *n.* species of sardine; (*slang*) liquor.

lapág: *n.* space below; ground level; **ilapág** *v.* to put down; dismount; **lumapág** *v.* to come down; **palapág** *adv.* downward; *n.* floor (story) of a building.

lapáng: *n.* hunk of meat; (*slang*) French kiss; **lapangín** *v.* to cut into hunks.

lapangga: (*slang*) *n.* sexual foreplay.

lapás: (Sp. *la Paz*) *n.* three days carnival before Ash Wednesday; species of fish, *Caesio* sp.

lapastangan: *adj.* disrespectful, sacrilegious; **lapastangin** *v.* to desecrate; break the rules.

lapat: *adj.* close fitting; adjusted; **maglapat** *v.* to administer; apply; adapt; **palapatin** *v.* to smooth out; flatten.

lapát: *n.* strips of bamboo; **maglapát** *v.* to tie down with bamboo strips.

lapaw: *n.* overgrowing of vines.

lapáy: *n.* pancreas, spleen.

lapì$_1$: *n.* affix; **gitlapì** *n.* infix; **hulapì** *n.* suffix; **unlapì** *n.* prefix; **lapian** *v.* attach, fasten; join.

lapì$_2$: *n.* political party; **lumapì** *v.* to join a political party.

lápida: (Sp.) *n.* gravestone.

lapíng: *n.* skin hanging from a bull's neck; wattle.

lapirát: *adj.* squashed.

lapirót: *adj.* squashed, crumpled (with the fingers).

lapis: *n.* pencil; stone slab; flagstone; graphite; leather jacket fish.

lapisâ: *adj.* kneaded; **lapisaín** *v.* to knead.

lapisák: *adj.* crushed; *n.* wallowing in mud; **maglapisák** *v.* to wallow in mud; walk in the mud.

lapit: *n.* nearness; **malapit** *adj.* near; **lumapit** *v.* to approach; **lumapit-lapit** *v.* to draw nearer, get a little closer; **magkalapit** *adj.* close together; **nalalapít** *adj.* oncoming, forthcoming.

lapláp$_1$: *n.* decortications; **laplapín** *v.* to remove the skin of.

lapláp$_2$: (*slang*) *n.* heavy kissing; flirting.

lapnís: *n.* stripped off bark; **lapnisán** *v.* to strip off bark.

lapnít: *adj.* decorticated; unglued; *n.* rind of bamboo used for tying.

lapnós: *adj.* peeled off; flayed; (*slang*) dead.

lapók: *adj.* rotten, decayed (wood).

lapóng: *n.* hunk of meat; (*slang*) sexual foreplay with the breasts.

lapongga: (*slang*) *n.* sexual foreplay.

lapot: **malapot** *adj.* dense; thick (liquid); **lumapot** *v.* to condense; thicken; congeal.

lapulapo: *n.* grouper fish; **lapulapung-liglíg** honey-combed grouper; **lapulapung-senyora** yellow margined grouper.

lapunaw: *n.* slush, mire; **lapunáw** *adj.* slushy.

lapurít: *adj.* crumpled (cloth).

lapyâ: *adj.* flattened.

lapyád: *adj.* flat nosed; **lapyarín** *v.* to hit with the flat side of a machete.

larang: **larangán** *n.* domain; field (of knowledge); stage, theater.

larawan: *n.* picture, drawing, illustration; reflection; figure; portrait; incarnation; **ilarawan** *v.* to depict, portray; reflect; represent; **málarawan** *v.* to be reflected; **mailarawan** *v.* to be portrayed; to represent; **mákalarawan** *v.* to typify; **nakalarawan** *adj.* illustrated, pictorial; **naglálarawan** *adj.* descriptive; figurative; **paglalarawan** *n.* portrayal; reflection; **pagsasalarawan** *n.* portrayal; **pagkakálarawan** *n.* description; **tagapaglarawan** *n.* figurative mirror (that which yields a description); **larawang-buhay** *n.* biographical sketch; **larawang-buháy** *n.* living image; **larawang-guhit** *n.* drawing.

larba: (Sp. *larva*) *n.* larva.

largá: (Sp.) *interj.* go ahead; **largahán** *v.* to slap; slacken; **lumarga** *v.* to go away, leave; go ahead.

largabista: (Sp. *larga vista*) *n.* binoculars.

largado: (Sp.) *adj.* free, loose; loosened (string of a kite); unrestricted, without limit.

largo: (Sp.) *n.* long trousers.

larís: *n.* stubbornness; odor of excreta.

larô: *n.* game; sport, event; gambling; trick; **láruan** *n.* playground; **laruán** *n.* toy; **kalarô** *n.* playmate; **larú-laruín** *v.* to toy with; **maglarô** *v.* to play; **malarô** *adj.* playful; **panlarô** *adj.* sporting, sporty; **paglaruán** *v.* to play with; play in; **makipaglarô** *v.* to join in a game; **manlalarò** *n.* athlete; **parehong-larô** *n.* sportsmanship; **naglalarô ng apóy** *id.* cheating on one's spouse (playing with fire).

larót: *adj.* frayed.

laróy: *adj.* crumpled; soft.

laryó: (Sp. *ladrillo*) *n.* brick.

lasa: *n.* taste; flavor; **lasahin** *v.* to taste; **malasa** *adj.* tasty, pleasing; **lumasa** *v.* to taste of; **magpalasa** *v.* to season, give flavor to; **pampalasa** *n.* condiment; flavoring; **panlasa** *n.* sense of taste; **waláng-lasa** *adj.* tasteless.

lasà: *n.* tiger grass weed.

lasak: *n.* rooster with red, black and white feathers.

lasáp: *n.* good flavor; **lumasáp** *v.* to relish food; **malasáp** *v.* to be able to taste, experience; **panlasáp** *n.* taste of a connoisseur.

lasaw: **lasáw** *adj.* thawed.

laseta: (Sp. *lanceta*) *n.* folding knife.

lasgás: *n.* hard core of timber.

lasì: *n.* crumbling; **lasiin** *v.* to break to pieces.

lasíng: *adj.* drunk; **malasíng** *v.* to get drunk; **nakalalasíng** *adj.* intoxicating; **lásingan** *n.* drinking spree; drinking party.

laslás: *n.* gash; slash; **laslasín** *v.* to gash; slash.

laso: (Sp. *lazo*) *n.* ribbon; bow.

lasò: *n.* blister on the tongue; inflammation of the lips.

lasóg: *adj.* pulled apart.

lason: *n.* poison; **lasunin** *v.* to poison; **nakakalason** *adj.* poisonous; **manlason** *v.* to poison people; **manlalason** *n.* poisoner.

laspág: (*slang*) *adj.* worn out.

latsay: (Ch.) *n.* cabletow; bamboo sieve used to smoke fish.

lástiko: (Sp. *elástico*) *n.* rubber band.

laswâ: *n.* lewd expression; **malaswâ** *adj.* vulgar; morally dirty.
lata: (Sp) *n.* can, tin; (*slang*) police badge; **de-lata** *adj.* canned; **latero** *n.* tinsmith.
latâ: *n.* softness, flabbiness; **malatâ** *adj.* weak and soft.
latak: *n.* residue, dregs.
latag: *n.* mantle, layer; something spread on the floor (carpet); **ilatag** *v.* to spread on a surface; **latág** *adj.* spread over; bedridden.
latang: *n.* bursting into flame; rise in temperature; **latáng** *adj.* very dry.
latay: (Ch.) *n.* weal, welt.
latero: (Sp. *hojalatero*) *n.* tinsmith.
lathalà₁: *n.* article; announcement; **ilathalà** *v.* to print, publish; **latháláan** *n.* communication media; **pagkakálathalà** *n.* publication; **palathalà** *n.* announcement; public notice.
lathalà₂: *n.* ferrying pole for boats.
lathî: *n.* mushy rice.
latì: *n.* marsh, swamp.
latík: *n.* scum of coconut milk.
látigo: (Sp. *látigo*) *n.* whip, lash; **latiguhín** *v.* to whip.
latok: (Ch.) *n.* low table.
latundán: *n.* species of banana.
latóy: (Ch.) **waláng-latóy** *adj.* tasteless.
laurél: (f. Spanish) *n.* bay leaf.
lawà: *n.* pool, pond; lake; **maglawâ** *v.* to turn into a pool.
lawaan: *n.* species of tree.
lawak: *n.* expanse; extent; area, field of research; **malawak** *adj.* extensive; vast, immense; with a wide range; **lumawak** *v.* to expand, spread.
lawagat: *n.* lagoon; small lake.
lawalawá: *n.* spider web; species of spider.
lawanít: *n.* coconut husk wall paneling.
lawas: *n.* cattail.
laway₁: *n.* saliva; **malaway** *adj.* full of spittle; **lawayan** *n.* long-finned cavalla; **tumútulò ang laway** *id.* mouth watering (saliva flowing); **laway lamang** *id.* gratuitous (just saliva).
laway₂: *n.* jackfish.
lawí: *n.* tail feather of roosters.
lawig: *n.* long duration; **lumawig** *v.* to prolong; **palawigin** *v.* to extend (in time), prolong; **pakálawigan** *v.* to take a long time in doing.
lawíg: (*Bats.*) *n.* migrant farm worker.
lawihan: *n.* banded slipmouth fish.
lawin: *n.* hawk; flying fish; **lawin-lawin** *n.* short-winged flying fish.
lawíng: *n.* tatters, rags.
lawingwíng: *n.* pendant.
lawis: *n.* curved blade attached to a pole used to pick coconuts.
lawiswís: *n.* top part of bamboo, named for the sound it makes in the wind; bamboo fish rake.
lawit: (*reg.*) *n.* sickle.
lawít: *adj.* suspended; **lumawít** *v.* to hang down; **palawít** *n.* something that hangs; pendant; **lawít ang pusod** *id.* selfish, stingy (protruding navel); **lawít ang dilà** *id.* exhausted.
lawláw₁: *n.* dangling; **ilawláw** *v.* to dangle; **malawláw** *adj.* too long.
lawláw₂: *n.* sardine; **maglawláw** *v.* to stir up (water) with the hands or feet.
lawláy: (*slang*) *n.* penis.
layà: *n.* freedom, liberty; **palayain** *v.* to emancipate, release, free; **kalayaan** *n.* independence, freedom; liberty; **malayà** *adj.* free, emancipated; **nakalálayà** *adj.* free, at large (criminals); **lumayà** *v.* to become free; **pagkápalayà** *n.* freedom; release; **pagpapalayà** *n.* liberation. **kalayaan sa pananampalataya** *n.* freedom of religion.
layâ: *adj.* licentious, free from moral restraints.
layák: *n.* flotsam; dry leaves.
layag: *n.* sail; **lumayag** *v.* to sail; **maglayág** *v.* to voyage, cruise; **paglalayág** *n.* cruise, passage.
layág: *n.* menopause; **malayagín** *adj.* prone to miss menstruation.
layáng: *n.* pruning.
layanglayang: *n.* Philippine swallow.
layas: *interj.* go away; **maglayás** *v.* to go from place to place; **lumayas** *v.* to run away; **layasan** *v.* to run away from someone; **palayasin** *v.* to chase away; banish, get rid of, oust.
layaw: *n.* freedom from parental control;

layáw *adj*. spoilt; **palayawin** *v*. to pamper; indulge; spoil; cuddle; **palayaw** *n*. nickname; pampering; **palayawan** *v*. to give a nickname to.
layíng: *n*. cutlass fish.
layláy: *adj*. hanging, drooping; **laylayan** *n*. hem; **lumayláy** *v*. to sag, droop; **layláy ang balikat** *id*. disappointed look (drooping shoulders).
layò: **malayò** *adj*. far, distant; **layuán** *v*. to ostracize; **lumayô** *v*. to avoid; **ilayô** *v*. to turn away; divert; **kalayuan** *n*. distance; **sa malayò** from afar; **malayò na ang naratíng** *id*. sound asleep (had gone far); **malayò sa tukâ** *id*. not in accordance with.
layog: *n*. elevation, altitude; **malayog** *adj*. high, elevated.
layon: *n*. intent, objective; purpose; **láyunin** *n*. aim, intention, objective, purpose. **palayón** *adj*. objective (grammar).
layót: *adj*. overripe; dried out before maturity.
laywán: *n*. species of honey bee.
lebadura: (Sp.) *n*. yeast.
lekat!: *interj*. exclamation of disappointment.
leég: *n*. neck.
lehia: (Sp. *lejía*) *n*. lye.
lente: (Sp.) *n*. lens.
lenteha: (Sp. *lenteja*) *n*. lentil.
lengguwá: (Sp. *lengua*) *n*. language, tongue.
lengguwahe: (Sp. *lenguaje*) *n*. language.
león: (Sp.) *n*. lion.
lepra: (Sp.) *n*. leprosy; **leproso** *n*. leper.
lesbya: (Sp.) *n*. lesbian.
leteng: *n*. cord, string.
letra: (Sp.) *n*. letter; script.
letse: (Sp. *leche*: milk → semen) *interj*. expresses disgust; ~ **ebaporada** *n*. evaporated milk; ~ **kondensada** *n*. condensed milk.
letseplán: (Sp. *leche flan*) *n*. custard.
letson: (Sp. *lechón*) *n*. roasted pig.
letsugas: (Sp. *lechuga*) *n*. lettuce.
ley: (Sp.) *n*. law.
leyenda: (Sp.) *n*. legend.
liâ: *n*. green scum on a pond.
liáb: *n*. blaze, flame.
liád: *adj*. bent backward with protruding stomach (like a pregnant woman).
liáng: *n*. cave.
liát: *n*. surface crack.
libák: *n*. insult; ridicule; **libakín** *v*. to ridicule.
libad: *n*. going from place to place.
libág: *n*. dirt on the skin.
liban: *n*. absence; *adj*. absent; **iliban** *v*. to procrastinate; delay; put off; **lumiban** *v*. to be absent; **libanan** *v*. to skip, omit; **liban sa** except; **mapagliban** *adj*. habitually procrastinating; **pagliban** *n*. absence; **pagpapaliban** *n*. postponement; **málíban kung** *conj*. unless, except; if not; **liban sa** *conj*. except.
libang: **libangan** *n*. consolation; entertainment; amusement; **maglibáng** *v*. to amuse oneself; **malibáng** *v*. to be entertained.
libát: *n*. recurrence of an illness; attack of a mental disorder.
libato: *n*. Malabar nightshade vine. (*alugbati*)
libay: *n*. female deer, doe.
libelo: (Sp.) *n*. libel.
libid: *n*. single coil; one trip around a track; **libíd** *adj*. wound round, encircled.
libído: (Eng.) *n*. sexual desire.
libíng: *n*. burial; **libingan** *n*. grave, cemetery; **ilibíng sa limot** *v*. to forget.
libís: *n*. slope; lower position of a place; **palibís** *adj*. sloping downwards.
liblíb: *adj*. hidden, secluded; heavier in front than in the back (cart).
libo: *n*. thousand; **libong-angaw** *n*. billion; **sampunlibo** *n*. ten thousand; **sandaanlibo** *n*. hundred thousand.
libog: **malibog** *adj*. lustful, sensual.
libot: **palibot** *n*. environment, surroundings; **libutan** *v*. to surround; **lumibot** *v*. to go around, tour; **maglibót** *v*. to tour, travel around; make rounds; **palibut-libot** *n*. going around and around; **palibut-sabi** *n*. message sent around; **sa palibot** around, on all sides of; **sangkalibután, sanlibután** *n*. universe.
libra: (Sp.) *n*. pound.
libre: (Sp.) *adj*. free; exempt; clear (traffic); **ilibre** *v*. to treat someone out, pay for someone's way.
libreta: (Sp.) *n*. bankbook, booklet.
librito: (Sp.) *n*. booklet.
libró$_1$: (Sp.) *n*. book; **tenedór-de-libro** *n*. ac-

countant, bookkeeper.

libró₂: (Sp.) *n.* tripe, third stomach of a ruminant.

libtóng: *n.* deep hole in a river bed.

libtós: *n.* blister.

libumbón: *n.* crowd.

likas: *n.* exodus; **lumikas** *v.* to evacuate, migrate. **palikasin** *v.* to cause to evacuate or migrate. **paglikás** *n.* evacuation; exodus; eruption of a rash.

likás: *adj.* natural, inherent; inbred; characteristic of; **kalikasán** *n.* nature. **pagkalikás** *n.* naturalness; inborn-ness.

likát: *n.* interruption, intermission.

likaw: *n.* coil; **ilikaw** *v.* to coil, wind around.

likhâ: *n.* creation; *adj.* created; **lumikhâ, likhain** *v.* to create; **mapanlikhâ** *adj.* ingenious, creative; **sanglinikhâ** *n.* universe, all creatures; **mga nilikhâ** *n.* creatures; **pagkamapanlikhâ** *n.* originality; **paglikhâ** *n.* creation; **tagalikhâ** *n.* producer, creator.

likit: *adj.* insistent, stubborn.

liklík: *n.* digressing, not coming straight to the point; **kaliklikán** *n.* digression.

likmík: *n.* smell of dirt or garbage; **malikmikán** *adj.* nauseated by the smell of dirt.

likmô: *n.* armchair, comfortable seat; **lumikmô** *v.* to sit down comfortably.

likô: *n.* bend, curve; *adj.* bent, turned; **likó-likô** *adj.* twisted, zigzag; crooked; **lumikô** *v.* to detour; curve; swerve; **palikú-likô** *adj.* zigzag; twisting; (*fig.*) erroneous.

likód: *n.* back; reverse side; **likód-bahay** *n.* backyard; **likurán** *n.* back, backside; place behind; background; **manalikód** *v.* to be on the toilet; **tumalikód** *v.* to turn one's back on; **palikód** *adv.* backward; **pálikuran** *n.* public toilet; **panlikód, panlikurán** *adj.* behind, posterior; **pagtalikód** *n.* departure; defection; renouncement; **waláng-lingúng-likód** without looking back. [See also *talikód*]

likom: *n.* collecting; **likumin** *v.* to gather, collect; withdraw, draw back.

likót: **malikót** *adj.* restless, mischievous, always moving; **likutín** *v.* to tamper with, meddle with; **kalikután** *n.* mischievousness; constant motion; prank; **malikót ang kamáy** *id.* thief (hand is restless); **malikót ang isip** *id.* without perseverance, inconstant.

liksí: **maliksá** *adj.* active, quick, agile.

likwád: **palikwád-likwád** *adj.* hesitating, evasive.

liderato: (Sp.) *n.* leadership.

liga: (Sp.) *n.* league, coalition.

ligalig: *n.* trouble; preoccupation; **ligalíg** *adj.* troubled; perplexed; **maligalig** *v.* to be worried, disturbed; confused; **lumigalig, ligaligin** *v.* to harass, disturb; **manligalig** *v.* to disturb, cause trouble; **panligalig** *n.* troublemaker; **panliligalig** *n.* general disturbance, causing trouble.

ligamento: (Sp.) *n.* ligament.

ligamgám₁: *n.* anxiety, perturbation, insecure feeling.

ligamgám₂: *n.* lukewarm temperature.

ligas: (Sp.) *n.* garter.

ligás: *n.* small tree with an edible fruit similar to the cashew.

ligasgás: *adj.* rough (skin).

ligat: **maligat** *adj.* with a delicious consistency (rice); gummy, viscous.

ligatà: *n.* itchy blotch on the skin.

ligaw: **ligawan, lumigaw** *v.* to court, woo; **manliligáw** *n.* suitor; **paligawin** *v.* to urge a man to court a woman; **ligaw-insík** *id.* giving gifts when courting (Chinese courting); **ligaw-tingín** *id.* bashful courting with the eyes only; **ligaw-kanto** *n.* courting a girl with no good intentions of marriage or meeting her parents (picking up on the corner); **ligaw-tapát** *id.* courting by standing in front of the lady's house.

ligáw: *adj.* wild; uncultivated; stray; **iligáw** *v.* to mislead; misdirect; **magligáw** *v.* to misdirect; lead astray; **máligáw** *v.* to lose one's way; stray; **malígáwin** *adj.* prone to get lost; having no sense of direction; **mapagligáw** *adj.* misleading; **paligáw-ligáw** *adj.* straying, losing one's way several times on a trip.

ligawgáw: **maligawgáw** *adj.* ticklish.

ligaya: *n.* happiness; **maligaya** *adj.* happy; **lumigaya** *v.* to cheer up, become happy;

magpakaligaya *v*. to strive to be happy.
ligelya: (*slang*) *adj*. exciting; arousing.
ligí: **ligihín** *v*. to pulverize.
ligid: **paligid** *n*. circumference; revolution; vicinity; **ligíd** *adj*. surrounded; encircled; **lumigid** *v*. to revolve, go around; **pumaligid** *v*. to encircle, surround.
ligís: *adj*. ground, crushed.
liglíg: *adj*. shaken.
ligò: *n*. bath; **maligò** *v*. to bathe, take a bath; **paliguan** *n*. bathroom; **ligong pato** *id*. taking a bath without wetting the head (duck bath).
ligoy: *n*. verbosity, wordiness; act of bypassing something; **maligoy** *adj*. rambling; redundant; indirect; roundabout.
ligpít: **iligpít** *v*. to put away, lay aside; kidnap; **lumigpít** *v*. to retire; **pagliligpít** *n*. retirement.
ligsá: *n*. evacuation.
ligtâ: **makaligtaán** *v*. to overlook, omit inadvertently.
ligtás: *adj*. saved, freed; exempt; redeemed; **makaligtás** *v*. to escape; get through a difficult situation; survive; **iligtás** *v*. to save, rescue; **pagliligtás** *n*. deliverance, redemption.
ligwák: *n*. spilling; **lumigwák** *v*. to spill.
liha: (Sp. *lija*) *n*. sandpaper.
lihà: *n*. segment of an orange; region in the hand bounded by lines.
liham: *n*. letter (written message); **iliham** *v*. to write in a letter; **lihaman** *v*. to write someone a letter.
lihí: *n*. act of becoming pregnant; **maglihí** *v*. to conceive; **paglihihán** *v*. to crave for (while in pregnancy).
lihim: *n*. secret; *adj*. secret, confidential; **kalihim** *n*. secretary; **ilihim** *v*. to hide, keep secret, cover up.
lihís: *adj*. devious; deflected; incorrect; **lumihís** *v*. to swerve; deviate; stray; **lihisan** *v*. to avoid; divert; **palihisín** *v*. to divert, deflect.
lihiyá: (Sp. *lejía*) *n*. lye.
lihò: *n*. deceit.
liíg: var. of *leég*: neck.
liíng: *n*. sidelong glance. (*sulimpát*)
liít: *n*. smallness, littleness; inadequacy; **liitán** *v*. to decrease, make smaller; **lumiít** *v*. to decrease; become small; **maliít** *adj*. small; unimportant, trivial; miniature; **maliitín** *v*. to belittle, take lightly; underestimate; **manliít** *v*. to feel small, cheap, embarrassed; shrink; **paliitín** *v*. to lessen, make smaller.
lila: (Sp.) *n*. lilac; broken piece of a clay pot.
lilik: *n*. blade of a sickle.
lilim: *n*. shade; shadow; **makalilim** *v*. to cast a shadow over; overshadow; **malilim** *adj*. shady; **maliliman** *v*. to be shaded. (*linong*)
liling: *n*. sullen look.
lilip: *n*. hem; **lilipan** *v*. to hem.
lilís: *adj*. rolled up (sleeve, skirt, pants).
lilít: *adj*. frayed.
liliw: *n*. kind of long-legged colorful bird.
lilo: *n*. renegade, traitor; *adj*. disloyal, unfaithful; **paglililo** *n*. treachery, disloyalty; infidelity; **pagliluhan** *v*. to be disloyal to.
lilok: *n*. sculptured work; **lumilok** *v*. to sculpt; **manlililok** *n*. sculptor.
lilom: *n*. shady place.
limá: *n*. five; **kalimá** *n*. one fifth; **lilimahin** *n*. five peso bill; **límáhan** *n*. quintet, group of five; **limahín** *v*. to make into five; **limampû** *n*. fifty; **makálimá** *adj*. five times; **makalimá** *v*. to get five of a kind; **panlimá** *adj*. fifth; **labinlimá** *n*. fifteen; **paglimahín** *v*. to multiply by five; make into five; **ikalimá, panlimá** *adj*. fifth; **sangkalimá** *n*. one fifth.
limák: *adj*. along the roadside; beside the point.
limahî: *adj*. untidy, messy.
limahid: *n*. shabbiness; **limahíd** *adj*. untidily dressed.
limang: *n*. mistake in counting, miscount; **malimang** *v*. to lose count.
limás: *n*. bailing water out of a boat; **maglimás** *v*. to bail out water.
limatik: *n*. leech.
limay: *n*. water left on the shore by a low tide.
limayón: **maglimayón** *v*. to gallivant.
limbág: *n*. printing; edition; **ilimbág** *v*. to print, imprint; **ipalimbág** *v*. to get something printed; **manlilimbág** *n*. printer; **nakalimbág** *adj*. printed; **pálimbagan** *n*. printing shop.
limbáng: **limbangín** *v*. to flirt with a woman

(insincerely).
limbás: *n.* bird of prey.
limbáy: *n.* gliding in the air (birds).
limbó: *n.* limbo; halo.
limbóng: **panlilimbóng** *n.* deceit; fraud.
limì: *n.* attention; **limiin** *v.* to pay attention to, heed.
limî: *n.* flower juice or extract.
limit: *n.* frequency; compactness; **malimit** *adj.* frequent, often; **limitan** *v.* to do frequently; put things closer together.
limlím: *n.* body warmth; impending darkness; **lumimlím** *v.* to get darken; **palimliman** *n.* brooder, incubator.
limón: (Sp.) *n.* lemon.
limonada: (Sp.) *n.* lemonade.
limonsito: (Sp. *limoncito*) *n.* kind of shrub.
limós: (Sp. *limosna*) *n.* alms; stipend; **maglimós** *v.* to give alms; **magpalimós** *v.* to ask for alms; **magpapalimós** *n.* beggar.
limot: *n.* oblivion; **kalimutan** *v.* to forget; **malimutan** *v.* to forget; neglect; **lumimot** *v.* to forget; **nakalimutan** *adj.* forgetful; **nakalimot** *v.* forgot; (*fig.*) took a nap.
limót: **manlimót** *v.* to pick up from the ground.
limpa: (Sp. *linfa*) *n.* lymph.
limpâ: *n.* spleen.
limpák: *n.* big piece of meat; large quantity of goods.
limpál: *n.* large piece.
limpáy: *n.* swaying, swinging.
limpî: *n.* barricade; stockade; act of resting with a group; *adj.* gathered together.
limpít: *n.* large jar with a wide mouth.
limpiyabota: (Sp. *limpiabotas*) *n.* shoe-shiner.
limpiyá: (Sp. *limpia*) **limpyahín** *v.* to clean.
limpiyesa: (Sp. *limpieza*) *n.* cleanliness.
limpyo: (Sp. *limpio*) *adj.* clean; neat.
lináb: *n.* greasy scum on the surface of liquids.
linagà: (*rt. lagà*) *n.* stew, boiled meat.
linamnám: *n.* flavor, savor, deliciousness; **malinamnám** *adj.* delicious.
lináng: *n.* farm; **kalinangán** *n.* cultivation; civilization; **maglináng** *v.* to cultivate.
linas: (Sp. *linaza*) *n.* linseed.
linás: *adj.* pressed and squeezed (lemon).
linatsáy: *n.* mackerel fry.
linaw: *n.* clearness of liquids; **malinaw** *adj.* clear; legible; **linawin** *v.* to clarify.
linay: **paglilinay** *n.* scrutinization of evidence.
lindayag: *n.* recovery of one's senses after a fright.
lindero: (Sp.) *n.* boundary.
lindî: *n.* affected gait or manner.
lindíg: **malindíg** *adj.* tall and elegant.
lindól: *n.* earthquake; shock; **lumindól** *v.* to quake, shake.
lineá: (Sp.) *n.* line; boundary; limit; row; rank; column.
liníb: *n.* small window for ventilation.
linimento: (Sp.) *n.* liniment.
lining: **liningin** *v.* to consider; reflect; meditate on.
linis: *n.* cleanliness; neatness; pureness; **malinis** *adj.* clean; neat; clear; hygienic; chaste; **linisin** *v.* to clean.
linláng: *n.* deceit, fraud; hoax; **linlangán** *v.* to fool, deceive.
linolyo: (Sp.) *n.* linoleum.
linsád: *adj.* dislocated; derailed.
linse: (Sp. *lince*) *n.* lynx.
linsíl: *adj.* improper; erroneous.
linsó: (Sp. *lienzo*) *n.* linen.
lintâ: *n.* leech; **lintáng-kati** *n.* slug; **parang lintâ** *id.* usurer.
linták: *interj.* expresses disgust or surprise.
lintík: *n.* lightning (*kidlát*); mild curse word.
lintóg: *adj.* swollen, blistered.
lintós: *n.* blister.
linugaw: (*rt. lugaw*) *n.* rice porridge.
linumot: *n.* variety of rice.
linya: (Sp. *línea*) *n.* line, boundary; limit; row; rank, column; **ilinya** *v.* to align; **nakalinya** *adj.* aligned; **mapalinya** *v.* to be cast in a certain role; put in line.
lingâ: **magpalingá-lingâ** *v.* to look from side to side; look here and there.
lingá: *n.* sesame.
lingál: **palingál-lingál** *adj.* rolling sideways (boats).
lingap: *n.* protective care.
lingas: *n.* blaze, flame; shine; boasting; pride; **~-kugon** *adj.* of short duration.
lingat: *n.* kind of fleshy herb with creepy, hairy

rootstock.
lingát: **malingát** *adj*. unaware; **pagkalingát** *n*. inadvertence; negligence.
lingaw: *n*. clamor; **lingáw** *adj*. confused.
lingawngáw: *n*. murmuring.
lingáy: *n*. slope of a mountain; **nakalingáy** *adj*. bent backwards.
lingkág: *adj*. opened with force; corrupt, wicked.
lingkáw: *n*. sickle.
lingkís: **lumingkís** *v*. to twine, coil around; **manlilingkís** *n*. boa constrictor.
lingkód: *n*. servant; **maglingkód** *v*. to serve; **palingkuran** *n*. service.
linggál: *n*. dim, clamor.
linggatong: *n*. perplexity; worry.
linggít: **malinggít** *adj*. tiny.
Linggó: (Sp. *domingo*) *n*. Sunday; week; **~-de-Ramos** *n*. Palm Sunday; **lingguhan** *n*. weekly newspaper; *adj*. weekly; **linggú-linggó** *adj*. weekly.
lingguwista: (Sp. *lingüísta*) *n*. linguist; person who speaks many languages.
lingguwístika: (Sp. *lingüística*) *n*. linguistics.
lingíd: *adj*. secret, hidden.
lingil: *n*. attention given to a task. (*asikaso*)
lingmíng: **nalingmíng** *adj*. confused.
lingó: **paglingó** *n*. assassination; **manglilingó** *n*. assassin.
lingón: *n*. looking back; esteem; **lumingón** *v*. to look back; to look around; **lingunín** *v*. to look back at something; **lingón-likód** *id*. looking back; **waláng lingón-likód** *id*. does not repay debts of gratitude (no looking back).
lingos: **lumingos** *v*. to look around.
lipá: *n*. nettle plant.
lipák: *n*. callus, corn on the hands or feet. (*kalyo*)
lipád: *n*. flight; **lumipád** *v*. to fly; take off; **lumipád-lipád** *v*. to hover; **páliparan** *n*. airfield; **maglípáran** *v*. to fly away together; **manlilipad** *n*. pilot; **lumílipád ang isip** *id*. straying from the topic (flying mind); **lumílipád pa sa alapaap** *id*. daydreaming (still flying in the clouds).
lipanà: *adj*. widespread; diffused.
lipás: *adj*. lapsed; old-fashioned; outdated; out of style; faded; **lumipás** *v*. to pass; elapse; pass by; **paglipas** *n*. passage.
lipat: *n*. transfer; **lumipat** *v*. to move, transfer; migrate; **palipát** *adj*. transitive; **paglilipat-kamáy** *n*. changing ownership.
lipay: *n*. species of plant with stinging hair; St. Thomas bean.
lipì: *n*. lineage, ancestry; race; **liping-mahal** *id*. from royal blood (costly clan).
lipol: *n*. extinction; destruction; **lipulin** *v*. to annihilate, wipe out; liquidate; get rid of.
lipon: *n*. crowd, gathering; assembly; **kalipunan** *n*. assembly; tribe; **panlípunan** *adj*. social. **lípunan** *n*. society; group gathered to converse. **makipaglipón** *v*. to join a conversation; **maglipón** *v*. to converse.
lipós: *adj*. covered with. **lipós-dálitâ** *adj*. very poor; heartbroken.
lipot: *n*. going over an obstacle; transferring.
lipstik: (Eng.) *n*. lipstick.
lipumpón: *n*. gathering; **magkalipumpón** *v*. to crowd around; collect, flock.
lira: (Sp.) *n*. lyre; lire (currency).
lirà: *n*. swollen eyelids.
lírika: (Sp. *lírica*) *n*. short poem.
liríng: *n*. second compartment of a fishing corral.
lirip: **liripin** *v*. to study carefully; try to understand; **paglilirip** *n*. understanding; careful scrutinization.
lirit: *adj*. torrential.
lirót: *adj*. scattered.
liróy: **maliróy** *adj*. of soft consistency.
liryo: (Sp. *lirio*) *n*. lily.
lisâ: *n*. nit.
lisan: **lumisan** *v*. to leave, depart; **lisanin** *v*. to depart, leave; abandon.
lisaw: **lumisaw** *v*. to swarm.
lisay: *n*. pounding of rice for the second time.
lisdíng: *adj*. plain, unadorned.
lisensiyá: (Sp. *licencia*) *n*. license.
lisik: **manlisik** *v*. to glare (angry eyes).
lislís: *adj*. lifted up (dress).
liso: (Sp. *liso*: flat) *adj*. simple, plain.
lisó: *adj*. confused. (*litó*)
lisô: *adj*. restless.

lisók: *adj*. dislocated, sprained.

listá: (Sp.) *n*. list; register; roll of names; **ilista** *v*. to list down; **pagpapalista** *n*. enrollment; **ilistá sa tubig** *id*. debt that will not be paid; gratuitous (list in the water).

listo: (Sp.) *adj*. alert; clever.

listón: (Sp.) *n*. hat band; ribbon; strip.

lisyâ: *adj*. wrong, incorrect; out of line; wayward.

liták: *n*. crack.

litania: (Sp.) *n*. litany.

litas: *n*. small split or cut.

litáw: *adj*. visible; well-known; noticeable; popular; **lumitáw** *v*. to appear; emerge; stand out; **paglitáw** *n*. appearance; occurrence.

literatura: (Sp.) *n*. literature.

litid: *n*. ligament; sinew, tendon.

litis: *n*. trial or investigation in court; careful examination; **litisin** *v*. to investigate judicially, try.

litmo: (Sp.) *n*. kind of dye used in chemical tests.

litó: *adj*. confused, puzzled; **lituhín** *v*. to confuse; **malitó** *v*. to be confused; **panlitó** *n*. red herring, something used to confuse.

litrato: (Sp. *retrato*) *n*. photograph, picture.

litro: (Sp.) *n*. liter.

litsón: (Sp. *lechón*) *n*. roasted pig; **litsunan** *n*. roasted pig party; place of cooking *litsón*.

litsugas: (Sp. *lechuga*) *n*. lettuce.

liwag: **maliwag** *adj*. slow to act; taking a long time to do things.

liwalas: **maliwalas** *adj*. spacious; fresh; breezy.

liwalíw: **magliwalíw** *v*. to go on a pleasure trip.

liwaló: *n*. climbing perch fish.

liwanag: *n*. light; shine; **maliwanag** *adj*. bright; clear; explicit; **lumiwanag** *v*. to clear up; brighten; **ipaliwanag** *v*. to explain, make clear; **paliwanag** *n*. explanation; solution.

liwás: *adj*. mistaken; deviating; out of line; **liwásan** *n*. plaza, park.

liwat: **iliwat** *v*. to pour a liquid several times between containers to mix or cool it well.

liwaywáy: *n*. dawn; **bukáng-liwaywáy** *n*. break of day.

liyâ: *n*. scum on a pond.

liyáb: *n*. blaze, flame.

liyabe: (Sp. *llave*) *n*. key, skeleton key; pliers; monkey-wrench; **~-inglesa** *n*. wrench; **~-de-tubo** *n*. pipe wrench; **liyabera** *n*. key chain; **~-maestra** *n*. master key. **liyabero** *n*. locksmith; key chain; key ring.

liyád: *n*. posture consisting of a protruding stomach and backwards bent back.

liyág: *n*. darling, beloved.

liyama: (Sp. *llama*) *n*. llama.

liyamada: (Sp. *llamada*) *n*. physician's visit or call.

liyamadista: (Sp. *llamadista*) *n*. one who always bets on the favored opponent.

liyamado: (Sp. *llamado*) *n*. favorite, favored opponent.

liyanera: (Sp. *llanera*) *n*. metal dish mold; pie pan.

liyano: (Sp. *llano*) *n*. plain, level land.

liyáng: *n*. top or outside surface.

liyát: *n*. slight crack in earthenware.

liyáw: *n*. act of spying; spy.

liyebo: (Sp. *llevo*) *n*. carrying over a figure in math.

liyebre: (Sp. *liebre*) *n*. hare.

liyempo: (Ch.) *n*. large cut of meat.

liyeno: (Sp. *lleno*) *adj*. full (vehicle).

liyó: *adj*. dizzy. (*hilo*, *lulà*)

liyók: *n*. movement of water in the stomach when shaken.

lobo: (Sp.) *n*. wolf; balloon.

loko: (Sp. *loco*) *adj*. madman; insane person; **manloloko** *n*. one who deceives, dishonest person; **kalokohan** *n*. foolishness; nonsense; **lokong-loko** *adj*. lunatic; **panloloko** *n*. racket; deceitfulness.

lóhika: (Sp. *lógica*) *n*. logic.

lola: (Sp. *abuela*) *n*. grandmother.

lolo: (Sp. *abuelo*) *n*. grandfather.

limilyo: (Sp. *lomillo*) *n*. small loin cut of meat.

lomo: (Sp.) *n*. loin; tenderloin.

lona: (Sp.) *n*. canvas, canvas floor of a boxing ring.

lonta: (*slang*, Sp. *pantalón*) *n*. long pants.

longganisa: (Sp. *langonisa*) *n*. pork sausage.

longsi: *n*. (*slang*) pork sausage and fried rice;

adj. drunk.

longsilog: (*coined: longganisa, sinangág, itlóg*) *n*. sausage, fried rice and fried egg.

loób$_1$: **kaloobán** *n*. will, volition; **kagandahang-loób** *n*. courtesy, kindness; generosity; **kapalagayang-loób** *adj*. intimate; **kagaanáng-loób** *n*. grace; **kababaang-loób** *n*. meekness; **kusang-loób** *adv*. willingly, voluntarily; **isaloób** *v*. to bear in mind; **sáloobín** *n*. attitude; disposition; **laban sa loób** against one's will; **lakás ng loób** *n*. courage; **lagáy ng loób** *n*. mood; **masasamáng-loób** *n*. underworld, criminals; **samaan ng loób** *n*. ill feeling; **utang na loób** *n*. debt of gratitude; **walâ sa loób** *adj*. indifferent, nonchalant.

loób$_2$: *n*. interior, inside; **palóob** *adj*. inward; **panloób** *adj*. interior; **sa loób** *adj*. inside; **tagaloób** *n*. insider; **ipaloób** *v*. to insert; encase; **looban** *n*. compound, premises; orchard; **mápasaloób** *v*. to occur in one's mind; **loób ng Mandaluyong** (*slang*) mental hospital.

loób$_3$: **kaloób** *n*. gift; **magkaloób** *v*. to give, donate; **ipagkaloób** *v*. to grant, give; **mapagkaloób** *adj*. generous; **pagkalooban** *v*. to give, bestow.

loób$_4$: **panloób, looban** *n*. robbery, burglary, pillaging; **manloloób** *n*. burglar.

loók: *n*. bay, harbor; gulf; **kalookan** *n*. region surrounding a bay.

loro: (Sp.) *n*. parrot; parrotfish; **parang loro** *id*. talkative (like a parrot).

loryat: (Ch.) **loryatan** *n*. Chinese banquet.

losa: (Sp.) *n*. porcelain; slab of tile.

losyáng: (*slang*) *adj*. sloppy.

lote: (Sp.) *n*. lot, parcel of land.

lotería: (Sp.) *n*. lottery.

luád: *n*. clay.

luáng: *see luwáng*.

luáy: **maluáy** *adj*. gentle, soft to the touch.

lubá: **lubahín** *v*. to remove husks by pounding.

lubák: *n*. pothole; hollow in the ground.

lubag: *n*. calming of emotions; end of a storm; lowering the sails of a sailboat; **lubág** *adj*. calm, tranquil; **lumubag** *v*. to calm down; **palubagin ang loób** *v*. to conciliate; **pampalubag-loób** *n*. balm; something used to please or calm.

lubalob: *n*. flathead fish; **maglubalób** *v*. to wallow in the mud.

lubang: *n*. hilly land.

lubáy: **lumubay** *v*. to become calm; become loose; **malubáy** *adj*. calm, relaxed; slack; **kalubayán** *n*. mildness; looseness; calmness; **waláng-lubáy** *adj*. persistent.

lubhâ: *adv*. extremely, very much; *n*. seriousness; **lumubhâ** *v*. to get worse, deteriorate; **malubhâ** *adj*. fatal.

lubid: *n*. rope; **lubirin** *v*. to twist strands of rope; **maglubid ng buhangin** *id*. to tell lies (make rope of sand).

lubig: **lubigan** *n*. species of aromatic herb.

lubíg: *n*. home run.

lubíng: (*slang*) *n*. homosexual male.

lublób: *n*. wallowing in mud; immersing; kind of fish trap; **lumublób** *v*. to wallow in mud; **ilublób** *v*. to immerse, duck, plunge into.

lubò: *n*. grouper fish.

lubó: *n*. dimple.

lubô: *n*. deep depression in the ground.

lubóg: *adj*. submerged, sunken; **ilubóg** *v*. to submerge, immerse; dip in water; **lumubóg** *v*. to sink; set (sun); **nilubugán ng araw** *id*. one who lost hope; abandoned; orphaned (sun set over); **lubóg sa utang** *id*. buried in debt.

lubós: *adj*. complete, perfect; entire, absolute, total; utter; *adv*. completely, entirely; wholly; **lubusín** *v*. to do completely.

lubyák: *n*. rut made in the road by wheels.

lukad: **lukarin** *v*. to remove coconut meat with a knife.

lukag: **pamamalukag** *n*. bristling of hair.

lukán: *n*. species of clam.

lukanót: *n*. effort, striving.

lukayo: *n*. clown, jester.

lukbán: *n*. pomelo; grapefruit.

lukbót: *n*. pouch; purse.

luklók: **luklukan** *n*. throne; seat of honor.

lukmô: *n*. act of sitting comfortably.

lukob: **paglukob** *n*. act of sheltering one's young (birds); **lukób** *adj*. sheltered, protected.

lukób: *n*. gouge, chisel; *adj*. convex; under the authority of.
lukóng: *n*. concavity; **malukóng** *adj*. bowl-shaped, concave.
lukop: *n*. shelter, support.
lukot$_1$: *n*. crease, wrinkle; **lukót** *adj*. wrinkled, crumpled.
lukot$_2$: *n*. species of honeybee.
luksâ: **magluksâ** *v*. to be in mourning; **panluksâ** *adj*. used in mourning.
luksó: *n*. jump, leap; **luksuhán** *v*. to jump over.
luktô: *n*. omission; interval.
luktón: *n*. young wingless locust; **luktóng dayupay** *id*. very greedy person.
lukulók: *adj*. melancholic.
ludlúd: *n*. glen; puddle; young deer with immature antlers.
lugà: *n*. secretion of earwax; **lugâ** earwax.
lugál: see *lugár*.
lugamì: **lugamî** *adj*. frustrated; **malugamì** *v*. to be frustrated; fallen into trouble.
lugamok: *adj*. fallen down drunk.
lug-ang: *n*. large crack in the ground.
luganggáng: *adj*. hollow, empty.
lugár: (Sp.) *n*. place, site; spot; **bigyáng-lugár** *v*. to give a chance to, give room to; **lumugár** *v*. to take one's place.
lugás: *adj*. fallen out; broken into bits; **malugás** *v*. to fall off; to fall out.
lugaw: (Ch.) *n*. gruel, rice porridge.
lugáy: *adj*. hanging loose.
lugaygáy: *adj*. disheveled.
lugi: (Ch.) *n*. financial loss; **malugi** *v*. to lose in a business deal. **lugíng-lugí** *adj*. at a great loss; having suffered a financial misfortune.
lugit: **palugit** *n*. handicap (sports); extension of time, extra allowance.
luglóg$_1$: *n*. kind of thick noodle from which *pansit palabok* is made.
luglóg$_2$: *n*. rinsing of clothes; **luglugín** *v*. to rinse clothes.
lugmók: *n*. bedridden state; helplessness. **malugmók** *v*. to collapse; fall down through weakness.
lugnás: *adj*. about to fall (fruit from a tree).
lugó: *adj*. very weak (birds).
lugód: *n*. pleasure, enjoyment; **malugód** *v*. to enjoy; **kalugúd-lugód** *adj*. delightful.
lugon: **malugon** *v*. to molt (shed feathers).
lugót: *adj*. wilted.
lugpô: *adj*. bedridden, unable to get up.
lugsô: *adj*. collapsed; deflowered (woman).
luhà$_1$: *n*. tear; **lumuhà** *v*. to cry, shed tears; **luhaán** *adj*. in tears; **lumuhà ng bató** *id*. to suffer much. **luhang-dalaga** *n*. bird cactus; Jew bush.
luhà$_2$: *n*. sap, resin.
luho: (Sp. *lujo*) *n*. luxury; **maluho** *adj*. luxurious.
luhoso: (Sp. *lujoso*) *adj*. luxurious; extravagant.
luhód: *n*. act of kneeling; kissing the hand of elders; **lumuhód** *v*. to kneel.
luhog: **lumuhóg** *v*. to implore, supplicate.
lulà: *n*. motion sickness; **lulâ** *adj*. dizzy, seasick.
lulan: *n*. load, cargo; **malulan** *v*. to be accommodated; **nakalulan** *adj*. aboard.
lulód: *n*. shin.
lulog: *n*. tinder.
lulón$_1$: **lulunín** *v*. to swallow; **hindî malulón** *id*. unacceptable to the conscience (can't be swallowed); **lulunín nang buô** *id*. to subdue.
lulón$_2$: *n*. roll of paper; **ilulón** *v*. to roll up.
lulóng: **mapalulóng** *v*. to be pushed into something against one's will.
lulos: **lumulos** *v*. to get through a difficult situation without hesitation.
lulót: *adj*. overripe; withered.
lulungi: *n*. halfbeak fish.
lumà: *adj*. old; second hand; former; **makalumà** *adj*. antique; old-fashioned; **lumang tugtugin** *id*. old news (old music).
lumahan: *n*. mackerel.
lumanay: *n*. gentleness, mildness; **malumanay** *adj*. gentle, mild.
lumat: *n*. slowness.
lumáy: *n*. love potion.
lumbá: *n*. continuous effort; drawing of water from a well.
lumbâ: *n*. gallop of a horse; black-finned shark.
lumbalumbá: *n*. dolphin.

lumbáng: *n*. species of tree.
lumbáy: **malumbáy** *adj*. sad, mournful, depressed.
lumbó: *n*. drinking cup made from a coconut shell.
lumbóy: *n*. Java plum.
lumì: **malumì** *adj*. with penultimate stress; *n*. kind of noodle dish; **kalumian** *n*. gentleness, softness.
luminaryo: (Sp. *luminario*) *n*. illumination festival.
lumitóg: *n*. mullet fish.
lumo: *n*. depression (feeling); **manlumó** *v*. to feel depressed.
lumó: *n*. fatigue.
lumog: *n*. eleotrid fish.
lumón: *adj*. very ripe.
lumot: *n*. moss; algae; **nilúlumot nang bató** *id*. obsolete; now longer useful (stone covered in moss).
lumpiyâ: (Ch.) *n*. egg roll.
lumpó: *adj*. paralyzed; crippled, lame.
lumpók: *n*. bundle of stalks ready for threshing.
lumpón: *n*. reunion, small gathering.
lumuluksó: *n*. milkfish spawner.
lunab: *n*. oil on the surface of a liquid.
lunak: *adj*. ripened on the tree.
lunademyél: (Sp. *luna de miel*) *n*. honeymoon.
lunán: **panlunán** *adj*. locative (grammatical).
lunas₁: *n*. cure, remedy; antidote; **lunasan** *v*. to cure, remedy.
lunas₂: *n*. kind of fern; kind of bamboo; bottom of a vase; basin; keel of a boat.
lunaw: *n*. soft mud.
lundág: *n*. jump, leap; **lumundág** *v*. to jump; **lundagan** *n*. hurdle.
lundáy: *n*. canoe.
lundô: *n*. slack, part hanging loose; **malundô** *adj*. slack, loose (not tight).
Lunes: (Sp.) *n*. Monday.
luningníng: *n*. sparkle, shine.
lunó: **maglunó** *v*. to molt, shed the skin.
lunók: *n*. swallow; **lumunók** *v*. to swallow.
lunod: **malunod** *v*. to drown; **lumurin** *v*. to drown someone; **kanluran** *n*. west.
lunos: **nakalulunos** *adj*. pitiful; touching; tragic, sad.
lunót: *adj*. overripe and soft.
lunoy: **maglunoy** *v*. to wade through a river.
lunsád: *n*. getting off a vehicle; **lumunsád** *v*. to get off a vehicle; dismount a horse; disembark; land. **ilunsád** *v*. to unload; launch; start a campaign.
lunsód: var. of *lungsód*: city; **tagalunsód** *adj*. urban.
luntî: (Ch.) *adj*. green; **luntián** *adj*. green; greenish; **kaluntián** *n*. greenness.
lungad: **maglungád** *v*. to vomit milk (babies).
lungangî: *adj*. with the head bent down on the chest.
lungás: *adj*. broken off (teeth).
lungáw: *n*. large hole in the ground.
lungayngáy: *adj*. with drooping head.
lungkág: *adj*. bulky.
lungkát: (*obs*.) *n*. wood molding.
lungkót: *n*. sadness, sorrow; gloom; grief; **malungkót** *adj*. sad, gloomy; depressed; miserable. **kalungkút-lungkót, nakalúlungkót** *adj*. sorrowful, lamentable; **ikalungkót** *v*. to sadden, depress. **lumungkót** *v*. to become sad. **malungkutin** *adj*. prone to sadness, melancholic; **pagkalungkót** *n*. sorrow; grief; **Ikinalulungkót ko** I'm sorry.
lunggâ: *n*. burrow in the ground (made by an animal).
lunggatî: *n*. fervent wish.
lungì: **mapalungì** *v*. to meet with misfortune.
lungíb: *n*. underwater cave.
lungó: **lulungú-lungó** *adj*. convulsing (when drowning).
lungos: *n*. cape (Geo. term).
lungóy: *adj*. ready to eat (*bagoóng*).
lungsód: *n*. city; **punung-lungsód** *n*. capital city; most important city of a region.
luog: *n*. lump of food stuck in the throat.
luóm: **naluóm** *adj*. enclosed with no access to fresh air; stuffy.
luóng: *n*. lowland at the base of a hill; mudfish trap.
luop: *n*. act of fumigating to cure sickness.
luóy: *adj*. withered.
lupà: *n*. earth, soil; ground; land; country; **lupain** *id*. to impoverish; **lupaín** *n*. land,

country; territory; estate, hacienda; **kalupaán** *n.* worldliness; **maglupà** *v.* to turn to soil; **panlupà** *adj.* ground; on the ground; **guhò ng lupà** *n.* landslide; **lamáng-lupà** *n.* root crops; **lupang-tinubuan** *n.* homeland; **makalupà** *adj.* worldly, earthly; material; materialistic; **maylupà** *n.* landowner; **sangkalupaán** *n.* the whole world; **kama ng lupà** *n.* plot of land; **katawáng lupà** *n.* earthly body; **lupang payapà** *id.* grave (peaceful earth). **lupang-tinubuan** *n.* mother country; **lupang-sarili** *n.* native land; **taong-lupà** *n.* mythological dwarf.

lupák: **lupakín** *v.* to pound rice; crush, beat.

lupagî: *adj.* squatting; sitting Indian style.

lupalop: *n.* vast expanse of land.

lupasáy: *adj.* squatting, sitting on the haunches.

lupaypáy: *adj.* prostrate; languid; with drooping wings; frustrated; **manlupaypáy** *v.* to droop; wilt.

lupî: *n.* fold; hem; *adj.* folded; **kalupî** *n.* folder.

lupíg: *adj.* conquered; **lupigin** *v.* to conquer, vanquish.

luping: *n.* dog ear (of a book). **lupíng** *adj.* dog-eared; with large, drooping ears.

lupít: *n.* cruelty; savageness; harshness; **lumupít** *v.* to become cruel; **malupít** *adj.* cruel, brutal; inhuman; **pagmamalupít** *n.* abuse, harsh treatment.

luplóp: *n.* squatting with the head bent low and the hands touching the ground. (*yupyóp*)

lupo: *n.* lump fish, poison fish; parrot fish.

lupog: *n.* rotting due to over watering (plants).

lupon: *n.* board, committee; commission.

lurâ: (var. of *durâ*) *n.* spit.

luray: *n.* mangling; mutilation. **luráy** *n.* mangled; mutilated. **luráy-luráy** *adj.* mutilated beyond recognition.

lurík: (*slang*) *adj.* insane.

lurit: *n.* insistence; persistence.

lusak: *n.* mud; slush. **lusak** *adj.* muddy. **lusakan** *n.* mire. **lusakin** *v.* to make muddy.

lusaw: *n.* melting; liquid state; beating (of eggs). **lusáw** *adj.* melted; diluted; beaten (eggs). *n.* fluid. **lusawán** *n.* beater; melting pot.

lusáy: *adj.* thin (hair); *n.* eel grass.

lusero: (Sp. *lucero*) *n.* morning star; star on a horse's forehead.

luses: (Sp. *luces*) *n.* sparkler, Roman candle.

luslós: *n.* hernia; *adj.* fallen, hanging down.

lusob: *n.* attack; **lusubin** *v.* to attack.

lusók: *adj.* blunt, dull pointed.

luság: *n.* health; **malusóg** *adj.* healthy, sound; robust.

lusong: *n.* descent; **palusóng** *adv.* downhill, downward.

lusóng: *n.* wooden mortar used for pounding grains.

lusót: *n.* passing through a narrow place; **lumusót** *v.* to go through.

luspád: *adj.* worn out by constant use. **lusparin** *v.* wear out; overuse.

lustáy: **lumustáy** *v.* to embezzle; **manlulustáy** *n.* embezzler.

lutád: *adj.* worn out by use and constant handling.

lutang: **lumutang** *v.* to float; **palutang** *n.* buoy, float; **lulutang-lutang** *adj.* adrift.

lutás: *adj.* solved; finished.

lutáy: *adj.* torn to shreds.

lutiin: *n.* parrot fish.

lutlót: **nalutlót** *adj.* very dry, withered; fallen from the stalk (dry grain); **nilutlót** *adj.* snatched.

luto: (Sp.) *n.* mourning clothes.

lutò: *n.* cooking, cuisine; (*slang*) cheating; frame up; game fixing; **maglutò** *v.* to cook; **tagapaglutò** *n.* cook; **lutong makáw** *id.* game fixing; **lutò sa Diyós** (*slang*) *n.* sexual intercourse.

lutok: *n.* snapping sound; brittleness of dry branches.

lutong: **lutong-makáw** *adj.* rigged.

lutóng: *n.* brittleness; crispiness; **malutóng** *adj.* brittle, crisp.

lutos: **lumutos** *v.* to collapse.

lutukán: *n.* species of rattan.

luwâ₁: **magluwâ** *v.* to belch out, eject from the mouth.

luwâ₂: *adj.* protruding, bulging.

luwág: **maluwág** *adj.* loose, not tight; roomy, spacious; lax; liberal; free; **luwagán** *v.* to relax, mitigate; ease up; **maluwág ang**

turnilyo *id.* crazy (screw is loose); **iluwág ng loób** *id.* to have peace of mind (loosen inside).

luwál: *adj.* exterior, outside; exposed; **lumuwál** *v.* to issue forth, come out; be born; **paluwál** *n.* disbursement; **paluwalán** *v.* to disburse.

luwalhatì: *n.* glory, splendor; **luwalhatiin** *v.* to glorify.

luwán: *n.* kind of river seaweed.

luwáng: *n.* width; **maluwáng** *adj.* wide; spacious; **maluwáng ang butas ng tainga** *id.* good listener (hole in ear is wide).

luwás₁: *n.* trip to town; **lumuwás** *v.* to go to town. **lúwasan** *n.* exodus of people from the country to the city.

luwás₂: *n.* export; **iluwás** *v.* to export.

luwát: *n.* long time. **maluwát** *adj.* taking a long time; **kaluwatán** *n.* long time.

luwáy: *n.* slow action, slow moving (when walking).

luwelang: *n.* large wicker basket.

luya: *n.* ginger; **luya-luyahan** *n.* zedoary, plant similar to ginger; **luyang-diláw** *n.* turmeric, plant that yields yellow dye for food coloring and broth.

luylóy: *adj.* flabby (flesh).

luyok: *n.* bending downward (heavy branch).

luyong: *n.* species of palm.

luyos: *n.* betel nut palm.

M

ma: *n.* species of mollusk.

ma-: *pref.* prefix forming adjectives or potentive verbs (expressing involuntary, coincidental, abilitative actions) → **mahulog** *v.* to fall accidentally, **maihî** *v.* to accidentally urinate; **mahinà** *adj.* weak, **malungkót** *adj.* sad.

maárì: *v.* possible, can.

maaga: (*rt. aga*) *adj.* early.

maanó: (*rt. anó*) *v.* to happen to; please; **Maanó sa akin kung panalo ka.** So what (I don't care) if you won.

maáng: *adj.* ignorant.

Mabuhay!: (*rt. buhay*) Long Live!

mabulo: *n.* species of sapodilla (*chico*).

mabuti: (*rt. buti*) *adj.* good; well.

maka- *pref.* Forms actor focus potentive verbs: **makabanggít** *v.* to happen to mention, be able to mention; **makahintô** *v.* to be able to stop; **makahindî** *v.* to be able to say no. 2. forms pro- adjectives **maka-Hapón** pro-Japanese; **makabayan** *adj.* nationalistic; 3. forms frequentatives: **makaitló** three times.

makabuhay: (*rt. buhay*) *n.* kind of spreading vine.

makahiyâ: (*rt. hiyâ*) *n. mimosa* plant that moves when touched.

makailán: *(rt. ilán) interrog.* How many times?

makaisá: (*rt. isá*) *n.* species of tree whose fruit is used in fish poisons.

makalawá *n.* the day after tomorrow; **makálawá** *adj.* twice.

makan: *n.* species of pig; kind of rice.

makapag- *pref.* used with *mag-* verbs to express the concept of unexpectedly having the chance to do the action denoted by the root: **makapagbili** *v.* to have the opportunity to sell; **makapag-alagà** *v.* to be able to care for.

makapagpa- *pref.* abilitative causative prefix.

makapál: *adj.* thick, dense.

makapunô: *n.* variety of coconut.

makatà: *n.* poet; **magmakatà** *v.* to be a poet.

makdô: (*slang*) *n.* McDonalds (restaurant).

maki- *pref.* 1. used to form social verbs → **makisayaw** *v.* to join in dancing; 2. also used in polite requests → **Makipuntá ka ngâ sa bahay niyá** Please go to her house.

mákina: (Sp. *máquina*) *n.* machine; motor.

makinarya: (Sp. *maquinaria*) *n.* machinery.

makinilya: (Sp. *maquinilla*) *n.* typewriter; **taga-makinilya** *n.* typist; **makinilyado** *adj.* typed.

makinista: (Sp. *maquinista*) *n.* machinist.

makipag- -an: *circumfix.* forms social or reciprocal verbs → **makipaginuman** *v.* to drink with others; **makipagsayáw** *v.* to dance with someone.

makipag-: *pref.* forms reciprocal social verbs

from *mag-* verbs → **makipagkamáy** *v.* to shake hands with; **makipag-usap** *v.* to converse with.

makopa: *n.* Malay rose apple tree, mountain apple, *Syzygium malaccense.*

maktól: *n.* grumbling; **magmaktól** *v.* to grumble.

makulít: (*rt. kulít*) *adj.* repetitious; persistent.

madâ: (*slang, madatóng*) *adj.* rich; wealthy.

madalíng-araw: *n.* dawn.

madatóng: (*slang*) *adj.* rich, wealthy.

madeha: (Sp. *madeja*) *n.* skein.

madlâ: *n.* public; people; *pron.* all, the public; **madláng tao** *pron.* anyone, the public.

madrastra: (Sp.) *n.* stepmother.

madre: (Sp.) *n.* nun.

madrokukáw: *n.* tree also known as *kukuwate.*

madrina: (Sp.) *n.* godmother.

madyák: (*slang*) *n.* marijuana.

madyóng: (Ch.) *n.* mahjong game; **madyongero** *n.* mahjong player.

maestra: (Sp.) *n.* female teacher.

maestro: (Sp.) *n.* male teacher.

mag- *pref.* 1. verbalizing prefix- **anák** child, **mag-anák** *v.* to give birth; **agahan** breakfast, **mag-agahan** *v.* to eat breakfast; 2. forms reciprocal nouns or verbs: **mag-iná** *n.* mother and child; 3. denotes occupations (with reduplication) **mag-iisdâ** *n.* fisherman.

magâ: *n.* swelling, swollen part; **mamagâ** *v.* to become swollen.

Magahat: *n.* ethnic group and language from SW Negros.

mag-amóy-. *pref.* (*mag-* + *amoy*) forms verbs which indicate the smell of the root → **mag-amóy-pawis** *v.* to smell like sweat, **mag-amóy-kandilà** *v.* to smell like a candle.

magka- *pref.* 1. prefix used to form reciprocal or sharing verbs **magkapartido** *adj.* to belong to (share) the same political party; **magkapareho** *v.* to be similar to each other; 2. prefix denoting possession: **magkapera** *v.* to have money.

magkano: *interrog.* How much?

magdalena: (*slang*) *n.* mistress; prostitute.

Magindanao: *n.* ethnic group and language from Mindanao.

magíng: *v.* to happen; become; **magigíng** *adj.* future, what is intended to be.

mago: (Sp.) *n.* magus, wise men of the Bible.

magpa- *pref.* forms causative verbs- **magpatakbô** *v.* to make someone run; **magpagandá** *v.* to beautify, make beautiful.

magpaka- *pref.* denotes that effort is involved in accomplishing the action of the verb, denotes intensity of adjectives → **magpakabuti** *v.* to do one's best; **magpakatiwalà** *v.* to have full trust in; **magpakalabis** *v.* to overindulge; **magpakapagod** *v.* to work very hard and tire oneself out.

magpati- *pref.* forms verbs expressing permissive reflexive actions → **magpatihulóg** *v.* to allow oneself to fall.

magsa- *pref.* 1. forms verbs meaning to imitate, or act the role of → **magsa-Pranses** *v.* to act like a Frenchman, do in a French way; 2. to translate **magsa-Ilokano** *v.* to translate into Ilocano.

magsi- *pref.* prefix which forms collective plural verbs (from *-um-* verbs) → **magsitulong** *v.* to cooperatively help.

magsipag- *pref.* designates collective or cooperative verbs, used with *mag-* verbs → **magsipagsimbá** *v.* to go to mass with others.

magsipagpa- *pref.* designates causative verbs with plural topics- **magsipagpagawâ** *v.* to have many people get something done.

magsipagpaka- *pref.* used for certain collective actions → **magsipagpakabaít** *v.* to try to be well-behaved, to all behave (said of many people).

magsipang- *pref.* form of *mang-* verbs specifying plural actors → **magsipang-isdâ** *v.* to go fishing together; **magsipangailangan** *v.* to need (plural).

magulang: *n.* parent.

mahablangka: (Sp. *maja blanca*) *n.* corn starch pudding.

mahadera: (*slang*) *adj.* talkative, noisy.

mahál$_1$: *n.* love; *adj.* dear; beloved, loved; **magmahál, mahalín** *v.* to love; **pagmamahál** *n.* love; **minámahál** *adj.* beloved, dear; **mahalín** *v.* to love; **pagmamáhálan** *n.*

bond of love; **mapagmahál** *adj.* affectionate; **mápamahál** *v.* to endear; **pakamahalín** *v.* to adore, cherish, worship; **pagmamahál** *n.* love; **Mahál kitá** I love you.

mahál₂: *adj.* expensive, costly; noble; **kamáhálan** *n.* nobility; majesty, highness; excellency; preciousness; expensiveness; **kámahál-mahálan** *adj.* sacred.

maharlikâ: *adj.* noble, aristocratic; **kamaharlikaán** *n.* nobility.

mahistrado: (Sp. *magistrado*) *n.* magistrate.

mahuwana: *n.* red porgy fish.

mai-: *pref.* forms involuntary or abilitative transitive verbs from *i-* verbs → **maibabà** *v.* to be able to lower; **maihanap** *v.* to be able to look for something for someone.

maiklî: (*rt. iklî*) *adj.* short; brief; (*slang*) *n.* pistol, handgun.

maipa-: *pref.* forms involuntary or abilitative causative verbs → **maipabukás** *v.* to be able to have someone open; **maipakita** *v.* to be able to show to someone.

maís: (Sp. *maíz*) *n.* corn; **binusáng maís** *n.* toasted corn, popcorn; **pusò ng maís** *n.* ear of corn.

maitines: (Sp.) *n.* midnight Mass.

mala- *pref.* expresses similarity, semi-, somewhat- **malagihay** *adj.* half-dry.

malabanos: *n.* moray, *Gymnothorax sp.*

malabató: *n.* rice grain beginning to show color.

maladyóng: *n.* Spanish mackerel.

malák: *n.* knowledge; consciousness.

Malakanyáng: (*Malacañan*) *n.* official residence of the President of the Philippines.

malakapas: *n.* mojarra fish.

malaguno: *n.* hardtail; mackerel scad.

malapando: *n.* Malabar cavalla fish.

malapito: *n.* jackfish, pampano.

malapní: *n.* herring fry.

malasakit: *n.* concern, interest; **mapagmalasakit** *adj.* concerned; **malasakitán** *n.* care for each other.

malasugi: *n.* swordfish; sailfish.

malarya: (Sp.) *n.* malaria.

malas₁: (Sp.) *n.* bad luck; *adj.* unlucky; **kamalasan** *n.* bad luck.

malas₂: *n.* intent look; **malasin** *v.* to observe, look intently at; **ipamalas** *v.* to show; prove one's ability.

malasado: (Sp. *mal asado*) *n.* soft-boiled egg.

malastigà: *n.* being tired of eating the same food all the time.

malatubà: *adj.* indifferent; unconcerned.

malatubâ: *adj.* with red feathers.

malasugì: *n.* swordfish.

malát: *adj.* hoarse (voice).

malaway: *n.* common slipmouth fish.

malay: *n.* consciousness; understanding; **kamalayán** *n.* knowledge; **waláng malay** *adj.* innocent; unconscious; unaware, ignorant; **malay-tao** *n.* consciousness; **papagkamaying-tao** *v.* to resuscitate; **mamalayan** *v.* to be aware of.

Maláy: *n.* Malay, Malayan.

Malaynon: *n.* ethnic group and language from NW Aklan Province, Panay.

malbás: (Sp. *malva*) *n.* kind of medicinal plant whose boiled leaves are used as a disinfectant or enema.

maldita: (Sp., *slang*) *n.* brat.

maleta: (Sp.) *n.* suitcase; **maletín** *n.* small suitcase.

malyete: (Sp.) *n.* mallet.

malî: **malî** *adj.* erroneous, false, wrong, untrue; **kamálían** *n.* defect, error, mistake, imperfection; **ipagkámalî** *v.* to confuse; **magkámalî** *v.* to make a mistake; **malí-malî** *adj.* full of mistakes; **máli-malì** *adj.* senile; **mámalî** *v.* to err; be mistaken; **maliín** *v.* to consider something wrong; **mápagkámalán** *v.* to misunderstand; to be mistaken for; **pagkakámalî** *n.* error, mistake; **pagkámalán** *v.* to mistake; **pamalí-malî** *adj.* erratic; **waláng-malî** *adj.* faultless.

malibanos: *n.* moray.

malikaskás: *adj.* peeling off (skin).

malimango: *n.* cavalla fish.

malikmatà: *n.* transfiguration; sleight of hand.

malinggá: *n.* kind of vine, known also as *kondól*.

maliputô: *n.* short person.

maliputó: *n.* jackfish, pompano; **maliputóng-laut** *n.* cavalla.

malisya: (Sp. *malicia*) *n.* malice; spite, ill will; **malisyoso** *adj.* malicious.
maliw: **magmaliw** *v.* to disappear; end; reduce in intensity or fervor; **pagmamaliw** *n.* disappearance; end, finish; diminishing of intensity or fervor; **waláng-maliw** *adj.* endless, never ceasing.
malmâ: *adj.* serious, grave.
malmál: (*slang*) *adj.* stoned, drugged.
maltrato: (Sp.) *n.* mistreatment.
malunggáy: *n.* horseradish plant.
malyete: (Sp.) *n.* mallet.
mam- *var.* of *mang-* prefix before labial consonants (*p*, *b*, *m*): **mambabae** *v.* to take on a mistress. The nasal *m* may replace the initial labial consonant: **mamuwís /maN-buwís/** *v.* to pay taxes.
mama-: *pref.* fused form of *maN-pa-*: **mamahayag** */maN-pa-hayag/* *v.* to attend a demonstration.
mamá: *n.* mother.
mamà: *n.* term of addressed for an unknown man.
mamâ: **magmamâ** *v.* to chew betel leaves.
mamák: *n.* rice straw.
mamád: *adj.* swollen from overexposure to water; not ironed well.
mamadera: (Sp.) *n.* breast pump (for nursing mothers).
mamadór: (Sp.) *n.* nursing bottle.
mamahagi: (rt. *bahagi*) *v.* to distribute in small portions.
mamahalà: (rt. *bahalà*) *v.* to direct; govern; be in charge.
mamahay: (rt. *bahay*) *v.* to reside in, live in; live independently from one's parents.
mamahò: (rt. *bahò*) *v.* to stink.
mamalakaya: (rt. *palakaya*) *v.* to fish with a *palakaya.*
mamalagì: (rt. *palagì*) *v.* to remain; stay permanently in one place or condition.
mamalahibo: (rt. *balahibo*) *v.* to have an inferiority complex.
mamalengke: (rt. *palengke*) *v.* to go to the market.
mamali: *n.* four fingered treadfin fish, *Eleutheronema tetradactylum.* **mamaling-bató** *n.* small-mouthed threadfin fish.
mamalít: (rt. *palít*) *v.* to exchange.
mamalità: (rt. *balità*) *v.* to spread gossip.
mamalò: (rt. *palò*) *v.* to beat, spank.
mamam: (*babytalk*) *n.* drink.
mámamakyáw: (rt. *pakyáw*) *n.* wholesale buyer.
mámamahayág: (rt. *pa-hayag*) *n.* newspaperman. (*peryodista*)
mámamalakaya: (rt. *palakaya*) *n.* *palakaya* fisherman.
mámamangkâ: (rt. *bangkâ*) *n.* boatman.
mámamatay-sunog: (rt. *patay-sunog*) *n.* fireman. (*bumbero*)
mámamatay-tao: (rt. *patay-tao*) *n.* murderer.
mámamayán: (rt. *bayan*) *n.* citizen; inhabitant of a place.
mamanata: (rt. *panata*) *v.* to take a religious vow.
mamanatag: (rt. *panatag*) *v.* to stay calm; have confidence in oneself; (*fig.*) die.
mamanhík: (rt. *panhík*) *v.* to make a formal marriage proposal (family of prospective groom); to implore, entreat.
mamansíng: (rt. *pansíng*) *v.* to fish with hook and line.
mamantál: (rt. *pantál*) *v.* to swell (from a bite); form a welt.
Mamanwa: *n.* ethnic group and language from Agusan del Norte and Surigao Provinces, Mindanao.
mamangkâ: (rt. *bangkâ*) *v.* to go by boat.
mamangláw: (rt. *pangláw*) *v.* to feel depressed, lonely.
mamaos: (rt. *paos*) *v.* to feel hoarse.
mamaraka: (rt. *baraka*) *v.* to go marketing.
mamarali: (rt. *parali*) *v.* to boast, brag.
mamarang: *n.* species of edible mushroom.
mamarati: (rt. *parati*) *v.* to stay, remain unchanged.
mamaríl: (*rt. baril*) *v.* to hunt with a gun; fire a gun at someone.
mamasahe₁: (rt. *masahe*) *v.* to be able to massage.
mamasahe₂: (rt. *pasahe*) *v.* to pay one's fare.
mámasan: (*slang*) *n.* madam of a prostitution house.

mamaskó: (rt. *paskó*) *v*. to ask for a Christmas gift.
mámasdán: (rt. *masíd*) *v*. to happen to observe closely.
mamaso: *n*. painful boil-like swelling.
mamasukan: (rt. *pasok*) *v*. to be employed; work as an employee.
mamasyál: (rt. *pasyál*) *v*. to take a walk, stroll.
mámaw: (*slang, Cebuano*) *n*. ghost.
mamay: (*reg*.) *n*. grandfather.
mamáy: *n*. wet nurse.
mámayâ: *adv*. soon; later; **pagpapamamayâ** *n*. postponement; **ipagpamamayâ** *v*. to postpone. **mámayá-mayâ** *adv*. later. **mámayáng gabí** tonight.
mamayabas: (rt. *bayabas*) *v*. to pick guavas.
mamayad: (rt. *bayad*) *v*. to pay one's debts.
mamayagpág: (rt. *payagpág*) *v*. to boast.
mamayan: (rt. *bayan*) *v*. to live in town.
mamayani: (rt. *bayani*) *v*. to prevail, predominate; triumph.
mamayapà: (rt. *payapà*) *v*. to pass away, die.
mamayat: (rt. *payat*) *v*. to become thin.
mamaybáy: (rt. *baybáy*) *v*. to follow the coast.
mamaywáng: (rt. *baywáng*) *v*. to stand with the arms akimbo.
mambo: (Sp.) *n*. mambo dance.
mameligro: (*rt. peligro*) *v*. to be in danger.
mameluko: (Sp. *mameluco*) *n*. children's overalls.
mamera: (rt. *pera*) *adj*. one centavo each.
mamerhuwisyo: (rt. *perhuwisyo*) *v*. to throw a temper tantrum; injure, cause trouble to.
mamì: (Ch.) *n*. flour noodles; noodle dish (usually with broth).
mamigáy: (rt. *bigáy*) *v*. to give for free.
mamihasa: (rt. *bihasa*) *v*. to be accustomed to.
mamilansík: (rt. *pilansík*) *v*. to splatter, splash.
mamiláy: (rt. *pilay*) *v*. to walk with a limp.
mamilayláy: *v*. to be uttered.
mamilí: (rt. *bilí*) *v*. to buy.
mamilì: (rt. *pilì*) *v*. to choose, pick.
mamiligro: (rt. *piligro*) *v*. to be in danger.
mamilipit: (rt. *pilipit*) *v*. to become twisted; squirm, writhe.
mamilit: (rt. *pilit*) *v*. to force.
mámimilí: (rt. *bili*) *n*. buyer; customer.
mámimintás: (rt. *pintás*) *n*. critic; fault finder.
mamín: *n*. betel pepper plant. (*ikmó*)
maminsalà: (rt. *pinsalà*) *v*. to injure, damage.
maminsán: (rt. *pinsán*) *v*. to be able to do all at once; **maminsán-minsán** *adv*. once in a while, now and then.
mamintakasi: (rt. *pintakasi*) *v*. to attend a cockfight festival.
mamintás: (rt. *pintás*) *v*. to criticize.
mamintô: (rt. *pintô*) *v*. to be on the threshold of.
mamintóg: (rt. *bintóg*) *v*. to swell, inflate.
mamintuhò: (rt. *pintuhò*) *v*. to show admiration for; ingratiate oneself by doing someone a favor.
maming: *n*. wrasse fish.
mamingit: (rt. *bingit*) *v*. to be on the verge of.
mamingwít: (rt. *bingwít*) *v*. to fish with hook and line; (*coll*.) obtain by trickery.
mamirinsá: (rt. *pirinsá*) *v*. to iron.
mamiseta: (rt. *piseta*) *adj*. twenty centavos each.
mamiso: (rt. *piso*) *adj*. one peso each.
mamistá: (rt. *pistá*) *v*. to attend a fiesta.
mamistâ: (rt. *pistâ*) *v*. to criticize.
mamitás: (rt. *pitás*) *v*. to pick (fruits).
mamiyapis: (rt. *piyapis*) *v*. to be defeated.
mamón: *n*. sponge cake.
mamsá: *n*. banded cavalla fish.
mamukadkád: (rt. *bukadkád*) *v*. to open (flowers).
mamuko: (rt. *buko*) *v*. to bud.
mamukód: (rt. *bukód*) *v*. to be different, distinctive.
mamukol: (rt. *bukol*) *v*. to bulge.
mamugad: (rt. *pugad*) *v*. to build a nest; settle permanently in a place.
mamuhay-: (rt. *buhay*) *pref*. to lead the life of: **mamuhay-mongha** *v*. to lead the life of a nun.
mamuhay: (rt. *buhay*) *v*. to live in a certain place.
mamuhunan: (rt. *puhunan*) *v*. to put up money as capital.
mamulà: (rt. *pulà*) *v*. to be critical of.
mamulá: (rt. *pulá*) *v*. to blush; redden.
mamulaklák: (rt. *bulaklák*) *v*. to bloom; (*fig*.)

be productive.

mamulot: (rt. *pulot*) *v*. to pick up; (*coll.*) *v*. to take for one's benefit.

mamulubi: (rt. *pulubi*) *v*. to live the life of a beggar.

mamulupot: (rt. *pulupot*) *v*. to twist, coil.

mámumuhunán: (rt. *puhunan*) *n*. capitalist.

mámumulót: (rt. *pulót*) *n*. picker.

mámumuna: (rt. *puná*) *n*. critic.

mámumuslít: (rt. *puslít*) *n*. smuggler.

mámumustá: (rt. *pustá*) *n*. bettor.

mámumursiyento: (rt. *pursiyento*) *n*. commission agent.

mámumuwís: (rt. *buwís*) *n*. taxpayer.

mamuná: (rt. *puná*) *v*. to criticize.

mamundók: (rt. *bundók*) *v*. to live in the mountains; pass through the mountains.

mamunò: (rt. *punò*) *v*. to lead; preside.

mamunú-munô: (rt. *punô*) *adj*. almost filled.

mamunga: (rt. *bunga*) *v*. to bear fruits; result.

mamungay: (rt. *pungay*) *v*. to become languid (eyes).

mamuô: (rt. *buô*) *v*. to harden; coagulate.

mamupô: (rt. *pô*) *v*. to speak respectfully using *pô*.

mamupól: (rt. *pupól*) *v*. to pick flowers.

mamurok: (rt. *burok*) *v*. to become chubby.

mamuról: (rt. *puról*) *v*. to become blunt.

mamursiyento: (rt. *pursiyento*) *v*. to sell on commission.

mamusangsáng: (rt. *busangsáng*) *v*. to be blunted.

mamusarga: (rt. *busarga*) *v*. to burst open (popped grains); become swollen.

mamutî: (rt. *putî*) *v*. to become white.

mamutlâ: (rt. *putlâ*) *v*. to become pale.

mamutók: (rt. *putók*) *v*. to break by cracking (dry skin).

mamuwís: (rt. *buwís*) *v*. to pay taxes. **mamuwisan** *v*. to enter a crop-sharing agreement.

mamuwisit: (rt. *buwisit*) *v*. to annoy.

mamuyat: (rt. *puyat*) *v*. to keep others awake all night.

man: *adv*. although, even if; with; too.

man- *pref*. variant of *mang-* prefix used before roots that begin with the apicals d, l, r, s, or t.

manCV-: *pref*. variant of *mangCV-*, forms frequentative nouns which specify occupation: **mándaragát** *n*. seaman; fisherman.

mana₁: *n*. inheritance; heritage; **ipamana** *v*. to bequeath; **magmana** *v*. to inherit; **pamana** *n*. inheritance; **tagapagmana** *n*. heir.

mana₂: (Sp.) *n*. manna.

manà: (*slang*) *n*. homosexual male.

maná: **maná pa'y** preferably.

manaan: (rt. *daán*) *adj*. one hundred pesos each.

manabako: (rt. *tabako*) *v*. to smoke cigars.

manabi: (rt. *sabi*) *v*. to tell on others; (*coll.*) defecate.

manabík: (rt. *sabík*) *v*. to be eager, enthusiastic.

manakalì: (rt. *sakalì*) *v*. to take a chance.

manaká-nakâ: *v*. occasionally; from time to time.

manakaw: (rt. *takaw*) *v*. to be able to steal. **manakawan** *v*. to be robbed, have something stolen from.

manakít: (rt. *sakít*) *v*. to ache; injure.

manakop: (rt. *sakop*) *v*. to conquer.

manakot: (rt. *takot*) *v*. to threaten; intimidate.

manaksák: (rt. *saksák*) *v*. to stab.

manada: (Sp.) *n*. herd; flock.

manadyâ: (rt. *sadyâ*) *v*. to do intentionally.

managalog: (rt. *tagalog*) *v*. to speak Tagalog.

managanà: (rt. *saganà*) *v*. to prevail, predominate.

managasà: (rt. *sagasà*) *v*. to force one's way; drive recklessly.

managát: *n*. red snapper.

managhilì: *v*. to be envious.

managhóy: (rt. *taghóy*) *v*. to lament.

managì: (rt. *sagì*) *v*. to hit lightly in passing.

managimpán: (rt. *panaginip*) *v*. to daydream, dream about.

managinip: (rt. *panaginip*) *v*. to dream.

managót: (rt. *sagót*) *v*. to be responsible for; reply; answer back. **manágutan** *v*. to be answerable for.

manahî: (rt. *tahî*) *v*. to sew.

manahimik: (rt. *tahimik*) *v*. to be silent; retire; (*fig.*) die.

manaíg: (rt. *daíg*) *v*. to prevail.

manainga: (rt. *tainga*) *v*. to hear, overhear.

manalakáb: (rt. *salakáb*) *v*. to fish with a

salakáb; find the truth by trick.
manalakay: (rt. *salakay*) *v*. to assault, attack.
manalamín: (rt. *salamín*) *v*. to look at oneself in the mirror; wear eyeglasses.
manalantâ: (rt. *salantâ*) *v*. to damage; harm physically.
manalangin: (rt. *panalangin*) *v*. to pray.
manalapî: (rt. *salapî*) *v*. fifty-centavos each.
manalát: (rt. *salát*) *v*. to be scarcely supplied.
manalaytáy: (rt. *talaytáy*) *v*. to flow, pass through a long tube (blood in the capillaries).
manaliksík: (rt. *saliksík*) *v*. to research.
manalig: (rt. *salig*) *v*. to believe; have faith in.
manalo: (rt. *talo*) *v*. to win.
manalot: (rt. *salot*) *v*. to damage; annihilate; cause massive destruction or death.
manaluntón: (rt. *taluntón*) *v*. to follow (road, example, etc.)
manansí: *n*. herring fry.
manambitan: (rt. *sambít*) *v*. to make a plea.
manambulat: (rt. *sambulat*) *v*. to be scattered.
manamít: (rt. *damít*) *v*. to wear (clothes).
manampál: (rt. *sampál*) *v*. to slap.
manampalasan: (rt. *tampalasan*) *v*. to damage, cause destruction; be wasteful.
manampalok: (rt. *sampalok*) *v*. to pick tamarind fruits.
manampalataya: (rt. *sampalataya*) *v*. to believe; have faith in.
mánanabas: (rt. *tabas*) *n*. pattern cutter.
mánanakop: (rt. *sakop*) *n*. conqueror; redeemer.
mánanagwán: (rt. *sagwán*) *n*. oarsman.
mánanahì: (rt. *tahî*) *n*. sewer; seamstress; tailor.
mánanalakáy: (rt. *salakáy*) *n*. invader.
mánanalaysáy: (rt. *salaysáy*) *n*. historian.
mánanaliksík: (rt. *saliksík*) *n*. researcher. **mánanaliksík-batás** *n*. legal researcher.
mánanalin: (rt. *salin*) *n*. translator.
mánanaló: (rt. *talo*) *n*. constant winner.
mánanalok: (rt. *salók*) *n*. water carrier.
mánanambáng: (rt. *tambáng*) *n*. waylayer.
mánananim: (rt. *taním*) *n*. planter; farmer.
mánanansô: (rt. *tansô*) *n*. cheater; swindler.
mánananggál: (rt. *tanggál*) *n*. evil being whose upper body roams at night for victims.
mánananggól: (rt. *sanggól*) *n*. defender.
mánanawíd: (rt. *tawíd*) *n*. ferryman.
mánanayà: (rt. *tayâ*) *n*. bettor.
mánanayáw: (rt. *sayáw*) *n*. dancer.
manandata: (rt. *sandata*) *v*. to take up arms, go to war.
mananid: *n*. species of large monkey.
manansô: (rt. *tansô*) *v*. to swindle, cheat.
manang: (Sp. *hermana*) *n*. elder sister; devotee.
mananghalì: (rt. *tanghalì*) *v*. to eat lunch.
mananghód: (rt. *tanghód*) *v*. to stay around idly waiting for something to happen.
manangis: (rt. *tangis*) *v*. to weep.
manaog: *v*. to descend, go down; get off a vehicle.
manaón: (rt. *taón*) *adv*. yearly; every year; one year each.
manapá: (*mana* + *pa*) *adv*. preferably.
manápatan: (rt. *tapat*) *v*. to serenade.
manapote: (rt. *sapote*) *v*. to cheat at cards.
manariwà: (rt. *sariwà*) *v*. to freshen up.
manás: *n*. beriberi; *adj*. afflicted with beriberi.
manata: *v*. to take a vow.
manatili: (rt. *tili*) *v*. to remain (stay unchanged).
manaw: *var*. of *pumanaw*: pass away; disappear.
manawà: (rt. *sawà*) *v*. to lose interest; overindulge.
manawagan: (rt. *tawag*) *v*. to appeal; call for help.
manáy: (*slang*) *n*. homosexual male.
manko: (Sp. *manco*) *adj*. lame in one hand.
mankwerna: (Sp. *mancuerna*) *n*. pair tied together (prisoners, cuff links, etc.).
manda: *var*. of *mando*: order, command.
mandarangkál: *n*. praying mantis.
mandalâ: *n*. stack of rice or straw.
mandamyento: (Sp. *mandamiento*) *n*. command, order; ~ **de aresto** *n*. arrest warrant; ~ **de rekisa** *n*. search warrant.
mandato: (Sp.) *n*. mandate.
Mandaya: *n*. ethnic group and language from Mindanao.
mandín: [Marinduque, *man* + *din*] *adv*. con-

firmatory particle.
mándirigmâ: (rt. *digmâ*) *n.* warrior; troops.
mando: (Sp.) *n.* command, order.
mandò: (*slang*, f. *mándurukot*) *n.* pickpocket.
mándurukot: (rt. *dukot*) *n.* pickpocket.
mándurugô: (rt. *dugô*) *n.* blood sucker, vampire.
mánduruwit: (rt. *duwít*) *n.* cheat; swindler.
maneho: (Sp. *manejo*) **magmaneho** *v.* to drive a car; to manage.
mánenekas: (*rt.* *tekas*) *n.* cheat; thief, pickpocket.
manhík: *var.* of *pumanhík*: go upstairs. **manhík-manaog** *v.* to go up and down.
manhíd: **manhíd** *adj.* numb, torpid; (*slang*) to take for granted; have no feelings about; **manmanhíd** *v.* to become numb; **pampamanhíd** *n.* local anesthetic; **manhíd ang utak** *id.* insensitive.
manî: (Sp. *maní*) *n.* peanut; (*slang*) easy; clitoris; **nagmámaní-manî** (*slang*) easy. **mánian** *n.* peanut plantation.
manibago: *v.* to be unfamiliar with, unaccustomed to.
manibaláng: *n.* mature fruit.
manibasib: (rt. *sibasib*) *v.* to rush forward (in attacking).
manibela: (Sp. *manivela*: crankshaft) *n.* steering wheel.
manibughô: *v.* to be jealous.
manibulos: *v.* to have confidence in; trust.
manik: *n.* mother or pearl beads; beads.
manikà. (Sp. *muñeca*) *n.* doll.
manikad: (rt. *sikad*) *v.* to kick someone.
maniketa: (Sp. *manigueta*) *n.* crank.
manikî, -kin (Sp. *maniquí*) *n.* mannequin.
manikíp: (rt. *sikíp*) *v.* to be tight.
manikís: (rt. *tikís*) *v.* to do intentionally (to annoy someone).
manikít: (rt. *dikít*) *v.* to stick, adhere.
manikluhód: (rt. *tikluhód*) *v.* to beg for forgiveness, appeal on bent knee.
manikmát: (rt. *sikmát*) *v.* to snatch, grab with the mouth.
manikó: (rt. *siko*) *v.* to hit with the elbow.
maniktík: (rt. *tiktík*) *v.* to watch closely, spy.
manigás: (rt. *tigás*) *v.* to become stiff, harden.
manigeta: (Sp. *manigueta*) *n.* crankshaft handle.
manigíd: (rt. *sigíd*) *v.* to pierce, penetrate (the cold, pain, etc.).
manigò: *adj.* fine, favorable; prosperous; fortunate, lucky. **Manigong Bagong Taón** Prosperous New Year.
manihalà: *n.* responsibility; charge; care; management.
maniîl: (rt. *siíl*) *v.* to treat cruelly; oppress.
Manila: *n.* capital of the Philippines; **Manilenyo** *n.* native or resident of Manila; **kamanilaan** *n.* metropolitan Manila.
manilà: (rt. *tilà*) *v.* to attack for food (predators).
maniláw: (rt. *diláw*) v. to become yellow. **maniláw-nilaw** adj. yellowish.
manilbihan: (rt. *silbi*) *v.* to do menial work, work as a servant.
manilip: (rt. *silip*) *v.* to peer.
manilò: (rt. *silò*) *v.* to trap, snare.
manilóng: (rt. *silong*) *v.* to peep under a house from under the bamboo flooring.
manimbáng: (rt. *timbáng*) *v.* to balance oneself; try to be compatible.
manimdím: (rt. *dimdím*) *v.* to feel sad, sorry.
manindahan: (rt. *tindahan*) *v.* to go shopping.
manindíg: (rt. *tindig*) *v.* to stand on end, bristle. **manìndigan** *v.* to stand pat; defend one's rights or beliefs; be responsible for.
máninilà: *n.* predatory animal.
máníningil: (rt. *singíl*) *n.* bill collector.
máninisíd: (rt. *sisid*) *n.* diver.
maningaláng-pugad: *v.* to begin to have interest in girls (said of boys at puberty).
maningáw: (rt. *singáw*) *v.* to emit steam; stink.
maningkád: (rt. *tingkád*) *v.* to be colorful.
maningkayád: (rt. *tingkayád*) *v.* to squat, sit on the heels.
maninghál: (rt. *singhál*) *v.* to shout at someone, snarl.
maningíl: (rt. *singíl*) *v.* to collect (bills).
maniobra: (Sp.) *n.* maneuver; operation.
manipesto: (Sp. *manifesto*) *n.* manifest.
manipà: (rt. *sipà*) *v.* to kick.
manipesto: (Eng.) *n.* manifesto, proclamation.
manipis: *n.* cavalla fish.

manipit: (rt. *sipit*) *v*. to grasp with the claws, pinch.
manipsíp: (rt. *sipsíp*) *v*. to sip, suck.
manirà: (rt. *sirà*) *v*. to damage; slander. **manirang-puri** *v*. to slander.
manirahan: (rt. *tirahan*) *v*. to stay at someone's house; live in a certain place.
manís: *var*. of *panís*: spoiled; stale.
manisid: (rt. *sisid*) *v*. to collect by diving.
maniwalà: (rt. *tiwalà*) *v*. to believe; trust.
maniyák: (rt. *tiyák*) *v*. to be sure.
manmán: *n*. spying. **manmanan** *v*. to spy on.
mantiní: (Sp. *mantener*) *n*. support, subsistence.
manitis: *n*. goatfish.
maniwalà: (rt. *tiwalà*) *v*. to believe; trust; have faith in.
mano: (Sp.) *n*. handful; kissing an elder's hand; quire of paper (24 sheets); right turn in traffic; person who is first in a game; **magmano** *v*. to kiss an elder's hand. **manuhán** *n*. contest to see who will go first in a game.
Manobo: *n*. ethnic group and language from Mindanao.
manók: *n*. chicken, fowl; **manukan** *n*. poultry yard; **tulog-manók** *n*. light sleep. **manukín** *v*. (*coll*.) to support a candidate.
manong: (Sp. *hermano*) *n*. older brother; devotee.
manoód: (*rt*. *noód*) *v*. to watch. **mánonoód** *n*. spectator; audience.
mansa: (Sp. *mancha*) *n*. stain.
Mansaka: *n*. ethnic group and language from Mindanao.
mansanas: (Sp. *manzana*) *n*. apple.
mansanilya: (Sp. *manzanilla*) *n*. chamomile.
mansanitas: (Sp. *manzanitas*) *n*. species of tree with a small apple-like fruit.
mansera: (Sp. *mancera*) *n*. plow handle.
manso: (Sp.) *adj*. meek, tame.
manta: (Sp.) *n*. woolen blanket.
manták! *interj*. What about that!
mantekado: (Sp.) *n*. vanilla ice-cream.
mantél: (Sp.) *n*. table cloth.
mantensiyón: (Sp. *manutención*) *n*. maintenance, support.
mantikà: (Sp. *manteca*) *n*. lard; **mamantikà** *adj*. greasy; **parang mantikà** *id*. deep sleep. **mantí-mantikà** *adj*. oily, fatty, greasy.
mantikilya: (Sp. *mantequilla*) *n*. butter.
mantilya: (Sp. *mantilla*) *n*. veil; saddlecloth.
mantiní: (Sp. *mantener*) **mantinihín** *v*. to maintain; persevere. **mantinido** *adj*. supported, provided for.
mantsa: (Sp. *mancha*) *n*. stain.
manubà: (rt. *subà*) *v*. to swindle.
manubíg: (rt. *tubig*) *v*. to urinate.
manubok: (rt. *subok*) *v*. to spy on; catch by surprise.
manubon: *n*. mojarras fish.
manukâ: (rt. *tukâ*) *v*. to peck with the bill; eat with the beak.
manukalà: *var*. of *panukalà* *n*. proposal, project; plan.
manugang: *n*. child-in-law. **manugang sa binyág** *n*. parent of one's godchild. **manugang sa pamangkín** *n*. wife of one's nephew; husband of one's niece.
manunog: (rt. *sunog*) *v*. to burn.
manuskrito: (Sp. *manuscrito*) *n*. manuscript.
manuksó: (rt. *tuksó*) *v*. to joke, tease.
manudyó: (rt. *tudyó*) *v*. to tease, joke.
manuhol: (rt. *suhol*) *v*. to bribe.
manulák: (rt. *tulak*) *v*. to push (through a crowd).
manulad: (rt. *tulad*) *v*. to imitate.
manuláy: (rt. *tuláy*) *v*. to flow on a long object; walk a tightrope.
manuligsâ: (rt. *tuligsâ*) *v*. to attack verbally, criticize.
manulót: (rt. *sulot*) *v*. to poke; tell on other's in order to ingratiate oneself.
manulsí: (rt. *sulsí*) *v*. to mend.
manulsól: (rt. *sulsól*) *v*. to incite; instigate.
manulungan: (rt. *tulong*) *v*. to volunteer.
manuluyan: (rt. *tuloy*) *v*. to board, stay temporarily.
manumbalik: (rt. *tumbalik*) *v*. to be restored.
manumpâ: (rt. *sumpâ*) *v*. to swear (an oath); curse, blaspheme.
manundô: (rt. *sundô*) *v*. to fetch people in a particular district (during elections).
manundót: (rt. *sundót*) *v*. to poke, thrust.
manunog: (rt. *sunog*) *v*. to set on fire.

manuntók: (rt. *suntók*) *v*. to hit with the fist.
mánunubà: (rt. *subà*) *n*. swindler.
mánunubos: (rt. *tubós*) *n*. savior, redeemer.
mánunukat: (rt. *sukat*) *n*. measurer. **mánunukat-lupà** *n*. land surveyor.
manunuklás: (rt. *tuklás*) *n*. explorer; inventor.
manunudlâ: (rt. *tudlâ*) *n*. marksman.
mánunuksó: (rt. *tuksó*) *n*. joker.
mánunugál: (rt. *sugál*) *n*. gambler.
mánunulà: (rt. *tulâ*) *n*. poet.
mánunulát: (rt. *sulat*) *n*. author; writer; journalist.
mánunulid: (rt. *sulid*) *n*. spinner.
mánunulsól: (rt. *sulsól*) *n*. instigator.
mánunog: (rt. *sunog*) *n*. arsonist; pyromaniac.
manununtok: (rt. *suntók*) *n*. boxer.
manungaw: (rt. *dungaw*) *v*. to look out the window.
manungayaw: (rt. *tungayaw*) *v*. to berate, scold, yell at.
manungkít: (rt. *sungkít*) *v*. to pick fruits with a pole.
manúngkulan: (rt. *tungkulan*) *v*. to hold an office.
manuót: (rt. *suot*) *v*. to penetrate, pierce.
manúparan: (rt. *tupad*) *v*. to fulfill a job; hold an office.
manura: (rt. *sura*) *v*. to annoy.
manurì: (rt. *surì*) *v*. to critique, criticize.
manurot: (rt. *surot*) *v*. to accuse, scold with the finger.
mánuskrito: (Sp. *manuscrito*) *n*. manuscript.
manuso: *n*. bandage wound around newborn babies.
mánusyâ: (*slang*) *n*. excrement.
manutok: (rt. *tutok*) *v*. hold up with a gun.
manuwág: (rt. *suwág*) *v*.to butt with the horns or head.
manuyâ: (rt. *tuyâ*) *v*. ridicule; make a sarcastic remark.
manuyò: (rt. *suyò*) *v*. to flatter; ingratiate oneself.
manwál: (Sp. *manual*) *adj*. manual.
manyakis: (*slang*) *n*. maniac.
manyanita: (Sp. *mañanita*) *n*. predawn serenade.
manyapa't: *conj*. just because.
manyari: *conj*. because; due to.
manyobra: (Sp. *maniobra*) *n*. maneuver.
manyémpo: (rt. *tiempo*) *v*. to take advantage of an opportune time to do something.
mang- *pref*. 1. verbalizing prefix → **gubat** forest, **manggubat** *v*. to hunt in the forest.
mangCV-: [maNCV] *pref*. forms frequentative nouns such as occupations: **mángingisdâ** *n*. fisherman. **manggagamot** *n*. physician. **mándudulà** *n*. playwright.
manga- *pref*. forms collective verbs (two or more subjects) → **mangawalâ** *v*. to disappear (many people), **mangagutom** *v*. to get hungry (many people).
mangadlít: *n*. surgeon fish.
mangag- *pref*. forms collective forms of *mag-* verbs: **mangagtawá** *v*. to laugh (several people).
mangagát: (rt. *kagát*) *n*. silver-spotted gray snapper; *v*. to bite.
mangagín-: *pref*. plural form of *magíng* → **mangagimpangit** *v*. to become ugly (plural topic); **mangagintao** *v*. to be born (a number of people).
mangahoy: (rt. *kahoy*) *v*. to collect firewood.
mangain: (rt. *kain*) *v*. to graze.
mangalakal: (rt. *kalakal*) *v*. to engage in business or trade.
mangalap: (rt. *kalap*) *v*. to recruit, enlist; cut logs.
mangalás: (rt. *kalás*) *v*. to unravel; become raveled.
mangalat: (rt. *kalat*) *v*. to distribute; scatter.
mangalawang: (rt. *kalawang*) *v*. to become rusty.
mangalay: (rt. *kalay*) *v*. to become fatigued.
mangalesa: (rt. *kalesa*) *v*. to ride in a buggy.
mangaligkíg: (rt. *kaligkíg*) *v*. to shiver, shake.
mangalisag: (rt. *kalisag*) *v*. to bristle, stand on end (hair).
mangalmót: (rt. *kalmót*) *v*. to attack with claws.
mangalót: (rt. *kalot*) *v*. to crunch, munch.
mangalumatá: (rt. *kalumatá*) *v*. to feel weak, fatigued.
mangalumbabà: (rt. *kalumbabà*) *v*. to rest the

chin on the palm.
mangálunyâ: (rt. *kalunyâ*) *v*. to have a concubine, commit adultery.
mangaluykóy: (rt. *kaluykóy*) *v*. to shiver.
mangamkám: (rt. *kamkám*) *v*. to appropriate another's possession.
mangampanya: (rt. *kampanya*) *v*. to campaign.
manganay: (rt. *panganay*) *v*. to give birth to the first child.
manganlóng: (rt. *kanlóng*) *v*. to take shelter.
manganyón: (rt. *kanyón*) *v*. to attack with cannons.
mángangalakál: (rt. *kalakal*) *n*. merchant, trader; businessman.
mángangantá: (rt. *kantá*) *n*. singer.
mángangathâ: (rt. *kathâ*) *n*. composer; novelist
mangapâ: (rt. *kapâ*) *v*. to grope in the dark; catch fish with the hands.
mangapál: (rt. *kapál*) *v*. to become thick, dense; increase in number.
mangapkáp: (rt. *kapkáp*) *v*. to frisk.
mangapit: (rt. *kapit*) *v*. to grasp, hold; cling to.
mangapós: (rt. *kapós*) *v*. to be lacking; to be hard of breathing.
mangaretela: (rt. *karetela*) *v*. to ride in a rig.
mangaromata: (rt. *karomata*) *v*. to ride in a *karomata*.
mangasera: (rt. *kasera*) *v*. to live in a boarding house.
mangastilà: (rt. *kastilà*) *v*. to speak Spanish.
mangatál: (rt. *katál*) *v*. to quiver, shake.
mangatí: (rt. *katí*) *v*. to itch.
mangatî: (rt. *katî*) *v*. to lure in to a trap using a decoy.
mangatóg: (rt. *katóg*) *v*. to shake, tremble.
mangkók: (Ch.) *n*. big bowl, saucer.
manggá: *n*. mango.
manggagamot: (*rt. gamót*) *n*. physician.
manggás: (Sp. *manga*) *n*. sleeve.
manggo: (Sp. *mango*) *n*. handle; butt of a gun; stem.
manggustán: (Sp. *mangostan*) *n*. mangosteen.
manghâ: **mamanghâ** *adj*. amazing, astonished; *v*. to wonder, be amazed; **kamanghá-manghâ** *adj*. wonderful, amazing.
mangilitî: (rt. *kilitî*) *v*. to tickle someone.
mangimî: (rt. *kimî*) *v*. to feel shy, timid.
manginain: (rt. *k[in]ain*) *v*. to graze.
manginíg: (rt. *kiníg*) *v*. to tremble, shake.
mángingisdâ: (rt. *isdâ*) *n*. fisherman.
mangipot: (rt. *kipot*) *v*. to become narrow or tighter.
mangirót: (rt. *kirót*) *v*. to sting (sharp pain).
mangisá-ngisá: (rt. *isá*) *adj*. few.
mangisáy: (rt. *kisáy*) *v*. to convulse.
mangitid: (rt. *kitid*) *v*. to become narrow.
mangiyakis: (rt. *kiyakis*) *v*. to rub the body against something (to relieve an itch).
mangmáng: *adj*. ignorant; uneducated; delirious from fever.
mangulót: (rt. *kulót*) *v*. to become curly.
mangulubót: (rt. *kulubót*) *v*. to wrinkle, become wrinkled.
mangumbidá: (rt. *kumbidá*) *v*. to invite.
mangumpáy: (rt. *kumpáy*) *v*. to cut with a sickle, cut grass for fodder.
mangumpisál: (rt. *kumpisál*) *v*. to confess.
mangumusta: (rt. *kumustá*) *v*. to inquire about the health of someone.
mangunót: (rt. *kunót*) *v*. to wrinkle.
manguntrata: (rt. *kuntrata*) *v*. to work under contract.
mángungulot: (rt. *kulot*) *n*. hairdresser; curler.
mángungultí: (rt. *kultí*) *n*. tanner.
mángungupit: (rt. *kupit*) *n*. pilferer.
mángunguwarta: (rt. *kuwarta*) *n*. swindler, racketeer; chiseler.
mangupas: (rt. *kupas*) *v*. to fade.
mangupete: (rt. *kupete*) *v*. to feel inferior to; be afraid to face (an enemy).
mangupit: (rt. *kupit*) *v*. to pilfer.
mangurakot: (rt. *kurakot*) *v*. to steal, loot; (*slang*) lose, be defeated.
mangurit: (rt. *kurit*) *v*. to pinch.
mangurót: (rt. *kurót*) *v*. to pinch.
mangursonada: (rt. *kursonada*) *v*. to select one's choice.
mangusinà: (rt. *kusinà*) *v*. to work in the kitchen.
Mangyán: *n*. group of related languages and ethnic groups from the island of Mindoro.
mangyari: (rt. *yari*) *v*. to happen, occur; **mangyari'y** *conj*. because.
maóng: *n*. denim.

maós: *var. of paos*: hoarse.
mapa: (Sp.) *n.* map.
mapa- *pref.* 1. used to form potentive causative verbs: **mapaalís** *v.* to (be able to) get someone to go away; 2. forms coincidental verbs **mapaiyák** *v.* to happen to cry.
mapaklá: *adj.* acrid.
mapag- *pref.* denotes fondness, habitual or incidental/ abilitative actions → **mapagbigay** *adj.* generous, prone to give; **mapagbasá** *adj.* fond of reading; **mapaghanap** *v.* to be able to search for; **mapagmasdán** *v.* to happen to observe; **mapagdaldál** *adj.* inclined to gossip; **mapaglakwatsa** *adj.* habitually truant.
mapang- *pref.* transitive form of *mapag*- **mapang-akit** *adj.* attractive (to others); **mapanganib** *adj.* dangerous (to others).
mapasa- *pref.* forms coincidental verbs: **mapasaisip** *v.* to happen to come to one's mind.
mapô: (*slang, maporma*) *n.* braggart.
Mapun: *n.* ethnic group and language from Cagayan del Sulu and Palawan Islands.
mapwáw: *n.* threadfin fish.
marabilya: (Sp. *maravilla*) *n.* marvel.
marahil: (rt. *dahil*) *adv.* maybe, perhaps; possibly.
Maranao: *n.* ethnic group and language from Mindanao.
marka: (Sp. *marca*) *n.* mark, brand.
marko: (Sp. *marco*) *n.* frame.
mare: (f. *kumare*) *n.* close female friend.
margaha: (Sp.) *n.* volcanic ash.
margarina: (Sp.) *n.* margarine.
marikita: (Sp. *mariquita*) *n.* lady bird.
marihuwana: (Sp. *marijuana*) *n.* marijuana.
marinero: (Sp.) *n.* sailor.
máriníg: (rt. *diníg*) *v.* to hear.
mariposa: (Sp.) *n.* butterfly; bow tie.
marmól: (Sp.) *n.* marble.
marpíl: (Sp. *marfil*) *n.* ivory.
Marso: (Sp. *Marzo*) *n.* March.
Marte: (Sp.) *n.* Mars.
Martes: (Sp.) *n.* Tuesday.
martilyo: (Sp. *martillo*) *n.* hammer.
martines: (Sp.) *n.* Chinese starling bird.
marinete: (Sp.) *n.* pile driver.
martiniko: *n.* climbing perch fish.
martír: (Sp.) *n.* martyr; **martirín** *v.* to martyr.
martiryo: (Sp. *martirio*) *n.* martyrdom.
maruyà: *n.* fritter.
mas: (Sp.) *adv.* more; **mas mabuti** better.
masa: (Sp.) *n.* dough; mash; pie dough; **masahin** *v.* to knead.
másakér: (Eng.) *n.* massacre.
masahe: (Sp. *masaje*) *n.* massage; **masahista** *n.* masseur.
Masbatenyo: *n.* ethnic group and language from Masbate Province.
maskada: (Sp. *mascada*) *n.* chewing tobacco.
máskara: (Sp. *máscara*) *n.* mask.
maskí: (Sp. *más que*) *adv.* even if.
maskulado: (corrupted English) *adj.* muscular.
masdán: (rt. *masíd*) *v.* to stare at; look at.
maseta: (Sp. *maceta*) *n.* flowerpot; small mallet; **masetera** *n.* flower pot.
masetas: (Sp. *maceta*) *n.* potted plant.
masíd: *n.* stare; **magmasíd** *v.* to watch; behold; see; **masdán, pagmasdán** *v.* to stare at; watch; eye; look at; **mapagmasíd** *adj.* observant; watchful; **pagmamasíd** *n.* stare; observation; **pangmasíd** *n.* observation; **pagmasdáng mabuti** *v.* to contemplate; scrutinize, examine; **tagapagmasíd** *n.* observer.
masilya: (Sp. *macilla*) *n.* putty.
maso: (Sp. *mazo*) *n.* mallet; sledge hammer.
masok: (f. *pumasok*) **labás-masok** *id.* more or less.
masón: (Sp.) *n.* Mason.
masyado: (Sp. *demasiado*) *adv.* excessive, too much.
matá: *n.* eye; sight; **abót ng matá** *adj.* within sight; **mangalumatá** *v.* to have rings around the eyes; **matahán** *adj.* big eyed; **pamatá** *n.* reproach; tenant's fee to a landlord; **matáng-baka** *n.* big-eyed scad fish; **matáng-pusà** *n.* sea bass; **mapangmatá** *id.* boastful, belittling (fond of eyeing); **mangmatá** *v.* to belittle, look down upon. **waláng matá** *id.* illiterate; **matáng-lawin** *n.* keen, sharp eyes.
mataan: *n.* mackerel.
matadero: (Sp.) *n.* slaughterhouse.

matadór: (Sp.) *n.* bullfighter.
matagál: (*rt. tagál*) *adj.* long (in time).
matalos: *n.* anchovy.
matangal: *n.* red snapper.
matapobre: (Sp. *mata pobre*: kill poor) *n.* one who despises or looks down upon others based on their inferior social standing.
materya: (Sp. *materia*) *n.* matter, subject in school.
mating: (*slang*) *n.* robber.
matón: (Sp.) *n.* bully, gang leader.
matríkula: (Sp. *matrícula*) *n.* tuition fee.
matrimonyo: (Sp. *matrimonio*) *n.* matrimony.
matrís: (Sp. *matriz*) *n.* womb; matrix.
matrona: (Sp.) *n.* matron, middle aged socialite.
matsete: (Sp.) *n.* machete.
matsíng: *n.* small monkey; (*slang*) *adj.* ugly; **parang matsíng** *id.* imitator.
matso: (Sp. *macho*, *slang*) *n.* sexy man.
matsora: (Sp. *machorra*) *adj.* infertile, barren.
maturan: (*rt. tuód*) *v.* to be able to mention; say, guess the answer.
matwíd: (rt. *tuwíd*) *n.* reason; common sense. **matwiranan** *v.* to explain, give the reason. **matwíranan** *n.* exchange of opinions.
matyág: *n.* surveillance; **matyagán** *v.* to observe.
mawalán: (rt. *walâ*) *v.* to lose.
mawaláng-: *pref.* to lose → **mawaláng-bisà** *v.* to lose potency; **mawaláng-halagá** *v.* to lose value.
mawò: *n.* pollen.
may: *exist.* there is, there are; has, have.
may- *pref.* used to express possession → **may-sakit** *adj.* having an illness, sick; **may-bantáy** *adj.* guarded, with a guard.
maya: *n.* sparrow; **mayang-bató** *n.* tree sparrow; **mayang-kosta**: *n.* Malayan gray sparrow; **mayang-dampól** *n.* Philippine weaver sparrow; **mayang-pakíng**: *n.* Luzon brown weaver sparrow.
mayabang: *adj.* boastful, proud.
mayahin: *n.* red feathered rooster.
mayamaya: *n.* red snapper.
mayana: *n.* kind of ornamental herb.
mayáng: *n.* speckled drepane fish.
mayaw: *n.* harmony; **di-magkamayaw** *adj.* disorderly.
maykapál: (*rt. kapál*) *n.* the Creator.
Mayo: (Sp.) *n.* May.
mayonesa: (Sp.) *n.* mayonnaise.
mayor: (Sp.) *n.* mayor; major.
mayordomo: (Sp.) *n.* majordomo, butler.
mayoría: (Sp.) *n.* majority.
mayroón: *exist.* There is, there are; see *may*; **mga mayroón** *n.* the wealthy.
mayukmók: *n.* fresh green rice mixed with sugar and grated coconut.
mekániko: (Sp. *mecánico*) *n.* mechanic.
medalya: (Sp. *medalla*) *n.* medal.
medikilyo: (Sp. *mediquillo*) *n.* herbalist.
médiko: (Sp. *médico*) *n.* medic, physician.
medida: (Sp.) *n.* tape measure.
medisina: (Sp. *medicina*) *n.* medicine.
medyanotse: (Sp. *media noche*) *n.* midnight.
medyas: (Sp.) *n.* stockings, hosiery.
medyo: (Sp. *medio*) *adj.* half, semi-, somewhat; rather; **medyo pangit** somewhat ugly.
meê: *n.* bleat of a sheep or goat.
mehora: (Sp. *mejora*) *n.* improvements (made on property).
melokotón: (Sp. *melocotón*) *n.* peach.
melón: (Sp.) *n.* melon.
membrete: (Sp.) *n.* letterhead.
memeng: (*baby talk*) go to sleep.
menór: (Sp.) *adj.* minor; younger; junior; ~ **de edád** *n.* minor (in age).
menos: (Sp.) *adj.* less; **menosin** *v.* to underestimate.
mensahe: (Sp. *mensaje*) *n.* message.
menta: (Sp.) *n.* mint.
mentól: (Sp.) *n.* menthol.
mentsi: (*slang*) *n.* female servant.
menú: (Sp.) *n.* menu.
menudensya: (Sp. *menudencia*) *n.* entrails (cooked in a dish).
menudo: (Sp.) *n.* tripe, dish with entrails, liver, pork, potatoes, tomatoes, and garbanzo beans.
merkadér: (Sp. *mercader*) *n.* merchant, trader; cloth dealer.
merkádo: (Sp. *mercado*) *n.* market.
merkansia: (Sp. *mercansia*) *n.* merchandise;

freight.
merkuryo: *n*. mercury.
merengge: (Sp. *merengue*) *n*. meringue.
meryenda: (Sp. *merienda*) *n*. snack between lunch and dinner.
mesa: (Sp.) *n*. table; plateau; **mesita** *n*. small table; **mesang-kainan** *n*. dining table; **mesang-sulatan** *n*. desk.
mestiso: (Sp. *mestizo*) *n*. mestizo, half-breed.
metál: (Sp.) *n*. metal; **metáliko** *adj*. metallic.
metápora: (Sp. *metáfora*) *n*. metaphor.
método: (Sp.) *n*. method.
metro: (Sp.) *n*. meter.
mga: *contr*. of **mangá**: 1. plural marker → **mga aso** dogs, **mga bahay** houses; 2. *adv*. about, approximately → **mga sampû** about ten, **mga alas tres** around three o'clock.
miki: (Ch.) *n*. kind of noodle.
mikmík: *adj*. tiny; finely pulverized.
mikrobyo: (Sp. *microbio*) *n*. microbe; germ.
mikrópono: (Sp. *micrófono*) *n*. microphone.
miga: (Sp.) *n*. crumb of bread.
mil: (Sp.) *n*. one thousand. (*libo*)
milagro: (Sp.) *n*. miracle; **milagroso** *adj*. miraculous.
milisya: (Sp. *milicia*) *n*. militia.
militár: (Sp.) *n*. military man; *adj*. military.
milya: (Sp. *milla*) *n*. mile; **milyahe** *n*. mileage.
milyón: (Sp. *millón*) *n*. million; **milyonaryo** *n*. millionaire.
mimbrete: (Sp. *membrete*) *n*. letterhead.
mímika: (Sp. *mímica*) *n*. sign language; pantomime.
mina: (Sp.) *n*. mine; **minero** *n*. miner.
minámahál: (*rt. mahál*) *adj*. dear; beloved.
minindál: *var. of* **meryenda**: afternoon snack.
ministeryo: (Sp. *ministerio*) *n*. ministry.
ministro: (Sp.) *n*. minister.
minoría: (Sp.) *n*. minority.
minsan: *adv*. once; **míminsán** *adv*. just once; **minsan pa** once more; **paminsan-minsan** *adv*. occasionally; now and then, sometimes.
minta: (Sp. *menta*) *n*. mint.
mintís: (Sp. *mentis*) *adj*. dud; failed to explode; hitting the target; inaccurate.
minudensiya: (Sp. *menudencia*) *n*. dish of entrails.
minúskula: (Sp. *menuscula*) *n*. small (lower case) letter.
minús-minós: (Sp. *menos*) *adj*. silly; foolish; mentally retarded to a slight degree.
minuta: (Sp.) *n*. minutes of a meeting.
minutero: (Sp.) *n*. minute hand.
minuto: (Sp.) *n*. minute.
minyatura: (Sp. *miniatura*) *n*. miniature.
mingkál: *adj*. full of milk.
mira: (Sp. *mirra*) *n*. myrrh.
miralya: *n*. slipmouth fish.
mirasól: (Sp.) *n*. sunflower.
mirindál: (Sp. *merienda*) *n*. light afternoon snack.
mirón: (Sp.) *n*. bystander, spectator.
misa: (Sp.) *n*. mass.
misál: (Sp.) *n*. prayer book (for mass).
misáy: *n*. moustache, beard.
mismís: *n*. remnants of food after a meal.
mismo: (Sp.) *n*. self, oneself; *adj*. very, actual.
misó: (Ch.) *n*. mashed beans for soup.
mistulà: *adj*. real, true; identical, same.
miswá: (Ch.) *n*. kind of very fine noodle similar to vermicelli.
misyón: (Sp. *misión*) *n*. mission; **misyonero** *n*. missionary.
mitád: (Sp.) *n*. half-and-half; half each.
mithî: *n*. ideal; ambition; **magmithî** *v*. to crave for; desire strongly.
mitig: **pamimitig** *n*. numbness.
miting: (Eng.) *n*. meeting; conference.
mito: (Sp.) *n*. myth.
mitolohía: (Sp. *mitología*) *n*. mythology
mitra: (Sp.) *n*. bishop's miter.
mitsá: (Sp. *mecha*) *n*. wick; (*carp*) tenon; spark; (*fig*.) immediate cause (of war); **mitsá ng buhay** *id*. cause of death.
mitsado: (Sp. *mechado*) *n*. dish of stuffed, rolled meat.
mitsero: (Sp. *mechero*) *n*. burner of a stove.
miyembro: (Sp. *miembro*) *n*. member. (*kasapì*)
miyentras: (Sp. *mientras*) *adv*. while. (*habang*)
miyerkules: (Sp. *miércoles*) *n*. Wednesday.
mo: *genitive pron*. your (singular, familiar); you (agent of transitive action). **Kunin mo na.** Take it. **Nasaán ang kapatíd mo?** Where is your sibling? [Polite form = *ninyó*]

moklô: (*slang*, Vis.) *n*. Muslim.
mokong: (*slang*) *n*. lousy dresser.
moda: (Sp.) *n*. fashion, style; **de-~** in style.
modelo: (Sp.) *n*. model.
moderno: (Sp.) *adj*. modern.
modista: (Sp.) *n*. dressmaker.
modo: (Sp.) *n*. manners, conduct.
mogadón: (*slang*) *n*. dope.
mohón: (Sp. *mojón*) *n*. landmark, cornerstone for marking property.
molà: (*slang*) *n*. big woman.
Molbog: *n*. ethnic group and language from Southern Palawan and Banggi Island.
molde: (Sp.) *n*. mold.
moldura: (Sp.) *n*. molding.
molestya: (Sp. *molestia*) *n*. bother, disturbance.
momya: (Sp. *momio*) *n*. mummy.
monarka: (Sp. *monarca*) *n*. monarch; **monarkía** *n*. monarchy.
monasilyo: (Sp. *monacillo*) *n*. acolyte.
monáy: *n*. bread roll; (*slang*) vagina.
monsateryo: (Sp. *monasterio*) *n*. monastery.
monopolyo: (Sp. *monopolio*) *n*. monopoly.
montadura: (Sp.) *n*. setting of jewels.
monte: (Sp.) *n*. card game.
monumento: (Sp.) *n*. monument.
mongha: (Sp. *monja*) *n*. nun; (*slang*) female that stays at home, stick in the mud.
monghe: (Sp. *monje*) *n*. monk.
morado: (Sp.) *n*. species of red-skinned banana; *adj*. purple.
morál: (Sp.) *n*. moral; **moralidád** *n*. morality.
moras: (Sp. *mora*) *n*. mulberry.
morkón: (Sp. *morcón*) *n*. large homemade sausage.
moreno: (Sp.) *n*. brunet. *adj*. brown, brunet.
morisketa-tostada: (Sp. *morisqueta tostada*) *n*. fried, toasted rice.
Moro: (Sp.) *n*. Moor; Muslim; (term applied to the Muslim inhabitants of Mindanao). **moro-moro** *n*. stage play depicting the war between the Christians and Muslims.
moralidád: (Sp.) *n*. morality.
morong: *n*. Caesio fish.
moroso: (Sp.) *adj*. delinquent in paying.
morpina: (Sp. *morfina*) *n*. morphine.
mortál: (Sp.) *adj*. fatal; mortal.
mortero: (Sp.) *n*. mortar.
mortwaryo: (Sp. *mortuario*) *n*. mortuary, funeral parlor.
moskada: *var. of muskada*: nutmeg.
moskatél: (Sp. *moscatel*) *n*. muscatel.
mosketero: (Sp. *mosquetero*) *n*. musketeer.
moskitero: (Sp. *mosquitero*) *n*. mosquito net.
mosyón: (Sp. *moción*) *n*. motion; proposal.
motibasyón: (Sp. *motivación*) *n*. motivation.
motibo: (Sp. *motivo*) *n*. motive.
motò: *var*. of *mutò*: stupid; dull.
motón: (Sp.) *n*. pulley.
motór: (Sp.) *n*. motor.
motorsiklo: (Eng.) *n*. motorcycle.
muál: *adj*. full (mouth when eating).
muáng: *n*. intelligence.
mukhâ: *n*. face; front; façade; **kamukhâ** *n*. someone with a similar face, look-alike; **magkamukhâ** *v*. to look identical; **dalawáng-mukhâ** *adj*. two-faced; **muhkaán** *v*. to recognize by the face; **múkhaan** *adj*. face to face; in one's presence. **Namumukhaan kitá** You look familiar; **pamukhaan** *adv*. face to face; **masamâ ang mukhâ** *id*. frowning (face is bad); **mukháng-Biyernes Santo** *adj*. gloomy faced; **mukháng-kuwalta/ salapî** *id*. materialistic; **mukháng-Paskó** *id*. happy.
mukháng-: (rt. *mukhâ*) *pref*. like, similar, resembling: **mukháng-anghel** like an angel; **mukháng-baboy** like a pig.
mukmók: *n*. sulkiness; **magmukmók** *v*. to sulk.
muktâ: *n*. knowledge.
muktô: *n*. swelling of eyes due to crying.
mudmód: *n*. distribution to all.
mugmóg: *adj*. softened by being beaten.
muhì: *n*. intense feeling of annoyance; **mamuhî** *adj*. to be annoyed; despise, scorn; **pagkamuhî** *n*. annoyance; detestation; dislike; **kamuhián** *v*. to detest, hate.
muhón: (Sp.) *n*. landmark, boundary stone.
mula: (Sp.) *n*. mule.
mulâ: **magmulâ** *v*. to originate, start from; stem from; **magsimulâ** *v*. to start, begin; **pinagmulán** *n*. source; origin; **magmulâ ngayón** from now on; **panimulâ, pan-**

simulâ *adj.* elementary; *n.* introduction. **mulá't-mulâ** from the very beginning; **mulâ rito** hence; from here; **mulâ roón** thence, from that place.

mulagà: **nakamulagà** *adj.* staring vacantly.

mulagat: *n.* gaze. **mamulagat** *v.* to have a blank stare; have one's eyes wide open.

mulalà: *n.* stupidity; ignorance. **mulalâ** *adj.* silly, foolish; ignorant; innocent.

mulambuhay: *n.* biogenesis.

mulán: (rt. *mulâ*) *v.* to begin; to originate from.

mulapì: *n.* prefix. (*unlapì*)

mulat: *n.* opening the eyes. **mulát** *adj.* with opened eyes; educated; trained; **imulat** *v.* to open; **mulatan** *v.* to train (while young). **kinamulatan** *n.* knowledge, skill.

mulawin: *n.* molave tree.

muláy: *n.* loose change. **mulayín** *v.* to break money into smaller denominations.

muleta: (Sp.) *n.* crutches.

mulí: (Sp. *moler*) *adj.* ground fine; **mulihan** *n.* grinder.

mulî: *adv.* again.

mulinero: (Sp. *molinero*) *n.* miller.

mulinilyo: (Sp. *molinillo*) *n.* coffee grinder.

mulino: (Sp. *molino*) *n.* windmill.

mulí't-mulî: (rt. *mulî*) *adv.* again and again.

mulmól: *n.* parrot fish; fluff, soft particles; unraveled, loose threads; **mamulmól** *v.* to fray.

mulós: **mamulós** *v.* to be spilled out of a sack.

multa: (Sp.) *n.* fine, penalty; **magmultá** *v.* to pay a fine; **multado** *adj.* fined; **pangmultá** *n.* money for the payment of a fine.

multiplisidád: (Sp. *multiplicidad*) *n.* multiplicity.

multó: (Sp. *muerto*: dead) *n.* ghost; **pinagmumultuhán** *adj.* haunted.

mumo: *n.* particles of cooked rice that fall off a plate.

mumò: (*baby talk*) *n.* ghost. (*multo*)

mumog: *n.* gargle; **magmumog** *v.* to gargle.

muna: *adv.* first; ahead of time; beforehand.

munakalà: [*muna* + *akalà*] *n.* plan, project; **magmunakalà** *v.* to speculate; consider.

munasilyo: (Sp. *monacillo*) *n.* acolyte.

munay: *n.* milk bread.

mundiyál: (Sp. *mundial*) *adj.* worldwide.

mundó: (Sp.) *n.* world, earth; **kamunduhán** *n.* worldliness; **makamundó** *adj.* mundane; **sanáy sa kamunduhán** *adj.* sophisticated.

muni: *n.* thought; idea; reflection. **magmunimuni** *v.* to speculate, reason; meditate, reflect; **pagmumuni** *n.* reasoning.

muninì: *n.* swarming; prevalence. (*mutiktík*) **namumuninì** *adj.* teeming with, abounding, swarming.

muníng: *n.* pussycat.

munisilyo: (Sp. *monacillo*) *n.* acolyte, assistant to a priest.

munisipyo: (Sp. *municipio*) *n.* municipality.

munisiyón: (Sp. *munición*) *n.* ammunition. (*bala*)

munsik: *adj.* tiny, very small.

muntî: *adj.* small; **kauntî** *n.* a little bit; small degree.

muntík: **muntík na** *adv.* almost, nearly.

munukalà: *n.* plan, project.

mungkahì: *n.* suggestion; offer; **imungkahì** *v.* to suggest; move, propose; **pagmumungkahì** *n.* proposal, suggestion.

munggó: *n.* mung bean.

mungláy: *adj.* smashed to pieces, shredded.

mungot: *n.* frown, sour face.

muók: *n.* hand-to-hand fight; **magmuók** *v.* to fight.

muóg: *n.* fort, fortification; den, hideout; bandfish; ~ **sa buról** *n.* rampart.

mura: *adj.* cheap, inexpensive; **ipagmura** *v.* to sell at a bargain; **mámurá** *v.* to become cheap; **nagmúmurang-kamatis** *id.* trying to look young (being an immature tomato); **mumurahin** *adj.* cheap, of little value. **murang isip** *id.* still young (immature mind).

mura: *n.* act of scolding; **murahin** *v.* to scold someone; **magmurahán** *v.* to quarrel, brawl; **murahán** *n.* noisy quarrel; **pakámurámuráhin** *v.* to scold; flay.

murà: *n.* young coconut; *adj.* unripe, immature; **kamuraan** *n.* immaturity; **murangilóng** *n.* threadfin fish; **nagmúmurang kamatis/kamiyás** *id.* elegant widow or spinster, trying to look young.

murado: (Sp. *morado*) *adj*. purple.
muralya: (Sp. *muralla*) *n*. rampart, wall of a fort.
musa: (Sp.) *n*. muse.
musang: *n*. wild cat.
musangsáng: *adj*. fully open (flowers); **mamusangsáng** *v*. to open (flowers), bloom.
museta: (Sp. *muceta*) *n*. short cape worn by doctoral candidates at graduation.
muskada: (Sp. *moscada*) *n*. nutmeg.
muskatél: (Sp. *moscatel*) *n*. muscatel wine.
muskulado: (*f. múskulo*) *adj*. muscular.
múskulo: (Sp. *músculo*) *n*. muscle.
muselina: (Sp.) *n*. muslin cloth.
museo: (Sp.) *n*. museum.
músika: (Sp. *música*) *n*. music; **músiko** *n*. musician.
muslák: *n*. sense; understanding.
musló: *n*. cavalla fish.
musmós: *adj*. immature; innocent; simple.
musón: *var. of* **muhón**: landmark.
mustasa: (Sp. *mostaza*) *n*. mustard.
mustra: *var. of* **muwestra**.
mutà: *n*. gummy secretion of the eyes.
mutawì: **mamutawì** *v*. to utter, pronounce.
mutiktík: **namumutiktík** *adj*. full, complete, laden with.
mutón: (Sp.) *n*. pulley.
mutsatsa: (Sp. *muchacha*: girl) *n*. housemaid.
mutsatso: (Sp. *muchacho*: boy) *n*. houseboy.
mutso: (Sp. *mucho*: much) *adj*. having plenty.
mutyâ: *n*. amulet; charm; pearl, jewel; **minumutyâ** *adj*. beloved.
muwál: *adj*. full of food (mouth).
muwáng: *n*. sense, grasp, understanding; big-eyed herring.
muwebles: (Sp. *muebles*) *n*. furniture; **inmuwebles** *n*. immovable property, fixtures.
muwelye: (Sp. *muelle*) *n*. wharf, pier; mechanical spring.
muwestra: (Sp. *muestra*) *n*. sample; pattern, model; sign, signal.
muyág: *adj*. spongy; loose (grains or soil); *n*. loose change.
muyangit: *n*. sticky liquid that sticks to the sides of a container, honey, molasses, etc.

N

na: *adv*. now, already → **Kumain na akó** I already ate; soon; marks perfective; variant of ligature *-ng* after consonants → **mahál na bahay** expensive house.
na- *pref*. realis form of *ma-*; forms verbal adverbs expressing existence → *naritó, nariritó, nariyán, naririyán, naroón, naróroón*.
nabe: (Sp. *nave*) *n*. ship.
nabigadór: (Sp. *navegador*) *n*. navigator.
naka- *pref*. 1. forms adjectives denoting possession → **nakabalabal** *adj*. wearing a shawl, **nakahikaw** *adj*. wearing earrings; 2. may indicate temporary states → **nakabukás** *adj*. open, **nakaluylóy** *adj*. hanging; 3. may indicate perfective possibility → **nakarubò** *adj*. was able to profit; 4. may form causative adjectives (involuntary) → **nakamamatáy** *adj*. fatal, **nakauuhaw** *adj*. causing thirst.
nakaka-: *pref*. forms causative statives and abilitatives → **nakákabasa** able to read; **nakákamatay** fatal, causing death; **nakákaawà** pitiful, causing pity.
nakapa-: *pref*. forms causative adjectives → **nakapapagod** *adj*. tiring (making one tired), **nakapagandá** *adj*. beautifying (making something beautiful).
nakapag-: *pref*. realis form of *makapag-*, forms causative adjectives from *mag-* verbs → **nakapagtataká** *adj*. surprising, causing surprise, **nakapagtuturò** *adj*. instructive.
nakapagpa-: *pref*. realis form of *makapagpa-*, forms causative adjectives from *magpa-* verbs → **nakapagpatulog** *adj*. causing sleep; **nakapagpapawis** *adj*. inducing sweat.
nakapaN-: *pref*. realis form of *makapaN-*, forms causative adjectives from *maN-* verbs → **nakapangíngilabot** *adj*. horrifying, causing horror.
nakar: (Sp. *nacar*) *n*. mother of pearl.
nakaraán: (*rt. daán*) *n*., *adj*. past.
nakaw: *n*. stolen item; **magnakaw** *v*. to steal;

magnanakaw *n*. thief; **panakáw** *adj*. surreptitious, stealthy; **pagnanakaw** *n*. burglary, larceny; stealing.
naki-: *pref*. realis form of *maki-*.
nakin: *part*. it seems to me.
nakipag-: *pref*. realis form of *makipag-*.
naknák: *n*. abscess; **magnaknák** *v*. to form an abscess.
Nakú!: *interj*. Oh my!
nag-: *pref*. realis form of *mag-*.
naga: *n*. dragon, species of narra tree; figurehead on ships.
nagka-: *pref*. realis form of *magka-*.
nagíng: [past of *maging*] *v*. became.
nagpa-: *pref*. realis form of *magpa-*.
nagpaka-: *pref*. realis form of *magpaka-*.
nagwas: (Sp. *enaguas*) *n*. half-slip, underskirt.
naik: *n*. surrounding countryside; suburb.
nais: *n*. desire, wish; **naisin** *v*. to wish for, desire; **pagnanais** *n*. desiring; preference; **kanais-nais** *adj*. desirable.
namán: *adv*. also, too; really.
namayabas: (*rt. bayabas, slang*) *v*. frustrated.
namî: *n*. species of plant with rootstocks that can be poisonous if not properly cooked, *Disocorea hispida Dennst*.
namin: *genitive pron*. our (exclusive); we (agent of transitive).
namnám: *n*. savor, taste; **malinamnám** *adj*. delicious.
namputsa: (*slang*) *interj*. damn!
nana: *n*. appellation for an aunt, or woman one generation older than the speaker.
nanà: *n*. pus; **magnanà** *v*. to discharge pus, form pus; **parang nanà** *id*. slow motion.
nanang: *n*. term of address for one's mother.
nanay: *n*. term of address for one's mother.
nang-: *pref*. realis form of *mang-*.
nang: *conj*. when; so that; denotes an adverb. [See also *na*]
nanga-: *pref*. realis form of *manga-*.
nangág-: *prep*. realis form of *mangag-*.
nangagín-: *pref*. realis form of *mangagín*.
nangálabasa: (*rt. kalabasa, slang*) *v*. failed in an exam.
nangkâ: *var. of* **langkâ**: jackfruit.
nangot: (*slang*) *n*. booger. (*kulangot*)
nápaka-: *pref*. forms superlative adjectives- **nápakagandá** very beautiful, **nápakabatà** very young. **nápakamahal** very dear, costly.
naptalina: (Sp.) *n*. naphthalene.
nara: *n*. narra tree.
narangha: (Sp. *naranja*) *n*. orange; **naranghado** *adj*. orange-colored, tangerine; **naranghita** *n*. species of orange tree.
naritó: (*rt. dito*) it is/was here.
naririyán: (*rt. diyan*) it is/was there.
naroroón: (*rt. doón*) it is/was there.
nars: (Eng.) *n*. nurse.
nasa: *prep*. in, at (expresses location as opposed to movement or direction.
nasà: *n*. wish, desire; **nasain** *v*. to wish.
nasaán: *interrog*. Where is (located)?
nasnás: *adj*. frayed.
nata₁: *pron*. postpositive of *ata* our, ours (dual).
nata₂: (Sp.) *n*. cream.
natin: *genitive pron*. genitive postpositive of *atin*, our (inclusive); we (agent of transitive).
naturalesa: (Sp. *naturaleza*) *n*. nature.
nawà: **kanawa-nawà** *adv*. naturally; as a matter of fact
nawâ: *interj*. expresses the optative. I wish. May it be so.
nawnáw: *n*. germination, taking root.
nayon: *n*. village, barrio; **kanayunan** *n*. center of a village.
nebera: (Sp. *nevera*) *n*. refrigerator.
neblina: (Sp.) *n*. fog, mist.
neknek: (*slang*) **neknek mo** *interj*. go to hell.
negosyante: (Sp. *negociante*) *n*. businessman; merchant.
negosyo: (Sp. *negocio*) *n*. trade, commerce; business.
Negrito: *n*. member of the indigenous race of people in the Philippines, named for their dark skin.
negro: (Sp.) *n*. black.
nenè: *n*. term of address for young girls.
nenok: (*slang*) **nenokin** *v*. to steal.
nepotismo: (Sp.) *n*. nepotism.
nerbiyo(s): (Sp. *nervio*) *n*. nerve; **nerbiyoso** *adj*. nervous; **makanerbiyos** *v*. to make someone nervous, be nerve wracking.

nesi: (*slang*) *adj*. annoyed.
neto: (Eng.) *n*. net income.
ni- *pref. var. of in-* before *l* or *w* → **nilagà** boiled, **nilason** poisoned, **niwaldás** destroyed, embezzled.
ni: *art*. singular actor/possessive personal article, plural is *niná*; **ni..ni..** *prep*. neither, nor.
nibél: (Sp. *nivel*) *n*. level; **nibelado** *adj*. leveled.
niki: (*slang*) *n*. cigarette lighter.
nikník: *n*. gnat; horsefly.
nido: (Sp.) *n*. edible bird's nest.
nigò: **manigò** *adj*. lucky, favorable; **kaniguan** *n*. fortune, good luck.
niíg: **pagniniíg** *n*. private conversation between two people.
nilá: *genitive pron*. postpositive of **kanilá**- their, theirs; they (agent of transitive).
nilà: *n*. indigo plant.
nilagà: (*rt. lagà*) *adj*. boiled.
nilay: **magnilay-nilay** *v*. to meditate; **mapagnilay-nilay** *adj*. meditative, contemplative.
nimbo: (Sp.) *n*. nimbus; halo.
nimpa: (Sp. *ninfa*) *n*. nymph.
nimpuhô: *adj*. seated flat on the haunches.
niná: *art*. plural of the personal article *ni*.
ninag: *n*. radiation.
ninang: *n*. godmother.
nino: *pron*. postpositive form of *kanino*- whose.
ninong: *n*. godfather; (*slang*) backer, promoter.
ninyo: (Sp. *niño*) *n*. child; **Santo** ~ *n*. Holy Child.
ninyó: *genitive pron*. your (plural/polite); you (plural/polite agent of transitive).
ningas: *n*. flame; **magniningas** *adj*. flaming; **ningas-bao, ningas-kugon** *adj*. quickly passing.
ningníng: *n*. shine, brilliance; **magningníng** *v*. to shine, radiate; **maningníng** *adj*. shiny, glittery; flamboyant; splendid; radiant.
nipa: *n*. East Indian palm.
nipís: *n*. thinness; **numipís** *v*. to become thin; **manipís** *adj*. thin; flimsy.
nirí: [*ng* + *irí*] *adj*. of this.
nisnís: *adj*. threadbare; **manisnís** *adj*. frayed, raveled.
niting: (Eng.) *n*. knitting.
nitó: [*ng* + *ito*] *adj*. of this.
nitò: *n*. species of fern.
nitso: (Sp. *nicho*) *n*. niche; tomb.
niyá: *genitive pron*. his, her, its (possessive); he, she it (agent of transitive).
niyán: [*ng* + *iyán*] *adj*. of that.
niyebe: (Sp. *nieve*) *n*. snow; **maniyebe** *adj*. snowy.
niyóg: *n*. coconut; **bao ng** ~ *n*. coconut shell; **bunót ng** ~ *n*. coconut husk; **gatâ ng** ~ *n*. coconut milk; **langís ng** ~ *n*. coconut oil.
niyón: [*ng* + *iyón*] *adj*. of that.
nobato: (Sp. *novato*) *n*. novice.
nobedád: (Sp. *novedad*) *n*. novelty.
nobela: (Sp. *novela*) *n*. novel.
nobena: (Sp. *novena*) *n*. nine day prayer, novena.
nobisyo: (Sp. *novicio*) *n*. novice in a religious congregation.
nobya: (Sp. *novia*) *n*. fiancée, sweetheart; bride.
Nobyembre: (Sp. *noviembre*) *n*. November.
nobyo: (Sp. *novio*) *n*. fiancé. sweetheart; bridegroom.
nognóg: (*slang*, from comic strip character) *n*. black person; person with a dark complexion.
nombrá: (Sp. *nombrar*) **nombrahán** *v*. to appoint, nominate; **nombrado** *adj*. nomination, appointment.
nómina: (Sp.) *n*. payroll.
nominado: (Sp.) *adj*. nominated.
nones: (Sp.) *adj*. odd (not even).
noó: *n*. forehead; **noóng-uróng** *n*. receding forehead.
noód: **manoód** *v*. to watch; **panoorín** *n*. show, sight; **manonoód** *n*. spectator, bystander, onlooker. [The root *noód* is not used alone].
noón: *adv*. then, at that time; formerly; ~ **din** immediately after that; ~ **pa** to date; ~ **pa man** even, even when; **noó'y** *adv*. at that time.
norte: (Sp.) *n*. north; **karne norte** *n*. corned beef.
nota: (Sp.) *n*. note; grade (in school).

notaryo: (Sp. *notario*) *n*. notary.
notas: (Sp.) *n*. annotations, records.
notisya: (Sp. *noticia*) *n*. notice.
Notsebuwena: (Sp. *nochebuena*) *n*. Christmas eve.
nugnóg$_1$: **kanugnóg** *adj*. adjoining, suburban.
nugnóg$_2$: (*coll.*) *adj*. dark skinned.
nulipiká: (Sp. *nulificar*) **nulipikahín** *v*. to nullify.
nulo: (Sp.) *adj*. null; annulled; **nuluhin** *v*. to annul.
numeradór: (Sp.) *n*. numerator.
númeró: (Sp.) *n*. number; symbol; figure; **pambuóng-~** *n*. integer.
nunál: *var. of lunár*: mole on the skin.
nunò$_1$: *n*. ancestor; grandparent; **~ sa tuhod** *n*. great grandparent; **~ sa talampakan** *n*. great, great grandparent; **kanunu-nunuan** *n*. ancestry; descent.
nunò$_2$: *n*. hobgoblin.
nunót: *adj*. softened; weakened.
nunsyó: (Sp.) *n*. nuncio, ecclesiastical representative.
nungka: (Sp. *nunca*) *adv*. never.
nutnót: *adj*. unraveled, frayed.
nuwáng: (Ilocano *nuang*) *n*. water buffalo.
nuwáy: (Sp. *no hay*: there is no..) **nuwáy na nuwáy** *id*. penniless.
nuwebe: (Sp. *nueve*) *n*. nine.
nuwés: (Sp. *nuez*) *n*. nut; **~ de nogal** *n*. walnut; **~ muskada** *n*. nutmeg.
nuynóy: **magnuynóy** *v*. to think seriously; **pagnuynóy** *n*. serious thought.

NG

-ng: (*lig.*) variant of enclitic ligature *-ng* after vowels or *n*. **ang bahay na bago** → **ang bago*ng* bahay** *n*. the new house.
ng: [*pron. nang*] 1. *art*. for impersonal (common) nouns, agentive marker of goal focus verbs, or patient marker of actor focus verbs; possessive marker → **Kumain akó *ng* saging** I ate a banana, **Kinain *ng* batà ang saging** The child ate the banana. 2. Genitive marker for common nouns: **ang hipag ng kaibigan ko** my friend's sister-in-law. [Plural: *ng mga*]
ngâ: *adv*. really, indeed; please.
ngabngáb: **ngabngabín** *v*. to bite off meat; gnaw.
ngadngád: *n*. falling on one's nose.
ngadyî: *n*. prayer.
ngakngák: *n*. loud crying.
ngalan: *n*. name; reputation; **pangalan** *n*. name; noun; **ka(pa)ngalan** *n*. namesake; **ipangalan** *v*. to name, call; **sa ~ ni** on behalf of, in the name of.
ngalandakan: **mangalandakan** *v*. to boast, brag, speak of with pride.
ngalangalá: *n*. palate, roof of the mouth.
ngalay: *n*. numbness; fatigue.
ngaligkíg: **mangaligkíg** *v*. to shiver from the cold.
ngalíngali: *adv*. almost, on the verge of.
ngalirang: **nangángalirang** *adj*. overdried, dried up; very thin.
ngalisag: **mangalisag** *v*. to bristle (hair).
ngalit: **mangalit** *v*. to grind the teeth.
ngalitngít: *n*. sound of gnashing, crunching.
ngalngál: *adj*. wailing; grumbling.
ngalò: *n*. numbness; fatigue.
ngalóg: **mangalóg** *v*. to tremble, quiver, shake.
ngalóg: *n*. extreme weakness; fatigue.
ngalót: *adj*. crunched; **magngalót** *v*. to crunch noisily.
ngalubakbák: **mangalubakbák** *v*. to become detached (skin, bark).
ngalukabkáb: *n*. peeling off (bark, plaster, etc.).
ngalubngób: *n*. noise of crunching brittle food.
ngaluktíng: **pangangaluktíng** *n*. clattering of teeth due to cold.
ngalumatá: *adj*. with dark rings under the eyes due to lack of sleep; with haggard looking eyes; gaunt.
ngalumbabà: **pangangalumbabà** *n*. pensive look (with the head supported by the palm).
ngalungkóng: *n*. depression.
ngalutngót: *n*. crunching sound.

ngamay: *n*. numbness (of the hands).
ngambá: **pangambá** *n*. doubt; apprehension; **mangambá** *v*. to be apprehensive about, to fear; to be alarmed.
nganay: **panganay** *n*. first born child.
ngandí: **mangandí** *v*. to be in sexual heat (animals).
nganì: var. of *ngâ*: indeed; please.
nganib: **panganib** *n*. danger; crisis; risk; **manganib** *v*. to be n danger; **mapanganib** *adj*. dangerous; critical; **panganganib** *n*. liability; **panganiban** *v*. to consider something dangerous; to be careful about something; **isapanganib** *v*. to threaten, endanger, jeopardize.
nganíngangí: *n*. apprehension.
ngangá: *adj*. with opened mouth, agape; **ngumangá sa hangin** *id*. hopeless.
ngangà: *n*. prepared betel nut for chewing.
ngángayón: (*rt. ngayón*) *adv*. just now.
ngapâ: **ngumapá-ngapâ** *v*. to grope in the dark; act clumsily; to be without help.
ngapós: *adj*. lacking; **mangapós** *v*. to lack; **mangapós ang hiningá** *v*. to be short of breath.
ngasáb: *n*. noise made of animals eating.
ngasiwà: **mangasiwà** *v*. to manage, direct; administer; **pangangasiwà** *n*. administration, management; control; reign; **pangasiwáan** *v*. to handle, manage, administer; transact; **tagapangasiwà** *n*. administrator, manager, boss.
ngasngás: *n*. scandal caused by gossip.
ngatâ: *n*. chewing the cud; **ngumatâ** *v*. to chew the cud, ruminate.
ngatál: **mangatál** *v*. to tremble, quiver, shake.
ngatngát: **ngatngatín** *v*. to gnaw, bite away bit by bit; (*slang*) finger sex.
ngawâ: **magngangawâ** *v*. to babble; **pagngawâ** *n*. babbling.
ngawil: *n*. twisting of lips while speaking.
ngawit: **mangawit** *adj*. tired or numb (from fatigue).
ngawngáw: *n*. empty talk.
ngayáw: *n*. act of refusing.
ngayngáy: *n*. continuous talk in monotone; (*reg*.) gnawing.
ngayón: *adv*. now; today; *adj*. present; **mulâ ~** from now on; **hanggáng ~** until now; still; **ngángayón** *adv*. just now, only now; **~ din** at once, right away.
ngayupapâ: *n*. humble submission. **mangayupapà** *v*. to humble oneself.
ngekngék: (*slang*) *adj*. high on drugs.
ngibá: *n*. tendency to cry when held by stranger (babies).
ngibì: *n*. pursing of lips (before crying).
ngibit: *n*. twisting of the mouth, grimace.
ngibngíb: *n*. nibbling. **ngibngibín** *v*. to nibble.
ngiki: *n*. chill; malaria. **ngikihin** *v*. to have the chills.
ngikngík: *n*. noise made by hungry pigs; **ngikngík mo** mild curse.
ngidngíd: *n*. gum (of teeth).
ngilin: **pangilin** *n*. abstinence; holiday; **mangilin** *v*. to observe and honor; **pistáng pangilin** *n*. holy day.
ngilngíl: *n*. whinnying.
ngiló: *n*. tingling sensation in the teeth. **mangiló** *v*. to feel a tingling sensation in the teeth; to have a nerve pain in the teeth.
ngima: *n*. food stuck between the teeth.
ngimay: *n*. numbness. **ngimáy** *adj*. numb. **mangimay** *v*. to become numb.
ngimbuló: *n*. feeling of inferiority. **mangimbuló** *v*. to envy.
ngimì: **ngimî** *adj*. shy, timid; **mangimì** *v*. to feel shy.
nginíg: **manginíg** *v*. to shake, tremble (from cold).
ngipin: *n*. tooth; **bukbók ng ~** *n*. cavity, tooth decay; **mangipin** *v*. to teethe; **~ ng tenedór** *n*. prong of a fork; **ngipin sa ngipin** a tooth for a tooth (retaliation); **ngipin ng gulóng** *n*. cog tooth; **ngiping dagâ** *id*. small teeth; **ngiping palakól** *id*. big teeth; **ngiping aso** *id*. sharp teeth.
ngisi: *n*. grin; broad smile. **ngisí** *adj*. fond of smiling, grinning.
ngisngís: *n*. grinning, showing the teeth; **ngumisngís** *v*. to grin.
ngita: (*rt. kita*) **pangita** *n*. meeting face to face; **pangitaín** *n*. vision; omen.
ngitî: *n*. smile; **ngitián** *v*. to smile at someone.

ngitngít: *n*. rage, fury; intensity.
ngitpá: (*slang*, < *pangit*) *adj*. ugly.
ngiwî: *adj*. wry, crooked, twisted (face); **ngumiwî** *v*. to contort the face, pucker the lips.
ngiwíd: *adj*. distorted; awry.
ngiyáw: *n*. meow; **ngumiyáw** *v*. to meow.
ngokngók: *n*. fool, idiot.
ngongò: *adj*. speaking nasally; (*slang*) ignorant.
ngubngób: *adj*. toothless and with sunken lips.
ngudngód: *n*. pushing with the snout.
ngulag: (*rt*. *kulag*) **mangulag** *v*. to have goose bumps; to have one's hair stand on end.
ngulag: **pangungulag** *n*. molting, shedding of feathers.
ngulila: **mangulila** *v*. to feel lonely.
ngulíng: (*rt*. *kuling*) **pangunguling** *n*. retraction of something promised.
ngulo: **ngumulo** *v*. to put both hand under the head when lying.
ngulngól: **pagngulngól** *n*. sulking and grumbling; sucking.
ngulughóy: (*rt*. *kulughóy*) **pangungulughóy** *n*. curling up.
nguni('t): *conj*. but; on the other hand.
ngunót: *n*. wrinkle.
ngungò: **ngumungò** *v*. to feed with premasticated food.
ngupinyo: (*rt*. *kupinyó*) **pangungupinyo** *n*. anger, grudge.
ngusngós: *n*. snout; tip of the nose; tips of string beans.
ngusò: *n*. snout; muzzle; (*slang*) informer; **ngusong-baboy** *n*. protruding upper lip.
ngutngót: *n*. noise of gnawing; whimper.
nguyâ: **manguyâ** *v*. to chew, masticate.
nguyapit: (*rt*. *kuyapit*) **pangunguyapit** *n*. climbing a tree, swinging from branch to branch.
nguyngóy: **pagnguyngóy** *n*. prolonged crying; crying with tantrums.

O

o: *conj*. or; **o kayá'y** or, otherwise; *interj*. expresses surprise, admiration.
óbalo: (Sp. *óvalo*) *n*. oval; **obalado** *adj*. oval.
obaryo: (Sp. *ovario*) *n*. ovary.
obeha: (Sp. *oveja*) *n*. sheep.)
obartura: (Sp. *overtura*) *n*. overture.
obelisko: (Sp. *obelisco*) *n*. obelisk.
obertura: (Sp. *overtura*) *n*. overture.
obispo: (Sp.) *n*. bishop.
obitwaryo: (Sp. *obituario*) *n*. obituary.
oblasyón: (Sp. *oblación*) *n*. oblation.
obligado: (Sp.) *adj*. obliged.
obligatoryo: (Sp. *obligatorio*) *adj*. obligatory.
obra: (Sp.) *n*. work; **~ maestra** *n*. masterpiece; **~ de mano** *n*. handwork; **obras públikas** *n*. public works.
obrerismo: (Sp.) *n*. labor movement.
obrero: (Sp.) *n*. worker.
obserbá: (Sp. *observar*) **obserbahín** *v*. to observe. **obserbadór** *n*. observer.
obserbatoryo: (Sp. *observatorio*) *n*. observatory.
obsesyón: (Sp. *obsesión*) *n*. obsession.
obstákuló: (Sp. *obstáculo*) *n*. obstacle.
okasyón: (Sp. *ocación*) *n*. occasion; opportunity; special event.
okey: (Eng.) *n*. okay.
okoy: (Ch.) *n*. Chinese dish of fried shrimps and pork with bean sprouts, green papaya, and squash.
okra: (Eng.) *n*. okra.
okráy: (*slang*) *adj*. corny, out of fashion.
okre: (Sp.) *n*. ochre.
oksíheno: (Sp. *oxígeno*) *n*. oxygen.
oktabo: (Sp. *octavo*) *adj*. eighth; *n*. octave.
Oktubre: (Sp. *octubre*) *n*. October.
okulista: (Sp. *oculista*) *n*. oculist, ophthalmologist.
okupado: (Sp. *ocupado*) *adj*. occupied; busy.
okupante: (Sp. *ocupante*) *n*. occupant.
okupasyón: (Sp. *ocupasión*) *n*. occupation; ownership.
oda: (Sp.) *n*. ode.
oeste: (Sp.) *n*. west. (*kanluran*)

ohales: (Sp. *ojal*) *n*. buttonhole.
ohetes: (Sp. *ojete*) *n*. eyelet (for buttons).
ohiya: (Sp. *ojear*) *n*. evil eye; **mauhiya** *v*. to be affected by the evil eye.
oído: (Sp.) *n*. ear for music.
ola: *n*. eagerness.
Olanda: (Sp. *holanda*) *n*. Holland, Netherlands.
Olandés: (Sp. *holandés*) *n*. Dutch; **olandés** *adj*. blond.
óleo: (Sp.) *n*. holy oil.
oliba: (Sp. *oliva*) *n*. olive.
oligarkía: (Sp. *oligarquía*) *n*. oligarchy.
omad: (*slang*) *n*. marijuana.
ombrang: (*slang*, f. *ombre*) *n*. male.
ombre: (*slang*, Sp. *hombre*) *n*. male stranger.
omi: *n*. macolor fish.
onda: (Sp.) *n*. wave; **ondá-ondá** *n*. ripples, tiny waves.
onsa: (Sp. *onza*) *n*. ounce.
onse: (Sp. *once*) *n*. eleven; **naonse** *id*. cheated; fooled.
oo: *adv*. yes; **oohan** *v*. to say yes.
onggo: (Sp. *hongo*) *n*. fungus.
ópalo: (Sp.) *n*. opal.
opas: (*slang*) *n*. cunnilingus.
ópera: (Sp.) *n*. opera; **opereta** *n*. operetta.
operá: (Sp.) **pag-ooperá** *n*. operation; **operado** *adj*. operated on; **operahín** *v*. to operate on.
opinyón: (Sp. *opinión*) *n*. opinion.
opisina: (Sp. *oficina*) *n*. office. (*tanggapan*)
opisyál: (Sp. *oficial*) *n*. official, officer; *adj*. official.
opisyo: (Sp. *oficio*) *n*. work, occupation.
opò: *adv*. yes sir (respectful).
oportunidád: (Sp.) *n*. opportunity.
oposisyón: (Sp.) *n*. opposition.
opsyión: (Sp. *opción*) *n*. option, choice.
optalmólogo: (Sp.) *n*. ophthalmologist.
óptiko: (Sp.) *n*. optician.
optómetra: (Sp.) *n*. optometrist.
opyo: (Sp. *opio*) *n*. opium. (*apyan*)
orákulo: (Sp. *oráculo*) *n*. oracle.
oradór: (Sp.) *n*. orator.
oras: (Sp.) *n*. hour; time; **hustó sa ~** *adj*. punctual; **isaoras** *v*. to time; **malayang ~** *n*. leisure time; **nasa ~** on time; **oras-oras** every hour; time after time; **talaorasán** *n*. timetable, schedule; **Anóng oras na?** What time is it? **Walâ akóng oras**. I don't have time.
orasyón: (Sp. *oración*) *n*. prayer; Angelus prayer.
orkesta: (Sp. *orquesta*) *n*. orchestra.
orden: (Sp.) *n*. order; arrangement; **ordenado** *adj*. ordained; **ordenansa** *n*. ordinance; **ordenasyón** *n*. ordination.
ordinaryo: (Sp.) *adj*. ordinary.
órgano: (Sp.) *n*. organ.
organdí: (Sp.) *n*. organdy.
orgániko: (Sp. *orgánico*) *adj*. organic.
organisá: (Sp. *organizar*) **organisahín** *v*. to organize; **organisado** *adj*. organized **organisasyón** *n*. organization.
organista: (Sp.) *n*. organist.
orgulyo: (Sp. *orgullo*) *n*. pride; boastfulness.
orihen: (Sp. *origen*) *n*. origin, source.
orihinál: (Sp. *original*) *adj*. original.
oriles: *n*. hardtail fish; scad.
orinola: (Sp. *orinal*) *n*. urinal; chamber pot.
ornitólogo: (Sp.) *n*. ornithologist.
oro: (Sp.) *n*. gold. (*gintô*)
oropél: (Sp.) *n*. tinsel; foil.
ortopédiko: (Sp.) *adj*. orthopedic.
oryente: (Sp. *oriente*) *adj*. orient.
osa: (Sp.) *n*. she bear; **~ mayór** *n*. Big Dipper; **~ menór** *n*. Little Dipper.
oso: (Sp.) *n*. bear.
ospisyo: (Sp. *hospicio*) *n*. asylum; orphanage.
ospitál: (Sp. *hospital*) *n*. hospital.
óstiya: (Sp. *hostia*) *n*. host (given in mass).
osyoso: (Sp. *ocioso*) *adj*. looking on; curiousness; **osyosero** *n*. curious person.
otél: (Sp. *hotel*) *n*. hotel.
otsenta: (Sp. *ochenta*) *n*. eighty.
otso: (Sp. *ocho*) *n*. eight.
oy!: *interj*. hey!

P

pa-: *pref.* 1. directional prefix → **pa-Maynila** going to Manila, **paroón** going there, to go there; 2. causative prefix → **paduguín** to cause to bleed, bleed, **pahalalín** to make someone vote; 3. prefix of manner → **pabantâ** in a threatening manner, **pahaláw** in a superficial manner, **paakyát** upwards, upstairs, **pakrús** crosswise. **paatrás** backwards. [The *pa* prefix forms stems and often participates in reduplications in place of the actual root].

pa₁: *adv.* more; still; even; **hindî** ~ not yet.

pa₂: *n.* the letter *p*.

paa: *n.* foot; let; **paahán** *adj.* with large feet; **paanán** *n.* foot, bottom, base; **bakás ng paá** *n.* footprint; **paá't kamáy** *id.* indispensable helper (foot and hand); **paáng-baliwis** *n.* species of hairy herb with yellow flowers.

paaga: *n.* kind of quick-growing rice.

paalam: (*rt. alam*) *interj.* goodbye.

pá- -an: *affix.* Locative circumfix **páaralán** *n.* school; **pálangoyan** *n.* swimming pool.

pa- -an: *affix.* Causative/Directional verbalizer: **paaralan** *v.* to send to school; finance the studies of another, **pagasolinahan** *v.* to provide someone with gasoline.

paano: *adv.* how, in what way; **kahit** ~ somehow.

paayap: *n.* cowpea.

paayón: *adj.* parallel; in conformity to.

pabalát-sibuyas: *n.* courteous invitation (not expected to be accepted).

pabangó: (*rt. bangó*) *n.* perfume.

pabilo: (Sp.) *n.* wick.

pablíng: (*slang*, f. *Pablo*) *n.* playboy; **pumapablíng** *v.* to try to do something difficult to gain recognition.

pabo: (Sp. *pavo*) *n.* turkey; **paboreal** *n.* peacock.

pabór: (Sp. *favor*) *n.* favor; **paborán** *v.* to favor; **paborable** *adj.* favorable; **paborito** *adj.* favorite.

pábrika: (Sp. *fábrica*) *n.* factory.

pabrikante: (Sp. *fabricante*) *n.* manufacturer.

pabukang-binhî: *n.* Moorish eel.

pabukó: (*slang*) *n.* homosexual male.

pábula: (Sp. *fábula*) *n.* fable.

pabuyà: *n.* reward; tip.

pakâ: *n.* species of mollusk.

pakakak: *n.* trumpet, bugle.

pakakas: *n.* boat decorations; plan, scheme.

pakán: **kapakanán** *n.* benefit; welfare; interest, affairs; **para sa iyóng kapakanán** for your own sake.

pak-án: *n.* hardtail fish.

pakanâ: *n.* plan, project; device; maneuver; **lihim na** ~ *n.* plot.

pakanlóg: *n.* wooden rattle.

pakang: *n.* dent on tools.

pakasam: *n.* native dish made of small shrimps and rice.

pakaskás: *n.* molasses and coconut candy.

pakas: *n.* nose ring; clasp for earrings.

pakawalâ: (*slang*) *adj.* wild.

pakawáy: *n.* bamboo outrigger.

pakay₁: *n.* purpose; aim; mission; errand; **pakayan** *v.* to request something from someone; **pakayin** *v.* to be the object of one's mission.

pakay₂: **pakayan** *n.* gold mine.

pakete: (Sp. *paquete*) *n.* package, parcel.

paki-: *pref.* denotes favors, please → **pakiabót** please hand over.

paki: (*slang*) *n.* short for *pakialám*.

pakialám: (*rt. alám*) *n.* interfering; **pakialamero** *n.* meddler.

pakiki- *pref.* denotes cooperation (mutual actions) or a request → **pakikiaway** *n.* quarreling with one another **pakikibagay** *n.* harmony (suiting one another), **pakikikamáy** *n.* shaking hands, **pakikisama** *n.* companionship, **pakikialám** *n.* interference.

pakíd: *adj.* knock-kneed.

pakilala: (*rt. kilala*) *v.* to introduce.

pakiling: *n.* kind of small tree with fragrant flowers and whose leaves may be used for sandpaper; small weight attached to maintain the balance of a kite; **pakilíng** *adj.* inclined to one side.

pakimkím: *n.* money given by a godparent.

pakinabang: *n.* profit, earnings; advantage;

interest; **kapakí-pakinabang** *adj.* profitable; advantageous; **makinabang** *v.* to gain, earn; profit; **tagapakinabang** *n.* beneficiary.
Pakinabang: *n.* Communion.
pakíng: *adj.* having poor hearing; **mayang ~** *n.* species of Philippine sparrow.
pakinggán: (*rt. kiníg*) *v.* to listen to.
pakipkíp: (*rt. kipkíp*) *n.* gift given by a godparent.
pakipot: (*rt. kipot*) *adj.* pretended unwillingness; playing hard to get.
pakiramdám: (*rt. damdám*) *n.* feeling; perception.
pakiskís: *n.* species of long-tailed sparrow.
pakit: *n. Dioscorea luzonensis*, wild vine.
pakiyáw: *n.* wholesale buying.
paklá: **mapaklá** *adj.* tart.
paklí: *n.* retort, rebuttal; **ipaklí** *v.* to retort, rebut.
paklóy: *adj.* swollen (lips).
paknít: *adj.* disattached (previously glued thing).
paknós: *adj.* stripped, denuded; with the skin off.
paknót: *adj.* peeled off (skin); stripped.
pakò: *n.* nail; spike; **ipakò** *v.* to nail; **magpakò ng tingín** *id.* to pay close attention (nail sight).
pakô: *n.* fern.
pakol: *n.* Chinese file fish.
pakpák: *n.* wing; applause; **panulat ng ~** *n.* quill; **may pakpák ang balità** *id.* the news spreads quickly (has wings); **waláng pakpák** *id.* penniless.
paksâ: *n.* topic; theme, subject; matter; object; target; **walâ sa ~** off-topic, not to the point; **malayò sa ~** beside the point, not relative.
paksáw: (*slang*) *n.* getting everything.
paksíw: *n.* fish or meat cooked in vinegar, garlic, and salt.
paktura: (Sp. *factura*) *n.* invoice, bill; price list.
pakubo: *n.* painted snipe bird.
pakulô: (*slang*) *n.* bragging.
pakultád: (Sp. *facultad*) *n.* faculty.
pakumbabâ: (*rt. kumbabâ*) *adv.* humbly; **magpa-kumbabâ** *v.* to be humble.
pakundangan: *n.* reverence.
pakupyâ: (*rt. kupyâ*) *n.* circumflex accent.
pakwán: *n.* watermelon.
pakyáw: *n.* wholesale buying, buying in large quantities; **magpapakyáw** *v.* to sell at wholesale; **mamakyáw, pumakyáw** *v.* to buy at wholesale.
padér: (Sp. *pared*) *n.* wall; **paderán** *v.* to wall up.
padpád$_1$: *adj.* carried by the tide; **maipadpád** *adj.* to flow with the wind or current; to be shipwrecked.
padpád$_2$: *adj.* cut off at the top; **padparín** *v.* to level by cutting, prune.
padrast(r)o: (Sp.) *n.* stepfather.
padre: (Sp.) *n.* priest.
padrino: (Sp.) *n.* godfather; male sponsor.
padrón: (Sp.) *n.* pattern, model.
padyák: **pumadyák** *v.* to stamp the feet; trample.
padyamas: (Eng.) *n.* pajamas.
pag: *conj.* if, whenever; *adv.* when, upon.
pag- *pref.* gerund forming prefix → **pag-abót** reaching, **paglabis** being excessive, **pagplantsá** ironing.
pagCV-: *pref.* nominalizing prefix for *mag-* verbs: **pagsasalunga** *n.* coming into conflict; **pagsasanay** *n.* rehearsing, practicing; **pagkukulambô** *n.* act of using or stealing mosquito nets.
pag- -an: *affix.* 1. Causative affixation for directional *-an* verbs: **paglabasán** *v.* to show something to someone. **pagbawalan** *v.* to forbid someone to do something. **pagwelgahán** *v.* to strike against, declare a strike against. 2. Instrumental verbalizer: **pagbayaran** *v.* to recompense, pay for. **paglabanan** *v.* to contend, vie for.
pag- -in: Causative affixation for patient focus verbs: **paghubarín** *v.* to force someone to undress. **paghirapan** *v.* to cause hardship. **paglakbayín** *v.* to allow one to travel.
paga: (Sp.) *n.* pay, wages.
pagá: *adj.* tired, exhausted; *n.* kind of bamboo loft attached to a ceiling.
pagâ: *adj.* swollen; **mamagâ** *v.* to swell.
pagák: *adj.* hoarse (voice).

pagakpák: *n.* flapping of wings; banging sound.

pagado: (Sp.) *adj.* paid.

pagadór: (Sp.) *n.* paymaster.

pagál: *n.* fatigue; assuming a burden on behalf of someone else; **gatimpagál** *n.* compensation.

pagalà: *adj.* at wild, on the loose; *n.* pelican.

pagalpál: *n.* dam; sound of pounding rice in a mortar; noise of wheels traveling over a rough road.

pagano: (Sp.) *n.* pagan.

pagáng: *adj.* lean, thin.

pagapa: *n.* milkfish.

pagaré: (Sp. *pagaré*: I will pay) *n.* IOU, promissory note.

pagarpár: (*slang*) *n.* nonsense; idle talk; braggart.

pagas: *n.* waning of the tide, rinsing in water.

pagás: *adj.* raucous.

pag-asa: (*rt. asa*) *n.* hope; trust.

pagaspás: *n.* flapping of wings.

pagat: **pagatin** *v.* to pursue, chase.

pagatpát: *n.* species of swift bird; kind of shrub.

pagaw: **pagáw** *adj.* hoarse.

pagawâ: (*rt. gawâ*) *adj.* made to order.

pagaya: *n.* single bladed paddle.

pagaypáy: *n.* flapping of wings; swaying in the wind (leaves).

pagbá: **pagbahín** *v.* to fire pottery.

pagka-: *pref.* after: **pagkabalík** after returning, **pagkahuli** after catching; **pagkasagót** after answering; **pagkaraán** after passing; **pagkaratíng** after arriving.

pagká(ka)-: *pref.* 1. forms gerunds and abstract nouns → **pagkatao** *n.* humanity, **pagkabuhay** *n.* means of livelihood, manner of living, **pagkaalam** *n.* knowledge, understanding; **pagkapuyat** *n.* inability to sleep; 2. denotes rank or office → **pagkapangulo** *n.* office of the President.

pagka: *conj.* when; if.

pagkâ: **pagká't** *conj.* because; whereas. (*sapagkâ*)

pagkakataón: (*rt. taón*) *n.* chance; opportunity.

pagkaraán: (*rt. daán*) *adv.* after.

pagkaraka: *adv.* suddenly, instantly.

pagkít: *n.* beeswax.

pagdaka: *adv.* at once; immediately; **kapagdaka** *adv.* as soon as.

pagi: *n.* sting ray; **paging-bulik** marbled ray; **paging-dahunan** marbled sting ray; **paging-paul** spotted eel ray; **paging-dalimanok** cow nosed ray.

pag-ibig: (*rt. ibig*) *n.* love.

pagikpík: *n.* pat.

pagíl: *n.* wild boar.

pagispís: *n.* flapping sound; swishing sound.

pagitan: *n.* intervening space; space between; aisle; interval; **mamagitan** *v.* to interpose, interfere; arbitrate; **pamamagitan** *n.* intervention; mediation; interceding; **sa pagitan ng** between; midway; **sa pamamagitan ng** by means of, through, upon; **tagapamagitan** *n.* mediator, intermediary, go-between.

pago: (Sp.) *n.* payment.

pagod: **mapagod** *v.* to tire; **pagód** *adj.* tired, weary; **pagurin** *v.* to tire, strain; **pamagod** *n.* tiresome thing, bore.

pagóng: *n.* small turtle; **magsapagóng** *id.* to make a false show.

pagpa-: causative affix used with *pa-* indirect stems. 1. It may be used to form nouns (frequently with the reduplication of *pa*, the gerunds of *magpa-* verbs:) **pagpapaapí** *n.* allowing oneself to be mistreated; **pagpapadangal** *n.* act of honoring; 2. Forms causative verbs with the suffixes *-in* or *-an*. **pagpahalataán** *v.* to make something obvious to someone; **pagpahingahín** *v.* to allow someone to rest, make someone rest.

pagpág: **magpagpág** *v.* to shake cloth.

pagpapa: *pref.* forms gerunds for *magpa-* verbs.

pagsasa: *pref.* forms gerunds for *magsa-* verbs.

pagsidlán: (rt. *silíd*) *n.* container.

pagumpóng: *n.* sound of beating something soft (pillow).

paha: (Sp. *faja; paja*) *n.* girdle; straw.

pahabela: (Sp. *paja vela*) *n.* sailfish.

pahaláng: *adv.* transversely.

pahám: *n.* genius; erudite person; *var. of paháng.*

paháng: *n.* potency of liquor or medicine.
pahás: *n.* species of turtle.
pahát: *adj.* meager; inadequate; not yet developed.
pahe: (Sp. *paje*) *n.* page.
pahid: **ipahid** *v.* to spread; rub on, smear on; **magpahid** *v.* to rub off, scrub away, wipe away; **pahiran** *v.* to coat, spread over; smear, daub; **pamahid** *n.* spread; ointment.
páhina: (Sp. *página*) *n.* page.
pahintulot: **magpahintulot** *v.* to permit.
pahingá: (*rt. hingá*) *n.* rest, relaxation; day off.
pahipan: (*rt. ihip*) *v.* blow out; **dî pahipan sa hangin** *id.* priceless.
pahit: *adj.* drained to the last drop.
pahò: *n.* species of small, sour mango.
pahuhutan: *n.* medium sized mango with large seeds.
pa- -in: *affix.* Causative/Directional circumfix for patient focus verbs: **patuwirín** *v.* to make something straight, straighten; make someone sit or stand in a straight manner. **pasauluhin** *v.* to make someone memorize.
pain: *n.* bait; **magpain** *v.* to set bait; lure; **pain sa bitag** *id.* coward.
painá: *n.* siding for steps of a staircase.
painás: *n.* live post (tree post).
pais: *adj.* compressed; **pinais** *n.* fish or meat wrapped in leaves and roasted; steamed fish.
páisdaan: *n.* fishpond.
pait: *n.* tripe, intestines of animals; cyprinid fish.
paít$_1$: *n.* chisel; **paitín** *v.* to chisel; **paráng paít** *id.* one who doesn't act without being prompted (like a chisel).
paít$_2$: *n.* bitterness; **mapaít** *adj.* bitter; **pumaít** *v.* to become bitter; **mapaít lunukín** *id.* humiliating disappointment (bitter to swallow).
palá- *pref.* 1. habitual prefix → **paláinóm ng arak** *n.* habitual drinker of wine; **palábigáy** *adj.* generous. 2. expresses a system or arrangement: **palábaybayan** *n.* spelling system; **palábigkasan** *n.* phonetics; prosody.
pala: (Sp.) *n.* shovel; blade of a windmill. **palápalahan** *v.* toy shovel.
palá: *interj.* interjection expressing sudden realization: **Ikáw pala** So it's you!
palà: **magpalà** *v.* to bless; **pagpapalà** *n.* grace, blessing.
palâ: **mapalâ** *v.* to gain by, benefit, profit.
palabâ: *n.* halo of the moon.
palábabahán: (*rt. babá*) *n.* windowsill; balustrade; seat of a *bangka.*
palábantasan: (rt. *bantás*) *n.* punctuation rules.
palábanghayan: (rt. *bangháy*) *n.* conjugation.
palabás: (*rt. labás*) *n.* show, entertainment. **palabás-dúlaan** *n.* stage play, drama.
palábatasan: (rt. *batas*) *n.* system of laws.
palábaybayan: (rt. *baybáy*) *n.* orthography.
palábigasan: *n.* granary; rice container; (*coll.*) backer, supporter.
palábigkasan: (rt. *bigkás*) *n.* phonetics; phonics; prosody.
palabok: *n.* thick sauce for noodles; flowery speech; **palabukan** *v.* to spice up, add flavor to.
palák: **di-palák** *adv.* by far, very much.
palabok: **pansít** ~ *n.* noodles cooked with shrimp, squid, pork rind, eggs, and a starchy sauce.
palabra: (Sp.) *n.* word; ~ **de honor** *n.* word of honor.
palakâ: *n.* frog; **mamalakâ** *v.* to catch frogs; **palakáng-kabkáb** *n.* bullfrog; **palakáng-langit** *n.* species of toad that appears during the rainy season; **palakáng-kati** *n.* toad; **parang palakáng kokak** *id.* talking constantly.
palakad: (*rt. lakad*) *n.* policy; regulation; administration, management.
palakat: *n.* shrill sound, scream.
palakáw: *n.* looped cord, lasso.
palakaya: *n.* trawl; **mamalakaya** *v.* to trawl (drag a fishnet).
palakól: *n.* ax; **palakulín** *v.* to chop with an ax.
palakpák: *n.* applause, clap.
palad$_1$: *n.* palm of the hand; *n.* luck, fate, destiny; **mapalad** *adj.* lucky; fortunate; **kapalaran** *n.* fate, destiny, luck; **kasamaáng-palad** *n.* misfortune; **ipagsapalarán** *v.* to risk money, stake; **magkapalad** *v.* to be lucky; **mapagsapalarán** *adj.* rash, inclined to take risks; **pakikipagsápalarán** *n.* venture, risk, adventure; **sápalarán** *n.* taking

a risk; **sa sápalarán** by chance, at random; **mapanganib na pakikipagsápalarán** *n.* adventure.

palad₂: *n.* flatfish.

palág: *n.* wiggling, jerking of the feet.

pálagarián: (rt. *lagarì*) *n.* sawmill; lumbershop.

palagáy: (*rt. lagáy*) *n.* opinion; judgment; conclusion; **ipalagáy** *v.* to conclude, suppose, imagine; **ipalagáy na bunga** *v.* to attribute; **pálagayang-loób** *n.* trust or confidence in each other; **masamáng-palagáy** *n.* complex, prejudice, bad opinion.

palágitlingan: (rt. *gitlíng*) *n.* hyphenation rules.

palaháw: *n.* howl, loud scream; outcry.

paláibunan: (rt. *ibon*) *n.* ornithology.

palairos: *n.* confection of dough, coconut milk, sugar and sago palm seeds.

paláisdaan: (rt. *isdâ*) *n.* fishpond; fishing ground.

paláisipan: (rt. *isip*) *n.* riddle; puzzle.

palalò: *adj.* proud, haughty, arrogant.

palalós: *adj.* inclusive, without exception.

pal-am: *n.* notch on a coconut tree.

palamám-inan: (*rt. mam-in*) *n.* betel leaf and nut container.

palamán: (*rt. lamán*) *n.* stuffing; (*coll.*) food to accompany an alcoholic drink.

palamara: *n.* traitor.

palamíg: (*rt. lamíg*) *n.* refreshment. **pálamigan** *n.* refreshment stand.

palamuti: *n.* decoration, ornament; garnish.

palamuymóy: *n.* tassel.

palanas: *n.* rocky shore; wide, level land.

palansák: *adj.* collective.

palantayan: *n.* stretcher; crosspiece (used for support).

paláng: *n.* butcher's knife.

palangan: *n.* heirloom, something esteemed but not used.

palangangâ: (*rt. ngangâ*) *adj.* fond of chewing betel nut.

palangka: (Sp. *palanca*) *n.* prayers offered to someone making the *kursilyo*.

palangká: (Sp. *palanca*) *n.* pole for carrying; lever.

palanggana: (Sp. *palangana*) *n.* washtub, washbasin; (*slang*) *adj.* true.

palangó: *n.* rattle; (*rt. langó*) intoxicant.

palapà: *n.* pulpy leaves or joint of palms and banana plants.

palapág: *n.* floor, story of a building; (*rt. lapág*) *adv.* downward; **páapagan** *n.* landing field; unloading.

palapala: *n.* gangplank; arbor, temporary shed.

palápantigan: (rt. *pantig*) *n.* rules of syllabification.

palarâ: *n.* tinsel, tin foil.

palas: **palás** *adj.* cut, lopped off.

palasak: **mamalasak** *v.* to become popular; **palasák** *adj.* popular, common, usual.

palasan: *n.* thick rattan.

palásintahan: *n.* collection of love stories.

palasingsingan: (*rt. singsíng*) *n.* ring finger.

palasô: *n.* arrow. (*tunod*)

palaspás: *n.* decorated palm leaves blessed for Palm Sunday.

palásurián: (rt. *surì*) *n.* analogy; semantics.

palasyo: (Sp. *palacio*) *n.* palace.

palaták: *n.* clicking of the tongue; **pangangalaták** *n.* hand sowing of seeds.

palátandaan: (rt. *tandâ*) *n.* sign; symbol; token; landmark.

palátauhan: (rt. *tao*) *n.* anthropogenesis.

palátayahan: (rt. *tayá*) *n.* calculus; system of calculation.

pálathalaán: (rt. *lathalà*) *n.* printing press; publishing house.

palatháw: *n.* hatchet, small ax.

palatikat: *n.* long-finned covalla.

palátitikan: (*rt. titik*) *n.* spelling, orthography.

palatol: *n.* grace period; allowance in measuring.

palatón: (*slang*, Sp. *platón*) *n.* large plate.

palatpát: *n.* long strip of bamboo.

palátulaan: (rt. *tulâ*) *n.* poetics.

palátuldikan: (rt. *tuldík*) *n.* rules of accentuation.

palátumbasan: (rt. *tumbás*) *n.* exchange rate.

palátuntunan: (rt. *tuntón*) *n.* program (of activities).

palátunugan: (rt. *tunog*) *n.* phonetics; phonemics.

paláugatan: (rt. *ugat*) *n.* etymology.

paláugnayan: (rt. *ugnáy*) *n.* syntax.
palawan: *n.* sleeper fish.
Palawano: *n.* ethnic group and language from Palawan Island.
palawingwíng: *n.* fringe.
palawis: *n.* small banner or flag (for boats).
palay: *n.* rice plant; unhusked rice; paddy.
palayaw: (*rt. layaw*) *n.* nickname.
palayók: *n.* earthen pot; **sampalayók** *n.* one potful. **palayúk-palayukan.** *n.* toy earthen pot.
paláypaláy: *adj.* gentle (breeze).
palaypáy: *n.* fin.
palbóg: *adj.* barren from overuse, over cultivated.
palko: (Sp. *palco*) *n.* balcony, gallery, upper floor of a theater; seat in the balcony.
palda: (Sp. *falda*) *n.* skirt; **nakapaldá** *adj.* wearing a skirt; (*coll.*) with business in a temporary slump.
paldák: *adj.* trampled over.
paldiyás: *n.* rim of a hat.
paldó: (Sp. *fardo*) *n.* bale, large bundle; (*slang*) *adj.* wealthy.
palengke: (Mex. Sp. *palenque*) *n.* market; **mamalengke** *v.* to market, go shopping at the market.
paleta: (Sp.) *n.* palette.
palî: *n.* spleen.
paliás: *n.* species of turtle.
palibhasà: *conj.* because; *n.* mockery; **kapalibhasaan** *n.* mockery, sarcasm; insult; **palibhasain** *v.* to mock, scorn.
palikero: (Sp. *palique* + *-ero*) *n.* playboy, ladies' man.
palikpík: *n.* fin of a fish.
paligpíg: **pamamaligpíg** *n.* shaking of the body.
paligsá: (*rt. ligsá*) *n.* test, exam.
palihán: *n.* anvil.
palimanok: *n.* cow-nosed ray.
palindayag: *n.* state of calmness after surprise.
palintâ: *n.* plowshare.
paling: *n.* slope, inclination; **palíng** *adj.* sloping.
palingâ: *adj.* with head turned sideways.
paliróng: *n.* shanty, hovel.
palis: **pamalis** *n.* tool used to level grain.
palís: *n.* whisk, small brush; act of wiping away, whisking.
palisan: *n.* kind of small tree.
palisán: (*reg.*) *n.* female water buffalo.
palispís: *n.* clearing of a field before planting; dusting.
palít: *n.* exchange, substitute; **kapalít** *adj.* reciprocal, in return; *n.* compensation; **kapalít ng** in place of, for; **ipagpalít** *v.* to swap, exchange; **magpalít** *v.* to exchange; substitute; **makipagpálítan** *v.* to interchange, exchange; **pakikipagpalít** *n.* exchange; **mapagpápalít** *adj.* interchangeable; **pagkakápalít** *n.* replacement; **pagpapalít** *n.* exchange; substitution; **pumalít** *v.* to make up for; supply; **bilang kapalít** in exchange; **mahinang pamalít** poor substitute, apology.
palitada: *n.* cement mortar; surface of concrete.
palitáw: *n.* rice cake.
palito: (Sp.) *n.* toothpick; matchstick; (*fig.*) thin person.
palma: (Sp.) *n.* palm tree, palm leaf.
palmo: (Sp.) *n.* pitching pennies.
palo: (Sp.) *n.* pole; mast of a ship.
paló: **palú-paló** *adj.* (*slang*) with big thighs.
palò₁: (Sp.) *n.* beating; spanking; **mamalò, pumalò** *v.* to beat, spank, whip; **pamamalò** *n.* beating, whipping, spanking; **palung-palò** *id.* whipped severely; (*fig.*) obsessed.
palò₂: *adj.* attracted to opposite sex; **palu-palò** (*slang*) *n.* large thighs.
palok: *n.* feathers growing on the back of the neck.
palók: *n.* working continuously; abstinence for a certain period due to a death of a relative.
palong: *n.* cockscomb; **magpalong** *v.* to grow a cockscomb; **palong-manók** *n.* an ornamental shrub used to make wreaths.
palós: *n.* large eel; (*slang*) escape artist; **palós-buhangin** *n.* conger eel.
palosebo: (Sp. *palo* + *cebo*) *n.* slippery bamboo pole climbing competition; the bamboo pole used in this competition.
palot: *n.* odor of soiled clothes; odor of evaporating urine.

palotsina: *n*. species of shrub, *Herpetica alata*.
palpák: (*slang*) *n*. failure, thwarted effort.
palpál: *n*. handful of food forced in the mouth.
palsipiká: (Sp. *falsificar*) **palsipikahín** *v*. to falsify; **palsipikado** *v*. to falsify.
palso: (Sp. *falso*) *adj*. false; (*slang*) defective; **palsó** (*slang*) failure.
palta: (Sp. *falta*) *n*. omission; blank.
palták: *n*. rivet; peg.
paltík: *n*. homemade gun; blow from a whip; (*slang*) *adj*. unreliable, untrustworthy.
paltók: *n*. sprout; sudden jerk; hit.
paltós: *n*. blister; *adj*. failed, missed; **pumaltós** *v*. to fail, miss the mark.
paludpód: *adj*. pruned.
palumpóng: *n*. shrub; cluster of flowers; plants that grow from fallen seeds.
palupalò: *n*. wooden mallet.
palupo: *n*. ridge of a roof.
palusì: *n*. post that holds the awnings of a small boat.
palutpót: *adj*. worn and uneven; corrugated.
paluwon: *n*. ornate eleotrid fish.
palyá: (Sp. *falla*) *n*. skip, omission; dud; **palyado** *adj*. dud, defective bullet.
palyát: *n*. bagasse (plant residue) of a coconut, copra.
palyó$_1$: (Sp. *pallo*) *n*. pall, canopy.
palyo$_2$: (Sp. *fallo*) *n*. decision by a board of judges.
palyók: *n*. clay pot.
pam- *var. of pang-* before labial consonants **pambanláw** water for rinsing, **pambuhók** for the hair.
pama: (Sp. *fama*) *n*. fame; profit.
pamaka: *n*. hand-to-hand combat; *adj*. for cows.
pamakalawá: (*rt*. *dalawá*) *v*. to wait for the day after tomorrow.
pamaki: *n*. anything used as a chip in some games.
pamakò: (*rt*. *pakò*) *n*. something used as a nail.
pamakod: (*rt*. *bakod*) *n*. material for fencing.
pamakpák: (*rt*. *pakpák*) *n*. materials needed to make a kite.
pámakuán: *n*. boards of structure to which wall boards are attached.
pamada: (Eng.) *n*. pomade.
pamadyák: (*slang*) *n*. fare (for a ride).
pamagát: *n*. title; caption, heading; **ipamagát** *v*. to title.
pamagitan: *n*. partition, dividing line; mediator, go between.
pamago: (*rt*. *bago*) *n*. first harvest; first fruits; **mamago** *v*. to use for the first time; harvest first crop.
pamagod: (*rt*. *pagod*) *n*. sleeping pill, something that causes tiredness.
pamaha: (*rt*. *paha*) *n*. something used as a girdle.
pamahalà: (*rt bahalà*) *n*. management
pamahalaán: (*rt*. *bahalà*) *n*. government.
pamahaw: (*obs*.) *n*. breakfast; light meal.
pamahay: (*rt*. *bahay*) *n*. something for household use; **pamamahay** household.
pamahayag: (*rt*. *pahayag*) *n*. proclamation; **pámamahayagán** *n*. journalistic ethics; journalism.
pamahayan: (*rt*. *bahay*) *n*. to live in, reside; become flooded; **pámahayán** *n*. residential place; **pamahayin** *v*. to let live in a place; let water lie low.
pamahid: (*rt*. *pahid*) *n*. rag, something used for wiping; **pámahirán** *n*. cloth for wiping; **~ ng paá** *n*. doormat.
pamahiín: *n* superstition; **mapamahiín** *adj*. superstitious.
pamahingá: (*rt*. *pahingá*) *n*. break time (for workers), **pamahingahan** *v*. to take a rest.
pamahulí: (*rt*. *pahulí*) *n*. hind quarter of an animal; habit of coming late; *adj*. usually late or last.
pamain: (*rt*. *pain*) *n*. something used as bait.
pamaít: (*rt*. *paít*) *n*. chisel.
pamala: (*rt*. *bala*) *n*. ammunition.
pamalá: **magpamalá** *v*. to dry in the sun (wet rice).
pamalakâ: (*rt*. *palakâ*) *n*. net for catching frogs.
pamalakad: (*rt*. *pa-lakad*) *n*. policy.
pamalakaya: (*rt*. *palakaya*) *n*. something used for trawling.
pamalagì: (*rt*. *palagì*) *n*. permanent position or situation; **pámalagián** *adj*. permanently;

pamamalagì *n*. permanence.
pamalas: *n*. act of showing; (*rt. malas*) something that brings bad luck.
pamalî: (*rt. malî*) *adv*. erroneously.
pamalík: (*rt. balík*) *n*. hand lever of a rudder.
pamalila: *n*. bamboo strips that support a nipa wall.
pamalís: (*rt. palís*) *n*. duster.
pamalità: (*rt. balità*) *n*. gossip, rumors.
pamalmák: *adj*. getting serious or worse.
pamalò: (*rt. palò*) *n*. bat, club, something used for hitting or whipping.
pamaltík: (*rt. baltík*) *n*. slingshot.
pamamalukag: (*rt. lukag*) *n*. bristling of hair; Goosebumps; **pamalukagan** *v*. to bristle; have Goosebumps.
pamamakyáw: (*rt. pakyáw*) *n*. wholesale buying.
pamamadyá: (*rt. badyá*) *n*. mimicking.
pamamagaw: (*rt. pagaw*) *n*. hoarseness of the voice.
pamamagitan: (*rt. pagitan*) *n*. intervention; mediation.
pamamago: (*rt. bago*) *n*. feeling of newness of being a novice.
pamamahagi: (*rt. bahagi*) *n*. distribution.
pamamahalà: (*rt. bahalà*) *n*. management; administration.
pamamahay: (*rt. bahay*) *n*. household; housekeeping; **pamamaháy** *n*. fondness for staying at home.
pamamahayag: (*rt. pahayag*) *n*. work of a journalist; public demonstration.
pamamahid: (*rt. pahid*) *n*. act of cleaning or wiping.
pamamahingá: (*rt. pahingá*) *n*. resting; retirement.
pamamahò: (*rt. bahò*) *n*. emission of a foul odor.
pamamalakâ: (*rt. palakâ*) *n*. catching frogs.
pamamalakad: (*rt. palakad*) *n*. management; administration.
pamamalengke: (*rt. palengke*) *n*. marketing.
pamamalità: (*rt. balità*) *n*. act of spreading information, gossip, etc.
pamamalò: (*rt. palò*) *n*. act of punishing, beating
pamamanà: (*rt. panà*) *n*. archery.
pamamanás: (*rt. panás*) *n*. beriberi; edema.
pamamanata: (*rt. panata*) *n*. vow, promise.
pamamanatag: (*rt. panatag*) *n*. rest; retirement; death.
pamamánhikan: (*rt. panhík*) *n*. custom of formally asking for the hand of a bride.
pamamanság: (*rt. banság*) *n*. act of boasting.
pamamantál: (*rt. pantál*) *n*. act of swelling or welting.
pamamangkâ: (*rt. bangkâ*) *n*. boating.
pamamangó: (*rt. bangó*) *n*. emission of fragrance.
pamamangós: (*rt. pangós*) *n*. chewing sugarcane.
pamamaos: (*rt. paos*) *n*. hoarseness of the voice.
pamamaraan: (*rt. daan*) *n*. system; method; process.
pamamarata: (*rt. barata*) *n*. act of bargaining.
pamamarati: (*rt. parati*) *n*. unchanged state or condition.
pamamaríl: (*rt. baríl*) *n*. shooting; hunting.
pamamasâ: (*rt. basâ*) *n*. wetting, splashing water; (*rt. pasâ*) *n*. bruise.
pamamasahe: (*rt. pasahe*) *n*. payment of a fare.
pamamaskó: (*rt. paskó*) *n*. act of visiting during Christmas.
pamamasukan: (*rt. pasok*) *n*. act of working as an employee.
pamamasyál: (*rt. pasyál*) *n*. promenading.
pamamatnubay: (*rt. patnubay*) *n*. guidance; leadership.
pamamayagpág: (*rt. payagpág*) *n*. flapping one's wings; (*fig*.) boastfulness.
pamamayan: (*rt. bayan*) *n*. living in a town.
pamamayani: (*rt. bayani*) *n*. prevalence; predominance.
pamamayapà: (*rt. payapà*) *n*. death, end of life.
pamamayát: (*rt. payát*) *n*. condition of being thin.
pamamaywáng: (*rt. baywáng*) *n*. placing the hands on one's hips; (*fig*.) doing nothing in the case of danger or need.
pamana: (*rt. mana*) *n*. heritage; inheritance;

pamanahin *v.* to leave an inheritance to.

pamanhík: (*rt. panhík*) *n.* entreaty, earnest request; **mamanhík** *v.* to entreat.

pamanhíd: (*rt. manhíd*) *n.* anesthetic; **pamanhirán** *v.* to feel numb in a certain part; anesthetize.

pamanihalaan: (*rt. panihalà*) *v.* to direct, manage; take charge of.

pamansá: *n.* boasting; *var.* of *pambansâ.*

pamanság: (*rt. banság*) *n.* declaration; public statement; **pamansagán** *v.* to declare; boast about.

pamansíng: (*rt. pansíng*) *n.* fishing line with hook and rod.

pámantasan: (*rt. taás*) *n.* university.

pámantayan: (*rt. pantáy*) *n.* standard; average, norm.

pamantíng: (*rt. pantíng*) *n.* steel used for striking fire with a flint.

pámantingin: *n.* broken pieces of chinaware.

pamantô: (*rt. bantô*) *n.* water used to adulterate something.

pamanyós: (*rt. banyós*) *n.* water used for a sponge bath.

pamangkín: *n.* niece, nephew; stepchild; ~ **sa pinsán** child of one's cousin; ~ **sa asawa** child of one's sibling-in-law.

pamangkól: *n.* bamboo pieces used to hold together a nipa roof.

pamanggít: (*rt. banggít*) *adj.* relative (grammatical).

pamanglawín: (*rt. pangláw*) *v.* to make lonely.

pamanguhín: (*rt bangó*) *v.* to make fragrant; use perfume.

pamao: (*rt. bao*) *n.* half a coconut shell used as a dipper.

pamaon: (*rt. baon*) *n.* money used to buy provisions.

pamara: (*rt. para*) *n.* somcthing used to stop or as a stop signal.

pamaraan: (*rt. paraan*) *n.* stratagem; method, manner.

pamaríl: (*rt. baríl*) *n.* gun used for hunting; **pámarilan** *n.* hunting ground.

pamarisan: (*rt. paris*) *v.* to imitatc.

pamasa: (*rt. basa*) *n.* reading lens.

pamasâ: (*rt. basâ*) *n.* bathing clothes; water used for soaking or wetting.

pamasak: (*rt. pasak*) *n.* something used as a plug; **pamasak-butas** *id.* substitute.

pamasadór: (*rt. pasadór*) *n.* sanitary napkin; moistened rag used for ironing.

pamasahe: (*rt. pasahe*) *n.* fare (for passage).

pamaskó: (*rt. paskó*) *adj.* for Christmas.

pamasò: (*rt. pasò*) *n.* something used to scald or burn.

pamasok: (*rt. pasok*) *n.* something used for school.

pamasta: (*rt. pasta*) *n.* filling for teeth.

pamasyál: (*rt. pasyál*) *n.* something used for promenading; **pámasyalan** *n.* promenade walk.

pamatá: (*rt. matá*) *n.* fee paid to work on good land; good advice; **pamatahán** *v.* to advise.

pamaták: (*rt. paták*) *n.* liquid dropper.

pamatag: (*rt. patag*) *n.* something used to level.

pamatáy: (*rt. patáy*) *n.* instrument used in slaughtering; extinguisher; off button or device; **~-kulisap** *n.* insecticide; **~-sunog** *n.* fire extinguisher; **~-tunóg** *n.* muffler, silencer; **~-uhaw** *n.* thirst quencher.

pamatbát: (*rt. batbát*) *n.* something used for binding.

pamatíd: (*rt. patíd*) *n.* tool for cutting; **~-alambre** *n.* wire cutter; **~-uhaw** *n.* thirst quencher.

pamatlíg: (*rt. patlíg*) *adj.* demonstrative (grammatical).

pamatnubay: (*rt. patnubay*) *n.* something used as a guide.

pamatnugutan: (*rt. patnugot*) *v.* to direct, supervise; manage; **pámatnugán** *n.* board of directors; editorial staff.

pamatò: *n.* cue, cue ball; star player of a team.

pamatok: (*rt. batok*) *n.* yoke.

pamatsí: (*slang*) *n.* fare (for a ride); massage. (*pamasahe*)

pamauna: (*rt. una*) *n.* front quarter of an animal; **pamáuná** *adj.* always coming early or first; *n.* partial advance payment.

pamawas: (*rt. bawas*) *n.* something used to reduce weight.

pamawi: (*rt. bawi*) *n.* eradicator; quencher;

eraser; **pamawing-uhaw** *n*. thirst quencher.
pamayák: *n*. coagulation.
pamayad: (*rt. bayad*) *n*. money set aside for paying loans, taxes, etc.
pamayan: *var*. of *pambayan*; **pámayanán** *n*. community.
pamayapà: (*rt. payapà*) *n*. something used to pacify.
pamaypáy: (*rt. paypáy*) *n*. something used as a fan.
pamayák: *n*. coagulation, curdling.
pamayo: (*rt. payo*) *n*. advice.
pamaypáy: (*rt. paypáy*) *n*. folding fan.
pambó: (*reg*.) *n*. bath.
pamigâ: (*rt. pigâ*) *n*. juice from a lemon; instrument used to extract citrus juice; **pamigaán** *v*. to add lemon juice to.
pamigáy: (*rt. bigáy*) *adj*. free; **pamigayán** *v*. to give for free.
pamigkás: (*rt. bigkás*) *n*. poem suitable for recitation
pamigkís: (*rt. bigkís*) *n*. girdle.
pamigô: (*rt. bigô*) *n*. something used to disappoint.
pamigtí: (*rt. bigtí*) *n*. something used to strangle.
pamihis: (*rt. bihis*) *n*. extra set of clothes.
pamilang: (*rt. bilang*) *n*. numeral.
pamilí: (*rt. bilí*) *n*. money for marketing; **pamilihán** *v*. to buy things from.
pamilo: (*rt. bilo*) *n*. something used for rolling things up.
pamilog: (*rt. bilog*) *n*. drawing compass, something used to make circles or round things.
pamilya: (Sp. *familia*) *n*. family.
pamimigát: (*rt. bigát*) *n*. slight illness.
pamimihasa: (*rt. bihasa*) *n*. being accustomed to.
pamimihilyá: (*rt. bihilyá*) *n*. abstinence; fasting.
pamimiláy: (*rt. piláy*) *n*. walking with a limp.
pamimilí: (*rt. bilí*) *n*. shopping, buying.
pamimilì: (*rt. pilì*) *n*. selecting, choosing.
pamimilipit: (*rt. pilipit*) *n*. condition of being twisted.
pamimilit: (*rt. pilit*) *n*. act of forcing.
pamimilog: (*rt. bilog*) *n*. becoming round or fat.
pamiminsalà: (*rt. pinsalà*) *n*. harming, injuring.
pamimintanà: (*rt. bintanà*) *n*. looking out the window.
pamimintás: (*rt. pintás*) *n*. criticizing, finding fault with others.
pamimintô: (*rt. pintô*) *n*. staying in the doorway; being near at hand.
pamimintóg: (*rt. bintóg*) *n*. inflating; state of being swollen; becoming fat.
pamimintuhò: (*rt. pintuhò*) *n*. admiring, veneration.
pamiminyagan: (*rt. binyág*) *n*. attending a baptism.
pamimingí: (*rt. bingí*) *n*. gradual deafness, slowly becoming deaf.
pamimingit: (*rt. bingit*) *n*. being at the threshold of.
pamimingwít: (*rt. bingwít*) *n*. act of fishing.
pamimirmé: (*rt. pirmé*) *n*. permanency, staying permanently.
pamimisâ: (*rt. pisâ*) *n*. hatching eggs.
pamimisík: (*rt. pisík*) *n*. splashing, spattering.
pamimistá: (*rt. pistá*) *n*. attending a fiesta.
pamimiták: (*rt. biták*) *n*. dawn, daybreak.
pamimitagan: (*rt. pitagan*) *n*. respect.
pamimitás: (*rt. pitás*) *n*. picking (fruits).
pamimitík: (*rt. pitík*) *n*. flicking.
pamimitig: (*rt. bitig*) *n*. muscular numbness.
paminsán: *adv*. all at one time; **paminsanín** *v*. to allow someone to do once.
pamintá: (Sp. *pimienta*) *n*. powdered pepper.
pamintón: (Sp. *pimentón*) *n*. paprika, red Cayenne pepper.
pamintosa: (*rt. bintosa*) *n*. cupping glass.
pamingkî: (*rt. pingkî*) *n*. something used as flint.
pamingkít: *n*. wild thistle.
páminggalan: *n*. cupboard, pantry; shelf for kitchen utensils.
pamingwít: (*rt. bingwít*) *n*. fishing rod with hook.
pamipî: (*rt. pipî*) *n*. pressboard; instrument for pressing.
pamipís: (*rt. pipís*) *n*. something used to press.
pamisâ: (*rt. pisâ*) *n*. incubator; **pamisaín** *v*. to

allow a hen to hatch her eggs.
pamispís: (*rt. pispís*) *n.* duster.
pamistá: (*rt. pistá*) *n.* thing used for a fiesta; best clothes reserved for a town fiesta.
pamitay: (*rt. bitay*) *n.* something used to hang, gallows; instrument used to carry out capital punishment, electric chair.
pamitík: (*rt. pitík*) *n.* cord attached to the nose ring of a water buffalo; carpenter's line maker.
pamitig: (*rt. bitig*) *n.* cramp, tingling pain; **pamitigan** *v.* to feel cramps.
pamitin: (*rt. bitin*) *n.* pendant, decorative hanging; fish hook; **pámitinan** *n.* hanger.
pamitpít: (*rt. pitpít*) *n.* something used to crush or flatten.
pamiyahe: (*rt. biyahe*) *n.* something used for travel; travel clothing.
pampa- *pref.* causative instrumental prefix, forms nouns that are used to perform causative actions, or adjectives expressing the use → **pampaandár** *n.* that which is used to start a motor or machine, **pampaantók** *n.* sleeping pill, that which induces sleep, **pampabahaw** *n.* that which is used to heal wounds, **pampabunga** *n.* that which induces trees to bear fruit; *adj.* inducing the bearing of fruits.
pampagana: (*rt. gana*) *n.* appetizer.
pampalamíg: (*rt. lamíg*) *n.* refreshment; *adj.* refreshing.
pampám: (*slang*) *n.* prostitute.
pampano: *n.* cavalla fish; **pampanung-riyál** *n.* threadfish.
pampáng: *n.* river bank.
Pampango: *n.* ethnic group and language from Pampanga, Tarlac and Bataan provinces, Luzon.
pamukot: (*rt. pukot*) *n.* dragnet.
pamukpók: (*rt. pukpók*) *n.* hammer, mallet.
pamuksâ: (*rt. puksâ*) *n.* exterminator, something used to eradicate.
pamukulan: (*rt. bukol*) *v.* to swell (said of the breasts of an adolescent girl).
pamugad: (*rt. pugad*) *n.* materials for making a nest; **pámugarán** *n.* nesting place; haunt; nesting season.
pamugbóg: (*rt. bugbóg*) *n.* club, cudgel; mallet.
pamugò: (*rt. pugò*) *n.* quail net.
pamugot: (*rt. pugot*) *n.* guillotine.
pamugtô: (*rt. bugtô*) **pamumugtô** *n.* swelling around eyes due to lack of sleep or crying.
pámuhatán: (*rt. buhat*) *n.* source, origin; etymology.
pamuhay: (*rt. buhay*) *var.* of *pambuhay*; **pamuhayan** *n.* means of livelihood.
pamuhunan: (*rt. puhunan*) *n.* money used as capital.
pámulaan: (*rt. mulâ*) *n.* starting place; origin; etymology.
pamulaklakán: (*rt. bulaklák*) *v.* to pick flowers from.
pamulahán: (*rt. pulá*) *v.* to blush (face); **pamulahín** *v.* to make someone blush.
pamulati: (*rt. bulati*) *n.* purgative drug to kill intestinal worms.
pamulî: (*rt. mulî*) *adv.* again.
pamulot: (*rt. pulot*) *n.* something used to pick up things.
pamulsá: (*rt. bulsá*) *n.* something used for the pocket or making pockets; pocket watch.
pamumukad: (*rt. bukad*) *n.* time when flowers open.
pamumukadkád: (*rt. bukadkád*) *n.* time when flowers are in full bloom.
pamumukaw: (*rt. pukaw*) *n.* inciting; waking up; arousing.
pamumukid: (*rt. bukid*) *n.* living in rural areas.
pamumuko: (*rt. buko*) *n.* budding season; gathering young coconuts.
pamumukó: (*rt. bukó*) *n.* opposing, contradicting; disappointing.
pamumukód: (*rt. bukód*) *n.* individuality; difference, distinction; singularity; **pamumukód-tangì** *n.* being different from all others.
pamumuksâ: (*rt. puksâ*) *n.* massacre.
pamumudbód: (*rt. budbód*) *n.* distributing sparingly.
pamumugad: (*rt. pugad*) *n.* building a nest; nesting season.
pamumugò: (*rt. pugò*) *n.* catching quails.
pamumuhay: (*rt. buhay*) *n.* way of life; live-

lihood.

pamumuhunan: (*rt. puhunan*) *n.* capitalization, investment of capital.

pamumulá: (*rt. pulá*) *n.* blushing; reddening.

pamumulà: (*rt. pulà*) *n.* criticizing.

pamumulaklák: (*rt. bulaklák*) *n.* blooming season.

pamumulítika: (*rt. pulítika*) *n.* politicking; talking politics.

pamumulot: (*rt. pulot*) *n.* picking up scattered things.

pamumulubi: (*rt. pulubi*) *n.* state of impoverishment.

pamumulupot: (*rt. pulupot*) *n.* coiling; winding.

pamumuná: (*rt. puná*) *n.* criticism.

pamumundók: (*rt. bundók*) *n.* hiding in the mountains.

pamumunò: (*rt. punò*) *n.* leadership; act of presiding.

pamumunga: (*rt. bunga*) *n.* bearing of fruits.

pamumuô: (*rt. buô*) *n.* coagulation; curdling.

pamumupô: (*rt. pô*) *n.* using *pô* to be polite.

pamumulpól: (*rt. pulpól*) *n.* picking flowers.

pamumuri: (*rt. puri*) *n.* praising.

pamumurnada: (*rt. purnada*) *n.* swindling others.

pamumursiyento: (*rt. pursiyento*) *n.* selling on commission.

pamumustá: (*rt. pustá*) *n.* act of betting.

pamumustura: (*rt. pustura*) *n.* dressing up.

pamumusyáw: (*rt. pusyáw*) *n.* fading; loss of color.

pamumuti: (*rt. puti*) *n.* picking; gathering.

pamumutî: (*rt. putî*) *n.* act of becoming white.

pamumutiktík: (*rt. butiktík*) *n.* swarming in great numbers.

pamumutlâ: (*rt. putlâ*) *n.* paleness.

pamumutók: (*rt. putók*) *n.* popping; cracking; breaking.

pamumutol: (*rt. putol*) *n.* cutting down.

pamumuwersa: (*rt. puwersa*) *n.* force; rape.

pamumuwís: (*rt. buwís*) *n.* paying taxes; working as a crop sharer.

pamumuwisit: (*rt. buwisit*) *n.* act of bringing bad luck; annoying someone.

pamumuyat: (*rt. puyat*) *n.* keeping others awake at night.

pamunas: (*rt. punas*) *n.* rag, something used to wipe.

pamunlâ: (*rt. punlâ*) *n.* seeds intended for planting.

pamunô: (*rt. punô*) *n.* something used to fill up, stuffing.

pamunot: (*rt. bunot*) *n.* tool used to uproot.

pamunsód: (*rt. bunsód*) *n.* instrument used for launching; *adj.* introductory, preliminary.

pámunuán: (*rt. punò*) *n.* board of officers.

pamungad: (*rt. bungad*) *n.* introduction; opening speech; frontispiece.

pamuô: (*rt. buô*) *n.* something used to complete something.

pamuók: *n.* hand to hand combat.

pamuód: (*rt. buód*) *n.* summary.

pamupoy: *n.* branch used as a stake for a fence.

pamupuán: (*rt. pô*) *v.* to speak respectfully to using *pô*.

pamurda: (*rt. burda*) *n.* embroidery materials.

pamusbós: (*rt. busbós*) *n.* surgical tool.

pamuso: (Sp. *famoso*) *adj.* famous.

pamusóg: (*rt. busóg*) *n.* food used to satisfy one's appetite.

pamutas: (*rt. butas*) *n.* instrument used to make holes, hole punch, borer.

pamutat: (*rt. putat*) *n.* appetizer, hors d'oevres.

pamutol: (*rt. putol*) *n.* cutting tool.

pamutong: (*rt. putong*) *n.* something used as a crown.

pamuuín: (*rt. buô*) *v.* cause something to solidify or coagulate.

pamuyat: (*rt. puyat*) *n.* something that keeps someone from sleeping.

pan: (Sp.) *n.* loaf of bread (*pan-amerikano*).

pan-: *pref.* forming instrumental words, *var. of* ***pang-*** before l, r, s, t, d → **panradyo** for the radio, **panlunsód** pertaining to the city, urban, **pandikít** something used as paste, **panlasa** sense of taste, taste bud, **pandamdám** sense of touch; interjection, exclamation, **pandaskól** something intended for everyday use.

panà: *n.* bow and arrow; **mamamanà** *n.* archer; **pumanà** *v.* to shoot with a bow;

namámanà sa dilím *id.* uncertain (shooting an arrow in the dark).
panaan: (*rt. taan*) *n.* reserves for future use.
panabaín: (*rt. tabâ*) *v.* to fatten up.
panabangán: (*rt. tabáng*) *v.* to lose one's interest or taste for.
panabas: (*rt. tabas*) *n.* tool used for cutting patterns; machete.
panabáw: (*rt. sabáw*) *n.* water used for broth.
panabáy: *adv.* simultaneously.
panabi: (*rt. sabi*) *n.* statement; (*rt. tabi*) material used to make an edge or border.
panabí: (*rt. tabí*). *n.* act of defecating; time of defecation; **pánabihan** public toilet; **panabihín** to tell someone to defecate.
panabik: (*rt. sabik*) *n.* eagerness.
panabil: (*rt. tabil*) *n.* temporary cover, screen.
panabing: (*rt. tabing*) *n.* sheet used as a curtain.
panabit: (*rt. sabit*) *n.* something used as a hook.
panablá: (*rt. tablá*) *adj.* ending in a draw.
panabò: (*rt. tabò*) *n.* scooper (made from a coconut).
panabong: (*rt. sabong*) *n.* cock used for cockfighting.
panaka: (*rt. saka*) *adj.* used for farming; **pánakahán** *n.* agricultural land.
panaká: (*rt. saká*) *n.* something used for tracing or copying.
panakál: (*rt. takal*) *n.* receptacle used for measuring grains; (*rt. sakál*) *n.* something used to strangle.
panakali: (*rt. sakali*) *n.* subjunctive.
panaká-nakâ: *adv.* once in a while.
panakaw: (*rt. takaw*) *n.* something that was ordered to be stolen; **panakawin** *v.* to order someone to steal.
panakíp: (*rt. takíp*) *n.* cover, lid; (*slang*) cover-up; **~-butas** *n.* filler for a hole; substitute worker; **~-matá** *n.* blindfold.
panakít: (*rt. sakít*) *n.* something used to hurt or sicken; **panakitán** *n.* having pains.
panakláb: (*rt. sakláb*) *n.* material used for fumigating a woman who has just given birth.
panakláng: (*rt. sakláng*) *n.* fork like frame used to keep a roof intact.
panakláw: (*rt. sakláw*) *n.* brackets, parenthesis.
panakláy: (*rt. sakláy*) *n.* crutch; saddle bag.
panakob: (*rt. takob*) *n.* something used for covering a surface.
panakot: (*rt. takot*) *n.* threat, frightful thing.
panaksák: (*rt. saksák*) *n.* stabbing instrument.
panaksí: (*rt. taksí*) *n.* money used for taxi fare.
panaderyá: (Sp. *panadería*) *n.* bakery.
panadero: (Sp.) *n.* baker.
panaderya: (Sp.) *n.* bakery.
panadlók: (*rt. sadlók*) *n.* scooper.
panag- *pref.* suitable for, for (used with seasons) → **panág-ulán** *n.* something used, done, etc. in the rainy season, **panág-aráw** *n.* something used, done, etc. in the summer.
panagâ: (*rt. tagâ*) *n.* hacking instrument; (*rt. dagâ*) *n.* mouse trap; rat poison.
panagál: (*rt. tagál*) *n.* head wind; difficult work.
panagán: (*rt. dagán*) *n.* paperweight.
panagano: *n.* mode, mood (grammar); dedication; **panaganong pasakalì** *n.* subjunctive mood; **panaganong paturól** *n.* infinitive mood; **panaganong pautós** *n.* imperative mood; **panaganong pawatás** *n.* infinitive mood.
panagap: (*rt. sagap*) *n.* small fish net; utensil used for skimming liquids.
panaghilì: *n.* envy; **mapanaghilì** *adj.* envious.
panaghóy: (*rt. taghóy*) *n.* lament.
panaginip: *n.* dream; ambition; aspiration; **managinip** *v.* to dream; **panagimpán** *n.* dream; ambition; **panaginipin** *v.* to dream about.
panagisag: (*rt. sagisag*) *n.* something used to symbolize.
panagót: (*rt. sagót*) *n.* something used as security, bond; prepared answer; **panagután** *v.* to be responsible for; **panágutan** *n.* responsibility; obligation; **panagutín** *v.* to hold someone responsible for.
panagupà: *n.* head-on collision; hand-to-hand combat.
panagurî: *n.* predicate.
panagután: (*rt. sagót*) *n.* duty; responsibility.
panahanán: (*rt. tahanan*) *v.* to use as one's

residence; be covered with stagnant water.

panahî: (*rt. tahî*) *n.* thread; something used to sew; **pánahian** *n.* tailor shop; sewing kit; **panahiín** *v.* to have someone sew.

panahíg: (*rt. sahíg*) *n.* materials for flooring.

panahod: (*rt. sahod*) *n.* receptacle for catching falling objects; receptacle for rain water.

panahóg: (*rt. sahóg*) *n.* seasoning ingredient.

panahón: (*rt. taón*) *n.* time; period, age; season; weather, era; **hindî panahón** *adj.* out of season; **habang-panahón** *adv.* forever; **magkapanahón** *v.* to have time; **kapanahón** *n.* contemporary; **kapanáhunan** *n.* season; **panahunín** *v.* to conjugate; **pánahunan** *n.* conjugation; **sapanahón** *n.* periodic menstruation; **pinapanahón** *adj.* having menstruation; **may panahón** *adj.* periodic; **nápapanahón** *adj.* opportune, timely; **walâ sa panahón** *adj.* inconvenient; inopportune; out of season; **panahóng háharapín** *n.* future time; **panahóng nakaraán** *n.* past time; **panahóng pandáratíng** *n.* future tense; future; **panahóng pangnagdaán** *n.* past; past tense.

panaíg: (*rt. daíg*) *n.* predominance; prevalence; **panaigán** *v.* to be overwhelmed.

panaing: (*rt. saing*) *n.* rice for cooking.

panalà: (*rt. salà*) *n.* filter, strainer.

panalab: (*rt. salab*) *n.* singing flame (for removing hair, feathers, of butchered animals).

panalabá: (*rt. talabá*) *n.* oyster net.

panalakay: (*rt. salakay*) *n.* weapon used to attack.

panalág: (*rt. salág*) *n.* hand held shield.

panalamín: (*rt. salamín*) *n.* something used as a mirror; **panalaminán** *v.* to look at oneself in a mirror; imitate, emulate.

panalangin: (*rt. dalangin*) *n.* prayer; **manalangin** *v.* to pray.

panali: (*rt. sali*) *n.* entry in a contest.

panalì: (*rt. talì*) *n.* binding string.

pánaliksikán: (*rt. saliksík*) *n.* research institution.

panalig: (*rt. salig*) *n.* trust, confidence; **manalig** *v.* to trust.

panalinghagà: (*rt. talinghagà*) *n.* metaphor; idiom; figure of speech.

panaling-sapatos: (*rt. taling-sapatos*) *n.* shoelaces; improvised shoelaces.

panalitâ: (*rt. salitâ*) *n.* word; part of speech.

panalo: (*rt. talo*) *n.* victor; winning; *adj.* victorious; **manalo** *v.* to win; **panalunan** *n.* winnings; trophy; *v.* to win as a prize.

panaló: (*rt. saló*) *n.* catcher's mitt; something used to catch.

panalok: (*rt. salok*) *n.* scooping device; bucket for bailing out water.

panalop: (*rt. salok*) *n.* peeler.

panalóp: (*rt. salóp*) *n.* measuring receptacle of three liters.

panamà: (*coll.*) *n.* chance, hope; compatibility.

panambák: (*rt. tambák*) *n.* soil used for filling.

panambíl: (*rt. tambíl*) *n.* temporary cover or shade.

panambíl: (*rt. tambíl*) *n.* awning; screen.

panambitan: (*rt. sambít*) *n.* supplication; lamentation.

panamból: (*rt. tamból*) *n.* drumstick.

panambót: (*rt. sambót*) *n.* something used to catch; articles sold to cover losses.

panamlayán: (*rt. tamláy*) *v.* to feel weak; lose interest in.

panampû: (*rt. sampû*) *adj.* tenth.

pananabâ: (*rt. tabâ*) *n.* gaining weight.

pananabako: (*rt. tabako*) *n.* smoking cigars.

pananabáng: (*rt. tabáng*) *n.* loss of interest; becoming tasteless or indifferent.

pananabi: (*rt. sabi*) *n.* telling on others.

pananabí: (*rt. tabí*) *n.* doing along the side; moving one's bowels.

pananabík: (*rt. sabík*) *n.* eagerness.

pananabotahe: (*rt. sabotahe*) *n.* sabotage.

pananakál: (*rt. sakál*) *n.* act of strangling.

pananakali: (*rt. sakali*) *n.* taking chances or risks.

pananakít: (*rt. sakít*) *n.* hurting others; feeling of pain.

pananakot: (*rt. takot*) *n.* scaring; intimidation.

pananaksák: (*rt. saksák*) *n.* act of stabbing.

pananadyâ: (*rt. sadyâ*) *n.* doing intentionally.

pananagâ: (*rt. dagâ*) *n.* stabbing with a knife.

pananaganà: (*rt. saganà*) *n.* abundance.

pananaghóy: (*rt. taghóy*) *n.* act of wailing.

pananagót: (*rt. sagót*) *n.* answering; talking

back rudely; taking responsibility; **pananagutan** *n.* responsibility; duty; **may-pananagutan** (*id.*) *adj.* married.

pananagumpáy: (*rt. tagumpáy*) *n.* success.

pananahî: (*rt. tahî*) *n.* act of sewing.

pananahimik: (*rt. tahimik*) *n.* keeping silent.

pananaíg: (*rt. daíg*) *n.* prevalence; predominance.

pananaingá: (*rt. tainga*) *n.* act of listening; growth of hangnails.

pananalakay: (*rt. salakay*) *n.* attack; raid; assault.

pananalamín: (*rt. salamín*) *n.* using a mirror or sunglasses.

pananalangin: (*rt. dalangin*) *n.* praying.

pananalapí: (*rt salapí*) *n.* finance; funds; currency.

pananalát: (*rt. salát*) *n.* depression, financial crisis; scarcity.

pananalaysáy: (*rt. salaysáy*) *n.* narrating.

pananalaytáy: (*rt. talaytáy*) *n.* passing along the side of; blood flow.

pananalikód: (*rt. talikód*) *n.* defecation.

pananaliksík: (*rt. saliksík*) *n.* research; act of searching.

pananalig: (*rt. salig*) *n.* confidence; trust; faith.

pananalitâ: (*rt. salitâ*) *n.* speech, diction; discourse.

pananalo: (*rt. talo*) *n.* chance of winning; winning.

pananamít: (*rt. damít*) *n.* dress, vestment; way a person dresses; dressing.

pananamláy: (*rt. tamláy*) *n.* feeling tired or depressed; losing interest.

pananampál: (*rt. sampál*) *n.* slapping in the face.

pananámpalasan: (*rt. tampalasan*) *n.* destruction; wasting money.

pananámpalataya: (*rt. sampalataya*) *n.* faith, believing; worship.

pananamsám: (*rt. samsám*) *n.* confiscation.

pananandata: (*rt. sandata*) *n.* revolt; use of weapons.

pananangá: (*rt. sangá*) *n.* growth of branches.

pananangan: (*rt. tangan*) *n.* taking hold; firm stand; depending on something.

panananggá: (*rt. sanggá*) *n.* defending, shielding oneself.

pananangaláng: (*rt. sanggaláng*) *n.* protecting oneself.

pananangól: (*rt. tanggól*) *n.* defending (as an attorney).

pananangháli: (*rt. tangháli*) *n.* eating lunch.

pananaghód: (*rt. tanghód*) *n.* waiting around for something to be given.

pananangis: (*rt. tangis*) *n.* weeping.

pananangos: (*rt. tangos*) *n.* becoming pointed (nose); taking pride in the flattery of others.

pananaog: (*rt. taog*) *n.* going downstairs; getting off; getting down; release from prison.

pananapak: (*rt. tapak*) *n.* stepping on.

pananapát: (*rt. tapát*) *n.* serenading.

pananapatos: (*rt. sapatos*) *n.* wearing shoes.

pananapaw: (*rt. sapaw*) *n.* first growth of a plant (rice).

pananariwà: (*rt. sariwà*) *n.* becoming fresh; improvement of one's health.

pananata: (*rt. panata*) *n.* taking a vow.

pananatili: (*rt. panatili*) *n.* prevalence; continuous existence.

pananaulì: (*rt. saulì*) *n.* return to a former state or condition.

pananáw: (*rt. tanáw*) *n.* eyesight; attitude, point of view; vision.

pananawà: (*rt. sawà*) *n.* satiation, being fed up.

pananawad: (*rt. tawad*) *n.* haggling.

pananayâ: (*rt. tayâ*) *n.* betting.

panandâ: (*rt. tandâ*) *n.* marker; sign used to indicate a location; (*fig.*) memory; **pánandaan** *n.* landmark; system of signs.

panandalán: (*rt. sandál*) *v.* to depend on; lean against; **pánandalan** *n.* something to lean on (back of a chair).

panandalî: (*rt. sandalî*) *adj.* brief in duration.

panandata: (*rt. sandata*) *n.* something used as a weapon.

pananib: (*rt. sanib*) *n.* something used to overlap.

pananím: (*rt. taním*) *n.* staple agricultural crop; seeds used for planting.

pananóng: (*rt. tanóng*) *n.* interrogation mark; *adj.* interrogative.

panansô: (*rt. tansô*) *n.* means to swindle

others.
panangan: (*rt. tangan*) *n.* something used to hold.
pananggá: (*rt. sanggá*) *n.* something used as a shield or covering.
pananggál: (*rt. tanggál*) *n.* device for removing.
pananggaláng: (*rt. sanggaláng*) *n.* something used for protection or defense, shield.
pananggól: (*rt. tanggól*) *n.* defense.
pananghál: (*rt. tanghál*) *n.* something suitable for exhibit.
pananghalì: (*rt. tanghalì*) *n.* food one eats for lunch; lunch money; **pananghalian** *n.* lunch time.
panangì: (*rt. tangì*) *adj.* for special use; (*grammatical*) proper, **pangngalang panangì** proper noun.
panangis: (*rt. tangis*) *n.* weeping; mourning; **panangisan** *v.* to weep about.
pananglâ: (*rt. sanglâ*) *n.* property to be mortgaged.
panangláw: (*rt. tangláw*) *n.* something used to illuminate; light, torch, candle.
panao: (*rt. tao*) *adj.* personal (grammar).
panaog: *n.* going downstairs, descending; discharge of the menses.
panaón: (*rt. taón*) *n.* coincidence; *adj.* simultaneous.
panapal: (*rt. tapal*) *n.* something used as a patch or poultice.
panapì: (*rt. sapì*) *n.* reinforcing material.
panapî: (*rt. tapî*) *n.* apron, something used to wrap around the lower body.
panapín: (*rt sapín*) *n.* something used as an underlayer or undergarment.
panapó: (*rt. sapó*) *n.* something used to support a structure, buttress.
panapók: (*rt. sapók*) *n.* punching; fist fight.
panapón: (*rt. tapón*) *n.* something used as a cork.
panapula: (*rt. sapula*) *n.* something used as a bib.
panará: (*rt. sará*) *n.* something used to close; shutters used to close windows; door lock.
panarak: (*rt. tarak*) *n.* something used for stabbing.
panarangka: (*rt. tarangka*) *n.* something used as a door latch.
panarì: (*rt. tarì*) *n.* spur of a gamecock.
panarili: (*rt. sarili*) *adj.* for one's personal use.
panarók: (*rt. tarók*) *n.* device for sounding depth.
panás: *n.* edema, beriberi; **mamanás** *v.* to have beriberi.
panasá: (*rt. tasá*) *n.* something used to sharpen.
panasilà: **nakapanasilà** *adj.* seated with the legs crossed.
panastás: (*rt. tastás*) *n.* something used to take away stitching.
panata: *n.* vow, promise; **ipanata** *v.* to make a vow; **panatang-makabayan** *n.* pledge to one's country.
panaták: (*rt. taták*) *n.* something used for sealing.
panatag: *adj.* tranquil, calm; **mamanatag** *v.* to be calm; **pumanatag** *v.* to settle down; **ipanatag mo ang loób mo** calm down.
panátiko: (Sp. *fanático*) *n.* fanatic, zealot.
panatili: *n.* permanence; prevalence; continuous stay; **panatilihan** *adj.* permanent.
panaugan: (*rt. taog*) *v.* bring downstairs; have menstrual flow; **pánaugán** *n.* unloading place; place of descent; **panaugin** *v.* go downstairs for something.
panauhan: (*rt. tao*) *n.* person (grammar); dramatis personae.
panauhin: (*rt. tao*) *n.* visitor, guest; **panauhing pandangál** *n.* guest of honor, **panauhing tagapagsalitâ** *n.* guest speaker.
panaulì: (*rt. saulì*) *n.* revival of one's health; return to a former condition.
pánaunan: (*rt. taón*) *n.* fiscal year.
panaw: *n.* sudden disappearance, departure; **panawan** *v.* to abandon; be deprived of; **pumanaw** *v.* to leave, depart; die; **panawan ng pag-asa** *v.* to lose hope.
panawag: (*rt. tawag*) *n.* term for; **panawagan** *n.* public appeal; **panawag-pansín** *n.* attention getter.
panawain: (*rt. sawà*) *v.* to satiate; gratify.
panawatâ: (*rt. sawatâ*) *n.* something used to check or restrain.
panawáy: (*rt. sawáy*) *n.* something used to

restrain or prohibit.

panawíd: (*rt. tawíd*) *n.* something used to carry across; **panawíd-buhay** *n.* something eaten in order to survive; **panawíd-gutom** *n.* something eaten to keep off hunger.

panáy: *adj.* all, every; steady, regular; unmixed, pure; **di-~** irregular; **panayan** *adv.* regularly; without interruption; **panayín** *v.* to do regularly; complete everything; **panáy ang kayod** *id.* working continuously.

panaya: (*rt. taya*) *n.* calculator.

panayâ: (*rt. tayâ*) *n.* money intended for betting; gambling chips; **panayaán** *v.* to place bets.

panayám: *n.* lecture; interview; conference; **magpanayám** *v.* to lecture; **pánayaman** *n.* lecture hall.

panayáw: (*rt. sayáw*) *n.* dance music.

pandaán ng lagarì: *n.* saw set.

pandadaki: *n. Tabernaemontana pandacaque* shrub with milky sap, white flowers, and red fruits.

pandák: *adj.* short (stature).

pandán: *n.* screw pine.

pandanggo: (Sp. *fandango*) *n.* fandango dance; **pandanggo sa ilaw** *n.* graceful dance by women balancing oil lamps.

pandarás: *n.* carpenter's adz.

pandáw: *n.* inspection of traps; **pandawín** *v.* to inspect traps.

pandawan: *n.* sergeant fish.

pandáy: *n.* blacksmith; **~-bakal** *n.* blacksmith; **~-kabán** *n.* locksmith; **~-gintô** *n.* goldsmith; **~-pilak** *n.* silversmith; **~-yero** *n.* tinsmith; **pandayín** *v.* to shape metal; to train someone very well.

panderetas: (Sp.) *n.* tambourine.

pandewang: (*rt. iwang*) *n.* toilet paper; something used to wipe the anus after defecating.

pandisál: (Sp. *pan de sal*) *n.* kind of sweet bread cooked in small loaves.

pandiwà: (*rt. diwà*) *n.* verb; **pandiwang kátawanín** *n.* intransitive verb; **pandiwang palipát** *n.* transitive verb; **pandiwang pangatníg** *n.* copula; linking verb.

pandiwarì: *n.* participle, gerund; *adj.* verbal.

pandóng: *n.* head covering; **~-ahas** *n.* species of poisonous fungus.

pandót: *adj.* sensual (women).

panhík: *n.* going upstairs; **mamanhík** *v.* to appeal; **panhikán** *v.* to take upstairs to someone; **panhikín** *v.* to go upstairs to meet someone; **pumanhík** *v.* to go upstairs; enter; **magpanhík** *v.* to bring upstairs; **panhík-panaog** *n.* going up and down continuously.

panibák: (*rt. sibák*) *n.* something used to chop wood.

panibág: (*rt. tibág*) *n.* something used to crush rocks.

panibago: (*rt. bago*) *adj.* renewed; **pagpapanibago** *n.* renewal; **panibaguhin** *v.* to renew.

panibát: (*rt. sibát*) *n.* something used as a spear.

panibukas: (*rt. bukas*) *n.* postponement; next day; tomorrow; **panibukasin** *v.* to postpone until tomorrow.

panibughô: *n.* jealousy.

panibulos: *n.* complete trust; **manibulos** *v.* to have complete trust in.

paniká: *n.* poor growth of plants.

panikad: (*rt. sikad*) *n.* something used for kicking.

panikalà: *n.* enterprise, scheme.

panikalâ: *n.* irony.

panikbí: *n.* eyetooth, upper canine tooth.

panikì: *n.* fruit bat; **parang panikì** *id.* sleeping all day.

panikluhód. (*rt. tikluhód*) *n.* falling on one's knees; entreaty.

paniksík: (*rt. siksík*) *n.* stuffing; something used to stuff or insert into an opening; **pániksikan** *n.* thick crowd of people; shoving one another; stuffing.

panig: *n.* side; panel; division, part, section; surface; **pagpanig** *n.* partiality; **panigan** *v.* to take the side of someone; panel; **kapanig** *n.* partisan, supporter; **pumanig** *v.* to support, side with; **may-pinápanigan** *adj.* biased; **waláng-pinápanigan** *adj.* unbiased; **panig-panig** *adj.* in groups.

paniga: (Sp. *fanega*) *n.* one and a half bushel container for measuring grains.

panigâ: (*rt. sigâ*) *n.* things used to start a

bonfire.

panigasán: (*rt. tigás*) *v.* to have an erection; **panigasín** *v.* to cause an erection.

panihalà: *n.* disposition; management; responsibility.

paniláb: (*rt. siláb*) *n.* something used to start a fire.

panilág: (*rt. silág*) *m.* magnifying glass.

panilán: *n.* beehive; honeycomb.

panilaw: (*rt. silaw*) *n.* something used to dazzle or dim the vision; **panilawán** *v.* to become jaundiced (eyes).

panilò: (*rt. silò*) *n.* something used as a lasso.

panimâ: (*rt. simâ*) *n.* small net used for fishing or shrimping.

panimbá: (*rt. simbá*) *n.* clothes for mass.

panimbâ: (*rt. timbâ*) *n.* something used as a bucket.

panimbáng: (*rt. timbáng*) *n.* weighing scale; counterbalance; **panimbangán** *v.* to balance oneself; try to get along with; **pánimbangan** *n.* seesaw; tightrope.

panimdím: *n.* misgivings; resentment, grudge.

panimót: (*rt. simót*) *n.* device for picking up things.

panimplá: (*rt. timplá*) *n.* condiment.

panimulâ: (*rt. simulâ*) *adj.* introductory; preliminary; *n.* start, beginning; **panimulán** *v.* to start.

paninág: (*rt. sinág*) *n.* magnifying glass.

panindá: (*rt. tindá*) *n.* goods for sale, merchandise; *adj.* for sale.

panindí: (*rt. sindí*) *n.* lighter; (*rt. tindí*) paperweight, something used to press down objects.

paninekas: (*rt. tekas*) *n.* swindling; stealing.

paninibago: (*rt. bago*) *n.* feeling of unfamiliarity.

paninibughô: (*rt. bughô*) *n.* jealousy.

paninikad: (*rt. sikad*) *n.* kicking.

paninikas: (*rt. tekas*) *n.* swindling; stealing (*paninekas*).

paninikíl: (*rt. sikíl*) *n.* act of oppressing.

paninikíp: (*rt. sikíp*) *n.* becoming tight.

paninikís: (*rt. tikís*) *n.* doing intentionally.

paninikít: (*rt. dikít*) *n.* sticking; adhesion.

paninikluhód: (*rt. tikluhód*) *n.* supplication.

paninikmát: (*rt. sikmát*) *n.* sudden bite or snatch.

paninikó: (*rt. sikó*) *n.* hitting or shoving with the elbow.

paniniksík: (*rt. siksík*) *n.* pushing through; stuffing.

paniniktík: (*rt. tiktík*) *n.* spying.

paninikwát: (*rt. sikwát*) *n.* stealing.

paninigarilyo: (*rt. sigarilyo*) *n.* smoking cigarettes.

paninigaro: (*rt. sigaro*) *n.* smoking cigars.

paninigás: (*rt. tigás*) *n.* becoming hard; erection of penis; ~ **ng katawán** *n.* laziness.

paninigáw: (*rt. sigáw*) *n.* shouting.

paniniíl: (*rt. siíl*) *n.* oppressing, oppressive treatment.

paninilbí: (*rt. silbí*) *n.* working as a servant.

paninilip: (*rt. silip*) *n.* peeping.

paninilò: (*rt. silò*) *n.* lassoing, snaring.

paninilóng: (*rt. silóng*) *n.* feeling inferior; peeping under a house.

paninimót: (*rt. simót*) *n.* picking up; consuming everything.

paninimpuhô: (*rt. timpuhô*) *n.* kneeling on one's feet.

panininđák: (*rt. sindák*) *n.* act of frightening, terrorizing.

panininingalâ: (*rt. tingalâ*) *n.* looking at things above; turning upward; **paninigaláng-pugad** *n.* period of time when a teenage boy starts courting girls.

paniningkád: (*rt. tingkád*) *n.* brightness of color.

paniningkayád: (*rt. tingkayád*) *n.* squatting.

paniningíl: (*rt. singíl*) *n.* collecting.

paninipà: (*rt. sipà*) *n.* kicking.

paniniphayò: (*rt. siphayò*) *n.* act of mistreating, disappointing.

paninipì: (*rt. sipì*) *n.* copying; quoting.

paninipit: (*rt. sipit*) *n.* grabbing with the claws; grasping.

paninirà: (*rt. sirà*) *n.* vandalism; destroying things; slander; **paninirang-puri** *n.* slander, defamation.

paninirá: (*rt. tirá*) *n.* act of residing.

paninisi: (*rt. sisi*) *n.* blaming.

paninisid: (*rt. sisid*) *n.* diving underwater.

paninitá: (*rt. sitá*) *n*. interrogating, interrogation.
paniniwalà: (*rt. tiwalà*) *n*. act of believing, trusting; faith; confidence.
paniniyák: (*rt. tiyák*) *n*. accusing; assuring.
paningá: (*rt. tingá*) *n*. something used as a toothpick.
paningas-kugon: (*rt. ningas-kugon*) *adj*. with sudden effort.
paningkáw: (*rt. singkáw*) *n*. something used to hitch or harness; animal used as a beast of burden.
paningín: (*rt. tingín*) *n*. opinion, view; sense of sight.
paningit: (*rt. singit*) *n*. filler, filling.
panipà: (*rt. sipà*) *n*. something used to kick; kicking foot.
panipat: (*rt. sipat*) *n*. target finder.
panipì: (*rt. sipì*) *n*. quotation marks; copy machine.
panipit: (*rt. sipit*) *n*. claw, nippers; hairclip; paper clip.
panipol: (*rt. sipol*) *n*. whistle, siren.
panirà: (*rt. sirà*) *n*. something used to destroy or ruin; defaming remark.
pánirahan: (*rt. tirahan*) *n*. housing site; den, lair; **panirahanin** *v*. to relocate people to a new housing site.
panís: *adj*. spoiled; stale; **mapanis** *v*. to become spoiled; **panis ang laway** *id*. absent-minded (sputum is spoiled).
panisid: (*rt. sisid*) *n*. something used for diving.
panit: *n*. tonsure; skin abrasion, shaved part of the head; **panít** *adj*. shaved; skinned; **panitan** *v*. to shave off; peel off.
panitik: (*rt. titik*) *n*. ability to write; **pánitikán** *n*. literature.
paniwalà: (*rt. tiwalà*) *n*. belief; confidence, trust; **paniwalaan** *v*. to believe in; have trust in; **paniwalain** *v*. to make someone believe, convince.
panlalaki: (*rt. lalaki*) *adj*. for men; masculine.
panlapì: (*rt. lapì*) *n*. affix.
panloloób: (*rt. loób*) *n*. plundering, pillage.
panós: *n*. squid.
panot: *n*. shaved part of the head; **panót** *adj*. close-cropped (hair); **panutan** *v*. to shave the hair off someone.
pansán: **kapansán** *n*. inconvenience; injury, accident.
pansín: *n*. notice, attention; recognition; **mapansín** *v*. to happen to notice; recognize; **mapapansín** *adj*. noticeable, perceptible; **pumansín** *v*. to pay attention to, observe, notice; **kulang sa pansín** *adj*. lacking attention.
pansíng: *n*. fishing hook with line and sinker; **pansingín** *v*. to catch fish with fishing tackle.
pansipít: *n*. kind of rat trap.
pansít: *n*. noodles.
pansól: *n*. spring of water.
pantál: *n*. welt, weal; hives; **mamantál** *v*. to become swollen.
pantalán: (Sp.) *n*. pier, wharf.
pantalón: (Sp.) *n*. pants, trousers.
pantalya: (Sp. *pantalla*) *n*. lamp shade; dummy, person acting as a front.
pantás: *n*. wise person, scholar; *adj*. scholarly, erudite; **~-wikà** *n*. linguist, philologist.
pantát: *n*. catfish.
pantáw: (Ch.) *adj*. on credit.
pantáy: *adj*. even, equal, level; flat; smooth; *n*. black-finned shark; **di-~** *adj*. unequal; **kapantáy** *adj*. level; *n*. equal; **magpantáy** *v*. to align; **pamantayan** *n*. standard, average, norm; unit; **pantayín** *v*. to even off, level; **waláng kapantáy** *adj*. unparalleled, without equal; incomparable; **pantáy-paá** (*id*.) dead; **pantay-pantayín** *v*. to make everything equal.
panti: (Eng.) *n*. panties; kind of gill net.
pantí: *n*. dragnet.
pantíg: *n*. syllable; resonant sound; **magpantíg** *v*. to syllabify.
pantíng: *n*. flint stroke; heightened anger; **nagpantíng ang tainga** *id*. angered (ear became hot).
pantiyón: (Sp. *panteón*) *n*. cemetery, pantheon, grave.
pantók: *n*. summit, top.
pantóg: *n*. bladder.
pantót: *n*. tedium, boredom.

pantukoy: (*rt. tukoy*) *n.* article (in grammar).
pantuto: (*rt. tuto*) *n.* ruler; moral guide; **kapanutuhán** *n.* discipline; **panutuhan** *v.* to discipline someone.
panubà: (*rt. subà*) *n.* act used to swindle.
panubali: (*rt. subali*) *n.* something used to object; adversative conjunction, i.e. *subali, nguni, dátapwâ.*
panubig: (*rt. tubig*) *n.* broth water.
panubíg: (*rt. tubig*) *n.* urination; **panubigán** *v.* to urinate into; **pánubigan** *n.* urinal; **pánubigín** *adj.* frequently urinating.
panubo: (*rt. tubo*) *n.* something used as a pipe.
panubós: (*rt. tubós*) *n.* ransom money; money for redeeming a mortgage.
panukà: (*rt. sukà*) *n.* something used as vinegar.
panukalà: *n.* plan, project; resolution; **magpanukalà** *v.* to plan; propose; sponsor; **panukalang-batas** *n.* bill, proposed law.
panukat: (*rt. sukat*) *n.* something used for measuring; **~-lupà** *n.* surveying instrument.
panukí: *n.* ear pick.
panukláy: (*rt. sukláy*) *n.* something used as a comb.
panuklí: (*rt. suklí*) *n.* change (lower denominations).
panukod: (*rt. tukod*) *n.* support for a structure.
panukól: *n.* chisel.
panudlóng: (*rt. sudlóng*) *n.* conjunction; something added in order to increase the size.
panuga: (*rt. suga*) *n.* tether.
panugál: (*rt. sugál*) *n.* gambling money.
panugat: (*rt. sugat*) *n.* instrument used for inflicting wounds.
panugpô: (*rt. sugpô*) *n.* something used to prevent or suppress.
panugpóng: (*rt. sugpóng*) *n.* something used to increase length or width.
panugtóg: (*rt. tugtóg*) *n.* something used in playing a musical instrument.
panuhay: (*rt. suhay*) *n.* prop; support.
panuhol: (*rt. suhol*) *n.* money to be used as a bribe.
pánulaan: (*rt. tulâ*) *n.* poetry.
punulat: (*rt. sulat*) *n.* writing materials; **panulatan** *n.* literature; style of writing.
pánulayan: (*rt. tulay*) *n.* conductor of electricity; channel.
pánuldikan: (*rt. tuldík*) *n.* accentuation rules.
panulok: (*rt. sulok*) *n.* corner; **panulukan** *n.* intersection.
panulog: (*rt. tulog*) *n.* sleeping clothes.
panuluyan: (*rt. tulóy*) *n.* lodging house.
panuma: (*rt. suma*) *n.* adding machine.
panumbalikin: (*rt. tumbalik*) *v.* to restore to the former condition.
pánumbasan: (*rt. tumbás*) *n.* rate of exchange.
panumpâ: (*rt. sumpâ*) *n.* words of an oath.
panundán: (*rt. sundó*) *v.* to follow an example.
panundól: (*rt. sundól*) *n.* hole puncher.
panundót: (*rt. sundót*) *n.* poking instrument.
panunód: (*rt. sunód*) *adv.* one after another.
panunog: (*rt. sunog*) *n.* something used to burn.
pánuntunan: *n.* guide, basis; regulation; principle.
panunugat: (*rt. sugat*) *n.* wounding.
panungkáb: (*rt. sungkáb*) *n.* device used to pry open a window.
panungkít: (*rt. sungkít*) *n.* pole with a hook used to gather fruits.
panuring: (*rt. turing*) *n.* modifier (grammar).
panurò: (*rt. turò*) *n.* pointer.
panursí: (*rt. sursí*) *n.* materials used for darning.
panuto: (*rt. tuto*) *n.* indicator; spiritual guide.
panutsá: (Sp. *panocha*) *n.* molasses cooked with peanuts in small cane; sugarcane molasses.
panuyô: (*rt. tuyô*) *n.* drying device.
panuyod: (*rt. suyod*) *n.* lice comb; harrow.
panyero: (Sp. *compañero*) *n.* colleague.
panyô: (Sp. *paño*) *n.* handkerchief; **panyudemano** *n.* hand cloth.
panyuelo: (Sp. *pañuelo*) *n.* shawl, shoulder kerchief.
panyuleta: (Sp. *pañoleta*) *n.* triangular shawl.
panyulón: (Sp. *pañolon*) *n.* large shawl.
pang-: *pref.* 1. forms instrumental nouns or adjectives → **pang-init** *n.* heater, device for heating, **pangwalís** *n.* something used for sweeping; 2. forms gerunds of goal focus or *mang-* verbs → **pang-uulo** hitting with the

head, **pang-unawà** understanding.
pangá: *n.* jaw; **pangahán** *adj.* with a big jaw.
pangakò: (*rt. akò*) *n.* promise.
pangahás: (*rt. ahás*) **mapangahás** *adj.* daring, rash, bold; daredevil; **pangahasán** *v.* to dare, venture; presume.
pangál: *adj.* blunt, dull; tired.
pang-al: *adj.* carried between the teeth.
pangalakal: (*rt. kalakal*) *adj.* commercial, having to do with business.
pangalan: (*rt. ngalan*) *n.* name.
pangalang: (*rt. kalang*) *n.* something used as a wedge.
pangalawá: (*rt. dalawá*) *adj.* second; *n.* assistant, associate; vice-; substitute.
pangalawit: (*rt. kalawit*) *n.* pole used to pick fruits.
pangaliskís: (*rt. kaliskís*) *n.* device used to scale fish.
pangalmót: (*rt. kalmót*) *n.* harrowing device.
pangalos: (*rt. kalos*) *n.* strickle used for leveling grain.
pangaltás: (*gram.*) *n.* sign of omission.
pangalubaybáy: (*rt. baybáy*) *n.* navigating close to shore.
pangama: (*rt. kama*) *n.* something for bed use.
pangamán: *n.* step relationship; **amáng** ~ *n.* stepfather; **anák na** ~ *n.* stepchild; **ináng** ~ *n.* stepmother.
pangambá: *n.* dread, fear, apprehension.
pangamot: (*rt. kamot*) *n.* scratching device.
panganák: (*rt. anák*) *n.* time of birth; **páng-anakan** *n.* delivery room.
panganay: *n.* first born child.
panganib: (*rt. nganib*) *n.* danger; **panganiban** *v.* to be in danger from; to fear.
panganino: *n.* inferiority complex.
panganurin: *n.* thin, high clouds.
pangangalap: (*rt. kalap*) *n.* recruitment; enlisting; logging; soliciting, collecting.
pangangandí: (*rt. andí*) *n.* estrus.
pangangapitál: (*rt. kapitál*) *n.* investing money.
pangangasiwà: (*rt. asiwà*) *n.* direction; management.
pangangatawán: (*rt. katawán*) *n.* physique.
pangangathâ: (*rt. kathâ*) *n.* composing literary works.
pangangatwiran: (*rt. tuwíd*) *n.* reasoning.
pangapit: (*rt. kapit*) *n.* hands (something used to hold).
pangaral: (*rt. aral*) *n.* teachings, parental advice; **pangaralan** *v.* to preach to.
pangarap: (*rt. arap*) *n.* dream; **mapangarapín** *adj.* dreamy.
pang-araw: (*rt. araw*) *adj.* for daytime use; day worker.
pangarera: (*rt. karera*) *n.* vehicle used for racing; race horse; money used for betting on the races.
Pangasinán: [*pron. pang.ga.si.nán*] *n.* ethnic group and language from Pangasinan Province.
pangat: **nakapangat** *adj.* exposed to danger.
pangát: *n.* fish cooked in water with vinegar and salt.
pangatahuan: (*rt. tahô*) *n.* omen, sign; superstition.
pangatang: (*rt. katang*) *n.* something used as a wedge.
pangatî: (*rt. katî*) *n.* decoy.
pangatló: (*rt. tatlo*) *adj.* third.
pangatníg: (*rt. katníg*) *n.* conjunction (grammar).
pangatwiranan: (*rt. ka-tuwid*) *v.* to justify, give reasons for.
pangaw: *n.* handcuffs; stocks; dungeon.
pangawíng: *adj.* linking, something used to hold.
pangawít: (*rt. kawít*) *n.* hook used for picking fruits.
pangayas: (*rt. kayas*) *n.* knife used for smoothing the edges of a stick.
pangayod: (*rt. kayod*) *n.* device used for grating or scraping.
pangkál: *adj.* slow-moving, lazy; muscular but simple; visible above ground (protruding roots).
pangkasalukuyan: *adj.* present (grammar).
pangkát: *n.* section, division; article; segment; crowd, mass; unit; **magpangkát** *v.* to join in a group, band together; **pangkatín** *v.* to classify, distinguish, separate into groups.
pangkista: (*slang*, Eng. punk) *n.* rocker.

pangkó: *n*. armful; *adj*. carried in the arms; **pangkuhín** *v*. to carry in the arms.
pangkól: *adj*. pressed together.
panggáp: **magpanggáp** *v*. to pretend; profess; disguise; **pagpapanggáp** *n*. pretense; **mapagpanggáp** *v*. to be pretentious.
panggás: **panggasín** *v*. to stroke the feathers of a rooster.
pangginggi: *n*. kind of card game.
panghál: *adj*. cold (food); tired of (waiting).
panghalíp: (*rt. halíp*) *n*. pronoun.
panghí: *n*. odor of fresh urine.
pangiki: *n*. chill, shaking.
pangikig: (*rt. kikig*) *n*. hen's feather; ear swab.
pangil: *n*. fang; tusk; **pangilán** *adj*. with large tusks or fangs.
pangilabot: (*rt. kilabot*) *n*. goose flesh.
pangilak: *n*. raising funds.
pangilin: *n*. abstinence; observation of a holy day; holiday.
pangimay: *n*. anesthetic. (*pamanhíd*)
panginoón: *n*. lord, master.
pangingkíl: (*coll.*) *n*. extortion.
pangingilíg: (*rt. kilíg*) *n*. twitching, act of being thrilled.
panginoón: (*rt. ginoó*) *n*. master, lord; boss.
pangingibig: (*rt. ibig*) *n*. courtship.
pangit: *adj*. ugly; **pumangit** *v*. to become ugly; **pinangitan** *n*. moray.
pangita: (*rt. kita*) *adj*. face to face; *n*. face to face meeting; **pángitain** *n*. omen, vision.
pangitî: *n*. smile; piping in dressmaking.
pangiwî: *adj*. distorted.
pangláw: *n*. melancholy, loneliness; **mamangláw** *v*. to feel lonely.
pangnán: *n*. small fishing basket.
pangngalan: (*rt. ngalan*) *n*. noun.
pangô: *adj*. snub-nosed.
pangód: *adj*. blunt, dull.
pangós: *n*. chewing sugarcane.
pang-ukol: (*rt. ukol*) *n*. preposition.
pang-ugnáy: (*rt. ugnáy*) *n*. conjunction.
pangulay: (*rt. kulay*) *n*. dye, coloring.
pangulo: (*rt. ulo*) *n*. president, leader, chief; **tagapangulo** *n*. chairman; **pangulong-lungsód** capital city; **panguluhan** *v*. to lead; preside.
pangulóng: (*rt. kulóng*) *n*. parenthesis; enclosure.
pangulót: (*rt. kulót*) *n*. hair curling device.
pangultí: (*rt. kultí*) *n*. device for tanning.
pangumpisalán: (*rt. kumpisál*) *v*. to confess.
panguna, pang-una: (*rt. una*) *adj*. first; **pángunahín** *adj*. first class; principal; chief, main.
pangungusap: (*rt. usap*) *n*. sentence, statement; promise.
pang-urì: (*rt. urì*) *n*. adjective.
pangusap: (*rt. usap*) *n*. reprimand.
pangwisík: (*rt. wisík*) *n*. sprinkler.
paód: *n*. yoke.
paos: *n*. hoarseness; **paós** *adj*. hoarse.
papa: (Sp.) *n*. pope; standard width of textiles.
papà: (*babytalk*) baby talk for food, eat.
papá: *n*. gentle slope.
papâ: *adj*. low and flat.
papák: (Ch.) *adj*. eaten without rice.
papakol: *n*. trigger fish.
papág-: *pref*. used with suffix *-in* or *-an* to form causative verbs → **papágpirasuhin** *v*. to make someone chop into pieces, **papágabugaduhin** *v*. to ask someone to get a lawyer, **papágmadliín** *v*. to have someone hurry up; **papág-ambagín** *v*. to make someone contribute.
papag: *n*. low bamboo bed.
papagayo: (Sp. *papagallo*) *n*. green parrot.
papalíd: *n*. scarecrow.
paparangga: (*slang*) *n*. prostitute.
papás: *adj*. unroofed.
papaw: *n*. species of wild duck.
papawirín: *n*. firmament.
papaya: (Sp.) *n*. papaya.
papél: (Sp.) *n*. paper; role of a character; reputation; ~ **de bangko** *n*. banknote; ~ **de liha** *n*. sandpaper; **papeles** *n*. legal papers, documents; **pangunahíng** ~ *n*. leading role; **pumapél** (*slang*) *v*. to make advances.
papeles: (Sp.) *n*. legal papers, documents.
papeleta: (Sp.) *n*. slip of paper; pass, permit.
papelito: (Sp.) *n*. small piece of paper.
para$_1$: *interj*. Stop!; **pumara** *v*. to stop; **parahán** *n*. stopping place; **parahanin** *v*. to reduce the speed of; **parahin** *v*. to stop (a

bus by waving the hand).
para$_2$: *conj.* for, on behalf of; so that; as if; *adv.* like, as; it seems.
pará: (Sp. *comparar*) **ipará** *v.* to compare.
paraán: (*rt.* *daán*) *n.* method, system; *adj.* about to pass; *v.* to have someone drop by a place to pick something up; (*imperative*) let me pass; **pamaraanán** *n.* ways and means; **paraanan** *v.* to go over, study, pass over; **paraán-daán** *adj.* passing back and forth.
parábola: *n.* parable.
parák$_1$: *n.* stamping of the feet; *adj.* flirtatious; meaningless.
parák$_2$: (*slang*) *n.* police.
parakaída: (Sp. *paracaída*) *n.* parachute.
parada$_1$: (Sp.) *n.* parade; **magparada** *v.* to parade.
parada$_2$: (Sp.) *n.* park, parking; unloading wholesale merchandise; **pumarada** *v.* to park; **nakaparada** *adj.* parked; **páradahán** *n.* parking lot; place of unloading wholesale merchandise.
parada$_3$: (Sp.) *n.* amount of bets put on a cock in cockfighting; **páradahán** *n.* usual amount of bets placed in a cockfight.
parado: (Sp.) *adj.* parked, stopped; spiritless.
paradusdós: *n.* ground sticky rice rolled in balls and cooked in coconut milk.
paragala: (Sp.) *n.* tip (for services).
paragat: (rt. *dagat*) *v.* to go to the sea; **paragát** *adv.* towards the sea.
paragatos: (Sp.) *n.* canvas sandal.
paragila: *n.* showing off, vanity.
paragos: (*rt.* *dagos*) *n.* sled, sledge; harrow.
paraíso: (Sp.) *n.* paradise.
parait: *n.* ally; alliance.
paralelo: (Sp.) *adj.* parallel.
parali: *n.* denunciation, accusation; boasting.
paralis: *n.* go-between; log placed under a heavy object to help move it.
paralisá: (Sp. *paralizar*) **pagkaparalisá** *n.* paralysis; **paralisahín** *v.* to paralyze, cripple; **paralisado** *adj.* paralyzed.
paraluman: *n.* muse; (*obs.*) magnetic needle.
param: **maparam** *v.* to disappear, vanish.
paramdám: (rt. *damdám*) *n.* hint, insinuation; **paramdamán** *v.* to insinuate, hint to; **paramdamín** *v.* to have someone feel or experience something.
parami: (rt. *dami*) *n.* amount added to increase quantity; **paramí** *adj.* increasing in quantity; **paramihin** *v.* to multiply; increase quantity.
paramin: *v.* to wipe out, get rid of.
paramít: (rt. *damít*) *n.* clothing allowance; paper used to cover a kite; *adj.* supplied with clothing.
paramtán: (rt. *damít*) *v.* to clothe, dress.
Paranan: *n.* ethnic group and language from Isabela Province, Luzon.
parang$_1$: [*para* + *-ng*] it seems, like.
parang$_2$: *n.* uncultivated field; **kaparangan** *n.* meadow, prairie.
parangál: (*rt.* *dangál*) *n.* honor; **parangalán** *v.* to honor.
parangparang: *n.* dorab fish.
parangyâ: **magparangyâ** *v.* to parade; display; **magpagparangyâ** *adj.* flamboyant, flashy; pompous; **karangyaán** *n.* ostentation.
paraos: (rt. *daos*) *n.* sponsored celebration; doing something to pass away the time; **pagparausan** *v.* to pass away the time.
parapâ: (rt. *dapâ*) *adj.* with the face and stomach down; **parapaín** *v.* to put someone flat on his stomach.
parapara: *n.* everything; everyone.
parapernál: (Sp. *parafernal*) *adj.* paraphernal.
parapina: (Sp. *parafina*) *n.* paraffin.
parapit: *n.* a kind of strong poultice.
párapo: (Sp. *párrafo*) *n.* paragraph.
pararak: **kapararakan** *n.* use, value; advantage.
pararayos: (Sp. *pararrayos*) *n.* lightning rod.
parás: *adj.* pungent, hot to the taste.
parasol: (Eng.) *n.* parasol, sun umbrella.
paratang: *n.* accusation, charge; complaint; **paratangan** *v.* to accuse, incriminate; **magparatang** *v.* to accuse.
parati: (*rt.* *dati*) *adv.* always; **páratihán** *adj.* permanent.
paratíng: (*rt.* *datíng*) *n.* gift; message sent; (*fig.*) bribe.
paratipus: (Sp. *paratifus*) *n.* paratyphoid.
paráw: *n.* kind of large sailboat.
parayâ: **magparayâ** *v.* to be tolerant; **mapag-**

parayâ *adj*. tolerant.
parayaw: *n*. false front, ostentation.
parkas: (Sp. *parca*) (*lit.*) *n*. goddess of faith.
parke: (Sp. *parque*) *n*. park.
pardilya: *n*. brim of a hat.
pardo: (Sp. *fardo*) *n*. bale.
pare: *abbrev*. of *kumpadre* → friend, mate.
parè: (Sp. *padre*) *n*. priest.
pareha: (Sp. *pareja*) *n*. couple, match; **kapareha** *n*. partner; **magpareha** *v*. to pair off, form in pairs; race with.
pareho: (Sp. *parejo*) *adj*. same; similar; equal; **kapareho** *n*. duplicate, match; **ipareho** *v*. to compare; **magpareho** *v*. to be equal; **pagkapareho** *n*. equality; **pumareho** *v*. to match (in a contest); be equal; **paré-pareho** *adj*. all the same; **parehong kaliwâ ang paá** *id.* with two left feet (cannot dance).
pares: (Sp.) *n*. pair; **pares-pares** *adj*. in pairs.
pargito: *n*. small snapper fish.
pargo: *n*. flame-colored snapper fish; **pargung-ilog** *n*. silver-spotted gray snapper.
parì: (Sp. *padre*) *n*. priest.
párián: (*obs.*) *n*. plaza; market place.
parikalâ: *n*. supposition; presumption.
parikít: *n*. decoration, adornment; kindling (for a fire); **parikít-ugit** *n*. remora fish; **parikít-bangkâ** *n*. sucking fish.
parihabâ: (*rt. habâ*) *n*. rectangle.
parihuwela: (Sp. *parihuela*) *n*. barrow.
paríl: *adj*. flat-nosed.
parilya: (Sp. *parilla*) *n*. grill; gridiron; (*coll.*) man's chest from shoulder to shoulder.
pariníg: (rt. *diníg*) *n*. allusion, innuendo, indirect reference; **parinigán** *v*. to say a derogatory remark to, make an indirect reference.
parinlas: *n*. species of small tree.
parípa: (*rt. ripa*) *n*. raffle.
paripá: *adj*. with the arms extended sideways.
parirala: *n*. phrase.
paris: (Sp. *pares*) *n*. pair, set; couple; *adj*. like, as, as well as; **kaparis** *n*. one of a pair, mate; equal; **waláng kaparis** *adj*. without equal.
parisidyo: (Sp.) *n*. parricide.
parisukát: *n*. square.
parisulok: *adj*. with all angles equal.
parito: (*rt. dito*) *interj*. come here; **paritó** *adj*. coming here.
pariugát: *n*. square root.
pariyán: (rt. *diyán*) *v*. to go there; *adj*. going there; *adv*. towards that place.
parlamento: (Sp.) *n*. parliament.
parmasya: (Sp. *farmacia*) *n*. pharmacy, drugstore.
pároko: (Sp. *parroco*) *n*. parish priest.
parokya: (Sp. *parroquia*) *n*. parish.
parokyano: (Sp. *parroquiano*) *n*. customer, client; parishioner.
parodya: (Sp. *parodia*) *n*. parody.
paról: (Sp. *farol*) *n*. lantern; street lamp; (Eng.) *n*. parole.
parola: (Sp. *farola*) *n*. lighthouse.
parolero: *n*. lighthouse keeper; lantern maker.
paroón: (rt. *doón*) *v*. to go there; *adj*. going there; *adv*. towards that place; **paroó't-parito** *adj*. back and forth, to and fro.
paróparó: *n*. butterfly; butterfly fish.
paros: *n*. species of clam with a black shell.
parsela: (Sp. *parcela*) *n*. parcel.
parte: (Sp.) *n*. part, portion; role in a play; share; **partihán** *v*. to give someone a share.
partida: (Sp.) *n*. departure; group of things taken as one; certificate; margin (of advantage); consignment of goods.
partidaryo: (Sp. *partidario*) *n*. partisan (usually used with a negative connotation).
partidista: (Sp.) *n*. partisan.
partido: (Sp.) *n*. party.
parugô: (*rt. dugô*) *n*. duel that ends at the first drop of blood; rapacity; blood letting; something that causes bleeding; **paruguín** *v*. to bleed.
párunungán: (rt. *dunong*) *n*. talent competition.
parunggít: (*rt. dunggit*) *n*. allusion, indirect reference; **párunggitan** *n*. exchange of innuendoes.
parúparó: *n*. butterfly; butterfly fish.
parusa: (*rt. dusa*) *n*. punishment; **maparusahan** *v*. to be punished; **párusahán** *n*. place where people are punished; **parusahan** *v*. to punish; require to pay a fine.
pasa- *pref.* prefix of direction → **pasa-Bulacan** *v*. to go to Bulacan.

pasa: *n.* cloth girdle; (Sp.) pass; **ipasa** *v.* to pass over, hand over something; **pasado** *adj.* passed, approved; **pagpasá** *n.* qualification, passing; **pumasá** (*coll.*) *v.* to win a girl; **pasáng-krus** *id.* unhappy.

pasâ: *n.* bruise; *adj.* bruised.

pasak: *n.* plug, stopper; dowel; **ipasak** *v.* to plug; **pamasak-butas** *id.* substitute (hole filler); **napasakan ang bibíg** *id.* bribed (mouth was stuffed).

pasakalì: (*rt. sakali*) *adj.* subjunctive (grammar).

pasakalye: (Sp. *pasacalle*) *n.* introductory notes before a song.

pasada: (Sp.) *n.* checking over; practice run; rehearsal.

pasado: (Sp.) *adj.* passed, approved; overdue; *n.* past.

pasadór: (Sp.) *n.* sanitary napkin; wet rag for ironing; bolt to lock a door.

paság: *n.* wriggle, wiggle; stamping of the feet; **pasagán** *v.* to stamp the feet in anger at someone.

pasahe: (Sp. *pasaje*) *n.* fare; journey, passage.

pasahero: (Sp. *pasajero*) *n.* passenger; **takas na ~** *n.* stowaway.

pasal: *n.* extreme hunger; plug, stopper; obstruction; **pasal sa bibíg** *n.* gag.

pasalap: *n.* dowry.

pasamano: (Sp.) *n.* window ledge, ledge; handrail.

pasán: *n.* burden, load; **pasanín** *v.* to carry on the shoulder; **magpápasán ng krus** *id.* suffering (carrying cross on the shoulder).

pasang: *n.* wedge; **pumasang** *v.* to enter a narrow passage; **magpasang** *v.* to wedge.

pasangit: *n.* anchor.

pasaporte: (Sp.) *n.* passport.

pasarì: *n.* insinuation.

pasas: (Sp.) *n.* raisin.

pasasà: *adj.* enjoying an abundance of something; **magpasasà** *v.* to satiate oneself.

pasatyempo: (Sp. *pasatiempo*) *n.* pastime, amusement.

pasaw: *n.* kind of shrub with resistant fibers, *Corchorus catharticus*.

pasáw: *n.* noise of wiggling fish in the water.

paskíl: (Sp. *pasquin*: lampoon) *n.* poster.

Paskó: (Sp. *pascua*) *n.* Christmas; **magpapaskó** *v.* to give a Christmas gift; **pamaskó** *adj.* for Christmas; **paskóng-tuyô** *id.* Christmas without gifts.

paskwa(s): (Sp. *pascua*) *n.* Christmas flower; poinsettia.

pase: (Sp.) *n.* pass; passing.

paseo: (Sp.) *n.* walk, drive.

pases: (Sp.) *n.* pass, permit; free ticket.

pasensiyá: (Sp. *paciencia*) *n.* patience; willing to forgive; **pasensiya ka na** sorry; bear with me.

pasikat: (*coll.*) *n.* gallant person; boastful person; bragging; *adj.* fond of showing off; boastful.

pasig: *n.* river that flows into the sea; **pasigan** *n.* sandy bank of a river.

pasil: *n.* game of spinning tops.

pasilyo: (Sp. *pasillo*) *n.* hall, corridor.

pásimundán: *n.* model, pattern; precedent.

pásimundín: *n.* the youngest child who is about to have a new baby sibling.

pasimunò: (rt. *punò*) *n.* perpetrator, one who leads an undesirable act. **pasimunuan** *v.* to lead others in committing an undesirable act.

pasinayà: *n.* installation; inauguration.

pasingáw: (*rt. singáw*) *n.* publication in a newspaper.

pasiyók: *n.* kind of whistle made from a reed or the stalk of a rice plant.

pasláng: *adj.* insolent, insulting.

paslít: *adj.* innocent, inexperienced.

pasmá: (Sp. *pasmo*) *n.* spasm.

paso: (Sp.) *n.* step, pace; passageway; **pumaso** *v.* to pace.

pasó: (Sp.) *adj.* expired, lapsed.

pasò: *n.* scald, burn; **pasô** *adj.* burned, scalded; **parang nagpápasò** *id.* in a hurry.

pasô: *n.* flowerpot.

pasok: *n.* entry, admission; school or work; **kapasukán** *n.* time for going to work or school; **ipasok** *v.* to cause to enter; **makapasok** *v.* to be able to enter; infiltrate; **magpapasok** *v.* to admit, permit entrance; **magpasok** *v.* to insert; bring into use; introduce; **mamasukan** *v.* to have a job;

enter a lowly kind of service; **mápapasukan** *n.* employment; **pápások** *adj.* incoming; **papasukin** *v.* to let someone enter; **pasukán** *n.* entrance; **pumasok** *v.* to enter; **pasukin** *v.* to enter; **pumasok na lamang** *v.* to barge into. [See also *himasok*]

pasol: *n.* irony.

paspás₁: *n.* gust of wind; attack; burst of speed; **paspasán** *v.* to attack; do fast; go fast. **páspasan** *n.* attack; burst of speed; sexual intercourse.

paspás₂: *n.* dusting; **pamaspás** *n.* duster.

pasta: (Sp.) *n.* paste; dough; plaster.

pastâ: *n.* tooth filling.

pastél: (Sp.) *n.* pie; pastel painting; **pastelería** *n.* pastry shop.

pasterisado: (Sp. *pasterizado*) *adj.* pasteurized. **pasterisasyón** *n.* pasteurization.

pastilyas: (Sp. *pastilla*) *n.* pastille; small tablet candy; lozenge.

pastól: (Sp. *pastor*) *n.* pastor, shepherd; **pastulan** *n.* land for grazing, pasture.

pastór: *var. of pastól.*

paswít: *n.* whistle.

pasyál: (Sp. *pasear*) *n.* stroll, promenade.

pasyente: (Sp. *paciente*) *n.* patient.

pasyón: (Sp. *pasión*) *n.* passion; drepane fish; **pasyonaria** *n.* passionflower plant.

pata: (Sp.) *n.* leg of an animal; game played with wooden blocks.

patâ: *adj.* fatigued, exhausted.

patabâ: (*rt. tabâ*) *n.* fertilizer.

paták: *n.* drop; spot; **pamaták** *n.* dropper; **pumaták** *v.* to fall, drop.

patakarán: (*rt. takad*) *n.* principle; regulation; policy; procedure.

patadyóng: *n.* butterfly sleeve dress.

patag: *adj.* even, flat, level; **pampatag** *n.* roller.

patagana: *n.* allowance, extra supply.

patál: (Sp. *fatal*) *adj.* fatal.

patanì: *n.* lima bean.

patas: *n.* stock, pile, heap; draw, tie in a game; **patás** *adj.* tied (in a game).

patatas: (Sp.) *n.* potato; smell of dirty socks.

pataw: *n.* handcuffs for two convicts; buoy; lien; hardship, suffering; ballast; burden; **ipataw** *v.* to put a burden on, impose.

patáy: *n.* dead person, corpse; **patáy** *adj.* dead; extinct; turned off; **kamatayan** *n.* death, doom; **himatáy** *n.* fainting, swooning; **ipapatáy** *v.* to have something killed; **mamatáy** *v.* to die; **magpatáy** *v.* to kill, slaughter; **nakamamatáy** *adj.* deadly, fatal; **pagkamatáy** *n.* death; **pumatáy**, **patayín** *v.* to kill; extinguish (light); **patay-patay** *adj.* sluggish; **patáy-gutom** *id.* poor, miserable person; **patáy na loób** *adj.* ungrateful; **patáy ang lente** *id.* all finished; **patáy na patáy** *adj.* crazy about something, obsessed; **patáy na parada** *id.* hopeless; **patáy na batà** (*slang*) *n.* nymphomaniac.

patdá: *n.* plant resin; bird lime.

patdín: (rt. *patíd*) *v.* to cut out of.

patela: (Eng.) *n.* kneecap, patella.

patente: (Sp.) *n.* patent.

paternidád: (Sp.) *n.* paternity.

pati: *n.* advice, warning.

patí: *adv.* including, also.

patì: *n.* interruption, interception.

patianak: *n.* goblin.

patibóng: *n.* snare, trap; pitfall.

patík: *n.* pick-axe.

patikî: *n.* species of kingfisher type bird; (*coll.*) concubine.

patid: **pumatid** *v.* to trick, stumble.

patíd: *adj.* cut off; **kapatíd** *n.* sibling; **kapatiran** *n.* brotherhood; **patíd-patíd** *adj.* disconnected; **patdán** *v.* to cut out; **patdín** *v.* to cut out of; **pumatíd ng uhaw** *v.* to quench one's thirst.

patilya: (Sp. *patilla*) *n.* sideburns.

patín: (Sp.) *n.* skate.

patintero: (Sp.) *n.* kind of children's game. (*tubigán*)

patíng: *n.* shark; (*slang*) ugly male; highway patrol; ~ **sa kati** *n.* usurer; **patíng-sudsód** *n.* guitar fish; **patíng-inglesa** *n.* black-finned shark.

patinga: *n.* down payment, deposit; charge in a gun.

patís: *n.* fish sauce.

patitís: *n.* plumb bob.

patiwakál: *n.* suicide.

patláng: *n.* interval, gap.
patláy: *n.* halfbeak fish.
patníg: *n.* quick reply, repartee.
patnubay: *n.* guide, companion; escort; **ipatnubay** *v.* to direct one's way, steer; **pumatnubay** *v.* to guide; accompany.
patnugot: *n.* manager, director; editor; **mamatnugot** *v.* to manage, direct; edit.
pato: (Sp.) *n.* duck.
patok: *n.* jump, leap.
patók: *n.* sure winner (in horseracing); success in a business deal.
patol: *n.* hardened mung bean; **patulan** *v.* to notice, pay attention to an unimportant person; **waláng patol** *id.* irresponsible.
patola: *n.* *Luffa acutangula* vine or fruit; (*coll.*) lower rank.
patólogo: (Sp.) *n.* pathologist.
patong: *n.* layer; fold; interest charged on a loan; **ipatong** *v.* to mount; put on top of; **ipatong ang singíl** *v.* to overcharge; **nakapatong** *adj.* lying; **patungan** *v.* to apply, put on.
patos: *n.* metal wedge; horseshoe.
patós: *adj.* dislodged; **patusín** *v.* to dislodge.
patpát: *n.* stick; **patpatín** *adj.* gaunt, thin; weak.
patriarka: (Sp.) *n.* patriarch.
patriota: (Sp.) *n.* patriot.
patrón: (Sp.) *n.* patron, patron saint.
patrulya: (Sp. *patrolla*) *n.* patrol.
patsada: (Sp. *fachada*) *n.* façade, front of a building; title page.
patsé: (Sp. *parche*) *n.* patch, plaster.
patubilíng: *n.* weathercock.
patumalmál: *adj.* petrified.
patumanggâ: *n.* consideration; attention.
patumapát: *n.* hypocrisy.
patuna: *n.* striped sea catfish.
patupat: *n.* cigarette holder.
patutot: *n.* prostitute.
patutsada: *n.* mockery.
patyò: (Sp. *patio*) *n.* courtyard, churchyard.
paul: *n.* spotted eagle ray.
paumanhín: *n.* toleration; meekness; **humingî ng ~** *v.* to apologize; **magpaumanhín** *v.* to pardon, excuse; accept an excuse.
pawà: *adj.* all, everyone; *adv.* purely, entirely.
pawì: **mapawì** *v.* to be erased; vanish; stop; **pagkapawì** *n.* abolition; **pamawì** *n.* eraser; **pawî** *adj.* erased, eradicated.
pawikan: *n.* sea turtle.
pawid: *n.* nipa palm.
pawis: *n.* sweat, perspiration; **magpawis** *v.* to sweat; **pampapawis** *n.* something that makes one sweat; **anák-pawis** *n.* child of the working class.
pawpáw: *adj.* level to the brim.
paya: *n.* tally, count; score card, record of winning numbers or cocks; act of gulping down (without swallowing).
payabat: *n.* spawning of fish.
payák: *adj.* simple; mere.
payag: *adj.* in agreement; **pumayag** *v.* to agree, consent; allow; accept; **pagpayag** *n.* approval, sanction; agreement.
payagód: *adj.* emaciated, skinny.
payagpág: *n.* flapping of wings.
payangitan: *n.* moray.
payapà₁: *adj.* peaceful, tranquil; placid; **kapayapaan** *n.* peace, tranquility; **mapayapà** *adj.* peaceful; **payapain** *v.* to pacify.
payapà₂: *n.* species of strangling fig tree.
payaso: (Sp.) *n.* clown.
payát: *adj.* thin, skinny, slender; barren (land); **mamayát, pumayát** *v.* to become thin; **páyatín** *adj.* prone to losing weight.
payatola: (*slang, payát*) *adj.* very slim.
payatot: (*slang, payát*) *adj.* skinny.
payì: *n.* extinction, eradication.
payikpík: *adj.* compressed.
payíd: *adj.* carried by the wind.
payimpín: *n.* grillwork; earthen dike; kind of trellis like corral for catching fish.
payupoy: *var. of payupoy*: wagging.
payo: *n.* advice; counsel; **ipayo** *v.* to advise; preach; **maipápáyo** *adj.* advisable; **payuhan** *v.* to advise; **tagapayo** *n.* counselor, adviser.
payola: (Eng.) *n.* payola, bribery.
payong: *n.* umbrella; **payungan** *v.* to hold an umbrella over someone; **payung-payungan** *n.* kind of lily, species of mushroom.
paypáy: *n.* fan; **paypayán** *v.* to fan someone.
payupoy: *n.* wagging of the tail.

pebre: (Sp. *pebrada*) *n*. sauce for roast pig.
Pebrero: (Sp. *febrero*) *n*. February.
pekas: (Sp. *pecas*) *n*. freckle; **mapekas** *adj*. freckled.
peklat: *n*. scar; **magkapeklat** *v*. to form a scar.
pekpek: (*coll.*) *n*. vagina. (*puki*)
pekwa: (*slang*) *n*. counterfeit money.
pedestál: (Sp.) *n*. pedestal. (*patungán, sálalayán*)
pedido: (Sp.) *n*. order of goods.
pedro: (*slang*) *n*. penis.
pelíkulá: (Sp. *película*) *n*. film, movie.
peligro, piligro: (Sp.) *n*. danger (*panganib*); **mamiligro** *v*. to be in danger; **peligroso** *adj*. dangerous; risky.
pelota: (Sp.) *n*. rubber ball; game of jai alai.
pelotaris: (Sp.) *n*. jai alai player.
peluka: (Sp. *peluca*) *n*. wig.
pelús, pelusa: (Sp. *vello*) *n*. velvet.
pemenidád: (Sp. *femenidad*) *n*. femininity.
pemenista: (Sp. *femenista*) *n*. feminist.
pena: (Sp.) *n*. penalty, punishment; **penahan** *v*. to penalize, fine.
pendeho: (Sp. *pendejo*) *n*. stealing another man's wife.
pendiyente: (Sp. *pendiente*) *adj*. pending.
péndolá: (Sp.) *n*. pendulum.
pendóng: (*slang*) *n*. bald spot.
peninsulares: (Sp., *obs.*) *n*. Spanish-born Spaniards in the Philippines. [Contrast *insulares*]
peniténsiya: (Sp. *penitencia*) *n*. penitence; purgatory.
penómeno: (Sp. *fenómeno*) *n*. phenomenon.
penoy: *n*. hard-boiled duck egg.
pens(i)yón: (Sp. *pensión*) *n*. pension; scholarship; **pens(i)yonado** *n*. pensioner; fellow.
penúltima: (Sp.) *adj*. penultimate.
peón: (Sp.) *n*. peon; unskilled laborer; (*chess*) pawn.
pepino: (Sp.) *n*. cucumber.
pepsín(a): (Eng.) *n*. pepsin; chewing gum (from trade name).
pera: (Sp.) *n*. money, cash; wealth; **mamera** *adj*. worth one centavo; **mapera** *adj*. wealthy; **perahin** *v*. to convert something into cash; **sampera** *n*. one centavo.
peras: (Sp.) *n*. pear.
perkál: (Sp. *percal*) *n*. percale cloth.
perdayà: *n*. unjustly collected money by government officials.
perdegana: (Sp. *pierde gana*) *n*. agreement in certain games whereby the loser wins.
perdigones: (Sp.) *n*. pellets; birdshot.
peregrino: (Sp.) *n*. pilgrim.
perehíl: (Sp. *perejil*) *n*. parsley.
pergamino: (Sp.) *n*. parchment; scroll.
perhuwisyo: (Sp. *perjuicio*) *n*. injury; harm; prejudice.
perimetro: (Sp.) *n*. perimeter.
perlas: (Sp.) *n*. pearl.
permiso: (Sp.) *n*. permission; permit.
pero: (Sp.) *conj*. but. (*nguni't, dátapwá't*)
perokaríl: (Sp. *ferrocarril*) *n*. railroad.
perpekto: (Sp. *perfecto*) *adj*. perfect.
persiyana: (Sp. *persiana*) *n*. window shade.
personahe: (Sp.) *n*. personage.
personalidád: (Sp.) *n*. personality.
pertilisá: (Sp. *fertilizar*) **pertilisahán** *v*. to fertilize.
perya: (Sp. *feria*) *n*. fair, exhibition.
peryodista: (Sp. *periodista*) *n*. newspaperman, journalist.
pesas: (Sp.) *n*. weights, dumbbell; weights.
peseta: (Sp.) *n*. twenty centavos.
peste: (Sp.) *n*. pest, plague; rot; epidemic.
pesteho: (Sp. *festejo*) *n*. festival, festivity; **pestehado** *n*. person honored in a feast.
petrolyo: (Sp. *petroleo*) *n*. petroleum.
petsa: (Sp. *fecha*) *n*. date; **petsadór** *n*. date stamping machine; **petsahán** *v*. to date.
petsáy: (Ch.) *n*. Chinese cabbage.
peynedora: (Sp. *peinadora*) *n*. hairdresser.
peyneta: (Sp. *peineta*) *n*. ornamental comb.
pika$_1$: (Sp. *pica*) *n*. irritation, annoyance; **pikahín** *v*. to provoke; irritate.
pika$_2$: *n*. tattoo. **pikahán** *v*. to tattoo.
pikadilyo: (Sp. *picadillo*) *n*. minced meat.
pikadura: (Sp. *picadura*) *n*. ready-cut pipe tobacco.
pikante: (Sp. *picante*) *adj*. pungent. (*maanghang*)
pikarát: (*slang*) *n*. flirt.

pikat: *n.* light scar; cavalla fish.
piké, pikí: (Sp. *piqué*) *n.* corduroy, piqué.
pikî: *adj.* knock-kneed.
pikít: *adj.* closed (eyes); **mapikít** *v.* to take a nap; **pumikít** *v.* to close the eyes; **pikitan** *v.* to wink at someone; **nagpikít ang matá** *v.* closed the eyes; (*fig.*) died.
piklát: *var. of peklát*: deep scar.
piko: (Sp. *pico*) *n.* spout; pickaxe; 75 kilos.
pikô: *n.* hopscotch.
pikolete: (Sp.) *n.* staple.
pikón: (Sp. *picón*) *adj.* touchy, oversensitive.
pikot: *n.* shotgun wedding; forced marriage; cornering into a difficult situation; act of surrounding an enemy; **pikutin** *v.* to force someone into a difficult situation (marriage); corner.
pikóy: *n.* species of parrot; (*coll.*) soldier in the Philippine constabulary.
pikpík: **pagpikpík** *n.* patting a child; *adj.* compressed; **pikpikín** *v.* to compress.
piksí: *n.* shrug; **pumiksí** *v.* to shrug.
pikul: (Eng.) *n.* picul, 75 kilos.
pideos: (Sp. *fideo*) *n.* vermicelli noodles.
pidpíd: *n.* piece of wood.
pigâ: **pumigâ** *v.* to squeeze out, wring out; **pigán, pigaán** *v.* to squeeze juice on.
pigapit: **pigapít** *adj.* under stress, compelled. **pigapitin** *v.* to compel, pressure; force someone into a tight situation.
pighatî: *n.* ache; woe; sorrow, grief.
pigî: *n.* rump, buttocks.
pigil: *n.* detention; holding back; control, restraint; **pigilin** *v.* to control, restrain, keep back, hold back; stop; obstruct; withhold; **pamigil** *n.* check, restraint; **pampigil** *n.* control, restraint; **magpigil** *v.* to abstain; refrain from; stop; **pumigil** *v.* to control, block, impede, prevent; stop; restrain.
piging: *n.* tightening a knot; **pigíng** *adj.* tight.
pigíng: *n.* feast, banquet.
pigipit: **pigipitin** *v.* to pressure, compel; force someone into a tight situation.
pigís: *adj.* pressed out, squeezed out (juices).
pigít: *adj.* glottal, guttural.
piglás: **pumiglás** *v.* to struggle to get free.
pigò: (*slang*) *n.* sleep.
pigsá: *n.* boil, tumor; **pigsáng-dagâ** *n.* small boil.
pigtâ: *adj.* soaked, drenched.
pigtál: **pigtalín** *v.* to detach.
pigtás: **mapigtás** *adj.* to be ripped, broken.
pigura: (Sp. *figura*) *n.* figure, shape.
pihâ: *n.* species of brightly colored snail.
pihado: (Sp. *fijado*) *adj.* sure, certain; **pihaduhin** *v.* to make sure.
pihik: *adj.* fastidious, choosy (with food).
pihit: *n.* turn; rotation; gyration; **pihít** *adj.* turned; **pihitán** *n.* crank; **mapihit** *adj.* to be turned.
piho: (Sp. *fijo*) *adj.* sure, firm; fixed. (*pamiho*)
piíng: *adj.* dented. (*yupî*)
piít: *adj.* cornered; imprisoned; pressed together; **mapiit** *v.* to be cornered, to be in a fix.
pila₁: (Sp. *fila*) *n.* line, row; clay.
pila₂: (Sp.) *n.* battery.
pilá: *adj.* chipped, broken off.
pilak: *n.* silver; money; **pinilakang-tabing** *n.* silver screen.
pilamento: (Sp. *filamento*) *n.* filament.
pilandót: *n.* spurt; awkward movements of a paralyzed person.
pilansík: *n.* splash.
pilantík: *n.* flip, flick.
pilantód: *adj.* walking with a limp.
pilántropo: (Sp. *filántropo*) *n.* philanthropist.
pilapil: *n.* small dike.
pilapís: *adj.* destroyed by the weather (crops).
pilár: (Sp.) *n.* pillar.
pilas: *n.* rip, tear; **kapilas** *n.* shred; **mapilas** *v.* to be torn.
pilat: *n.* scar; **pumilat** *v.* to form a scar.
pilay: *n.* limp; sprain; **piláy** *adj.* lame; crippled; sprained.
píldoras: (Sp.) *n.* pill.
pileges: (Sp. *pliegue*) *n.* pleat, plait.
pilì: *n.* almond nut; choice, selection; **mamilì** *v.* to choose; **pilì** *adj.* choice, select; **pilián** *adj.* choosy; **piliin** *v.* to choose; **mapagpípililan** *n.* choice, alternative; **mapilì** *adj.* choosy, fussy; **pamiliin** *v.* to be given a choice; **pumilì** *v.* to choose, select; **waláng-pilì** *adv.* by chance, at random; not discriminating;

promiscuous.
pilí: *n.* twist; ply (of rope); **pilihín** *v.* to twist, twine.
pilík: *n.* eyelashes.
pilikáw: *adj.* deformed in the legs.
pilík-matá: *n.* eyelash.
pilíg: *n.* shaking the body to get water off; shaking of the head.
piligro: *see peligro*: danger.
piling: *n.* side; **ipiling** *v.* to put beside; **kapiling** *n.* person close to oneself; *adj.* near, at the side of; **pumiling** *v.* to get close to another.
pilíng: *n.* cluster of bananas.
pilipig: (*rt. pipig*) *n.* immature rice grains that are toasted and pounded.
Pilipina: (Sp. *filipina*) *n.* Filipina, Philippine female.
Pilipinas: (Sp. *Filipinas*) *n.* Philippines.
Pilipino: (Sp. *filipino*) *n.* Filipino; Filipino language (Tagalog).
pilipisán: *n.* temple.
pilipit: *n.* wring, squeeze, twist; **mamilipit** *v.* to writhe, squirm; convulse; **pilipít** *adj.* twisted, awry, contorted; *n.* kind of spiral cookie.
pilipitin: *n.* anchovy.
pilipot: *n.* back part of the head.
pilit: **ipilit** *v.* to force; insist; impose; **pilít** *adj.* forced; **ipilit** *v.* to impose; force; insist. **magpilit** *v.* to strive, try hard for. **makapilit** *v.* to be able to get by force; **magpumilit** *v.* to persist; try very hard. **ipagpilitan** *v.* to laboriously force. **pamimilit** *n.* persistence; compulsion; force; **pilitin** *v.* to force, compel; oblige; urge; **mapilit** *v.* to get through effort; be able to force. **mapilitan** *adj.* to be forced, obliged; **pagpilitan** *v.* to make an effort; attempt; strive for. **pagpipilit** *n.* insistence. **pagpupumilit** *n.* struggle, great effort; persistence. **sápilitán** *adj.* compulsory, required; forced.
pilók: *adj.* twisted (arm, ankle or foot).
pilón: (Sp.) *n.* lump of sugar.
pilosopía: (Sp. *filosofía*) *n.* philosophy.
pilósopó: (Sp. *filósofo*) *n.* philosopher; (*fig.*) smart aleck. **mapagpilósopó** *adj.* pedantic; tediously learned.
pilote: (Sp.) *n.* pile, beam.
piloto: (Sp.) *n.* pilot.
pilpíl: *n.* refuse left by the tide; *adj.* compressed.
piltro: (Sp. *filtro*) *n.* filter, strainer.
pilús: (Sp. *pelusa*) *n.* velvet.
pilyán: *n.* lactarid fish.
pilyo: (Sp.) *adj.* naughty; mischievous. **kapilyuhán** *n.* mischief; bad behavior.
pilyego: (Sp. *pliego*) *n.* sheet of paper.
pimbrera: (Sp. *fiambrera*) *n.* lunch pail.
pimentón: (Sp.) *n.* paprika, ground red pepper.
pimiento: (Sp.) *n.* pepper.
pimpóng: (Eng.) *n.* Ping-Pong.
pina-: *pref.* perfective form of *pa-*.
pinak: *n.* footprint of a water buffalo; shallow lagoon present in the rainy season.
pinaka- 1. *pref.* forms superlative adjectives: **pinakamagandá** *adj.* most beautiful. 2. with nominal roots, connotes serving: **pinakahepe** *n.* one serving as a chief.
pinakbét: (Ilk.) *n.* stewed vegetables with pork and shrimp paste.
pinag-: *pref.* perfective form of *pag-*.
pinais: (*rt. pais*) *n.* steamed fish.
pinál: (Sp. *final*) *adj.* final.
Pináy: *n.*, *adj.* Filipino woman.
pindán: *n.* kind of shade.
pindáng: *n.* jerked beef.
pindanga: *n.* black pike eel.
pindanggâ: *n.* silver pike eel.
pindól: (Sp. *pendon*) *n.* banner, standard.
pindóng: *n.* head covering (for women).
pindót: **pindutín** *v.* to squeeze, press with the fingers.
pinesa: (Sp. *fineza*) *n.* fineness.
pinid: **piníd** *adj.* closed; **ipinid** *v.* to close.
pininsulares: (*Sp. peninsulares, slang*) *n.* socialite.
pinipig: (*rt. pipig*) *n.* rice crispies made from toasted green rice.
pinlák: *adj.* in whole groups; **pinlakín** *v.* to finish a job without rest.
pino₁: (Sp. *fino*) *adj.* fine; refined; polite.
pino₂: (Sp.) *n.* pine tree.
Pinóy: *n.* Filipino.
pinpín: *n.* frame of a plow.

pinsalà: *n.* damage, losses; harm; **bayad-pinsalà** *n.* damages, reparations; **mapinsalà** *v.* to be damaged; crippled; **nakapípinsalà** *adj.* harmful, injurious; **pinsalain** *v.* to injure, do harm to; hurt; **sa kapinsalaán ng** at the expense of.

pinsán: *n.* cousin; **pinsang-buô** *n.* first cousin.

pinsél: (Sp.) *n.* artist's paint brush.

pintá: (Sp.) *n.* paint; **pintahán** *v.* to paint.

pintakasi: *n.* patron saint; cockfighting session during a fiesta.

pintál: *n.* warp, bend; **mapintál** *v.* to warp.

pintás: *n.* fault, defect; **pintasán** *v.* to find faults in others; **mámimintás** *n.* critic; **mapamintás** *adj.* prone to criticizing; **pamimintás** *n.* faultfinding.

pintíg: *n.* throb, pulse.

pintíng: *n.* light throb, pulse.

pintô: *n.* door; **namimintô** *adj.* on the threshold; expected to happen; within sight; **pintuan** *n.* doorway.

pintóg: *n.* swelling; **mamintóg, pumintóg** *v.* to swell.

pintón: *n.* tall bamboo basket.

pintóng: *n.* warehouse.

pintór: (Sp.) *n.* painter; artist; **~-kulapol** *n.* novice painter.

pintuhò: **pamimintuhò** *n.* admiration; showing admiration; paying homage to; **mamintuhò** *v.* to pay a tribute to, show admiration.

pintura: (Sp) *n.* paint; painting.

pinyá: (Sp. *piña*) *n.* pineapple; pineapple cloth.

pingá: *adj.* warlike, quarrelsome.

pingal: **pingál** *adj.* broken off, disattached; nicked.

pingas: *n.* chip, nick; **pingás** *adj.* notched, nicked; chipped.

pingkás: (Sp. *finca*) *n.* real estate.

pingkáw: (Ch.) *adj.* crooked, twisted (arm).

pingkî: *n.* friction fire; **pamingkî** *n.* stone used in kindling.

pingkít: (Ch.) *adj.* slant-eyed; with one eye smaller than another; cavalla fish.

pingkók: *adj.* crooked in the forearm; claw-handed.

pingga: (Ch.) *n.* carrying pole; lever; **magpinggá** *v.* to carry on a pole.

pinggán: *n.* plate, dish.

ping-il: *adj.* full of fruits.

pingód: *adj.* with only one ear.

pingol: **pingulin** *v.* to twist the ears of; **kapingulan** *n.* earlobe; **pingól** *adj.* without ears.

pingót: *adj.* slightly nicked (plate).

pipa: (Sp.) *n.* pipe.

pipi: *adj.* dumb, mute; inarticulate.

pipí: *adj.* barren (women).

pipî: *adj.* pressed, flattened.

pipikat: *n.* cavalla fish.

pipikaw: *n.* leather jacket fish.

pipino: (Sp. *pepino*) *n.* cucumber.

pipís: *adj.* pressed, flattened, rolled thin.

pipitsugin: *adj.* easily taken advantage of; cheap; inexpensive; *n.* small time person; beginner; (*coll.*) thin person.

piral: *n.* pinch of the ears.

piralî: *n.* lime. (*apog*)

pirámide: (Sp.) *n.* pyramid.

piranggót: **kapiranggót** *n.* very small piece.

piraso: (Sp. *pedazo*) . piece, bit; fragment; portion; **mapiraso** *v.* to be broken in pieces; **pirasó** *adj.* broken in pieces.

pirát: *adj.* flattened (cotton).

pirata: (Sp.) *n.* pirate.

pirinsá: (Sp. *prensa*) *n.* clothes iron.

piríng: *n.* blindfold.

pirito: (Sp. *frito*) *adj.* fried.

pirma: (Sp. *firma*) *n.* signature; **pumirmá**, **pirmahán** *v.* to sign; **pirmado** *adj.* signed.

pirme: *var.* of *pirmí*: fixed, permanent.

pirmí: (Sp. *firme*) *adj.* fixed; permanent; always; **mamirmí** *v.* to become fixed, take root; **magpirmí** *v.* to keep something steady, fixed; **nakapirmí** *adj.* in a fixed position; sitting still; **pirmihan** *adj.* fixed, set; permanent; **pumirmí** *v.* to settle, become fixed.

pirot: *n.* act of pinching and twisting.

pisâ: (Sp. *pisar*) *adj.* crushed, pressed; hatched (eggs); **mamisâ** *v.* to hatch; **pumisâ** *v.* to squeeze, press; **pisaín** *v.* to squeeze, crush, apply pressure to something.

pisák: *adj.* blind in one eye.

pisan: *adj.* staying together; **kapisanan** *n.* club, organization; society; **makipamisan** *v.* to request permission to live with; **magkapisan** *v.* to live together; **mapisan** *v.* to be brought together; converge; **pumisan** *v.* to live together.

pisara: (Sp. *pizarra*) *n.* blackboard.

pisáw: *n.* long, thin kind of machete.

piskál: (Sp. *fiscal*) *n.* fiscal; **piskalyá** *n.* fiscal's office.

piskante: (Sp. *fiscante*) *n.* driver's seat.

pisík: *n.* splash; **pisikán** *v.* to splash someone.

písika: (Sp. *física*) *n.* physics.

pisíg: *n.* solid bamboo; **pisigán** *adj.* stout, robust.

pisíl: *n.* squeeze; **pisilín** *v.* to squeeze.

pisngí: *n.* cheek.

piso: (Sp. *peso*) *n.* peso; floor of a building.

pisón: (Sp.) *n.* steam roller, roller.

pisót: *adj.* flattened (with the foot); (*slang*, Ceb.) uncircumcised.

pispís: *adj.* left over scraps of food; act of dusting; **pamispís** *n.* duster.

pistá: (Sp. *fiesta*) *n.* fiesta, festivity; holiday; ~ **ng bayan** *n.* town fiesta.

pistâ: **pumistâ** *v.* to undervalue.

pistola: (Sp.) *n.* pistol.

pistón: (Sp.) *n.* piston; primer of a gun; crease.

pístula: (Sp. *fístula*) *n.* fistula, tubelike sore.

pita: *n.* intense desire.

pitâ: *n.* lowland, watery land.

pitak: *n.* division, section; portion.

pitakà: (Sp. *petaca*: tobacco pouch) *n.* wallet; pouch.

pitagan: *n.* respect; reverence; **mamitagan** *v.* to respect; **mapitagan** *adj.* reverent.

pitás: *adj.* picked (fruits, flowers); snatched.

pitáw: *adj.* detached; fallen (leaves).

pithayà: *n.* fervent desire.

pitik: **mamitik** *v.* to become numb.

pitík: *n.* flick, toss; jerk; carpenter's line for marking; rein; (*slang*) pickpocket; **pitikín** *v.* to flick, flip.

pitis: *n.* pint.

pitís: *adj.* tight-fitting.

pitlág: *n.* dodge; **pumitlág** *v.* to dodge.

pito: (Sp.) *n.* whistle; flute.

pitó: *n.* seven; **labimpitó** *n.* seventeen; **makapitó** *adj.* seven times; **pipitó** seven only.

pitóng-bukó: *n.* scorpion.

pitpít: *adj.* beaten, pounded; **pintipít na luya** *id.* dumbfounded (pounded ginger).

pitsa: (Sp. *ficha*) *n.* chip (in gambling).

pitsél: (Sp. *pichel*) *n.* pitcher; jug.

pitsó: (Sp. *pecho*) *n.* breast of a chicken.

pitsón: (Sp. *pichón*) *n.* squab, young pigeon.

piyák: *n.* squawk, cry of fowls.

piyadór: (Sp. *fiador*) *n.* guarantor.

piyais: **piyaisin** *v.* to attack in great numbers.

piyait: **piyaít** *adj.* crushed between two heavy objects.

piyambre: (Sp. *fiambre*) *n.* tiered lunch container.

piyambrera: (Sp. *fiambrera*) *n.* tiered lunch container.

piyano: (Sp. *piano*) *n.* piano.

piyansa: (Sp. *fianza*) *n.* bail; bond, surety.

piyangâ: (*slang*) *adj.* greedy; selfish.

piyangót: **kapiyangót** *n.* particle, small bit.

piyapís: *adj.* defeated; overpowered.

piyé: (Sp. *pie*) *n.* foot (measurement).

piyér: (Eng.) *n.* pier.

piyesa: (Sp. *pieza*) *n.* piece of music; bolt of cloth.

piyesta: (Sp. *fiesta*) *n.* fiesta, festival; feast.

piyô: *n.* gout.

piyók: *n.* complete turn.

piyón: (Sp. *peón*) *n.* pawn; unskilled laborer.

piyonít: (*slang*) *adj.* hot.

piyorea: (Sp. *piorrea*) *n.* disease of the gums.

plaka: (Sp. *placa*) *n.* disk; record; plaque.

plahelante: (Sp.) *n.* flagellant.

pláhiyo: (Sp. *plagio*) *n.* plagiarism.

plais: (Eng.) *n.* pliers. (*bukaypato*)

plamengko: (Sp. *flamenco*) *n.* flamingo.

planeta: (Sp.) *n.* planet; **planetaryo** *n.* planetarium.

plano: (Sp.) *n.* plan, design; sketch; **iplano** *v.* to plan.

planta: (Sp.) *n.* plant, factory.

plantilya: (Sp. *plantilla*) *n.* payroll, list of employees.

plantsa: (Sp. *plancha*) *n.* iron, flatiron; scaffold; **magplantsa** *v.* to iron.

plasa: (Sp. *plaza*) *n.* square, plaza.

plaso: (Sp. *plazo*) *n.* installment payment.

plastado: (Sp. *aplastado*) *adj.* crushed; lying flat; bedridden; tight-fitting; well-dressed; prone.
plata: (Sp.) *n.* silver; **plateria** *n.* silversmith's shop; **platero** *n.* silversmith.
plataporma: (Sp. *plataforma*) *n.* platform.
platilyo: (Sp. *platillo*) *n.* pan of a scale; small plate, saucer.
platina: (Sp.) *n.* bedplate in printing; microscope slide.
platino: (Sp.) *n.* platinum.
platito: (Sp.) *n.* small plate, saucer.
plato: (Sp.) *n.* plate, dish.
plauta: (Sp. *flauta*) *n.* flute.
plebe: (*slang*) *n.* fourth class freshman cadet.
plebisito: (Sp.) *n.* plebiscite, direct vote.
plebo: *var.* of *plebe*.
plegarya: (Sp. *plegaria*) *n.* prayer; tolling of church bells for the dead.
plehe: (Sp. *fleje*) *n.* iron hoop used for packing.
plema: (Sp. *flema*) *n.* phlegm. (*kanaghalâ*)
plete: (Sp. *flete*) *n.* fare (passenger).
pletsa: (Sp. *flecha*) *n.* arrow, dart. (*panà*)
plomero: (Sp.) *n.* plumber. (*tubero*)
plorera: (Sp. *florera*) *n.* flower vase; female florist.
plorete: (Sp. *florete*) *n.* swordsmanship; fencing.
plota: (Sp. *flota*) *n.* fleet of ships; **plotilya** *n.* small fleet.
pluma: (Sp.) *n.* writing pen; feather.
plumahe: (Sp. *plumaje*) *n.* plumage.
plumero: (Sp.) *n.* feather duster.
pô: *part.* respect particle; **opô** yes sir; **mamupô** *v.* to address respectfully with *pô*.
poblasyón: (Sp. *población*) *n.* population; center of town.
pobre: (Sp.) *adj.* poor. (*mahirap*)
poknát: (*slang*) *adj.* bald.
pokpók: (*slang*) *n.* prostitute.
podér: (Sp.) *n.* power, authority.
poesía: (Sp.) *n.* poetry. (*tulâ*)
poeta: (Sp.) *n.* poet.
pogi: (*coll.*) *adj.* handsome.
pohas: (Sp. *fojas*) *n.* sheet (of paper).
polaynas: (Sp. *polaínas*) *n.* leggings.
polbera: (Sp. *polvera*) *n.* powder box.
polbo(s): (Sp. *polvo*) *n.* face powder.
polido: (Sp. *pulido*) *adj.* neat, tidy.
polilya: (Sp. *polilla*) *n.* moth.
pólisa: (Sp. *póliza*) *n.* policy.
polítika: (Sp. *política*) *n.* politics.
polyeto: (Sp. *folleto*) *n.* pamphlet.
pomada: (Sp.) *n.* pomade, hair grease.
pomento: (Sp. *fomento*) *n.* compress, pad of wet cloth.
pomes: (Sp. *pomez*) *n.* pumice.
pompiyáng: *n.* cymbal; (*slang*) lesbian; masculine female.
pondo: (Sp. *fondo*) *n.* fund; background.
pontípise: (Sp.) *n.* pontiff, pope.
pontse: (Sp. *ponche*) *n.* liquor punch.
ponggayan: (*slang*) *n.* drinking spree.
pongka: (*slang*) *n.* prostitute.
poók: *n.* place; section; quarter; **kapookán** *n.* center of a place; **pampoók** *adj.* local, regional; **poók na malapit** *n.* neighborhood.
poón: *n.* lord, master; **poonín** *v.* to deify.
poót: *n.* hatred, ill will; spite; **kapootán** *v.* to hate, abhor; **nakapopoót** *adj.* hateful, odious.
popa: (Sp.) *n.* poop, stern of a ship.
populasyón: (Hispanicized English) *n.* population.
por: (Sp.) *adj.* by; ~ **ora** by the hour.
porké: (Sp. *por qué*) *conj.* because.
pordiyós: (Sp. *por dios*) *interj.* By God!
porma: (Sp. *forma*) *n.* form.
pormál: (Sp. *formal*) *adj.* formal; **pormalidád** *n.* formality.
pórmula: (Sp. *fórmula*) *n.* formula; **pormularyo** *n.* formulary; form to be filled in; pharmaceutical prescriptions.
Porohanon: *n.* ethnic group and language from Camotes Islands.
porsado: (Sp. *forzado*) *adj.* forced.
porselana: (Sp. *porcelana*) *n.* porcelain; (*fig.*) fine skin; (*slang*) clean work.
porsiyento: (Sp. *porciento*) *n.* percent; percentage.
porsoso: (Sp. *forzoso*) *adj.* obligatory.
portada: (Sp.) *n.* portal, gate.
portal: (Sp.) *n.* portal; entrance; gate; doorstep.
portamoneda: (Sp.) *n.* purse, wallet.

portero: (Sp.) *n.* porter; doorkeeper.
pórtiko: (Sp.) *n.* porch, covered entrance.
portpolyo: (Eng.) *n.* portfolio.
portuna: (Sp. *fortuna*) *n.* fortune.
posas: (Sp. *esposas*) *n.* handcuffs.
posesyón: (Sp. *posesión*) *n.* possession.
posible: (Sp.) *adj.* possible; **posibilidád** *n.* possibility.
poso: (Sp. *pozo*) *n.* well; ~ **negro** *n.* septic tank.
pósporo: (Sp. *fósforo*) *n.* match.
póste: (Eng.) *n.* post.
posteridád: (Sp.) *n.* posterity.
postre: (Sp.) *n.* dessert.
postura: (Sp.) *n.* posture; *adj.* well-dressed.
potógrapo: (Sp. *fotógrafo*) *n.* photographer.
potro: (Sp.) *n.* colt, goal.
pranela: (Sp.) *n.* flannel.
Pransés: (Sp. *francés*) *n.* French.
prangkisya: (Sp. *franquicia*) *n.* franchise.
prangko: (Sp. *franco*) *adj.* frank; sincere.
prayle: (Sp. *fraile*) *n.* friar.
predikadór: (Sp.) *n.* preacher.
prehuwisyo: (Sp. *prejuicio*) *n.* prejudice, bias.
prelado: (Sp.) *n.* prelate, high ranking clergyman.
premyo: (Sp. *premio*) *n.* prize, award; **premyado** *adj.* awarded. **premyadór** *n.* prize giver.
prenda: (Sp.) *n.* pledge; hostage.
preno: (Sp. *freno*) *n.* brake; **waláng preno ang bibíg** *id.* talkative (mouth has no brake).
prente: (Sp. *frente*) *n.* front; forepart.
preparado: (Sp.) *adj.* prepared.
prepasyo: (Sp. *prefacio*) *n.* preface.
presas: (Sp. *fresas*) *n.* strawberries.
presko: (Sp. *fresco*) *adj.* fresh, cool (weather); (*slang*) rude, coarse.
preserba: (Sp. *preservar*) **preserbahín** *v.* to preserve; **pampreserbá** *n.* preservative; **preserbado** *adj.* preserved.
presidente: (Sp.) *n.* president.
presinto: (Sp. *precinto*) *n.* precinct; voting district.
presiyón: (Sp. *presión*) *n.* pressure; **alta** ~ *n.* high blood pressure.
preso: (Sp.) *n.* prisoner; **ipreso** *v.* to imprison.
prestíhiyo: (Sp. *prestigio*) *n.* prestige.
presupuwesto: (Sp. *presupuesto*) *n.* budget.
presyo: (Sp. *precio*) *n.* price.
presyón: (Sp. *preción*) *n.* pressure.
presyoso: (Sp. *precioso*) *adj.* precious.
pribado: (Sp. *privado*) *adj.* private.
pribiléhiyo: (Sp. *privilegio*) *n.* privilege.
pridyider: (Eng. *frigidaire*) *n.* refrigerator.
prima: (Sp.) *n.* premium; female cousin.
primado: (Sp.) *n.* primate.
primo: (Sp.) *n.* cousin.
primarya: (Sp. *primaria*) *n.* primary school; *adj.* primary.
primero: (Sp.) *adj.* first.
prinsa: (Sp. *presa*) *n.* dam.
prinsesa: (Sp. *princesa*) *n.* princess.
prinsipál: (Sp. *principal*) *n.* principal; *adj.* main, principal.
prínsipe: (Sp. *príncipe*) *n.* prince.
prinsipyo: (Sp. *principio*) *n.* beginning, origin; principle.
prisintá: **iprisintá** *v.* to apply; come unwanted; volunteer; **prisintado** *adj.* offered; volunteered.
prito: (Sp. *frito*) *adj.* fried.
proa: (Sp.) *n.* bow of a boat, prow.
probabilidád: (Sp.) *n.* probability.
probado: (Sp.) *adj.* proved.
probetso: (Sp. *provecho*) *n.* benefit, profit.
probi: (*slang*) *n.* hick, person from the province.
probinsiya: (Sp. *provincia*) *n.* province.
problema: (Sp.) *n.* problem.
proklamá: (Sp. *proclamar*) **iproklamá** *v.* to proclaim, announce; **proklamado** *adj.* proclaimed.
produkto: (Sp. *producto*) *n.* product.
programa: (Sp.) *n.* program.
prólogo: (Sp.) *n.* prologue.
promdi: (*slang*, Eng. *from the*) *n.* hick, unsophisticated person from the provinces.
propaganda: (Sp.) *n.* propaganda.
propeso: (Sp. *profeso*) *adj.* professed.
propesór: (Sp. *profesor*) *n.* professor.
propeta: (Sp. *profeta*) *n.* prophet.
proplas: (*slang*) *n.* stag party.
propyedád: (Sp. *propiedad*) *n.* property; **propyetaryo** *n.* landlord.

prosa: (Sp.) *n*. prose.
prostituta: (Sp.) *n*. prostitute.
protehido: (Sp. *protegido*) *adj*. protected.
protestante: (Sp.) *n*. Protestant.
prototipo: (Sp.) *n*. prototype.
proyekto: (Sp. *proyecto*) *n*. project.
prusisyón: (Sp.) *n*. procession; **parang nagpuprusisyón** *id*. numerous.
pru(w)eba: (Sp.) *n*. proof; test, trial.
prutas: (Sp. *fruta*) *n*. fruit; **prutera** *n*. fruit basket; **pruteria** *n*. fruit stand.
-pû: *suf*. ten → **sampû** ten, **dalawampû** twenty (two tens).
públiko: (Sp. *público*) *n*. public.
publisidád: (Sp. *publicidad*) *n*. publicity.
pukâ: *adj*. rotten.
pukás: *n*. open space between towns.
pukaw: **pumukaw** *v*. to arouse, excite; **pamukaw** *n*. incitement; **makapukaw** *v*. to incite; inspire; provoke; excite.
pukengkay: (*slang*) *n*. vagina.
puki: *n*. vagina; vulva.
pukinggán: *n*. blue pea vine.
puklô: *n*. groin.
puknát: *adj*. unglued, detached; **puknatín** *v*. to detach, unglue; **walang-puknát** *adj*. endless, without stopping.
pukól: *n*. throw, toss; shot; **ipukól** *v*. to toss, throw; **pukulan** *n*. hitting end to end.
pukpók: *n*. bang; hammering sound; **pukpukin** *id*. lazy.
puksâ: *adj*. exterminated; **pagpuksâ** *n*. massacre; complete defeat, annihilation.
puktô: *adj*. swollen (*pugtô*), *n*. portion, part; **puktú-puktô** *adj*. in small pieces.
pukyót: *n*. honeybee.
pudáy: (*slang*) *n*. vagina.
pudpód: *adj*. stubby; blunt; worn on the ends; **pudpurín** *v*. to wear out at the ends, make blunt.
puga: (Sp. *fuga*) *n*. escape; (*slang*) leaving a restaurant without paying the bill; female prostitute.
pugá: *n*. roe, eggs or fish or crabs.
pugák: *n*. sound of honking.
pugad: *n*. nest; **magpugad** *v*. to make a nest; **mamugad** *v*. to infest; be nestled in; **namugad sa dibdíb** *id*. in the mind and heart (nestled in the chest); **paniningaláng-pugad** *id*. starting to court girls (looking up in the nest); **pugad-aliwan** *n*. place of entertainment.
pugal: **ipugal** *v*. to tie, fasten; **nakapugal** *adj*. tied down, fastened.
pugante: (Sp. *fugante*) *n*. fugitive.
pugay: **magpugay** *v*. to take off one's hat.
pugità: *n*. cuttlefish, octopus.
pugnáw: *adj*. razed, completely destroyed.
pugo: (*slang*) *n*. hostage.
pugò: *n*. quail; **mamugò** *v*. to hunt for quail.
pugók: *adj*. short-necked; *n*. wringing the neck of a big fish.
pugonero: (Sp. *fogonero*) *n*. stoker, furnace tender.
pugong: *n*. cord, twine; hair ribbon; kerchief tied around the hair.
pugot₁: **pugutan** *v*. to decapitate; **pugót** *adj*. decapitated.
pugot₂: *n*. Negrito; black man.
pugtô: *n*. swelling of the eyes after crying; *adj*. cut off, severed.
puhág: *adj*. castrated.
puhunan: *n*. capital in business; investment; interest; **pamumuhunan** *n*. investment; **mamuhunan** *v*. to invest; **sa puhunan** at cost.
puil: *n*. coccyx.
pulá: *n*. red; *adj*. red; **kapulahán** *n*. redness; **magpulá** *v*. to wear red; **mamulá** *v*. to blush; **mamulá-mulá** *v*. to glow; look warm; **namúmulá** *adj*. reddening; bloodshot; **pampapulá** *n*. rouge; **pamulahín** *v*. to inflame; scorch; **pamumulá** *n*. glow, shine; blush; **pulá ng itlóg** *n*. yolk; **pumulá** *v*. to become red; **pulahán** *n*. Malabar red snapper; **puláng-matá** *n*. cavalla fish; **puláng magulang** *n*. deep red; **puláng-ngusò** *n*. sardine fingerling.
pulà: *n*. criticism; **mamulà** *v*. to criticize, find fault with; **mapamulà** *adj*. critical.
pulak: **pulakin** *v*. to cut off branches; clear away trees.
pulád: *n*. feather vane of an arrow; sprouting of feathers.
pulag: *n*. glare.

pulandít: *n.* spurt; squirt; (*coll.*) flirtatious woman.
pulanggós: *n.* escaping to freedom, slipping free.
pulás: *n.* departure; escape.
puláw: *n.* keeping watch over a sick person; **kapulawán** *n.* (*fig.*) loneliness.
pulbera: (Sp. *polvera*) *n.* powder box.
pulbó(s): (Sp. *polvo*) *n.* powder; (*slang*) winning a competition; beating to a pulp; **pulbos de mesa** *n.* person lucky in gambling.
pulburá: (Sp. *polvora*) *n.* gunpowder.
pulburón: (Sp. *polvorón*) *n.* kind of milk cookie.
pulea: (Sp. *polea*) *n.* pulley.
pulekos: (Sp. *flecos*) *n.* fringe.
pulgada: (Sp.) *n.* inch.
pulgás: (Sp.) *n.* flea.
puli: **pampuli, pamuli** *n.* replacement; **pulihan** *v.* to replace.
pulí: **pinamulihán** *n.* tradition.
pulikat: *n.* spasm, body cramps.
pulido: (Sp.) *adj.* neat; well-behaved; polished.
pulilan: *n.* lagoon; southwest direction.
pulín: *n.* roller placed under heavy objects to move them.
pulinas: (Sp. *polaínas*) *n.* leggings.
pulís: (Eng.) *n.* police; policeman; **pulís pito** *n* traffic cop; **pulís-kotong** *n.* corrupt cop.
pulisyá: (Sp. *policía*) *n.* police, police force.
pulmón: (Sp.) *n.* lung. (*bagà*)
pulò: *n.* isolated place.
pulô: *n.* island; **kapuluán** *n.* archipelago; **taga-pulô** *n.* islander.
pulók: *n.* feathers on the neck of fowls; pecking with the beak.
pulon: **pulunín** *v.* to wind, coil; **pulunán** *n.* reel, spool, bobbin.
pulong: *n.* meeting; **kapulungan** *n.* assembly, meeting; **magpulong** *v.* to meet; talk a matter over.
pulós: (Sp. *puro*) *adj.* completely, fully; entirely; all of the same kind.
pulot: *n.* picking up from the ground; (*coll.*) one who picks up balls at a tennis court; **mamulot** *v.* to pick up things; glean; **makápúlot** *v.* to happen to pick up, find; **pulutan** *n.* appetizers taken with alcohol (pick-up food); **pulutin** *v.* to pick up.
pulót: *n.* molasses; syrup; **pulót-gatâ** *n.* honeymoon; **pulót-sasá** *n.* nipa palm honey.
púlpito: (Sp.) *n.* pulpit.
pulpól: *adj.* blunt, dull.
pulseras: (Sp.) *n.* bracelet.
pulso: (Sp.) *n.* pulse, heartbeat.
pulubi: (*corruption of pobre*) *n.* poor person, beggar; pauper.
puluhan: *n.* handle.
pulupón: *n.* small group.
pulupot: *n.* turn, twist; **puluputin** *v.* to wind, twist, coil.
pulutan: (*rt. pulot*) *n.* appetizers taken with alcohol.
pulutóng: (Sp. *peloton*) *n.* platoon; group.
pumada: (Sp. *pomada*) *n.* pomade, hair grease.
pumarito: (*rt. dito*) *v.* to come here; **pumariyán** *v.* to go there; **pumaroón** *v.* to go there (distal).
pumento: (Sp. *fomento*) *n.* fomentation.
pumpiyáng: (Ch.) *n.* cymbals.
pumpón: *n.* bunch, cluster of flowers.
puná: *n.* remark, observation; criticism; **punahín** *v.* to remark; observe, notice.
punas: *n.* sponge bath, wiping; **punasan** *v.* to wipe; **pamunas** *n.* rag, something used to wipe.
pundá: (Sp. *funda*) *n.* pillowcase.
pundakán: *adj.* full, replete.
pundadór: (Sp. *fundador*) *n.* founder.
pundár: (Sp. *fundar*) **ipundár** *v.* to found, establish.
pundí₁: (Sp. *fundir*) **mapundí** *adj.* to burn out; **pundido** *adj.* burnt out; cast (metals).
pundí₂: (*slang*) *adj.* angry, irritated.
pundilyo: *var. of pundió*: seat of pants.
pundió: (Sp. *fondillos*) *n.* seat of pants.
pundiyá: *n.* seat of the pants.
pundó: (Sp. *fondo*) *n.* lodging place; landing place; parking place; **pumundó** *v.* to lodge in a place; beach a boat; park; **punduhan** *n.* boarding place, anchorage.
punebre: (Sp. *funebre*) *n.* funeral march.
punerarya: (Sp. *funeraria*) *n.* funeral parlor.

punit: *n.* tear, rip; **pumunit, punitin** *v.* to tear, rip.

punlâ: *n.* seedling; **punlaan** *n.* seed bed; **pumunlâ, punlaán** *v.* to sow.

punò$_1$: *n.* chief, leader; superior; **mamunò** *v.* to head, lead; conduct; preside over; **pinunò** *n.* official, officer; **punong-gurò** *n.* head teacher, principal; **pamunuan** *v.* to lead; preside; **pámunuán** *n.* regime, board of officers; **pagpunuan** *v.* to preside, act as chief; **pagpupunò** *n.* leadership. **pasimunò** *n.* perpetrator; **pinakapunò** *n.* chief; **punong-katawán** (*slang*) *n.* penis. [See also *simunò*]

punò$_2$: *n.* origin, beginning, source; base; **puno't dulo** *id.* beginning and end (trunk and end).

punò$_3$: *n.* tree. (*punong-kahoy*)

punô: *adj.* full, filled; **kapunuán** *n.* fullness; what must be added to fill; **magpunô** *v.* to compensate for; **mapunô** *v.* to be filled; **pumunô** *v.* to cram, make full, fill up; **punuán, punán** *v.* to fill; add to; **punuín, punín** *v.* to fill something; **púnuán** *adj.* fully loaded.

punsó: *n.* ant hill; hillock.

punsón: (Sp. *punzón*) *n.* awl, ice-pick; punch.

punsóy: *n.* feng shui.

punsyón: (Sp. *función*) *n.* function; social gathering.

punta: (Sp.) *n.* point; aim, purpose; headland; direction, destination; **kápuntahán** *v.* to end up, result as; **magpuntá** *v.* to go to, head towards; **pumuntá** *v.* to go to; **papuntá** *adj.* bound for; **papuntahín** *v.* to send; **púntahan** *n.* destination; **puntahán** *v.* to go to a place; **puntahin** *n.* aim, purpose.

puntablangko: (Sp. de *punta en blanco*) *adj.* direct; *n.* target practice.

puntás: (Sp.) *n.* lace, lacework.

puntero: (Sp.) *n.* pointer; hand of a clock.

puntiryá: (Sp. *punteria*) *n.* target practice; aim; **ipuntiryá** *v.* to aim; **puntiryahan** *n.* aim, target.

punto: (Sp.) *n.* period; point scored; accent, intonation.

puntók: *n.* cone; apex of a cone.

puntód: *n.* mound; tomb; tee in golf; sandbank.

puntós: (Sp.) *n.* point, score.

punyagî: **magpunyagî** *v.* to struggle, try hard; **pagpupunyagî** *n.* determination, struggle, hard effort.

punyál: (Sp. *puñal*) *n.* dagger.

punyemas: *var. of punyetas.*

punyetas: *interj.* mild curse word, damn!

punyós: (Sp. *puños*) *n.* cuff.

pungás: *adj.* half-asleep (just woken up).

pungát: *adj.* having one eye half-closed.

pungay: **mapungay** *adj.* languid.

pungká: *n.* hitting someone on the coccyx with the fingers clasped together; partially raising a heavy object with a lever.

pungkâ: (Ch.) *n.* intrigue; **mamumungkâ** *n.* one prone to intrigue.

pungkól: *adj.* armless, handless; deformed in the arm.

pungga: *n.* living or hiding in a den; **pungggahan** *n.* den; lair.

punggál: *adj.* cut off above the root.

punggî: *adj.* tailless; blunted; *n.* bobtail.

punggók: *adj.* tailless; stubby, stumpy, short and thick.

punggós: **punggusín** *v.* to wrap in a handkerchief.

punglô: (Ch.) *n.* bullet.

pungól: *adj.* blunt.

pungos: **pungós** *adj.* cut off; lopped off; with the ear cut off; **magpungos** *v.* to cut the tops off, prune.

puol: *n.* wavy-lined grouper

puón: *n.* lord, master.

pupás: *adj.* faded in color.

pupitre: (Sp.) *n.* desk.

pupó: *adj.* cut off near the base.

pupô: **mamupô** *v.* to address someone respectfully using *pô*.

pupók: (*slang*) *adj.* busy.

pupog: **pupugin** *v.* to peck at, smother with kisses.

pupól: *n.* picking flowers.

pupóg: *adj.* pampered, spoiled; putting the finger over the lips; **magpupót** *v.* to put a finger across the lips to request silence.

pupos: *n.* young taro leaves; (*slang*) prostitute.

pupót: *n.* shredding, tearing to shreds; putting

the finger across the mouth to ask for silence.

purás: *n.* orange or lemon blossoms.

purát: **kapurát** *n.* particle, small piece.

purbado: (Sp. *probado*) *adj.* proved, tried.

purgá: (Sp.) *n.* purgative; **pamurgá** *n.* purgative.

purgatoryo: (Sp. *purgatorio*) *n.* purgatory.

purgón: (Sp. *furgon*) *n.* baggage on a railway train.

puri: *n.* praise, fame, honor; name, reputation; **kapurihán** *n.* honor, credit; **kasiraáng-puri** *n.* scandal, disgrace; **magbangong-puri** *v.* to save face; **magpuri** *v.* to praise, bless; compliment; exalt; **papuri** *n.* praise, commendation, compliment; **papurihan** *v.* to praise, applaud; **may-papuri** *adj.* complimentary.

puríl: (Sp. *pueril*) **puríl** *adj.* stunted in growth.

puripiká: (Sp. *purifica*) **puripikahán** *v.* to purify; **puripikadór** *n.* purifier.

purista: (Sp.) *n.* purist.

purít: **kapurít** *n.* particle, small piece or amount.

puritano: (Sp.) *n.* Puritan.

purmás: (Sp. *forma*) *n.* unconsecrated host.

purnada: (Sp.) *n.* swindling; wasted efforts; failure to follow through; **mapurnada** *v.* to be swindled; wasted, unrealized (efforts).

puro: (Sp.) *adj.* pure.

purók: *n.* district, place; neighborhood; region.

puról: **mapuról** *adj.* blunt, dull; **mapuról ang ulo** *id.* with a poor memory.

pururot: *n.* sound of a fart.

púrpura: (Sp.) *adj.* purple.

pursigido: (Sp.) *adj.* diligent, with initiative.

purtuna: (Sp. *fortuna*) *n.* fortune, fate.

purunggô: *n.* broken crystals; short-necked bottle.

pusà: *n.* cat; (*slang*) informer; **magpusà** *v.* to play the cat (use foul means to gain support); **kapusaan** *n.* (*fig.*) act of a traitor.

pusak: **mamusak** *v.* to break out (skin disease).

pusakál: *adj.* addicted.

puság: *n.* wriggling of fish.

pusalì: *n.* mire under the bamboo platform of a house.

pusáw: *n.* wriggling movement.

pusible: (Sp. *fusible*) *n.* electric fuse.

pusikít: *adj.* intense darkness.

pusít: *n.* squid.

puslít: *n.* smuggling; squirt, spurt.

pusò: *n.* heart; center; **taós-pusò** *adj.* sincere, heartfelt; **wasák ang pusò** broken hearted; **magandáng pusò** *adj.* kind hearted.

pusók: **mapusók** *adj.* aggressive, impetuous; excited.

pusod: *n.* navel; hub; deepest part of a river or ocean.

pusód: *n.* bun, topknot; auger, borer; arrow point; **pusudán, pusdán** *v.* to knot the hair of someone.

pusón: *n.* abdomen.

pusong: *n.* foolishness.

pusóy: *n.* poker.

puspás: *n.* dish of rice gruel and chicken.

puspós: *adj.* full, replete; **puspusán** *v.* to complete.

pustá: (Sp. *posta*) *n.* bet, wager; **mamustá** *v.* to bet; **pustahán** *v.* to bet on.

pustiso: (Sp. *postizo*) *n.* artificial teeth, denture.

pustura: (Sp.) *n.* posture; elegant dressing; **pusturyoso** *adj.* stylish, always well-dressed.

pus(u)welo: (Sp. *pozuelo*: small pit) *n.* small cup or bowl; measuring cup.

pusyáw: (Ch.) *n.* tarnish; discoloration.

puta: (Sp.) *n.* prostitute.

putak: *n.* cackle of hens, squawk; **puták nang puták** *adj.* always nagging; **nagpúputák** *id.* talking to much.

putakî: *n.* state of being scattered in small quantities.

putaktí: *n.* wasp, hornet; **parang pinutaktí** *id.* being swarmed.

putahe: (Sp. *potaje*) *n.* viand; course of a meal.

putál: *n.* small amount in excess of round figures.

putat: **pamutat** *n.* appetizer, tidbits taken with alcohol.

putatsíng: (*slang*) *n.* prostitute.

putbol: (Eng.) *n.* football; **putbolista** *n.* football player.

putháw: *n.* hatchet, small ax.

puti: *n.* picking of flowers; **pagputi ng buhay** *n.* taking the life of (kill).

putî: *adj.* white; **mamutî** *v.* to become white; **paputiín** *v.* to make white; **putián** *adj.* whitish; *v.* to color white; **pumutî** *v.* to whiten, become white; **putíng-tabing** *n.* silver screen; **putíng-tainga** *n.* white ear (stingy); **pag putî ang uwák** *id.* never (when the crow turns white); **putî ang tainga** *id.* selfish (ear is white).

putik: *n.* mud; **magputik** *v.* to become muddy; **putikan** *n.* muddy place.

putlâ: *n.* paleness; **maputlâ** *adj.* pale, pallid; pasty, white.

putlán: (rt. *putol*) *v.* to cut off from.

puto: *n.* kind of rice flour cake; (*slang*) *adj.* easy; **~-soko** *n.* dry biscuits made from rice starch; **~-maya** *n.* rice cake made from sticky rice.

putók₁: *n.* blast, report; bang; (*slang*) body odor; **mamutók** *v.* to burst; explode; **pagputók** *n.* explosion; eruption; **paputók** *n.* explosive; **paputukán** *v.* to detonate, discharge; blow up, explode; **pumutók** *v.* to explode; bounce (check); **máputukán** *v.* to suffer an explosion; (*fig.*) to be held responsible unexpectedly; **magputók ang dibdíb** *id.* to experience great sorrow (break the chest); **nagpúputók ang butsé** *id.* jealous, angry (crop is breaking); **nagpúputók sa tao** *id.* very compact;.

putók₂: *n.* crack in wood, crack in the ground; **putók sa buhò** *n.* illegitimate child.

putol: *n.* cut; **putól** *adj.* cut off; **pamutol** *n.* something that cuts; **putulan, putlán** *v.* to cut down, prune; amputate, cut off from; **putlín** *v.* to cut off; **kaputol** *n.* fragment, cut piece; **maputol** *adj.* cut; **pagkaputol** *n.* cutting off; severance.

putong: *n.* turban; crown.

putós: *adj.* crammed; replete.

putót: *adj.* burdened with work; short, cut short; with a twisted or broken neck; *n.* short pants.

putpót: *n.* sound of a car horn.

putrangka: (Sp. *potranca*) *n.* filly, young mare.

putsa: (*slang*) *excl.* damn.

putsero: (Sp. *puchero*) *n.* meat stew.

puwá: (Sp. *pua*) *n.* plectrum (for playing stringed instruments).

puwáng: *n.* gap, space between; way.

puweblo: (Sp. *pueblo*) *n.* township, town.

puwede: (Sp. *puede*) *v.* can, possible.

puwera: (Sp. *fuera*) *interj.* get out!; *prep.* except; **puwerahin** *v.* to exclude.

puwersa: (Sp. *fuerza*) *n.* force, strength; pressure; **mamuwersa** *v.* to force; **mapuwersa** *v.* to be forced; **pamumuwersa** *n.* pressure, using force; **puwersahín** *v.* to force something.

puwerte: (Sp. *fuerte*) *adj.* strong; loud; vigorous.

puwerto: (Sp. *puerto*) *n.* port, harbor.

puwés: (Sp. *pues*) *conj.* therefore.

puwesto: (Sp. *puesto*) *n.* place; position; employment; **nakapuwesto** *adj.* in position; **ipuwesto** *v.* to install, establish in a place; **pumuesto** *v.* to take a position.

puwíng: *n.* dust in the eye; **mapuwíng** *adj.* with foreign matter in the eyes; **puwingín** *v.* to throw dust in someone's eyes; (*fig.*) contradict.

puwít: *n.* buttocks, rump; **puwitán** *n.* rear, seat; bottom; **puwít ng palayók** *id.* refers to something not understood or clear (bottom of pot); **pumuwít** *v.* to turn one's buttocks to; **sa puwitán** at the rear.

puyat: *n.* lack of sleep; insomnia; **magpuyát** *v.* to stay awake all night; **mapagpuyát** *adj.* prone to staying up late; **pagpupuyát** *n.* night vigil; **puyatin** *v.* to keep someone up late at night (or all night).

puyaw: *n.* fresh juice of sugar cane.

puyo: *n.* climbing perch.

puyó: *n.* cowlick; whirling motion; **puyó ng bagyó** *n.* eye of the storm; **puyó ng tubig** *n.* eddy; **puyó sa pisngí** *n.* dimple; **may puyó sa talampakan** *id.* wanderer (has a cowlick in the sole).

puyók: *n.* wringing the neck of fowls; group of gossipers in a circle.

puyód: *n.* topknot.

puyós: *n.* friction; **magpuyós** *v.* to start a

friction fire.
puyupoy: *n.* wagging of the tail.
puyupóy: *n.* pickets of a fence.
pwe: *interj.* expresses disgust (sound of spitting).

R

ra: *n.* the letter *r*.
raán: *var. of daán* after a vowel.
raketa: (Sp. *raqueta*) *n.* racket.
rakitis: (Sp. *raquitis*) *n.* rickets.
radyá: *n.* species of banana, rajah banana.
radyo: (Sp. *radio*) *n.* radio; radium.
ragasâ: *var.* of *dagasâ*: rush, hasty action.
ragid: (*slang*) *n.* bum; dressing too informally.
rahuyo: *n.* enticement, inducement.
rambol: (Eng. *rumble*) *n.* gang fight.
rambután: *n.* lychee type fruit.
rantso: (Sp. *rancho*) *n.* ranch; **rantsero** *n.* ranchman.
ranggo: (Sp. *rango*) *n.* rank; grade.
rangyâ: see under *parangyâ*.
rasón: (Sp. *razón*) *n.* reason.
raspa: (Sp.) *n.* rasp, curette.
rasyón: (Sp. *ración*) *n.* ration; allowance.
Ratagnon: *n.* ethnic group and language from the southern tip of Western Mindoro.
ratók: (*slang*) *adj.* feeble-minded.
ratrát: *n.* sound of rapid gunfire; **ratratín** *v.* to fire bullets on.
ratsa: (*slang*) *n.* requesting help.
ratsada: (*coll.*, Sp. *racha*) *n.* streak, run of luck; **rumatsada** *v.* to enjoy a (winning) streak.
raw: *var. of daw* after vowels.
ray: (Eng.) *n.* rye.
raya: (Sp.) *n.* line.
rayág: **karayagán** *adj.* more important; right side of.
rayama: *n.* private conversation. **karayama** *n.* intermingling; constant companion.
rayos-ekis: (Sp. *rayo equis*) *n.* x-ray.
rayuma: (Sp.) *n.* rheumatism.
rebaha: (Sp. *rebaja*) *n.* discount, reduction.
rebálida: (Sp. *reválida*) *n.* oral examination for post-graduate students.
rebelde: (Sp.) *n.* rebel. (*manghihimagsík*)
rebentadór: (Sp. *reventador*) *n.* firecracker.
rebesino: (Sp. *revesino*) *n.* old card game.
rebisado: (Sp. *revisado*) *adj.* revised; **rebisadór** *n.* reviewer; inspector; auditor.
rebokado: (Sp. *revocado*) *adj.* revoked; withdrawn.
rebosado: (Sp.) *adj.* cooked with batter.
rebulto: (Sp.) *n.* statue.
rekargo: (Sp. *recargo*) *n.* additional tax; increase of a sentence.
rekisa: (Sp. *requisa*) *n.* inspection. **rekisahin** *v.* to inspect.
rekisisyón: (Sp. *requisición*) *n.* requisition.
rekisito: (Sp. *requisito*) *n.* requisite, requirement.
reklamado: (Sp. *reclamado*) *adj.* reclaimed.
reklamadór: (Sp. *reclamador*) *n.* reclaimer; complainant.
reklamo: (Sp.) *n.* complaint; claim; reclamation.
rekluta: (Sp. *recluta*) *n.* recruit. **reklutahín** *v.* to recruit.
reklutadór: (Sp. *reclutador*) *n.* recruiter.
rekobeko: (Sp. *recoveco*) *n.* roundabout way; unnecessary details. (*kuskus balungos*)
rekodo: (Sp. *recodo*) *n.* angle.
rekomenda: (Sp.) **irekomenda** *v.* to recommend. (*itagubilin*)
rekonosido: (Sp. *reconocido*) *adj.* recognized; acknowledged; accepted.
rekonosimyento: (Sp. *reconocimiento*) *n.* recognition; acknowledgement.
rekonsilyado: (Sp. *reconciliado*) *adj.* reconciled. (*nagkakásundô na*)
rekorida: (Sp. *recorrida*) *n.* regular round of a policeman.
rekorte: (Sp. *recorte*) *n.* newspaper clipping.
rekreo: (Sp. *recreo*) *n.* recreation.
rek(u)wa: (Sp. *recua*) *n.* multitude; **sangrekwa(ng)** *n.* bunch of, pack of.
rekwerdo: (Sp. *recuerdo*) *n.* remembrance.
redoma: (Sp.) *n.* flask. (*prasko*)
regadera: (Sp.) *n.* sprinkler. (*pandilíg*)
regalo: (Sp.) *n.* gift. (*kaloób, handóg*)

regalya: (Sp. *regalia*) *n.* royal pomp.
regla: (Sp.) *n.* rule; ruler; menstruation; **regladór** *n.* ruler; **reglamento** *n.* regulation.
rehas: (Sp. *rejas*) *n.* grating, grill.
rehimyento: (Sp. *regimiento*) *n.* regiment.
rehistro: (Sp. *registro*) *n.* register, registry; **registradór** *n.* registrar; cash register.
relebo: (Sp. *relevo*) *n.* relief, substitute.
relihión: (Sp. *religión*) *n.* religion.
reló: (Sp. *reloj*) *n.* clock, watch; **relohero** *n.* watchmaker; **relohería** *n.* watch shop.
relyebe: (Sp. *relieve*) *n.* relief, raised work.
relyeno: (Sp. *relleno*) *adj.* stuffed (food).
rematá: (Sp.) *n.* foreclosure; sale of mortgaged property; **rematado** *adj.* foreclosed; auctioned off.
rematse: (Sp. *remache*) *n.* rivet.
remedyo: (Sp.) *n.* remedy; relief.
remolke: (Sp. *remolque*) *n.* towing.
remontados: (*obs.*, Sp.) *n.* indigenous hill people (used during the Spanish regime).
renasimyento: (Sp. *renacimiento*) *n.* renaissance. (*mulíng-pagsilang*)
renda: (Sp. *rienda*) *n.* rein.
rendí: (Sp. *rendir*) **rendihín** *v.* to confuse, tire out.
rentas: (Sp.) *n.* government income; revenue; **rentas internas** *n.* internal revenue.
reparo: (Sp.) *n.* notice, observation.
repaso: (Sp.) *n.* review.
repike: (Sp.) *n.* peal of bells.
repinado: (Sp. *refinado*) *adj.* refined.
repolyo: (Sp. *repollo*) *n.* cabbage.
reporma: (Sp. *reforma*) *n.* reform.
repositoryo: (Sp. *repositorio*) *n.* repository.
resada: (Sp. *rezada*) *n.* recited prayers.
reserba: (Sp. *reserva*) *n.* reserve.
resetaryo: (Sp. *recetario*) *n.* doctor's prescription pad.
resibaryo: (Sp. *recibario*) *n.* stub book.
resibo: (Sp. *recibo*) *n.* receipt.
resma: (Sp.) *n.* ream.
respeto: (Sp.) *n.* respect.
respiradór: (Sp.) *n.* respirator.
restaurán: (Sp.) *n.* restaurant; ~ **de banggáw** third class restaurant.
resulta: (Sp.) *n.* result.
retaso: (Sp. *retazo*) *n.* remnant, scrap; one's child; small piece of cloth.
retirado: (Eng.) *adj.* retired.
reto: (Sp.) *n.* challenge.
retoke: *n.* retouch; **retokado** *adj.* retouched.
retrato: (Sp.) *n.* photo, portrait; picture.
reyna: (Sp. *reina*) *n.* queen.
reyno: (Sp. *reino*) *n.* kingdom.
ribál: (Sp. *rival*) **karibál** *n.* rival.
ribete: (Sp.) *n.* trimming for a dress; ornamental edge.
rikado: (Sp. *recado*) *n.* spices, condiments.
rikonsí: (Sp. *reconocer*) **rikonosihín** *v.* to diagnose.
rigadera: (Sp.) *n.* water sprinkler. (*pandilíg*)
rigodón: (Sp.) *n.* rigodon dance; lactarid fish.
riles: (Sp. *carriles*) *n.* rails. (*daáng-bakal*)
rima: (Sp.) *n.* rhyme. (*tugmâ*)
rimarim: **marimarim** *v.* to feel disgusted.
rimas: (Sp.) *n.* breadfruit.
rimatse: (Sp. *rematse*) *n.* rivet.
rin: *var. of din* after vowels.
ripa: (Sp.) *n.* raffle. **ripahin** *v.* to raffle.
ripike: (Sp. *repique*) *n.* peal of bells.
ritmo: (Sp.) *n.* rhythm.
rito: (Sp.) *n.* rite.
riyesgo: (Sp. *riesgo*) *n.* risk.
robot: (Eng.) *n.* robot.
rodilyo: (Sp. *rodillo*) *n.* roller; rolling pin.
rolyo: (Sp. *rollo*) *n.* roll. **rolyohín** *v.* to roll. **roly-rolyo** *adj.* in rolls.
romansa: (Sp. *romanza*) *n.* romance, love affair.
romanse: (Sp. *romance*) *n.* romance; tale.
Romblomanon: *n.* ethnic group and language from Romblon and Sibuyan Islands.
romero: (Sp.) *n.* rosemary.
ronda: (Sp.) *n.* patrol; round of cards or drinks. **róndahan** *n.* small fire brigade station. **rondahán** *v.* to patrol.
rondalya: (Sp. *rondalla*) *n.* string orchestra.
rondilyo: (Sp. *rondillo*) *n.* roller.
roón: *var.* of *doón* after a vowel.
ropero: (Sp.) *n.* hamper.
rosa: (Sp.) *n.* rose.
rosál: (Sp.) *n.* gardenia.
rosario: (Sp.) *n.* rosary. (*dásalang kuwintas*)

rosas: (Sp.) *n.* rose; pink.
roskas: (Sp. *rosca*) *n.* thread of a screw.
rosilyo: (Sp. *rosillo*) *n.* roan-colored (horses).
rota: (Eng.) *n.* route.
rotaryo: (Eng.) *n.* Rotary, Rotary Club.
rotonda: (Sp.) *n.* circular intersection.
rubí: (Sp.) *n.* ruby.
ruleta: (Sp.) *n.* roulette.
rumpí: *n.* barracuda.
rupike: (Sp.) *n.* peal of a church bell.
rurok: *n.* highest point, acme.
Ruso: (Sp.) *n.* Russian.
ruta: (Sp.) *n.* route, routine.
ruweda: (Sp. *rueda*) *n.* wheel.
ruwibarbo: (Sp.) *n.* rhubarb.
ruwina: (Sp. *ruina*) *n.* ruins.
ruwisenyór: (Sp. *ruiseñor*) *n.* nightingale.

S

sa₁: *prep.* to, at in, on (marks locative case); **para sa** for; **sa abâ ko** woe to me.
sa₂: *n.* the letter *s*.
saab: *n.* burning superficially over a flame.
saák: *adj.* split lengthwise.
saád: **isaád** *v.* to relate; state.
saán: *interrog.* where; from what place; **taga-saán** from where?; **saanmán** *adv.* everywhere; **kahit saán** anywhere, wherever.
saát: *n.* hook attached to the end of a pole.
sabá: *n.* species of banana.
sabák₁: *n.* notch on a post used to support a beam.
sabák₂: *n.* blind attack; **sumabak, sabakan** *v.* to attack blindly; (*fig.*) to undertake something suddenly and vigorously.
sabád: **makisabád** *v.* to interrupt.
Sábado: (Sp.) *n.* Saturday.
sabagay: *adv.* after all.
sabal: *n.* embankment.
sabalás: *n.* northeast wind; northeast.
sábalo: *n.* spawner of milkfish.
sabanyón: (Sp. *sabañon*) *n.* swelling caused by the cold.
sabang: *n.* advance scouting patrol.
sabáng: *n.* intersection.
sabat: *n.* design woven into cloth.
sabát: *n.* dowel, peg; interruption; meddling; unexpected answer; **sabatín** *v.* to interrupt; cut across someone's path.
sabáw: *n.* broth; **masabáw** *adj.* with broth.
sabáy: *adj.* simultaneous, at the same time; concurrent; **magkasabáy** *v.* to happen at the same time; **kasabayín** *v.* to have a person accompany oneself; **makisabáy** *v.* to go at the same time; **panabáy** *adv.* simultaneously; **sabayán** *v.* to accompany; **sabáy-sabáy** *adj.* at the same time; in unison; **sumabáy** *v.* to accompany; do or happen at the same time.
sabi: *n.* statement; *v.* to say; **kasabihán** *n.* saying, expression; *adj.* famous; **sabihin** *v.* to say, tell; **sabí-sabihin** *v.* to mention repeatedly; **ipagsabí, ipanabi** *v.* to tell to many; **pasabi** *n.* message sent; **pakisabi** *v.* please tell; **pasabihan** *v.* to notify; **makisabi** *v.* to request someone to relay a message; **magsabi** *v.* to say, tell; state; **magpasabi** *v.* to get someone to say; **makapagsabi** *v.* to be able to tell; **pagsabihan** *v.* to reprimand; **sabihan** *v.* to notify; reprove; **sinabi** *v.* said; *adj.* professed; **tagapagsabi** *n.* spokesperson; **waláng sinásabi** *id.* without importance or ability (saying nothing); **may sinásabi** *id.* intelligent; **ibig sabihin** *v.* to mean; **páunáng-sabi** *n.* official notice; **sabí-sabí** *n.* rumor, hearsay; **sa madalíng sabi** in short.
sabík: *adj.* eager, keen; **manabík** *v.* to be anxious, yearn for.
sabíd: **isabíd** *v.* to coil, entangle; **masabíd** *v.* to get entangled in.
sabila: *n.* kind of ornamental plant.
sabit: *n.* hanging; getting caught doing something bad; **sabitan** *v.* to hang with a nail; **sabitán** *n.* hanger; **sumabit** *v.* to latch on; (*fig*) be dependent on; **násabit ng pantáy** *id.* met one's match; **may sabit** *id.* to be inconvenienced.
sabláy: *n.* blow with the fist; innuendo, indirect hint; speed and swiftness; **pasabláy** *adj.* indirect; oblique; **sumabláy** *v.* to miss the

target.

sable: (Sp.) *n*. saber.

sablót: **sablutín** *v*. to snatch suddenly.

sabnáw: *n*. small pool, puddle.

sabo: *n*. large flock; **sabuhín** *adj*. attractive (people).

sabog: *n*. scattering; **magsabog** *v*. to scatter, strew; **isabog** *v*. to scatter, spread about, disseminate; **pasabugin** *v*. to blow up, blast; **sabugan** *v*. to sprinkle about. **pagsabog** *n*. explosion, blast; **sumabog** *v*. to explode; scatter; **tagapagsabog** *n*. seed sower.

sabóg: (*slang*) *adj*. high on drugs; *n*. wreck.

sabón: (Sp. *jabón*) *n*. soap; **sumabón, sabunán** *v*. to soap; **nasabón** *adj*. soaped; (*coll*.) scolded, reprimanded. **sábúnan** *n*. soap dish; soap factory; (*coll*.) reprimanding.

sabong: *n*. cockfight; (*slang*) *n*. sexual intercourse.

sabotahe: (Sp. *sabotaje*) *n*. sabotage. **sabutahihin** *v*. to sabotage.

saboy: *n*. splash, splatter; **magsaboy** *v*. to splash.

sabsáb: *n*. noisy eating; manger, crib; **sumabsáb** *v*. to eat like a pig.

sabúkay: *n*. slap in the face; beating of the waves; combed backward by the fingers (hair).

sabukót: *n*. red-winged concal bird.

sabunot: *n*. pulling the hair.

sabungol: *n*. act of pulling one's own hair.

sabután: *n*. screwpine.

sabwát: *n*. accomplice, partner in a crime; **magkasabwát** *v*. to connive with, plot; **sabwatan** *n*. plot, conspiracy.

saka: *n*. agriculture; **magsasaká, magsasáka** *n*. farmer; **magsaka** *v*. to farm; **sakahan** *n*. farm land.

sakâ: *adv*. and then; besides; afterwards; **sakâ na** some other time.

sakáb: *n*. kind of basket-like fish trap; getting someone to tell the truth by tricky questioning.

sakada: (Sp. *sacada*) *n*. laborers hired from the outside that work for cheaper pay.

sakág: *n*. fishing net mounted between two poles.

sakál: *adj*. choked, strangled; **sakalín** *v*. to choke; **sinasakál ang bituka** *id*. economizing.

sakalì: *adv*. in case, if; perhaps; **bakasakalì** by chance; **pabakasakalì** *adj*. random, haphazard; **pasakalì** *n*. subjunctive mode; **saká-sakalì** just in case.

sakáng: *adj*. bowlegged.

sakarina: (Sp.) *n*. saccharin.

sakate: (Sp. *zacate*) *n*. hay, grass fodder; (*slang*) marijuana.

sakáy$_1$: *n*. passenger, load; **kasakáy** *n*. fellow passenger; **makisakáy** *v*. to ask for a ride; ride with; **nakasakáy** *adj*. riding; on board; **pasakáy** *adj*. by riding; *n*. someone requested or allowed to ride; **sasakyán** *n*. vehicle; transportation; **sakáyan** *n*. loading place; **sumakáy** *v*. to ride; go aboard, get on; **magpasakáy** *v*. to allow others to ride; **makapagsakáy** *v*. can carry (passengers); **nasakyán** *v*. was able to ride; (*fig*.) understood; **sakyán** *v*. to ride; get on, go aboard; mount; **tagapagsakáy** *n*. commercial driver.

sakáy$_2$: *n*. typesetting, font.

sakbát: *n*. shoulder band; *adj*. slung from the shoulder.

sakbáy: *adj*. with an arm around the waist of another (for support); **sakbayán** *v*. to guide by the waist.

sakbibi: *adj*. carried in a sling; carried in the arms (baby).

sakbót; **sakbutín** *v*. catch something falling.

sakdál$_1$: *n*. accusation, charge; suit; **isakdál** *v*. to charge in court, sue; impeach; **magsakdál** *v*. to file a complaint; **pagsasakdál** *n*. denunciation.

sakdál$_2$: *adj*. extreme; very great; **kasakdalán** *n*. perfection, excellence.

sakil: **pakikisakil** *n*. overabundance of passengers.

sakím: **masakím** *adj*. greedy, selfish, avaricious.

sakintà: (*slang*) *pro*. mine.

sakit$_1$: *n*. pain; sorrow; grief; **magsakit** *v*. to make a great effort; **pagpapakasakit** *n*. sacrifice; abnegation.

sakit$_2$: **malasakit** *n*. concern, interest; de-

votion; **magmalasakit** *v.* to show concern.
sakít: *n.* disease, sickness; pain, suffering; grudge; **manakít** *v.* to hurt others; **masakít** *adj.* sore, painful; hurtful; **magkasakít** *v.* to fall ill; **masaktán** *v.* to be hurt; **may-sakít** *adj.* sick; **sakitin** *adj.* sickly; **sakít ng ulo** *n.* headache; **sakít ng tiyán** *n.* stomach ache; **sakít sa bató** *n.* kidney problem; (*slang*) lazy.
saklâ: *n.* metal ring around handles of knifes; sitting astride an animal; kind of gambling card game.
sakláng: *n.* yoke; trestle horse.
sakláp: *n.* acrid taste; **masakláp** *adj.* bitter, acrid.
sakláw: *n.* degree, amount; limits; range; *adj.* included, inclusive; extensive, vast; **kasaklawán** *n.* generality; comprehensiveness; **saklawín** *v.* to include, contain, embrace; **panakláw** *n.* brackets; parenthesis.
sakláy: *n.* yoke; shawl; crutch.
saklít: *n.* loop of rope around the neck of jars to help carry them; entanglement of rope.
saklób: *n.* concave lid; *adj.* face to face; **magsaklób** *v.* to cover the head, put on a hat; cover a pot; **sumaklób** *v.* become superimposed; (*cards*) put a share of capital with the banker.
saklolo: *n.* aid, succor; **pasaklolo** *v.* to ask for help; **sumaklolo** *v.* to help, aid.
saklóng: *n.* share in a harvest; bracket, parenthesis; **saklungán** *v.* to help someone in his work.
saklót: *n.* grabbing; **saklutín** *v.* to grab, snatch.
sakmál: *n.* quick bite; *adj.* held in the mouth; **sakmalín** *v.* to snap at; grab with the mouth.
sakmát: *var.* of *sakmál*: grab with the mouth.
sakmatá: *n.* wastefulness.
saknóng: *n.* stanza; section of a ricefield assigned to a worker; **saknungán** *v.* to help someone in his work.
sako: (Sp. *saco*) *n.* sack.
sakob: **pansakob** *n.* cover, covering.
sakol: *n.* cutting of sugarcane.
sakól: *n.* quantity of food that the fingers can put in the mouth; **sakulín** *v.* to put food in the mouth with the fingers.
sakong: *n.* heel; **apo sa** ~ great great grandchild.
sakop: *n.* conquest, subject (under control); **masakupan** *v.* to occupy a place; be under the jurisdiction of; **pagsakop** *n.* occupation; **sakupin** *v.* to conquer; seize; occupy.
sakote: (*slang*) *n.* catching; arresting; **masakote** *v.* to be caught, apprehended; arrested.
sakramento: (Sp. *sacramento*) *n.* sacrament.
sakré: *adj.* selfish; greedy, avaricious.
sakriléhiyo: (Sp. *sacrilegio*) *n.* sacrilege.
sakripisyo: (Sp. *sacrificio*) *n.* sacrifice.
sakristán: (Sp. *sacristán*) *n.* sacristan, acolyte.
saksâ: *adj.* abundant; **sumaksâ** *v.* to become abundant.
saksák$_1$: *n.* pierce, stab; **saksakan** *n.* to stab someone.
saksák$_2$: *n.* stuffing, tight packing; **isaksák** *v.* to cram, stuff into.
saksí: *n.* eyewitness; **saksihán** *v.* to testify.
saktán: (*rt. sakít*) *v.* to hurt, harm; injure.
sakunâ: *n.* accident; mishap; misfortune.
sakwá: *n.* stump, base of a banana plant.
sakwîl: *n.* denial, refusal.
sakyád: *adj.* carried inside the belt.
sakyán: (*rt. sakáy*) *v.* to ride; get on, mount.
sakyód: *n.* net for catching insects; **pagsakyód** *n.* sideswipe; swinging motion of using a net; **panakyód** *n.* pouch net.
sákyutib: (*slang*, Eng.) *n.* executive, big person in business.
sadlák: *n.* falling into disgrace.
sadlók: **sadlukín** *v.* to scoop out with a dipper.
sadsád: **isadsád** *v.* to beach, ground; **sumadsád** *v.* to run aground; **masadsád** *v.* to be grounded; stranded.
sadyâ: *n.* purpose, aim; *adv.* on purpose, intentionally; **sinadyâ** *adj.* intentional; **magsadyâ** *v.* to do on purpose; **pasadyâ** *adj.* custom made, made to order.
sagà: *n.* kind of vine with red and black seeds.
sagaák: *n.* cracking noise of breaking wood.
sagabal: *n.* barrier, obstacle; hindrance; hurdle; **sumagabal** *v.* to hinder, interfere; oppose; **masagabal** *adj.* full of impediments; **sagabalan** *v.* to impede, block.
sagakán: *n.* bamboo mats used as hot pots.

sagad: *adj*. at the height of fame.
sagád$_1$: *adj*. reaching the limit; sunk to the bottom; completely exhausted; completely broke; **isagád** *v*. to carry to completion; push through until finished; do until the end; **sagaran** *adj*. from end to end; from the beginning to the end.
sagád$_2$: *n*. snare for birds.
sagadsád: *n*. skidding, dragging.
sagal: *n*. slowness due to an obstacle.
sagala: (Sp. *zagala*) *n*. costumed maiden of a Lenten Procession.
sagalsál: *n*. spurt; jerk.
sagalwák: *n*. gush of water; spilling.
saganà: **masaganà** *adj*. abundant; plentiful; **kasaganaan** *n*. abundance; *adj*. plenty; **pasaganaan** *v*. to give abundantly.
sagansán: *n*. row; **sagansanín** *v*. to arrange in rows.
sagap: *n*. scoop net; something inhaled; (*fig*.) rumor picked up accidentally; **sagapin** *v*. to inhale; scoop off; **magpasagáp ng alimuom** *id*. spread false news, gossip (inhale vapor).
sagapák: *n*. sound of a small splash.
sagapsáp: *adj*. tasteless.
sagasà: **masagasà** *v*. to be run over; **sagasain** *v*. to run over; **sagasâ** *adj*. reckless; *n*. (*slang*) connections.
sagasáp: *adj*. insipid.
sagat: *n*. fishhook.
sagawsáw: *n*. gurgling sound.
sagay: *n*. coral.
sagayad: *n*. train of a gown.
sagkâ: *n*. shackle; **sagkaán** *v*. to shackle, restrain.
sagì: *n*. light touch; **masagì** *v*. to be touched lightly in passing; **sumagì** *v*. to touch lightly, graze.
sagila: **sumagila** *v*. to occur to one's mind; drop in at a house.
sagilap: *n*. thin bubbles (in liquor).
sagimpót: *n*. spurt of water; sudden start of a bird.
sagimsím: *n*. presentiment, premonition.
saginsín: *adj*. closely woven; dense (growth, population).
saging: *n*. banana; **sagingsaging** *n*. goatfish.
sagíp: **sag(i)pín** *v*. to save, salvage; **masagíp** *v*. to be saved.
sagisag: *n*. emblem; symbol; monument; **sumagisag** *v*. to symbolize; typify; **maysinásagisag** *adj*. symbolic.
sagisod: *n*. pushing on the floor with the foot.
sagison: *n*. pushing things closer together or in the corner.
sagitsít: *n*. hissing, fizz, sizzle; (*slang*) *adj*. hurried.
saglít: *n*. instant, moment; **saglitan** *adj*. brief; **isaglít** *v*. to do in a hurry.
sago: *n*. drip.
sagó: *n*. sago palm, tapioca.
sagô: (*slang*) *n*. nipple; **sagu-sagô** *n*. semen.
sagót: *n*. answer; reply; **managót** *v*. to answer for, assume responsibility; **panagot** *n*. voucher, surety; **panagután** *v*. to answer for; assume responsibility; **pananágútan** *n*. responsibility; liability; **kaságútan** *n*. answer, solution; **isagót** *v*. to give as an answer; **masagutan** *v*. to be guaranteed; **makasagót** *v*. to be able to answer; **makipagságútan** *v*. to answer back; **magságútan** *v*. to debate, have a heated argument; **magsasagót** *v*. to answer back continuously; **pagsagót** *n*. answering; assuming responsibility; **pagsaságútan** *n*. debate; angry words; **papanagutín** *v*. to be held responsible; **pasagutín** *v*. to request someone to answer; **pinapanánagót** *adj*. under fire; blamed; **ságútan** *n*. quarrel; controversy; **sagután** *v*. to guarantee; **sumagót**, **sagutín** *v*. to answer; be responsible for; **ságútin** *n*. responsibility; **tagapanagót** *n*. guarantor; **sagutan** *n*. controversy; dialogue; **may pananagutan sa buhay** *id*. married (have responsibility in life); **waláng-kapananágútan** *adj*. not responsible, unaccountable.
sagóy: *n*. light touch.
sagpák: *n*. noise of breaking waves; falling flat on one's stomach.
sagpáng: *n*. snatching with the mouth.
sagpî: **kasagpî** *n*. ally.
sagpín: (rt. *sagíp*) *v*. to save, rescue.
sagrado: (Sp.) *adj*. sacred; **sagrario** *n*. taber-

nacle.

sagság: *adj*. blunt at the point; sagging; split lengthwise; slipped (bone); **sagsagan** *adj*. rushed, hasty; **sumagság** *v*. to go somewhere in a hurry.

sagubáng: *n*. small hut.

sagunsón: *n*. neat pile; tracing, following up; **sagunsunín** *v*. to follow up; arrange in a neat pile.

sagupà: **magsagupà** *v*. to meet each other; **sagupain** *v*. to attack; collide with; **sagupaán** *n*. encounter; conflict.

sagupsóp: *n*. absorbing; sucking.

sagutsót: *n*. noise of sucking or sipping.

sagwâ: **masagwâ** *adj*. vulgar, indecent; immodest; obscene; **sumagwâ** *v*. to act indecently.

sagwák: *n*. sudden gush; **sagwakán** *v*. to splash someone.

sagwán: (Sp. *zagual*) *n*. paddle.

sagwíl: *n*. obstacle, hindrance; problem.

sahà: *n*. sheath of a banana plant.

sahang: *n*. strength of alcoholic drinks.

sahíg: *n*. floor.

sahing: *n*. species of tree. (*pilì*)

sahô: *adj*. subjugated; insufficient, lacking; **di-masahô** *adj*. invincible, unbeatable.

sahod: *n*. open hands used to catch a falling object; salary, wage; **isahod** *v*. to catch something falling; get a salary from. **pasahurin** *v*. to pay the wage of; **sumahod** *v*. to catch in the hands; receive a salary. **kasahurán** *n*. payday; full salary.

sahóg: *n*. mixture; **isahóg** *v*. to add an ingredient; **masahóg** *adj*. mixed with many ingredients.

sahól: **sahulín** *v*. to subdue, subjugate; **masahól**. adj. worse than; v. to be able to defeat or subdue; **sahól** *adj*. subdued; **kasahulán** *n*. deficiency; lacking. **masahól pa sa basáng upós** *id*. obstinate.

saíd: *adj*. completely consumed; **sairín** *v*. to strip bare. **kasairán** *n*. complete consumption.

saikapát: *n*. one fourth.

saikatló: *n*. one third.

saikwaló: *n*. one eighth; 7.5 centavo coin.

saíd: *adj*. exhausted, consumed; nothing left.

sainete: *n*. one act farce.

saing: *n*. steamed rice; **sinaing** *n*. steamed rice; **magsaing** *v*. to steam rice.

sala$_1$: *n*. error, mistake; blame; sin; **kasalanan** *n*. fault, blame; **makasalanan** *adj*. wrong; guilty; sinful; **magbigáy-sala** *v*. to blame; **pagkakasala** *n*. guilt.

sala$_2$: *n*. miss, failure to hit; **salahan** *v*. to miss a target; **waláng-sala** *adj*. not missing the target, accurate; **sumásala sa oras** *id*. indigent; not eating three meals a day due to poverty (missing the time).

sala(s): (Sp. *sala*) *n*. living room.

salà$_1$: **magsalà** *v*. to sieve, filter; **panalà** *n*. filter.

salà$_2$: **salâ** *adj*. broken, dislocated (bones); **salà sa init, salà sa lamíg** *id*. referring to a seasoned person that can withstand the heat or cold.

salá: **salá-salá** *adj*. interwoven; *n*. lattice.

salab: *n*. scorching; dried coconut leaf; **isalab** *v*. to scorch.

salabat: *n*. obstruction; **magkasalá-salabat** *v*. to entwine, entangle, be criss-crossed.

salabát: *n*. ginger tea.

salabay: *n*. octopus. (*pugità*)

salabíd: *n*. something that entangles; **isalabíd** *v*. to coil, twist around; **sumalabíd** *v*. to become entangled.

salabsáb: **isalabsáb** *v*. to smoke meat or fish.

salakáb: *n*. fishtrap; **salakabín** *v*. to fool someone into telling the truth.

salakasan: *n*. use of superior force.

salakát: *n*. kind of trap.

salakatâ: *n*. liveliness, jolliness.

salakay: *n*. attack, assault; **sumalakay** *v*. to attack.

salakbát: *n*. crossband (shoulder to hip); **salakbatín** *v*. to carry something hanging over the shoulder.

salakhatì: *n*. suffering, affliction.

salakóp: *n*. encircled, surrounded.

salakót: *n*. kind of native hat.

salaksák: *n*. probing.

salakuban: *n*. wooden jar.

salag: *n*. midwife's assistant.

salág: **salagín** *v.* to parry, ward off.
salaghatì: *n.* displeasure; resentment.
salagimsím: *n.* premonition; foreboding.
salágintô: *n.* goldbug.
salagíp: *n.* act of catching a falling object.
salagmák: **sumalagmák** *v.* to settle oneself comfortably.
salagóy: *n.* light touch.
salágubang: *n.* June beetle.
salahilo: *adj.* stubborn.
salalak: *n.* crosspiece; forklift.
salalay: *n.* container; flat thing put under another object, rack, support; **kinasasalalayan** *n.* pivot; **salalayan** *v.* to provide with a temporary support; **nakasalalay** *adj.* conditional, contingent, dependent upon something else.
salamangka: *n.* magic; juggling; **salamangkero** *n.* magician, juggler.
salamat: *n.* thanks; **pasalamatan** *v.* to thank; ~ **sa** thanks to.
salambáw: *n.* kind of fishing net; *adj.* heavier at the rear.
salamín: *n.* mirror; glass; crystal; eyeglasses; **magsalamín** *v.* to wear glasses; **salamíng babasagín** *id.* referring to delicate ladies (fragile glass).
salamisim: *n.* recollection, memory.
salampák: **masalampák** *v.* to fall on one's buttocks; plump down.
salampáy: *n.* neckerchief.
salamuhà: **makisalamuhà** *v.* to hobnob with other people.
salansán: *n.* file, stack; **salansanín** *v.* to pile; file.
salantâ: *n.* cripple; injury; *adj.* crippled; injured.
salang₁: **isalang** *v.* to put on the stove, over the fire; **isalang na ang palayók** *id.* the cat's in the bag, victory is sure (put the pot on the stove).
salang₂: (*slang*) *n.* assignment; share of work.
salang₃: *n.* light touch; **salangín** *v.* to lightly touch, to touch on; (*fig.*) to make an injurious remark.
salangà₁: *n.* species of ray, spineless devil ray.
salangà₂: *n.* hooked pole for picking fruits.
salangsáng: *n.* objection; protest; *adj.* contrary, opposite; **salansangín** *v.* to oppose.
salangat: *n.* hook attached to a pole for picking fruit; **napasalangat** *adj.* caught between branches.
salanggapáng: *adj.* mischievous.
salangsáng: *n.* objection; opposition.
salap: *n.* small fishing net; tip (for service).
salapáng: *n.* harpoon, trident.
salapáw: *adj.* superficial; skin deep; **salapawín** *v.* to do superficially.
salapî: *n.* money; currency; fifty centavo coin; **pananalapî** *n.* finances; treasury; **masalapî** *adj.* rich. **pampananalapî** *adj.* financial; **mukháng salapî** *id.* worshipping money (looks like money). **salaping-papel** *n* paper money. **manalapî** *adj.* costing fifty centavos each.
salapíd: *n.* plait, strip of braided hair.
salapóng: *n.* forked harpoon, trident; juncture.
salapsáp: *adj.* superficial.
salapyáw: *adj.* superficial (wound).
salarín: *n.* criminal; offender.
salaryo: (Sp. *salario*) *n.* salary. (*sahod*)
salas: (Sp.) *n.* living room; parlor.
salasà: *n.* compressed-bodied garfish; **panalasà** *n. adj.* abreast; evenly matched.
salásalá: *adj.* interwoven.
salát₁: *n.* palpitation, touch; **pagsalát** *n.* feeling, touching.
salát₂: *adj.* in need; scarce; **pananalát** *n.* depression, financial crisis, scarcity; **tagsalát** *n.* famine, time of need.
salatan: *n.* southwest.
salaulà: *adj.* filthy, dirty; nasty.
salawá: *adj.* taking on too many things without finishing any.
salawák: *n.* spilling.
salawag: *n.* supports for a thatch roof.
salawahán: *adj.* fickle, inconstant; **salawahan** *n.* doubt.
salawál: *n.* trousers.
salawikaín: (*rt. wikà*) *n.* proverb, saying.
salawsáw: *n.* turmoil.
saláy: *n.* bird's nest; small branch.
salaysaláy: *n.* crevalle fish (*Caranx* sp.); **salaysaláy-aso** *n.* deep-bellied crevalle; **salay-**

saláy-batang *n.* yellow-striped crevalle; **salaysaláy-buntutan, salaysaláy-dikyâ** *n.* species of crevalle; **salaysaláy habagat-/lalaki** *n.* even-bellied crevalle.

salaysáy: (Ch.) *n.* story, narration; deposition; **isalaysáy** *v.* to relate, narrate.

salbabida: (Sp. *salvavidas*) *n.* lifesaver.

salbadór: (Sp. *salvador*) *n.* savior.

salbahe: (Sp. *salvaje*) *adj.* savage, wild; *n.* savage; **salbasiyón** *n.* salvation.

saldo: (Sp.) *n.* balance in an account; **saldado** *adj.* paid; balanced.

salero: (Sp.) *n.* salt shaker.

sali: **sumali** *v.* to participate; share in; take part in; **kasali** *n.* participant; *adj.* included (as a participant); **masali** *v.* to be included as a participant; **saling-pusà, salimpusà** *adj.* not really included, not a true member.

salì: *n.* saliva reddened by betel or chewing tobacco.

salibád: *n.* swooping.

salibát: *n.* interruption of a conversation.

salik: *n.* element; basic part; (*gram.*) syllable.

salikbubo: *n.* upward jump; bubbling up.

salikop: *n.* junction; intersection.

salikóp: *adj.* surrounded; encircled.

saliksík: *n.* research, search; **magsaliksík** *v.* to search carefully for; **tagapagsaliksík** *n.* researcher.

salida: (Sp.) *n.* exit; going out on call; emergency call (for doctor's); expenditures.

salig: *adj.* based on; **kapanalig** *n.* friend, ally; **magsalig** *v.* to base on; **másalig** *v.* to be based on; **pananalig** *n.* confidence, trust; faith; **saligan** *n.* basis; *adj.* basic, fundamental; **isalig** *v.* to base on; **saligáng-batás** *n.* constitution; **waláng-saligán** *adj.* without basis, unjustifiable.

saligawgáw: *adj.* mischievous.

saligawsáw: *n.* bustle, commotion.

saligutgót: *adj.* complicated, intricate.

salilong: *n.* shelter, sheltering.

salimaó: *n.* tusk.

salimbangaw: (*sali-ng bangaw*) *n.* person who does not really belong with those he is with, not a true member.

salimbáy: *n.* swoop; **salimbayán** *v.* to swoop down on.

salimbibíg: *adj.* oral, orally transmitted; **tradisyóng salimbibíg** *n.* oral tradition.

salimol: *n.* licking the lips.

salimpusà: (*sali-ng pusà*) *n.* asking someone to participate in a game to appease him, although he is not necessarily wanted; person who is not a true member.

salimuót: **masalimuót** *adj.* complex, intricate; entangled; **salí-salimuót** *adj.* very complicated.

salin₁: *n.* translation; copying; **isalin** *v.* to translate, copy.

salin₂: *n.* pouring; transferring of cargo.

salin₃: *n.* endorsement; turnover; **magsalin** *v.* to hand over; transfer to, hand down; pass on.

salindayaw: *n.* young stag with horns.

salinlahì: *n.* generation; posterity.

salinwikà: *n.* language translation.

saling-án: (*slang*) *num.* one hundred.

salingbo: (*slang*) *num.* one thousand.

salingít: *adj.* hidden; **isalingít** *v.* to insinuate; sneak in; **salingitán** *v.* to do something surreptitiously.

salingsíng: *n.* curtain rings; ingrown toenail.

salipadpád: *n.* fluttering.

salipanyâ: *adj.* impertinent.

salipot: **isalipot** *v.* to cover up, conceal.

salipsíp: *adj.* superficial.

salisí: *adj.* alternately; in opposite directions; (*slang*) snatcher; **magsalisí** *v.* to do in terns, alternate; **magsalisihán** *v.* to come towards each other from opposite directions; **salisihín** *v.* to alternate doing with someone; **salí-salisí** *adj.* arranged alternately; **salí-salisihín** *v.* to arrange in an alternating manner.

salisig: **salisigin** *v.* to probe a wound; scrape wax from the ears.

salisod: *n.* dragging the feet when walking.

salisol: *n.* scraping off dirt with a swab.

salít: *n.* interspersing; alternation; **masalít** *adj.* interspersed; **salitan** *adj.* alternating.

salitâ: *n.* word; language; talk; **masalitâ** *adj.* talkative; to be able to say; **magsalitâ** *v.* to talk, speak; **pagsasalitâ** *n.* speech, talking;

salitain *v.* to put into words; **salí-salitaan** *n.* rumor, common talk; **tagapagsalitâ** *n.* spokesperson; **talasalitaan** *n.* vocabulary; **salitáng-ipis** *n.* high pitched talk; (*slang*) gay talk; **salitáng-kantó** *n.* street talk.
salitre: (Sp.) *n.* saltpeter.
salíw: *n.* musical accompaniment; **isaliw** *v.* to accompany; **tagasaliw** *n.* accompanist.
salíw: *n.* accord, harmony.
saliwâ: *adj.* reverse; left-handed; contrary; (*slang*) disrespectful; **kasaliwâ** *adj.* opposite, contrary; **pagsaliwâ** *n.* reversal, reverse; **pasalí-saliwâ** *adj.* missing the beat; **saliwaín** *v.* to invert, reverse; **kasaliwaang-palad** *id.* misfortune (reversed luck).
salmo: (Sp.) *n.* psalm.
salmón: (Sp.) *n.* salmon; runner fish.
salmunete: *n.* nemipterid, goatfish.
salmuwera: (Sp. *salmuera*) *n.* brine.
salo: *adj.* eating together; **makisalo** *v.* to join others in eating; **magsalo** *v.* to share food; **sumalo** *v.* eat with others; **isalo** *v.* to let a person share one's food.
saló: *n.* catch of a ball; lower support; **makasaló** *v.* to be able to catch; **panaló** *n.* something used to catch (mitt); support; **tagasaló** *n.* catcher.
salók: *n.* scoop net; fetching water; **sumalok** *v.* to draw water from a well.
salog: *n.* puddle.
salón: (Sp.) *n.* large hall, salon.
salong: **isalong** *v.* to sheathe; surrender one's arms; **isalong na ang sandata** *id.* stop fighting (sheathe the weapon).
salóp: *n.* ganta (3 liters dry measure); (*slang*) snob.
salot: *n.* plague, epidemic.
saloy: *n.* current of a stream; overflowing.
salpák: **sumalpák** *v.* to fall plump on something; carelessly fit into.
salpók: *n.* bump, collision, hit; **salpukan** *n.* crash.
salsa: (Sp.) *n.* sauce, gravy.
salsál: *adj.* dull, blunt; **magsalsál** *v.* to masturbate.
saltá: (Sp.) *n.* leap, jump; omission; (*coll.*) coming in (money); **isaltá** *v.* to bring up; **bagong saltá** *n.* newcomer.
saltík: *n.* slingshot.
salto: (Sp.) *n.* omission, skip.
salubong: *n.* welcome; reception; **magsalubong** *v.* to converge; meet along the way; **kasalubong** *n.* person who is met along the way; **pasalubong** *n.* gift given by an arriving visitor or relative; **pasalubóng** *adj.* meeting each other from different directions; **ipasalubong** *v.* to give a gift (when arriving from a trip); to get someone to meet along the way; **magkásalubong** *v.* to meet along the way; **sálubungán** *n.* encounter; **sumalubong, salubungin** *v.* to meet; welcome; **tagasalubóng** *n.* welcome host; **di-napagsásalubungán** *adj.* one-way.
salubsób: *n.* splinter.
salukbít: *adj.* tucked in at the waist.
salukót: *n.* wide brimmed buri leaf hat.
salukoy: **kasalukuyan** *adj.* current; present; **sa kasalukuyan** at the present time.
saluksók: *adj.* inserted at the waist; *n.* probing.
saludo: (Sp.) *n.* salute; salvo.
saludsód: *n.* basting stitch; weeding tool; **saludsudín** *v.* to scrape off by pushing (with the feet).
salugsóg: *n.* sliver in the hand or foot; detailed investigation.
salulò: *n.* bamboo water conduit.
salumbabâ: *n.* sling for a broken arm; bandage that supports the chin or a corpse.
salumpóng: *n.* head-on collision.
salumpuwít: [*saló-ng puwít*] *n.* seat.
salunò: *n.* person sent to meet someone.
salunga: **sumalungá** *v.* to go against (current, etc.); **pasulangá** *adv.* going against; upward; uphill; upstream.
salungát: *adj.* contrary, adverse; against; **kasalungatín** *v.* to go against, oppose; **magkasalungát** *v.* to interfere with each other; clash; **pasalungát** *adj.* contradictory; opposing (side); **pagsalungát** *n.* opposition; **pagsasálungatán** *n.* contradiction; inconsistency; **sálungátan** *n.* conflict; clash; dispute; **salungatín** *v.* to deny, disagree; contradict; **sumalungát** *v.* to deny, oppose; contradict; **tagasalungát** *n.* member of the opposition

party.

salungkawit: *n.* curved support; curved blade.

salungkít: *n.* fruit hook (attached at the end of a pole).

salungsóng: *n.* gangplank; **pasalungsóng** *n.* against the current or wind; **pagsasalungsóng** *n.* folding betel leaves after putting the lime on the leaf.

salupinít: *adj.* missed; spoilt, stale; knotty (wood).

saluysóy: *n.* spring of water; rivulet.

salwák: *n.* spilling liquid out of a container.

salya: *n.* pushing away forcibly; (*slang*) pawn.

sam- *pref.* var. of *sang-* before labial consonants, p, b, m: **sambuwán** one month; **sambayanán** *n.* the whole town; *adj.* public.

sama: **sumama** *v.* to accompany; join; **kasama** *n.* companion; partner; **kasá-kasama, kásamahín** *n.* constant companion; **kasamahán** *n.* colleague; professional companion; **kasamahin** *v.* to take someone along; **kasama-sama** *n.* tag-along; **isama** *v.* to include; insert; take someone along; **makisama** *v.* to unite, join; **magkasama** *adj.* together (two people); **magkakasama** *adj.* together (more than two); **magkásama** *v.* to be together; live together; be associated with; **magsama** *v.* to unite; blend; consolidate; **magsama-sama** *v.* to stay in a group; **pakikisama** *n.* company, society; getting along with others; **pakisamahan** *v.* to get along well with; request that something be accompanied of included; **pagkakásáma** *n.* embodiment; union; **pagka-kasama** *n.* partnership; **pagsamahin** *v.* to combine; unite; merge; **pagsasama** *n.* inclusion; companionship; **pagsasamahán** *n.* dealings, connections; **samahan** *v.* to accompany, conduct; **sama-sama** *adj.* all together; united; **sumama sa agos** *id.* to go with the flow, agree.

Sama: *n.* ethnic group and language from Northwest Samar (*Abaknon*) or Sulu Province (*Balangingi, Panguaran*).

samá: *n.* share of capital stock; **kasamá** *n.* tenant farmer; business partner; **samahán** *n.* association; union; partnership; **magkasamá** *n.* landlord and tenant.

samâ: *adj.* evil, bad; wicked; **makasamâ** *v.* to effect; be bad for, harm; be hurtful; disagree with; **masamâ** *adj.* bad, evil, harmful; **masamaín** *v.* to condemn, regard as wrong; **makasamâ** *v.* to affect (negatively); harm, damage; **magpakasamâ** *v.* to go from bad to worse; **kásamá-samaan** *adj.* worst; **magpasamâ** *v.* to corrupt; deprave; **masamáng-loób** *n.* criminal; **nakasásamâ** *adj.* harmful; **pagsamâ** *n.* deterioration; **di-makasásamâ** *adj.* harmless; **pasamaín** *v.* to make worse; mislead; make dirty; **samaín** *v.* to fail; be unlucky; **sumamâ** *v.* to become worse; **lalong masamâ** *adj.* worse; **samâ ng katawán** *n.* slight illness; **samâ ng loób** *n.* hurt feeling; bad blood; dissatisfaction; **magkasamaang-loób** *v.* to disagree; quarrel; **masamáng damó** *id.* bad man; **masamâ ang tubò ng dilà** *id.* with a foul mouth; **pasamaín ang loób** *v.* to offend; **ubod ng samâ** *adj.* depraved; vicious; wretched.

samakalawá: *adv.* on the day after tomorrow.

samakatuwíd: *conj.* therefore.

samantala: *conj.* meanwhile; while, whereas.

samantalá: **magsamantalá** *v.* to capitalize; take advantage of; abuse; impose; **samantalahín** *v.* to take advantage of; **pagsasamantalá** *n.* exploitation; opportunism.

samaral: *n.* siganid fish.

samat: *n.* leaf of the betel plant. (*ikmó*)

samatá: *n.* blinder for a horse; blinker.

sambá: *n.* worship; **sambahín** *v.* to worship, love very much; **sumambá** *v.* to adore; worship.

sambaháy: [*isang bahay*] *adj.* living under the same roof; **sambahayán** *n.* household; group of houses.

sambál: *n.* crossing.

Sambál: *n.* language and ethnic group from Zambales Province.

sambalilo: (Sp. *sombrero*) *n.* hat.

sambasambá: *n.* praying mantis.

sambát: *n.* forking point (of road or river).

sambayanán: (*rt. bayan*) *n.* the whole town; public.

sambeles: *n.* small coin during Spanish occupation.

sambeses: [*isang beses*] *adv*. once.

sambigà: *n*. dagger with a carved figure on the handle.

sambilat: *n*. grabbing, snatching.

sambít: *n*. mention; reference.

sambitlâ: *n*. sudden utterance.

sambóng: *n*. tall kind of herb, *Blumea balsamefera*.

sambót: *n*. catching; **sambutín** *v*. to catch; save from falling.

sambuhat: *n*. lifting something heavy together.

sambulat$_1$: *n*. scattered things; **magsambulat** *v*. to scatter.

sambulat$_2$: *n*. burst, explosion.

samíd: **masamid** *v*. to choked (food going into trachea).

samil: *n*. nipa awning for small boats.

saming: (*slang*) *n*. bad first impression.

samláng: *adj*. unclean, dirty; **samlangín** *v*. to do haphazardly.

samò: *n*. appeal, supplication; **isamò** *v*. to beg, beseech; **sumamò** *v*. to beg, pray; coax, persuade.

samot: **samut-samot** *adj*. diverse; heterogeneous.

sampá: **sampahín** *v*. to climb over; (*slang*) make love to; ride an animal, **isampá** *v*. to carry over; **pasampá** *adj*. rising, climbing.

sampák: *n*. jasmine; **sampagita** *n*. Philippine jasmine.

sampál: *n*. slap on the face.

sampalataya: **pagsampalataya** *n*. faith, believing; **manampalataya** *v*. to have faith; **pasampalatayahin** *v*. to convert one's faith.

sampalok: *n*. tamarind.

sampáy: *n*. hanging clothes; **sampayan** *n*. clothesline; **isampáy** *v*. to hang clothes to dry; **sampáy-bakod** *id*. worthless.

sampíd: *adj*. clinging; (*slang*) outsider; *adj*. carefree.

sampilóng: *n*. slap on the face (nose, mouth, etc.).

sampít: (*slang*) *n*. cousin.

sampiyád: *n*. idler, loafer.

samporado: *n*. rice porridge with chocolate.

sampót: *n*. accidental acquisition.

sampóy: (Ch.) *n*. salted or sweetened dry fruit.

sampû: *n*. ten; **makasampû** ten times; **ikasampû** tenth; **sampúng piraso ang mukhâ** *id*. angry (face has ten parts).

samsám: **pagsamsám** *n*. confiscation; **samsamán** *v*. to confiscate.

samuol: *n*. mouthful.

samyô: (Ch.) *n*. aroma, fragrance; **masamyô** *adj*. sweet smelling.

san- *var. of sang-* before, t, d, l, r, and s: one.

sana: *adv*. expresses optative; If only, I wish; should.

sanà: *n*. aromatic species of taro.

sanâ: *adj*. devastated.

sanáp: *adj*. covered to the top in liquid; drenched.

sanatoryo: (Sp. *sanatorio*) *n*. sanatorium.

sanaw: *n*. puddle, pool.

sanay: **magsanay** *v*. to practice; exercise; **kasanayan** *n*. skill, practice, proficiency; **sanáy** *adj*. skilled; expert; experienced, proficient; **sanayán** *n*. place for rehearsal or practice; **sumanay** *v*. to train someone; **tagapagsanay** *n*. trainer.

sanaysáy: *n*. essay.

sandaán: *n*. one hundred; **sandaántaón** *n*. one hundred years.

sandakót: *n*. handful.

sandál: *n*. reclining, leaning back; **sandalan** *n*. back of a chair; **sumandál** *v*. to recline; **nakasandál sa padér** *id*. person with good financial support (leaning on the wall).

sandalî: *n*. moment, instant; second; **pansandalî** *adj*. momentary.

sandalyás: (Sp. *sandalia*) *n*. sandal.

sandamák: (*isáng* + *damák*) *n*. width of the open palm of the hand.

sandampót: (*isáng* + *dampót*) *n*. single picking up of.

sandangkál: (*isáng* + *dangkál*) *n*. distance between the extended tip of the index finger and thumb.

sandapal: (*isáng* + *dapal*) *n*. the width of four fingers laid flat and pressed together.

sandát: *adj*. satisfied (after eating), full.

sandata: *n*. arm, weapon; **masandata** *adj*. armed; **sandatahan-lakás** *n*. armed forces.

sandíg: *n.* leaning, reclining; **pasandíg** *adj.* tilted, leaning; **sandigan** *n.* person who 'leans' or relies on other people for help; basis; back of a seat; basis; **sandigán** *v.* to lean against; depend on; **sandiganbayan** *n.* Court of Appeals.

sandipá: (*isáng* + *dipá*) *n.* arm span.

sandó: (Jap.) *n.* sleeveless undershirt.

sandók: *n.* coconut shell scoop; **sandukán** *v.* to scoop out; give someone food.

sandosena: (*isáng* + *dosena*) *n.* one dozen.

sandugô: (*isáng* + *dugô*) *n.* blood compact; alliance, coalition.

sanduyong: *n.* variety of reddish-purple sugarcane.

sanhî: *n.* cause, motive, reason.

sanib: *n.* overlapping part; joining together; underlayer; **masanib** *adj.* overlapped; joined with; **saniban** *v.* to join; provide with an underlayer (support); **kasanib** *n.* affiliate, member.

sanidád: (Sp.) *n.* sanitation; **sanitario** *n.* sanatorium.

sanlaksâ: (*isáng* + *laksá*) *n.* ten thousand.

sanlibo: (*isáng* + *libo*) *n.* one thousand.

sanlibután: *n.* universe.

sanlíng: *n.* red ochre; yellow gold.

sanliggó: (*isáng* + *linggó*) *n.* one week; *adv.* for a week.

sanô: *adj.* stupid, dull.

sanog: *n.* small stream.

san pedro: (*slang*) *n.* good boy.

sansalà: *n.* interruption; prohibition; prevention.

sansalitâ: (*isáng* + *salitâ*) *n.* one word.

sansán: *adj.* arranged neatly; *adv.* repeatedly.

sansáw: *n.* species of woody twine used in fish poisons and making ropes.

sansé: (Ch.) *n.* third eldest sister.

santán: *n.* coconut milk cooked with molasses; kind of shrub.

santaón: (*isá-ng taón*) *n.* one year.

santasa: (*isáng* + *tasa*) *n.* one cupful.

santíng: *n.* becoming intense.

santo: (Sp.) *adj.* holy; **santísimo** *adj.* very hold; **santo-santito (corazón maldito)** *id.* pretending to be a good.

santól: *n.* sandor tree, sandor fruit.

santukâ: *n.* one feeding (of fowls); one peck.

santuwaryo: (Sp. *santuario*) *n.* sanctuary.

sang- *prep* [*isa-* + *-ng*] one **sang-angaw** *n.* one million; (with *-an-* the whole), changes to *sam-* before labial consonants (p, b, m), and *san-* before dentals and liquids (t, d, s, d, l, r) → **sandaigdíg** *n.* the whole world; **sandagatan** the entire sea .

sangá: *n.* branch; fork; offshoot; **sumangá** *v.* to branch; fork, divide; **magsangá** *v.* to grow branches; **sangá-sangá** *adj.* ramified; **sangá-sangáng-dilà** *id.* talkative (branched tongue).

sangab: *n.* inhalation of medicine.

sangág: *adj.* fried; roasted; *n.* fried rice; **isangág** *v.* to fry.

sangál: *adj.* cut off.

sangáp: *n.* sipping; inhaling; **sangapín** *v.* to sip; inhale.

sangat: *n.* notch; ball and socket joint; support.

sangát: *n.* division of a company, branch of a firm, chapter.

sangáy: **kasangáy** *n.* namesake.

sang-ayon: *adj.* based on; in conformity with.

sangka- *pref.* used as *sang-* with certain roots → **sangkalangitán** *n.* heavens; **sangkapuluán** *n.* the whole archipelago; **sangkatauhan** *n.* all of humanity.

sangkâ: *n.* ditch, canal; dam.

sangkaka: (Sp. *chancaca*) *n.* brown molasses molded into a coconut shell.

sangkál: *adj.* hardened (mother's breast with too much milk).

sangkalan: *n.* chopping block; (*fig.*) *n.* scapegoat; **isangkalan** *v.* to use a block for chopping; give an excuse for; **sinangkalan** *n.* scapegoat.

sangkáp: *n.* part, element; ingredient; **kasangkapan** *n.* tool, instrument; furniture; implement; organ; **isangkáp** *v.* to outfit, equip; use as an ingredient; **panangkáp** *n.* raw material.

sangkawan: *n.* flock of birds; herd; school (of fish).

sangkî: (Ch.) *n.* star anise spice.

sangkó: (Ch.) *n.* appellation for the third eldest

brother.

sangkô: (*slang*) *n.* fifty pesos.

sangkót: *n.* implication; involvement; **kasangkót** *adj.* implicated, involved; **isangkót** *v.* to involve, implicate.

sangkutsá: (Sp. *sancochar*) **sangkutsahín** *v.* to boil meat until partially cooked in a little fat.

sanggá$_1$: **sumanggá** *v.* to defend, shield; **pananggá** *n.* shield, protection; **sanggahán** *v.* to protect someone using oneself as a shield or cover.

sanggá$_2$: **pagsasanggahan** *n.* taking sides; **kasanggá** *n.* team mate.

sanggaláng: *n.* protection, defense; **magsanggaláng** *v.* to protect, defend, shield.

sánggano: (Sp. *zangano*) *n.* loafer; parasite.

sanggî: *n.* light touch in passing.

sanggól: *n.* baby, infant; **kasanggulán** *n.* infancy.

sanggunì: *n.* consultation, advice; **kasanggunì** *n.* consultant; **isanggunì** *v.* to consult; **sumanggunì** *v.* to consult; **sanggunián** *n.* consultation; reference; **sumanggunì** *v.* to consult; refer to; **tagapagsanggunì** *n.* person who seeks advice on behalf of another; **talasanggunián** *n.* bibliography, list of references.

sanggumay: *n.* species of yellow orchid.

sangháp: *n.* inhalation.

sanghayà: *n.* honor, dignity.

sanghíd: *n.* rank odor.

sanghód: *n.* bad odor (stronger than *sanghíd*).

sangì: *n.* part in the hair.

Sangil, Sangir(e): *n.* ethnic group and language from Balut Island, off Mindanao

sangít: **mapasangít** *v.* to get hooked onto while falling.

sanglâ: *n.* pledge, bond; mortgage; **isanglâ** *v.* to mortgage; **sánglaan** *n.* pawnshop; **sanglaán** *v.* to pawn to, mortgage to; **tagasanglâ** *n.* pawn broker; **sangláng-bilí** *n.* mortgage with a purchase option in case of default.

sangláy: *n.* Chinese merchant.

sangmaliwanag: (*fig.*) *n.* the world as a creation.

sangód: *var.* of *sang-ód*.

sang-ód: *n.* protrusion on a surface; hitting a protrusion on a surface.

sangsáng: *n.* strong odor (not unpleasant).

sangtaón: *var.* of *santaón*: one year.

sanyawà: *n.* sulfur. (*asupre*)

sangyód: *n.* odor, smell. (*amóy*)

sangyutà: *n.* one hundred thousand.

saó: *n.* mooring cable for boats.

saog: *n.* spring, small river.

saóy: *n.* polishing gold.

sapá: *n.* bagasse, residue after chewing sugarcane; **sapahín** *v.* to chew to a pulp.

sapà: *n.* brook, small stream.

sapak: **sapák** *adj.* broken off (branches); *n.* punch.

sapák: (*coll.*) *adj.* excellent, very good.

sapakát: *n.* intrigue; conspiracy; **sapakatín** *v.* to get an accomplice in a conspiracy; **sápakatan** *n.* conspiracy; **magsapakatan** *v.* to be an accomplice.

sapád: *adj.* flat, flattened.

sapagkâ('t): *conj.* because, since.

sapal: *n.* pulp, residue; *adj.* having no chance for defeat.

sapalà: **di-sapalà** *adj.* impossible.

sápalarán: (*rt. palad*) *adj.* involving risks; *n.* game of chance.

sapanahón: (*rt. panahon*) *n.* menstruation; **sa panahón** *adv.* on time.

sapantahà: *n.* suspicion, presumption; impression; **sapantahain** *v.* to presume, suppose; **sapantahaan** *v.* to suspect someone.

sapáng: *n.* sappanwood tree.

sapát: *adj.* enough; adequate; sufficient; *adv.* sufficiently; **sumapát** *v.* to suffice, be enough; **makasapát** *v.* to meet the needs of, be enough for.

sapatero: (Sp. *zapatero*) *n.* shoemaker, cobbler; moonfish; **sapateríya** *n.* shoe store.

sapatilya: (Sp. *zapatilla*) *n.* slipper; washer (of a faucet).

sapatos: (Sp. *zapato*) *n.* shoe; **magsapatos** *v.* to wear shoes.

sapaw: *n.* first fruits of a tree; skin disease; *adj.* bearing fruits early.

sapì$_1$: *n.* ply; reinforcement; **sapian** *v.* to reinforce.

sapì₂: *n.* business stocks; **pagsapì** *n.* membership; **kasapì** *n.* member; **magsapì** *v.* to join together; **sumapì** *v.* to join.

sapid: *n.* sticking to the lid of a container.

sápilitán: (rt. *pilit*) *adj.* required, compulsory.

sapín: (Sp. *chapin*) *n.* pad, cushion; clogs; **sapín-sapín** *adj.* layer upon layer; *n.* layered cake; **sasapnán** *n.* upper part of the buttocks curving to the back.

sapiro: (Sp. *zafiro*) *n.* sapphire.

sapisapì: *n.* kind of kite.

sapit: **kasapitan** *n.* luck, fate; *v.* to result in; **sumapit** *v.* to come, arrive (at a certain time); **pasapitin** *v.* to send to; **sapitin** *v.* to reach a place; result in; experience; **makasapit** *v.* to be able to reach.

saplád: *n.* kind of embankment to keep grain from spreading; dike.

sapláng: *n.* sudden attack.

saplót: *n.* tattered clothes.

sapnán: [*sapin* + *-an*]: to protect or support with an underlayer.

sapnít: *n.* slight cut or wound.

sapnót: *var. of saplót*: tattered clothes.

sapó₁: **isapó** *v.* to use the hands to support or carry; use a prop for support; **pasapó** *adj.* supported from underneath with the hands; **sapuhín** *v.* to hold with the hands.

sapó₂: *n.* red ochre; gilding.

sapó₃: (*slang*) *n.* handing a culprit over to the police.

sapók: (*Bicolano*) *n.* uppercut (closed fist punch).

sapól: *adv.* ever since; at the beginning; *adj.* straight, direct; **isapól** *v.* to start at the beginning; **sapulín** *v.* to hit hard (face); **sapulán** *v.* to begin something; be present at the very start.

sapot: *n.* black shroud for the dead.

sapote₁: (Sp. *zapote*) *n.* kind of native plum tree, marmalade tree, *Calocarpum sapote*.

sapote₂: *n.* cheating while shuffling the cards.

sapsáp: *n.* slipmouth fish (Family *leiognathidae*).

sapsúy: (Ch.) *n.* chop suey.

sapula: *n.* baby's bib.

sapupo: *adj.* held in the hands; **sinapupunán** *n.* lap, womb; bosom.

sapyáw: *n.* kind of dragnet; superficial wound; **pasapyáw** *adj.* sketchy; superficial.

sará: (Sp. *cerrar*) *adj.* closed; **isará** *v.* to shut, close; **panará** *n.* fastener, catch; **sarhán** *v.* to close; **tagasará** *n.* doorman (job is to close the door); **sarado** *adj.* closed; ended; clogged (nose); **saraduhan** *v.* to shut, close.

sarada: (Sp. *cerrada*) *n.* close-neck coat.

sarado: (Sp. *cerrado*) *adj.* closed; finished.

saráng: *n.* brilliance, shine.

saragate: (Sp. *zaragate*) *n.* rascal.

saramulyete: *n.* goatfish.

saramulyo: *adj.* mischievous; disrespectful.

saranggola: *n.* kite.

saráp: *n.* tastiness; comfort; **masaráp** *adj.* delicious; comfortable (sleep); **kasarapán** *n.* climax, height of satisfaction; **sarapán** *v.* to make tasty.

sarát: *adj.* flat (nose); snub-nosed.

saray: *n.* floor of a building; layer; honeycomb; beehive.

sardinas: (Sp.) *n.* sardines.

sarhán: (rt. *sará*) *v.* to close.

sarhento: (Sp.) *n.* sergeant; **sarhento-de-mesa** *n.* desk sergeant.

sari: *n.* Indian female gown, sari.

sarì: *n.* kind, class; **kasarian** *n.* gender; **sari-sarì** *n.* all kinds, variety.

sarili: *n.* self; *adj.* own; exclusive; private; sole; independent; original; **kasarinlán** *n.* independence, individuality; **kasarilinan** *n.* selfishness; **makasarili** *v.* to be able to get for oneself; *adj.* selfish; **magkasarili** *v.* to have one's own; **magsarilí** *v.* to become independent; **mapagsarilí** *adj.* independent; **magsárilinan** *v.* to act independently of one another; **mapagsarilí** *adj.* independent; **masarili** *v.* to monopolize; **pagkamakasarili** *n.* self-esteem; individuality; egotism; **pagsasarilí** *n.* being on one's own; **pansarili** *adj.* domestic; personal; private; **sarilihin**, **sarilinin** *v.* to monopolize, take as one' own; **sárilinan** *adj.* each one's own; **sárilinán** *adv.* privately; secretly; **tiwalà sa sarili** *n.* self-confidence; **yaring-sarili** *adj.* homemade; **sarilihin** *v.* to do alone; appropriate something for oneself alone; **may-kasa-rinlán** *adj.* autonomous; **sariling pugad** *id.* one's own home (own nest); **walâ sa kanyáng sarili** *id.* absent minded (not in own self).

sarinlán: *see sarili.*

saríng: *n.* deflected impact; indirect remark.

sarisarì: *adj.* assorted; various; *n.* small native store.

sariwà: *adj.* fresh; new; **manariwà** *v.* to revive; becoming refreshed; **pasariwà** *n.* freshener; **kasariwaán** *n.* freshness.

sarna: (Sp.) *n.* mange, scabies.

saro: (Sp. *jarro*) *n.* water jug.

saról: (Sp. *charol*) *n.* patent leather.

sarsa: (Sp. *salsa*) *n.* gravy, sauce.

sarsalida: *n.* kind of bitter herb.

sarsaparilya: (Sp. *zarzaparrilla*) *n.* sarsaparilla plant.

sarsuwela: (Sp. *zarzuela*) *n.* traditional Spanish musical drama.

sartén: (Sp.) *n.* frying pan.

sasà: **pasasà** *n.* abundance; **kasasaan** *n.* abundance, over-indulgence; **magpasasà** *v.* to enjoy to the full; **masasaan** *v.* to bear the brunt of, suffer the most.

sasá: *n.* nipa palm. (*pawid*)

sasak: *n.* sound made by house lizards.

sasakyán: (*rt. sakay*) *n.* vehicle.

saság: *n.* split bamboos for walling; **sasagin** *v.* to split bamboos.

sasál: *n.* sudden attack of pain; fury.

sasambá: (*rt. samba*) *n.* praying mantis.

sasáng: *n.* candle; taper; **sasangan** *n.* candlestick.

saserdote: (Sp. *sacerdote*) *n.* priest.

sastre: (Sp.) *n.* tailor, seamstress; **sastreryá** *n.* tailor's shop.

satanás: (Sp.) *n.* Satan.

satè: *n.* string (used in spinning tops).

satín: (Sp.) *n.* satin.

sátira: (Sp.) *n.* satire. (*tuyâ, uyám*)

satiyán: *n.* girth; strap that keeps the saddle in place.

satok: (Ch.) *n.* hammer.

satsát₁: (Ch.) *adj.* closed-cropped (hair).

satsát₂: (Sp. *chacharear*) *n.* gossip.

saubát: *n.* conspiracy, intrigue.

saulado: (*rt. ulo*) *adj.* memorized.

saulì: (*rt. ulì*) *n.* return; **isaulì** *v.* to return; **masaulì** *v.* to be returned; **manaulì** *v.* to return; **pagsasaulì** *n.* returning; restoration; **pagsaulian** *v.* to return to someone; **papanauliin** *v.* to restore; revive; **sáulián** *n.* returning (borrowed things) to each other; **nagsaulian ng kandilà** *id.* quarreled (returned candles).

sauna: (*rt. una*) *adj.* old fashioned.

sawá: *n.* python, boa; (*slang*) policeman.

sawà: *adj.* satiated, fed up; **magsawà** *v.* to do to excess; get tired of; be fed up with; **sawâ** *adj.* tired of, fed up.

sawalì: *n.* woven bamboo strips used for walling.

sawan: **masawan** *adj.* dizzy; prone to heart ailments.

sawang: (*slang*) *interj.* so what?

sawatâ: *n.* checking, prevention; **masawatâ** *v.* to obstruct; put an end to; **sumawatâ** *v.* to restrain someone from doing.

sawáy: *n.* restraint, prohibition; **sumawáy** *v.* to prohibit.

sawî: **masawî** *v.* to die, meet misfortunes; **kasawian** *n.* misfortune, death; **sawing-palad** *adj.* unlucky, unfortunate; **sawiin** *v.* to frustrate, disappoint; **ibong sawî** *id.* unfortunate person (disappointed bird).

sawíl: *adj.* embarrassed.

sawímpalad, sawíng-palad: *adj.* unlucky, unfortunate; unsuccessful.

sawò: *n.* anchor.

sawong: *n.* hut in the mountains.

sawsáw: *n.* dipping; (*slang*) husband; foreplay; **isawsáw** *v.* to dip (in a sauce); immerse; **sawsawan** *n.* dipping sauce; **sawsáw sukâ** *id.* to disappear suddenly.

saya: (Sp.) *n.* skirt.

sayà: (*slang*) *n., adj.* Visayan.

sayá: *n.* joy, happiness; **masayá** *adj.* happy, glad; **ipagsayá** *v.* to celebrate; **sumayá** *v.* to cheer up, become happy.

sayad: *n.* bottom of a skirt; **sayád** *adj.* dragging on the ground; aground; **sumayad** *v.* to drag; run aground.

sayang: *n.* pity; wasting; *interj.* too bad, what a shame, what a waste; **masayang** *v.* to waste away; **sayangin** *v.* to waste.
sayáp: *adj.* exact.
sayat: **pananayat** *n.* exploring enemy territory.
sayáw: *n.* dance; (*slang*) reckless driving; **sumayáw** *v.* to dance; **pasayáw** *n.* benefit dance, ball.
sayì: **sumayì** *v.* to accomplish in the rain or storm.
sayíd: *adj.* consumed, exhausted supply.
saymót: *var.* of *simót*.
saynát: *n.* slight fever.
saynete: (Sp. *sainete*) *n.* humorous farce.
sayód: *adj.* consumed.
sayote: (Sp. *chaiote*) *n.* kind of vine that bears a delicious pear shaped vegetable.
saysáy: *n.* statement; **isaysáy** *v.* to declare, state; attest; **makasaysayan** *adj.* eventful; historic; **kasaysayan** *n.* history; **pangkasaysayan** *adj.* historical; **waláng-saysáy** *adj.* empty, meaningless; **may kasaysayan** *adj.* historical.
sayusay: *n.* effective use of words in speaking, articulateness.
sebo: (Sp. *cebo*) *n. n.* fat; shoe polish; cavalla fish.
sebra: (Eng.) *n.* zebra.
sekante: (Sp. *secante*) *n.* blotting paper.
sekreta: (Sp. *secreta*) *n.* secret agent; **sekretarya** *n.* secretary.
sekreto: (Sp. *secreto*) *adj.* secret.
seksi: (Eng.) *adj.* sexy.
sekundaryo: (Sp. *secundario*) *adj.* secondary; high school.
seda: (Sp.) *n.* silk; (*slang*) *adj.* numerous.
sedatibo: (Sp. *sedativo*) *n.* sedative.
sédula: (Sp. *cédula*) *n.* personal tax.
segida: (Sp. *seguida*) *adj.* in succession; *adv.* immediately.
seglár: (Sp.) *adj.* secular; *n.* layman.
según: (Sp.) *prep.* according to.
segundo: (Sp.) *n.* second; (*-a-* also); **segunda klase** second class; **segundahán** *v.* to second a motion.
segurado: (Sp.) *adj.* insured; sure.
seguridád: (Sp.) *n.* safety.
seguro: (Sp.) *n.* certainty, assurance; insurance; **segurista** *n.* person who only does things if he is sure of success; **masiguro** *v.* to be sure of.
seís: *var. of saís*: six.
seisiyentos: (Sp. *seiscientos*) *n.* six hundred.
selang: *n.* delicacy; fastidiousness; **maselang** *adj.* delicate; fastidious; hard to please; **napakaselang** *adj.* prudish; **selang-baboy** *id.* eating without washing one's hands.
selda: (Sp. *celda*) *n.* cell.
selos: (Sp. *celos*) *n.* jealousy; **seloso** *adj.* jealous.
selyo: (Sp. *cello*) *n.* stamp, seal; **selyado** *adj.* stamped, sealed.
semana: (Sp.) *n.* week; ~ **santa** *n.* Holy (Easter) Week.
semento: (Sp. *cemento*) *n.* cement; **sementado** *adj.* cemented.
sementeryo: (Sp. *cementerio*) *n.* cemetery.
semestre: (Sp.) *n.* semester; **semestrál** *adj.* semestral.
sempláng: (*slang*) *n.* fall; **sumempláng** *v.* to fall.
sempot: (*slang*) *n.* coitus.
senado: (Sp.) *n.* senate; **senadór** *n.* senator.
senaryo: (Sp. *escenario*) *n.* scenario; scenery.
senepa: (Sp. *cenefa*) *n.* decorative trimming, edging; lining.
sensilyo: (Sp. *sencillo*) *adj.* simple; plain; loose change; **sensilyuhín** *v.* to change into smaller coins.
sensura: (Sp. *censura*) *n.* censorship.
senténsiya: (Sp. *sentencia*) *n.* sentence, verdict; **sentensyado** *adj.* convicted; sentenced.
sentido: (Sp.) *n.* sense; meaning; temple of the head; ~ **komún** *n.* common sense.
séntimos: (Sp. *centimo*) *n.* centavo.
sentimyento: (Sp. *sentimiento*) *n.* sentiment, feeling; displeasure.
sentro: (Sp. *centro*) *adj.* center, middle.
senyál: (Sp. *señal*) *n.* signal, sign.
senyás: (Sp. *seña*) *n.* signal, sign.
senyór: (Sp. *señor*) *n.* sir; **senyorito** *n.* master; aristocratic young man; (*fig.*) lazy man.
senyora: (Sp. *señora*) *n.* ma'am, madam; **senyorita** *n.* miss; aristocratic lady; species

of finger-like banana; (*fig.*) lazy woman.
senglot: (*slang*) *adj.* drunk.
sepilyado: (Sp. *cepillado*) *adj.* planed (lumber).
sepilyo: (Sp. *cepillo*) *n.* toothbrush.
sepo: (Sp. *cepo*: block) *n.* truss, beam to support a roof.
septiyembre: (Sp. *setiembre*) *n.* September.
sepya: (Sp.) *n.* sepia.
sera: (Sp. *cera*) *n.* wax.
seradura: (Sp. *cerradura*) *n.* lock.
serbesa: (Sp. *cerveza*) *n.* beer. **serbesahán** *n.* brewery; beer stand.
serbí: (Sp. *servir*) *n.* service. **serbihán** *v.* to serve.
serbidór: (Sp. *servidor*) *n.* waiter.
serbilyeta: (Sp. *servilleta*) *n.* napkin.
serbisyo: (Sp. *servicio*) *n.* service; chamber pot.
seremonia: (Sp. *ceremonia*) *n.* ceremony.
serenata: (Sp.) *n.* serenade; concert.
sereno: (Sp.) *n.* night watchman; *adj.* serene.
seresa: (Sp. *cereza*) *n.* cherry.
sermón: (Sp.) *n.* sermon; speech; (*coll.*) scolding.
sero: (Sp. *cero*) *n.* zero.
serpyente: (Sp. *serpiente*) *n.* serpent.
sertipikado: (Sp. *certificado*) *adj.* certified.
serutso: (Sp. *serrucho*) *n.* carpenter's saw.
serye: (Sp. *serie*) *n.* series; episode.
seryo: (Sp. *serio*) *adj.* serious; grave.
sesante: (Sp. *cesante*) *adj.* dismissed (employee).
sesenta: (Sp.) *n.* sixty.
sesyón: (Sp. *sesión*) *n.* session.
setenta: (Sp.) *n.* seventy.
setro: (Sp. *cetro*) *n.* scepter.
si: *art.* personal topic marker. **Si Maria** Maria.
siasi: (*slang*) *n.* masturbation.
sibà: *n.* gluttony; **masibà** *adj.* greedy, gluttonous.
sibák: *n.* chopping wood; (*slang*) coitus; *adj.* split, chopped.
sibakóng: (Ch.) *n.* kind of medicinal small tree with milky sap whose leaves occur in whorls.
sibad: *n.* dart; sudden movement; spurt; **sumibad** *v.* to dart; spurt.
siban: *n.* delay; wasting time.
sibasib: *n.* attack of an animal.
sibát: *n.* spear; lance; (*slang*) scram; **sumibát** *v.* to spear.
sibáy: (*slang*) *n.* call boy, gigolo.
sibi: *n.* balcony; lean-to shed; awning.
sibì: *n.* pouting the lips.
sibig: *n.* stopping a row boat with oars.
sibilisá: (Sp. *civilizar*) **masibilisá** *v.* to become civilized; **sibilisado** *adj.* civilized.
sibò: *n.* attack of a large fish.
sibóg: *n.* noisy scolding.
siból: *n.* spring of water; growth, sprout; **magpasiból** *v.* to germinate; **sibulán** *v.* to grow over, overgrow; **sumiból** *v.* to germinate; **tagsiból** *n.* spring (season).
siboy: *n.* starting to simmer.
sibsíb: *adj.* set (sun); *n.* sunset.
sibungin: *n.* spotted gruntfish.
sibuyas: (Sp. *cebolla*) *n.* onion; **balát-sibuyas** *id.* smooth skin (onion skin).
sikad: *n.* back kick; energy; **sikaran** *v.* to kick someone.
sikada: (Eng.) *n.* cicada.
sikal: *n.* rising of the tide; rising fever.
sikamod: *n.* pout, sour look on the face.
sikante: *var. of sekante*: *n.* blotting paper.
sikang: *n.* crosspiece between posts of a house; keeping the eyes from sleeping; suppressing passion.
sikap: *n.* diligence; **masikap** *adj.* diligent, industrious; **magsikap** *v.* to endeavor, make an effort to; **magsumikap**, **pagsumikapan** *v.* to strive; **pagsikapan** *v.* to try, attempt; **pagsisikap** *n.* attempt; effort; enthusiasm; zeal; **sikapin** *v.* to try; seek; **sariling sikap** (*slang*) *n.* masturbation.
sikat: *n.* splendor; rising (sun, stars); **kasikatan** *n.* heyday; **magpasikat** *v.* to show off; **pasikat** *n.* rising of the sun, stars; showing off; bragging; **sumikat** *v.* to rise; shine; **sikát** *id.* well known, famous. **sikatán** *n.* east horizon.
sikatsikat: *n.* young crab.
sikdó: *n.* vibration; feeling of dread (heart palpitation).
sikháy: (Ch.) *n.* diligence, zeal.

sikî: *adj*. crowded; in a tight situation.
sikíg: *adj*. short-necked; tight fitting around the neck or armpits.
sikíl: *n*. push of a paddle or oar in rowing.
sikíl: *adj*. oppressed; **sikilín** *v*. to oppress.
sikíp: *n*. tightness; congestion; **masikíp** *adj*. tight; **nagsísikíp ang hiningá** *id.* angry (breath is choked).
sikitíng: (Sp. *chiquitó*) *n*. very small child.
sikláb: *n*. flame, blaze; spark; **magsikláb** *v*. to flare up, kindle; **sumikláb ang digmaan** *id.* war broke out; **pasikláb** (*slang*) *n*. gimmick; *adj*. boastful; loud-mouthed.
siklát: *adj*. split open.
siklo: (Sp. *ciclo*) *n*. cycle; **siklista** *n*. cyclist.
siklót: *n*. game of jacks; tossing. (*fig*.) *adj*. affected by a misfortune; **sumiklót, siklutín** *v*. to toss; **siklút-siklutín** *v*. to toss about.
sikmát: *n*. snap, bite; rebuke.
sikmurà: *n*. stomach; (*fig*.) sense of shame. **waláng sikmurà** *id.* insensitive, unsympathetic; shameless (no stomach).
siko: *n*. elbow; **sikó** *n*. nudge; **sumikó** *v*. to elbow.
sikolo: (*obs*.) *var*. of *saikwaló*: 7.5 centavo coin.
sikólogo: (Sp. *psicólogo*) *n*. psychologist.
sikot: **pasikut-sikot** *adj*. roundabout, indirect.
sikoy: *n*. banded pomadasid fish.
sikpáw: *n*. dip net used in fishing.
siksík: *adj*. crammed, tightly packed; (*slang*) fat; **isiksík** *v*. to cram, pack; wedge; assert; **paniksík** *n*. stopper, plug; **siksikan** *adj*. crowded.
sikwán: *n*. spindle for making nets.
sikwát: *n*. raising with a lever; pilfering; **sikwatín** *v*. to pilfer; **sikwátan** *n*. robbery.
sikyò: (*slang*) *n*. security guard.
sidhâ: **kasidhaán** *n*. diligence, industriousness.
sidhî: *n*. intensity; effectiveness; **masidhî** *adj*. intense.
sidlán: (rt. *silíd*) *v*. to fill (a container).
sidra: (Sp. *cidra*) *n*. cider.
sidronela: (Sp.) *n*. citronella.
sidsíd: *adj*. excessive; very much.
sigà: (*slang*) *adj*. in style; part of the act; **siga-sigà** *adj*. tough; boastful; proud.
sigâ: *n*. blaze, bonfire; (*slang*) cigarette; tough guy; conceited guy; **sígaan** *n*. incinerator; **sigaán** *v*. to make into a bonfire; **sigá-sigâ** *id.* progressing.
sigabó: *n*. sudden burst, outburst.
sigalbó: *n*. sudden burst; **sumigalbó** *v*. to surge, rise suddenly (waves); break forth.
sigalót: *n*. quarrel, dispute.
sigám: *n*. tuberculosis.
sigáng: **magsigáng** *v*. to place cooking utensils on a stove prior to cooking; **sinigáng** *n*. sour stew; **sigangan** *n*. stove.
sigapo: *n*. grouper fish.
sigarilyás: *n*. winged beans.
sigarilyo: (Sp. *cigarillo*) *n*. cigarette.
sigaro: (Sp. *cigarro*) *n*. cigar.
sigasig: *n*. diligence; enthusiasm; effort; **masigasig** *adj*. diligent, energetic; enterprising; earnest; zealous.
siga-sigaro: (Sp. *cigarro*: cigar) *n*. barracuda.
sigáw: *n*. shot, scream; **sumigáw** *v*. to scream.
sigay: *n*. cowry.
sigbó: *n*. diving head first; dousing fire with water.
sigé: (Sp. *sigue*) *interj*. Go ahead!; **sumige** *v*. to go ahead.
sigî: (*slang*) *n*. cigarette.
sigík: *adj*. short-necked. (*sikíg*)
sigíd: **masigíd** *adj*. piercing, stinging (pain).
sigido: (Sp. *seguido*) *adj*. consecutive.
sigíng: *n*. pride, arrogance; breaking out of a disease.
sigít: *n*. light shining through a crack.
siglá: *n*. liveliness, energy; cheerfulness; **magpasiglá** *v*. to liven up, uplift the spirits of; **masiglá** *adj*. eager, enthusiastic, vivacious; energetic, active.
sigláp: *n*. glimpse, accidental glance.
sigláw: *n*. glimpse.
siglo: (Sp.) *n*. century. (*dantaón*)
sigók: *n*. hiccup.
sigsá: *n*. lively enthusiasm.
sigsíg: *n*. bamboo torch.
sigurado: (Sp. *segurado*) *adj*. sure, certain; **sigurista** *n*. person who doesn't take chances.
siguro: (Sp. *seguro*: sure) *adv*. perhaps, maybe;

siguruhin *v.* to be sure of.

sigwá: *n.* storm, heavy rain; **sigwahan** *n.* rainy season.

sihà: *n.* space between fingers or toes.

sihâ: *n.* area marked off by the palms of the hands; interior section of a section of an orange.

sihang: *n.* jawbone.

siíd: *n.* bamboo catfish trap

siíl: *adj.* oppressed; **maniíl** *v.* to oppress.

siít: *n.* thorny bamboo; twig.

silá: *pron.* they; you (very polite); *art.* colloquial version of *siná.*

silà: **silain** *v.* to prey upon; devour; hunt for.

siláb: *n.* blaze, fire; **masiláb** *v.* to catch on fire.

sílaba: (Sp.) *n.* syllable. (*pantíg*)

silakbó: *n.* fit, outburst; spasm; surge; **pagsilakbó** *n.* outbreak; **sumilakbó** *v.* to burst forth.

silág: *n.* myopia; **silagin** *v.* to see through a translucent object.

silahis: (Sp. *celajes*) *n.* ray (of sunlight); (*coll.*) bisexual.

silam: *n.* skin blemish; irritation of the eyes.

silambáng: *n.* haphazard hit or answer.

silan: *var. of selang.*

silang: *n.* appearance; rising; **silangan** *n.* east; birthplace; **Silanganan** *n.* Far East; **isilang** *v.* to be born, bring forth; **sumilang** *v.* to come forth; be born; **isinilang na may kakambál na bituín** *id.* born lucky (with a twin star).

siláng: *n.* mountain pass.

silát: *n.* slit, crack in a bamboo floor; (*slang*) losing in gambling.

silaw: *n.* glare from a bright light; **siláw** *adj.* dazzled; **nasilaw sa salapî** *id.* influenced by money.

silay: *n.* brief glimpse or appearance.

silbato: (Sp.) *n.* whistle.

silbí: (Sp. *servi*) *n.* use, utility; **magsilbí** *v.* to serve, be of use to; **maninilbihan** *n.* server; **magsilbíng-kanin** *id.* to work for food.

silensyo: (Sp. *silencio*) *n.* silence; **silensyadór** *n.* silencer.

sili: *n.* hot pepper; **siling-labuyò** *n.* small person who is brave or great.

silíd: *n.* room; **isilíd** *v.* to enclose in a container; **pagsidlán, sisidlán** *n.* container; **sumilíd** *v.* to enter, go in; **sidlán** *v.* to fill a container; **silíd-aralán** *n.* classroom; **silíd-aklatan** *n.* library room; **silíd-basahán** *n.* reading room; **silíd-kainán** *n.* dining room; **silíd-dasalan** *n.* oratory; **silíd-tulugán** *n.* bedroom; **sumilid** *v.* to enter; **magsilíd na mulî** *v.* to refill.

silim: *n.* dusk; **takíp-silim** *n.* twilight.

silindro: (Sp.) *n.* cylinder; harmonica.

silinyasì: *n.* immature herring.

silip: *n.* peep; peeping; (*slang*) cheating on an exam; **silipán** *n.* peephole; **manilip** *v.* to peep; **nakasilip ng butas** *id.* found a reason to argue (saw a hole).

siliw: *n.* halfbeak fish.

silò: *n.* loop; noose; **manilò** *v.* to snare.

silok: *n.* spoon; ladle.

silong: *n.* basement; ground floor; **isilong** *v.* to take animals in to shelter; **silungán** *n.* shelter; haven.

silóng: **pagkasilóng** *n.* inferiority complex; **nasisilóng** *adj.* having an inferiority complex.

silópono: (Sp. *xilopono*) *n.* xylophone.

silsíl: *adj.* blunted, flattened.

silweta: (Sp. *silhueta*) *n.* silhouette.

silya: (Sp. *silla*) *n.* chair; left turn; ~ **maygulóng** *n.* wheel chair; **silyang tumba-tumbá** *n.* rocking chair; **silyeta** *n.* small chair, folding chair; **silyón** *n.* large chair.

sim- *pref.* var. of *(ka)sing-* prefix before labial consonants, p, b, and m, forming equalitative adjectives → **simpayát** as thin as; **simpangit** as ugly as.

simà: *n.* barb; feather at the end of an arrow.

simâ: *n.* dip net; pot for catching fish.

simangot: *n.* frown; **simangutan** *v.* to frown at, scowl.

simarón: (Sp. *cimarrón*) *adj.* wild, unruly.

simawar: *n.* ornate electric fish, *Ophiocara aporos.*

simbá: **magsimbá** *v.* to go to Mass; **simbahan** *n.* church; **simbang-gabí** *n.* early morning mass before the nine days of Christmas.

simbád: *n.* swooping; plundering; cavalla fish.

simbergwensa: (Sp. *sin vergüenza*) *adj*. shameless.
símbolo: (Sp.) *n*. symbol; **simbóliko** *adj*. symbolic.
simburyo: (Sp. *cimborrio*) *n*. dome; cockpit.
simenteryo: (Sp.) *n*. cemetery.
simetría: (Sp.) *n*. symmetry.
simì: *n*. remnants of food after a meal.
similya: (Sp. *semilla*) *n*. embryo.
simoníya: (Sp.) *n*. simony, selling church things.
simót: *adj*. completely consumed; **magsimót** *v*. to collect everything left; **simutín** *v*. to pick up everything around.
simoy: *n*. breeze; **simuyan** *v*. to expose to the wind.
simpán: *n*. thrift, saving; savings; **magsimpán** *v*. to be thrifty.
simpatíya: (Sp. *simpatía*) *n*. friendliness; sympathy; **simpátiko** *adj*. friendly; good-looking.
simpî: *n*. sulking.
simple: (Sp.) *adj*. simple, homely; innocent; natural; plain.
simponía: (Sp. *sinfonía*) *n*. symphony.
simpók: *n*. surge of the sea; **simpukan** *n*. breakers (waves).
simsím: *n*. enjoying little by little (tasting, etc.).
simulâ: *n*. origin, beginning, start; onset; nucleus; **magsimulâ** *v*. to begin, commence; **pagpapasimulâ** *n*. promotion; **panimulâ** *adj*. primary; fundamental; **pasimulâ** *n*. rudiment; beginning; dawn; **sa simulâ pa** at first; beforehand; **simulain** *n*. principle.
simunò: see *pasimunò*.
sin- *pref*. var. of *sing-* used before t, d, l, r, or s → **sintabâ** as fat as.
siná: *art*. Plural of the personal topic marker *si*.
sinákulo: (Sp. *cenaculo*) *n*. Cenacle, place of the Last Supper.
sinadobo: (*slang*, *sinangág* + *adobo*) *n*. fried rice and *adobo*.
sinag: *n*. ray of light; beam, gleam; **suminag** *v*. to beam, gleam; **sinag-araw** *n*. sunshine; ray of sunlight; **sinag-buwán** *n* moonlight; **sinag-talà** *n*. star ray.
sinagoga: (Sp.) *n*. synagogue.
sinagtalâ: *n*. star ray.
sinala: *n*. flowerpot.
sinalog: (*slang*, *sinangág* + *itlóg*) *n*. fried rice and eggs.
sinamóng: (Ch.) *n*. large china jar.
sinangág: (*rt*. *sangág*) *n*. fried rice.
sinap: *n*. overflowing of water.
sinat: *n*. slight fever; kind of woody vine.
sinauna: (*rt*. *una*) *adj*. old fashioned.
sinayà: *n*. tasting for the first time; **pasinayà** *n*. inauguration.
sindák: *n*. terror, awe, fright; **masindák** *adj*. terrified, stunned; **pagkasindák** *n*. terror.
sindál: *n*. contrary current or flow.
sindí: (Sp. *encender*) **magsindí** *v*. to light (fire); **panindí** *n*. lighter; **sindihán** *v*. to light.
sindikato: (Sp. *sindicato*) *n*. syndicate.
sine: (Sp. *cine*) *n*. movies; cinema.
sinelas: (Sp. *chinelas*) *n*. slippers.
sinigáng: (*rt*. *sigáng*) *n*. sour stew.
sinigwelas: (Sp. *ciruelas*) *n*. Spanish plum, *Spondias furpurea*.
sinilí: *n*. hip, hip joint.
sining: *n*. art; **masining** *adj*. artistic.
sinipete: (Sp.) *n*. anchor.
sinisa: (Sp. *ceniza*) *n*. ash; **sinisado** *adj*. ash colored, gray.
sino: *pron*. who; ~ **man** anybody; whomever, anyone; **walang sinuman** nobody.
sinók: *n*. hiccup.
sinop: **isinop** *v*. to file (documents); **masinop** *adj*. orderly; economical; **sinupan** *n*. file cabinet.
sinsá: (Sp. *cincha*) *n*. girth for a saddle.
sinsáy: *adj*. deflected; missing the mark; opposed; **suminsáy** *v*. to deviate; oppose; drop by (visiting).
sinsél: (Sp. *cincel*) *n*. chisel; wedge.
sinsero: (Sp. *sincero*) *adj*. sincere; **sinseridád** *n*. sincerity.
sinsilyo: (Sp. *sencillo*) *n*. loose change; coins; *adj*. simple.
sinsín: *n*. density of growth; closeness of weaving; **suminsín** *v*. to become dense.
sinsoro: (Sp. *chinchorro*) *n*. dragnet (general term).

sinta(s): (Sp. *cinta*) *n.* ribbon.
sintá$_1$: **sumintá** *v.* to rise on the hind legs.
sintá$_2$: *n.* love; **kasintahan** *n.* sweetheart; **manintá** *v.* to love; **sintahan** *n.* love affair.
sintabì: **pasintabì** *n.* asking permission to do; giving due respect to.
sinták: *n.* jackstones; jerky motion; pulsation.
sintás: (Sp. *cinta*) *n.* ribbon; tape; ~ **sa baywáng** *n.* sash.
sintido: (Sp. *sentido*) *n.* sense; temple of the head.
sintô: **sintú-sintô** *adj.* crazy; imbecile; abnormal.
sintóg: *n.* sudden jerk, pull, palpitation.
sintunis: (*Batangas*) *n.* mandarin orange.
sintura: (Sp. *cintura*) *n.* waistline measurement.
sinturera: (Sp. *cinturera*) *n.* belt supports sewn on the waistline.
sinturón: (Sp. *cinturón*) *n.* belt.
sinungaling: *n.* liar; lie; *adj.* false, untruthful; **magsinungaling** *v.* to lie; **pasingungaling** *n.* counterproof.
sing-: *var. of kasing-* expressing an equalitative relationship → **singlapit** as near as; **singlapad** as broad as.
singá: *n.* blowing the nose; **sumingá** *v.* to blow the nose.
singáp: **sumingáp** *v.* to gasp for breath.
singasing: *n.* snorting; panting.
singáw: *n.* vapor, steam; skin eruption around the mouth; **sumingáw** *v.* to evaporate, steam, emit from; **pasingáw** (*coll.*) *n.* publication in a newspaper; **sumingáw ang bahò** *id.* revealed a secret.
singkaban: *n.* temporary arch built for Easter celebrations.
singkád: *adj.* whole, full; exact.
singkál: **singkalín** *v.* to split with a wedge.
singkamás: (Sp. *jícama*) *n.* jicama, turnip.
singkáw: *adj.* hitched, yoked.
singkî: (Ch.) *n.* novice, beginner.
singkíl: *n.* elbowing, elbow nudge; kind of native dance.
singkít: (Ch.) *adj.* with slanted eyes.
singko: (Sp *cinco*) *n.* five; **alas** ~ five o'clock.
singkól: *adj.* twisted (arms).
singkóm: (Ch.) *n.* species of citrus tree (like tangerine).
síngkopa: (Sp. *sincopa*) *n.* syncopation; syncope.
singkuwenta: (Sp. *cincuenta*) *n.* fifty.
singgá: *n.* recurrence of an illness or craving.
singgalong: *n.* bamboo wine cup.
singgî: *n.* stingy person.
singgleta: (Sp. *cingleta*) *n.* float for a fishing net.
singguwatse: (Ch.) *n.* dried, salted melon seeds.
singhál: *n.* snarl, growl; outburst of anger.
singháp: *n.* gasping for breath.
singhót: *n.* sniffing; sniffling.
singíl: *n.* collection of a payment, charge; **sumingíl** *v.* to collect, charge; **tagasingíl** *n.* collector; **maningíl sa hangin** *id.* debt that can't be paid (collect from the air); **maningíl ng buhay** *id.* kill (collect life).
singit: *n.* slit; groin; **isingit** *v.* to insert between, tuck in.
singlot: (*slang*) *adj.* drunk.
singsíng: (Ch.) *n.* ring; **palasingsingan** *n.* ring finger.
sipà: *n.* kick; hackey sack; **sumipà** *v.* to kick.
sipák: *adj.* cracked; split; **sumipák** *v.* to split, crack.
sipag: **masipag** *n.* diligent, hard working; **masipagsayáw** *v.* to dance energetically.
sipat: **sipatán** *n.* sight, view finder; **pagsipat** *n.* act of sighting or aiming; **sipatin** *v.* to aim, line up by sight.
sipaw: *n.* pied chat bird, *Pratincola caprata*.
sipháw: *n.* persecution.
siphayò: *n.* oppression, mistreatment; **siphayuin** *v.* to mistreat; disappoint; frustrate.
sipì: *n.* copy; **pagsipì** *n.* reproduction, copying; **panipì** *n.* quotation marks; **sipiin** *v.* to copy, quote.
sipilyo: (Sp. *cepillo*) *n.* toothbrush, brush.
siping: *adj.* side by side; **isiping** *v.* to put beside; **sumiping** *v.* to come near someone; **magsiping** *v.* to be at one's side, lie next to.
sipit$_1$: *n.* claw, pincer; **panipit** *n.* tongs, forceps; hairclip.
sipit$_2$: **isipit** *v.* to insert between.

sipò: **sipuin** *v.* to look for something lost.
sipók: *n.* bundle of rice stalks with the grain.
sipol: (Sp. *chiflo*) *n.* whistling; siren.
sipón: *n.* cold (sickness); siphon.
sipót: *n.* arrival; **sumipot** *v.* to appear, arrive.
sipoy: **sipuyin** *v.* to drag with a rope.
siprés: (Sp. *cipres*) *n.* cypress.
sipsíp: *n.* sip; sucking; (*coll.*) sycophancy; bootlicker; **sumipsíp** *v.* to sip; suck; absorb.
sirà: *n.* break, damage; **sirâ** *adj.* broken, damaged, ruined; torn; hurt; crazy; **makipagsirâ** *v.* to quarrel; **mapanirà** *adj.* destructive; **masirà** *v.* to spoil, damage; break down; **may-sirà** *adj.* diseased; **nakasisirà** *adj.* belittling, derogatory; **nasirà** *adj.* late (deceased); **pagsirà ng loób** *n.* discouragement; **waláng-sirà** *adj.* flawless, perfect; **mapanirang-puri** *id.* fault-finding (destroying honor); **nasirà ang tiyán** *id.* with indigestion; **sirâ ang baít** *id.* insane; **nasirang amá** *id.* deceased father; **sirâ ang tuktók** *id.* unreasonable; lunatic; **waláng sumísirà sa bakal kundî ang kalawang** *id.* refers to a person who destroys the reputation of a relative or friend (nothing destroys the iron but the rust).
sirbyente: (Sp. *sirviente*) *n.* servant; waiter.
sirkero: (Sp. *cirquero*) *n.* circus person, acrobat.
sirko: (Sp. *circo*) *n.* circus.
sírkulo: (Sp. *círculo*) *n.* circle; social group.
sirena: (Sp.) *n.* mermaid; siren.
siripít: (*slang*) *n.* making love.
sirit: *n.* sizzling; hissing; squirt; ~ **na** expression used when one gives up when attempting to solve a riddle.
sirok: *n.* diving in the air (birds).
sirol: *n.* poking with a stick.
siruhano: (Sp. *cirujano*) *n.* surgeon; **siruhía** *n.* surgery.
siryo: (Sp. *cirio*) *n.* long, thick wax taper.
sisi₁: *n.* regret; remorse; **magsisi** *v.* to repent, be sorry for. **pagsisihan** *v.* to be sorry for, regret.
sisi₂: *n.* blame; reprimand, reproach; **isisi** *v.* to blame; **paninisi.** *n.* reprimand; blame. **manisi, sumisi, sisihin** *v.* to blame; upbraid.
sisid: *n.* diving; **máninisid** *n.* diver; **sisirin** *v.* to dive for. **sumisid** *v.* to dive.
sisidlán: (rt. *silíd*) *n.* container.
sisíl: **panisíl** *n.* brush used in cleaning yarn.
sisíp: *n.* long-handed knife used in rattan work.
sisíw: *n.* chick, young chicken; (*slang*) easy. **sisiwán** *n.* hatchery.
sisiwa: *n.* wet nurse.
sisiyo: (Ch.) *n.* fig tree, fig. (*igos*)
sismis: *var.* of *tsismis*: gossip.
sisne: (Sp. *cisne*) *n.* swan; outstanding poet.
sisté: (Sp. *chiste*) *n.* joke.
sistema: (Sp.) *n.* system; **sistemátiko** *adj.* systematic.
sisterna: (Sp. *cisterna*) *n.* cistern, water tank.
sita: (Sp. *cita*) *n.* appointment, engagement; citation; hiring for a service (lawyers, musicians, etc.).
sitá: **sitahín** *v.* to interrogate.
sitado: (Sp. *citado*) *adj.* cited, mentioned; hired for a service.
sitasyón: (Sp. *citación*) *n.* citation; mention.
sitaw: *n.* string bean; (*slang*) rank, stripes on a uniform.
sitrón: (Sp.) *n.* lemon.
sitsâ: (Sp. *chicha*) *n.* fermented drink made from corn.
sitsaró: (Sp. *chicharo*) *n.* pea.
sitsarón: (Sp. *chicharrón*) *n.* crispy pork rind.
sitsirika: (Sp. *chichirica*) *n.* pink periwinkle.
sitsít: (Ch.) *n.* gossip; calling someone by hissing; *adj.* fond of gossiping.
situwasyón: (Sp. *situación*) *n.* situation.
sityo: (Sp. *sitio*) *n.* site; district.
siwà: (*obs.*) *n.* excuse for breaking a promise.
siwal: **masiwal** *adj.* wicked, perverse.
siwalat: **isiwalat** *v.* to disclose, reveal, confess.
siwang: *n.* crevice, gap; tear.
siway: *n.* divergence, deviation.
siwî: *n.* corners of the mouth.
siya: (Sp. *silla*) *n.* saddle. **siyahan** *v.* to saddle.
siyá₁: *pron.* he, she, it; the one; ~ **na** Stop it! ~ **nawâ** Amen!; **Siyangâ** Indeed!; of course.
siyá₂: **kasiyá** *adj.* enough, sufficient; **magkasiyá** *v.* to be enough.
siyá₃: **pasiyá** *n.* decision; judgment; **kapasiyahán** *n.* decision reached, finding; **ipa-**

siyá *v.* to decide, resolve; **magpasiyá** *v.* to decide; reason; **mapagsiyá** *v.* to distinguish.
siyá₄: (Ch.) **kasiyá-siyá** *adj.* appreciable; pleasing; pleasant; **kasiyahán** *n.* satisfaction, pleasure; **makasiyá** *v.* to please, satisfy; **masiyá** *v.* to approve; be satisfied.
siyaho: (Ch.) *n.* term for one's elder sister's husband.
siyám: *n.* nine; **labinsiyám** *n.* nineteen; **siyaman** *n.* novena, nine days prayer for the dead; **siyamnapû** *n.* ninety.
síyan: *interj.* used in driving away dogs.
siyansí: (Ch.) *n.* cooking tong (for turning things).
siyangâ: *adv.* of course; indeed.
siyáp: *n.* chirping.
siyasat: *n.* investigation; enquiry; **pagkakasiyasat** *n.* survey; **siyasatin** *v.* to examine, investigate; scrutinize.
siyasi: (*slang*) *n.* masturbation.
siyasik, siyasig: *n.* careful research; meticulousness.
siyasip: **masiyasip** *n.* prudent, careful.
siyempre: (Sp. *siempre*: always) *adv.* of course, certainly.
siyénsiya: (Sp. *ciencia*) *n.* science. (*aghám*)
siyento: (Sp. *ciento*) *n.* one hundred; **siyentobeinte** one hundred twenty; (*slang*) *adj.* semi-conscious.
siyerto: (Sp. *cierto*) *adj.* certain, sure.
siyesta: (Sp. *siesta*) *n.* nap, siesta.
siyete: (Sp. *siete*) *n.* seven; **siyete kartas** (*slang*) *n.* group.
siyók: (Ch.) *n.* frightened cry of a chicken.
siyokè: (Ch.) *n.* hermaphrodite; effeminate man.
siyoktóng: (Ch.) *n.* rice wine.
siyongá: (*slang*) *adj.* stupid.
siyopaw: (Ch.) *n.* steamed rice bun.
siyukoy: (Ch.) *n.* merman.
siyudád: (Sp. *ciudad*) *n.* city.
siyumay: (Ch.) *n.* meatballs wrapped in noodles.
siyuting: (Eng.) *n.* shooting, filming.
soberano: (Sp.) *n.* sovereign; monarch.
soberanya: (Sp. *soberanía*) *n.* sovereignty.
sobérbiyó: (Sp. *soberbio*) *adj.* stubborn.
soborno: (Sp.) *n.* bribe.
sobra: (Sp.) *adj.* excess; *adv.* too much, excessive; extremely; **sobrado** *adj.* excessive.
sobre: (Sp.) *n.* envelope.
sobrekama: (Sp. *sobrecama*) *n.* bedspread.
sobrekarga: (Sp. *sobrecarga*) *n.* overload.
sobrenaturál: (Sp.) *adj.* supernatural.
sobrepaga: (Sp.) *n.* extra pay.
sobresalyente: (Sp. *sobresaliente*) *adj.* excellent, outstanding.
sokoro: (Sp. *socorro*) *n.* succor, help.
soda: (Eng.) *n.* soda; sodium carbonate.
soga: (Sp.) *n.* tether.
solapa: (Sp. *solapa*: flap) *n.* coat lapel.
solbáng: (*slang*) *adj.* OK; high on drugs; drunk.
soldado: (Sp.) *n.* soldier (*sundalò*); (*coll.*) follower.
soldadór: (Sp.) *n.* soldering iron, solderer.
soldadura: (Sp.) *n.* solder.
soleras: (Sp.) *n.* joist.
solidaridád: (Sp.) *n.* solidarity.
solihiyá: *n.* rattan work.
solo: (Sp.) *n.* solo; *adj.* alone; **solohán** *adj.* single; **soloista** *n.* soloist.
solomilyo: (Sp. *lomillo*) *n.* loin, sirloin.
solpeo: (Sp. *solfeo*) *n.* solfeggio; solfa.
soltero: (Sp.) *n.* unmarried person.
solusyón: (Sp. *solución*) *n.* solution.
sombra: (Sp.) *n.* shade; (*coll.*) joke; criticism.
sombrero: (Sp.) *n.* hat.
sona: (Sp. *zona*) *n.* zone.
sonámbulo: (Sp.) *n.* sleepwalker.
sonda: (Sp.) *n.* plummet, sounder; catheter; **sondahín** *v.* to measure the depth of with a probing instrument; insert a catheter.
sondo: (*slang*, Jap.) *n.* peso.
soó: (Eng.) *n.* zoo; **soolohía** *n.* zoology.
sopá: (Sp. *sofá*) *n.* sofa, couch.
sopas: (Sp.) *n.* soup; **sopera, sopero** *n.* soup bowl.
Sor: (Sp., *eccles.*) *n.* sister (title for nuns).
soro: (Sp. *zorro*) *n.* fox.
sorbetes: (Sp.) *n.* ice-cream; **sorbetero** *n.* ice-cream vendor.
sorpresa: (Sp.) *n.* surprise.
Sorsogón: *n.* language of Sorsogon Province,

Bikol.

sorteo: (Sp.) *n.* raffle, drawing.

sosi: (*slang*) *n.* elite, social person; classy person.

sospetsa: (Sp. *sospecha*) *n.* suspicion; **sospetsoso** *adj.* suspicious.

sosyál: (Sp. *social*) *adj.* social; elite; (*coll.*) classy person; **sosyal gubat** *n.* social climber; **sosyalada** *n.* high society girl.

sosyedád: (Sp. *sociedad*) *n.* society

sosyo: (Sp. *socio*) *n.* partner (in business).

sosyolohiya: (Sp. *sociología*) *n.* sociology.

sota: (Sp.) *n.* groom; man in charge of horses; jack (in cards).

sotanghón: (Ch.) *n.* mung bean noodle.

sotsoá: (Ch.) *n.* straw paper.

súag: *n.* stomach ache; rise of the tide.

suág: **masuág** *v.* to be gored (by horns).

suál: *n.* lever; moving something inside the mouth with the tongue; **panuál** *n.* lever.

suám: (Ch.) *n.* kind of garlic and ginger stew; **isuám** *v.* to poach (an egg).

suát: *n.* reprimand, reproach.

suáy: **suayín** *v.* to disobey.

subá: **subahán** *v.* to put out a fire with water.

subà₁: **masubà** *v.* to be cheated, swindled; **mánunubà** *n.* cheat; swindler; **sumubà, subain** *v.* to swindle; cheat; **panunubà** *n.* swindling.

subà₂: *n.* fit of convulsion; **panunubà** *n.* convulsions.

subabang: *n.* falling on the face.

subalì: **pasubalì** *n.* objection; reservation about something; **pasubalian** *v.* to object to.

subali't: *conj.* but; only.

Subanon: *n.* ethnic group and language from Mindanao.

subará: (*slang*) *n.* cigarette. [Alt: *subaratsi, subaru*]

subasób: *adj.* fallen face-downwards.

subasta: (Sp.) *n.* auction.

subaybáy: **sumubaybáy** *v.* to keep track of, observe closely.

subida: (Sp.) *n.* ascent, rice; doctor's visit.

subido: (Sp.) *adj.* deep (color); very bright.

sublî: *n.* folk dance.

subò: (Ch.) *n.* mouthful, morsel; **isubò** *v.* to put in the mouth; **subuan** *v.* to feed someone; **isubò sa basag-ulo** *v.* to put in trouble.

subó: *n.* tempering of metal; fit of anger; seething; **sub(u)hán** *v.* to temper metal.

subô: *adj.* inserted too deep; bold.

subok₁: *n.* trial, test; experiment; **subukin** *v.* to try, test; **subukan** *v.* to try out, taste something.

subok₂: **manubok** *v.* to spy; **mánunubok** *n.* spy; **subukan** *v.* to spy on.

subsób: **nakasubsób** *adj.* with the head bent down touching a surface.

subyáng: *n.* splinter under the skin.

suka: (Ch.) *n.* spew; vomit; **sumuka** *v.* to spew, vomit; **isuka** *v.* to spew out; **makásuká** *v.* to nauseate; **nakakásuká** *adj.* disgusting, offensive; **pampasuka** *adj.* causing vomiting.

sukà: *n.* vinegar; **magsukà** *v.* to make vinegar; **sukaan** *v.* to add vinegar to.

sukáb: *adj.* treacherous; **sukabín** *v.* to pry open an oyster.

sukal₁: *n.* garbage; flotsam; dirt; ~ **ng loób** *n.* ill feeling.

sukal₂: **masukal** *adj.* savage, wild.

sukarón: (Sp. *socarrón*) *adj.* sly, crafty.

sukat₁: *interj.* expresses wonder, surpass, Imagine!

sukat₂: *n.* measurement; size; tract, area; **kasukát** *adj.* proportional; **isukat** *v.* to try on; **sukatin** *v.* to measure; survey; **panukat** *n.* measuring tool; **sukatán** *n.* scale; model used for measuring; **sukat na** *adj.* enough; **nagsukatán ng lakás** *id.* fought with bare fists (measured the strength).

sukbít: (Ch.) **isukbít** *v.* to tuck under one's belt.

sukdán: *conj.* even if, although.

sukdól: **kasukdulán** *n.* climax; *adj.* utmost, extreme; **panukdulan** *n.* superlative; **sukdulan** *n.* extremity.

sukì: (Ch.) *n.* faithful customer.

sukíng: *n.* loose-fitting shirt for men.

suklám: *n.* disgust; hatred; **masuklám** *v.* to hate, detest; **naksusuklám** *adj.* disgusting, repulsive.

sukláy: (Ch.) *n.* comb.

suklî: (Ch.) *n.* change (of money).
suklô: *adj.* pressed down.
suklób: *n.* covering, casing (movable, like a sheath).
suklót: *n.* protective cover for the tip of something.
sukò: *n.* surrender; **sumukò** *v.* to surrender, give up.
sukó: *adj.* reaching the tip or top.
sukob₁: *adj.* sharing cover, shelter; **makisukob** *v.* to ask to share shelter or cover; **sumukob** *v.* to join others in taking shelter.
sukob₂: *n.* mudfish net.
sukól: *adj.* enclosed; surrounded; **daáng** ~ *n.* dead end street.
sukong: *n.* bundle of rattan strips.
sukot: **sumukot** *v.* to cringe, cower
suksók: *n.* shuffling of playing cards; repairing woven things; reserving something for future use; sheathing a weapon; inserting into a tight space; **panuksók** *n.* old style hair clip; **magsuksók** *v.* to shuffle; reserve money for future use.
sudasod: *var. of sulasod.*
sudián: *n.* spindle.
sudlóng: *n.* juncture; something added to increase the length.
sudsód: *n.* plowshare; blade of a plow; guitar fish; **sudsuran** *n.* quarrel.
suga: (Sp. *soga*) *n.* cardinal fish; **panuga** *n.* tether.
sugabang: *n.* greed, avarice.
sugál: (Sp. *jugar*) *n.* gambling, **manunugal** *n.* gambler.
sugapà: *adj.* addicted; *n.* addiction; small fishing net.
sugaról: (Sp. *jugador*) *n.* gambler.
sugasog: **magsugasog** *v.* to explore.
sugat: *n.* wound; cut; sore; **magsugat** *v.* to develop into a wound; **sumugat, sugatan** *v.* to wound; **sugatán** *n.* wounded person, casualty; *adj.* covered with wounds.
sugaygáy: *n.* keeping track of; spying.
sugbá: **sumugbá** *v.* to rush into danger.
sugbó: **sumugbó** *v.* to dive head first, plunge into.
sugíd: **masugíd** *adj.* active, diligent.
sugigì: *n.* shaking the finger at; forcing into the mouth of.
sugnáy: *n.* clause.
sugò: *n.* sending someone on an errand; delegate; messenger, envoy; ambassador; **sumugò, suguin** *v.* to send off; dispatch; **mga sugò** *n.* mission.
sugók: *adj.* short-necked; second plowing of a field.
sugod: *n.* plunge, dash; **sumugod** *v.* to dash, lunge, plunge; **sugód** *adj.* impulsive; **magsúgúran** *v.* to stampede; **súgúran** *adj.* headlong; **sugurin** *v.* to rush; move forward, lunge.
sugpô₁: *n.* lobster; prawn; crayfish.
sugpô₂: *n.* suppression; **sumugpô** *v.* to prevent, check, suppress.
sugpóng: **sugpungan** *n.* juncture; joint.
suhà: *n.* pomelo.
suhay: *n.* brace, prop, support.
suheto: (Sp. *sujeto*: subject) *n.* discipline; **suhetado** *adj.* disciplined; controlled.
suhî: *adj.* breech baby; lying with the head next to the feet of another.
suhol: *n.* bribe.
sulà: *n.* bright red gem; inflamed swelling.
sulák *adj.* simmering; **sumulák** *v.* to simmer.
sulam: *n.* design on mats or fabrics.
sulambî: *n.* eaves; annex to a house.
sulapa: (Sp. *solapa*) *n.* lapel of a coat.
sulár: (Sp. *solar*) *n.* lawn, residential lot.
sulasi: **sulá-sulasihan** *n.* kind of fragrant herb, *Leucas aspera.*
sulasod. **sulusurin** *v.* push forward along the surface.
sulat: *n.* writing, letter; **kasulatán** *n.* correspondent; **kasulátan** *n.* deed; document; **isulat** *v.* to write down; **magsulát** *v.* to write continuously; **magsulatán** *v.* to correspond, write to each other; **manulat** *v.* to write professionally; **mánunulát** *n.* writer, author; **sulatan** *v.* to write to; **sulatán** *adj.* used for writing; **pagkakásúlat** *n.* handwriting; **pagsulat** *n.* writing; **pansulat** *n.* writing instrument; **panulat** *n.* pen, style of writing; **panunulat** *n.* professional writing; **sulatin** *v.* to write; **sumulat** *v.* to write; **tagasulat** *n.*

clerk.
suldá: (Sp. *solda*) *n*. solder.
suleras: (Sp.) *n*. crossbeam, joist.
sulíb: *n*. small secret compartment; space between double walls; species of shellfish.
sulikap: *n*. cloven-hoofed foot.
sulid: *n*. flax for a spinning wheel; Caesio fish; **suliran** *n*. spinning wheel, spool, spindle; **sinulid** *n*. thread; **suliranin** *n*. problem.
suligì: *n*. dart, small spear; awl; **sumuligì** *v*. to pierce with a dart.
sulihiá: (Sp. *celosia*) *n*. split rattan, wickerwork.
sulilíng: **pasulilíng** *adv*. sideways; *n*. sudden twisting of the neck.
sulimpát: *adj*. squinty-eyed.
sulindíng: *var. of sulilíng*.
suling: **sumuling-suling** *v*. to do to and fro.
suliranin: (*rt. sulid*) *n*. problem; issue, question.
sulit: *n*. test; explanation; report; **ipagbigáy-sulit** *v*. to account for; **isulit** *v*. to give, turn over; **magsulit-tanong** *v*. to cross question; **makasulit** *v*. to pass a test; **pagsusulit** *n*. report; explanation; returning something; test; **magsulit** *v*. to account for; **sulít na** *adj*. recovered (capital).
suló: **masuló** *adj*. to be dazzled by a strong light.
sulô: *n*. lighted torch.
sulok: *n*. corner; angle; **panulukan** *n*. street corner; **tatsulok** *n*. triangle.
Sulod: *n*. ethnic group and language from Capiz Province, Panay.
sulong: *n*. turn (in a game); partial payment, installment; *interj*. Go ahead! Move!; **isulong** *v*. to push forward; **pagsulóng** *adv*. forward; **sumulong** *v*. to advance, progress.
sulot: **magsulót** *v*. to insert; **magpasulót** *v*. to outwit; play a trick on someone; replace someone at work using foul means.
suloy: *n*. sprouting of plants.
sulpák: *n*. toy popgun; forcing something into a hole or one's mouth; indiscriminate use of clothes.
sulpato: (Sp. *sulfato*) *n*. sulfate.
sulpít: *n*. spurt; jet of liquid.
sulpót: **sumulpót** *v*. to emerge, appear unexpectedly.
sulsí: (Sp. *zurcir*) *n*. mend, stitch; **sulsihán** *v*. to darn, mend clothes.
sulsól₁: **sumulsól** *v*. to incite, instigate, stir up.
sulsól₂: **isulsól** *v*. to put out a candle by jabbing.
sultada: (Sp. *soltada*) *n*. round of cockfighting.
sultán: (Sp.) *n*. sultan.
sultera: (Sp. *soltera*) *n*. spinster, old maid.
sultero: (Sp. *soltero*) *n*. bachelor.
sulukasok: *n*. disgust, loathing.
sulupikâ: *adj*. traitorous; *n*. traitor, liar.
sulyák: *n*. eyesore; *adj*. offensive to the sight.
sulyáng: *n*. large bamboo fish trap.
sulyáp: *n*. glance, glimpse; **sumulyáp** *v*. to glance.
sulyasid: *n*. duck-like bird.
sulyáw: (Ch.) *n*. large bowl.
suma- *pref*. [*sa*- + -*um*-] verbalizing prefix for intransitive *sa* verbs → **sumalangit** to go to heaven; **sumakamáy** put on the hand.
suma: (Sp.) *n*. sum, total; **sumahin** *v*. to sum up, total.
sumà: *n*. species of vine whose roots are used as a fish poison, *Anamirta cocoulus*.
sumalapaw: *n*. poison fish.
suman: *n*. rice cake.
sumáng: **sumangín** *v*. to contradict.
sumásainyó: [*s-um-a CV inyó*] yours truly; yours.
sumbabaáy: *adj*. carried on the back, piggy-back.
sumbá: (Sp. *zumba*) *n*. device made of buri leaf that hisses in the wind.
sumbál: **sumumbál** *v*. to back out of an agreement.
sumbalilo: (Sp. *sombrero*) *n*. hat.
sumbáng: *n*. rooting with the snout (pigs).
sumbát₁: *n*. reproach, upbraiding.
sumbát₂: **sumumbát** *v*. to mix silver and gold.
sumbî: *n*. punch in the face.
sumbilang: *n*. salt water catfish.
sumbó: *n*. light of a candle or lamp.
sumbol: *n*. flower of reed grass.
sumbóng: *n*. complaint; accusation; **ipagsumbóng** *v*. to denounce, accuse; **magsumbóng** *v*. to tell on someone.

sumbrero: (Sp. *sombrero*) *n.* hat; **magsumbrero** *v.* to wear a hat.

sumpâ: *n.* oath, vow; **isumpâ** *v.* to condemn; protest; **kasumpá-sumpâ** *adj.* hateful; **manumpâ** *v.* to swear to; take an oath; **sumumpâ** *v.* to swear; curse.

sumpák: *n.* blowgun.

sumpál: *n.* plug, stopper.

sumpíng: *adj.* carried behind the air; with the hair combed back without a part in the middle; *n.* game of hooking fingers to test one's strength.

sumpít: *n.* blowgun; enema apparatus; enema.

sumpóng₁: *n.* caprice, whim; **sumpungin** *adj.* cranky, moody; fickle.

sumpóng₂: **makasumpong** *v.* to stumble on to, find accidentally.

sundalo: (Sp. *soldado*) *n.* soldier; **sundalong-kanin** *id.* cowardly soldier.

sundán: (rt. *sunód*) *v.* to follow.

sundáng: *n.* dagger; **sundangín** *v.* to stab with a dagger.

sundín: (rt. *sunód*) *v.* to obey.

sundô₁: *n.* fetcher, one who fetches another person; **sumundô** *v.* to fetch; **sunduín** *v.* to fetch someone; **súnduan** *n.* fetching; time when people are fetched (children at school).

sundô₂: **kasundô** *n.* betrothed person; friendly person, ally; **kasunduan** *n.* agreement; pact, treaty; **magkásundô** *v.* to agree; reconcile; **magkasundô** *adj.* on good terms, friendly; **mákasundô** *v.* to get along with; agree; **makipagkásundô** *v.* to make a contract; agree to do, promise; **mapagkakásundô** *adj.* reconcilable; **nápagkásunduán** *adj.* arranged by agreement; **pagkakasundô** *n.* harmony, unity, reconciliation; **papagkásunduín** *v.* to reconcile others; **pinagkásunduán** *n.* point of agreement; **kásunduang magpakasál** *n.* engagement; **ipakipagkásundóng pakasál** *v.* to promise in marriage.

sundóng: *n.* forked pole.

sundót: *n.* poke, jab; (*slang*) impregnating; getting someone to bed; making someone confess.

sunò: **isunò** *v.* to give someone a ride; **sunuan** *v.* to ride with someone.

sunók: *n.* surfeit; loss of interest; **makasunók** *v.* to be tired of.

sunód: **susunód** *adj.* next, following; **kasunód** *n.* next, following; sequence; **magkakasunód** *adj.* consecutive; **magkasunód** *adj.* one after the other; **magpasunód** *v.* to set, arrange (for others to follow); **magpapasunód** *adj.* lenient; **masúnúrin** *adj.* obedient; submissive; **pagkakásumundán** *n.* precedent; **pagkakásunúd-sunód** *n.* order; series; sequence; succession; **pagkamasúnúrin** *n.* obedience; **pagsunód** *n.* obedience; compliance; submission; **pagsunúd-sunurín** *v.* to rank; **sundán** *v.* to follow someone; **palasunód** *adj.* amenable; submissive; **pasimundín** *n.* youngest child about to be followed by a newborn baby; **sumunód-sunód** *v.* follow behind, tag along; **sumúsunód** *adj.* next; following; **sundán** *v.* to follow someone; **sundín** *v.* to follow; obey; **sunúd-sunúran** *adj.* easily influenced; servile; **tagasunód** *n.* follower; **bilang pagsunód** in compliance with; **sumunód sa bakás ng amá** *id.* followed in the father's footsteps, inherited father's character.

sunog₁: *n.* fire; (*slang*) deadline; **sunóg** *adj.* burnt; sunburnt; **masunog** *v.* to burn; **panununog** *n.* arson; **magsunog ng kilay** *id.* to study late at night (burn eyebrow).

sunog₂: *n.* flatfish; **susunog** *n.* species of fish, *Butis amboinensis*.

sunong: *n.* load on the head.

sunót: (*slang*) *n.* taking illegal drugs.

suntók: *n.* fist punch; **magsuntukan** *v.* to box; **suntók sa buwán** *id.* useless effort (punching the moon) **sumuntók sa hangin** *id.* hoped for nothing (punched the air).

sungangà: *n.* stroke under the chin.

sungabà: *n.* falling face down.

sungál: *n.* with the upper lip protruding over the lower; tap under the chin; push of tongue against teeth; **sungalín** *v.* to push upward (mouth); push with tongue; (*coll.*) contradict.

sungalngál: **isungalngál** *v.* to force something into the mouth of someone else.

sungangà: *n.* push on the mouth or chin.
sungaw: *n.* peeping out; **isungaw** *v.* to thrust out.
sungáw: *adj.* uncircumcised. (*supót*)
sungay: *n.* horn; **magsungay** *v.* to grow horns; **sungayán** *adj.* horned; (*fig.*) disrespectful; rebellious.
sungay-sungayan: *n.* hornfish.
sungkâ: *n.* native game played by dropping shells into holes.
sungkád: *n.* check mark; **sungkarín** *v.* to check.
sungkál: *n.* uprooting with the snout, digging with the snout.
sungkî: *adj.* uneven.
sungkít: *n.* fruit picking hook attached to a pole.
sungkô: *n.* recruit; **masungkô** *v.* to be drafted.
sungkól: *n.* blow with the elbow or knuckles.
sunggáb: *n.* snatch, seizure; **sunggabán** *v.* to grasp, seize, snatch; tackle.
sunggô: *n.* light bump.
sungì: *n.* harelip; **sungî** *adj.* hare lipped.
sungilngíl: **isungilngíl** *v.* to force into the mouth of.
sungit: **masungit** *adj.* grouchy, ill-tempered; unfriendly.
sungó: *adj.* dejected; crestfallen.
sungót: *n.* antenna; pointed end of unhusked grains.
sungsóng: *n.* going against the current of wind; north of the monsoon.
suób: **suubín** *v.* to burn incense; fumigate; **suób-kabayo** *n.* bush-tea bush.
suóng: *n.* determined effort; **sumuóng sa panganib** *v.* to face danger.
suót: *n.* clothes; **isuót** *v.* to wear, put on; **suután** *v.* to dress someone; **magsuót** *v.* to wear; **sumuót** *v.* to enter, penetrate; **suót pamburol** *id.* most elegant apparel (dead person's clothing).
supá: (Sp. *sofá*) *n.* sofa, couch.
supalpál: **supalpalán** *v.* to force into the mouth of; (*coll.*) interrupt.
supang: *n.* sprout, bud; offshoot.
superyor: (Sp. *superior*) *adj.* superior.
superyora: (Sp. *superiora*) *n.* female head of a convent, mother superior.
superyoridád: (Sp. *superioridad*) *n.* superiority.
supí: *interj.* interjection used to drive cats away.
supil: **mánunupil** *n.* bully; **mapanupil** *n.* bully, one who terrorizes others; **panunupil** *n.* domination, control; repression; **manupil** *v.* to terrorize; **masupil** *v.* to be controlled, dominated; **sumupil** *v.* to tame, subdue.
supitra: (*slang*) *v.* end something quickly; get rid of somebody.
suplá: (Sp. *sopla*) **supladór** *n.* blowpipe; **suplado** *adj.* conceited, snobbish; **suplahán** *v.* to inflate, blow up; prompt someone (reciting).
suplemento: (Sp.) *n.* supplement.
suplente: (Sp.) *n.* substitute; alternate.
suplete: (Sp. *soplete*) *n.* blowtorch; blowpipe.
suplíng: *n.* offspring, offshoot.
suplóng: **magsuplóng** *v.* to denounce; **suplungán** *v.* to report an irregularity.
supo: *n.* act of contradicting; (*slang*) catching someone in the act; game similar to *tatsing*.
supók: *adj.* burnt to cinders.
supositoryo: (Sp.) *n.* suppository.
supot: *n.* paper bag, pouch; pocket; (*slang*) catching someone red-handed; **manunupot** *n.* mythological creature that kidnaps children (putting them in bags); **supút-suputan** *n.* pocket; pocket of a billiard table.
supót: (Ch.) *n.* uncircumcised.
supremo: (Sp.) *adj.* supreme.
supsóp₁: (Sp. *chupar*) **sumupsóp** *v.* to suck.
supsóp₂: (*slang*) *n.* addict.
sur: (Sp.) *n.* south.
sura: **surahán** *v.* to annoy.
suray: *n.* swaying, staggering, tottering.
surì₁: *n.* test, analysis; examination. **magsurì** *v.* to examine, review; probe into; **mapanurì** *adj.* critical, analytical; **pagkakasurì** *n.* examination. **surián** *n.* institute; place where examinations or investigations are done. **suriin** *v.* to analyze; examine; investigate. **suring-aklát** *n.* book review. **suring-bangkáy** *n.* autopsy.
surì₂: *n.* crease, fold in cloth.

suriso: (Sp. *chorizo*) *n*. pork sausage.
surò: *n*. pointed tube used to probe in rice sacks to sample grains; act of puncturing a sack.
surot$_1$: *n*. bedbug. **surutin** *v*. to be infested with bedbugs.
surot$_2$: *n*. scolding with the finger; poking a finger at.
surtido: (Sp.) *adj*. assorted.
sus: *interj*. Contraction of *Jesús*, used to show disapproval.
suskribí: (Sp. *suscribir*) **sumuskribí** *v*. to subscribe.
suskritór: (Sp. *suscritor*) *n*. subscriber.
susì$_1$: (Ch.) *n*. key; **susian** *v*. to lock; **susián** *n*. keyhole; **nasusian ang mga labì** *id*. dumbfounded (lips locked); **waláng susì ang bibíg** *id*. could not keep a secret (mouth has no key); **magsusì ang bibíg** *id*. to remain silent (lock mouth).
susì$_2$: **masusì** *adj*. detailed, minute.
susmaryosép: *interj*. Contraction of *Jesús, María, Josep*, shows disapproval.
suso$_1$: *n*. breast; **sumuso** *v*. to suckle.
suso$_2$: **susuhan** *v*. to set fire to fireworks.
susô: *n*. snail (general term); (*slang*) ugly person.
susog: *n*. amendment, change; following the trail of.
susón: *n*. extra layer; **magsusón** *v*. to double, fold over.
susóp: *adj*. in a hurry, pressed for time.
susót: *adj*. fed up.
suspendí: (Sp. *suspender*) **suspendihín** *v*. to suspend; **suspendido** *adj*. suspended.
sustansya: (Sp. *sustancia*) *n*. substance; nutrient; **masustansya** *adj*. substantial; nutritious; wholesome.
sustantibo: (Sp. *sustantivo*) *n*. noun.
sustento: (Sp.) *n*. maintenance, support, alimony; **magsustento** *v*. to support, sustain, provide; **sustentuhán** *v*. to support.
susulbót: *n*. kingfisher bird.
sutana: (Sp. *sotana*) *n*. cassock.
sutil: (Sp.) *adj*. subtle; cunning.
sutíl: *adj*. stubborn, undisciplined.
sutlâ: *n*. silk. (*seda*)
sutsót: *n*. hiss; whistle.
sutura: (Sp.) *n*. surgical thread or stitch.
suwabe: (Sp. *suave*) *adj*. suave, smooth; mellow.
suwág: *n*. bunt, butt with the horns.
suwagan: *n*. long-finned gizzard shad.
suwahe: *n*. species of fresh-water shrimps.
suwaíl: *adj*. disobedient; rebellious; wayward.
suwál: **suwalín** *v*. to push the teeth with the tongue; raise with a lever.
suwám: (Ch.) *n*. dish of fish, eggs, garlic and ginger.
suwangit: (*slang, suwapang + pangit*) *n*. ugly snob.
suwapang: *adj*. avaricious.
suwát: **suwatán** *v*. to quarrel.
suwatò: *n*. friendly relations; harmony. **isuwatò** *v*. to reconcile; **magkasuwatò** *adj*. compatible, agreeing, in harmony.
suwáy: **sumuwáy** *v*. to disobey; violate a rule; **pagsuwáy sa húkúman** *n*. contempt of court; **pagsuwáy sa nakatátaás** *n*. insubordination.
Suweko: (Sp. *sueco*) *n*. Swede, Swedish; **suwekos** *n*. clogs.
suwelas: (Sp. *suelas*) *n*. soles of shoes.
suweldo: (Sp. *sueldo*) *n*. salary, wages, allowance; **suwelduhan** *adj*. salaried, **suwelduhán** *v*. to pay a salary to.
suwelo: (Sp. *suelo*) *n*. floor.
suwelto: (Sp. *suelto*) *adj*. loose; separate, single; disconnected.
suwerdo: *var*. of *suweldo*: salary.
suwero: (Sp. *suero*) *n*. serum; hypodermic needle.
suwerte: (Sp. *suerte*) *n*. luck, fortune.
suweter: (Sp. *suéter*) *n*. sweater.
suwí: *n*. sucker, subordinate shoot that grows from the bud on the root or stem.
suwî: *adj*. breech (baby).
suwisidyo: (Sp. *suicidio*) *n*. suicide.
suwitik: *adj*. cunning, sly; cheating; **suwitikin** *v*. to swindle.
suyà: (Ch.) *n*. disgust, dissatisfaction; **masuyà** *v*. to feel disgust; be fed up with; **suyain** *v*. to annoy; bore; surfeit.
suyak: *n*. spike; prong.

suyò: *n.* affection; **kasuyò** *n.* sweetheart.
suyò: (Ch.) **masuyò** *adj.* obsequious; **suyuin** *v.* to patronize, flatter; woo; **panunuyò** *n.* ingratiating.
suyod: (Ch.) *n.* nit comb; harrow; **suyurin** *v.* to harrow.
suysóy: (Ch.) **suysuyín** *v.* to encourage, prod.
syana/o: (*slang*) *n.* provincial person; (*fig.*) unsophisticated rural person.
syete: (*slang*, Sp. *siete*) *n.* gossip.
syoki: (*slang*) *n.* homosexual male.
syogal: (*slang*) *interj.* how long!
syondak: (*slang*) *adj.* short.
syontót: (*slang*) *n.* sexual intercourse.
syongág: (*slang*) *adj.* high on drugs.
syota: *n.* boyfriend, girlfriend.
syoyot: (*slang*) *n.* homosexual male.
syukab: (*slang*) *n.* taxicab.

T

't: *contr.* contracted form of *at* used as a suffix → **bawa't** each, **nguni't** but, **ibá't-ibá** varied, various.
ta: *n.* the letter *t*.
taab: *n.* tapering.
taad: *n.* sugarcane cutting for planting.
taál: *adj.* native, original.
taán1: *n.* long fishing line; kind of fish trap.
taán2: *n.* reservation for future use; **nakataán** *adj.* reserved; **pataán** *n.* leeway; allowance to make up for something.
taás: *n.* height; **mataás** *adj.* tall; high; **mataasán** *v.* to outgrow; **itaás** *v.* to hoist, raise, lift; **magmataás** *v.* to act proudly; **mapagmataás** *adj.* arrogant, haughty; **nakatátaás** *adj.* preeminent; senior (in rank); **naitátaás** *adj.* liftable, movable; **pagkakátaás** *n.* exaltation; **pagmamataás** *n.* pride; **pagmataasán** *v.* to act proudly to; **pagpapataás** *n.* exaltation; causing an increase or raise; **pagtaás** *n.* rising; promotion; advancement; **pa(i)taás** *adv.* upward; **pátaasan** *n.* contest; **pataasín** *v.* to raise; exalt; **sa itaás** *adj.* above, overhead; **tumaás** *v.* to rise, increase; ascend; **tumaás** *v.* to go up, rise; advance; **itaás ang putíng watawat** *id.* surrender (raise the white flag); **mataás ang lipád** *id.* over ambitious, dreamer (flight is high); **mataás ang noó** *id.* proud (forehead is high).
tabâ: *n.* fat; lard; grease; **matabâ** *adj.* fat; greasy; oily; rich, fertile; **katabaán** *n.* fatness, obesity; **patabâ** *n.* fertilizer; **pampatabâ** *adj.* fattening; *n.* fertilizer; vitamin; **tumabâ** *v.* to become fat; **pampatabáng-pusò** *id.* something that makes one happy (fattens the heart); **patabaing baboy** *id.* lazy person (pig to be fattened); **tabáng-lamíg** *id.* weak although big bodied (cold fat); *n.* dropsy; beriberi; **tabáng-baboy** *n.* pig's fat; obesity; **matabâ ang bulsa** *id.* with plenty of money.
tabák: *n.* cutlass.
tabako: (Sp. *tabaco*) *n.* tobacco; cigar; **magtabako** *v.* to smoke a cigar; deal in tobacco; **tabakero** *n.* cigar maker; tobacconist; **tabakería** *n.* cigar store; **tabakalera** *n.* tobacco dealer.
tabad: *n.* chaser, water that dilutes an alcoholic drink.
tabád: *n.* bloodletting; phlebotomy.
tabag: *n.* something added to make up for loss (in cooking or building).
tabal: *n.* excessive foliage resulting in infertility.
taban: **itaban, tabnán** *v.* to hold onto.
tabáng: **matabáng** *adj.* tasteless, insipid.
tabangongo: *n.* species of large sea catfish.
tabas: *n.* moonfish, *Mene maculata*.
tabas: *n.* cut, style, pattern; **magtabas** *v.* to cut cloth in a pattern; **tabás** *adj.* cut down, lopped off; **pinagtabasán** *n.* remnants of cloth.
tabatsóy: (*coll.*) *adj.* very fat.
tabátuból: (*slang*) *n.* constipation.
tabaw: *n.* ferry.
tabayag: (*Batangas*) *n.* bottle gourd. (*upo*)
tabayág: *adj.* sleeping without a cover.
tabengkalasing: (*slang*) *n.* twenty-five pesos.
taberna: (Sp. *taverna*) *n.* tavern, bar.
tabì: *interj.* Out of the way!; **pasintabì** *n.* asking pardon.
tabí: *n.* side; edge, margin; border; **katabí** *adj.*

next to, adjacent; **itabí** *v.* to put beside; **mag-tabí** *v.* to set aside; **magkatabí** *adj.* side by side, beside one another; **manabí** *v.* to go along the side of; (coll.) move one's bowels; **sa tabí** *adv.* aside, beside; **tábíhan** *n.* place for safekeeping; **tumabí** *v.* to step aside; **sa tabí tabí** *id.* no special place; modest surroundings; **tabíng-tabí** *adj.* at the very edge.

tabikì: (Sp. *tabique*) *n.* thin dividing wall.

tabig: *n.* smack with the back of the hand, push with the elbow.

tabigì: *n.* species of tree with bitter bark, *Xylocarpus granatum.*

tabíl: **matabíl** *adj.* talkative, vocal.

tabing: *n.* curtain, screen; veil; **itabing** *v.* to screen; **tabingan** *v.* to screen, protect.

tabingî: *adj.* uneven, unbalanced; twisted; lop-sided.

tabíng-daán: *n.* roadside.

tabíng-dagat: *n.* beach, shore.

tablá: *n.* board, timber; tie in a game; **tablá ang mukhâ** *id.* shameless (face is a board); **tablá-manalo** *n.* handicap in a game.

tablán: (rt. *taláb*) *v.* to take effect, respond to (medicine).

tabláw: *adj.* exposed to the elements.

tableryá: *n.* lumberyard.

tablero: (Sp.) *n.* chessboard.

tabletas: (Sp.) *n.* tablet; **tabliya** *n.* chocolate tablet.

tabnán: (rt. *taban*) *v.* to hold on to.

tabò: *n.* scoop, dipper; **tabuin** *v.* to scoop out.

tabód: *n.* semen.

tabog: *n.* stamping the feet.

tabol: *n.* flatus, gas in the stomach (*kabag*); increase in volume due to boiling.

tabon: *n.* heap; dike; megapod bird; **itabon** *v.* to fill a hole with earth; **tumabon** *v.* to fill up; engulf.

tabóy: **itabóy** *v.* to drive away, chase out, dispel; **ipagtábúyan** *v.* to rebuff; **pagkaká-pagtabóy** *n.* repulse; **pantabóy** *n.* goad.

tabsák, tabsáw, tabsík: *n.* splash.

tabsíng: *n.* brackish taste of sea water.

tabsíng: **matabsíng** *adj.* brackish, salty.

tabsô: **tabsuín** *v.* to unhook.

tabsóng: **matabsóng** *v.* to sink into deep mud.

tabtáb: **tabtabín** *v.* to hem, trim.

tabú: (Eng.) *n.* taboo.

tabubok: *n.* sponge gourd, *Luffa cylindrica.*

tabugí: *n.* coccyx.

tabulog: *n.* species of small shellfish.

taburete: (Sp.) *n.* stool.

tabyó: *n.* bend of a river.

tabyós: *n.* goby fish, *Mistickthys luzonensis.*

taka: *n.* bamboo sticks placed over rice sprouts at angles.

taká: *n.* surprise; *adj.* surprised; **magtaká** *v.* to be surprised; **nakapagtátaká** *adj.* magical; **pagtakhán** *v.* to marvel at, be amazed at.

takà: *n.* imprint, impression; stamping machine.

takad: **patakarán** *n.* base, foundation.

takád: *n.* stomping the feet in anger.

takal$_1$: **itakal** *v.* to measure liquids or grains; **takalán** *n.* measuring device.

takal$_2$: (*slang*) *n.* beating, whipping; torture.

takám: **tumakám** *v.* to lick one's chops (when seeing tasty food); **takamín** *v.* to tantalize.

takáp: *n.* insulting language; smacking one's chops.

takas: *n.* runaway, fugitive; refugee; *adj.* runaway; **magtakas** *v.* to escape with; **takasan** *v.* to escape from; **tumakas** *v.* to escape, flee, desert.

takaták: *n.* sound of rain on a roof; plants growing from fallen seed.

takaw: *n.* greed; **matakaw** *adj.* greedy; **takaw-mata (takaw-tingín)** *n.* passing fancy; **matakaw ang matá** *id.* wanting to eat more than one can handle (eyes are greedy); **takaw-apóy** *id.* inflammable (greedy fire); **takaw-tingín** *id.* attractive (greedy look).

takbá: *n.* native clothes chest made of bamboo.

takbó: *n.* run; drift; direction; tide; **itakbó** *v.* to run away with; **matakbó** *v.* to be able to run a certain distance; **magpánakbuhan** *v.* to scamper; **magpatakbó** *v.* to make run, set in motion; drive; **mapatakbó** *v.* able to run or manage; **pátakbuhan** *n.* runaway; **patakbuhín** *v.* to make something run; **pátakbuhin** *n.* poorly made goods; **takbuhan** *n.* running competition; **takbuhin** *n.* one who runs away from a challenge; **tumakbó** *v.* to run.

takdâ: *n.* measure; limitation, limit; restriction; *adj.* stated; limited, restricted; **itakdâ** *v.* to assign, settle; provide; restrict; **takdáng-aralín** *n.* assignment; **magtakdâ** *v.* to set, assign; provide; **matakdaán** *v.* to be able to set a limit to; **nakatakdâ** *adj.* set; fixed; arranged; **natátakdaán** *adj.* limited; qualified; **takdaán** *v.* to limit; restrict; **takdáng-araw** *n.* assigned date; **takdáng-oras** *n.* time limit; death; **waláng-takdâ** *adj.* limitless; absolute; indefinite.

takdáng: *adj.* short (skirts).

takid: **matakid** *v.* to trip over; stub the toe.

takígrapo: (Sp. *taquígrafo*) *n.* stenographer.

takigrapía: (Sp. *taquigrafía*) *n.* shorthand, stenography.

takilya: (Sp. *taquilla*) *n.* box office, ticket booth; **takilyero** *n.* teller; ticket salesman.

takín: *n.* bark of a puppy; **tumakín** *v.* to bark.

takíp: *n.* cover, lid; **itakíp** *v.* to use as a cover; **magtakíp** *v.* to cover, patch; **matakpán** *v.* to hide; block, obstruct; **pagtakpán** *v.* to cover up, suppress; **pagtatákípan** *n.* covering up (one's faults); **panakíp** *n.* something used for covering; **takpán** *v.* to cover, put a lid on; **tumakíp** *v.* to block (the view); **takip-matá** *n.* eyelid; **takip-butas** *n.* substitute; **takip-silim** *n.* twilight; **kawaláng-takíp** *n.* bareness.

takitaki: *n.* imagination.

takláb: *n.* granary.

takláng: *n.* raising the hind leg to urinate (dog); bending the knee to defecate.

taklás: *adj.* consumed.

taklíp: *n.* scratch, slight wound.

taklís: **magtaklís** *v.* to sharpen tools.

taklób: *n.* cover, covering; **taklubán** *v.* to cover; **pinagtaklubán ng langit at lupà** *id.* saddened (covered by heaven and Earth).

taklobo: *n.* mother of pearl; species of clam.

tako: (Sp. *taco*) *n.* billiard cue; plug, wad.

takob: *n.* thin covering.

takóng: (Sp. *tacón*) *n.* heel.

takot: *n.* fear; **takót** *adj.* afraid; **katakutan** *n.* fear; *v.* to fear; **katakut-takot** *adj.* terrible, fearful, dreadful; **kinatátakutan** *adj.* dreadful; **matakot** *adj.* afraid; **makatakot** *adj.* frightful; **manakot** *v.* to scare; **matakutín** *adj.* easily frightened; **nakatátákot** *adj.* fearful, frightful, horrible; **panakot** *n.* scarecrow; **pananakot** *n.* scaring, intimidation; **takutin** *v.* to frighten, scare; intimidate; **tumakot** *v.* to scare, frighten.

takpán: (*rt. takíp*) *v.* to cover, put a lid on.

taksán: *n.* quire (of betel leaves).

taksáy: *n.* slipmouth fish.

taksi: (Eng.) *n.* taxi.

taksíl: *n.* traitor; *adj.* disloyal, faithless, treacherous; **kataksilán** *n.* treason; **magtaksíl** *v.* to betray.

takták: **itakták** *v.* to shake out the contents.

táktika: (Sp. *táctica*) *n.* tactics, tact.

takuko: *n.* nipa leaf covering for the head.

takukóng: *n.* kind of palm leaf helmet.

takupis: *n.* husk (of corn), calyx.

takurî: *n.* teakettle.

takusa: (*slang*) *n.* hen-pecked husband.

takuyan: *n.* basket carried on the hip (during harvest).

takwar: (*slang*) *n.* money.

takwíl: *n.* renunciation; **itakwíl** *v.* to renounce; disown, repudiate.

takyád: *n.* stilt.

tadhanà: *n.* fate, destiny; nature; **magtadhanà, itadhanà** *v.* to arrange in an agreement, stipulate; **pagtatadhanà** *n.* predetermination; including a certain provision in an agreement; **birò sa tadhanà** *id.* misfortune; mishap.

tadó: (*slang*) *adj.* stupid, foolish.

tadtád: *adj.* minced; thickly covered; **tadtarín** *v.* to hack, chop up; **panadtád** *n.* chopping knife; **tadtaran** *n.* chopping block.

tadyák: *n.* backward kick.

tadyáng: *n.* rib.

Tadyawan: *n.* ethnic group and language from East central Mindoro.

tae: *n.* feces, excreta; **magtae** *v.* to have loose bowels; **tae ng bituín** *n.* meteor, shooting star; **tumae** *v.* to defecate; **pagtae** *n.* defecation; **pagtatаé** *n.* diarrhea; **nagtátaé ng salapî** *id.* rich (defecating money); **taé** *adj.* defecating often; **taeng-hayop** *n.* manure; **parang taeng aso** *id.* useless.

taeb: *n.* high tide.

tag- *pref.* denotes time or season → **tag-init** *n.* summer, hot season; **tag-ani** *n.* harvest time.

taga- *pref.* 1. denotes origin → **taga-Baguio** from Baguio, **tagabaryo** from the barrio. **tagababâ** *n.* lowlander; 2. may express occupation → **tagalutò** *n.* cook, **tagaadorno** *n.* decorator, **tagahilot** *n.* massage therapist; midwife. **tagabalità** *n.* reporter.

tagâ: *n.* cut with a big knife; fishhook; (*slang*) overpriced; commission; **matagâ** *v.* to be cut with a machete; **tagâ sa panahón** *id.* mature (cut in time).

tagababá: (*rt. babá*) *n.* male quadruped used for inbreeding; carrier of the children or sick (piggyback).

tagák: *n.* cattle egret; seagull.

tagakták: *n.* downpour; flow of tears; dripping of sweat.

tagál: *n.* duration; **matagál** *adj.* long in time; for a long time, all along; long ago; **katagalán** *n.* long duration; **kátagalan** *adj.* longest in duration; **kátagalán** *v.* to delay for a long time; **itagál** *v.* to delay; **makatagál** *v.* to be able to last; **magtagál** *v.* to last; take a long time; **magpatagál** *v.* to prolong; **matagalán** *v.* to be able to endure, withstand; **pangmátagálan** *adj.* lasting a long time, perennial; **pátagalan** *n.* test in endurance; **patagalín** *v.* to prolong; **tumagál** *v.* to endure, last.

Tagalista: *n.* specialist in Tagalog.

Tagalog: *n.* Tagalog (Pilipino) language; **Katagalugan** *n.* Tagalog region; **magtagalog** *v.* to speak Tagalog; **managalog** *v.* to speak Tagalog well; **mánanagalóg** *n.* Tagalist; **Tagalista** *n.* specialist in Tagalog. **tágalugán** *n.* speaking in Tagalog; Tagalog section; **tagalugin** *v.* to say in Tagalog.

tagán: *n.* small-toothed sawfish.

taganás: *adv.* purely, fully.

tagapag- *pref.* denotes duty or occupation → **tagapag-taním** *n.* planter, one whose duty is to plant; **tagapagtingî** *n.* retailer; **tagapag-masahe** *n.* masseur, **tagapagsalitâ** *n.* speaker, guest speaker, **tagapagsumpít** *n.* person whose duty is to give enemas.

tagas: *n.* silvery pomfret fish; leakage; **tumagas** *v.* to leak out, ooze.

tagatao: (*rt. tao*) *n.* person who remains at home or office to watch over it; house sitter.

tagatoy: *n.* kind of tree that grows near the seashore.

tagay: *n.* toast (in drinking); drinking session; **tagayán** *n.* wineglass.

tagaytáy: *n.* mountain ridge; drops of honey or sap; **managaytáy** *v.* to scale a mountain ridge.

Tagbanwa: *n.* ethnic group and language from Northern Palawan.

tagbisî: *n.* bad season, i.e. heat wave; crop failure; famine.

tagdán: *n.* staff, pole; shaft.

taghán: *var. of tagán*: sawfish.

taghikaw: *n.* nose ring for cattle.

taghók: *n.* violent coughing.

taghóy: *n.* lament.

tagibáng: *adj.* tilted, leaning; unequal.

tagibuhól: *n.* slipknot.

tagibus: *n.* banded snake eel.

tagikaw: *n.* nose ring for cattle.

tagiktík: *n.* patter, ticking of a clock; sound of dripping.

tagihabâ: *adj.* elongated.

tagihabol: *n.* addendum; appendix; postscript.

tagihawat: *n.* pimple, blackhead; **tágihawatín** *adj.* pimply.

tagilíd: *adj.* tilted, inclined; **tagiliran** *n.* side of; **tumagilid** *v.* to become tilted, lean.

tagiló: *n.* pyramid.

tagimpán: *n.* illusion, dream; aspiration.

tagimtím: *n.* seepage, ooze; feeling of satisfaction.

tag-init: (*rt. init*) *n.* summer.

tagintíng: *n.* jingling sound; twang; vibration.

tagipós: *n.* dry, flammable timber.

tagís: *n.* whetstone; **nagkátagisan ang parehong talím** *id.* matched their strengths.

tagisang-lawin: *n.* scolopsid fish.

tagisi: *n.* nemipterid fish.

tagistís: *n.* dripping, leaking.

tagisuyò: *n.* gift given to win favor; sycophant.

taglagás: (*rt. lagás*) *n.* fall (season).

taglamíg: (*rt. lamíg*) *n.* winter, cold season.

tagláy: *adj.* possessing, possessed; **magtagláy, taglayín** *v.* to have in one's possession; maintain.

tagnî: *n.* piece of cloth used in mending or patching; **magtagní-tagnî** *v.* to do patchwork.

tagò: **itagò** *v.* to hide; **ipagtagò** *v.* to reserve; **taguán** *n.* hiding place; hide and seek; **tagô, nakatagò** *adj.* hidden; **magtagò** *v.* to hide; **magtaguán** *v.* to hide from each other, play hide and seek; **patagò** *n.* something given to another for safekeeping; **patagô** *adj.* secret, covert; **taguán** *n.* place for hiding or keeping things; harbor; hide and seek; **tinagò** *adj.* hidden; **tumagô** *v.* to hide oneself; **tagong-bayawak** *id.* hiding with the head seen (lizard hiding); **waláng tinagong bola** *id.* without a secret.

tagók: *n.* gulping, swallowing; **tatagukan** *n.* windpipe.

tagóp: *n.* union; touching end to end; meeting.

tagós: *adj.* penetrating; **tagusán** *v.* to pierce.

tagpás: *adj.* slashed; **tagpasín** *v.* to slash.

tagpî: *n.* patch; **tagpián** *v.* to patch, mend; **tagpí-tagpî** *adj.* covered with patches.

tagpô: *n.* scene; circumstances; **pagtatagpô** *n.* meeting; appointment; **makatagpô** *v.* to discover, come across; **magtagpô** *v.* to meet, converge; **matagpuán** *v.* to happen to find, discover; **tagpuan** *n.* meeting place; rendezvous; **tagpuín** *v.* to go and meet.

tagpós: **tumagpós** *v.* to penetrate, pierce through.

tagsiból: *n.* spring, blooming season.

tagsô: *adj.* detached; unfastened.

tagtág: *adj.* unfastened; loosened; dismissed; **matagtág** *adj.* bumpy, jerky; *v.* to be loosened, unfastened.

tagubanà: *n.* leakage; seeping of water.

tagubilin: *n.* advice, counsel; recommendation; **ipagtagubilin** *v.* to recommend; entrust; **magtagubilin** *v.* to recommend, advise; **maitátagubilin** *adj.* advisable.

taguktók: *n.* clack of the heels.

tagudtód: *n.* isthmus; **tumagudtód** *v.* to keep going along a path.

tagulabáy: *n.* hives, skin blotches.

tagulamín: *n.* mold formed on dirty clothes.

tagulawáy: *n.* woody vine, *Parameria laevigata.*

tagulayláy: *n.* monotonous style singing.

tagulimot: *n.* forgetfulness.

tagulíng: *n.* irrigation canal.

tagumanák: *n.* last state of pregnancy; nesting season of birds.

tagumpáy: *n.* victory, success; **magtagumpáy** *v.* to succeed, prosper; **mapanagumpáy** *adj.* frequently successful; **mapagtagumpáy** *adj.* successful, triumphant; **matagumpáy** *adj.* successful; **pagtagumpayán** *v.* to defeat, overcome; conquer; **papagtagumpayín** *v.* to give success to, help to succeed.

tag-unós: *n.* typhoon season.

taguntón: *n.* file, row, line; species of small shrimp.

taguntóng: *n.* metallic sound.

tagunggóng: *n.* piggy bank, bank of winnings.

tagupák: *n.* banging sound.

tagurî: *n.* darling; predicate (grammar) (*panagurî*); **magtagurî** *v.* to caress, be fond of.

tagustós: *adj.* hanging down.

taguyod: **itaguyod** *v.* to support, help forward; **tagapagtaguyod** *n.* supporter, follower.

tagwáy: **matagwáy** *adj.* tall and thin.

tahak: **tahakin** *v.* to take a shortcut; go across (a difficult path); **tahák** *adj.* passed (land); explored.

tahada: (Sp. *tajada*) *n.* slice; **tahadera** *n.* cutting knife.

tahado: (Sp. *tajado*) *adj.* sliced.

tahán₁: **tahanan** *n.* home; **tahanán** *v.* to live in a certain place; **tumahán** *v.* to abide, live, reside; **matátahanán** *adj.* livable.

tahán₂: **tahán!** Stop!; **tumahán** *v.* to cease; calm down; **patahanín** *v.* to stop, calm, pacify.

tahás: *adj.* direct; frank; straightforward; *adv.* directly; **táhásan** *adj.* definite, clear; (*gram.*) active (voice).

tahaw: *n.* clearing in a forest; **taháw** *adj.* exposed, clear; public.

tahî: *n.* sewing, stitch; **tumahî** *v.* to sew; **maytahî** *adj.* showing seams; **ipatahî** *v.* to have sewn; **mánanahì** *n.* dressmaker; **táhian** *n.* tailor's shop; **pananahì** *n.* sewing; **táhían** *n.*

tailor's shop; **tahiín**, **tahín** *v.* to sew; **tinahî** *adj.* sewn; *v.* sewed; **tahíng-kamáy** *adj.* hand-sewn; **tahíng-mákina** *adj.* machine-sewn.

tahik: *n.* dry land.

tahíd: *n.* spur, cockspur; **tahid-labuyò** *n.* spur of a wild cock; species of woody vine.

tahilan: *n.* joist for supporting a crossbeam.

tahimik: *adj.* calm, quiet, peaceful; serious; **manahimik** *v.* to be peaceful, silent; **pagpapatahimik** *n.* pacification; **pananahimik** *n.* retirement; **patahimikin** *v.* to calm, pacify; **tumahimik** *v.* to become quiet, keep quiet; relax.

tahíp$_1$: **magtahíp** *v.* to winnow; **táhípan** *n.* winnowing basket.

tahíp$_2$: **tumahíp-tahíp** *v.* to palpitate, heave.

tahiyuyo: *n.* rooster that does not grow spurs.

tahó: (Ch.) *n.* sweet dish made from mung beans and syrup.

tahô: *adj.* known; understood; **pagkatahô** *n.* understanding; information, knowledge.

tahól: *n.* bark of a dog; **tumahól** *v.* to bark.

tahóng: *n.* mussel.

tahór: *n.* person who places bets in cockfighting.

táhurí: *n.* salted fermented soybean curd.

tai: *var. of tae*: excrement; **taing-bakal** *n.* rust; **taing-bituín** *n.* meteor.

taimtím: *adj.* sincere; heartfelt.

tainga: *n.* ear; **manainga** *v.* to listen; **putíng-tainga** *n.* stingy or selfish person; **salamín ng tainga** *n.* eardrum; **taingang dagâ** *n.* kind of edible fungus, wood ear; **taingang-kawalì** *n.* handle of a skillet; person who turns a deaf ear (pretends not to hear); **waláng tainga** *id.* deaf.

tala- *pref.* denotes a list or record of → **tala-aklatan** *n.* book list; **talaarawan** *n.* diary; **talababaan** *n.* footnotes.

tala: *n.* species of herb used in flavoring, *Limnophila rugosa*.

talà: *n.* planet; bright star.

talâ: **talâ**, **talaán** *n.* list; registry; record; entry; note; memorandum; **ipatalâ** *v.* to enroll; **italâ** *v.* to list, register, note, record; **magtalâ** *v.* to tally; list; **pagpapatalâ** *n.* registration; **patalaan** *n.* registry; **tagapagtalâ** *n.* registrar; **talaang-itím** *n.* blacklist.

talaarawán: (*rt. araw*) *n.* diary, journal.

taláb: *adj.* effective (medicine); *n.* act of cutting (knives); **di-tinatalaban** *adj.* immune; invulnerable; **talabán**, **tablán**, **talbán** *v.* to take effect; respond to (medicine).

talabá: *n.* oyster.

talababâ: (*rt. babà*) *n.* footnote.

talabing: *n.* protection against the elements.

talabís: *n.* slope; inclination.

talabóg: *n.* kind of fishtrap made from twigs.

talák: **magtatalák** *v.* to shout continuously.

talakay: *n.* term; **tálakayan** *n.* discussion; **tumalakay** *v.* to discuss; dwell on a subject.

talakitilyo: *n.* immature cavalla fish.

talakitok: *n.* species of cavalla fish.

talakop: *n.* wall; fence; **pananalakop** *n.* encircling movement of troops; encounter of opposing forces.

talaksán: *n.* bundle; stack; **italaksán** *v.* to pile up; **magtalaksán** *v.* to stack.

talakták: **manalakták** *v.* to navigate; **tumalakták** *v.* to cross a place with obstacles.

talád: (Sp. *talar*) **magtalád** *v.* to fight hand to hand.

taladro: (Sp.) *n.* drill.

talag: **pagtatalag** *n.* beating metal sheets to flatten them.

talagà: *n.* well, spring. (*bulón*)

talagá$_1$: *adv.* really, truly, indeed.

talagá$_2$: **katalágáhan** *n.* law of nature; **magtalagá** *v.* to assign; appoint; detail; **italagá** *v.* to devote, dedicate, design; **nakatalagá** *adj.* determined, resolute; prepared, ready; **nátatalagá** *adj.* determined, in earnest; **pagtatalagá** *n.* dedication; **tumalagá** *v.* to dedicate oneself to; prepare; yield, submit; resign; **katalágáhan** *n.* law of nature; **italagá sa kasáwían** *v.* to doom beforehand; **italagá sa tungkulin** *v.* to induct, inaugurate.

talagháy: **katalaguhayán** *n.* enduring courage.

talahib: *n.* kind of coarse grass.

talahuluganan: *n.* vocabulary, dictionary.

talalán: *n.* first steps of a child.

talamák: *adj.* serious, critical; fallen; prostate; addicted; drenched, infused.

talambuhay: (rt. *buhay*) *n.* biography.
talamitam: *n.* close friend; **talamitamán** *n.* intermingling.
talampák: *adj.* frank, open; direct; flat, blunt (knife).
talampakan: *n.* sole of a foot, 12 inches.
talampás: *n.* plateau, plain.
talampunay: *n.* thorn apple shrub.
talán: *adj.* carried on the head; first attempt to talk.
talandáng: *n.* scattering in small pieces (explosion).
talandî: *n.* coquette, flirtatious woman.
talang: *n.* species of tree; red skies at sunset.
talangà: *n.* quiver, arrow container.
talangás: *adj.* serious looking.
talangkâ: *n.* small, edible crab; (*fig.*) moodiness, irrational behavior.
talangkás: *n.* gracefulness in gait.
talangkáw: *n.* bamboo rake.
talangtalang: *n.* leather jacket fish.
talaok: *n.* crowing of a rooster.
talapyâ: *adj.* flat (nose); adult leather jacket fish.
talarô: *n.* scales, balance; weight.
talarok: *n.* instrument used for measuring the depth of water.
talas: **matalas** *adj.* sharp; keen; **matalas ang ulo** *id.* keen, intelligent.
talás: *n.* scraping palm leaves from the rib.
talásalitaan: (rt. *salitâ*) *n.* vocabulary.
talasanggunián: (rt. *sangguni*) *n.* bibliography, list of references.
talasok: *n.* fastener (of a door).
talasók: *n.* diarrhea.
talastás: *adj.* known, informed; **ipatalastás** *v.* to inform, tell, announce; **patalastás** *n.* advice; notice; **patalastasán** *v.* to advise, notify.
talatà: *n.* line of printing or writing; **talataan** *n.* paragraph.
talátinigan: *n.* pronouncing dictionary.
talaw: *n.* exceptional height; **talawan** *v.* to surpass in height.
talaytáy: *n.* flowing (blood, saliva).
talbóg: *n.* bounce; (*coll.*) bounced check; **talbóg** *adj.* rejected; unsuccessful; **tumalbóg** *v.* to bounce; **magpatalbúg-talbóg** *v.* to dribble; **pagtalbóg** *n.* rebound.
talbós: *n.* young shoot or leaf, edible tips; **tumalbós** *v.* to cut the tops off.
talko: (Sp. *talco*) *n.* talcum powder.
taldík: *n.* killing lice between the fingers.
talento: (Sp.) *n.* talent.
talhák: *n.* clearing of the throat; persistent coughing.
talì: *n.* string, cord; **italì** *v.* to tie, fasten; **maytalì** *adj.* tied; **táling-kurbata, táling-husô** *n.* slip knot. **táling-sapatos** *n.* shoestring, shoelace. **makataling-pusò** *id.* able to marry (tie heart); **magkataling pusò** *n.* couple; **may talì sa bibíg** *id.* unable to speak; **may talì sa ilóng** *id.* controlled.
talí: **di-matalí** *adj.* restless, anxious.
talibà: *n.* guard, sentinel; **talibaan** *v.* to guard.
talibád: *adj.* reversed, inside out; **talibarín** *v.* to reverse, invert.
talibadbád: *n.* error, mistake; disagreement.
talibás: *adj.* slanting, oblique.
talibatab: *n.* wetting the lips with the tongue.
talibóng: *n.* long dagger.
talibugsô: *n.* bow knot, slipknot; snare.
talik: **matalik** *adj.* close, intimate; familiar; **pagtatalik** *n.* coitus, sexual intercourse; **pagkamatalik** *n.* intimacy.
talík: *n.* movements of the hands in dancing; **magtalík** *v.* to enjoy.
talikakás: *n.* great effort, diligence.
talikbâ: *n.* deceit, fraud.
talikdán: (*rt. talikód*) *v.* to leave, abandon, turn one's back to; disown, renounce.
talikód: **tumalikód, talikurán** *v.* to turn one's back on, abandon; **tálikuran** *adj.* back to back; **pagtalikód** *n.* departure; defection; renouncement.
talikop: **matalikupan** *v.* to be besieged, surrounded.
taliktík: *n.* boundary, limit; sonority of the voice.
talikwás: *adj.* tilted; upside down; turned over; **tumalikwás** *v.* to pry, turn over; tilt.
talihabsô: *adj.* loosely tied, easily untied.
talihalat: *n.* black mole.
talilís: **tumalilís** *v.* to escape; evade; **patalilís** *adv.* secretly.

talilong: *n.* mullet fingerling, *Mugilidae* Family.
talím: *n.* blade; edge; **matalím** *adj.* sharp.
talima: *n.* compliance; **tumalima** *v.* to comply with, obey.
talimáng: *adj.* lost count; **talimangín** *v.* to mislead.
talimangmáng: *n.* deceit, hoax.
talimbilao: *n.* species of banded sea snake.
tálimbuhay: (*coll., talì-ng buhay*) *n.* marriage.
tálimbuhól: *n.* engagement of a couple, betrothal.
talimuáng: *n.* pretense of ignorance; giving the responsibility to someone else; **talimuangín** *v.* to feign ignorance.
talimundós: *adj.* pointed.
talimusák: *n.* long-finned goby fish, *Oxyurichthys microlepis*.
talimusód: *adj.* spiral and pointed at one end.
talimuwáng: *var. of* ***talimuáng***.
talindáw: *n.* ancient boat song.
talindíg: (*rt. tindíg*) *n.* bristling (hair).
talinduwâ: (*obs.*) *n.* paying three cavans of rice for every two borrowed (tenant to landlord).
talino: *n.* talent; intelligence; **matalino** *adj.* intelligent, bright; cunning.
taling: *n.* mole on the skin.
talingan: *n.* one-spotted gray snapper; toothless cavalla.
talinghabâ: *adj.* oval.
talinghagà: *n.* parable, figure of speech; metaphor; mystery.
talingíd: *adj.* secret; unknown.
talipá: *n.* young of the yellow jacket fish.
talipà: *adj.* out of step; with the shoe on the wrong foot.
talipandás: *adj.* hypocritical; bold; flirtatious.
talipapâ: *n.* temporary fish market.
taliptíp: *n.* barnacle; detached chips of paint.
talipuspós: *adj.* thorough, complete.
talipyâ: *adj.* flat on the top; unbalanced.
talirik: *n.* standing perpendicular; erection of penis; perpendicularity.
taliris: *n.* spurt of water forced out a hole.
talisain: *n.* unlicensed firearm.
talisay: *n.* species of shade tree.
talisik: **matalisik** *adj.* witty, keen, intelligent.
talisod: **matalisod** *v.* to trip, stumble.
talisuyò: *n.* good relations between individuals (exchanging mutual favors); work done by a man to win a lady's hand.
talitis: *n.* small intestines.
taliwakás: *n.* abandonment; breaking up of a relationship.
taliwás: *adj.* opposed to; deviating from; opposite.
talo: *adj.* lost; defeated; *n.* loss; defeat; loser; **taló** *adj.* lost; **katalo** *n.* opponent; **pagkatalo** *n.* defeat; **magtalo** *v.* to argue, debate; **magpatalo** *v.* to give in; admit defeat; **magtalo ang kalooban** *v.* to be undecided; **manalo** *v.* to win; **matalo** *v.* to lose, be defeated; **mapagtátalunan** *adj.* debatable; controversial; **nanánálo** *adj.* winning; **makipagtalo** *v.* to argue with; **pagtatalo** *n.* argument, debate; controversy; **pagtalunan** *v.* to argue; debate, discuss; dispute; **pinagtátalunan** *adj.* controversial; **panalo** *n.* winnings; victor; winner; **panalunan** *n.* winnings; **talunin** *v.* to defeat; **talunan** *adj.* defeated; *n.* underdog; **tumalo** *v.* to defeat, beat; **magtátalo-sirà** *id.* to take back one's word (argue the broken); **talo-salíng** *id.* sensitive; **di-manánalo** *adj.* losing, without a chance to win; **maááring pagtalunan** *adj.* debatable.
talob: *n.* covering of soft materials.
talón: *n.* jump; stub of a checkbook, waterfall; **tumalón** *v.* to jump; **tumalún-talón** *v.* to tumble.
talonaryo: (*Sp. talonario*) *n.* checkbook; receipt book.
talóng: *n.* eggplant, aubergine; **talóng-aso** *n.* species of shrub with velvetlike leaves; **talóng-pipít** *n.* Indian night shade shrub; **talóng-suso** *n.* woody shrub which bears pear shape fruits with nipples; **talóng-gubat** *n.* species of prickly, hairy weed; **talóng-punay** *n.* datura plant.
talop: **magtalop** *v.* to peel, skin; **talóp** *adj.* peeled; **parang tinalupang bunga** *id.* defeated in gambling (like a peeled betel nut).
talós: *adj.* known, informed; **matalós** *v.* to understand; penetrate; **tumalós** *v.* to learn, get information about.

talunin: (rt. *talo*) *v.* to defeat.
talpák: *n.* speaking frankly and openly; **talpakan** *adj.* frank, without reservation of fear.
talpók: *adj.* reduced to ashes; beaten (clothes); carbonized.
talpóg: *adj.* pulverized.
talsík: *n.* splash; dismissal from office; leap of a spark.
talsók: *n.* splinter, thorn; piercing.
talták: *n.* clicking sound of the tongue.
taltál: *n.* quarrel, dispute; babble.
talubanát: *adj.* tight-fitting; stretched.
talubatâ: *adj.* mid-aged (25-35 years old).
talukab: *n.* hard shell of crustaceans; loose or detached scab.
talukap: *n.* eyelid; sheath of palm leaves.
talukbóng: *n.* head veil.
taluktók: *n.* tip, apex, peak.
taludtód: *n.* row, line, file; **taludturan** *n.* stanza; paragraph.
taluhabâ: *n.* rectangle.
talulo: *n.* species of rattan.
talulô: *n.* bud of a flower; cone.
talulot: *n.* petal of a flower.
talumpatì: *n.* speech; oration; **magtalumpatì** *v.* to address, give a speech; **mánanalumpatî** *n.* speaker.
talumpók: *n.* heap of unthreshed rice stalks, sand, or gravel.
taluntón: *n.* line, row; path; rule, regulation; **talátuntunan** *n.* index; **tumaluntón** *v.* to follow, trace.
talungkás: **italungkás** *v.* to tuck in.
talungkô: **nakatalungkô** *adj.* sitting flat on the floor in a relaxed manner; sitting idly.
talungtóng: *n.* granary, barn.
talupak: *n.* sheathing on the upper part of palms; leather jacket fish.
talurang: *n.* staircase landing.
talurok: *adj.* very steep; *n.* precipice.
talusalíng: *adj.* easily offended.
talusirà: *n.* breach of an agreement or promise.
talya: (Sp. *talla*) *n.* posture; sculpture; **talyada** *adj.* cut; engraved.
talyasì: (Ch.) *n.* iron vat.
talye: (Sp. *talle*) *n.* form, shape, figure.
talyér: (Sp. *taller*) *n.* workshop, repair shop.
tamà: *adj.* correct, right; exact; accurate; precise; fitting; **di-tamà** *adj.* not fitting, improper, wrong, unjust, not right; **patamà** *n.* solution to a problem; hint; winning number in a lottery; **pagtamà** *n.* getting the correct answer; hitting the target; **pagtamain** *v.* to make two things agree or correspond; **tamà na** That's enough; all right; **tamà sa** in accordance to; **makatamà** *v.* to be able to hit a target, do correctly; **magtamà** *v.* to be correct; agree, correspond; **magkátáma-tama** *v.* to fit together exactly; **matamaan** *v.* to hit the mark; (*slang*) get high on drugs **itamà** *v.* to place correctly; to set the time of; **magtamà** *v.* to agree; correct; **tumama** *v.* to hit the mark; fit in size; guess correctly; **tamaan** *v.* to answer correctly, hit the mark; **tamà sa padér** *id.* failed, lost.
tamák: *adj.* soaked; serious.
tamád: *adj.* lazy; idle; sluggish; **katámáran** *n.* laziness; **tamarisya** *n.* lazy girl. **tamád-tamaran** *n.* pretending to be lazy; overall laziness; **tumamád** *v.* to become lazy.
tamales: (Sp.) *n.* tamale.
tamán: **katamanán** *n.* perseverance, persistence.
tamanyo: (Sp. *tamaño*) *n.* size, measurement.
tamaráw: *n.* wild water buffalo found in Mindoro.
tamarindo: (Sp.) *n.* tamarind.
tamarisya: (*coll.*) *n.* lazy girl.
tamasa: *n.* enjoying wealth or health.
tamasok: *n.* gray borer, bug destructive to sugarcane.
tamaulì: *n.* change of mind.
tambaás: *n.* direct, frank talk.
tambák: *n.* pile, mound; embankment; **matambák** *v.* to be piled up; **mátambakán** *v.* to be blocked up, oversupplied; (*fig.*) overwhelmed; **santambák** *n.* heap, pile; **tambakan** *n.* dump; **tambakán** *v.* to fill a place with rubbish; load.
tambakol: *n.* yellow-fin tuna; (*fig.*) obese person.
tambád: *adj.* exposed to view.
tambág: *n.* substitute, proxy.
tambál: *n.* pair; *adj.* paired; **katambál** *n.*

partner.

tambán: *n.* Indian sardine, *Sardinella longiceps*; **tambáng-lapad** *n.* deep-bodied herring; **tambáng-bató** *n.* herring, sardine.

tamban-tambán: *n.* small waves in the sea.

tambáng: *n.* trap for catching wild game; peg to which a fighting cock in tied; ambush.

tambanggalán: *n.* overload.

tambáw: *n.* howling of dogs.

tambay: (Eng. stand by) *n.* hanging out, being idle.

tambáy: *adv.* immediately, instantly; *adj.* consumed, finished; *n.* sudden killing. **tambayín** *v.* to kill in a single blow or shot.

tambikí: *n.* ovate sole fish, *Solea humilis*.

tambíl: *n.* temporary shade.

tambilang: *n.* digit, digital number (0-9).

tambilawan: *n.* round-bodied garfish.

tambilíng: *n.* dizziness due to turning.

tambilogan: *n.* ellipse.

tambíng: *adv.* immediately, at once; *n.* insinuation.

tambís: *n.* indirect statement; *adv.* indirectly.

tambisî: *adv.* half-heartedly, lacking enthusiasm.

tambiyolo: (Sp. *tambiolo*) *n.* lottery drum.

tambô: *n.* reed.

tambobong: *n.* rice granary, barn.

tambók: *n.* bulge, swelling; **matambók** *adj.* bulging; **katambukan** *n.* bulkiness.

tambóg: *n.* loud splash; whipping.

tamból: (Sp. *tambor*) *n.* drum; **tambolero** *n.* drummer.

tambóng: *n.* slipmouth fish.

tambuko: *n.* pommel; handgrip behind a shield.

tambukulan: *n.* young stag.

tambugák: *adj.* obese (woman).

tambulì: *n.* bugle, horn.

tambulilid: *n.* dwarf coconut tree.

tambulok: *n.* toupee.

tambulukan: *adj.* rotten (fish).

tambulog: *n.* species of elongated clam.

tamburín: (Sp.) *n.* tambourine.

tambusto: *n.* exhaust pipe.

tambyolo: (Sp. *tambiolo*) *n.* lottery drum.

tamì: *n.* puckering of the lips.

tamilmíl: *adj.* lacking an appetite. (*tumilmíl*)

tamindák: *n.* mud skipper fish.

tamís: **matamís** *adj.* sweet; *n.* dessert; **minatamís** *adj.* candied; **magpatamís** *v.* to sweeten; **patamisán** *v.* to sweeten; **mátamisan** *n.* dessert bowl; friendly relationship; **matamisán** *adj.* sweet-toothed; **matamisín** *v.* to consider sweeter or better; make into dessert; **tumamís** *v.* to become sweet; **matamís ang dilà** *id.* fluent, glib (tongue is sweet).

tamláy: **matamláy** *adj.* downhearted; listless; languid; looking tired, without energy; **magpatamláy** *v.* to depress; weaken; **panamlayán** *v.* to lose interest in; feel weak; **tumamláy** *v.* to feel depressed; lose interest in.

tamnán: (rt. *taním*) *v.* to plant.

tamó: **magtamó** *v.* to obtain, acquire; gain; **pagkátamó** *n.* acquisition; **tamuhín** *v.* to take, acquire.

tamód: *n.* semen.

tampá: *n.* bid; advance payment.

tampák: *adj.* evident; patent; exposed to elements.

tampál: *n.* slap with the open hand, spank; flatfish.

tampalasan: *adj.* wicked, destructive; *n.* rascal; **katampalasanan** *n.* crime, villainy; **manampalasan** *v.* to harm, damage.

tampát: *adj.* deserving.

tampáy: *n.* serenity.

tampî: *n.* light slap, tap.

tampipi: *n.* bamboo chest.

tampisák: *adj.* covered with mud.

tampisáw: **magtampisáw** *v.* to play in water; wallow; **nagtátampisáw sa putik** *id.* expresses infidelity of women (wading in the mud).

tampó: *n.* sulking; resentment; **magtampó** *v.* to sulk, be ill-tempered, be grouchy; **matampuhin** *adj.* prone to sulk; **támpúhin** *adj.* grouchy, sulky.

tampók₁: *n.* elevation; center of attraction; **magtampók** *v.* to feature; **matampók** *v.* to be featured.

tampók₂: *n.* stem, stalk.

tampól: *n.* dashing of waves; **tampulan** *n.*

breakwater; focus.
tamták: (Eng.) *n.* thumbtack.
tamtám: **katamtaman** *adj.* normal, average; middle, ordinary; medium; **katamtaman** *adv.* just right; fairly well.
taná: (*coll.*) *abbrev.* for *katá na*: let's go.
tanaga: *n.* Philippine haiku.
tanan: *n.* escapee; **tumanan** *v.* to escape; elope; **tananan** *v.* to escape from; **makatanan** *v.* to be able to escape.
tanán: *pron.* all, everyone; *adj.* entire, whole.
tanáp: **katanapan** *n.* sufficiency (of taste or temperature).
tanáw: *adj.* in view; **abót-tanáw** *n.* horizon; **mátanawán** *v.* to see, look at from a distance; **pananáw** *n.* vision, sight; **tanawán** *v.* to look at something from afar; **tánáwin** *n.* view, outlook; landscape, scenery; **tumanáw** *v.* to view, look into the distance; **di-nagtátanáw-tamà** *id.* have not seen or met in a long time (did not see the mark); **tumanáw ng utang-na-loób** *v.* to be grateful to; **waláng tinátanáw na bukas** *id.* no bright future in sight.
tanda: (Sp.) *n.* work shift; turn.
tandâ₁: *n.* sign, mark; signal; evidence; **itandâ** *v.* to jot down, mark, record, list; use as a marker; **magtandâ** *v.* to mark; **panandâ** *n.* marker; **palátandaan** *n.* landmark; **panandâ ng pagbabawas** *n.* minus sign; **tandáng pandamdám** *n.* exclamation point.
tandâ₂: **matandâ** *adj.* old, grown-up; **magmatandâ** *v.* to play the role of an old person; act as an elder; **matandain** *adj.* aging quickly; **nakatátandâ** *adj.* older, senior; **patandaín** *v.* to age; **tumandâ** *v.* to age, get old; **tumátandâ nang pauróng** *id.* referring to someone who ages but does not progress.
tandâ₃: **pantandâ** *n.* ability to remember; **magtandâ** *v.* to remember; **makatandâ** *v.* to be able to remember; **matandaán** *v.* to remember; identify; **matandain** *adj.* having a good memory; **pakatandaán** *v.* to remember; keep in mind; **tandaán** *v.* to keep in mind remember; record.
tandakíl: *adj.* flat-headed.
tandáng: *n.* rooster; **magtandáng-tandangan** *v.* to be proud like a rooster.
tandayag: *n.* whale.
tandipil: *n.* mullet fish.
tandís: *adj.* certain, sure.
tandók: *n.* dry cupping. (*bentosa*)
tandós: *n.* lance, spear.
tanikalâ: *n.* chain. **tanikalaán** *v.* to chain.
tanigì: *n.* Spanish mackerel.
taním: *n.* plant; **magtaním** *v.* to plant, grow; **tagtaním** *n.* planting season; **mapagtaním, matánimin** *id.* holding a grudge for a long time; **pananím** *n.* crop; food plants; **pátaniman** *n.* plot for planting; planting season; **tagtaním** *n.* planting season; **tamnán** *v.* to plant. **tániman** *n.* planting season; agricultural land; plantation; (*fig.*) ill feeling between friends.
taning: *n.* limit; time limit; **lampás sa ~** *adj.* overdue; **magtaning** *v.* to number; fix a limit or date for; **waláng-taning** *adj.* not limited, indefinite.
taníng: (*slang*) *n.* devil, evil person.
tanod: *n.* guard; **tanuran** *v.* to guard, defend; **matanuran** *v.* to be guarded.
tanóng: *n.* question; **katánúngan** *n.* question; **magtanóng** *v.* to question, ask a question; **matanóng, palatanóng** *adj.* inquisitive; **nagtátanóng** *adj.* interrogative; **tagapagtanóng** *n.* interrogator; **palatánúngan** *n.* questionnaire; **pananóng** *n.* question mark; **tanungín** *v.* to ask, question; **ipinagtátanóng ng barbero** *id.* needs a haircut (being asked by the barber).
tansán: *n.* bottle cap.
tansô₁: *adj.* bronze; brass; (*coll.*) trick, scam; **manananansô** *n.* swindler; **manansô** *v.* to swindle; **taing-tansô** *n.* verdigris.
tansô₂: *n.* removing off a hook.
tantán: **tumantán** *v.* to cease, stop.
tantáw: *n.* slight understanding of something heard.
tantiyá: (Sp. *tantear*) *n.* estimate; **tantiyado** *adj.* estimated.
tanto: (Sp.) **tanto-porsyento** *n.* percentage.
tantô: **tumantô** *v.* to realize; understand.
tanyág: *adj.* prominent, well-known, famous; **katanyagán** *n.* prominence, popularity; **mápatanyág** *v.* to distinguish oneself.

tang: (*slang*) *n.* old man.
tangà: (Ch.) *n.* potato bug; clothes moth.
tangá: *adj.* stupid, idiotic; **matangá** *v.* to gape at; **katangahán** *n.* stupidity; **nakatangá** *adj.* open mouthed; **tumangá** *v.* to gape at, stare; **may-pagkatangá** *adj.* simple minded.
tangab: *n.* slanting cut.
tangáb: *n.* harelip.
tangad: *n.* center part of a water source where the water is pure and motionless.
tangan: *adj.* held; **tangnán** *v.* to hold; **tanganán** *n.* handle; **tumangan** *v.* to take hold of; **tangantangan** *n.* castor oil plant.
tangáy: **natangáy** *adj.* carried away by the wind; **tumangáy** *v.* to carry off, snatch away; **parang may tangáy na butó** *id.* does not stop murmuring (as if carrying a bone).
tangkâ: *n.* plan, intention, **magtangkâ** *v.* to offer, intend; try; **tangkaíng abutín** *v.* to reach for.
tangkáb: **mapatangkáb** *v.* to fall on one's mouth; **tangkabán** *v.* to hit in the mouth.
tangkakal: *n.* support, protection, defense.
tangkád: **matangkád** *adj.* tall and slender.
tangkál: *n.* coop.
tangkalág: *n.* pulley.
tangkás. *n.* bundle of leaves.
tangkáy: *n.* stalk, stem.
tangke: (Sp. *tanque*) *n.* tank; vat.
tangkíl: *n.* annex, light touch in passing; preliminary roofing.
tangkilik: *n.* patronage; protege; **tumangkilik** *v.* to help, support, patronize; **tagatangkilik** *n.* patron; sponsor.
tangkô: *n.* light touch.
tangkulók: *n.* wide-brimmed hat.
tangengot: (*slang*) *adj.* stupid. [Alt: *tangé*]
tangga: *n.* game of pitching coins.
tanggál: *adj.* unfastened; off; **pagtanggál** *n.* removal, detachment; dismissal from office; **tanggalín** *v.* to detach, loosen; take off; **tumanggál** *v.* to detach, separate.
tanggáp: *adj.* accepted; **mátanggáp** *v.* to accept; admit; **mananggáp** *v.* to admit (the truth of something); **tanggapín** *v.* to accept; take, receive; allow; **tanggapán** *v.* to accept from, take from; **ayaw tanggapín** *v.* to deny; **pagtanggáp** *n.* acceptance; reception; **pagkatanggáp** *adv.* after receiving; **pananggapán** *v.* to admit (truth); **punong-tanggapan** *n.* main office; headquarters; **tanggapan** *n.* office; **tumanggáp** *v.* to receive; **tinanggáp ng dalawáng kamáy** *id.* welcomed someone who wasn't welcome before (receive with two hands).
tanggí: *n.* refusal, denial; negation; **itanggí** *v.* to deny; **patanggí** *adj.* negative; **tanggihán** *v.* to refuse; reject; deny; negate; **tumanggí** *v.* to refuse; deny; negate; **tumanggíng pagtibayin** *v.* to disapprove.
tanggigi: *n.* Spanish mackerel.
tanggo: (Sp. *tango*) *n.* tango dance.
tanggól: *n.* defense; **ipagtanggól** *v.* to defend; uphold, fight for; **tanggulan** *n.* defense, **magtanggól** *v.* to defend; **pananggól** *n.* protection, defense; *adj.* protective; **tagapagtanggól** *n.* defender; bulwark.
tanggunggóng: *n.* piggy bank.
tanghál: **itanghál** *v.* to exhibit, display; **matanghál** *adj.* to be shown, on display; **tanghalan** *n.* exhibition.
tanghalì: *n.* midday; noon; **katanghalian** *n.* meridian, twelve o'clock sun; heyday; **mananghalì** *v.* to eat lunch; **tanghalian** *n.* lunch; **tumanghalì, tanghaliin** *v.* to be late in the morning.
tanghás: *n.* josh stick (Chinese temple).
tanghód: **tumanghód** *v.* to wait for something to happen.
tangì: *adj.* only, particular; exceptional, special; *adv.* exclusively; **katangian** *n.* special ability; accomplishment; attribute, characteristic; trait; **katangi-tangì** *adj.* extraordinary; unique; unusual; **itangì** *v.* to distinguish; **matangì** *prep.* except; **pagtatangì** *n.* distinction; **pagtatangi-tangì** *n.* discrimination; **pantangì** *adj.* exclusive; occasional.
tangî: *adj.* keeping to oneself.
tangilì: *n.* species of mahogany
tangis: *n.* weeping; **tumangis** *v.* to mourn; lament; **manangis** *v.* to weep, wail; **panangis** *n.* wailing.
tangląd: *n.* lemon grass, *Andropogon citratus.*
tangláw: (Ch.) *n.* light; **tanglawán** *v.* to il-

luminate.

tangnán: (rt. *tangan*) *v*. to hold.

tangô: *n*. nod; **tumangô** *v*. to nod; **tanguán** *v*. to nod to.

tangos: *n*. cape; physical prominence; **matangos** *adj*. pointed, prominent; **tangos-ilóng** (*fig*.) pride for being praised.

tanguyngóy: *n*. sobbing, sulking.

tangtáng: *n*. jerking of a rope.

tangwá: (Ch.) *n*. edge of a cliff; precipice.

tangwáy: *n*. peninsula.

tao: *n*. human, man, person; **kapwa-tao** *n*. fellow human; **kilaláng-tao** *n*. celebrity; **makatao** *adj*. humane, humanitarian; **matao** *adj*. peopled, crowded with people; **matauhan** *v*. to revive; recover consciousness; **pagkatao** *n*. character, personality; **panao** *adj*. personal; **sangkatauhan** *n*. humanity; **tauhan** *n*. character in a play; vassal; personnel; *v*. fill a position; stand guard; furnish with personnel; **tauhin** *v*. to treat as a human; **tauhín** *n*. sex of a newborn baby. **tumao** *v*. to be on guard temporarily; **pagsasatao** *n*. personification; **magpakatao** *v*. to act with good manners (as a human); **magpatao** *v*. to staff, provide with employees; **pagtao** *n*. treating another like a human; house-sitting, occupying another's residence; **pánauhan** *n*. person (grammar); **panauhin** *n*. guest, visitor; **patao** *n*. supplying manpower; **pantao** *adj*. human; **katauhan** *n*. personality; reputation. **taú-tauhan** *n*. puppet; toy human figure; effigy; **taong-lupà** *n*. mythological dwarf; **taong-makalupà** *n*. materialist.

taób: *n*. tipping over; bankruptcy; (*slang*) murder; *adj*. upside down; bankrupt; (*slang*) murdered; beaten; **itaób** *v*. to turn upside down; **magtaób** *v*. to capsize; **pataób** *adj*. upside down; **tumaób** *v*. to turn upside down, overturn.

taog: *n*. high tide.

taól: *n*. disease of infants causing convulsions.

taón: *n*. year; **táúnan** *adj*. annual; yearly; **pagkakátaón** *n*. chance, opportunity; coincidence; **kátaón** *adj*. incidental; **itaón, taunín** *v*. to make coincide; **magkátaón** *v*. to happen, occur accidentally; **mátaón** *adj*. concurrent, happening at the same time; **mátaunán** *v*. to meet by chance; **nagkátaón** *adj*. accidental, by chance; **tumaón** *v*. to take advantage of the opportune time; **táunan**, **manaón** *adj*. yearly; **taóng-pánuusán** *n*. fiscal year.

taong: *n*. black veil used in mourning.

taóng: *n*. container for water.

taóp: *n*. arranged meeting, appointment.

taós: *adj*. profound, sincere, deep-felt; **taóspusò** *adj*. heart-felt.

tapa: (Sp.) *n*. jerked meat; **tapá** *adj*. smoked, cured (meat); **tápahan** *n*. smokehouse, kiln.

tapak: *n*. footstep; **tapák** *adj*. barefoot; **tapakan** *v*. to step on; **tapakán** *n*. footrest; treadle; foothold; footing; **tumapak** *v*. to step.

tapadera: (Sp.) *n*. cover for a pot.

tapal: *n*. patch; **itapal** *v*. to patch, plaster; **panapal** *n*. plaster, something used for patching.

tapaláng: *n*. species of mussel.

tapaludo: (Sp.) *n*. mudguard.

tapang: **matapang** *adj*. brave, bold, valiant; **katapangan** *n*. bravery; **tumapang** *v*. to become brave; **pagtatapáng-tapangan** *n*. pretending to be brave; **matapang ang hiyâ** *id*. shameless.

tapas: *n*. lopping of trees, de-husking of coconuts.

tapát$_1$: *adj*. direct, straight; *n*. last price; **katapát** *adj*. opposite; **itapát** *v*. to put exactly opposite, above or beneath; **magtápátan** *v*. to place opposite one another; **tápátan** *n*. short cut; **tapatín** *v*. to take a shortcut; **tapát-tapát** *adj*. facing each other; **tumapát** *v*. to be in front of; go in front of.

tapát$_2$: **matapát** *adj*. loyal, faithful, sincere; **katápátan** *n*. honesty; integrity; loyalty; **katapatang-loób** *n*. confidant; sincerity; **ipagtapát** *v*. to confide; confess, tell the truth; **magtapát** *v*. to tell the truth, confess; **pagtapatán** *v*. to confess to someone; **pagtapatín** *v*. to make someone else confess; **tapatín** *v*. to tell the truth to; **nang tápátan** *adv*. frankly, openly; truly.

tapaw: *n*. surpassing; **tapawan** *v*. to surpass.

tapay: *n*. dough; **tinapay** *n*. bread.

tapayan: *n*. large earthenware jar; **taingang-**

tapayan *id.* pretending not to hear (ear of jar).
tapeta: (Eng.) *n.* taffeta.
tapete: (Sp.) *n.* rug.
tapî: *n.* apron.
tapík: *n.* light tap; **tapikín** *v.* to tap; **katápikang-balikat** *id.* friend (shoulder-tapping mate).
tapil: *n.* short digging stick.
tapíl: *adj.* flat-nosed; with a flat forehead.
tapilók: **matapilók** *v.* to sprain the ankle.
taping: *n.* animal pest.
tapíng: *n.* facial dirt.
tapis: (Sp.) *n.* sash worn around the skirt of a *mestisa* dress; **tapiseryá** *n.* tapestry.
tapon: *n.* waste material; exile; **itapon** *v.* to throw away, get rid of; reject; **ipagtapon** *v.* to deport, exile, banish; **magtapon** *v.* to junk; deport; **mapagtapón** *adj.* wasteful; **pagkakátápon** *n.* banishment; **panapón** *n.* garbage; castoff; dregs; **tapunán** *n.* garbage dump; place of banishment; **tumapon** *v.* to throw away; **tapunan ng habág** *id.* sympathize (throw pity).
tapón: (Sp.) *n.* cork, plug, stopper.
tapóng: **katapóng** *adj.* inclusion of a non-family member in the preparation or cooking of food.
tapos: *n.* end; **magtapós** *v.* to finish; result in; **katapusán** *adj.* last; **kátapús-tapúsan** *n.* the very end, the very last; **ipatapos** *v.* to have something completed; **matapos** *v.* to end, be completed; accomplish; **pagkatapos** *n.* end, completion; *adv.* after, afterwards; since; subsequently; **pagtatapós** *n.* graduation; accomplishment; **tapós** *adj.* done, complete, finished; **tapusan** *v.* to finish off, pay last installment of a bill; **tapusin** *v.* to complete, terminate.
tapsák: *n.* sound of falling and splashing water.
tapsáw: *n.* chipping wood; wood chips; **tumapsáw** *v.* to scatter (chopped wood).
tapsi: (*coined: tapa + sinangág*) *n.* rice and barbecued beef breakfast.
tapsigaw: (*coined: tapa + sinangág + lugaw*) *n.* dish of fried rice, beef and porridge.
tapsilóg: (*coined: tapa + sinangág + itlóg*) *n.* rice, egg, and barbecued beef.
tapwe: (*slang*) *n.* fifty pesos.
tapyás: *n.* slanted cut on the tip of a tendon; facet of a cut gem; oblique cut; *adj.* cut.
tapyók: **matapyók** *v.* to trip; twist one's ankle.
tapyoka: (Eng.) *n.* tapioca.
tara: (Sp.) *n.* tare, weight of a container which is deducted from the total weight.
tará: (*coll.*) let's go. (*taná*)
tarabilya: (Sp. *tarabilla*) *n.* fastener, catch.
tarak: **itarak** *v.* to stab; **tarakan** *v.* to stab; stake out.
tarakán: *n.* dwarf coconut tree.
tarantá: **katarantahán** *n.* confusion, bewilderment; **matarantá** *v.* to be confused, puzzled; **tarantahín** *v.* to confuse, baffle, bewilder.
tarantado: (Sp. *atarantado*) *adj.* shameless; foolish.
taráng: *n.* rapid stamping of the feet.
tarangká: (Sp. *tranca*) *n.* bolt (to lock a door); **tarangkahan** *n.* gate.
tarapál: *n.* tarpaulin.
tarás: *n.* frankness in speech; boldness.
tarát: *n.* long-tailed sparrow.
tarátitat: *n.* female pimp.
taraumpalit: *n.* species of plant with purple flowers.
taray: *n.* arrogance or contemptuousness in speech (used for women); **mataray** *adj.* snobbish.
tarká: *n.* confused state; annoyance; **tarkado** *adj.* confused; annoyed; **tarkahin** *v.* to confuse.
tardíng: (*slang*) *adj.* retarded.
tarheta: (Sp. *tarjeta*) *n.* calling card.
tarì: *n.* gaff, blade attached to a fighting cock; **hindî nagpapatuyô ng tarì** *id.* tireless.
tarík: **mataríк** *adj.* steep.
tariktík: *n.* woodpecker.
tarima: (Sp.) *n.* low bench, low platform; bed; formation with five rows.
taríng: *adj.* elegant.
taripa: (Sp. *tarifa*) *n.* tariff, charge.
tariya: (Sp. *tarea*) *n.* number of games to be played before a winner is declared.
tara: *n.* confused state; **tarkado** *adj.* confused.

tarkók: (*slang*) *n.* coward.
tarlák: *n.* species of cane.
taro: (Sp. *tarro*) *n.* mug, jar.
tarók: **tarukín** *v.* to understand thoroughly; fathom.
tarol: *n.* sounding gauge; gauze inserted in a wound.
taróng: *n.* comprehension; *adj.* understood.
tarós: **waláng-tarós** *adj.* wild, uncontrolled; reckless.
tartanilya: (Sp. *tartanilla*) *n.* two wheeled horse-drawn carriage with a round top.
tartaró: (Sp.) *n.* cream of tartar.
tarugo: (Sp.) *n.* peg or latch for fastening a door or window; (*slang*) penis. **taruguhan** *v.* to fasten with a latch.
tarundón: *n.* pathway between rice paddies.
tasa₁: (Sp. *taza*) *n.* drinking cup.
tasa₂: (Sp. *tasación*) **magtasa** *v.* to assess; **tasadór** *n.* assessor; **tumasa** *v.* to estimate, appraise.
tasa₃: **magtasa** *v.* to diet; limit expenses; **tasado** *adj.* limited; controlled; on a diet.
tasá: (Sp. *tazar*) **tasahán** *v.* to sharpen a pencil.
tasak: *n.* stabbing.
tasado: *adj.* under diet; controlled, limited; appraised.
tasadór: *n.* assessor; appraiser.
tasi: (*slang*) *n.* brave man.
tasik: *n.* brine, salt-water.
tasok: *n.* sliver; peg.
tasón: (Sp. *tazón*) *n.* bowl, bowlful; large cup.
tastás: *n.* rip, run (in a stocking); **tastasín** *v.* to unseam, undo; rip; **tumastás** *v.* to detach; become dismantled, disassembled.
tata: *n.* daddy.
tatà: *n.* sign or symbol carved with a knife.
taták: *n.* imprint; marker; **tatakán** *v.* to seal, stamp, mark; **taták-dalirì** *n.* fingerprint; **taták ng kadalisayan** *n.* hallmark; **taták-kalakal** *n.* trademark.
tatag: *n.* establishment; stability; **itatag** *v.* to establish; set up; organize, form; **matatag** *adj.* immovable; uncompromising; **patatagín** *v.* to establish firmly; consolidate; **pagkamatatág** *n.* solidarity; **tagapagtatág** *n.* founder; **tatagán** *v.* to establish, found; make firm; **waláng-tatág** *adj.* not reliable, shaky.
tatagukán: (*rt.* *tagók*) *n.* Adam's apple.
tatal: *n.* wood shavings, splinters.
tatampál: *n.* flatfishes.
tatang: *n.* dad, daddy.
tatangnán: (*rt.* *tangan*) *n.* handle.
tatáp: **matatap** *v.* to understand, learn about.
tatás: **matatás** *adj.* fluent and clear (speech).
tataw: *n.* hazy understanding; slight vision of something.
tatáw: *n.* doll; mannequin.
tatay: *n.* dad, daddy.
tatê: (*slang*) *n.* United States.
tatló: *n.* three; **ikatló** *adj.* third; **makatatló, makaitló** *adv.* three times; **pangatló** *adj.* third; **tatluhín** *v.* to triple; divide into three parts; **tatlumpû** *n.* thirty; **tatlóng-harì** *n.* Feast of Epiphany. **tatlóng-baraha** *n.* trick card game using only three cards. **tatlóng-kapat** *n.* three fourths.
tatsá: (Sp. *tachar*) *n.* opposition; fault-finding; contradiction. **tatsahín** *v.* to contradict; object; find fault.
tatsíng: *n.* coin tossing game.
tatso: (Sp. *tacho*) *n.* metal casserole dish.
tatsulok: *n.* triangle. **tatsulók** *adj.* triangular.
tatú: (Eng.) *n.* tattoo.
tatwâ: *n.* denial; repudiation; **itatwâ** *v.* to deny; repudiate; disclaim.
tatyaw: (Ch.) *n.* breeding cock.
tauhan: (rt. *tao*) *n.* employees; followers; character in a play. *v.* to fill up (a position); furnish with workers; stand guard.
taumbahay: (*tao* + *bahay*) *n.* housekeeper.
taumbayan: (*tao* + *bayan*) *n.* public, people.
taumpiskál: (*taón* + *piskal*) *n.* fiscal year.
taumpánuusán: (*taón* + *pánuusán*) *n.* fiscal year.
taún: *var.* of *taón*: year.
táupû: (*tao* + *pô*) *n.* greeting used when entering, knocking at a door.
Tausug: *n.* ethnic group and language from the Sulu Islands.
tawa: *n.* laugh, laughter; **katatawanán** *n.* joke, humor; **katawá-tawá** *adj.* ridiculous; laughable; **ikátawá** *v.* to amuse; **makatawá** *v.* to be able to laugh; **magtawá** *v.* to laugh

out loud; **nakakátawá** *adj.* funny, comic; **pagtawanán** *v.* to make fun of, laugh at; tease, joke; ridicule; **palátawá** *adj.* prone to laughter; **tawanan** *v.* to laugh at; **táwánan** *n.* laughter; **tumawa** *v.* to laugh; **tawang malutóng** *n.* hearty laugh; **tawang-aso** *n.* mockery; **ugaling mapagpatawá** *n.* sense of humor.

tawák: *n.* quack doctor with magic saliva; **parang tawák** *id.* staring or stopping at everything.

tawad₁: *n.* discount, bargain; **tawaran** *v.* to bid; haggle; **tawarán** *n.* common price offered by the majority of buyers; **tawarin** *v.* to request a discount; **itawad** *v.* to offer as a price for; **magpatawad** *v.* to give a discount to; request a better deal; **mánanawad** *n.* bidder; **manawaran** *v.* to bargain; **makipagtawarán** *v.* to haggle with each other; **matawad** *adj.* discountable; **patawad** *n.* discount given; **patawaran** *v.* to request someone to ask for a discount; **palátáwad** *adj.* prone to haggling; **tumawad** *v.* to haggle; bid; propose a price for.

tawad₂: *n.* forgiveness; **kapatawarán** *n.* forgiveness; **ipatawad** *v.* to pardon, condone; **ipagpatawad** *v.* to pardon, excuse; **magpapatawad** *adj.* forgiving; **maipagpápatawad** *adj.* excusable; **mapatátáwad** *adj.* pardonable; **pagpapatawad** *n.* forgiving; **patawarin** *v.* to forgive; **humingî ng tawad** *v.* to apologize.

tawag: *n.* call, name, term; summons; announcement. **tumawag, tawagan** *v.* to call; **panawagan** *n.* appeal; **magpatawag** *v.* to call for a doctor; **katawagán** *n.* term; terminology; **ipatawag** *v.* to page, call for; **magpatawag** *v.* to send for, summon; **itawag** *v.* to call, summon; **magtawagán** *v.* to call each other; **manawagan** *v.* to issue a call for help; **patawag** *n.* summons; call; **patawagin** *v.* to request someone to call; **panawag-pansín** *n.* something that attracts attention.

tawas: *n.* alum.

tawatawa: *n.* kind of orchid.

tawáy: *n.* range; swing of the arm.

Tawbuid: *n.* ethnic group and language from Central Mindoro.

tawgi: (Ch.) *n.* mongo bean sprouts. (*toge*)

tawíd: *n.* crossing; **magtawíd** *v.* to carry across; **tumawíd** *v.* to cross; **maipagtátawíd-buhay/gutom** *id.* money intended for food (able to cross life); **patawirín** *id.* cross over, die. **tawíd-dagat** *n.* crossing the sea; going abroad; **magtawíd-dagat** *v.* to go abroad; **táwiran** *n.* crossing point; pedestrian lane.

tawig: *n.* protruding length of something extending horizontally.

tawîl: *n.* pendant, something hanging loosely.

tawilís: *n.* fresh water sardine.

tawilwîl: *adj.* extended too long horizontally.

tawíng: **tumawíng-tawíng** *v.* to hang on a hinge.

tawisî: *adj.* awry; unbalanced.

tawo: (*reg.*) *var.* of *tao*: person.

tawpe: (Ch.) *n.* bean skin edible wrapping.

tawsî: (Ch.) *n.* soy beans preserved in soy sauce.

tawtáw: *n.* jerking a fishing rod; guess; touching or inserting just the tip of.

taya: *n.* estimate, calculation; **tayahin** *v.* to calculate, figure out.

tayâ: *n.* bet, stake; **magtaya** *v.* to bet on, **itayâ** *v.* to bet (a specific amount); **tay(a)án** *v.* to bet on.

tayabak: *n.* jade vine.

tayabutab: *n.* damp, soggy soil.

tayakad: *n.* stilt; portable *nipa* shed.

tayamutan: *n.* garbage, rubbish; scrapings, shavings.

tayangkád: **matayangkád** *adj.* long-legged.

tayangtáng: *adj.* overheated; too dry.

tayo: *pron.* we (inclusive); **pantayu-tayo** *adj.* informal; **Tayo na** Let's go.

tayô: **magtayô** *v.* to build, set up; **magpatayô** *v.* to have something built; **nakatayô** *adj.* placed; straight up, standing; **patayô** *adj.* vertical; perpendicular; **táyúan** *n.* stand; **tumayô** *v.* to stand up, position oneself; **katayuan** *n.* location, site; position; condition, state; rank; **kinátatayuán** *n.* position; location; standpoint; **tumayú-tayô** *v.* to loiter; **tumayô ang mga balahibo** *id.* scared (hair bristled).

tayód: *n.* square piece of cloth used for wrapping grains.
tayog: *n.* loftiness; boastfulness.
tayom: *n.* indigo plant.
tayon: *n.* pendulum swinging.
tayong: *n.* temporary suspension of work.
taytáy: *n.* bamboo bridge.
tayubák: *n.* species of green bird with a yellow beak.
tayubasi: *n.* metal fillings.
tayubay: **tinayubay** *adj.* smoked (meat, fish).
tayukod: *n.* forked pole; **tayukód** *adj.* standing with the body bent forward.
tayuntóng: *n.* ridge of a roof; crest of a wave.
tayungkód: *n.* improvised walking stick.
tayutáy: *n.* figure of speech.
tayutô: *adj.* rotten, decayed.
taywanák: *n.* thornless bamboo, *Bambusa monogyna*.
Tboli: *n.* ethnic group and language from South Cotabato, Mindanao.
teatro: (Sp.) *n.* theater.
teka: (Sp. *teca*) *n.* teak; *interj.* wait!
tekas: **manenekas** *n.* swindler; **matekas** *v.* to be swindled; **tekasin** *v.* to swindle.
tekla: *n.* teak tree.
teklado: (Sp. *teclado*) *n.* keyboard.
tékniko: (Sp. *técnico*) *n.* technician; *adj.* technical.
teksas: (*slang*) *n.* Texan gamecock; bum.
teham: (Ch. *tè hám*: sole join) *n.* cut in outer sole of shoe into which stitches are made.
tehero: (Sp. *tejero*) *n.* tile maker.
tehuwelo: (Sp. *tejuelo*) *n.* small tile.
tela: (Sp.) *n.* cloth, fabric.
telareho: (Sp. *telarejo*) *n.* small room.
telebabad: (*slang*) *n.* talking on the phone for a long time.
telembáng: *n.* toll of a bell.
telépono: (Sp. *teléfono*) *n.* telephone.
teleskopyo: (Sp. *telescopio*) *n.* telescope.
telón: (Sp.) *n.* curtain (in a play).
tema: (Sp.) *n.* theme.
temahan: (*coll.*) *n.* slight mutual resentment.
temperatura: (Sp.) *n.* temperature.
templo: (Sp.) *n.* temple.
tenedór: (Sp.) *n.* fork; ~ **de libro** *n.* bookkeeper, accountant; **teneduría** *n.* bookkeeping.
tensyón: (Sp. *tensión*) *n.* tension, stress.
tentákulo: (Sp. *tentáculo*) *n.* tentacle.
tentasyón: (Sp. *tentación*) *n.* temptation.
tenya: (Sp. *tenia*) *n.* tapeworm.
tenyente: (Sp. *teniente*) *n.* lieutenant. **tenyente-koronél** *n.* lieutenant colonel.
tenga: *var. of tainga*: ear.
teoría: (Sp.) *n.* theory.
tepok: (*slang*) **nátepok** *adj.* caught; killed.
terasa: (Sp. *terraza*) *n.* terrace.
terko: (Sp. *terco*) *adj.* stubborn.
terenál: (Sp. *terrenal*) *adj.* mundane, earthly.
término: (Sp.) *n.* term; condition of a contract.
terno: (Sp.) *n.* three piece suit; set of things.
tersero: (Sp. *tercero*) *adj.* third.
tesis: (Sp.) *n.* thesis.
tersiyopelo: (Sp. *terciopelo*) *n.* velvet.
tesauro: (Sp.) *n.* thesaurus.
tesorero: (Sp.) *n.* treasurer.
tesoro: (Sp.) *n.* treasure.
testadór: (Sp.) *n.* testator (of a will).
testamento: (Sp.) will, testament.
testíkulo: (Sp. *testículo*) *n.* testicle, testes.
testigo: (Sp.) *n.* witness.
testimonyo: (Sp. *testmonio*) *n.* testimony.
testo: (Sp. *texto*) *n.* text.
tétano: (Sp. *tétano*) *n.* tetanus.
tetilya: (Sp. *tetilla*) *n.* nipple of a bottle.
teybol: (*slang*, Eng. *table*) **iteybol** *v.* to engage the services of a dancer at one's table at a nightclub.
tía: (Sp.) *n.* aunt. (*tiya*)
tianak: *n.* elf, goblin.
tibà: **tiba-tibà** *adj.* full of anything.
tibâ: **tumibâ** *v.* to cut down a banana tree or bunch; to gain in a business deal.
tibák: *n.* foot disease.
tibadbád: *n.* false alarm, wrong news.
tibág: *n.* landslide; demolition; excavation; native stage play based on the search for the cross; **matibág** *v.* to break up, disintegrate, crumble.
tibalaw: *n.* species of herb used as a fish poison.
tibalbál: *adj.* chubby, flabby.

tibalsík: *n.* sputtering of hot embers.
tibalyáw: *n.* verified (true) news.
tibatib: *n.* pockmarks; dirt on the skin.
tibaw: *n.* feast in memory of a dead relative.
tibay: *n.* vitality; lasting quality; **matibay** *adj.* durable, sturdy, firm; hardy; rigid; secure; strong; **magpatibay** *v.* to strengthen; approve; confirm; **pagpapatibay** *n.* settlement; approval; confirmation.
tibí: *n.* constipation.
tibò: *n.* pointed organ in fish or insects which pricks.
tibô: *n.* lesbian, tomboy.
tibók: *n.* pulse, beat of the heart; (*fig.*) feeling of love; **tumibók** *v.* to beat (heart).
tibong: **nakatibong** *adj.* steep.
tibóng: **patibóng** *n.* trap, snare.
tibór: *n.* large China jar.
tibtíb: *n.* sugarcane cuttings.
tibubos: *adj.* true; genuine.
tibuhos: *n.* full length (of bamboo, cane, etc.).
tibulos: *n.* becoming involved unwittingly.
tiburín: (Sp. *tilburí*) *n.* sulky, two-wheeled carriage.
tibusok: *n.* perpendicular dive; sinking to the bottom.
tika: **pagtitika** *n.* intention; determination; **magtika** *v.* to determine; resolve.
tikà: *n.* ashy crane with a yellow beak.
tikâ: *n.* slight limp.
tikáb: *n.* gasping for breath (dying person).
tikál: **paninikál** *n.* tiredness of the feet.
tikám: *n.* gasping of a dying person.
tikán: *n.* species of mussel.
tikáng: *n.* loss of enthusiasm; slight limp.
tikáp: *n.* sudden gasp; glimmer of a weak light.
tikas: *n.* species of tuber, Indian bread shot, *Canna indica*; physical bearing, manner of carrying oneself; **tikas-tikas** *bandera española* flower.
tikatík: *adj.* light but continuous (rain).
tikbalang: *n.* centaur; long-legged mythological creature that makes people lose their way.
tikbe: *n.* species of wild grass with gray seeds that are used as necklace beads.
tiket: (Eng.) *n.* ticket; **tikitan** *v.* to issue a ticket to.
tikhá: *n.* subject; theme.
tikhím: *n.* hem; gentle cough (to attract attention).
tikhô: *n.* resounding cough (person with tuberculosis).
tikím: *n.* taste; experimenting; **matikmán** *v.* to experience; **tumikím**, **tikmán** *v.* to taste; sample; experiment; **hindî nagtítikím-idlíp** id didn't sleep a wink (taste a nap).
tikin: (Ch.) *n.* pole.
tikís: *adj.* intentionally; **tikisín** *v.* to do intentionally against someone.
tikitiki: *n.* rice bran extract.
tikiw: *n.* species of herb, *Scirsus grossus*.
tikláp: *adj.* detached, disjoined; *n.* flake.
tiklíng: *n.* Philippine rail bird; **tiniklíng** *n.* native dance.
tiklís: *n.* deep, wide-mouthed basket.
tikló: (*slang, Cebuano*) *adj.* caught in the act.
tiklóp: *n.* fold; **paniklóp** *n.* folder; **tiklóp tuhod** *id.* humble (bent knee).
tikluhód: **manikluhód** *v.* to appeal (on bent knee).
tikmâ: **tikmaan** *n.* agreement; conspiracy.
tikmán: (*rt. tikím*) *v.* to taste.
tikô: (*slang*) *n.* lesbian.
tikód: *n.* limp; **tumikód** *v.* to limp.
tikóm: *adj.* closed, shut; **magtikom ng bibíg** *v.* to keep quiet.
tikong: *n.* puffer, globefish.
tikoy: (Ch.) *n.* kind of fried cake; (*slang*) dope; stingy.
tiktak: *n.* ticking.
tiktík: *n.* spy, detective; **paniniktík** *n.* espionage; **maniktík** *v.* to spy.
tiktikò: *n.* male quail.
tikwád: *adj.* slightly tilted.
tikwál: **tikwalín** *v.* to pry with a lever.
tikwás: *adj.* tilted; **itikwás** *v.* to tilt; raise with a lever.
tidô: (*slang*) *n.* tomboy.
tig- *pref.* forms distributive numbers → **tig-isá** one each; **tigapat** four each.
tigá-: *pref.* (*coll.*) variant of *tagá-*: from.
tigáb: *n.* weak gasping for breath.
tigad: *n.* bamboo basked used for chickens.

tigagal: *n.* restlessness; uneasiness.
tigám: *adj.* dehydrated.
tigáng: *adj.* dry; barren; (*coll.*) old maid.
tigás: **matigás** *adj.* hard, stiff; **magpatigás** *v.* to harden; **tigasin** *adj.* strong; **matigás ang butó (katawán)** *id.* lazy (bone is hard); **matigás ang loób** *id.* courageous (inside is hard); **matigás ang mukhâ/sikmurà** *id.* shameless (face/stomach is hard); **matigás na ang butó** *id.* can live independently already; **matigás pa sa kulíg** *id.* fell unconscious (as hard as a baby pig).
tigatig: **matigatig** *v.* to trouble, worry; be disturbed.
tigatló: [*tig- tatlo*] three for each.
tigbak: (*slang*, Vis.) *n.* murder.
tigbakay: (Vis.) *n.* illegal cockfight.
tigbalang: *var.* of *tikbalang*: centaur-like creature.
tigbí: *n.* kind of berry yielding shrub, *Coix lachrymajobi*.
tigbín: *n.* species of crocodile.
tigbuhól: *n.* word puzzle.
tigkakalahatì: *adj.* half each.
tigkál: *n.* lump, clod.
tigdâ: **nakatigdâ** *adj.* tiptoe.
tigdás: *n.* measles.
tigdáy: *n.* improvised scarecrow.
tigirgír: (*slang*, Ilk. *tigergér*) *adj.* nervous.
tighabâ: (*rt. habâ*) *adj.* oval.
tighaból: *adj.* late; *n.* postscript.
tigháw: *adj.* not intense, alleviated; **tumigháw** *v.* to mitigate.
tighím: *n.* gentle cough; **tighimán** *v.* to cough at someone (to call the attention).
tighóy: *n.* lessening in strength; mitigation.
tigi: *n.* deep-bodied anchovy.
tigì: **pagtigì** *n.* testing the temperature of a liquid.
tigíb: *adj.* overflowing; loaded.
tigidíg: (*slang*) *n.* pimple.
tig-iilán: *interrog.* how many each?
tigil: *n.* stop, pause; **tigíl** *adj.* sleepy, not active; **patigilin** *v.* to stop, make stop; **tigilán** *n.* stop; haunt (frequently visited place); **tumigil** *v.* to stop; halt.
tigilán: *interrog.* How many for each?
tigis: *n.* pouring liquids; **tigís** *adj.* emptied to the last drop; **tigisán** *n.* drip pan.
tigiti: *n.* young sea catfish.
tigmák: *adj.* saturated.
tignás: *adj.* melted (butter, fat).
tigók: *n.* swallowing sound; (*slang*) *adj.* arrested; dead; **tiguk-tigukan** *n.* glottis.
tigpás: *n.* cutting off in one slash.
tigpáw: *n.* nightmare; dipper-shaped crab net.
tigpô: *n.* target.
tigre: (Sp.) *n.* tiger.
tigsál: *n.* barbed fish spear.
tigsó: *n.* barracuda.
tigtíg: **matigtíg** *adj.* jerky.
tigyawat: *n.* pimple. (*tagihawat*)
tihayà: **tumihayà** *v.* to lie on the back.
tiheras: (Sp. *tijeras*: scissors) *n.* folding cot.
tihò: (Ch. *té hò*: best) *n.* bar of gold.
tiíg: *n.* barracuda.
tiím: *adj.* clenched in the jaws; (Ch.) steamed; soaked.
tiín$_1$: *n.* pressure; pressing down. **itiín** *v.* to press down on in order to get up.
tiín$_2$: **tiíntiín**. *n.* forked pole that supports the outriggers of a boat.
tiís: **magtiís** *v.* to suffer, bear; persevere; **mapagtitiisán** *adj.* tolerable, bearable; **matiís** *v.* to be able to endure; **tiisín** *v.* to put up with.
tila: *adv.* it seems, perhaps, it appears to be; somewhat.
tilà: *adj.* ended, stopped (rain).
tilabsík: *n.* splash of hot liquid; stain made by a spattering of mud.
tilabso: *adj.* detached from a hook.
tilád: *n.* bits, small pieces; **tilarín** *v.* to chop, split.
tiladusdós: *n.* downward slope.
tilagós: *adj.* pierced through.
tilagpák: *n.* loud crashing sound.
tilalay: *n.* distant call; exposing the defects of another.
tilamsík: *n.* splash. **tumilamsík** *v.* to splash, spatter.
tilandáng: *n.* scattering in small pieces.
tilandóg: *n.* spurt of water.
tilandóy: *n.* upward spurt.
tilaó: *n.* uvula.

tilaok: *n.* crowing of a rooster.
tilapon: *n.* throw; **tilapunan** *v.* to hit by throwing.
tilapyâ: *n.* leather jacket fish.
tilaris: *n.* jet of water.
tilarok: *n.* spurt.
tilas: *n.* cocoon.
tilasithâ: (*obs.*) *n.* triangle.
tilasók: *n.* diarrhea.
tilay: *n.* slight burn, scald.
tilburí: (Sp.) *n.* light carriage, tilbury.
tildí: (Sp. *tilde*) *n.* tilde (~).
tilhák: *n.* hiccup, choking sound.
tili: (root not used alone) **manatili** *v.* to remain, continue, persist, stay; exist; **mapanatili** *v.* to retain; **pagpapanatili** *n.* retention; **panatilihan** *adj.* permanent.
tilí: **matilihan** *v.* to be flabbergasted.
tilî: *n.* shriek, loud sound; **tumilî** *v.* to screech.
tililíng: *n.* continuous ringing of a bell.
tilin: *n.* clitoris.
tilís: *n.* lye.
tilitíng: (*slang*) *adj.* crazy.
tilos: *n.* sharp point.
tiltíl: *n.* nibbling.
tilyadora: *n.* threshing machine.
tiím: (Ch.) *adj.* steamed (food).
timák: *n.* lowland with a humid climate.
timáng: *adj.* simple, somewhat dense.
timawà: *n.* freeman; despicable person
timayok: *n.* chewed cud.
timbâ: *n.* bucket, pail.
timbabalák: *n.* species of small lizard.
timbanin: *n.* low stool.
timbáng: *n.* weight; *adj.* balanced; **katimbáng** *adj.* equal in weight; equivalent; **manimbáng** *v.* to balance; **matimbáng** *adj.* heavy; **timbangan** *n.* weighing scales; **timbangín** *v.* to weigh.
timbáw: *n.* something extra added.
timbók: *n.* hollow canes immersed in rice deposits as outlets of heat; height of a mound.
timbóg: *n.* splashing while swimming; dying with indigo.
timból: *adj.* floating; **timbulan** *n.* float, lifesaver.
timbón: *n.* pile of dirt, garbage, etc.
timbre: (Sp.) *n.* seal, stamp; doorbell.
timbuwáng: *adj.* fallen on one's back.
timik: *n.* silence.
timig: *n.* humidity.
timlo: (Ch.) *n.* kind of Chinese dish.
timò: **timuan** *v.* to pierce, penetrate.
timog: *n.* south; **patimóg** *adv.* southward.
timón: (Sp.) *n.* rudder, helm; steering wheel; **timonél** *n.* helmsman.
timos: **tumimos** *v.* to taste broth.
timpalák: *n.* contest, competition. **timpalákpánulatán** *n.* literary contest.
timpáng: *adj.* somewhat bow-legged.
timpî: *n.* moderation, temperance, control of one's emotion; **matimpî** *adj.* reserved, sober, sensible; *adv.* calmly, sensibly.
timplá: (Sp. *templar*) *n.* blend, mixture; **magtimplá** *v.* to mix, concoct, prepare food by mixing, marinate; **panimplá** *n.* marinade, condiment; **timplado** *adj.* moderate, tempered; seasoned.
timpuhò: *adj.* squatting.
timsím: (Ch.) *n.* wick of an oil lamp.
timtím: *n.* tasting without swallowing; **matimtiman** *adj.* modest, prudent; **matimtimang birhen** *id.* woman with mature judgment.
timurò: *n.* unit of length approximately one inch long.
timyás: **matimyás** *adj.* genuine, pure (love).
tinà: (Sp. *tinta*) *n.* dye.
tinag: *n.* move; **di-matinag** *adj.* immovable; motionless; **matinag** *v.* to be able to be moved; **tuminag** *v.* to budge.
tinaha: (Sp. *tinaja*) *n.* large earthen jar; **tinahón** *n.* large water jug.
tinapá: (*rt. tapá*) *n.* smoked fish.
tinapay: (*rt. tapay*) *n.* bread.
tinasa: (Sp. *tenaza*) *n.* tongs, pincers.
tináw: *n.* clean liquid.
tindá: (Sp. *tienda*) *n.* merchandise; **magtindá** *v.* to sell in a store or market; **magtitindá** *n.* shopkeeper; **panindá** *n.* merchandise, stock; wares; **patindá** *n.* consigned goods; **ipatindá** *v.* to consign; **itindá** *v.* to sell; **tindahan** *n.* store, shop; **tindá-tindahan** *n.* children's game of shop keeping; **tindero** *n.* vendor, seller.

tindág: *n.* skewered meat; **tindagan** *n.* skewer.
tindalô: *n.* species of tree.
tindayag: *n.* whale.
tindí: **katindihán** *n.* intensity; stress, pressure; **itindí** *v.* to tighten (a grip); **matindí** *adj.* severe, intense; extreme; **pagtindí** *n.* intensification; **nápakatindí** *adj.* intense; profound; **pagkamatindí** *n.* intensity; **pagtindí** *n.* intensification; **patindihín** *v.* to intensify; **tumindí** *v.* to become serious, intense.
tindíg: *n.* posture; bearing; **itindíg** *v.* to stand; erect; **magtindíg** *v.* to stand up; **manindíg** *v.* to stand on end, bristle; **maníndigan** *v.* to stand pat; defend one's belief; guarantee; **panindigán** *v.* to affirm, allege; uphold; **paninindigan** *n.* position, viewpoint; **patindíg** *adv.* in an upright manner; **tindigán** *v.* to erect (a building) in a certain place; **tumindíg** *v.* to stand, rise up.
tindók: *n.* species of banana, horse plantain.
tinedyer: (Eng.) *n.* teenager.
tiniblás: (Sp. *tiniebla*) *n.* tenebrae.
tiník: *n.* thorn; fishbone; (*slang*) *adj.* excellent; **magtiník** *v.* to grown thorns; **tinikán** *v.* to dethorn, debone; **tiník ng pusò** *id.* ill-feeling (thorn of the heart); **tinikán** *n.* climbing perch.
tiniklíng: (*rt. tiklíng*) *n.* popular dance.
tinidór: *var. of tenedór*: fork.
tinig: *n.* voice; **katinig** *n.* consonant; **isatinig** *v.* to express, voice one's opinion; **patinig** *n.* vowel; **palatinigan** *n.* phonetics; **talatinigán** *n.* pronouncing dictionary.
tining₁: *n.* dregs, sediment.
tining₂: **matining** *adj.* tranquil, peaceful.
tiníp: *adj.* having little to say.
tinís: **matinís** *adj.* shrill, piercing (voice).
tinlóy: *n.* burry love-grass, *Adrapgon aciculatus*.
tinô: **matinô** *adj.* sensible, sane; **katinuán** *n.* sense; seriousness; integrity.
tinola: *n.* stewed chicken with papaya and bottle gourd.
tinta: (Sp.) *n.* ink; **tintero** *n.* inkwell.
tinte: (Sp.) *n.* tint.
tintinpiyé: (Sp. *tente en pie*) *n.* buffet; light meal.
tinto: (Sp.) *n.* port wine; **tintodulse** *n.* sweet red wine.
tintura: (Sp.) *n.* tincture.
tingá: *n.* bits of food between the teeth.
tingadngád: *adj.* with one end higher than the other; tilted upward (tail of scorpion).
tingalâ: **itingalâ** *v.* to turn upward, raise upward; **maningaláng-pugad** *v.* to start courting girls; **tumingalâ** *v.* to look up.
tingarò: *n.* erection of the penis; **tingarô** *adj.* erect.
tingáy: **matingáy** *adj.* neglected; lost sight of.
tingka: *n.* crop of fowls.
tingkáb: *adj.* forced open (locks).
tingkád: *n.* brightness of color; intensity of heat.
tingkál: *n.* clod, lump of earth.
tingkalâ: *n.* understanding; **di-matingkalâ** *adj.* incomprehensible.
tinkayád: **tumingkayád** *v.* to squat.
tinggâ: *n.* lead (metal); **nátinggá** *id.* cheated; swindled.
tinggál: *n.* store, storage; *adj.* stored up.
tinghád: *adj.* with a strained neck from stretching.
tingháw: *adj.* exposed to view, visible.
tinghóy: (Ch.) *n.* wick oil lamp.
tingî: *n.* retain selling: *adj.* retailed.
tingín: *n.* look, view; sight; estimate, calculation; big-eyed scad fish; **patingín** *n.* seeing; estimation; **paningín** *n.* sense of sight; eyes, view; consultation (of a doctor); **tingnán** *v.* to see, look at; notice; **sundán ng tingín** *v.* to keep one's eyes on; **matingnán** *v.* to happen to see.
tingnán: (*rt. tingín*) *v.* to look at, view.
tingní: *v.* look (*imperative*).
tingsím: (Ch.) *n.* lamp wick.
tingtíng: *n.* midrib of a palm leaf; (*fig.*) thin person; **walís-tingtíng** *n.* broom made out of palm midribs.
tio: (Sp. *tío*) *n.* uncle. (*tiyo*)
tipà, tipa: (Eng.) *n.* typing; *n.* key (of a typewriter); **tipaan** *n.* keyboard; **pagtipa** *n.* typing.
tipák: *n.* piece, lump, chunk, chip; **tumipák** *v.* to chop off; **pagtipák** *n.* chopping; (*coll.*) big

profit of success; **tipakan** *n.* quarry.

tipaklóng: *n.* species of grasshopper.

tipán: *n.* appointment, engagement; betrothal; **tipanan** *n.* appointment.

tipas: *n.* escape; avoidance.

tipás: *adj.* cut off in one stroke.

tipî: *adj.* compressed, pressed; solid.

tipík: *n.* small particle.

tipíd: *n.* conservation, thrift; **magtipíd** *v.* to save, economize, do sparingly; **matipíd** *adj.* economical; frugal, thrifty.

tipíl: *n.* particle; **tipilín** *v.* to shorten; mold into particles.

tipíng: **tipingín** *v.* to taste without swallowing.

tipläg: *n.* nervous jerk of the body.

tiplás: *n.* escape.

tiple: (Sp.) *n.* treble, soprano voice.

tipo: (Sp.) *n.* type, kind; style; (*slang*) preferred kind.

tipò: *n.* dent, notch; **tipô** *adj.* notched; missing a tooth.

tipol: *n.* species of crane-like bird.

tipon: *n.* collection; **katipunan** *n.* assembly; federation; **magtipon** *v.* to collect; gather; **pagtipún-tipunin** *v.* to bring together, assemble; **tipunán** *n.* place of assembly; *v.* gather, collect.

tipos: (Sp. *tifus*) *n.* Typhoid fever; (slang) adj. dead.

tiptíp: *n.* flake, chip.

tipunò: **matipunò** *adj.* robust.

tipus: (Sp. *tifus*) *n.* typhoid fever.

tipyáo: **tipyaoán** *v.* to make a slanting cut.

tira: (Sp. *tirar*) *n.* throwing; move in a game; hitting, beating up; (*slang*) having sex; **tirahan** (*slang*) sex.

tirá$_1$: **pagtirá** *n.* residence; occupation; **manirá** *v.* to reside; **nakatirá** *adj.* resident, living in; **tinitirahán** *n.* residence; **tirahan** *n.* residence; address; habitat; **tir(a)hán** *v.* to live in; **tumirá** *v.* to live in a place.

tirá$_2$: *adj.* leftover; residue; **itirá** *v.* to set aside; **tirhán, tirán** *v.* to set aside, spare, leave for someone.

tirà: **matirà** *adj.* able to endure; **pagkamatirà** *n.* endurance.

tirabusón: (Sp. *tirabuzón*) *n.* corkscrew.

tiradór: (Sp.) *n.* slingshot; alternate route, bypass; emissary; **tiradores** *n.* marksmen.

tiranía: (Sp.) *n.* tyranny; **tiránico** *adj.* tyrannical.

tirano: (Sp.) *n.* tyrant.

tirante: (Sp.) *n.* suspenders; bra strap.

tirapâ: (*rt.* *dapâ*) **mapatirapâ** *v.* to fall prostrate in pleading; **nagpápatirapâ sa paanán** *id.* admiring a girl (falling prone at the foot).

tirera: (*slang*) *n.* go go dancer.

tirhán: *see tirá.*

tirik: **magtirik** *v.* to build, construct; **tirikán ng kandilà** *n.* candle stand; **patirík** *adj.* in an upright position; **ipinagtirik ng kandilà** *id.* prayed for (lighted candle for).

tirintás: (Sp. *trenzas*) *n.* braid; pigtail.

tirirít: (*slang*) *n.* marijuana.

tirís: (Sp. *triza*) *n.* crushing lice between thumbnails.

tirtír: (*slang*) *n.* pickpocket.

Tiruray: *n.* ethnic group and language from Cotabato, Mindanao.

tirya: *n.* attack; vengeance.

tisà: (Sp. *tiza*) *n.* chalk; (Sp. *teja*) *n.* roof tile.

tisáy: *n.* fair skinned lady.

tisis: (Sp.) *n.* tuberculosis; **tísiko** *adj.* tubercular.

tisod: **matisod** *v.* to trip, stumble; **tísuring bató** *id.* person often insulted or teased (stone stepped upon).

tisóy: *n.* fair skinned man.

tistís$_1$: *n.* surgical operation.

tistís$_2$: **magtistis** *v.* to trim wood into long strips; remove fibers from.

tita: *n.* auntie.

titatita: *n.* go-between, procurer of a prostitute.

titi: (*baby talk*) *n.* milk, bottle.

titì: *n.* penis.

titî: *adj.* well-drained.

titik: *n.* letter; writing; lyrics; **ititik** *v.* to write down; **panitikán** *n.* literature; **pagkakatitik** *n.* lettering; **nakatitik** *n.* written.

titig: *n.* stare, gaze; **titigán** *v.* to stare at.

titis: *n.* ash; **titisán** *n.* ash tray.

titís: **magtitís** *v.* to flow continuously.

título: (Sp.) *n.* title; degree; deed; **titulado** *adj.* titled; with a degree.

tiwa: *n.* intestinal worm.
tiwal: *n.* hookworm.
tiwakál: **magpatiwakál** *v.* to commit suicide.
tiwalà: **pagtitiwalà** *n.* trust, faith; **katiwalà** *n.* manager, foreman; **kapaní-paniwalà** *adj.* believable; reliable; conclusive; **kapaniwalaán** *n.* traditional belief; **i(ka)tiwalà** *v.* to entrust; confide; commit; **maniwalà** *v.* to believe; **mag(ká)tiwalà** *v.* to have faith in, trust; **mapagtiwalà** *adj.* trusting; **mapagkakátiwalaan** *adj.* trustworthy; reliable; **mapaníniwalaan** *adj.* trustworthy, reliable; **mapaniwalaín** *adj.* trustful, trusting; gullible; **paniwalà** *n.* belief; faith; trust; **paniwalaan** *v.* to belief; have trust in; **pagtitiwalà** *n.* trust; **pagtiwalaan** *v.* to trust; rely on; **tiwalaan** *v.* to trust someone; entrust to; **kawaláng-paniwalà** *n.* disbelief; mistrust.
tiwalág: *adj.* discharged; separated; dismissed; **tumiwalág** *v.* to resign; quit; **magtiwalág** *v.* to dismiss; impeach; **matiwalág** *adj.* to be dismissed.
tiwalî: *adj.* incorrect; inverted; abnormal; absurd; **katiwalián** *n.* irregularity; **tiwaliín** *v.* to do the opposite.
tiwalwál: *adj.* neglected; abandoned.
tiwangwáng: *adj.* wide-open.
tiwarík: *adj.* inverted; upside-down.
tiwás: *adj.* not level, tilted; **patiwasín** *v.* to tilt upward; **magtiwasan** *v.* to seesaw.
tiwasáy: **matiwasáy** *adj.* calm, quiet; peaceful.
tiyá: (Sp. *tía*) *n.* aunt; stepmother; **tiyang-kabayo** *n.* cavalla fish.
tiyáb: *n.* notch cut in posts to help climb.
tiyák: *adj.* sure, certain; definite; **tumiyák** *v.* to ensure; **pagtiyák** *n.* certainty.
tiyakád: *n.* bamboo stilts.
tiyád: **tumiyád** *v.* to tiptoe.
tiyagâ: **matiyagâ** *adj.* diligent, persevering.
tiyán: *n.* belly, abdomen; **tiyanín** *v.* to have a stomach ache; **tiyán ng lupà** *id.* grave (belly of ground).
tiyanak: *n.* goblin.
tiyanì: (Ch.) *n.* tweezers, pincers.
tiyangge: (Ch.) *n.* market.
tiyáp: **magtiyáp** *v.* to agree to; **tiyapín** *v.* to arrange an appointment with; **tiyapan** *n.* appointment, agreement; **katiyáp** *n.* accomplice; person meeting another.
tiyara: (Sp.) *n.* tiara, triple crown.
tiyáw: *n.* mocking; scoffing.
tiyempo: (Sp. *tiempo*) *n.* timing; time; **magkatiyempo** *v.* to have the chance to do; **tiyempuhán** *v.* to do at the opportune time; **patiyempo** *adj.* through proper timing; **matiyempuhán** *v.* to be caught in the act.
tiyó: (Sp. *tío*) *n.* uncle; stepfather.
tiyobibo: (Sp. *tiovivo*) *n.* merry-go-round.
tiyopè: *n.* cowardly cock in cockfighting; (*slang*) *adj.* stupid.
tiyukà: (Ch.) *n.* stick used for threshing grains.
toka: (Sp. *tocar*) *n.* turn to do; **itoka** *v.* to assign; **tokadór** *n.* dresser; chest of drawers.
tokayo: (Sp. *tocayo*) *n.* namesake.
toke: (Sp. *toque*) *n.* touch, artistic touch.
tokis: (*slang*) *n.* soundtrack of a movie.
toknát: (*slang*) *adj.* horny, lustful.
tokneneng: (*slang*) *adj.* unaware; uninformed.
tokoy: (Ch.) *n.* goldsmith's working table.
tokrat: (*slang*) *n.* scar on the head.
tokwa: (Sp.) *n.* tofu, soybean curd.
todas: (Sp.) *adj.* finished, completely consumed; exterminated; broken, worn-out; (*slang*) dead; desperate, in trouble; **todasin** *v.* to consume everything; (*slang*) murder; **todas ang tayâ/ lahì** *id.* consumed.
todo(s): (Sp.) *adj.* all; the whole of; **pagtodo** *n.* full exertion of strength; betting all one's money in one game; **todohin** *v.* to include all; do to the fullest; **Todos Los Santos** *n.* All Saint's Day. **todo-todo** *adj.* all; without exception.
toga: (Sp.) *n.* judicial robe; graduation gown.
togè: *n.* bean sprouts.
'tol: (*short for utol*) *n.* sibling; bro, sis.
tolerá: (Sp. *tolerar*) *n.* tolerance.
tolerasyón: (Eng.) *n.* toleration.
tolda: (Sp. *toldo*) *n.* tent.
tolók: (*slang*) *adj.* stupid. [Alt: *tolonggés*]
tomá: (Sp., *slang*) *n.* drinking session; **tomadór** *n.* alcoholic.
tomadór: (Sp.) *n.* alcoholic.
tomaposesyón: (Sp. *toma posesión*) *n.* induction; taking the position of a new office.

tomboy: (Eng.) *n.* tomboy; lesbian.
tomo: (Sp.) *n.* volume.
tonelada: (Sp.) *n.* ton; **tonelahe** *n.* tonnage.
tono: (Sp.) *n.* tone; tune; pitch.
tonsilitis: (Eng.) *n.* tonsillitis.
tonsura: (Sp.) *n.* tonsure; shaving the crown of the head.
tonto: (Sp.) *adj.* silly, stupid.
tong: (Ch.) *n.* bribe; percentage of winnings taken by the casino; collection of money.
tongaling: (*slang*) *n.* sexual intercourse.
tongô: (*slang*) *adj.* foolish.
tongók: (*slang*) *adj.* crazy.
topasyo: (Sp. *topacio*) *n.* topaz.
tore: (Sp. *torre*) *n.* tower.
toreadór: (Sp.) *n.* bullfighter.
torero: (Sp.) *n.* bullfighter; (*slang*) male go go dancer.
torete: (Sp.) *n.* young bull.
tormento: (Sp.) *n.* torment.
tornabiyahe: (Sp. *tornaviaje*) *n.* return trip.
tornasól: (Sp.) *n.* litmus paper.
torneo: (Sp.) *n.* tournament.
tornilyo: (Sp. *tornillo*) *n.* screw; bolt.
torno: (Sp.) *n.* windlass; lathe.
toro: (Sp.) *n.* bull; (*slang*) stud; penis; **toro-toro** (*slang*) *n.* live sex show; **toro't-kara** (*slang*) *n.* fellatio.
torotot: (*slang*) *n.* wife with an unfaithful husband; child's trumpet; penis.
torpe: (Sp.) *adj.* timid, shy (with the opposite sex); stupid.
torsido: (Sp. *torcido*) *adj.* twisted; crooked.
torta: (Sp.) *n.* omelet.
tortilya: (Sp. *tortilla*) *n.* small omelet.
tosi: (*tosino* + *sinangág*) *n.* bacon and fried rice.
tosilog: (*tosino, sinangág, itlóg*) *n.* bacon, fried rice, and egg.
tosino: (Sp. *tocino*) *n.* bacon; smoked meat.
tosperina: (Sp. *tos ferina*) *n.* whooping cough.
tostado: (Sp.) *adj.* toasted.
tostadora: (Sp.) *n.* toaster.
totál: (Sp.) *n.* total; as a matter of fact, to sum up.
totalidád: (Sp.) *n.* totality.
toto: **katoto** *n.* close friend.
totò: *n.* appellation for a small boy.
totoó: *adj.* true, real; genuine; *adv.* quite, very; **katotóhánan** *n.* truth, fact; **makatotóhánan** *adj.* realistic; **magkatotoó** *v.* to be true; realize; **magtotóhánan** *v.* to compete with each other; be frank with each other; **pagkamakatotóhánan** *n.* realism; **patotoó** *n.* proof; **patotóhánan** *v.* to prove, confirm; **pagpapatotoó** *n.* proving; assurance; **totohanin** *v.* to be sincere; **totoóhin** *v.* to be truthful, sincere.
totoy: *n.* appellation used in addressing a young boy.
totso: (Ch.) dish of fish with tofu.
totwák: (*slang*) *n.* sexual intercourse.
toyò: (Ch.) *n.* soy sauce; (*slang*) irrational behavior, mood swings; **toyò sa ulo** *id.* irrational, demented.
trabaho: (Sp. *trabajo*) *n.* work; job; employment; **magtrabaho** *v.* to work; **trabahadór** *n.* worker.
trabisanyo: (Sp. *travesaño*) *n.* crossbar, tie.
trabyesa: (Sp. *traviesa*) *n.* crosstie; sleeper in a railway track.
trak: (Eng.) *n.* truck; **magtrak** *v.* to go by truck.
trakoma: (Sp. *tracoma*) *n.* trachoma.
traktilyo: *n.* immature cavalla fish.
tradisyón: (Sp. *tradición*) *n.* tradition.
traduksiyón: (Sp. *traducción*) *n.* translation.
tradusí: (Sp. *traducir*) **tradusihín** *v.* to translate.
trahe: (Sp. *traje*) *n.* suit; **trahe de boda** *n.* wedding dress.
tráhikó: (Sp. *trágico*) *adj.* tragic.
traidór: (Sp.) *n.* traitor.
traisyón: (Sp. *traición*) *n.* treason; treachery.
trambía: (Sp. *tranvía*) *n.* streetcar.
tramo: (Sp.) *n.* section of a bridge of railroad track.
trampolina: (Sp.) *n.* trampoline.
transkri(p)to: (Sp. *transcrito*) *n.* transcript.
trangá: (Sp.) *n.* crossbar.
trangkaso: (Sp. *trancazo*) *n.* flu, influenza.
trangkilya: (Sp. *tranquilla*) *n.* small latch.
trapál: *n.* oilcloth.

trapesoda: (Eng.) *n.* trapezoid.
trápiko: (Sp. *tráfico*) *n.* traffic; **trapikante** *n.* trafficker, trader.
trapitse: (Sp. *trapiche*) *n.* sugar mill.
trapo: (Sp.) *n.* rag.
tratado: (Sp.) *n.* treaty.
trato: (Sp.) *n.* contract; treatment; **tratuhin** *v.* to treat.
treinta: (Sp.) *n.* thirty.
trementina: (Sp.) *n.* turpentine.
tren: (Sp.) *n.* train; **magtren** *v.* to go by train.
trepilya: *var.* of *tripilya*: innards used as food.
tres: (Sp.) *n.* three.
trese: (Sp. *trece*) *n.* thirteen.
tresyentos: (Sp. *trescientos*) *n.* three hundred.
triánggulo: (Sp.) *n.* triangle.
tribu: (Sp.) *n.* tribe.
tribuna: (Sp.) *n.* tribunal; board of judges; stage; dais.
tribunál: (Sp.) *n.* court of justice.
trigo: (Sp.) *n.* wheat. **triguhan** *n.* wheat field.
trilyadora: (Sp. *trilladora*) *n.* threshing machine.
trinidád: (Sp.) *n.* trinity.
trinsera: (Sp. *trinchera*) *n.* trench.
trintas: (Sp. *trenzas*) *n.* braid; pigtail.
trip: (*slang*, Eng.) *adj.* arousing, stimulating; *n.* enjoyment; liking; want; plan; idea; **mapagtripán** *v.* to enjoy, get off on; feel like doing, desire; **pinagtripán** *v.* messed with; tricked, cheated; took advantage of.
tripa: (Sp.) *n.* tripe; entrails.
tripilya: (Sp. *tripilla*) *n.* tripe dish.
triple: (Sp.) *adj.* triple; **triplikado** *adj.* triplicate.
tripulante: (Sp.) *n.* crew.
trole: (Sp.) *n.* trolley.
trombon: (Sp.) *n.* trombone.
trompeta: (Sp.) *n.* trumpet. **trompetero** *n.* trumpeter.
trono: (Sp.) *n.* throne; (*slang*) toilet.
tropa: (Sp.) *n.* troop; gang; (*slang*) close friends, social group.
tropeo: (Sp.) *n.* trophy.
tropikál: (Sp. *tropical*) *adj.* tropical.
trópikó: (Sp. *trópico*) *n.* tropics.
trosilyo: *var. of tursilyo*: small barracuda.
troso: (Sp. *trozo*) *n.* log.
trote: (Sp.) *n.* trot; gallop.
tsa: (Ch.) *n.* tea.
tsabita: *n.* moonfish, *Mene maculata.*
tsaka: (*coll.*) *n.* ugly girl.
tsaketa: (Sp. *chaqueta*) *n.* jacket; **tsaketilya** *n.* vest.
tsaleko: (Sp. *chaleco*) *n.* vest.
tsamba: (*coll.*) *n.* fluke; chance.
tsambwá: (Ch.) *n.* gold shavings.
tsampaka: (Sp. *champaca*) *n.* ornamental shrub, *Michelia champaca.*
tsamporado: (Sp. *champorado*) *n.* rice porridge with chocolate.
tsampóy: *n.* bay berry, Chinese strawberry, box myrtle.
tsansa: (Eng.) *n.* chance. (*pagkakátaón*)
tsáng: (*slang, f. tiya*) *n.* aunt; girlfriend.
tsapa: (Sp. *chapa*: metal plate) *n.* badge.
tsáperón: (Eng.) *n.* chaperon.
tsarera: (Sp. *charera*) *n.* teapot.
tsaról: (Sp. *charol*) *n.* patent leather.
tsasko: (Sp. *chasco*) *n.* failure; disappointment.
tsasis: (Eng.) *n.* chassis.
tsata: (Sp. *chata*) *adj.* flat; *n.* bedpan; **urinola-~** *n.* flat, metal bedpan.
tsato: (Sp. *chato*) *adj.* flat-nosed; flat.
tsatsa: (Sp. *chacha*) *n.* chacha dance.
tsaubinismo: (Sp. *chauvinismo*) *n.* chauvinism. **tsaubinista** *n.* chauvinist.
tseke: (Sp. *cheque*) *n.* check.
tsekung, tsekwa: (*slang*) *n., adj.* Chinese.
tsedéng: (*slang*) *n.* Mercedes Benz.
tsibak: (*slang*) *v.* to eat.
tsibúg: (*coll.*) *v.* eat; **tsibugán** eating place.
tsika: (*slang*, Sp. *chica*) *n.* girl; female friend; gossiper; **tsika-tsika** *n.* gossip.
tsikitíng: (Sp. *chiquitín*) *adj.* tiny.
tsikito: (Sp. *chiquito*) *n.* young child.
tsiko: *n.* sapodilla fruit, *Achras zapota*; young boy; **amóy-tsiko** *id.* drunk (smell of *chico*).
tsikot: (*slang*) *n.* car.
tsimáy: (*coll.*) *n.* female servant.
tsimenea: (Sp.) *n.* chimney.
tsimóy: (*coll.*) *n.* male servant, house boy.
Tsina: (Sp. *china*) *n.* China; Chinese; **Tsino** Chinese.

tsinelas: (Sp. *chinelas*) *n.* slippers.
Tsináy: (*slang*) *n.*, *adj.* Chinese-Filipino (woman).
Tsinóy: (*slang*) *n.*, *adj.* Chinese-Filipino.
tsismís: (Sp. *chisme*) *n.* gossip; **tsismoso** *adj.* gossipy.
tsitsaró: (Sp. *chicharrón*) *n.* pea.
tsítsarón: (Sp. *chicharrón*) *n.* crispy fried pork rind.
tsitsirika: *n.* tropical periwinkle.
tso Pablo: (*slang*) *n.* homosexual male.
tsok: (Eng.) *n.* chalk.
tsokarán: (*slang*) *n.* gangmate.
tsoke: (Sp. *choque*) *n.* crash, collision.
tsokolate: (Sp. *chocolate*) *n.* chocolate.
tsong: (*slang, f. tiyo*) *n.* uncle; dude; buddy.
tsongkî: (*slang*) *n.* marijuana.
tsopi: (*slang*) *adj.* effeminate.
tsotsò: *n.* children's term for dog.
tsupa: (Sp. *chupa*, *slang*) *n.* oral sex.
tsupér: (Sp. *chófer*) *n.* chauffeur, driver.
tsupón: (Sp. *chupón*) *n.* nipple of a bottle.
tsuriso: (Sp. *chorizo*) *n.* pork sausage.
tsutserias: (Sp. *chucherías*) *n.* trifles, little unimportant things.
tsutsu: (*slang*) *n.* informer, big mouth; sycophant.
tuba: *n.* croton oil shrub, *Croton tiglium.*
tubâ: *n.* sugarcane alcohol.
tubal: *n.* dirty clothes; dirt and sweat.
tubayan: *n.* dark skinned sweet potato.
tuberiya: (Sp.) *n.* plumbing; **tubero** *n.* plumber.
tubig: *n.* water; **manubíg** *v.* to urinate; **pantubig** *adj.* aquatic, referring to water; **patubig** *n.* irrigation; **bulutong-tubig** *n.* chicken pox; **natútubigan** *id.* kept silent (was watered); **tubíg-tubíg** *adj.* watery; **tubig-ulán** *n.* rainwater.
tubo: (Sp.) *n.* pipe, tube; conduit.
tubò$_1$: *n.* gain, profit; interest; **matubò** *adj.* profitable; **patubuan** *n.* lending money with interest; **papatubò** *n.* usury; **magtubò** *v.* to profit; gain; **tubong-nilugaw** *n.* excessive profits.
tubò$_2$: *n.* sprout; growth; **tumubò** *v.* to grow; **magpatubò** *v.* to plant;
tubò$_3$: *n.* native; **katutubò** *adj.* native; natural; instinctive; characteristic; **katutubong-ugalì** *n.* instinct; nature; **lupang-tinubuan** *n.* fatherland.
tubó: *n.* sugarcane.
tubóg: *n.* pool of water; **itubóg** *v.* to dip in water; plate with metal.
tubós: *n.* ransom; redeeming; **mánunubós** *n.* redeemer; **katúbúsan** *n.* redemption; **matubós** *v.* to be able to redeem; **pagkátubós** *n.* redemption; **pan(t)ubós** *n.* ransom; **tumubós, tubusín** *v.* to redeem; ransom; free someone.
tukâ: (Ch.) *n.* bill, beak; **manukâ** *v.* to peck; **matukâ** *v.* to be pecked; **patukâ** *n.* poultry feed; **parang nátukâ ng ahas** *id.* speechless; crest-fallen (as if bitten by a snake); **tukaín** *v.* to peck; (*coll.*) to kiss.
tukakì: **tukakî** *adj.* with nodding head due to drowsiness.
tukáng: *n.* featherless bird.
tukaról: *n.* baby's bonnet; monk's hood.
tukas-tukas: *n.* *bandera española* flower.
tukatók: *n.* nodding of the head when sleepy.
tukil: *n.* short bamboo container.
tukláp: *adj.* peeled off; detached; **tuklapín** *v.* to detach, separate.
tuklás: *n.* discovery, find; **makatuklás** *v.* to discover; find out; **manunuklás** *n.* discoverer.
tukláw: *n.* snakebite.
tuklóng: *n.* barrio chapel; temporary shrine.
tukmô: *n.* small heap or pile.
tukmól. *n.* inland turtledove; (*fig.*) ugly person; coward.
tuko: *n.* whale shark, *Rhineodon typus.*
tukô; *n.* gecko; measles.
tukod: *n.* support, prop; brace; **tukuran** *v.* to prop up; **tukod ng yaman** *id.* wealthiest family in an area; **tukod-langit** *n.* kind of vegetable used in salads; **tukod-ilóng** *n.* bone that supports the nose.
tukól: *n.* overripe rice grains; *adj.* even (numbers).
tukong: **tukóng** *adj.* tailless.
tukop: **tukóp** *adj.* covered with the palm of the hand.
tukoy: *n.* mention, reference; **pantukoy** *n.*

article (grammatical); **tukuyin** *v.* to mention, cite.

tukóy: *adj.* well-experienced; accurate (shooting).

tuksayan: *n.* large fresh-water shrimp.

tuksó: *n.* temptation; seduction; joke; **ituksó** *v.* to tease (a woman); **magtuksuhan** *v.* to joke with one another; **manuksó** *v.* to tempt; tease; **panunuksó** *n.* temptation.

tuktók: *n.* top, peak, summit; crown of the head; knocking sound; (*fig.*) brain; **tumuktók** *v.* to knock.

tudlâ: *n.* shooting, aiming; **tudlaan** *n.* target; **panudlaan** *n.* shooting range; **matudlâ** *adj.* to be shot; **manunudlâ** *n.* marksman.

tudláng: *n.* prop to keep a window open.

tudlík: *n.* apostrophe.

tudlíng₁: *n.* furrow; **magtudlíng** *v.* to furrow.

tudlíng₂: *n.* newspaper column; **pangulong tudlíng** *n.* editorial.

tudlók: *n.* puncture, prick; dot, period.

tudyó: *n.* joke, jest; **manudyó** *v.* to tease, joke.

tugá: *adj.* stupid; gullible.

tugâ: *adj.* true, correct; right; *n.* telling the truth; confession.

tugák: *n.* species of frog; *adj.* stupid.

tugagà: *adj.* change for the better; amazement.

tugahók: (*slang*) *adj.* stupid.

tugatog: *n.* peak; height, summit; top.

tugaygáy: **tugaygayán** *v.* to follow behind, trail; keep track of.

tugdâ: *n.* spear for catching fish.

tugdáy: *n.* pole used to hold up nets.

tugkâ: *adj.* dislodged.

tugdâ: *n.* kind of spear.

tugî: *n.* wild yam, *Dioscorea esculenta.*

tugis: *n.* pursuit, chase; **tugisin** *v.* to chase, pursue.

tugmâ: **tugmaan** *n.* verse; rhyme; **magtugmâ** *v.* to harmonize; rhyme; be correct; **katugmâ** *adj.* on good terms with; in rhyme with; **pagkakatugmâ** *n.* harmony; going well together.

tugnás: *adj.* thawed, melted; humid.

tugnáw: *adj.* completely burnt.

tugnô: *n.* brine, filtered salt water.

tugón: **tugunín** *v.* to answer; greet; reply; **katugón** *adj.* corresponding, equivalent; **tugunan** *n.* exchange of views.

tugot: *n.* stopping; **tugutan** *v.* to stop doing to.

tugoy: *n.* swing.

tugpá: **pagtugpá** *v.* going down; **mapatugpá** *v.* to be driven by the wind or fate.

tugtóg: **pagtugtóg** *n.* music; touch; **manunugtóg** *n.* musician; **tugtugin** *n.* music; **tugtugín** *v.* to play (a musical instrument).

tugyâ: *n.* swaying motion.

tuhák: *n.* egret, night heron.

tuhod: *n.* knee; ~ **manók** *n.* chicken knee; species of medicinal shrub.

tuhog: *n.* string of beads; skewer; **tuhugin** *v.* to string (beads); skewer; (*fig.*) collect girlfriends (courting many girls at once).

tula: *n.* kind of mouth disease in babies; distemper in fowls.

tulâ: *n.* poem; **manunulà** *n.* poet; **tumulâ** *v.* to write a poem.

tulak₁: *n.* push, shove; (*slang*) pusher; **itulak** *v.* to push, shove; **itinulak sa bangín** *id.* driven to danger (pushed down cliff); **magtulák ng alon** *id.* to remain idle (push the wave); **tulak ng bibíg, kabig ng dibdíb** *id.* pretending to dislike an esteemed thing (pushed by the mouth, pulled by the chest); **waláng itulak-kabigin** *id.* can't choose between the two (nothing pushes or pulls); **tulak-kabig** *n.* push and pull.

tulak₂: *n.* departure of vehicles; **tumulak** *v.* to depart.

tulakbahalà: *n.* ballast.

tulakís: *n.* worthless poetry.

tulad: *n.* imitation; **katulad** *adj.* like, similar; **itulad** *v.* to compare; conform; **magtulad** *v.* to coincide; parallel; **tularán** *n.* model; pattern to copy; **tularan** *v.* to copy, imitate; model; **walang-katulad** *adj.* incomparable; without equal.

tulág: *n.* lance, spear.

tulagâ: *n.* kind of small fish net.

tulalâ: *adj.* stupid, silly; astonished.

tulalí: *adj.* unique; only, alone.

tulas: *n.* watery feces; gonorrhea.

tulasók: *n.* severe diarrhea.

tulatód: *n.* coccyx.

tuláw: **tulawín** *v.* to kill an animal by smashing

the head.
tuláy: *n.* bridge, overpass; (*fig.*) go-between; **manuláy** *v.* to keep one's balance.
tuldík: *n.* accent mark.
tuldók: *n.* period, dot; **tutuldók** *n.* colon; **tuldók-kuwít** *n.* semi-colon.
tulì: **tuliin** *v.* to circumcise; **tulî** *adj.* circumcised.
tulík: *adj.* multicolored; **tulikán** *n.* multicolored rooster.
tulíg: *adj.* deafened by noise, stunned.
tuligsâ: *n.* verbal attack; **manunuligsâ** *n.* critic; **tumuligsâ** *v.* to attack in words; censure.
tulin: *n.* speed; **magmatulin** *v.* to move fast; **matulin** *adj.* fast; **tumulin** *v.* to accelerate.
tulingág: *adj.* stunned; stupefied; stupid.
tulingan: *n.* tuna type fish, *Thunnidae* family; **tulingan-puti** *n.* Oceanic bonito.
tulingaw: **makitulingaw** *v.* to be at ease with, be familiar with a person.
tuliró: *adj.* confused; stunned.
tulis: *n.* point, sharp end; round herring; **tulisan** *v.* to sharpen.
tulís: (*slang*) *n.* playboy.
tulisán: *n.* bandit, robber; **tulisáng-dagat** *n.* pirate; **tulisáng-pulpól** *id.* not a true bandit.
tulò: *n.* drip; leak; (*slang*) venereal disease; **patuluin** *v.* to drain; **tumulò** *v.* to drip; **magpatulò ng pawis** *id.* to work (drip sweat); **tumutulò ang laway** *id.* mouth watering (saliva dripping); **tulò-laway** *id.* stupid; **tumulò ang patís** *id.* cried.
tulók: *n.* earwax discharge due to infection.
tulod: *n.* young shoot of a banana tree.
tulog: *n.* sleep, rest; **matulog** *v.* to sleep; **magpatulog** *v.* to put to sleep; **pampatulog** *n.* sleeping aid; **tulugán** *n.* sleeping place.
tulong: *n.* help, aid; support; **tulungan** *v.* to help someone; **katulong** *n.* helper; maid; associate; **magtulong** *v.* to help one another; **matulungín** *adj.* helpful; cooperative; **pagtutulungán** *n.* cooperation; **tumulong** *v.* to help.
tulos: *n.* stake; **tulusan** *v.* to stake out a place.
tulot: **pahintulot** *n.* approval, sanction; permission; **pahintulutan** *v.* to allow, permit; approve.
tuloy: **tumuloy** *v.* to stay in a house; **manuluyan** *v.* to stay in someone else's place; **bahay-panuluyan** *n.* boarding house; **patuluyin** *v.* to accommodate, put up (for some time); **pánuluyan, tuluyan** *n.* lodging.
tulóy: *interj.* Come in! (**Tuloy po kayó**); **itulóy** *v.* to continue, proceed; **magtulóy** *v.* to go ahead, move forward, proceed; **pagtulóy** *n.* progress; **pagtutulóy** *n.* continuation; **patuloy** *adj.* constant, continuous; **ipag-patulóy** *v.* to proceed; pursue; keep on, continue; **túlúyan** *n.* prose; *n.* direct, continual; **patulúy-tulóy** *adv.* continuously; **tulóy-tulóy** *adj.* continual; **tumulóy** *v.* to go ahead, move forward; progress.
tulsók: *n.* piercing; small hole made by piercing.
tultól: *n.* plumbline used for leveling; guidance.
tulyá: *n.* species of small clam.
tuma: *n.* pubic louse.
tumà: **tumain** *v.* to thin thread before threading a needle.
tulyapis: *n.* useless things; undeveloped rice grains.
tumal: **matumal** *adj.* slow (business).
tumali: *n.* bamboo stud used in the framework of a wall.
tumalula: *n.* species of long, thin rattan.
tumanà: *n.* farmland, highly arable land.
tumáng: (*slang*) *n.* idiot, fool.
tumba: (Sp.) *n.* tomb.
tumbá: (Sp. *tumbar*) *adj.* fallen down; (*slang*) beat up; **tumbá-tumbá** *n.* rocking chair; **matumbá** *v.* to fall down; become bankrupt.
tumbado: (Sp.) *adj.* fallen down; bankrupt.
tumbaga: *n.* copper and gold alloy.
tumbalík: *adj.* inverted; upside down; ironic.
tumbalilong: *n.* somersault.
tumbás: *adj.* sufficient, enough; **katumbás** *adj.* equal; **tumbasán** *v.* to math, put in an equal amount; **tumbasan** *n.* ratio; exchange of an equal amount.
tumbók: *adj.* directly hit; **katumbukán** *n.* focus.
tumbóng: *n.* rectum; swollen anus; puff ball mushroom; **tumbóng-aso** *n.* species of

medicinal plant.

tumok: *n.* thick growth of tall grass; **katumukan** *n.* savanna.

tumór: (Sp.) *n.* tumor.

tumpá: **pagtumpá** *n.* route, course.

tumpák: *adj.* proper; justified; deserved; faithful; **katumpakán** *n.* accuracy; correctness.

tumpík: **pagpapatumpík-tumpík** *n.* prudishness; squeamishness.

tumpók: *n.* heap, pile, mound.

tumurò: *n.* span between the thumb and forefinger.

tuna: *n.* tuna fish.

tunâ: *adj.* sunk, submerged; collapsed.

tunaw: **matunaw** *v.* to melt; dissolve; **pantunaw** *adj.* solvent; **panunaw** *n.* laxative; digestion; **tumunaw** *v.* to liquefy, melt; thaw out; **natunaw na parang asín** *id.* disappeared immediately (melted like salt).

tunay: *adj.* true, correct; pure, real, genuine; sincere; *adv.* truly, really, in fact; **magpatunay** *v.* to prove, testify; **patunay** *n.* proof, testimony; **patunayan** *v.* to prove, testify, verify; **tunay na lalake** *n.* true man; (*slang*) heavy drinker.

tundâ: **manundâ** *v.* to fish with hooks.

tundô: **tumundô** *v.* to prick.

tundók: **tumundók** *v.* to pierce with a skewer.

tunél: (Sp.) *n.* tunnel.

túnika: (Sp. *tunica*) *n.* tunic, gown.

tunod: *n.* arrow; shaft; candle-like shoot of a banana plant.

tunóg: *n.* sound; tone; **matunóg** *adj.* resonant; sonorous; famous; easily informed; **katunugán** *n.* resonance.

tunsóy: *n.* fimbriated sardine, *Sardinalla fimbriata.*

tuntón₁: *n.* tracing the path of; tracing the source, origin; **tuntunan** *n.* basis.

tuntón₂: **pagtutuntón** *n.* giving guidance at the start; **itintón** *v.* to guide at the start; **palatuntunan** *n.* regulation; **tuntunin** *n.* rule, principle.

tuntóng₁: **tumuntóng** *v.* to step on; **nakatuntóng sa guhit** *id.* on the brink of death; **nakatuntóng sa número** *id.* having difficulty dealing with others.

tuntóng₂: *n.* lid, cover of a cooking pot.

tungág: *adj.* stupid, dull.

tungangà: *adj.* agape; **tumungangà** *v.* to state at stupidly (agape).

tungáw: *n.* mite, small red chicken tick.

tungayaw: **magtungayaw** *v.* to swear, curse, use bad language.

tungkáb: *adj.* forced opened, forced out of place.

tungkî: *n.* tip, point.

tungkô: *n.* tripod; tripodal stove; trivet; **tungkóng-kalán** *n.* stove with tripodal base.

tungkód: *n.* cane, walking stick; **tungkód-parì** *n.* shrub that grows from tuberous roots.

tungkól sa: *prep.* concerning, about, regarding.

tungkól: **tungkulin** *n.* duty; work; function, role; **manungkulan** *v.* to practice a profession; hold the office of.

tungkós: *n.* bouquet; bundle; tuft.

tunggâ: **tumunggâ** *v.* to gulp down; **patunggâ** *adj.* drinking in gulps; *n.* toast (in honor of someone); **tunggá-tunggâ** *n.* rocking chair.

tunggák: *adj.* stupid, foolish (women).

tunggalî: *n.* conflict, debate; **katunggaliín** *v.* to oppose; dispute; **magtunggalî** *v.* to vie compete.

tunggól: *adj.* beheaded, decapitated.

tunghán: (rt. *tungó*) *v.* to look down to see; read a newspaper.

tungháy: **itungháy** *v.* to raise the head to look up; **tumungháy** *v.* to look up; **nakatungháy** *adj.* looking up.

tungo₁: *n.* goal, purpose; direction; **patungo** *adj.* going to a certain place; *prep.* toward; **patunguhan** *v.* to go to a certain place; **patunguhin** *v.* to send to a certain place; **patútunguhan** *n.* destination; **tumungo** *v.* to go to; **tunguhán** *n.* destination; place where people usually go.

tungo₂: (*reg.*) **makitungo** *v.* to deal with, act toward; **pakikitungo** *n.* dealing with others; attitude; **madalíng pakitunguhan** easy to get along with; **mahusay na pakikitungo** *n.* diplomacy, skill in dealing with people.

tungó: *adj.* with the head bent; stooped; **tumungó** *v.* to bow, look down; **panunghán** *v.* to view from above; overlook; **tunghán** *v.* to look down on; look down.

tungod: **itungod** *v.* to refer to someone's attention; **matungod** *v.* to appertain to, concern; **tungod sa** *prep.* concerning, pertaining to.

tung-ol: *n.* pennant, banner; *adj.* decapitated.

tungtóng: *n.* cover for pots.

tuód: *n.* stump of a tree; answer of a puzzle or riddle; goby; **katuturán** *n.* definition; **parang tuód** *id.* standing firmly.

tuón: *n.* pressure point; **tuunán** *v.* to press down on.

tuón: **katuón** *n.* accomplice; **magkatuón** *v.* to conspire with one another.

tuóng: *n.* bucket, pail, round water tank.

tuóp: *n.* covering with the palm.

tuos: *n.* computation; **tuós** *adj.* computed; **tumuós** *v.* to compute; **tagatuós** *n.* accountant.

tupa: *n.* sheep.

tupâ: **tumupâ** *v.* to press the keys (piano, typewriter); **tupaan** *n.* keyboard.

tupák: *n.* large china jar.

tupád: **tumupád** *v.* to fulfill; carry out; perform, accomplish; **ipatupád** *v.* to enforce, have something performed; **katúpáran** *n.* accomplishment, fulfillment; **matupád** *v.* to be able to comply; to fulfill; consummate; become true; **matúpárin** *adj.* observant; faithful in fulfilling; **pagkatupád** *n.* realization; **pagtupád** *n.* accomplishing, fulfilling; **panunúpáran** *n.* performance (of one's duties); **patuparín** *v.* to order someone to fulfill (a duty); **tagatupád** *n.* executor; **tuparín, tupdín** *v.* to obey an order; fulfill.

tupada: (Sp. *topada*) *n.* illegal cockfighting; picnic.

tupdín: (rt. *tupád*) *v.* to fulfill; obey an order.

tupé: (Eng.) *n.* toupée, small wig.

tupî: *n.* fold, pleat; **tumupî** *v.* to fold.

tupok: **tupukin** *v.* to burn up; **tupók** *adj.* completely burned.

turan: (*rt. tuód*) *v.* to mention; guess the answer of a riddle; **maturan** *v.* to be able to mention; **katuturán** *n.* meaning, importance; term; use, utility; answer to a riddle.

turbante: (Sp.) *n.* turban.

turbina: (Sp.) *n.* turbine.

turkesa: (Sp. *turquesa*) *n.* turquoise.

Turko: *n., adj.* Turk, Turkish.

turing$_1$: **magturing** *v.* to give the answer to a riddle.

turing$_2$: **panuring** *n.* modifier; **tumuring** *v.* to modify (grammar).

turing$_3$: *n.* price offered, quote; remark, name, mention; **ituring** *v.* to name, mention; consider; **waláng-turing** *id.* doesn't reciprocate the debt of gratitude (no bargain).

turismo: (Sp.) *n.* tourism; **turista** *n.* tourist.

turnilyo: (Sp. *tornillo*) *n.* screw; **turnilyo sa utak** *id.* abnormal behavior.

turno: (Sp.) *n.* turn, rotation; lathe; **magturno** *v.* to alternate with each other, take turns.

turò: *n.* teaching, instruction; **magturò** *v.* to teach, tutor; **pagtuturò** *n.* education, teaching; **turuan** *v.* to teach someone, educate; train someone.

turò: *n.* pointing; **hintuturò** *n.* index finger; **iturò** *v.* to show, point, direct; indicate; **panurò** *n.* pointer, indicator; **turu-turò** *n.* kind of restaurant where one points out what one wants; **turuán** *n.* student; teaching; **turuan** *v.* to teach; educate.

turók: *n.* young male deer; small puncture; (*slang*) needle using drug addict; **iturók** *v.* to pierce, inject; **turukán** *v.* to give an injection to; **turukan** *n.* pin cushion.

turól: **paturól** *adj.* (*gram.*) affirmative, indicative.

turón: (Sp. *turrón*) *n.* fritter.

turong: *n.* nipa leaf hat.

tursál: (Sp. *torzal*) *n.* twisted silk cord.

tursido: (Sp. *retorcido*) *adj.* crooked, twisted.

tursilyo: *n.* small barracuda.

turumpó: (Sp.) *n.* spinning top.

tusak: *adj.* more than enough, oversupplied.

tusino: (Sp. *tocino*) *n.* bacon; salted pork.

tusing: **tusíng** *adj.* satiated from overeating.

tuso: *adj.* clever, cunning; sly; astute.

tusok: *n.* piercing, perforating; (*slang*) drug addict; **tusukán** *n.* pin cushion; **tusukan** *v.* to pierce, perforate.

tusol: (*slang*) *n.* stabbing.

tuspirina: (Sp. *tos ferina*) *n.* whooping cough.

tustá: (Sp.) **tustahín** *v.* to toast; **tustado** *adj.*

toasted.

tustós: **tustusán** *v.* to support financially; **panustós** *n.* support, allowance, maintenance; supply.

tutà: *n.* puppy; (*fig.*) blind follower; crony; favorite; spy.

tután: (*slang*) *n.* two pesos.

tuto: *n.* learning; **mátúto** *v.* to learn; **mátutuhan** *v.* to find out; learn; **pagkátúto** *n.* learning; **panuto** *n.* guide; **patuto** *n.* guide; **kapanutuhán** *n.* education; guidance; discipline; propriety.

tutok: *n.* aim; (*slang*) bandit; hold up, point a gun at; **itutok** *v.* to aim; **manutok** *v.* to hold up at the point of a gun; **tutukan** *v.* to aim at someone.

tutog: **magtutog** *v.* to snuff out candles; **panutog** *n.* candle extinguisher.

tutol: *n.* objection, disapproval; opposition; protest; **katutulan** *n.* objection to something; **tutól** *adj.* habitually opposing others; **itutol** *v.* to object to; **tumutol** *v.* to disagree with, object; rebel; **tutulan** *v* to dispute; disagree with; **di-matútutulan** *adj.* indisputable.

tutóng: *n.* rice sticking to the bottom of the pot; (*fig.*) thick dirt on skin.

tutóp: *n.* lining; trimming at the edges; *adj.* caught in the act; covered with the hand; **tutupán** *v.* to line, trim.

tutos: *n.* basting (temporary) stitch; tacking.

tutot: *n.* convex-lined therapon fish.

tutsáng: (Ch. *t^haú cang*: head queue) *n.* very short hair.

tutubí: *n.* dragonfly.

tutulí: *n.* earwax; **tutulihán** *v.* to clean out earwax.

tutyál: (*slang*) *adj.* high-class.

tuwâ: *n.* joy, happiness, fun; **matuwâ** *v.* to enjoy, have fun; **nakatutuwâ** *adj.* funny, amusing; **ikatuwâ** *v.* to amuse, make someone happy; **katuwaan** *n.* fun, merriment.

tuwabak: (Ch.) *n.* big-eyed herring.

tuwakang: (Ch.) *n.* Indian anchovy, *Stolephorus commersoni.*

tuwád: **ituwád** *v.* to bend over (with buttocks up); **nakatuwád** *adj.* bending over with raised buttocks; **tuwaran** *n.* bending down with raised buttocks; (*fig.*) team defeat.

tuwalya: (Sp. *toalla*) *n.* towel; **tuwalyita** *n.* small towel.

tuwáng: *adj.* coordinate (grammar); supported on both sides; **katuwáng** *n.* partner; **tumuwáng** *v.* to help carry a load; **tuwáng-tuwáng** *adj.* in pairs.

tuwás: *adj.* unbalanced; **pantuwás** *n.* weight added to create a balance.

tuwatwa: *n.* white spots on the skin.

tuwáy: *n.* exchange; favor; **tuwayán** *v.* to return a favor.

tuwerka: (Sp. *tuerca*) *n.* nut (carpentry).

tuwî: *adv.* whenever; *adj.* every; **tuwî na** *adv.* always; *conj.* whenever.

tuwíd: *adj.* straight, erect; direct; **ituwíd** *v.* to straighten, correct; **makatwiran** *adj.* rational, reasonable; just; **katwiran** *n.* reason, argument; **matwíd** *adj.* fair, just; legitimate; straight; **tuwiran** *adj.* direct, straight; **walâ sa matwíd** *adj.* unreasonable, irrational.

tuwina: (*tuwî na*) *adv.* always; whenever.

tuyá: *n.* species of herb whose leaves are used to cure gangrenous ulcers.

tuyâ: *n.* sarcastic remark, sarcasm; slur; **pagtuyâ** *n.* sarcasm; **tumuyâ** *v.* to slur, insult, taunt, tease.

tuyo: *n.* goatfish, Family Mullidae.

tuyô$_1$: *adj.* dry; *n.* dried, salted fish; **magpatuyô** *v.* to dry (under the sun); **patuyuan** *n.* dryer.

tuyô$_2$: *n.* tuberculosis.

tuyong: *n.* water added to make up for water lost (in cooking).

tuyót: *adj.* extremely dry; withered; **tagtuyót** *n.* drought; **tuyutín** *v.* to overdry, make wither.

tuytóy: *n.* flask; slowness of action.

U

ubà: *n.* voracious eating.

ubak: *n.* sheath of banana plant; bark.

ubad: *n.* dowry (given by father to his daughter).

uban: *n.* gray hair.

ubaob: *n.* falling of the face; *adj.* face down; vanquished; with the face buried in a pillow.
ubas: (Sp. *uva*) *n.* grape; **ubasán** *n.* vineyard.
ubás$_1$: *n.* woman's first bath after menstruation
ubás$_2$: *n.* residue of *gugò* after juice is extracted; **mag-ubas** *v.* to wear again something already used.
ubayà: *n.* relinquishment; **ipaubayà** *v.* to relinquish.
ubi: *n.* species of purple yam, *Sioscorea alata*; *adj.* purple.
ubò: *n.* act of transplanting.
ubó: *n.* cough; **umubó** *v.* to cough.
ubod: *n.* core; pith; pulp; gist; center.
ubos: *n.* consuming; **ubós** *adj.* consumed, all gone; **ubusin** *v.* to consume; destroy; eat up; **ubus-lakás** *adj.* in full operation or strength
ubrá: *var.* of *obra*; loose bowel movement after taking a laxative or enema; *adj.* possible; useable, acceptable.
ukà: *n.* cavity, shallow hole; engraving, carving; **ukain** *v.* to dig out, hollow out; **ukáukâ** *adj.* full of holes.
ukab: *n.* big bite; **ukabin** *v.* to take a big bite of.
ukang: *n.* slow body movements.
ukáy: *n.* crawling (of a snake).
ukbót: *n.* sitting lazily.
ukilkíl: *n.* persistent questioning or talking; **maukilkíl** *adj.* persistent (in asking or questioning).
ukit: *n.* groove; carving; **ukitan** *v.* to engrave.
uklô: *adj.* stooped from a heavy load.
ukô: **iukô** *v.* to duck the head; bow the head.
uk-ók: *adj.* worn out on the inside (by worms, etc.); sunken in, depressed.
ukód: *n.* bending the head, stooping down.
ukol: *adj.* intended for, destined; *prep.* concerning, regarding; **iukol, mag-ukol** *v.* to intend, set aside for; allot; concern, relate to; **kaukulán** *n.* reference, relation; purpose; grammatical case; suitability; **iniúúkol** *adj.* sacred; dedicated to a certain purpose; **máúkol** *v.* to pertain to; be appropriate; concern, be intended for; **pag-uukol** *n.* application; **pang-ukol** *n.* preposition; **pag-ukúl-ukulin** *v.* to apportion according to suitability; **ukulan** *v.* to set aside (something for a particular purpose); put time into; **sa kináuukulan** to whom it may concern.
ukót: *adj.* slightly bent (body).
ukráy: (*slang*) *adj.* ugly.
ukyabit: **ukyabitin** *v.* to scramble; climb up laboriously.
udlót: *n.* sudden stop or drawing back.
udyók: *n.* urge, incitement; inducement; **mag-udyók** *v.* to urge, prompt, incite, instigate.
ugà: **maugà** *adj.* wobbly, loose; **umugà** *v.* to sway back and forth, be loose.
ugák: *adj.* foolish, stupid; sound of deflation.
ugagà: **di-makaugagà** *adj.* not able to move or cope with; incapacitated.
ugalì: *n.* custom, habit; tradition; style; way;; manners; **nakaugalián** *adj.* usual, customary, **ugaliin** *v.* to make a custom of; **kinaugalián** *adj.* accustomed, ordinary; **makiugalì** *v.* to adopt the custom of; **ugaling-hayop** *id.* with a despicable character, animal instinct.
ugaog: *n.* act of shaking.
ugát: *n.* root; origin; vein, artery; **salitáng-ugát** *n.* root word; **kaugát** *adj.* sharing the same root (grammatical); **mag-ugát** *v.* to grow roots; **ugatin** *v.* to trace the origin or source of.
ugáw: *n.* large ape; *adj.* stupid.
ugit: *n.* rudder, helm; **umugit** *v.* to steer; manage.
ugmâ: *n.* connection; *adj.* well-adjusted; fit, proper; **iugmâ** *v.* to join, fit; **kaugmaán** *n.* harmony.
ugnáy: *n.* connection, relation; relevance; **iugnáy** *v.* to relate, associate; **palaugnayan** *n.* syntax; **pang-ugnáy** *n.* conjunction.
ugók: *n.* rumbling sound of a hungry stomach; *adj.* stupid.
ugód: *adj.* decrepit; **umugúd-ugód** *v.* to walk like an old person.
ug-óg: **ug-ugín** *v.* to shake violently.
ugong: *n.* roaring; howling; reverberating sound.
ugoy: **ugoy-ugoy** *n.* prostitute; taxi-dancer; slow dance movement; (*slang*) rock and roll; marijuana.
ugóy: *n.* swing, cradle, sway; dangling.

uguna: *n.* Philippine weaver bird.
ugwâ: *n.* overflowing of boiling water.
ugwák: *n.* bubbling, gushing up.
uhâ: *n.* cry of a newborn infant.
uhales: (Sp. *ojal*) *n.* buttonhole.
uhaw: *n.* thirst; **mauhaw** *adj.* thirsty.
uhay: *n.* ear of grain; **mag-uhay** *v.* to bear grain.
uhetes: (Sp. *ojete*) *n.* eyelets (in clothes).
uhiya: (Sp. *ojear*) *n.* evil eye (witchcraft).
uhô: **mag-uhô** *v.* to pour out; dump.
uhog: *n.* snivel, nasal mucus; **mag-uhóg** *v.* to snivel, have a nose run; **malauhog** *adj.* mucuslike; **uhugin** *adj.* with a runny nose; (*fig.*) immature child.
ulabát: **mangulabát** *v.* to walk around by holding onto things (babies).
ulak: *n.* reel, spool.
ulag: *n.* molting of fowls.
ulalò: *n.* sweet potato grub. (*tangà*)
ulam: *n.* viand, something eaten with rice.
ulán: *n.* rain; **tag-ulán** *n.* rainy season; **umulán** *v.* to rain; **umúulán-ulán** *v.* raining on and off; **mag-uulán** *v.* to rain continuously; **maulanán** *v.* to get wet by the rain; **pang-ulán** *adj.* for the rainy season; **paulanán ng bala** *v.* to shower with bullets; **uláng-tikatík** *n.* light, continuous rain.
Ulandés: (Sp. *holandés*) *n.* Dutch; blond.
uláng: *n.* lobster; crayfish.
ulaol: *n.* pushing with the tip (i.e. tongue).
ulap: *n.* cloud; fog; mist; **maulap** *adj.* cloudy, misty, hazy; **pagkamaulap** *n.* cloudiness; **papag-ulapin** *v.* to cloud, fog.
ulapihan: *n.* scorpion. (*alupihan*)
ulapot: *n.* small bag.
ulasiman: *n.* water hyssop.
ulat: *n.* report, account; statement; record; **mag-ulat** *v.* to report, tell, give an account of; declare; **iulat** *v.* to report, recount; **di-maulatan** *adj.* unable to be expressed in words.
ulay: *n.* intestinal worm.
ulayaw: *n.* intimate conversation, tête-à-tête.
ulbô: *n.* pigsty.
ulbók: *n.* bulge, protuberance.
uldóg: *n.* member of a religious order; (*coll.*) *adj.* stupid.
ule: (Sp. *hule*) *n.* oil cloth.
ulì: *n.* wandering; **paulí-ulì** *adv.* to and fro, going and returning; **mang-ulì** *v.* to be restored to a former position.
ulî: *adv.* again; **umulî** *v.* to do again; **iulî** *v.* to return to the original place; restore; put back. **isaulì** *v.* to return, give back; **manaulì** *v.* to return, revert; **sumag-ulì** *v.* to return to a former state. [See also *saulì*]
ulián: (*rt.* *ulî*) *adj.* eccentric; senile; **pagka-ulian** *n.* senility.
ulik: *n.* hesitation; **ulik-ulik** *adj.* hesitant; doubtful.
ulikbâ: *n.* fowl with dark meat.
ulik-ulik: *adj.* uncertain; hesitant.
ulila: *n.* orphan; **mangulila** *v.* to feel like an orphan, miss one's parents; **maulila** *v.* to be orphaned; **ulilang-lubós** *id.* without father or mother.
ulinig: *n.* sense of hearing; **ulinigin** *v.* to listen to; **maulinigan** *v.* to happen to hear.
uling: *n.* charcoal; soot.
ulipás: *adj.* oblique; slanting; biased.
ulipores: *n.* obsequious followers.
ulirán: (*rt.* *ulid*) *n.* model, standard, norm; pattern; example; **uliranín** *v.* to imitate (a model); idealize.
ulirát: *n.* sense, consciousness; **waláng-ulirát** *adj.* unconscious.
ulit: *n.* repetition; *adj.* done in return; **káuulit** *n.* continuous repetition; **maulit** *adj.* repetitious; insistent; **mag-ulit** *v.* to repeat; **paulit-ulit** *adj.* continual; repeated; constantly; **ulitin** *v.* to repeat; reproduce; **ulít-ulitin** *v.* to keep repeating; **umulit** *v.* to repeat, do over.
uliuli: *n.* eddy. (*alimpuyó*)
ulo: *n.* head; chief; heading; **mangulo** *v.* to head; preside; **pangulo** *n.* chief, president; **magpaulo** *v.* to overfill; **magsaulo, sauluhin** *v.* to memorize; **mang-ulo** *v.* to butt with the head; **pagkapangulo** *n.* presidency; **pampánguluhán** *adj.* presidential; **paulo** *adj.* heaping; **tagapangulo** *n.* chairman; **uluhin** *v.* to butt with the head; **ulunán** *n.* head (of a bed, table, etc.); **basag-ulo** trouble, fight; **katigasán ng ulo** *n.* stubbornness; **mainit**

ang ulo *adj.* grumpy, quick tempered; **may ulo** *id.* intelligent.
ulok: **umulok** *v.* to coax, induce; urge.
ulóg: **naulóg** *adj.* deserted; evacuated.
ulól: *adj.* crazy, insane; foolish; **ululín** *v.* to fool.
ulong: *n.* intimate conversation.
ulop: *n.* fog; mist.
ulos: **ulusin** *v.* to pierce with a long, pointed weapon.
ulót: *n.* provocation.
ulpót: *n.* sticking out (over the surface).
úlsera: (Sp. *úlcera*) *n.* ulcer.
ultáw: *adj.* sticking out (with head over the surface).
último: (Sp.) *adj.* last.
ultók: (*slang*, f. *ulo* + *katók*) *adj*. crazy.
ulumbayan. [*ulo-ng-bayan*] *n.* capital; head of a town.
ulumbubóng [*ulo-ng-bubóng*] *n.* ridge of a roof.
ulunán: (*rt. ulo*) *n.* head of a bed.
ulupóng: *n.* Philippine cobra; (*fig.*) treacherous person, traitor.
ulupót: *n.* sticking out (head over surface).
ulúuló: *n.* tadpole, polliwog.
ul(u)wâ: *adj.* sticking out; bulging out.
ulyabid: *n.* tapeworm.
ulyáw: *n.* reverberation.
-um-: *infix.* Verbalizing infix placed before the first vowel of a root, may express simple acts, natural phenomena, bodily functions, and inchoative states → **gumandá** to become beautiful; **umihì** to urinate, **umamà** to become tame, **pumuntá** to go, **humiwalay** to separate, divorce, **umulán** to rain.
umaga: (*rt. aga*) *n.* morning; **kaumagahan** *n.* next morning; **umagahin** *v.* to be overtaken by the morning.
umanó: (*rt. anó*) *v.* to do (used interrogatively); **di-umanó** they say, it is said.
umang: *n.* trap, snare.
umat: **pagpaumat** *n.* slowness.
umay: **maumay** *v.* to be tired of (a certain food).
umbág: (*slang, Cebuano*) *n.* punch, beating up; **umbagero** *n.* brave man.
umbáng: *n.* rooting with the snout; **umbangín** *v.* to push or root with the snout.
umbáw: (*slang*) *n.* dominant male.
umbók: *n.* bulge; swelling; lump; convex surface; **umumbók** *v.* to swell, bulge.
umbóng: **maumbóng** *adj.* overflowing.
umboy: (Ch.) *n.* smoking meat or fish; (*slang*) beating up.
umbrera: (Sp. *hombrera*) *n.* yoke.
umedád: (Sp. *humedad*) *n.* humidity.
úmido: (Sp. *humedo*) *adj.* humid.
umento: (Sp. *aumento*) *n.* raise; increase in salary.
umíd: *adj.* speechless.
umis: *n.* slight smile; **umisan** *v.* to smile slightly at.
umít: *n.* theft, pilfering; pickpocketing.
umok: *n.* small worm found in grains.
umog: *n.* attack by a group of persons on an individual.
umpís: *adj.* deflated.
umpisá: (Sp. *empezar*) *n.* start, beginning.
umpók: *n.* small group of people, gathering.
umpóg: *n.* bumping; collision.
una: *adj.* first; primary, chief; previous; former; *adv.* ahead; in the beginning; **kaunahán** *n.* primacy; **kauná-unahan** *adj.* first; earliest; **makauna** *v.* to be able to be or do first; **magpáuná** *v.* to advance, precede; lead; **mag-uná** *v.* to make down payment; **mag-unahán** *v.* to try to get ahead of others, compete to be first; **manguna** *v.* to do better than, lead; precede; excel; **iuna** *v.* to put before; prefix; **ipáuná** *v.* to do first; **máuná** *v.* to do before; precede; **máunahan** *v.* to get ahead; take possession; **pagkáuná** *n.* priority; **páuná** *adj.* preliminary; *adv.* beforehand; **pag-una** *n.* start; **panguna** *adj.* initial; first; **pangunahan** *v.* to start, spearhead; advise beforehand; **pángunahín** *adj.* main, principal; foremost; major; **pangunguna** *n.* precedence; initiative; **sa una, sinauna** ancient, antiquated, archaic; **sáunahín** *adj.* primitive; simple; **tagapagpáuná** *n.* forerunner; **tagapanguna** *n.* spearhead; **unahán** *n.* front, forepart; **umuna** *v.* to go before, do ahead of; **unahin** *v.* to do first; **una-una** *adv.*

one by one; primarily; principally; **mangu-nang-baít** *v.* to give advice without being asked; **nang káuná-unahan** for the first time; **pángunahíng urì** first class; **páunáng salitâ** *n.* foreword; preface.

unab: *n.* fatty substance; **unaban** *v.* to remove the fatty substance from the surface of a liquid.

unan: *n.* pillow; **unan-unanan** *n.* a small pillow.

unano: (Sp. *enano*) *n.* dwarf.

unang-: *pref.* first → **unang-benta** first sale, **unang-una** the very first.

unat: **umunat** *v.* to straighten out; **unát** *adj.* straight, stretched; **mag-unat** *v.* to stretch out; straighten out; **mag-umunat** *v.* to stretch oneself to the limit.

unawà: *n.* understanding; notion, idea; perception; **ipaunawà** *v.* to get someone to understand; **makáunawà** *v.* to understand; **mag-únawaan** *v.* to come to an understanding; **máunawaan** *v.* to understand; perceive; realize; figure out; **maunawaín** *adj.* understanding; broad minded; **pagkamaunawaín** *n.* broad mindedness; **pang-unawà** *n.* comprehension; intelligence; **paunawà** *n.* notice, notification; warning; **umunawà** *v.* to understand; **únawaán** *n.* mutual understanding; **unawain** *v.* to heed, pay attention to.

unay: **mag-unay** *v.* to crush lice between the fingernails.

undáp: *n.* flickering of light.

undás: *var.* of *undrás*: All Saints' Day.

undayon: *var. of indayon*: swing.

undók: *n.* oscillation.

undót: *n.* falling back when startled.

undrás: (Sp.) *n.* All Saints' Day.

unibersál: (Sp. *universal*) *adj.* universal.

universidád: (Sp. *universidad*) *n.* university.

uniporme: (Sp. *uniforme*) *n.* uniform. **unipormado** *adj.* wearing a uniform.

unipormidád: (Sp.) *n.* uniformity.

unlák: **paunlakán** *v.* to oblige; favor; give in to a request.

unlád: **pag-unlád** *n.* growth, progress, improvement; **magpaunlád** *v.* to develop, promote, foster; **maunlád** *adj.* progressive, prosperous; **paunlarín** *v.* to develop, foster, promote; **umunlád** *v.* to prosper, improve; progress.

unlapì: *n.* prefix. **unlapian** *v.* to prefix.

unó: **umunú-unó** *v.* to stammer.

uno: (Sp.) *n.* one.

unós: *n.* squall, strong wind with rain; wood borer, weevil.

unsí: (Sp. *uncir*) **iunsi** *v.* to harness a horse.

unsík: *adj.* tiny, miniscule.

unsiyamî: *adj.* frustrated; unsuccessful; stunted in growth. **unsiyamiín** *v.* to frustrate.

unsóy: (Ch.) *n.* coriander.

unsyón: (Sp. *unción*) *n.* unction, ointment.

untág: *n.* reminder; **untagín** *v.* to remind.

untáy: *adj.* twisted (rope).

untî: **kauntî** *n.* bit, small amount; **kauntián** *n.* smallness, littleness; **muntî** *adj.* little, small; **kaú-kauntî** *adv.* a little at a time; **pinakakauntî** *adj.* minimum; **umuntî** *v.* to decrease, diminish; **untián** *v.* to make less, smaller; **untí-untî** *adv.* little by little; **untí-untiín** *v.* to do little by little; use sparingly.

untík: *n.* closeness; **untík-untík** *adv.* in small bits.

untóg: *n.* bump on the head.

untól: *n.* sudden stop; temporary stop; **umuntól** *v.* to suddenly stop; be retarded.

untós: *n.* decrease; **umuntós** *v.* to decrease; diminish; subside.

unyón: (Sp. *unión*) *n.* union; unity.

ungâ: **umungâ** *v.* to moo (cows).

ungab: *n.* big hole, cavity; big bite.

ungág: *adj.* stupid; foolish.

ungal: *n.* howling, roar of animals.

ungás: *adj.* stupid; rude, crude.

ungkát: *n.* mention of something forgotten. **umungkát** *v.* to recall; bring up again.

ungkô: *n.* sitting with the back bent forward.

ungkót: **pag-ungkót** *n.* sitting around idly.

unggî: *adj.* tailless (cats, dogs).

unggô, unggóy: *n.* monkey.

unggók: (*slang*) *adj.* stupid.

ungguwento: (Sp. *unguento*) *n.* ointment.

ungî: *adj.* tilted; (*reg.*) harelipped.

ungol: *n.* growl; grumble.

ungós$_1$: *n.* snout; upper lip.

ungós$_2$: *n.* ledge, projection; advantage, superiority.
ungót: *n.* mumbling; whining; whimpering.
ungóy: (*slang*) *n.* fight, quarrel.
uód: *n.* worm, grub; maggot; **may uod sa katawán** *id.* restless.
uóm: *n.* nightmare; **uumín** *v.* to have a nightmare; be suffocated while sleeping.
upa: *n.* rent; hire; wage; **magpaupa** *v.* to rent out; **mangupahan** *v.* to rent; be a tenant; **mángungupahan** *n.* tenant; **mapaupahan** *v.* to be rented; **pag-upa** *n.* hire; lease; **pagpapaupa** *n.* hiring; **paupahan** *v.* to hire out; lease; charter; **pinaúupahan** *adj.* for rent; **umupa** *v.* to rent; hire; **upahan** *v.* to lease, rent out; **kaupahán** *n.* actual compensation for work done.
upak$_1$: *n.* bark; husk, sheathing.
upak$_2$: **upakan** *v.* to eat with relish; attack cruelly, punch.
upang: *conj.* in order to; in order that; so; whereby; **upang dî** *conj.* lest.
upas: **upasan** *v.* to remove all the leaves.
upasalà: *n.* berating; abusive language; **upasalain** *v.* to berate; use abusive language against.
upat: **umupat** *v.* to instigate, urge on by intrigue.
upaw: **upáw** *adj.* bald; **upawín** *v.* to shave off all hair.
upisina: (Sp. *oficina*) *n.* office.
upisiyo: (Sp. *oficio*) *n.* employment, occupation; trade.
uplak: **kauplakán** *n.* extreme hunger.
upo: *n.* bottle gourd, *Lagenaria siceraria*).
upô: *n.* sitting; **umupô** *v.* to sit; **iupô** *v.* to seat; **palaupô** *adj.* sedentary; **paupuín** *v.* to have someone sit down; **úpúan** *n.* seat; **upuán, upán** *v.* to sit on.
upód: *adj.* worn out.
upong: *n.* end point.
upóng: **upungán** *v.* to feed a fire (with wood).
upós: *n.* cigar butt; butt of a candle, stub; *adj.* consumed to the butt; submerged to the bottom; **naúupós na kandilà** *id.* losing consciousness (melted candle).
uralì: *n.* instigation through intrigue or deception.
Urano: (Eng.) *n.* Uranus.
uranyo: (Sp. *uranio*) *n.* uranium.
urang: *n.* picket, stake (for fencing).
uráng: (*slang*) *n.* house help.
uraw: *n.* loud cry.
uray: *n.* thorny amaranth weed.
urbanidád: (Sp.) *n.* urbanity; good manners.
urì: *n.* kind, class; sort; species; type; **kaurì** *adj.* of the same kind; **makaurì** *adj.* adjectival; **magkaurì** *v.* to be the same, of the same kind; **mag-urì** *v.* to classify; **pang-urì** *n.* adjective; **uri-urì** *adj.* of all kinds, various.
urikál: *n.* ringing of bells.
uríg: (*slang*) *n.* made-to-order clothing; *adj.* spiffy, dressed well.
uriles: *n.* hardtail fish
urirà: *n.* teasing; joke; inquisitiveness; **maurirà** *adj.* inquisitive.
urirat: *var. of urirà*: persistent asking.
uriraw: *n.* kind of small black bird with a blue breast.
uriya: (Sp. *orilla*) *n.* selvage; edge of a fabric that is finished off to prevent unraveling.
urna: (Sp.) *n.* urn; ballot box.
urong: **pag-urong** *n.* retreat, backward movement; recoil; postponement; **umurong** *v.* to retreat, recede, withdraw; retract; go back; **mangurong** *v.* to shrink; **maurong** *v.* to be revoked; postponed; **pagkakapaurong** *n.* repelling; repulse; **pauróng** *adv.* backward; **urong-sulong** *adj.* indecisive, hesitation.
urót: (*slang*) *n.* teaser.
uróy: *n.* mockery.
urtikarya: (Sp. *urticaria*) *n.* urticaria; rash.
usá: *n.* deer; **usáng reno** *n.* reindeer.
usád$_1$: **pag-usad** *n.* moving along on one's buttocks; **usad-uód** *n.* slow moving.
usád$_2$: *n.* review; **usaran** *n.* simultaneous review.
usál: **usalín** *v.* to say repeatedly in whispers or chants.
usang: *n.* dripping of candle wax.
usap: **usap, úsápan** *n.* conversation; talking to each other; **kumausap, kausapin** *v.* to speak with, converse; **makiusap** *v.* to request, ask for; plead; **makipag-usap** *v.* to converse,

communicate with; **nangúngúsap** *adj.* expressive, verbally eloquent; **pakikipag-usap** *n.* conversation; **pakikiusap, pakiusap** *n.* request, plea; **pakiusapan** *v.* to beg, entreat; **pag-usapan** *v.* to discuss; talk about; **pag-uusap** *n.* conversation; **pangungusap** *n.* remark; expression; sentence; **pinag-úusapan** *n.* point (subject of conversation); court case; *adj.* in question, at hand, at issue; **usapín** *n.* lawsuit, case; **usáp-úsapan** *n.* circulating news; gossip, rumors; **labis na pangungusap** *n.* exaggeration; overstatement; **usapang-maginoó** *id.* gentleman's agreement.

usbíng: (*slang*) *n.* peeping Tom.

usbóng: *n.* sprout, bud; (*fig.*) progress; **umusbóng** *v.* to sprout.

usig: **umusig** *v.* to prosecute; persecute; **taga-usig** *n.* prosecutor; **pag-uusig** *n.* investigation; persecution.

usisà: *n.* inquiry, investigation; **mausisà** *adj.* curious; inquisitive; **usisain** *v.* to inquire; examine, investigate; **usisero** *adj.* inquisitive.

uslak: *adj.* silly, foolish.

uslî: *n.* projection; bulge; *adj.* protruding, projecting; prominent; **umuslî** *v.* to protrude, jut out.

usngál: *adj.* protruding (teeth).

uso: (Sp.) *n.* style, fashion; **mauso** *v.* to be in style.

usok: *n.* smoke, fumes, vapor; (*slang*) marijuana; **mausok** *adj.* smoky; **umusok** *v.* to smoke, fume; **pausok** *n.* cigarette lighter, matches; **umúusok ang tuktók** *id.* braggart.

usog: *n.* stomach gas, flatulence. **usugín** *adj.* prone to flatulence.

usong: *n.* mutual carrying of a load.

us-ós: *n.* slipping, sliding down.

usuos: *n.* fresh-water garfish.

usura: (Sp.) *n.* usury; high rate of interest.

usurero: (Sp.) *n.* usurer.

usurpadór: (Sp.) *n.* usurper.

usurya: (Sp.) *n.* usury; **usurero** *n.* usurer.

utab: *var. of kutab*: mortise made on the side of a board.

utak: *n.* brain; **mautak** *adj.* brainy, clever; ~ **sa butó** *n.* marrow; **utak-biyâ** *id.* stupid (goby brain); **waláng utak** *id.* stupid, with a poor memory; **utak-lamók** *id.* stupidity.

utál: *adj.* stuttering, stammering; **umutál-utál** *v.* to stutter, stammer; **mápautál-utál** *v.* to falter; **pagkautál** *n.* stuttering.

utan: *n.* species of weed.

utang: *n.* debt; debit; bill; loan; **mangutang** *v.* to borrow; **umutang** *v.* to borrow, get a loan; **utangin** *v.* to borrow; **pautang** *n.* loan; **pa-utangin** *v.* to lend; **pagkautangan** *v.* to be in debt to someone; **utang-na-loób** *n.* debt of gratitude; **waláng-utang-na-loób** *adj.* ungrateful; **umutang ng buhay** *id.* murder (borrow life).

utangero: *n.* debtor.

utás: *adj.* terminated, finished; dead; obsessed.

utaw: *n.* soybean.

utáw: (*slang*) *n.* man.

utáy-utáy: *adv.* little by little; gradually. **utay-utayín** *v.* to do little by little.

utdó: **umutdó** *v.* to be short, lack the required length. **utduhán** *v.* to shorten.

útero: (Sp.) *n.* uterus.

util: (Sp.) *adj.* useful; **utilidád** *n.* utility.

utin: *n.* penis.

utità: *var. os usisà*: inquisitive.

utitab: *n.* species of small spider; mucus film on the eyeball.

utô: (Ch.) *n.* simpleton; fool; **utó-utô** (*slang*) *n.* blindly following someone.

utód: *adj.* cut off at the end; worn-off at the end.

utog: *n.* libido, sexual urge.

utol: (*coll.*) *n.* term for one's sibling.

utóng: *n.* nipple, teat.

utos: *n.* command, order; **utusan** *v.* to order, command; assign; **utusán** *n.* servant; **pala-utós** *adj.* bossy; **pautós** *adj.* imperative; **iutos** *v.* to command, order; tell to do; **kautusán** *n.* order, mandate; commandment; rules; **utos-harì** *n.* strict order.

utót: *n.* fart, anal gas; **umutót** *v.* to fart.

ut-ot: **umut-ót** *v.* to suck the teat of; **ka-ututang-dilà** *id.* friend (tongue sucking mate).

utúutô: *adj.* idiotic, foolish.

uúm: *n.* nightmare; dying in one's sleep.

uwák: *n.* crow, raven.

uwáng: *n.* horned beetle.
uwáy: *n.* species of rattan used in wickerwork.
uwî: *n.* something brought home; **pag-uwî** *n.* returning home; **umuwî** *v.* to go home; **ma-uwî** *v.* to develop into; happen as a result; **pauwî** *adj.* on the way home; **pauwiín** *v.* to send home; **uwián** *n.* usual time to go home, dismissal time.
uwido: (Sp. *oído*) *n.* ear for music.
uya: (Sp. *olla*) *n.* earthen jar with a narrow mouth.
uyad: **pauyad-uyad** *adj.* walking awkwardly.
uyám: *n.* mocking; sarcasm; **uyamín** *v.* to mock, taunt.
uyan: *n.* compensation.
uyaw: *n.* ridicule.
uyayi: *n.* lullaby.
uyóg: **uyugán** *v.* to incite, induce (to do something bad).
uyót: *n.* frustration; loss of balance; **uyutín** *v.* to frustrate; cause one to lose his balance.

W

wa₁: *interj.* expresses surprise; Shoo!
wa₂: *var.* of *walâ* used in certain colloquial expressions: **wa-datúng** having no money, flat broke; **wa-epék** having no effect; **wa ka na** you're hopeless.
wa₃: *n.* the letter *w*.
waak: *n.* large tear or rip.
waág: *adj.* open, clean (space).
waang: *n.* big gaping hole; long rip.
wakaak: **iwakaak** *v.* to isolate, exile.
wakás: *n.* end, conclusion; **magwakás** *v.* to terminate, end; **pawakás** *adj.* about to end; **wakasán** *v.* to end, stop; wind up, settle; **wa-kasan** *adv.* finally, once and for all; **pang-wakás** *adj.* final, conclusive; last.
wakawak: *adj.* exposed to danger of the elements; falling into disrepute.
wakiwak: **pagwawakiwak** *n.* hoisting up.
waklás: *n.* ripping; *adj.* ripped open.
waklî: **mawaklî** *v.* to be out of sight; be misplaced.
waksi: **iwaksí** *v.* to shake off; drive away, get rid of.
wakwák: *n.* long tear or rip.
wakyâ: *n.* tidiness, neatness.
wadá: (*slang*) *adj.* having nothing at all.
wadwád: *adj.* exposed, uncovered.
wagás: *adj.* pure; perfect.
wagawag: **iwagawag** *v.* to shake in order to clean.
wagaywáy: **iwagaywáy** *v.* to wave about; **wumagaywáy** *v.* to flutter, wave about; flaunt.
wagí: *n.* winning; **magwagí** *v.* to win, triumph; **mapagwagí** *adj.* triumphant.
waglít: **mawaglít** *adj.* to be misplaced, mislaid; **iwaglít sa alaala** *v.* to erase from one's memory.
wagwág: *n.* variety of rice; wagging motion; shaking in order to dry or clean.
wahak: *n.* long rip or tear.
wahì: *n.* part (dividing line); dispersal of smoke, clouds, etc; **wahiin** *v.* to part (hair); disperse.
wahíl: **magwahíl** *v.* to divide up property of a deceased person without a will.
wail: *n.* slight turn (in a boat).
waíng: (*slang*) *adv.* none at all.
waís: (*slang*) *n.* boyfriend; girlfriend.
walâ: *pron.* none, no, nothing, not any; without; lacking; absent; **kawalán** *n.* loss, lack; absence; negation; need; default; **iwalâ** *v.* to misplace, miss; lose; **makawalâ** *v.* to miss, lose; escape, get free; **mawalâ** *v.* to be lost; disappear; **mawalán** *v.* to lose, miss; **mapawalán** *v.* to set free; deny, refuse to give what someone asks; annul; **nawalâ** *adj.* missing, lost; gone; **nakakawalâ** *adj.* loose; free; **pagkawalâ** *n.* disappearance; **pagkawa-láng-kamátáyan** *n.* immortality; **ipagsa-waláng-bahalà, ipagsawaláng-kibô** *v.* to ignore.
walandyó: (*slang*) *exp.* good.
waláng-: (rt. *walâ*) *pref.* privative prefix, without → **waláng-alam** *adj.* ignorant, without knowing; **waláng-kusà** *adj.* without initiative; **waláng-pusò** *adj.* heartless; **waláng-malay-tao** *adj.* unconscious;

magwaláng-bahalà *v.* to not pay attention to; **waláng-antala** *adj.* without delay; **waláng-kasya** *adj.* with no suitable size.

walas: *n.* open, clear space.

walastík: *interj.* wow!

walat: **walát** *adj.* destroyed, demolish; **walatin** *v.* to destroy.

walawalà: *n.* distracting one's attention; pretending ignorance or indifference.

walay: *n.* separating; weaning; **mawalay** *v.* to be separated; be weaned; **magwalay** *v.* to separate from.

waldás: **magwaldás** *v.* to waste money, squander.

waligwíg: **waligwigán** *v.* to sprinkle water on.

walíng-bahalà: *v.* to disregard.

waling-waling: *n.* wild orchid.

walís: *n.* broom; **walisín** *v.* to sweep away; **magwalís** *v.* to sweep; **waliswalisan** *n.* broom weed; **walís-tingtíng** *n.* palm leaf broom; *id.* thin as a rod.

walís-haba: *n.* common weed, *Sida rhombifolia.*

waliswís: *n.* swishing sound of branches in the wind.

waliwali: *adj.* close to the time of delivery (pregnant woman); *n.* defective eyesight caused by hunger.

walnâ: *n.* varicolored cloth.

waló: *n.* eight; **walumpû** *n.* eighty; **labingwaló** *n.* eighteen.

walúng-kuwarta: *n.* five centavos.

walwál: *adj.* spread out; wide open.

waní: *n.* manner of doing; help; **kawaní** *n.* employee; **kawanihán** *n.* bureau.

wansóy: (Ch.) *n.* coriander.

wangkî: *adj.* similar in appearance.

wangga: (*slang*) *n.* mother.

wanggo: (*slang*) *n.* father.

wangis: **kawangis** *adj.* similar, resembling; **magkawangis** *v.* to resemble.

wango: (*slang*) *adj.* drunk.

wangwáng: *adj.* wide-open.

warák, warát: (*slang*) *adj.* high on drugs.

waráy: *adj.* dilapidated.

Waráy: *n.* native of Samar-Leyte; **Waráy-waray** *n.* the language of the *Waráy.*

wardí: **wardihín** *v.* to do carelessly.

warì: *n.* opinion, estimation; *adv.* it seems; **wari-warì** *n.* idea, vague opinion; **magwari-warì** *v.* to meditate, reflect upon.

wasák: *n.* ruin; **wasák** *adj.* ruined, destroyed; **iwasák** *v.* to ruin, destroy.

wasiwas: *n.* waving in the air.

wasò: (Ch.) *adj.* not properly done or made.

wastô: *adj.* correct, proper; **kawastuán** *n.* correctness; justice; **pagwawastô** *n.* revision; redress; **magwastô** *v.* to correct, put in order.

waswás: **magwaswás** *v.* to wave in the air continuously.

waswit: (*slang*) *n.* wife.

waták: **waták-waták** *adj.* scattered; disunited.

watas: **mawatasan** *v.* to be understood; **pawatás** *adj.* infinitive.

watawat: *n.* flag, banner.

watíng-watíng: *adj.* blurred, dim (eyesight).

watiwat: (*slang*) *n.* wife.

watók: (*slang*) *adj.* child-like; soybeans.

watot: (*slang*) *n.* spouse.

watusi: (*slang*) *n.* firecrackers.

wawà: *see awà.*

wawà$_1$: *n.* mouth of a river.

wawà$_2$: (Ch.) *n.* meaning; **kawawaan** *n.* real meaning; point; **waláng-kawawaan** *adj.* pointless, meaningless.

waywáy: *n.* act of waving the hand to signal someone; entire length.

wayukak: (Ch.) *n.* bronze container which holds borax and water for welding.

webera: (Sp. *huevera*) *n.* egg cup.

welga: (Sp. *huelga*) *n.* workers' strike; **welgista** *n.* striker.

wengweng: (*slang*) *n.* short person.

wenggól: (*slang*) *adj.* drunk.

weyter: (Eng.) *n.* waiter. (*serbidór*)

weytres: (Eng.) *n.* waitress. (*serbidora*)

wikà: *n.* language; dialect; **kawikaán** *n.* saying, proverb; **magwikà** *v.* to say; **pagwikaan** *v.* to insult someone with words; **wikain** *v.* to express verbally; **wikaín** *n.* idiomatic expression; **salawikaín** *n.* proverb, saying; motto; **dalubwikà** *n.* linguist. **wikang banyagà, wikang dayuhan** *n.* foreign language; **wikang katutubo** *n.* native language;

wikang pampánitikán *n.* literary language; **wikang pandaigdíg** *n.* international language.

wiklás: *adj.* tore off. **wiklasín** *v.* to pull apart forcibly.

wiklát: *adj.* dilated. **wiklatín** *v.* to dilate.

wigwíg: **wigwigán** *v.* to sprinkle water on clothes before ironing.

wili: *n.* enjoyment; *adj.* interesting, absorbing; **kawili-wili** *adj.* interesting, pleasing, entertaining; **wilihin** *v.* to keep one's interest; **wilíng-wilí** *adj.* with one's full attention and interest.

wilíg: *n.* sprinkling. **iwilíg** *v.* to sprinkle water; **pangwilíg** *n.* sprinkler.

wiliwíd: *adj.* awry; askew.

wilwíl: *n.* shaking something violently.

windang: *adj.* torn apart; **windangín** *v.* to tear to bits.

wingkág: *n.* prying open; **wingkagín** *v.* to pry open.

wingkî: *adj.* slanting, oblique.

wisík: **wisikán** *v.* to spray or sprinkle on.

wisít: (Ch.) *n.* mascot (kept for good luck).

wiswís: *n.* species of grasshopper; *var. of wagiswís.*

witwít: **witwitán** *v.* to shake the finger at.

Y

'y: *contr.* Contraction of *ay* after vowels and sometimes after a dropped *n*.

ya: *n.* the letter *y*.

yaang: *n.* threatening gesture of the hand.

yabág: *n.* step; sound of footsteps.

yabang: **mayabang** *adj.* boastful, proud; **yumabang** *v.* to boast, brag; **mapagmayabáng** *adj.* boastful, arrogant.

yabó: *n.* looseness of the soil; sponginess of tubers.

yabong: **mayabong** *adj.* leafy, luxuriant (foliage).

yabúl: (*slang*, German *ja wohl*) *adj.* beautiful.

yakà: (*slang*) **yakang-yakà** can do, no problem.

yakag: *n.* invitation; persuasion; **magyakág** *v.* to invite, persuade to do.

yakál: *n.* kind of lumber tree, *Hopea flagata.*

Yakan: *n.* ethnic group and language from Basilan Island.

yakap: *n.* embrace, hug; **yumakap** *v.* to embrace, hug; **yakap-Hudas** *n.* treachery; pretense.

yakbí: (*slang*) *n.* half-sibling; equal profit sharing.

yakis: *n.* friction, rubbing against; sharpening blades.

yakyák: *n.* foolish talk; act of trampling or crushing.

yagang: *n.* emaciation, extreme thinness.

yagbán: *n.* route.

yagít: *n.* vagrant; flotsam, rubbish; *adj.* poor; dirty.

yago: *n.* sap; juice.

yagong: *n.* extreme thinness, emaciation.

yagpág: **pamamayagpág** *n.* flapping, fluttering of wings.

yagyág: *n.* trot; jogging gait.

yahod: **yumahod** *v.* to rub with pressure.

yamâ: *n.* sense of touch.

yaman: *n.* wealth, treasure, riches; **mayaman** *adj.* rich, wealthy; **payamanin** *v.* to enrich; treasure, value highly; **yumaman** *v.* to become rich.

yamang: *conj.* since, because.

yamás: *n.* bagasse, plant residue.

yambâ: *n.* threatening gesture; **yambaán** *v.* to threaten.

yamò: *n.* stubble (of beard or cuttings).

yamót: *n.* annoyance; disgust; boredom; *adj.* irritated, annoyed; **yamutín** *v.* to annoy, irritate, harass.

yamukmók: *n.* annoyance caused by waiting.

yamungmóng: *n.* luxuriant foliage; shade; **yamungmungán** *v.* to place under one's care; cast a shadow on.

yamutmót: *n.* rubbish; frayed ends of thread.

yandatíg: (*slang*) *n.* variety store.

yaníg: *n.* tremor, shaking; vibration; (*slang*) *adj.* surprised, shocked.

yano: (Sp. *llano*) *n.* plain; *adj.* level.

yanot: *n.* coconut husk fibers; frayed threads.

yansumí: (*slang*) *adj*. beautiful.
yantadíg: (*slang*) *n*. variety store.
yantás: *n*. rim of a wheel; *adj*. thin and dried up.
yantáw: (*slang*) *adj*. handsome.
yantók: *n*. rattan palm.
yangá: (*obs*.) *n*. flowerpot.
yangasngás: *n*. gritting the teeth; tingling discomfort in the teeth.
yangkáw: *n*. stride, big step.
yangga: (*slang*) *n*. sexual intercourse.
yanggi: (*slang*) *n*. the shakes, experience of withdrawal from drugs.
yangít: *n*. fallen dried twigs.
yangót: *n*. thick beard.
yangutngót: *n*. sound of hard chewing, brittle crunching.
yangyáng$_1$: **iyangyáng** *v*. to dry in the air; **yangyangan** *n*. clothesline.
yangyáng$_2$: (*slang*) *n*. homosexual.
yao: **yumao** *v*. to leave, depart; die.
yaon: **pagyaon** *n*. departure.
yaón: *pron*. that (distal). (*iyón*)
yapá: *n*. tastelessness. **mayapá** *adj*. tasteless, insipid; with little juice.
yapak: *n*. footstep, footprint; **iyapak** *v*. to set one's foot on; **yapakán** *n*. footboard; **yumapak** *v*. to trample on, stamp on.
yapák: *adj*. barefoot.
yapáng: (*slang*) *adj*. fragrant, good-smelling.
yapáw: **yapawín** *v*. to crush under the feet; trample.
yapo: (*slang*) *adj*. handsome.
yapós: *n*. embrace, hug; **yumapós** *v*. to embrace; clench.
yapyáp: *n*. small fish or shrimp sold in large quantities.
yarda: (Eng.) *n*. yard.
yari$_1$: **mangyari** *v*. to happen, occur, take place; **pangyayari** *n*. event; affair; incident.
yari$_2$: **kapangyarihan** *n*. power, might; control, authority; right; **nakapangyayari** *adj*. dominant, governing; **makapangyari** *v*. to dominate; rule, govern; predominate; **pagsasakapangyarihan** *n*. empowerment; authorization.
yarì: *n*. something made or manufactured; *adj*. made, built of; **yarî** *adj*. finished, completed; (*slang*) dead, met one's downfall; **mangyarî** *v*. to make, manufacture; **mayarì** *v*. to be able to make; **yumarì** *v*. to manufacture; **yarián** *n*. place of manufacture; (*slang*) sex; **pagkakayarì** *n*. construction, manufacturing. **yáring-makina** *adj*. machine made. **yáring-pábrika** *adj*. factory made. **yáring-kamáy** *adj*. handmade.
yarí: *pron*. this; **niyarí** of this.
yaros: *n*. sudden, impatient departure.
yasak: **yumasak** *v*. to trample on (plants).
yasang: **yasáng** *adj*. rough; dry and brittle.
yasyás: **magyasyás** *v*. to scrape; **yasyasín** *v*. to scrape off.
yatà: *adv*. maybe, perhaps.
yatab: *n*. short hand-sickle.
yate: (Sp.) *n*. yacht.
yatyát: *n*. partial corrosion.
yawe: (Sp. *llave*) *n*. key. (*susì*)
yaya: *n*. wet nurse; nursemaid.
yayà: **yumayà** *v*. to invite to do.
yayát: *adj*. very thin, emaciated.
yeba: (*slang*, Sp. *lleva*) *interj*. okay; wow.
yedra: (Sp. *hiedra*) *n*. poison ivy.
yelo: (Sp. *hielo*) *n*. ice; **magyelo** *v*. to freeze; make ice; **yeluhán** *n*. ice plant.
yema: (Sp.) *n*. egg yolk.
yerbabuwena: (Sp. *yerbabuena*) *n*. peppermint.
yero: (Sp. *hierro*) *n*. galvanized iron.
yeso: (Sp.) *n*. chalk; plaster of Paris.
yibók: **magyibók** *v*. to fatten animals for food.
yodo: (Sp. *iodo*) *n*. iodine.
Yogad: *n*. ethnic group and language from Isabela Province, Luzon.
yonggá: (*slang*) *n*. making love.
yosi: (*slang*) *n*. cigarette.
yoyò: *n*. yoyo toy; (*slang*) wrist watch.
yukayók: *adj*. with drooping head; crestfallen; fallen headlong; **magyukayók** *v*. to nod; droop the head.
yukdó: **yumukdó** *v*. to bend the knee.
yukô: *n*. bending the body, inclination; **yumukô** *v*. to bend; stoop; droop.
yukód: **yumukód** *v*. to bow one's head; slouch.
yukós: *adj*. bent; wrinkled.

yukyók: **yumukyók** *v.* to crouch, stoop down.
yugayog: *n.* violent shaking.
yugtô: *n.* act (in a drama); part of a series; part; installment.
yugyóg: **yumugyóg** *v.* to shake; (*slang*) make love; dance to rock-and-roll music; **yugyugan** *n.* dance party.
yumì: **mayumì** *adj.* tender, soft; delicate; refined (in manners).
yunit: (Eng.) *n.* unit.
yungíb: *n.* cave.
yungyóng: **yumungyóng** *v.* to hang over, shelter; loom over, dominate.
yupapà: **mangayupapà** *v.* to submit humbly; bow, fall prostrate.
yupì: *n.* dent; **yupî** *adj.* dented.
yupyóp: **yumupyóp** *v.* to cover up; sit on one's eggs; (*coll.*) delay.
yurak: *n.* treading, trampling; infringement. **yurakan** *v.* to tread on, trample on.
yutà: *n.* hundred thousand. (*sandaanlibo*)
yutyót: *n.* intermittent shaking (in the wind); sagging; *adj.* sagging; sinking from too much weight; overloaded.

ENGLISH – TAGALOG

INGGLÉS – TAGALOG

ENGLISH-TAGALOG

A

a: *indefinite article*. ang isá, isá; (*noun markers*) sa, ng.
abandon: *v*. magpabayà, pabayaan, layasan; lisanin; tumalikód.
abasement: *n*. paghamak, pagpapababà.
abate: *v*. humulaw; pahupaín, humupâ.
abattoir: *n*. katayán ng hayop, matadero.
abbreviate: *v*. daglatín; magpaiklî, paikliín.
abbreviation: *n*. daglát; pagpapaiklî, pagdaglát.
abdicate: *v*. magbitíw (ng kaharian).
abdomen: *n*. tiyán; **lower ~** pusón.
abduct: *v*. umagaw, dumukot; kidnapín.
aberration: *n*. pagkaligáw.
abhor: *v*. mapoót, masuklám; **~rent** *adj*. kasuklám-suklám.
abide: *v*. sundín, manatiling tapát; mamalagì.
ability: *n*. kaya, kakayahán.
abjure: *v*. magtakwíl.
able: *adj*. may-kaya; malakás; **~ bodied** malakás.
abnormal: *adj*. alangán, hindî karaniwan, di-pangkaraniwan.
aboard: *adj*. nakalulan, lulan, sakáy.
abode: *n*. tahanan, tinitirahán.
abolish: *v*. pumawì, bigyáng-wakás.
abominable: *adj*. kasuklam-suklám, nakapopoót.
aboriginal: *adj*. taál, katutubò.
abortion: *n*. pagpapalaglág, pagpapaagas; (*have miscarriage*) makunan, maagasan.
abound: *v*. makapál; managanà.
about: *prep*. (*nearly*) halos; (*concerning*) tungkól sa; sa buóng paligid.
above: *prep*. nasa itaás; sa ibabaw; higít sa.
abreast: *adv*. magkatabí, magkaagapay.
abridge: *v*. magpaigsî, magpaiklî.
abroad: *adj*. nasa ibáng bansá.
abrupt: *adj*. biglâ.
abscess: *n*. pigsá, naknák; magâ; (*glandular*) kulanì.
absent: *adj*. liban, walâ; **~ minded** lumilipád ang isip, limut-limót.
absolute: *adj*. buô, lubós, ganáp; waláng-takdâ.
absolve: *v*. kalagán, kalagín.
absorb: *v*. sumipsíp.
abstain: *v*. mangilin, mag-abstinénsiya, di-lumahók.
abstinence: *n*. abstinénsiya.
abstract: *adj*. basal; *v*. hugutin; iwalay; dukutin; lagumin.
absurd: *adj*. balighô, kakatuwâ; **~ity** kabalighuán.
abundant: *adj*. saganà, pasasà.
abuse: *n*. abuso, pagmamalabís; *v*. magmalabís.
abyss: *n*. kailaliman.
acacia: *n*. akasya.
academy: *n*. akadémiya.
accelerate: *v*. patulinin, magpabilís.
accent: *n*. diín; **~ mark** tuldík; (*way of speaking*) puntó.
accentuate: *v*. magpatingkád; bigyáng-diín.
accentuation: *n*. pánuldikan, palátuldikan.
accept: *v*. tumanggáp; (*consent*) pumayag.
access: *n*. daán, daanán, paglapit.
accessory: *n*. (*to a crime*) kasabuwát, kasapakát.
accident: *n*. disgrasya, sakunâ; **~ally** dî kina sadyâ, dî kinukusà.
acclaim: *v*. magbunyî, pumalakpák.
acclimatize: *v*. masanay, mahirati.
accolade: *n*. parangál, akolado.
accommodate: *n*. maglamán; magpatulóy.
accommodation: *n*. tulúyan, mapapanuluyan.
accompaniment: *n*. (*musical*) salíw.
accompanist: *n*. tagasalíw.
accompany: *v*. sumama, samahan.
accomplice: *n*. kasabuwát, kasapakát; katiyáp.
accomplish: *v*. tumupád, tuparín; ganapín; **~ment** *n*. paggawâ; katúparan.
accord: *n*. kaisá, kasang-ayon; **~ance**: *n*. pagkaakma, pag-ayon, pasang-ayon; **in ~ance with** ayon sa, alinsunod sa.
according: *prep*. ayon sa, sang-ayon sa.
account: *n*. halagá; dahilán; (*narrative*) salaysáy; (*bank*) kuwénta.
accountant: *n*. tagatuós, tenedor-de-líbro, kontadór.
accumulate: *v*. magtipon, mag-ipon; **accu-**

mulation *n.* pagtitipon, pagkaipon.

accurate: *adj.* tamang-tamà, wastong-wastô, tumpák, waláng malî.

accusation: *n.* paratang, bintáng.

accuse: *v.* magparatang, paratangan; (*in court*) magsakdál, ipagsakdál, ihablá, idemanda.

accustom: *v.* ihigig, igawî; magawî; **~ed** *adj.* bihasá, sanáy.

ace: *n.* batikán; (*in cards*) alás.

ache: *n.* sakít, pananakít, kirót, panghahapdî; *v.* kumirót, sumakít.

achieve: *v.* makagawâ, makatapos, kamtán.

acid: *n.* ásido, asim.

acidity: *n.* kaasiman, pangangasim.

acknowledge: *v.* kumilala; tumanggáp; magbigáy-alám; **~ment** *n.* pagkilala, pagtanggáp, pag-amin, pagsagót.

acme: *n.* rurók, tugatog.

acne: *n.* tagihawat.

acorn: *n.* bunga ng *oak*.

acoustics: *n.* akústika.

acquaint: *v.* mabatíd; makilala; sanayin, hiratihin, bihasahin; **~ance**: *n.* kakilala; **mutual ~ance** pagkikilala.

acquisce: *v.* sumang-ayon, pumayag, payagan, mapahinuhod.

acquire: *v.* magtamó; (*by inheritance*) mamána.

acquit: *v.* magpawaláng-sala.

acrid: *adj.* maaskád.

acrobat: *n.* sirkéro.

across: *prep.* sa kabilâ, sa ibayo.

act: *n.* gawâ, akto; (*of play*) yugtô; (*decree*) batás; *v.* umanyô, kumilos; mag-asal; (*role*) gumanáp; **~ion** *n.* gawâ, pagkilos; (*conduct*) asal; (*of verb*) pagganáp, pangyayari.

active: *adj.* maliksí; masúgid, masipag; masiglá.

activity: *n.* kilos, kilusán; gawáin.

actor: *n.* artísta, aktór, manlalabás.

actress: *n.* artistang babae, manlalabás.

actual: *adj.* tunay, totoó, talagá.

acute: *adj.* (*keen*) matalas; (*severe*) matindí; **~ accent** *n.* pahilís.

adage: *n.* sáwikaín, kasabihán, saláwikaín.

adamant: *adj.* matatág, matibay.

Adam's apple: *n.* lalagukán, tatagukán, gulúng-gulungan.

adapt: *v.* bumagay, maibagay; umagpáng.

add: *v.* maglagáy, lagyán; isama; (*in speech*) idugtóng.

addendum: *n.* ang nadagdág.

addict: *n.* adik; sugapà.

addicted: *adj.* gumón; pusakál.

addition: *n.* dagdág, dugtóng; **~al** *adj.* karagdagan.

address: *n.* tiráhan; (*speech*) talumpatì; **~ with respect** *v.* mamupô.

adept: *adj.* dalubhasà.

adequate: *adj.* sapát, hustó.

adhere: *v.* dumikít, kumapit, manikít.

ad hoc: *n.* tangì.

adjacent: *adj.* katabí, kanugnóg, kalapít.

adjective: *n.* pang-urì.

adjure: *v.* mag-utos.

adjust: *v.* isaayos, iayos; (*adapt*) iakmâ, itamà.

administer: *v.* mamahalà, mangsiwà.

administration: *n.* (*government*) pangasiwaán; pamamahalà.

admire: *v.* humangà.

admit: *v.* magpapasok; (*confess*) umamin, tanggapín.

admonish: *v.* magbalà, pagsabihan.

ado: *n.* ingay, linggál; kuskos-balúngos.

adolescence: *n.* kabataan; (*male*) pagbibinatâ; (*female*) pagdadalagá.

adopt: *v.* umangkín; mag-ampón, kumupkóp.

adorable: *adj.* kaibig-ibig.

adore: *v.* pakamahalín; sumambá.

adorn: *v.* maggayák, mag-adorno; palamutihan.

adrift: *n.* nakalutang, lutáng.

adult: *n.* mayór-de-edád, nasa gulang.

adulterate: *v.* magbantô, maghalò.

adultery: *n.* pakikiapíd, pangangalunyâ.

advance: *v.* sumugod, sumulong, umuna; (*progress*) sumulong, umunlád; *n.* (*forward movement*) pagsulong, pag-unlád; (*money*) pauná.

advantage: *n.* kapakinabangán, pakinabang; kahigtán; **take ~ of** *v.* samantalahín, kumikil; **have an ~ over** *v.* lumamáng; dumaíg; **~ous** *adj.* makabúbúti, mabuti; (*profitable*) kapaki-pakinabang.

advent: *n.* Adbiyento; (*coming*) pagdatíng.

adventure: *n*. abentúra; pambihirang karanasán, pakikipagsápalarán.
adverb: *n*. pang-abay; **~ial phrase** *n*. malapang-abay na parilala.
adversary: *n*. kaaway, kagalít.
adverse: *adj*. salungát, pasalungát.
advertise: *v*. magbabalâ, mag-anunsiyó; **~ment** *n*. anunsiyó.
advice: *n*. payo, pangaral, paalaala, tagubilin.
advisable: *adj*. maipápáyo, mabuti, marapat.
advise: *v*. magpayo, ipayo, mangara, ipangaral, ipaalaala, mag-abisá; (*inform*) magpatalastás; **~er** *n*. tagapayo.
advocate: *n*. abugádo, mánananggól; tagataguyod, tagatangkilik.
adze: *n*. darás.
afar: *adj*., *adv*. sa malayò.
affable: *adj*. magalang, mapitagan.
affair: *n*. bagay; (*concern*) kapakanán, suliranin, pangyayari.
affect: *v*. magkabisà, tumaláb; umantíg.
affection: *n*. pagmamahál, pag-ibig; **~ate** *adj*. mapagmahál, magiliw.
affidavit: *n*. apidabit, sinumpaang pahayag.
affiliate: *v*. umanib; *n*. kaanib.
affiliation: *n*. pag-anib, pagkakaanib, pagsapì.
affinity: *n*. hilig; pagkakahawig; kaugnayan.
affirm: *v*. magpatibay; magsabi na totoó; **~ative** *adj*. sang-ayon, katig.
affix: *v*. magdikít; *n*. (*grammatical*) panlapì.
affliction: *n*. dalamhatì; lungkót; hapdî.
affluent: *adj*. mayaman.
afford: *v*. makaya.
affront: *n*. paghamak, pagdustâ.
aflame: *adj*., *adv*. nagaalab, nagliliyáb.
afloat: *adj*., *adv*. lulutang-lutang; (*going around*) kumakalat.
afoot: *adj*., *adv*. lakád.
aforementioned: *adj*. nabanggít, nasabi, naturan.
afraid: *adj*. matakot, takót.
after: *adv*., *prep*. pagkatapos, pagkaraán; kasunód; **~ all** kung sabagay; **~-effect** kinahinatnán.
aftermath: *n*. resúlta, bunga.
afternoon: *n*. hapon; **~ meal** meriyénda.
afterwards: *adv*. pagkatapos, pagkaraán.
again: *adv*. ulî, mulî; minsán pa, ulit.
against: *prep*. laban sa, kontra; salungát.
agape: *adj*. nakangangá, nakatungangà.
age: *n*. edád, taón; panahón; **old ~** katandaán; *v*. tumandâ.
agency: *n*. ahénsiyá; tanggapan; sangáy.
agenda: *n*. adyenda, tálaan ng pag-úusapan.
agent: *n*. ahénte; alagád; kinatawán.
aggravate: *v*. magpalubhâ; (*annoy*) yumamót.
aggregate: *n*. kabuuán.
aggressive: *adj*. mapusók, mabalasik, palaawáy.
aghast: *adj*. nangihilakbót, takót.
agile: *adj*. maliksí, mabilís; masiglá.
agitate: *v*. bumagabag, mangguló; kalugín.
agnostic: *n*. agnóstiko.
ago: *adj*., *adv*. noóng matagál na.
agony: *n*. pag-aágaw-buhay, paghihingalô.
agrarian: *adj*. pangkabukiran.
agree: *v*. pumayag; magkasundô; maging-hiyáng; **~ment** *n*. kasunduan; pagkakasundô.
agriculture: *n*. pagsasaka, pagbubukid.
aground: *adj*. nakasadsád, nakasayad.
ahead: *adv*. una, nauuná; **go ~** *v*. mauná, umuna; *excl*. sigé.
aid: *n*. tulong, saklolo; *v*. tulongan, sumaklolo.
ailment: *n*. sakít, diperénsiya.
aim: *n*. layon, balak, tungukin; (*in firing*) puntíriya; *v*. pumuntíriya.
air: *n*. hangin; *v*. isahihimpawíd; **on the ~** *adj*. nasa himpapawíd; **~-mail** koreong-panghimpapawíd; **~craft** *n*. eruplano; **~field** páliparan; **~ force** hukbóng panghimpapawíd.
airplane: *n*. eruplano.
air plant: *n*. dapò.
airport: *n*. páliparan, himpilan ng eruplano, pálapagan.
aisle: *n*. pasíliyo, pagitan, daanán.
ajar: *adj*. nakakawang.
akimbo: *adj*. nakapamaywáng.
akin: *adj*. kamag-anak; katulad; kaurì.
alarm: *n*. babalâ, hudyát, alarma; **~ clock** *n*. despertadór.
alas: *excl*. abâ.
albacore: *n*. albakora.
albino: *n*. anak-araw, sarka.
albumen: *n*. pulá ng itlóg.

alcohol: *n*. alkohól; **~lic**: *n*. maglalasing, may-alkohól.
ale: *n*. serbesa.
alert: *adj*. listó, alistó; mabilís, maliksí; naka-handâ; *v*. pahandaín.
algebra: *n*. álhebra.
alibi: *n*. dahilán, sangkalan.
alien: *n*. dayuhan, banyagà.
alight: *v*. bumabâ; umibís.
align: *v*. magpantáy, humanay, ipila.
alike: *adj*. magkamukhâ.
alimony: *n*. sustento.
alive: *adj*. buháy.
all: *n*., *adj*. lahát; parapara, taganás; bawa't isá; buô; ~ **Saints' Day** Todos los Santos; ~ **right** ayos, tamà; **above** ~ sa ibabaw ng lahát; **after** ~ sa kabilá ng lahát; ~ **the same** pareho; gayón man; ~ **the way** habang daán; **not at** ~ hindî sa anúmang paraán; **is that** ~? iyón lamang ba?
allay: *v*. magbawas; pagaanín; payapain; ba-wahan.
allegation: *n*. ang pinagsásabí.
allege: *v*. manindigan, magsabi, sabihin.
allegiance: *n*. katapatan, pagkamatapát.
alleviate: *v*. magpabawa, magpakalmá.
alley: *n*. eskina, eskinita; kalyehón.
alliance: *n*. pagkakaisá, alyansá.
alligator: *n*. buwaya.
allot: *v*. mamahagi, ipamahagi.
allow: *v*. matiís, atimín; magpahintulot, tulutan, pumayag; magbigáy; tumanggáp; **~ance** *n*. pataán; panggastós; suwéldo.
alloy: *n*. magkahalong metál.
allude: *v*. magpariníg, magpahiwatig; tumukoy.
allure: *v*. tumuksó; humikayat; bihagin.
allusion: *n*. tukoy, pagtukoy.
ally: *n*. kaanib, kapanalig, kapanig.
almighty: *adj*. makapangyarihan.
almost: *adv*. halos, muntík na.
alms: *n*. limós.
aloft: *adj*. nasa itaás.
alone: *adj*. nag-iisá; **leave** ~ bayaan, hayaan.
along: *prep*. habang-daán; sa tabí; **take** ~ i-sama; **get** ~ mamuhay.
aloof: *adj*. layô.
aloud: *adv*. malakás.
alphabet: *n*. abakáda; baybayin.
already: *adv*. na.
also: *adv*. rin, din; patí, pa.
altar: *n*. altár, dambanà.
alter: *v*. bumago; mag-ibá; **~ation** *n*. pag-babago.
altercation: *n*. balitaktakan, taltalan.
alternate: *v*. maghalilí; magsalisí; *adj*. tuwíng ikalawá, maka-makalawá; **alternative** *n*. pamimilì.
although: *conj*. kahit na, maskí, bagamán.
altitude: *n*. taás.
altogether: *adv*. ganáp, lubós.
alum: *n*. tawas.
aluminum: *n*. alumíniyo.
always: *adv*. lagì, parati.
am: first person singular present tense of ***be*** is represented by a pronoun in Tagalog→ akó; akó'y.
amalgamate: *v*. pag-isahín.
amaranth weed: *n*. uray, bayambáng.
amass: *v*. tipunin, impukin.
amateur: *n*. baguhan, bagito.
amaze: *v*. humangà, magtaká.
amazing: *adj*. kataka-taká, kagulat-gulat.
ambassador: *n*. embahadór; sugò.
ambiguous: *adj*. hindî tiyák, may dalawáng magkaibáng kahulugán; pang-alangán.
ambition: *n*. adhikâ, hangárin.
ambitious: *adj*. mapaghangád, mapagpita, ma-paglunggatî, mapag-adhikâ.
ambulance: *n*. ambulánsiya.
ambush: *v*. bakayan, tambangán.
ameliorate: *v*. mapagbuti, makapagpaunlád.
amen: *interj*. siyá nawâ.
amenable: *adj*. palasunód.
amend: *v*. magsusog; bumago; iwastô.
amendment: *n*. pagbabago, susog.
amends: *n*. bayad-pinsalà.
America: *n*. Amérika; **United States of** ~ Estados Unidos.
American: *adj*. Amerikáno; (*coll.*) Kanó.
amicable: *adj*. mabaít.
amid: *prep*. sa gitnâ ng.
amity: *n*. pagkakasundô, pagmamabutihán.
ammunition: *n*. bala, munisiyón.
amnesty: *n*. amnéstiya, pagpapatawad.

among: *prep*. sa gitnâ ng, kasama ng.
amorous: *adj*. mapagmahál; masintahin.
amount: *n*. dami; (*sum of money*) halagá.
amphibian: *n*. ampibyán.
ample: *adj*. sapát, hustó; malakí, malawak.
amplifier: *n*. palakás-tunóg.
amplify: *v*. laksán; dagdagán, punán.
amputate: *v*. pumutol, putulin.
amuck: *adv*. huramentádo.
amulet: *n*. anting-antíng, agimat; mutyâ.
amuse: *v*. lumibáng, makalibáng; magpasayá; **~ment** *n*. áliwan, libangan.
an: *indefinite article used before vowel-initial nouns, see* ***a***.
anaesthetic: *n*. pampamanhíd, pampatulog.
analogy: *n*. pagkakatulad, pagkakáhawig; palásurián.
analysis: *n*. pagsusurì, pagkakasurì, pánurian.
analyze: *v*. suriin, analisahín.
anarchy: *n*. anarkiyá, kagúluhang-bayan.
anatomy: *n*. anatomiyá; **anatomical** *adj*. pangkatawán.
ancestor: *n*. nunò, ninunò.
ancestry: *n*. kanunununuan.
anchor: *n*. sinipete, angkora, angkla; *v*. dumaóng.
anchovy: *n*. dilis.
ancient: *adj*. napakatandâ.
and: *conj*. at.
anemic: *adj*. kuláng sa dugô; putlain; anémiko.
anesthesia: *n*. pampamanhíd.
anesthetic: *adj*. pamanhíd.
anesthetize: *v*. pamanhirán.
anew: *adv*. ulî, ulit.
angel: *n*. anghel.
Angelus: *n*. Orasiyón.
anger: *n*. galit, kagalitan.
angle: *n*. ánggulo, panulukan; **with all ~s equal** *adj*. parisulok.
angling: *n*. pamimingwít, pamamansíng.
angry: *adj*. galít, magalit.
anguish: *n*. hapis, sakit, dalamhatì.
animal: *n*. háyop.
animate: *v*. magbigáy-buhay, mapasiglá; **~d** *adj*. buháy, masiglá.
animosity: *n*. poót.
ankle: *n*. bukung-bukong.
annex: *n*. dugtong, dagdag, datig.
annihilate: *v*. pumuksâ, puksaín.
anniversary: *n*. kaarawán, anibersáryo; **silver wedding ~** boda de pláta; **golden wedding ~** boda de oro; **death ~** araw ng pagkamatáy.
announce: *v*. ihayág, magpatalos, magpabatid; **~ment** *n*. patalastás, babalâ; **~r** *n*. tagapagbalitá.
annoy: *v*. mayamót, mabagót, mabuwísit; magpagalit, galitin.
annual: *adj*. taunan, taun-taón.
annul: *v*. pawaláng-bisà.
anoint: *v*. magpahid.
anomalous: *adj*. tiwalî.
anomaly: *n*. katiwalián, pambihirà.
anonymous: *adj*. waláng-lagdâ, waláng-pangalan.
another: *adj*. ibá; (*one more*) isá pa.
answer: *n*. sagót, tugón; *v*. sumagót, sagutín; **~ for** managót.
ant: *n*. langgám; **flying ~** gamugamó; **kind of small ~** apanas, kuwitib; **big ~** hantík; **~ hill** punsó.
antagonistic: *adj*. magkaaway, magkagalít, kalaban, kasalungát.
antagonize: *v*. mapagalit, pagalitin, kalabanin.
Antarctic: *n*. Antártikó.
antecedent: *adj*. nauná; **~s** *n*. pinagmulán, kasaysayan.
antedate: *v*. paagahin ang petsa.
antenna: *n*. sungót, antena.
anthem: *n*. awit; **National ~** Pambansáng Awit.
anthology: *n*. antolohiyá.
anthropology: *n*. antropolohía, palátauhan.
anti- *pref*. kóntra, salungát, laban sa.
anticipate: *v*. umasa, umasám; umasa, mauná.
antics: *n*. katawá-tawáng kils, kalokohan.
antidote: *n*. pamatáy-bisà, panlunas, panremedyo.
antipathy: *n*. pagkainís, antipatíya.
antiquated: *adj*. sa una, sinauna; lipás na.
antique: *adj*. sa una pa, antigo.
antiseptic: *n*. antiséptikó.
antithesis: *n*. katumbalikán, kabaligtarán.
antler: *n*. sungay.
anus: *n*. butas ng puwít.

anvil: *n*. palihán.
anxiety: *n*. pag-áalaalá, pag-áalalá; balisa; pananabík.
anxious: *adj*. balisá, sabík, mag-alalá.
any: *adj*. kahit anó, alinman, sínuman; ~ **longer** pa.
anybody: *pron*. sínumán.
anyhow: *adv*. sa papaano, paano't paano man.
anyone: *pron*. sínumán, maskí sino.
anything: *adv*. man lamang, anumán.
anyway: *adv*. sa anót-anó man, anumán.
anywhere: *adv*. kahit saán, saán man.
apart: *adv*. bukód, tangì; pagitan; **set** ~ ibukód, itabí; **take** ~ pagtanggál-tanggalín.
apartment: *n*. aksesóriyá, apartamento.
apathetic: *adj*. waláng-siglá.
apathy: *n*. kawaláng-interés, kawaláng-pagpapahalagá.
ape: *n*. bakulaw.
aperture: *n*. butas, siwang.
apex: *n*. taluktók, tugatog, tuktók.
aphaeresis: *n*. mayputot.
aphid: *n*. dapulak.
aphorism: *n*. talinghagà.
aphrodisiac: *n*. pampalibog, gayumà.
apiece: *adv*. sa bawa't-isá; ang isá.
apocalypse: *n*. pahayag.
apocope: *n*. maypungos.
apologize: *v*. humingî ng tawad.
apology: *n*. paghingî ng tawad.
apostle: *n*. alagád, apostól.
apostrophe: *n*. kudlít, apóstrope.
appall: *v*. pangilabutan, mangilabot; **~ing** nakapanlúlumó.
apparatus: *n*. kasangkapan, kagamitán, aparato.
apparel: *n*. damít, kasúután.
apparent: *adj*. maliwanag, malinaw; madalíng mapansín; **~ly** *adv*. tila, mukhâ, warì; parang.
apparition: *n*. pangitáin; (*ghost*) multó.
appeal: *n*. panawagan, samò, pagsamò; (*court*) apela, paghahabol; *v*. mamanhík, ipamanhík, hilingín; ~ **to** *v*. hibikán; samuan, pamanhikán, pakiusapan; **Court of ~s** *n*. Húkuman sa Paghahabol.
appear: *v*. magpakita, lumitáw, lumabás; (*seem*) magmukhâ; **~ance** *n*. mukhâ, anyô, hitsura; paglitáw, pagpapakita; paglabás.
appease: *v*. magpalubag, magpahinahon, payapain.
append: *v*. magdagdág, maglakip, isama.
appendicitis: *n*. apendisitis.
appendix: *n*. dagdág (ng aklát); apendiks.
appertain: *v*. itungod, iukol.
appetite: *n*. gana.
appetizer: *n*. pampagana.
appetizing: *adj*. nakagágana, nakatátakám.
applaud: *v*. pumalakpák; pumuri.
applause: *n*. palakpák, papuri.
apple: *n*. mansanas.
appliance: *n*. aparato, kasangkapan, kagamitán.
applicable: *adj*. tumutukoy, bagay; magagamit.
application: *n*. pagpapahid, paglalagáy; paguukol.
apply: *v*. magpatong, ipatong, maglagáy; (*for work*) magprisintá.
appoint: *v*. magtakdâ, maglaán; humirang; **~ment** *n*. tipanan, tipán, usapan; (*position*) tunguklin, puwesto, katungkulan.
apportion: *v*. magbahagi, magpartí, paghatíhatiin.
appraise: *v*. maghalagá, tumasa, tasahan.
appreciate: *v*. magpasalamat, matuwâ, malugód; (*in value*) magíng-mahál.
apprehend: *v*. humuli, dumakíp; dakpín, hulihin.
apprehensive: *adj*. takót, nag-aalaalá.
apprentice: *n*. manggagawang nagsasanay.
approach: *v*. lumapit.
approbation: *n*. patibay; papuri.
appropriate: *adj*. bagay, angkóp, akmâ, wastô.
approval: *n*. pagpayag, pagsang-ayon.
approve: *v*. pumayag, sumang-ayon; masiyahán; magpatibay.
approximate: *adj*. humigít-kumulang; *v*. halos pumantáy.
approximately: *adv*. halos, malapit sa, mga.
apricot: *n*. albarikoke.
April: *n*. Abríl.
apron: *n*. epron, dilantál, tapî, tapis.
apropos: *adj*. bagay, akmâ, angkóp.
apt: *adj*. maáarì, malamáng.
aptitude: *n*. kakayahán, hilig.
aquamarine: *n*. agwamarina.

aquarium: *n*. akwaryum, akwario.
Aquarius: *n*. mang-iigib.
aquatic: *adj*. pantubig.
aquiline: *adj*. hugis-tukâ (ilóng).
Arab: *n*., *adj*. Arabo.
arable: *adj*. maáararo, masásáka, mapagháhalamanan.
arbitrate: *v*. magpasiyá; mamagitan; magpahatol.
arbor: *n*. balag.
arch: *n*. arko; (*of foot*) bubóng ng paá; *v*. iarko; maghubog.
archaic: *adj*. sa una, matandâ.
archbishop: *n*. arsobíspo.
archipelago: *n*. kapuluán.
architect: *n*. arkitekto; **~ure** *n*. arkitektura.
ardent: *adj*. marubdób, maalab; masiglá.
ardor: *n*. kasiglahán, sigasig.
arduous: *adj*. mahirap, nakapapapagod.
are: *see* ***be***.
area: *n*. purók, poók; lawak.
argue: *v*. magtalo, makipagtalo; (*shouting*) magtaltalan.
argument: *n*. pagtatalo; (*reasoning*) pangangatwiran, pagmamatwíd.
argumentative: *adj*. mapágmatwíd, palákontra.
arid: *adj*. tuyô, tigáng.
Aries: *n*. tupang lalaki (sa langit).
arise: *v*. tumindíg, tumayô, magbangon.
aristocrat: *n*. aristókratá.
arithmetic: *n*. palátuusan, aritmétiká.
ark: *n*. daóng.
arm: *n*. bráso, bisig; (*weapon*) armas; **crooked** ~ pingkáw, komang.
armament: *n*. sandata.
armchair: *n*. silyón.
armful: *n*. pangkó.
armistice: *n*. pagtigil ng labanán, armistisyo.
armor: *n*. balutì, kutamaya.
armpit: *n*. kilikili.
army: *n*. hukbó.
aroma: *n*. bangó, samyó, halimuyak; **~tic** *adj*. mabangó, masamyó.
around: *adv*., *prep*. sa palibot; (*about*) humigít-kumulang.
arouse: *v*. pumukaw, pukawin; magsulsól.
arraign: *v*. isakdál, ipagsakdál, ihablá.
arrange: *v*. mag-ayos, isaayos; (*prepare*) maghandâ; **~ment** *n*. pagsasaayos, pakikipag-ayos; pagkakaayos.
array: *n*. tanghál; ayos.
arrears: *adj*. atrasádo, atraso.
arrest: *v*. humuli, damakíp, pigilin.
arrival: *n*. datíng, pagdatíng.
arrive: *v*. dumatíng, sumipót; dumatál.
arrogance: *n*. pagmamataás.
arrogant: *adj*. hambóg, napakapalalò, mapagmataás.
arrogate: *v*. kumamkám.
arrow: *n*. palasô, tunod; **bow and** ~ panà.
arson: *n*. panununog, paniniláb.
art: *n*. sining, arte; (*skill*) kasanayán.
artery: *n*. artéryá, malakíng ugát.
artesian well: *n*. poso (artisyano).
article: *n*. lathalain; artikulo; bagay; (*gram.*) pantukoy.
articulate: *v*. bumigkás nang maliwanag; *adj* nakapagsásalitâ.
artifice: *n*. pakanâ.
artificial: *adj*. hindî tunay, di-likás.
artillery: *n*. artileryá.
artist: *n*. artista; pintór; **~ic** *adj*. masining, maarte. **~ry** *n*. kaartihán, pagkamakasinig.
as: *adv*., *prep*., parang, katulad, kaparis; warì; *conj*. samantala; ~ **if** parang; (*in the capacity of*) bilang; (*while*) habang; **as** __ **as** kasing-.
asbestos: *n*. asbesto.
ascend: *v*. umakyát, pumaitaás.
ascension: *n*. pag-akyát, pagtaás.
ascent: *n*. pag-akyát, pagtaás, pag-ahon.
ascertain: *v*. tumiyák; (*find out*) umalám.
ascribe: *v*. dahilanin, idahilán.
ash: *n*. abó; ~ **Wednesday** Miyérkules ng Abó; ~ **tray** siniséro, titisan, ábuhan.
ashamed: *adj*. nahihiyâ, napapahiyâ.
ashen: *adj*. maputlâ, abuhín, malaabó.
ashore: *adj*., *adv*. nasa dalampasigan, nasa kati, sa pampáng.
Asia: *n*. Asya; **~tic** Asyátiko.
aside: *adv*. bukód sa, sa isáng tabí.
asinine: *adj*. tangá, gago, hangál.
ask: *v*. magtanóng; ~ **for** humingî; (*invite*) anyayahan.
askew: *adj*. nakatagilid, baluktót.

asleep: *adj*. tulóg; **fall ~** maidlíp, makatulog; **half-~** alimpungát.
asparagus: *n*. aspáragus.
aspect: *n*. hitsura, ayos, anyô, astâ.
asperity: *n*. gasláw, karahasán, dahás, kalupitán.
asphalt: *n*. aspálto.
aspirant: *n*. aspirante.
aspiration: *n*. nais, nasà, hangád, lunggatî.
aspire: *v*. hangarín, magmithî, maghangád.
aspirin: *n*. aspirína.
ass: *n*. asno; (*coll: rump*) puwít.
assail: *v*. sumalakay, daluhungin; lumusob.
assassin: *n*. mamamatay-tao; **~ate** *v*. pumatáy nang pataksíl.
assault: *v*. sumalakay, lumusob; gumahasà; *n*. panggagahasà.
assemble: *v*. magtipon, mag-ipon; magbuô, magkabit-kabít.
assembly: *n*. pagtitipon.
assent: *n*. pahintulot, pagpayag; pasang-ayon; *v*. pumayag, magpahintulot.
assert: *v*. magpahayag, magsaysáy; igiít; isiksík.
assess: *v*. tayahin, tasahan; **~or** *n*. tasadór, tagatasa; **~ment** tasa.
asset: *n*. bagay na may halagá, propyedád.
assiduous: *adj*. masigasig, mapagsumikap, matiyagâ.
assign: *v*. magtalagá; iutos; magtakdâ, itadhanà; **~ment** *n*. gawain, trabáho.
assimilate: *v*. lumagom, lagumin; mátutuhan, maging bahagi.
assist: *v*. tumulong, sumaklolo; **~ant** *n*. kawaní, katulong, pangalawá.
associate: *n*. kasama, kabakas.
association: *n*. samahán, kalipunán, pagsasama-sama.
assort: *v*. pagbukúd-bukurin, piliin; **~ed** *adj*. sari-sari, halu-halò, ibá-ibá, surtidos; **~ment** *n*. urí, kláse.
assume: *v*. ipalagáy, mag-akalà; (*an office*) manungkól.
assumption: *n*. palagáy, pagkukunwarî.
assure: *v*. tumiyák, sumiguro.
asterisk: *n*. asterisko.
astern: *adj*. nasa hulihán ng bapór.
asthma: *n*. hikà, asma.
astonish: *v*. magpataká, mamanghâ.
astound: *v*. magpataká.
astray: *adj*. ligáw, náliligáw.
astrology: *n*. astrolohiyá.
astronomer: *n*. astronomó.
astronomy: *n*. astronomiyá.
astute: *adj*. matalino, tuso, matalas.
asylum: *n*. asílo, ampunan.
at: *prep*. sa, nasa; **~ all costs** anó man ang mangyari; **~ first** nang uná; **~ last** sa wakás; **~ most** pinakamalakí; **~ once** agad-agád; **~ least** kahit man lamang; **~ times** kung minsan.
atheist: *n*. ateo, ateista.
athlete: *n*. manlalarò, atleta; **~'s foot** alipungá.
atlas: *n*. atlas.
atmosphere: *n*. alangaang; kapaligirán, atmospera.
atom: *n*. átomo; **~ic** atómiko.
atone: *v*. magbayad-puri; pagsisihan.
atop: *adv*., *prep*. nasa itaás, nasa dulo, nasa ibabaw.
atrocious: *adj*. napakasamâ, buktót; mabagsík, mabangís.
atrophy: *n*. atropyá, pagkasayang, pagkaaksayá.
attach: *v*. magkabít, kabitán; magdikít; isama; **~ment** pagkakábít, pagkágiliw; panalì.
attaché: *n*. embahadór; lalagyán ng mga papeles.
attack: *n*. salakay, lusob, atake; sumpóng; *v*. sumalakay, lumusob, dumaluhong, manibasib.
attain: *v*. umabót, magtamó, magkamít.
attempt: *n*. tangkâ, pagsubok; (*effort*) sikap; *v*. magtangkâ; magpilit.
attend: *v*. dumaló; **~ to** *v*. harapín, malingkód, mag-alaga.
attention: *n*. pansín; paglilimì, pag-aasikaso, asikaso; **pay ~ to** makiníg, pakinggán.
attentive: *adj*. maasikaso, masigasig.
attest: *v*. magpatotoó, magpatunay; ibunyág.
attire: *n*. kasuutan, damít.
attitude: *n*. palagáy, saloobín, pagtingín; kilos.
attorney: *n*. abugádo, manananggól.
attract: *v*. mabalanì; akitin, umakit; **~tion** *n*.

pang-akit, pantawag-pansín; **~ive** *adj.* kaakit-akit, kahalí-halina.
attribute: *n.* katángían; *v.* magpalagáy, ipalagáy, iukol.
auction: *n.* subasta; *v.* magsubasta; **~ off** isubasta.
audacious: *adj.* matapang, marahás, pangahás.
audible: *adj.* naririníg.
audience: *n.* mga nakikiníg, tagapanoód.
audit: *v.* magtuós, sumurì (ng kuwenta); **~or** tagasurì; (*student*) tagapakiníg.
auditorium: *n.* bulwagan, auditoryum.
auger: *n.* baréna, balibol, pambutas.
augment: *v.* magdagdág; magpalakí, palakihín.
auger: *n.* manghuhulà; *v.* magbabalâ.
augury: *n.* hulà, babalâ.
August: *n.* Agosto.
aunt: *n.* tiyá.
auspices: *n.* tangkilik.
austere: *adj.* mahigpít, mabagsík.
authentic: *adj.* kapní-paniwalà, mapanánaligan; **~ate** *v.* patunayan, magpatotoó.
author: *n.* maykathâ, may-akdâ, autór; **~ity** *n.* kapangyarihan, autoridád; karapatán; **~ize** *v.* mag-autorisá; magpahintulot.
authoritative: *adj.* makapangyarihan; mapanghâhawakan.
autobiography: *n.* sariling talambuhay.
autograph: *n.* pirma, autograp.
automatic: *adj.* automátikó, kusà, pakusâ; **~ally** *adv.* pakusâ.
automobile: *n.* kótse.
autonomous: *adj.* nagsásarilí, may-kasarinlán.
autonomy: *n.* pagsasarili.
autopsy: *n.* autopsiyá, súring-bangkáy.
autumn: *n.* taglagás.
auxiliary: *n.* katulong; (*verb*) pandiwang pantulong.
avail: *v.* makatulong; mapakinabangan.
available: *adj.* maáarì, magágamit, makukuha.
avalanche: *n.* pagguhò ng yelo.
avaricious: *adj.* masikím, matakaw.
avenge: *v.* maghigantí; **~r** *n.* tagapaghigantí.
avenue: *n.* abenída.
average: *adj.* karaniwan, pangkaraniwan; pámantayan, pámantungan.
aversion: *n.* pag-ayáw, kaayawán.
avert: *v.* ilayò; umiwas.
aviator: *n.* abiyadór, manlilipad.
avid: *adj.* sabík, napakamahilig.
avocado: *n.* abukádo.
avoid: *v.* umiwas, iwasan, ilagan; lihisán.
await: *v.* maghintáy, mahandâ.
awake: *adj.* gisíng; **half-~** pupungás-pungás, naáalimpungatan; **~n** *v.* gumising, pumukaw.
award: *n.* gantimpalà, premyo.
aware: *adj.* alám, nalalaman, batíd.
away: *adv.* walâ; malayò; **give ~** ipamigáy; **go ~** umalís.
awe: *n.* sindák, pitagan, alang-alang; **~some** *adj.* kasindak-sindák.
awful *adj.* masamâ, nakasísindák
awhile: *adv.* sandalî, saglít.
awkward: *adj.* saliwâ, lampá, asiwâ, waláng-kabikas-bikas.
awl: *n.* balibol, pambutas.
awning: *n.* sibi, pasibi, ambî.
awry: *adj.* pilipít, palíng.
ax: *n.* palakól; (*small*) putháw.
axis: *n.* éhe.
axle: *n.* éhe ng gulóng.
azure: *n., adj.* bugháw, asúl, kulay-langit.

B

babble: *v.* ngumawâ, magngángangawâ.
baboon: *n.* tsonggo, unggóy na malakí.
baby: *n.* sanggól; (*young child*) batà.
bachelor: *n.* binatà, bagong-tao, soltéro.
back: *n.* likód; likurán; (*of chair*) sandalan, *v.* tumulong, itaguyod, managót; **come ~** bumalík; **give ~** isaulì; **turn one's ~** tumalikód; **behind one's ~** sa tálikuran; **~ country** liblíb na bayan; **hold ~** pigilin.
backbone: *n.* gulugód.
background: *n.* likurán; (*experience*) karanasán.
backhand: *n.* aldabís, sampál.
backing: *n.* tulong, tangkilik.
backside: *n.* puwít, puwitán; hulihán.
backstage: *n.* likód ng entablado.
backward: *adv.* pauróng, patalikód; (*not progressive, slow*) atrasado, mahinà.
backyard: *n.* looban, bakuran, likód-bahay,

duluhan.
bacon: *n*. tusino.
bacteria: *n*. bakterya.
bad: *adj*. masamâ; (*rotten*) bulók, panís; (*fish*) bilasâ; (*evil*) samâ.
badge: *n*. tsapa, sagisag.
baffle: *v*. tumarantá, malitó.
bag: *n*. supot; bayóng; kustál; (*suitcase*) maléta.
bagasse: *n*. bagaso, yamás, sapal.
baggage: *n*. bagahe, maleta, mga balutan, dalá-dalahan; ~ **carrier** *n*. kargadór.
baggy: *adj*. maluwáng; maumbók, nakaumbók.
bail: *n*. piyansa, lagak; *v*. maglimás.
bailiff: *n*. opisyál ng batas; tagapamahalà.
bait: *n*. pain.
bake: *v*. ihurnó.
baker: *n*. panadero, magtitinapáy.
bakery: *n*. panaderyá, tinapayán.
baking powder: *n*. pampaalsá.
balance: *n*. timbangan, timbáng; balanse; (*of a debt*) hulihan; **keep one's** ~ *v*. manimbáng; **loss of** ~ *n*. uyót.
balcony: *n*. asutea, balkón, balkonahe.
bald: *adj*. kalbó, panót.
bale: *n*. paldó, bastâ.
balk: *v*. tumigil, humadláng.
ball: *n*. bola; (*dance*) bayle.
ballast: *n*. tulakbahalà.
balloon: *n*. lóbo.
ballot: *n*. baluta.
balm: *n*. pang-alò, bálsamo.
balustrade: *n*. balustrada, barandilya.
bamboo: *n*. kawayan.
ban: *v*. magbawal, ipagbawal; *n*. pagbabawal.
banana: *n*. saging.
band: *n*. banda; (*group*) pangkát; (*girdle*) paha; **rubber** ~ lástiko; **hat** ~ listón.
bandage: *n*. bendahe, benda, talì; *v*. bendahán.
bandfish: *n*. muog.
bandit: *n*. tulisán, manghaharang.
bandstand: *n*. gloriyeta.
bandy-legged: *adj*. sakáng.
bang: *n*. putók, kalampág, kalantóg.
bangle: *n*. pulseras, galáng.
banish: *v*. magpalayas, magtabóy; itapon, i-waksi.
banister: *n*. balustre; pasamano.
banjo: *n*. bandyo.
bank: *n*. bangko; (*of river*) pampáng; **~book** libreta; **~er** *n*. bangkero; **~rupt** *adj*. bangkarota, bagsák, tumbado; hikahós.
banner: *n*. estandarte, bandilà.
banquet: *n*. bangkete, pigíng, salu-salo.
banter: *v*. tuksuhín.
baptism: *n*. binyág, bautismo.
baptize: *v*. magbinyág, magpangalan.
bar: *n*. baras, kabilyá; rehas; (*obstacle*) hadláng, sagabal; *v*. magbawal, maghadláng.
barb: *n*. simà; **~ed wire** alambreng may-tiník.
barbarian: *n*. bárbaró.
barbarity: *n*. kalupitán, kabangisán.
barbecue: *n*. ihaw, bárbikyú; *v*. mag-ihaw, mag-litsón, magbárbikyú.
barber: *n*. barbero, manggugupit; **~shop** págupitan.
barbituate: *n*. gamót na pampatulog.
bare: *adj*. hubád, lantád, waláng-gayák; *v*. maglahad, maglantád, magbukás; (*reveal*) isiwalat; **~foot** *adj*. nakayapák, yapák, tapák; **~ly** *adv*. bahagyâ na; halos.
bargain: *n*. (*agreement*) kasunduan; (*sale*) baratílyo; *v*. makamura; manawaran, tumawad.
barge: *n*. lantsa.
baritone: *n*. barítono.
bark: *n*. (*of tree*) balát ng kahon, banakal; (*of dog*) tahól, kahól; *v*. tumahól.
barley: *n*. sebáda.
barn: *n*. kamalig, bangán, baysá.
barnacle: *n*. taliptíp.
barracks: *n*. kuwartél, barak.
barracuda: *n*. asugon, balyos, bikuda, rompe kandado, trosilyo.
barrel: *n*. baríl.
barren: *adj*. (*arid*) tigáng; (*sterile*) baóg; (*not bearing fruit*) hindî namumúnga.
barricade: *n*. hadláng, halang, sagabal.
barrier: *n*. sagabal, hadláng, salabíd.
barrow: **wheel-~** karetílya, parihuwela.
barter: *v*. magpalitan, magtuwayán, tuwayán.
base: *n*. patungán; punò; pundasiyón; (*headquarters*) himpilan; *adj*. napakaimbí, napakahamak, nakapasamâ; *v*. magbatay, magsalalay, isalig.

baseball: *n.* beisbol.
basement: *n.* silong.
bashful: *adj.* mahihiyáin, madungô, mahiyâ.
basic: *adj.* saligán, batayán; mahalagá; pansímulain.
basin: *n.* palanggana; lababo; lunas.
basis: *n.* batayán, pamantungan, saligán.
bask: *v.* magpainit.
basket: *n. kinds:* bilao, buslô, takuyan, tiklís, kaíng.
bass: *adj.* malagong, mababà
bastard: *n.* bastardo, anák sa labás.
baste: *v.* mantikaan; (*sew*) maghilbana; tutusan.
bat: *n.* (*animal*) kabág, bayakan, panikì; (*club*) pamalò.
batch: *n.* bungkós, talaksán, buntón; pulutóng.
bath: *n.* paligò; (*room*) banyo; ~ **robe** bata; **take a** ~ maligò.
bathe: *v.* maligò; paliguan; **~ing suit** damítpampaligò.
bathroom: *n.* banyo.
bathtub: *n.* banyera.
battalion: *n.* batalyón.
batter: *v.* humampás, gumulpí, bumugbóg.
battery: *n.* bateryá; (*violence*) pambububugbóg.
battle: *n.* labanán; digmâ, gera; *v.* ipaglaban; **~ship** bapor-pandigmâ.
bawl: *v.* umangal; sumigáw.
bay: *n.* loók.
bay leaf: *n.* laurel.
bayonet: *n.* bayoneta; *v.* bayonetahin.
B.C.: *abbrev.* panahóng bago ipinanganák ni Hesukristo.
be: *copular verb.* There is no copular verb in Tagalog, however, referents preceding predicates are followed by the inverse particle *ay* (*'y*). *Matalino siya* = *Siya'y matalino* = He/she is intelligent.
beach: *n.* aplaya, tabíng-dagat; *v.* isadsád.
beacon: *n.* parola.
bead: *n.* butil; (*glass*) manik, abaloryo.
beak: *n.* tukâ.
beam: *n.* sinag, silahis.
bean: *n.* patanì; **string** ~ sitaw; **mungo** ~ balátong; **kidney** ~ abitsuwelas.
bear: *n.* oso; *v.* magtiís, tiisín; madalá; (*give birth*) manganák; ~ **fruit** magbunga.
beard: *n.* balbás.
bearing: *n.* tikas, bikas, tindíg, kiyás.
beast: *n.* hayop.
beat: *v.* pumalò, bumugbóg; (*win*) manalo, tumalo; (*heart*) tumibók; *n.* (*music*) kumpás, tiyempo.
beater: **egg~** pambatí ng itlóg.
beating: *n.* pamamalò; pagkatalo.
beautiful: *adj.* magandá.
beautify: *v.* pagandahín.
beauty: *n.* gandá, kagandahan; ~ **parlor** pákulutan.
became: *past of become*: naging-.
because: *conj.* kasí, dahil, sapagká't, palibhasà; (*since*) yamang.
beckon: *v.* kawayán.
become: *v.* magíng, -um-.
becoming: *adj.* bagay.
bed: *n.* kama, katre; **bamboo** ~ papag; **put to** ~ patulugin, ihigâ.
bedbug: *n.* surot.
beddings: *n.* kumot.
bedridden: *adj.* nararatay sa baníg, nakaratay.
bedroom: *n.* silíd-tulugán.
bedspread: *n.* kubrekáma.
bee: *n.* pukuyutan, laywán, bubuyog; **~hive** bahay-pukyutan.
beef: *n.* karneng-baka; **~steak** bistik.
beer: *n.* serbesa.
beeswax: *n.* pagkít.
beet: *n.* rimulatsa.
beetle: *n.* salagúbang, salagintô, uwáng.
befall: *v.* mangyari, datnán.
before: *prep., adv.* bago; (*in front of*) sa haráp; (*ahead*) una; **-hand** *adv.* muna, antimano.
befriend: *v.* kaibiganin.
beg: *v.* magpalimós, humingî, magmakaawà, sumamò; **-gar** *n.* magpapalimos, pulubi.
begin: *v.* magsimulâ, mag-umpisá; **~ner** *n.* baguhan, bagito; **~ning** *n.* simulâ, pinagsimulán.
beguile: *v.* magdayà, luminláng.
behalf: *n.* alang-alang, sa ngalan ng.
behave: *v.* kumilos, magpakatao, magpakabaít.
behavior: *n.* kilos, gawî.
behead: *v.* pumugot ng ulo, pugutan.

behind: *prep*. sa likód, sa hulí; (*in time*) atrasádo, mahulí.
behold: *v*. tumingín.
being: *n*. tao; *v*. *present participial of* **be**; **for the time ~** samantala.
belated: *adj*. hulí, naatraso.
belch: *v*. dumigháy, dumighál.
belfry: *n*. kampanaryo.
Belgium: *n*., *adj*. Bélhiká.
belief: *n*. paniniwalà, pananampalataya; paniwalà.
believe: *v*. maniwalà, paniwalaan.
belittle: *v*. maliitín, mangmatá, menosin, muntiín.
bell: *n*. kampanà, batingáw, kulilíng; **~ tower** kampanaryo, tore.
belligerent: *adj*. mapanlabán.
bellow: *v*. umungal, pumalaháw; **~s** *n*. bulusan, alulusan.
belong: *v*. may pag-aarì; (*be a member of*) sumapì; **~ings** arí-arian, gawá-gawaan.
beloved: *adj*. minamahál.
below: *adv*. sa ibabâ, sa ilalim ng.
belt: *n*. sinturón; (*machine*) korea.
bench: *n*. bangkô; (*court of law*) hukuman.
bend: *v*. yumukô, humubog; **~ over** *v*. matuwád.
beneath: *adv*. sa ibabâ, sa ilalim ng.
benediction: *n*. bendisyón; basbás.
benefactor: *n*. tagapagpalà, tagapag-ampón.
beneficial: *adj*. mabuti, nakabubúti.
beneficiary: *n*. benepisyaryo, ang makíkinabang.
benefit: *n*. pakinabang, kapakinabangán; buti, benepisiyo; *v*. mahitâ, mapalâ, mapakinabang.
benevolent: *adj*. mabaít, mapagkawanggawâ.
bent: *adj*. baluktót, balikukô; (*stooping*) tungó.
bequeath: *v*. magpamana, ipamana, mag-iwan.
bequest: *n*. pagpapamana.
bereave: *v*. maulila.
beriberi: *n*. manás, panás.
Bermuda grass: *n*. kawitan, kulatáy.
berry: *n*. beri (presa, sasamora, arandano, atb).
beside: *prep*. sa tabí, katabí; **~s** *adv*., *prep*. bukód sa, tangì sa.
besiege: *v*. makubkób, kumubkób.
besmear: *v*. magdumí, dumihán.
best: *adj*., *adv*. pinakamabuti; **~ man** abay.
bestial: *adj*. makahayop.
bestow: *v*. magkaloób, pagkaloobán.
bet: *n*. pustá, pustahan; *v*. pumustá, pustahán.
betamax: *n*. betamaks.
betel: *n*. hitsó, itsó; ikmó; **~-leaf pepper** buyo-anís.
betray: *v*. magdayà, dumayà; magtaksíl.
betrothal: *n*. pagpapakasál.
better: *adj*. mas mabuti, lalong mauti; *v*. pagalingín; **get ~** gumalíng, bumuti.
between: *adv*., *prep*. sa gitnâ, sa pagitan ng.
beverage: *n*. inumin.
beware: *v*. mag-ingat, mangilag.
bewilder: *v*. guluhín, magulahán.
bewitch: *v*. ingkantuhín, umingkanto; mangulam, kumulam.
beyond: *prep*. lagpás, lampás; di-abót.
bias: *n*. pagkiling, pagkampí; **~ed** kampí, makiling; makásarili.
bib: *n*. babero, baberón.
Bible: *n*. Bíbliyá.
bibliography: *n*. talasanggunián.
bicep: *n*. dagá-dagaan.
bicker: *v*. magsuwatan, suwawán.
bicycle: *n*. bisikleta.
bid: *n*. alók, tawad; tasa; halagá; *v*. tumawad, tawaran, magtasa; (*command*) mag-utos.
bier: *n*. kalandra; karo ng patáy.
big: *adj*. malakí; (*important*) mahalagá.
bigot: *n*. panátiko.
bigwig: *n*. maimpluénsiyang-tao.
bike: *n*. bisikleta.
bile: *n*. apdó.
bill: *n*. kuwenta; utang; (*proposed law*) panukalang-batás; (*banknote*) papel-de-bangko; (*beak*) tukâ; *v*. ilistá.
billboard: *n*. paskilan, kábitan ng kartelón.
billfold: *n*. pitakà, kartera, portamoneda.
billiards: *n*. bilyár.
billion: *num*. libong angaw.
bind: *v*. gapusin, igapos, italì; bigkisín; (*bandage*) bendahihan; (*oblige*) atasan.
binder: *n*. pambigkís; (*of books*) magbabalát ng aklát.
binding: *n*. tahì; (*of book*) pabalát; (*bandage*)

benda, bendahe.
biographer: *n.* mananalambuhay.
biography: *n.* talambuhay, dulámbuhay.
biology: *n.* biyolohiyá.
bird: *n.* ibon; **~ of prey** ibong máninilà; **~cage** *n.* hawla; **~'s eye** *adj.* tanáw-ibon.
birth: *n.* kapangánakan, pagkaluwál, pagsilang, pagluwál; **~ control** *n.* pagpigil sa panganganák; **give ~** *v.* manganák, magsilang; **~day** *n.* kaarawán, kapanganakan, kumpleanyo; **~mark** *n.* bálat; **~place** *n.* bayang pinanganakán.
biscuit: *n.* galyetas.
bisect: *v.* biyakín, maghatì.
bishop: *n.* obispo.
bit: *n.* kauntî; kapiraso; (*of horse's bridle*) bokado.
bitch: *n.* asong babae.
bite: *n.* kagát; *v.* kumagát, kagatín; **~ the lips** *v.* mapakat-labì.
bitter: *adj.* mapaít.
bizarre: *adj.* kakaibá; kagila-gilalas.
blab: *v.* magdaldál, magtsismis.
black: *n.* itím; *adj.* maitím; (*dark night*) madilím; **wear ~ for mourning** *v.* magluksâ; **~list** *n.* tálaang-itím.
blackberry: *n.* (*Java plum*) lumbóy, duhat.
blackboard: *n.* pisara.
blackjack: *n.* blákdiyák.
blacken: *v.* paitimín.
blacksmith: *n.* panday, magbabakál.
bladder: *n.* pantóg.
blade: *n.* talím; (*of shovel*) dahon.
blame: *n.* kasalanan, paninisi; *v.* isisi, manisi.
bland: *adj.* matabáng.
blank: *adj.* waláng-sulat, blangko, palta.
blanket: *n.* kumot, mantá; *v.* balutin.
blare: *v.* umingay.
blast: *n.* putók, pagsabog; *v.* pasabugin.
blatant: *adj.* waláng patumanggá; lantád; bastós.
blaze: *n.* liyáb, dingas, alab; *v.* magliyáb.
bleach: *v.* paputiín, ikulá.
bleak: *adj.* mapangláw, malungkót.
bleed: *v.* dumugô; duguín; **nose ~** balinguyngóy.
blemish: *n.* pilat, peklat; mantsá; depekto.
blend: *v.* magtimpla, maghalò, maglahók, magsama.
bless: *v.* benditahin, magbendita.
blessed: *adj.* banál, sagrado; mapalad.
blessing: *n.* bendisión; biyayà.
blind: *adj.* bulág; *v.* bulagin; **~er** panakíp sa matá.
blindfold: *v.* piringán, takpán ang matá.
blink: *v.* kumuráp, mapakisáp.
bliss: *n.* kaligayahan.
blister: *n.* paltós; lintós; *v.* magpaltós.
blizzard: *n.* bagyó ng yelo.
bloat: *v.* mamagâ.
bloated: *adj.* namamagâ, magâ.
block: *n.* bloke, tipák; *v.* bumará, magharang; pigilan; **~head** tangá, galgál.
blockade: *n.* bangkulóng.
blond: *adj.* Olandés.
blood: *n.* dugô; **high ~ pressure** altapresiyón; **~shed** pagdanak ng dugô; **~shot** namumulá.
bloody: *adj.* marugô, dugu-duguán.
bloom: *v.* mamulaklák, mamukadkád.
blossom: *n.* bulaklák.
blot: *n.* bahid, mantsá; dungis.
blotter: *n.* sekante.
blouse: *n.* blusa.
blow: *v.* bumugá; (*one's nose*) sumingá; (*wind*) humangin, umihip; **~ up** pumutók; *n.* (*punch*) dagok; (*whip*) hampás, palò, bugbóg; (*wind*) ihip ng hangin.
blowfly: *n.* bangaw.
blow-out: *n.* bloaut, handâ, salu-salo.
blue: *n.* asúl, bughāw; **feel ~** malungkót; **navy ~** *n.* asúl-marino.
bluff: *v.* magkunwarî; *n.* dalisdís, talampás.
blunder: *n.* malakíng pagkakámalî.
blunt: *adj.* mapuról, pudpód.
blur: *v.* lumabò; **blurry** *adj.* malabò, ulap-ulap.
blurt: *v.* bumulalás.
blush: *v.* mamulá, mapamulá; *n.* pamumulá.
boa: *n.* sawá, manlilingkís.
boar: *n.* bulugan, baboy-damó, barakong-baboy.
board: *n.* tablá; (*council*) konseho; (*ironing*) pamalantsahan; **~er** nangángasera; *v.* tumulóy, tumirá; **~ing house** bahay-pangaserahán; **~ of directors** pangasiwaan, pamat-

nugutan, pamahalaan.
boast: *v*. maghambóg, magyabáng; **~ful** *adj*. hambóg, palalò, mapágmayabáng.
boat: *n*. bapór, bangkâ, paraáw, lantsa.
bob: *v*. lumubóg-lumitáw; (*hair*) magpabáb, magpa-putol.
bobbin: *n*. bobina, pulunán ng sinulid.
bobtail: *n*. punggî.
body: *n*. katawán; (*structure*) kabahayan.
bodyguard: *n*. guwardiyá, buntót; talibà.
bog: *n*. lusak, balahô, kuminóy.
bogus: *adj*. huwád; palso.
boil: *n*. (*with pus*) pigsá; *v*. (*water*) kumulô; (*in cooking*) maglagà.
boiler: *n*. kaldera.
boisterous: *adj*. maingay.
bold: *adj*. matapang, pangahás; (*rude*) bastós.
bolo: *n*. iták, gulok.
bolt: *n*. kandádo; trángka, perno; *v*. itarangká.
bomb: *n*. bomba; *v*. bombahín; **~er** *n*. eruplanong pambomba.
bond: *n*. bigkís, gapos, talì; (*guarantee*) garantiyá, panagót, akò; (*pledge*) sanglâ.
bondage: *n*. pagkaalipin.
bone: *n*. butó; (*of fish*) tiník.
bonfire: *n*. sigâ.
bonnet: *n*. bonete, gora; tukaról.
bony: *adj*. (*fish*) matiník; (*thin*) payát.
booby prize: *n*. nakatutuyáng gawad.
booby trap: *n*. patibóng.
book: *n*. libro, aklát; **~case** aparadór ng mga aklát; **~keeper** *n*. tenedór-de-libro; **~let** *n*. librito.
boom: *n*. (*sound*) ugong, hugong, dagundóng; (*in business*) bigláng paglakás ng negosyo.
boomerang: *n*. bumiráng.
boost: *v*. magtulak, itulak, isulong; magdagdág.
boot: *n*. bota; **~black** limpiyabota.
booth: *n*. kuból, tanghalan; puwesto.
bootlegger: *n*. kontrabandista ng alak.
booty: *n*. ang ninakaw.
booze: *n*. alak.
border: *n*. gilid, pagilid; (*boundary*) hangganan; (*brink*) bingit; (*margin*) palugit.
bore: *v*. (*hole*) butasan; (*tire*) yamutín, mainís.
boring: *adj*. makayamót, mainíp.
born: *adj*. ipinanganák, isinilang.
borrow: *v*. humirám, manghirám; **~ed** *adj*. hirám.
bosom: *n*. dibdíb; kaloobán; (*breast*) suso.
boss: *n*. hepe, punò.
bossy: *adj*. dominante, palautós, mapag-amúamuhan.
botany: *n*. botánika, paláhalamanan.
botch: *v*. sumirà.
both: *adj*., pron. kapwà, dalawá.
bother: *v*. abalahin, maabala, mang-istorbo.
bottle: *n*. bote, botelya; **~cap** *n*. tansán.
bottom: *n*. kailaliman, ilalim; (*buttocks*) puwít; **~less** dî maarók.
bough: *n*. sangá.
boulder: *n*. malaking bató.
boulevard: *n*. búlebar(d).
bounce: *v*. tumalbóg; *n*. talbóg.
bound: *adj*. nakatalì; (*certain*) tiyák; (*leap*) talón, luksó.
boundary: *n*. hangganan.
bountiful: *adj*. mapagbigáy; saganà.
bouquet: *n*. pumpón, tungkós.
bout: *n*. labanán.
bow: *v*. (*stoop*) yumukô; (*yield*) isukò; *n*. (*for ribbon*) laso; (*of violin*) panghilis, arko; (*for archery*) busog; **~ and arrow** panà.
bowels: *n*. bituka; **move the ~** dumumí, tumae.
bowl: *n*. mangkók, tasón; tagayán; *v*. (*sport*) magboling.
bowlegged: *adj*. sakáng.
bowling: *n*. boling.
box: *n*. kahón; káha; *v*. sumampál, sumuntók; **~ office** takílya
boxer: *n*. boksingero.
boy: *n*. batang lalaki.
boycott: *n*. layô, boykoteo; *v*. boykoteuhín.
boyhood: *n*. kabataan ng lalaki.
brace: *n*. suhay; *v*. suhayan.
bracelet: *n*. pulseras.
braces: *n*. tirantes.
bracket: *n*. panaklóng.
brackish: *adj*. maalát-alát.
brag: *v*. maghambóg, magmayabáng.
braggart: *n*. hambóg, hambugero.
braid: *n*. tirintás; *v*. magtirintás.
brain: *n*. utak; **~ child** bungang-isip.
braise: *v*. magkulob, kulubin.

brake: *n*. preno; *v*. magpreno.
bran: *n*. darák.
branch: *n*. sangá; **drooping ~** dukláy; *v*. sumangá.
brand: *n*. marká, taták; (*on cattle*) hero; (*kind*) urì, klase; **~-new** bagung-bago.
brass: *n*. tansô.
brat: *n*. pilyong batà.
brave: *adj*. matapang; *v*. mangahás; sagupain.
brawl: *n*. murahán.
brawny: *adj*. malakás, matipunò, muskulado.
brazen: *adj*. waláng-hiyâ, bastós.
breach: *n*. butas, pagkakasirâ; paglabág.
bread: *n*. tinapay; **~fruit** rimas.
breadth: *n*. luwáng, kaluwangan.
break: *v*. sumirà, madurog, mabasag, mabalì, malagót; **~ up with** makipagkasirâ; **~down** panlulupaypáy, pagbagsák.
breakable: *adj*. marupók, madalíng mabasag.
breakdown: *n*. pagkasirà; panlulupaypáy.
breakfast: *n*. almusál, agahan; **eat ~** mag-almusál.
breakwater: *n*. harang sa alon.
breast: *n*. suso; dibdíb.
breath: *n*. hiningá; **out of ~** humíhíngal.
breathe: *v*. humingá; (*inhale*) suminghót.
breed: *v*. magparami, magpaanák; *n*. lahì, kasta.
breeze: *n*. hangin, simoy.
brevity: *n*. kaiklián, kaigsián.
brew: *v*. ilutò; gumawâ ng serbesa.
brewery: *n*. serbeseriya.
bribe: *n*. lagáy, suhol, paratíng; *v*. sumuhol, magpabagsák.
bribery: *n*. pagsuhol, panunuhol, pagparating, paglalagáy, pagpapabagsák.
brick: *n*. ladrilyo, laryo.
bride: *n*. nobya, babaing ikákasál; **~groom** nobyo, lalaking ikákasál.
bridesmaid: *n*. abay na babae.
bridge: *n*. tuláy; (*of nose*) balingusan.
bridle: *n*. kabisada; *v*. pigilin.
brief: *adj*. maiklî, maigsî; *n*. (*legal*) alegato; **~case** porpolyo.
brigand: *n*. tulisán, mandarambóng.
bright: *adj*. maliwanag, matingkád; (*shining*) makináng.
brighten: *v*. magpaliwanag, lumiwanag.
brilliance: *n*. kaningningán; katalinuhan.
brilliant: *adj*. makináng; (*smart*) matalíno, nápakatalino.
brim: *n*. labì, bibíg.
brimstone: *n*. asupre.
brine: *n*. tasik.
bring: *v*. magdalá, dalhán; magsama; **~ up** (*raise*) magpalakí; **~ home** iuwî.
brink: *n*. bingit, gilid, labì.
briny: *adj*. maalat.
brisk: *adj*. mabilís, matulin, maliksí.
bristle: *v*. mangalisag; *n*. balahibo.
brittle: *adj*. madalíng mabasag; malutóng.
broach: *n*. pambutas.
broad: *adj*. malapad, maluwáng; (*general*) pangkalahatán; **~ minded** malawak ang isipan.
broadcast: *v*. magsahimpapawíd, isahimpapawíd; magkalát, ibalità.
broil: *v*. mag-ihaw.
broke: *adj*. saíd na saíd, waláng-walâ; **~n** *adj*. sirâ, basag; **~n hearted** nawasák.
bronze: *n*. tansô, bronse.
brood: *v*. lumimlím; malungkót na isipin; *n*. mga sisiw.
brook: *n*. sapà, batis.
broom: *n*. walís; **~stick** tankáy ng walís.
broth: *n*. sabáw.
brother: *n*. kapatíd na lalaki; **elder ~** kuya; **second oldest ~** diko; **third eldest ~** sangkó; **~hood** *n*. kápatiran, pagkamagkapatíd; **~-in-law** *n*. bayáw.
brow: *n*. noó; kilay; gilid.
browbeat: *v*. sindakin; bulasın.
brown: *adj*. kayumanggí.
browse: magbasá nang palakdáw-lakdáw, magbasá-basá.
bruise: *n*. pasâ; *v*. magíng-pasâ.
brunette: *n*. kuláy-kapé (buhók).
brunt: *n*. lakás, bagsík, tindí, bigát, sidhî.
brush: *n*. iskoba, sipilyo; **tooth ~** sipilyo; **paint ~** brotsa; *v*. magsipilyo, mag-iskoba; (*wipe away*) magpahid.
brusque: *adj*. bastos.
brutal: *adj*. malupít; mabangís.
brute: *n*. bruto, taong malupít; hayop.

bubble: *n.* bulubók, kulô; bulâ; *v.* bumulâ.
buck: *n.* usáng lalaki; ~ **tooth** sungkî; *v.* magalmá.
bucket: *n.* balde, timbâ; **kick the** ~ (*slang*) mamatáy.
buckle: *n.* hebilya.
bud: *n.* buko, usbóng; *v.* mamuko, magusbóng.
budge: *v.* mapakilos, maigaláw.
budget: *n.* badyet, laáng-gugulín.
buffalo: *n.* kalabáw-ramó; tamaráw; **water** ~ kalabáw-damulag.
buffer: *n.* nagpapahinà ng lakás.
buffet: *n.* páminggalan; bupéy.
buffoon: *n.* luko-lukó, komikero.
bug: *n.* insekto, kulisap; **bed**~ surot.
bugle: *n.* korneta.
build: *v.* gumawâ; magpagawâ; (*form*) anyô, yarì; (*body*) pangangatawán; ~**ing** *n.* gusalì.
bulb: *n.* bombilya.
bulge: *n.* tambók, uslî, umbók.
bulk: *n.* lakí, karamihan; ~**y** *adj.* malakí, mahirap hawakan.
bull: *n.* toro.
bulldoze: *v.* maninghál, singhalín, mambulas.
bullet: *n.* bala, punglô.
bulletin: *n.* ulat, bulitín, patalastás, paunawà; páhayagán.
bullfight: *n.* huwego-de-toro.
bullfighter: *n.* torero, toreadór.
bullock: *n.* kopang toro.
bull's-eye: *n.* gitnâ ng tudlaan.
bully: *n.* mapang-apí, matón, mapanupil; *v.* bulasin.
bulwark: *n.* tagapagtanggól, tagapangsanggaláng.
bum: *n.* palaboy, hampas-lupà; (*buttocks*) puwít.
bumblebee: *n.* bubuyog.
bump: *v.* bumanggâ, bumundól; ~**er** *n.* depensa, bamper; ~**y** *adj.* bakú-bakô.
bun: *n.* ban; (*hair*) pusód.
bunch: *n.* grupo; (*of bananas*) buwíg; (*of people*) lipón, langkáy; (*of grapes*) kumpól.
bundle: *n.* balutan; *v.* magbigkís, magbungkós.
bungalow: *n.* bunggaló.
bunion: *n.* bukol sa paá.
bunt: *v.* pumintíg, kantiín.
bunny: *n.* kuneho.
buoy: *n.* boya, palutang.
buoyant: *adj.* nakalulutang, lumulutang.
burden: *n.* pasán, dalá; *v.* magkargá, magpapasán.
bureau: *n.* (*government*) kawanihán; (*chest of drawers*) aparadór, kómoda.
bureaucracy: *n.* burukrasya.
burglar: *n.* magnanakaw.
burial: *n.* libíng.
burlap: *n.* estopa.
burly: *adj.* malakí, matipunô.
burn: *v.* sumunog, manunog; ~ **incense** magsuób; ~**er** *n.* metsero.
burst: *v.* magputók, pumutók.
bury: *v.* maglibíng; magbaón.
bus: *n.* bus.
bush: *n.* palumpóng; **beat around the** ~ magpaliguy-ligoy.
bushel: *n.* panega; busel.
bushy: *adj.* malagô.
business: *n.* negosyo, gawain, trabaho; (*right*) karapatán; ~ **man** negosyante, mangangalakál; **none of your** ~ walâ kang pakialám (pakí).
bust: *n.* busto; dibdíb; *v.* paputukín.
bustle: *v.* mag-apurá, magdalás-dalás.
busy: *adj.* okupado, matrabaho.
busybody: *n.* mapakialám; mapanghimasok.
but: *conj.* pero, ngunít, dátapuwá't, subali't.
butcher: *n.* magpapatay; *v.* magpatáy.
butler: *n.* mayordomo.
butt: *n.* (*buttocks*) puwít, pigî; (*of cigarette*) upós, beha; (*of gun*) kulata; (*target*) paksâ; *v.* sumuwág, uluhin; ~ **in** makialám, sumabád.
butter: *n.* mantikilya.
butterfly: *n.* paruparó; ~ **fish** paru-paro, barobaro; ~ **sleeve dress** balintawák.
buttocks: *n.* puwít, pigî, puwitán.
button: *n.* butones; *v.* ibutones.
buttonhole: *n.* uhales.
buttress: *n.* pansaló, panapó ng gusalì.
buy: *v.* bilhín, bumilí; ~ **wholesale** pumakyáw; ~**er** *n.* tagapamilí.
buzz: *n.* ugong, hugong, higing.
by: *adv.*, *prep.* sa piling, sa tabí; (*by means of*)

sa pamamagitan ng; (*made by, done by*) ni, ng.
bygone: *n.* nakaraán, nakalipas.
bylaw: *n.* álituntuning-panloób.
bystander: *n.* manonoód, mirón.
byword: *n.* káwikaán, karaniwang sabihin.

C

cab: *n.* taksi, kab.
cabaret: *n.* kabarét.
cabbage: *n.* repolyo.
cabin: *n.* kubo, dampâ; (*boat*) kamarote.
cabinet: *n.* gabinete, aparadór.
cable: *n.* kable; **~gram** kablegrama, pahatíd-kawad.
cabletow: *n.* lastáy.
cacao: *n.* kakáw.
cackle: *n.* kakak, puták.
cactus: *n.* hagdambató.
cadaver: *n.* bangkáy.
cadence: *n.* ritmo, indayog, alíw-iw.
cadet: *n.* kadete.
cage: *n.* kulungan; (*birds*) hawla; (*chickens*) tangkál; *v.* ihawla, itangkál.
cajole: *v.* humikayat, hikayatin, mang-akit, akitin.
cake: *n.* puto, bibíngka.
calamity: *n.* kalamidád, sakunâ, kapahamakán.
calcium: *n.* kálsiyum.
calculate: *v.* kalkulahín, tantiyahín.
calculus: *n.* palátayahan.
calendar: *n.* kalendaryo.
calf: *n.* (*of leg*) bintî; (*young cow*) bulô, guyà.
caliber: *n.* kalibre.
call: *n.* tawag; *v.* tawagan, tawagin; (*name*) ipangalan; ~ **off** itigil; **close** ~ pinagmuntík-muntikanan.
callus: *n.* kalyo, lipák.
calm: *adj.* tahimik, kalma, payapà.
calumnious: *adj.* mapanirang-puri.
calumny: *n.* paninirang-puri.
calyx: *n.* takupis.
camaraderie: *n.* pagkakaibiganán.
cambric: *n.* kambráy.
came: *v.* *irregular past tense of* **come**: dumatíng.
camel: *n.* kamelyo.
camera: *n.* kodák, kámera.
camouflage: *n.* balatkayô, pagtatakíp.
camp: *n.* kampo; **~ing** kampíng.
campaign: *n.* kampanya, kilusán; *v.* kumampanya; ~ **manager** *n.* punong-tagakampanya.
camphor: *n.* alkampór.
can: *v.* (*be able to*) maka-, ma-; maáarì; (*know how*) marúnong; (*preserve in a can*) ilata; *n.* lata.
canal: *n.* kanál, bambáng.
canary: *n.* kanaryo.
cancel: *v.* alisín, kumaltás, kaltasín, kanselahín; **~lation** pagkaltás; pawaláng-bisà.
cancer: *n.* kanser.
candid: *adj.* matapát.
candidate: *n.* kandidáto.
candied: *adj.* minatamisán.
candle: *n.* kandilà, sasáng; **~stick** kandelero.
candy: *n.* kendi.
cane: *n.* (*stick*) bastón, tungkód; (*sugar*) tubó; *v.* bastunín.
canine: *n.* aso.
cannibal: *n.* kanibal.
cannon: *n.* kanyón.
cannot: *v.* dî maáarì.
canny: *adj.* tuso; maingat.
canon: *n.* batás (ng iglesia).
canopy: *n.* palyo, kulandóng.
cantaloupe: *n.* milóng bilóg.
cantine: *n.* kantína.
canter: *v.* yumagyág.
canvas: *n.* lona, kambás, balindáng.
canvass: *v.* manghingî ng boto; magsiyasat, siyasatin, saliksikín.
cap: *n.* (*head*) gora; (*bottle*) takíp.
capability: *n.* kakayahán.
capable: *adj.* kaya, may-kaya.
capacious: *adj.* malulan.
capacity: *n.* kapasidád, malalamán.
cape: *n.* kapa, balabal; (*land*) lungos.
capital: *n.* kapitál; ulong-bayan; ~ **letter** malakíng titik; (*city*) kabesera; **~ist** *n.* kapitalista, mamu-muhunán.
caprice: *n.* sumpóng; **capricious** *adj.* kapritsoso, bisyoso, makapritso, sumpungin.
Capricorn: *n.* kambíng (sa zodiac).

capsize: *v*. tumaób, mataób.
capsule: *n*. kápsula.
captain: *n*. kapitán.
caption: *n*. pamagát, título.
captivate: *v*. makabighanì, magayuma, bihagin, maakit.
captive: *adj*. bihag.
captivity: *n*. pagkabilanggô, pagkabihag.
capture: *v*. bumihag; dakpín, bihagin.
car: *n*. kotse, awto; **dining ~** kotseng kainán; **freight ~** bagón; **sleeping ~** kotseng tulugán.
carabao: *n*. kalabáw; **male ~** damulag.
caramel: *n*. karamélo.
carapace: *n*. talukab, bahay ng alimango.
card: *n*. (*playing*) baraha; (*postcard*) tarhéta postál.
cardboard: *n*. kartón.
cardinal: *n*. kardinál; **~ fish** bungka, dangat, suga.
care: *v*. alagaan, tumingín; **take ~ of** alagaan; **take ~** mag-ingat; *n*. pag-aalagà; pag-iingat; **~taker** *n*. katiwalà; **I don't ~** walâ akóng pakialám.
career: *n*. karera.
careful: *adj*. maingat.
careless: *adj*. pabayâ; waláng-ingat.
caress: *v*. humaplós, yumakap; himasin.
cargo: *n*. karga, dalá, merkansiya.
caricature: *n*. karikatura.
carillon: *n*. karilyón.
carnal: *adj*. mahalay; pangkatawán.
carnival: *n*. karnabál.
carnivorous: *adj*. mahilig sa karne.
carousel: *n*. tiobibo.
carpenter: *n*. karpintero, alwagi, anluwagi; **~'s file** *n*. kikil.
carpet: *n*. alpombra, karpet.
carriage: *n*. karwahe; tikas.
carrier: *n*. tagapagdalá, tagapaghatíd.
carrot: *n*. karot.
carry: *v*. magdalá; (*in one's arms*) pumangkó; (*in the hands*) bitbitín; (*on the back*) babahín; (*on the hip*) kilikin, kumilik; (*on the head*) magsunong, sunungin; (*on shoulder*) magpasán, pasanín; **~ out** gawín, isagawâ.
cart: *n*. (*horse drawn*) kalésa, karitela.
cartilage: *n*. kartilago.
cartoon: *n*. kartún, larawang katatawanán; **~ist** karikaturista.
cartridge: *n*. kartutso.
carve: *v*. maglilok, ililok.
carving: *n*. inukit, lilok; **~ knife** kutsilyong pang-hiwà.
case: *n*. (*box*) kahón; (*lawsuit*) asunto, usapín; (*instance*) kaso; (*suitcase*) maleta; (*situation*) lagáy, tayô; (*grammar*) kaukulán; **genitive ~** *n*. kaukuláng paarî; **nominative ~** *n*. kaukuláng palagyô; **objective ~** *n*. kaukuláng palayón; **vocative ~** *n*. kaukuláng panawag.
cash: *n*. perang hawak, salapî; **~ier** *n*. kahero.
cashew: *n*. kasóy, balubad.
casino: *n*. kasino, sugalán.
cask: *n*. bariles.
casket: *n*. ataúl; kabaong; kahita, estutse.
cassava: *n*. kamoteng-kahoy, kasaba; **~ starch** *n*. gawgáw.
cassock: *n*. sutana.
cast: *v*. ihagis, iitsá; imolde; tauhan ng dulà.
castanet: *n*. kastanyedas.
castigate: *v*. magparusa, kastiguhin.
castle: *n*. kastilyo.
castor oil: *n*. langís ng lansinà.
casual: *adj*. di-ináasahan, nagkataón.
casualty: *n*. nadisgrasya; sakunâ.
cat: *n*. pusà; **wild ~** musang, alamíd.
catacomb: *n*. katakúmba.
catalogue: *n*. katálogo.
catapult: *n*. tiradór.
cataract: *n*. bilíg ng matá, kulabà.
catarrh: *n*. sipón, kataro.
catastrophe: *n*. malakíng sakunâ.
catch: *v*. hulihin, dakpín; saluhín; **~ a disease** mahâwa, malainan.
catechism: *n*. katesismo.
category: *n*. kaurián, urì, pangkát.
caterpillar: *n*. higad, uod.
catfish: *n*. pantát, hito.
cathedral: *n*. katedrál.
catheter: *n*. kalilya, sunda.
Catholic: *adj*. Katóliko.
catsup: *n*. ketsap.
cattail: *n*. lawas.
cattle: *n*. mga baka.
caught: *v*., *adj*. nahuli; dinakíp; **~ red handed**

adj. mabukíng. [Past of *catch*]
cauldron: *n*. talyasì, kalderón.
cauliflower: *n*. koliplór, kolis.
cause: *n*. dahilán, sanhî; *v*. magbigán, dulutan, pa-.
cauterize: *v*. pasuin, pumasò.
caution: *n*. balà, babalâ, ingat; *v*. magbalà, pagsabihan.
cautious: *adj*. napakaingat.
cavalry: *n*. kabalyeriya, kalbaryo.
cave: *n*. kuweba, yungíb, lunggâ.
caviar: *n*. mga itlóg ng mga isdâ, pugá.
cavity: *n*. butas.
cayenne pepper: *n*. pamintón.
cease: *v*. tumigil, humintô; ~ **raining** tumilà.
ceiling: *n*. kísame, taluktók.
Celcius: *adj*. Sentigrado.
celebrate: *v*. magdiwang, ipagbunyî.
celebrity: *n*. tanyág na tao, bantóg na tao.
celibate: *adj*. waláng-asawa.
cell: *n*. sélda; (*plant or animal*) sélula.
cellar: *n*. bodega.
cello: *n*. tselo.
cellophane: *n*. selopín.
cement: *n*. simento.
cemetery: *n*. sementeryo, kamposanto, libingan.
censor: *v*. suriin, sensurahin; *n*. sensura.
census: *n*. senso.
cent, centavo: *n*. séntims.
centaur: *n*. tikbalang.
centenary: *n*. sentenaryo, anibersario ng sandaang taón.
center: *n*. gitnâ, sentro; *v*. isentro; **very** ~ *n*. kalagitnaan, pinakagitnâ.
centimeter: *n*. sentimetro.
centipede: *n*. alupihan.
central: *adj*. nasa gitnâ; punò; pangunahín.
century: *n*. siglo, isáng daáng taón, dantaón.
ceremony: *n*. seremonya.
certain: *adj*. sigurado, tiyák.
certificate: *n*. katibayan, sertipiko, alusithâ.
certify: *v*. magpatunay, magpatotoo; panagután.
chafe: *v*. magkuskós.
chain: *n*. tanikalâ, kadena.
chair: *n*. silya, upuan; **rocking** ~ silyang tumba-tumbá; **~man** *n*. tagapangulo.
chalk: *n*. yeso, tisà.
challenge: *n*. hamon, reto; *v*. hamunin.
chamber: *n*. kapulungán; kámara; **~maid** kamarera.
chameleon: *n*. kamaleón, hunyangò, bangkaláng.
chamois: *n*. gamusa.
chamomile: *n*. mansanilya.
champagne: *n*. tsampán.
champion: *n*. kampeón, mananaló; **~ship** *n*. kampeonato.
chance: *n*. pagkakataón; (*luck*) palad, kapalaran; **by** ~ dî sinasadyâ.
chandelier: *n*. aranyas.
change: *v*. magbago, bumago; suklián; palitán; (*dress*) magbihis; *n*. pagbabago; (*when buying*) suklî, **loose** ~ sinsilyo.
channel: *n*. kanál, bambáng.
chaos: *n*. guló, pagkakagulóm saligutgót.
chapel: *n*. kapilya.
chaperon: *n*. kasama, tsaperón.
chap: *v*. pumutók-putók; **~ped** lipák, putukputók.
chapter: *n*. kabanatà, kapítulo; sangáy.
character: *n*. pagkatao; tauhan; **~istic** *n*. likás, katutubò.
charcoal: *n*. uling.
charge: *v*. singilín, halagahán; (*attack*) salakayin; (*in court*) magsakdál; *n*. halagá, singil.
charity: *n*. karidád, kawanggawâ, kagandahang-loób.
charm: *n*. pang-akit, panghalina, alindóg; *v*. humalina, mang-akit; **~ing** *adj*. kalugudlugód, kahalí-halina.
chart: *n*. talángguhit; tsart.
charter: *v*. umalkilá, umupa; magpaupa.
chase: *v*. humabol, humagad, tumugis; palayasin, itabóy.
chasm: *n*. bangín.
chaste: *adj*. malinis, mahinhín.
chat: *v*. mag-usap, magdadaldál.
chatter: *v*. dumaldál, magsasatsát.
chauffeur: *n*. tsupér.
cheap: *adj*. (*inexpensive*) mura; (*bad quality*) mumurahin; ~ **talk** úsapang waláng ka-

buluhán.
cheat: *v.* luminláng, manloko, subain; *n.* magdarayà, manunubà; ~ **sheet** (*slang*) *n.* kódigó.
check: *n.* tseke, tsek; *v.* magsiyasat; magrepaso; magmarká.
checkerboard: *n.* damahán.
checkers: *n.* dama.
cheek: *n.* pisngî.
cheer: *n.* tuwâ, galák; *v.* sumigáw nang masayá, pumalakpák.
cheese: *n.* keso.
chemical: *n.* kímiko.
chemise: *n.* kamisón.
chemist: *n.* kímiko.
chemistry: *n.* kímika.
cherish: *v.* mahalín, pakamahalín.
cherry: *n.* seresa.
cherub: *n.* kerubín.
chess: *n.* ahedrés.
chest: *n.* dibdíb; pitso; (*box*) kahón.
chestnut: *n.* kastanyas.
chew: *v.* ngumuyâ, ngumatâ; (*sugar cane*) magpangós; (*betel nut*) ngumangà.
chick: *n.* sisiw.
chicken: *n.* manók; ~ **pox** bulutung-tubig; **wild** ~ labuyò.
chief: *n.* hepe, punò; *adj.* pinakamahalagá; ~ **justice** *n.* punong-mahistrado; ~ **of police** *n.* pamunuan ng kapulisan.
child: *n.* batà; **youngest** ~ bunsô; **eldest** ~ panganay; ~**hood** kabataan; kamusmusán; ~**birth** panganganák; ~**ish** *adj.* batang-batà; ~**ren** *n.* mga anák.
chill: *n.* ngiki, gináw; ~**y** *adj.* maginám, malamíg.
chime: *n.* rupike, rupikál, dupikál.
chimney: *n.* tsimenea.
chin: *n.* babà; **double** ~ kabil.
china: *n.* losa, porselana.
Chinese: *n.*, *adj.* Insík.
chink: *n.* biták, gahak.
chip: *n.* tatal; piraso; *v.* matapyás, mapingas.
chirp: *v.* humuni, sumiyáp.
chisel: *n.* paít, panukól.
chocolate: *n.* tsokolate.
choice: *n.* pagpilì, pamimilì, pilì.
choir: *n.* koro.
choke: *v.* sumakál, sakalín.
cholera: *n.* kólera.
choose: *v.* pumilì, mamilì; (*decide*) magpasiyá.
chop: *v.* tumagâ, magtilád, tilarín, hapakín; maglabrá; ~**ing block** sangkalan, tadtaran; ~**sticks** *n.* sipit ng Insík.
chord: *n.* kuwerdas.
chore: *n.* gawain.
chorus: *n.* koro.
chosen: *adj.* pinilì.
Christ: *n.* Kristo; ~**ian** *adj.* Kristiyano, binyagan; ~**ianism** *n.* Kristiyanismo.
Christmas: *n.* Paskó; ~ **gift** pamaskó.
chronic: *adj.* matagál na.
chronological: *adj.* sunúd-sunód.
chrysanthemum: *n.* krisántemo.
chubby: *adj.* mabintóg, maburók.
chuck: *v.* ipukól.
chuckle: *v.* umalik-ík.
chum: *n.* kaibigan, katoto, karayama.
chunk: *n.* tipák.
church: *n.* simbahan, iglesia; ~ **yard** patyò.
cicada: *n.* kuliglíg.
cicatrice: *n.* peklát.
cigar: *n.* sigaro, tabako.
cigarette: *n.* sigarilyo; ~ **holder** pipa, patupak.
cinder: *n.* baga; ~**s** *n.* abó.
cinema: *n.* sine, pelíkula.
cinnamon: *n.* kanela.
circle: *n.* sírkulo, bilog.
circuit: *n.* paligid, palibot; ~**ous** *adj.* paikut-ikot; maligoy.
circular: *adj.* bilóg, pabilóg.
circulate: *v.* kumalat, lumaganap; ikalat.
circumcise: *v.* magtulì, tuliin; ~**d** *adj.* tulî, kugít.
circumcision: *n.* pagtutulì, pagsusunat.
circumference: *n.* palibot, paligid, kabilugan.
circumflex: *n.* tuldík na pakupyâ.
circumstance: *n.* bagay-bagay, pangyayari, kalagayan.
circus: *n.* sirko.
citadel: *n.* kutà, muóg.
citation: *n.* banggít, sipì.
cite: *v.* bumanggít, sipiin.
citizen: *n.* mamamayán; ~**ship** *n.* pagkama-

mamayán.
city: *n.* lun(g)sód, siyudád.
civic: *adj.* pambayan, pangmámamayán.
civil: *adj.* sibíl, pambayan; pangmámamayán; **~ian** *n.* sibilyan, paysano; **~ized** *adj.* sibilisado, bihasa; **~ization** *n.* sibilisasiyón, kabihasnán.
clack: *n.* taguktók.
claim: *n.* kahilingan, pahayag, pag-angkín.
clam: *n.* kabyâ, lukán, paros.
clamor: *n.* kaingayan, hiyawan.
clan: *n.* angkán, lipì.
clandestine: *adj.* lihim, lingíd.
clang: *n.* kalatóng.
clap: *v.* pumalakpák.
clarify: *v.* ipaliwanag, ipalinaw.
clarinet: *n.* klarinete.
clash: *n.* pag-aaway, salungatán; kalatóng.
clasp: *v.* pisilín; mag-ipit; yakapin; *n.* kawit.
class: *n.* urì; klase; ~ **mate** kaklase; **~room** *n.* silíd-aralán.
classical: *adj.* klásiko.
classify: *v.* magbukúd, bukód, mag-urí-urì.
clause: *n.* sugnáy.
clavicle: *n.* balagat.
claw: *n.* pangalmót, kukó (ng ibon), sipit (ng uláng); *v.* kumalmot.
clay: *n.* luwád
clean: *adj.* malinis; **~ing** *n.* paglilinis.
cleanse: *v.* linisin.
clear: *adj.* maliwanag, (*transparent*) malinaw; (*without obstructions*) tahaw; (*traffic*) libre; *v.* magliwanag.
clearance: *n.* pagpapaliwanag; pagpapalinaw.
cleavage: *n.* biyák, baák, biták.
cleave: *v.* magbiyák.
clemency: *n.* awà, habág.
clench: *v.* maghawak, magkimkím.
clergy: *n.* mga parì.
clerk: *n.* eskribiyente, kawaní.
clever: *adj.* matalas, matalino.
click: *n.* lagitík; tunóg.
client: *n.* kliyente; **regular** ~ sukì.
cliff: *n.* talampás; matarík na dalisdís.
climate: *n.* klima.
climax: *n.* rurok, kasukdulán, karurukan, kahayunán.
climb: *v.* umakyát; *n.* pag-akyát; ~ **down** bumabâ.
clinch: *v.* yapusín; magrimatse; magpasiyá.
cling: *v.* ikapit, kumapit.
clinic: *n.* dispensaryo, klínika.
clip: *v.* gupitín; *n.* sipit, ipit; **newspaper ~ping** *n.* rekorte.
clipper: *n.* panggupít, pamputol; **fingernail** ~ panghinukó.
clique: *n.* pangkát, grupo ng mga kaibigan.
cloak: *n.* balabal, kapa, manto.
clock: *n.* relós, orasan; **~wise** *adv.* paikót sa kanan.
clog: *v.* bumará; *n.* hadláng; (*shoe*) bakyâ; **~ged** *adj.* barado.
close: *v.* magsará, magpinid; (*finish*) magtapós; ~ **eyes** pumikít; **come** ~ lumapit; **~d** *adj.* sarado.
close: *adj.* (*near*) malapit.
closet: *n.* dispensa; **water** ~ kubeta.
closure: *n.* pagpipinid, pagsasará; pagwawakás.
clot: *n.* namuóng dugô; *v.* mamuô, makultá.
cloth: *n.* tela, kayo; **table~** mantél.
clothe: *v.* damitán, damtán; magpadamít.
clothes: *n.* mga damít; **~line** sampayan; **~pin** pang-ipit ng damít.
clothing: *n.* damít, pananamít.
cloud: *n.* ulap; **cirrus** ~ alapaap; **rain** ~ dagím; *v.* mag-ulap; **~y** *adj.* maulap.
clown: *n.* komikero, payaso, lakayo.
club: *n.* kapisanan, klub, samahán; (*cudgel*) garote, pambambó; (*police cudgel*) batutà.
cluck: *n.* kurók, kurukutók.
clue: *n.* tandâ, bakás, himaton, palatandaan.
clump: *n.* kimpál, tigkál, kumpól.
clumsy: *adj.* padaskúl-daskól, asiwâ; malamyâ.
cluster: *n.* kumpól; (*of coconuts*) balaybáy.
clutch: *v.* sunggabán, dakmaín; *n.* klats.
clutter: *v.* ikalat, magkalat; *n.* kalat.
coach: *n.* tagasanay; (*railroad*) kotse; **~man** *n.* kutsero.
coagulate: *v.* makultá, mamuô.
coal: *n.* karbón.
coalesce: *v.* magsanib.
coalition: *n.* pagsasanib, pagsasama.
coarse: *adj.* magaspáng, maligasgás; magaslâw.

coast: *n*. babáy-dagat, baybayin; aplaya; *v*. magpadausdós.
coat: *n*. amerikana; ~ **of arms** eskudo.
co-author: *n*. kamánunulát.
coax: *v*. isamò, manuyò, suyuin.
cob: *n*. busal.
cobalt: *n*. kobalto.
cobbler: *n*. sapatero.
cobra: *n*. ulupóng.
cobweb: *n*. bahay ng gagambá.
coccyx: *n*. kuyukót, tulatod.
cock: *n*. (*rooster*) tandáng; **cry of** ~ talaok, tilaok; **~pit** sabungán; **~fight** *n*. sabong; **illegal ~fight** tupada; **~scomb** *n*. palong.
cock-a-doodle-do: *n*. tiktilaok.
cockle: *n*. sigay.
cockroach: *n*. ipis.
cockspur: *n*. tahíd.
cocktail: *n*. kaktel.
cocoa: *n*. kakáw.
coconut: *n*. niyóg; **young** ~ buko, murà; ~ **husk** bunót; ~ **milk** gatâ; ~ **shell** bao; ~ **toffee** bukayò; ~ **oil** langís ng niyóg.
cocoon: *n*. bahay-uód, kukún.
cod: *n*. bakaláw.
code: *n*. kódigó; **penal** ~ *n*. kódigó penál.
coerce: *v*. pumilit, pumuwersa.
coffee: *n*. kapé; **~pot** kapetera.
coffin: *n*. kabaong, ataúl.
cognate: *adj*. magkaugnáy.
cognizance: *n*. kamalayán.
cognizant: *adj*. nalalaman, batíd.
cohere: *v*. magdikít.
coherent: *adj*. magkakaugmâ, magkakaugnáy.
cohort: *n*. pangkát.
coil: *n*. rolyo, likaw, ikid; *v*. pumulupot, iikid.
coin: *n*. baryá, sinsilyo; **~ed** *adj*. likhâ.
coincide: *v*. mapasabáy, magkataón, mátapát.
coincidence: *n*. pagkakataón, panaón.
coitus: *n*. hindót, pagtatalik.
colander: *n*. salaan, panalà.
cold: *adj*. malamíg; maginàw; *n*. lamíg; (*sickness*) sipón.
collaborate: *v*. magtulong, tumulong sa trabaho.
collapse: *v*. gumuhò, bumagsák.
collar: *n*. kuwelyo; **~bone** balagat.
collateral: *n*. garantíya; kaanak.
colleague: *n*. paniyero, kasamahán.
collect: *v*. tipunin, ipunin; magkatipon; **~ion** *n*. pagtitipon; (*of debts*) paniningíl; (*of church*) kolekta; **~ive** *adj*. palansák.
collector: *n*. tagasingíl, kobradór, máníningil.
college: *n*. koléhiyo, dálubhasaan.
collide: *v*. bumanggâ, magkabunggô.
colloquial: *adj*. palasak, pangkaraniwan, pang-araw-araw, pantalakayan.
colon: *n*. tutuldók.
colonel: *n*. koronél.
colony: *n*. kolóniya.
color: *n*. kulay, kolór; *v*. magkulay, kulayan; **~-blind** bulág sa kulay; **~ful** *adj*. makulay.
colt: *n*. potro, bisiro.
column: *n*. haligi, kulumna.
coma: *n*. kawaláng-malay.
comb: *n*. sukláy; **lice-~** suyod; (*ornamental*) peineta; (*of fowl*) palong; *v*. suklayán, magsukláy.
combat: *n*. labanán, paglalaban.
combination: *n*. pagkasasama, pagkakahalò.
combine: *v*. magsama, maghalò.
come: *v*. dumatíng; (*approach*) lumapit, dumulóg; (*attend*) dumaló; ~ **from** galing, taga-; ~ **here** pumarito; ~ **home** umuwî; ~ **in** pumasok; ~ **back** bumalík; ~ **on!** halá na; ~ **out** lumabás; ~ **upon** mátagpuán.
comedy: *n*. komedya, katatawanán.
comet: *n*. buntalà, kometa.
comfort: *n*. ginhawa, kaginhawahan, kaluwagán; alíw; *v*. umalíw; **~able** *adj*. maginhawa, nakagiginhawa.
comic: *adj*. kómiko, katawá-tawá.
comma: *n*. kuwít, koma.
command: *n*. utos, mando; kapangyarihan; *v*. mag-utos, magmando; mag-atas; **~ment** *n*. utos, kautusán.
commemorate: *v*. magpagunitâ, gunitaín, ipaalaala.
commence: *v*. magsimulâ.
commend: *v*. pumuri, papurihan; **~ation** *n*. papuri, parangál.
commensurate: *adj*. katimbáng, kasukát.
comment: *n*. komentaryo, puná, pansín; *v*. magkomentaryo; **~ator** *n*. komentarista.

commerce: *n*. kalakal, pangangalakal, komérsiyo.
commercial: *adj*. pangkalaka, kumersiyál.
commercialize: *v*. kumalakal.
commissary: *n*. komisaryo.
commission: *n*. komisiyón, porsiyento, kaparte; **~er** komisyonado.
commit: *v*. mangakò, ipasiyá; magkatiwalà.
committee: *n*. lupon, komité.
commodity: *n*. kalakal, panindá.
common: *adj*. karaniwan, pangkaraniwan, kaugalian; laganap, palasak; (*public*) pangmadlâ, pambayan; **~place** pangkaraniwan; **~ sense** sentido komún, likás, na pagkukurò; **~wealth** *n*. sam-pámahalaán.
commotion: *n*. pagkakaguló.
communicate: *v*. magbalità, sumulat, makipag-usap.
communication: *n*. pahatíd; liham.
communion: *n*. komunyón; pakikipagniíg.
communist: *n*. Komunista.
community: *n*. taong-bayan.
compact: *adj*. siksík, masinsín, pikpík; *n*. kasunduán.
companion: *n*. kasama, kasamahán.
company: *n*. kompanyá; mga kasama; **keep ~** sumama.
comparable: *adj*. maiwawangis, maipaparis, maitu-tulad.
comparative: *adj*. panulad, pánularan.
compare: *v*. maghambíng, magtulad, magparis.
comparison: *n*. pagtutulad, katulad, pagpaparis.
compass: *n*. aguhon, kumpas, bruhula.
compassion: *n*. pakikiramay, pagkahabág, awà.
compatible: *adj*. magkasuwatò, magkasundô.
compatriot: *n*. kababayan.
compel: *v*. magpilit.
compensate: *v*. magbayad, ibayad, tumbasán.
compete: *v*. sumali, maglaban.
competence: *n*. kakayahán.
competent: *adj*. may-kakayahán.
competition: *n*. paglalaban, paligsahan, kompeténsiya; **beauty ~** timpalák-kagandahan.
compile: *v*. ilistá, italâ.
complacent: *adj*. nasisiyahán.
complain: *v*. dumaíng, magsumbóng, magreklamo.
complaint: *n*. reklamo, sumbóng.
complement: *n*. kapupunán.
complete: *adj*. buô, lahát, tapós; **~ly** *adv*. lubós, lahát.
complex: *adj*. mahirap, salí-salimuot, maguló.
complexion: *n*. kutis.
complicate: *v*. magpaguló.
complication: *n*. pagkamaguló, kaguluhan.
compliment: *n*. papuri; **~ary** *adj*. kaloób, bigáy; may-papuri.
comply: *v*. sumunód, talimahin, tumalima, tumupád, tuparín, pumayag.
composure: *n*. hinahon, kahinahunan.
compound: *n*. timplada; looban; *v*. magtimplá.
comprehend: *v*. unawain, umunawà, maintindihán.
compress: *v*. magpikpík, pikpikín; magsiksík.
comprise: *v*. bumuô, buuín.
compromise: *v*. magkasundô, magbigayan; *n*. kasunduan, pagbibigayan.
compulsory: *adj*. sapilitán, puwersahan.
compute: *v*. tuusín, kuwentahín; **~r** *n*. tuusán, kuwentahan; tagatuós; tagataya; kompyuter.
comrade: *n*. kasama, kaibigan.
con: *adv*. kontra; *v*. dumayà.
concave: *adj*. malukóng, hungkág.
conceal: *v*. magtagò, ikublí.
concede: *v*. tanggapín, magkaloób, payagan.
conceited: *adj*. mkaakó, mapagmataás, palalò, mapagpahalagá.
conceive: *v*. akalain, isipin; (*pregnancy*) maglihí.
concentrate: *v*. pag-isiping matamán, paglimiin; magtipon.
concept: *n*. kuro-kurò.
concern: *n*. pagmamalasakit, malasakit; tungkulin; pagkabahalà; **~ed** *adj*. mabahalà; **~ing** *prep*. tungkól sa, ukol sa, hinggíl sa.
concert: *n*. konsiyerto.
concise: *adj*. maiklî, maigsî.
conclude: *v*. tapusin; ipalagáy.
conclusion: *n*. wakás; hinuhà; pasiyá.
concord: *n*. kasunduan, pagkakasundô.
concrete: *n*. kongkreto; tunay.
concubine: *n*. kerida, kalunyâ, babae.
concurrent: *adj*. sabáy, magkasabáy.

condemn: *v*. sumpaín, isumpâ; (*sentence*) hatulan.
condense: *v*. paikliín, magpaiklî.
condescend: *v*. magpakababà.
condiment: *n*. pampalasa, rekado.
condition: *n*. lagáy, kalagayan, kondisiyón; batayán, saligán; **on ~ that** sa kondisyóng.
conditional: *adj*. may-pasubalì.
condolence: *n*. pakikiramay, pakikidalamhatì.
condom: *n*. goma.
condominium: *n*. kondominyum.
condone: *v*. kalimutan, magpatawad.
conduct: *n*. asal, kilos, ugalì; *v*. mamunò, mang-asiwà.
conductor: *n*. (*guide*) patnubay, giya; (*of band*) konduktor.
conduit: *n*. tubo, padaluyán.
cone: *n*. kono, balisungsóng.
confer: *v*. sumanggunì, magkonsulta.
conference: *n*. komperénsiya, panayám, kapulungán.
confess: *v*. tumanggáp, umamin, magtapát; (*to a priest*) mangumpisál; **~sion** *n*. kumpisál, pag-amin.
confide: *v*. ipagtapát, magkatiwalà; **~nce** *n*. kom-piyansa, tiwalà; pagtitiwalà; **~nt** *adj*. nagtitiwalà, nananalig; natitiyák; **~ntial** lihim; pinagka-kátiwalaan.
confine: *v*. magkulóng, ikulóng; *n*. hanggahan.
confirm: *v*. magpatotoó, magpatunay; magpatibay.
confiscate: *v*. umilit, kumpiskahín, samsamín.
conflict: *n*. labanán, salungatán.
conform: *v*. sumunód, talimahin.
confound: *v*. lituhín, tarantahín.
confront: *v*. humaráp, harapín.
confuse: *v*. tarantahín, lituhín; **~d** *adj*. maguló, litó, tarantá.
congeal: *v*. mamuô.
congenial: *adj*. kasundô, kalugúd-lugód.
congratulate: *v*. batiin.
congratulations: *n*. batì, pagbatì.
congregate: *v*. mag-umpók-umpók, magtipuntipon.
congress: *n*. batasan, kongreso; kapulungán.
conjugate: *v*. magbangháy.
conjugation: *n*. pagbabangháy ng pandiwà.
conjunction: *n*. pangatníg, pang-ugnáy.
conjurer: *n*. salamangkero.
connect: *v*. magkabít, magdugtóng; **~ion** *n*. pagkakabít, pag-uugnáy.
connive: *v*. makipagsabwatan, kasabwatín, kasapakatín.
connoisseur: *n*. dalubhasà, eksperto.
connote: *v*. mangahulugán din.
conquer: *v*. gahisín, sumakop, magtagumpáy.
conquest: *n*. pagsakop, pananakop, pagtalo.
conscience: *n*. budhî, konsiyénsiya.
conscious: *adj*. alám, nalalaman, may-malay; **~ness** *n*. malay-tao, ulirat, kamalayán.
consecrate: *v*. konsagrahín, italagá; gawíng banál.
consecutive: *adj*. sunúd-sunód, magkasunód.
consensus: *n*. pinagkaisahán.
consent: *n*. pahintulot, permiso.
consequence: *n*. bunga, resulta, ang káuuwián.
consequently: *adv*. samakatuwíd, kayâ.
conservative: *adj*. makalumà, konserbatibo; maingat.
conserve: *v*. mag-alagà, alagaan; mag-imbák.
consider: *v*. isipin, ipalagáy; (*count as*) ituring, ibilang; **~ate** *adj*. mapagbigáy, maunawaín, mabaít; **~ation** *n*. pag-iisip, pagsasaalang-alang; konsiderasiyón.
consign: *v*. ipatindá.
consignment: *n*. patindá; pagpapadalá.
consist: *v*. binubuó ng.
consistent: *adj*. di-nagbábago; náaalinsunod.
console: *v*. mag-alíw, aliwín.
consolidate: *v*. magsama, mapisan, pag-isahín, pagpisanin.
consonant: *n*. katinig, konsonante.
consort: *n*. konsorte; asawa.
conspiracy: *n*. sabwatan, pagsasabuwatan, sapakatan.
conspire: *v*. magsabwatan.
constant: *adj*. hindî nagbabago, palagian; patuloy; **~ly** *adv*. lagì, palagì.
constipated: *adj*. tinitibí, hindî mapadumí.
constituent: *n*. sangkáp, bahagi.
constitute: *v*. bumuô, buuín.
constitution: *n*. Konstitusiyón; pangangatawán, saligáng-batás.
contraception: *n*. pagpipigil sa pagbubuntís.

constrain: *v.* pumilit, pumuwersa.
constrict: *v.* hapitin, humapit.
construct: *v.* magtayô, yariin, yumarì.
construe: *v.* ipakahulugán, pakahuluganán.
consul: *n.* Konsúl.
consulate: *n.* konsulado.
consult: *v.* sangguniin, isanggunì, magkonsulta; **~ant** *n.* tagapayo; kasanggunì; **~ation** *n.* konsulta, pagsanggunì.
consume: *v.* maubos; tumupok; magsayáng.
consummate: *v.* tumupád, taparín, malubós.
consumption: *n.* paggamit; (*tuberculosis*) tisis, tuyô.
contact: *n.* pagdiít, pagkakalapat, paghipò, paglapat; *v.* makipag-alam, humipò.
contagious: *adj.* nakakáhawa, nakakalalin.
contain: *v.* maglamán; makapaglamán; maylamán; (*restrain*) pumigil; **~er** *n.* sisidlán, lalagyán.
contaminate: *v.* magparumí, dumhán.
contemplate: *v.* niláy-nilayin, pagniláy-nilayin, magdilidili, magbulay-bulay.
contemporaneous: *adj.* kapanahón.
contempt: *n.* pagdustâ, pag-upasalà, paghamak.
contend: *v.* maglaban, magtalo; imatwíd; ipakipagtalo.
content: *n.* (*contained substance*) lamán; *adj.* (*happy*) nasisiyahán, nalulugód; **~s** *n.* lamán, nilálamán.
contentious: *adj.* mapágmatuwíd.
contest: *n.* paligsahan, timpalák, labanán.
continent: *n.* kontinente, lupalop, sanlupaín.
contingent: *adj.* nakasalalay, nababatay.
continually: *adv.* lagì na, waláng-tigil.
continuation: *n.* karugtóng.
continue: *v.* magpatuloy, itulóy.
contort: *v.* pilipitin, ipilipit.
contour: *n.* hugis; ayos.
contraband: *n.* kontrabandong kalakal.
contract: *n.* (*agreement*) kontrata, kasunduan; *v.* (*become smaller*) lumiít; **~ion** *n.* pag-iklî; may-angkóp; **~or** *n.* kontratista, mangongontrata.
contradict: *v.* sumalangsáng, sumalungát, magka-kontra; **~ory** *adj.* nagkakásalungatán.
contrary: *adj.* salungát, laban sa.
contrast: *n.* kaibhán, pagkakaibá; *v.* ihambíng, itulad.
contribute: *v.* mag-abuloy, mag-ambág.
contrive: *v.* lumikhâ, umimbento.
control: *v.* mamahalà, magpigil; *n.* pamamahalà, kapangyarihan.
controversy: *n.* pagtatalo, álitan.
contusion: *n.* pasâ.
convalescence: *n.* pagpapalakás.
convenience: *n.* kalúwagan, kaginhawahan.
convenient: *adj.* nápapanahón; maginhawa, maluwág, madalî; magalíng; nakatutulong; magaán.
convent: *n.* kumbento.
convention: *n.* kombensiyón, kapulungán.
converge: *v.* magtagpô, mapisan, matipon.
conversation: *n.* pag-uusap, pagsasalitaan.
converse: *v.* mag-usap, pag-usapan.
convert: *v.* gawín, ipalít; (*religious belief*) magpasampalataya.
convex: *adj.* kukób, lukób.
convey: *v.* magdalá, ihatíd.
convict: *n.* preso, bilanggô; *v.* mapatunayang may sala.
convince: *v.* kumbinsihín, papaniwalain, pasang-ayunin.
convoke: *v.* tawagin, tumawag.
convoy: *n.* kumbóy, eskolta.
convulsion: *n.* kumbulsiyón, pagkisáy, subà, pag-iihít.
cook: *n.* tagapaglutò, kusinero; *v.* maglutò, lutuin; **~ rice** magsaing.
cookie: *n.* galyetas, kukis.
cool: *adj.* malamíg-lamíg, presko; *v.* magpalamíg.
coop: *n.* tangkál, kulungán.
cooperation: *n.* pagtutulungán, pagdadamayán.
coordinate: *v.* magtugmâ, iugmâ.
cope: *n.* makaya, kayahin.
copper: *n.* tansô, tumbaga.
copra: *n.* kopra, kalibkíb, palyát.
copula: *n.* pandiwang pangatníg.
copulate: *v.* maghindót.
copy: *n.* kopya, sipì; *v.* kumopya, tularan.
coquettish: *adj.* haliparót, kirí, talandí.
cord: *n.* lubid, pisì.
cordial: *adj.* tapát, mataimtím, taós-pusò.

core: *n.* (*fruit*) ubod; (*central part*) kaibuturan, buód, kalagitnaan, pusod.
coriander: *n.* kulantro, unsóy.
cork: *n.* tapón; **~screw** tribusón.
cormorant: *n.* kurbihón, maninisid-isdâ..
corn: *n.* maís; (*on skin*) lipák, kalyo; **~starch** gawgáw; **~cob** *n.* busal.
corner: *n.* sulok, kanto; *v.* mapikot, masukól.
cornet: *n.* kornetín, korneta.
corporation: *n.* korporasyón, samahán.
corpse: *n.* bangkáy.
corpulent: *adj.* matabâ.
corral: *n.* kurál; **fish ~** *n.* bungsód.
correct: *adj.* tamà, wastô, tumpák; *v.* magtumpák, iwastô; **~ion** *n.* pagwawastô.
correlate: *v.* magkaugnáy, iayon.
correspond: *v.* bumagay, magkabagay, makatulad; **~ent** *n.* kasulatán, kalihamán; **~ence** *n.* kaisahán; pagsusulatán; **~ing** *adj.* katugón, kaukulán.
corridor: *n.* pasílyo, kuridór.
corroborate: *v.* patunayan, patotohanan.
corrode: *v.* agnasín, kaning untí-untî.
corrupt: *adj.* bulók, makasalanan; *v.* magpasamâ, pasamaín.
corruption: *n.* kasamaán, katiwalián, kabulukán.
corsage: *n.* kurpinyo.
corset: *n.* korset, paha.
cost: *n.* halagá; (*expenses*) gastos, kostas, gugol; **~ly** *adj.* mahál, mahalagá.
costume: *n.* kasuutan.
cot: *n.* tiheras, katre.
cottage: *n.* maliít na bahay.
cotton: *n.* bulak; algodón.
couch: *n.* sopá.
cough: *n.* ubó; *v.* umubó.
council: *n.* konseho, kapulungán, sanggunián; **~or** *n.* konsehál.
counsel: *n.* payo; abugado; *v.* magpayo, pagpayuhan; **~or** *n.* tagapayo.
count: *v.* bumilang, magbilang; (*consider*) ibilang; (*nobleman*) konde; (*include*) ibilang, isama.
countenance: *n.* bukás ng mukhâ.
counter: *n.* pambilang; despatso; *v.* sumalungát.
counterfeit: *adj.* palsipikado, huwád.
counterpart: *n.* kapilas, kamukáng-mukhâ.
countess: *n.* kondesa.
countless: *adj.* dî mabilang.
country: *n.* bansâ, bayan; (*rural*) probinsiyá, lalawigan; **~man** kababayan.
coup d'état: *n.* sápilitáng pag-agaw sa gobyerno, kudetá.
couple: *n.* dalawá, isáng pares; *v.* ikabít.
coupon: *n.* kupón.
courage: *n.* tapang, giting, lakás; **~ous** *adj.* matapang, magiting.
course: *n.* kurso; daán; hakbáng; (*meal*) potáhe.
court: *n.* hukuman; *v.* lumigaw; **~-martial** *n.* hukumáng militár; **~ hearing** bista. **~ of Appeals** *n.* Húkuman sa Paghahabol.
courteous: *adj.* magalang, mapitagan.
courtesy: *n.* galang, paggalang, pitagan.
court-martial: *n.* hukumang-militár.
courtship: *n.* pagligaw, panliligaw.
cousin: *n.* pinsán; **first ~** pinsán-buô; **second ~** pinsán-pangalawá.
covenant: *n.* kasunduan, tipán.
cover: *n.* (*of book*) balát; (*container*) takíp, panakíp; (*pot*) tungtóng, suklób; *v.* magtakíp, magtaklób.
covert: *adj.* tagô, lihim, lingíd, kublí.
covet: *v.* mag-imbót, magnasà; **~ous** *adj.* masakím, mapag-imbót.
cow: *n.* baka; **~ fish** baka-baka; **~-nosed ray** palimanok.
coward: *n.* duwág; **~ice** karúwagan; **~ly** *adj.* duwág.
cowboy: *n.* koboy, bakero.
cowlick: *n.* puyó.
co-worker: *n.* kamánggagawà, katrabaho.
cowrie: *n.* kaligay.
coy: *adj.* kimî, mahiyain.
cozy: *adj.* maginhawa.
crab: *n.* alimango; (*kinds*) katáng, talangkâ, alimasag.
crack: *n.* putók, biták; basag, lamat.
cracker: *n.* biskuwít.
crackle: *v.* kumaluskós.
cradle: *n.* kuna, duyan.
craft: *n.* kasanayán, kagalingán; **~y** *adj.* tuso, magdarayà.

cram: *v*. magsiksík.
cramp: *n*. pulikat, kalambre.
crane: *n*. (*bird*) bakáw, tagák; (*machine*) grua.
cranium: *n*. bungô.
crank: *n*. pihitán, maniketa.
cranky: *adj*. magagalitín, sumpungin.
crash: *v*. bumagsák, magbanggá, maglagapák.
crate: *n*. malakíng kahón, kanastro.
crater: *n*. hukay, bungangà ng bulkán.
crave: *v*. magmithî, manabík.
crawfish: *n*. uláng, kokomo.
crawl: *v*. gumapang.
crayfish: *n*. uláng.
crayon: *n*. krayola.
crazy: *adj*. balíw, ulól, sirâ.
creak: *v*. lumangingít.
cream: *n*. krema, gatas; **~ of the crop** kakanggatâ.
crease: *n*. lukot, tupî, lupî.
create: *v*. lalangín, lumikhâ.
creative: *adj*. mapanlikhâ; malíkhain.
creature: *n*. nilikhâ, tao o hayop.
credence: *n*. paniwalà.
credible: *adj*. kapaní-paniwalà.
credit: *n*. utang, pautang; paniwalaan; *v*. maniwalà.
credulity: *n*. kamápaniwalaín.
creed: *n*. pananampalataya, pananalig, kredo, doktrina.
creek: *n*. ilúg-ilugan, sapà; batis.
creep: *v*. gumapang; **It gives me the ~s** kinikilabutan akó.
cremate: *v*. sunugin ang bangkáy.
crepe: *n*. krep, krispón.
crescent: *n*. gasukláy (ng buwán).
crest: *n*. taluktók, tuktók.
crevice: *n*. biták, siwang.
crew: *n*. tripulante.
crib: *n*. kuna, aluyan; sabsaban.
cricket: *n*. kuliglíg, kamaksî, túrurukan, kerwè.
crime: *n*. krimen.
criminal: *n*. salarín, kriminál.
crimson: *adj*. puláng-pulá.
cringe: *v*. sumukot.
cripple: *v*. lumpuhín, pilayin; **~d** *adj*. salantâ, lumpó.
crisis: *n*. peligro, krisis, panganib.
crisp: *adj*. malutóng; sariwà.
critic: *n*. krítiko, mámumuná.
critical: *adj*. mapamulà, mapamintás; mápamuná.
criticism: *n*. pagsusurì, pulà, pintás, puná.
criticize: *v*. suriin, mamulà, pintasán, punahín.
croak: *n*. kukak; *v*. kumukak; **~er fish** abo, ibot.
crochet: *n*. gansilyo.
crocodile: *n*. buwaya.
crony: *n*. kaibigan, katoto.
crook: *n*. manloloko, manggagantso, estapadór.
crooked: *adj*. kilô, likô, balikukô.
crop: *n*. ani, mga taním.
cross: *n*. krus; *v*. krusán; *adj*. galít; **~-eyed** *adj*. dulíng.
crouch: *v*. yumukyók, sumukot.
crow: *n*. (*of rooster*) tilaok; (*bird*) uwák.
crowbar: *n*. barreta.
crowd: *n*. karamihan ng tao; *v*. dumagsâ, mapunô.
crown: *n*. putong, korona.
crucial: *adj*. napakamahalagá, napakaimportante.
crucifix: *n*. krusipiho.
crucify: *v*. ipakò sa krus.
crude: *adj*. krudo, magaspáng.
cruel: *adj*. malupít, mabagsík; **~ty** kalupitán.
cruise: *n*. paglalayág.
crumb: *n*. mumo, karampót, napakaliít na peraso; **~y** *adj*. sirà, samâ.
crumble: *v*. lumugsô, gumuhò.
crumple: *v*. lamukusin, kusutín.
crunch: *v*. ngumalót, ngalutín.
crupper: *n*. batikola.
crusade: *n*. kilusán, krusada.
crush: *v*. durugin, lumigís, kuyumusin; kusutín, lurayín.
crust: *n*. balát ng tinapay.
crutch(es): *n*. muleta, sakláy, panakláy.
cry: *v*. umiyák, lumuhà; *n*. (*loud call*) sigáw, hiyáw.
crystal: *n*. kristál, bubog.
cube: *n*. kubo.
cucumber: *n*. pipino.
cuddle: *v*. pangkuhín, kandúng-kandungín.
cue: *n*. hudyát; tako.

cuff: *n*. punyós; ~ **link** hemelo.
cuisine: *n*. lutò.
culminate: *v*. humanggá, humantóng.
culprit: *n*. maykasalanan.
cult: *n*. kulto.
cultivate: *v*. lumináng, linangín, bungkalín; (*improve*) payamanin.
culture: *n*. kultura, kalinangán.
culvert: *n*. alkantarilya.
cumbersone: *adj*. mahirap, nakasasagabal.
cunning: *adj*. tuso.
cup: *n*. tasa, kopa.
cupboard: *n*. aparadór, páminggalan, banggerahán; platera.
curb: *n*. gilid ng bangketa; *v*. sugpuín, pigilin.
curdle: *v*. mamuô, makultá.
cure: *v*. magpagalíng, gamutín, pagalingín; *n*. gamót, lunas, panlunas.
curfew: *n*. karpiyó.
curious: *adj*. usisero, usyoso, mausisà.
curl: *n*. kulót; *v*. kulutín.
currency: *n*. kuwalta, pera.
current: *n*. agos, kuryente; *adj*. malaganap.
curry: *n*. kari.
curse: *n*. sumpâl; (*swearing*) pagtutungayaw; *v*. sumpaín; magtungayaw.
curtail: *v*. magpaiklî.
curtain: *n*. kurtina.
curve: *n*. kurba, kurbada; **~d** *adj*. baluktót, balikukô, pabalantók.
cushion: *n*. almuhadón.
custard: *n*. lestseplán; ~ **apple** atis.
custodian: *n*. tagapag-alagà.
custom: *n*. kaugalian, kostumbre; **~ary** *adj*. kaugalian, karaniwan;
customer: *n*. mamimili; **regular** ~ sukì; **~s** *n*. aduwana; impuwesto.
cut: *n*. hiwà; (*wound*) sugat; (*of dress*) tabas; **short** ~ daáng tuwiran, daáng tapatan; *v*. humiwà, hiwain; (*reduce*) bawasan; (*divide*) hatiin; ~ **off** putulín; gupitín; ~ **off head** pugutan.
cute: *adj*. magandá, guwapo.
cuticle: *n*. patáy na balát sa kukó.
cutlass fish: *n*. laying.
cutlery: *n*. kubiyertos, mga panghiwà.
cuttlefish: *n*. pugità.
cyanide: *n*. siyanuro.
cycle: *n*. bisikleta.
cyclist: *n*. siklista.
cyclone: *n*. bagyó, unós, buhawì, ipuipo.
cylinder: *n*. silindro.
cymbal: *n*. pumpiyáng.
cynic: *n*. mangungutyâ, mapangutyâ.
cynical: *adj*. nakauuyám.
cyst: *n*. suron, katô; bukol.

D

dab: *v*. dampián, idampî.
dabble: *v*. iwilíg.
dad: *n*. tata, amá, tatay.
dagger: *n*. daga, balaráw.
daily: *adj*. araw-araw.
dainty: *adj*. delikado, maselan.
dally: *v*. mag-ansikót, magpatigil-tigil.
dam: *n*. prinsa, saplád.
damage: *n*. sirà, pinsalà.
damn: *v*. sumpaín, mapahamak; ~ **it!** diyablo! damuho! letse!
damp: *adj*. malagihay, basá-basâ; **~en** *v*. basaín.
dance: *n*. sayáw, bayle; *v*. sumayáw; **~r** *n*. mananayáw.
dandelion: *n*. amargón, ngiping-león.
dandruff: *n*. balakubak.
danger: *n*. peligro, panganib; **~ous** *adj*. mapang-anib, peligroso.
dangle: *v*. lumawít-lawít, paugúy-uguyín.
dare: *v*. hamunin, mangahás; *n*. hamon; **~devil** *n*. pangahás, kaskasero.
daring: *adj*. waláng-takot, matapang.
dark: *adj*. madilím; (*skin*) maitím; ~ **meat** ulikbâ.
darling: *n*. mahál, sintá.
darn: *v*. magsulsí; *interj*. punyeta.
dart: *n*. (*weapon*) tunod, suligì; (*swift movement*) sibad, kaskás, hagibís.
dash: *v*. sabuyan, magpukól.
data: *n*. datos.
date: *n*. (*calendar*) petsa; (*fruit*) dátiles; (*appointment*) tipanan; ~ **stamper** petsadór.
daub: *v*. tapalan, itapal, ipatsí.
daughter: *n*. anák na babae; ~ **in-law** manu-

gang na babae.
daunt: *v*. takutín, sumirà.
dawn: *n*. liwaywáy, madalíng-araw.
day: *n*. araw; ~ **before yesterday** kamakalawá; ~ **after tomorrow** sa makalawá; **~break** *n*. bukáng-liwaywáy; **~dream** *v*. mangarap nang gisíng.
dazed: *adj*. matulingág, matuliró, masilaw.
dazzle: *v*. silawin; makamanghâ.
dazzling: *adj*. nakasísilaw.
deacon: *n*. diyakonó.
dead: *adj*. patáy; **~line** *n*. hulíng araw; **~ly** *adj*. nakamamatáy.
deadlock: *v*. máhintô, mátigil; *n*. pagkatigil; pagkáhintô.
deaf: *adj*. bingí; **~-mute** *adj*. bingí't-pipi.
deal: *n*. panukalà; *v*. magtindá, magbilí; makisama; ipamigáy; **~er** *n*. mangangalakál.
dean: *n*. dekano.
dear: *adj*. mahál, sinisintá, ginigilíw.
death: *n*. kamátayan, pagkamatáy.
debase: *v*. magpababà.
debate: *n*. pagtatalo, debate.
debauchery: *n*. kahayupan, kahalayan.
debilitate: *v*. pahinain.
debility: *n*. kahinaan.
debris: *n*. mga labí, basura.
debt: *n*. utang.
debut: *n*. pasinayà.
decade: *n*. dekada, sampúng taón.
decadence: *n*. pagbabà.
decapitate: *v*. pugutin ang ulo.
decay: *v*. mabulók; huminà; **~ed** *adj*. mabulók.
deceased: *adj*. patáy.
deceit: *n*. kasinungalingan, kabulaanan.
deceive: *v*. linlangín, dayain, lokohin.
December: *n*. Disyembre.
decent: *adj*. mahinhín, dî masagwâ.
decide: *v*. pasiyahán, ipasiyá, magpatibay.
decipher: *v*. unawain, intindihín.
decision: *n*. pasiyá, kapasiyahán.
deck: *n*. (*ship*) palapág, kubyerta; (*cards*) balasa (ng baraha).
declaration: *n*. pagpapahayag.
declarative: *adj*. paturól.
declare: *v*. sabihin, magsabi, magpahayag.
declension: *n*. páukulan, pag-uukol.
decline: *v*. (*lose power*) huminà; (*refuse*) tanggihán; (*gram.*) mag-ukul-ukol.
decompose: *v*. mabulók.
decorate: *v*. gayakán, palamutihan.
decoration: *n*. palamuti, dekorasyón, gayák.
decoy: *n*. pangatî, pain.
decrease: *v*. magbawas, bawasan; bumabâ, umiklî; *n*. pagliít, pag-iklî.
decree: *n*. batás, utos, atas.
decrepit: *adj*. hukluban, matandâ at mahinà.
dedicate: *v*. italagá, ilaán, iukol.
deduce: *v*. huluin, hinuhain.
deduct: *v*. bawasin, awasán.
deduction: *n*. pagbabawas; pangangatwiran; paghuhulò.
deed: *n*. gawâ.
deem: *v*. ipalagáy.
deep: *adj*. malalim; **~-rooted** di-mapápaknít; **~en** *v*. palalimin; lumalim.
deer: *n*. usá; **female** ~ libay.
deface: *v*. sirain ang anyô.
defame: *v*. manirà, sirrang-puri.
default: *n*. kakulangán, kawalán; *v*. sumala sa pagtupád.
defeat: *v*. matalo, talunin; *n*. pagtalo, pagkatalo.
defecate: *v*. tumae, dumumí, manalikód, tumaklâ.
defect: *n*. kamalian, pagkakamalî, diperénsiya, depekto; **~ive** *adj*. may sala, may depekto.
defend: *v*. ipagtanggól, ipag-adyá, ipagsanggaláng; **~ant** *n*. ang nasasakdál.
defense: *n*. pagtatanggól, pananggól.
defer: *v*. ipagpaliban, bumalam, balamin, antalahin; **~ence** *n*. galang, pitagan, pakundangan.
defiance: *n*. paglaban, pagsuwáy.
defiant: *adj*. mapanlabán.
deficient: *adj*. kulang, di-sapát.
deficit: *n*. kulang.
defile: *v*. magparungis, makamantsá.
define: *v*. ipaliwanag; magtakdâ.
definite: *adj*. tiyák, maliwanag, tahás; **~ly** *adv*. tiyakan, tahasan.
deflate: *v*. mag-alís ng hangin.
deflect: *v*. ilihís, palihisín.
deform: *v*. sirain ang hugis.
deformity: *n*. kapangitan, depormidád.

defraud: *v*. dumayà.
deft: *adj*. sanáy, maliksí.
defunct: *adj*. patáy na, lipás na.
defy: *v*. labanan, salungatín.
degenerate: *v*. sumamâ, lumubhâ.
degradation: *n*. pagkababâ.
degrade: *v*. ibabâ, magpasamâ.
degree: *n*. título, katibayan; (*gram*.) kaantasán.
deity: *n*. diwatà, bathalà.
dejected: *adj*. malumbáy, mapangláw.
delay: *v*. maantala, ihulí, balamin, atrasuhin.
delegate: *n*. sugò, delegado, kinatawán.
delete: *v*. kumaltás, alisín, burahín.
deliberate: *adj*. kusà, sadyâ, tikís; *v*. bulay-bulayin.
delicate: *adj*. mahinà, pino, masasaktín.
delicious: *adj*. masaráp, malinamnám.
delight: *n*. tuwâ, katuwaan; *v*. matuwâ; **~ful** kalugúd-lugód.
delinquent: *adj*. pabayâ; (*bad*) masamâ.
delirious: *adj*. nahihibáng, hibáng.
delirium: *n*. hibang.
deliver: *v*. dalhín, magdalá; (*give birth*) isilang, iluwál.
delivery: *n*. pagdadalá, paghahatíd; (*giving birth*) panganganák.
delta: *n*. delta.
deluge: *n*. gunaw, pagkagunaw, bahâ; *v*. dumagsâ.
delusion: *n*. paglinláng, pagliligáw.
delve: *v*. pakasaliksikín.
demand: *v*. hingíng pautós, kailanganin; *n*. kailangan, pangangailangan; habol.
demeanor: *n*. kilos, pagkilos.
demijohn: *n*. damahuwana.
democracy: *n*. demokrasya.
democratic: *adj*. demokrátiko.
demolish: *v*. gibaín.
demon: *n*. diyablo, demóniyo.
demonstrate: *v*. itanghá, ipakita; magpatunay.
demonstrative: *adj*. hayág, halatâ; pamatíg; ~ **pronoun** *n*. panghalíp pamatlíg, panurò.
demote: *v*. ibabâ, magbabà.
demure: *adj*. mabini, mahinhín.
den: *n*. yungíb, kuweba.
denial: *n*. pagtanggí.
denim: *n*. maóng.
denote: *v*. ipakilala, mangahulugán.
denounce: *v*. tumuligsâ, batikusin.
dense: *adj*. makapál, masinsín, masukal.
dent: *n*. kupì, yupì; *v*. yupián.
dentist: *n*. dentista.
deny: *v*. itakwil, itanggí, ikailâ, ikaít.
deodorant: *n*. pamawing-amóy, pang-alís-bahò.
depart: *v*. umalís; yumao; **~ment** *n*. kagawarán, departamento; **~ure** *n*. alís.
depend: *v*. umasa, manghawak, mabatay, pagtiwa-laan; magdepende; **~able** *adj*. mapaniniwalaan, mapagtitiwalaan; **~ence** *n*. pagpapasustento, pagpapaarugâ; **~ent** *n*. sustentado, pakainín.
depict: *v*. maglarawan, ilarawan.
deplete: *v*. umubos, ubusin.
deplore: *v*. ikalungkót, ikalumbáy.
deport: *v*. itapon, matapon.
depose: *v*. itiwalág, alisín (sa trabaho).
deposit: *v*. magdepósito; ilapág; *n*. pauná, depósito.
deprave: *v*. pasamaín.
depraved: *adj*. napakasamâ.
deprecate: *v*. itakwíl.
depreciate: *v*. pababain ang halagá.
depress: *v*. panamlayín; **~ed** *adj*. malumbáy, malungkót; **~ion** *n*. pananamláy, panlulungkót.
deprive: agawan, bawian, bumawì.
depth: *n*. lalim.
deputy: *n*. kinatawán, representante.
deranged: *adj*. loko, sirâ.
derivation: *n*. pinagmulán, pinanggalingan.
derivative: *adj*. hangò.
derive: *v*. manggaling, magmulâ; tamuhín.
derogatory: *adj*. nakasisirà, mapanirà.
descend: *v*. bumabâ, manaog; **~ant** *n*. inapó, suplíng.
descent: *n*. pagbabâ, paglapág; dalisdís.
describe: *v*. ilarawan.
description: *n*. paglalarawan.
descriptive: *adj*. palarawán.
desecrate: *v*. lumapastangan.
desert: *n*. disyerto, iláng; *v*. tumanan, tumakas; magpabayà; **~r** *n*. takas.
deserve: *v*. marapat.

deserving: *adj*. karapat-dapat.
design: *n*. disenyo, dibuho, plano; tangkâ, balak, panukalà.
designate: *v*. iturò, hirangin, piliin.
desirable: *adj*. kanais-nais.
desire: *n*. nais, ibig, gustó, nasà; *v*. gusto, mithiín, pitahin.
desk: *n*. pupitre, eskritoryo.
desolate: *adj*. mapangláw, ulila; waláng tao.
despair: *n*. kawalán ng pag-asa.
desperate: *adj*. walâ nang pag-asa; gipít.
despicable: *adj*. kalait-lait, kakutyá-kutyâ.
despise: *v*. humamak, matahín, mamuhî.
despite: *prep*. kahit na, sa kabilâ ng.
dessert: *n*. matamís, himagas.
destination: *n*. paroroonán, pupuntahán.
destiny: *n*. destino, tadhanà; hantungan; kapalaran.
destitute: *adj*. hikahós, salát, sayuád, dukhâ.
destroy: *v*. sirain, pinsalain, wasakín.
destruction: *n*. paninirà, pagsirà.
destructive: *adj*. mapanirà.
detach: *v*. magtanggál, alisín, tuklapín, baklasín.
detail: *n*. bahagi, detalye; *v*. isá-isahín.
detain: *v*. pigilin, bibinín.
detect: *v*. tiktikán, manubok, subukan, hulihin; pansinín; **~ive** *n*. tiktík, sekreta.
deter: *v*. humadláng, masansalà.
deteriorate: *v*. lumubhâ, sumamâ.
determination: *n*. pagtitika, pagpupunyagi.
determine: *v*. tumiyák, itakdâ, pasiyahán, hatulan.
detest: *v*. mapoót, masuklám.
detonate: *v*. paputukín.
detour: *n*. likô, baling, likuan.
detract: *v*. ialís, bawasan.
detriment: *n*. pinsalà, kapinsalaán; **~al** *adj*. nakapipinsalà, nakasasamâ.
deuce: *n*. tablá, patas.
devastate: *v*. iwasák, lurayín.
develop: *v*. tumubò, bumuti, lumakás, lumakí; **~ment** *n*. pagtubò, paglakí; (*progress*) pagsulong, pag-unlád.
deviate: *v*. lumihís.
device: *n*. kagamitán, kasangkapan, aparato.
devil: *n*. diyablo, satanás, demonyo.
devious: *adj*. palihís, maligoy.
devise: *v*. magbalangkás, isipin.
devoid: *adj*. hubád, walâ.
devote: *v*. italagá, iukol, maglaán.
devoted: *adj*. matapát, maalalahanín; mairugin.
devour: *v*. sumilâ, lumamon.
devout: *adj*. banál, relihiyoso.
dew: *n*. hamóg; **~drop** paták ng hamóg.
dewlap: *n*. lambî.
dexterous: *adj*. mahusay ang kamáy.
diabetes: *n*. diyabitis.
diabolic: *adj*. napakasamâ, nakadedemonyo.
diadem: *n*. diyadema, koronang bulaklák.
diagnose: *v*. kumilala, tingnán, suriin, magrikonosí.
diagnosis: *n*. rikonosí, pagsurì.
diagram: *n*. krokis, bangháy, plano.
dial: *n*. pihitán, (*of a watch*) mukhâ, *v*. dumayal.
dialect: *n*. diyalekto, wikà, salitâ.
dialog: *n*. diyálogo.
diameter: *n*. diyametro, bantód.
diamond: *n*. brilyante.
diaper: *n*. lampín.
diarrhea: *n*. kursó, bululós, pagtataé.
diary: *n*. aklát-taláarawán.
dice: *n*. dais.
dictate: *v*. magdiktá, idiktá.
dictator: *n*. diktadór; **~ship** diktadura.
diction: *n*. panalitâ.
dictionary: *n*. diksiyonáryo, talátinigán, talahuluganan.
die: *v*. mamatáy, yumao.
diet: *n*. diyeta; *v*. magdiyeta.
differ: *v*. magkaibá; **~ence** *n*. kaibhán, diperénsiya; di-pagkakaunawaán; **~ent** *adj*. ibá, ibá-ibá; di katulad; **~entiate** *v*. ikaibá.
difficult: *adj*. mahirap; **~ty** *n*. pinagkakahirapan, kahirapan.
diffuse: *v*. lumaganap.
dig: *v*. hukayin, maghukay.
digest: *v*. tumunaw, tunawin; *n*. haláw, lagom; **~ible** natútunaw; **~ion** panunaw.
digit: *n*. (*finger*) dalirì; (*number*) tambilang.
dignified: *adj*. marangál, kapita-pitagan.
dignify: *v*. magpadakilà.
dignity: *n*. dignidád, dangál, karangálan, pag-

kamarangál, kadakilaan.
digress: *v*. lumayô sa paksâ.
dike: *n*. pilapil, hapilà, saplád.
dilapidated: *adj*. sirá-sirâ, wasák-wasák.
dilate: *v*. palakhín.
dilemma: *n*. mahirap na kalagayan.
diligent: *adj*. masipag, masikap.
dilute: *v*. magbantô, maghalò.
dim: *adj*. hindî maliwanag, malamlám.
dimension: *n*. sukat; lakí.
diminish: *v*. paliitín; magbawas; umuntî.
diminutive: *adj*. maliít, muntî.
dimple: *n*. biloy, puyó sa pisngî.
dine: *v*. magtanghalian, mananghalî.
dingy: *adj*. marumí.
dinner: *n*. tanghaalian; hapunan.
dip: *v*. isawsáw.
diphthong: *n*. kambál-patinig.
dipper: *n*. tabò, panabò.
diplomacy: *n*. diplomasya.
diplomat: *n*. diplomátiko; **~ic** *adj*. mahusay makibagay, diplomátiko.
direct: *v*. pamahalaan, mamatnugot, mangasiwà; mag-atas; umakay; *adj*. turiran, deretso, tulúy-tulóy; **~ion** *n*. pamamahalà; gawî, dako; **~or** *n*. tagapamahalà, patnugot; **~ object** *n*. túwirang layon.
dirge: *n*. punebre, tugtóg-patáy, sambitan.
dirt: *n*. dumí; (*on face*) amos dusing, dungis; (*on body*) bail, libág; **~y** *adj*. marumí, marungis.
disability: *n*. kawaláng-lakás, pagkabaldá.
disabled: *adj*. baldado, salantâ.
disadvantage: *n*. kasahulán, desbentaha.
disagree: *v*. hindî magkasundô, magkaibá; **~ment** *n*. pagkakaibá ng palagáy, hidwaan.
disappear: *v*. mawalâ, maparam, mapawi; **~ance** pagkawalâ; paglubóg.
disappoint: *v*. hindî makasiyá, bumigô; **~ment** *n*. pagkabigô.
disapprove: *v*. dî mabutihin, dî pagtibayin.
disarrange: *v*. guluhín.
disaster: *n*. malakíng kapahamakán, desastre; sakunâ.
disband: *v*. maglanság, bumuwág.
discard: *v*. itapon, iwaksí.
discern: *v*. aninawin, pagwariin, pansinín.
discharge: *v*. itiwalág, mag-alís, paputukín; labasán; *n*. (*from ears*) lugà; (*from wound*) nanà; (*of menses*) panaog (ng sapanahón).
disciple: *n*. alagád, disípulo.
discipline: *n*. disiplina, parusa; *v*. parusahan.
disclose: *v*. magbunyág, isiwalat.
discomfort: *n*. kahirapan, kakulangán sa ginhawa.
disconnect: *v*. alisín, tanggalín, ihiwaláy.
discontinue: *v*. tumigil, ihintô.
discord: *n*. salungatan, pagsasalungatan.
discount: *n*. tawad, diskuwento, bawas.
discourage: *v*. magpahinà ng loób.
discourse: *n*. talumpatì, panayám.
discover: *v*. tumuklás, madiskubre.
discovery: *n*. pagkatuklás.
discredit: *v*. pasinungalingan.
discreet: *adj*. mahinahon, maingat.
discrepancy: *n*. pagkakaibá, kaibhán.
discriminate: *v*. itangì.
discuss: *v*. mag-usap, talakyin; **~ion** *n*. pagtalakay, pag-uusap.
disease: *n*. sakít; karamdaman.
disembark: *v*. ilunsád, bumabâ, iahon.
disentangle: *v*. kalasín, kalagín.
disfigure: *v*. magpapangit.
disgrace: *n*. desgrasiya, kahihiyán; *v*. magdulot ng kahihiyán, hiyaín.
disguise: *v*. magbalatkayô, ikublí.
disgust: *n*. pagkainís, pagkasuyà, pagkasuklám; **~ting** *adj*. nakaíinís, nakamumuhî.
dish: *n*. pinggán, plato.
disheveled: *adj*. lukót, lugaygáy.
dishonest: *adj*. hindî tapát.
dishonor: *n*. paninirà; *v*. siraan ng puri, manirà.
disinfect: *v*. disimpektahín; **~ant** *n*. disimpektante.
disintegrate: *v*. matibág, mabagbág, mabuwág.
dislike: *v*. ayawán; *n*. pag-ayaw.
dislocate: *v*. luminsád, palinsarín.
dismal: *adj*. mapangláw.
dismantle: *v*. magkalás, magtanggál-tanggál.
dismay: *n*. bagabag, balisa.
dismember: *v*. magputúl-putól.
dismiss: *v*. magpaalís, paalisín; **~al** *n*. pagpaalís, pagtitiwalág; pagpapatalsík.
dismount: *v*. bumabâ sa kabayo; ilapág.

disyllabic: *adj*. dadalawahíng pantíg.
disobey: *v*. sumuwáy, suwayín.
disorder: *n*. kaguluhan, guló; **~ly** *adj*. maguló.
disown: *v*. itakwíl, itatuwâ.
disparity: *n*. pagkakaiba.
dispatch: *v*. magsugò, suguin.
dispense: *v*. ipamigáy, ipamahagi, pamudmód.
disperse: *v*. ikalat, papaghiwá-hiwalayín.
displace: *v*. galawín, tinagín; palitán; alisín.
display: *v*. magpakita, ipakita, itanghál; *n*. tanghál.
displeasure: *n*. yamót, hinanakít, galit.
disposal: *n*. pagtatapon.
dispose: *v*. itapon, magtapon.
disposition: *n*. kaloobán; kaugalian.
disprove: *v*. magpabulaan, magpasinungaling.
dispute: *v*. makipagtalo, magdebate; *n*. pagtatalo, debate.
disqualification: *n*. pag-aalís sa karapatán.
disqualify: *v*. magpawaláng-karapatán.
disregard: *v*. walíng-bahalà, magpabayà; *n*. pagpa-pabayà.
disrespect: *v*. kawaláng-pitagan.
disrobe: *v*. maghubád.
disrupt: *v*. lansagín, sirain.
dissatisfied: *adj*. nayayamót.
dissect: *v*. katayin, hiwain, lapain.
disseminate: *v*. isabog, ikalat, palaganapin.
dissent: *n*. pagtutlo.
dissimilar: *adj*. magkaiba.
dissipate: *v*. mapawi, pawiin, pumaram, paramin.
dissolution: *n*. pagkabuwág, pagkalanság.
dissolve: *v*. matunas, magtunaw; maglahò.
distance: *n*. agwát, pagitan, distánsiya.
distant: *adj*. malayò.
distaste: *n*. suyà, sunók.
distil: *v*. dalisayin, magdistilá.
distillery: *n*. alakán, distileryá.
distinct: *adj*. ibá; **~ion** *n*. pagtatangì, katangian.
distinctive: *adj*. pagkakakilanlán, pansarili.
distinguish: *v*. mapatanyág, mapabantóg, itangì, ibukód.
distinguished: *adj*. dakilà, bantóg, tanyág, litáw, sikát.
distort: *v*. pilipitin ang porma, magpapangit.
distract: *v*. umabala, abalahin, gumambalà.
distraction: *n*. paggambalà.
distress: *n*. pagaalaalá, pagkabalisa, pagkabahalà.
distribute: *v*. mamigáy, manudmód, mamahagi; ikalat.
distributive: *n*. (*gram.*) pang-uring paayaw-ayaw.
distributor: *n*. tagapamahagi, mámamahagi.
district: *n*. poók, distrito.
distrust: *v*. mawaláng-tiwalà.
disturb: *v*. bulabugin, gambalain; pakialamán, galawín.
ditch: *n*. bambáng, kanál.
dive: *v*. tumalón sa tubig, sumisid; *n*. sisid, bulusok.
diver: *n*. maninisid.
diverge: *v*. maghiwaláy, magkaibá; **~nce** *n*. pagkakaibá, pagkakalayô.
diverse: *adj*. ibá-ibá.
diversify: *v*. pag-ibá-ibahín.
diversity: *n*. kaibhán, pagkakibá.
divert: *v*. maglihís, palihisín; iligáw.
divest: *v*. alisán; hubarán.
divide: *v*. humatì, hatiin, biyakín.
dividend: *n*. tubò, pakinabang, dibidendo.
divine: *adj*. dibino, banál.
divisible: *adj*. maháhatì.
division: *n*. paghahatì, pagbabahagi; hatì.
divisor: *n*. panghatì.
divorce: *n*. diborsiyo, paghihiwaláy.
divulge: *v*. ibunyág, isiwalat.
dizzy: *adj*. mahilo, hiló; lulâ.
do: *v*. gawin, gumawâ; **~ away with** alisín, patayín; **have nothing to do with** waláng kinálaman sa.
docile: *adj*. maamò; masunurin.
dock: *n*. pantalán, daungán, atrakadero muwelye; *v*. dumaóng; ipundó.
dockyard: *n*. baradero; atrakadero.
doctor: *n*. manggagamot, médiko, doktór.
doctrine: *n*. doktrina, paniniwalà.
document: *n*. dokumento, kasulatan.
dodge: *v*. umigtád, iwasan, tiplagán.
doe: *n*. libay, usang babae.
dog: *n*. aso.
dogma: *n*. dogma.
doing: *n*. gawâ, kagagawán.

doldrums: *n*. katamlayán, lumbáy.
doll: *n*. manyikà, manikà.
dollar: *n*. dolyár, dolar.
dolphin: *n*. dolpín. lumbá-lumbá.
dolt: *n*. tangáng tao.
dome: *n*. kúpola, simboryo.
domestic: *adj*. maamò, ng mag-anak; **~ate** *v*. magpaamò.
domicile: *n*. tírahan, bahay, táhanan.
dominant: *adj*. nangingibabaaw, nakapangyáyari; pangunahín.
dominate: *v*. makapangyari, mapangibabawan.
domineering: *adj*. dominante, mapagharíharian.
dominion: *n*. kapangyarihan, pamamahalà.
domino: *n*. dómino.
don: *v*. magsuót.
donate: *v*. magbigáy, mag-abuloy.
donation: *n*. pagbibigáy, paghahandóg.
done: *adj*. tapós, yarì.
donkey: *n*. asno, buriko.
donor: *n*. ang nagbigáy, ang nagkaloób.
don't: *v*. huwág.
doom: *n*. kamátayan; tadhanà, kapalaran.
door: *n*. pintô; **~bell** *n*. timbre; **~keeper** *n*. portero; **~ mat** *n*. kuskusan ng paá; **~step** *n*. portál, bungad ng pingô; **~way** *n*. pintuan.
dope: *n*. apyan; gamót na pampatulog; tangáng tao.
dormitory: *n*. dormitoryo.
dose: *n*. dosis.
dot: *n*. tuldók; *v*. tuldukán.
dote: *v*. mahalíng, kahalingán.
double: *adj*. doble, ibayo, dalawá; *v*. magdoble; doblihín; **~-cross** *v*. manloko, luminláng, linlangín, dumayà; **~ breasted** doble karera.
doubt: *n*. alinlangan, duda; *v*. mag-alinlangan; **~ful** *adj*. dudoso, nag-aalinglangan.
dough: *n*. masa.
douse: *v*. sabuyan, magbuhos.
dove: *v*. kalapati.
down: *adv*. pababâ, paibabâ; *n*. (*soft feathers*) balahibo.
downcast: *adj*. malungkót.
downfall: *n*. pagbagsák, pagkalagpák.
downgrade: *n*. pagbabâ; pagsamâ.
downhill: *adv*. palusóng, pababâ.
downpayment: *n*. páunáng bayad.
downpour: *n*. buhos ng ulán.
downright: *adv*. lubós, ganáp, talagá.
downstairs: *adv*. pababâ ng hagdanan.
downtown: *adv*. sa kabayanan.
downward: *adv*. pababâ.
dowry: *n*. dote, bilang, bigáy-kaya.
doze: *v*. maidlíp.
dozen: *n*. labindalawá, dosena.
drab: *adj*. nakababagót, mapangláw.
draft: *n*. hihip ng hangin; (*rough copy*) buradór; (*sketch*) plano, krokis; *v*. bumalangkás; mangalap.
drag: *v*. kaladkarín, hilahin.
dragnet: *n*. lambát, sinsoro.
dragon: *n*. dragón; **~fly** *n*. tutubí.
drain: *v*. patuyuín, umubos; *n*. alulód, paagusán; **~age** *n*. páagusán, desagwe.
drama: *n*. dulà, drama; **~tic** *adj*. pandulà, pandrama, dramátiko; **~tize** *v*. isadulà.
drape: *v*. balutin, magkurtina; **~ry** *n*. kurtinahín.
drastic: *adj*. marahás.
draw: *v*. (*attract*) maakit, akitin, kayagin; (*pull out*) bumunot, dukutin; (*sketch*) gumuhit, magdrowing; *n*. (*tie in a game*) patás, tablá; **~back** *n*. balakíd, sagabal, sagwíl; **~er** *n*. kahón; **~ing** *n*. dibuho, drowing.
dread: *v*. masindák, matakot; **~ful** nakasísindák.
dream: *n*. pangarap, panaginip; *v*. mapangarap, pangarapin.
dreary: *adj*. waláng-siglá; malungkót.
dredge: *n*. draga; *v*. dragahin.
dregs: *n*. latak, tining.
drench: *v*. pigtaín, basaín.
dress: *n*. bestido, barò, damít; *v*. magbihis, magdamít; **~ maker** mananahì; **~er** *n*. tokadór; **~ing** *n*. (*sauce*) sarsa; (*bandage*) bendahe; **~ed up** nakapustura, bihis.
dribble: *v*. tumulò, tumagas.
dried: *adj*. tuyô.
drift: *v*. maanod, matangáy; *n*. takbó, tungo.
drill: *n*. balibol, barena, taladro, pambutas.
drink: *v*. inumín, uminóm; *n*. inóm.
drip: *v*. pumaták-paták, tumulu-tulò.
drive: *v*. magmaneho; maghatíd; *n*. lakás,

puwersa.
drivel: *v*. maglawáy.
driver: *n*. tsupér; kutsero.
drizzle: *n*. ambón; *v*. umambón.
droll: *adj*. katawá-tawá.
drone: *v*. gumiging, umugong.
droop: *v*. lumayláy, iyukô.
drop: *n*. paták; tulò; *v*. malaglág, mabagsák; ~ **by** dumalaw, bisitahin, dumaán.
dropsy: *n*. pamamanás.
drought: *n*. tagtuyót, tagbisî.
drown: *v*. malunod; lunurin.
drowsy: *adj*. maantók, antók.
drudgery: *n*. mahirap na trabaho.
drug: *n*. gamót; bawal na gamót; **~store** parmasya, botika.
druggist: *n*. botikaryo.dug
drum: *n*. tamból; **~stick** *n*. panamból.
drummer: *n*. tambulero, bombista.
drunk: *adj*. lasíng, langó; **~ard** *n*. maglalasing, lasenggo, boratsero.
dry: *adj*. tuyô; (*land*) tigáng; ~ **dock** dahikan, baradero.
dual: *adj*. dálawahan.
dub: *v*. ipalayaw, itagurî.
dubious: *adj*. nakapagaalinlangan.
duchess: *n*. dukesa.
duck: *n*. pato; *v*. yumukóng biglâ, maglubóg.
duckling: *n*. sisiw ng pato.
due: *adj*. bagay, nararapat, marapat, angkóp; ~ **to** dahil sa.
duel: *n*. duwelo, disapyo.
dues: *n*. butaw.
duet: *n*. duweto, dálawahang-tinig.
dugout: *n*. lungáw.
dull: *adj*. mapuról, pulpól; (*cloudy*) kulimlím, maulap; (*not shiny*) di-makintáb.
duly: *adv*. gaya ng nárarapat.
dumb: *adj*. (*stupid*) tangá; (*unable to speak*) pipi.
dumbfound: *v*. matilihan, matigilan.
dummy: *n*. manikí; pantalya.
dump: *v*. magtambák, ibuntón; *n*. basurahán.
dumpling: *n*. bola-bola.
dunce: *n*. tangáng tao.
dung: *n*. tae ng hayop.
dungeon: *n*. bartolina, kalabós.
dupe: *v*. manloko, mandayà, linlagín.
duplicate: *v*. kopyahín, dalawahín.
durable: *adj*. matibay, pangmatagalan.
duration: *n*. tagál.
during: *prep*. habang, samantalang.
dusk: *n*. dapit-hapon, takíp-sílim, agaw-dilím.
dust: *n*. alikabók; *v*. magpaspás, palisán; **~ter** *n*. plumero, pamunas; **~y** *adj*. maalikabók.
Dutch: *adj*. Olandés.
dutiful: *adj*. masunurin.
duty: *n*. tungkulin, katungkulan; (*tax*) buwís.
dwarf: *n*. burít, bulilít, unano; *v*. papanliitín.
dwell: *v*. tumahán, tumirá; **~ing** *n*. tírahan, táhanan.
dwindle: *v*. umuntî, lumiít; maubos.
dye: *v*. tinain, kolorán, magtinà; *n*. pangulay.
dynamite: *n*. dinamita.
dynamo: *n*. dínamo.
dynasty: *n*. dinastiya.
dysentery: *n*. disinteriya, iti, pag-iiti.

E

each: *adj*., *pron*. bawa't isá.
eager: *adj*. sabík.
eagle: *n*. ágila, banoy.
ear: *n*. tainga; (*of corn*) pusò ng maís; **~wax** *n*. tutulí; ~ **infection** *n*. tulók.
eardrum: *n*. salamín ng tainga.
early: *adv*. maaga.
earn: *v*. gumana, ganahin, kitain; maging-dapat; **~ing** *n*. kita.
earnest: *adj*. masigasig; maalab.
earring: *n*. hikaw, arilyos, aritos.
earth: *n*. mundó, daigdíg, lupà; **~quake** *n*. lindól; **~worm** *n*. bulati.
ease: *v*. magbawas; luwagán; *n*. alwán; ginhawa, kariwasaán.
easel: *n*. kabalyete.
east: *n*. silangan; **~ern** *adj*. sílanganín; **~ward** pa-silangán.
Easter: *n*. Mulíng Pagkabuhay, Paskó ng Pagkabuhay.
easy: *adj*. magaán, madalî; ~ **going** *adj*. mapag-waláng-bahalà.
eat: *v*. kumain, kainin.
eaves: *n*. sulambî, ambî, medya-agwa.

eavesdrop: *v*. makiníng nang pasubók.
ebb: *v*. umuntî, lumiít.
eccentric: *adj*. katuwâ, katakataká.
echo: *n*. alingawngáw.
eclipse: *n*. paglalahò, eklipse.
economic: *adj*. pangkabuhayan; **~s** *n*. ekonómiko.
economize: *v*. magtipíd.
economy: *n*. pamamalakad, kabuhayan, pamamalakad ng pangkabuhayan; ekonomiya; pagtitipíd.
ecstasy: *n*. lubós na kagalakan.
edge: *n*. gilid, bingit; tabí, baybáy; talím.
edible: *adj*. nakakain.
edict: *n*. útos, kautusán.
edifice: *n*. gusalì, edipisyo.
edition: *n*. labas, limbág, edisiyón.
editor: *n*. patnugot, editór; **~ial** editoryál; pangulong tudlíng.
educate: *v*. turuan; paaralan.
education: *n*. karunungan, pinag-aralan.
eel: *n*. igat; (*kinds*) palós, balila; **black pike ~** pindanga; **~ grass** lamon, lusay, yaay.
effect: *n*. bunga, resulta; bisà, epekto.
effective: *adj*. mabisà.
effeminate: *adj*. binabae.
efficient: *adj*. sanáy, may-kakayahán.
effort: *n*. pagpupunyagî, pagpipilit, pagsisikap.
egg: *n*. itlóg; **duck ~** penoy; **duck ~ with embryo** balút.
eggplant: *n*. talóng.
ego: *n*. sarili, pagkamakaako; kaakuhan.
egotism: *n*. pagkamakasarili, kasarilinan.
eight: *n*. waló, otso; **~een** *n*., *adj*. disiotso, labingwaló; **~y** *n*. ikawaló, pangwaló.
either: *adj, pron*. otsenta, walumpû.
ejaculate: *v*. bumulwák.
eject: *v*. bumugá, iluwâ.
eke out: *v*. magdagdág nang kauntî.
elaborate: *adj*. detalyado, maguló, magusót; *v*. magpabuti, painamin.
elapse: *v*. lumipas, dumaán.
elastic: *adj*. lástiko, napaháhabà.
elated: *adj*. nápapaangát.
elbow: *n*. siko; kodo; *v*. sikuhín.
elder: *adj*. nakatatandâ.
elect: *v*. piliin, maghalál; **~ion** hálalan, eleksiyón; **~or** maghahalal.
electric: *adj*. eléktriko, de-koryente.
electricity: *n*. koryente, elektrisidád.
electrocute: *v*. koryentihín.
elegance: *n*. kisig, gilas, tikas, dingal.
elegant: *adj*. makisig, magilas, mabigas, elegante.
element: *n*. bahagi, elemento, salik, sangkáp.
elementary: *adj*. panimulâ, elementaryo.
elephant: *n*. elepante, gadyá.
elevate: *v*. itaás.
elevation: *n*. kataasan, pagkakátaás.
elevator: *n*. asensór, elebeytor.
eleven: *n*. labing-isá, onse.
elf: *n*. duwende.
elicit: *v*. tamuhín, magtamó.
eligible: *adj*. mapilì, mahirang, mahalál.
eliminate: *v*. alisín.
elite: *adj*. pilì, hirang.
ellipse: *n*. tambilugan.
elongated: *adj*. habâ, talinghabâ.
elope: *v*. itanan; tumakas, lumayas.
eloquent: *adj*. maliwanag; magalíng magsalitâ.
else: *adj*. pa; ibá; (*instead*) kung di, kung hindî.
elsewhere: *adv*. sa ibáng dako.
elude: *v*. umiwas, iwasan; tumalilís.
elusive: *adj*. madulás; mailáp
emaciated: *adj*. payát, yayát.
emancipate: *v*. magpalayà, palayain.
embalm: mag-embalsamo, embalsamuhín.
embargo: *n*. embargo; pagbabawal, pagpigil.
embark: *v*. sumakáy sa bapór, magsimulâ.
embarrass: *v*. hiyaín, mapahiyâ.
embassy: *n*. embahada, pasuguán.
embellish: *v*. gayakán, magpagandá.
ember: *n*. alipato, baga.
embezzle: *v*. lustayín, lumustáy; magdespalko; **~ment** paglustáy.
emblem: *n*. sagisag, símbulo.
embody: *v*. maglangkáp, magsama.
emboss: *v*. magpalamuti.
embrace: *v*. yumakap, yumapós; (*include*) sumakláw; (*enclose*) magpaligid.
embroider: *v*. magburdá; **~y** *n*. burdá.
embryo: *n*. similya, bilíg, binhî.
emerald: *n*. esmeralda.
emerge: *v*. lumabás, lumitáw.

emergency: *n.* kagipitan.
emery paper: *n.* papél-de-liha.
emigrant: *n.* dayuhan, nandárayuhan.
emigrate: *v.* dumayo (sa ibang bansâ).
eminent: *adj.* dakilà, mabunyî, tanyág.
emissary: *n.* sugò.
emit: *v.* magbugá, bigyán.
emotion: *n.* damdamin; **~al** *adj.* maramdamin.
emperor: *n.* emperadór.
emphasis: *n.* diín; pagpapahalagá.
emphasize: *v.* bigyáng-diín.
emphatic: *adj.* mariín.
empire: *n.* imperyo.
employ: *v.* upahan; (*use*) gamitin; **~ee** *n.* empleado, kawaní; **~er** maypagawâ; **~ment** *n.* gawain, trabaho, empleo.
empower: *v.* magbigáy ng kapangyarihan; **~ment** *n.* pagsasakapangyarihan.
empress: *n.* emperatrís.
empty: *adj.* basyó, waláng-lamán.
emulate: *v.* tumulad, tularan, parisan.
enable: *v.* itulot; makaya; maka-.
enamel: *n.* enamel, esmalte.
encage: *v.* ikulóng, kulungín.
encase: *v.* balutin, mabalot.
enchant: *v.* gayumahin, marahuyò; **~ing** *adj.* kaakit-akit, kabigha-bighanì.
encircle: *v.* lumigid, pumalibot, bangkulungín.
enclose: *v.* kulungín, palibutan.
enclosure: *n.* bakod; (*of letter*) kalakip, kasama.
encompass: *v.* pumaligid, paligiran.
encounter: *v.* magkasagupà, makatagpô.
encourage: *v.* mapasiglá, pasiglahín; himukin.
encroach: *v.* manghimasok.
encyclopedia: *n.* ensiklopedya.
end: *n.* tapos, pagkatapos, wakás; (*last part*) dulos; *v.* matapos, magwakás; **at the ~ of** sa wakás ng; **put an ~ to** tapusin.
endanger: *v.* isapanganib, ilagáy sa panganib.
endeavor: *v.* magsikap, magpunyagî; pagsikapan.
endless: *adj.* waláng katapusán, waláng hanggán.
endorse: *v.* sumang-ayon, pagtibayin; **~ment** paglilipat; pagsang-ayon.
endow: *v.* pagkaloobán; **~ment** *n.* kaloób.
endurance: *n.* tatág, tibay, pagtitiís.
endure: *v.* makapagtiís, mapagtiisán; tumagál.
enema: *n.* labatiba.
enemy: *n.* kaaway, kalaban; katunggalî.
energetic: *adj.* masipag, masigasig; masikap; masiglá.
energy: *n.* siglá, sigasig, sipag.
enforce: *v.* magpatupád; **~ment** pagpapatupád; **law ~r** *n.* tagapagpatupád ng batás.
engage: *v.* ipangakò; **~ment** kompromiso, tipán.
engaged: *adj.* may kasunduang pakasál.
engine: *n.* motór, mákina.
engineer: *n.* inhinyero; *v.* bumalangkás; gumawâ.
England: *n.* Inglatéra.
English: *n.* Inglés.
engrave: *v.* ukitin, iukit.
engulf: *v.* lamunin, sakmalín.
enhance: *v.* magdagdág ng gandá.
enigma: *n.* talinghagà, palaisipán.
enjoy: *v.* malugód, ikatuwâ; **~ment** katúwaan.
enlarge: *v.* magpalakí, lakhán; **~ment** pagpapalakí.
enlighten: *v.* paliwanagin, liwanagan.
enlist: *v.* magpalista; **~ment** pagpapatalâ.
enormous: *adj.* malakí; napakalubhâ.
enough: *adj.* husto, tamà; sapát.
enquire: *v.* magtanóng.
enrage: *v.* galitin, pagalitin.
enrich: *v.* magpayaman.
enroll: *v.* ilistá; isapì; magpatalâ; magmatríkula; **~ment** pagpapatalâ, pagpapalistá.
enslave: *v.* alipinin, alilain.
ensure: *v.* tiyakin, siguruhin.
entangle: *v.* másangkót.
enter: *v.* pumasok.
enterprise: *n.* gawain, proyekto, negosyo.
entertain: *v.* libangín, aliwín, istimahín; **~ment** líbangan; pag-istimá.
enthusiasm: *n.* sigasip, siglá.
enthusiastic: *adj.* masiglá, masigasig.
entice: *v.* umakit, rahuyuin.
entire: *adj.* buô.
entitle: *v.* magbigáy-karapatán.
entomb: *v.* ilibíng.
entomologist: *n.* entomólogo, dalúbkulisap.

entomology: *n*. entomolohiya, aghám-kulisap.
entrails: *n*. lamáng-loób.
entrance: *n*. pagpasok; pasukán.
entrap: *v*. pikutin, hulihin sa bitag; linangín.
entreat: *v*. samuin, sumamò.
entrust: *v*. ipagkatiwalà, pagkátiwalaan; **~ed** *adj*. nakatiwalà.
entry: *n*. pagpasok, daán, pasukán.
entwine: *v*. pumulupot, pamuluputan.
enumerate: *v*. isá-isahín.
enunciate: *v*. bumigkás ng salitâ.
envelop: *v*. kubkubín.
envelope: *n*. sobre.
envious: *adj*. mainggitin, mapanghilì.
environment: *n*. paligid, kapaligirán, kagiliran.
environs: *n*. mga paligid-ligid.
envoy: *n*. sugò.
envy: *n*. inggít, hilì, pagkahilì.
epenthesis: *n*. maypaningit.
epidemic: *n*. salot, peste.
epithet: *n*. banság.
epoch: *n*. panahón, kapanahunan.
equal: *n*. kapantáy, kapareho.
equality: *n*. pagkakapareho.
equator: *n*. ekwadór.
equiangular: *adj*. parisulok.
equip: *v*. magbigáy; **~ment** *n*. kagamitán, kasangkapan.
equivalent: *adj*. katumbás, katimbáng, katapát.
equivocal: *adj*. may dalawáng magkaibáng kahulugán.
era: *n*. kapanáhunan.
eradicate: *v*. lumipol, puksaín.
erase: *v*. bumurá, pumawì; **~r** pamburá; pamawì.
erect: *adj*. tuwíd; *v*. magtayô; **~ion** (*of penis*) *n*. tingarò, paninigás, garol, talirik, pagtayô.
erode: *v*. maagnás.
err: *v*. magkamalî.
errand: *n*. sadyâ; nilálákad; **send on an ~** utusan.
erratic: *adj*. malí-malî.
erroneous: *adj*. malî.
error: *n*. kamálian, pagkakamalî.
erudite: *adj*. marunong.
erupt: *v*. pumutók, bumugá.
escalator: *n*. eskaladór; hagdáng gumagaláw.
escape: *v*. tumakas; makakawalâ.
escort: *n*. bantáy, konsorte, abay.
esophagus: *n*. lalamunan.
especially: *adv*. lalò na; sadyâ.
espionage: *n*. ispiyonahe, paniniktík.
espouse: *v*. ikasál.
essay: *n*. sanaysáy.
essence: *n*. diwà, esensiya.
essential: *adj*. kailangan, mahalagá.
establish: *v*. matatag, magtatág, itayô; **~ment** pagtatatag, pagkakátatag.
estate: *n*. arí-arian, propyedád.
esteem: *v*. magpahalagá, tingnán.
estimate: *v*. magtasa, tasahan; *n*. palagáy, tasà, tantiyá.
estrus: *n*. pangangandí.
estuary: *n*. wawà.
etc.: (*et cetera*) at ibá pa.
etch: *v*. iukit; **~ing** *n*. ukit; grabado.
eternal: *adj*. waláng hanggán.
eternity: *n*. kawaláng-katapusán.
ethics: *n*. étika.
etiquette: *n*. etiketa, magandáng kaugalian.
etymology: *n*. etimolohiyá, paláugatan, pámuhatán, pinagmulan ng salitâ.
eulogy: *n*. parangál.
evacuate: *v*. lumisan, mag-iwan.
evade: *v*. iwasan, talilisán.
evaluate: *v*. tumasa, tasahan, halagahán.
evaporate: *v*. sumingáw, matuyô.
evaporation: *n*. singáw, pagsingáw.
eve: *n*. bísperas.
even: *adj*. (*level*) patag, pantáy; (*equal*) pareho; amanos; **~ so** kahit na; **get ~ with** gumantí.
evening: *n*. gabí; *adj*. panggabí.
event: *n*. pangyayari; **in the ~ of** sakalì.
eventually: *adv*. sa wakás, sa hulí.
ever: *adv*. lagì, kailanmán, kahit minsan.
every: *adj*. bawá't isá, lahát.
everyday: *adv*. araw-araw.
everyone: *pron*. bawa't isá.
everything: *n*. lahát.
everywhere: *adv*. saanmán, kahit saán.
evict: *n*. magpaalís, magpalayas.
evidence: *n*. ebidénsiya, katunayan, katibyan; tandâ.
evident: *adj*. maliwanag, malinaw.

evil: *adj*. masamâ, makasalanan.
evolution: *n*. ebolusiyón.
evolve: *v*. bumalangkás.
ex- *pref*. dati.
exact: *adj*. tamà, wastô, tumpák.
exactly: *adv*. tamang-tamà.
exaggerate: *v*. magpalabis, palakihín.
exalt: *v*. itaás, purihin.
exam: *n*. eksamen.
examine: *v*. suriin, siyasatin; alamín.
example: *n*. huwaran, modelo, ulirán; halimbawà.
excavate: *v*. humukay, hukayin.
exceed: *v*. labisan, humigít, higtán; **~ing** *adj*. higít; **~ingly** *adv*. lubhâ.
excel: *v*. lumampás, higtán, lampasán.
excellence: *n*. kagálingan, kahusayan.
excellent: *adj*. napakagalíng, napakahusay, mabuti.
except: *prep*. maiban sa, matangì sa; *v*. ihiwaláy.
exception: *n*. kataliwasán; paghihiwaláy; **~al** *adj*. pambihirà.
excerpt: *n*. haláw, hangò.
excess: *n*. labis, sobra, kalabisán.
excessive: *adj*. labis-lais, sobra.
exchange: *v*. ipagpalít, magpalít.
excite: *v*. pumukaw, gumising; biglaín.
exciting: *adj*. nakapupukaw, nakabibiglâ, nakagugulat.
exclaim: *v*. isigáw, ibulalás.
exclamation: *n*. bulalás.
exclude: *v*. palayasin.
exclusive: *adj*. malíban; tangì, sarili.
excommunicate: *v*. itiwalág.
excommunicated: *adj*. eskolmulgado.
excrement: *n*. tae, dumí.
excursion: *n*. pagliliwalíw, iskursiyón.
excuse: *n*. dahilán, katwiran; *v*. ipagpatawad; **~ me** maabalà kita; kompermiso; (*to pass*) pakiraán pô.
execute: *v*. (*carry out*) isagawâ, ganapín; (*put to death*) bitayín.
executive: *adj*. pampangasiwaán; *n*. tagapagpaganáp; punò.
exemplify: *v*. magpakitang-halimbawà.
exempt: *v*. palibrihín; *adj*. di-sakláw.
exercise: *n*. pagsasanay, hersisyo.
exert: *v*. magsikap, pilitin; **~ion** pagsisikap; pag-pupunyagî.
exhale: *v*. humingá nang palabás.
exhaust: *v*. ubusin; maubos; *n*. pásingawan; **~ pipe** tambutso; **~ion** hapò; pagkaubos.
exhausted: *adj*. pagód, patâ.
exhibit: *v*. magtanghál, magpakita; *n*. katibayan, tanghál.
exhibition: *n*. tanghalan.
exhilirate: *v*. magpasayá.
exile: *n*. pagtatapon; *v*. ipatapon.
exist: *v*. mabuhay; mayroón; umiral; **~ence** *n*. pagkakaroón; pag-iral.
exit: *n*. lábasan, paglabás.
exodus: *n*. paglálábsan.
exonerate: *v*. pawaláng-sala.
exorcise: *v*. magpalayas, magtawas.
exotic: *adj*. kakaibá; banyagà.
expand: *v*. lumawak, lumakí.
expanse: *n*. lawak, kalawakan.
expansion: *n*. pagpapalakí.
expect: *v*. asahan, asamín; hintayín.
expedient: *adj*. nábabagay, nápapanahón.
expedite: *v*. pabilisín, dalí-daliín.
expedition: *n*. paglalayág, ekpedisiyón.
expel: *v*. ibugá, ilabás.
expenditure: *n*. gastos; paggugol.
expense: *n*. gastos; **at the ~ of** sa kapinsalaán ng.
expensive: *adj*. mahál, magastos.
experience: *n*. karanasán, kasanayán; *v*. magdanas, dumanas.
experienced: *adj*. bihasá, sanáy, may-karanasán.
experiment: *n*. pagsubok; *v*. subukin.
expert: *n*. sanáy, eksperto, dalubhasà, bihasa.
expire: *v*. mataos, lumpias, magwakás.
explain: *v*. ipaliwanag, ipalinaw.
explanation: *n*. paliwanag; katwiran.
explicit: *adj*. malinaw, maliwanag.
explode: *v*. pumutók.
exploit: *v*. magsamatalá, kasangkapanin; **~-ation** *n*. pagpapaunlád, pagsasamantalá.
explore: *v*. galugarin; siyasatin; **~r** manggagalugad.
explosion: *n*. putók, pagsabog.

explosive: *n*. paputók, púlbura.
export: *n*. luwás, kalakal-panluwás; *v*. iluwás (sa ibáng bansâ).
expose: *v*. ibunyág, ihayág, ilantád; ~ **to the sun** ibilád, magpaaráw.
exposé: *n*. pagbubunyág.
exposed: *adj*. nakabunyág; nakalantád; (*to the elements*) nakatiwangwáng, nakawakawak
exposition: *n*. tanghalan; paglalahad.
exposure: *n*. pagbubunyág, pagkátampák, paghahayág.
express: *v*. ipahayag, sabihin, ipahiwatig; **~ion** *n*. pananalitâ, kasabihán, pangungusap; **~ive** nagpápahayag, pagpápakilala; **~way** ekpreswey.
expulsion: *n*. pagpalabás; pagtitiwalág, pagkátiwalág.
exquisite: *adj*. marikít, katangi-tangì, marilág.
extemporaneous: *adj*. di-inihandâ.
extend: *v*. (*reach*) umabót; (*grant*) igawad; (*lengthen in time*) magpatagál, magpatuloy, magpalawig.
extension: *n*. pagpapahabà, pagpapatuloy; (*extra time alloted*) palugit.
extensive: *adj*. malawak, masakláw.
extent: *n*. lawak, sakláw; lakí.
exterior: *n*. labás, panlabás.
exterminate: *v*. lipulin, puksaín.
external: *adj*. panlabás.
extinct: *adj*. lipól na, walâ na.
extinction: *n*. pagkamatáy, pagkalipol.
extinguish: *v*. patayín.
extort: *v*. mangikil, manghuthót, kikilan; **~ion** *n*. panghuhuthót, pangingikil.
extra: *adj*. ekstra, dagdág, labis.
extract: *v*. katasín, bunutin; *n*. hangò, haláw; katás; sipì.
extradite: *v*. magpabalík.
extraordinary: *adj*. pambihirà, di-karaniwan, ka-hanga-hangà.
extravagant: *adj*. gastadór, mapagtapon, marangyâ; labis, sobra; maaksayá.
extreme: *adj*. dakilà; masidhî; *n*. sukdulan; kaduluhan.
extremity: *n*. dulo, kaduluhan; paá't kamáy.
exude: *v*. gumitî, tumagas.
exult: *v*. magpakasayá, magpakagalák.
eye: *n*. matá; ~ **of a needle** butas ng karayon; **black** ~ pasâ sa matá; **open the ~s wide** dumilat; **close the ~s** pumikít; ~ **of the sea fish** matáng-dagat; **~brow** kilay; **~glasses** *n*. salamín sa matá; **~lash** pilikmatá; **~let** *n*. uhetes; **~sight** *n*. tingín, pa-ningín; **~witness** saksí, testigo.

F

fable: *n*. pábula, katakatà, alamát.
fabric: *n*. tela, kayo.
fabricate: *v*. magtayô, kathaín, magkata-katà.
façade: *n*. patsada, haráp ng gusalì; delantera.
face: *n*. mukhâ; *v*. humaráp, harapín.
facet: *n*. tapyás.
facetious: *adj*. mabirô, masisté.
facilitate: *v*. magpadalî, padaliín.
facility: *n*. dalî, gaán; kakayahán.
fact: *n*. katotohanan, katunayan.
faction: *n*. pangkát.
factor: *n*. dahilán, sanhî, salik.
factory: *n*. pábrika, págawaan.
factual: *adj*. tunay, totoó.
faculty: *n*. pakultád, kagawarán; kapangyarihan.
fad: *n*. pasamantaláng uso.
fade: *v*. lumabò, kumupas.
fag: *adj*. mapagod; *n*. (*coll.*) baklâ.
fail: *v*. mabigô, lumagpák, bumagsák; **~ure** *n*. pagkabigô, pagkabagsák.
faint: *v*. himatayín, mahilo, malulà; *adj*. bahagyâ.
fair: *adj*. makatarungan, husto; (*complexion*) maputî; *n*. perya.
fairy: *n*. engkanto, duwende.
faith: *n*. tiwalà, pananalig; (*religious*) pananampalataya; **~ful** *adj*. matapát; **~less** *adj*. taksíl, hindî tapát.
fake: *adj*. huwád, palsipikado; *n*. dayà, pagdarayà; *v*. huwarán; magkunuwâ.
falcon: *n*. palkón.
fall: *v*. mahulog; ~ **on one's back** matimbuwáng; *n*. (*act of falling*) pagkahulog; (*autumn*) taglagás.
fallacy: *n*. kamálían, pagkakámalî, malíng akalà.

fallible: *adj*. maááring magkámalî.
fallow: *adj*. binugkál.
falls: *n*. talón.
false: *adj*. hindî tamà, malî, sala; ~ **alarm** *n*. tibadbád.
falsification: *n*. panghuhuwád, palsipikasiyón.
falsify: *v*. palsipikahín, huwarán.
falter: *v*. matigilan, mag-atubilì.
fame: *n*. kabantugán, kabunyián.
familiar: *adj*. kilalá, alám; magkalapit; ~**ize** *v*. sanayin; palaganapin.
family: *n*. pamilya, mag-anak.
famine: *n*. pagkakagutóm, taggutóm, tagsalát.
famish: *v*. magutom na lubhâ.
famous: *adj*. bantóg, tanyág.
fan: *n*. (*for cooling*) pamaypáy; abaniko; (*electric*) bentiladór; (*of sports*) apisiyonado; *v*. magpaypáy.
fanatic: *n*. panátiko.
fancy: *adj*. kaakit-akit; magarà.
fanfare: *n*. tokata; **without** ~ waláng kiyáw-kiyáw.
fantastic: *adj*. kakatuwâ, hindî tuwâ.
fantasy: *n*. pantasíya.
far: *adj*. malayò; *adv*. higít, mas; ~ **East** Dulong Silangan.
faraway: *adj*. malayò.
farce: *n*. saynete, komedya.
fare: *n*. plete, upa, bayad.
farewell: *n*. paalam na, adiyós; ~ **party** despedida.
farm: *n*. bukid, sakahán, lináng; *v*. magsaka; ~**er** *n*. magsasaká, maglilináng; ~**house** kubo.
fascinate: *v*. halinahin, gayumahin, bighaniin.
fascination: *n*. pagkabighanì, pagkahalina.
fashion: *n*. moda, uso; kaugalian; *v*. gumawâ, hugisan; ~**able** pusturyoso; sunód sa moda.
fast: *adj*. mabilís, matulin; *v*. mag-ayuno; *n*. ayuno.
fasten: *v*. mag-ugnáy; isará; ikandado, isusì; ~**er** *n*. pantalì, pangkabít, pansiper.
fastidious: *adj*. maselan, delikado.
fat: *n*. tabâ; (*lard*) mantikà; *adj*. matabâ.
fatal: *adj*. nakamamatáy, nakakasawî.
fate: *n*. kapalran, palad, tadhanà, suwerte.
father: *n*. amá, tatay, tatang; (*priest*) parì; ~-**in-law** biyenáng-lalaki; ~**hood** pagiging-amá; ~**land** bayang-tinubuan.
fathom: *v*. tarukín, huluin, unawain, maunawaan, matarók; *n*. lalim na anim na talampakan.
fatigue: *n*. pagod, pagál, hapò, pagkahapò.
fatten: *v*. magpatabâ, patabaín.
fatty: *adj*. matabâ; (*oily*) malangís.
faucet: *n*. gripo.
fault: *n*. kasalanan, sala; (*defect*) sirà; (*mistake*) malî, kamalian; ~**y** *adj*. may-sirà, may-depekto; ~**finding** *adj*. palápintasin, mápamintás.
fauna: *n*. palahayupan.
favor: *n*. tulong, kabutihang-loób; *v*. tangkilikin, mabutihin, magalingín; ~**able** paayón; sang-ayon; ~**ite**: *adj*. paborito, pinakamahál, pinakatangì, ~**itism** *n*. pagkampí, pagtatangì.
fawn: *n*. muntíng usa.
fear: *n*. takot, sindák; *v*. matakot, ipangambá, ikasindák.
feasible: *adj*. magágawâ, maisasagawâ.
feast: *n*. piyesta, bangkete, handaan.
feat: *n*. kahang-hangang gawâ.
feather: *n*. balahibo, plumahe.
feature: *n*. katangian; tampók na palabás; ~**s** *n*. pagmumukhâ.
February: *n*. Pebrero.
fed up: *n*. suyáng-suyâ.
fee: *n*. bayad, butaw, kota.
feeble: *adj*. mahinà; ~-**minded** sirá-sirâ.
feed: *v*. pakanin; (*farm animals with fodder*) kumpayán.
feel: *v*. hipuin; maramdamán, madamá; ~**ing** *n*. pandamdám; pagsalát, hipò; damdamin.
feign: *v*. magkunwarî.
felicitate: *v*. batiin, bumatì.
fell: *v*. patumbahín, putulin.
fellow: *n*. tao, kasama.
felt: *n*. piyeltro.
female: *n*. babae.
feminine: *adj*. pambabae.
fence: *n*. bakod; *v*. bakuran.
fencing: *n*. eskrima, estukada, plorete; arnís.
fender: *n*. depensa.
feng shui: *n*. punsóy.

ferment: *v*. mangasím, umasim; *n*. ligalig.
fern: *n*. pakô, eletso.
ferocious: *adj*. mabangís, mabagsík.
ferocity: *n*. kabangisán, bagsík; kalupitán.
ferry: *n*. badeo, bangkáng pantawíd, táwiran.
fertile: *adj*. mabunga; palaanák.
fertilizer: *n*. abuno, patabâ.
fervent: *adj*. maalab, taimtím.
fervor: *n*. kataimtimán, kaalaban.
fester: *v*. magnaknák, magnanà.
festival: *n*. piyesta, pagdiriwang, pagsasayá.
festschrift: *n*. parangál.
fetch: *v*. kumuha, kunin; ~ **water from a well** umigíb, sumalok.
fetid: *adj*. mabantót, mabahò.
fetter: *n*. tanikalâ sa paá.
fetus: *n*. bilig, similya.
feud: *n*. matandáng alitan.
fever: *n*. lagnát.
few: *adj*. kakauntî.
fiance(e): *n*. nóbiyo(a).
fiasco: *n*. tsasko, ganáp na kabígúan.
fib: *n*. maliít na kasinungalingan.
fiber: *n*. himaymáy, hilatsá, hiblá.
fickle: *adj*. salawahán, pabagu-bago.
fiction: *n*. likhâ, kathâ, kathambuhay.
fiddle: *n*. biyolín.
fidelity: *n*. katapatan, pagkamatapát.
field: *n*. lináng, bukid.
fiend: *n*. napakahayop na tao.
fierce: *adj*. mabangís, malupít, mabagsík, mabalasik.
fiery: *adj*. maapóy, napakainit; maangháng.
fiesta: *n*. piyesta.
fifteen: *n*. kinse, labinlimá.
fifth: *adj*. ikalimá, panlimá.
fifty: *n*. singkuwenta, limampû; **~-fifty** tigkalahatì, hatì.
fig: *n*. igos.
fight: *v*. maglaban, mag-away; **fist** ~ suntukan.
figment: *n*. guni-guní.
figurative: *adj*. patalinghagà.
figure: *n*. anyô, itsura, pigura, hugis; (*body*) pangangatawán; (*picture*) larawan; ~ **out** tayahin; ~ **of speech** talinghagà.
figurehead: *n*. tau-tauhan; (*of ship*) roda.
filch: *v*. umitín.
file: *n*. kikil; (*row*) pila, hilera, hanay; (*of papers*) salansán; *v*. kikilin, ihilera, ipila, magsalansán.
filibuster: *n*. pilibusterismo, pagsusuwaíl; *v*. magsuwaíl.
fill: *v*. magpunô, punuín; **~ing** *n*. pamasak, pastá, palamán.
filly: *n*. bisiro.
film: *n*. pilm, kodal; (*movie*) pelíkula; (*membrane*) balok; (*of eyes*) kulabà.
filter: *n*. panalà, salaán, piltro; *v*. magsalà.
filthy: *adj*. marumí, napakarumí.
fin: *n*. palaypáy, palikpík.
final: *adj*. hulí, panghulí; **~ly** *adv*. sa wakás; ~ **decision** pangwakás na pasiyá.
finance: *n*. pananalapî; *v*. magpagastos, magpapuhunan.
financial: *adj*. náuukol sa pananalapî.
find: *v*. mahanap, makapulot, makatagpô, matagpuán; (*discover*) tumukás, madiskubre; ~ **out** umalám, alamín; *n*. tuklás.
fine: *n*. multá; *adj*. pino, napakaliít, napakapino; mabuti. ~ **arts** *n*. belyas artes.
finger: *n*. dalirì; **index** ~ hintuturò; **middle** ~ datò, hinlalatò; **ring** ~ palasingsingan; **little** ~ kalingkingan; *v*. hipuin; **~nail** *n*. kukó; **~print** *n*. taták ng dalirì, bakás ng dalirì.
finish: *v*. magwakás, tapusin.
finite: *adj*. may-wakás.
fire: *n*. apóy, sunog; *v*. (*dismiss from work*) mag-alis sa trabaho; (*a gun*) magpaputók; ~ **engine** bomba sa sunog; ~ **escape** takasán sa sunog; ~ **hydrant** *n*. boka-inséndiyo.
firearm: *n*. armás, putók.
firecracker: *n*. rebentadór.
firefly: *n*. alitaptáp.
fireman: *n*. bombero, bantáy-sunog, mámamatay-sunog.
fireplace: *n*. páusukán; tsimineá.
firewood: *n*. panggatong.
firm: *adj*. matigás; matibay, matatág.
first: *adj*. pang-una, una; **at** ~ sa simulâ; *adv*. muna; ~ **aid** pangunang lunas; ~ **class** primera klase.
first-rate: *adj*. primera klase.
fiscal: *n*. pánuusán, piskál; ~ **year** *n*. taóng-pánuusán; **~'s office** *n*. piskalyá.

fish: *n.* isdâ; *v.* mangisdâ; ~ **bone** tiník; **~erman** *n.* mángingisdâ; **~hook** *n.* tagâ; **~trap** *n.* baklád; **~ing line** pansíng.
fissure: *n.* biták, putók.
fist: *n.* kamaó.
fit: *adj.* karapat-dapat, bagay, angkóp; *v.* magagpáng, bumagay; magkasya; maghusto; *n.* (*emotional*) sikláb, simbuyó; **ting** *adj.* tamà, akmâ, angkóp.
five: *n.* limá; **~fold** makálimá.
fix: *v.* mag-ayos, maghusay; magkabít, magtakdâ; ipakò; **~ed** *adj.* nakapirmí, matibay, matatág; **~er** tagaayos, tagaareglo; **~ture** *n.* kakabít.
fizzle: *v.* sumagitsít; ~ **out** mabigô.
flabby: *adj.* luylóy; malambót, mahinà.
flag: *n.* bandilà, watawat; *v.* hudyatán.
flagellate: *v.* humampás, pumalò, magpenenténsiyá.
flagpole: *n.* tagdán ng bandilà.
flail: *n.* panlugas, panggiík.
flake: *n.* tikláp na maliít, taliptíp.
flamboyant: *adj.* matingkád, nakasisilaw; mabulaklák.
flame: *n.* liyáb, lagabláb, ningas, alab.
flank: *n.* gilid, giliran, libís, tagiliran.
flannel: *n.* pranela.
flap: *v.* pumayagpág, pumagaspás; **~per** kirí, talandî; turít.
flare: *n.* sikláb; *v.* sumikláb.
flash: *n.* kisláp; silakbó; *v.* humagibis, sumalimbáy; **~light** lente, plaslait.
flashy: *adj.* marangyâ.
flask: *n.* prasko.
flat: *adj.* patag, pantáy, makinis; lapád; ~ **tire** putók na goma; **~fish** palad-palad, darapa, tatampál; **~ten** *v.* patagin, pantayín; unatin.
flatboat: *n.* gabara.
flattery: *n.* panghihibò, panghihibok, labis na papuri.
flatulence: *n.* utót, kabag, kabagan, usugan.
flatulent: *adj.* ututin.
flatus: *n.* kabag, tabol, usog.
flaunt: *v.* magmarangyâ, magpasikat; itanghál.
flavor: *n.* lasa, linamnám; *v.* magtimplá, magpa-lasa; **~ing** *n.* panimplá, pampalasa.
flaw: *n.* sirà, depekto.
flay: *v.* bakbakán, bakbakín.
flea: *n.* pulgás.
fleck: *n.* batík.
fleet: *n.* plota.
flesh: *n.* karne, lamán.
flex: *v.* magbaluktót.
flexible: *adj.* nababaluktót.
flick: *v.* pitikín; *n.* kisáp; **~er** *v.* umandápandáp, kumutí-kutitap.
flight: *n.* paglipád; pagtakas; (*of stairs*) hagdanan.
flimsy: *adj.*s manipís, marupók.
flinch: *v.* umurong, umudlót.
fling: *v.* ihagis, ipukól, pukulín.
flint: *n.* batóng kiskisan, puyusan.
flip: *v.* ipitík, pilantikín; *n.* paltík, pitík.
flirt: *n.* kirí; *v.* lumandî, kumirí, umalembong; **~ation** ligaw-birò, pakikipagkírihan.
float: *v.* lumutang; *n.* balsa.
flock: *n.* kawan; *v.* magsama-sama, magkalipumpón.
flog: *v.* pumalò, humagupít, latiguhín.
flood: *n.* bahâ; *v.* bumahâ; apawan.
floor: *n.* sahíg; (*story*) palapág, grado.
flop: *v.* magkakawág; sumalagmák, sumalampák; *n.* kabiguan, pagkabigô.
florid: *adj.* mabulaklák; mapalamuti.
florist: *n.* plorero, magbubulaklák.
flotilla: *n.* plotilya, muntíng plota.
flounce: *n.* borlas.
flounder: *v.* magkumayod, *n.* dapa, isdáng kitang.
flour: *n.* harina; **rice** ~ galapóng.
flourish: *v.* lumagô, umunlád.
flow: *v.* umagos; *n.* agos, tulò.
flower: *n.* bulaklák; *v.* mamulaklák; **~pot** *n.* pasô, masetera; **~y** *adj.* mabulaklák; **~ing** *n.* pamumulaklák.
flu: *n.* trangkaso, flu.
fluctuate: *v.* tumaás-bumabâ, magbagu-bago.
fluent: *adj.* mahusay na magsalitâ, madulás; (*unexpected* ~) matatás.
fluff: *n.* mulmól, himulmól.
fluid: *n.* líkido, tubig; *adj.* lusáw, sunudsúnuran.
flunk: *v.* bumagsák sa iksamen.
flush: *n.* bugsô; *v.* mamulá.

fluster: *v*. tarantahín, lihuhín.
flute: *n*. plauta, bansî.
flutter: *v*. magwagaywáy, ipagaypáy, ikampáy.
fly: *n*. (*housefly*) langaw; (*blowfly*) bangaw; *v*. lumipád; **~ing ant** gamugamó; **~ing fish** buladór, balang, iliw.
foam: *n*. bulâ; *v*. bumulâ.
focus: *n*. katumbakán; *v*. ipokus, itumbók, ipakò ang matá; tampulan, pokus.
foe: *n*. kaaway, kalaban.
fog: *n*. ulap, ulop; **~gy** *adj*. maulap; malabò.
foil: *v*. biguín, bumigô; *n*. palarâ.
fold: *v*. magtiklóp; *n*. tiklóp, lupî.
folder: *n*. polder.
foliage: *n*. mga dahon.
folk: *n*. mga tao; lipì; **~ song** kantahing-bayan, awiting-bayan; **~ tale** kuwentong-bayan.
follow: *v*. sumunód, sundán; taluntunín; (*understand*) umanawà; **~er** *n*. tagasunód; **~ing** *adj*. sumunód; *n*. mga tagasunód.
folly: *n*. kaululán, kahangalán.
foment: *v*. magsulsól, sulsulán.
fond: *adj*. mahilig, mairog, magiliw; minimithî.
fondle: *v*. kumarinyo.
food: *n*. pagkain; (*for fowls*) patukâ.
fool: *n*. luku-lukó, gago, ulól; *v*. lokohin, linlangín; **~ish** *adj*. ulól, hangál, tangá; loko; **~hardy** *adj*. waláng hunusdilì.
foot: *n*. paá; (*lowest part*) paanán, punò; (*measurement*) talampakan, piyé; **~ball** *n*. putbol; **~ing** *n*. tapakán, tuntungan; **~note** *n*. talábabâ; **~print** *n*. bakás ng paá; **~rest** *n*. tapakán; **~step** *n*. bakás ng paá; **~wear** *n*. sapatos.
for: *prep*. para; (*in place of*) kapalít ng, bilang kapalít; (*because*) dahil sa; **~ the sake of** alang-alang kay.
forage: *v*. maghanáp.
foray: *v*. dambungín.
forbid: *v*. ipagbawal, pagbawalan, sawayín; **~den** *adj*. bawal.
force: *n*. lakás, puwersa; bisà; *v*. pumilit, pilitin, puwersahín; **~ful** malakás, mabisà.
forceps: *n*. tiyanì, pansipit, panipit.
forearm: *n*. bisig, baraso.
foreboding: *n*. kabá, kutób, salagimsím.
forecast: *v*. manghulà, humulà.
forefather: *n*. nunò, ninunò.
forefinger: *n*. hintuturò.
forego: *v*. ipagpaubayà.
forehead: *n*. noó.
foreign: *adj*. dayuhan, banyagà; panlabás; **~er** *n*. dayo, dayuhan, banyagà, estranghero.
foreman: *n*. kapatás.
foremost: *adj*. nauuná, pangunahín.
forerunner: *n*. tagapagpagpáuná; hudyát, tandâ.
foresee: *v*. humulà.
foreshadow: *v*. magbabalâ.
foreskin: *n*. busisì; **roll up ~** *v*. buratín
forest: *n*. gubat, kagubatan; **~ry** *n*. panggugubat.
foretell: *v*. manghulà.
forever: *adv*. magpakailán mán, nang waláng-hanggán.
forewarn: *v*. mag-abiso, magbabalâ.
foreword: *n*. pambungad.
forefeit: *v*. matalo dahil sa isáng pagkukulang.
forge: *v*. magpandáy.
forgery: *n*. paghuwád, pagpalsipká.
forget: *v*. kalimutan, limutin; makaligtâ; **~ful** *adj*. malilimutín.
forgive: *v*. magpatawad, ipagpatawad; **~ness** patawad.
forgo: *v*. tumalikód, tumigil.
fork: *n*. tenedór; sangá; *v*. magsangá.
form: *v*. hubugin, magtatag; *n*. itsura, anyô, hugis; tabas.
formal: *adj*. pormál.
former: *adj*. una, nauna, dati.
formula: *n*. pórmula; **~te** *v*. magpanukalà; bumalangkás.
forsake: *v*. iwan, pabayaan, talikdán.
fort: *n*. kutà, muóg.
forthcoming: *adj*. daratíng, nalalapít.
fortification: *n*. kutà.
fortify: *v*. magpalakás, magpatibay; kutaan.
fortnight: *n*. dalawáng linggó.
fortress: *n*. muóg, tanggulan, kutà.
fortunate: *adj*. masuwerte, mapalad.
fortune: *n*. palad, kapalaran, suwerte, tagumpáy; (*money*) kayamanan; **~ teller** magpahulà.
forty: *n*. kuwarenta, apatnapû.

forward: *adv*. pasulóng; *adj*. sa unahán.
foster: *v*. magpaunlád, payamanin, paunlarín; ~ **child** anák-anakan; ~ **father** amá-amahan; ~ **mother** iná-inahan.
foul: *adj*. napakarumí, mabahò; masamâ.
found: *v*. itatag, itayô; ~**ation** *n*. saligán, batayán, pundasyón; ~**er** *n*. pundadór, tagapagtatag; ~**ling** *n*. batang-pulot.
fountain: *n*. bukál.
four: *n*. kuwatro, apat; ~**teen** *n*. labíng-apat, katorse; ~**th** *adj*. ikaapat, pang-apat.
fowl: *n*. manók; ibon; **wild** ~ labuyò.
fox: *n*. soro.
foxtrot: *n*. pakstrát.
fraction: *n*. bahagi, kapiraso.
fracture: *n*. balì; *v*. mabalì; málinsád.
fragile: *adj*. marupók, mahinà.
fragment: *n*. kaputol, pamantingin; retaso.
fragrance: *n*. bangó, samyó, halimuyak.
fragrant: *adj*. mabangó, mahalimuyak.
frail: *adj*. mahinà, marupók.
frame: *n*. bangháy, balangkás; (*picture*) kuwadro; *v*. ikuwadro; ~ **up** sábuwatan.
franchise: *n*. prangkisya.
frank: *adj*. tapát, prangko, tahás.
frantic: *adj*. balisáng-balisá.
fraternal: *adj*. pangkapatid, pangkapatiran.
fraternity: *n*. kapatiran.
fratricide: *n*. pagpatáy sa sariling kapatíd, pratrisidyo.
fraud: *n*. dayà, huwád, ~**ulent** *adj*. magdarayà.
fray: *n*. away, babág, labanán; ~**ed** *adj*. nisnís.
freak: *adj*. pambihirà; *n*. taong kakatuwá.
freckle: *n*. pekas.
free: *adj*. (*independent*) malayà, libre; (*gratuitous*) libre, waláng-bayad; (*loose*) malayà; *v*. magpaka-walâ, iligtás; ~**dom** *n*. layà, kalayaan; ~**lance** malayang trabahadór.
freeze: *v*. magyelo.
freight: *n*. kargada, bagahe; *v*. ikarga.
French: *n*., *adj*. Pransés; ~ **kiss** *n*. lapáng.
frenzy: *n*. sikláb ng galit; pagka-ulól; diliryo.
frequent: *adj*. malimit, madalás.
frequentative: *n*. paralás.
fresh: *adj*. sariwà; bago; (*water*) tabáng.
fret: *v*. maligalig, mabalisa, mabahalà; (*of stringed instrument*) bidyá, traste.
friar: *n*. prayle.
friction: *n*. pagkikiskís, pagpipingkî.
Friday: *n*. Biyernes.
fried: *adj*. prito.
friend: *n*. kaibigan, katoto; ~**ly** *adj*. magiliw, mabaít; ~**ship** *n*. pagkamagkaibigan, pagkakaibigan.
fright: *n*. bigláng takot; ~**en** *v*. takutin, sindakín; ~**ful** *adj*. nakatatakot, nakasisindák.
frigid: *adj*. nápakalamíg; matamláy.
fringe: *n*. lamuymóy, palawít.
frisk: *v*. kumapkáo; sumayáw-sayáw.
fritter: *v*. mag-aksayá; *n*. maruyà.
frivolous: *adj*. parák, hangál, tunggák.
frizzle: *v*. sumagitsít.
frock: *n*. sutana.
frog: *n*. palakâ.
frolic: *v*. magsayá, magkátuwaan.
from: *prep*. taga-; mulâ sa, galing sa; simulâ; **from .. to..** mulâ.. hanggáng..
front: *n*. unahán, haráp; larangan; ~ **seat of a cart** *n*. piskante.
frontier: *n*. hanggahan.
frost: *n*. namuóng hamóg.
froth: *n*. bulâ.
frown: *v*. sumimangot; *n*. simangot.
frozen: *adj*. nagyelo, namuô sa lamig.
frugal: *adj*. matipíd, masimpán.
fruit: *n*. prutas, bunga; ~**ful** *adj*. mabunga.
fruition: *n*. kaganapan, katupara; pagbubunga.
frustrate: *v*. bumigô, siphayuin.
frustration: *n*. kabiguan, pagkabigô, pagkasiphayò.
fry: *v*. magprito; *n*. anák na isdâ.
frying pan: *n*. kawalì.
fuck: (*vulg*.) *v*. magkantót, maghindót.
fuel: *n*. gatong, pampasikláb.
fugitive: *n*. pugante, takas.
fulfill: *v*. tumupád, tupdín, ganapín.
fulfillment: *n*. pagkaganáp.
full: *adj*. punô; (*entire*) buô; ~ **moon** kabilugan ng buwán; ~**ly** *adv*. lubós, ganáp.
fumble: *v*. makabitíw, umapuhap.
fume: *n*. usok, asó, singáw.
fumigate: *v*. magpausok.
fun: *n*. sayá, kasayahan, katuwaan, libangan; **just for** ~ katuwaan lang.

function: *n*. tungkulin, ginagawâ; pagdiriwang.
fund: *n*. ponde, laáng-gugulín.
fundamental: *adj*. napakahalagá, kailangan; *n*. simulain, saligán, batayán.
funeral: *n*. libíng.
fungus: *n*. halamang-singáw.
funnel: *n*. imbudo; **~-shaped** balisungsóng.
funny: *adj*. nakakatawá, nakatutuwâ.
fur: *n*. balahibo.
furious: *adj*. nagngángálit.
furl: *v*. magbalumbón, maglulón, tiklupín.
furnace: *n*. pugón.
furnish: *v*. maglagáy ng muwebles, pagkaloobán, bigyán.
furniture: *n*. muwebles.
furrow: *n*. tudlíng, kulubót; guhit.
further: *adj*. pa, lalong malayò; **~more** *adv*. at sakâ, bukód sa roón.
fury: *n*. matindíng galit, bangís, kabangisán.
fuse: *n*. mitsá, piyús; *v*. tunawin, magsanib.
fusion: *n*. pagtutunaw, paghahalò, pagsasanib.
fuss: *n*. kuskus-balungos, kuririÌ.
fussy: *adj*. delikado, maselán.
futile: *adj*. waláng-saysáy, waláng-halagá; waláng kasaysayang pagtatalo.
future: *n*. haharapín, kinabukasan; (*verb form*) panghinaharáp, pandaratíng; *adj*. magigíng, daratíng.
fuzzy: *adj*. di-malinaw; malabò.

G

gab: *v*. dumaldál, sumatsát; **~bler** daldalero.
gabardine: *n*. gabardín.
gable: *n*. kabalyéte.
gadfly: *n*. bangaw.
gaff: *n*. tarì; kalawit; tagâ.
gag: *n*. pasal sa bibíg; birò; *v*. sikangan; busalán.
gage: *n*. panukat; *v*. sukatin; tayahin.
gaiety: *n*. pagkatuwâ; pagkagalák; (*coll.*) pagkabaklâ.
gain: *n*. tubò, pakinabang; *v*. magtubò, kunin; abutin; **~ful** kapakí-pakinabang.
gainsay: *v*. itanggí; salungatín.
gale: *n*. unós, malakás na hangin.
gall: *n*. apdó; samâ ng loób; gasgás.
gallant: *adj*. galante, matapang; **~ry** *n*. galantirya, pagkamáginoó, kaginoohán.
galleon: *n*. galyón, barkong pangkalakalan.
gallery: *n*. palko, galeriya.
gallon: *n*. galón.
gallop: *v*. umiskape, kumaskás, mag-iskape.
gallows: *n*. bibitayán.
galvanize: *v*. galbanisahín.
gamble: *v*. pumusta, magsugál, maghuwego; **~r** *n*. hugadór, manunugal, sugaról.
gambol: *v*. lumuksú-luksó, magpatalún-talón.
game: *n*. larô, huwego; **~cock** sasabungín.
gander: *n*. lalaking gansâ.
gang: *n*. barkáda, pangkát.
gangplank: *n*. túlayan, andamyo.
gangrene: *n*. kanggrena.
gangster: *n*. butangero, mambubutáng.
gap: *n*. siwang, puwáng; patláng.
gape: *v*. maghigáb.
garage: *n*. garahe; (*repair shop*) talyér.
garb: *n*. pananamít; suót.
garbage: *n*. basura.
garden: *n*. hardín, hálamanán; **~er** hardinero, maghahalamán.
gardenia: *n*. rosál.
garfish: *n*. haba, kambabalò.
gargle: *v*. magmumog.
garland: *n*. kuwentas na bulaklák.
garlic: *n*. bawang.
garment: *n*. damít, pananamít.
garnish: *n*. adorno, dekorasyón.
garter: *n*. ligas.
gas: *n*. gas, gasolina; (*flatulence*) kabag.
gash: *n*. laslás.
gasket: *n*. sapatilya.
gasoline: *n*. gasolina.
gasp: *v*. sumingáp.
gate: *n*. tarangkahan.
gather: *v*. tipunin, magkalipumpón.
gaudy: *adj*. matingkád, masagwâ.
gauge: *n*. panukat, tarol, pang-arók; *v*. sukatin.
gaunt: *adj*. payát, yayát; hapís; patpatin.
gauze: *n*. gasa.
gavel: *n*. malyete.
gawk: *v*. tumunganga̖, tumangá.
gay: *adj*. (*homosexual*) baklâ; (*happy*) masayá,

maligaya.
gaze: *n.* titig; *v.* tumitig; titigan.
gear: *n.* engranahe; **shift ~s** magkámbiyo.
gecko: *n.* butikî.
gelding: *n.* kabayong kinapón.
gem: *n.* alahas, hiyás.
Gemini: *n.* Kambál (sa zodiac).
gender: *n.* kasarian; **neuter ~** kasariang pambalakì.
genealogy: *n.* talaangkanan, palaangkanan.
general: *adj.* panlahát, kalahatán, laganap; **in ~** karaniwan; *n.* henerál.
generate: *v.* lumikhâ.
generation: *n.* salinlahì, henerasyón.
generic: *adj.* panlahát; (*gram.*) pangmadlâ.
generosity: *n.* pagkamapagbigáy.
generous: *adj.* magandáng-loób, mapagbigáy.
genial: *adj.* masayá, magiliw.
genitals: *n.* maselang bahagi ng katawán.
genitive: *adj.* paarî; **~ case** *n.* kaukuláng paarî.
genius: *n.* henyo.
genteel: *adj.* makisig, magalang.
Gentile: *n.* Hentíl.
gentle: *adj.* marahan, mahinay, mayumì; **~man** maginoó.
genuine: *adj.* tunay, totoó.
geography: *n.* heograpiya.
geology: *n.* heolohiya; **geologist** heólogo.
geometry: *n.* heometriya.
germ: *n.* mikrobiyo.
German: *n.* Alemán.
germinate: *v.* sumibol, tumubò.
gerund: *n.* pandiwang makangalan, pangngalang-diwà.
gesticulate: *v.* magkukumpás.
gesture: *n.* kumpás; pagpapahayag; *v.* kumumpás.
get: *v.* kumuha, kunin; (*become*) maging; (*understand*) maintindihán; **~ up** tumayô; bumangon; **~ away** lumayas; **~ down** bumabâ; **~ in** pumasok; **~ off** bumabâ; **~ out** lumabás; **~ along** magkakáayos; **~ together** magtipon-tipon.
ghastly: *adj.* nakatatakot.
ghost: *n.* multo.
giant: *n.* higante, dambuhalà; **~ grouper fish** kerapo, kugtóng.
gibberish: *n.* satsát, daldál.
gibe: *v.* manuyâ, tuyaín.
giddy: *n.* hiló, lulâ.
gift: *n.* regalo, alaala, handóg; (*talent*) likás ng talino.
gig: *n.* kalesa, karetela.
gigantic: *adj.* napakalakí.
giggle: *v.* bumungisngís.
gild: *v.* gintuín, duraduhin.
gill: *n.* hasang.
gilt: *adj.* durado.
gimmick: *n.* pakulô, pakwela, gimik, pakanâ.
gin: *n.* hinebra.
ginger: *n.* luya; **~ tea** *n.* salabát.
girdle: *n.* sintás, sinturón, bigkís.
girl: *n.* batang babae; **~friend** nobya.
girth: *n.* kabilogan.
gist: *n.* buód, kakanggatâ, diwà.
give: *v.* bigyán, ihandóg; **~ away** ipamigáy; **~ back** isaulì; **~ in** mapatalo; **~ up** sumukò; **~ a hand** tulungan.
gizzard: *n.* balumbalunan.
glad: *adj.* masayá, natutuwâ, nagágalák.
glamour: *n.* halina, gayuma.
glamorous: *adj.* kaakit-akit, kahalí-halina.
glance: *n.* sulyáp; *v.* sumulyáp.
gland: *n.* glándula.
glare: *n.* pandidilat; *v.* sumilaw; mandilat.
glass: *n.* salamín; (*drinking*) baso; **broken ~** bubog; **~ fish** langaray.
glasses: *n.* salamín.
glaze: *n.* kintáb, kináng.
gleam: *n.* kisláp, sinag, banaag; *v.* kumisláp.
glean: *v.* manghimalay.
glee: *n.* tuwa, galák.
glib: *adj.* magalíng magsalitâ.
glide: *v.* dumausdós.
glimmer: *v.* umandáp-andáp.
glimpse: *n.* sulyáp.
glitter: *v.* kumináng, kumisláp; *n.* kináng, kisláp.
gloat: *v.* titigan; ikatuwâ.
globe: *n.* globo; **~ fish** butete.
gloom: *n.* lungkót, pangláw, lumbáy; **~y** mapangláw.
glorify: *v.* purihin, luwalhatiin.
glorious: *adj.* maluwalhatì.

glory: *n*. kaluwalhatian, dakilang karangalan; kalangitán.
gloss: *n*. kintáb.
glossary: *n*. taláhulunganán.
glossy: *adj*. makintáb.
glottal: *adj*. pigít, paimpít; **internal ~ stop** *n*. malaw-aw.
glove: *n*. guwantes, glab.
glow: *n*. pagbabaga, pamumulá; *v*. magbaga, mamulá; magliwanag.
glue: *n*. kola, pangola; *v*. ikola, idikít ng kola.
glum: *adj*. malungkót, mapangláw.
glutton: *n*. taong matakaw; **~ous** *adj*. matakaw, mayamò; masibà; **~y** kayamuan, katakawan, kasibaan.
gnarl: *v*. umangil, angilan.
gnash: *v*. magngalit.
gnat: *n*. nikník.
gnaw: *v*. ngumatngát.
gnome: *n*. duwende.
go: *v*. pumuntá, umalís; **~ ahead** sige; **~ away** umalís; **~ back** bumalík; **~ back on** bawiin; umurong; **~ home** umuwî; **~ on** magpatulóy; **~ over** magsiyasat.
goad: *v*. sundutín; magbunsód.
goal: *n*. hanggahan, hantungan; (*sport*) gol.
goat: *n*. kambíng; **~fish** amarilis, kapon; saramulyete.
gobble: *v*. kumukók, kumurukók.
go-between: *n*. taga-pamagitan, tuláy.
goblin: *n*. tiyanak, duwende.
goby: *n*. bakuli, biya, tuod; **~ fry** dulong.
go-cart: *n*. karetilya.
God: *n*. Diyós, Bathalà, ang Lumikhâ.
godchild: *n*. anák sa binyág.
goddess: *n*. diyosa, diwatà.
godfather: *n*. ninong, padrino, inaamá.
godly: *adj*. banál, maka-Diyós.
godmother: *n*. ninang, madrina, iniiná.
goggle: *n*. salamín de-kolór; *v*. mamulagat.
going: *n*. pag-alís.
goiter: *n*. bosyò, bukláw.
gold: *n*. gintô **~en**: *adj*. gintô; **~en jack fish** garapetse.
goldfinch: *n*. kardelina.
goldsmith: *n*. pandáy-gintô.
golf: *n*. golp.
gone: *adj*. walâ na, nakaalís na.
gong: *n*. agong, batingáw.
gonorrhea: *n*. tulas, tulò, gonorea.
good: *adj*. mabuti, mahusay, magalíng; **~bye** paalam na; diyán ka na; maiwan na kitá; **~ Friday** Biyernes Santo; **~ looking** magandá, guwapo; **~ness** kabutihan.
goods: *n*. kalakal, panindá; arí-arihan.
goodwill: *n*. mabuting pakikisama, mabuting kaloobán.
goose: *n*. gansâ.
gore: *v*. manuwág, suwagín.
gorge: *n*. bangín.
gorgeous: *adj*. napakaringal, napakarilág; napakagandá.
gorilla: *n*. gorila, bakulaw.
gory: *adj*. madugô.
gosh: *interj*. susmaryosep, sus.
gosling: *n*. sisiw ng gansâ.
gospel: *n*. ebanghelyo.
gossip: *n*. tsismis, sitsít.
gouge: *n*. lukób; *v*. maglukób.
gourmet: *n*. krítiko sa pagkain.
govern: *n*. pamahalaaan, gubyernohán, pamunuan; **~ment** *n*. gubyerno, pamahalaán; **~nor** *n*. gubernadór.
gown: *n*. barò, bestido, bata; **wedding ~** damit pangkasál.
grab: *v*. saklutín, sunggabán.
grace: *n*. grasya, biyayà, pagpapalà, parangalán; **~ful** marikít; kaaya-aya.
gracious: *adj*. magiliw, mapagmahál.
grade: *n*. grado, ranggo, klase; marká; *v*. magmarká.
gradual: *adj*. banayad; untí-untî, baí-baitáng; **~ly** *adv*. untí-untî, atay-atay.
graduate: *v*. magtapós; *n*. ang nagtapós.
graduation: *n*. pagtatapós, graduwasiyón.
graft: *n*. pangunguwalta.
grain: *n*. butil; haspé; (*direction of lines*) gisok.
gram: *n*. gramo.
grammar: *n*. balarilà, gramátika.
grammatical: *adj*. pambalarilà.
granary: *n*. kamalig, bangán, takláb, baysá.
grand: *adj*. dakilà, maringal, pagkálaki-lakí.
grandchild: *n*. apó.
grandeur: *n*. kadakilaan, kamahalan, kama-

harlikaán.
grandfather: *n*. lolo, ingkóng, lelong, apò, abuwelo.
grandmother: *n*. lola, impó, lelang, abwela.
grandparent: *n*. nunò; ninunò.
grant: *v*. aprobahán, ipagkaloób, magbigáy; *n*. kaloób.
granular: *adj*. butil-butíl.
grape: *n*. ubas.
grapefruit: *n*. suhà, lukbán; kahél.
graph: *n*. grap, talángguhit.
grapple: *v*. magbunô, sunggabán, makipagbunô.
grasp: *v*. sumunggáb, dumakmál, dakmaín.
grass: *n*. damó; **~land** damuhán.
grasshopper: *n*. típaklóng, balang, luktón.
grassland: *n*. damuhán.
grassy: *adj*. maramó.
grate: *v*. rehasan; magkayod; kudkurin; magkaskás; *v*. parilya, rehas.
grateful: *adj*. nagpapasalamat.
gratify: *v*. magbigáy-lugód, makalugód.
grating: *n*. rehas, parilya; *adj*. magaralgál.
gratis: *adj*. libre, waláng-bayad.
gratitude: *n*. pasasalamat.
gratuity: *n*. bigáy-palà, pabuyà.
grave: *n*. libíng, puntód, hukay; *adj*. maselan, malubhâ; **~stone** *n*. lápida; **with a ~ accent** *adj*. malumì; **~ accent** *n*. paiwà.
gravel: *n*. graba, kaskaho.
graveyard: *n*. libingan, kamposanto, semen teryo.
gravity: *n*. grabidád; kalubhaán.
gravy: *n*. sawsawan, sarsa.
gray: *n*. gris, senisado, kulay-abó, abuhín; **~ hair** uban; **~ snapper fish** butangal, alsó.
graze: *v*. (*eat grass*) magpastól; (*touch lightly*) dumaplís.
grease: *n*. tabâ, sebo, mantikà; *v*. grasahan.
greasy: *adj*. masebo, mamantikà.
great: *adj*. napakalakí; malawak; mahalagá.
great-grandchild: *n*. apó sa tuhod.
great-grandfather: *n*. lolo sa tuhod.
great-grandmother: *n*. lola sa tuhod.
greatly: *adv*. masyado, labis, sobra, lubhâ.
greed: *n*. kasakimán, kayamuan; **~y** *adj*. matakaw, masakím.
Greek: *n*. Griyego.
green: *adj*. berde; luntî, luntián; **~house** punlaán, pasibulán; **~ mango** manggáng hiláw.
greenhorn: *n*. baguhan, bagito.
greet: *v*. batiin, sumalubong; **~ting** *n*. batì, pagbatì.
gregarious: *adj*. mahilig magsasama.
grenade: *n*. granada.
grey: *n*. gris, kulay-abó.
grid: *n*. parilya.
grief: *n*. lungkót, dalamhatì, hapis.
grievance: *n*. karáingan, reklamo.
grieve: *v*. magdalamhatì, mamighatî, mahapis, malumbáy.
grill: *v*. mag-ihaw; *n*. parilya.
grim: *adj*. mabalasik, malupít.
grimace: *n*. ngibit, ngiwî; *v*. ngumiwî; sumimangot.
grime: *n*. dumí, dungis.
grin: *v*. ngumisi, ngumisngís; *n*. ngisi, ngitî.
grind: *v*. gilingin; durugin, dikdikín; **~er**: *n*. (*person*) tagagiling; (*machine*) gilingán; **~stone** *n*. hasaán, panghasà; panggiling.
grip: *n*. sunggáb, pagsunggáb.
gripe: *v*. magreklamo; *n*. reklamo, hinanakít.
groan: *v*. humalinghíng, dumaíng, maghinagpís.
grocery: *n*. groseri.
groggy: *adj*. liyó, grogi, nahihilo, hiló.
groin: *n*. singit.
groom: *v*. mag-alagà, mag-almuhasa.
groove: *n*. kanál, ukit, ukà, bakat.
grope: *v*. maghagiláp; mag-apuháp, apuhapin, kapain.
gross: *n*. kabuuán; grosa; *adj*. malubhâ, napakalakí; **~ income** buóng kita.
grotesque: *adj*. napakatakot.
grotto: *n*. groto; yungíb; lunggâ.
grouch: *v*. umungol; magreklamo.
grouchy: *adj*. tampuhin.
ground: *n*. lupà; (*basis*) batayán, saligán; **stand one's ~** manindigan; **~ floor** silong; **~work** batayán, saligán.
group: *n*. grupo, pangkát, pulutóng; urì; **~er fish** lapu-lapo, garopa, kaltáng, kulapo, sigapo.
grovel: *v*. sumukot; maggapáng.

grow: *v.* lumakí; lumagô.
growl: *v.* umungol, angilan.
growth: *n.* paglakí.
grub: *n.* uód; *v.* kukayin.
grudge: *n.* hinanakít, samâ ng loób, pagtatanín.
gruel: *n.* lugaw, nilugaw.
gruesome: *adj.* nakatatakot, kakilá-kilabot.
grumble: *v.* umungol, magmaktól, bumulúngbulóng.
grumpy: *adj.* galít, sumpungin.
grunt: *n.* igík, ungol; ingít; ~ **fish** babansí, gunggóng, baraongan, dukuson.
guarantee: *n.* garantíya, panagót; *v.* garantiyahán.
guarantor: *n.* piyadór, tagapanagót.
guard: *n.* bantáy, tanod; *v.* magtanod, tanuran, bantayán.
guardian: *n.* tagapag-alagà; ~ **angel** *n.* anghél na tagatanod.
guava: *n.* bayabas.
guerilla: *n.* gerilya.
guess: *n.* hulà; *v.* hulaan.
guest: *n.* bisita, dalaw, panauhin; ~ **of honor** panauhing pandangál.
guffaw: *n.* halakhák.
guidance: *n.* pag-akay, pagpatnubay, pamamatnubay.
guide: *n.* giya; *v.* pumatnubay; akayin.
guild: *n.* samahán.
guile: *n.* lansí, laláng, katusuhan.
guillotine: *n.* gilotina, pamugot.
guilt: *n.* kasalanan, pagkakásala.
guilty: *adj.* may-sala, may-kasalanan.
guinea pig: *n.* dagáng-putî, kunehilyo; taong ginagamit sa eksperimento.
guise: *n.* balatkayô, pagkukunwarî.
guitar: *n.* gitara; ~ **fish** sudsód.
gulf: *n.* golpo, malakíng loók.
gullet: *n.* lalamunan.
gullibility: *n.* kamápaniwalaín.
gullible: *adj.* lokohín, mapaniwalaín.
gulp: *v.* lumunók.
gum: *n.* (*chewing*) pepsin; (*around teeth*) gilagid; (*of trees*) kola, pandikít.
gun: *n.* baríl; ~**point** *n.* tutok ng baríl.
gunpowder: *n.* púlbura.
gurgle: *v.* bumulubók, lumaguklók.
guru: *n.* gurong Hindú.
gush: *v.* bumulwák.
gust: *n.* bugsô ng hangin.
gusto: *n.* gana, saráp.
gut: *n.* bituka.
gutter: *n.* kanál, bambáng.
guy: *n.* tao, lalaki.
guzzle: *v.* lumaklák.
gymnasium: *n.* dyim, himnasyo.
gymnastics: *n.* himnástiko.
gyp: *v.* subain, dayain.
gypsy: *n.* hitano.
gyrate: *v.* umikot.

H

habit: *n.* ugalì, gawî, asal, kinágawián.
habitat: *n.* tirahan (ng mga ayup).
habitual: *adj.* karaniwan; kinaugalián.
hacienda: *n.* asyenda.
hack: *v.* tadtarín.
hag: *n.* huklubang babae.
haggard: *adj.* hapís, nangangalumatá.
haggle: *v.* pagtalunan, magtawarán, makipagtawarán.
haiku: *n.* tanaga.
hail: *v.* batiin; *n.* nayelong ulán.
hair: *n.* buhók; **grey** ~ uban; ~**cut** gupít; ~**dresser** barbero, tagapaggupít; mangungulot; ~**pin** ipit sa buhók; ~**tail fish** pak-án, uriles, atulay; ~**y** *adj.* mabuhók.
hairbreadth: *n.* gabuhók.
half: *adj.* kalahatì; ~ **breed** mestiso; ~**-hearted** bantulót; ~ **way** nasa kalahatian.
hall: *n.* pasilyo; salas; bulwagan; ~ **of fame** bulwagan ng kabantugán.
hallmark: *n.* taták ng kadalisayan.
hallucination: *n.* guniguní, kinikinitá.
halo: *n.* (*of moon*) limbo; (*of saint*) sinag.
halt: *v.* tumigil.
halve: *v.* hatiin.
ham: *n.* hamón.
hammer: *n.* martilyo; ~**head shark** krusan, bingkungan.
hammock: *n.* duyan, hamaka.
hamper: *n.* rupero; *v.* hadlangán; makapigil.

hand: *n*. kamáy; ~ **down** ilipan, ipamana; ~ **grenade** granada; **shake ~s** kumamáy; ~ **over** ibigáy, iabot; **~ful** sandakót; **on** ~ *adj*. nasa kamáy; **~made** yaring-kamáy; ~ **woven** *adj*. hábing-kamáy; (*of clocks*) *n*. puntero; **minute** ~ *n*. minutero; **second** ~ *n*. segundaryo; **hour** ~ *n*. oraryo.
handcuff: *n*. posas; *v*. posasan.
handful: *n*. sandakót.
handicap: *n*. lamáng, palugit, palamáng.
handkerchief: *n*. panyô.
handle: *v*. hawakan, hipuin, tangnán; mamahalà.
handrail: *n*. gabáy (ng hagdán).
handshake: *n*. pagkamáy.
handsome: *adj*. guwapo.
handwriting: *n*. sulat-kamáy.
handy: *adj*. gamitín; handâ.
hang: *v*. ibitin, ikabít; ~ **around** umalí-aligíd.
hangar: *n*. garahe ng eruplano.
hanger: *n*. sabitán.
hangman: *n*. tagabitay, berdugo.
hangnail: *n*. taingang-dagâ.
haphazard: *adj*. pabaká-sakalì, padaskúl-daskól.
happen: *v*. mangyari; magkátaón.
happy: *adj*. maligaya, nasisiyahán.
harass: *v*. ligaligin, guluhín, yamutín.
harbor: *n*. puwerto; silungán.
hard: *adj*. (*not soft*) matigás; (*difficult*) mahirap; ~ **up** mahirap; ~ **working** masipag; ~ **headed** matigás ang ulo.
harden: *v*. magpatigás; tumigás.
hardly: *adv*. bahagyâ na.
hardship: *n*. paghihirap, hirap.
hardy: *adj*. matibay, matipunò.
hare: *n*. liyebre.
harelip: *n*. bingot, bungì.
harlot: *n*. patutot, puta, masamáng babae.
harm: *v*. sumir puminsalà.
harmonica: *n*. silindro.
harmonize: *v*. itugmâ, isuwatò.
harmony: *n*. pagkakaisá, pagkakasundô.
harness: *n*. gurnasyón; *v*. isingkáw.
harp: *n*. alpa.
harpoon: *n*. salapáng; *v*. manalapáng.
harquebus: *n*. astinggál.
harrow: *n*. suyod, kalmót, paragos.
harsh: *adj*. magaspáng, maligasgás.
harvest: *n*. pag-aani, gapasán.
has: *third person singular present tense form of* ***have*** > She has a house. *May bahay siyá.*
hashish: *n*. marihuwana.
haste: *n*. pag-aapurá, pagmamadalî.
hasty: *adj*. mabilís, madalian, madalî.
hat: *n*. sumbrero.
hatch: *v*. pumisâ, pisaín; **~ery** *n*. pámisaan.
hatchet: *n*. putháw, palatáw.
hate: *v*. mapoót, mamuhî.
hatred: *n*. pagkapoót, pagkamuhî.
haughty: *adj*. palalò, mapagmataás.
haul: *v*. hilahin, batakin, remorkihín.
haunch: *n*. pigî.
haunt: *n*. tigilán, pugad.
have: *v*. may, mayroón; ~ **no** walâ; ~ **on** suót.
haven: *n*. silungán, kanlungan.
havoc: *n*. kaguluhán, kalituhán.
hawk: *n*. lawin; **~er** *n*. maglalakò.
hay: *n*. tuyóng damó, dayami; **~stack** mandalâ ng dayami.
hazard: *n*. panganib, risko; **~ous** *adj*. mapanganib, peligroso.
haze: *n*. asó.
hazel: *n*. kastanyo; **~nut** kastanyas.
hazing: *n*. pagmamalabís sa baguhang estudyante.
hazy: *adj*. malabò; maasó, maulap; kulimlím.
he: *pron*. siyá.
head: *n*. ulo; **~ache** sakít ng ulo; **~line** ulo ng balità.
heading: *n*. pamuhatan, pamagát, pámulaan.
headman: *n*. punò, pinunò.
headquarters: *n*. kuwartél, punong-tanggapan.
headway: *n*. pagkásulong, pagsulong.
heal: *v*. lumunas, magpagalíng.
health: *n*. kalusugan.
healthy: *adj*. malusóg, pampalusóg.
heap: *n*. buntón, tambák; *v*. magbuntón.
hear: *v*. makiníg, pakinggán, mariníg.
hearing: *n*. pandiníg; paglilitis.
hearsay: *n*. sabi-sabí, bulung-búlungan; ~ **evidence** katibayang sabi-sabí.
heart: *n*. pusò; **~ache** pighatî, salaghatî; ~ **attack** atake sa pusò; **~broken** nagdada-

lamhatì.
hearten: *v*. pasiglahín.
hearth: *n*. dapóg, tahanan.
hearty: *adj*. taós-pusò.
heat: *n*. init; *v*. magpainit; **in ~** mangandí; **~ wave** tag-init.
heave: *v*. buhatin, ihagis.
heaven: *n*. langit.
heavy: *adj*. mabigát; **~weight** hébiweyt.
heckle: *v*. kantiyawán, mangantiyáw.
hectare: *n*. ektarya.
hectic: *adj*. napakahirap, tísiko.
hedge: *n*. bakod na halaman.
hedgehog: *n*. parkupino; baboy kalisag.
heed: *v*. unawain.
heel: *n*. sakong.
hegemony: *n*. pananakop.
heifer: *n*. bakang-dumalaga.
height: *n*. taás.
heinous: *adj*. kasuklám-suklám; buktót.
heir: *n*. tagapagmana, eredero.
helicopter: *n*. elikóptero.
helium: *n*. helyo.
hell: *n*. impiyerno.
hello: (*greeting*) kumustá, hoy.
helm: *n*. timón; ugit; **~sman** *n*. timonél.
helmet: *n*. balutì sa ulo.
help: *n*. tulong; *v*. tumulong, tulungan, sumaklolo.
hem: *n*. lupî, tupî.
hemisphere: *n*. háting-globo, háting-daigdíg.
hemoglobin: *n*. pulá ng dugô.
hemorrhage: *n*. pagdurugô, emoráhiya; **have a ~** dinúrugô.
hemorrhoids: *n*. almuranas.
hemp: *n*. abaká.
hen: *n*. inahíng manók, inahín.
hence: *adv*. kayâ.
henceforth: *adv*. mulâ ngayón.
henchman: *n*. kampón; kabig; tauhan.
henpecked: *adj*. ander, dominado ng asawa.
hepatitis: *n*. sakít sa atáy.
her: *adj*. niyá.
herald: *n*. tagapagbando, mensahero.
herb: *n*. damóng-gamót; **~ doctor** erbularyo, albularyo.
herd: *n*. ganado, kawan; *v*. mag-ipun-ipon.
here: *adv*. dito, rito; **~ it is** narito, heto; **come ~** halika.
hereby: *adv*. sa pamamagitan nitó.
hereditary: *adj*. námamana, násasalin.
heredity: *n*. pagmamana.
heresy: *n*. erehiyá.
heretic: *n*. erehe.
heritage: *n*. mana, pamana, namana.
hermaphrodite: *n*. baklâ; binalaki, bínabaé.
hermetic: *adj*. mahigpít; ermétiko.
hermit: *n*. ermitanyo; **~age** ermita.
hernia: *n*. luslós.
hero: *n*. bayani; **~ic** *adj*. magiting.
heroism: *n*. kabayanihan.
heron: *n*. tagák; kandurô; **white ~** kandangaok; **purple ~** bakaw.
herpes: *n*. buni.
herring: *n*. tunsóy, tambán, silinyasì; **~ fry** malapní, manansí.
hers: *pron*. sa kanyá.
hesitant: *adj*. natitigilan, nag-aatubilì.
hesitate: *v*. mag-alaala; mag-atubilì, magpaulik-ulik.
hew: *v*. labrahín, tabtabín.
heyday: *n*. kapanáhunan, kasikatan.
hibernate: *v*. matulog sa panahón ng taglamíg.
hiccup: *n*. sinók.
hidden: *adj*. tagô, kublí.
hide: *v*. itagò, takpán.
hideous: *adj*. napakapangit, kahindík-hindík.
hierarchy: *n*. herarkiya.
high: *adj*. mataás; dakilà; **~ blood pressure** altapresiyón; **~land** kataasán, paltók; **~-lander** tagapaltók, tagabundók; **~ ness** kataasán; (*royal*) kamáhalan; **speak ~ly of** papurihan; **~ seas** kalautan ng dagat; **~way** lansangang-bayan, daáng-bayan.
hijack: *v*. haydyakin, kumanderin ang eroplano.
hike: *v*. maglakád nang mahabà.
hilarious: *adj*. masayáng-maingay.
hill: *n*. buról; **ant~** punsó.
hilly: *adj*. maburól.
hilt: *n*. puluhán.
him: *pron*. sa kanyá, siyá.
hind: *adj*. hulí; **~most** pinakahulí.
hinder: *v*. hadlangán; makasagabal.

hindrance: *n*. abala, hadláng, balakíd.
Hindu: *n., adj*. Hindú; **~ism** Hinduísmo.
hinge: *n*. bisagra.
hint: *n*. pahiwatig, paramdám; *v*. magparamdám.
hip: *n*. balakáng.
hire: *v*. umupa, umarkilá.
his: *adj., pron*. niyá, sa kanyá.
hiss: *n*. sirit, sagitsít, sutsót.
historian: *n*. mananalaysáy.
historic: *adj*. makasaysayan, pangkasaysayan.
history: *n*. kasaysayan, istorya.
hit: *v*. humampás, bumuntál; paluin; *n*.. suntók, palò, hampás.
hitch: *v*. italì, igapos, isingkáw.
hive: *n*. bahay-pukyutan.
hives: *n*. tagulabáy, pantál, pamamantál, utikarya.
hoard: *v*. itinggál; magtipon.
hoarse: *adj*. malát, paós, pagáw.
hoax: *n*. laláng, dayà, panloloko.
hobble: *v*. umikâ, umingkód.
hobby: *n*. kinágigiliwang líbangan.
hobnob: *v*. makisalamuhà, makihalubilo.
hobo: *n*. palaboy, hampaslupà.
hoe: *n*. asada, asaról.
hog: *n*. baboy; **eat like a ~** sumabsáb.
hoist: *v*. itaás.
hold: *v*. humawak, tumangan; (*contain*) maglamán; **~ on** kumapit, mangapit; **~ up** *n*. panghaharang.
hole: *n*. butas; hukay, lubák; **~ puncher** pamutas.
holiday: *n*. pistá, bakasyón.
holiness: *n*. kabánalan.
hollow: *adj*. hungkág, may-guwáng, humpák.
holocaust: *n*. pagkapuglsáw, malakíng pinsalà.
holy: *adj*. banál, santo; **~ water** agwa-bendita; **~ week** semana santa.
homage: *n*. paggalang, pagsambá, pintuhò.
home: *n*. tahanan, bahay; **go ~** umuwî; **~land** lupang-tinubuan; **~less** waláng-bahay; **~ly** pambahay; pantahanan; **~ward** pauwî.
homemade: *adj*. yaring-bahay.
homesick: *adj*. sabík sa pag-uwî.
homeward: *adj*. pauwî.
homework: *n*. aralíng-bahay.
homicide: *n*. homisidyo.
homogeneous: *adj*. magkakaurì, magkatulad.
homonym: *n*. salitáng kasintunóg.
homosexual: *n*. bakla; (*lesbian*) tombóy.
hone: *n*. hasaán.
honest: *adj*. matapát, tunay, di-madayà, mapagtotoó.
honey: *n*. pulút-pukyutan; **~bee** pukyutan; **~comb** saray; **~moon** pulút-gatâ, luna-de-miyél; **~ combed grouper fish** alatan, lapulapung liglíg.
honk: *v*. magpugák; magbusina.
honor: *n*. dangál, karangalan, paggalang, puri; *v*. igalang; parangalán; **~able** *adj*. marangál; **~ary** *adj*. pandangál.
hood: *n*. kaputsa, talukbóng.
hoodlum: *n*. butangero, basagulero.
hoodwink: *v*. dayain, linlangin
hoof: *n*. kukó.
hook: *n*. kawit, sabitán; tagâ; *v*. ikawit.
hookworm: *n*. bulati, tiwal.
hooligan: *n*. bagamundo; butangero, basagulero.
hoop: *n*. buklód, pagulong.
hoot: *n*. huni.
hooter: *n*. (*owl*) kuwago; (*coll., breast*) susò.
hooves: *Plural of hoof*. mga kukó.
hop: *v*. magkandirít, lumuksó, lumundág.
hope: *n*. pag-asa.
hopeless: *adj*. waláng-pag-asa.
hopscotch: *n*. pikô.
horizon: *n*. abót-tanáw; guhit-tagpuan, kagiliran.
horizontal: *adj*. pahigâ, pahaláng.
hormone: *n*. hormón.
horn: *n*. (*of cattle*) sungay; (*horn instrument*) tambulì; (*brass instrument*) torotót; (*car horn*) busina; **~fish** sungay-sungayan; **~y** masungay; (*sexually excited*) malibóg.
hornet: *n*. putaktí.
horny: *adj*. (*slang*) malibóg.
horoscope: *n*. oroskopyo.
horrible: *adj*. kakilá-kilabot, kasuklám-suklám.
horrid: *adj*. kasindák-sindák.
horrify: *v*. katakutan, sindakín.
horror: *n*. pagkamuhî, malakíng takot.
horse: *n*. kabayo; **~fly** nikník; **~man** mángang-

abayó; ~**play** kalokohan, magulóng larô; ~**power** lakás-kabayo; ~**shoe** bakal ng kabayo; ~**whip** látigo.
horseradish: *n*. malunggáy.
horticulture: *n*. paghahalaman, hortikultura.
hose: *n*. gomang pandilíg.
hosiery: *n*. medyas.
hospitable: *adj*. mapagbigáy sa pakikitungo.
hospital: *n*. págamutan, ospitál; ~**ity** mabuting pakikitungo.
host: *n*. may-anyaya, may-handâ, punong-abala; (*wafer*) ostiyá.
hostage: *n*. prenda.
hostile: *adj*. kalaban, kaaway.
hot: *adj*. mainit; (*and humid*) maalinsangan.
hotel: *n*. otél.
hound: *n*. asong pangaso.
hour: *n*. oras; **every** ~ oras-oras.
house: *n*. bahay, tahanan; ~ **of Representatives** Kapulungán ng mga Kinatawán.
housefly: *n*. langaw.
household: *n*. sambahayán; *adj*. pambahay.
housekeeper: *n*. tagapangasiwà, taong bahay.
housemaid: *n*. katulong nga babae, alilang babae.
housewife: *n*. maybayay, taong-bahay.
housework: *n*. gawaing-bahay.
housing: *n*. pagpapabahay.
hover: *v*. lumipád-lipád, umali-aligid.
how: *adv*. paanó, papaano; gaano; ~ **are you** kumustá; ~ **fat**? gaanong katabâ?
however: *adv*. gayunmán, sa paanóng paraán.
howl: *v*. humagulhól, mag-alulóng.
hub: *n*. masa; pusod; lunduyan.
hubbub: *n*. pagkakaingáy.
huddle: *n*. pagsasang-usapan; *v*. mag-umpukan; sumiksík.
hue: *n*. kulay.
hug: *v*. yumapós, yumakap; *n*. yapós, yakáp.
huge: *adj*. napakalakí, malakíng-malakí.
hum: *v*. humiging.
human: *n*. tao; ~**kind** sangkatauhan.
humane: *adj*. makatao.
humanitarian: *n*. taong mapagkawanggawâ; *adj*. makatao.
humanity: *n*. sangkatauhan, katauhan.
humble: *adj*. mapagpakumbabâ; mababà.
humid: *adj*. basá-basâ, malagihay.
humiliate: *v*. manghiyâ, hiyaín, hamakin.
humility: *n*. kababaang-loób, kapakumbabaán.
humor: *n*. katatawanán, pampatawá; **sense of** ~ ugaling mapagpatawá.
humorous: *adj*. nakakatawá.
hump: *n*. umbók; ~**back** kubà; ~**ed red snapper** dapak.
hunch: *n*. kutón, sapantahà, hinuhà, agam-agam.
hunchback: *n*. kubà; bukót.
hundred: *n*. daán, siyento; ~**th** ikasandaán; ~ **thousand** yutà.
hunger: *n*. gutom, pagkagutom; (*strong desire*) pananabík.
hungry: *adj*. gutóm, nagugutom.
hunk: *n*. lapáng, kimpál; (*coll.*) maskuladong lalake.
hunt: *n*. paghahanap; pangangaso, pamamaríl; *v*. maghanáp.
hunter: *n*. mángangasó, mamamaril.
hurdle: *v*. luksuhín, lundagín; *n*. lundagán.
hurl: *v*. ipukól, ihagis.
hurrah: *interj*. mabuhay!
hurricane: *n*. bagyó, buhawi.
hurry: *v*. mag-apurá, daliín.
hurt: *v*. saktán, masugatan; sumakít; ~ **the feelings of** saktán ang loób.
husband: *n*. asawang lalake; ~**ry** pagsasaka, pagbubukid; **animal** ~**ry** paghahayupan.
hush: *v*. magpatahimik.
husk: *n*. upak, talupak; *v*. bunután, tapasan.
huskiness: *n*. (*muscular*) pagkatipunô; (*hoarse*) pamamalát, pamamaós, pamamagaw.
husky: *adj*. (*muscular*) matipunô; (*hoarse*) malát, paós.
hussy: *n*. puta, bastós na babae.
hustle: *v*. magmadalî, magtabóy.
hut: *n*. kubo, barongbarong.
hybrid: *n*. mestiso; hibrido; halumbinhî.
hydrant: **fire** ~ *n*. boka-inséndiyo.
hygiene: *n*. ihiyene, pangangalagà sa kalúsugan.
hymn: *n*. imno, awit, dalít.
hyphen: *n*. gitlíng.
hyphenate: *v*. gitlingán.
hyphenation: *n*. palágitlingan.

hypnotic: *adj*. pampatulog, ipnótiko.
hypnotism: *n*. ipnotismo.
hypnotize: *v*. hipnotismuhín, patulugin.
hypocrite: *n*. ipókrita, mapagkunwâ, mapagpaimbabáw.
hypocrisy: *n*. pagkukunwâ, pagpapaimbabáw.
hypotenuse: *n*. hipotenusa; bagtás.
hypothesis: *n*. teorya, ipótesis, hakà, hinuhà.
hysterical: *adj*. istériko; masayáng-maingay.

I

I: *pron*. akó.
ice: *n*. yelo; **~box** palamigan; **~ cream** sorbetes.
iced: *adj*. elado.
icicle: *n*. yelong bitin.
icon: *n*. bultó, imahen.
icy: *adj*. nagyeyelo, mayelo.
idea: *n*. palagáy, idea, kurukurò.
ideal: *adj*. tamang-tamà.
identical: *adj*. magkamukhâ.
identification: *n*. pagkakákilanlán; pagkilala.
identify: *v*. kumilala, kilalanin; iturò.
identity: *n*. pagkakakilanlán.
ideology: *n*. idcolohiyá, kaisipán.
idiom: *n*. kawikaán.
idiosyncrasy: *n*. katangi-tanging ugalì.
idiot: *n*. tangá, tulalâ, gagong tao.
idle: *adj*. nakatigil, tamád, waláng-ginagawâ.
idol: *n*. anito, ídolo, diyús-diyusan; **~atry** idolatriyá; **~ize** *v*. pakaibigin, pakamahalín.
if: *conj*. kung, kapág, pag-; **what ~** paano kung.
ignite: *v*. pag-apuyín; sumikláb.
ignorance: *n*. kamangmangán, kawaláng-pinag-aralan.
ignorant: *adj*. mangmáng, waláng-nalalaman.
ignore: *v*. huwág pansinín.
iguana: *n*. bayawak.
ill: *adj*. may-sakít; masamâ; **~ feeling** samâ sa loób.
illegal: *adj*. bawal, ilegál.
illegitimate: *adj*. (anák) sa labás.
illicit: *adj*. bawal, ipinagbabawal.
illiterate: *adj*. hindî makabasa.
illness: *n*. sakít, karamdaman.
illogical: *adj*. waláng matwíd.
illuminate: *v*. ilawan.
illusion: *n*. guniguní, malikmatà; kahibangán.
illustrate: *v*. ilarawan; (*exemplify*) halimbawaan.
illustration: *n*. larawan.
illustrious: *adj*. tanyág, bantóg.
image: *n*. larawan, imahen; anino.
imaginary: *adj*. nasa isip, haka-hakà, likhâ.
imagination: *n*. likháng-isip, guniguní.
imaginable: *adj*. mailálarawan sa isip.
imagine: *v*. hagapin, ipalagáy, mag-akalà.
imbecile: *n*. tangang tao.
imbue: *v*. pumunô.
imitate: *v*. tularan, parisan; huwarán.
imitation: *n*. panggagaya, panunulad, paghuwád.
immature: *adj*. batà pa, hiláw, murà.
immediate: *adj*. kagyát, madalî.
immediately: *adv*. kaagád, kagyát, daglî.
immense: *adj*. napakalakí.
immerse: *v*. ilubóg.
immigrant: *n*. dayo, mandarayuhan.
immigrate: *v*. dumayo, mandayuhan.
immigration: *n*. pandarayuhan, imigrasyón.
immolate: *v*. isakripisyo.
immoral: *adj*. masamâ, mahalay, malaswâ.
immortal: *adj*. waláng-kamatayan; **~ity** *n*. kawaláng-kamátayan; **~ize** *v*. magpapanatiling-buhay.
immune: *adj*. dî tinatablan; ligtás.
immunity: *n*. kaligtasan (sa sakít o sa huli).
immunize: *v*. ibakuna.
imp: *n*. pilyong batà.
impact: *n*. banggâ, salpók.
impair: *v*. magpasamâ, puminsalà.
impale: *v*. tusukin, tuhugin.
impartial: *adj*. waláng kiníkilingan.
impatient: *adj*. mainipin, waláng-pasyensiya.
impede: *v*. pigilin, hadlangán.
impediment: *n*. hadláng, sagabal, bakakíd.
impel: *v*. pilitin, itabóy.
impenetrable: *adj*. di mapápasok, di-mapaglálagusán.
imperative: *adj*. kailangan; pautós.
imperfect: *adj*. kulang, dî ganáp.
imperil: *v*. isapanganib.
impersonal: *adj*. waláng pinatátamaan, waláng tinútukoy.

impersonate: *v*. ganapín, katawanín.
impertinent: *adj*. salipanyâ.
impetuous: *adj*. mapusók, marahás.
impetus: *n*. laksá, puwersa; siglá.
implement: *v*. isagawâ, isakatuparan; **~ation** *n*. pagsasagawâ, pagsasakatuparan.
implicate: *v*. isangkót, idamay, iramay.
implicit: *adj*. pahiwatig.
implore: *v*. isamò, sumamò, ihulóg.
impolite: *adj*. bastos, waláng-galang.
import: *n*. angkát; *v*. umangkát.
importance: *n*. halagá, bigát.
important: *adj*. mahalagá, mataás.
impose: *v*. ipataw, ilapat, utusan; magpataw.
impossible: *adj*. dî maaarì, imposible.
impostor: *n*. impostór, manlilinláng.
impotence: *n*. kawalán ng lakás, kainutilán.
impotent: *adj*. unutil, waláng-lakás; (*sexually*) baóg.
impoverish: *v*. ipaghirap, ipamulubi.
impractical: *adj*. di-maisásagawâ.
impregnate: *v*. papagbinhiín, papaglamnín.
impress: *v*. ikintál, iukit, magkabisà.
impression: *n*. impresiyón, sapantahà; bakás.
impressive: *adj*. makabagbag-pusò, maringal.
imprint: *v*. itaták.
imprison: *v*. ibilanggô, ipiít.
impromptu: *adj*. biglaan, di-inihandâ.
improper: malî, dî tamà.
improve: *v*. magpabuti, mapaayos, isaayos; **~ment** pagpabuti; paghusay; paggalíng.
improvised: *adj*. pansamantalá.
imprudent: *adj*. waláng-ingat.
impudent: *adj*. pusóng, waláng-galang.
impulse: *n*. salpók, pusók, udyók.
impulsive: *adj*. mapusók, pabiglá-biglâ.
impurity: *n*. dumí, kahalayan.
in: *prep*. nasa, sa.
inaccurate: *adj*. dî tamà.
inadequate: *adj*. sahól, kulang.
inanimate: *adj*. waláng-buhay.
inappropriate: *adj*. dî tamà.
inarticulate: *adj*. pipi, dî makapagsalitâ.
inattentive: *adj*. waláng-bahalà.
inaugurate: *v*. pasinayaan.
inauguration: *n*. pasinayà.
incapable: *adj*. dî kaya.
incapacity: *n*. pagkawaláng-kaya.
incarcerate: *v*. ibilanggô, ipiít.
incase: *v*. magpaloób.
incense: *n*. insenso, kamanyáng.
incentive: *n*. pampasiglá.
incessant: *adj*. patuloy, waláng humpáy.
inch: *n*. pulgada, dalì.
incident: *n*. pangyayari.
incidental: *adj*. kaugnáy, nauugnáy, kataon.
incision: *n*. hiwà.
incisor: *n*. ngiping pangalís.
incite: *v*. gisingin, pukawin.
inclination: *n*. pagkakagustó, hilig; dahilig.
incline: *n*. dahilig, talibís, dalisdís.
include: *v*. sumakláw, sakupin.
including: *prep*. patí, kabilang, kasama.
incognito: *adj*. nagbabalatkayô.
incoherent: *adj*. maguló, halu-halò.
income: *n*. kita, kinikita.
incoming: *adj*. dumaratíng, pápasok.
incomparable: *adj*. waláng-kaparis, dî matutularan.
incompatible: *adj*. magkalaban, nalalaban.
incompetence: *n*. kawaláng-kaya.
incompetent: *adj*. dî sanáy, waláng kaya.
incomplete: *adj*. dî tapós.
inconsiderate: *adj*. dî maalalahanín.
inconsistent: *adj*. pabagu-bago, paibá-ibá, di-nagkakátugón.
inconspicuous: *adj*. di-mahahalatâ.
incontinence: *n*. kapusukán, kawalán ng pagpipigil; **incontinent** *adj*. ihî, di mapigil ng pagdumí.
inconvenient: *adj*. nakaaabala, nakasasagabal, dî bagay.
incorporate: *v*. isama, ilangkáp, ilakip.
incorrect: *adj*. dî tamà, dî wastô; tuwalî.
increase: *v*. dumami, damihan, lakhán.
incredible: *adj*. dî mapaniniwalaan.
increment: *n*. dagdág; paglakí, pagdami.
incriminate: *v*. idawit, isangkót.
incubator: *n*. pagpapapisâ ng mga itlóg, pámisaan.
incumbent: *adj*. kasalukuyang nanúnungkulan.
incur: *v*. kapasukan, mapalâ.
indebtedness: *n*. pagkakautang.
indecent: *adj*. masagwâ, malaswâ, mahalay.

indecision: *n*. kawaláng-pasiyá, pag-aatubilì.
indeed: *adv*. sa katunayan, talagá, totoó.
indefatigable: *adj*. di-marunong mapagod.
indefinite: *adj*. waláng-katiyakan; dî malinaw; ~ **pronoun** *n*.panghalíp panakláw.
indemnify: *v*. magbayad-pinsalà.
indent: *v*. iurong, ipasok.
independence: *n*. kalayaan, kasarinlán.
independent: *adj*. malayà, nagsasarilí.
index: *n*. índise, talátuntunan; ~ **finger** hintuturò.
Indian: *n*. Indyo, Bumbáy; ~ **anchovy** tuwakang; ~ **sardine** tambán.
indicate: *v*. iturò, ipakilala; ipahiwatig.
indication: *n*. babalâ, hudyát, tandâ.
indicative: *adj*. nagpapakilala, nagpapahiwatig; (*grammar*) paturól; ~ **mood** *n*. panaganong paturól.
indifferent: *adj*. waláng-bahalà, dî interesado.
indigent: *adj*. dukhâ, maralitâ, mahirap.
indigestion: *n*. impatso.
indignant: *adj*. nagágalit; napópoót.
indignity: *n*. kawaláng-dangál.
indigo: *n*. anyíl, tinang asúl.
indirect: *adj*. dî tuwiran, maligoy; ~ **object** *n*. di-túwirang layon.
indiscretion: *n*. kawaláng-ingat.
indisposition: *n*. kauntíng karamdaman.
indistinct: *adj*. malabò, di-malinaw.
individual: *n*. tao, isáng tao; ~**ly** *adv*. isa-isá; ~**ism** pagkamakasarili; ~**ity** kakanyahán, sariling katángian.
indivisible: *v*. dî mahahatì.
indolent: *adj*. tamád, batugan.
indoors: *adj*. nasa bahay.
induce: *v*. hikayatin, humimok, ulukan; ~**ment** panghikayat.
indulge: *v*. magpakasawà, palayawin.
indulgent: *adj*. mapagpalayaw, magpasunód, mapagbigáy.
industrial: *adj*. pang-industriya.
industrious: *adj*. masipag.
industry: *n*. industriya; kasipagan.
inebriated: *adj*. lasíng.
inedible: *adj*. dî makakain.
ineffective: *adj*. dî mabisà; waláng-kuwenta, waláng-saysáy, waláng-gaanong saysáy.
inefficiency: *n*. kawaláng-kaya.
inequality: *n*. dî pagkakapareho.
inevitable: *adj*. dî maiiwasan.
inexcusable: *adj*. di-maipagpápaumanhín.
inexpensive: *adj*. murà.
inexperienced: *adj*. bagito, waláng-karanasán.
infallible: *adj*. dî maááring magkamalî.
infamous: *adj*. kalait-lait, kadustá-dustâ.
infamy: *n*. kabuktután.
infancy: *n*. kasanggulán, kamusmusán; simulâ.
infant: *n*. sanggól, musmós, paslít.
infantile: *adj*. batang-batà, pambatà.
infantry: *n*. hukbóng-lakad.
infatuation: *n*. pagkahibáng, kahalingán.
infect: *v*. lalinan; ~**ed** *adj*. nalalinan.
infection: *n*. impeksiyón, pagkahawa.
infer: *v*. huluin, hinuhain.
inferior: *adj*. mababà kaysa, mas mababà; ~**ity** *n*. pasahól.
infertile: *adj*. baóg.
infernal: *adj*. makademonyo.
infest: *v*. pamugaran.
infidelity: *n*. pagliliho, pagtataksíl.
infiltrate: *v*. lumusót, pumasok.
infinite: *adj*. waláng-hanggán.
infinitive: *n*. pawatás.
infirmary: *n*. págamutan, dispensaryo.
infix: *n*. gitlapì; *v*. igitlapì; isaksák; itaním.
inflame: *v*. pag-alabin; mag-apóy.
inflammable: *adj*. madalíng magningas, siklabin.
inflate: *v*. papintugín; (*puff up*) mamayagpág.
inflation: *n*. implasiyón; pagpapapintóg, pamímintóg.
inflict: *v*. ipabatá; pahirapan.
influence: *n*. bisà, impluho; *v*. hikayatin, akitin.
influential: *adj*. makapangyarihan.
influenza: *n*. trangkaso, flu.
influx: *n*. dagsâ, pag-agos, paghugos, saksâ.
inform: *v*. ipaalám, pabatirán, sabihin, magbigáy-alám; ~**ative** nakapagtúturò.
informal: *adj*. dî pormál.
information: *n*. kaalaman, kabatiran; balità.
infrequent: *adj*. bihirà, madalang.
infringe: *v*. lumabág, labagín, makialám.
infuriate: *v*. pagalitin.
ingenious: *adj*. mahusay, matalino.

ingenuity: *n*. katalinuhan, mapangathâ.
ingot: *n*. bara ng metál.
ingratiate: *v*. magmagalíng, manuyò, magmapurí.
ingratitude: *n*. kawalán ng utang-na-loób.
ingredient: *n*. sangkáp, sahóg.
inhabitant: *n*. nananahanan.
inhale: *v*. lumangháp, samyuín.
inherent: *adj*. likás, katutubò.
inherit: *v*. manahin. mamana.
inheritance: *n*. pagkamana, pagmamana; mana.
inhibit: *v*. pigilin, hadlangán.
initial: *adj*. kauna-unahan, panguna; *n*. unang titik.
initiate: *v*. magpasimulâ, simulán.
initiation: *n*. pagtanggáp bilang kasapì.
inject: *v*. paturukán; mag-inyeksiyón; **~ion** *n*. inyeksiyón, iniksiyón.
injure: *v*. sumakít, saktán; manirà.
injury: *n*. pinsalà, kapinsalaan.
injustice: *n*. kawaláng-katárungan.
ink: *n*. tinta.
in-laws: *n*. mga pinagbiyanan.
inlay: *v*. ikalupkóp.
inmate: *n*. preso, bilanggô.
inn: *n*. bahay-panuluyan.
innards: *n*. lamanloób, isaw.
innate: *adj*. katutbò, likás.
inner: *adj*. sa dakong loób; matalik.
innocence: *n*. kawalán ng kasalanan.
innocent: *adj*. waláng-sala; waláng-kamalayán.
innuendo: *n*. patutsada, pasaríng, parunggít.
inoculation: *n*. pagbabakuna.
inopportune: *adj*. dî napapanahón.
input: *n*. ang nailagáy, ang naipasok.
inquire: *v*. itanóng, magsiyasat.
inquiry: *n*. tanóng.
inquisition: *n*. pag-uusisà, pagtatanóng.
inquisitive: *adj*. maurirà, mausisà.
insane: *adj*. loko, sirâ, baliw.
insanity: *n*. pagkabaliw, pagkaulók; kalokohan.
insect: *n*. insekto, kulisap.
insecticide: *n*. pamatáy-kulisap.
insecure: *adj*. di-matatág.
insensitive: *adj*. dî maramdamin.
insert: *v*. ipasok, isuót, ipaloób.
inside: *n*. loób; *adv*. nasa loób; **~-out** baligtád.
insight: *n*. kabatirán, maliwanag na pagkáunawà.
insignificant: *adj*. dî mahalagá.
insincere: *adj*. dî matapát; magdarayà.
insinuate: *v*. pagpapahiwatig.
insinuation: *n*. pahiwatig, paramdám, pariníg, pagsaríng.
insipid: *adj*. matabáng, sagapsáp, waláng-lasà.
insist: *v*. ipilit, igiít.
insolent: *adj*. pusóng, bastós.
insomnia: *n*. di-pagkakatulog.
inspect: *v*. suriin, siyasatin.
inspector: *n*. tagasurì, tagasiyasat.
inspiration: *n*. pampasiglá.
inspire: *v*. magbigáy-siglá; pukawin.
instability: *n*. kawaláng-tatág; pagkapabagubago.
install: *v*. ikabít, ipuwesto; italagá; iluklók; **~ation** *n*. instalasyón, pagkakakabít; **~ment** hulog; hurnál; yugtô.
instance: *n*. halimbawà, pagkakataón; **for ~** halimbawà.
instant: *n*. sandalî, saglít.
instantaneous: *adj*. biglâ.
instead: *adv*. sa halíp ng.
instep: *n*. balantók ng sakong.
instinct: *n*. likás na hilig; katutubong simbuyó.
instigate: *v*. magsulsól.
instill: *v*. itaním.
instinct: *n*. katutubong ugalì.
institute: *n*. paaralán, paturuán, surián, instituto.
institution: *n*. institusyón.
instruct: *v*. turuan, iturò; ipatalastás; **~ion** turò.
instructor: *n*. gurò, tagapagturò.
instrument: *n*. kasangkapan, gamit; instrumento; paraán.
insubordination: *n*. pagsuwáy sa punò.
insufficient: *adj*. kulang, kapós, dî hustó.
insulate: *v*. insulahín; mag-insulá.
insult: *n*. insulto, pag-alipustâ, paghamak, pagdustâ, paglait; *v*. hamakin, insultuhín, dustaín.
insurance: *n*. seguro, pagpapaseguro.
insure: *v*. tiyakín; ipaseguro.
insurgency: *n*. paghihimagsík, pagbabangon.
insurrection: *n*. paghihimagsík, pagbabangon,

pag-aalsá.
integral: *adj*. mahalagá, kailangan.
integrate: *v*. pagsamahin, totalín, buuín.
integrity: *n*. integridád, katápatan, kalinisang-budhî.
intellect: *n*. isip, pang-unawà.
intellectual: *n*. taong marunong; *adj*. pang-kaisipán.
intelligence: *n*. katalinuhan.
intelligent: *n*. matalino, marunong.
intelligible: *adj*. máuunawaan.
intend: *v*. balakin; magtangkâ; ilaán.
intended: *adj*. hangád, layon; sinasadyâ.
intense: *adj*. napakatindí, napakalakí; marub-dób.
intensify: *v*. patindihín, pasidhiín, palalaín.
intensity: *n*. sidhî, tindí.
intensive: *adj*. masidhî; másinsinan.
intent: *n*. layon, hangád, tangkâ, balak.
intention: *n*. (*purpose*) hangád, layon; (*plan*) balak, tangkâ.
intentional: *adj*. sadyâ, kusà.
intercede: *v*. mamagitan.
intercept: *v*. maharang, harangin; sugpuín.
interchange: *v*. magpalít, maghalili.
intercourse: *n*. pagsasamahán, unawaán; paha-tiran; (*sexual*) pagtatalik.
interdependent: *adj*. nagtutulungán.
interest: *n*. interés; (*profit*) kapakanán; (*share in property*) puhunan; (*bank*) tubò, paki-nabang; *v*. mawili, akitin.
interesting: *adj*. kawili-wili, nakakawili, ka-akit-akit.
interfere: *v*. manghimasok, magkasalungát; hadlangán; **~nce** panghihimasok, pakiki-alám.
interim: *adj*. pansamantalá.
interior: *adj*. loób, panloób.
interjection: *n*. bulalás, pandamdám.
interlace: *v*. magsalá-salabat, ilala.
interlock: *v*. magsalabíd, magkawíng.
intermarry: *v*. mangagkapangasawawhán.
intermediary: *n*. tagapamagitan.
intermediate: *adj*. nasa pagitan, panggitnâ.
intermingle: *v*. makihalò, makilahók.
intermission: *n*. pahingá, pagitan ng mga tag-pô.
intermittent: *adj*. paulit-ulit, patigil-tigil.
intern: *n*. interno.
internal: *adj*. panloób.
international: *adj*. internasiyonál, pandaigdíg.
interpret: *v*. ipaliwanag; ipakahulugán; **~ation** pakahulugán.
interpreter: *n*. tagapagsalin.
interrogate: *v*. magtanóng; tanungín.
interrogative: *adj*. nagtatanóng, patanóng; |**~ particle** *n*. katagáng pananóng; **~ pronoun** *n*. panghalíp pananóng.
interrupt: *v*. umabala, abalahin; (*conversation*) makisabád.
intersect: *v*. bumugtás, magsalikop.
interval: *n*. patláng, pagitan.
intervene: *v*. pumagitan, mamagitan.
intervention: *n*. pamamagitan; pakikihalò.
interview: *n*. pakikipanayám; **~er** tagapaki-nayám.
intestine: *n*. bituka.
intimacy: *n*. pagpapálagayang-loób.
intimate: *adj*. kapalagayang-loób, kilaláng-kilala.
intimidate: *v*. takutin.
into: *prep*. sa; sa loób ng.
intolerable: *adj*. di-matátagalán, di-matítiís.
intolerance: *n*. kawaláng-parayâ, di-pagpapa-hintulot.
intonation: *n*. tono; himig.
intoxicate: *v*. lasingín, langulín; **~d** *adj*. lasíng, langó.
intransitive: *adj*. kátawanín, di-palipát.
intrepid: *adj*. malulóng.
intricate: *adj*. masalimuót, magulô.
intrigue: *n*. sabuwatan, pakanâ, intriga.
introduce: *v*. ipakilala; iharáp.
introduction: *n*. pauna, pagpapakilala.
intrude: *v*. makisabád, pakialamán.
inundate: *v*. bumahâ; bahaín.
invade: *v*. lusubin, salakayin; labagín.
invalid: *adj*. waláng-bisà; *n*. masasaktíng tao, salantâ.
invalidate: *v*. magpawaláng-halagá, pawaláng-bisà.
invaluable: *adj*. nápakamahalagá.
invasion: *n*. paglusob, pagsalakay.
invent: *v*. likhaín, imbentuhín; kathaín.

invention: *n*. pagkathâ, imbensiyón, paglikhâ.
inventor: *n*. mangangathâ, imbentór.
invert: *v*. itaób, itiwarík; baligtarín; saliwaín.
invest: *v*. puhunanin, mamuhunan.
investigate: *v*. siyasatin, imbestigahín, suriin.
investigation: *n*. pagsisiyasat, paglilitis, pag-uusig.
investor: *n*. mamumuhunán.
invigorate: *v*. magbigáy-lakás, palakasín.
invigorating: *adj*. pampalakás.
invincible: *adj*. di-magagapì.
invisible: *adj*. di-maaaring makita.
invitation: *n*. anyaya, paanyaya.
invite: *v*. anyayahan; halinahin.
invoice: *n*. paktura, talaan.
involuntary: *adj*. di-kusà; di-sadyâ.
involve: *v*. magsangkót; mapaloób; **~d** *adj*. masalimuót, maligoy; mádalakit; mápahalò; mápasabit.
iodine: *n*. yodo.
irate: *adj*. galít.
Irish: *n*. Irlandés.
irk: *v*. yamutin, ikabuwisit.
iron: *n*. (*metal*) bakal; (*pressing ~*) plantsa, prinsá; *v*. plantsahín.
ironic: *adj*. tumbalík, mapanuyâ, baligtád.
irony: *n*. ironiya, pambabaligtád, panunuyâ.
irrational: *adj*. di-nakapagmamatwíd.
irreconcilable: *adj*. di-mapagkakásundô.
irregular: *adj*. di-panáy, di-pantay; labág sa batás; **~ity** katiwalián, di-pagkapanáy; **~ verb** *n*. pandiwang di-karaniwan.
irrelevant: *adj*. walâ sa paksâ, di-kaugnáy.
irresponsible: *adj*. waláng-pananagutan, di-mapagkakátiwalaan.
irreverent: *adj*. waláng-pitagan, waláng-galang.
irrigate: *v*. magpatubig.
irrigation: *n*. patubig.
irritable: *adj*. magagalitín, bugnutin, mayayámutin.
irritate: *v*. ikagalit, galitin; yamutín.
irritation: *n*. katí; yamót.
is: see **be**.
island: *n*. pulô, isla; **~er** taong-pulô.
islet: *n*. muntíng pulô.
isolate: *v*. ihiwaláy, ibukód.
isolation: *n*. paghihiwaláy, pagbubukód.
issue: *n*. isyu, bilang; suliranin; paksâ; *v*. maglathalà; bigyán.
isthmus: *n*. tangwáy.
it: *pron*. iyán, iyón; siyá.
Italian: *n*. Italiano, tagá-Italya.
itch: *n*. katí, pangangatí; *v*. magpakatí; kumatí.
itchy: *adj*. makatí.
item: *n*. bagay; kasangkapan.
itinerary: *n*. itineraryo.
its: *pron*. nitó, niyón.
itself: *pron*. kanyáng sarili.
ivory: *n*. garing.
ivy: *n*. lanat; **poison ~** yedra

J

jab: *v*. sundutín, idurò.
jack: *n*. diyák; (*in cards*) sota; **~ off** magsalsál; **~fish** malapito, malaputó; **~s** (*game*) siklót; *v*. gatuhin.
jackass: *n*. buriko; hangál, utó-utô.
jacket: *n*. diyaket, tsaketa.
jackfruit: *n*. langkâ.
jacknife: *n*. kortapluma, lanseta.
jade: *n*. batóng ihada; **~ vine** tayabak.
jail: *n*. bilangguan, piitan, kulungán, kalaboso.
jam: *v*. maipit, mapasingit; sumiksík; *n*. halayá; **traffic ~** siksikan ng sasakyán.
jamboree: *n*. diyamborí.
janitor: *n*. tagapaglinis, diyánitor.
January: *n*. Enero.
Japanese: *n*. Hapón; **~ mackerel** lumahan.
jar: *n*. taro, garapón, galong.
jasmine: *n*. hasmín, sampagita, kampupot.
jaundice: *n*. paniniláw ng balát.
javelin: *n*. habelina.
jaw: *n*. pangá, sihang.
jazz: *n*. diyás.
jealous: *adj*. seloso, naninibughô; naiinggít; **~y** *n*. panibughô, pagseselos.
jeans: *n*. maóng.
jeep: *n*. dyip.
jelly: *n*. halayá.
jellyfish: *n*. dikyâ.
jeopardize: *v*. mamiligro, isapanganib.
jerk: *n*. halták, kalóg, udlót; *v*. baltakín, hal-

takín, iudlót; **~ed meat** *n.* tapa.
jest: *n.* birò, sisté.
Jesus: *n.* Hesús.
jet: *n.* tilarok, sagitsít, pampasirit.
Jew: *n.* Hudiyó.
jewel: *n.* hiyás, alahas; **~ry** mga alahas.
jeweler: *n.* alahero.
jingle: *v.* kumalansíng, kumililíng.
jinx: *n.* buwisit, malas, kasaykasay.
jitters: *n.* nérbiyos, malabis na pagkatakot.
job: *n.* trabaho, gawain, hanap-buhay.
jockey: *n.* hinete; mandaya, manlinláng.
jocund: *adj.* masayá.
join: *v.* magkabít; mag-isá; makisama, sumali.
joint: *n.* dugtóng, hugpóng.
joist: *n.* suleras.
joke: *n.* birò, sisté; **~r** taong mapagbirô; (*in cards*) ang kalabisán.
jolt: *n.* alóg, kalóg.
jostle: *v.* manikó.
jot: *v.* italâ.
journal: *n.* talaarawán, aklát tuusán; diyaryo; **~ism** peryodismo; **~ist** mamamahayág, peryodista.
journey: *n.* paglalakbáy, biyahe.
jovial: *adj.* masayá, masiglá.
joy: *n.* tuwâ, galák; **~ful** maligaya, masayá, nagagalák; **~ous** nakalúlugód, nakalíligaya.
jubilation: *n.* pagkakatuwâ, pagsasayá.
judge: *n.* huwés, tagahatol, hukóm; *v.* hatulin, hukumán; **~ment** paghuhukóm, paghuhusgá.
judo: *n.* diyudo.
juggle: *v.* magsalamangka.
juice: *n.* dyus, katás; **juicy** makatás.
July: *n.* Hulyo.
jumble: *v.* guluhín, paghalú-haluin.
jump: *v.* tumalón, lumuksó, lumundag; **~ing goby** talimusak; **~y** magugulatín, matatakutín.
junction: *n.* salikop.
June: *n.* Hunyo.
jungle: *n.* gubat, kagubatan.
junior: *adj.* nakababatà.
junk: *n.* basura.
junta: *n.* hunta.
Jupiter: *n.* Húpiter.
jurisdiction: *n.* huridiksyon, sakop.
jurist: *n.* hurista.
jury: *n.* hurado, inampalán.
just: *adj.* tamà; *adv.* lamang; (*barely*) bahagyâ.
justice: *n.* katarungan, katwiran, katumpakán; **~ of the Peace** *n.* Hukóm-Tagapamayapà.
justifiable: *adj.* mapangángatwiranan, karapat-dapat.
justified: *adj.* makatarungan, náalinsunod sa batás.
justify: *v.* mangatwiran, magbigay-matwíd.
jut: *v.* umuslî, pausliín, umungós.
juvenile: *adj.* batà; pambatà; *n.* batà.
juxtaposition: *n.* pagtatabí-tabí, pagkakahanay.

K

kaleidoscope: *n.* kaleydoskopo.
kangaroo: *n.* kanggaró.
karma: *n.* karma; tadhanà, destino.
keel: *n.* kilya.
keen: *adj.* matalas, matalím, mahayap.
keep: *v.* itagò, iligpít; mag-alagà; **~ from** pigilin; (*continue*) ipagpatuloy; **~sake**: *n.* alaala; **~ off** umiwas; **~ an eye on** magbantáy; **~ on** magpatuloy.
keeper: *n.* tagapag-ingat; nangángasiwà.
keg: *n.* maliít na bariles.
kerchief: *n.* panwelo, alampáy; bandana.
kernel: *n.* butil, lamán.
kerosene: *n.* petrolyo.
ketchup: *n.* katsap, ketsap.
kettle: *n.* kaldero, kawa.
key: *n.* susì; **~board** teklado; **~note** saligán, batayán, tono.
keyhole: *n.* susian.
khaki: *n.* kaki.
kick: *v.* manipà, sipain, tadyakán.
kid: *n.* batà, paslít.
kidnap: *v.* dumukot, dukutin.
kidney: *n.* bató.
kill: *v.* patayín, pumatáy.
kiln: *n.* tapahan, ápuyang pátuyuan.
kilogram: *n.* kilo.
kilometer: *n.* kilómetro.
kilowatt: *n.* kilowát.
kimono: *n.* kimono.
kin: *n.* kaanak, kaangkán.

kind: *adj*. mabaít, matulungín; *n*. klas, urì; **~hearted** mahábangin, maawaín.
kindle: *v*. magningas, sindihán.
kindling: *n*. pamparikít, pampaningas.
kindred: *n*. kamag-anakan.
king: *n*. harì; **~dom** kaharian; **~fisher** piskadór, susulbót; **~ship** pagkaharì.
kink: *n*. pulupot, pilipit.
kinky: *adj*. kulót.
kipper: *n*. tinapa.
kitchen: *n*. kusinà.
kite: *n*. buladór, guryón, saranggola.
kitten: *n*. kutíng.
kleptomaniac: *n*. makatíng-kamáy.
knapsack: *n*. mutsila, tampipì; alporhas.
knead: *v*. magmasa, masahin.
knee: *n*. tuhod; **~cap** bayugo ng tuhod.
kneel: *v*. lumudód.
knell: *n*. agunyas.
knife: *n*. kutsilyo; lansita; *v*. saksakín; **~ point** duló ng patalim.
knight: *n*. kabalyero.
knit: *v*. magniting; ikunót.
knob: *n*. tatangnán ng pintô.
knock: *v*. tumuktók, kumatók; **~-kneed** pikî, pingkî.
knot: *n*. buhól; (*wood*) bukó.
know: *v*. (*person*) kilala; (*thing*) alam.
knowingly: *adv*. kusà, sadyâ.
knowledge: *n*. kaalamán, nalalaman, malay.
knuckle: *n*. bukó ng dalirì.
Koran: *n*. Kurán.

L

label: *n*. etiketa, taták.
labor: *n*. trabaho; (*childbirth*) magdamdám sa panganganák.
laboratory: *n*. laboratoryo.
lace: *n*. puntás; enkahe.
lacerate: *n*. sugatan.
lack: *v*. mangailangan; *n*. kakulangán.
lacquer: n barnís.
lactarid fish: *n*. algodón, pelyán, rigodón.
laden: *adj*. may-kargá.
ladle: *n*. kutsarón.
lady: *n*. babae, binibini.
lag: *n*. pagkaantala, pagkakahulí.
lagoon: *n*. lawà, danaw.
laissez faire: *n*. hindî pakikialám sa pamahalaan.
lake: *n*. dagat-dagatan, lawà.
lamb: *n*. kordero.
lame: *adj*. piláy; **~ duck** baldado, mahinang tao.
lament: *v*. itangis, ipagdalamhatì, ipanangis; *n*. pagdaíng, taghóy.
lamp: *n*. lamparaá, ilawán; **~shade** pantalya.
lance: *n*. sibát.
land: *n*. lupà; bansâ; *v*. lumunsád, bumabâ; **~ owner** *n* maylupà.
landlady: *n*. kasera; propiyetarya.
landlord: *n*. propyetaryo; kasero.
landmark: *n*. tandâ; muhón; palátandaan.
landscape: *n*. paysahe, tanawin.
landslide: *n*. guhò; nápalakíng kalamangán (*overwhelming defeat*).
language: *n*. salitâ, wikà, pananalitâ.
languid: *adj*. matamláy, lupaypáy.
lanky: *adj*. matangkád at payát.
lantern: *n*. paról.
lap: *n*. kandungan.
lapel: *n*. sulapa.
lard: *n*. mantikà.
large: *adj*. malakí; **at ~** *adj*. nakalálayà.
lark: *n*. ruwisenyór.
larva: *n*. tilas; uod; anák ng insekto; **mosquito ~** *n*. kikinsót, kitikití.
laryngitis: *n*. laringhitis, pamamagâ ng babagtingan.
larynx: *n*. babagtingan.
lascivious: *adj*. malibóg, mahalay.
lash: *n*. látigo; **eye~** pilikmatá; *v*. hagupitín.
last: *adj*. hulí, katapusán, pinakahulí; nakaraán, nagdaán; *v*. matagál; itagál; **~ farewell** *n*. hulíng-paalam; **~ will** *n*. hulíng-habilin; **~ word** *n*. hulíng-salitâ.
lasting: *adj*. magtatagál, matibay.
latch: *n*. aldaba, trangká.
late: *adj*. hulí, naantala.
lathe: *n*. lalik.
lather: *n*. bulâ ng sabón.
Latin: *n*. Latín.
latter: *adj*. panghulí, magtatapós.

latticework: *n*. dawa-dawa, sala-salá.
laugh: *v*. tumawa; **~ingly** *adj*. patawá.
launch: *n*. lantsa; *v*. ibunsód, ilunsád.
laundry: *n*. labada; **~person** labandero.
lava: *n*. laba, kumúkulóng putik.
lavender: *n*. labanda.
lavish: *adj*. masyado; labis-labis.
law: *n*. batás; ordenansa; **~maker** *n*. mambabatás; **~suit** usapín, kaso; **~ enforcement officer** *n*. tagapagpatupád ng batás.
lawn: *n*. damuhán.
lax: *adj*. maluwág; pabayà.
laxative: *n*. laksante; pamurga.
lay: *v*. ilapág, ibabâ; ilatag, itabí; **~-off** alisín sa trabaho, kaltasín, bawasin, tanggalín.
layer: *n*. patong, susón; patong.
layout: *n*. kaayusan, plano; pagkakálatag.
lazy: *adj*. tamád, batugan.
lead: *n*. tinggâ (*metal*).
lead: *v*. umakay; manguna; pangunahan; **leader** punò, pasimunò.
leaf: *n*. dahon; **~ fish** bayang, dahung gabi, darapugan.
leafy: *adj*. madahon, mayabong.
league: *n*. unyón, kapisanan, liga.
leak: *v*. tumulò; tumagas.
lean: *adj*. payát, di-matabâ; *v*. humilig, humapay; **~-to** sibi.
leap: *v*. lumuksó, lumundág; **~ year** taóng bisyesto
learn: *v*. matuto, mag-aral; **~èd** *adj*. marunong.
lease: *n*. pag-upa; *v*. magpaupa.
leash: *n*. talì.
least: *adj*. pinakamaliít, pinakakauntî.
leather: *n*. katad, balát, kuwero; **~ jacket fish** durado, talapyá.
leave: *v*. umalís, lumakad; yumao; **~ alone** pabayaan, hayaan; **~ behind** nalimutang dalhín; **~ out** hindî naisama.
leaven: *n*. lebadura.
lecture: *n*. panayám; *v*. magpanayám.
ledge: *n*. pasamano.
leech: *n*. lintâ.
leeway: *n*. pataán, pasobra, palabis, plaso.
left: *adj*. (*not right*) kaliwâ; **~-handed** *adj*. kaliwete; **~ over** tirá, labí.
leg: *n*. paá; bintî.
legacy: *n*. pamana, legado.
legal: *adj*. legál, pambatás.
legend: *n*. alamát.
legible: *adj*. mababasa, nababasa, malinaw.
legislation: *n*. pagbabatás.
legislative: *adj*. pambátásan.
legitimate: *adj*. matuwíd, marapat.
leisure: *n*. malayang oras.
lemon: *n*. limón; **~grass** *n*. tanglád.
lemonade: *n*. limonada.
lend: *v*. magpahirám, magpautang.
length: *n*. habà; (*of time*) tagál.
lengthwise: *adv*. pahabà.
lenient: *adj*. maamò; di-mahigpít;.
lens: *n*. lente.
Lent: *n*. Kuwaresma.
lentil: *n*. lenteha.
leopard: *n*. leopardo.
leprosy: *n*. ketong, lepra.
lesbian: *n*. tombóy, binalaki.
less: *adj*. mas maliít, kakauntî.
lessen: *v*. magbawas; bumabâ; umiklî.
lesser: *adj*. lalong maliít; mababà.
lesson: *n*. aralín, liksiyón.
lest: *conj*. upang dî.
let: *v*. pumayag, magpahintulot, bayaan.
lethal: *adj*. makamamatáy.
lethargic: *adj*. nag-aantók; pampaantók.
letter: *n*. (*symbol*) titik, letra; (*correspondence*) sulat, liham.
lettuce: *n*. litsugas.
level: *adj*. patag, pantáy; *v*. pagpantayín.
lever: *n*. pinggá, panikwás.
levy: *n*. buwis.
lewd: *adj*. mahalay, masagwâ, malaswâ.
liable: *adj*. nananagót, may-pananagutan.
liar: *n*. sinungaling, bulaan.
libel: *n*. paninirang-puri, libelo; **~ous** *adj*. mapanirang-puri.
liberal: *adj*. di-mahigpít, maunawaín; mapagbigáy; maluwág.
liberate: *v*. palayain, pakawalán.
liberty: *n*. kalayaan.
libido: *n*. libog, utog.
Libra: *n*. timbangan (sa zodiac).
librarian: *n*. kátiwalà ng aklatan.
library: *n*. aklatan, libreria, biblioteka.

lice: *n*. mga kuto.
license: *n*. lisensiya.
lick: *v*. umimid, himurin, dilaan.
licorice: *n*. regalis; anís.
lid: *n*. takíp, panakíp, taklób.
lie: *n*. (*untrue*) kasinungalingan, kabulaanan; *v*. (*flat position of body*) humigâ; ~ **on one's back** tumihayà; ~ **face down** dumapâ; ~ **prostrate** humandusáy; (*deceive*) magsinungaling.
lieutenant: *n*. tenyente.
life: *n*. buhay; ~**long** *adj*. habang-buhay; ~ **preserver** *n*. salbabida; ~**time** buóng buhay.
lifeboat: *n*. lantsang salbabida.
lift: *v*. itaás, iangát; (*elevator*) asensór.
ligament: *n*. litid.
ligature: *n*. panalì, talì; (*gram*.) pang-angkóp.
light: *n*. liwanag; ilaw; *adj*. magaán.
lighter: *n*. pansindí, panindí; (*gram*.) pang-angkóp.
lighthouse: *n*. parola.
lightning: *n*. kidlát.
likeable: *adj*. kalugúd-lugód, kaibig-ibig.
like: *adj*. katulad, kamukhâ; *v*. maibigan, magustuhán, gustó.
likely: *adj*. maáarì, malamáng.
likewise: *adv*. gayón din.
lily: *n*. liryo; **water** ~ baino.
limb: *n*. bisig; paá; sangá.
lime: *n*. (*burning limestone*) apog; (*lemon*) dayap.
limit: *n*. hangganan, hanggá; sakláw; *v*. magtakdâ, magtasa.
limitation: *n*. pagtatakdâ, tasa.
limp: *v*. tumikód, humingkód; *adj*. malatâ.
line: *n*. linya, guhit, raya; hanay, hilera; pila; (*of poetry*) taludtód; (*of drama*) pangungusap; *v*. tutupán; guhitan; **stand in** ~ pumila; **clothes**~ sampayan.
lineage: *n*. angkán, lahì.
linen: *n*. de-ilo, linen.
linger: *v*. magtagál, tumayú-tayô; umalí-aligíd.
linguist: *n*. lingguwista, dalubwikà; ~**ic** *adj*. pangwikà; ~**ics** lingguwístika, palawikaan.
lining: *n*. aporo.
link: *n*. kawíng, kawíl; *v*. isangkót, iugnáy, ikawíl.
linotype: *n*. linotipya.
lion: *n*. león.
lip: *n*. labì; ~**stick** lipistík.
liquefy: *v*. tunawin, lusawin.
liquid: *n*. líkido; *adj*. tunáw, lusáw.
liquidate: *v*. lipulin; likidahín.
liquor: *n*. alak, pampainit.
lisp: *v*. mautál.
list: *n*. talâ, listahan.
listen: *v*. makiníg, pakinggán.
literary: *adj*. pampánitikán, kamulatán.
literate: *adj*. marunong bumasa at sumulat.
literature: *n*. literatura, pánitikán.
litigant: *n*. kausáp.
litigation: *n*. pagsasakdál, pagdedemanda.
litter: *n*. kalat; (*animals*) kamada.
little: *adj*. maliít, muntî.
live: *v*. mabuhay; mamuhay; *adj*. buháy.
livelihood: *n*. pagkabuhay, kabuhayan, ikinabúbuhay.
lively: *adj*. masiglá.
liver: *n*. atáy.
livestock: *n*. hayupan.
livid: *adj*. nangingitím-ngitím.
living: *adj*. buháy; *n*. ikinabubuhay; ~ **room** salas.
lizard: *n*. butikî; tukô; bayawak; ~ **fish** bubule, kalaso, kamutihan.
load: *n*. karga; *v*. magkargá.
loaf: *n*. pandeunan; *v*. maglimayón; maglakwatsa.
loan: *n*. utang; *v*. ipautang.
loathe: *v*. masuklám, mamuhî, mapoót.
lobby: *n*. bulwagan; lobi; *v*. maglobi.
lobbyist: *n*. maglolobi.
lobster: *n*. uláng.
local: *adj*. pampoók; lokál; ~**ity** poók.
locate: *v*. humanap, matagpuán.
location: *n*. kinalalalgyán, lugár.
locative: *adj*. panlunán.
lock: *n*. kandado, seradura, susián; *v*. isusì.
lockjaw: *n*. tétano.
locksmith: *n*. magsususì, pandáy-susì, pandáykabán.
locust: *n*. balang, luktón.
lodge: *n*. tirahan; *v*. tumirá.
lofty: *adj*. napakataás, napakatayog; palalò.

log: *n*. troso.
logging: *n*. pagtotroso.
logic: *n*. lóhika, pangangatwiran.
loin: *n*. lomo; **~cloth** *n*. baház.
loiter: *v*. magpatigil-tigil, magpasabit-sabit.
lollipop: *n*. lolipap.
lone: *adj*. nag-iisá, bugtóng, kabutó.
lonely: *adj*. nag-iisá, nalulungkót, nalulumbáy, namamangláw.
long: *adj*. mahabà; (*in duration*) matagál; **as ~ as** basta.
longshoreman: *n*. estibidór.
look: *v*. tumingín, tingnán, masdán; **~ out!** mag-ingat ka!; **~ for** hanapin; **~ forward to** umasa; **~ into** mag-usisa; **~ing glass** salamín; **~s** *n*. astâ, mukhâ; kiyás; **~out** *n*. bantayan, pagbabantáy.
loom: *n*. panghabi, habihán.
loop: *n*. silò; **~hole** butas.
loose: *adj*. kalág, tanggál; (*in morals*) halagháq, pabayâ; **~n** pakawalán; buhaghagín.
loot: *v*. mandambóng, magnakaw.
lopsided: *adj*. tagibáng, kabilán.
loquacious: *adj*. daldál, matabíl.
lord: *n*. poón, panginoón.
lose: *v*. (*no longer have*) mawalán; (*not win*) matalo; **~ face** *v*. mapahiyâ.
loss: *n*. pagkawalâ; pagkatalo, kawalán.
lost: *adj*. nawalâ, nawáwalâ.
lot: *n*. kalipunán, katipunan, bahagi; lote; **a ~** marami.
lotion: *n*. losyón.
lottery: *n*. loteriya, sápalarán.
lotus: *n*. lotus, baino.
loud: *adj*. malakás, maingay.
lounge: *n*. pahingahan, silíd-pahingahan.
louse: *n*. kuto; **~ egg** lisâ.
lousy: *adj*. kinukuto; masagwâ; waláng-kuwenta.
love: *n*. pagmamahál, pag-ibig, pagsintá; *v*. ibigin, mahalín, sintahín, irugin; **~ song** *n*. kundiman.
lovely: *adj*. kaibig-ibig; kaakit-akit; magandá.
lover: *n*. mangingibig; (*outside of marriage*) kalaguyò.
low: *adj*. mababà; **~ tide** *n*. hibás, kati; **~land** *n*. kapatagan, kababaan; **~ spirited** matamláy, malumbáy.
lower: *v*. ibabâ; hinaan.
loyal: *adj*. matapát.
lubricant: *n*. lubrikante, pampadulás, langís.
lubricate: *v*. langisán.
lucid: *adj*. maliwanag, maningníng; malinaw.
luck: *n*. kapalaran, suwerte; **bad ~** *n*. malas; **good ~** *n*. buenas.
lucky: *adj*. masuwerte, mapalad.
lucrative: *adj*. pinakikinabangan, kapípakinabang.
ludicrous: *adj*. katawá-tawá.
luggage: *n*. bagahe, dalá-dalahan.
lukewarm: *adj*. malahiningá, maligamgám.
lullaby: *n*. hele, kantáng pampatulog.
lumbago: *n*. lumbago.
lumber: *n*. mga tablá, kahoy; **~jack** magtotroso; **~ yard** tableriya.
lump: *n*. bukol; umbók; tipák; **~fish** lupo.
lunatic: *n*. balíw, loko.
lunch: *n*. tanghalian, pananghalian.
lung: *n*. bagà.
lunge: *v*. sumugod, dumaluhong.
lure: *v*. tumuksó, bumighanì, umakit.
lurk: *v*. mangublí, kumublí.
luscious: *adj*. kalugúd-lugód; malinamnám.
lush: *adj*. malagô, malusóg, malabay, malambô.
lust: *n*. kalibugan; kasakimán, katakawan; **~ful** malibóg; maiyág.
luster: *n*. kintáb, kináng.
lustful: *adj*. malibog, mahalay; masakím.
luxurious: *adj*. marangyâ, maluho.
luxury: *n*. luho, rangyâ.
lye: *n*. lihiya, sosa.
lymph: *n*. limpa.
lyre: *n*. lira, kudyapî.
lyric: *n*. líriko; **~al** lirikál.

M

ma'am: *n*. ginang.
macadamia: *n*. makadamya.
macaroni: *n*. makaroni.
machine: *n*. mákina; **~ gun** masinggán.
machinery: *n*. makinarya.
mackerel: *n*. alumahan, mataán; kabalyá; **~ fry** linatsáy; **~ scad** balangwán.

mad: *adj*. (*crazy*) loko, balíw; (*angry*) galít.
madam: *n*. ginang.
made: *v*. gawâ, yarì.
magazine: *n*. rebista, magasín.
maggot: *n*. uód.
magic: *n*. salamangka, máhiya.
magician: *n*. salamangkero.
magistrate: *n*. mahistrado.
magistry: *n*. pagkamahistrado, hudikatura, pagkahukóm.
magnet: *n*. batubalanì; **~ic needle** *n*. paraluman.
magnificent: *adj*. maringal, dakilà; kahangahangà.
magnitude: *n*. halagá, kalakhán.
mahogany: *n*. kamagóng, tangilì.
maid: *n*. katulang, alilang babae.
maiden: *n*. dalagita, dalagindíng, dalaga; **~ name** *n*. apelyido sa pagkadalaga.
maidenwort: *n*. kamariya, damóng-mariya.
mail: *n*. koreo; **~ box** *n*. busón; **~ man** *n*. kartero.
maim: *v*. makapinsalà, baldahín.
main: *adj*. pinakamahalagá, pangunahín; **~ office** *n*. punong-tanggapan.
maintain: *v*. magpanatili; sustentuhán.
majesty: *n*. kamahalan, kamaharlikaán.
major: *n*. medyor, komandante; *adj*. lalong malakí, pangunahín.
majority: *n*. karamihan, mayoria.
make: *v*. gawín, iyarì; *n*. yarì, urì; marka; **~-believe** *n*. pagkukunwarî; *adj*. pakunwari; **~-up** *n*. pampagandá, meykap; *v*. (*after a fight*) magkasundô; **~ a living** kumíkita ng ikinabúbuhay; **~ love** lumigaw; **~ room for** bigyáng-lugár; **~ sense** magkaroón ng kahulugán; **~ sure** tiyakín; **~ up one's mind** magpasiyá; **~ way** magparaán.
maker: *n*. manggagawâ, pabrikante.
malady: *n*. sakít, karamdaman.
malaria: *n*. malarya.
male: *n*. lalaki.
malevolent: *adj*. mapaghangád ng masamâ.
malice: *n*. malisya.
malignant: *adj*. napakasamâ, mapagpahamak.
mallet: *n*. maso.
malt: *n*. malta.
maltreat: *v*. magmalupít, magmalabís; **~ment** pagmamalupít, pagmamalabís.
mamma: *n*. nanay, ináy.
mammal: *n*. hayop na nagpapasuso.
man: *n*. lalaki, tao; mamà; **~hood** pagkalalaki, kalalakihan.
manacle: *n*. posas; *v*. posasan.
manage: *v*. mamahalà, mamatnugot, pumatnubay; **~ment** pángasiwaán, patnugután; **~r** *n*. tagapamahalà, tagapangasiwà; mayordomo.
mandate: *n*. kautusán, orden, atas.
mandatory: *adj*. sapilitán.
mane: *n*. kilíng.
manuever: *n*. maniobra; pakanâ.
mange: *n*. dusdós, galís-aso.
manger: *n*. sabsaban.
mangle: *v*. sirain, papagsugát-sugatín.
mango: *n*. manggá.
mangrove: *n*. bakawan.
manhood: *n*. kahusuháng-gulang, pagkalalaki.
mania: *n*. sumpóng, hangál na pagnanasà.
maniac: *n*. loko, balíw.
manifest: *v*. magpahalatâ, magpakilala; magpatunay.
manifesto: *n*. pahayag.
manioc: *n*. kamoteng kahoy.
manipulate: *v*. humawak, patakbuhín, magpaandár.
mankind: *n*. sangkatauhan.
manly: *adj*. parang lalaki, panlalaki.
mannequin: *n*. manekín, estatwá.
manner: *n*. paraán, pamamaraán, kilos, asal, gawî; ugalì.
manpower: *n*. lakás-tao.
mansion: *n*. malakíng bahay.
mantis: *n*. sasambá.
mantle: *n*. manta.
manual: *n*. manwál; *adj*. pangkamáy.
maunfacture: *v*. yumarì, gumawâ; lumikhâ.
manure: *n*. abono, patabâ.
manuscript: *n*. manuskrito.
many: *adj*. marami, napakarami; **~ many** magkano; **too ~** labis-labis; **twice as ~** ibayong dami.
map: *n*. mapa.
mar: *v*. sumirà, puminsalà; pagpangitin.

marauder: *n*. mandarambóng, magnanakaw.
marble: *n*. marmól; (*game*) holen; **~d ray** paging bulik.
march: *n*. (*month*) marso; (*marching*) martsa.
margarine: *n*. margarina.
margin: *n*. palugit; gilid, paligid.
marijuana: *n*. marihuwana.
marine: *adj*. ng dagat; *n*. marinero.
marital: *adj*. ng kasál.
mark: *n*. tandâ; gatlâ; guhit, marka.
marker: *n*. panandâ.
market: *n*. palengke, merkada, pamilihan; **~ price** *n*. presyo sa palengke; paktura.
marksman: *n*. manunudlâ; **~ship** *n*. punta-blangko.
marmalade: *n*. marmelada.
maroon: *v*. mápadpád; *adj*. kastanyáng ma-gulang.
marriage: *n*. pagkakasál, kasál.
married: *adj*. may-asawa, kasado.
marrow: *n*. utak sa butó.
marry: *v*. magkasál; magpakasál.
Mars: *n*. Marte.
marsh: *n*. latian, latì.
marshall: *n*. mariskál. **field ~** *n*. mariskál de kampo.
martyr: *n*. martír, mapagtiís; **~dom** pagma-martír.
marvelous: *adj*. kagilá-gilalás, kataká-taká.
mascot: *n*. wisit, maskot.
masculine: *adj*. parang lalaki, panlalaki.
mash: *v*. ligisín, masahin.
mask: *n*. máskara, balatkayô.
mason: *n*. kantero, masón.
masquerade: *n*. pagbabalatkayô.
mass: *n*. (*church*) misa; (*large quantity*) *n*. tumpók, buntón; (*of people*) pangkát; (*size*) lakí.
massacre: *n*. pagpuksà, pamumuksâ.
massage: *n*. hilot, masahe, himas, hagod.
massive: *adj*. malakí at mabigát.
mast: *n*. albór, palo ng bapór.
master: *n*. panginoón, punò; *v*. magpaka-dalubhasà, magpakasanay.
masterpiece: *n*. pinakamahusay ng gawâ, obra maestra.
masticate: *v*. ngumuyâ, ngumatâ.
masturbate: *v*. magsalsál.
mat: *n*. (*floor*) baníg; (*door*) kuskusan ng paá.
match: *n*. (*pair that fits*) pareha, tambál; (*game*) labanán; (*for lighting*) kasapuwego, pósporo; (*equal*) kasukát, kapareho; *v*. magpareha; bumagay; pagpaparis-parisin.
mate: *n*. kasama, katoto; asawa.
material: *n*. materyál, sangkáo, kagamitán; **~ist** *n*. taong-makalupà.
materialize: *v*. mangyari, maganáp, magka-totoó.
maternal: *adj*. makainá; sa iná.
maternity: *n*. pagka-iná.
math: *n*. matemátika.
matineé: *n*. panghapong palabás.
matriculation: *n*. matríkula.
matrix: *n*. matrís, bahay-batà.
matron: *n*. ginang; matrona.
matter: *n*. bagay; paksâ; halagá; kapakanán; *v*. mahalagahín; **it doesn't ~** dî bale; **no ~ what** kahit na anó.
mattress: *n*. kutsón.
mature: *adj*. ganáp na, hinóg; *v*. mahinog, gu-mulang.
maturity: *n*. kagánapan sa gulang; kahinugán; pagkatapós.
maul: *v*. mambugbóg, manggulpí.
maxim: *n*. salawikaín, kasabihán.
maximum: *adj*. pinakamarami, pinakamataás.
may: *n*. Mayo; *v*. maáarì, maka-; bakâ.
maybe: *adv*. bakâ, maáarìì, yatà, tila.
mayonnaise: *n*. mayonesa.
mayor: *n*. alkalde.
maze: *n*. kalituhán, kataranatahán.
me: *pron*. sa akin, akó.
meadow: *n*. parang, kaparangan; pastulan.
meager: *adj*. kakauntî, pahát.
meal: *n*. pagkain.
mean: *adj*. (*cranky*) magagalitín; (*stingy*) ku-ripot, maramot; *v*. mangahulugán.
meander: *v*. magpalikú-likô, lumibut-libot.
meaning: *n*. kahulugán; **~ful** makahulugán.
means: *n*. paraán, kaparaaanán, dahilán.
meantime: *adv*. samantala, habang.
meanwhile: *adv*. samantala.
measles: *n*. tigdás, tukô.
measure: *v*. sukatin, sukatan; *n*. hakbáng, pa-

nukat; medida.
measurement: *n.* pagsukat, sukat.
meat: *n.* karne.
meaty: *adj.* makarne, malamán; makahulugán.
mechanic: *n.* mekániko; **~al** yaring-mákiná.
mechanism: *n.* mekanismo, kayarian, kabuuán.
medal: *n.* medalya.
meddle: *v.* makialám, manghimasok; **~some** pakiálamin, mapanghimasok.
median: *n.* panggitnâ, kalahatián.
mediate: *v.* mamagitan; magnilay-nilay.
mediator: *n.* tagapamagitan.
medicinal: *adj.* panggamót, naigagamót.
medicine: *n.* gamót, medisina; panlunas.
mediocre: *adj.* kainaman, katamtaman; karaniwan.
meditate: *v.* magnilaynilay, magmuni-munì.
medium: *adj.* kaayusan, katamtaman, katatagán.
medley: *n.* halu-halong klase, samut-sarì.
meek: *adj.* maamò, mababang-loób.
meet: *v.* magkasalubong; magtagpô; magkakilala; magpulong.
meeting: *n.* pagtatagpô, pagkikita; pagkikilala.
melancholy: *adj.* malumbáy, malungkót, mapangláw.
mellow: *adj.* malambót; lunót.
melody: *n.* himig, melodya.
melon: *n.* melón.
melt: *v.* matunaw, malusaw.
member: *n.* kasapì, kaanib, miyembro; kagawad; **~ship** pagkakásapì; pag-anib.
membrane: *n.* lamad.
memoir: *n.* talaarawán.
memorial: *adj.* alaala, pang-alaala.
memorize: *v.* sauluhin, isaulo, memoryahín.
memory: *n.* memorya, alaala, gunitâ.
men: *n.* mga lalaki, mga tao.
menace: *n.* panganib, bantâ.
mend: *v.* magkumpuní, magsulsí; (*net*) maghayuma.
mendicant: *n.* pulubi, nagpapalimos.
menopause: *n.* ménopós.
menses: *n.* regla, sapanahón.
menstruation: *n.* regla, sapanahón.
mental: *adj.* pang-isip; pandiwà; **~ity** *n.* pagiisip, kaisipán.
mention: *v.* bumanggít, tumukoy.
mentor: *n.* tagapayo.
menu: *n.* mga putahe, menú.
meow: *n.* ngiyáw; *v.* ngumiyáw.
merchandise: *n.* kalakal, panindá.
merchant: *n.* komersyante, mangangalakál, magtitingì.
merciful: *adj.* maawaín, mahábagin.
mercury: *n.* asoge, merkuryo.
mercy: *n.* awà, habág; **have ~** *v.* maawà.
mere: *adj.* lamang, galos lamang.
merge: *v.* isama, ipisan; mag-isá.
merger: *n.* pag-iisá, pagsama-sama.
merit: *n.* kabutihan, kagalingan, mérito; *v.* marapat, marapatin.
mermaid: *n.* sirena.
merry: *adj.* masayá, maligaya; **~-go-round** *n.* tiyubibo.
mesh: *n.* butas, matá.
mesmerize: *v.* hipnotismuhín.
mess: *n.* guló; marumíng ayos.
message: *n.* pahatíd, pasabi, bilin, mensahe.
messenger: *n.* mensahero, sugò.
messy: *adj.* maguló, waláng-ayos.
mestizo: *n.* mestiso.
metabolism: *n.* metabolismo, pagsunog ng pagkain sa katawán.
metal: *n.* metál.
metaphor: *n.* talinghagà, metápora.
metaplasm: *n.* pagbabagu-bago.
metathesis: *n.* maylipat.
meteor: *n.* bululakaw, taeng-bituín.
meter: *n.* metro.
method: *n.* paraán, pamamaraán, kaparaanán.
meticulous: *adj.* maselang, delikado; mabusisì, makurirì.
mezzanine: *n.* entresuwelo.
miaow: *n.* ngiyáw; *v.* ngumiyáw.
microbe: *n.* mikrobiyo.
microscope: *n.* mikroskopyo.
mid: *adj.* panggitnâ; **~day** tanghalì.
middle: *n.* gitnâ, kalagitnaan; kalahatián; **~ aged** nasa katamtamang gulang.
midget: *n.* bulitít, unano.
midnight: *n.* hatinggabí.
midst: *n.* gitnâ.
midway: *adj.* sa pagitan, hating-daán.

midwife: *n*. komadrona, hilot.
might: *n*. lakás, kapangyarihan; *v*. maárì, bakâ; **~y** *adj*. napakalakás, napakalakí.
migrant: *n*. dayuhan; *adj*. galâ.
migrate: *v*. dumayo, magibáng-bayan.
mild: *adj*. maamò, mahinahon; kainaman; malumanay.
mildew: *n*. amag, tagulamín.
mile: *n*. milya.
militant: *adj*. mapanlabán, mapandigmâ.
military: *n*. hukbó; *adj*. pandigmâ, panghukbó.
milk: *n*. gatas; **coconut ~** gatâ; *v*. gatasan; **~y Way** pulóng-bituín, ariwanas.
milkfish: *n*. bangós, banglós.
milkman: *n*. maggagatás.
mill: *n*. gilingán, kiskisan, kabyawan.
millet: *n*. dawa.
million: *n*. angaw, milyón.
mimic: *v*. tumulad, gumaya.
mimosa: *n*. makahiyâ, mimosa.
minaret: *n*. minarete.
mince: *v*. magtadtád; **~meat** pikadilyo; tinadtád na karne.
mind: *n*. isipan, isip; katalinuhan; *v*. mag-ingat; mag-alagà, asikasuhin; **change one's ~** magbago ng isip; **keep in ~** tandaan; **on one's mind** nasa isip.
mine: *pron*. sa akin, ko; *n*. mina; *v*. magmina, minahin.
miner: *n*. minero.
mingle: *v*. humalò, makisalamuhà, makisama, makiharáp, makihalò, makihalo-bilò.
miniature: *adj*. maliít, muntî
minimum: *adj*. pinakakauntî, pinakamaliít.
minister: *n*. ministro; pastór.
minor: *adj*. di-lubháng mahalagá; *n*. menor.
minority: *n*. minoryá, kakauntî.
minstrel: *n*. trobadór; manganganta, kantór.
mint: *n*. menta; gawaán ng salapî.
minus: *adj*. may-bawas, kulang.
minute: *n*. minuto; *adj*. muntíng-muntî; **-s** (*of meeting*) katitikan, akta.
miracle: *n*. milagro, kababalaghán.
mirage: *n*. malikmatà.
mire: *n*. pusalì, burak, lusak, putikan.
mirror: *n*. salamín.
mis- *prep*. malí, masamâ.
misappropriate: *v*. lumustáy, lustayín.
misbehave: *v*. magmasamáng-asal.
miscarriage: *n*. agas, pagkakuha, pagkalaglág.
miscellaneous: *n*. halu-halò.
mischief: *n*. kapílyuhán, kalikután.
mischievous: *adj*. malikó, pilyo, mapagbirô.
miser: *n*. kuripot na tao.
miserable: *adj*. abáng-abâ, kulang-palad.
misery: *n*. kahirapan, pagdaralitâ.
misfit: *n*. di-kasukát.
misfortune: *n*. sakunâ; kasawian.
mishap: *n*. aksidente, kapahamakán, kasawian, sakunâ.
misjudge: *v*. humatol nang pamalî; magkámalî ng tantiyá.
misinterpretation: *n*. malíng pakahulugán.
mislead: *v*. magligáw; magpasamâ; dumayà.
misplace: *v*. iwaklî, iwaglít.
misrepresent: *v*. maglarawan nang pamalì.
miss: *v*. di-tumamà; di-makuha; di-umabot; *n*. binibini; sala, mintís; di-pag-abot.
missing: *adj*. kulang, nagkukulang; nawawalâ.
mission: *n*. pakay, misyón, sadyâ.
missionary: *n*. misyonero.
mist: *n*. dagím, ulap, ambón.
mistake: *n*. kamalî, malî.
mister: *n*. ginoó.
mistreat: *v*. taratuhin nang masamâ.
mistress: *n*. maybahay; kerida.
mistrust: *n*. alinlangan, duda, kawalán ng tiwalà; *v*. mawalán ng tiwalà, paghinalaan.
mitigate: *v*. magpagaán, magpahupâ, bawahan.
mitigating: *adj*. nagpápagaán; **~ circumstances** mga pangyayaring nagpápagaán.
mitten: *n*. guwantes.
mix: *v*. haluin, isama; magkahalò; **~-up** kagúluhan, kagúsutan.
mixture: *n*. timplá, pinaghalò; paglalahók, paghahalò.
moan: *v*. humalinghíng, tumaghóy, humaluyhóy.
mob: *n*. makapál na tao; *v*. pagkaguluhán; dumugin.
mobile: *adj*. napakikilos, napagagaláw.
mobilize: *v*. magtipun-tipon, mag-ipun-ipon; pakilusin.
mock: *v*. manggagád, gagarín; magtawá.

mockery: *n.* panunuyâ, pangungutyâ, katatawanán; pagkutyâ.
modal: (*gram.*) *n.* anyóng pamaraán.
mode: *n.* paraán; kalakarán; (*grammar*) panagano.
model: *n.* modelo, huwaran, tularán; *v.* imolde, ihugis.
moderate: *adj.* kainanman, katamtaman, mahinahon.
modern: *adj.* moderno, makabago.
modest: *adj.* mababang-loób, mahiyain, kaigihan; mahinhín; mapágpakumbabâ; **~y** *n.* pagkamahinhín, kahinhinán.
modifier: *n.* (*gram.*) panturing, panuring.
modify: *v.* bumago; tumuring.
moist: *adj.* mamasá-masâ, malagihay.
moisture: *n.* halumigmíg.
molar: *n.* bagáng.
molasses: *n.* pulót.
mold: *n.* molde, hulmá; hugis; amag, tagulamín; *v.* móldihín; hubugin; **~ing** *n.* moldura; paghuhulmá; paghubog.
moldy: *adj.* amagin, may-amag.
mole: *n.* nunál, lunár, taling.
molest: *v.* abalahin, istorbohín.
mollusk: *n.* molusko.
molly fish: *n.* bubuntís.
molt: *v.* malugon; maghunos.
moment: *n.* sandalî, saglít.
monarch: *n.* monarka, harì.
monastery: *n.* monsteryo.
Monday: *n.* Lunes.
monetary: *adj.* ng salapî.
money: *n.* kuwarta, salapî; ~ **box** alkansiyá; ~ **order** hiro postál.
monitor: *n.* mónitor.
monk: *n.* monghe.
monkey: *n.* tsunggo, unggóy; ~ **wrench** liyabe.
monopolize: *v.* sarilinin, monopolisahín.
monopoly: *n.* monopolyo, pagsarili.
monosodium glutamate: *n.* betsín.
monosyllabic: *adj.* sampantíg.
monosyllable: *n.* íisáng pantíg.
monster: *n.* napakalakíng hayop; (*sea*) dambuhalà; (*wild beast*) halimaw.
monstrous: *adj.* kasindák-sindák, nakatátakot; nápakalakí.
month: *n.* buwán.
monument: *n.* bantayog, monumento.
moo: *v.* umungâ, umungal.
mood: *n.* lagáy ng loób, kalagayan, kalooban; (*grammar*) panagano.
moody: *adj.* sumpungin.
moon: *n.* buwán; **full** ~ kabilugan ng buwán.
mop: *n.* lampaso, panlampaso.
mope: *v.* manamláy.
moral: *n.* aral, liksiyón; (*morals*) ugalì, kilos, asal.
morality: *n.* moralidád; kalinisang-asal.
moray: *n.* malabanos, payangitan, pinangitan.
morbid: *adj.* di-mabuti, masamâ; may-sakít.
more: *adj.* lalò, mas, higít.
moreover: *adv.* bukód diyán; tangì sa riyán.
morgue: *n.* morge.
morning: *n.* umaga.
moron: *n.* tangá, tunggák.
morose: *adj.* malumbáy, sumpungin.
morphine: *n.* morpina.
morsel: *n.* subò, kapiraso.
mortal: *adj.* malubhâ, nakamamatáy; **~ity** pagkakamatáy.
mortar: *n.* lusóng, almirés.
mortgage: *n.* sanglâ, pagkakasanglâ; *v.* isanglâ.
mortuary: *n.* morge, punerarya.
mosquito: *n.* lamók; ~ **larva** *n.* kikinsót, kitikití; ~ **net** kulambô, moskitero.
moss: *n.* lumot; **~y** *adj.* malumot, lúmutin.
most: *adj.* pinaka-, ang karamihan.
motel: *n.* motél.
moth: *n.* gamugamó, tangà.
mother: *n.* iná, ináy, mamá; **~hood** pagka-iná; ~ **of pearl** nakar.
motion: *n.* kilos, galáw; mungkahì; **~less** *adj.* di-gumágaláw.
motivate: *v.* ibuyós, udyukán, ganyakín.
motivation: *n.* pagganyák, pangganyák.
motive: *n.* motibo, layon, hángarin.
motor: *n.* motor, mákina; **~boat** bangkang demotór.
motorcycle: *n.* motorsiklo.
motto: *n.* sawikaín, kasabihán.
mound: *n.* buntón, tambák.
mount: *v.* umakyá, sumakáy; magdikít; *n.* bundók.

mountain: *n.* bundók; **~ous** bulubundukin, mabundók; **~ bass** damagan, lamayan; **~ climbing** *n.* barangka.
mourn: *v.* magdalamhatì, mamighatî, mahapis; ikalumbáy.
mouse: *n.* dagâ; **~trap** panhuli ng dagâ.
moustache: *n.* bigote.
mouth: *n.* bibíg; bungangà; **~ful** sansubò; **~piece** bokilya, ilipán, pambibíg.
movable: *adj.* nagagaláw, napagagaláw.
move: *v.* ilipat; bumago; gumaláw; *n.* kilos, galáw, kulusán; (*in games*) tira, sulong; **~ment** galáw, kibô, kilos.
movie: *n.* sine, pelíkula.
mow: *v.* magtabás, gumapas.
much: *adj.* marami, malakí.
mucus: *n.* uhog.
mud: *n.* putik; **~dy** maputik; **~guard** tapaludo.
muddle: *v.* lituhín, guluhín.
muffle: *v.* balutan, balutin, suklubán; **~r** *n.* bupanda; mapler, pamatáy-tunóg.
mug: *n.* taro, saro, tabò.
muggy: *adj.* maalinsangan.
mugwort: *n.* kamariya, damóng-mariya.
mule: *n.* mula.
mullet: *n.* banak; agwás, asubi, bilugan, kapak, lumitog, tandipil.
multiple: *adj.* napakarami.
multiplicative: (*gram.*) *n.* pang-uring palambál.
multiply: *v.* multiplikahín; dumami.
multitude: *n.* karamihang tao; kawan.
mumble: *v.* bumulúng-bulóng.
mummy: *n.* mómiya.
mumps: *n.* baikì, bikì.
munch: *v.* ngumalót.
mundane: *adj.* makalupà, makamundó.
municipality: *n.* munisipyo, bayan.
munition: *n.* armás, kagamitáng-digmâ.
mural: *n.* miyural.
murder: *n.* pagpatáy sa tao; *v.* pumatáy ng tao; **~er** *n.* mamamatay-tao; **~ous** makamamatáy, pamatáy.
murky: *adj.* madilím.
murmur: *n.* lagaslás, aliw-iw; *v.* bumubulóng, umanás.
murrel fish: *n.* bundaki, bundalag, dalag, bakuli.
muscle: *n.* lamán, kalamnán.
muscular: *adj.* maskulado, malamán, matipunô.
muse: *n.* paraluman, diwatà, lakambini.
museum: *n.* museo.
mush: *n.* lugaw.
mushroom: *n.* kabuté; *v.* sumulpót.
music: *n.* músika; tugtugin; **~al** ng músika; **~ian** musikero, manunugtóg.
mussel: *n.* tahóng, paros, kabyâ.
must: *v.* kailangan, nararapat.
mustache: *n.* bigote; misáy.
mustard: *n.* mustasa.
muster: *v.* ipunin; gisingin.
mute: *adj.* pipi; waláng-imík.
mutilate: *v.* putulin ang paá; sumirà.
mutineer: *n.* manghihimagsík.
mutiny: *n.* pag-aalsá, paghihimagsík.
mutter: *v.* magbubulóng.
mutton: *n.* karne ng tupa.
mutual: *adj.* damayán, nagdadamayán; sa isá't isá.
muzzle: *n.* ngusò; busál.
my: *pron.* ko, sa akin; **~self** aking sarili.
myrrh: *n.* mira.
mysterious: *adj.* mahiwagà; kataká-taká.
mystery: *n.* hiwagà, lihim.
mystify: *v.* papagtakhín.
myth: *n.* alamát, kathá-kathâ; **~ical** *adj.* likhâ, gawá-gawâ; **~ology** *n.* palaalamatán, mitolohiya.

N

nab: *v.* sunggabán; dakpín.
nadir: *n.* pinakamababang lugár.
nag: *v.* murahin, yamutín.
nail: *n.* (*peg*) pakò; (*finger, toe*) kukó; *v.* magpakò.
naive: *adj.* musmós, waláng-malay; **~te** *n.* kamusmusán.
naked: *adj.* hubó't-hubád; waláng-takíp; **~ness** pagkahubót't-hubád, kahubuán, kahubarán, kahubdán; **~ truth** payák na katotóhanan.
name: *n.* ngalan, pangalan; tawag; pamagát; **~less** waláng-ngalan; di kilalá; **~sake** *n.*

tokayo, kapangalan.
nap: *n*. idlíp, siyesta.
nape: *n*. batok.
napkin: *n*. serbilyeta.
narcotic: *n*. narkótiko.
narrate: *v*. magkuwento, magsalaysáy; **narrative** *n*. salaysáy, kuwento.
narrator: *n*. tagapagsalaysáy.
narrow: *adj*. makitid, makipot; ~ **minded** makitid ang isip; ~**ness** kakiputan, kakitiran.
nasal: *adj*. ng ilóng, galing sa ilóng.
nastiness: *n*. kadirihan, pandidiri.
nasty: *adj*. nakapandidiri, napakarumí, masagwâ, karimá-rimarim.
nation: *n*. bansá, bayan, nasyón; ~**al** *adj*. pambansâ; ~**alism** *n*. pagkamakabayan; ~-**alist** nasyonalista, taong makabansâ; ~**ality** *n*. kabansaán; ~**alize** *v*. magsabansâ; ~-**wide** sa buóng bansâ; ~**ization** *n*. pagsasabansâ; ~**hood** pagkabansâ.
native: *n*. tubò sa isáng bansâ, katutubò, taál.
natural: *adj*. likás, naturál; ~**ize** *v*. naturalisahín; ~ **resources** likás na kayamanan, rekursos naturales; ~**ist** naturalista.
nature: *n*. kalikasan; sariling katangian.
naughty: *adj*. malikót, pilyo, saragate, masuwayin.
nausea: *n*. alibadbád, alimbukáy, pagkáduwál; ~**te** makapagpaalibadbád.
naval: *adj*. pandagat; nabál.
navel: *n*. pusod.
navigate: *v*. umigit, mamiloto; maglayág.
navigator: *n*. nabigadór, nabigante, piloto.
navy: *n*. hukbóng-dagat; ~ **blue** asúl marino.
nay: *adv*. hindî.
near: *adj*. malapit; ~**ly** *adv*. halos; ~**by** malapit; ~ **sightedness** *n*. korta-bista.
neat: *adj*. maayos; ~**ness** kaayusan, kalinisan.
nebulous: *adj*. malabò.
necessary: *adj*. kailangan.
necessity: *n*. pangangailangan, kailangan.
neck: *n*. leég.
neckerchief: *n*. bupanda.
necklace: *n*. kuwintás.
nectar: *n*. nektár.
necktie: *n*. kurbata.
need: *n*. kawalán, kakulangán; *v*. kailangan; ~-**less to say** sabihin pa.
needle: *n*. karayom.
needlework: *n*. pananahî; pagbuburda.
needy: *adj*. nangángailangan; maralitâ, dukhâ, dahóp; mahirap.
nefarious: *adj*. kasuklám-suklám, karumaldumal.
negate: *v*. itanggí, ipagkailâ.
negation: *n*. pagtanggí, pagkakailâ.
negative: *n*. pagtanggí; *adj*. negatibo; salungát; tutol.
neglect: *v*. pabayaan, pagkulangan; ~**ful** *adj*. pabayâ.
negligent: *adj*. mapagpabayâ.
negotiate: *v*. makipag-ayos, makipag-areglo, makipagkasundô.
Negrito: *n*. Ita.
neigh: *n*. halinghíng.
neighbor: *n*. kapitbahay, kahanggá; ~**ing country** kapitbansâ; ~**hood** magkakapitbahay.
neither: *adv*. alinmá'y hindî; ~**... nor...** ni.. ni...
neophyte: *n*. bagito, baguhan.
nephew: *n*. pamangkíng-lalaki.
nepotism: *n*. nepotismo.
nerve: *n*. nerbyos; lakás ng loób.
nervous: *adj*. ninenerbiyos, kinakabahán.
nest: *n*. pugad; ~**egg** paing-itlóg; *v*. magpugad.
nestle: *v*. sumalagmák.
nestling: *n*. inakáy.
net: *n*. lambát; *v*. tubuin; magtubò; **mosquito** ~ kulambô, muskitero; **insect** ~ sakyód; ~ **profit** neto; ~**ting** lalambatin, alambreng matá-matá.
nettle: *n*. kulitis.
neuralgia: *n*. neuralhiyá.
neuter: *adj*. waláng-kasarian; (*gram*.) balakì.
neutral: *adj*. neutral, waláng-kinikilingan.
never: *adv*. hindî kailanmán; ~**theless** gayunmán.
new: *adj*. bago; ~**born** kasisilang; ~**comer** bagong-datíng.
news: *n*. balità.
newspaper: *n*. peryódiko, diyaryo, pahayagán; ~ **clipping** *n*. rekorte.
next: *adj*. kasunód, sumusunód; ~ **door** sa kahanggá.
nibble: *v*. magkukót.

nice: *adj*. kalugúd-lugód, angkóp; mahusay.
niche: *n*. nitso, butas.
nick: *v*. bumingaw, pumingas; *n*. gatlâ; **in the ~ of time** hustung-hustó sa oras.
nickel: *n*. nikél; *v*. magnikelá.
nickname: *n*. palayaw; *v*. palayawan.
nicotine: *n*. nikotina.
niece: *n*. pamangkíng-babae.
night: *n*. gabí; *adj*. panggabí; **every ~** gabí-gabí; **~fall** takíp-silim.
nightingale: *n*. ruwisenyór.
nightmare: *n*. bangungot, uóm.
nil: *n*. walâ.
nimble: *adj*. mabilís, maliksí.
nine: *n*. siyám, nuwebe; **~teen** labinsiyám; **~ty** siyamnapû, nobenta.
nip: *v*. kitilín; kagatín; kumurót.
nipple: *n*. (*bottle*) tetilya, tsupón; (*teat*) utóng.
nit: *n*. lisâ.
no: *adv*. hindî, dî; walâ.
nobility: *n*. kamaharlikaán; pagkamaharlikâ.
noble: *adj*. maharlikâ, marangál; **~ness** *n*. kamarharlikaán.
nobody: *pron*. waláng sinumán.
nocturnal: *adj*. panggabí.
nod: *v*. tumangô; *n*. tangô.
node: *n*. bukó, bukol.
noise: *n*. kaingayan, linggál, inggay; **noisy** *adj*. maingay.
nomad: *n*. pagalà, lagalág, layás.
nominal: (*gram*.) *adj*. makangalan.
nominate: *v*. hirangin.
nominative: *adj*. palagyô; **~ case** *n*. kaukuláng palagyô.
nonchalant: *adj*. waláng-bahalà, walâ sa loób.
none: *pron*. walâ.
nonplus: *v*. malitó.
nonsense: *n*. kalokohan, katarantaduhan.
nonstop: *adj*. waláng-hintô.
noodle: *n*. pansít, miki, bihon; **~ house** *n*. pansitiryá, pansitan.
nook: *n*. sulok.
noon: *n*. tanghalì.
noose: *n*. silò.
nor: *conj*. ni.
norm: *n*. pamantayan, karaniwan.
normal: *adj*. karaniwan, katamtaman.
north: *n*. hilagà; **~ernmost** *adj*. kahila-hilagaan; **~ward** pahilagâ.
nose: *n*. ilóng; *v*. mangamóy, magmanmán; **~bleed** balinguyngóy; **~dive** bulusok; **~fish** isdáng-ilóng.
nostril: *n*. butas ng ilóng.
not: *adv*. hindî.
notable: *adj*. tanyág, litáw; dakilà.
notary: *n*. notaryo.
notch: *n*. gatgát, gatlâ, kutab.
note: *n*. talâ, nota; puná; **~book** kuwaderno, aklát-sulatán.
nothing: *pron*. walâ.
notice: *v*. pumansin, pansinín, pumuná; *n*. pansín; **~able** kapansín-pansín.
notify: *v*. magbigáy-alam, magpatalastás.
notion: *n*. pagkaunawà, hakà; palagáy.
notorious: *adj*. bantóg sa kasamaán.
notwithstanding: *prep*. sa kabilâ ng.
noun: *n*. pangngalan; **common ~** *n*. pangngalang pambálana; **proper ~** *n*. pangngalang pantangì; **verbal ~** *n*. pangngalang pandiwarì; **~ phrase** *n*. pangngalang pariralà.
nourish: *v*. buhayin, palusugín; pakanin; **~ment** pagkain.
novel: *n*. nobela, kathambuhay; **~ist** mangangat-hambuhay.
November: *n*. Nobyembre.
novice: *n*. bagito, baguhan.
now: *adv*. ngayón; **~adays** sa panahóng itó.
nowhere: *adv*. walâ saanmán.
noxious: *adj*. nakakalason; nakapipinsalang lubhâ.
nozzle: *n*. bakilya; ngusò ng gripo.
nude: *adj*. hubó't hubád.
nudge: *v*. sikuhín.
nudist: *n*. kakalók.
nugget: *n*. tipák.
nuisance: *n*. kayamut-yamót; buwisit.
null: *adj*. waláng-bisà, waláng-halagá; **~ify** *v*. magpawaláng-bisà.
numb: *adj*. manhíd, waláng-pakiramdám; **~ness** pamamanhíd.
number: *n*. bilang.
numerous: *adj*. napakarami, marami.
nun: *n*. madre, mongha.
nuncio: *n*. núnsiyo; sugò ng Papa.

nuptial: *adj.* ng kasál.
nurse: *n.* nars; *v.* magpasuso; mag-alagà ng maysakít.
nursemaid: *n.* yaya.
nurture: *n.* pagpapalakí, pag-aalagà.
nut: *n.* nuwés; **~shell** balát ng nuwés.
nutmeg: *n.* nuwés moskada.
nutrient: *n.* pagkaing nakapagpálusóg.
nutritious: *adj.* pampalusóg, masustansiya.
nuzzle: *v.* sumungkál.
nylon: *n.* naylon.
nymph: *n.* nimpa, diwatà.

O

oaf: *n.* tunggák, ungás.
oar: *n.* gaod.
oasis: *n.* oasis.
oat: *n.* obena; **~meal** otmíl, nilugaw na obena.
oath: *n.* sumpâ, panunumpâ.
obedient: *adj.* masunurin; **obedience** *n.* pagsunód, pagtalima.
obese: *adj.* napakatabâ.
obey: *v.* sumunód, sundín; talimahin.
obituary: *n.* obitwaryo.
object: *n.* bagay; paksâ; (*gramm.*) layon; *v.* tuutol, sumalungát.
objective: *n.* layon, nilalayon.
oligate: *v.* ubligahín; **obligation** *n.* ubligasiyón, katungkulan; **obligatory** *adj.* sapilitán, kinakailangan.
oblige: *v.* ubligahín; pilitin.
oblique: *adj.* pahiwíd, pahilíg, tagilíd, pairáp.
obliterate: *v.* burahín, pawiin.
oblivion: *n.* paglimot.
oblivious: *adj.* di-alintana, di-alumana.
oblong: *adj.* pahabâ.
obnoxious: *adj.* nakasusuklám, nakasusuyà.
obscene: *adj.* masagwâ, mahalay.
obscure: *adj.* malabò; tagô; madilím.
obsequious: *adj.* napaalipin, masuyò, mapagmapurí, sipsip.
observe: *v.* pumansín, pumuná; siyasitin, bantayán; **observance** *n.* pagtupád, pagmamasíd, pagmamatyág; **observant** *adj.* mapagmasíd, mapagmatyág, mapúnahin, mapánsinin.
obsession: *n.* himaling.
obsolete: *n.* lipás na, laós na.
obstacle: *n.* hadláng, halang, sagwíl, sagabal.
obstinate: *adj.* matigás ang ulo, sutíl.
obstruct: *v.* hadlangán, harangan, barahan, sagwilán.
obtain: *v.* kunin, kamtán, tamuhín.
obvious: *adj.* maliwanag, halatâ, nauunawaan.
occasion: *n.* pagkakataon, okasyón, pagdiriwang.
occasionally: *adv.* paminsan-minsan, manakánakâ.
occidental: *adj.* kanluranín, ng kanluran.
occiput: *n.* kukote, pilipot.
occult: *adj.* lihim, mahiwagà.
ocupant: *n.* nakatirá.
occupation: *n.* tungkulin, hanap-buhay; okupasyón.
occupied: *adj.* may-tao, may-nakatirá; okupado.
occupy: *v.* sumakláw, umokupá; sumakop.
occur: *v.* mangyari, maganáp, mataón; **~rence** *n.* pangyayari.
ocean: *n.* dagat, karagatan.
o'clock: *adj.* alas-
October: *n.* Oktubre.
octopus: *n.* pugità, salabay.
odd: *adj.* kabiyák, waláng-kaparis; kakaibá, kakatwâ; butál.
odds: *n.* kahigtán, kalamangán.
ode: *n.* oda.
odious: *adj.* nakapopoót, kamuhí-muhî.
odor: *n.* amóy; **~ous** may-amoy, maamóy.
of: *prep.* ni; ng; sa, yarì sa.
off: *adv.* mulâ sa; walâ sa; tanggál; **~ and on** manaká-nakâ; **turn ~** patayín; **wear ~** magasgás; **lay ~** magbawas; **see someone ~** maghatíd.
offend: *v.* sumugat ng damdamin; galitin; **~er** *n.* makasalanan, maysala.
offense: *n.* kasalanan, paglabág.
offensive: *adj.* nakagagalit, pampagalit; pansalakay, pang-atake.
offer: *v.* maghandóg, ialay; *n.* paghahandóg, pag-aalók.
offering: *n.* paghahandóg, pag-aalay, abuloy.
offhand: *adj.* biglaan; di-inihandâ.

office: *n.* tungkulin; opisina; **~r** pinunò, pamunuán.
official: *adj.* opisyál, pantungkulin; *n.* punò, opisiyál.
officiate: *v.* tumupád ng tungkulin.
offing: *n.* laot.
offset: *v.* magpagaán, magpaginhawa, magpaluwág.
offshoot: *n.* suplíng, supang, suloy.
offshore: *adj.* malayò sa pampáng.
offspring: *n.* mga anák; suplíng.
often: *adv.* malimit, madalás.
ogre: *n.* halimaw, dambuhalà.
oil: *n.* langís; **~ cloth** uli; **~er** asetera; **~y** malangís.
oilstone: *n.* hasaán (ng labaha).
ointment: *n.* ungguwento, pamahid.
o.k.: *adj.* ayos.
okra: *n.* okrá.
old: *adj.* matandâ; lumà; (*former*) dati; **~ fashioned** makalumà, lipás; **~-timer** datihan.
oligarch: *n.* oligarka.
olive: *n.* oliba.
omelette: *n.* torta.
omen: *n.* babalâ, tandâ, pangitain.
omission: *n.* nakaligtaán, di-pagsasama.
omit: *n.* laktawán, iwan, kaligtaán.
omnipotence: *n.* waláng-hanggáng kapangyarihan.
omnipotent: *adj.* makapangyarihan.
on: *prep.* nasa, sa ibabaw.
once: *adv.* minsan; **~ in a while** paminsan-minsan; **~ upon a time** minsan, noóng araw.
oncoming: *adj.* palapit; dumarating.
one: *n.* isá, uno; **~ each** tig-isá; **~ness** kaisahán; **~ sided** may-kinikilingan; **~ way** waláng-salubong.
oneself: *n.* sarili.
onion: *n.* sibuyas; lasuná.
onlooker: *n.* ang nanónoód.
only: *adv.* lamang; tangì; bugtóng.
onset: *n.* simulâ; lusob.
onslaught: *n.* mabangís na salakay.
onto: *prep.* sa.
onward: *adv.* pasulóng, patuloy.
ooze: *v.* dumaloy, tumagas.
opal: *n.* ópalo.
open: *v.* buksán; bumukás; *adj.* bukás, buká; **~er** pambukás; **~ing** *n.* butas, puwáng; **~ minded** bukás ang isip.
opera: *n.* ópera.
operate: *v.* magpaandár, magmaneho; umandár.
operation: *n.* andár, takbó; (*medical*) operasiyón.
operator: *n.* aparatista; tagapamahalà.
opinion: *n.* palagáy, kuru-kurò.
opium: *n.* apyan, opyo.
opponent: *n.* kalaban, katalo, katunggalî.
opportune: *adj.* nápapanahón.
opportunity: *n.* pagkakataon, oportunidád.
oppose: *v.* sumalungát, kontrahín, tutulan.
opposite: *adj.* kasalungát, kalaban; katapát.
opposition: *n.* pakikilaban, paglaban.
oppress: *v.* maniíl, apihín; pagmalupitán; **~ive** *adj.* mapagpahirap, malupít; **~ion** *n.* pagmamalupít, pagsiíl, pang-aapí.
opt: *n.* pumilì.
optical: *adj.* ng matá.
optician: *n.* óptiko.
optimist: *n.* optimista; **~ism** *n.* optimismo.
option: *n.* opsiyóng, karapatán.
optional: *adj.* opsiyonál, di-sapilitán.
opulent: *adj.* mayaman, mariwasâ.
or: *conj.* o; **~ otherwise** o kayá'y.
oracle: *n.* orákulo.
oral: *adj.* pasalitâ; ng bibíg; binibigkás; **~ tradition** *n.* tradisyong salimbibíg.
orange: *n.* dalandán, kahél.
orangutan: *n.* oranggutáng.
oration: *n.* talumpatì, diskurso.
orbit: *n.* landás ng mundó.
orchard: *n.* laguerta.
orchestra: *n.* orkestra.
orchid: *n.* dapò, orkidia.
ordain: *v.* ordenán, ilagdâ, iatas.
ordeal: *n.* mahigpít na pagsubok.
order: *v.* utusan, atasan, ordenán; *n.* orden, utos; (*arrangement*) pagkakasunúd-sunód; **~ly** maayos; **put in ~** ayusin.
ordinal: (*gram.*) *n.* pang-uring pánunuran.
ordinance: *n.* ordenansa, kautusán.
ordinary: *adj.* karaniwan.
organ: *n.* (*musical instrument*) órgano; (*func-*

tional part of animal) bahagi, sangkáp.
organdy: *n*. organdí.
organization: *n*. pagbuô; kapisanan, samahán.
organize: *v*. itatag, ipundár, itayô.
orgy: *n*. kawaláng-habas, lasingan; paglalabis sa pagtatalik.
orient: *n*. silangan; *v*. mamihasa; bihasahin; **~al** *adj*. sílanganín; **~ation** pag-aangkóp.
origin: *n*. simulâ, umpisá; dahilán; ninunò; **~ate** magsimulâ; manggaling.
original: *adj*. kauna-unahan; bago; *n*. orihinál, pinagparisan; **~ity** *n*. orihinalidád, kasarilinan.
ornament: *n*. palamuti; dingal; **~al** pampalamuti, pang-adorno.
ornate: *adj*. gayák, maadorno, mapalamuti.
ornithology: *n*. paláibunan.
orphan: *n*. ulila; **~age** bahay-ampunan; pagkaulila.
orthodox: *adj*. tinatanggáp, kinikilala.
orthography: *n*. palabaybayan, ortograpía, palátitikán.
oscillate: *v*. umugóy, dumuyan-duyan.
ostentatious: *adj*. mapagparangyâ, mapagpasikat, mapágpakitang-tao.
ostracize: *v*. ipatapon; layuán, itakwíl.
ostrich: *n*. abestrús.
other: *adj*. ibá; **every ~** tuwíng ikalawá; **~wise** ibá; sa ibáng pagkakátaón; **~ than** bukod sa; **on the ~ hand** sa isáng bandá.
ouch: *interj*. aráy!
ought: *v*. dapat, kailangan.
ounce: *n*. onsa.
our: *adj*. atin, natin; namin, amin.
ours: *pron*. atin; amin.
ourselves: *pron*. aming sarili, ating sarili.
oust: *v*. palayasin, tanggalín.
out: *adj*. walâ sa; malî; (*in the open*) litáw; **~bound** paalís; **~ of fashion** ilpás sa moda; **~ and ~** pusakál; **~ dated** lipás sa panahón.
outbreak: *n*. silakbó, pagsikláb.
outburst: *n*. pagbulalás.
outcast: *n*. tapon, palaboy.
outcome: *n*. bunga, resulta, kinahinatnán, kinahantungán.
outcry: *n*. palaháw, sigawan.
outdated: *adj*. lipás na sa moda.
outdo: *v*. madaíg, mahigtán, tumalo.
outdoors: *adj*. sa labás.
outer: *adj*. panlabás; **~most** pinakamalayò, nasa kalayuan.
outfit: *n*. gamit, sangkap; pangkáp.
outgrow: *v*. mapagkalakhán, malakihán, makaiwan; **~th** *n*. bunga.
outlandish: *adj*. kakaibá, kakatuwâ.
outlaw: *n*. tulisán, manliligalig, salarín.
outlay: *n*. gugol, paggugol.
outlet: *n*. labasan, lagusan.
outline: *n*. guhit-balangkás; bangháy.
outlook: *n*. hinaharáp, tanawin; kurò.
outnumber: *v*. higtán, laluan.
outpost: *n*. himpilan, bantayan.
output: *n*. buhos, pagbubuhos.
outrage: *n*. lupít, kalapastanganan; **~ous** *adj*. nakapangingilabot, napakasamâ; mapamalibhasà.
outrigger: *n*. katig.
outright: *adj*. ganáp, tahás; kagyát.
outrun: *v*. maunahan, malampasan.
outset: *n*. pasimulâ, simulâ.
outside: *adj*. sa labás; **~r** *n*. tagalabás.
outskirts: *n*. labás ng bayan.
outstanding: *adj*. litáw; mahalagá.
outstretched: *adj*. nakaladlád, nakadipá.
outward: *adv*. palabás, paalís.
outwit: *v*. luminláng, lokohin, dayain.
oval: *n*. habilóg, óbalo; *adj*. tabas-itlóg.
ovary: *n*. bahay-itlóg, obaryo.
oven: *n*. hurno, tapahan.
over: *adv*. sa itaás; sa ibayo, sa kabilâ; mahigít sa; masyado; **all ~** tapós na; **~ and ~** paulit-ulit; **~ there** sa dako roón.
overall: *n*. óberol.
overbearing: *adj*. mapanupil, dominante, mapaghari-harian.
overcast: *adj*. maulap, kulimlím.
overcharge: *v*. singilín ng labis.
overcoat: *n*. gaban, abrigo, sobretodo.
overcome: *v*. dumaíg, sumupil, mapanaigán, mapagtagumpayán.
overdo: *v*. magmalabís, magpakasobra; lumabis.
overdose: *n*. labis na dosis.
overdue: *adj*. lampás sa taning, hulí.
overflow: *v*. umapaw.

overgrown: *adj*. labis ang lakí.
overhead: *adj*. sa itaás; pangkalahatán.
overhear: *v*. máulinigan.
overjoyed: *adj*. tuwaáng-tuwâ.
overland: *adv*. sa katihan.
overlap: *v*. magsanib.
overlay: *v*. magkalupkóp; latagan; *n*. kalupkóp.
overload: *v*. magkargá nang labis.
overlook: *v*. di makita, makaligtaán; tunghayán.
overnight: *adj*. magdamág.
overpass: *n*. tuláy; óberpas; *v*. lumampás.
overpower: *v*. magapì, mapipilan.
override: *v*. manaíg, magpawaláng-bisà.
overrule: *v*. panaigín; magpawaláng-bisà.
overseas: *adj*. sa ibayo ng dagat.
oversee: *v*. mamahalà, mangasiwà.
overtake: *v*. abutan, abutin.
overthrow: *v*. ibagsák, lupigin, igupò, magpapabagsák, pabagsakín.
overtime: *n*. higít na oras, lamay.
overture: *n*. obertura.
overturn: *v*. tumaób, magbagsák.
overwhelmed: *adj*. mapuspós; magapì.
owe: *v*. may utang, mangutang; **owing to** dahil sa.
owl: *n*. kuwago.
own: *v*. magkaroón; mag-arì; **~er** may-arì; **~ership** pagkamay-arì.
ox: *n*. kapóng baka.
oxygen: *n*. oksíheno.
oxytone: *adj*. maríin.
oyster: *n*. talabá.
ozone: *n*. osono.

P

pace: *n*. bilís; hakbáng.
pacific: *adj*. mapayapà; ~ **Ocean** Dagat Pasípiko.
pacify: *v*. magpatahimik, magpapayapà; payapain.
pack: *n*. balutan, bastâ; *v*. mag-impake, magbastâ.
package: *n*. pakete, balutan.
pact: *n*. pagkakasundô; **blood** ~ sanduguan.
pad: *n*. almohadón.
padding: *n*. palamán, pampakapál.
paddle: *n*. sagwán; palupalò.
paddock: *n*. kurál ng kabayo.
paddy: *n*. palayan.
padlock: *n*. kandado.
pagan: *adj*. pagano; **~ism** paganismo.
page: *n*. páhina; mukhâ; *v*. magpatawag.
pageant: *n*. palabás, pagtatanghál.
pagoda: *n*. pagoda.
pail: *n*. timbâ, baldé.
pain: *n*. sakít, hapdî; **~ful** *adj*. mahapdî, makirót, masakít.
painstaking: *adj*. maingat.
paint: *n*. pintá; *v*. pintahán; **~er** *n*. pintór; **~ing** *n*. pintura, larawan, kuwadro; pagpipintá.
pair: *n*. pares, pareha.
pajamas: *n*. padyama.
pal: *n*. kaibigan, katoto; kalarô.
palace: *n*. palasyo.
palate: *n*. ngalangalá.
palatial: *adj*. malapalasyo.
pale: *adj*. maputlâ; barák; mapusyáw.
palette: *n*. paleta.
palindrome: *n*. palindromya.
pall: *n*. kulumbóng, lambóng.
pallete: *n*. paleta.
palliative: *n*. pampatigháw, pampaginhawa.
pallid: *adj*. maputlâ, barák.
pallor: *n*. kaputlaán, pamumutlâ.
palm: *n*. (*of hand*) palad; (*tree*) pawid, sasá; ~ **leaves** palaspás; ~ **Sunday** *n*. Domingo de Ramos, Linggó ng Palaspás.
palpitate: *v*. tumibók.
palpitation: *n*. tahíp, tibók, sikdó.
pampano: *n*. bitilya, maliputó.
pamper: *v*. magpalayaw, magpamihasa.
pamphlet: *n*. polyeto, muntíng aklát.
pan: *n*. kawalì.
pancreas: *n*. lapáy.
panda: *n*. panda.
pandemonium: *n*. kaguluhan.
panel: *n*. panel; hurado.
pang: *n*. matindíng kirót.
panic: *v*. magkaguló, magkagulát.
panorama: *n*. tánawin; panorama.
pant: *v*. humingal, mahapò.
pantheism: *n*. panteismo.

pantomine: *n*. dulang waláng salitâ.
pantry: *n*. dispensa, paminggalan.
pants: *n*. pantalón.
papa: *n*. amá, papá, tatay.
papacy: *n*. pagka-Papa.
paper: *n*. papél; dokumento; **news~** pahayagán, diyaryo.
paprika: *n*. pamintón.
par: *n*. pagkakapantáy, pagkakapareho.
parable: *n*. parábula, talinghagà.
parachute: *n*. parakaida; *v*. magparakaida.
parade: *n*. parada; *v*. magparada.
paradigm: *n*. halimbawang bangháy; paradaym, húwaran, tularán.
paradise: *n*. paraiso; langit.
paradox: *n*. kabalintunaan, kabalighuán.
paragon: *n*. ulirán, huwaran.
paragraph: *n*. párapo, tálataán.
parakeet: *n*. muntíng loro.
parallel: *adj*. magkahilera, magkabalalay; *n*. pagpaparis, pagtutulad.
paralysis: *n*. pagkaparalisá, paralisis.
paralyze: *v*. lumpuhín, paralisahín.
paraphernalia: *n*. kagamitán, kasangkapan.
parasite: *n*. paraásito.
parasol: *n*. payong.
parcel: *n*. parsela, balutan, pakete.
parch: *v*. ibilád, idaráng, tigangín.
pardon: *n*. patawad; *v*. magpatawad; **~able** *adj*. mapatatawad.
pare: *v*. balatán, talupan.
parent: *n*. magulang; **~age** *n*. kaangkanán, lipì; **~-in-law** biyanán.
parenthesis: *n*. saklóng, panaklóng.
parish: *n*. parokya.
parity: *n*. pagkakapareho.
park: *n*. parke, liwasan; **~ing lot** *n*. paradahán; *v*. pumarada.
parliament: *n*. parlamento.
parlor: *n*. salas, silíd-tanggapan.
parody: *n*. parodya.
parole: *n*. paról, paglayang may-pasubalì.
parricide: *n*. parisidyo, pagpatáy sa sariling amá.
parrot: *n*. loro; **~ fish** loro, mulmúl, lutiin.
parry: *v*. manalág, salagín, sanggahín, iwasan, ilagan.
parsimony: *n*. karamutan, kakuriputan.
parsley: *n*. perehíl.
part: *n*. bahagi, parte; (*hair*) hatì, hawì, biyák; (*in a play*) papél; *v*. humiwaláy; maghatì; **take ~** makihalò, makisali, makilahók; **~ing** paghihiwaláy; *adj*. pahimakás, pamaalam.
partake: *v*. makisali, makilahók.
partial: *adj*. bahagi; kumakampí, pumapanig; **~ity** pagkatig, pagkampí, pagkiling.
participate: *v*. makisali, makisama, makilahók.
participle: *n*. pandiwarì.
particle: *n*. katitíng, kapurít; (*gram*.) katagâ.
particular: *adj*. pansarili; tangì; maselang.
partisan: *n*. partidista, partidaryo, kapanig.
partition: *n*. pagbabahagi, pagkabahagi; dindíng.
partitive: (*gram*.) *adj*. pahatî.
partner: *n*. kasama; kasosyo; kapareha; **~ship** pagkakasosyo, pagkakasama; **dance ~** *n*. kasayáw.
part-time *adj*. pansamantalá.
party: *n*. pangkát; pagtitipon, parti; salu-salo.
pass: *v*. dumaán, daanán; lumipas; *n*. landás, daán; pases; **~ out** mawalán ng malay-tao; **~ by** magdaán; **~ around** ilibot; **~ away** mamatáy.
passage: *n*. daanán; paglipas.
passé: *adj*. lipás, laós.
passenger: *n*. pasahero, sakáy.
passion: *n*. pag-iibigan, pagsisintahan, kahalingán, pagkahumaling; **ate** *adj*. makabagbág-pusò, mainapóy.
passive: *adj*. waláng-kibô, waláng-tutol, pasibo; *n*. (*gram*.) balintiyák.
passport: *n*. pasaporte.
password: *n*. hudyát, kontrasenyas.
past: *adj*. nagdaán, nakalipas; lampás; **~ tense** pangnagdaáng panahunan.
paste: *n*. pandikít, kola.
pastime: *n*. aliwan, líbangan.
pastor: *n*. kura, pastór.
pastry: *n*. pasteleryá.
pasture: *n*. damuhán, pastulan.
pat: *v*. tumapík; *n*. tapík.
patch: *n*. tagpî; tapal; **eye ~** tapal.
paté: *adj*. atáy na dinurog.
patella: *n*. bayugo (ng tuhod).

patent: *n*. patente; *adj*. patentado.
paternal: *adj*. makaamá; ng amá.
paternity: *n*. pagka-amá.
path: *n*. landás; pagdaraanán; (*between rice paddies*) pilapil, tarundón.
pathetic: *adj*. kaawa-awà, kalunus-lunos.
pathology: *n*. patolohiya.
patience: *n*. pasyensiya, pagtitis, paumanhín.
patient: *n*. (*hospital*) pasyente, maysakít; (*with patience*) matiisin, matiyagâ.
patriarch: *n*. patriyarka.
patriot: *n*. bayani; **~ic** makabayan; **~ism** kabayanihan.
patrol: *n*. patrulya; *v*. magpatrulya.
patron: *n*. patron, tagapagtaguyod; parokyano, sukì; **~age** tangkilik, pagtataguyod; **~ize** *v*. tumangkilik, magtaguyod; manuyò.
pattern: *n*. dibuho, disenyo; tularán.
paunch: *n*. sikmurà, tiyán.
pauper: *n*. pulubi, mahirap na tao.
pause: *v*. huumintóng sandalî.
pave: *v*. latagan, aspaltuhan; **~ment** palitada, aspalto.
pavilion: *n*. pabilyón; gusaling-pamistá.
paw: *n*. paá; *v*. kalmutín.
pawn: *n*. sanglâ; peón; *v*. isanglâ; **~broker** maypásanglaan; **~shop** sanglaan.
pay: *v*. magbayad; *n*. bayad; **~ attention to** mag-asikaso, pag-ukulan ng pansín; **~master** *n*. tagapagbayad, pagadór; **~ment** *n*. bayad, kabayarán; **~ roll** peyrol, taláupahán.
pea: *n*. gisantes.
peace: *n*. kapayapaan; katahimikan; **~ful** *adj*. mapayapà, tahimik.
peach: *n*. melokotón.
peacock: *n*. paboreál.
peak: *n*. tuktók, taluktók; tugatog.
peal: *n*. repike, dagundóng.
peanut: *n*. manî.
pear: *n*. peras.
pearl: *n*. perlas; **mother of ~** nakar.
peasant: *n*. magbubukíd, magsasaká.
pebble: *n*. maliít na bató.
peck: *v*. tukaín, tumukâ.
peculiar: *adj*. kakatwâ, kakaibá, kataká-taká.
pedagogy: *n*. pagtuturò.
pedal: *n*. pedál.
pedantic: *adj*. mapagmaalam.
peddle: *v*. maglakò, magtindá-tindá; **~r** maglalakô, manlalakò.
pedestal: *n*. pedestál, patungán.
pedestrian: *n*. taong naglálakád.
peek: *v*. silipin, sulyapán; sumilip.
peel: *v*. talupan; *n*. balát; **~er** pambalát, panalop.
peep: *v*. sumilip, sumulyáp.
peer: *n*. kapareho, kapantáy, kaurì.
peg: *n*. talasok, panipit; pakong kahoy.
pelican: *n*. pelikano.
pelt: *n*. balát, katad; *v*. pumukól, bumató.
pelvis: *n*. balakáng.
pen: *n*. pluma, bolpen; (*for animals*) kulungan, tangkál; **~knife** kortaplúma; **~ name** sagisag-panulat.
penal: *adj*. ng parusa; **~ code** kódigo penál; **~ize** parusahan; **~ty** parusa, multá.
penance: *n*. penitensiya, pagpapakasakit.
pencil: *n*. lapis.
pendant: *n*. palawít.
pending: *adj*. nakabitin, hindî pa tapós.
pendulum: *n*. péndulo, palawít.
penetrate: *v*. bumaón; lumagós; tumagós.
penguin: *n*. penguwín, ibong dagat.
peninsula: *n*. tangwáy, península.
penis: *n*. titì.
penitent: *adj*. nagsisisi; **~iary** bilangguan.
penmanship: *n*. sulat-kamáy.
penny: *n*. séntimos, pera.
pension: *n*. pensiyón, sustento; **~er** pensionado.
penultimate: **with ~ stress** *adj*. malumay.
people: *n*. mga tao; lahì.
pepper: *n*. pamintá, sili; **~y** maanghang
peppermint: *n*. yerbabuwena, menta.
per: *prep*. sa bawa't isá, para sa isá; **~ capita** para sa isáng tao.
perceive: *v*. mahiwatigan, mahalatâ.
percent: *n*. porsiyento, bahagdán; **~age** porsiyento, bahagi.
perception: *n*. pang-unawà, pagkaunawà.
perch: *v*. dumapò, humapon.
percolate: *v*. tumagós.
perennial: *adj*. santaunan; pangmatagalan.
perfect: *adj*. waláng-malî, perpekto; *v*. pabutihin, magpakasanay; **~ion** *n*. kawastuan,

katumpakán, kasakdalan.
perforate: *v*. bumutas, butasin.
perform: *v*. gumanáp; gawín, tumupád; **~ance** *n*. paggawâ, pagpapalabás.
perfume: *n*. bangó, halimuyak, pabangó.
perhaps: *adv*. marahil, malamáng, siguro.
peril: *n*. panganib; **~ous** mapanganib.
perimeter: *n*. paikot, paligid, buóng gilid.
period: *n*. tuldók, puntó; panahón; **~ic** *adj*. paulit-ulit; paná-panahón.
perish: *v*. mamatáy, malipol, mawalâ; **~able** *adj*. siraín, bulukin.
perk: *v*. sumiglá.
permanent: *adj*. pirmihan, palagian, permanente.
permeate: *v*. tumagós; lumaganap, kumalat.
permission: *n*. pahintulot, permiso.
permit: *v*. pahintulutan, tulutan, payagan; *n*. permiso, pahintulot.
perpendicular: *adj*. patayô, patindíg, patiník.
perpetrate: *v*. isagawâ, isakatuparan.
perpetrator: *n*. pasimunò; promutór.
perpetual: *adj*. waláng-hanggáng; pálagian.
perpetuate: *v*. magpanatili, magpamalagì; pamalagiin.
perplex: *v*. lituhín; **~ity** bagabag, kabalisahan; kalituhán.
persecute: *v*. magmalupít, mang-apí; umusig.
perseverance: *n*. pagtitiyagâ, pagkamatiyagâ.
persevere: *v*. magtiyagâ.
persist: *v*. magpilit, magpumilit; manatili, magtagál; **~ent** *adj*. matiyagâ, waláng-puknát.
person: *n*. tao; katao; **~al** *adj*. personál, pansarili; panao; **~ality** personalidád, katauhan; **~ify** *v*. kumatawán, ilarawang tao; **~ification** *n*. pagsasatao.
personnel: *n*. mga empleado.
perspiration: *n*. pawis; pagpapawis.
perspire: *v*. magpawis.
persuade: *v*. hikayatin, himukin, akitin.
persuasion: *n*. paghikayat, paghimok.
pertain: *v*. tumukoy, maukol.
pertinence: *n*. kaugnayan, kaangkupán.
pertinent: *adj*. may-kinalaman.
perturb: *v*. ligaligin, tigatigin, balisahin.
peruse: *v*. bumasa.
perverse: *adj*. balakyót, napakasamâ; salungát.
pervert: *n*. masamáng tao; **~ed** *adj*. masamâ.
peso: *n*. piso.
pessimist: *n*. pesimista; **~ic** *adj*. pesimista.
pest: *n*. peste, maninirà.
pester: *v*. guluhín, buwisitin.
pestle: *n*. halo, pambayó.
pet: *n*. paboritong hayop; *v*. haplús-haplusín.
petal: *n*. talulot; pétalo.
petition: *n*. kahilingan, petisyón; *v*. humilíng.
petrify: *v*. magíng bató.
petroleum: *n*. petrolyo.
petticoat: *n*. nagwas, kamisón.
petty: *adj*. di-mahalagá.
pew: *n*. bangkô.
phantasm: *n*. malikmatá, multó.
phantom: *n*. multó.
pharmacist: *n*. botikaryo, parmasyútiko.
pharmacy: *n*. parmasya, butika.
pharynx: *n*. lalaugan.
phase: *n*. pagbabago; anyô.
pheasant: *n*. benggala.
phenomenal: *adj*. kahanga-hangà; napakapambihirà.
phenomenon: *n*. kababalaghán; palatandaan.
philander: *v*. magbirô sa pag-ibig; **~er** *n*. babaero, palikero.
philanthropist: *n*. pilántropo, mapagkawanggáwang tao.
Philippines: *n*. Pilipinas.
philosopher: *n*. pilósopo.
philosophy: *n*. kaisipan; pilosopiya.
phlegm: *n*. kala(n)ghalâ, plema.
phone: *n*. telépono; *v*. teleponohán, tumawag.
phonetics: *n*. palátinigan, palátunugan, ponétika.
photo: *n*. larawan, ritrato; **~copy** larawang sipì; **~graph** *n*. retrato; *v*. retratuhin, **~grapher** *n*. retratista, potógrapo; **~graphy** *n*. potograpiya.
phrase: *n*. prase, pariralà.
physical: *adj*. pangkatawán, ng katawán.
physician: *n*. médiko, doktór, manggagamot.
physique: *n*. pangangatawán, tikas ng katawán.
pianist: *n*. piyanista.
piano: *n*. piyano.
pick: *v*. (*choose*) pumilì; (*flowers*) pupulín, pumitás; *n*. pilì; **~ax** piko; **~ out** piliin; **~ on**

sisihin; ~ **up** pumulot.
picket: *n*. istakà, tulos, urang.
pickle: *n*. atsara; *v*. atsarahin.
pickpocket: *n*. mandurukot.
picnic: *n*. piknik.
picture: *n*. ritrato, larawan; panoorín; **~sque** maringal, parang larawan, mapaglarawan.
pidgin: *n*. magkakahalong salitâ.
pie: *n*. pastél, empanada.
piebald: *adj*. hubero.
piece: *n*. piraso; bahagi, kaputool.
pier: *n*. pantalán, daungan.
pierce: *v*. lumagós, tumagós; butasin.
piety: *n*. kabanalan.
pig: *n*. baboy; **young ~** biík; **roasted ~** litsón; **~sty** ulbô.
pigeon: *n*. kalapati; **wild ~** batu-bató; **~-toed** *adj* pingkáw ang paá
pigment: *n*. pangulay, pangolór.
pigpen: *n*. kulungan ng baboy, ulbô.
pigtail: *n*. tirintás.
pike: *n*. istakà.
pile: *n*. salansán, talaksán, buntón; *v*. magbuntón; magsalansán.
pilfer: *v*. kumupit, umumít.
pilgrim: *n*. peregrino; **~age** *n*. peregrinasyón.
pill: *n*. píldoras.
pillage: *v*. loóban, dambungín.
pillar: *n*. haligi, paste.
pillow: *n*. unan; **~case** pundá.
pilot: *n*. piloto, abyadór; *v*. magpiloto; umugit.
pimple: *n*. tagihawat.
pin: *n*. aspilí; alpilér; **bowling ~** bulilyo; **hair ~** panuksók; **safety ~** imperdíble; **~ down** *v*. ipitin, daganán; **~ cushion** *n*. turukan, duruán, tusukán.
pincers: *n*. pansipit; tiyanì.
pinch: *v*. maipit, mangurót, mamingol.
pine: *n*. pino; ~ **wood** palutsina.
pineapple: *n*. pinya.
pink: *n*. kulay-rosas.
pinnacle: *n*. karurukan, kaitaasan; taluktók.
pioneer: *n*. tagapagbunsód, tagapanguna, tagapaglawag-landás.
pious: *adj*. banál, relihiyoso.
pipe: *n*. tubo; pito; **smoking ~** kuwako.
piquant: *adj*. maangháng, mahangháng.
piracy: *n*. pandarambóng.
pirate: *n*. tulisáng-dagat, pirata, mandarambóng.
pisces: *n*. isdâ (sa zodiac).
pistol: *n*. baríl, pistola.
pit: *n*. hukay; balón; **cock~** sabungán.
pitch: *v*. ihagis, ibató; **~er** *n*. pitsél; pitser.
pitfall: *n*. umang, pakanâ, patibóng.
pith: *n*. ubod; buód.
pitiful: *adj*. kaawa-awà, kahabág-habág.
pittance: *n*. kauntî.
pity: *n*. awà, habág.
pivot: *n*. paikután, ikután; kinasasalalayan.
pixie: *n*. duwende.
placard: *n*. paskíl, kartelón, kartél.
placate: *v*. suyuin, payapain.
place: *n*. lugár; puwesto; dako; *v*. ilagáy; **out of ~** walâ sa lugár; **take ~** mangyari; **in ~ of** sa halíp ng.
placid: *adj*. payapà; **~ity** kapayapaan.
plagiarism: *n*. pamamláhiyo.
plagiarize: *v*. mamlahiyó, pumlahiyó.
plague: *n*. salot, peste; *v*. mameste; manggambalà.
plain: *adj*. simple, payák; maliwanag; karaniwan; pantáy.
plaintiff: *n*. nagsasakdál, maysakdál.
plait: *n*. tirintás.
plan: *n*. plano, balak; panukalà; *v*. magbalak, magpanukalà.
plane: *n*. pantáy; kalagayan; eroplano; **carpenter's ~** katám.
planet: *n*. planeat.
plank: *n*. makapál na tablá.
plant: *n*. halaman, taním; planta; *v*. tamnán; **~er** magtatanim, mananaim.
plantation: *n*. asyenda; **~ owner** asyendero.
plaster: *n*. pamasta, pasta; panapal.
plate: *n*. plato, pinggán.
plateau: *n*. talampás, patag na kataasan.
platform: *n*. plataporma, entablado.
platinum: *n*. platino.
platter: *n*. bandehado.
plausible: *adj*. maaarì; mapaniniwalaan.
play: *n*. larô; sulong; dulâ; *v*. maglarô; (*music*) tugtugín; **~er** manlalarò; **~ful** *adj*. mapaglarô; **~ground** *n*. palaruán; **~mate** kalarô;

~**thing** laruán; ~**wright** mandudulà, dramaturgo.
plaza: *n*. plasa, liwasan.
plea: *n*. pakiusap, samò, panawagan.
plead: *v*. magmatwíd, mangatwiran, ikatwiran, pakisuapan.
pleasant: *adj*. kawili-wili; nakalulugód.
please: *v*. ikasiyá, ikalugód; *adv*. ngâ.
pleasing: *adj*. kalugúd-lugód, nakakawili.
pleasure: *n*. kaluguran, lugód, gakák.
pleat: *n*. pileges; ~**ed** may-pileges.
plebiscite: *n*. plebisito.
plectrum: *n*. puwá.
pledge: *n*. pangakò; garantiyá; *v*. mangakò.
plentiful: *adj*. marami, saganà.
plenty: *adj*. saganà, labis-labis, marami.
pliant: *adj*. hutukin, malambót.
pliers: *n*. bukay-pato.
plight: *n*. suliranin, kalagayan.
plot: *n*. balangkás; masamámg balak, sabuwatan, sapakatan; *v*. bumalangkás; ~ **of land** kapirasong lupà; **vegetable** ~ kamang gulayán.
plow: *n*. araro; *v*. mag-araro.
pluck: *v*. bumunot; maghimulmól.
plug: *n*. pamasak, pasak, tapón; *v*. pasakan, tapunán.
plum: *n*. sirwelas.
plumage: *n*. plumahe, balahibo.
plumb: *n*. pabigát, palawít sa panghulog; ~**line** panghulog.
plumber: *n*. tubero.
plumbing: *n*. tuberiyas; pagtutubero.
plume: *n*. balahibo; *v*. mag-ayos ng balahibo.
plump: *adj*. mapintóg, mabilog.
plunder: *v*. loobán, dambungín.
plunge: *v*. magtubóg, maglublób, sumisid, lumundág.
plural: *n*. pangmarami; ~**ity** pagkamarami, karamihan.
plus: *adj*. higít; ~ **sign** tandâ ng pagdaragdág.
ply: *n*. sapì, patong; *v*. gamitin; panayín.
pneumonia: *n*. pulmunyá.
poach: *v*. mangaso nang waláng karapatán; magsuám.
pock: *n*. pilat; bulutong; ~**marked** *adj*. bulutunggó.
pocket: *n*. bulsa, lukbutan; *v*. ibulsa; ~**book** portamoneda, kartera, pitakà; ~**knife** lanseta, kortapluma.
pod: *n*. balát, supot ng butó.
poem: *n*. tulâ.
poet: *n*. manunulà, makatà; ~**ics** *n*. palátulaan. ~**ry** tulain; **bad poetry** tulakís.
poignant: *adj*. masidhî; matindí; masangsáng, makirót.
poinsettia: *n*. paskuas.
point: *n*. tulis, dulo; punto; ~ **out** *v*. ipakita, iturò; ~ **blank** tuwiran, tahasan; ~**ed** *adj*. tulís, matulis; ~**less** *adj*. waláng-tulis, waláng-bisà; ~ **of view** *n*. pagkukurò, palagáy. ~ **of no return** *n*. dulo ng waláng-hanggán.
poise: *n*. katatagán.
poison: *n*. lason; *v*. maglason; ~**ous** nakakalason; ~ **fish** lupu, sumalapaw; ~ **ivy** yedra.
poke: *v*. sumundót, dumuldól.
poker: *n*. pusóy.
pole: *n*. haligi, poste; polo.
police: *n*. pulís, pulisyá; ~**man** pulís; ~ **force** *n*. kapulisan.
policy: *n*. pólisa; palakad, patakarán.
polish: *v*. pakintabín, bulihin; *n*. pakintáb.
polite: *adj*. magalang, mapitagan, marangál.
political: *adj*. pampulítika.
politician: *n*. pulítiko.
politics: *n*. pulítika.
poll: *n*. paghahalál, pagbobotohán.
pollute: *v*. marumhán, salaulain.
polygamy: *n*. poligamyá.
polygonal: *adj*. binalimbíng.
pomade: *n*. pumada.
pomegranate: *n*. granada.
pomp: *n*. rangyâ, dingal; ~**ous** *adj*. mapagparangyâ, mapagmataás; magarbo.
pond: *n*. lawà.
ponder: *v*. magisip-isíp, magbulay-bulay.
ponderous: *adj*. napakabigát.
pony: *n*. buriko.
poodle: *n*. asong-delanas.
pooh: *interj*. puwé.
pool: *n*. lawà; languyan; magkabakas.
poor: *adj*. mahirap, dukhâ, pobre, maralitâ; ~**ly** *adv*. masamâ.
pop: *n*. putók; *v*. bumusá; ~**gun** baríl-barilan.

popcorn: *n.* binusáng maís, papkorn.
pope: *n.* papa.
poppy: *n.* amapola.
populace: *n.* madlâ, mga tao.
popular: *adj.* bantóg, sikát; populár; kilalá, matunóg; **~ity** katanyagán, kabantugán, pagkapopulár.
populate: *v.* panirahán; tumirá.
population: *n.* populasyón.
porcelain: *n.* porselana.
porch: *n.* pórtiko, balkón.
porcupine fish: *n.* buteteng laot.
pore: *n.* napakaliít na butas.
porgy: *n.* bitilya, bukawal, kanuping, abo, gaud-gaod.
pork: *n.* karne ng baboy.
pornography: *n.* pornograpiya.
porridge: *n.* lugaw, nilugaw.
port: *n.* daungan, puwerto.
portable: *adj.* bitbitin.
porter: *n.* pahinante; portero; bantáy-pintô, tanod-pintô; mángangargá, kargadór.
portfolio: *n.* portpolyo.
portion: *n.* kabahagi, kapiraso.
portly: *adj.* matabâ; mabigát.
portrait: *n.* larawan, retrato.
portray: *v.* gumuhit; ilarawan; gumanáp ng papél; **~al** *n.* pagsasalarawan, pagguhit.
pose: *n.* tindíg, tikas, tayô; *v.* pumuwesto, umayos.
position: *n* kalagayan; kinatatayuán, lagáy; empleo, puwesto.
positive: *adj.* tiyák, sigurado; mapaniyák.
possess *v.* mag-arì, mag-angkín; **~ion** pagkamay-arì; **~ive** *adj.* paarî; mapang-ankín; **~or** *n.* may-arì; **~ive case** *n.* kaukuláng paarî.
possibility: *n.* posibilidád, pagkamaaarì.
possible: *adj.* maaarì, posible, marahil.
post: *n.* poste, haligi; *v.* ipaskíl, idikít; **~man** kartero; **~ card** tarheta postál; **~mark** tatákkoreo; **~ office** tanggapan ng koreo, posopis, pádalahang-liham; **~script** pahabol, tagihabol.
postage: *n.* bayad sa koreo; **~ stamp** selyo.
postal: *adj.* pangkoreo.
poster: *n.* paskíl, kartelón.
posterior: *adj.* panlikód, panghulí; *n.* puwít.
posterity: *n.* angkáng susunód; inapó.
posthumous: *adj.* póstumó, nangyari pagkamatáy.
postpone: *v.* iliban, ipagpaibáng-araw; **~ment** pagpapaliban, pagtatayong.
postscript: *n.* dagdág, habol (sa sulat).
postulate: *v.* maghaka-hakà, magkuro-kurò.
posture: *n.* pustura, tindíg.
post- *pref.* pagkatapos ng.
pot: *n.* palayók; anglít; **flower ~** masetera, pasô.
potassium: *n.* potasyo, potasa.
potato: *n.* patatas.
potency: *n.* kabisaan; (*of liquor*) tapang, sahang.
potent: *adj.* makapangyarihan, mabisà.
potential: *adj.* maaarì, puwede; *n.* (*gram.*) paarì.
potpourri: *n.* sari-sarì.
potter: *n.* magpapalayók.
pottery: *n.* mga palayók, pagpapalayók.
pouch: *n.* supot; lukbutan.
poultry: *n.* mga manók.
pounce: *v.* sunggabán, sagpangín, sumagpáng.
pound: *n.* libra; kabóg, kalampág; *v.* kumalampág, pumukpók.
pour: *v.* isalin, ibuhos; umagos, bumulos.
pout: *v.* ngumusò, lumabì.
poverty: *n.* kahirapan, karukhaán, pagdaralitâ.
powder: *n.* pulbós; púlbura; *v.* magpulbós.
power: *n.* lakás, kapangyarihan; bisà; **~ful** *adj.* malakás.
practical: *adj.* magagawâ, mapakikinabangan.
practice: *n.* pagsasanay, kasanayán; *v.* magsanay; ugaliin
prairie: *n.* parang, kaparangan.
praise: *n.* puri; *v.* purihin; **~worthy** *adj.* kapuripuri.
prank: *n.* kalikután, kapilyuhán.
prattle: *v.* maggagugaguhan, ngumawâ; magdadaldál.
prawn: *n.* sugpô, hipon; uláng.
pray: *v.* magdasál, manalangin; **~er** *n.* dasál, panalangin.
praying mantis: *n.* sasambá, sasambá-ahas.
preach: *v.* magsermon, mangaral; **~er** *n.* tagapang-aral.

precaution: *n*. pag-iingat.
precede: *v*. umuna, mauná; tumaás; **~nce** *n*. pangunguna, pagpapauná; **~nt** *n*. pasimundán, bantayán, saligán.
preceding: *adj*. nauuná, nakalipas.
precinct: *n*. presinto; sakláw.
precious: *adj*. mahalagá, mamahalin.
precipice: *n*. bangín.
precipitate: *v*. padaliín, ikadalî.
precipitation: *n*. ulán.
precise: *adj*. tamà, wastô; maalagà, tiyák.
precision: *n*. katiyakán, katumpakán.
preconceive: *v*. maghakà.
predatory: *adj*. maninilà.
predicament: *n*. suliranin.
predicate: *n*. panagurî.
predict: *v*. hulaan; **~ion** hulà.
predispose: *v*. ihantád.
predominance: *n*. pangíngibabaw; pamámayani.
predominant: *adj*. pinakamakapangyarihan, pinakaharì.
predominate: *v*. mangibabaw, manaíg; dumaíg.
preface: *n*. paunáng salitâ.
prefer: *v*. mas gustó; mabutihin; **~ence** pagtatangì; higít na pagkakagustó.
prefix: *n*. unlapì; *v*. iuna; iunlapì.
pregnancy: *n*. pagbubuntís, kabuntisán.
pregnant: *adj*. buntís, nagdadaláng-tao.
prejudice: *n*. di-matwíd na palagáy; pinsalà, prehuwisyo, masamáng palagáy.
prelate: *n*. prelado.
preliminary: *adj*. pauná, pamauná.
prelude: *n*. pambungad, pasimulâ, umpisá.
premature: *adj*. walâ pa sa panahón.
premeditate: *v*. maghandâ.
premier: *adj*. kauná-unahan; pangunahín.
premise: *n*. saligán, batayán.
premium: *n*. gatimpalà.
premonition: *n*. agam-agam, kutób ng loób, salagimsím.
preparation: *n*. paghahandâ.
prepare: *v*. maghandâ, ihandâ.
preponderance: *n*. pananaíg, pangingibabaw.
preposition: *n*. pang-ukol.
prerequisite: *n*. unang kailangan.
prerogative: *n*. kaukuláng karapatán.
prescribe: *v*. ireseta, ihatol.
prescription: *n*.. reseta, hatol; kautusán.
presence: *n*. pagkadaló, pagkaharáp; harapán.
present: *n*. regalo; *adj*. (*now*) ngayón; ~ **tense** panahóng kasalukuyan; *v*. ibigáy; ipakilala; **~able** *adj*. handâ; karapat-dapat; **~ation** *n*. paghaharáp; pagpapakilala; pagtatanghál.
presentiment: *n*. hinalà, kutób.
preservation: *n*. pangangalagà; pag-iimbák, pagtitinggál.
preservative: *n*. pampreserbá; pangusilbá.
preserve: *v*. preserbahín; mangalagà, ingatan.
preside: *v*. mangulo; mamunò.
presidency: *n*. pagkapangulo.
president: *n*. pangulo, presidente; **~ial** pampánguluhán.
press: *v*. dumiín; pigaín; (*iron*) magplantsá; *n*. imprenta; **~ed** *adj*. pipî; **~board** pamipî; ~ **release** *n*. palathalà; **printing ~** *n*. pálathalaán.
pressure: *n*. tindí, presyón, puwersa, bigát; pamimilit.
prestige: *n*. katanyagán, pagkakilalá.
presume: *v*. mag-akalà; magpalagáy; mangahás.
presumption: *n*. sapantahà, akalà.
pretend: *v*. magkunwarî, magkunwâ.
pretense: *n*. pagkukunwarî; karangyaán.
pretentious: *adj*. pasikat; marangyâ, mapágpanggáp.
preterite: *n*. panahóng pangnagdaán.
pretext: *n*. pagdadahilán, pagkukunwâ.
pretty: *adj*. magandá, marikít, kaakit-akit.
prevail: *v*. umiral; manaíg; himukin; managumpáy; **~ing** *adj*. nagháharì; nanánaíg; umíiral; nanánatili; nangíngibabaw.
prevalence: *n*. paglaganap, pagkalat.
prevalent: *adj*. laganap, kalát.
prevent: *v*. humadláng, sumansalà; pumigil; **~able** mapipigilan; **~ion** paghadláng.
preview: *n*. prebista, prebyu.
previous: *adj*. dati, nauuná.
prey: *n*. hauop na sisilaín; *v*. manilâ.
price: *n*. presyo, halagá; bayad.
prick: *n*. tulis; durò; *v*. magdurò.
prickly: *adj*. matiník; ~ **heat** bungang-araw.

pride: *n*. kayabangan, karangalan, kapurihán.
priest: *n*. parì, saserdote; **~hood** pagkaparì.
primary: *adj*. pang-una, pasimulâ; primarya.
primate: *n*. primado.
prime: *adj*. kataás-taasan; pinakamahusay; pangunahín.
primer: *n*. panimuláng aklát.
primitive: *adj*. kauná-unahan; saunahín.
prince: *n*. prínsipe; **~ss** *n*. princesa.
principal: *n*. prinsipál, punong-gurò; *adj*. pangunahín, pinakapunò; **~ verb** *n*. pandiwang pamadyá.
principle: *n*. tuntunin, panuntunan, prinsipyo, simulain.
print: *n*. taták, bakás; *v*. maglimbág, maglathalà; **~er** manlilimbág; **~ing press** limbagan; **~ing shop** *n*. pálimbangan.
prior: *adj*. nauuna; **~ity** karapatáng mauna, kaunahan.
prism: *n*. prisma.
prison: *n*. bilangguan, kulungan, karsél; **~er** bilanggô, preso.
privacy: *n*. nang sarilinán, palihím; pag-iisá.
private: *adj*. pansarili, pribado; palihím.
privilege: *n*. pribilehiyo, tanging karapatán.
prize: *n*. gatimpalà, premyo; *v*. pahalagahán.
pro: *adv*. para kay, sang-ayon sa; maka-.
probability: *n*. probabilidád, pagkakataón.
probable: *adj*. malamáng, maáarì.
probably: *adv*. malamáng, bakâ, marahil.
probe: *v*. magsuring mabuti; *n*. pagsusurì.
problem: *n*. suliranín, problema; **~atic** di-tiyák; na kapag-aálinlangan.
procedure: *n*. paraán, kaparaanán, palakarán, palakad.
proceed: *v*. magtulóy; magpatuloy; **~ing** *n*. hakbáng; **~ings** paglilitis.
process: *n*. paraán; pagpapatuloy; paglakad.
procession: *n*. prosesyón.
proclaim: *v*. magpahayag, magproklamá; ipahayag.
procrastinate: *v*. magpabukas-bukas; magpaliban.
procure: *v*. kumuha, humanap.
prod: *v*. mag-udyók, sumundót.
prodigal: *n*., *adj*. alibughâ.
prodigy: *n*. himalâ, kababalaghán.
produce: *v*. magbigáy; gumawâ; magbunga; **~r** tagalikhâ.
product: *n*. yarì, produkto; gawâ; **~ion** paggawâ, paglikhâ; **~ive** *adj*. nagbubunga; matubò.
profane: *adj*. di-banál.
profanity: *n*. kalapastanganan; pagkawaláng-galang, tungayaw, mura.
profess: *v*. ipahayag; ipagpanggáp; **~ion** hanapbuhay, propesyón.
professional: *adj*. propesyonál.
professor: *n*. propesór; gurò.
proficiency: *n*. kasanayán, kahusayan, kadalubhasaan.
proficient: *adj*. sanáy, bihasá; may-kaya.
profit: *n*. tubò, pakinabang; bentaha; *v*. tumubò, makinabang; **~eer** *v*. manghuthót.
profound: *adj*. malalim, mahimbíng; masidhî.
profundity: *n*. kalaliman.
profuse: *adj*. napakarami, saganà, masaganà.
progeny: *n*. suplíng, anák.
program: *n*. programa; palátuntunan.
progress: *n*. pagtulóy, pagsulong, pag-unlád; *v*. sumulong, umunlád, magtulóy; **~ive** *adj*. maunlád, umaasenso, progresibo.
prohibit: *v*. ipagbawal; pigilin; **~ion** *n*. pagbabawal.
project: *n*. plano, panukalà, balak; *v*. umuslî, umungós; **~ion** uslî; pagtudlâ.
projectile: *n*. panudlâ.
proletariat: *n*. ang mga manggagawà.
prolific: *adj*. mabunga; palaanák.
prologue: *n*. prólogo, paunáng salitâ.
prolong: *v*. tagalán, ipagpatuloy, pahabain.
promenade: *n*. pasyál; pasyalan; *v*. magpasyál.
prominence: *n*. katanyagán, kabantugán.
prominent: *adj*. tanyág, kilalá; bantóg; uslî.
promiscuous: *adj*. waláng-delikadesa, makatí.
promise: *n*. pangakò; *v*. mangakò.
promissory: *adj*. may-pangakò; **~ note** *n*. pagaré, kasulatan sa pagbabayad ng utang.
promote: *v*. itaás sa ranggo; magpaunlád.
promotion: *n*. pagsisimulâ, pagkakataás.
prompt: *v*. udyukán; diktahán; *adj*. madalî; maagap.
promulgate: *v*. magpalaganap.
prone: *adj*. mahilig; makiling; nakataób.

pronoun: *n*. panghalíp; **demonstrative** ~ *n*. panghalíp na pamatlíg; **indefinite** ~ *n*. panghalíp na panakláw; **interrogative** ~ *n*. panghalíp na pananóng; **relative** ~ *n*. panghalíp sa pamanggít..
pronounce: *v*. bumigkás; maggawad.
pronunciation: *n*. bigkás, pagbigkás.
proof: *n*. pruweba; patibay, patunay; pangontra; **bullet~** dî tinátablán ng bala.
prop: *n*. tukod, suhay, gabáy; *v*. itukod, suhayan.
propaganda: *n*. pagpapalaganap.
propagate: *v*. paramihin, papag-anakín.
propel: *v*. itulak, ibunsód; **~ler** élise.
propensity: *n*. likás na hilig.
proper: *adj*. wastô, tamà; tumpák; ~ **noun** *n*. pangngalang panangì.
property: *n*. ari-arian; katangían.
prophecy: *n*. paghulà, hulà.
prophesy: *v*. hulaan.
prophet: *n*. manghuhulà, propeta.
proportion: *n*. katimbáng, kasukát; bahagi; **~al** *adj*. kasukát, katapát; ukol.
proposal: *n*. panukalà; mungkahì.
propose: *v*. imungkahì; ipanukalà.
proposition: *n*. mungkahì; balak.
proprietor: *n*. may-arì, propiyetaryo.
proscribe: *v*. ipahayag na labág sa batás.
prose: *n*. túluyan, prosa.
prosecute: *v*. ipagsakdál, mag-usig.
proselytize: *v*. mangumbertí.
prosody: *n*. palábigkasan.
prospect: *n*. pag-asám; hinaharáp; tanawin; **~ive** inaasahan, nalalapit.
prosper: *v*. magtagumpáy; lumagô; umunlád; **~ity** tagumpáy, kasaganaan; **~ous** *adj*. nabubuhay, naunlád, matagumpáy.
prostitute: *n*. puta, patutot, burikák.
prostitution: *n*. pagpuputa, prostitusyón.
prostrate: *adj*. nakadapâ, nakarapâ.
protect: *v*. ikanlóng, ikublí; ipagsanggaláng, ipagtanggól, kalingain; **~ion** pagkalingà, pagkupkóp; **~ive** *adj*. panaggaláng, panananggól; **~or** tagapagtanggól, tagapagsanggaláng.
protegé: *n*. tangkilik, protehido.
protest: *n*. pagtutol; *v*. tutulan, sumalungát; **~ant** Protestante.
prototype: *n*. prototipo, tularan.
protract: *v*. lumabás, humabà; lumawig.
protrude: *v*. magpauslî; umuslî.
protuberance: tambók, bukol, umbók.
proud: *adj*. kapuri-puri; maipagkakapuri; mapagmataás, palalò.
prove: *v*. magpatunay, magpatotóo; patunayan.
proverb: *n*. saláwikaín, kasabihán.
provide: *v*. bigayán, pagkaloobán; sustentuhán; **~d** *conj*. kung, sa kondisyón.
province: *n*. lalawigan, probínsiyá.
provision: *n*. baon, panustós; **~al** *adj*. pansamantalá.
provocation: *n*. pagpapagalit.
provoke: *v*. pagalitin; pukawin.
prow: *n*. proa, daóng.
prowess: *n*. kagitingan, kadalubhasaan.
prowl: *v*. umalí-aligid; magpalabuy-laboy; **~er** pagala-galang-tao.
proximity: *n*. kalapitan.
proxy: *n*. paghalili, pagkatawán.
prude: *n*. napakaselang tao; **~nt** *adj*. maingat; maalám; masinop.
prune: *n*. prun; *v*. putulan, pungusan.
pry: *v*. talikwasín; *n*. panikwát, panikwás.
pseudo: *adj*. huwád.
pseudonym: *n*. sagisag-panulat.
psychological: *adj*. ng isip, pangkaisipán.
psychologist: *n*. sikólogo.
psychology: *n*. sikolohiyá.
puberty: *n*. pagbibinatâ, pagdadalagá.
pubic: *adj*. ng singit; ~ **hair** *n*. bulból.
public: *adj*. ng madlâ; públiko; lathalà; *n*. mga tao, madlâ; ~ **school** paaraláng-bayan; ~ **works** mga gawaing-bayan.
publication: *n*. publikasyón, paglilimbát.
publicity: *n*. pahayag, palathalà.
publish: *v*. ipalathalà, ilathalà. **~ing house** *n*. pálathalaán.
pucker: *v*. humibî, magkunót.
pudding: *n*. puding.
puddle: *n*. lusak, sanaw.
pudgy: *adj*. matabáng-pandák, balisaksakan; punggók.
puff: *v*. bumugá, umihip; mamintóg; **~y** *adj*. pugtô, mapintóg, magâ.
puffer fish: *n*. butete.

pug nose: *n*. sarát na ilóng.
pugnacious: *adj*. palaawáy.
pugnacity: *n*. pagkapalaawáy.
pull: *v*. hilahin, batakin; dukutin; bunutin.
pulley: *n*. kalô.
pulmonary: *adj*. ng bagà.
pulp: *n*. ubod, kalamnán, lamukot, sapal.
pulpit: *n*. púlpito.
pulsate: *v*. tumibók; kuminíg; pumintíg.
pulse: *n*. pulso; *v*. tumibók.
pulverize: *v*. pulbusín, ligisín.
pumice: *n*. batóng pampakintáb.
pump: *n*. bomba; *v*. magbomba.
pumpkin: *n*. kalabasa.
punch: *n*. (*drink*) pontse; (*hit*) suntók; **hole ~** pambutas; *v*. sumuntók; butasan.
punctual: *adj*. nasa oras; maagap.
punctuate: *v*. magbantás.
punctuation: *n*. pagbabantás; palábantasan.
puncture: *v*. butasin; *n*. butas.
pungency: *n*. (*taste*) kaanghangán; (*smell*) kasangsangán; (*fig*.) katalasan.
pungent: *adj*. (*taste*) maanghang; (*smell*) masangsáng; (*fig*.) matulis, matalas.
punish: *v*. magparusa; parusahan; **~ment** *n*. parusa.
punitive: *adj*. pamparusa.
puny: *adj*. bulilít, bansót; waláng kabuluhán.
pupil: *n*. estudyante, mag-aarál; disípulo; (*of eye*) balintatáw.
puppet: *n*. manikà, tau-tauhan.
puppy: *n*. tutà, kuwâ.
purblind: *adj*. aninág; malabò ang matá.
purchase: *v*. mamilí, bilhín; *n*. binilí.
pure: *adj*. puro; tunay, lantáy; **~ly** *adv*. pawà, pulos, ganáp.
purgative: *n*. purgá, pampurgá.
purgatory: *n*. purgatoryo.
purify: *v*. maglinis, magdalisay.
purist: *n*. purista.
puritan: *n*. puritano.
purity: *n*. kalinisan, kadalisayan.
purple: *adj*. habán, lila, murado, kulay-ube.
purport: *n*. diwà.
purpose: *n*. tangkâ, hangád; layon; **on ~** sadyâ; **~ly** *adv*. kusà, sadyâ.
purse: *n*. portamoneda; pitakà; lukbutan.
pursuant: *adj*. alinsunod sa, sang-ayon sa, ayon sa.
pursue: *v*. sumundó, habulin, tugisin.
pursuit: *n*. pagtugis, paghabol.
purview: *n*. sakláw.
pus: *n*. nanà.
push: *v*. magtulak; magbaón; **drug ~er** puser.
pusillanimous: *adj*. duwág.
pussy: *n*. pusà.
pustule: *n*. bubas, pústula, pigsá.
put: *v*. ilagáy; **~ away** iligpít; **~ off** magpaliban; **~ on** magsuót; **~ up with** magtiís; **~ under** *v*. ipasailalim.
putrefy: *v*. mabulók.
putrid: *adj*. sirâ, bulók, bilasâ.
putty: *n*. masilya.
puzzle: *n*. suliranin; paláisipán, bugtóng; *v*. lituhín.
pygmy: *n*. unano; bululít na tao.
pyramid: *n*. pirámide, tagiló.
pyre: *n*. sigâ.
pyjamas: *n*. padyama.
python: *n*. sawá.

Q

quack: *n*. (*duck sound*) kakak; (*doctor*) albularyo; *adj*. di-tunay, huwád; **~ery** panlilinláng, pandarayà; *v*. kumakak.
quadruped: *n*. apatáng paá.
quadruple: *v*. lumakí nang apat na beses; pag-apatin.
quagmire: *n*. latì, putikan, kuminóy.
quail: *n*. pugò.
quaint: *adj*. kakaibá, kakatuwâ.
quake: *v*. mangatál, lumindól.
qualification: *n*. katángian, kakayahán.
qualified: *adj*. bagay, may-kaya, angkóp.
qualify: *v*. magíng-marapat.
quality: *n*. husay, kabutihan; katangian.
qualm: *n*. pagkabalisa, tigatig; alinlangan.
quantity: *n*. dami.
quarantine: *n*. kuwarentenas.
quarrel: *n*. away, pagbababág, pag-aalít; *v*. mag-away, magkagalít; **~some** palaawáy.
quarry: *n*. silyaran.
quarter: *n*. kuwarto; sangkapat.

quartet: *n.* grupong apatán.
quash: *v.* pawaláng-saysáy.
quaver: *v.* manginíg; mangatál.
quay: *n.* pantalán, muelye.
queen: *n.* reyna.
queer: *adj.* kakatuwâ, kakaibá; baklâ.
quell: *v.* sugpuin, apulain.
quench: *v.* wakasán, apulain, sawataín; patayín.
querulous: *adj.* mareklamo, palaangíl.
query: *n.* tanóng; *v.* magtanóng.
quest: *n.* paghanap; *v.* humanap.
question: *n.* tanóng; *v.* magtanóng; mag-alinlangan; **~able** *adj.* nakapag-aalinlangan; **~ mark** pananóng.
questionnaire: *n.* kuwestiyonaryo, palatánúngan.
queue: *n.* pila, hanay, hilera; (*hair*) tirintás.
quick: *adj.* mabilís; biglâ; **~en** *v.* bumilís; **~ly** *adv.* madalî; **~sand** *n.* kumінóy.
quiescent: *adj.* tahimik.
quiet: *adj.* tahimik, waláng-ingay; payapà.
quill: *n.* pakpák na panulat.
quilt: *n.* kubrekama.
quinine: *n.* kinina.
quintet: *n.* limahan.
quit: *v.* tumiwalág; tumigil; humintô.
quite: *adv.* lubós, talagá.
quits: *adj.* amanos; tablá.
quiver: *v.* manginíg, mangatál; *n.* talangà; pangangatál; pangangatóg.
quiz: *n.* pagsusulit, iksamen.
quorum: *n.* korum.
quota: *n.* kota, takdâ.
quotation: *n.* sinipì; **~ marks** panipì.
quote: *v.* ulitin, sipiin.
quotient: *n.* kusyente.

R

rabbi: *n.* rabi, gurong Hudyo.
rabbit: *n.* kuneho.
rabid: *adj.* ulól, bangáw; masugíd.
rabies: *n.* rabis, kamandág ng aso.
rabble: *n.* hamak.
raccoon: *n.* alamíd.
race: *n.* (*contest*) karera, takbuhan, patulinán; (*of people*) lahì; **~ horse** kabayong pangarera; *v.* magtumulin; makipagkarera.
racial: *adj.* panlahì, panlipì.
rack: *n.* bastagan, suksukan, taasan.
racket: *n.* raketa; linggál; pangungulimbát; **~eer** manlilinláng, mángngungulimbát.
racy: *adj.* may kasagwaán; makináng.
radiance: *n.* liwanag, ningníng.
radiant: *adj.* maningníng, makináng.
radiate: *v.* mamanaag.
radiator: *n.* radiadór.
radical: *adj.* sukdulan, labis; radikál.
radio: *n.* radyo.
radish: *n.* labanós.
radius: *n.* radyo, radius; paikót na sukat.
raffia: *n.* tingtíng.
raffle: *n.* ripa, paripa; *v.* pagripahan.
raft: *n.* balsá.
rafter: *n.* kilo.
rag: *n.* trapo; pira-pirasóng damít, basahan.
rage: *n.* pagkapoót.
ragged: *adj.* sirá-sirâ, punít-punít.
raid: *n.* salakay, paglusob; *v.* sumalakay, lumusob.
rail: *n.* baranda, riles.
railing: *n.* barandilya, rehas.
railroad: *n.* perokaríl, daáng-bakal.
rain: *n.* ulán; *v.* umulán; **~coat** kapote; **~ drop** paták ng ulán; **~y** *adj.* maulán; **~y season** tag-ulán; **~fall** pag-ulán.
rainbow: *n.* bahagharì, balangáw.
raise: *v.* itaás, itayô; itaním; *n.* umento.
raisin: *n.* pasas.
rajah: *n.* raha.
rake: *n.* kalaykáy; *v.* magkalaykáy.
rally: *n.* magtulung-tulong; pagtipun-tipunin.
ram: *n.* lalaking tupa; *v.* mag-umpóg; isagasà.
ramble: *v.* magsalitâ nang halu-halò, magpasikut-sikot; **~r** *n.* palalakád.
ramify: *v.* magsangá-sangá.
ramp: *n.* rampa, deklibe.
rampage: *n.* pandadaluhong.
rampant: *adj.* kalát, palasák, laganap.
rampart: *n.* kutà, balwarte; muralya.
ranch: *n.* rantso; **~r** rantsero.
rancid: *adj.* bulók, panís, sirâ.
rancor: *n.* samâ ng loób.

random: *adj*. pasumalá, palambáng; waláng tiyák na láyunin.
range: *n*. pastulan; kalán; layò, agwát; **~r** tanod-gubat; *v*. ihanay; gumala-galà.
rangy: *adj*. galâ.
rank: *n*. ranggo; *v*. ihanay.
ransack: *v*. maghalungkát, maghalughóg, humukay.
ransom: *n*. panubós, pagtubós.
rant: *v*. maghumiyáw; *n*. paghuhumiyáw.
rap: *n*. katók, tuktók; *v*. kumatók.
rapacious: *adj*. mánanagpáng, mapanagpáng.
rape: *v*. manggahís, gahisín, gumahasà.
rapid: *adj*. mabilís, matulin.
rapture: *n*. masidhíng kagalakan.
rare: *adj*. bihirà, madalang.
rarity: *n*. pagkapambihirà; pambihirà.
rascal: *n*. tampalasan; pilyo.
rash: *adj*. padalus-dalos; waláng-hinahon; *n*. butlíg-butlíg; pantál.
rasp: *v*. kumakas.
raspberry: *n*. prambuwesas.
rat: *n*. dagâ.
rate: *n*. halagá; bayad; urì, klase; *v*. halagahán; **at any ~** gayunman. **~ of exchange** *n*. palátumbasan.
rather: *adv*. lalò pa, higít pa; médyo; manapá; tila mandín; warì; **would ~** mas gugustuhin.
ratification: *n*. pagpapatibay.
ratify: *v*. pagtibayin.
rating: *n*. marka, grado.
ratio: *n*. panumbasan, tumbasan.
ration: *n*. rasyón.
rational: *adj*. makatwiran, nasa katwiran.
rattan: *n*. uwáy, yantók, palasan.
rattle: *n*. kalansíng, alug-alóg; *v*. kumalantóg, gumaralgál; kalampagín.
raucous: *adj*. piyaós, pagáw, maragalgál, malát.
ravage: *v*. wasakín, magwasák; pinsalain.
rave: *v*. magsisigáw, magmalakí, humaging.
ravel: *v*. makalás.
raven: *n*. uwák.
ravenous: *adj*. dayukdók, dayupay; mapanagpáng.
ravine: *n*. bangin.
ravish: *v*. kalugdán, hangaan; saklutín.
raw: *adj*. hiláw, di-lutò; **~ material** panangkáp.
rawhide: *n*. balát ng baka.
ray: *n*. sinag, silahis, banaag; (*fish*) pagi.
rayon: *n*. rayon.
raze: *v*. wasakín, gibaín, iguhò.
razor: *n*. labaha.
re-: *pref*. ulî, mulî.
reach: *v*. dumatíng; umabót; iabót; sumapit; **~ for** dukwangín; **within ~** abót.
react: *v*. magbunga, gumantí; **~ion** gantí, sagót.
read: *v*. bumasa, basahin; **~er** mambabasa, bumabasa.
ready: *adj*. handâ, nakahandâ.
real: *adj*. tunay, totoó; **~ism** realismo, pagkamakatotohanan; **~ity** katotohanan.
realize: *v*. umunawà, mahulò, matantô; mapaghulò; maisakatúparan.
really: *adv*. talagá, tunay ngâ.
realm: *n*. kaharian, lupaín.
ream: *n*. resma.
reap: *v*. gumapas; mag-ani.
rear: *n*. likód; hulihán; *v*. magpalakí.
reason: *n*. layon, dahilán; *v*. magpasiyá, lumutás, mangatwiran; **~able** makatwiran; **~ing** pangangatwiran.
reassure: *v*. magbigáy-tiwalang mulî.
rebate: *n*. diskuwento, bawas.
rebel: *n*. rebelde; *v*. maghimagsík, magrebelde; **~lion** paghihimagsík; **~lious** mapanghimagsík.
rebirth: *n*. mulíngpagsilang.
rebuff: *n*. tanggihán.
rebuke: *v*. bumulyáw, pagwikaan.
rebut: *v*. sumalangsáng, tumugón, tugunín, **~tal** paklí; ganting-matwíd.
recalcitrant: *adj*. ayaw sumunód, suwaíl.
recall: *v*. maalaalang mulî.
recant: *v*. bawiin; itakwíl.
recapitulate: *v*. lagumin.
recede: *v*. mag-urong; bumalík, umurong.
receipt: *n*. resibo; pagtanggáp.
receive: *v*. tumanggáp; matamó; **~r** tumanggáo, tipunán, panahod; **telephone ~r** awditibo.
recent: *adj*. bago, kamakailán lamang.
receptacle: *n*. lalagyán, sisidlán.
reception: *n*. pagtanggáo; pagsalubong.
recess: *n*. risés, pahingá.

recession: *n*. pag-urong; paglayô.
recipe: *n*. résipe, paraán ng paglulutò.
recipient: *n*. ang tumanggáo.
reciprocal: *adj*. kapalít, katugón, katumbás; tugunan; (*gram*.) *n*. tambingan.
reciprocate: *v*. tumugón, gumantí.
recital: *n*. pagsasalaysáy, paglalahad.
recite: *v*. magsalaysáy, magbida; bumigkás.
reckless: *adj*. waláng-tarós, waláng-ingat.
reckon: *v*. kumilala; magpalagáy; tuusín.
reclaim: *v*. bumawì, magpasaulì.
recline: *v*. humilig; sumandál, sumandíg.
recognition: *n*. pagkilala; pagtanggáp; pagpapahalagá.
recognize: *v*. kilalanin; mákilala; tanggapín, pumansín.
recoil: *v*. mápaurong; sumikad.
recollect: *v*. maalaala.
recommend: *v*. magrekomendá, itagubilin; ipayo; **~ation** *n*. tagubilin.
recompense: *v*. makinabang.
reconcile: *v*. magkasundô; tumalagá.
reconnaissance: *n*. pagmamatyág.
reconnoiter: *v*. magmatyág.
record: *n*. plaka; talâ; kasulatan; *v*. magtalâ.
recount: *v*. ikuwento; mulíng bilangin.
recourse: *n*. pagdulóg, dulugan.
recover: *v*. manumbalik; makabawì.
recreation: *n*. libangan, aliwan, pagaalíw.
recrimination: *n*. ganting-paratang.
recruit: *n*. rekluta, bagong kaanib; *v*. mangaláp.
rectangle: *n*. rektánggulo.
rectification: *n*. pagtutuwíd, pagwawastô, pagtutumpák.
rectify: *v*. iayos, iwastô, itumpák, tuwirín.
rectory: *n*. tírahan ng kura.
rectum: *n*. tumbóng.
recuperate: *v*. magpalakás, magpagalíng.
recur: *v*. magbalík, umulit; **~rence** pagbalík, pag-ulit.
red: *n*. pulá; ~ **cross** Krus Roha; ~ **handed** huli sa akto; ~ **herring** pampalitó, pampaligáw; ~ **snapper** *n*. maya-maya, bambangon, managat, matangal; ~ **porgy** bisugong tabo, mahuwana; **~-tailed cavalla** puláng-buntót.
redden: *v*. mamulá; papulahín.
reddish: *adj*. mamulá-mulá, mapula-pulá.
redeem: *v*. tumubós; humangò, magligtás.
redemption: *n*. pagtubós, pagkatubós.
redress: *v*. lunasan; *n*. lunas.
reduce: *v*. magbawas, magpaliít.
reduction: *n*. pagbabawas, bawas.
redundant: *adj*. kalabisán.
reduplicate: *v*. umulit, ulitin; **~d** *adj*. inuulit.
reduplication: *n*. pag-uulit; **partial** ~ *n*. báhagihang pag-ulit; **full** ~ *n*.búuang pag-ulit.
reed: *n*. tambô.
reef: *n*. bahura; batuhán.
reek: *v*. mangamóy; umalingasaw.
reel: *n*. ulakan, ikirán; karete.
refer: *v*. sumanggunì; ikonsulta; tumukoy.
referee: *n*. tagahatol, reperí.
reference: *n*. sanggunián; reperénsiya, sangguniáng babasahín.
refill: *v*. lamnáng mulî, puníng mulî.
refine: *v*. dalisayin; malantáy; **~d** repinado, dalisay; **~ment** kayumian, hinhín.
reflect: *v*. humunáb, pabalikín; maglarawan; **~ion** paglalarawan, panganganinag.
reflexive: *adj*. (*gram*.) pasarilí.
reform: *v*. pabutihin, bumuti; *n*. pagbabago.
refractory: *adj*. sutíl, masuwayin.
refrain: *v*. pigilin ang sarili; *n*. koro, reprán.
refresh: *v*. papanariwain; **~ment** *n*. pagpapapresko, pampalamíg, pamawing-gutom.
refrigerate: *v*. eladuhin, palamigín.
refrigerator: *n*. palamigan, pridyedér.
refuge: *n*. kublihan, kanlungan, taguán.
refugee: *n*. takas.
refund: *n*. pagsasaulì ng ibinayad; *v*. ibalík (salapî).
refusal: *n*. pag-ayáw, pagtanggí.
refuse: *v*. tanggihán, ayawán, magpahindî; *n*. basura, dumí.
refute: *v*. pabulaanan, pasinungalingan.
regain: *v*. magpanag-ulî.
regal: *adj*. makaharì.
regard: *v*. magpalagáy; tingnáng mabuti; masdán; malasin; *n*. pagmamasíd, pagtitig; alang-alang; **~ing** *prep*. tungkól sa, hinggíl sa.
regatta: *n*. karera ng paggaod o paglalayag.
regent: *n*. rehente, pansamantaláng-punò.

regime: *n.* pamunuán, pamamahalà.
regiment: *n.* rehimyento.
region: *n.* lugár, dako, poók, panig; **~al** pampoók.
register: *v.* ilistá, ipatalâ; *n.* listahan, talaan, rehistro.
registrar: *n.* tagapagtalâ.
registration: *n.* pagtatalâ, paglilistá.
registry: *n.* pátalaan; rehistro.
regress: *v.* umurong.
regret: *n.* pagsisisi; *v.* magsisi, magdamdám, manghinayang; **~ful** nagsisisi.
regular: *adj.* palagian, pirmihan; karaniwan; katamtaman; maayos; pantáy-pantáy.
regulate: *v.* mamahalà, kontrolahín.
regulation: *n.* palakad, reglamento, kautusán; álintuntunin.
rehabilitation: *n.* pagpapanibagong-buhay; pagbabagong-tatag.
rehearsal: *n.* pag-eensayo; pagsasanay; pagsasalaysáy.
rehearse: *v.* mag-insayo; isalaysáy.
reign: *n.* pangangasiwà, panahón ng kapangyarihan; *v.* magharì.
rein: *n.* renda; *v.* rendahán.
reindeer: *n.* usáng reno.
reinforce: *v.* palakasín, patibayin; **~ment** pampatibay, pampalakás.
reinstate: *v.* ibalík sa dating tungkulin.
reiterate: *v.* umulit, ulitin.
reject: *v.* tanggihán, di-tanggapín, itapon; **~tion** pagtanggí.
rejoice: *v.* magsayá, magalák.
rejuvenate: *v.* magpabatà, magbagong-sibol.
relapse: *n.* binat; *v.* mabinat.
relate: *v.* isalaysáy, ikuwento; magkaugnáy; **~d** *adj.* kaugnáy; magkamag-anak.
relation: *n.* kaugnayan; relasyón; magkamag-anak; **~ship** kaugnayan.
relative: *n.* hinlóg, kamag-anak; *adj.* kaugnáy; bagay-bagay; **~ pronoun** *n.* panghalíp pamanggít.
relax: *v.* lumuwág; magpahingá; manahimik; **~ation** pagpapahí-pahingá; pagluluwág.
relay: *v.* ihatíd; *n.* riléy.
release: *v.* bitiwan; palayain; *n.* pagpapalayà.
relevant: *adj.* nauugnáy, nauukol sa paksâ.
reliable: *adj.* mapagtitiwalaan; mapaniniwalaan.
reliance: *n.* pagtitiwalà.
relic: *n.* relikya, labí, banál na alaala.
relief: *n.* ginhawa, kaluwagán; abuloy; panaklolo.
relieve: *v.* paginhawahin, papagbawahin, pahupaín.
religion: *n.* relihiyón, pananampalataya.
religious: *adj.* may relihiyón, tungkól sa relihiyón.
relinquish: *v.* isukò; lisanin; iwan.
relish: *n.* kasarapán; *v.* magkagustó; máibigan.
reluctant: *adj.* atubilì, urong-sulong; bantulót.
rely: *v.* asahan, iasa; itiwalà.
remain: *v.* manatili; matirá, maiwan; **~der** *n.* ang natitirá; **~s** labí, tirá.
remark: *n.* pangungusap; puná; *v.* magsabi, bumanggít; **~able** *adj.* kapansín-pansín; di-karaniwan.
remedy: *n.* remedyo, panlunas; *v.* magremedyo; lunasan.
remember: *v.* maalaala, magunitâ; isaalaala.
remembrance: *n.* gunitâ, alaala.
remind: *v.* ipaalaala, ipagunitâ; **~er** *n.* paalaala.
reminisce: *n.* alalahanin.
remission: *n.* pagbabawa, pagbabawas; patawad.
remit: *v.* magpadalá; bawahan; **~tance** *n.* pagpadalá.
remnant: *n.* retaso, pinagtabasan.
remonstrate: *v.* tumutol.
remorse: *n.* mataós na pagsisisi.
remote: *adj.* malayò.
removal: *n.* pag-aalís.
remove: *v.* mag-alís, ialís; itiwalág; pawiin; kumaltás; **~ ash from cigarette** *v.* titisan, abuhán; **~ bark** *v.* bakbakán; **~ earwax** *v.* hinulihán; **~ from top** *v.* hapawin; **~ skin** *v.* laplapín; **~ weeds** *v.* himamatan.
remunerate: *v.* gantimpalaan, bayaran.
renaissance: *n.* mulíng-pagsilang.
render: *v.* ibigáy, gawín; isulit; magkaloób.
rendezvous: *n.* tipanan, tagpuan.
rendition: *n.* pagganáp, pagtugtóg; pagsasalin.
renegade: *n.* taksíl, lilo.
renew: *v.* baguhin; papanumbalikin; magpani-

bago; **~al** pagkakabago, pag-uulit.
renounce: *v*. tumalikód; magtakwíl.
renovate: *v*. baguhin, kumpunihín.
renowned: *adj*. bantóg, mabunyî, kilalá.
rent: *n*. upa, renta, arkilá; *v*. umarkilá, umupa; **~al** upa.
renunciation: *n*. pagtatakwíl, pagtiwalág.
repair: *v*. kumpunihín; isaasyos; **~ nets** *v*. maghayuma.
reparation: *n*. pagbabayad-puri.
repast: *n*. pagkain.
repay: *v*. gantihín, bayaran.
repeal: *v*. pawaláng-bisà; *n*. pagpapawaláng-bisà.
repeat: *v*. ulitin; **~ed** *adj*. inulit, mulî; **~edly** *adv*. paulit-ulit.
repel: *v*. itabóy, ikasuklám; **~lent** *adj*. naka-súsuklám.
repent: *v*. magsisi; **~ance** *n*. pagsisisi; **~ant** *adj*. nagsisisi.
repercussion: *n*. alingawngáw.
repertory: *n*. repertoryo.
repetition: *n*. pag-ulit, pagkaulit.
replace: *v*. palitán; isaulì; humalili, pumalít; **~ment** *n*. pagpapalít, paghahalili.
replenish: *v*. lagyáng mulî, punuing mulî.
replete: *adj*. punô, putós, hitík.
replica: *n*. salin, kopya, sipì.
reply: *n*. sagót, tugón; *v*. sagutín, sumagót.
report: *n*. balità; ulat, report; *v*. iulat, magbigáy-ulat; **~er** *n*. tagapagbalità.
repose: *v*. humigâ; *n*. pamamahingá.
repository: *n*. repositoryo, lalagyán.
reprehend: *v*. pagwikaan; kagalitan; sisihin.
represent: *v*. katawanín; sumagisag; kumaka-tawán; **~ation** *n*. pagkatawán; **~ative** *n*. kinatawán, sugò, representante.
repress: *v*. pumigil; sumupil; sansalain.
reprieve: *n*. pansamantaláng kamátayan.
reprimand: *v*. kagalitan, pagsabihan; pagwi-kaan.
reprint: *n*. ikalawáng limbág, panibagong limbág.
reprisal: *n*. higantí, gantíng-pinsalà.
reproach: *n*. pagsisi; *v*. manisi.
reproduce: *v*. kopyahín, tularan; mag-anak.
reproduction: *n*. pamumunga, pagpaparami; pag-ulit.
reproof: *n*. pagsisi, pagwiwikà.
reprove: *v*. sisihin, pagwikaan.
reptile: *n*. reptilya.
republic: *n*. repúblika.
repudiate: *v*. itakwíl; itatuwâ.
repugnant: *adj*. nakasusuklám, nakaririmarim.
repulse: *v*. mapaurong; *n*. paurungin.
repulsive: *adj*. nakasusuklám, nakamumuhî, nakaíinís, nakákainís.
reputable: *adj*. kapuri-puri, marangál, kaga-lang-galang.
reputation: *n*. reputasyón, pangalan, kapu-rihán.
request: *v*. ipakiusap; *n*. pakikiusap; pama-manhík.
require: *v*. kailanganin, hingín, utusan; **~ment** *n*. pangangailangan.
requisite: *n*. kahíngian; *adj*. hinihingî; kina-kailangan.
requisition: *n*. kahílingan.
rescind: *v*. pawaláng-bisà; iurong.
rescue: *v*. iligtás, sagipín, hanguin.
research: *n*. pananaliksík; *v*. manaliksík.
resemble: *v*. makatulad, matulad; mákamukhâ; mákahawig.
resent: *v*. magalit, magdamdám, masamaín; **~ment** *n*. galit, poót.
reservation: *n*. pagpapareserba; pasubalì.
reserve: *n*. reserba, panlaán, patagana; **~s** (*mil.*) panlaang kawal; *v*. maglaán, magreserba.
reservoir: *n*. sisidlán, depósito.
reside: *v*. manirá, tumahán; **~nce** *n*. táhanan, tírahan; **~nt** *n*. naninirahan; **~ntial** *adj*. pan-tahanan.
residual: *adj*. labí, tirá.
residue: *n*. natitirá; latak, nálalabí.
resign: *v*. magbitíw sa tungkulin; **~ation** *n*. pagbibitíw.
resin: *n*. resina, dagtâ.
resist: *v*. lumaban, tumutol; mapigil; **~ance** *n*. paglaban, pagtutol; pagtatanggól.
resolute: *adj*. disidido, matigás, natatalagá.
resolution: *n*. pagpapasiyá, pagtitika.
resolve: *v*. lumutás; magpatibay; ipasiyá.
resonant: *adj*. matunóg, maugong, matagin-tíng.

resort: *n.* bakasyunan, pahingahan; takbuan; *v.* mangailangan; magtungo; dumulóg.
resound: *v.* umalingawngáw.
resource: *n.* rekurso, mapagkukunan, pinagkukunan; kakayahán; kayamanan; **~ful** *adj.* maparaán, mapamaraán.
respect: *n.* paggalang, pagpipitagan; *v.* igalang, mamitagan; **~able** *adj.* kapita-pitagan, kagalang-galang; **~ful** *adj.* magalang; mapítagan.
respective: *adj.* ukul-ukol, kaní-kanyá.
respiration: *n.* paghingá.
respire: *v.* humingá.
respite: *n.* pahingá, pamamahingá.
resplendent: *adj.* makináng.
respond: *v.* sagutín, tugunín.
response: *n.* sagót, tugón.
responsibility: *n.* responsibilidád, tungkulin; pananagutan.
responsible: *adj.* nananagót; mapagkakatiwalaan.
rest: *n.* pahingá; *v.* magpahingá; **~less** galawgáw, balisá, di-mapakalí.
restaurant: *n.* restaurán, karihan; **small ~** karinderiya.
restitution: *n.* pagsasaulì; paggantíng-bayad, pagpapanumbalik.
restive: *adj.* balisá.
restless: *adj.* balisá; di mapalagáy.
restore: *v.* magbalík sa dating kalagayan; isaulì.
restrain: *v.* pigilan, sawayín; magpigil.
restraint: *n.* sawáy, pagpigil.
restrict: *v.* itakdâ, higpitán; **~ion** *n.* kabawalan, paghihigpít.
result: *n.* bunga, resulta; *v.* humantóng sa.
resume: *v.* magpatuloy, ipagpatuloy.
resumé: *n.* buód, kabuuran; lagom.
resumption: *n.* pagpapatuloy.
resurrection: *n.* pagpapanag-ulî, pagkabuhay mulî.
resuscitate: *v.* magpamalay-tao, buhayin.
retail: *n.* tingî; *adj.* tingian; **~er** magtitingì.
retain: *v.* panatilihin, pamalagiin; matandaán.
retake: *v.* mulíng kunan; bawiin.
retaliate: *v.* gumantí, maghigantí.
retaliation: *n.* pagganti.
retard: *v.* magpatagál, bumalam.
retch: *v.* dumuwál.
retention: *n.* pagpapanatili, pamamalagì.
reticent: *adj.* waláng kibô; di-masalitâ.
retinue: *n.* mga abay.
retire: *v.* magretiro; lumigpít; lumikom; **~ment** *n.* pagpapahingá sa trabaho.
retort: *v.* ipaklí.
retouch: *v.* retokihin.
retrace: *v.* tuntuning pabalík, gunitain; alalahanin.
retract: *v.* bumawà, mag-urong; bawiin.
retreat: *v.* umurong, bumalík; *n.* urungán.
retribution: *n.* gantí; pagpaparusa.
retrieve: *v.* bawiin, kuning mulî.
retrogression: *n.* pag-urong; pagbabà sa urì.
retrospect: *adj.* sa paggunitâ.
return: *v.* magsaulì; ibalík; bumalík; *adj.* pabalík; **in ~** bilang kapalít.
reunion: *n.* mulíng pagtitipon.
reunite: *v.* mulíng pagsamahin; mulíng magsama.
revamp: *v.* ayusin, kumpunihin.
reveal: *v.* magpakita, magbunyág, magtapát; ihayág.
revel: *v.* magsayá.
revelation: *n.* paghahayág, pagsisiwalat.
revenge: *n.* higantí, gantí; **~ful** mapaghigantí.
revenue: *n.* kinita; rentas internas.
reverberate: *v.* umalingawngáw.
revere: *v.* magpitagan, gumalang; sumambá; **~nce** *n.* paggalang, pítágan; pakundangan; pahalagá; **~nt** *adj.* magalang.
reversal: *n.* pagbaligtád, pagtumbalík.
reverse: *n.* kabaligtarán, kasaliwaán; likód; *v.* sumaliwâ; bumaligtád; ibaligtad; *adj.* baligtád, tumbalík.
revert: *v.* manumbalik, manaulî.
review: *n.* repaso; *v.* magrepaso; magsuring mulî.
revile: *n.* alimurahin.
revise: *v.* baguhin; pabutihin.
revision: *n.* pagbabago, rebisyón.
revival: *n.* paglakás; pagbabagong-buhay; mulíng pagsilang.
revive: *v.* magpamalay-taong mulî; magpasiglá.
revoke: *v.* bumawì; magpawaláng-bisà.
revolt: *n.* pag-aalsá, paghihimagsík.

revolution: *n*. hímagsikan, pag-aalsá, rebolusiyón; pagligid; pag-ikot; **~ary** *adj*. mapanghimagsík; *n*. manghihimagsík, rebolusyonista.
revolve: *v*. umikot; lumigid.
revolver: *n*. rebolbér, baríl.
reward: *n*. gantimpalà; *v*. gantihín.
rhetoric: *n*. retórika; sayusay.
rhetorical: *adj*. pantalumpatì, ng retórika.
rheumatism: *n*. reuma, rayuma.
rhubarb: *n*. ruwibarbo.
rhyme: *n*. rima, tugmâ; *v*. magrima, magtugmâ.
rhythm: *n*. ritmo, indayog, aliw-iw; **~ics** *n*. palátugmaan.
rib: *n*. tadyáng.
ribald: *adj*. lapastangan; malaswâ; mahalay.
ribbon: *n*. laso, sintas; ~ **garfish** kambabalo, salasa.
rice: *n*. palay; **husked** ~ bigás; **cooked** ~ kanin; **burnt** ~ tutóng; **fried** ~ sinangág; ~ **field** palayan; **~mill** bigasan, gilingán ng palay.
rich: *adj*. mayaman; (*fertile*) matabâ.
rickety: *adj*. mahinà, umaalóg.
rid: *v*. paalisín, pawalán.
riddle: *n*. palisipán, bugtóng.
ride: *v*. sumakáy, magsakáy.
ridge: *n*. tagaytáy; palupo; buról.
ridicule: *v*. tawanan, libakín; kutyaín, tuyaín.
ridiculous: *adj*. nakakatawá, kakatuwá, katawá-tawá, balighô.
rifle: *n*. riple, baríl.
rift: *n*. siwang, awang, biták, puwáng; hidwaan.
rig: *n*. kalesa; *v*. sangkapán.
right: *adj*. tamà, matwíd; wastô, hustó; totoó; *n*. (*right side*) kanan; (*privilege*) karapatán; ~ **of way** karapatáng dumaán; ~ **away** kaagád; ngayón din; ~ **angle** panulukang tumpák; **~eous** banál, tapát, tumpák, makatárungan. **human ~s** *n*. karapatáng pantao.
rigid: *adj*. matigás, mahigpít; matibay.
rigor: *n*. kahigpitán, kalupitán; **~ous** mahigpít, mabalasik; mabagsík.
rim: *n*. gilid; (*of a hat*) pardiyás, dahon.
rind: *n*. balát; banakal.
ring: *n*. (*finger*) singsíng; (*hoop*) argulya; (*circle*) bilog; (*boxing*) ruweda; (*sound*) tunóg, kulilíng; *v*. tumugtóg, kumililíng; **~leader** pinunò; ~ **bush** akapulko.
ringleader: *n*. pasimunò, kapural.
ringworm: *n*. buni.
rinse: *v*. magbanláw, mag-anláw; (*mouth*) magmumog.
riot: *n*. kaguluhan; *v*. mangguló.
rip: *v*. pumunit, pumilas.
ripe: *adj*. hinóg; **~n** *v*. mahinóg.
ripple: *n*. alun-alón; onda-ondá.
ripsaw: *n*. lagaring panistís.
rise: *v*. tumaás, lumakí; (*sun*) sumikat.
risk: *n*. panganib, peligro; *v*. ipagbakásakalì, itayâ, ipagsápalarán; **~y** *adj*. mapanganib.
rite: *n*. rito, seremonya.
ritual: *n*. ritwál, seremonya.
rival: *n*. karibál, kaagáw; *v*. mapaligsahan; maglaban; **~ry** labanán; kompetensiya, pagpapangagáw.
river: *n*. ilog.
rivet: *n*. rimatse.
rivulet: *n*. ilug-ulugan, batis.
road: *n*. daán, lansagan, karsada, kalye.
roam: *v*. magpagala-galà, magpalibut-libot.
roar: *v*. umungal; *n*. ungal, ugong, dagundóng.
roast: *v*. iihaw, ihurnó; ~ **pork** litsón.
rob: *v*. manloób, magnakaw, agawan; **~ber** *n*. manloloób, magnanakaw; **~bery** *n*. looban, nakawán.
robe: *n*. bata; *v*. damtán.
robot: *n*. robot.
robust: *adj*. matipunô, malusóg.
rock: *n*. bató; *v*. tumgóy, umugâ, gumiwang; iugóy; yanigín; **~ing chair** tumba-tumba; **~y** mabató; ~ **goby** biyang bató.
rocket: *n*. kuwitis.
rod: *n*. baras; gabilya; (*fishing*) baliwasan.
roe: *n*. itlóg ng isdâ, pugá.
rogue: *n*. pusong.
role: *n*. papél; tungkulin sa bahay.
roll: *v*. gumulong; magpulupot; *n*. gulong; (*of coins*) kartutso; ~ **up** maglihís; *n*. balumbón, bilot; **~er** pampatag, pamipís, pisón; **~ing pin** rodilyo; ~ **up dress** *v*. bulislisán.
romance: *n*. romansa, pag-iibigan.
romantic: *adj*. romántiko.
roof: *n*. bubóng; *v*. mag-atíp; **~ing** pag-aatíp.

rookie: *n*. bagito, baguhan; singkî.
room: *n*. silíd, kuwarto; (*space*) lugár; **~mate** kakuwarto; **~y** *adj*. maluwáng.
roost: *n*. pagdapuán; *v*. dumapò.
rooster: *n*. tandáng; tatyaw, katyaw.
root: *n*. ugát; **~ word** salitáng-ugát; **square ~** *n*. pariugát.
rope: *n*. lubid; *v*. igapos.
rosary: *n*. rosaryo.
rose: *n*. rosas.
rosemary: *n*. romero.
roster: *n*. talaan, listahan.
rostrum: *n*. plataporma, entablado.
rot: *v*. masirà, mabulók.
rotate: *v*. umikot, uminog; pagturnu-turnuhín.
rotation: *n*. pag-ikot, pag-inog.
rotten: *adj*. bulók, sirâ.
rotund: *adj*. bilóg; matambók.
rouge: *n*. kolorete, pampapulá ng pisngí.
rough: *adj*. bakú-bakô, magaspáng; magasláw.
roulette: *n*. ruleta.
round: *adj*. bilóg; **~about** paligid-ligid; pasikut-sikot; paliguy-ligoy; **~ trip** balikang paglalakbáy; **~-up** pagsasama-sama, tipunin; **~-bodied garfish** tambilawan; **~ herring** tulis; **~ scad** galunggóng.
rouse: *v*. gisingin; **~ to action** pakilusin.
route: *n*. daanan, ruta.
routine: *n*. karaniwang gawain, karaniwang palakad.
rove: *v*. magpagala-galà, maglibót; maglagalág.
rover: *n*. galà; lagalág.
row: *n*. hanay, pila, hilera; álitan; *v*. gumaod.
rowdy: *adj*. maguló, magasláw, maligalig; na pakaingay.
royal: *adj*. ng harì, pangharì, makaharì.
rub: *v*. magkiskís; magkuskós; **~ off** hilurin.
rubber: *n*. goma; **~ band** lástiko.
rubbish: *n*. basura; yagít.
rubble: *n*. iskombro, kaskaho.
ruby: *n*. rubí.
rucksack: *n*. alporhas.
rudder: *n*. timón, ugit; **~ fish** ilak.
ruddy: *adj*. namumulá-mulá.
rude: *adj*. bastós; magaspáng; **~ness** kabastusán.
rudiment: *n*. pasimulâ; **~ary** *adj*. panimulâ.
rue: *v*. pagsisihan.
ruffle: *n*. rapol, pangitî; *v*. gumusót.
rug: *n*. alpombra.
rugged: *adj*. bakú-bakô; mabagsík.
ruin: *v*. sirain, wasakín; *n*. guhò; wasák.
rule: *n*. tuntunin; kautusán; pamamahalà; *v*. mamahalà; **~r** *n*. (*leader*) pinunò; (*for measuring*) regladór, panraya.
ruling: *n*. pasiyá.
rum: *n*. ram, rhum.
rumble: *v*. dumagundóng.
ruminate: *v*. ngumatâ.
rummage: *v*. halughugín; maghalungkát; magbungkál.
rumor: *n*. higing, bulúng-bulungan, tsismis.
rump: *n*. puwitán, pigî.
rumple: *v*. gusutín; *n*. tupî.
rumpus: *n*. káguluhan; awayan.
run: *v*. tumakbó; (*manage*) mamahalà; **~ across** magkatagpô; **~ out of** maubusan; **~ away** tumakas; *n*. takbó; **~away** *n*. takas, puga, tanan; **~-down** *adj*. sirá-sirâ; **~ over** makásagasà.
runaway: *n*. takas.
rung: *n*. baitang.
runt: *n*. bulilit.
runway: *n*. patakbuhan, daanán (ng eroplano).
rupture: *v*. pumutók, malagót; *n*. pagkalagót; álitan.
rural: *adj*. pambukid, rurál.
ruse: *n*. lansí; laláng; dayà.
rush: *v*. magmadalî, magpadalu-dalos, madaliín; *n*. pagmamadalî.
Russian: *n*., *adj*. Ruso
rust: *n*. kalawang; *v*. magkakalawang; **~y** *adj*. makalawang, kálawangín.
rustic: *adj*. pambukid, tagabukid.
rustle: *v*. kumaluskós, pumagaspás; **~r** *n*. magnanakaw ng baka.
rut: *n*. daán ng gulóng.
ruthless: *adj*. waláng-awà, malupít, waláng habág.
rye: *n*. senteno; ray.

S

Sabbath: *n*. Sábado (ng mga Hudyó), araw ng pangilin.
saber: *n*. sable.
sabotage: *v*. sabutahihin; *n*. pagpapahamak, paninirà, sabotahe.
saccharin: *n*. sakarina.
sack: *n*. sako; kostál; *v*. dambungín.
sacrament: *n*. sakramento.
sacred: *adj*. sagrado.
sacrifice: *n*. pag-aalay, sakripisyo.
sacrilegious: *adj*. lapastangan.
sacrosanct: *adj*. napakasagrado.
sad: *adj*. malungkót, malumbáy; **~den** ikalungkót; **~ness** *n*. lungkót.
saddle: *n*. upuan, sintadera; si(l)yá.
sadist: *n*. sadista.
safe: *adj*. ligtás, matibay; *n*. kaha-de-yero; **~ty** kaligtasan.
safeguard: *v*. iligtás, iadyá.
sag: *v*. lumayláy, lumuylúy.
saga: *n*. alamát, leyenda.
sagacious: *adj*. matalino.
sage: *n*. pahám, pantás.
Sagittarius: *n*. mámamanà (sa zodiac).
sail: *n*. layag; *v*. maglayág; **~or** *n*. magdaragát, marinero; **~fish** pahabela.
saint: *n*. santo; **~hood** *n*. pagkasanto.
sake: *n*. kapakanán; **for your ~** alang-alang sa iyo.
salable: *adj*. mabilí, maipagbíbilí.
salacious: *adj*. malaswâ, mahalay.
salad: *n*. ensalada.
salary: *n*. suweldo, sahod, kita.
sale: *n*. pagbibilí, benta; **~sman** *n*. tindero, tagapagbilí; **for ~** ipinagbíbilí.
salient: *adj*. halatáng-halatâ; namúmukód.
saline: *adj*. ng asín, maasín.
saliva: *n*. laway.
sallow: *adj*. nanínіláw.
sally: *v*. dumaluhong; *n*. bulalás; pagdaluhong.
salmon: *n*. salmón.
salon: *n*. sala, salón.
saloon: *n*. bulwagan, salón.
salt: *n*. asín; *v*. asinán; **~y** *adj*. maasín, maalat.
salubrious: *adj*. pampalusóg, nakapagpápalusóg.
salutation: *n*. pagbatì.
salute: *v*. saluduhan, magpugay; batiin; *n*. saludo, batì.
salvage: *v*. sagipín; *n*. pagsagíp.
salvation: *n*. pagliligtás.
salvo: *n*. saludong naputók, pasalbá.
same: *adj*. din, pareho, kagaya.
sample: *n*. muwestra, halimbawà; *v*. tikmán.
sanctify: *v*. pabanalín.
sanction: *n*. pahintulot, pagpapatibay.
sanctity: *n*. kabánalan, pagkabanál.
sanctuary: *n*. santuwaryo, banál na lugár.
sand: *n*. buhangin; **~y** *adj*. mabuhangin.
sandal: *n*. sandalyas; sándalo.
sandpaper: *n*. liha; *v*. lihahin.
sandwich: *n*. sanwits, emparadados.
sanitary: *adj*. malinis; **~ napkin** pasadór.
sanity: *n*. katinuán, hustóng pag-iisip.
sap: *n*. katás, dagtâ.
sapling: *n*. suwí; batang punungkahoy.
sapodilla: *n*. tsiko.
sapphire: *n*. sápiro.
sarcasm: *n*. tuyâ, panununyâ; uyám.
sarcastic: *adj*. nakakatuyâ, mapanuyâ,
sardine: *n*. sardinas, lawlaw, karis-karis; **transparent ~** bulinaw.
sash: *n*. sintás, laso.
Satan: *n*. satanás; **~ic** *adj*. makademonyo.
satchel: *n*. maletín.
satiate: *v*. busugín, suyain.
satin: *n*. satín.
satire: *n*. tuyâ, pagtuyâ, tudyó.
satisfaction: *n*. kasiyahan, kaluguran.
satisfy: *v*. bigyáng-kasiyahan, pawiin.
saturate: *v*. tigmakín, babarin.
Saturday: *n*. Sábado.
sauce: *n*. sarsa; **~pan** *n*. kasirola.
saucer: *n*. platito.
saunter: *v*. lumakad-lakad.
sausage: *n*. longganisa, batutay, tsoriso.
savage: *n*. taong-gubat, salbahe.
savant: *n*. marunong na tao; pantás.
save: *v*. iligtás; sakupin; tipirín.
savior: *n*. tagapagligtás.
savor: *n*. laso; *v*. lasapín, lasahin; **~y** malinamnám.

saw: *n.* lagarì; *v.* maglagarì; **~dust** kusot, pinaglagarian; **~fish** barasan, tagán.
say: *v.* sabihin, wikain, bigkasín; sabi; **~ing** pananalitâ, saláwikaín, kasabihán.
scab: *n.* langíb; (*strikebreaker*) eskiról.
scabbard: *n.* kaluban, baina.
scaffold: *n.* andamyo; plantsa.
scald: *v.* banlián; *n.* banlî, pasò.
scale: *n.* (*of reptiles*) kaliskís; (*balance*) timbangan; (*calibrated marks*) grado; *v.* akyatín.
scalp: *n.* anit.
scalpel: *n.* iskalpel.
scaly: *adj.* makaliskís.
scamper: *v.* kumarimot.
scan: *v.* suriing mabuti; tingnáng pahapyáw.
scandal: *n.* iskándalo, alingasngás; **~ous** *adj.* maiskándalo, nakasisirang-puri.
scant: *adj.* maliít, bahagyâ; **~y** katitíng; kákarampót.
scapegoat: *n.* sangkalan, kasangkapan, hantungan ng sisi.
scar: *n.* peklat, pilat; *v.* magkapeklat.
scarce: *adj.* bihirà, madalang; manalát.
scare: *v.* takutin; **~crow** panakot.
scarf: *n.* bupanda, bandana.
scarlet: *n.* iskarlata.
scatter: *v.* isabog, ibudbód, ikalat; maghiwáhiwaláy.
scavenger: *n.* basurero.
scene: *n.* tagpô, pinangyarihan; **~ry** *n.* tanawin, senaryo.
scent: *n.* amóy, pabangó.
scepter: *n.* setro.
schedule: *n.* palatuntunan, talaan; *v.* itakdâ.
scheme: *n.* panukalà, balak; *v.* magbalak.
scholar: *n.* dalub-aral; mag-aarál, iskolár.
scholarship: *n.* pensiyón; karunungan; kaálaman.
school: *n.* eskuwelahán, paraalán; (*of fish*) kawan.
science: *n.* aghám, siyénsiya.
scientific: *adj.* makaaghám, siyentípiko.
scientist: *n.* siyentípiko.
scintilla: *n.* bakás; bahid.
scissors: *n.* guntíng.
scoff: *v.* kutyaín; *n.* pagkutyâ.
scold: *v.* murahin, pagsabihan.
scoop: *n.* tabò, sandók; maghukáy; maglimás.
scoot: *v.* sumibad.
scope: *n.* abót ng isip.
scorch: *v.* pasuin.
score: *n.* puntós, bilang; *v.* makapuntós, umiskór; magtalâ.
scorn: *v.* humamak, uyamín; **~ful** mapanlibák.
scorpion: *n.* alakdán.
Scotch: *n., adj.* Eskosés, tagá-Eskosya.
Scotland: *n.* Eskosya.
scoundrel: *n.* salbahe, taong buhóng.
scour: *v.* isisín, saliksikínn.
scourge: *v.* hagupitín, paluin, hampasín; bugbugín.
scout: *n.* tagapanubok, iskaut.
scowl: *v.* sumimangot.
scramble: *v.* mag-ukyabít, magpangagawán.
scrap: *n.* kapiraso, labí; *v.* ibasura.
scrape: *v.* kayurin, kaskasín.
scratch: *v.* gasgasán, kalmutín, kahigin; *n.* gasgás, grulís, galos; **up to ~** nasa pámantayan.
scrawny: *adj.* payát at mahinà.
scream: *n.* tilî, sigáw; *v.* tumilî; humiyáw.
screech: *n.* palaháw, matinís na sigáw.
screen: *n.* tabing, tela-metálika; *v.* tabingan.
screw: *n.* tornilyo; *v.* magroskas; **~driver** distornilyadór; **cork~** tirabusón.
scribble: *v.* sumulat nang padalus-dalos.
scribe: *n.* tagasulat, iskribyente; tagasipì.
scrimpy: *adj.* nápakauntî.
script: *n.* titik, sulat-kamáy; **~ure** banál na kasulatan.
scroll: *n.* balumbón, pergamino.
scrub: *v.* magkuskós, magiskoba.
scruple: *n.* pag-aatubilì, pag-aalangan.
scrupulosity: *n.* diwarà, kakuririan, kabusian.
scrutinize: *v.* aninawin, suriing mabuti.
scuffle: *v.* magkaguló; magpánunggaban.
sculptor: *n.* eskultór, manlililok.
sculpture: *n.* lilok, eskultura; *v.* maglilok.
scum: *n.* iskoma, lináb.
scurf: *n.* balakubak.
scurry: *v.* magmadalî, maghumangos; magkumamot.
scurvy: *n.* iskarbi.
scythe: *n.* karit; lilik.
sea: *n.* dagat; **~food** pagkaing-dagat; **~man**

marinero, mandaragát; ~ **bass** katuyot, matáng-pusà; ~ **catfish** arahan, kanduli; **~port** dáungang-dagat; ~ **urchin** susóng-dagat na may kalisag.
seagull: *n*. tagák.
seahorse: *n*. kabayo-kabayohan.
seal: *n*. (*animal*) poka; (*stamp*) selyo, taták; *v*. magselyo.
seam: *n*. tahî, datig; **~stress** *n*. mananahì, modista.
sear: *v*. pasuin.
search: *v*. hanapin, kapaán; magsaliksík; *n*. paghanap; ~ **warrant** mandamyento de rekisa; **~light** lente.
seashore: *n*. dalampasigan, baybayin, tabíng-dagat.
seasick: *adj*. lulâ, hiló, liyó.
season: *n*. panahón, tag-; *v*. timplahán; sanayin; **~able** *adj*. napapanahón; **~al** *adj*. panápanahon; **~ing** *n*. pampalasas, panimplá.
seat: *n*. upuan, likmuan; *v*. upuán.
seaweed: *n*. damóng-dagat; gulaman.
secede: *v*. tumiwalág, magbitíw.
secluded: *adj*. tagô, liblíb.
second: *adj*. ikalawá, pangalawá; **~ary** *adj*. sekundaryo, pangalawá; ~ **class** segunda klase; ~ **hand** segunda mano, galing sa ibá; ~ **nature** pinagkaugalian; ~ **person** ikalawáng panauhan, kasálitaan.
secrecy: *n*. lihim, pagkasekreto.
secret: *adj*. lihim, sekreto; *n*. sekreto; **~ive** *adj*. malihim; ~ **service** sangáy ng mga tiktík.
secretariat: *n*. kálihimán.
secretary: *n*. kalihim, sekretarya.
sect: *n*. pangkát, sekta.
section: *n*. bahagi; purók.
secular: *adj*. seglár.
secure: *adj*. tiwasáy; matatág, ligtás; *v*. magpatibay, iligtás.
security: *n*. kaligtasan; katiwasayán; panagót.
sedate: *adj*. mahinahon, tahimik.
sedative: *n*. pampakalma, kalmante.
sedentary: *adj*. palaupô.
sediment: *n*. tining, latak.
seduce: *v*. manghikayat, magligáw, mang-upat; rahuyuín.
seduction: *n*. panunulsól, pang-uupat, pang-aakit.
see: *v*. makita, tumingín; (*make sure*) tiyakín.
seed: *n*. binhî, butó, similya.
seedling: *n*. punlâ.
seek: *v*. humanap, maghangád.
seem: *v*. magtila, magmukhâ, parang; tila; warì.
seep: *v*. tumulò, tumagas; tumagós.
seer: *n*. manghuhulà; propeta.
seethe: *v*. magbubulâ; kumulô; sumulák.
segment: *n*. putol, kaputol, bahagi; pangkát; lihà.
segregate: *v*. ibukód, ilayô.
seismic: *adj*. panlindól.
seize: *v*. sunggabán, hawakang biglâ; samsamín.
seizure: *n*. pagsamsám; pagsunggáb.
seldom: *adv*. bihirà, madalang.
select: *v*. pumilì, humirang; *adj*. hirang, pilì; **~ion** *n*. pilì.
self: *n*. sarili; ~ **respect** paggalang sa sarili, amór propyo; **~-conscious** mahíyain; **~-confidence** tiwalà sa sarili; **~-control** pagtitimpî, pagpipigil sa sarili; ~ **esteem** *n*. pagpapahalagá sa sarili, pagpuri sa sarili, pagkamakasarili; ~ **sacrifice** *n*. pagpapakasakit sa sarili.
selfish: *adj*. masakím, maramot, makamkám; makasarili.
sell: *v*. magbilí; maglakò.
semantics: *n*. palásurián, semántika.
semaphore: *n*. semáporo.
semblance: *n*. pagkakaháwig.
semen: *n*. tabód.
semester: *n*. semestre; hatintaón.
semicolon: *n*. tuldók-kuwit.
senate: *n*. Senado; **Senator** *n*. Senadór.
send: *v*. ipadalá; papuntahín.
senile: *adj*. huklób, matandâ na, mahulí.
senility: *n*. katandaán, pag-uúlianin.
senior: *adj*. nakatatandâ; **~ity** katandaán.
sensation: *n*. paningín, pakiramdám; **~al** *adj*. nakagulat, kahindík-hindík.
sense: *n*. sentido, karamdaman; pakiramdám; **common** ~ sentido komún; *v*. dumamá, damahín, maramdamán; ~ **of humor** *n*. ugaling mapagpatawá.
sensible: *adj*. may-katwiran; matinô.

sensitive: *adj*. madalíng kahalataán; maramdamin; **~ness** pagkamaramdamin.
sensual: *adj*. pangkatawán; malibóg.
sentence: *n*. pangungusap; (*in court*) hatol; *v*. hatulan; **complex** ~ *n*. pangungusap na hugnayan; **compound** ~ *n*. pangungusap na tambalan; **declarative** ~ *n*. pangungusap na pasaysáy; **imperative** ~ *n*. pangungusap na pautos; **interrogative** ~ *n*. pangungusap na patanóng; **simple** ~ *n*. pangungusap na payák.
sentiment: *n*. damdamin; **~al** *adj*. sentimentál, madamdamin.
sentinel: *n*. tanod, bantáy.
sentry: *n*. tanod, bantáy; talibà.
sepal: *n*. sépalo.
separable: *adj*. maihíhiwaláy.
separate: *v*. maghiwaláy; magtanggál; ibukód, hatiin.
separation: *n*. paghihiwaláy.
September: *n*. Septiyembre.
sequel: *n*. kinalabasán, karugtóng.
sequence: *n*. pagkakasunúd-sunód.
serenade: *n*. harana; *v*. magharana.
serene: *adj*. tahimik, mapayapà.
serf: *n*. busabos, alipin.
sergeant: *n*. sarhento; ~ **fish** dalag-dagat, gile, pandawan; **~-at-arms** masero; tagapamayapà.
serial: *n*. serye; *adj*. sunúd-sunód.
series: *n*. serye, hanay.
serious: *adj*. seryo; di-nagbibirô; **~ness** pagkawaláng-kibô; **~ly** mataimtím.
sermon: *n*. sermón, pangaral.
serpent: *n*. ahas, serpiyente.
serum: *n*. suwero.
servant: *n*. alilà, bataan, utusán, katulong; alagád.
serve: *v*. magsilbí; maglingkód; **~r** serbidór, tagapagsilbí.
service: *n*. serbisyo, paglilingkód, pagtulong.
serviette: *n*. serbilyeta.
servitude: *n*. pagkaalipin; pagkabusabos.
session: *n*. sesyón, kapulungán, pagpupulong.
set: *v*. lagyán; ayusin; (*sun*) lumubóg; *adj*. nakatakdâ, nakahandâ; *n*. huwego, pulutóng, buhat.
setback: *n*. hadláng, sagabal, sagwíl.
setting: *n*. tagpô; enggaste.
settle: *v*. magpasiyá; mag-ayos; tumirá; **~ment** *n*. kasunduan, pagsasaayos; paninirahan.
seven: *n*. pitó; **~teen** labimpitó, disisiyete; **~ty** pitumpû.
sever: *v*. putulin, tagpasín; papaghiwalayín; **~ance** *n*. pagkaputol, pagkapatíd, pagkalagót.
several: *adj*. mga ilán, iba-ibá.
severe: *adj*. mahigpít, mabagsík; marahás.
severity: *n*. kahigpitán; kabigatán; kabalasikan.
sew: *v*. tumahî, manahî; tahiín; **~ing** pananahî; tahî.
sewage: *n*. dumí sa imburnál.
sewer: *n*. imburnál, alkantarilya.
sewing: *n*. pagtahî; ~ **machine** makináng-panahî.
sex: *n*. kasarian, tauhin; (*coitus*) pagtatalik, hindót; **~y** *adj*. malibóg, maiyág.
sexton: *n*. kampanero; sakristán.
shabby: *adj*. nanlilimahid.
shack: *n*. kubo, dampâ.
shackle: *n*. posas, kadena.
shade: *n*. lilim, tabing; **lamp** ~ pantalya ng lámpara; *v*. magtabing, takpán.
shadow: *n*. anino; *v*. kumanlóng; subaybayán; ~ **play** karilyo.
shaft: *n*. baras, katawán ng poste.
shaggy: *adj*. mabuhók, balhón.
shake: *v*. magkalóg, umugâ; ~ **hands** makipagkamáy, ~ **off** iwagwág.
shaky: *adj*. mabuwáy; umáalóg; umúugâ.
shallow: *adj*. mababaw, malandáy.
sham: *n*. pagkukunwarî.
shame: *n*. hiyâ; kahihiyán; **~ful** *adj*. kahiyâ-hiyâ; **~less** waláng-hiyâ.
shampoo: *n*. siyampú, panggugò; *v*. maggugò.
shank: *n*. bintî.
shanty: *n*. barungbarong, kubo.
shape: *n*. anyô, hugis; kórtehán; *v*. humugis; mabuô.
share: *n*. kabahagi, kaparte; (*in stock*) aksiyón; *v*. magbahagi, maghatì.
shark: *n*. patíng; bagsák.
sharp: *adj*. matalas, matalím; matalino; **~en** magpatalas; **~er** pantasá, hasaán.

shatter: *v*. bumasag; madurog; durugin.
shave: *v*. mag-ahit; **~r** *n*. pang-ahit.
shawl: *n*. panyolón, alampáy, balabal.
she: *pron*. siyá (babae).
shear: *v*. gupitín; **~s** *n*. guntíng.
sheath: *n*. kaluban, baina; (*of banana plant*) sahà.
sheathe: *v*. isalong.
shed: *n*. kamalig, bangán; habong; *v*. maghunos; ~ **tears** malagląg ang luhà.
sheen: *adj*. makintáb; ningníng.
sheep: *n*. tupa; kordero.
sheer: *adj*. napakanipís.
sheet: *n*. kumot; pilyego.
sheik: *n*. pinunò ng mga Arabo.
shelf: *n*. istante, salansanan.
shell: *n*. balát, kabibi.
shelter: *n*. kanlungan, taguán; *v*. tangkilikin, mag-adyá.
shelve: *v*. ilagáy sa istante.
shepherd: *n*. pastól, tagapag-alagà ng tupa.
sherry: *n*. alak-herés (Jerez).
shield: *n*. kalasag; pansanggá; *v*. ipagsanggaláng.
shift: *v*. magbago, lumipat; *n*. pagbabago, rilyebo; **night** ~ panggabí.
shimmer: *v*. magpaandáp-andáp; kumisláp; kumisáp.
shin: *n*. lulód.
shine: *v*. magningníng; sumikat; kumináng; *n*. kinang, kintáb.
shingle: *n*. tisà.
shiny: *adj*. maningníng; makináng, makintáb, makinis.
ship: *n*. barko, bapór; *v*. maglulan sa bapór.
shipment: *n*. pagluluan sa bapór.
shipwreck: *n*. pagkawasák ng bapór.
shipyard: *n*. dáhikan, baradero, gáwaan ng bapór.
shirk: *v*. umiwas.
shirt: *n*. kamisa, kamiseta.
shit: (*vulgar*) *n*. tae.
shiver: *v*. mangaligkíg.
shoal: *n*. banlík, buhanginán.
shock: *n*. yaníg, dagok; *v*. makabiglâ, gulatin; **~ing** kagulat-gulat.
shoe: *n*. sapatos; **horse~** bakal ng kabayo; **~maker** sapatero; **~string** sintás ng sapatos.
shoelace: *n*. talíng-sapatos.
shoo: *v*. bugawin; paalisin.
shoot: *v*. bumaríl; magpaputók; *n*. tubò, sibol; **~ing star** bulalakaw.
shop: *n*. tindahan; *v*. mamilí; **~per** mamimili; **~keeper** tagapagtindá, tindero.
shoplift: *v*. manekas (sa tindahan).
shore: *n*. tabíng-dagat, pasigan; pampáng.
short: *adj*. pandák; maiklî, maigsî; **~age** *n*. kakulangán; ~ **cut** tuwirang daán; **~en** paikliín, paigsiín.
shortcoming: *n*. pagkukulang, kamálían, kapintasan.
shorthand *n*. takigrapiya, iklilat.
shorts: *n*. korto, putót.
shot: *n*. baríl, tudlâ; putók; **long** ~ pakikipagsapalarán.
should: *v*. dapat; nárarapat.
shoulder: *n*. balikat; ~ **blade** *n*. paypáy.
shout: *v*. sumigáw, humiyáw; *n*. sigáw.
shove: *v*. magtulak, magsalyá.
shovel: *n*. pala; *v*. magpala.
show: *v*. ipakita, iturò; *n*. palabás; ~ **off** *v*. magparangyâ; **~case** eskaparate; **just for** ~ pakitang-tao lang.
shower: *n*. dutsa; ambón.
show-off: *n*. taong magpasikat.
showy: *adj*. masagwâ.
shred: *n*. pilas, kapiraso; *v*. maggutáy.
shrewd: *adj*. tuso, maulo, matalino; suwitik.
shriek: *n*. huni, tilî; *v*. tumilî.
shrill: *adj*. matinís, nakatutulíg.
shrimp: *n*. hipon; **dried ~s** hibi; **~fish** isdáng laring-laring, isdáng sikwán.
shrine: *n*. dambanà, templo.
shrink: *v*. umurong, umiklî; magpaurong; **~age** pag-urong.
shrivel: *v*. matuyô, malantá; mangulubót.
shrub: *n*. palumpóng.
shrug: *v*. magkibít ng balikat.
shudder: *v*. manginíg, mangaligkíg.
shuffle: *v*. magbalasa; maghalungkát.
shun: *v*. umilag, layuán.
shush: *v*. patahimikin.
shut: *v*. isará, magsará; mapinid.
shutter: *n*. persiyana, pananggá sa bintanà.

shy: *adj*. mahiyain, nahihiyâ; kimî; tigil; umíd; **~ness** pagkamahihíyain.

sibling: *n*. kapatíd.

sick: *adj*. may-sakít; **~ly** masasaktín; **~ness** sakít.

sickle: *n*. lilik, karit.

side: *n*. tagiliran; tabí; mukhâ; paligid; **take ~s** *v*. kumampí; **sideswipe** *v*. dagilin; **~walk** *n*. bangketa; **~ways** *adv*. pataligíd.

siege: *n*. pagkubkób, paglusob.

sieve: *n*. salaán, panalà; *v*. salain.

sift: *v*. salain; bistayín, magbistáy, magbitháy; **~er** panalà.

siganid: *n*. barangan, indongan, samaral; **~ fry** kuyog

sigh: *n*. buntóng-hiningá, himutók.

sight: *n*. paningín; pananáw; **~seeing** *n*. pagliliwalíw.

sign: *n*. tandâ, karátula; senyas; *v*. lumagdâ, **~board** karátula; **~ of omission** *n*. pangaltás.

signal: *n*. hudyát; senyas, babalâ; *v*. humudyát; sumenyas.

signature: *n*. lagdâ, pirma.

significance: *n*. kahulugán, katuturán, kabuluhán.

significant: *adj*. makahulugán, may-kahulugán.

signify: *v*. mangahulugán.

silence: *n*. katahimikan; **silent** *adj*. tahimik, waláng-ingay.

silhouette: *n*. silweta.

silicon: *n*. sílikon.

silk: *n*. seda, sutlâ; **~y** *adj*. maseda, malasutlâ.

sill: *n*. pasamano, palababahán.

sillago fish: *n*. asuhos, asuos.

silly: *adj*. ulók, luku-lukó; tunggák, hangál.

silt: *n*. banlík.

silver: *n*. plata, pilak; **~smith** platero, pandáy-pilak; **~ware** *n*. kubyertos na pilak; **~ barfish** balila; **~ grunt** ikuran; **~ perch** ayungin; **~side fish** guno, langaray papako; **~ sea bass** apahap.

similar: *adj*. magkatulad, magkawangis; **~ity** *n*. pagkakapareho, pagkakatulad.

simile: *n*. simil, pagtutulad.

simmer: *v*. magpakulô, kumulô.

simple: *adj*. magaán, madalíng gawín; simple; (*gram.*) payák; **~ton** *n*. hangál, utô, bobo, gago.

simplicity: *n*. kapayakán, kalantayán, kasimplihán.

simplify: *v*. pagaanín.

simulate: *v*. tularan; magkunwarî.

simultaneous: *adj*. magkasabáy, sabáy-sabáy.

sin: *n*. kasalanan (sa Diyós); **~ful** *adj*. makasalanan; **~ner** *n*. makasalanan.

since: *adv*. mulâ noón; buhat pa.

sincere: *adj*. matapát, dalisay, taós-pusò.

sinew: *n*. litid; lakás.

sing: *v*. kumantá, umawit; **~er** mangangantá, kantór.

singe: *v*. isalab.

single: *adj*. iisá, tangì, bugtóng; **~-handed** nag-íisa (waláng katulong).

singsong: *adj*. nakayayamót.

singular: *adj*. pang-isá; di-karaniwan, pambihirà.

sinister: *adj*. masamâ, nakapangángambá.

sink: *n*. lababo, hugasán; *v*. lumubóg; **~er** *n*. pabigát, pabató.

sip: *v*. humigop; *n*. higop, sipsíp.

siphon: *n*. tubong panghigop.

sir: *n*. Ginoó.

siren: *n*. sirena.

sirloin: *n*. sirloya; hiwà ng karneng baka.

sissy: *adj*. binabae.

sister: *n*. kapatíd na babae; **~-in-law** hipag.

sit: *v*. umupô; **~ting room** tanggapan ng panauhin.

site: *n*. lugár, kinátatayuán.

situated: *adj*. nakatayô.

situation: *n*. tayô; kinalalagyán, puwesto.

six: *n*. anim, saís; **~teen** labing-anim; didisaís; **~th** pang-anim, ika-anim; **~ty** animnapû.

size: *n*. lakí.

sizzle: *v*. sumagitsít; *n*. sagitsít.

skate: *n*. isketing; *v*. mag-isketing.

skein: *n*. madeha, labay.

skeleton: *n*. kalansáy; (*of house*) balangkás.

skeptical: *adj*. nagdududa, may-pagaalinlangan, mapag-alinlangan

sketch: *n*. dibuho, krokis; maiklíng kasaysayan; balangkás, bangháy; *v*. idibuho; **~y** *adj*. pahapyáw.

skewed: *adj*. balikukô.

skewer: *n*. tuhog, tuhugan, duruan; *v*. tuhugin.
skid: *v*. dumulás na patibí; *n*. sagkâ.
skill: *n*. kasanayán, kadalubhasaan; **~ed** *adj*. bihasá, sanáy, dalubhasà.
skillet: *n*. kawalì.
skim: *v*. sagapin; hapawín.
skimp: *v*. magtipíd; **~y** *adj*. kakauntî, salát.
skin: *n*. balát; (*leather*) kuwero, balát; *v*. talupan, balatán.
skinny: *adj*. payát, patpatin.
skip: *v*. luksuhín, lundagín; talunín; **~jack tuna** gulyasan.
skirmish: *n*. maiklíng labanán.
skirt: *n*. palda, saya.
skit: *n*. maikling palabás.
skulk: *v*. manubok; magtagò.
skull: *n*. bungô, bao ng ulo.
sky: *n*. langit, himpapawíd; **~rocket** *n*. kuwitis; *v*. bigláng tumaás; **~scraper** *n*. napakataás na gusalì.
slab: *n*. piraso; tilád; tipák.
slack: *adj*. maluwág, malubáy.
slam: *v*. ibagsák, isará nang malakás; *n*. kalabóg ng pintô.
slander: *n*. paninirang-puri.
slang: *n*. salitáng balbál.
slant: *v*. humilig, humilís; **~ing** *adj*. hilíg; **~wise** *adv*. pahilíg.
slap: *n*. sampál, tampál; *v*. sampalín.
slash: *v*. laslasín, iwaan.
slate: *n*. muntíng pisara.
slaughter: *v*. katayin; magpatáy, pumatáy; **~-house** *n*. matadero, katayán.
slave: *n*. alipin; **~ry** pagkaalipin; pagkabusabos.
slay: *v*. patayín, kitlan ng buhay.
sled: *n*. paragos, kareta.
sledge hammer: *n*. maso, malakíng martilyo.
sleep: *v*. matulog; *n*. tulog; **~y** *adj*. nag-aantók; **~er fish** biyang-tulog, bakulihan, dalagan, kaple, palawan.
sleeve: *n*. manggás; **~less shirt** sandó.
slender: *adj*. mahagwáy, patpatin, balingkinitan.
sleuth: *n*. tiktík; sekreta.
slice: *n*. hiwà, putol; *v*. maghiwà.
slick: *adj*. makinis, makintáb.
slide: *v*. dumulás, dumausdós; **land~** guhò.
slight: *adj*. kakauntî; **~ly** *adv*. di-masyado, bahagyâ.
slim: *adj*. payát, balingkinitan.
slime: *n*. lusak, burak.
sling: *n*. tiradór; sakláy; **~shot** tiradór.
slip: *v*. umus-ós, dumaus-ós; dumulás; *n*. malî; kamisón; **~ knot** buhól na talibugsô, tagibuhól; **~mouth fish** hiwas, bakagan, miralya, sapsáp, taksáy, tambóng, yapyáp.
slipper: *n*. tsinelas.
slippery: *adj*. madulás.
slit: *n*. punit, laslas; bitas; *v*. hiwain, laslasín.
slither: *v*. dumulás.
slobber: *v*. maglawáy.
slogan: *n*. pamanság, sawikaín.
slope: *n*. dahilig, talibís.
sloppy: *adj*. burarâ, busalsál.
slot: *n*. butas.
sloth: *n*. katamaran; kaalisagaan.
slouch: *v*. yumukyók, humukót.
sloven: *adj*. burarâ.
slow: *adj*. mabagal, maluwát; matagál; **~ly** untî-untî; dahan-dahan.
slug: *n*. lintáng-kati; *v*. hambalusin; bumambó; sumuntók.
sluggish: *adj*. tamád, tigíl; makuyad.
slum: *n*. kaiskwaterán, poók ng mga dukhâ.
slumber: *n*. pagtulog.
slump: *v*. mápasadlák; *n*. pagkásadlák; pagbabâ.
slur: *n*. tuyâ; paninirang-puri; *v*. bumigkás nang malabò.
slut: (*vulgar*) *n*. puta.
sly: *adj*. tuso, napakatuso; palihím.
smack: *v*. tumampál.
small: *adj*. muntî; kauntî; maliít.
small intestine: *n*. isaw.
smallpox: *n*. bulutong.
smart: *adj*. matalino, listo.
smash: *v*. basagin, durugin, wasakín.
smear: *v*. pahiran, kulapulan; dungisan.
smell: *v*. amuyín, maamuyán; mangamóy; *n*. amóy; **~y** nangangamóy.
smelt: *v*. tunawin (metál).
smile: *n*. ngitî; *v*. ngumitî.
smirch: *v*. dungisan; kulapulan.

smirk: *n*. ngisi.
smite: *v*. bumagabag.
smoke: *n*. usok, asó; *v*. umusok; magsigarilyo, magtabako; paasuhán; **~house** *n*. tapahan.
smoky: *adj*. mausok, maasó.
smolder: *v*. magbaga.
smooth: *adj*. makinis; **~ness** kinis.
smother: *v*. inisín.
smudge: *v*. dungisan; pausukan.
smuggle: *v*. magpuslít; maglusót; **~r** *n*. kontrabandista.
smutty: *adj*. mahalay, masagwâ.
snack: *n*. merienda, minindál.
snail: *n*. susô; kuhól.
snake: *n*. ahas; **~ eel** palos.
snap: *v*. (*break*) lumagót; (*quick bite*) sakmalín; **~per** *n*. alsís, pargito.
snare: *n*. patibóng; silò, bitag; *v*. umangan.
snarl: *v*. umangil, umungol.
snatch: *v*. sambilatin, sumaklót, dumaklót.
sneak: *v*. sumubuk-subok.
sneer: *v*. umismíd, lumabì.
sneeze: *n*. bahín; *v*. bumahín.
snicker: *n*. paghagikgík; *v*. humagikgík.
sniff: *v*. suminghót; *n*. singhót.
sniffle: *n*. pagsisininghót.
snigger: *v*. ngumisngís; humagikhík.
snip: *v*. gupitín.
snivel: *v*. mag-uhóg.
snob: *n*. supladong tao, isnabero; **~bish** *adj*. suplado, mapagmataás.
snoop: *v*. maunubok; *n*. panunubok.
snore: *n*. hilík, harok; *v*. maghilík.
snorkel: *n*. hingahan (nasa ilalim ng tubig)
snort: *v*. suminghál, sumingasing.
snout: *n*. ngusò.
snow: *n*. niyebe; busilak; *v*. magniyebe; **~y** *adj*. maniyebe; busilak.
snuff: *v*. suminghót.
snuffle: *v*. magsisinghót.
snug: *adj*. maginhawa, maayos.
snuggle: *v*. kalung-kalungin, yumakap.
so: *adv*. kayâ; ganyán, gayón; pagayón; **~ and so** si kuwán.
soak: *v*. magpigtâ; ibabad.
soap: *n*. sabón; *v*. magsabón; **~y** *adj*. masabón.
soar: *v*. pumailangláng.
sob: *v*. humikbî, humibík.
sober: *adj*. di-lasíng; mahinahon.
sociable: *adj*. palakaibigan, sosyál.
social: *adj*. panlipunan, sosyál; **~ist** sosyalista; **~ism** sosyalismo; **~ circle** *n*. sírkulo ng pakikipagkapwà.
society: *n*. lipunan, samahán, kapisanan.
sock: *n*. medyas, kalsetín; *v*. buntalín.
socket: *n*. saket.
soda: *n*. soda, sosa.
sodden: *adj*. babád.
sofa: *n*. sopá.
soft: *adj*. malambót; makinis; mabini; **~en** *v*. palambutín; lumambót; **~ water** tubig tabáng.
soggy: *adj*. babád, basâ.
soil: *n*. lupà; *v*. dumihán.
solace: *n*. ginhawa, alíw, kaáliwan.
soldier: *n*. sundalo, kawal, **~ fish** baga-baga.
sole: *adj*. tangì, kaisá-isá; *n*. (*of foot*) talampakan; (*of shoes*) suwelas.
solemn: *adj*. waláng-kibô, taimtím.
solicit: *v*. manghingî; mangilak; mangalap.
solid: *adj*. buô; matibay, matatág; **~ify** buuín.
solidarity: *n*. pagkakaisá, kaisahán.
soliloquy: *n*. pagsasalitâ nang nag-íisá.
solitaire: *adj*. nag-íisá, solitaryo.
solitary: *adj*. iisá, bugtóng, tangì.
solitude: *n*. pag-iisá; kapanglawán.
solo: *n*. solo, *adj*. nag-iisá.
solution: *n*. kalutasán, katuusan.
solve: *v*. sagutín; lumutás; lutasín.
somber: *adj*. kulimlím; madilím; malamlám.
some: *adj*. sinumán; alinmán; ilán; kauntî.
somebody: *pron*. may, isáng tao; **Did somebody call?** May tumawag?
someday: *adv*. balang araw.
somehow: *adv*. sa paanumán.
somersault: *n*. sirko, tiwarik, pagbaligtád.
something: *n*. may, isáng bagay.
sometime: *adv*. sa ibáng araw.
sometimes: *adv*. paminsan-minsan.
somewhat: *adv*. medyo; tila.
somewhere: *adv*. kung saán; sa tabí-tabí.
son: *n*. anák na lalaki; **~-in-law** manugang na lalaki.
song: *n*. awit, kantá.

sonnet: *n.* soneto.
sonorous: *adj.* matunóg; matagintíng.
soon: *adv.* sa madalíng panahón; mamayâ.
soot: *n.* uling, agiw.
soothe: *v.* patahimikin, aliwín.
sop: *v.* ilubóg; **~py** *adj.* babád.
sophisticated: *adj.* sanáy sa kamunduhán.
sorcerer: *n.* mangkukulam, manggagaway.
sorcery: *n.* pangkukulam.
sordid: *adj.* imbí; marumí; nakapandídiri; hamak.
sore: *adj.* masakít, mahapdî; *n.* sugat.
sorrow: *n.* lumbáy, pighatî, dalamhatî; **~ful** *adj.* malungkót.
sorry: *adj.* nagsisisi; kaawa-awà; nagdáramdám, nalúlungkót.
sort: *n.* klase, urì; *v.* isaayos, magbukúd-bukód.
soul: *n.* káluluwá; **body and ~** katawá't káluluwá.
sound: *n.* tunóg, ingay; (*of water*) kipot; *v.* umingay.
soundtrack: *n.* tugtóg sa sine.
soup: *n.* sopas; sabáw.
sour: *adj.* maasim.
source: *n.* pinanggagalingan; bukál; (*of river*) inantubig, hulò, pámulaan.
south: *n.* timog; **~ward** *adv.* patimóg.
souvenir: *n.* alaala; tagapagpaalaala.
sovereign: *adj.* malayà; pinakadakilà; **~ty** kapangyarihan.
sow: *n.* inahíng baboy; *v.* magpunlâ; ihasík.
soy: *n.* balatong; **~ sauce** *n.* toyò; **dry, salted ~** tawsî.
space: *n.* lugár; alangaang, kalawakan; agwát.
spacious: *adj.* maluwáng.
spade: *n.* pala; ispada; **~fish** kikiro, kitang.
spaghetti: *n.* ispageti.
Spain: *n.* Espanya.
span: *n.* dangkál; agwát; *v.* dangkalín.
Spanish: *n. adj.* Espanyól, Kastila; **~ mackerel** maladyóng, tanggigi, tanigi
spank: *v.* pumalò sa puwít; *n.* palò sa puwít.
spare: *v.* patawarin; ipagtagò.
sparingly: *adv.* matipíd; maawaín.
spark: *n.* alipato, tilamsík; kutitap; *v.* kumisláp.
sparkle: *v.* kumináng; mamilansík.
sparrow: *n.* maya.
sparse: *adj.* kakauntî; kalát.
spasm: *n.* pulikat, hilab.
spasmodic: *adj.* pasumpúng-sumpóng.
spastic: *adj.* malamyâ.
spatter: *v.* sabuyan, mamilamsík.
spatula: *n.* ispátula.
spawn: *v.* umitlóg; mangitlóg.
speak: *v.* magsalitâ; magsabi; **~er** nagtatalumpatì, nagsasalitâ.
spear: *n.* sibát.
spearhead: *n.* tagapanguna.
special: *adj.* espesyál; di-pangkaraniwan; sadyâ; **~ist** *n.* dalubhasà, espesiyalista; **~ize** *v.* magpakatangì, magpakadalubhasà; **~ty** *n.* espesyalidád, pinagdalubhasaan.
species: *n.* urì ng hayop.
specific: *adj.* partikulár, tiyák; **~ation** *n.* detalye; pagpapaliwanag.
specify: *v.* tiyakín, banggitín.
specimen: *n.* muwestra, halimbawà.
speck: *n.* batik; mantsá.
spectacle: *n.* panoorín, tanawin; **~s** salamín sa matá.
spectacular: *adj.* kahindík-hindík.
spectator: *n.* mirón, manonoód.
spectrum: *n.* espektro.
speculate: *v.* magmunukalà, mag-isíp-isíp; nuynuyín.
speech: *n.* talumpatì; pagsasalitâ; **part of ~** bahagi ng panalitâ; **deliver a ~** magtalumpatì.
speed: *n.* bilís, tulin; *v.* bumilís; **~ maniac** kaskasero; **~y** *adj.* mabilís.
speedometer: *n.* belosimetro, panukat-tulin.
spell: *v.* magbaybáy, baybayín; *n.* bulóng; gayuma; **~ing** *n.* pagbaybáy, palábaybayan.
spellbound: *adj.* nagágayuma; nabíbighanì.
spend: *v.* gumastós, gumugol; **~thrift** *n.* gastadór.
spent: *adj.* ubós na.
sperm: *n.* esperma; tamúd.
spew: *v.* isuka; sumuka; *n.* suka.
sphere: *n.* globo; kalipunán.
sphinx: *n.* espinghe.
spice: *n.* pampalasa.
spicy: *adj.* maangháng.
spider: *n.* gagambá; **~ web** bahay-gagambá.

spike: *n*. malakíng pakò.
spill: *v*. ibubô; lumigwák; padanakin.
spin: *v*. iikid, sulirin; paikutin.
spinach: *n*. espinaka.
spinal column: *n*. gulugód.
spindle: *n*. ikirán, kidkirán.
spine: *n*. gulugód; (*fish bone*) tiník.
spinster: *n*. matandáng dalaga; soltera.
spiny: *adj*. matiník.
spiral: *adj*. papilipít; *n*. ikid, likaw.
spirit: *n*. káluluwá, espíritu; siglá; **~ual** *adj*. pangkáluluwá, espirituwál.
spit: *v*. lumurâ, dumurâ, maglaway.
spite: *n*. pagkagalit, pagkayamót; *v*. inisín; **in ~ of** kahit na, kulób; **~ful** mapangyamót.
spittle: *n*. laway, lurâ.
spittoon: *n*. iskupidór, luraan.
splash: *v*. magsaboy, magwisík; tumilamsík.
splatter: *v*. magsaboy
spleen: *n*. palî.
splendid: *adj*. maluningníng, maluwalhatì, kahanga-hangà; maringal.
splendor: *n*. luwalhatì; kaningningán; dingal.
splice: *v*. magdugtóng.
splint: *n*. balangkát; lapát.
splinter: *n*. salubsób, subyáng, pinagkalisán.
split: *v*. hatiin; tipakín, biyakín.
spoil: *v*. masirà; (*child*) palayawin; **~ed** *adj*. sirâ, bulók; **easily ~ed** *adj*. mapanisín, masiraín.
spoke: *n*. rayos ng gulóng.
spokeshave: *n*. katám.
spokesperson: *n*. tagapagsalitâ.
sponge: *n*. espongha; **~ bath** banyos; **spongy** *adj*. buhaghág.
sponsor: *n*. padrino, may-panukalà; *v*. tumangkilik, magtaguyod.
spontaneous: *adj*. bukál, kusang-loób, kusà.
spook: *n*. multo.
spool: *n*. karete, ikirán.
spoon: *n*. kutsara; *v*. kutsarahin.
sporadic: *adj*. kalát-kalát; manaká-nakâ, pabugsú-bugsô.
sport: *n*. larô, palakasan; **~smanship** pagkamaginoó, kakayahán sa paglalarô, parehonglarô.
spot: *n*. batik, mantsa; **~ted cavalla** banlóg; **~ted eagle ray** paging paul; **~ted goatfish** babayaw; **~ted grunt** sibungin.
spotless: *adj*. waláng dumí.
spouse: *n*. asawa.
spout: *n*. alulód; piko; *v*. magbugá; pumulandít.
sprain: *v*. mapilay; *n*. pilay, pagkapuwersa.
sprawl: *v*. humilatà; humandusáy, mátimbuwáng
spray: *v*. wiligán, wisikán; *n*. tilamsík, wisík.
spread: *v*. iunat, ibuká, ikalat.
sprig: *n*. supang; suwí.
spring: *n*. lukső; muwelye, paigkás; (*season*) tagsibol; *v*. lumuksó; bumukál.
sprinkle: *v*. sabugan, diligín; *n*. wilíg; ambón; **~r** *n*. pangwilíg, rigadera, pangwisík.
sprite: *n*. ada, engkanto.
sprout: *v*. sumibol; tumubò; *n*. suplíng, supang; tubò.
spry: *adj*. mabilís; masiglá.
spume: *n*. espuma; bulâ.
spur: *n*. tarì, espuewclas; pampasiglá.
spurt: *v*. pumuslít; tumilamsík.
sputter: *v*. pumisík, bumusá.
sputum: *n*. laway, lurâ.
spy: *n*. espiya, tiktík; *v*. maniktík.
squab: *n*. inakáy; pitsón.
squabble: *v*. magbangay, magtalu-talo.
squad: *n*. pangkát, pulutóng, iskuwád, kuwadrilya.
squalid: *adj*. hamak; marumí, nanlílimahid.
squall: *n*. unós, sigwada.
squalor: *n*. dumí, panlilimahid.
squander: *v*. aksayahín, lustayín.
square: *n*. parisukát, kuwadrado; **~ inch** pulgadang kuwadrado; **~ root** *n*. pariugát.
squash: *n*. kalabasa; *v*. pumipî, pipiín.
squat: *v*. tumingkayád, lumupagì.
squatter: *n*. iskuwater.
squawk: *v*. pumiyák, sumiyók; *n*. siyok.
squeak: *v*. umagitít, lumangitngít.
squeal: *v*. tumilî; magsumbóng; humiyáw.
squeamish: *adj*. madalíng maalibadbarán, maselan.
squeeze: *v*. ipitin, pipiín; pumisíl, pisilín.
squid: *n*. pusít.
squint: *v*. umaninag; sulimpatín; **~y** *adj*. dulíng, sulimpát.

squire: *n*. eskudero.
squirm: *v*. mamilipit, umalumpihít.
squirrel: *n*. ardilya.
squirt: *v*. papulanditín, papuslitín.
stab: *v*. sumaksák, tarakan.
stability: *n*. katatagán.
stabilize: *v*. magpatatág, magpatibay.
stable: *adj*. matatág, matibay; *n*. kabalyerisa.
stack: *n*. salansán, buntón; *v*. magtalaksán, magsalansán.
stadium: *n*. istadyo.
staff: *n*. tungkód, bastón; pangkát, patnugután.
stag: *n*. usáng barako; ~ **party** salu-salo ng mga lalaki.
stage: *n*. yugtô; entablado; **~coach** karwahe; **~show** bodabíl.
stagger: *v*. sumuray-suray; humapay-hapay; gumiray-giray.
stagnant: *adj*. waláng-pag-unlád, waláng kilos.
staid: *adj*. pormál; seryo.
stain: *n*. mantsá; *v*. magmantsá.
stair: *n*. baitáng; **~s** hagdanan; **~case** hagdanan.
stake: *n*. tulos, istakà; tayâ; premyo; *v*. tulusan; itayâ.
stalactite: *n*. estalaktita.
stalagmite: *n*. estalagmita.
stale: *adj*. sirâ; lumà, dati.
stalk: *n*. tangkáy; sumubaybáy nang palihím.
stall: *n*. tindahan; *v*. abalahin.
stallion: *n*. kabayong lalaki.
stalwart: *adj*. matipunô; matatág.
stamina: *n*. lakás, tibay.
stammer: *v*. umutál-utál.
stamp: *n*. pantaták, timbre; taták; selyo; *v*. selyuhán; (*feet*) tapakan, pumadyák.
stampede: *n*. pagdaluhong, pagsusugurán; magpánakbuhan.
stand: *n*. puwesto; kinatatayuán; paninindigan; *v*. tumayô; tumindíg; ~ **by one's word** pinaníninindigán ang kanyáng salitâ; ~ **up for** ipagtanggól; ~ **up to** harapín.
standard: *n*. tularán, modelo, ulirán, huwaran, pámantayan; **up to** ~ nasa pámantayan.
standpoint: *n*. kinatatayuán; paninindigan.
standstill: *n*. pagkahintô; pagkatigil.
stanza: *n*. estropa, saknóng.
staple: *n*. pikolete, panará, pakong baluktót; pángunahíng bílihin; *adj*. pangunahín.
star: *n*. bituín, talà; estrelya; **~ry** mabituín; **~ry goby** dulong; ~ **player** pamatò.
starboard: *n*. estribór.
starch: *n*. gawgáw, almiról; *v*. mag-almiról.
starfish: *n*. isdáng bituín.
stare: *n*. titig, dilat; *v*. tumitig, dumilat.
stark: *adj*. ganáp, panáy.
start: *n*. simulâ; kilos; *v*. magsimulâ; (*engine*) magpaandár.
startle: *v*. gulatin, sindakín; **be ~d** mágulatán.
starvation: *n*. paggutom.
starve: *v*. gutumin.
state: *n*. estado; tayô; lagáy; bansâ; *v*. ipahayag, ilahad; **~ment** *n*. pahayag, ulat; **~sman** estadista.
stateroom: *n*. kamarote.
station: *n*. istasyón; lugár; *v*. itayô.
stationary: *adj*. nakapirmé.
stationery: *n*. mga sobre at papél.
statistics: *n*. estadístika.
statue: *n*. istatuwá, rebulto, bantayog.
stature: *n*. taás.
status: *n*. kalágayan, lagáy; tayô; ~ **quo** dating kalágayan; ~ **symbol** sagisag ng katángian.
statute: *n*. batás.
statutory: *adj*. ayon sa batás, takdâ ng batás.
staunch: *v*. ampatín ang dugô.
stay: *v*. manatili; matirá; ~ **put** pumirmí.
stead: *n*. lugár; halíp; **in~** embés, sa halíp ng.
steady: *adj*. matibay, matatág.
steak: *n*. bistík; karnéng hiniwà.
steal: *v*. nakawin, kupitin.
stealthily: *adv*. pailalím; panakáw; patalilís.
steam: *n*. singáw; **~boat** bapór; ~ **roller** pisón.
steed: *n*. kabayo.
steel: *n*. asero, bakal.
steep: *adj*. matarík.
steeple: *n*. kampanaryo.
steer: *v*. ugitan, mamiloto; kabigin; mamatnubay; **~ing wheel** manibela.
stem: *n*. tangkáy; *v*. manggaling.
stench: *n*. bahò, alinagasaw.
stenography: *n*. takigrapiya.
step: *n*. hakbáng; antás, grado; *v*. hakbangín, tumapak; **~ladder** hagdán.
stepbrother: *n*. kinakapatíd na lalaki.

stepchild: *n*. anák sa una ng isáng asawa.
stepfather: *n*. amaín.
stepladder: *n*. hagdán.
stepmother: *n*. ináng pangumán.
steppe: *n*. kapatagan.
sterile: *adj*. isterilisado; baóg.
sterling: *n*. esterlina.
stern: *adj*. mahigpít, mabagsík.
stethoscope: *n*. isteteskopyo.
stevedore: *n*. estibadór.
stew: *n*. nilagà; sinigáng; *v*. ilagà; **~pan** kasirola.
steward: *n*. serbidór; **~ess** serbidora.
stick: *n*. kahoy; **walking ~** bastón; *v*. magdikít; **~ out** umuslî; **~ up for** magtaguyod; ipagtanggól; **~ up** (*buttocks*) *v*. ituwád; **~y** *adj*. madikít, malagkít.
stiff: *adj*. matigás; **~en** *v*. magpatigás.
stifle: *v*. pigilin; inisín.
stigma: *n*. dungis sa karángalan, estigma.
stiletto: *n*. panusok.
still: *adj*. waláng-kibô; *adv*. pa, pa rin.
stilt: *n*. tayakád, takyaran.
stimulant: *n*. pampasiglá; pampalakás-loób.
stimulate: *v*. pasiglahín.
stimulus: *n*. pampasiglá.
sting: *v*. mangagát; *n*. durò, kagát.
stingy: *adj*. kunipot; maramot.
stink: *v*. bumahò, bumantót; mangamóy.
stipend: *n*. suweldo; limós; sahod.
stipulate: *v*. itadhanà, itakdâ.
stipulation: *n*. pagtatadhanà, pagtatakdâ.
stir: *v*. haluin, batihín; pagalawín.
stirrup: *n*. estribo.
stitch: *n*. tahî; *v*. tumahî.
stock: *n*. (*of company*) aksiyón, agkán, panindá; *v*. magtustós; mag-imbák; **~ exchange** *n*. pamilihan ng sapì; **~holder** aksiyonista; kasapì.
stockade: *n*. tanggulan, istakada.
stockings: *n*. medyas.
stocky: *adj*. matipunô.
stomach: *n*. tiyán; sikmurà.
stone: *n*. bató; *v*. batuhín; **stony** *adj*. mabató.
stool: *n*. bangkito; tae.
stoop: *v*. tumungó; magyukô; **~ed** *adj*. uklô; bayukós.
stop: *v*. tumigil; humintô; *n*. tigilán, hintuan; **~per** *n*. tapón, pansará; **~over** pansamantaláng paghintô.
storage: *n*. pag-iimbák.
store: *n*. tindahan; **~house** bodega; *v*. mag-imbák, itinggál.
stork: *n*. tagák.
storm: *n*. bagyó; **~y** *adj*. mabagyó, binábagyó.
story: *n*. kuwento, salaysáy.
stout: *adj*. matabâ; matatág.
stove: *n*. kalán, pugón.
stowaway: *n*. takas na pasahero.
straddle: *v*. bumukakà.
straggler: *n*. taong-ligaw; taong napag-iiwanan.
straight: *adj*. matuwíd; matwíd; **~en** *v*. ituwíd, tuwirín; **~forward** tapát.
strain: *n*. pagkapuwersa; *v*. mabanat; puminsalà; pagurin; **~er** *n*. panalà, salaán
strait: *n*. kipot.
strand: *n*. hiblá; *v*. sumadsád.
strange: *adj*. kataká-taká; kakaibá; **~r** *n*. taong di-kilalá; banyagà.
strangle: *v*. sakalín, bigtihín.
strap: *n*. bigkís, panalì; *v*. talian, bigkisán.
stratagem: *n*. laláng, panlinláng; pandarayà.
strategy: *n*. estratehiya.
stratosphere: *n*. estratospera.
straw: *n*. dayami; balanggót; panghithít.
strawberry: *n*. presa, istroberi.
stray: *v*. gumalà, lumaboy; *adj*. palaboy, kawalâ.
streak: *n*. bahid, guhit; **~ of insanity** bahid ng pagkabalíw.
stream: *n*. sapà; agos, daloy; **~r** *n*. palawit.
street: *n*. lansangan, kalye; **~car** trambiya.
strength: *n*. lakás, puwersa; bisà; **~en** magpatibay, magpalakás.
strenuous: *adj*. mahirap, mabigát, nakapapagod.
stress: *n*. tindí; diín; lundô; *v*. bigyáng-diín.
stretch: *v*. mag-inát; magbanat; **~er** *n*. kamilya.
strew: *v*. isabog; magsabog.
strict: *adj*. mahigpít, mabagsík, istrikto.
stride: *n*. mahanang hakbáng.
strike: *n*. welga; hampás; *v*. manghampás; magwelgá; **~r** *n*. welgista, mag-aaklás.

string: *n*. talì, pisì; *v*. magtuhog; tuhugin.
strip: *n*. mahabang piraso; *v*. maghubó't-hubád.
stripe: *n*. guhit; haplít; **~d grunt** gunggóng; **~d mackerel** alumahan, lumahan; **~d sea catfish** patuna, sumbilang.
stripling: *n*. bintilyo.
strive: *v*. magsumikap, magpunyagî.
stroke: *n*. tunóg; hagod; hampás; kampáy; *n*. atake serebrál.
stroll: *n*. pasyál; *v*. mamasyál.
stroller: *n*. andadór.
strong: *adj*. malakás; **~hold** *n*. muóg.
structure: *n*. balangkás; gusalì; pagtatayô.
struggle: *n*. pagpupumilit, pagsisikap; labanán; *v*. magpunyagî, magsumikap; maglaban.
stub: *n*. upós, beha; talón.
stubble: *n*. pinaggapasan.
stubborn: *adj*. sutíl; matigás ang ulo; **~ness** kasutilán.
stubby: *adj*. punggók; pudpód.
stuck-up: *adj*. suplado.
stud: *n*. (*clothes*) hemelo, butón; (*animal*) ganadór, palahing kabayo.
student: *n*. estudyante, mag-aarál.
studio: *n*. istudyo.
study: *n*. pag-aaral, pagsusurì; *v*. mag-aral.
stuff: *n*. mga bagay, sangkáp; *v*. palamanán, paloobán; rilyenuhin; **~ing** *n*. palamán, rilyeno.
stuffy: *adj*. luóm.
stumble: *v*. matapyók, matapilók, matisod.
stump: *n*. tuód; **~y** *adj*. punggók.
stun: *v*. lituhín; tuligín; magpawaláng-malay; **~ning** *adj*. nakatatarantá, nakalilitó, kagilagilás.
stunt: *v*. sumugpó sa paglakí.
stupefaction: *n*. pagkabaghán.
stupefy: *v*. mabaghán; mawalán ng ulirát.
stupendous: *adj*. kagulat-gulat, kataká-taká.
stupid: *adj*. tangá, gago, hangál, ungás, gunggóng; **~ity** *n*. katangahán.
stupor: *n*. kawalán ng pandamdám; kabaghanán.
sturdy: *adj*. malakás, matibay.
stutter: *v*. umutál-utál.
sty: *n*. korál; gulitî, kulitì.
style: *n*. uso, moda; estilo; paraán.
stylish: *adj*. de-moda; pusturyoso, sunód sa moda.
suave: *adj*. pinong kumilos; napakagalang.
subdue: *v*. pasukuin, lupigin.
subject: *n*. paksâ; simunò; asignatura; sakop, alagád; *v*. isailalim, ipailalim; **~ive** pasakali.
subjugate: *v*. supilin; gahisín.
subjunctive: *n*. panakalì.
sublime: *adj*. marilág, maringal.
submarine: *n*. submarino.
submerge: *v*. ilubóg, ilublób.
submission: *n*. pagsukò, pagpapasakop.
submissive: *adj*. masunurin, mapagpakumbabâ.
submit: *v*. pailalim; sumukò; ibigáy; iharáp.
subordinate: *adj*. mas mababà; *v*. ipailalim.
subpoena: *n*. subpena.
subscribe: *v*. sumuskribí; **~r** *n*. suskritór.
subscription: *n*. suskrisyón, pagpapahatíd; abuloy.
subsequent: *adj*. susunód, sumúsunód.
subservient: *adj*. sunud-sunuran; ugalingalipin.
subside: *v*. umurong; humupâ; humulaw.
subsidiary: *n*. sukursál, sangáy.
subsidize: *v*. tulungan ng salapî.
subsidy: *n*. tulong na salapî.
subsist: *v*. magpatuloy, mabuhay.
subsoil: *n*. ilalim ng lupà.
substance: *n*. sustansiya; buód.
substantial: *adj*. mahalagá; tunay; matibay.
substantiate: *v*. patibayan.
substitute: *n*. kapalít; *v*. ipalít.
subterfuge: *n*. laláng; pakanâ.
subterranean: *adj*. sa ilalim ng lupà.
subtle: *adj*. pino; mapaglaláng; matalisik.
subtract: *v*. bawasin, alisán; **~ion** *n*. pagbabawas.
suburb: *n*. arabál, paligid-lungsod.
subway: *n*. daán sa ilalim.
succeed: *v*. magtagumpáy; (*in order*) sumunód; humalili.
success: *n*. tagumpáy; **~ful** *adj*. matagumpáy.
succession: *n*. pagkakasunúd-sunód; paghalili.
successive: *adj*. sunúd-sunód.
successor: *n*. kahalili.
succinct: *adj*. maiklî ngunit masakláw.
succor: *n*. saklolo.
succumb: *v*. sumukò.

such: *adj*. ganyán; ganoón.
suck: *v*. sumipsíp; susuhin; **~ling** pásusuhín.
suckle: *v*. pasusuhin, magpasuso.
suction: *n*. pagsipsíp; pagsupsóp.
sudden: *adj*. biglâ; kagyát; **~ly** *adv*. pabiglâ; kagyát.
sue: *v*. isakdál, idemanda.
suede: *n*. gamusa.
suet: *n*. sebo.
suffer: *v*. magtiís; magdusa; malasin; **~ing** *n*. pagdurusa, paghihirap.
suffice: *v*. maghustó, magkásiyá; sumapát.
sufficient: *adj*. sapát, hustó.
suffix: *n*. hulapì; *v*. ihulapì, hulapian.
suffocate: *v*. inisín, sagkaán ang paghingá.
suffrage: *n*. supráhiyo; karapatáng bumoto.
sugar: *n*. asukal; *v*. asukalan; **~cane** tubó; **~mill** kabyawan.
suggest: *v*. imungkahì; ipahiwatig; **~ion** *n*. pagmumungkahì; payo; **~ive** *adj*. nagpápahiwatig.
suicide: *n*. pagpapakamatáy, pagpapatiwakál, pagbibigtí; **commit ~** magpakamatáy.
suit: *n*. terno; (*lawsuit*) sakdál, paghahablá; *v*. iangkóp, magbagay; **~able** *adj*. angkóp, bagay; akmâ; **~ability** *n*. kaangkupán; pagkaakmâ.
suitcase: *n*. maleta.
suitor: *n*. manliligaw, talisuyò; mángingibig.
sulfur: *n*. asupre.
sulk: *v*. magtampó; **~y** nagtátampó.
sullen: *adj*. nagtatampó.
sulphur: *n*. asupre, sangyawà.
sultan: *n*. sultán.
sultana: *n*. sultana.
sum: *n*. kabuuán, suma, totál; *v*. buuín.
summarize: *v*. buurín, lagumin.
summary: *n*. buód, lagom.
summer: *n*. tag-aráw; *adj*. pantag-aráw.
summit: *n*. taluktók, tuktók.
summon: *v*. tawagin; **~s** *n*. patawag; abiso.
sumptuous: *adj*. marangyâ, maringal.
sun: *n*. araw; *v*. paarawan; **~ny** *adj*. maaraw; **~burn** sunog ng araw; **~rise** pagsikat ng araw; **~light** liwanag ng araw; **~set, ~down** paglubóg ng araw; **~tan** kulay mulâ sa araw.
sundae: *n*. sorbetes.
Sunday: *n*. Linggó.
sundry: *adj*. sarisarì.
sunflower: *n*. mirasól.
superb: *adj*. napakagandá; marangyâ.
superficial: *adj*. panlabás, sa ibabaw.
superior: *adj*. nakahihigít; napakagalíng, napakahusay; **~ity** kahigtán; kataasán.
superlative: *adj*. panukdulan, pasukdól; pinakamataás.
supernatural: *adj*. sobrenaturál, kahimá-himalâ.
supersede: *v*. halinhán.
superstition: *n*. pamahiín.
superstitious: *adj*. mapámahiín.
supervise: *v*. mamahalà, magmaneho; pangasiwaan.
supine: *adj*. nakatihayà.
supper: *n*. hapunan.
supplant: *v*. palitán.
supple: *adj*. malambót.
supplement: *n*. dagdág, kapupunán, suplemento.
supply: *n*. panustós; *v*. tustusán.
support: *n*. pagtulong, taguyod; sustento; *v*. suhayan; tukuran; magtaguyod; tustusán.
suppose: *v*. ipalagáy.
suppress: *v*. sawataín, sugpuín; hadlangán; **~ion** pagsugpô.
supreme: *adj*. pinakamataás; sukdulan; **~ Court** Kataás-taasang Hukuman.
surcharge: *n*. dagdág-bayad.
sure: *adj*. tiyák, sigurado, piho; **~ty** panagót; nanánagót.
surely: *adv*. tiyák, sigurado.
surf: *n*. daluyong.
surface: *n*. ibabaw, labás; karayagán; kalatagan.
surfeit: *v*. magpakabundát.
surge: *v*. umalon, gumulong; *n*. paggulong; pag-akyát.
surgeon: *n*. siruhano, maninistís; (*fish*) indangan, labahita, yapot, mangadlít.
surgery: *n*. pagtistís, siruhiya, paninistís.
surmise: *v*. sapantahain; ipalagáy.
surmount: *v*. mapagtagumpayán; lagyán ang ibabaw.
surname: *n*. apelyido.

surpass: *v.* dumaíg, higtán.
surplus: *n.* sobra, labis.
surprise: *n.* gulat, gitlá, manghâ; *v.* biglaín; gumulat.
surrender: *v.* sumukò; *n.* sukò.
surreptitious: *adj.* palihím; patagô.
surround: *v.* pumaligid, kulungín; pumikot; paligiran.
surroundings: *n.* kagiliran.
surveillance: *n.* pagbabantáy, pagmamatyág.
survey: *n.* pagtingín, pagsurì, pagsisiyasat; *v.* tingnán, siyasatin; **~or** *n.* agrimensór.
survival: *n.* kaligtasan ng buhay.
survive: *v.* makaligtás, manatili.
suspect: *n.* pinaghihinalaan; *v.* maghinalà; magsapantahà.
suspend: *v.* magbitin; magpatigil; **~ers** *n.* tirante.
suspense: *n.* pag-aalinlangan; kapanabikán.
suspension: *n.* pagtigil; pagbinbín.
suspicion: *n.* hinalà, sapantahà.
suspicious: *adj.* nakapaghihinalà.
sustain: *v.* magpatuloy; magdalá; manindigan.
sustenance: *n.* sustento; pagkain.
suture: *n.* tahî.
swab: *n.* pamunas; panlampaso.
swaddle: *v.* pahahan; *n.* paha.
swagger: *v.* kumayangkáng.
swallow: *v.* lumunók; lumulón; *n.* (*bird*) layang-layang; golondrina.
swamp: *n.* latian.
swan: *n.* sisne.
swap: *v.* ipagpalít, magpálitan.
swarm: *n.* kawan, kuyog, kulupón; *v.* magkulumpón.
swash: *n.* ligwák, sagwák.
swat: *v.* humampás; *n.* hampás.
swathe: *v.* bendahan; balutin.
sway: *v.* umugâ; umugóy; gumiwang.
swear: *v.* (*oath*) sumumpâ; (*with profanity*) manungayáw.
sweat: *n.* pawis; *v.* magpawis; **~y** *adj.* pawisan; **~er** suweter.
sweep: *v.* magwalís; **~er** *n.* magwawalís.
sweet: *adj.* matamís; **~en** *v.* patamisín; **~ness** tamís; **~ potato** *n.* kamote; **purple sweet ~** *n.* tubayan.
sweetheart: *n.* nobyo, katipán, kasuyò, syota.
swell: *v.* mamagâ; mamukol; lumakí; **~ing** *n.*pamamagâ.
swerve: *v.* lumihís; *n.* paglihís.
swift: *adj.* mabilís, matulin.
swim: *v.* lumangóy; **~er** *n.* manlalangóy.
swindle: *v.* tansuín, dayain, subain; **~r** *n.* manunubà, manananso̕.
swine: *n.* baboy.
swing: *v.* umugóy, magduyan; *n.* duyan; ugóy; imbáy.
swirl: *v.* umikot; umikit.
switch: *n.* pamalò; paglipat; *v.* magbago, maglipat, magpalít.
swivel: *v.* magpaikot.
swollen: *adj.* magâ.
swoon: *v.* himatayín; maghimatáy.
swoop: *v.* sumalimbáy, dumagit.
sword: *n.* espada, sable; tabák.
swordfish: *n.* malasugi.
sycophant: *n.* manghihibò; **~ic** *adj.* sipsíp.
syllable: *n.* sílaba; pantíg.
syllogism: *n.* silohismo.
symbol: *n.* tandâ, sagisag, símbolo; **~ic** *adj.* nasasagisag, may-sinásagisag; makahulugán; **~ize** *v.* sumagisag, katawanín.
symmetry: *n.* simtería.
sympathetic: *adj.* nahahabág, nakikiramay, maawaín.
sympathize: *v.* mahabág, makiramay, kaawaan.
sympathy: *n.* pakikiramay, pagdamay, pakikidalamhatì.
symptom: *n.* síntomas, palatandaan.
synchronize: *v.* pagparelohin.
syncope: *n.* pagbabawas, pagkakaltás.
syncopated: *adj.* maybawas, maykaltás.
synopsis: *n.* sinopsis, lagom.
syndicate: *n.* sindikato.
synonym: *n.* singkahulugán; **~ous** *adj.* kasingkahulugán.
syntax: *n.* paláugnayan.
synthetic: *adj.* sintétiko; gawâ ng tao.
syphilis: *n.* sípilis, sakít sa babae.
syringe: *n.* hiringgilya.
syrup: *n.* pulót, arnibal; harabe.
system: *n.* paraán, kaparaanán, pamamaraán; tuntunin, sistema; **~atic** *adj.* may-sistema;

maparaán.

T

tab: *n.* magtalâ.
tabernacle: *n.* tabernákulo, dálanginán.
table: *n.* mesa, lamesa; hapág; **low ~** dulang; **~cloth** mantél; tapete; **~spoon** kutsara.
tablet: *n.* tableta.
taboo: *adj.* bawal; *n.* pagbabawal.
tabulate: *v.* ihanay; italâ.
tacit: *adj.* di-ipinaháhayag, pahiwatíg.
taciturn: *adj.* di-masalitâ.
tack: *n.* pakong uluhán; *v.* ikabít.
tackle: *v.* sumunggáb; harapín; *n.* kagamitán, aparato; (*fishing*) bingwít, pansíng.
tact: *n.* táktika, kaparaanán; **~ful** magalíng makitungo.
tactics: *n.* táktika, pamamaraán.
tadpole: *n.* ulouló, kikinsót, kitikití.
tag: *n.* etiketa, panandâ; *v.* sundán-sundán.
tail: *n.* buntót; **~less** punggî; **~piece** pabuntót.
tailor: *n.* sastre.
taint: *v.* sirain, bumulók; lalinan; hawalan.
take: *v.* kunin, humawak; hulihin; **~ off** tanggapín; **~ advantage of** pagsamantalahán; **~ back** bawiin; **~ care** mag-ingat; **~ effect** magkabisà; umiral; **~ for granted** ipagpalagáy; **~ off** alisin; hubarin; (*airplane*) lumipád; **~ place** manyari; **~ time** magdahan-dahan; **~-off** pagtaás (ng eruplano).
talcum: *n.* talko.
tale: *n.* kuwento; salaysáy.
talent: *n.* katlinuhan, talino.
talisman: *n.* agimat, anting-anting, galíng.
talk: *v.* magsalitâ; mag-usap; **~ative** *adj.* masalitâ, daldál.
tall: *adj.* mataás, matangkád.
tallow: *n.* sebo.
tally: *n.* bilang; talaan; *v.* bilangin.
talon: *n.* kukó.
tamale: *n.* tamales.
tamarind: *n.* sampalok.
tambourine: *n.* tamburín, panderetas.
tame: *adj.* maamò; *v.* magpaamò.
tamper: *v.* likutín.
tan: *v.* (*leather*) kultihín; (*under sun*) magpaitím; **~nery** *n.* kultihan.
tang: *n.* sangsáng.
tangible: *adj.* nadaramá, nahihipò.
tangle: *v.* pagsalí-salimuutín; gumuló.
tango: *n.* tanggo.
tank: *n.* tangke.
tantalize: *v.* takamín; papanabikin.
tantamount: *adj.* katumbás; para na rin.
tantrum: *n.* alboroto.
tap: *v.* tumapík; kumatók; *n.* (*faucet*) gripo.
tape: *n.* sintás; **~ measurer** medida, panukat; **~ recorder** kintaláng tinig.
taper: *v.* tumulis.
tapestry: *n.* tapiscryá.
tapeworm: *n.* ulyabid, bulati, tiwa, ulay.
tar: *n.* alkitrán.
tarantula: *n.* tarántula, malakíng gagambá.
tardiness: *n.* pagkáhulí.
tardy: *adj.* atrasado, hulí.
target: *n.* patamaán; tudlaan; **~ practice** *n.* puntablangko; **~ range** *n.* puntablangkuhan.
tariff: *n.* taripa, buwís.
tarnish: *v.* magpapusyáw.
tarpaulin: *n.* tarapál.
tarry: *v.* magtagál; magpalumagak.
taro: *n.* gabi.
tarpaulin: *n.* ule, tarapál.
tarpon: *n.* buán-buán.
tart: *adj.* maasim, maaskád; mahayap.
task: *n.* gawain, trabaho.
tassel: *n.* borlas, palawít.
taste: *n.* lasa; *v.* tikmán; **~less** matabáng; waláng-lasa; **tasty** *adj.* malasa, masaráp.
tattered: *adj.* gulá-gulanít, punít-punít.
tatting: *n.* tating.
tattle: *v.* ngumawâ; sumitsít; *n.* katakatà; salitáng batà.
tattoo: *n.* tatú.
taunt: *v.* uyamín, tuyaín.
Taurus: *n.* toro (sa zodiac).
taut: *adj.* banát; maigtíng, haták.
tavern: *n.* taberna.
tawny: *adj.* kayumanggí.
tax: *n.* buwís; *v.* magpabuwís.
taxi: *n.* taksi.
taxpayer: *n.* mámumuwisan.

tea: *n*. tsa; **~cup** tasa ng tsa; **~spoon** kutsarita
teach: *v*. magturò; **~r** *n*. gurò, maestro.
team: *n*. koponán; pangkát; *v*. itambál; **~ up** magtambál.
tear: *n*. luhà; *v*. punitin, pilasin, gutayín.
teargas: *n*. tirgas, gas na nakapagpapaluhà.
tease: *v*. tuksuhín, tudyuhín; lokohin.
teat: *n*. utóng.
technical: *n*. téknikal.
technology: *n*. teknolohiya.
tedious: *adj*. nakabábagót, nakayáyamót.
teem: *v*. managanà, mapunô.
teeth: *n*. mga ngipin; **~e** *v*. magkangipin.
telegram: *n*. telegrama; pahatíd-kawad.
telegraph: *n*. telégrapo.
telephone: *n*. telépono.
telescope: *n*. teleskopyo.
television: *n*. telebisyón.
tell: *v*. sabihin; **~ on someone** isumbóng; **~ a lie** magsinungaling.
teller: *n*. takilyero; tagabayad.
temper: *n*. kaloobán; *v*. pahinahunin, pahinain.
temperament: *n*. pag-uugalì.
temperate: *adj*. kainaman, katamtaman.
temperature: *n*. temperatura.
tempest: *n*. bagyó, sigwá.
temple: *n*. templo, sambahan.
temporal: *adj*. pamanahón.
temporary: *adj*. pansamantalá, temporero.
tempt: *v*. tuksuhín, udyukán; hikayatin; **~ation** *n*. pagtuksó, pannuksó; **~ing** *adj*. nakatutuksó.
ten: *n*. sampû, diyés.
tenable: *adj*. mapanínindigán.
tenacious: *adj*. mahigpít kumapit.
tenant: *n*. nangungupahan, ingkilino.
tend: *v*. mag-alagà, tumingín, mamahalà; **~-ency** *n*. pagkahilig, kaugalian.
tender: *adj*. malambót; magiliw.
tenderloin: *n*. lomo.
tendon: *n*. litid.
tendril: *n*. pangkuyapit.
tenement: *n*. tírahan.
tenet: *n*. símulain; doktrina; kuro-kurò.
tennis: *n*. tenis.
tense: *adj*. banát; malubhâ; *n*. panahón; *v*. bumanat; **present ~** *n*. panahóng pangkasalukuyan; **past ~** *n*. panahóng pangnagdaán; **future ~** *n*. panahóng panghinaharáp.
tension: *n*. pagbanat, pag-igtíng; pagkakáhigpitan.
tent: *n*. tolda, kulandóng.
tentacle: *n*. galamáy.
tentative: *adj*. pansamantalá.
tenth: *adj*. pansampû, ikasampû.
tenure: *n*. panunungkól.
tepid: *adj*. malahiningá.
term: *n*. katawagán, término; tadhanà; **~s of the agreement** mga hiníhingî sa kásunduan; **come to ~s** magkaayos.
terminal: *adj*. pandulo.
terminate: *v*. tapusin, lutasín, hintuán.
terminology: *n*. terminolohiya.
termite: *n*. anay.
terrace: *n*. terasa, baí-baitang na lupà.
terrain: *n*. kalupaán.
terrestrial: *adj*. panlupà.
terrible: *adj*. nakapanghíhilakbót; kasindák-sindák, napakahirap.
terrific: *adj*. nakakikilabot.
terrify: *v*. sindakín, tumakot.
territory: *n*. lupaín; teritoryo.
terror: *n*. sindák, kilabot; **~ism** *n*. pananakot na lubhâ; **~ize** *v*. takutin nang lubhâ.
terse: *adj*. maiklî at malamán.
test: *n*. iksamen, pagsusulit; *v*. subukin, suriin.
testament: *n*. testamento; tipán.
testify: *v*. patunayan, ipahayag; saksihán.
testimony: *n*. patotoó, patunay, pahayag.
tetanus: *n*. tétano.
tether: *n*. panuga, suga; *v*. isuga.
text: *n*. teksto; **~book** aklát-pampáaralán.
textile: *n*. tela, kayo.
texture: kayarián; pagkakahabi.
than: *conj*. kay, kaysa.
thank: *v*. magpasalamat; **~ful** nagpápasalamat; **~s** Salamat; **~sgiving** pagpapasalamat.
that: *adj*. iyán, iyón; *conj*. na.
thatch: *n*. atíp.
thaw: *v*. tumunaw; lumusaw.
the: *art*. ang; yung.
theater: *n*. dulaan, teatro.
theft: *n*. pagnanakaw.
their: *pron*. (*gen*.) nilá; (*obl*.) sa kanilá.

them: *pron.* (*nom.*) silá; (*obl.*) sa kanilá.
theme: *n.* tema, paksâ.
themselves: *pron.* kaniláng sarili.
then: *adv.* noón; sakâ.
theology: *n.* teolohiyá.
theorem: *n.* teorama.
theory: *n.* teoriya, paliwanag, kuru-kurò.
there: *adv.* diyán; doón; **~after** *adv.* mulâ noón.
thereby: *adv.* sa gayóng paraán.
therefore: *adv.* samakatwíd, kayâ; dahil doón.
thermometer: *n.* termómetro.
these: *adj.* mga itó.
thesis: *n.* tisis.
they: *pron.* (*nom.*) silá; (*gen.*) nilá.
thick: *adj.* makapál; (*liquids*) malapot; **~en** *v.* lumapot; magpalapot; **~ness** *n.* kapál; kakapalán; kalaputan.
thicket: *n.* kasukalan, palumpungán.
thief: *n.* magnanakaw.
thigh: *n.* hità.
thimble: *n.* didál.
thin: *adj.* manipís; payát; (*liquids*) malabnáw; *v.* magpadalang, magpanipis.
thing: *n.* bagay.
think: *v.* mag-isip; akalà; magdilidili.
third: *adj.* pangatló, ikatló; **~ person** ikatlóng panauhan, pinagsasálitaan, pinag-úusapan.
thirst: *n.* uhaw; **~y** nauuhaw, uháw.
thirteen: *n.* labintatló, trese.
thirty: *n.* tatlumpû, treinta.
this: *pron.* itó; **like ~** ganitó; **of ~** nitó.
thorn: *n.* tiník; **~y** *adj.* matiník.
thorough: *adj.* ganáp; lubós; **~ly** *adv.* lúbusan; puspusan; paikáy, pasaíd, pasimót.
thoroughbred: *adj.* dinalisay na lahì.
those: *adj.* mga iyán, mga iyón.
though: *conj.* kahit na, bagamán.
thought: *n.* isip, akalà; **~ful** *adj.* maalalahanín; maasikaso; **~less** *adj.* waláng pagtingín.
thousand: *n.* libo, mil.
thraldom: *n.* kaalipinán.
thrash: *v.* bugbugín, hagupitín.
thread: *n.* sinulid; hiblá, himulmúl; **~bare** *adj.* gulanít; **~fin fish** murang-ilóng, damis lawin, kuwa-kuwa, lawiha, mapwáw.
threat: *n.* bantâ; pananakot; **~en** *v.* bantaán, balaan.
three: *n.* tatló, tres.
thresh: *v.* giikín; lugasín.
treshold: *n.* pintuan; pasimulâ; bukana.
thrice: *adv.* makatatló, tatlóng beses.
thrift: *n.* pagtitipíd; **~y** *adj.* matipíd; **~iness** pagkamatipíd, pagkamaimpók.
thrill: *n.* pangingilíg sa tuwâ.
thrive: *v.* umunlád; lumakás.
throat: *n.* lalamunan.
throb: *v.* tumibók; pumintíg; *n.* tibók.
throne: *n.* trono.
throng: *n.* karamihan ng tao.
throttle: *n.* bálbula; *v.* sakalín, hadlangán.
through: *adv.* mulâ sa punò hanggáng sa dulo; sa; tapós na; **~ thick and thin** sa hirap at ginhawa.
throughout: *adv.* sa buóng itinagál.
throw: *v.* iható, ihagis; **~ away** itapon, ibasura.
thrust: *v.* itulak, isalyá; itarak; ulusin.
thud: *n.* kalabóg, lagapák; kalabóg.
thug: *n.* butangero; mambubutáng.
thumb: *n.* hinlalakí; **under my ~** nasa ilalim ng kapangyarihan ko.
thump: *v.* humampás, dumagok.
thunder: *n.* kulóg; hugong.
Thursday: *n.* Huwebes.
thus: *adv.* sa ganyán; kayâ, samakatwíd.
thwart: *v.* biguín; salungatín; hadlangán.
thyroid: **~ gland** *n.* tiroydeo.
tick: *n.* tikták; gurlít; (*blood sucking insect*) garapata.
ticket: *n.* tiket, bilyete.
tickle: *v.* kilitiín; **ticklish** *adj.* makilitíin.
tidbit: *n.* maliit na piraso.
tidal wave: *n.* agwahe.
tide: *n.* taás ng tubig; **low ~** kati; **high ~** lakí ng tubig.
tidings: *n.* balità.
tidy: *adj.* maayos, malinis; *v.* iayos.
tie: *v.* magbuhol; talian; gapusin; *n.* (*necktie*) kurbata; (*in a game*) patas; (*bond*) pagkakaugnáy.
tier: *n.* baitang, andana.
tiff: *n.* bangayán, muntíng sigalót.
tiger: *n.* tigre.
tight: *adj.* masikíp; mahigpít; banát; **~en** *v.*

pahigpitín, palapatin; **~wad** *n*. kuripot.
tilbury: *n*. tiburín.
tile: *n*. baldosa; tisà.
till: *prep*. hanggáng; *v*. mag-araro; maglináng.
tilt: *v*. itagilid, ikiling.
timber: *n*. kahoy; kahuyan.
time: *n*. panahón; oras; *v*. orasan; **from ~ to ~** sa paná-panahón; **long ~** matagál; **behind the ~s** makalumà; **~ keeper** tagapagtalâ ng oras; **~less** waláng-hanggáng; **~ limit** *n*. takdáng-oras; **~table** *n*. talaorasán; **what ~ is it** Anóng oras na?
timely: *adj*. nápapanahón.
timid: *adj*. mahiyain; kimî.
timing: *n*. pagsasaoras; tiyempo.
tin: *n*. lata; **~foil** *n*. palarâ; **~smith** *n*. latero, pandáy-yero, maghihináng.
tinge: *v*. bahiran, lahiran.
tingle: *v*. mangilíg; mangilabot.
tinker: *v*. magkutí-kutiltíl.
tinkle: *v*. kulilingín; kumalansíng.
tinsel: *n*. palarâ.
tint: *n*. urì ng kulay; bahid.
tiny: *adj*. napakaliít, muntî.
tip: *n*. tulis; dulo; kantî; (*money*) pabuyà; *v*. tumagilid; angatín; ibubô; **~ of the tongue** tungkî, dulo ng dilà; **~-off** lihim na pabalità.
tipsy: *adj*. mabuwáy, lasíng.
tiptoe: *v*. lumakad nang patiyád, tumiyád.
tirade: *n*. tuligsâ; batikos.
tire: *v*. magpapagod; humapò; makasawà; **~some** *adj*. nakapápagod; **~d** *adj*. pagód, hapô; panghál; *n*. goma.
tissue: *n*. himaymáy; tisyu.
tit: *n*. utóng.
title: *n*. pamagát, título.
to: *prep*. sa; **~ and fro** pabalík-balik; **from.. ~..** mulâ.. hanggáng...
toad: *n*. palakâ.
toadstool: *n*. kabutíng-ahas, kabutíng-lason.
toast: *n*. tustadong tinapay; brindis; *v*. tumagay; magtustá; **~r** *n*. toster; ihawán.
toastmaster: *n*. tagapagpakilala.
tobacco: *n*. tabako.
today: *adv*. ngayón.
toddler: *n*. batà, sanggól.
together: *adv*. magkasama.
toil: *n*. mabigát na trabaho.
toilet: *n*. kasilyas, pálikuran; **~ paper** pang-iwang, pandewang.
token: *n*. palatandaan, sagisag; alaala.
tolerable: *adj*. matitiís.
tolerance: *n*. pagpaparayâ; pagpapaubayà, pagpapahintulot.
tolerant: *adj*. mapagparayâ, mapag-alintana.
tolerate: *v*. pahintulutan, payagan, ipaubayà.
toll: *n*. bayad, tol; *v*. tugtugín ang kampanà.
tomato: *n*. kamatis.
tomb: *n*. puntód, líbingan; nitso.
tomboy: *n*. tombóy, bínalaki.
tomcat: *n*. lalaking pusà.
tombstone: *n*. lápida.
tomorrow: *adv*. bukas.
ton: *n*. tonelada; **~nage** *n*. tonelahe.
tone: *n*. tono, tunóg.
tongs: *n*. sipit, panipit.
tongue: *n*. dilà; **~ fish** dapa, darapang habâ; **~-tied** *adj*. umíd.
tonic: *adj*. tóniko; **~ water** tónikong tubig.
tonight: *adv*. sa gabíng itó.
tonnage: *n*. tonelahe.
tonsil: *n*. tonsil.
tonsure: *n*. tonsura; satsát.
too: *adv*. din, rin; patí.
tool: *n*. kagamitán, kasangkapan.
toot: *v*. magbusina, magpatunóg ng busina.
tooth: *n*. nigpin; **molar ~** bagáng; **~ache** sakít ng ngipin; **~brush** sipilyo; **~less** bungî; waláng-ngipin; **~paste** kremang pansipilyo; **~pick** palito, pantingá.
top: *n*. tuktók; kaitaasan; (*of plant*) talbós; (*toy*) turumpó; (*peak*) tugatóg; **~soil** lupà sa ibabaw.
topaz: *n*. topasyo.
topic: *n*. paksâ; tema.
topknot: *n*. pusód.
topmost: *adj*. pinakamataás.
topography: *n*. topographiya.
topple: *v*. bumuwág; lumagpák.
topsy-turvy: *adj*. maguló.
torch: *n*. tangláw, sulô, sigsíg.
torment: *v*. papagdusahin.
torn: *adj*. napunit; punít.
tornado: *n*. buhawi.

torpid: *adj*. matamláy; ngimáy.
torpor: *n*. pagkangimay; katamlayan.
torrent: *n*. malakás na agos.
torrid: *adj*. nakatítigáng na init.
torso: *n*. katawán (ng tao).
tortoise: *n*. pagóng.
torture: *n*. labis na pagpapahirap.
toss: *v*. ipukól, ihagis.
total: *adj*. buô, kalahatán, totál; *v*. buuín; **~ly** *adv*. lubós, ganáp; **~itarian** *adj*. totalitaryo.
totter: *v*. sumuray-suray, humapay-hapay.
touch: *v*. humipò, hipuin; (*affect*) tumimò; **~y** *adj*. masyadong maramdamin.
tough: *adj*. makunat; malakás, matatág; mahirap.
toupee: *n*. piluka, tambulok.
tour: *n*. paglalakbáy, paggalà; **~ist** turista, manlalakbáy.
tournament: *n*. tornea, paligsahan.
tow: *v*. hilahin; **~boat** bangkáng panghila.
toward: *prep*. patungo, sa gawî; pa-.
towel: *n*. tuwalya; **face ~** labakara.
tower: *n*. tore; *v*. mamukód sa kataasán.
town: *n*. bayan; **~ hall** munisipyo; **~sman** tagabayan; **~ fiesta** pista ng bayan.
toxic: *adj*. may-lason.
toxin: *n*. lason.
toy: *n*. laruán; *v*. paglaruán.
trace: *n*. bakás; palatandaan; bakasín.
trachea: *n*. tatagukan, lalagukan.
track: *n*. riles; bakás; karerahán; landás; *v*. bakasín; **keep ~ of** subaybayán; **~ down** tugisin.
tractor: *n*. traktora.
trade: *n*. kalakalán, komersiyo, pangangalakal; *v*. makipagpalít, magnegosyo; **~mark** tatákpangkalakal; **~r** *n*. negosyante, mangangalakál.
tradition: *n*. tradisyón, kaugalian; **~al** *adj*. kinaugalian.
traffic: *n*. trápiko; **~ light** ilaw trápiko.
tragedy: *n*. trahedya, kapahamakán.
tragic: *adj*. kalunus-lunos.
trail: *n*. buntót; bakás; daán, landás; *v*. bumuntót; tugaygayán; makaladkád.
train: *n*. tren; (*of dress*) buntót, kola; *v*. turuan, mahersisyo; palakihín; sanayin; **~er** *n*. tagasanay, tagapagturò; **~ing** *n*. pagsasanay, pagaaral.
trait: *n*. katángian, kaugalian.
tram: *n*. trambiyá.
tramp: *n*. bagamundo; *v*. lumakad nang padyák.
trample: *v*. yapakan, yurakan, tapakan.
trampoline: *n*. trampolín; palundagan.
trance: *n*. kawalán ng malay-tao.
tranquil: *adj*. payapà, tiwasáy; **~ity** *n*. katahimikan.
transact: *v*. humaráp, gawín; **~ion** *n*. bilihan, unawaán.
transcend: *v*. humigít, lumampás.
transcribe: *v*. isulat; kopyahín.
transcription: *n*. salin, sipì.
transfer: *v*. ilipat, isalin; sumalin.
transfigure: *v*. magbagong-anyô.
transfix: *v*. tuhugin.
transform: *v*. magbagong-anyô.
transfusion: *n*. pagsasalin ng dugô.
transgress: *v*. labagín; suwayín; **~ion** paglabág, pagsuwáy.
transient: *adj*. lumilipas, napaparam.
transit: *n*. pagdadalá, paghahatíd.
transition: *n*. pagbabago.
transitive: *adj*. palipát.
transitory: *adj*. lumílipas.
translate: *v*. magsalin sa; isalin.
translation: *n*. pagsasalinsa, traduksiyón.
translator: *n*. tagasalin, traduktór.
transmission: *n*. paghahatíd.
transmit: *v*. magpadalá, ihatíd.
transom: *n*. trabesanyo.
transparent: *adj*. naaaninag; malinaw.
transpire: *v*. maganáp; mangyari.
transplant: *v*. maglipat, ilipat.
transport: *v*. iluluan, ihatíd; *n*. pagdadalá; **~ation** *n*. paglilipat, paglululan.
transverse: *adj*. pahaláng; nakahaláng.
trap: *n*. panghuli; silò, umang; *v*. máhuli; mápikot; patibungán; umangan.
trash: *n*. basura; yagít; kahangalán.
travel: *v*. maglakbáy; **~er** *n*. biyahero; manlalakbáy; **~ agency** ahénsiya ng paglalakbáy.
traverse: *v*. bagtasín.
trawl: *v*. mamalakaya; *n*. palakaya.

tray: *n*. bandeha, bandehado.
treacherous: *adj*. taksíl, lilo.
tread: *v*. lakarin, tapakan, yapakan.
treason: *n*. kataksilán, kasukabán.
treasure: *n*. kayamanan; *v*. mahalagahín; **~r** *n*. tesorero, tagaingat-yaman.
treasury: *n*. tesoreryá, ingatáng-yaman.
treat: *v*. makitungo, tratuhin, makisama; *n*. handóg, parangál; **~ment** *n*. pakikisama, trato, pagtrato.
treaty: *n*. kásunduan.
treble: *v*. pagtatluhín.
tree: *n*. punò, punungkahoy.
trek: *n*. paglalakbáy.
trellis: *n*. balag.
tremble: *v*. kuminíg, manginíg.
tremendous: *adj*. napakalakí; pambihirà.
tremor: *n*. yaníg; ugâ.
tremulous: *adj*. nangínginíg; nangángatál.
trench: *n*. trinsera; bambáng.
trenchant: *adj*. matalisik; matalím.
trend: *n*. hilig, pagkahilig; lakad; takbó.
trepidation: *n*. pagkabalisa; pangambá.
trespass: *v*. magkasala; manghimasok; lumabág sa batás.
trial: *n*. pagsubok; litis, paglilitis, bista.
triangle: *n*. triyánggulo, tatsulok; (*musical instrument*) batingtíng.
tribe: *n*. lipì, tribu; angkán.
tribulation: *n*. malubháng sigalót.
tribunal: *n*. husgado, húkuman.
tributary: *n*. ilog na pasangá.
tribute: *n*. parangál, papuri.
trick: *n*. dayà, laláng; *v*. magdayà.
trickle: *v*. tumulò, pumaták, tumagas.
tricolor: *adj*. tatlóng-kulay.
tricycle: *n*. trisiklo, traysikél.
trident: *n*. salapáng.
trifle: *n*. maliít na bagay.
trigger: *n*. gatilyo, gato, kálabitan; **~ fish** papakol.
trillion: *n*. sangangaw na angaw.
trilogy: *n*. trilohiya, tatlóng akdâ.
trim: *v*. pantayín, gupitín, pakinisin; **~ming** *n*. palamuti.
trinity: *n*. pagkatatló.
trinket: *n*. mumurahing hiyás.
trio: *n*. tiryo, tatluhan.
trip: *n*. paglalakbáy; *v*. matisod, madupilas, matalisod.
tripe: *n*. labót, tripa.
triple: *adj*. tatlóng beses; *v*. tatluhín; **~-tail** kapkáp-bató.
triplet: *n*. tatlóng magkakambál.
tripod: *n*. tungkô.
trisyllabic: *adj*. tatatluhíng pantíg.
triumph: *n*. tagumpay, panalo; *v*. magtagumpáy; **~ant** *adj*. matagumpáy.
trivial: *adj*. di-mahalagá.
trolley: *n*. troli.
trombone: *n*. trombón.
troop: *n*. pangkát, tropa; mga kawal.
trophy: *n*. tropeo, katibayan, gantimpalà.
tropic: *adj*. trópiko; **~al** pantrópiko.
trot: *n*. trote, paso; *v*. yumagyág, pumaso.
trouble: *n*. guló; bagabag, kabalisahan, hilahil; *v*. tigatigin; guluhín; gambalain; mabahalà; **~-maker** basag-uluero; **~some** *adj*. mapangguló; nakayáyamót.
trough: *n*. labangán, sabsaban, pákakanán.
troupe: *n*. tropa.
trousers: *n*. salawá, pantalón.
trout: *n*. isdáng tabáng.
trowel: *n*. dulós.
truant: *adj*. bulakbulero, bulakból.
truce: *n*. pahingá ng labanán.
truck: *n*. trak.
true: *adj*. totoó, tunay.
truism: *n*. katotohanan.
trump: *v*. magkatakatà, umimbento.
trumpet: *n*. torotot, trumpeta; tambulì.
trunk: *n*. (*tree*) punò; (*car*) baúl; ngusò ng elepante; **~fish** baka-bakahan.
trust: *n*. tiwalà, pananalig; utang; *v*. magtiwalà; **~worthy** *adj*. mapagtítiwalaan.
trustee: *n*. tagapangalagà, katiwalà.
truth: *n*. katotohanan, totoó; **~ful** matapát.
try: *v*. sumubok, subukin; magtangkâ; magpilit; *n*. subok, pagsubok; pagtatangkâ.
tryst: *n*. tagpuan, pagtatagpô; típanan, pakikipagtipán.
tsar: *n*. sar.
tub: *n*. batyâ; banyera; taóng.
tube: *n*. tubo.

tuber: *n.* lamáng-lupà.
tuberculosis: *n.* tisis, pagkatuyô.
tuck: *v.* isuksúk; isukbít; ililís.
Tuesday: *n.* Martes.
tuft: *n.* bungkós, borlas.
tug: *v.* humatak, bumatak, hilahin.
tuition: *n.* pagtuturò, matríkula.
tumble: *v.* magpabalí-baligtád, magpabilíng-bilíng; mabuwál; *n.* pagkabuwál, pagkárapâ.
tumor: *n.* bukol, tumór, bagâ.
tumult: *n.* guló; kaingayan.
tuna: *n.* tuna, using, tulingan; **yellowfin ~** albakora, badlaan, buyo, tambakol.
tune: *n.* tono; himig, tugtugin; *v.* itono.
tungsten: *n.* tangsten.
tunnel: *n.* tunél.
turban: *n.* turbante.
turbid: *adj.* maputik, malabò.
turbine: *n.* turbina.
turbulent: *adj.* waláng-kaayusan.
turkey: *n.* pabo; karne ng pabo.
turmoil: *n.* pagkakaguló; ligalig.
turn: *v.* umikot; magpaikot; bumaling, pabalingin; lumikô; *n.* likô; pagkakataón, turno; **~ one's back** tumalikód; **~ down** itanggí; **~ out** lumitáw, lumabás; **~ over** itaób, baligtarín; **~ off** patayín; **~ on** buksán.
turnabout: *n.* pagtalikód.
turncoat: *n.* tumiwalág.
turner: *n.* tornero.
turnip: *n.* singkamás.
turnkey: *n.* bastonero.
turnout: *n.* ang nagawâ; ang nayarì.
turnover: *n.* paglilipat, pagsambót ng puhunan
turntable: *n.* páikutan.
turpentine: *n.* trementina, agwarás.
turquoise: *n.* turkesa; berdéng-asúl na kulay.
turtle: *n.* pagóng; **sea ~** pawikan; **~dove** *n.* punay, tukmól, batubató.
tusk: *n.* pangil, salimaó.
tussel: *v.* magbunô.
tutelage: *n.* pagtuturò; pag-aalagà.
tutor: *n.* pribadong gurò.
tuxedo: *n.* tuksedo.
twang: *n.* kahumalán; tagintíng, haging; kumalabít.
tweak: *v.* lumabnót, sumabunot.
tweezers: *n.* tiyanì.
twelfth: *adj.* ikalabindalawá.
twelve: *n.* labindalawá; dose.
twenty: *n.* dalawampû; beinte.
twice: *adv.* makalawá, dalawáng beses.
twig: *n.* maliít na sangá.
twilight: *n.* silim, takíp-silim.
twin: *n.* kambál.
twine: *n.* leteng; pisì; *v.* magpulupot, ipilipit.
twinkle: *v.* kumutitap, kumisláp.
twirl: *v.* umikit; magpaikut-ikot.
twist: *v.* magtabingî; bumaluktót; umikot; magpalikú-likó.
twitch: *v.* magpakibót; kumislót.
two: *n.* dalawá, dos; **~fold** *adv.* dalawá; **~-finned bonito** kuringdíng.
twotime: *v.* kaliwaín, mangaliwâ.
tycoon: *n.* kasike; taykon, makapangyarihang mangangalakal.
type: *n.* tipo; klase; urì.
typesetter: *n.* kahista.
typewrite: *v.* magmakinilya; **~r** *n.* makinilya.
typewritten: *adj.* makinilyado.
typhoid: *n.* tipus.
typhoon: *n.* bagyó.
typical: *adj.* kaugalian.
typify: *v.* mákalarawan; sumagisag.
typist: *n.* tagapagmakinilya.
typography: *n.* pagkakálimbág.
tyranny: *n.* kalupitán, paniniíl.
tyrant: *n.* punong malupít.
tyro: *n.* bagito, bahuhan.

U

ubiquitous: *adj.* nasa lahát ng poók.
udder: *n.* suso.
ugliness: *n.* kapangitan.
ugly: *adj.* pangit.
ulcer: *n.* úlsera.
ulterior: *adj.* lihim, di-hayág; **~ motive** lihim na hángarin.
ultimate: *adj.* hulí, pangwakás.
ultimatum: *n.* ultimatum.
ultra: *n.* labis, sobra; sukdulan.
ultraviolet: *adj.* ultrabiyoleta; ultrayolado.
umbilical cord: *n.* pusod.

umbrella: *n*. payong.
umpire: *n*. reperí, tagahatol.
un-: *pref*. dî, hindî, di-; waláng.
unable: *adj*. di-kaya, waláng-kaya.
unaccompanied: *adj*. waláng kasama.
unaccustomed: *adj*. di-bihasá, di-hiratí.
unanimous: *adj*. buóng pagkakaisá.
unarmed: *adj*. waláng-armas.
unavoidable: *adj*. di-maíiwasan.
unaware: *adj*. di-alám, waláng-malay.
unbalanced: *adj*. di-timbáng; tabingî.
unbiased: *adj*. waláng-pinápanigan.
unbutton: *v*. tanggalín sa pagkakabutones.
uncanny: *adj*. kataká-taká; mahiwagà.
uncertain: *adj*. di-tiyák.
unchain: *v*. alisán ang tanikalâ.
unchaste: *adj*. malaswâ, mahalay, masagwâ.
uncircumcised: *adj*. supót.
uncle: *n*. amaín, tiyo.
unclean: *adj*. di-malinis, marumí, marungis.
unclothed: *adj*. waláng-suot.
uncomfortable: *adj*. di-maginhawa.
uncommon: *adj*. bihirà, di-karaniwan.
unconscious: *adj*. waláng-malay-tao; **~ness** kawalán ng malay-tao.
uncontrollable: *adj*. di-mapigil.
uncouth: *adj*. masagwâ; bastós; kákaibá.
uncover: *v*. ihayág, buksán, isiwalat.
undeniable: *adj*. di-matatanggihán.
under: *prep*. sa ilalin ng; *adv*. mababà pa sa; *adj*. mas mababà.
underdog: *n*. talunan, apí-apihan, dehado.
underestimate: *v*. maliitín, hamakin, abaín.
undergo: *v*. magdanas, tumikím, magbatá.
underground: *adj*. sa ilalim ng lupà.
underhand: *adj*. palihím; pataksíl.
underline: *v*. guhitan sa ilalim, salungguhitan.
underlying: *adj*. batayán.
undermine: *v*. parupukín, papanghinain.
underneath: *adj*. sa ilalim, sa ibabâ.
underpants: *n*. karsonsilyo.
underscore: *v*. salungguhitan.
undershirt: *n*. kamiseta.
understand: *v*. maintindihán, maunawaan, matarók; **~ing** *n*. pagkaalám, pag-unawà; *adj*. maunawaín.
understood: *adj*. talastás, batíd.
undertake: *v*. magtangkâ, magsagawâ; **~r** *n*. ang may-punerarya.
undervalue: *v*. maliitín; tayahin sa mababang halagá.
underwear: *n*. kasuutang pang-ilalim, damít na panloób.
underworld: *n*. impiyerno; ang masasamáng-loób.
underwriter: *n*. ahente ng siguro.
undo: *v*. kalagán, kalasín; pawaláng-bisà; tastasín.
undoubtedly: *adv*. waláng-alinlangan, sigurado.
undress: *v*. maghubád, maghubo't-hubád.
undue: *adj*. di-kailangan; labis-labis.
undulate: *v*. mag-alún-alón.
unearth: *v*. hukayin, bungkalín.
uneasy: *adj*. nababalisa, di-mapakalí.
uneducated: *adj*. di-nag-aral, mangmáng.
unemployed: *adj*. waláng-trabaho, waláng-kita, di kumíkita.
unequal: *adj*. di-pantáy, di-pareho; di-timbáng.
uneven: *adj*. di-patag; di-pareho.
unexpectedly: *adv*. di-inaasahan.
unfair: *adj*. di-tapát, marayà.
unfaithful: *adj*. taksíl, lilo, alibughâ; **be** ~ *v*. pagtaksilán (ang asawa), kaliwaín.
unfamiliar: *adj*. di-kilalá; di-maalam.
unfasten: *v*. kalagín, kalasín.
unfit: *adj*. di-nababagay, di-akmâ.
unfold: *v*. magbukadkád; magbuká.
unforgettable: *adj*. di-malílimot.
unfortunate: *adj*. waláng-suwerte, kapús-kapalaran; **~ly** *adv*. sa kasawiang-palad.
unfriendly: *adj*. mailáp, salugát.
unfurl: *v*. magladlád.
ungainly: *adj*. kakatuwâ; kakaibá.
ungrateful: *adj*. waláng-utang-na-loób.
unhappy: *adj*. malungkót.
unification: *n*. pag-iisá, pagbubuklód.
uniform: *n*. uniporme; *adj*. magkakapareho; waláng-pagbabago.
unify: *v*. pag-isahín, papagkáisahín.
unimaginable: *adj*. di-akalain.
unimportant: *adj*. di-mahalagá.
uninhabited: *adj*. waláng-nakatirá, di-tinítirahán.

unintelligible: *adj*. di-maintindihán.
unintentional: *adj*. di-sinasadyâ.
union: *n*. unyón, pagkakaisá, pagsasama, samahan.
unique: *adj*. waláng-katulad; bugtóng.
unit: *n*. yunit, isáng bagay.
unite: *v*. isahín, pagsamá-samahin; maging-isá; **~d** *adj*. nagkakaisá, magkaisá; sama-sama; **~d States** *n*. Estados Unidos.
unity: *n*. pagkakaisá; pagkakasundô.
universal: *adj*. ng daigdíg, ng lahát, pandaigdíg.
universe: *n*. santinakpán, sandaigdigan, sandinukob.
university: *n*. pamantasan, unibersidád.
unkempt: *adj*. di-malinis at maayos, gusót.
unkind: *adj*. masungít, malupít.
unknown: *adj*. di-kilalá.
unlawful: *adj*. labág sa batás, bawal.
unless: *conj*. maliban kung, maliban sa.
unlike: *adj*. di-katulad; *prep*. ibá sa; **~ly** *adv*. di-tiyák.
unlimited: *adj*. waláng-hanggán.
unload: *v*. magdiskargá, diskargahán.
unlock: *v*. magbukás (ng kandado).
unlucky: *adj*. waláng-kapalaran.
unmask: *v*. alisán ngmáskara; ilantád.
unmerciful: *adj*. waláng-awà.
unmistakable: *adj*. di-mapagkakámalán.
unnatural: *adj*. balintunà; labág sa kalikasan, di-likás.
unnecessary: *adj*. di-kailangan.
unobtrusive: *adj*. mahinhín, mayumì.
unoccupied: *adj*. bakante, waláng-nakatirá.
unpack: *v*. alisán ng lamán.
unparalleled: *adj*. waláng-kapantáy.
unprofitable: *adj*. di-kapaki-pakinabang.
unqualified: *adj*. di-karapat-dapat.
unquestionable: *adj*. di-mapagdududahan.
unravel: *v*. kalasín, tastasín; matastás.
unreasonable: *adj*. waláng-katwiran.
unrelenting: *adj*. waláng-bawa.
unrest: *n*. guló, pagkabalisa.
unrighteous: *adj*. masamâ, waláng-katarungan.
unripe: *adj*. hiláw, dî pa hinóg.
unroll: *v*. ikadkád, ilatag.
unruly: *adj*. simarón, di-masupil.
unsafe: *adj*. mapanganib.
unsanitary: *adj*. marumí.
unsatisfied: *adj*. di-nasisiyahán.
unsheathe: *v*. humugot sa kaluban.
unskilled: *adj*. di-bihasa, di-sanáy; **~ laborer** manggagawang waláng kadalubhasaan.
unsophisticated: *adj*. simple; waláng pagkukunwarî.
unspeakable: *adj*. napakasamâ; di-masabi.
unstable: *adj*. di-matatág, di-matibay.
unsteady: *adj*. mabuwáy, di-matatág.
unstitch: *v*. tastasín.
unsuccessful: *adj*. nabigô, bagsák.
unsuitable: *adj*. di-bagay.
unsung: *adj*. di-napararangalán; limót.
untamed: *adj*. simarón, mailáp.
untangle: *v*. kalasín; lutasín.
untidy: *adj*. waláng-ayos; marungis.
untie: *v*. kalasín, kalagín.
until: *prep*. hanggáng sa.
untimely: *adj*. walâ sa oras.
untouched: *adj*. di-nakibô, di-nagaláw.
untrue: *adj*. di-totoó.
untrustworthy: *adj*. di-mapagkakatiwalaan.
unused: *adj*. di-gamít.
unusual: *adj*. di-karaniwan.
unveil: *v*. mag-alís ng tabing.
unwelcome: *adj*. di-kinagigiliwan, kinasusuyaan.
unwilling: *adj*. aayáw, ayaw; bantulót.
unwind: *v*. magkalás sa pagkakaikid.
unworthy: *adj*. di-karapat-dapat.
unwrap: *v*. mag-alís ng balot.
up: *adv*. pataás; *prep*. sa itaás ng; *adj*. patayô; **get ~** *v*. bumangon; **stand ~** *v*. tumayô, **it's ~ to you** bahalà ka; **~s and downs** tagumpáy at kabiguán.
upbraid: *v*. sisihin, murahin; pagsalitáan.
upgrade: *v*. iasenso; itaás.
upbringing: *n*. pagpapalakí.
uphill: *adj*. paakyát, pasalungá, pataás.
uphold: *v*. ipagtanggól; pagtibayin.
upholstery: *n*. tapeseriya.
upkeep: *n*. pangangalagà.
upland: *n*. kataasán, bakood.
uplift: *v*. pataasín.
upmost: *adj*. pinakamataás.

upon: *prep*. sa ibabaw ng, sa.
upper: *adj*. itaás; **~most** *adj*. pinakamataás.
upright: *adj*. patayô, patindíg.
uprising: *n*. pag-aalsá, paghihimagsík.
uproar: *n*. pagkakaingáy, kaingayan, hiyawan.
uproot: *v*. bunutin; sungkalín.
upset: *n*. pagkabigô; *v*. guluhín; itaób; *adj*. balisá; taób.
upside: *n*. ibabaw.
upside down: *adj*. pataób, tiwarík, baligtád.
upstairs: *adj*. sa itás (na palapág).
upstream: *adj*. salungát sa agos.
upward: *adj*. pataás, paitaás.
uranium: *n*. uranyo.
Uranus: *n*. Urano.
urban: *n*. ng lunsód; tagalunsód.
urbane: *adj*. magalang; mapítagan.
urchin: *n*. batang pilyo; **sea ~** lamang-dagat, susúng-dagat na may kalisag.
urge: *v*. kimukin, pakiusapan; igiít, ipilit.
urgent: *adj*. madalian, mahalagá, kailangang-kailangan, ápurahan.
urinal: *n*. orinola; ihián.
urinate: *v*. umihì, manubíg.
urine: *n*. ihì; **odor of ~** *n*. palot, panghí; **smelling like ~** *adj*. mapalot, mapanghí.
urn: *n*. urna; (*container for liquids*) nona, initan ng tubig.
urticaria: *n*. tagulabáy.
us: *pron*. (*nom*.) kamí, (*gen*.) amin (*exclusive*); (*nom*.) tayo, (*gen*.) atin (*inclusive*).
usable: *adj*. magagamit.
usage: *n*. paggamit; kaugalian.
use: *n*. paggamit; *v*. gumamit, gamitin; **~ful** nakatutulong, nagagamit; **~less** waláng-silbí, inutil, waláng-kagamitán.
usher: *n*. tagahatíd; *v*. ihatíd.
usual: *adj*. karaniwan, kaugalian; nápagkágawián; **~ly** *adv*. karaniwan.
usurer: *n*. usurero.
usurious: *adj*. labis na patubò.
usurp: *v*. kumamkám, mang-agaw.
usury: *n*. usura, labis na pagpapatubò.
utensil: *n*. kagamitán, kasangkapan.
uterus: *n*. bahay-batà, matrís, útero.
utility: *n*. palingkurang-bayan; pagigíng mahalagá; kagamitán.
utilize: *v*. gamitin.
utmost: *adj*. pinakamalakít, pinakamataás; **of ~ importance** mahalagáng-mahalagá.
utter: *v*. bumigkás, magwikà; magbitíw; *adj*. lubós, ganáp; **~ly** *adv*. lubós, ganáp.
uvula: *n*. tilaó.

V

vacancy: *n*. bakante, pagkawaláng-tao.
vacant: *n*. puwáng, bakante, waláng-lamán.
vacate: *v*. alisán, iwan, lisanin.
vacation: *n*. bakasyón, pagpapahingá.
vaccinate: *v*. magbakuna; bakunahan.
vaccination: *n*. pagbabakuna.
vaccine: *n*. bakuna, pagbabakuna.
vacillate: *v*. mag-atubilì, mag-urong-sulong.
vacuum: *n*. bakyúm; **~ cleaner** panlinis na humihigop ng dumí
vagabond: *n*. bagamundo.
vagina: *n*. kaluban; puki.
vagrancy: *n*. bagansiya, pagpapagala-galà.
vague: *adj*. malabò, di-maliwanag.
vain: *adj*. banidoso; waláng-kapararakan; **in ~** waláng kabubuluhán, waláng-bisà; **~glorious** *adj*. hambóg, mayabang.
valet: *n*. kamarero.
valiant: *adj*. matapang.
valid: *adj*. mabisà, bálido; **~ity** *n*. bisà; katumpakán.
validate: *v*. magbigáy-bisà.
valise: *n*. maleta.
valley: *n*. lambák; libís.
valor: *n*. tapang; **~ous** *adj*. matapang, magiting.
valuable: *adj*. mahalagá, mamahalin.
value: *n*. kahalagahan, saysáy; kabuluhán; *v*. halagahán, tasahan.
valve: *n*. bálbula.
vampire: *n*. mandurugô.
vandal: *n*. taong maninirà; **~ism** *n*.paninirà, katampalasanan.
vane: *n*. pulád; banog-lawin, girimpulá.
vanguard: *n*. pangunang hanay.
vanish: *v*. mawalâ, maglahò.
vanity: *n*. banidád, kapalaluan.
vanquish: *v*. lupigin, talunin.
vapid: *adj*. matabáng; matamláy.

vapor: *n*. singáw; hamóg.
variable: *adj*. pabagu-bago; *n*. nagpapabagu-bago.
variant: *n*. ibáng anyô; *adj*. ibá.
variation: *n*. kaibhán, pag-iibá-ibá.
varicose vein: *n*. bárikós; ugat na bukul-bukól.
varied: *adj*. sarisarì, ibá-ibá.
variety: *n*. pagkakaibá-ibá; sarisaring urì.
various: *adj*. ibá't ibáng (klase); marami.
varnish: *n*. barnís; *v*. barnisán.
vary: *v*. mag-ibá-ibá; ibahín.
vase: *n*. saro, plorera.
vassal: *n*. kampón, basalyo.
vast: *adj*. malawak.
vaudeville: *n*. bódabíl.
vault: *n*. kaha-de-yero; *v*. lumuksó, umigpáw.
veal: *n*. karné ng guyà.
veer: *v*. pumihit, pumaling.
vegetable: *n*. gulay.
vehemence: *n*. kapusukán; pagngangalit.
vehement: *adj*. masidhî, marubdób; nagngangalit; mapusók.
vehicle: *n*. sasakyán.
veil: *n*. belo, talukbóng, pindóng; lambóng.
vein: *n*. ugát; (*in marble*) hilatsá, gisok.
velocity: *n*. kabilisán; tulin; belosidád.
velvet: *n*. pelús, tersiyopelo.
vendetta: *n*. benggansa, paghihigantí.
vendor: *n*. tindero, magtitindá, maglalakò.
veneer: *n*. tapal; kalupkóp.
venerate: *v*. igalang, magpitagan.
venereal: *adj*. makalamán; ~ **disease** *n*. sakít sa babae, sakít na nakuha sa pakikipagtalik.
vengeance: *n*. higantí.
vengeful: *adj*. mapaghigantí.
venison: *n*. karné ng usá.
venom: *n*. lason, kamandág; **~ous** *adj*. may-lason.
vent: *n*. labasan; *v*. ibulalas.
ventilate: *v*. pahanginan; **ventilator** *n*. bentiladór.
ventricle: *n*. bentríkulo.
venture: *n*. pakikipagsapalarán, pangangahás.
Venus: *n*. Benus.
veracious: *adj*. mapagtapát; may katotóhanan.
veracity: *n*. katotóhanan; katápatan.
veranda: *n*. beranda.
verb: *n*. pandiwà, berbo; **copulative** ~ *n*. pandiwang pangatníg; **intransitive** ~ *n*. pandiwang kátawanín; **transitive** ~ *n*. pandiwang palipát.
verbal: *adj*. malapandiwà; ~ **noun** *n*. pandiwaring pangngalan; ~ **adjective** *n*. pandiwaring pang-urì; ~ **affix** *n*. panlaping makadiwà.
verbatim: *adj*. waláng-bawas ang mga salitâ.
verdant: *adj*. luntî.
verdict: *n*. pasiyá, hatol ng hurado.
verdigris: *n*. taing-tansô.
verge: *n*. bingit, gilid; **be on the** ~ of **bumingit**.
verify: *v*. magpatunay; magsiyasat.
vernacular: *n*. karaniwang salitâ.
versatile: *adj*. maraming nálalaman, maraming nagagawâ.
verse: *n*. berso, tulâ.
version: *n*. ulat, pahayag; salin.
versus: *prep*. laban sa.
vertebra: *n*. butó sa gulugód.
vertex: *n*. tuktók, tugatog.
vertical: *adj*. patayô, patindíg.
vertigo: *n*. pagkahilo.
verve: *n*. siglá; kasiglahán.
very: *adv*. lubhâ, napaka-; talagá.
vespers: *n*. orasyón.
vessel: lalagyán; sasakyáng-dagat.
vest: *n*. tsaleko; *v*. bihisan.
vestige: *n*. palatandaan, bakás.
vestry: *n*. sakristiyá.
veteran: *n*. beterano.
veterinarian: *n*. beterinaryo, manggagamot ng hayop.
veto: *n*. beto; *v*. betohan.
vex: *v*. yamutín, inisín; pagalitin; **~ation** pagkayamót; pagkainís.
via: *prep*. sa pamamagitan ng daán sa.
viand: *n*. ulam.
vibrate: *v*. mayaníg; mangatál.
vicar: *n*. bikaryo.
vice: *n*. bisyo, kasamaán; *pref*. bise-; ~ **versa** gayón din namán, kabaligtarán.
vicinity: *n*. paligid, kalapitan.
vicious: *adj*. bisyoso, masamâ.
victim: *n*. bíktima; **~ize** *v*. biktimahín.
victor: *n*. nagtagumpáy; **~ious** *adj*. mapana-

gumpáy; **~y** *n.* tagumpáy.
video: *n.* bidyo.
vie: *v.* makipagtunggalian.
view: *n.* pagtingín; tingín; pagtanáw; kabatirán; *v.* ipalagáy; manoód; **~point** *n.* palagáy, kurò.
vigil: *n.* bihilya; pagpupuyát; **~ant** *adj.* maingat, mapagbantáy.
vignette: *n.* binyeta.
vigor: *n.* lakás; **~ous** *adj.* malakás, malusóg.
vile: *adj.* napakasamâ; hamak; imbí.
vilify: *v.* siraan ng puri.
villa: *n.* bilya.
village: *n.* nayon, baryo; **~r** *n.* taong-nayon.
villain: *n.* kontrabida, belyako.
vindicate: *v.* magpawaláng-sala.
vindictive: *adj.* mapaghigantí, bengatibo.
vine: *n.* baging.
vinegar: *n.* sukà.
vineyard: *n.* ubasán, bagingan.
violate: *v.* lumabág, sumuwáy; kumontra.
violence: *n.* dahás, karahasán, kalupitán; kapinsalaán.
violent: *adj.* marahás; malupít.
violet: *n.* biyoleta, lila.
violin: *n.* biyolín; ~ **player** biyolinista.
viper: *n.* ulupóng, bíbora.
virgin: *n.* birhen, dalaga, donselya; **~ity** *n.* pagkadonselya, pagkabirhen.
Virgo: *n.* birhen (sa zodiac).
virile: *adj.* may-pagkalalaki.
virtual: *adj.* tunay, totoó.
virtue: *n.* kabutihan, birtúd, kabanalan.
virtuous: *adj.* mabuti, mabaít.
virulent: *adj.* lubháng nakapípinsalà.
virus: *n.* birus.
visa: *n.* bisa.
viscera: *n.* lamáng-loób.
viscount: *n.* biskonde.
viscous: *adj.* maligat.
vise: *n.* gato.
visible: *adj.* nakikita, natatanáw.
vision: *n.* paningín, pananáw; pangmalas; tanáw.
visit: *v.* dumalaw, bumisita; *n.* bisita, pagdalaw; **~or** *n.* dalaw, panauhin, bisita.
visual: *adj.* pangmatá, ng paningín; **~ize** maglarawan sa isip.
vital: *adj.* kailangan, napakahalagá; **~ity** *n.* katibayan, kalakasán.
vitamin: *n.* bitamina.
vivacious: *adj.* masiglá, bibo.
vivid: *adj.* buháy na buháy; matingkád.
vocabulary: *n.* bokabularyo, talasalitaan.
vocal: *adj.* pantinig, ng tinig; maingay; **~ist** *n.* mang-aawit, kantór.
vocation: *n.* gawain, trabaho; **~al** bokasyonál; náuukol sa hanapbuhay.
vocative: *adj.* panawag; ~ **case** *n.* kaukuláng panawag.
vociferous: *adj.* mabungangà, maingay.
vodka: *n.* bodka.
vogue: *n.* moda, uso.
voice: *n.* tinig, boses; (*gram.*) tingig; *v.* magpahayag, magsabi.
void: *adj.* waláng-bisà; *v.* pawaláng-bisà.
volatile: *adj.* sumpungin.
volcano: *n.* bulkán.
volition: *n.* pagpapasiyá, pagkukusà.
volleyball: *n.* báliból.
volt: *n.* boltahe; **~age** *n.* boltahe.
volume: *n.* bolumen; libro, tomo; lakí.
voluntary: *adj.* kusà, kinusà, kusang-loób, pakusâ.
volunteer: *n.* boluntaryo; *v.* magboluntaryo.
voluptuous: *adj.* makamundó; makalamán; kaakit-akit (katawán ng babae).
vomit: *n.* suka; *v.* magsuká, magbugá.
voracious: *adj.* masibà, matakaw.
vote: *n.* boto, halál; *v.* bumoto; **~r** *n.* botante, manghahalal.
vouch: *v.* gumarantiyá, managót; **~er** butser; katibayan sa nagugol.
vow: *n.* sumpâ, panata; *v.* magpanata, magsumpâ.
vowel: *n.* bokál, patinig.
voyage: *n.* paglalayág, biyahe; *v.* maglayág.
voyeur: *n.* bosero.
vulgar: *adj.* bastós, magaspáng, mahalay; masagwâ; **~ity** *n.* kabastusán, kasagwaán.
vulnerable: *adj.* masugatan, masasalakay.
vulture: *n.* buwitre.
vulva: *n.* puki, bilát, kikì.
vying: *adj.* nag-aagawán.

W

wabble: *v*. sumuray-suray.
wad: *n*. balumbón, tungkós.
waddle: *v*. lumakad nang lakad-pato; *n*. lakad-pato.
wade: *v*. lumakad sa tubig.
wafer: *n*. biskuwít; (*cone*) apa; (*host*) ostiyá.
wag: *v*. magwasiwas, kumawág, magpagpág, magwagwág; ipaypáy, ikawág.
wage: *n*. kita, sahod, suweldo, pasahod; **minimum ~** pinakamababang pasahod; **~ war** digmaín.
wager: *n*. pustá, tayâ; *v*. pumustá.
wagon: *n*. bagón, karitón.
wail: *v*. humagulhól, tumaghóy; manangis.
waist: *n*. baywáng.
wait: *v*. maghintáy, mag-abáng; *n*. paghihintáy; **~ on** *v*. magsilbí; **~ing room** *n*. hintayan; **~ing list** talaan ng naghihintáy.
waiter: *n*. serbidór, tagapagsilbí; tagapaglingkód.
waitress: *n*. serbidora, tagapagsilbí.
waive: *v*. magpaubayà; kusang talikdán.
wake: *v*. gumising; gisingin; *n*. (*for the dead*) lamay, lamayán.
wale: *n*. latay; *v*. latayan.
walk: *v*. maglakád, lumakad; *n*. lakad; **~ing stick** tungkód, bastón; **~out** *n*. welga, aklasan; **~ the dog** ipapasyál ang aso.
wall: *n*. padér; tabikì, dingdíng; *v*. paderán; **~flower** (*coll*.) pamutas-silya; mahiyaing tao sa pistá.
wallet: *n*. pitakà, kartera, kalupî.
wallop: *v*. bumugbóg.
wallow: *v*. maglublób; maglunoy; lunuyán.
walrus: *n*. bokang dagat.
waltz: *n*. balse.
wan: *adj*. maputlâ; matamláy.
wand: *n*. batón.
wander: *v*. gumalà; maglibót; magpalakad-lakad.
wane: *v*. huminà; lumiít.
want: *v*. gustó, ibig; *n*. gustó; **~ed dead or alive** pinagháhanap patáy man o buháy.
wanton: *adj*. mahalay; masamâ; waláng habas.
war: *n*. digmâ, gera; **~like** *adj*. paladigmâ, gerero; **declare ~** magpahayag ng pakikidigmâ.
ward: *n*. alagà, ampón; **~ off** *v*. ilagan, salagín.
warden: *n*. alkayde, bantáy ng mga bilanggô.
wardrobe: *n*. (*clothes*) mga damít; (*chest*) aparadór.
ware: *n*. panindá.
warehouse: *n*. bodega, kamalig; pintungan.
warfare: *n*. digmaan, labanán.
warm: *adj*. mainit; *v*. painitan; **~th** *n*. init; **~ up the spirits** pasiglahín ang loób.
warn: *v*. balaan, babalaán; papag-ingatin; **~ing** *n*. babalâ, balà, paalaala.
warp: *v*. pumintád, pumintál; mamilipit.
warrant: *n*. mandamyento; utos; *v*. magbigáy-katwiran; garantiyahan; hingín; **~ of arrest** mandamyento de aresto, utos ng pagpaparakíp.
warranty: *n*. garantiya.
warrior: *n*. gerero, mandirigmâ.
warship: *n*. bapór-de-gera.
wart: *n*. kulugó.
wary: *adj*. maingat.
wash: *v*. maghugas; hugasan; **~ face** maghilamos; **~ clothes** maglabá; *n*. paghuhugas; labahin; **~out** *n*. pagkabagbág, pagkaagnáw; **mouth ~** pangmumog; **~room** banyo at kasilyas; **~ing machine** mákinang panlabá.
washer: *n*. (*ring*) sapatilya; (*one who washes*) labandero, tagapaghugas.
wasp: *n*. putaktí.
waste: *v*. mag-aksayá, sumayang; *n*. pagsayang, pag-aaksayá, basura; **~land** iláng, kaparangan; **~ful** *adj*. aksayá, gastadór.
watch: *v*. manoód, magmasíd, tumingín; magbantáy; *n*. (*guard*) pagtanod; (*time instrument*) relós; **~dog** *n*. asong tagapagbantáy; **~word** hudyát; **~maker** relohero; **~ out!** mag-ingat ka!.
water: *n*. tubig; *v*. diligín; (*mouth*) maglawáy; **~ closet** kumón, kubeta, palikuran; **~fall** talón; **~proof** *adj*. di-tinatagusán ng tubig; **~y** *adj*. matubig; **~ spinach** kangkóng; **~lily** baino.
waterfall: *n*. talón.
watermelon: *n*. pakwán.
waterway: *n*. daanán ng bangkás sa tubig.
watt: *n*. wat.
wattle: *n*. lambî.

wave: *n.* alon; daluyong; *v.* pumagaspás; kumawáy; magwagaywáy; **~length** habâ ng daluyong.
waver: *v.* umandáp-andáp; mangatál; mag-atubili; mag-alinlangan.
wavy: *adj.* alún-alón; kulót; **~-lined grouper** abo-abo, buluan, puol.
wax: *n.* pagkít, waks.
way: *n.* paraán; kalakarán, uso; daán, landás; pamumuhay; **under ~** *adj.* kasalukuyang ginagawâ; **out of the ~** malayò sa daanán; **by the ~** máibá akó; **give ~** magparaán; bumagsák; magbigáy-daán; **~s and means** mga para-paraán.
waylay: *v.* abatan, harangin.
wayward: *adj.* suwaíl, masuwayin.
we: *pron.* tayo (*inclusive*); kamí (*exclusive*).
weak: *adj.* mahinà; **~en** *v.* magpahinà, papanghinain; **~ness** *n.* hinà.
wealth: *n.* kayamanan; kasaganaan; **~y** *adj.* mayaman, masalapî.
wean: *v.* magwalay; mag-awat sa iná.
weapon: *n.* armás, sandata.
wear: *v.* gumamit, magsuót; **~ out** *v.* masirà; pagurin; mapudpód.
wearisome: *adj.* nakapápagod; nakapanghíhinawà.
weary: *adj.* pagód, hapô; pagál.
weather: *n.* panahón; klima; **~cock** *n.* girimpulá, banog-lawin, patubilíng.
weave: *v.* maghabi; lumala.
web: *n.* bahay-gagambá.
wed: *v.* ikasál; magsama; pakasalán; **~ding** *n.* kasál, pagkakasál.
wedge: *n.* sinsél, kalang, kalsó.
wedlock: *n.* matrimonyo.
Wednesday: *n.* Miyerkulés.
wee: *adj.* napakaliít.
weed: *n.* damó; *v.* gamasin.
week: *n.* linggó; **~ly** *adj.* lingguhan, linggúlinggó; **~end** Sábado at Linggó.
weep: *v.* umiyák, lumuhà; tumangis; humagulgól.
weevil: *n.* bukbók, unós.
weigh: *v.* magtimbáng; tumimbáng.
weight: *n.* timbáng; talarô; bigát.
weir: *n.* tambák; pilapil.
weird: *adj.* mahiwagà, kakatuwâ, kaibá.
welcome: *v.* bumatì nang malugód, sumalubong; *interj.* maligayang pagdatíng; **you-'re ~** waláng anumán; **Welcome!** Maligayang pagdatíng.
weld: *v.* ihinang; pag-isahín.
welfare: *n.* kabutihan, kapakanán; kagálingan.
well: *adv.* mahusay, mabuti; lubós; *n.* balón, bukál; **~-being** *n.* kagalingan, kabutihan; **~-dressed** mabikas; **~-known** laganap, kalát, kilalá; **~-to-do** mariwasâ; **~ off** mayaman.
welt: *n.* latay; ribete.
west: *n.* kanluran; *adv.* pakanlurán; **~ern** *adj.* pakanlurán; **~erner** *n.* tagakanluran; **~ward** pakanlurán.
wet: *adj.* basâ; *v.* basaín; **~ nurse** sisiwa, mamáy.
whack: *v.* humambalos, bumuntál.
whale: *n.* balyena, dambuhalà; **~ shark** isdángtuko.
wharf: *n.* daungan, muwelye, pantalán.
what: *pron.* anó; **~ever** anumán; **~ if** paano kung.
wheat: *n.* trigo.
wheel: *n.* reweda, gulóng; **~barrow** karetilya.
wheeze: *v.* umagahas; sumingasing.
when: *adv.* kailán; (*before adverbial clauses*) nang; **~ever** *adv.* kailanmán; kapág.
where: *adv.* saán; nasaán; **~ever** kung saán, saanmán.
whereabouts: *n.* kinaroroonán.
whereas: *conj.* subali't, datapwá't.
whereby: *adv.* upang.
wherefore: *adv.* kayâ, sa ganyán.
whet: *v.* ihasà; **~ting** *n.* paghahasà; **~ stone** hasaáng bató.
whether: *conj.* kung.
which: *pron.* alín; **~ever** alinmán.
whiff: *n.* hihip, simoy; *v.* amuyín.
while: *conj.* habang, samantala, noóng; **worth~** *adj.* kapakí-pakinabang; *n.* panahón.
whim: *n.* kapritso; **~sical** *adj.* kapritsoso.
whimper: *v.* umungót, magnguyngóy.
whine: *v.* umugót, ngumulngól, umungol.
whinny: *n.* halinghíng; *v.* humalinghíng.
whip: *n.* látigo, pamalò; *v.* paluin, latiguhín; haplitín; (*eggs*) magbatí.

whir: *n*. kagalgál.
whirl: *v*. uminog; umikot; **~pool** *n*. alimpuyó ng tubig; **~wind** ipuipo.
whisk: *n*. pamalís; sibad; *v*. magpalís; sumibad.
whiskers: *n*. balbás; **~ed croaker** kabang.
whiskey: *n*. wiskí, agwardiyente.
whisper: *n*. bulóng; *v*. bumulóng, ibulóng.
whistle: *n*. silbato; sipol; sutsót; *v*. sumipol, sumutsót; sumilbato.
white: *adj*. putî; **~-collar** *adj*. pang-opisina; **~n** *v*. paputiín; **~ goby** biyang putî, dapal.
whiting fish: *n*. usuos; **~ ant** anay.
whiz: *n*. haging, hagibis.
who: *pron*. sino; **~ever** sinumán.
whole: *adj*. buô; lahát.
wholesale: *adj*. sa pakyáw; *n*. pakyawan.
wholesome: *adj*. masustansiya.
wholly: *adv*. lubós, ganáp.
whom: *pron*. sino.
whooping cough: *n*. tuspirina.
whore: *n*. burikák, puta.
whose: *pron*. kanino.
whosoever: *pron*. sinumán, kahit sino.
why: *adv*. bakit; kung bakit.
wick: *n*. mitsá.
wicked: *adj*. masamâ, makasalanan.
wicker: *n*. pansulihiyá.
wide: *adj*. malapad; malawak; maluwáng; **~n** *v*. palaparin, paluwangín; **~spread** *adj*. laganap, kalát.
widow: *n*. biyuda, balong babae; **~hood** pagkabalo.
widower: *n*. balong lalake.
width: *n*. lapad, luwáng
wield: *v*. maghawak; gumamit.
wife: *n*. asawang babae, maybahay.
wig: *n*. peluka.
wiggle: *v*. kumawág, kumislót.
wild: *adj*. (*not tame*) mabangís, mailáp; (*plants*) ligáw; **~ boar** baboy-ramó; **~cat** musang, alamíd; **~ chicken** labuyò; **~life** hayop-gubat.
wilderness: *n*. kagubatan; iláng.
wile: *v*. luminláng.
will: *n*. kaloóban; nais, hangád; testamento; **~ful** sadyâ.
willing: *adj*. maluwág sa kaloóban, sabík.
wilt: *v*. malantá, maluóy.
wily slipmouth: *n*. dalupani.
win: *v*. tumalo, manalo; kamtán; *n*. panalo; **~ner** ang nanalo; **~ning** *adj*. nananalo; **~nings** panalunan, panalo.
wince: *v*. mángiwî.
wind: *n*. hangin; **~y** *adj*. mahangin; *v*. ipulupot, iikid; magkuwerdas.
winded: *adj*. hapô, humihingal.
window: *n*. bintanà, dúrungawán; **~ pane** salamín ng bintanà; **~ sill** pasamano.
windpipe: *n*. tatagukan.
windshield: *n*. pananggáng-hangin; **~ wiper** pangkayod ng tubig.
wine: *n*. alak; **coconut ~** lambanóg; tubâ; **sugarcane ~** basì.
wing: *n*. pakpák, bagwís.
wink: *v*. kumuráp; kumindát; *n*. kuráp, kisáp; kindát.
winnow: *v*. magtahíp; magbitháy.
winsome: *adj*. kaakit-akit; mapanghalina.
winter: *n*. taglamíg, tagginâw.
wipe: *v*. magpunas, magkuskús; **~ anus** iwangan.
wire: *n*. kawad, alambre; **~ mesh** *n*. tela dealambre.
wisdom: *n*. karunungan, dunong, talino.
wise: *adj*. marunong, matalino; **~crack** *n*. birò.
wish: *n*. nais, nasà; *v*. naisin, ibigin; **~ful** *adj*. mapágnais, mapágnasà, mapághangád.
wisp: *n*. tintíng, hiblá; piraso.
wit: *n*. kisláp ng talino; pagpapatawa.
witch: *n*. mangkukulam, maggagaway; **~craft** *n*. panggagaway, pangkukulam.
with: *prep*. kay, sa; kalakip; magkasama.
withdraw: *v*. magurong, iurong, lumayô; maglabás.
wither: *v*. malantá, maluóy; tumuyô.
withhold: *v*. magkaít, pumigil; bumimbín.
within: *prep*. nasa loób ng.
without: *prep*. walâ; sa labás ng.
withstand: *v*. tumagál, magtiís.
witness: *n*. testigo, saksí; *v*. saksihán.
witty: *adj*. mapagbirô, nakakatawá.
wizard: *n*. salamangkero; pantás.
wobble: *v*. humapay-hapay, sumuray-suray.
wobbly: *adj*. umaalóg, gumigiwang, umuugâ.

woe: *n*. pighatî, lungkót; *excl*. sa abâ.
wolf: *n*. lobo; **cry** ~ magbigáy ng malíng alarma.
woman: *n*. babae; **young** ~ dalaga; **~hood** kababaihan.
womb: *n*. matrís, bahay-batà.
wonder: *n*. kababalaghán, himalâ; *v*. gustóng malaman, alamín; magtaká; **~ful** *adj*. kahanga-hangà; kataká-taká.
woo: *v*. lumigaw, ligawan.
wood: *n*. kahoy; **~s** gubat, kahuyan; **~cutter** mamumutol ng kahoy, magtotroso; **~ed** *adj*. makahoy; **~en** *adj*. yarì sa kahoy; **~en shoes** bakyâ; **~lands** kakahuyan, kagubatan.
woodpecker: *n*. batuktók, tariktík.
woof: *n*. tahól, kahól.
wool: *n*. lana.
word: *n*. salitâ; pangakò; balità; **~ing** *n*. pagsasalitâ; ~ **of honor** pangakò, sumpâ; **~y** *adj*. masalitâ; **in other ~s** sa ibáng salitâ; **eat one's ~s** bawiin ang sinabi.
work: *n*. trabaho, paggawâ; hanapbuhay; (*literary*) akdâ; *v*. magtrabaho; (*operate*) umandár, tumakbó; **~er** *n*. trabahadór, manggagawâ; **~shop** *n*. gawaan, talyér.
workmanship: *n*. pagkakágawâ, pagkakáyarì, kahusayan ng yarì.
world: *n*. daigdíg, mundo; **~liness** *n*. pagkamakamundó; **~-wide** kalát sa buóng mundó.
worm: *n*. uod, bulati; **earth** ~ bulating-lupà.
worn: *adj*. ukâ; sirâ; ~ **out** siráng-sirâ.
worry: *v*. mag-alaala, mabahalà, mabalisa.
worse: *adj*. mas masamâ; **~n** *v*. lalong sumamâ.
worship: *n*. pagsambá; *v*. sambahín.
worst: *adj*. pinakamasamâ.
worth: *n*. halagá; pakinabang; **~less** *adj*. waláng-halagá; **~y** *adj*. karapat-dapat; may-halagá.
would: *v*. conditional verb form.
wound: *n*. sugat; *v*. sugatan.
wrangle: *v*. mag-away, magbangay.
wrap: *v*. magbalot; bumalot; *n*. balabal, balot; **~per** *n*. balutan, balot, pambalot.
wrasse fish: *n*. bungat, maming.
wrath: *n*. matindíng poót.
wreath: *n*. korona (ng mga bulaklák).
wreck: *v*. magwasák; (*ship*) mabagbág; *n*. pagkabagbág ng bapór; **~age** pagwawasák; pagsirà; paglanság.
wrench: *n*. liyable, biradór; **pipe** ~ liyabe de tubo.
wrestle: *v*. magbunô; **~r** *n*. mambunuò; **wrestling** pakikipagbunô.
wretch: *n*. waláng-palad; **~ed** *adj*. kahabág-habág.
wriggle: *v*. kumislót, kumisáy-kisáy.
wring: *v*. mamilpit, magpigâ; pilipitin.
wrinkle: *n*. kunót, kulubót; *v*. magkulubót, kumunót; **~d** *adj*. malukot; gusót.
wrist: *n*. pulso, galánggalangán, pupulsuhan.
writ: *n*. kasulatan; utos.
write: *v*. sumulat, isulat; **~r** *n*. sumusulat, manunulát.
writhe: *v*. mamilipit, magalumpihít.
writing: *n*. sulat; pagsulat; akdâ.
written: *adj*. nakasulat.
wrong: *adj*. malî, di-tamà, lisyâ.
wrought: *adj*. nilabrá, pinandáy.
wry: *adj*. ngiwî, pangiwî.

X

xenophobia: *n*. sinpobya, takot o galit sa mga banyagà.
xerox: *n*. seroks; *v*. magseroks.
x-ray: *n*. rayo-ekis.
xylophone: *n*. silópono.

Y

yacht: *n*. yate; **~ing** pagyayate; **~sman** mangyayate.
yak: *n*. bakang may mahabang buhók.
yam: *n*. tugî; namî.
yank: *v*. baltakín, haltakín.
yap: *v*. magdadaldál, sumatsát.
yard: *n*. yarda; bakuran, loóban.
yarn: *n*. estambre, sinulid; hilatsá.
yawn: *v*. humigáb, humikáb.
year: *n*. taón; **~ly** taún-taón; santáunan.
yearn: *v*. manabík, magnasà; **~ing** pananabík, pagnanasà.
yeast: *n*. pampaalsá, lebadura.

yell: *n*. hiyáw, sigáw; *v*. humiyáw, sumigáw.
yellow: *n*. diláw, amarilyo; **~ish** *adj*. madiláw-diláw; **~-finned tuna** albakora, badlaan, buyo; **~ fever** sakít na paniniláw.
yelp: *n*. angal, atungal.
yes: *adv*. oo; (*with respect*) opò, ohò.
yesterday: *adv*. kahapon.
yet: *adv*. di pa; pa.
yield: *v*. mamunga, bigyán; sumukò; pag-anihan; *n*. ani.
yoga: *n*. yoga.
yogurt: *n*. yogúr(t).
yoke: *n*. pamatok; umbrera; paód.
yolk: *n*. pulá ng itlóg.
yonder: *adv*. doón, roón.
you: *pron*. ikáw (*familiar*); kayó (*plural, polite*).
young: *adj*. batà; bago; **~ster** *n*. batà.
your: *pron*. iyo, mo (*familiar*); inyo, ninyo (*plural, polite*).
yourself: *pron*. sarili mo, sarili ninyó.
yourselves: *pron*. sarili ninyó.
youth: *n*. kabataan; **~ful** batà.
yoyo: *n*. yoyò.
Yuletide: *n*. Paskó.

Z

zany: *adj*. luku-lukó, komikero.
zeal: *n*. pagsisikap, sigasig, sipag; **~ot** *n*. panátiko; **~ous** *adj*. masipag, masikap, masikháy.
zebra: *n*. sebra.
zenith: *n*. taluktók, kaitaasan.
zephyr: *n*. simoy, hanging palay-paláy.
zero: *n*. sero, walâ.
zest: *n*. linamnám, gana.
zigzag: *adj*. palikú-likô.
zinc: *n*. sink.
zip: *n*. haging, hagibis; **~per** *n*. siper.
zither: *n*. sitara.
zodiac: *n*. sodyak; sagisag ng mga pangkát ng bituín.
zone: *n*. sona; *v*. sonahin.
zoo: *n*. su, soolóhiko.
zoologist: *n*. soólogo, dalubhasà sa soolohiya.
zoology: *n*. soolohiya.
zoom: *v*. pumaimbulóg; *n*. imbulóg.

REFERENCES AND PILIPINO RESOURCES

Alejandro, Rufino. 1947. *Handbook of Tagalog Grammar with Exercises*. Manila: University Publishing Co.

Arsenio, M. E. 1971. A lexicographic study of Tayabas Tagalog of Quezon Province. Quezon City: University of the Philippines Press.

Blake, F. R. 1925. *A Grammar of the Tagalog Language*. New Haven: American Oriental Society.

Bloomfield, L. 1917. *Tagalog texts with Grammatical Analysis*. Urbana: University of Illinois.

Bowen, J. Donald. 1965. *Beginning Tagalog*. Berkeley: University of California Press.

---- (editor). 1968. *Intermediate Readings in Tagalog*. Berkeley: University of California Press.

Brichoux, Robert. 1972. *Acoustic correlates of stress in Tagalog: Spectrographic studies of relative amplitude, relative frequency, and length.* M.A. thesis. California State College. 87 p.

Chan Yap, G. 1980. *Hokkien Chinese borrowings in Tagalog*. Canberra: Pacific Linguistics.

Conklin, Harold C. 1956. Tagalog Speech Disguise. *Language* 32:136-39.

Constantino, E. 1971. 'Tagalog and other major languages of the Philippines', in T.A. Sebeok (ed.) *Current Trends in Linguistics* 8:1:112-154, The Hague: Mouton

Cruz, E.L. 1975. A subcategorization of Tagalog verbs. *The Archive*, Special Monograph No.2, Quezon City: University of the Philippines.

De Guzman, Videa. 2001. Tagalog. In Garry, Jane and Carl Rubino (eds.) *Facts About the World's Languages: An Encyclopedia of the World's Languages Past and Present*. New York/Dublin: H. W. Wilson.

English, Leo James. 1977. *English-Tagalog Dictionary*. Quezon City, Philippines, Kalayaan Press Marketing Enterprises, Inc.

----. 1986. *Tagalog-English Dictionary*. Quezon City, Philippines: Kalayaan Press Marketing Enterprises, Inc.

Eugenio, Damiana L. 1975. *Philippine Proverb Lore*. Quezon City: Philippine Folklore Society.

Gonzales, Andrew B. 1970. Acoustic correlates of accent, rhythm, and intonation in Tagalog. *Phonetica* 22:11-44.

----. 1981. Tagalog accent revisited: Some preliminary notes. In Andrew Gonzalez and David Thomas (eds.), *Linguistics across continents: Studies in honor of Richard S. Pittman* , 27-45. Linguistic Society of the Philippines Monograph, 2. Manila: Summer Institute of Linguistics and Linguistic Society of the Philippines.

Hendrickson, Gail R. and Leonard Newell. 1991. *A bibliography of Philippine language dictionaries and vocabularies*. Manila: Linguistic Society of the Philippines.

Herre, Albert W., and Agustin F. Umali. 1948. *English and local common names for Philippine fishes*. Washington DC: U.S. Government Printing Office, United States Dept. of the Interior, Fish and Wildlife Service, Circular 14.

Himmelmann, Nikolaus. 2000. Lexical categories and voice in Tagalog. In P. Austin and S. Musgrave (eds) *Grammatical relations and voice in Austronesian*, Stanford: Center for the Study of Language and Information.

----. *in press*. Tagalog. In Himmelmann, N., and S. Adelaar (eds.) *The Austronesian Languages of Asia and Madagascar*. London: Curzon.

Institute of Natl. Language and Instructional Materials Corporation. 1960. *English-Filipino Dictionary*. Philippines: Dept. of Education, Culture and Sports.

Kroeger, Paul R. 1993. *Phrase structure and grammatical relations in Tagalog*. Dissertations in Linguistics. Stanford, CA: Center for the Study of Language and Information.
Laktaw, Pedro Serrano. 1914. *Diccionario Tagalog-Hispano*. Manila: Imp. y Lit. de Santos y Bernal.
Lendoyro, Constantino. 1909. *The Tagalog Language*. Manila: Juan Fajardo.
Llamzon, T. A. 1976. *Modern Tagalog: A functional-structural description*. The Hague: Mouton.
Lopez, C. 1937. Preliminary Study of the Affixes in Tagalog. In E. Constantino (ed.) (1977) *Selected writings of Cecilio Lopez in Philippine linguistics*, 28-104, Diliman: University of the Philippines Press.
----. 1970. On the Boak Tagalog of the island of Marinduque. *The Archive* (University of the Philippines) I/2:1-53.
Lopez, Cecilio. 1974. Comparative Philippine word-list. *The Archive,* Special Monograph Issue No. 1.
McFarland, C. D. 1976. *A provisional classification of Tagalog verbs*. Tokyo: Institute for the Study of Languages and Cultures of Asia and Africa.
----. 1989. *A Frequency Count of Pilipino*. Manila: Linguistic Society of the Philippines.
Muyargas, Wilfredo, Rosa Soberano, and Frank Flores. 1968. *Tagalog for Non-Filipinos* (2 volumes). Manila: Interchurch Language School.
Naylor, P. B. 1995. Subject, topic, and Tagalog syntax. In D. Benett, T. Bynon and G.B. Hewitt (eds) *Subject, voice and ergativity*, 161-201. London: School of Oriental and African Studies.
Quisumbing, Eduardo. 1947. Philippine plants used for arrow and fish poisons. *Philippine Journal of Science* 77:2:127-177.
Panganiban, Jose Villa. 1972. *Diksyunario-tesauro Pilipino-Ingles*. Quezon City: Manlapaz.
----. 1969. *Concise English-Tagalog dictionary*. Tokyo: Charles E. Tuttle Co.
Pittman, Richard S. 1966. Tagalog *-um-* and *mag-*: An interim report. *Linguistic Circle of Canberra Publications* A8: 9-20.
Ramos, Teresita V. 1971. *Tagalog Structures*. Honolulu: University of Hawaii Press.
----. 1985. *Conversational Tagalog. A Functional-Situational Approach*. Honolulu: University of Hawaii Press.
Ramos, Teresita V., and Maria Lourdes Bautista. 1986. H*andbook of Tagalog Verbs: Inflections, Modes, and Aspects*. Honolulu: University of Hawaii Press.
Ramos, Teresita V., and Resty M. Cena. 1990. *Modern Tagalog*. Honolulu: University of Hawaii Press.
Ramos, Teresita V. and Videa de Guzman. 1971. *Tagalog for Beginners*. Honolulu: University of Hawaii Press.
Ramos, Teresita V. and Rosalina M. Goulet. 1981. *Intermediate Tagalog: developing cultural awareness through language*. Honolulu: University of Hawaii Press.
Rubino, Carl. 1998. The Tagalog Derivational Clitic. *Linguistics* 36:5:1147-1166.
----. 2000. *Ilocano Dictionary and Grammar*. Honolulu: University of Hawaii Press.
San Miguel, Rachel M. Ligaya. 1975. *Beginning Tagalog*. Quezon City: JMC Press.
Santiago, Alfonso O. 1984. The *elaboration of a technical lexicon of Pilipino.* Manila: Linguistic Society of the Philippines and Summer Institute of Linguistics.
Santos, Vito C. *Pilipino-English Dictionary*. 1978. Caloocan City, Philippines: Philippine Graphic Arts, Inc.
Schachter, Paul. 1987. Tagalog. in B. Comrie (ed.) *The world's major languages*, 936-958. London: Croom Helm.
Schachter, Paul, and Fe T. Otanes. *Tagalog Reference Grammar*. 1972. Berkeley: University of California Press.

Sebastian, Federico B., and Antonio D. G. Mariano. *Idiomatic Expressions in the Tagalog Language*. 1954. Manila: Committee on the National Language Textbook Preparation.

Soberano, R. 1980. *The dialects of Marinduque Tagalog*. Canberra: Pacific Linguistics.

Surian ng Wikang Pambansa. 1971. *Pinaglakip na Talasalitaan (Composite vocabulary)*. Quezon City: JMC Press, Inc., ix and 211 pp. [Eight major Philippine languages]

Wolfenden, Elmer and Rufino Alejandro, editors. 1957. *Intensive Tagalog conversation course*. Manila: Summer Institute of Linguistics and Institute of National Language.

Wolff, J. U. 1972. *A Dictionary of Cebuano Visayan*. Ithaca: Cornell University.

----. 1976. Malay borrowings in Tagalog. In C. D. Cowan and O. W. Wolters (eds) *Southeast-Asian history and historiography: essays presented to D.G.H. Hall*, 345-367. Ithaca: Cornell University Press.

Wolff, J. U. with M.T.C. Centeno and D.V. Rau. 1991. *Pilipino through self-instruction*, 4 vols. Ithaca: Cornell Southeast Asia Program.

Yap, Gloria Chan. 1980. *Hokkien Chinese borrowings in Tagalog*. Canberra: Pacific Linguistics Series B, No. 71, Australian National University.

Zorc, R. David Paul, and Rachel San Miguel (compilers); Annabelle M. Sarra, Patricia O. Afable (editors). 1993. *Tagalog Slang Dictionary*, 3rd edition. Manila: De La Salle University Press.

Zorc, R. David. 1994. Tagalog. in D.T. Tryon (ed.) *Comparative Austronesian dictionary*, vol. 1:335-341, Berlin. Mouton de Gruyter.

APPENDIX

Supplementary vocabulary lists for travelers to the Philippines and students of Tagalog

Numbers (Mga bilang)

isá	one
dalawá	two
tatló	three
apat	four
limá	five
anim	six
pitó	seven
waló	eight
siyám	nine
sampû	ten
labing-isá	eleven
labindal(a)wá	twelve
labintatló	thirteen
labíng-apat	fourteen
labinlimá	fifteen
labíng-anim	sixteen
labimpitó	seventeen
labíngwaló	eighteen
labinsiyám	nineteen
dalawampû	twenty
dalawampú't isá	twenty-one
dalawampú't waló	twenty-eight
tatlumpû	thirty
ápatnapû	forty
limampû	fifty
animnapû	sixty
pitumpû	seventy
walumpû	eighty
siyámnapû	ninety
sandaán	one hundred
sandaá't isá	one hundred one
dalawandaán	two hundred
sanlibo	one thousand
sanlaksâ, sampúng libo	ten thousand
sangyutà, sandaáng libo	hundred thousand
sang angaw	one million

Ordinal Numbers

una	first
ikalawá, pangalawá (ika-2)	second
ikatló, pangatló (ika-3)	third
ikapat, pang-apat (ika-4)	fourth
ikalimá, panlimá (ika-5)	fifth
ikaanim (ika-6)	sixth
ikapitó (ika-7)	seventh
ikawaló (ika-8)	eighth

Calendar terms (Kalendaryo)

araw	day
linggó	week
buwán	month
taón	year
ngayón	today
bukas	tomorrow
kahapon	yesterday
kamakalawá	day before yesterday
samakalawá	day after tomorrow
Lunes	Monday
Martes	Tuesday
Miyérkoles	Wednesday
Huwebes	Thursday
Biyernes	Friday
Sábado	Saturday
Linggó	Sunday
Enero	January
Pebrero	February
Marso	March
Abríl	April
Mayo	May
Hunyo	June
Hulyo	July
Agosto	August
Setyembre	September
Oktubre	October
Nobyembre	November
Disyembre	December

Seasons (Mga panahón)

tagsibol	spring
tag-aráw, tag-init	summer
taglagás	autumn, fall
tagginàw, taglamíg	winter
tag-ulán	rainy season

Telling Time (Oras)

relós	watch
oras	time; hour
minuto	minute
saglít	second
sandalî	moment
Anóng oras na?	What time is it?
Las singko na; Ikalimá na.	It is five o'clock.
Las siyete y medya na.	It is seven thirty.

Directions (Direksiyón)

hilagà	north
timog	south
silangan	east
kanluran	west

Wind Direction (Tungo ng hangin)

amihan	northeast wind
habagat	west wind, monsoon
hilagà	north wind
timog	south wind
balaklaót	northwest wind

Celestial bodies (Mga bagay nasa langit)

araw	sun
hangin	air
buwán	moon
bahag-harì	rainbow
bituin, talà	star
bulalakaw	meteor
kometa	comet
paglalahò	eclipse
ulap	cloud

Natural Elements and Occurrences

hamóg	dew
ambón	drizzle
alikabók	dust
lindól	earthquake
salot, peste	epidemic
apóy	fire
bahâ	flood
kidlát	lightning
putik	mud
lahár	mudflow
ulán	rain
buhangin	sand
lupà	ground, soil
bató	stone
asó, usok	smoke
kulóg	thunder
bagyó	storm
tubig	water
alon	wave
alimpuyó	whirlpool
ipuipo, buhawi	whirlwind

Day (Araw)

araw	day, daytime
umaga	morning
tanhalì	noon
hapon	afternoon
dapít-hapon	late afternoon
gabí	night
hatíng-gabí	midnight
magdamág	the whole night
maghapon	the whole day
takíp-silim	twilight
bukáng-liwaywáy	daybreak
madalíng-araw	dawn

Holidays (Pistá)

Paskó	Christmas
Bagong-Taón	New Year
Paskó ng Pagkabuhay	Easter
Kurismá	Lent
Huwebes Santo	Holy Thursday

Biyernes Santo	Good Friday
Araw ng Pasasalamat	Thanksgiving
Araw ng mga Banál	All Saint's Day
Todos los Santos	"
Araw ng Pag-aalaala	Memorial Day
Kaarawán	Birthday
Maligayang Paskó!	Merry Christmas!
Masaganang Bagong-Taón!	Prosperous New Year!
Maligayang batì!	Congratulations!
Maligayang batì sa iyóng kaarawán!	Happy birthday!
Mabuhay!	Long Live!

Parts of the Body (Mga bahagi ng katawán)

bukung-bukong	ankle
bisig	arm
kilikili	armpit
likód	back
katawán	body
suso	breast
pigî	buttock
puwít	buttocks
bintî	calf of leg
pisngí	cheek
dibdíb	chest
babà	chin
tainga (tenga)	ear
siko	elbow
matá	eye
kilay	eyebrow
pilik-matá	eyelash
mukhâ	face
dalirì	finger
kukó	fingernail
noó	forehead
singit	groin
buhók	hair
kamáy	hand
ulo	head
sakong	heel
balakáng	hip
alak-alakán	hock
tuhod	knee
labì	lower lip, lip
bibíg	mouth
batok	nape

leég	neck
ilóng	nose
palad	palm
titì	penis
balikat	shoulder
tagiliran	side
talampakan	sole
ngusò	snout, upper lip
pilipisan	temple
hità	thigh
dalirì ng paá	toe
dilà	tongue
pukì	vagina
baywáng	waist
pulsó	wrist

Kinterms (Pagkakamag-anak)

ale, tiyá	aunt
kapatíd na lalaki	brother
bayáw	brother-in-law
pinsán	cousin
pinsán buô	first cousin
anák na babae	daughter
mag-anak	family
amá	father
apó	grandchild
lolo, lelong, ingkóng, abuwelo	grandfather
lola, lelang, impó, abuwela	grandmother
iná	mother
biyanán	mother/father-in-law
pamangkíng lalaki	nephew
pamangkíng babae	niece
kamag-anak	relative
kapatíd	sibling
kapatíd na babae	sister
hipag	sister-in-law
asawa	spouse
mag-asawa	husband and wife
anák na babae	son
manugang	son/daughter-in-law
amaín, tiyó	uncle
panganay	first born
bunsô	youngest child
kuya	oldest brother

diko	second eldest brother
ate	oldest sister
dete	second eldest sister

Occupations (Mga hanap-buhay)

antropólogo	anthropologist
bangkero	banker
pandáy	blacksmith
mángangalakál, negosyante	businessman
alawagi	carpenter
tsupér	chauffeur
sapatero	cobbler, shoemaker
mángangathâ, kompositór	composer
mánanayáw	dancer
dentista	dentist
manggagamot, doktór	doctor
elektrista	electrician
inhinyero	engineer
magsasaká	farmer
mángingisdâ	fisherman
mángungulot, tagapagkulót	hairdresser, curler
mánanalaysáy, istoryadór	historian
abugado, mánananggól	lawyer
tagapamahalà, tagapangasiwà	manager
manghihilot, masahista	masseur
mekániko	mechanic
komersyante, mángangalakál	merchant
hilot, komadrona	midwife
músiko	musician
nars	nurse
pintór	painter
manggagamot, doktór	physician, doctor
piloto	pilot
tubero	plumber
pangulo, presidente	president
propesór	professor
sikólogo	psychologist
mánanaliksík	researcher
mánanahì	seamstress
mángangantá, mang-aawit	singer
aksiyonista	stockbroker
tindero	storekeeper
estudyante, mag-aarál	student
siruhano	surgeon
agrimensór	surveyor

sastre, modista	tailor
latero	tinsmith
mánanalin, tagasalin	translator
reluhero	watchmaker
manggagawà	worker, laborer
gurò	teacher
manggagamot-hayop	veterinarian

Colors (Mga kulay)

kulay	color
itím	black
bugháw, asúl	blue
malabugháw	bluish
kayumanggí	brown (skin)
kulay-kapé	brown, coffee colored
ginintuán	golden
kulay-abó, gris	gray
lintián, berde	green
kaki	khaki
berdeng murà	light green
berde-lumot	dark green (moss)
maputlâ	pale
rosas	pink
lila	purple
pulá	red
pinilakan	silver colored
putî	white
putián	whitish
diláw	yellow

Topographical Terms (Topograpiya)

tabíng-dagat, dalámpasígan	beach
sapà	brook
lungos	cape
yungíb, kuweba	cave
lungsód, siyudád	city
disyérto	desert
búkid	field; farm
gúbat	forest
buról	hill
pulò	island
lawà	lake
tanawin	landscape, scenery

parang	meadow
bundók	mountain
dagat	ocean, sea
tangwáy	peninsula
kapatagan	plain
lusak, sanaw	puddle
ilog	river
daán	street
bayan	town
lambák, libís	valley
nayon	village
bulkán	volcano
talón	waterfall
daungan	wharf

Playing Cards

alás	ace
baraha	card
diyák	jack
dyoker	joker
harì	king
reyna	queen
turno	turn
pagtayâ, pusta	wager, ante
ipamigáy ang baraha	deal the cards
magbalasa	shuffle
magdayà	cheat
magsugál	gamble
manalo	win
matalo	lose
pumustá, tumayâ	bet

Philippine/Spanish deck suits:

bastós	clubs
kopas	goblets
ispada	swords
oros	gold coins

Court terms (Sa húkuman)

húkuman	court
hukóm	judge
kasabuwát	accomplice
ang pinagbíbintangán	the accused

paghahabol	appeal
lagak, piyansa	bail
usapin	case
bintáng	charge, accusation
sakdál	complaint, charge
gantíg-sakdál	counter complaint
násasakdál	defendant
katibayan	evidence
multá	fine
piskál	fiscal
ang maysala	guilty party
bista	case, hearing
pagkábilanggô	imprisonment
abugado, mánananggól	lawyer
tutlo	objection
tagausig	prosecutor
hatol	sentence, decision
patotoó	testimony
paglilitis	trial
saksí	witness

Antonym List of common adjectives

mabuti / masamâ	good / bad
magandá / pangit	beautiful / ugly
malakí / maliít	big / small
batà / matandâ	young / old (person)
bago / lumà	new / old (thing)
malakás / mahinà	strong / weak
malinis / marumí	clean / dirty
murà / mahál	cheap / expensive
malamíg / mainit	cold / warm, hot
mayaman / mahirap	rich / poor
maputî / maitím	light / dark (complexioned)
maingay / tahimik	noisy / quiet
lutò / hiláw	cooked / raw
totoó / malî, sinungaling	true / false
malalim / mababaw	deep / shallow
madalî / mahirap	easy / difficult
magaán / mabigát	light / heavy
maáwain / malupít	kind / cruel
maluwáng / makítid	wide / narrow
maluwáng / masikíp	loose / tight
marunong / mangmáng	wise / ignorant
makinis / magalás	smooth / rough
matigás / malambót	hard / soft

mataás / mababà	high / low
mabangó / mabahò	fragrant / foul smelling
matangkád / pandák	tall / short
mahabà / maiklî	long / short
matalino / bobo	intelligent / stupid
matapang / duwág	brave / cowardly
masipag / tamád	hardworking / lazy
maligaya / malungkót	happy / sad
matabâ / payát	fat / thin
pangó / matangos	flat nosed / long nosed
magaspáng / pino	coarse / fine
hinóg / bubót	ripe / immature
maasim / matamís	sour / sweet
maliwanag / madilím	bright / dark
matalím / mapuról	sharp / dull
bukás / sarado	open / closed
basâ / tuyô	wet / dry
matuwíd / kilô, likô	straight / crooked
patáy / buháy	dead / alive
maaga / mahulí	early / late
maangháng / matabáng	spicy / bland
mayabang / mapakumbabâ	boastful / humble
magalang / bastós	polite / rude
mabilís / mabagal	fast / slow

Food (Pagkain)

Vegetables (Mga gulay)

bamboo shoots	labóng
banana blossom	pusò ng saging
banana (for cooking)	sabá
beans	bins
lima, kidney	patanì
mung	munggó
snap	abitsuwelas
soy	balatong
string	sitaw
winged	sigarílyas
beet	remolatsas
bittermelon	ampalayá
bottle gourd	upo
cabbage	repolyo
Chinese cabbage	petsáy
swamp cabbage	kangkóng
carrot	karot

cassava	kamoténg-kahoy
cauliflower	koliplór
chaiote	sayote
chickpeas	garbansos
Chinese celery	kintsáy
coconut pith	ubod
corn	maís
cucumber	pipino
eggplant	talóng
gourd	upo
bottle gourd	upo
wax gourd	kondól
horseradish leaves	malunggáy
Jew's mallow (Ilocano)	saluyot
jicama	singkamás
leaves	mga dahon
lentils	lentehas
lettuce	letsugas
mung bean	munggo
mushroom	kabutí
okra	okra
onion	sibuyas
peas	gisantes
pea pods	sitsaró
pepper	síli
chili pepper	labuyò
radish	labanós
scallions	sibuyas na murà
spinach	kulitis
sponge gourd	patola
sprouts	togè
squash	kalabasa
sweet potato	kamote
taro	gabi
tomato	kamatis
tree ears	taingang dagâ
turnip	singkamás
water chestnut	apulid
wax gourd	kondól
yam	kamote
purple yam	ube
yam bean (jícama)	singkamás

Noodles (Mga pansít)

bean noodle	sótanghón
dried yellow Chinese noodle	pansít kantón
rice noodle	bíhon
wheat noodle	míki
wheat noodle (fine)	míswa

Condiments (Mga rekado)

anise	anís
bay leaf	lawrél
butter	mantekilya
cheese	keso
cinnamon	kanela
coconut milk	gatâ
coriander	kulantro
fish paste	bagoóng
fish sauce	patís
garlic	bawang
ginger	luyà
honey	pulót-pukyutan
horseradish	malunggáy
ketchup	katsap
mayonnaise	mayonesa
monosodium glutamate	betsin
mustard	mostasa
nutmeg	nues moskada
oregano	orégano
pepper	pamintá
red Cayenne pepper	pamintón
spicy pepper	síli, sili labuyo
salt	asín
sesame seeds	lingá
soy sauce	toyò
soy beans	tausi
soy bean curd (fermented)	tahurí
sugar	asukal
crude sugar	panocha (panutsa)
sweet and hot sauce	tamís-angháng
syrup	pulót
turmeric	diláw
vanilla	banílya
vinegar	sukà
worcestershire sauce	salsa perín

Poultry (Manukan)

chicken	manók
duck	pato, bibe
egg	itlóg
duck egg (fertilized)	balót
duck egg (unfertilized)	penoy
gizzard	balún-balunan
quail	pugò
squab	kalapati
turkey	pabo

Meat (Karne)

bacon	tusino
beef	baka
belly	liyempo
feet	pata
goat	kambíng
ham	hamón
meat	karne
rind	sitsarón
roast pork	letsón
skin	balát
spare ribs	tadyáng
steak	bisték
tenderloin	lomo
tripe	góto

Seafood

anchovy	dilis
caesio fish	dalagang-bukid
catfish (freshwater)	hitò
catfish (saltwater)	kandulì
cavalla fish	talakitok
clam	halaán
cod	bakaláw
crab	
large, black	alimango
with speckled shell	alimásag
small	talamangkâ
cuttlefish	pugità
dried fish	tuyô
goby	biá
grouper	lapu-lapu

herring	tambán
jellyfish	dikyâ
lobster	uláng
mackerel	tanggigi
mullet	talílong
young	kapak
adult	banak
mussel	tahóng
octopus	pugità
oyster	talabá
pompano	pampanó
porgy	bakoko
prawn	sugpô
salmon	salmón
salted fish paste	bagoóng
sardines	sardinas
seaweed	damóng-dagat
shark	patíng
shrimp	hipon
very small	alamáng
smoked fish	tinapa
snapper	maya-maya
sole	dapâ
squid	pusít
surgeon fish	labahita
tilapia	tilapya
tuna	tulingan

Fruits (Prutas)

apple	mansanas
mountain apple	makupa
sugar apple	atis
velvet apple	mabolo
apricot	albarikoke
avocado	abukado
banana	saging
cooking	sabá
breadfruit	rimas
cantaloupe	milón
cherry	seresa
coconut	niyóg
young	buko
soft meat	makapunô
durian	duryán
grape	ubas

guamachile	kamatsilé
guava	bayabas
jackfruit	langkâ, nangkâ
lemon	limón
lime	dayap
small lime	kalamansî
lychee	letsiyas
mango	manggá
mangosteen	manggustín
nuts	
almond	almendras
cashew	kasúy
chestnut	kastanyas
palm	kaong
peanut	manî
orange	naranghita, dalanghita, dalandán
papaya	papaya
peach	melokotón
pear	peras
pineapple	pinyá
plum	duhat, sinigwelas
pomelo	suhà
rambutan	rambután
sandorium indicum	santól
sapodilla	tsiko
soursop	guyabano
star-apple	kaimito
starfruit	balimbíng
tamarind	sampalok
watermelon	pakwán

Beverages (Mga inumin)

beer	serbesa
black beer	serbesa negra
chocolate	tsokolate
coconut wine	tubâ
coffee	kapé
gin	hinebra
ginger tea	salabát
juice	dyús
liquor, wine	alak
milk	gatas
sherry	herés
tea	tsa, tsaá
water	tubig

wine	alak
anise wine	anisado

A Philippine Menu (description of various Philippine dishes)

Entrées and Entrée terms

Menus in the Philippines will usually adhere to old Spanish spellings, as those given below. Where applicable, Tagalog spelling is rendered in parentheses.

adobo	Philippine national dish, pork or chicken marinated with garlic, soy, vinegar, and bay leaf
afritada (apritada)	pork stew with liver, green pepper, garlic, onion, tomatoes, soy, vinegar, and potatoes
alimango	crab
almóndigas	meat balls
arroz caldo (aroskaldo)	rice porridge with chicken, garlic, ginger, onion, and fish sauce
arroz valenciana (aros balensiana)	paella
asado	roast
bachóy (batsóy)	pork parts cooked in garlic, onions, ginger, and *patis*
bopis	pig innards (liver, lungs, and heart) cooked in garlic with onion, tomatoes and pepper
bulangláng	horseradish leaves cooked in various ways, (with pork, squash, fish, etc.)
camarón rebosado (kamarón)	breaded shrimps
cardillo (kardilyo)	fish stew with eggs
chuletas (tsuletas)	pork chops
cocido (kosido)	Spanish stew
kaldereta	goat stew with potatoes, tomatoes, onions, garlic, and peas
kalyos	ox tripe dish with garbanzos
kare-kare	ox tail stew with banana blossoms, annatto, cooked in a peanut sauce
kilawín	raw (fish or meat)
daing	dried fish
dinengdéng (Ilocano)	boiled vegetables with bagoóng
dinuguán	blood pudding cooked with internal organs
embutido	porkloaf sausage
escabeche (eskabetse)	sweet and sour fish dish
estofado (estopado)	beef stew with beans, carrots, tomatoes, onion, and vinegar
ginataán	cooked in coconut milk (gatâ)
gulay	vegetables
humbâ	var. of *umbâ*
inihaw	barbecued

laing	taro leaves cooked in coconut milk
lengua	tongue
litsón	roast pork
longaniza (longganisa)	sweet and sour pork sausage
lumpia	meat roll, fresh or fried (egg roll)
lumpia shanghai	ground beef roll
mechado (metsado)	beef and onions cooked with tomato sauce, potatoes, bay leaf and paprika
menudo	cow tail stew with garbanzos
misua	thin noodle dish
morcón (morkón)	Philippine meat loaf
paella (paelya)	rice dish with seafood, chicken and vegetables
paksíw	fish or pork marinated in vinegar, brown sugar, ginger, pepper and salt
palabok	garnishing (for noodles) made from ground shrimps
pansít	noodles
pansít guisado	sautéed noodles
pansít luglúg	noodles with shrimps and sauce
pansít mami	noodle soup with meat
pesa	chicken (or fish) soup with potatoes, onion, cabbage, and onions
picadillo (pikadilyo)	ground meat and diced vegetables
pinakbét (Ilocano dish)	vegetable dish cooked with bagoóng
pinais	shrimps with coconut milk
pinangat	fish dish
pochero (putsero)	chicken and pork stew with bananas and vegetables
pusít	squid
rebosado	breaded
relyeno	stuffing
relyenong bangós	stuffed milk fish
sarsiado	sauce (used with fish)
sinaing	boiled rice
sinangág	fried rice
sinangláy	catfish with taro leaves, coconut, and *bagoóng*
sinigáng	fish stew with tamarind
sitaw	string beans
tapa	seasoned dried meat
tinola	chicken stew with papaya
tokua	tofu
torta	omelet
tortilla (tortilya)	omelet
ukoy	fried shrimp cakes
umbâ	*adobo* with sugar

Desserts (Matamís)

barquillos (barkilyos)	rolled wafers
bibingka	rice cake
bombones de arroz	rice cakes with coconut milk
buchi (butsi)	mongo paste buns rolled in sesame
budín	pudding
bukayo	coconut bars
buko pie	coconut pie
cassava cake	rice cake with cassava
champorado (tsampurado)	chocolate porridge
churros (tsurros)	fried long donuts
cuchinta (kutsinta)	annato rice cake
empanadas	small pies
ensaymada	sponge cake
espasól	sticky rice grounded with sugar, coconut milk, vanilla and salt
ginataán	coconut sweet soup
gulaman	sweet seaweed gelatin
halayá	jelly made from ube
halo-halò	sweet beans with coconut milk and shaved rice
kalamay	thin sweet coconut cakes
lecheflán (letseplán)	custard
maja blanca (mahablangka)	wet corn and flour cake
makapuno	young coconut
palitáw	rice cake in small balls
pastillas (pastilyas)	sweet flavored milk tablets
pinipig	rice crispies (green)
polvorón (polborón)	milk powder cake
puto	small milk cakes
puto maya	rice cake with grated coconut
sapín-sapín	layered coconut and ube cake
sinukmani	rice cooked in coconut milk with a caramel-like topping
sorbetes	ice cream (sherbet)
suman	sticky rice cake with coconut milk
tamarindo	tamarind (sampalok)
turrón	fritter
ube	purple yam (used to make various confections)
yema	milk, egg, and sugar confection

Selected Tagalog folk songs

Bahay Kubo

Bahay kubo, kahit muntî
Ang halaman doón ay sari-sari
Singkamás at talóng
Sigarilyas at manî
sitaw, bataw, patanì
Kundól, patola, upo't kalabasa
At saká mayroón pang labanós, mustasa
Sibuyas, kamatis, bawang at luya
sa paligid-ligid ay puro lingá

Bayan Ko

Ang bayan kong Pilipinas
Lupain ng gintó't bulaklák
Pag-ibig ang sa kanyáng palad
Nag-alay ng gandá't dilág
At sa kanyáng yumì at gandá
Dayuhan at nahalina
Bayan ko! Binihag ka
Nasadlák sa dusa.
Ibong mang may layang lumipád
Kulungin mo at umiiyák
Bayan pa kayang sakdál dilág
Ang di magnasang makaalpás
Pilipinas kong minumutyâ
Pugad ng luha ko't dalitâ
Aking adhikâ
Makita kang sakdál layà.

Sitsiritsít

Sitsiritsít, alibangbáng,
Salagintô at salagubang.
Ang babae sa lansangan,
Kung gumiri'y parang tandáng
Santo Niño sa Pandakan,
Putoseko sa tindahan,
Kung ayaw mong magpautang,
Uubusin ka ng langgám.
Mama, mama, namamangkâ,
Pasakayín yaring batà.

Pagdatíng sa Maynila,
Ipagpilit ng manikà.
Ale, ale, namamayong,
Pasukubin yaring sanggól
Pagdatíng sa Malabon,
Ipagpilit ng bagoóng.
Sitsiritsít, alibangbáng....

Dahil sa Iyo

Sa buhay ko'y labis, ang hirap at pasakít
Ng pusong umiibig, mandi'y walâ nang langit.
At nang lumigaya, hinangò mo sa dusa
Tanging ikáw sintá, ang aking pag-asa.
Dahil sa iyó, nais kong mabuhay,
Dahil sa iyó, hanggáng mamatáy
Dapat mong tantuín, walâ nang ibáng gilíw
Pusò ko'y tanungín, ikáw at ikáw rin.
Dahil sa iyó, akó'y lumigaya
Pagmamahál, ay alayan ka
Kung tunay mang akó ay alipinin mo
Ang lahát ng itó'y dahil sa iyó

Leron-Leron Sintá

Leron-Leron sintá, umakyát sa papaya
Dalá-dalá'y buslô, sisidlán ng bunga
Pagdatíng sa dulo'y nabalì ang sangá
Kapós kapalaran, humanap ng ibá.
Halika na Neneng, tayo'y manampalok
Dalhín mo ang buslô, sisidlán ng hinog
Pagdatíng sa dulo'y uunda-undayog
Kumapit ka Neneng, baka ka mahulog.
Halika na Neneng at tayo'y magsimbá
At iyóng isuot ang barò mo't saya
Ang barò mo't sayang pagkagandá-gandá
Kay gandá ng kulay-berde, putî, pulá.
Akó'y ibigin mo, lalaking matapang
Ang baríl ko'y pitó, ang sundáng ko'y siyám
Ang lalakarin ko'y parte ng dinulang
Isáng pinggáng pansít ang aking kalaban.

Magtaním ay di birò

Magtaním ay di birò
Maghapong nakayukô

Di ka man makatayô
Di ka man makaupô
Sa umagang pagkagising
Lahát ay iisipin
Kung saán may pataním
May masaráp na pagkain.
Halina, Halina
Mga kaliyág
Tayo'y magsipag-unat-unat
Magpanibago tayo ng lakás
Para sa araw ng bukas

Sarung Banggí (Bicol song, Tagalog version)

Isáng gabí, maliwanag
Akó'y naghihintáy
Sa aking magandáng dilág
Namamangláw, ang pusò ko
At ang diwa ko'y laging nangangarap.
Malasin mo gilíw
Ang saksí ng aking pagmamahál
Bituing nagniningníng
Kisláp ng tala't liwanag ng buwán
Ang siyáng nagsasabing
Pag-ibig ko'y sadyáng tunay
Araw-gabí, ang panaginip ko'y ikáw.
Magbuhat nang ikáw ay aking mamalas
Akó ay natutong gumawâ ng awit
Patí ng pusò kong dati'y matahimik
Ngayó'y dumadalás
Ang tibók ng dibdíb

Paruparong Bukid

Paruparong bukid, na lilipad-lipád
Sa gitnâ ng daán, papagapagaspás
Isáng bara ang tapis
Isáng dangkál ang manggás
Ang sayang de kola
Isáng piyesa ang sayad.
May payneta pa siyá... uy!
May sukláy pa mandín... uy!
Nagwas de ohetes ang palalabasín
Haharáp sa altár, at mananalamín
At saká lalakad nang pakendeng-kendéng

Lulay

Anóng laking hirap kung pagkaiisipin
Ang gawáng umibig sa babaing mahinhín
Lumuluhod ka na'y di ka pa mandin pansín
Sa hirap iká'y kaniyáng susubukin.
Ligaya ng buhay, babaing sakdál inam
Ang halagá niyá'y
Di matutumbasan
Kahinhinan niyá'y tanging kayamanan

Harana

Dungawin mo hirang
Ang nananambitan
Kahit sulyáp mo man lamang
Iyóng idampulay
Sapagkát ikáw lamang
Ang tanging dalanginan
Ng pusò kong dahil sa iyó'y
Nabubuhay

Kataka-taká

Kataka-takáng mahibáng ang katulad ko sa iyó
Biru-birò ang simulâ, ang wakás palá ay anó
Aayaw-ayáw pa akó ngunit iyáy ay di totoó
Dahil sa iyó, pusò kong itó'y binihag mo.
Alaala ka magíng gabí't araw
Alipinin ma'y waláng kailangan
Mariníg ko lang sa labi mo hiráng
Na akó'y iibigin, habang nabubuhay

Ang dalagang Pilipina

Ang dalagang Pilipina
Parang tala sa umaga
Kung tanawín ay nakaliligaya
May ningníng na tangì at dakilang gandá
Magíng sa ugali, magíng sa kumilos
Mayumì, mahinhín, mabinì ang lahát ng ayos
Malinis ang pusò, magíng sa pag-irog
May tibay at ningníng ng loób
Bulaklák na tanging marilág
Ang bangó ay humahalimuyak
Sa mundó'y dakilang panghiyás

Pang-aliw sa pusong may hirap
Batis ng ligaya at galák
Hantungan ng madláng pangarap
Iyán ang dalagang Pilipina
Karapat-dapat sa isáng tunay na pagsintá

National Anthem, Tagalog Version (Pambansang Awit)

Bayang Magiliw
Perlas ng Silanganan
Alab ng pusò
Sa dibdíb mo'y buháy

Lupang hinirang,
Duyan ka ng magiting,
sa manlulupig
Di ka pasisiíl

Sa dagat at bundók
Sa simoy at sa langit mong bugháw;
may dilag ang tulâ
at awit sa paglayang minamahál
Ang kisláp ng watawat mo'y
Tagumpáy na nagniningning
Ang bituin at araw niyá
Kailán pa ma'y di magdidilím

Lupà ng araw, ng luwalhati't pagsintá,
Buhay ay langit sa piling mo,
Aming ligaya na pag may mang-aapí
Ang mamatáy nang dahil sa iyó

SELECTED TAGALOG PROVERBS

MGA PINILING SALAWIKAING TAGALOG

Ang lakí sa layaw, karaniwa'y hubád.
One who is reared pampered is usually naked (lacks good sense).

Anák na pinaluhà, kayamanan sa pagtandâ.
A child who is made to cry will be his parents' wealth in their old age.

Pagkamatáy nang sinag, waláng pintarong bayawak.
After the sun beams are gone, there is no colored iguana. [At night all cats are grey.]

Huwág kang magtiwalà sa guhit hanggáng walâ ka sa langit.
Don't trust in fortune until you are in heaven.

Kung nagbibigáy ma't mahirap sa loob, ang pinakakain ay di mabubusog.
Alms given grudgingly will not appease the hunger of the recipient.

Makikilala sa labì ang palanganga't hindî.
Whether one chews betel nut is shown by his mouth.

Kung magagawâ rin lang ng paupô, ay huwág na sanang gawín ng patayô.
What can be done sitting shouldn't be done standing (negotiations before violence).

Sa karamihan ng paá ng alupihan, ay nalalaglág din.
For all its feet, the centipede still falls.

Ang palay ay parisan, habang nagkakulamán ay lalong nagpupugay.
Imitate the rice stalk, the more grains it bears, the lower it bows.

Ang tumutulad sa langgám, hindî manghihiram ng ikabubuhay.
Whoever follows the ant will not have to borrow his means of livelihood.

Ang sungay ng usáng mahalò sa garing, sa malabong matá'y garing na rin.
A deer horn mixed with ivory will pass for ivory to one with poor eyesight.

Batóng buhay ka man na sakdál ng tigás, sa paták ng tubig lamang naaagnás.
Even the hardest stone may be eroded by dripping water.

Mabuti lamang sa kahigan, masamâ na sa bitawan.
The cock is good before the fight, but poor in actual combat.

Ang taong mapanaghilì sa kayamanan at arì, ay hindî luluwalhatì sa hirap at sakít lalagì.
He who is envious of others' possessions will always be in poverty and suffering.

Natutuksó kahit banál, pag nakabukás ang kabán.
Even a saintly man is tempted by an open chest.

Mabuti pa ang kubo na ang lamán ay tao, kaysá bahay na bató, na ang lamán ay kuwago.
Better a hut with a good man in it than a stone house with an owl in it.

Anumáng gawín ng tao, nararamay patí inapó.
The consequences of one's acts are even felt by the grandchildren.

Ang tulin ng bangkâ di sa kahoy galing, kundî sa piloto't sa hihip ng hangin.
The speed of the boat depends on the wind and pilot, not the wood of which it is made.

Mamatáy ng gutom na nakalala'y mabuting higít sa aliping matabâ.
It's better to starve and be free than to be a fat slave.

Masubali't sugat na mahapdî, sa masamáng batì ng katotong pilì.
We can better endure the pain of a wound than the treachery of a friend.

Katotong di mautangan, at di makahiwang sundáng, aanhín ko masirâ man?
A friend who doesn't lend and a knife that doesn't cut, who cares if they're lost?

Mabuti ang sampál ng kaibigan kaysá halík ng kaaway.
Better the blow of a friend than the kiss of a traitor.

Mga biyayà at handóg, bató man ay pinalalambót.
Gifts can soften even stone.

Ang may gawáng buktót, nagtatabo't sumusukot, nagdadaláng takot, waláng sumusubok.
A guilty conscience runs and hides even when not chased.

Waláng magaling na lalaki pag nasubukan sa pagtae.
No man can maintain his dignity when caught defecating.

Mahanga'y ang paít ng pag-aaral kaysa paít ng kamangmangán.
The bitterness of studying is preferable to the bitterness of ignorance.

Ang pag-ibig at pagmamahal, parang tiník sa lalamunan, habang kinakamot, makatíng malinamnám.
Love is like a fishbone in the throat, the more you scratch it the more it feels deliciously itchy.

Tumandâ man ang damulag, murang damó rin ang hanap.
Even when a water buffalo gets old, it still seeks young grass. (Old men still want young girls.)

Waláng matimtimang birhen sa matiyagang manalangin.
There is no steadfast virgin to the persevering devotee.

Hanggáng maiksi ang kumot, magtiís na mamaluktót, Kung humabà na't lumapad, sakâ na namán umunat.
Live within your means (when your blanket is short, you must cuddle in it; when it becomes long, you may stretch).

Waláng karneng tinangáy ng aso na di nalawayan.
No meat carried away by a dog remains undefiled by its saliva.

Huwág kang mangahas bumuhat ng bató, kung natatakot kang madurog ang butó.
Don't dare to lift a heavy stone if you are not afraid to break your bones.

Kapág tunay ang anyaya, sinasamahan ng hila.
If the invitation is sincere, it will be accompanied by a pull.

Ang kamalian ng mahirap napupuná ng lahát, ang kamalian ng mayaman pinaparang waláng anumán.
The mistakes of the poor are noticed, those of the rich are overlooked.

Ang bibíg ng ilog, iyóng masasarhán, ang bibíg ng tao'y di mo matatakpán.
You can stop the mouth of a river, but not the mouth of a man.

Lahát ng ulo ay may buhók, nguni't hindî lahát ay may utak.
All heads have hair, but not all have brains.

Ang kita sa bulábulâ, sa bulâ rin nawawalâ.
That which was acquired from foam disappears in the foam.

Waláng mahirap na gisingin na gayà ng nagtutulog-tulugan.
The hardest person to awaken is he who is already awake.

Waláng palayók na di may kasukát na tuntóng.
There is no pot that doesn't have a matching lid.

Ang dati sa bahág, magsalawál ma'y aliswág
He who is accustomed to loincloths feels uncomfortable in pants.

Ang sugat ng kaloobán, ay mahirap na mabahaw, kung sakaling gumalíng man, ay magnanaknák din balang araw.
Hurt feelings are difficult to mend, they may improve for a time but will fester again one day. (Hurt feelings never heal completely.)

Other Philippine Interest Titles from Hippocrene Books

Ilocano-English/English-Ilocano Dictionary & Phrasebook
7,000 entries • 268 pages • 5½ x 8½ • $16.95pb • 0-7818-0642-9 • (718)

Pilipino-English/English-Pilipino Concise Dictionary
5,000 entries • 389 pages • 4 x 6 • $12.95pb • 0-87052-491-7 • (393)

Pilipino-English/English-Pilipino Dictionary & Phrasebook
2,200 entries • 186 pages • 3¾ x 7 • $11.95pb • 0-7818-0451-5 • (295)

Other Titles of Regional Interest…

China: An Illustrated History
154 pages • 5 x 7 • $14.95hc • 0-7818-0821-9 • (542)

Beginner's Chinese with Two Audio CDs
Two 80-Minute Audio CDs • 192 pages • 5½ x 8½ • $25.95pb • 0-7818-1095-7 • (192)

Intermediate Chinese with Audio CD
One 80-Minute Audio CD • 320 pages • 5½ x 8½ • $21.95pb • 0-7818-0992-4 • (193)

English-Chinese Pinyin Dictionary
10,000 entries • 500 pages • 4 x 6 • $19.95pb • 0-7818-0427-2 • (509)

Chinese-English Frequency Dictionary
A Study Guide to Mandarin Chinese's 500 Most Frequently Used Words
500 entries • 240 pages • 5½ x 8½ • $18.95pb • 0-7818-0842-1 • (277)

Japanese Home Cooking
140 pages • 5½ x 8½ • b/w photographs • $19.95hc • 0-7818-0881-2 • (27)

Japan: An Illustrated History
232 pages • 5 x 7 • $14.95pb • 0-7818-0989-4 • (469)

Japanese-English/English-Japanese Concise Dictionary
Romanized
8,000 entries • 235 pages • 4 x 6 • 0-7818-0162-1 • $11.95pb • W • (474)

Japanese-English/English-Japanese Dictionary & Phrasebook
2,300 entries • 231 pages • 3¾ x 7½ • $12.95pb • 0-7818-0814-6 • (205)

The Best of Korean Cooking
196 pages • 5½ x 8½ • b/w illustrations • $22.50hc • 0-7818-0929-0 • (55)

Korea, From Ancient Times to 1945: An Illustrated History
168 pages • 5 x 7 • $12.95pb • 0-7818-0873-1 • (354)

Korean-English/English-Korean Dictionary & Phrasebook
5,000 entries • 312 pages • 3¾ x 7½ • $12.95pb • 0-7818-1029-9 • (565)

Korean-English/English-Korean Practical Dictionary
8,500 entries • 358 pages • 4¼ x 8¼ • $19.95pb • 0-87052-092-X • (399)

Korean-English/English-Korean Handy Dictionary
4,000 entries • 184 pages • 5 x 8 • $8.95pb • 0-7818-0082-X • (438)

Simple Laotian Cooking
236 pages • 6 x 9 • b/w photographs • $24.95hc • 0-7818-0963-0 • (522)

Lao-English/English-Lao Dictionary & Phrasebook
2,500 entries • 207 pages • 3¾ x 7 • $12.95pb • 0-7818-0858-8 • (470)

Mongolian-English/English-Mongolian Dictionary & Phrasebook
3,300 entries • 286 pages • 3¾ x 7½ • $12.95pb • 0-7818-0958 • (158)

The Best of Taiwanese Cuisine
132 pages • 5½ x 8½ • b/w illustrations & photos • $24.95hc • 0-7818-0855-3 • (46)

The Best of Regional Thai Cuisine
236 pages • 6 x 9 • b/w illustrations & photos • $24.95hc • 0-7818-0880-4 • (26)

Thai-English/English-Thai Dictionary & Phrasebook
1,800 entries • 200 pages • 3¾ x 7 • $12.95pb • 0-7818-0774-3 • (330)

A Vietnamese Kitchen
2-Color • 175 pages • 6 x 9 • $24.95hc • 0-7818-1081-7 • (115)

Vietnam: An Illustrated History
184 pages • 5 x 7 • $14.95hc • 0-7818-0910-X • (302)

Vietnamese-English/English-Vietnamese Dictionary & Phrasebook
3,000 entries • 248 pages • 3¾ x 7 • $11.95pb • 0-7818-0991-6 • (104)

Vietnamese-English/English-Vietnamese Standard Dictionary
12,000 entries • 506 pages • 5⅜ x 8 • $24.95 • 0-87052-924-2 • (529)

Beginner's Vietnamese
517 pages • 7 x 10 • $19.95pb • 0-7818-0411-6 • (253)

All prices are subject to change without prior notice. **To order Hippocrene Books**, contact your local bookstore, call (718) 454-2366, visit www.hippocrenebooks.com, or write to: **Hippocrene Books, 171 Madison Avenue, New York, NY 10016**. Please enclose check or money order adding $5.00 shipping (UPS) for the first book and $.50 for each additional title.